ROBERT DALLEK

John F. Kennedy

An Unfinished Life 1917–1963

PENGUIN BOOKS

PENGUIN BOOKS

Published by the Penguin Group
Penguin Books Ltd, 80 Strand, London WC2R ORL, England
Penguin Group (USA) Inc., 375 Hudson Street, New York, New York 10014, USA
Penguin Group (Canada), 90 Eglinton Avenue East, Suite 700, Toronto, Ontario, Canada M4P 2Y3
(a division of Pearson Penguin Canada Inc.)
Penguin Ireland, 25 St Stephen's Green, Dublin 2, Ireland (a division of Penguin Books Ltd)
Penguin Group (Australia), 707 Collins Street, Melbourne, Victoria 3008, Australia
(a division of Pearson Australia Group Pty Ltd)
Penguin Books India Pvt Ltd, 11 Community Centre, Panchsheel Park, New Delhi – 110 017, India
Penguin Group (NZ), 67 Apollo Drive, Rosedale, Auckland 0632, New Zealand
(a division of Pearson New Zealand Ltd)
Penguin Books (South Africa) (Pty) Ltd, Block D, Rosebank Office Park, 181 Jan Smuts Avenue,
Parktown North, Gauteng 2193, South Africa

Penguin Books Ltd, Registered Offices: 80 Strand, London WC2R ORL, England

www.penguin.com

First published in the United States of America by Little, Brown and Company 2003
First published in Great Britain by Allen Lane 2003
Published in Penguin Books 2004
This edition published 2013

002

Copyright © Robert Dallek, 2003, 2013

978-0-141-97658-7

www.greenpenguin.co.uk

Penguin Books is committed to a sustainable
future for our business, our readers and our planet.
This book is made from Forest Stewardship
Council™ certified paper.

Contents

PART FOUR The President

Preface

Why another Kennedy book? I was asked repeatedly during the five years I worked on this biography. The availability of new materials — written contemporary documents, telephone and Oval Office tapes, and entire oral histories or parts thereof — seemed ample reason to revisit Kennedy's personal and public lives. I also took guidance from science writer Jacob Bronowski: "Ask an impertinent question and you are on your way to a pertinent answer." As I worked my way through the records, I was startled by how many fresh things could be said based on the combination of old and new files about the man, his family, and his political career. To cite just a few examples, new documents reveal more clearly the cause of the accident that killed Joseph Kennedy Jr. in World War II, how Bobby Kennedy became attorney general in 1960, and what JFK thought of U.S. military chiefs, their plans for an invasion of Cuba, the American press corps in Saigon, and the wisdom of an expanded war in Vietnam.

As with all our most interesting public figures, Kennedy is an elusive character, a man who, like all politicians, worked hard to emphasize his favorable attributes and hide his limitations. He and those closest to him were extraordinarily skillful at creating positive images that continue to shape public impressions. My objective has not been to write another debunking book (these have been in ample supply in recent years) but to penetrate the veneer of glamour and charm to reconstruct the real man or as close to it as possible. The result is not a sharply negative portrait but a description of someone with virtues and defects that make him seem both exceptional and ordinary — a man of uncommon intelligence, drive, discipline, and good judgment on the one hand, and of lifelong physical suffering and emotional problems on the other. I have not emphasized one aspect over the other but have tried to bring them into balance. Learning, for example, a great deal more than any biographer has previously known about Kennedy's medical history allowed me to see not only the extent to which he hid his infirmities from public view but also the man's exceptional strength of character. In addition, I have tried to understand his indisputable womanizing, including previously unknown instances of his compulsive philandering. More significant, I have ventured answers to questions about whether his health problems and behavior in any way undermined his performance of presidential duties.

I have also tried to judiciously assess the negative and positive family influences on his character, the record of his navy service, his House and Senate careers, and, most important, his presidential policies on the economy, civil rights, federal aid to education, health insurance for seniors, and poverty, and, even more consequentially, on dealings with Russia, nuclear weapons, space, Cuba, and Vietnam. I have not hesitated to say what I believe Kennedy might have done about the many ongoing problems certain to have faced him in a second term, however open to question these conclusions may be. "It is better to debate a question without settling it than to settle a question without debating it," said Joseph Joubert, a French philosopher of the eighteenth and nineteenth centuries.

I believe this biography provides the most authoritative discussion to date on Kennedy the man and his political career. Nonetheless, however much it may be a significant advance in understanding, I have no illusion that I am recording the last word on John F. Kennedy. The economist Thorstein Veblen was surely right when he cautioned that "the outcome of any serious research can only be to make two questions grow where one question grew before." Add to this the man's almost mythical importance to Americans and hundreds of millions of people around the globe and you can be certain that future generations will be eager for renewed attention to him in the context of their own times.

R.D.
February 2003

PART ONE

Growing Up

*Every man had to test himself, and if he was courageous
and lucky he found maturity. That was all the reward
you could ask for, or were entitled to: growing up.*

— Ward Just, *The Translator* (1991)

CHAPTER 1

Beginnings

George Bernard Shaw, speaking as an Irishman, summed up an approach to life: . . . "I dream things that never were — and I say: Why not?"

— John F. Kennedy before the Irish Parliament, June 28, 1963

IN AUGUST 1947, John F. Kennedy traveled to Ireland. The trip was notable for several reasons. Kennedy was first and foremost a "good New Englander," an American — so said the Irish ambassador to the United States — who had all but lost his connection to the old country. Indeed, recalling how often Jack Kennedy had visited England in the 1930s and early 1940s without going to Ireland, the ambassador archly described Kennedy as "an English American." "Many people made much of his Irish ancestry," one of Kennedy's English friends said. But he was "a European . . . more English than Irish." Now, at long last, he was going home. That was not, however, how his father saw it. For Joseph Patrick Kennedy, whose drive for social acceptance shadowed most of what he did, being described as an "Irishman" was cause for private rage. "Goddamn it!" he once sputtered after a Boston newspaper identified him that way. "I was born in this country! My children were born in this country! What the hell does someone have to do to become an American?"

But his son had if not formed a deep emotional attachment, at least taken his cue from his mother's father, John F. Fitzgerald. "There seems to be some disagreement as to whether my grandfather Fitzgerald came from Wexford, Limerick or Tipperary," Kennedy would later recall. "And it is even more confusing as to where my great[-]grandmother came from — because her son — who was the Mayor of Boston — used to claim his mother came from whichever

Irish county had the most votes in the audience he was addressing at that particular time." And indeed, when the twenty-nine-year-old had first run for Congress the year before, Irish Americans in his district had been hesitant to support Kennedy because of his lack of ethnic identification, let alone pride.

Officially, Kennedy was on a fact-finding mission to study the potential workings of the Marshall Plan in a Europe still reeling from the devastation wrought by the Second World War. Unofficially, it was a chance to relax with Kathleen Kennedy Hartington, Jack's favorite younger sister, who was even more "English American" than he was. Though her husband, William Cavendish Hartington, who was in line to become the next duke of Devonshire, had died in the war, Kathleen had stayed in England, where the Devonshires treated her with fond regard. They gave her free run of their several great estates, including Lismore Castle in southern Ireland's County Waterford, a twelfth-century mansion once owned by Sir Walter Raleigh. Kathleen called it the "most perfect place" in the world.

Kathleen asked Jack to join her for a vacation at Lismore, where she promised to bring him together with former Foreign Secretary Anthony Eden; Pamela Churchill, the divorced wife of Winston's son, Randolph; and other prominent English social and political lions. "Anthony Eden arrives today," Kathleen wrote an American friend, "so by the end of the week he and Jack will have fixed up the state of the world."

Like Kathleen, Jack Kennedy had been schooled to move comfortably in privileged circles. Jack and Kathleen did not think of themselves as anything but American aristocrats. Wit, charm, and intelligence added to the cachet he carried as a congressman and the son of one of America's wealthiest entrepreneurs who himself was a former ambassador to Britain.

Yet those who met John Kennedy for the first time in 1947 found little assurance in his appearance. Though having passed his thirtieth birthday in the spring, he looked like "a college boy," or at best a Harvard Ph.D. candidate in political science. He contributed to the impression with his casual attire, appearing sometimes on the House floor in khaki pants and a rumpled seersucker jacket with a shirttail dangling below his coat or in the House cafeteria line in sweater and sneakers. At six feet and only 140 pounds, his slender body, gaunt and freckled face, and full head of tousled brown hair made him seem younger than his thirty years. Even when he dressed in formal suits, which was not often, it did not make him look older or like a congressman. "He wore the most godawful suits," Mary Davis, his secretary, said. "Horrible looking, hanging from his frame." Unlike so many members of the House who self-consciously dressed the part, Kennedy reflected his sense of entitlement in his informal dress. But it did not encourage an impression of maturity, and it was difficult for most colleagues to take him seriously. He initially struck veteran congressmen as the son of a famous family who had inherited his office rather than earned it. Sometimes he didn't impress them at all. "Well, how do you like that?" he asked his congressional office staff one morning. "Some people got into the elevator and asked me for the fourth floor." During his first week in the House, a veteran congressman who mistook him for a page demanded a copy of a bill until Jack informed the astonished member that they were colleagues.

Nevertheless, he offended almost no one. Although he conveyed a certain coolness or self-control, his radiant smile and genuine openness made him immediately likable. "The effect he has on women voters was almost naughty," *New York Times* columnist James Reston later wrote. "Every woman either wants to mother him or marry him." Another columnist saw something in his appearance that suggested "to the suggestible that he is lost, stolen or strayed — a prince in exile, perhaps, or a very wealthy orphan."

A visit to New Ross, a market town on the banks of the Barrow River fifty miles east of Lismore, filled some of Jack's time in Ireland. Kathleen, who spent the day playing golf with her guests, did not join him. Instead, Pamela Churchill, whom Jack asked "rather quietly, rather apologetically," went along. They drove for five hours in Kathleen's huge American station wagon over rutted roads along Ireland's scenic southeastern coast before reaching the outskirts of the town.

New Ross was not casually chosen. As they approached, with only a letter from his aunt Loretta, his father's sister, to guide him, Jack stopped to ask directions to the Kennedy house. ("Which Kennedys will it be that you'll be wanting?" the man replied.) Jack tried a little white farmhouse on the edge of the village with a front yard full of chickens and geese. A lady surrounded by six kids, "looking just like all the Kennedys," greeted him with suspicion. After sending for her husband, who was in the fields, the family invited Jack and Pamela for tea in their thatched-roof cottage with a dirt floor. Though Pamela was impressed with the family's simple dignity, she compared the visit to a scene from Erskine Caldwell's *Tobacco Road*.

Jack believed that he had discovered his third cousins and seemed to enjoy himself thoroughly. Asking if he could do anything for them, the cousins proposed that he "drive the children around the village in the station wagon," which he did to their pleasure and his. For her part, Pamela clearly did not understand "the magic of the afternoon." Neither did Kathleen, who was angry when Jack returned late for dinner. "Did they have a bathroom?" she asked snidely.

The successful striving of her great-grandparents, grandparents, and parents — the unceasing ambition of the Fitzgeralds and the Kennedys — had catapulted the family into another realm, an ocean and a century apart from the relatives left behind in Ireland. In America anything was possible — the Fitzgeralds and the Kennedys were living proof. For most of the family, these Kennedys of New Ross were something foreign, something best ignored or forgotten. But not for Jack.

JACK HAD ONLY RUDIMENTARY KNOWLEDGE about his distant ancestors. He knew that his great-grandfather Patrick Kennedy had come to East Boston during the great potato famines of the late 1840s, worked as a cooper making wagon staves and whiskey barrels, married Bridget Murphy, and fathered three daughters and a son before he died of cholera in 1858 when only thirty-five.

Jack also knew that his great-grandfather on his mother's side, Thomas Fitzgerald, had clung to his farm in Ireland until 1854, when the famine drove him to America as well. Initially settling in Acton, twenty-five miles west of Boston, his impoverishment as a farmer forced him to take up life in Boston's North End Irish ghetto, a crowded slum of wooden tenements. One contemporary described it as a "dreary, dismal" desolate world in which all was "mean, nasty, inefficient [and] forbidding," except for the Catholic Church, which provided spiritual comfort and physical beauty.

In 1857 Thomas married Rosanna Cox, with whom he had twelve children — nine of whom reached maturity, an amazing survival rate in a time when infant mortality was a common event. Thomas, who lived until 1885, surviving Rosanna by six years, prospered first as a street peddler of household wares and then in a grocery business, which doubled as a North End tavern in the evenings. Income from tenements he bought and rented to Irish laborers made his family comfortable and opened the way to greater success for his offspring.

The limits of Jack's knowledge about his Irish relatives was partly the result of his parents' upward mobility and their eagerness to replace their "Irishness" with an American identity. Rose Fitzgerald Kennedy, Jack's mother, took pains to instill American values in the children, ignoring their Irish roots and taking them to the storied landmarks of the country's Revolutionary past around Boston. This attitude differed little from that of other ethnic groups, who tried to meet the demands of being an American by forgetting about their Old World past, but in stratified Boston it took on special meaning. Rose and Joe were understandably eager to insulate the family from the continual snubs that Irish Americans suffered at the hands of local Brahmins, well-off Protestant Americans whose roots went back to the earliest years of the Republic. Although Rose and Joe enjoyed privileged lives, their tangible sense of being outsiders in their native land remained a social reality they struggled to overcome.

The Boston in which Joe and Rose grew up was self-consciously "American." It was the breeding ground for the values and spirit that had given birth to the nation and the center of America's most famous university where so many of the country's most influential leaders had been educated. Snobbery or class consciousness was as much a part of the city's landscape as Boston Common. Coming from the wrong side of the tracks in most American cities was no fixed impediment to individual success. But in Boston, where "the Lowells speak only to the Cabots and the Cabots speak only to God," rising above one's station was an enterprise for only the most ambitious.

What vivid sense of family history there was began with Jack's two grandfathers — Patrick Joseph Kennedy and John F. Fitzgerald, both impressively successful men who achieved local fame and gave their children the wherewithal to enjoy comfortable lives. Patrick Joseph Kennedy was born in 1858, the year his father died. In an era when no public support program came to the aid of a widow with four children, Bridget Murphy Kennedy, Patrick's mother, supported the family as a saleswoman and shopkeeper. At age fourteen, P.J., as he was called, left school to work on the Boston docks as a stevedore to help support his mother and three older sisters. In the 1880s, with money he had saved from his modest earnings, he launched a business career by buying a saloon in Haymarket Square. In time, he bought a second establishment by the docks. To capitalize on the social drinking of upper-class Boston, P.J. purchased a third bar in an upscale hotel, the Maverick House.

With his handlebar mustache, white apron, and red sleeve garters, the stocky, blue-eyed, red-haired P.J. cut a handsome figure behind the bar of his taverns. By all accounts, he was a good listener who gained the regard and even affection of his patrons. Before he was thirty, his growing prosperity allowed him to buy a whiskey-importing business, P. J. Kennedy and Company, that made him a leading figure in Boston's liquor trade.

Likable, always ready to help less fortunate fellow Irishmen with a little cash and some sensible advice, P.J. enjoyed the approval and respect of most folks in East Boston, a mixed Boston neighborhood of upscale Irish and Protestant elite. Beginning in 1884, he converted his popularity into five consecutive one-year terms in the Massachusetts Lower House, followed by three two-year terms in the state senate. Establishing himself as one of Boston's principal Democratic leaders, he was invited to give one of the seconding speeches for Grover Cleveland at the party's 1888 national convention in St. Louis.

But campaigning, speech making, and legislative maneuvering were less appealing to him than the behind-the-scenes machinations that characterized so much of Boston politics in the late-nineteenth and early-twentieth centuries. After leaving the senate in 1895, P.J. spent his political career in various appointive offices — elections commissioner and fire commissioner — as the backroom boss of Boston's Ward Two, and as a member of his party's unofficial Board of Strategy. At board meetings over sumptuous lunches in room eight of the Quincy House hotel near Scollay Square, P.J. and three other power brokers from Charlestown and the South and North Ends chose candidates for local and statewide offices and distributed patronage.

There was time for family, too. In 1887 P.J. married Mary Augusta Hickey, a member of an affluent "lace curtain" Irish family from the upscale suburb of Brockton. The daughter of a successful business-man and the sister of a police lieutenant, a physician with a Harvard medical degree, and a funeral home director, Hickey had solidified Kennedy's move into the newly emerging Irish middle class, or as legendary Boston mayor James Michael Curley mockingly called them, "cut glass" Irish or FIFs ("First Irish Families"). By the time he died in 1929, P.J. had indeed joined the ranks of the cut-glass set, holding an interest in a coal company and a substantial amount of stock in a bank, the Columbia Trust Company. His wealth afforded his family of one son, Joseph Patrick, and two daughters an attractive home on Jeffries Point in East Boston.

John F. Fitzgerald was better known in Boston than P.J. and had a greater influence on Jack's life. Born in 1863, John F. was the fourth of twelve children. As a boy and a young man, his father's standing as a successful businessman and his innate talents gained him admission to Boston's storied Latin School (training ground for the offspring of the city's most important families, including the Adamses, John, John Quincy, and Henry), where he excelled at athletics and compiled a distinguished academic record, graduating with honors. Earning a degree at Boston College, the city's Jesuit university, John F. — or Johnnie Fitz or Fitzie, as friends called him — entered Harvard Medical School in 1884. When his father died in the spring of 1885, he abandoned his medical education, which had been more his father's idea than his own, to care for his six younger brothers. Taking a job in the city's Customs House as a clerk, he simultaneously converted an affinity for people and politics into a job as a secretary to Matthew Keany, one of the Democratic party's North End ward bosses.

In 1891 Fitzie won election to a seat on Boston's Common Council, where he overcame resistance from representatives of more affluent districts to spend $350,000 on a public park for his poor North End constituents. The following year, when Keany died, Fitzgerald's seven-year apprenticeship in providing behind-the-scenes services to constituents and manipulating local power made him Keany's logical successor.

He was a natural politician — a charming, impish, affable lover of people who perfected the "Irish switch": chatting amiably with one person while pumping another's hand and gazing fondly at a third. His warmth of character earned him yet another nickname, "Honey Fitz," and he gained a reputation as the only politician who could sing "Sweet Adeline" sober and get away with it. A pixielike character with florid face, bright eyes, and sandy hair, he was a showman who could have had a career in vaudeville.

But politics, with all the brokering that went into arranging alliances and the hoopla that went into campaigning, was his calling. A verse of the day ran: "Honey Fitz can talk you blind / on any subject you can find / Fish and fishing, motor boats / Railroads, streetcars, getting votes." His gift of gab became known as Fitzblarney, and his followers as "dearos," a shortened version of his description of his district as "the dear old North End."

Fitzgerald's amiability translated into electoral successes. In 1892 he overcame internal bickering among the ward bosses to win election to the state senate. Compiling a progressive voting record and a reputation as an astute legislator eager to meet the needs of every constituent, Fitzgerald put himself forward in 1894 for the only sure Democratic congressional seat in Massachusetts, Boston's Ninth District. His candidacy pitted him against his fellow bosses on the Strategy Board, who backed incumbent congressman Joseph O'Neil. Running a brilliant campaign that effectively played on suffering caused by the panic of 1893 and the subsequent depression, Fitzgerald's torchlight parades and promises of public programs produced an unprecedented turnout. Also helped by a division among the bosses, who responded to his candidacy by failing to unite against him, the thirty-one-year-old Fitzgerald won a decisive primary victory.

During three terms in Congress, Fitzgerald voted consistently for measures serving local and statewide needs, for laws favoring progressive income taxes over higher protective tariffs, and for a continuation of unrestricted immigration. Massachusetts' senator Henry Cabot Lodge, a tall slender Brahmin who, with his Vandyke beard and courtly manner, could not have been more of a contrast to Fitzgerald, once lectured the Irishman on the virtues of barring inferior peoples — indigestible aliens — from corrupting the United States. "You are an impudent young man," Lodge began. "Do you think the Jews or the Italians have any right in this country?" Fitzgerald replied: "As much right as your father or mine. It was only a difference of a few ships."

At the end of three terms as one of only three Catholics in the House, Fitzgerald announced his decision not to run again. It was a prelude to gaining the post he wished above all, mayor of Boston. During the next five years, while he waited for a favorable moment to run, he prospered as the publisher of a local newspaper, *The Republic*. Demonstrating a keen business sense, Fitzgerald substantially increased department-store advertising in his pages by running stories of special interest to women.

One of the city's leading political power brokers as the boss of the North End's Ward Six, despite having moved to Concord and then Dorchester, Fitzgerald was in a strong position to become mayor when the incumbent died in 1905. But another round of opposition from his fellow bosses, including P.J., put his election in doubt. In response, he devised a shrewd anti-boss campaign that appealed to current progressive antagonism to undemocratic machine politics. Despite a bruising primary fight and another closely contested race against a formidable Republican, Fitzgerald gained the prize, chanting, "The people not the bosses must rule! Bigger, better, busier Boston." Within hours of winning the election, he showed up at P. J. Kennedy's East Boston office to say that there were no hard feelings about P.J.'s opposition to him. It was, two family biographers later said, "a first hurrah for the dynasty to come."

HONEY FITZ HAD COMPLEMENTED his political and business successes with marriage to his second cousin, Mary Josephine Hannon, or Josie, as intimates called her. They had met first in Acton at the Hannons' farm in September 1878, when Fitzgerald was fifteen and Josie thirteen. As he remembered it, he immediately fell in love with the beautiful girl to whom he would be married for sixty-two years, but Fitzgerald had to wait eleven years before Josie's family put aside their concerns about the consequences of having Josie marry a blood relative, however distant. The union produced six children, three sons and three daughters.

The eldest of the Fitzgerald children, Rose Elizabeth, was Fitz's favorite. Praying for a daughter who might fulfill his dreams of winning acceptance into polite society, Honey Fitz envisioned Rose's life as a storybook tale of proper upbringing and social acclaim. As Rose later viewed it, her father succeeded: "There have been times when I felt I was one of the more fortunate people in the world, almost as if Providence, or Fate, or Destiny, as you like, had chosen me for special favors."

From her birth in the summer of 1890, she led a privileged life. When Rose was seven, Fitz and Josie moved the family to the Boston suburb of West Concord, where Rose remembers "a big, old rambling . . . wonderfully comfortable house" and the traditional pleasures and satisfactions of life in a small New England town: "serenity, order, family affection, horse-and-buggy rides to my grandparents' nearby home, climbing apple trees, picking wild flowers." There was the excitement of a father coming home on weekends from Washington, where, in Rose's limited understanding, he was something called a "congressman" doing important things. Whatever her sadness at his frequent absences, she remembered "the absolute thrill" of driving to the Concord train station to meet him and his affectionate greeting, with "a wonderful present" always pulled from his bags. She also recalled a trip to the White House at age seven with her father, where President William McKinley warmly greeted them and gave her a carnation. "There was no one in the world like my father," she said. "Wherever he was, there was magic in the air." There were also the memories of the matched pair of beautiful black horses that pulled the family carriage and of her own rig that at twelve she began driving to the Concord library to borrow books.

There were also the summers in Old Orchard Beach, Maine, where Boston's prominent Irish families would seek the pleasure of one another's company and relief from the heat. A beachfront crowded with hotels, cottages, and gregarious folks strolling, sunning themselves, swimming, fishing, shopping, playing cards, and eating together in the Brunswick Hotel's huge dining room, Old Orchard was described as "the typical watering place for those who detest the name of solitude." Rose remembered the joy of playing with other children and being surrounded by relatives and family friends who "visited back and forth constantly."

In 1904, having grown affluent on the returns from *The Republic*, the Fitzgeralds moved to suburban Dorchester, where their growing family of three girls and two boys lived in a sprawling fifteen-room house with a "scrollwork porch, mansard turret, and stained-glass insert in the front door portraying what Fitzie insisted was the family's coat of arms." Rose attended the Dorchester High School for Girls and, like her proper Bostonian Beacon Hill counterparts, rounded out her education with private lessons in French, dancing, piano, and voice.

Dorchester's remove from the center of Boston allowed Fitz to insulate Rose and the family from the rough-and-tumble politics of his 1905 mayoral campaign. Though now fifteen, Rose had only "a hazy idea of what was happening." This was a good thing, for it was a contest with much name-calling and ugly innuendoes about her father's private life and public dealings that would have offended any loving daughter, especially one as starry-eyed as Rose.

Rose's sheltered life extended into her twenties. At seventeen, as the mayor's vivacious, intelligent daughter, Rose had become something of a Boston celebrity, in attendance at "all manner of political and social events." Wellesley was an ideal college choice for so talented and prominent a young woman: It represented the chance to enter an exciting universe of intellectual and political discourse in the country's finest women's college. But believing her too young and impressionable, Fitz enrolled her in an elite Catholic school, Boston's Convent of the Sacred Heart, where she received instruction in deportment and feminine virtues promising to make her a model wife and mother.

At the close of Rose's year in Sacred Heart, the Fitzgeralds took their two eldest daughters on a grand European tour. Ostensibly, it was to broaden the girls' education. But Fitz, who had lost a reelection bid as mayor in 1907 and was under suspicion of lining his pockets during his two-year term, saw the summer trip as a chance to shield Rose and her sister Agnes from press coverage of his wrongdoing. To keep them away from the unpleasant public gossip and discourage a budding romance with Joseph Patrick Kennedy, P.J.'s son, the child of a family with less social standing, Fitz also decided to enroll Rose and Agnes for the 1908–09 academic year in a Sacred Heart convent school in Holland. Attended mainly by the daughters of French and German aristocrats and well-off merchant families, it was a more cosmopolitan version of its Boston counterpart.

After coming home in the summer of 1909, Rose took refuge from the political wars with another year of schooling at the Sacred Heart Convent in Manhattanville, New York. At the close of that year, she returned to Boston ready to assume a large role in her father's second term, which ran from 1910 to 1912. With two small children to care for and little patience for the duties of a political first lady, Josie left the part to Rose, who filled it with a style and grace reflecting her advantaged upbringing and education. She became Honey Fitz's constant "hostess-companion-helper," traveling with him to Chicago and Kansas on city business, to the Panama Canal to consider its effect on Boston's future as an international trade center, to western Europe to advance Boston's commerce with its principal cities, to meet President William Howard Taft at the White House, and to attend the 1912 Democratic National Convention in Baltimore that nominated New Jersey governor Woodrow Wilson for president. As one biographer records: "Fitzgerald delighted in the good looks of his daughter, in her intelligence, her presence of mind and superb social skills. . . . She proved to be her father's equal in conversation, curiosity, dancing, athletic ability and powers of endurance and even in the capacity for fascinating reporters," who gave her front-page coverage in Boston's newspapers.

Nothing more clearly marked Rose as a local leading light than her coming-out party in January 1911. The state's most prominent figures were counted among the 450 guests in attendance. Even the normal social barriers between Protestants and Catholics fell away for the occasion: Massachusetts' governor-elect, two congressmen, Boston's district attorney and city councilmen — who declared the day a holiday — rubbed shoulders with wealthy and fashionable bankers, businessmen, attorneys, physicians, and clergymen.

By the conventions of the time, Rose's debut at age twenty was a prelude to courtship and marriage. She certainly did not lack for suitors, but by accepted standards, they did not include Protestants. The "mistrust" and "resentment" between Boston's Brahmins and its Irish Catholics caused them to have "as little as possible to do with each other." And even though her father had fostered better relations by joining with Brahmin James Jackson Storrow to establish the Boston City Club, a place where both sides could meet in "a neutral and socially relaxed atmosphere," Rose saw the divide as "one of those elementary facts of life not worth puzzling about." Besides, there were enough eligible Catholic men who could measure up to her status, including, she believed, P.J.'s son, Joe, whom she had known almost her entire life and who impressed her — if not her own father — as a most desirable mate.

DESPITE BOSTON'S CULTURAL DIVIDE, Joe, like Rose, had no sense of inhibition about reaching the highest rungs of the country's economic and social ladders. His parents and their families had gained material comforts and social standing that had put them in the upper reaches of the American middle class. And like the business titans of the late-nineteenth century — Diamond Jim Brady, Andrew Carnegie, Jim Fisk, Jay Gould, J. P. Morgan, John D. Rockefeller — whose backgrounds and middle-class beginnings had acted as no bar to their acquisition of vast wealth and international fame, Joe Kennedy could entertain similar dreams.

Born in 1888, Joe grew up in an era when America's greatest heroes were daring entrepreneurs who not only enriched themselves but greatly expanded the national wealth by creating the infrastructure of an industrial society — steel, cheap energy, railroads, and financial instruments to grow the economy. Never mind that many were left behind in the rush to affluence: The social Darwinian code of the time, by which Joe was guided throughout his life, gave legitimacy to the view that the innately talented and virtuous succeeded while the less deserving made only modest gains or fell by the wayside. It was the natural order of things, and no sense of injustice need attach to wide gaps between the richest and poorest Americans. Of course, there was nothing against the fortunate sharing some of their largesse with needy Americans; indeed, the most well off were obliged to help the least advantaged. But to impute any inhibition on the accumulation of wealth from this obligation was never a part of Joe's outlook or that of other contemporary self-made men. As a boy, Joe had an oak bookcase stacked with the works of Horatio Alger Jr., which one of his sisters said he read avidly. Although Alger's stories were more attuned to the world of a rural pre–Civil War America, his rags-to-riches theme held a constant appeal to ambitious, up-and-about boys and young men like Joe Kennedy. Similarly, "mind power," or a belief in self-manipulation or success through positive thinking, which began to have a strong hold on the popular imagination at the turn of the century, captivated Joe. As he made his way in the world, Joe never tired of reminding people that anyone with God-given talents could figure out how to succeed; it was largely a matter of will.

As a teenager, Joe had already made clear that he was determined to rise above the ordinary. There were the usual things boys did then to make a little money: sell newspapers on the docks and candy and peanuts to tourists on a harbor excursion boat, light gas lamps and stoves in the homes of Orthodox Jews on holy days, deliver hats for a haberdasher, work as an office boy in his father's bank. But Joe had an urge to make money in a more inventive way. At the age of fifteen, he organized a neighborhood baseball team, the Assumptions. As the team's business manager, coach, and first baseman, he bought uniforms, rented a ball field, scheduled the games, and collected enough money from spectators to make a profit. When some of his teammates complained that he was too domineering and that they had no say about anything, Joe made it clear he didn't care. There could be only one boss, and he would settle for nothing less. Summing up his personal philosophy, Joe told his sister: "If you can't be captain, don't play."

Because she believed that Joe was special, his mother decided to use the family's social standing and affluence to move her son from East Boston's Catholic Xaverian School to Boston Latin. It was not unheard-of for aspiring Catholic families to seek and win admission for a son to Boston Latin; Rose's father had of course been a student there in the 1870s. But when Joe attended the school in September 1901, the redheaded, freckled-faced, muscular thirteen-year-old Irish kid from across the harbor was in a distinct minority among the scions of Beacon Hill and Back Bay families.

It did not stop Joe from making a special mark at the school. Although he never stamped himself out as an especially good student, he excelled in extracurricular activities and athletics, becoming the colonel on a drill team that won a citywide competition, captain of the baseball team, and in his senior year, the player with the city's highest high school batting average, for which he won the Mayor's Cup, presented by His Honor John F. Fitzgerald. Admired by his fellow students for his accomplishments on the diamond and for his warm personality and loyalty to his friends, Joe was also elected president of his senior class.

Reflecting the drive and self-help outlook that dominated his thinking, Joe later said that Boston Latin "somehow seemed to make us all feel that if we could stick it out we were made of just a little bit better stuff than the fellows our age who were attending what we always thought were easier schools." Joe's self-assurance rested not simply on the cultural milieu in which he grew to manhood but also on the special affection that his parents had showered on him as their only son and that his two sisters gave him as an adored elder brother.

After Boston Latin, in 1908 Joe moved on to Harvard, which, in response to nationwide pressure for more institutional and political democracy and less concentration of wealth and power, was ostensibly committed to diversifying its student body. Yet old habits of social stratification remained as intense as they had been in the nineteenth century. Despite coming from Boston Latin, Joe had no claim on social status at Harvard, where the "golden boys" from the elite private schools such as Groton, St. Mark's, and St. Paul's, many of them the sons of millionaires, arrived at the college with servants and lived in luxurious residence halls with private baths, central heating, swimming pools, and squash courts. Joe joined the less affluent majority in drab, poorly heated dormitories with primitive plumbing. Characteristically, he had no sense of fixed inferiority from the sharp divisions he met at the university. Instead, he built a congenial social world on friendships with former Boston Latin classmates and ties to athletes, including some who came from the elite circle closed to someone of Joe's background. Within limits, Joe gained a measure of acceptability that spoke volumes about his potential for reaching heights not yet scaled by Boston's Irish. In his sophomore year he and his closest friends became class leaders, serving on the student council, organizing all major class events, and winning entrance into significant clubs such as the Institute of 1770, the Dickey, and Hasty Pudding, which conferred high status on their members. Yet admission to the innermost circle of student standing through membership in the most prestigious clubs, such as Porcellian and AD, was denied him. For such appointments, one's pedigree still made all the difference.

On the ball field Joe had his frustrations as well. After making the freshman baseball team, a number of injuries kept him from the varsity until his junior year, and then another injury consigned him to the bench through most of his senior year. Only when team captain and starting pitcher Charles McLaughlin asked the coach to put Joe in the final Yale game did he manage to earn a coveted varsity letter, and later stories that Joe's father had arranged the substitution by threatening to withhold a license McLaughlin wanted to operate a movie theater in Boston diminished the accomplishment of having gained the prize. Other accounts describing Joe's refusal to give McLaughlin the game ball, which Joe caught for the final out, further tarnished his standing with classmates.

Only in the realm of business did Joe have an unmitigated sense of triumph while at Harvard. During the summers of his junior and senior years, he and a friend bought a tour bus from a failing business. Boldly approaching Mayor Fitzgerald for a license to operate from a bus stand at South Station, the city's choice location for such an enterprise, Joe turned an unprofitable venture into a going concern. With Joe acting as tour guide and his partner driving, they converted a $600 investment into an amazing $10,000 gain over two years.

After graduating in 1912, Joe decided on a career in banking, the "basic profession" on which all other businesses depended, as Joe put it. This was not the product of study in a Harvard economics or business course. (He later enjoyed describing how he had to drop a banking and finance course because he did so poorly in it.) Instead, Joe came to this conclusion through keenly observing contemporary American financial practices. That spring, congressional hearings had described how the "astounding" power and influence of bankers over the national economy gave anyone ambitious for wealth on a grand scale a model to imitate. And Joe Kennedy was nothing if not ambitious. Whereas progressives turned the power of the bankers into a justification for democratizing reform, Joe saw it as a competitive challenge. He wanted to be the first Irish American to penetrate a preserve of some of Boston's wealthiest and most prominent old-school families.

Harvard degree in hand, Joe became a clerk in his father's Columbia Trust. There, during the summer of 1912, he worked as an apprentice under Alfred Wellington, the bank's thirty-nine-year-old treasurer. Recognizing that his pupil had uncommon talent and ambition, Wellington urged him to become a state bank examiner as a way to learn the essentials of the industry. After he passed the civil service exam and was placed on a list of potential examiners, Joe persuaded Mayor Fitzgerald to lobby the governor by pointing out that the state had no Irish Catholic bank examiners. The political pressure combined with Joe's merits to win him an appointment. For a year and a half he traveled around the state, learning the intricacies of the industry and impressing senior executives as a brilliant banker in the making.

As a consequence, when a downtown Boston bank threatened a takeover of Columbia Trust, Joe knew what he had to do to sustain the autonomy of one of the city's few Irish-owned financial institutions: He needed to raise enough money to outbid the rival bank, which had made an offer that a majority of stockholders wanted to accept. He also knew that appeals to local pride could strengthen his case. But money was key, and the president of the city's mainline Merchants National Bank, who saw a Columbia Trust run by Joe as a good risk, provided it.

Joe's success on fending off the takeover won him, at age twenty-five, the presidency of Columbia and taught him the advantages of good publicity. Joe's victory and appointment to Columbia's top job became the subject of local and national newspaper accounts that grew in the telling. Encouraging — or at least not discouraging — exaggeration with each reporter who came calling, Joe Kennedy went from being the youngest bank president in Boston to the youngest in the country to the youngest in the world, and the small neighborhood Columbia magically became not a local depository but a mainstay of the national banking industry. All the positive accounts nearly doubled Columbia's deposits and increased loans by more than 50 percent during the three years Joe served as president. He planned to be a millionaire by the age of thirty-five, he told a reporter. At this rate, it seemed possible.

* * *

IN THE SUMMER OF 1906, when Joe was eighteen and Rose sixteen, the two fell in love. Except for Rose, who saw Joe as a complement in every way to her life's ambitions, the Fitzgeralds considered the young man and his family a step down. And between 1906 and 1914 Honey Fitz had done all he could to discourage the courtship. He forbade Rose from accompanying Joe to a Boston Latin dance or the Harvard junior prom, and would not even allow Joe in the Fitzgerald house. And, of course, Rose's years in Holland and New York were partly aimed at keeping Joe and Rose apart.

But the attraction between Rose and Joe endured. They were smitten with each other. "I was never seriously interested in anyone else," Joe later said. Rose was more effusive: She remembered the young Joe Kennedy as "tall, thin, wiry, freckled," with blue eyes and red hair, "not dark red, orange red, or gold red, as some Irish have, but sandy blond with a lot of red lights in it." His "open and expressive" face conveyed a "youthful dignity," which bespoke self-reliance and self-respect. He was serious, "but he had a quick wit and a responsive sense of humor." His "big, spontaneous, and infectious grin . . . made everybody in sight want to smile, too." They arranged to meet at friends' homes, always with "a responsible adult on the premises." And in 1914 the romance blossomed into promises of marriage that Honey Fitz could no longer resist. Forced to abandon another run for the mayor's office by rumors of his affair with "Too-dles" Ryan, a beautiful cigarette girl, Fitzgerald had lost enough public standing to make Joe, the successful young banker, a worthy — or at least tolerable — addition to the Fitzgerald family. After a four-month engagement lasting from June to October 1914, Rose and Joe were married in a relatively subdued ceremony in William Cardinal O'Connell's private chapel, followed by a wedding breakfast for seventy-five guests at the Fitzgerald house. Fitz's diminished stature and a lingering reluctance about establishing ties with the Kennedys made Rose's matrimony a less celebrated event than her coming-out.

In November the young couple, Joe twenty-six and Rose twenty-four, moved into a comfortable two-and-a-half-story house on a quiet tree-lined street in Brookline, a Boston Protestant enclave made up of second- and third-generation lower-middle-class laborers and middle-class professionals. The seven-room Kennedy house on Beals Street, a gray wooden structure with clapboard siding, a large porch, sloping roof, and dormer windows, put Joe $6,500 in debt. The $2,000 personal loan and $4,500 mortgage was a heavy financial burden, but Joe could not imagine a bank president living in a rented apartment. Moreover, he had every confidence that he was on an ascending financial trajectory that would allow him to pay off his loans and entitled him and Rose to drive a new Model T Ford, which he also bought with borrowed funds. A seven-dollar-a-week maid who cooked, cleaned, laundered, and served meals was also considered appropriate to their lifestyle.

The following summer their first child was born at Nantasket Beach in Hull, Massachusetts, where Joe rented a house next to his in-laws. Two doctors, a trained nurse, and a housemaid attended the birth of the nearly ten-pound boy. Though speculation was rife that the child would be named after his maternal grandfather, John Fitzgerald, Joe insisted that his firstborn son be christened Joseph Patrick Jr. Despite Honey Fitz's disappointment at not having his first grandson named after him, he expected the boy to have an extraordinary future: "He *is* going to be President of the United States," the ex-mayor told a reporter, "his mother and father have already decided that he is going to Harvard, where he will play on the football and baseball teams and incidentally take all the scholastic honors. Then he's going to be a captain of industry until it's time for him to be President for two or three terms. Further than that has not been decided. He may act as mayor of Boston and governor of Massachusetts for a while on his way to the presidential chair." Fitzgerald's tongue-in-cheek description was the true word said in jest: ambition and unlimited confidence were central features of the Fitzgerald and Kennedy outlook.

Less than two years later, the birth of Rose and Joe's second child was greeted with less fanfare. John Fitzgerald Kennedy, a healthy boy named after his irrepressible grandfather, came into the world on the afternoon of May 29, 1917. Born in an upstairs bedroom in the Beals Street home with the same contingent of doctors and helpers as attended Joe Jr.'s birth, Jack, as the new baby was called, received his first notice in the press from a proud grandfather "wearing a pleased smile." Against the backdrop of an America that had entered the First World War, in which so many young men seemed certain to die, predictions about Jack's future were left unspoken.

THE SAME DAY Jack was born, his father was elected to the board of the Massachusetts Electric Company, making him at twenty-eight one of the youngest trustees of a major corporation in America. It was the start of Joe's meteoric climb in the business world, which, paradoxically, the war would serve. World War I, which millions of Americans saw as an idealistic crusade to end national conflicts and preserve democracy, elicited little enthusiasm from Joe. The idea of sacrificing his life or that of any of his generation seemed absurd. He was too cynical about human nature and Europe's traditional strife to believe that anything particularly good could come out of the fighting. Though this put him at odds with most of his Harvard friends, many of whom volunteered for military service, Joe saw nothing to be gained personally or nationally by enlisting. The war, he said, was a senseless slaughter that would ruin victor and vanquished alike. Looking down at Joe Jr. in his crib after hearing the news that tens of thousands of British troops had died in the unsuccessful 1916 Somme offensive, Joe told Rose, "This is the only happiness that lasts."

Joe's response to the First World War set a pattern that would repeat itself in other international crises faced by the United States. Whereas he was more often than not brilliantly insightful about domestic affairs, particularly the country's economic prospects, Joe consistently misjudged external developments. He understood world problems not on moral or political grounds but rather on how he felt they might inhibit his entrepreneurial ventures and, worse, cut short his life or, later, that of his sons. These personal fears would make him a lifelong isolationist.

Joe's rapid accumulation of wealth began with his departure from the bank and appointment as assistant general manager of Bethlehem Steel's Fore River shipbuilding plant in Quincy, Massachusetts. Though a salary of $15,000 a year was not enough to make Joe a wealthy man, his defense work assuaged his conscience about avoiding military service. More important, the experience, business contacts, and, most of all, the chance to demonstrate his effectiveness in managing a multimillion-dollar enterprise were invaluable in opening the way to bigger opportunities. During his eighteen months at Fore River, beginning in September 1917, Joe worked constantly, sometimes sleeping in his office for only one or two hours a night. Others worked as hard as Joe, but they lacked the inventiveness for efficiency and effectiveness he brought to every task. When he left Bethlehem in the summer of 1919, he received a bonus check "for services rendered at a time when no one else could have done what you did."

Joe converted his wartime success as a manager at Bethlehem

into a job as a stockbroker with the prestigious Boston firm of Hayden, Stone and Company. Believing that the greatest possibility to accumulate wealth in the coming decade would be in the stock market, Joe used his $10,000-a-year job to turn "inside" information into disciplined speculation that netted him nearly two million dollars over the next six years. Joe had made good on his promise to make his first million before he turned thirty-five, and after leaving Hayden, Stone in 1923 to open his own office, he made millions more trading stocks and in the movie industry, by buying first movie theaters in Massachusetts and then an English-owned Hollywood production company. After selling all his movie holdings in 1930, he made another fortune in the liquor trade when Prohibition ended in 1933.

Joe's growing wealth allowed him and Rose to have several more children. In 1918 Rosemary, a tragically retarded child, was the first of four successive daughters: Kathleen, born in 1920; Eunice, in 1921; and Patricia, in 1924. Three more children — Robert Francis, born in 1925; Jean Ann, in 1928; and Edward Moore, in 1932 — would make Joe and Rose the parents of nine children over a seventeen-year span. Joe and Rose took great joy in their large contingent; it distinguished them in an era when most upwardly mobile families had abandoned the tradition of having many children. Joe enjoyed telling the story of how he had missed Patricia's birth because of nonstop business negotiations in New York. On his return home, the five elder children, ranging in age from two to nine, greeted him at the train station with shouts: "Daddy! Daddy! Daddy! We've got another baby! We've got another baby!" Joe remembered other passengers on the platform probably thinking: "What that fellow there certainly doesn't need right now is *another baby*."

Joe loved that his large family made him and Rose an object of public attention. He also loved the message sent by his being able to provide lavishly for so large a brood. In 1921 he had moved the family into a larger Brookline house only a five-minute walk from Beals Street at the intersection of Naples and Abbotsford Roads. The twelve-room two-and-a-half-story house with a long enclosed front porch, where the Kennedy children could play, provided enough room not only for the whole family but also for a hospital-trained live-in nursemaid and a separate room for Rose, where she could have a small measure of privacy from the daily challenge of raising so many children. It was a challenge at which neither Joe nor Rose could claim unqualified success.

* * *

FOR ALL THE FAMILY'S WEALTH, status, and outward appearance of unity and good cheer, Joe and Rose had personal issues that strained their marriage and burdened their children. Rose's religious education, the intense requirements of her orthodoxy, left limited room for the joy her comfortable existence opened to her. For Joe, the harshness of the social slights he had suffered at Harvard, at their summer homes, and in the banking and business worlds from folks contemptuous of upstarts like him rankled throughout his life and drained some of the pleasure from his rise to prominence.

To be sure, they were a well-matched couple — similar backgrounds, similar aspirations for wealth and prominence — but they were also decidedly different: complementary opposites. Rose was the consummate conformist. She meticulously followed the social mores of the day, whether set down by her church or by the larger society around her. Joe, too, was a great conformist — striving to achieve a kind of universal acceptability — but he also prided himself on being unconventional: bolder, more adventurous than everyone else, and, if need be, a rule breaker. Innovation, thinking imaginatively, would be a hallmark of his business career and a trait he passed along to a few — though not all — of his children.

Joe's independence and willingness to defy accepted standards partly expressed itself in compulsive womanizing. Speculation abounds that Rose's unresponsiveness to a man with normal appetites drove him into the arms of chorus girls, starlets, and other casual lovers. A mainstay of Kennedy family biographies is the story of Joe teasing Rose in front of friends about her sexual inhibitions. "Now listen, Rosie," he would say. "This idea of yours that there is no romance outside of procreation is simply wrong. It was not part of our contract at the altar, the priest never said that and the books don't argue that. And if you don't open your mind on this, I'm going to tell the priest on you." But Rose apparently remained unresponsive to Joe's desires. According to one family friend, after their last child was born in 1932, Rose declared, "No more sex," and moved into a separate bedroom.

But even if Rose had not denied him her favors, Joe would have been a compulsive philanderer. For someone who needed to win, win, win, who could never be content with great success in one arena, who spent his life seeking new challenges in business — banking, liquor, movies, stocks, real estate — and politics, it is difficult to imagine that he would have been content with one woman.

Joe made little effort to hide his womanizing. In 1921, for example, he brazenly wrote a theatrical manager in New York: "I hope you will have all the good looking girls in your company looking forward with anticipation to meeting the high Irish of Boston because I have a gang around me that must be fed on wild meat." A political reporter who knew Joe thought that for him women "were another thing that a rich man had — like caviar. It wasn't sex, it was part of the image . . . his idea of manliness." Joe even brought mistresses into the Kennedy home, the young women eating meals with the family and becoming part of the daily household routine. Betty Spalding, the wife of one of Jack's closest friends, who witnessed the process, exclaimed, "And the old man — having his mistresses there at the house for lunch and supper! I couldn't understand it! It was unheard of." Joe served propriety by describing the young women to visitors as friends of his daughters.

But there were some limits. An affair with movie actress Gloria Swanson in the late 1920s almost broke up the Kennedy marriage. The romance was an open secret, with one Boston newspaper reporting that Joe's phone calls to Gloria in California from New York amounted to "the largest private telephone bill in the nation during the year 1929," even though Joe had taken precautions to ensure that the affair was never so obvious that Rose would be unable to deny its existence to herself and others. But there is evidence that Honey Fitz argued with Joe over the affair, threatening to tell Rose if Joe did not end it. Stubbornly, Joe refused, warning his father-in-law that he might then divorce Rose and marry Gloria. Though Joe eventually broke off the relationship with Swanson when he left the movie industry in 1929–30, it scarred the Kennedy household and made for difficulties with the children that never disappeared.

Like Joe, Rose was an imperfect parent. Part of her difficulty was Joe's insistence that she confine herself to "women's work" in the family. Generally, she played the good wife and repressed her irritation at being inhibited by her overbearing husband. "Your father again has restricted my activities and thinks the little woman should confine herself to the home," she complained to the children in February 1942. Rose was also unhappy with Joe's many absences attending to business in New York and California, which threw the burden of child rearing largely on her. Despite a large retinue of household help, she was under constant pressure to attend to the needs of so many small children during repeated pregnancies. Indeed, between 1914 and 1932, the eighteen years after she and Joe married, Rose was with child nearly 40 percent of the time. Moreover, a sense of isolation from her previously glamorous life as the mayor's favorite daughter and a prominent Boston debutante joined with Joe's philandering to drive her into a brief separation from him early in 1920. Pregnant with her fourth child and exhausted by mothering three others between the ages of one and five, she returned to her father's home for three weeks before he insisted that she "go back where you belong." Moved by her father's insistence that she make her marriage work, as well as her attendance at a religious retreat on the obligations of a Catholic wife and mother, Rose returned to her Brookline house with a renewed determination to succeed at the job of building a successful family.

As part of an agreement with Joe on how to sustain their marriage and serve the children's well-being, Rose regularly traveled around the United States and abroad as a way to free her from constant household demands. In the mid-thirties, she made seventeen trips to Europe, where she shopped for the latest fashions and enjoyed sight-seeing excursions. Assured that Joe, who arranged to be at home during her absences, or at least close enough in case of an emergency, would attend to the children, Rose took special pleasure in the freedom and stimulation reminiscent of her premarital travels. During their respective separations from the family, Rose and Joe agreed that neither would burden the other with current family problems. Joe, for example, never reported an outbreak of measles in the household while Rose was away in California for six weeks. "He didn't want to worry me and perhaps cause me to cancel part of my trip," Rose recalled. Similarly, when Joe called from California during one of his frequent trips to Hollywood, Rose told him nothing about a car accident that had her lying down with "a good-sized gash in my forehead. . . . I spoke naturally, gave him news of the children and told him what a fine day it was: a perfect day for golf. Then I drove to the hospital where the doctor took five stitches in my forehead." It was an accommodation that allowed them to keep their family intact and enjoy a privileged life. But it never eliminated the many difficulties that would belie the picture of a well-adjusted, happy family.

CHAPTER 2

Privileged Youth

*Youth [is] not a time of life but a state of mind . . .
a predominance of courage over timidity, of the appetite
for adventure over the love of ease.*

— Robert F. Kennedy (1966), borrowing from
Samuel Ullman, "Youth" (1934)

AS HE GREW UP, Jack Kennedy came to understand that being the second son of one of America's richest and most famous families set him apart from the many other privileged youths he knew. The Cabots, Lodges, and Saltonstalls were better-known Boston clans; the Carnegies, Rockefellers, and Vanderbilts were wealthier; and the Adamses, Roosevelts, and Tafts were more prominent as political dynasties. But the Kennedys were also a recognizable national force, a next generation ready to take on the world. And if Joe Kennedy were ever to become president, *Life* magazine said in 1938, his appealing children would have played a significant part. "His bouncing offspring make the most politically ingratiating family since Theodore Roosevelt's." They were a symbol of hope to the country's millions of ethnics and its more established middle class who remained wedded to the belief — even in the worst of economic times — that anyone with exceptional talent and drive could still realize material opulence and public eminence exceeding the ordinary promise of American life.

JACK'S FIRST MEMORIES from 1922–23 were associated with the Naples Road house and attendance at the local public school, Edward Devotion. In 1924, Joe Jr., now nine, and Jack, age seven, were sent to a local private school, Dexter, where — unlike Devotion, which had shorter hours — they would be supervised from 8:15 in the morning until 4:45 in the afternoon. This schedule freed Rose to give more attention to Rosemary, whose retardation mandated home tutoring. The boy's mother also saw Dexter as a guard against the mischief — the "state of quixotic disgrace," she called it — for which Joe Jr. and Jack had an obvious affinity. To their father, Dexter, the successor to the discontinued lower school of the prestigious Noble and Greenough School, would bring his sons together with their Beacon Hill counterparts, the offspring of *Social Register* families such as the Storrows, Saltonstalls, and Bundys.

Jack's first ten years were filled with memories of Grandpa Fitz taking him and Joe Jr. to Red Sox games, boating in Boston's Public Garden, or on the campaign circuit around Boston in 1922, when the old man made a failed bid for governor. There were also the childhood illnesses from bronchitis, chicken pox, German measles, measles, mumps, scarlet fever, and whooping cough that confined him to bed, where he learned the pleasure of being read to by Rose or reading on his own about the adventures of Sinbad the Sailor, Peter Pan, and Black Beauty. His favorites were *Billy Whiskers* — the escapades of a billy goat that traveled the world and "which Jack found vastly interesting" — and Reddy Fox, one of various animals "mixed up in a series of simple, but . . . exciting adventures." Jack was also drawn to the stories of adventure and chivalry in Sir Walter Scott's Waverley novels, to biographies of prominent characters, and to histories, "so long as they had flair, action, and color," Rose recalled. He read and reread *King Arthur and the Round Table*.

Young Jack regularly took morning walks with Rose and one or two of his siblings to the local shopping area, the five-and-ten, and the parish church, which Rose explained was not only for Sunday or special holidays but part of a good Catholic's daily life. And there were the summers away from Boston, first at Cohasset, a Protestant enclave on the South Shore, where the family met a wall of social hostility in 1922, including Joe's exclusion from membership in the town's country club, then at the Cape Cod villages of Craigville Beach in 1924 and Hyannis Port, beginning in 1926, both more welcoming. Traveling to the Cape in Joe's chauffeur-driven Rolls-Royce, the Kennedys rented a two-and-a-half-acre estate overlooking the Hyannis Port harbor. There, Jack learned to swim and enjoy the outdoor activities that became a constant in the family's life.

"It was an easy, prosperous life, supervised by maids and nurses, with more and more younger sisters to boss and to play with," Jack told his 1960 campaign biographer, James MacGregor Burns. When later asked if anything really bothered him as a child, Jack could only think of his competition with Joe. Their games and roughhousing on the front porch occasionally descended into hostilities that disrupted their strong mutual attachment. "He had a pugnacious personality," Jack said about his brother. "Later on it smoothed out, but it was a problem in my boyhood." A young woman Jack dated as a teenager remembered that whenever they were alone, Jack would talk about his brother. "He talked about him all the time: 'Joe plays football better, Joe dances better, Joe is getting better grades.' Joe just kind of overshadowed him in everything."

Joe Jr., bigger and stronger than Jack, bullied him, and fights between the two — often fierce wrestling matches — terrified younger brother Bobby and their sisters. Jack particularly remembered a bicycle race Joe suggested. They sped around the block in opposite directions, meeting head-on in front of their house. Never willing to concede superiority to the other, neither backed off from a collision that left Joe unhurt and Jack nursing twenty-eight stitches. Joe Jr. patiently instructed all his younger siblings in the rules and techniques of various games, except for Jack. A football handoff became an opportunity to slam the ball into Jack's stomach "and walk away laughing as his younger brother lay doubled up in pain." Jack, who refused to be intimidated, developed a hit-and-run style of attack, provoking Joe into unsuccessful chases that turned Jack's flight into a kind of triumph.

But for all the tensions, Jack thought Joe hung the moon. When Joe went to summer camp in 1926, the nine-year-old Jack briefly enjoyed his temporary elevation to eldest sibling. But as Joe Sr. noted, Jack was soon pining for his brother's return and made his father promise that he could accompany Joe Jr. the following summer. Jack later remembered that there was no one he would "rather have spent an evening or played golf or in fact done anything [with]." Still, a rivalry remained. In November 1929, when Joe Jr. returned home for Thanksgiving from his first term at boarding school, Jack took special pleasure in recording his triumphs over his dominant brother. "When Joe came home he was telling me how strong he was and how tough," Jack wrote their father. "The first thing he did to show me how tough he was to get sick so that he could not have any Thanksgiving dinner. Manly youth. He was then going to show me how to Indian wrestle. I then threw him over on his neck." Jack also crowed over the paddling the sixth formers (the seniors) at the school gave Joe, who "was all blisters. . . . What I wouldn't have given to be a sixth former."

The backdrop for all this was no longer Brookline. In September 1927, when Jack was ten, the family had moved to Riverdale, New York, a rural Bronx suburb of Manhattan. Joe had become a force in the film industry, and his ventures took him between New York and Los Angeles, so there were sensible business reasons for the relocation.

But Joe's frustration with Boston's social barriers had as much to do with the move to New York as convenience. Boston "was no place to bring up Irish Catholic children," Joe later told a reporter. "I didn't want them to go through what I had to go through when I was growing up there." But unwilling to completely sever ties to the region that both he and Rose cherished, Joe bought the Hyannis Port estate they had been renting, ensuring that the family would continue to spend its summers on the Cape.

The move to New York was not without strain. Despite being transported in a private railway car and moving into a thirteen-room house previously owned by former Secretary of State Charles Evans Hughes in a lovely wooded area overlooking the Hudson River, Rose remembered the change as "a blow in the stomach. For months I would wake up in our new house in New York and feel a terrible sense of loss." Her distance from familiar surroundings, friends, and family made for a painful transition. The ancestors in the North End tenements would have puzzled over her hardship. A second move in 1929 into a mansion on six acres in the village community of Bronxville, a few miles north of Riverdale, where the average per capita income of its few thousand residents was among the highest in the country, was more to Rose's liking.

Jack had quickly settled into the private Riverdale Country Day School, where he excelled in his studies in the fourth and fifth grades. In the sixth grade, however, when Joe Jr. went to the Choate boarding school in Wallingford, Connecticut, Jack's work suffered, falling to a "creditable" 75, a February 1930 report stated. Despite his undistinguished school record, or possibly because of it, Joe and Rose decided to send Jack to boarding school as well. But instead of Choate, Rose enrolled Jack in the Canterbury School in New Milford,

Connecticut, an exclusive Catholic academy staffed by fourteen Catholic teachers for ninety-two students. Of the twenty-one students in the school's 1930 graduating class going to college, seven went to Yale, seven to Princeton, and one to Harvard.

Although attending a boarding school marked Jack as a privileged child, he did not appreciate being sent so far away from home. (It would not be the last time Jack felt the burdens of privilege.) "It's a pretty good place," he wrote a relative, and "the swimming pool is great," but he saw little else to recommend the school. He was "pretty homesick the first night" and at other times thereafter. The football team looked "pretty bad." Worse, "you have a whole lot of religion and the studies are pretty hard. The only time you can get out of here is to see the Harvard-Yale and the Army-Yale [games]. This place is freezing at night and pretty cold in the daytime." His attendance at chapel every morning and evening would make him "quite pius [sic] I guess when I get home," he grudgingly told Rose. He also had his share of problems with his classes. English, math, and history were fine, but he struggled with science and especially Latin, which drove his average down to a 77. "In fact his average should be well in the 80's," the headmaster recorded. Jack admitted to his mother that he was "doing a little worrying about my studies because what he [the headmaster] said about me starting of[f] great and then going down sunk in."

In the fall of 1930, when he was thirteen and a half, Jack was more interested in current events and sports than in any of his studies. Football, basketball, hockey, squash, skating, and sledding were Jack's first priorities, but feeling closed off in the cloistered world of a Catholic academy made him increasingly eager to keep up with the state of the world. He wrote Joe from Canterbury: "Please send me the Litary [sic] Digest, because I did not know about the Market Slump until a long time after, or a paper. Please send me some golf balls." A missionary's talk one morning at mass about India impressed Jack as "one of the most interesting talks that I ever heard." It was all an early manifestation of what his later associate Theodore C. Sorensen described as "a desire to enjoy the world and a desire to improve it; and these two desires, particularly in the years preceding 1953, had sometimes been in conflict."

In 1930, however, pleasure seeking clearly stood first. In 1960, when *Time* journalist Hugh Sidey asked Jack, "What do you remember about the Great Depression?" he replied, "I have no first-hand knowledge of the depression. My family had one of the great fortunes of the world and it was worth more than ever then. We had bigger houses, more servants, we traveled more. About the only thing that I saw directly was when my father hired some extra gardeners just to give them a job so they could eat. I really did not learn about the depression until I read about it at Harvard."

He was insulated by money but also by nurture. Charles Spalding, one of Jack's close childhood friends, who spent weekends and holidays with the family, noted, "You watched these people go through their lives and just had a feeling that they existed outside the usual laws of nature; that there was no other group so handsome, so engaged. There was endless action . . . endless talk . . . endless competition, people drawing each other out and pushing each other to greater lengths. It was as simple as this: the Kennedys had a feeling of being heightened and it rubbed off on the people who came in contact with them. They were a unit. I remember thinking to myself that there couldn't be another group quite like this one."

If Jack understood that he was part of an unusual family, it also bred a certain arrogance. Joe Sr. could be abrupt and unfriendly, even disdainful of anyone he considered unworthy of his attention, especially those who did not show him proper regard. He saw some of this as payback for the humiliating slights inflicted on him for being an Irish Catholic.

Most victims of Joe's disdain were not ready to forgive and forget. They saw Joe and the family as pretentious and demanding. At Cape Cod, for example, where renovations had turned the original cottage on the Kennedy property into a house with fourteen bedrooms, nine baths, a basement theater wired to show talking pictures, and an outdoor tennis court, Joe had a reputation as "opinionated," "hard as nails," and "an impossible man to work for." The family was notorious for its casualness about paying its bills or carrying cash to meet obligations in a timely fashion. Shopkeepers and gas station attendants lost patience with giving the family credit and having to dun servants for payment. "We're Kennedys," a carful of kids told a gas station owner who refused to accept a promise to pay later for a fill-up. A call to the Kennedy compound brought a chauffeur with a can of gasoline to get the car back to the estate.

Jack came to his maturity with an almost studied indifference to money. He never carried much, if any, cash. Why would someone so well-off need currency to pay for anything? Everyone knew or should have known that he was good for his debts, be it a restaurant check, a clothing bill, or a hotel tab. He was always asking friends to pick up the bill, not because he expected them to pay but because his handlers, his father's moneymen, would square accounts later. And they usually did, though occasionally some of Jack's creditors would have to make embarrassing requests for payment of loans or debts that he had overlooked.

The self-indulgence of the Kennedy children was often on public display. Stepping off one of the Kennedy boats onto the Hyannis Port pier, the children would shed articles of clothing as they marched along, expecting "that someone else would pick up after them." Kennedy maids particularly complained about Jack's slovenliness: "the wet towels in a heap on the floor, the tangle of ties in one corner, the bureau drawers turned over and emptied in the middle of the bed in a hurried search for some wanted item."

The children also had little sense of being confined to a place and time. One of Jack's childhood friends remembered them this way: "They really didn't have a real home with their own rooms where they had pictures on the walls or memorabilia on the shelves but would rather come home for holidays from their boarding schools and find whatever room was available. . . . 'Which room do I have this time?'" Jack would ask his mother. He did not feel he had to live by the ordinary rules governing everyone else. He was always arriving late for meals and classes, setting his own pace, taking the less-traveled path; he was his father's son. With the Kennedys, Jack's friend recalled, "life speeded up."

There was also a remarkable sense of loyalty. Joe taught his children, particularly Jack and Joe Jr., to rely on family unity as a shield against competitors and opponents. On a crossing to Europe in 1935, Joe called Jack away from a game of deck tennis to meet Lawrence Fisher, one of the brothers who had gained fame and fortune designing autos for General Motors. "Jack, I sent for you because I want you to meet Mr. Lawrence Fisher, one of the famous Fisher Body family. I wanted you to see what success brothers have who stick together." It was a lesson that none of the Kennedy children ever forgot. Once, when Joe Jr. and Jack argued with each other and one of Jack's friends tried to take his side, Jack turned on him angrily, saying, "Mind your own business! Keep out of it! I'm talking to Joe, not you!"

* * *

AFTER A YEAR at Canterbury School, Jack was not keen to return, wishing instead to follow Joe Jr. to Choate. Joe acquiesced to his son's request, and in September 1931 Jack joined his brother at the storied New England academy. Joe and Rose were less interested in the distinctive education the boys would receive than in the chance to expose them to the country's power brokers, or at least the sons of America's most influential families. Choate was not quite on a par with the older, more elite prep schools of Andover, Exeter, St. Mark's, or St. Paul's, but it was distinctive enough — part of a wave of boys' boarding schools founded in the 1880s and 1890s. Association with the best and the brightest, Joe and Rose believed, would ultimately come at Harvard, but the prelude to admission there was an education at a school like Choate. As Jack would soon learn, membership in the world of privilege carried lifelong responsibilities that would both attract and repel him.

An IQ of 119 and strong scores on the English and algebra parts of Jack's Choate entrance exams had helped ease his admission, though the desire to have Jack Kennedy at the school was decidedly mutual. Choate, which had a keen interest in the sons of a family so wealthy and, by 1930, publicly visible, had in fact courted first Joe's and then Jack's attendance. Jack had actually failed the Latin part of Choate's entrance exam in the spring of 1931, but the school was more than happy to let him retake the test after some summer tutoring. And even if he did not measure up on his next Latin test, Choate intended to enroll him in the fall term; the only question was whether he would start "a straight Third Form schedule," which he did when he met the Latin requirement in October.

The difficult transition from teenager to young adult characterized Jack's four years at Choate. Not the least of his difficulties was a series of medical problems that baffled his doctors and tested his patience. From the time he was three, not a year passed without one physical affliction or another. Three months before his third birthday, he came down with a virulent case of scarlet fever. A highly contagious and life-threatening illness for so small a child, he had to be hospitalized for two months, followed by two weeks in a Maine sanatorium. To get Jack proper care at the Boston medical center best prepared to treat the disease, Joe had to exert all his influence, including that of his father-in-law. With 600 local children suffering from scarlet fever and only 125 beds available at Boston City

Hospital, arranging Jack's admission was no small feat. But when it came to medical attention for his children, Joe was as aggressive as in any of his business dealings: He not only got Jack into the hospital but also ensured that one of the country's leading authorities on contagious diseases would care for him. During the 1920s, Jack's many childhood maladies included chicken pox and ear infections. They compelled him to spend a considerable amount of time in bed or at least indoors, convalescing.

At Canterbury in the fall of 1930, at age thirteen, he began to suffer from an undiagnosed illness that restricted his activities. Between October and December he lost nearly six pounds, felt "pretty tired," and did not grow appropriately. One doctor attributed it to a lack of milk in his diet, but the diagnosis failed to explain why during a chapel service he felt "sick dizzy and weak. I just about fainted, and everything began to get black so I went out and then I fell and Mr. Hume [the headmaster] caught me. I am O.K. now," he declared bravely in a letter to his father. In April 1931, he collapsed with abdominal pains, and the surgeon who examined him concluded that it was appendicitis and that an operation was necessary at the nearby Danbury Hospital. Later notes on Jack's school attendance describe him as "probably very homesick during his time at Canterbury. He wrote a great deal of letters home. In May, he left school with appendicitis and did not return." But having completed his year's work with the help of a tutor at home, he was able to move on to Choate in the fall.

There, his medical problems became more pronounced. Several confinements in the infirmary marked his first year at the school. In November, "a mild cold" cost him two nights in the hospital, and when he went home for Thanksgiving, Joe remarked on how thin he looked. In January, he was confined again for "a cold," which did not clear up quickly, turned in to "quite a cough," and kept him in the infirmary for more than a week. Although administered regular doses of cod liver oil and enrolled in a bodybuilding class, his weight remained at only 117 pounds — less than robust for a fourteen-and-a-half-year-old boy — and he continued to suffer fatigue. In April, he had to return to the infirmary because of another cold, swollen glands, and what was described as an abnormal urine sample.

More puzzling medical problems punctuated Jack's second year at Choate. In January and February 1933, "flu-like symptoms" plagued him, as well as almost constant pain in his knees. "Jack's winter term sounded like a hospital report," a fiftieth-anniversary remembrance of his attendance at the school recounted, "with correspondence flying back and forth between Rose Kennedy and Clara St. John [the headmaster's wife]. Again, eyes, ears, teeth, knees, arches, from the top of his head to the tip of his toes, Jack needed attention." X rays showed no pathology in his knees, and so his doctor attributed his difficulties to growing pains and recommended exercises and "built-up" shoes.

Matters got worse the following year. Over the summer of 1933, after he had turned sixteen, he gained no weight. It precluded him from playing football, but more important, it stimulated fresh concerns about his health, which now went into a sharp decline in January and February 1934. "We are still puzzled as to the cause of Jack's trouble," Clara St. John wrote Rose early in February. "He didn't look at all well when he came back after Christmas, but apparently had improved steadily since then." But at the end of January he became very sick and had to be rushed by ambulance to New Haven Hospital for observation. Mrs. St. John told Jack: "I hope with all my heart that the doctors will find out in the shortest possible order what is making the trouble, and will clear it out of the way even quicker than that." His symptoms were a bad case of hives and weight loss; but the doctors now feared that he had life-threatening leukemia and began taking regular blood counts. "It seems that I was much sicker than I thought I was," Jack wrote classmate LeMoyne Billings after he got out of the hospital, "and am supposed to be dead, so I am developing a limp and a hollow cough." He complained that his rectum was "plenty red after the hospital. Yours would be red too if you had shoved every thing from rubber tubes to iron pipes up it. When I crap I don't even feel it because it's so big." By March, Jack's symptoms had largely disappeared, but his doctors remained uncertain about the cause of his difficulties.

In addition to his illnesses, Jack now struggled with normal adolescent problems about identity and sexuality, as well as having to live in the shadow of a highly successful and favored elder brother. By the time Jack arrived at Choate, Joe Jr. had established himself as, in the words of the headmaster's wife, "one of the 'big boys' of the school on whom we are going to depend." Rose had already signaled George St. John, the headmaster, that Jack was not Joe Jr. — unlike Joe Jr., Jack did not acclimate easily to either academic or social regimens. Mindful of their concern, the headmaster told Joe, "Jack sits at a nearby table in the Dining Hall where I look him in the eye three times a day, and he is fine."

But Joe Jr.'s success on the playing fields and in the classroom took its toll on Jack. A tall, skinny boy of fourteen, whom his classmates called Rat Face because of his thin, narrow visage, Jack was too slight to gain distinction in athletics, which he badly wanted. When his brother won the school's coveted Harvard Trophy at his graduation in 1933, an award to the student who best combined scholarship and sportsmanship, it confirmed in Jack the feeling that he could never win the degree of approval his parents — and, it seemed, everyone else — lavished on his elder brother. Jack told Billings that he believed he was as intelligent as his brother, and probably even as good an athlete, but he had little confidence that his family would ever see him as surpassing Joe Jr.

In addition to feeling too much in his brother's shadow, Jack wrestled with the strains of uncommonly high parental expectations, pressures to live up to "Kennedy standards," to stand out not just from the crowd but from the best of the best. The overt message, especially from his father, was "second best will never do." Whether in athletics, academics, or social standing, there was an insistent demand that the Kennedy children, especially the boys, reach the top rung. The lesson Jack now learned was that privilege had its advantages and pleasures, but it also had its demands and drawbacks. As one Kennedy family biographer said: "[Joe] stressed to his children the importance of winning at any cost and the pleasures of coming in first. As his own heroes were not poets or artists but men of action, he took it for granted that his children too wanted public success. . . . All too often, his understanding about their desires . . . were fruits of *his* experience and *his* dreams, not necessarily theirs."

Joe Jr., with a robust constitution, a temperament much like his father's, and a readiness to follow his lead, was Joe's favorite. Yet despite this and whatever Jack's antagonism toward Joe, an understanding that his father would do anything for him, that his overpowering dad was motivated by an intense desire to ensure his well-being, established surpassing lifelong ties of affection. Jack also identified with Joe's iconoclasm, with his talent for seeing opportunities conventional businessmen missed, making independent judgments at variance with prevailing wisdom, and setting social standards that ignored accepted rules for married life.

For all the love and attention he lavished on his second son, Joe resented the many medical problems that plagued Jack's early life. "Jack was sick all the time," one of his friends recalled, "and the old man could be an asshole around his kids." In the late 1940s, during a visit to the Kennedys' Palm Beach, Florida, home, the friend, Jack, and a date bade Joe good night before going out to a movie. Joe snidely told Jack's girlfriend: "Why don't you get a live one?" Angered by the unkind reference to Jack's poor health, afterward the friend made a disparaging remark about Joe. But Jack defended his father: "Everybody wants to knock his jock off," he said, "but he made the whole thing possible."

It was typical of Jack to see the best in people and outwardly not take umbrage at Joe's occasional hostility toward him for his physical limitations. But Joe's hectoring did make Jack wonder whether the pressure was worth the many privileges his father's wealth and status conferred on him. "We all have our fathers," Jack said resignedly to a friend complaining about his parent. At a minimum, Joe's allusion to Jack's health problems struck a painful chord. Jack was self-conscious about his physical problems and worked hard to overcome and ignore them. One friend said, "[Jack's] very frame as a light, thin person, his proneness to injury of all kinds, his back, his sickness, which he wouldn't ever talk about . . . he was heartily ashamed of them, they were a mark of effeminacy, of weakness, which he wouldn't acknowledge." When this friend upbraided Jack for being too concerned about improving his appearance by getting a tan, Jack replied, "Well, . . . it's not only that I want to look that way, but it makes me feel that way. It gives me confidence, it makes me feel healthy. It makes me feel strong, healthy, attractive."

Within sharply delineated bounds, Jack rebelled against school and, indirectly, parental authority at Choate. His schoolwork continued to be uneven — strong in English and history, in which he had substantial interest, and mediocre at best in languages, which required the sort of routine discipline he found difficult to maintain. His low grades in Latin and French compelled him to attend summer session in 1932, at the end of his freshman year. Rose later remarked on how concerned they were about Jack's health during his Choate years. But "what concerned us as much or more was his lack of diligence in his studies; or, let us say, lack of 'fight' in trying to do well in those subjects that didn't happen to interest him. . . . Choate had a highly 'structured' set of rules, traditions, and expectations into which a boy was supposed to fit; and if he didn't, there was little or no 'permissiveness.' Joe Jr. had no trouble at all operating within this system; it suited his temperament. But Jack couldn't or wouldn't conform. He did pretty much what he wanted, rather than what the school wanted of him."

During his years at Choate, Jack remained more interested in contemporary affairs than in his classes. But although he "conspicuously failed to open his schoolbooks," Choate's headmaster recalled, he "was the best informed boy of his year." One classmate remembered that Jack was able to answer between 50 and 60 percent of the questions on the popular radio quiz show *Information, Please,* while he himself could only get about 10 percent of them right. Jack's limited grasp of the Great Depression suggests that he did not have much interest in economic affairs, but he became a regular subscriber to the *New York Times,* reading it, or at least glancing at it, every morning. He also began a lifelong fascination with the writings of Winston Churchill.

Although Jack's academic work was good enough in his junior and senior years to allow him to graduate in the middle of his class, and although he enjoyed considerable popularity among his peers, winning designation from his senior classmates as the "most likely to succeed," he still refused to fit in. "I'd like to take the responsibility for Jack's constant lack of neatness about his room and person, since he lived with me for two years," Jack's housemaster wrote. "But in the matter of neatness . . . I must confess to failure." Jack's sloppiness was seen as symbolic of his disorderliness "in almost all of his organization projects. Jack studies at the last minute, keeps appointments late, has little sense of material value, and can seldom locate his possessions."

In November 1933, Joe Sr. wrote George St. John: "I can't tell you how unhappy I was in seeing and talking with Jack. He seems to lack entirely a sense of responsibility. His happy-go-lucky manner with a degree of indifference does not portend well for his future development." Joe urged his eldest son to help in any way he could to encourage Jack's commitment to his work. Joe worried that Jack might end up as a ne'er-do-well son ruined by an indulged childhood. "We have possibly contributed as much as anybody in spoiling him by having secretaries and maids following him to see that he does what he should do," Joe told Choate's assistant headmaster.

In his final year at Choate, Jack pushed the school's rules to the limit. Organizing a Muckers Club, the headmaster's term for Choate boys who defied the rules and did not meet their obligations to the school, Jack and several of his friends aimed to "put over festivities in our own little way and to buck the system more effectively."

LeMoyne Billings and Ralph (Rip) Horton, Jack's two closest friends, were "co-conspirators" in the "rebellion." Jack and Billings had a natural affinity for each other. Both had more successful elder brothers who had set seemingly insurmountable standards at Choate for their younger siblings. Like Jack, Lem loved practical jokes and was irreverent about the school's many rules regulating their daily lives. Billings, the son of a Pittsburgh physician, and Horton, the child of a wealthy New York dairy business family, deferred to Jack, who enjoyed higher social standing and, like his father, insisted on being the leader.

Although the Muckers represented no more than a small rebellion on Jack's part, in the cloistered atmosphere of a rural private school, where such defiance took on a larger meaning, St. John responded angrily. He "let loose" at the thirteen club members in chapel, naming names and denouncing their corruption of the school's morals and integrity. Privately, he described the Muckers as "a colossally selfish, pleasure loving, unperceptive group — in general opposed to the hardworking, solid people in the school, whether masters or boys." He wired Joe Kennedy to come "for a conference with Jack and us which we think a necessity." Choate English teacher Harold Tinker later admitted that St. John enjoyed the thought of humiliating Jack's father: St. John was anti-Catholic — something he made quite clear at faculty meetings — and "resented having Catholics at his school," especially any related to someone as rich and prominent as Joe Kennedy. But St. John also understood that the well-being of the school partly depended on giving no overt expression to his bias. Though Jack had no evidence that the head-master would act on his anti-Catholicism, he nevertheless feared that St. John might expel him and destroy whatever approval he still enjoyed from his parents. The episode, however, blew over when Jack promised to disband the club and take his punishment of a delayed Easter vacation.

In acting as he had, Jack played out several impulses that dominated his early life. He tested the rules so boldly at Choate because he believed he could get away with it. As the son of a wealthy and prominent family — Joe had become the chairman of Franklin Roosevelt's Securities and Exchange Commission in the summer of 1934 — Jack felt some invulnerability to St. John's strictures. But he also understood that the limits to what St. John would allow might be influenced by Jack's own powers to ingratiate himself with both his elders and his peers. He was very well liked by most of the other boys at the school, as their willingness to vote him most likely to succeed demonstrates. St. John himself readily acknowledged that Jack had a winning way that endeared him to most everyone: "In any school he would have got away with some things, just on his smile. He was a very likeable person, very lovable." Writing Joe in November 1933, St. John concluded that "the longer I live and work with him and the more I talk with him, the more confidence I have in him. I would be willing to bet anything that within two years you will be as proud of Jack as you are now of Joe." In another letter that month, St. John went so far as to declare: "I never saw a boy with as many fine qualities as Jack has, that didn't come out right . . . in the end." The following February, during a health crisis Jack weathered, St. John told Joe, "Jack is one of the best people that ever lived — one of the most able and interesting. I could go on about Jack!" He may not have liked Catholics, but he certainly liked this Catholic, a testament to Jack's remarkable charm.

In his limited rebellion at Choate, Jack was also playing out a trait Joe Sr. had consciously worked to instill in his children. Joe was not entirely blind to the fact that he was an overbearing, demanding, insistent character who dominated almost everyone and everything he touched. Because he sensed how destructive this could be to his offspring, especially the boys, he made a point of encouraging a measure of independence and even irreverence. Visitors to the Kennedy home who watched Joe's interactions with Joe Jr. and Jack remembered how he would push them to argue their own point of view, make up their own minds, and never slavishly follow accepted wisdom. Lem Billings recalled that mealtime conversations at the Kennedys' never consisted of small talk. Joe Sr. "never lectured. He would encourage them [the children] completely to disagree with him, and of course they did disagree with him. Mr. Kennedy is, I'd say, far right of his children, and yet he certainly didn't try to influence them that way."

And perhaps if Joe Sr. saw in his eldest son what could be, he saw in Jack more who he was. When St. John interrupted a conversation between him, Jack, and Joe to take a phone call, Joe leaned over and whispered to Jack, "My God, my son, you sure didn't inherit your father's directness or his reputation for using bad language. If that crazy Mucker's Club had been mine, you can be sure it wouldn't have started with an M!" Joe's irreverence was not lost on Jack, who inscribed a graduation photo to one of the other leading lights in the club, "To Boss Tweed from Honest Abe, may we room together at Sing Sing."

When Joe Jr. graduated from Choate, his father sent him to study in England for a year with Harold Laski, a prominent socialist academic. Rose considered this "a little wild and even dangerous," but Joe, convinced it would encourage greater independence and sharpen his son's ability to argue the case for a more conservative outlook, ignored his wife's concern. And when Joe Jr. returned after a summer trip to Russia with Laski and described the advantages of socialism over capitalism, Joe told Rose, "If I were their age I would probably believe what they believe, but I am of a different background and must voice my beliefs." Joe made it clear that he cared much less about their different outlooks than that they had reached independent judgments.

St. John saw even more of this sort of constructed independence in Jack's behavior. "Jack has a clever, individualist mind," he told Joe. "It is a harder mind to put in harness than Joe [Jr.]'s. . . . When he learns the right place for humor and learns to use his individual way of looking at things as an asset instead of a handicap, his natural gift of an individual outlook and witty expression are going to help him. A more conventional mind and a more plodding and mature point of view would help him a lot more right now; but we have to allow, my dear Mr. Kennedy, with boys like Jack, for a period of adjustment . . . and growing up; and the final product is often more interesting and more effective than the boy with a more conventional mind who has been to us parents and teachers much less trouble." The mature John Kennedy would fulfill St. John's prediction.

DESPITE BEING SIXTY-FIFTH in a class of 110, Jack was assured a place at Harvard. In 1935, as the son of so prominent an alumnus, with an elder brother in good standing at the university, and Harry Hopkins, FDR's welfare administrator, and Herbert Bayard Swope, the prominent journalist/editor, listed as nonacademic references, Jack had few doubts about his admission. But reluctant once more to be directly in Joe Jr.'s shadow, he chose to go to Princeton with Lem Billings and other Choate friends. Joe Sr. accepted his son's decision as a welcome demonstration of Jack's independence — though he may have smiled when the son who so wanted to diverge from his elder brother's path asked to follow Joe Jr. in spending a year in England under Harold Laski's tutelage.

In the conflict between self-indulgence and worldly interests, the former gave little ground to the latter in Jack's eighteenth year. And in fact, in the summer and fall of 1935, when he traveled to Europe for the first time, Jack was less interested in studying with Laski at the London School of Economics than in making acquaintances and enjoying the social life in London. Rising European tensions over the Rhineland and Italy's invasion of Ethiopia registered less on Jack as a significant moment in history than simply as reasons to go home.

In October, when one of Jack's bouts of illness added to concerns about keeping him abroad, he returned to America, where he quickly seemed to recover and petitioned for late admission to Princeton's fall term. When the university denied it, Joe arranged through a prominent Princeton alumnus for Jack's enrollment at the beginning of November. He lasted only until December, when illness again interrupted his studies and sent him to Peter Bent Brigham Hospital in Boston. Recuperating from his still-undiagnosed maladies in Palm Beach, Florida, Jack accepted his father's suggestion that he go to Arizona for two months beginning in April. There, the warm climate and relaxed pace at a ranch seemed to restore Jack's health. With time to reflect, Jack changed his mind about college. Princeton's cloistered environment and spartan living quarters in South Reunion Hall had disappointed him, so he decided to renew his application to Harvard in July 1936, receiving admission to the fall term within three days of applying.

During his first two years at Harvard, Jack largely continued the pattern he had established at Choate. His academic record was unimpressive: a B-minus in government the first year and a B in English the second were offset by grades of C and C-plus in French, history, and a second government course, his major interest. "Exam today," he wrote Billings during his first finals period in January 1937, "so have to open my book & see what the fucking course is about." When he got too far behind in his work, Jack occasionally relied on a tutoring service or an outside "cram school," which charged a fee for bringing unprepared students up to speed for an exam. Jack's freshman adviser predicted that he would probably do better in time, but in his sophomore year he had still not lived up to his talent or promise. "Though his mind is still undisciplined," his tutor wrote, "and will probably never be very original, he has ability, I think, and gives promise of development."

Jack's classmates and teachers remember a charming, irreverent young man with a fine sense of humor and a passion for sports and the good life. He certainly showed no overt interest in the campus activism provoked by the Depression, FDR's New Deal, and the challenges to democracy and capitalism from fascism, Nazism, and communism. There is no indication that he read any of the popular progressive journals of the day, such as The Nation, the New Republic, or New Masses, or gave much, if any, heed to the parades and protest demonstrations organized by students eager to have a say in public affairs. He had little use for doctrinaire advocates who "espoused their causes with a certitude which he could never quite understand." Indeed, after only two months at Harvard, he privately vented his irritation with the political clichés he had been hearing in a whimsical letter to Billings. "You are certainly a large-sized prick to keep my hat," he complained to Lem, "as I can't find my other one and consequently am hatless. Please send it as I am sending yours. . . . Harvard has not made me grasping but you are getting a certain carefree communistic attitude + a share the wealth attitude that is rather worrying to we who are wealthy."

His focus remained on the extracurricular and social activities he found more enjoyable, and stamped him as one of the many students at Harvard more interested in earning the social standing that attendance and graduation provided than in the book learning needed to advance a career. Although James Bryant Conant, Harvard's president beginning in 1933, stressed the importance of "meritocracy," a university focused more on the intellect and character of its students than on their social origins, social snobbery continued to dominate the undergraduate life of the university. Jack's first two years on campus were a reflection of these mores. Football, swimming, and golf, and service on the Smoker and Annual Show committees occupied his freshman year, while junior varsity football, varsity swimming, the Spee and Yacht Clubs, and service on the business board of the Harvard Crimson filled his second year.

Jack put a premium on succeeding at these chosen activities. He was a fierce competitor. "He played for keeps," the football coach recalled. "He did nothing half way." Swim practice often occupied four hours a day sandwiched between classes. The athletic competitions gave him some gratifying moments: the freshman swim team went undefeated, and an intercollegiate championship in sailing for the boat he commanded sophomore year was a high point.

Yet, as at Choate, his brother continued to eclipse him. Joe Jr. was the best-known member of his class, and "Jack was bound to play second-fiddle," a Harvard contemporary and later dean of admissions said. Whereas Joe was big enough and strong enough to play varsity football, Jack, at six feet and 150 pounds, was too slight to make more than the sophomore junior squad. Moreover, his fragile health undermined his success as a backstroke specialist, contributing to his failure to beat out a classmate for the starting assignment in the Yale swim meet.

His brother's success in campus politics also reduced any hopes Jack may have had of making a mark in that area. Under an unstated family rule of primogeniture, the eldest son had first call on a political career. And Joe Jr. left no doubt that this was already his life's ambition. Economist John Kenneth Galbraith, one of Joe's tutors, remembered him as keenly interested in politics and public affairs and quick to cite his father as the source of his beliefs. "When I become President, I will take you up to the White House with me," he liked to tell people. Joe's quick rise to prominence on campus gave resonance to his boasts. He won elections as chairman of the Winthrop House committee, as a class representative to the student council, as an usher for Class Day, and as business manager of the class album. He also enjoyed prominence as an outspoken anti-interventionist in the emerging troubles abroad.

Although very much in his brother's shadow during his freshman and sophomore years, Jack also gave indications that he had more than a passing interest in public issues. A failed bid for a student council seat suggested that he was not content to leave politics entirely to his father and brother or that he was focused solely on high jinks. Moreover, his academic work began to demonstrate a substantial engagement with political leadership and how influential men changed the world. Economics, English, history, and government courses formed the core of his first two-year curriculum. In March 1937, his freshman adviser noted that Jack "is planning to do work in Gov. He has already spent time abroad studying it. His father is in that work." He read several books on recent international and political history, and more revealing, he wrote papers on King Francis I of France and Enlightenment philosopher Jean-Jacques

Rousseau. His essays focused on the uses of political and intellectual power to alter human relations, Francis I being notable to Jack as someone who had made himself the "undisputed and absolute" ruler of France and the architect of the French Renaissance, and Rousseau was the author of works that Jack saw as "the seeds of the revolution that took place in 1789."

JACK'S GREATEST SUCCESS in his first two years at Harvard was in winning friends and proving to be "a lady's man." He made a positive impression on almost everyone he met. "A gangling young man with a slightly snub nose and 'a lot of flap in his reddish-brown hair,'" Jack etched himself in the memory of one classmate who saw him climbing the stairs of the *Crimson* building "with his long coltish stride." One professor remembered "his bright young face which stood out in the class." According to the master of John Winthrop House, who interviewed Jack and reviewed his request for a transfer there in 1937 from Weld Hall, he was a "good boy," one of the "most popular at Weld," and "one of [the] most popular men in his class." John Kenneth Galbraith remembered Jack as "handsome . . . gregarious, given to various amusements, much devoted to social life and affectionately and diversely to women."

"We are having one hell of a fine time," Jack wrote Billings after arriving on campus and reconnecting with some Choate friends. "I am now known as 'Play-boy,'" he wrote again in October. Jack was "very humorous, very bright, very unassuming," said Torbert Macdonald, his closest Harvard friend, who became a star back on the football team. "Anytime you were with Jack Kennedy you would laugh," another athlete friend recalled. Lem Billings agreed: "Jack was more fun than anyone I've ever known, and I think most people who knew him felt the same way about him." His irreverence particularly endeared him to classmates, who shared a certain distaste for the social hierarchy of which they themselves were so much a part.

Jack's discovery that girls liked him or that he had a talent for charming them gave him special satisfaction. As early as the summer of 1934, when he was seventeen, he had become aware that young women were attracted to him, reporting to Billings that the girl next door on the Cape had called from Cleveland to ask about his health. "I can't help it," he declared with evident self-pleasure. "It can't be my good looks because I'm not much handsomer than anybody else. It must be my personality."

His letters to Billings over the next few years, especially through his sophomore year at Harvard, contain numerous references to his sexual exploits. Some of this was adolescent bragging. "I had an enema given by a beautiful blonde," he wrote Billings during a hospital stay in June 1934. "That, my sweet, is the height of cheap thrills." "The nurses here are the dirtiest bunch of females I've ever seen," he wrote a few days later. "One of them wanted to know if I would give her a work out last night. . . . I said yes but she was put off duty early." During his first two years at Harvard, Jack had a series of conquests he graphically described to Billings. He worried that one of his weekend outings might mean "a bundle from heaven. Please keep all this under your skin and I wish now I had kept mine under my skin if you know what I mean. I would have less worries." But it did not deter him. "I can now get my tail as often and as free as I want which is a step in the right direction," he told Billings a few months later.

In rereading this correspondence years later, Billings categorized the letters as "dirty," "very dirty," or "not so dirty." But he understood that there was more here than some adolescent rite of passage by a young man with a strong sexual appetite. "He was interested, very interested, in girls," Billings remembered. But it was also "a form of being successful at something." It was "important to him," because it was an area in which he held an advantage over his brother and Billings and most of his other peers. At a wedding reception, Lem wrote Jack's sister Kathleen, "brother John was right in his element as he found Dotty Burns & Missy Greer there — all anxious to hear about how Marlene Dietrich thinks he's one of the most fascinating & attractive young men she's ever met."

When Billings told him that he was so successful with women only "because he was Joseph P. Kennedy's son, since his father was pretty well known as a very rich man," Jack was determined to prove him wrong. He insisted that they take out blind dates and change identities. "I was to be Jack Kennedy and he was LeMoyne Billings. He went so far as to get his father's Rolls for the occasion. We had one very competitive night trying to see who would do better and I'm afraid, as I recall, he was satisfied with the results."

A normal adolescent appetite and the competitive advantage over brother Joe and other rivals are only part of the explanation for Jack's preoccupation with sexual conquests. Although it is impossible to know exactly how much Jack knew about Joe's extramarital affairs, or when he first learned of them, it is clear that by the time he was at Harvard, Jack had a pretty good idea that his father, who was often away in New York, Hollywood, and Europe on business, was quite the man about town. Certainly by the time he was twenty-three, according to one girlfriend, Jack knew about his father's infidelities. "He said his father went on these long trips, was gone so much of the time, and that he'd come back and give his mother some very lavish presents — a big Persian rug or some jewelry or something like that. Obviously, Jack knew everything that was going on in [his parents'] marriage."

Stories about his grandfather Fitzgerald further buttressed Jack's understanding of how elastic certain rules might be. At the very least, it is evident that Joe had no objection to Jack's active social life and even facilitated it. In October 1936, Jack told Billings that he "went down to the Cape with five guys from school — EM [Edward Moore, Joe Sr.'s administrative assistant and confidant] got us some girls thru another guy — four of us had dates and one guy got fucked 3 times, another guy 3 times (the girl a virgin!) + myself twice — they were all on the football team + I think the coaches heard as they gave us all a hell of a bawling out." This enthusiastic defiance of public standards of sexual behavior would be another link between father and son. Jack told "locker room stories about his father's conquests." Jack once described how Joe tried to get into bed one night with one of his sisters' friends, whispering to her as he began removing his robe, "This is going to be something you'll always remember." Jack, with an amused smile, would tell female visitors to Palm Beach or Hyannis Port, "Be sure to lock the bedroom door. The Ambassador has a tendency to prowl late at night."

Of course, Joe's sexual escapades were an abuse of someone as devout and conventional as Rose. She took exception to even the slightest off-color story. Any acknowledgment of infidelity carried on under her roof before the eyes of her children was impossible. But Jack and his siblings were more sympathetic to Joe than to Rose in this family conflict. They not only accepted their father's philandering at Palm Beach and Hyannis but facilitated it away from home. A Washington, D.C., socialite recounted the occasion in the 1940s when Joe Sr., Jack, and Robert Kennedy invited her to their table in a posh restaurant. The boys explained that Joe would be in town for a few days and "needed female companionship. They wondered whom I could suggest, and they were absolutely serious." Similarly, when Joe visited Hollywood in the 1950s, his daughter

Patricia, who was married to actor Peter Lawford, would ask the wife of a television producer to get the names and phone numbers of female stars her father might call.

Certainly the risk taking was part of the appeal for Jack. The fact that the football coaches gave him and his friends hell did not deter him from planning to go "down next week for a return performance." In fact, in response to Jack's "little party," the coaches demoted him to the third team, which angered him but did not alter his social life. Nor did the possibility that he and his friends might have gotten one or more of the girls pregnant or contracted a sexually transmitted disease hold him back. "One guy is up at the doctor's seeing if he has a dose," he wrote Billings, "+ I feel none too secure myself." Yet taking chances and breaking rules were partly what made life fun; and at age nineteen, he was enjoying himself too much to stop.

Jack's easy conquests compounded the feeling that, like the member of a privileged aristocracy, of a libertine class, he was entitled to seek out and obtain what he craved, instantly, even gratefully, from the object of his immediate affection. Furthermore, there did not have to be a conflict between private fun and public good. David Cecil's *The Young Melbourne*, a 1939 biography of Queen Victoria's prime minister, depicted young British aristocrats performing heroic feats in the service of queen and country while privately practicing unrestrained sexual indulgence with no regard for the conventional standards of monogamous marriages or premarital courting. Jack would later say that it was one of his two favorite books.

One woman reporter remembered that Jack "didn't have to lift a finger to attract women; they were drawn to him in battalions." After Harvard, when he spent a term in the fall of 1940 at Stanford (where, unlike at Harvard, men and women attended classes together), he wrote Lem Billings: "Still can't get use to the co-eds but am taking them in my stride. Expect to cut one out of the herd and brand her shortly, but am taking it very slow as do not want to be known as the beast of the East."

But restraint was usually not the order of the day. He had so many women, he could not remember their names; "Hello, kid," was his absentminded way of greeting a current amour. Stories are legion — no doubt, some the invention of imagination, but others most probably true — of his self-indulgent sexual escapades. "We have only fifteen minutes," he told a beautiful co-ed invited to his hotel room during a campaign stop in 1960. "I wish we had time for some foreplay," he told another beauty he dated in the 1950s. One of Jack's favorite sayings, one male friend said, was "slam, bam, thank you, ma'am." A woman friend described him as "compulsive as Mussolini. Up against the wall, Signora, if you have five minutes, that sort of thing." At a society party in New York he asked the artist William Walton how many women in the gathering of socialites he had slept with. When Walton gave him "a true count," Jack said, "Wow, I envy you." Walton replied: "Look, I was here earlier than you were." And Jack responded, "I'm going to catch up."

JACK'S DEVIL-MAY-CARE ATTITUDE found a fresh outlet in the summer of 1937 when his father sent him and Billings on a grand European tour. Because Billings could not afford the trip, Jack financed it. The journey was a kind of obligatory excursion for young gentlemen, an extension of the formal education they were getting at the best colleges in America. A firsthand acquaintance with the great sites of western Europe was a prerequisite for high social status. And Jack and Lem left few architectural wonders and major museums unvisited. Moreover, both of them took genuine satisfaction from schooling themselves in the great landmarks of the Old World. Their travels, as the old saw has it, were broadening. Ironically, Jack remained closed off from entire strata of society — blue-collar workers and African Americans — he would not glimpse until much later. Even then, he would find them difficult to viscerally understand.

Perhaps most important, the trip deepened Jack's interest in foreign affairs. A diary he kept of the two months they spent abroad is largely a running commentary on public events and national character. They went first to France, where they spent the month of July touring in a convertible Jack brought across the Atlantic on the SS *Washington*. Taking in the sights of Beauvais, Rouen, Paris, Versailles, Chartres, Orléans, Amboise, Angoulême, St.-Jean-de-Luz, Lourdes, Toulouse, Carcassonne, Cannes, Biarritz, and Marseille, they also made a point of visiting World War I battlefields. Jack spoke as often as possible with Frenchmen about current events. He sounded them out on developments in America under Roosevelt's New Deal and in Europe, where Nazi Germany and Fascist Italy raised concerns about another European war. Jack gained the impression "that while they all like Roosevelt, his type of government would not succeed in a country like France which seems to lack the ability of seeing a problem as a whole. They don't like [Premier Léon] Blum as he takes away their money and gives it to someone else — that to a French-man is *tres mauvais*. The general impression also seems to be that there will *not* be a war in the near future and that France is much too well prepared for Germany. The permanence of the alliance of Ger-many and Italy is also questionable." Billings later remembered that they spent a lot of time visiting churches and museums and "inter-viewing French peasants in schoolboy French. We wanted to see what they thought of the Germans. They were so confident of the Maginot Line," the fortresses on the Franco-German border.

"The distinguishing mark of the Frenchman," Jack noted in his diary, "is his cabbage breath and the fact that there are no bath-tubs." He was even more annoyed by their readiness to exploit American tourists for everything they could get. When they had din-ner with a French officer they had picked up on their drive to Paris, Jack noted that he had "succeeded in making him pay for part of it." He was particularly incensed by the efforts of hotels to squeeze higher rates out of them. "Have now acquired the habit," he wrote on their fourth day in France, "of leaving the car around the block to keep the [hotel] price from going up. Had the lights [on the car] fixed and got another screwing. These French will try & rob at every turn." "France," he concluded, "is quite a primitive nation."

He had no better opinion of the Spanish. The stories of atroci-ties in the Spanish civil war between Francisco Franco's fascist rebels and the republican government in Madrid told to them by refugees in France seemed all too believable after they witnessed the bar-barism of a bullfight in Biarritz on the Franco-Spanish border. "Very interesting but very cruel," Jack recorded, "especially when the bull gored the horse. Believe all the atrocity stories now as these south-erners, such as these French and Spanish, are happiest at scenes of cruelty. They thought funniest sight was when horse ran out of the ring with his guts trailing." Billings later said, "Of course, we didn't understand this temperament at all, and we were disgusted by it."

The Italians made a better first impression on Jack. Their "streets are much more full and lively than those of France — and the whole race seems more attractive. Fascism seems to treat them well," he wrote after two days in Italy. He was also "very impressed by some of the [twelve-year-old] children [his brother] Bobby's age and by the fact that they all seem regimented." Billings remembered that "Italy was cleaner and the people looked more prosperous than we had anticipated." Within a few days, however, Jack was complaining that "the Italians are the noisiest race in existence — they have to be [in] on everything — even if it is only Billings blowing his nose." By the time he left Italy, Jack saw the Italians as being as exploitive as the French. A battle with their hotel proprietor over the bill marked their departure from Rome. The man "turned out to be a terrific crook despite," Jack wrote sarcastically, "[being] an Italian and a gentleman. Left Rome amidst the usual cursing porters."

The Germans were even worse. Though they picked up some young German hitchhikers in Italy who seemed attractive enough, a conceit and near contempt for Americans in Germany offended them. "We had a terrible feeling about Germany," Billings recalled, "and all the 'Heil Hitler' stuff. . . . They were extremely arrogant — the whole race was arrogant — the whole feeling of Germany was one of arrogance: the feeling that they were superior to us and wanting to show it." The Germans were "insufferable," Billings also said. "We just had awful experiences there. They were so haughty and so sure of themselves." To mock them, Jack and Lem would answer Nazi salutes of "Heil Hitler" by throwing back their hands and saying, "Hi ya, Hitler."

Of greater interest to Jack than the flaws he saw in each of these countries was the state of current relations among them and the likely course of future events. He also began to see how easy it was to fall into a distorted view of public affairs based more on personal bias than on informed understanding. In this he was starting to distance himself from his father, who saw the outside world primarily in personal terms.

Questions about international relations and Europe's future intrigued Jack. He understood that the Spanish civil war was a focus for national rivalries between England, France, Italy, Germany, and Russia. England did not want the Mediterranean to become "a Fascist lake," he noted. But how far it or any of the other countries would go to advance their respective interests seemed open to question. Because the competing nations seemed so intolerant of one another, Jack believed it likely that they would fight another war. He also pondered the comparative evils of fascism and communism. Whatever the advantages of one over the other, he concluded that "Fascism is the thing for Germany and Italy, Communism for Russia, and democracy for America and England."

His curiosity about European power politics moved him to seek out Arnaldo Cortesi, the *New York Times* correspondent in Rome. Jack thought him "very interesting and [he] gave me some very good points." Cortesi believed a war "unlikely as if anyone had really wanted war there had been plenty of excuses for it. . . . Said Europe was too well prepared for war now — in contrast to 1914." Jack also read John Gunther's 1937 book *Inside Europe,* which he found illuminating, especially with regard to the Spanish civil war. But Jack did not take Cortesi's or Gunther's opinions as gospel. His trip showed him that Europe was in flux and that the continent's political future was uncertain. At the end of his diary, he posed a series of questions to himself. Would Mussolini's current popularity hold up after invading Ethiopia in 1935 and provoking widespread international criticism? Would Franco be able to win his civil war without Italo-German support? Could Germany and Italy, which had divergent interests, maintain an alliance? Did British military strength make a war less likely? And would fascism be possible in as wealthy and egalitarian a country as the United States?

Jack's queries were as sophisticated as those of professional journalists and diplomats in Europe. They were also part of an understandable search by a bright, inquiring young man for a niche that separated him from his father and elder brother and satisfied an affinity for critical thinking about public affairs. Joe Sr. was the family's moneymaking genius and Joe Jr. might be slated for a meteoric career in U.S. domestic politics, but Jack could imagine himself as the *New York Times* man in a major European capital, probing current realities and educating isolationist Americans about a world they wished to ignore.

Given how much the French, Germans, Italians, and Spanish offended him, it is puzzling that Jack did not embrace the prevailing isolationism of his father and most Americans. This may have been a way to separate himself from his brother. But more likely, the trip to Europe schooled him in the satisfaction of forming independent judgments rather than giving in to easier clichés about those "foreigners." He understood that despite the physical and institutional distance between the United States and Europe, European affairs had a large impact on the Americas. An affinity for analyzing and explaining current conditions trumped feelings of antagonism and bias, which he believed informed the way his father and other isolationists saw the world.

The trip also strengthened Jack's sense of privileged status. He and Billings ended their travels in Britain, where Joe arranged for them to stay at palatial English and Scottish homes. "Terrific big castle with beautiful furnished rooms," Jack said of Sir Paul Latham's residence in Sussex. (One bedroom was forty yards long.) Likewise, the estate of Scottish nobleman Sir James Calder impressed Jack and amazed Lem, who spent their visit fly-fishing and shooting rabbit and grouse.

For Jack, the lifestyle of these British aristocrats was not so removed from that of his father. From July 1934 to September 1935, when he served as chairman of the Securities and Exchange Commission, Joe had lived in a sumptuous 125-acre Maryland estate half an hour's drive from Washington. The thirty-three-room rented mansion had been built by a multimillionaire Chicago businessman, Samuel Klump Martin III, and rivaled the great homes of English aristocrats. The living room was the size of a hotel lobby, and the dining room was modeled after one built for King James I of England. Twelve master bedrooms, a recreation room with several billiard tables and three Ping-Pong tables, a hundred-seat movie theater, and a large outdoor swimming pool surrounded by guest bath houses provided all the modern amenities.

In 1937–38, at the age of twenty, Jack saw himself and his family as a kind of American nobility. On returning home in September, Jack learned that *Fortune* magazine had published a cover article about his father, who since March had been serving as the chairman of a newly created U.S. Maritime Commission. Then, during the fall term, Jack had a personal victory when he received an invitation to the Spee, one of Harvard's eight elite clubs that included only about a hundred out of the thousand students in the class of 1940. It was an honor neither his father nor Joe Jr. had managed to win. "It was a status symbol for him," one of Jack's classmates believed, "that at last the Kennedys were good enough."

And then, in December 1937, President Roosevelt appointed Joseph Kennedy ambassador to Great Britain, America's most prestigious diplomatic post. By choosing a self-made Irish American as his envoy, Roosevelt assumed that he would not become a captive of England's conservative government and its appeasement policy toward Hitler's Germany.

Whatever the president's political purposes, the appointment gave Joe and his family an uncommon degree of social prominence. "The moment the appointment was proposed," Rose said, "Joe accepted. It was the kind of appointment he had been waiting for all along." Indeed, he had lobbied Roosevelt for it. When the president tried to get him to become secretary of commerce instead, Joe told Roosevelt's son James: "London is where I want to go and it is the only place I intend to go." Interior Secretary Harold Ickes asked White House insider Thomas Corcoran why Kennedy was so eager for the London post. "You don't understand the Irish," Corcoran answered. "London has always been a closed door to him. As Ambassador of the United States, Kennedy will have all doors open to him." Joe, who was not sure how long the assignment would last, told an aide who accompanied him, "Don't go buying a lot of luggage. We're only going to get the family in the *Social Register*. When that's done we come on back."

Joe's appointment also gave Jack an uncommon opportunity to be, however temporarily, a part of English high society. In July 1938, at the end of his sophomore year, he traveled to London to spend the summer working at the U.S. embassy. The work itself was less memorable than the social whirl Jack enjoyed. He found a warm welcome from England's aristocracy and had ready access to the teas, balls, dances, regattas, and races that were part of their summer ritual. Although Jack looked "incredibly young for his age at 21," he engaged his English friends with his bright, quick mind, highly developed sense of humor, and vitality about everything. In August, the family fled London for a villa in the south of France near Cannes, where they socialized with members of the English royal family. A final few days in London at the end of August gave Jack a close-up view of an evolving European crisis over Czechoslovakia, which Hitler had provoked by demanding that Prague give up its Sudetenland territory. In August, with the crisis unresolved, Jack returned to the States for his junior year at Harvard.

His summer in Europe had fired Jack's imagination, and he was determined to return to the Continent. He asked and received permission from his advisers to take six courses in the fall term of 1938 and a semester's leave in the spring of 1939, which he planned to spend in Europe working on an honor's thesis about contemporary affairs. He promised his Harvard adviser that during his time abroad, he would read several assigned books on political philosophy, including Walter Lippmann's *The Good Society*. He also pledged to gather material for a senior thesis on some aspect of international law and diplomacy or the history of international relations, which were listed as his special fields of interest. As impressive, he turned from a C into a B student and excelled in his government classes during the fall term.

A. Chester Hanford, the dean of Harvard College and Jack's instructor in Government 9a, a course on American state government, remembered "a rather thin, somewhat reserved but pleasant young man with an open countenance which often wore an inquisitive look. He . . . took an active part in classroom discussion in which he made pertinent remarks." But much to Hanford's surprise, the grandson of Honey Fitz showed little interest in state politics. He "was more interested in the changing position of the American state, in federal-state relations and state constitutional development." Jack's examination papers gave evidence of independent thought and made Hanford "wonder if he [Jack] might not become a newspaper man."

Jack made an even stronger impression on Professor Arthur Holcombe, whose Government 7 focused on national politics and the workings of Congress in particular. Holcombe "tried to teach . . . government as if it were a science." Each student was required to study a congressman and assess his method of operation and his performance. Holcombe urged the class to substitute objective analysis for personal opinions, and this "scientific method" greatly appealed to Jack, who believed that politics should rest less on opinion than on facts.

Holcombe assigned Jack to study Bertram Snell, an upstate New York Republican whose principal distinction was his representation of the electric power interests in his region. Holcombe said that Jack "did a very superior job of investigating, and his final report was a masterpiece." Of course, Jack had some advantages. As Holcombe noted, "When Christmas vacation came, he goes down to Washington, meets some of his father's friends, gets a further line on his congressman and on Congress."

When he finished the fall term, Jack made plans to sail for Europe at the end of February. First, however, he flew to New Orleans for Mardi Gras, where he was met at the airport by a girl he was dating and a Princeton friend, who was impressed that Jack had come by plane: "Not many people flew in those days," the friend recalled. But Jack did, and then flew back to New York before boarding a luxury liner for Europe.

Although his father's public image had taken a downturn in the fall of 1938, when he publicly expressed favor for Prime Minister Neville Chamberlain's appeasement of Nazi Germany at Munich, Jack felt no discomfort with his father's political pronouncements or his family identity. Although his father's pro-Chamberlain speech "seemed to be unpopular with the Jews, etc.," he wrote his parents, "[it] was considered to be very good by everyone who wasn't bitterly anti-Fascist." A new play, which he saw in New York and included several references to the Kennedys, greatly amused Jack. "It's pretty funny," he reported in the same letter, "and jokes about us get the biggest laughs whatever that signifies."

As soon as he arrived in London, Jack resumed "having a great time," he wrote Billings. He was working every day and "feeling very important as I go to work in my new cutaway." He met the king "at a Court Levee. It takes place in the morning and you wear tails. The King stands & you go up and bow. Met Queen Mary and was at tea with the Princess Elizabeth with whom I made a great deal of time. Thursday night — am going to Court in my new silk breeches, which are cut to my crotch tightly and in which I look mighty attractive. Friday I leave for Rome as J.P. has been appointed to represent Roosevelt at the Pope's coronation."

When he returned from Rome in late March, Jack reported to Billings that they had had "a great time." His youngest brother, Teddy, had received Communion from the new pope, Pius XII, "the first time that a Pope has ever done this in the last couple of hundred years." The pope then gave the Sacrament to Joe, Jack, and his sister Eunice "at a private mass and all in all it was very impressive." For all the sense of importance Jack gained from his father's prominence and influence, he kept an irreverent sense of perspective that allowed him to see the comical side of his family's social climbing. He wrote Billings: "They want to give Dad the title of Duke which will be hereditary and go to all of his family which will make me Duke John of Bronxville and perhaps if you suck around sufficiently I might knight you." (In fact, Joe had a sense of limits about what an American public official could do and had no intention of asking the required permission of Congress to accept a title of nobility.)

Jack's letters to Billings over the next several months describe a young man enjoying his privileged life. On the way back from Rome, he had stopped at the Paris embassy, where he had lunch with Carmel Offie, Ambassador William Bullitt's principal aide, and was invited by them to stay at Bullitt's residence. He "graciously declined," as he wanted to get back to London for the Grand National steeplechase before returning to Paris for a month and then traveling to "Poland, Russia, etc." As of this writing in March, he was not doing "much work but have been sporting around in my morning coat, my 'Anthony Eden' black Homburg and white gardenia."

Two weeks later, he told Billings that he was "living like a king" at the Paris embassy, where Offie and he had become "the greatest of pals" and Bullitt had been very nice to him. He had lunch at the embassy with the famed aviator and isolationist Charles Lindbergh and his wife, Anne, "the most attractive couple I've ever seen." He was "going skiing for a week in Switzerland which should be damn good fun." Apparently, it was: "Plenty of action here, both on and off the skis," he told Billings in a postcard. "Things have been humming since I got back from skiing," he next wrote Lem. "Met a gal who used to live with the Duke of Kent and who is as she says 'a member of the British Royal family by injections.' She has terrific diamond bracelet that he gave her and a big ruby that the Marajah [sic] of Nepal gave her. I don't know what she thinks she is going to get out of me but will see. Meanwhile very interesting as am seeing life." And he was still living "like a king" at the embassy, where Bullitt "really fixes me up," and Offie and he were served by "about 30 lackies." Bullitt, Jack wrote, was always "trying, unsuccessfully, to pour champagne down my gullett [sic]."

But however welcoming Bullitt and Offie were, Jack did not like feeling dependent on their hospitality. He must have also sensed some hostility from Offie, who remembered "Jack sitting in my office and listening to telegrams being read or even reading various things which actually were none of his business but since he was who he was we didn't throw him out." Jack privately reciprocated the irritation: "Offie has just rung for me," he wrote Lem, "so I guess I have to get the old paper ready and go in and wipe his arse."

For all the fun, Jack had a keen sense of responsibility about using his uncommon opportunity to gather information for a senior thesis. Besides, the highly charged European political atmosphere, which many predicted would soon erupt in another war, fascinated him. However much he kept Lem Billings posted on his social triumphs, his letters to Lem and to his father in London were filled with details about German intentions toward Poland and the likely reactions of Britain, France, Russia, Romania, and Turkey. "The whole thing is damn interesting," he told Billings. He found himself in the eye of the storm, traveling to Danzig and Warsaw in May, where he spoke to Nazi and Polish officials, and then on to Leningrad, Moscow, Kiev, Bucharest, Turkey, Jerusalem, Beirut, Damascus, and Athens. He received VIP treatment from the U.S. diplomatic missions everywhere he went, staying at a number of embassies along the way and talking with senior diplomats, including Ambassador

Anthony Biddle in Warsaw and Charles E. Bohlen, the second secretary in Moscow.

Jack spent August traveling among England, France, Germany, and Italy in pursuit of more information for his senior thesis. He and Torbert MacDonald, his Harvard roommate who had come to England for a track meet, met fierce hostility in Munich from storm troopers who spotted the English license plates on their car. Against the advice of the U.S. embassy in Prague, Joe Kennedy arranged a visit by Jack to Czechoslovakia. The diplomat George F. Kennan, who was serving as a secretary of the legation, remembered how "furious" members of the embassy were at the demand. Joe Kennedy's "son had no official status and was, in our eyes, obviously an upstart and an ignoramus. The idea that there was anything he could learn or report about conditions in Europe which we . . . had not already reported seemed . . . wholly absurd. That busy people should have their time taken up arranging his tour struck us as outrageous." Jack saw matters differently, believing a firsthand look at Prague, now under Nazi control, would be invaluable, and his sense of entitlement left him indifferent to the complaints of the embassy.

In keeping with the peculiar way in which he moved between the serious and the frivolous at this time of his life, Jack spent part of August on the French Riviera, where his family had again rented a villa for the summer at Antibes. There he socialized with the famous movie actress Marlene Dietrich and her family, swimming with her daughter during the day and dancing with Marlene herself at night.

But the good times came to an abrupt end in September when Hitler invaded Poland and the British and the French declared war. Jack joined his parents and his brother Joe and sister Kathleen in the visitor's gallery to watch Prime Minister Neville Chamberlain and members of Parliament, including Winston Churchill, explain Britain's decision to fight. Churchill's speech, giving evidence of the powerful oratory that would later inspire the nation in the darkest hours of the war, left an indelible impression on Jack. To Joe, the onset of war was an unprecedented disaster. He became tearful when Chamberlain declared that "everything that I have believed in during my public life has crashed in ruins." In a telephone call to FDR, the inconsolable Joe Kennedy moaned, "It's the end of the world . . . the end of everything."

Jack now also got his first experience of hands-on diplomacy. His father sent him to Glasgow to attend to more than two hundred American citizens rescued by a British destroyer after their British liner carrying 1,400 passengers from Liverpool to New York had been sunk by a German submarine. More than a hundred people had lost their lives, including twenty-eight U.S. citizens. The surviving Americans were terrified at the suggestion that they board a U.S. ship without a military escort to ensure their safety, and Jack's assurances that President Roosevelt and the embassy were confident that Germany would not attack a U.S. ship did not convince them. Although Jack recommended to his father that he try to meet the passengers' demand, Joe believed it superfluous, and an unescorted U.S. freighter returned the citizens to the United States. Meanwhile, Jack flew on a Pan Am Clipper to Boston in time for his senior fall term.

More than anything, Jack's travels encouraged an intellectual's skepticism about the limits of human understanding and beliefs. When he returned to America in September, he asked a Catholic priest: "I saw the rock where our Lord ascended into Heaven in a cloud, and [in] the same area, I saw the place where Mohammed was carried up to Heaven on a white horse, and Mohammed has a big following and Christ has a big following, and why do you think we should believe Christ any more than Mohammed?" The priest urged Joe to get Jack some "instruction immediately, or else he would turn into a[n] . . . atheist if he didn't get some of his problems straightened out." When a friend at Harvard who thought Jack less than pious about his religion asked why he was going to church on a holy day, Jack "got this odd, hard look on his face" and replied, "This is one of the things I do for my father. The rest I do for myself."

It was all part of Jack's affinity for skepticism, which Payson S. Wild, one of his instructors in the fall of 1939, helped foster in a tutorial on political theory. Wild urged him to consider the question of why, given that there are a few people at the top and masses below, the masses obey. "He seemed really intrigued by that," Wild recalled.

Jack gave expression to his independence — to his developing impulse to question prevailing wisdom — in an October 1939 editorial in the Harvard *Crimson*. Responding to the impression that "everyone here is ready to fight to the last Englishman," Jack published a counterargument in the campus newspaper that essentially reflected the case his father was then making privately to President Roosevelt and the State Department. As much an expression of loyalty to Joe as of pleasure in running against majority opinion and

presenting himself as someone with special understanding of international conditions, Jack urged a quick, negotiated end to the fighting through the good offices of President Roosevelt. Because it
would require a third party to mediate a settlement, Jack thought
that the "President is almost under an obligation to exert every office
he possesses to bring about such a peace."

Jack believed that both Germany and England were eager for an
agreement. And though such a settlement would mean sacrificing
Poland, it would likely save Britain and France from probable defeat. But it would have to be a "peace based on solid reality," Jack
asserted, which meant giving Germany a "free economic hand" in
eastern Europe and a share of overseas colonies. Hitler would have
to disarm in return for these conditions, but Jack did not think this
was out of reach.

Jack's misplaced hopes seem to have been more a case of taking
issue with current assumptions than an expression of realism about
European affairs developed in his recent travels. Nevertheless, his
interest in exploring political questions — in honing his skills as a
student of government — is striking. "He seemed to blossom once
Joe was gone [to law school] and to feel more secure himself and to
be more confident as his grades improved," Wild said. As another
token of Jack's interest and vocational aspirations in 1939, he tried
to become a member of the *Crimson*'s editorial board; but it already
had a full complement of editors and he had to settle for a spot on
the paper's business board. He also occasionally wrote for the paper.
An editorial in the *Crimson* and a speech before the YMCA and YWCA
on how to restore peace made him feel like "quite a seer around
here." He also joked with his father that being an ambassador's son
who had spent time in Europe with prominent officials gave him
added cachet with the girls. "I seem to be doing better with the girls
so I guess you are doing your duty over there," he wrote his father,
"so before resigning give my social career a bit of consideration."

In the fall of 1939, Jack's interest in public affairs reflected itself
in his course work. In four government classes, he focused on contemporary international politics. "The war clinched my thinking on
international relations," he said later. "The world had to get along
together." In addition to a course with Wild on elements of international law, he took Modern Imperialism, Principles of Politics,
and Comparative Politics: Bureaucracy, Constitutional Government,
and Dictatorship. Some papers Jack wrote for Wild's course on neu-

tral rights in wartime on the high seas made Wild think that Jack might become an attorney, but Jack displayed a greater interest in questions about power and the comparative workings and appeal of fascism, Nazism, capitalism, communism, and democracy. The challenge of distinguishing between rhetoric and realism in world affairs, between the ideals of international law and the hard actualities of why nations acted as they did, particularly engaged him.

THE PRINCIPAL OUTCOME of Jack's travels and course work was a senior honor's thesis on the origins of Britain's appeasement policy. The history of how Jack wrote and published the thesis provides a microcosm of his privileged world. During Christmas vacation 1939 at Palm Beach, he spoke with British ambassador Lord Lothian, a guest at his father's Florida home. In January, Jack stopped at the British embassy in Washington for a conversation with Lothian that, as Jack later wrote him, "started me out on the job." Taking advantage of his father's continued presence in London, Jack received invaluable help from James Seymour, the U.S. embassy press secretary, who sent him printed political pamphlets and other Conservative, Labour, and Liberal publications Jack could not obtain in the United States. His financial means also allowed him to use typists and stenographers to meet university deadlines.

Although the papers Jack wrote for his senior-year courses show an impressive capacity for academic study and analysis, it was the contemporary scene that above all interested him — in particular, the puzzle of how a power like Great Britain found itself in another potentially devastating war only twenty years after escaping from the most destructive conflict in history. Was it something peculiar to a democracy that accounted for this failure, or were forces at work here beyond any government's control?

With only three months to complete the project, Jack committed himself with the same determination he had shown in fighting for a place on the Harvard football and swimming teams. Some of his Harvard friends remembered how he haunted the library of the Spee Club, where he worked on the thesis. They teased him about his "book," poking fun at his seriousness and pretension at trying to write a groundbreaking work. "We used to tease him about it all the time," one of them said, "because it was sort of his King Charles head that he was carrying around all the time: his famous thesis. We got so sick of hearing about it that I think he finally shut up."

Seymour proved a fastidious research assistant who not only persuaded the English political parties to provide the publications Jack requested but also chased down books and articles on the subject at Chatham House, the Oxford University Press, and the British Museum Reading Room. Seymour's efforts initially produced six large packages sent by diplomatic pouch to the State Department and then to Joe's New York office. But Jack was not content with Seymour's initial offering and pressed him for more: "Rush pacifist literature Oxford Cambridge Union report, etc.," he cabled Seymour on February 9, "all parties business trade reports bearing on foreign policy[,] anything else." "Dear Jack, your cables get tougher," Seymour replied, but by the end of the month Jack had an additional twenty-two volumes of pamphlets and books.

The thesis of 148 pages, titled "Appeasement at Munich" and cumbersomely subtitled ("The Inevitable Result of the Slowness of Conversion of the British Democracy to Change from a Disarmament Policy to a Rearmament Policy"), was written in about two months with predictable writing and organizational problems and an inconsistent focus. The thesis was read by four faculty members. Although Professor Henry A. Yeomans saw it as "badly written," he also described it as "a laborious, interesting and intelligent discussion of a difficult question" and rated it magna cum laude, the second-highest possible grade. Professor Carl J. Friedrich was more critical. He complained: "Fundamental premise never analyzed. Much too long, wordy, repetitious. Bibliography showy, but spotty. Title should be British armament policy up to Munich. Reasoning re: Munich inconclusive. . . . Many typographical errors. English diction defective." On a more positive note, Friedrich said, "Yet, thesis shows real interest and reasonable amount of work, though labor of condensation would have helped." He scored the work a cut below Yeomans as cum laude plus.

Bruce C. Hopper and Payson Wild, Jack's thesis advisers, were more enthusiastic about the quality of his work. In retrospective assessments, Wild remembered Jack as "a deep thinker and a genuine intellectual" whose thesis had "normal problems" but not "great" ones; Hopper recalled Jack's "imagination and diligence in preparedness as outstanding as of that time." On rereading the thesis twenty-four years later, Hopper was "again elated by the maturity of judgment, beyond his years in 1939/1940, by his felicity of phrase, and graceful presentation."

Yeomans and Friedrich were closer to the mark in their assessments. So was political scientist James MacGregor Burns, whose campaign biography of JFK in 1960 described the thesis as "a typical undergraduate effort — solemn and pedantic in tone, bristling with statistics and footnotes, a little weak in spelling and sentence structure." Yet it was an impressive effort for so young a man who had never written anything more than a term paper.

Had John Kennedy never become a prominent world figure, his thesis would be little remembered. But because it gives clues to the development of his interest and understanding of foreign affairs, it has become a much discussed text. Two things seem most striking about the work: First, Jack's unsuccessful effort at a scientific or objective history, and second, his attempt to draw a contemporary lesson for America from Britain's failure to keep pace with German military might.

His objective, he states throughout the thesis, was to neither condemn nor excuse Prime Ministers Stanley Baldwin and Neville Chamberlain, but rather to get beyond assertions of blame and defense in order to understand what had happened. Yet Jack's reach for objectivity is too facile. Though his thesis is indeed an interesting analysis of what caused Britain to act as it did at Munich, it is also quite clearly a defense of Baldwin, Chamberlain, and the appeasers. Jack argues that Britain's failure to arm itself in the thirties forced it into the appeasement policy at Munich but that this failure was principally the consequence not of weak leadership on the part of the two prime ministers but of popular resistance led by the pacifists, advocates of collective security through the League of Nations, opponents of greater government spending, and shortsighted domestic politicians stressing narrow self-interest over larger national needs. No one who knew anything about Joe Kennedy's pro-Chamberlain, pro-Munich views could miss the fact that the thesis could be read partly as a defense of Joe's controversial position. Carl Friedrich privately said that the thesis should have been titled "While Daddy Slept."

Yet dismissing the thesis as simply an answer to Joe's critics is to miss Jack's compelling central argument — one originally made by Alexis de Tocqueville over a hundred years before: Popular rule does not readily lend itself to the making of effective foreign policy. Democracies, Jack asserts, have a more difficult time than dictatorships in mobilizing resources for their defense. Only when a pervasive fear of losing national survival takes hold can a democracy like Britain or the United States persuade its citizens "to give up their personal interests, for the greater purpose. In other words, every group [in Britain] wanted rearmament but no group felt that there was any need for it to sacrifice its privileged position. This feeling in 1936 was to have a fatal influence in 1938" at Munich.

Jack saw his thesis as a cautionary message to Americans, who needed to learn from Britain's mistakes. "In this calm acceptance of the theory that the democratic way is the best . . . lies the danger," Jack wrote. "Why, exactly, is the democratic system better? . . . It is better because it allows for the full development of man as an individual. But . . . this only indicates that democracy is a 'pleasanter' form of government — not that it is the best form of government for meeting the present world problem. It may be a great system of government to live in internally but it's [sic] weaknesses are great. We wish to preserve it here. If we are to do so, we must look at situations much more realistically than we do now."

What seems most important now about Kennedy's thesis is the extent to which he emphasizes the need for unsentimental realism about world affairs. Making judgments about international dangers by ignoring them or wishing them away is as dangerous as unthinking hostility to foreign rivals who may be useful temporary allies. Personal, self-serving convictions are as unconstructive as outdated ideologies in deciding what best serves a nation's interests. Although he would not always be faithful to these propositions, they became mainstays of most of his later responses to foreign challenges.

The exploding world crisis encouraged Jack to turn his thesis into a book. It was not common for a Harvard undergraduate to instantly convert his honor's paper into a major publication. As Harold Laski told Joe, "While it is the book of a lad with brains, it is very immature, it has no structure, and dwells almost wholly on the surface of things. In a good university, half a hundred seniors do books like this as part of their normal work in their final year. But they don't publish them for the good reason that their importance lies solely in what they get out of doing them and not out of what they have to say. I don't honestly think any publisher would have looked at that book of Jack's if he had not been your son, and if you had not been ambassador. And those are not the right grounds for publication."

However accurate Laski's assessment of the thesis, he missed something others in America saw — namely, that international developments made Jack's analysis a timely appeal to millions of Americans eager to consider a wise response to the European war. The collapse of France had made Americans feel more vulnerable to external attacks than at any time since the Franco-British abuse of neutral rights during the Napoleonic Wars.

New York Times columnist Arthur Krock, to whom Jack showed the thesis, thought "it was amateurish in many respects but not, certainly not, as much so as most writings in that category are." "I told him," Krock said, "I thought it would make a very welcome and very useful book." And so Krock helped Jack with stylistic revisions and suggested a title, *Why England Slept*, mirroring Churchill's *While England Slept*. Krock also gave Jack the name of an agent, who arranged a contract with Wilfred Funk, a small publishing house, after Harper & Brothers and Harcourt Brace both turned it down. Harpers thought the manuscript already eclipsed by current events, and Harcourt thought "sales possibilities too dim" and "things moving too fast" for a book on the British failure at Munich to command much interest in the United States.

They were wrong, but partly because Jack made revisions to the manuscript that gave it more balance and greater timeliness than the original. In deciding to try for publication, Jack understood that he needed to do it "as soon as possible, as I should get it out before . . . the issue becomes too dead." He also accepted the recommendation of several English readers that he not place so much more blame on the public than on Baldwin and Chamberlain for Munich. Most important, he saw the need to say less about the shortcomings of democracy and more about its defense in present circumstances. Hitler's victories in Europe and the feeling that Britain might succumb to Nazi aggression made it more appealing for Jack to emphasize not democracy's weakness in meeting a foreign crisis but what America could do to ensure its national security in a dangerous world.

The book, which received almost uniformly glowing reviews and substantial sales in the United States and Britain, demonstrated that Jack had the wherewithal for a public career. No one, including Jack, was then thinking in terms of any run for office. But his success suggested that he was an astute observer of public mood and problems, especially as they related to international affairs. Neither Jack nor Joe foresaw the precise direction Jack's life would now take, but Joe saw the book as a valuable first step for a young man reaching for public influence. "I read Jack's book through and I think it is a swell job," he wrote Rose. "There is no question that regardless of whether he makes any money out of it or not, he will have built himself a foundation for his reputation that will be of lasting value to him." And to Jack he wrote: "The book will do you an amazing amount of good. . . . You would be surprised how a book that really makes the grade with high-class people stands you in good stead for years to come."

For his part, Jack had few, if any, illusions about the book. He understood that circumstances more than his skill as a writer and analyst had given the book its resonance. But he also understood that seizing the main chance when it presented itself was not to be despised; he was more than happy, then, to devote his summer to publicizing and selling *Why England Slept*.

Kennedy friend Charles Spalding remembers visiting Jack at the Cape shortly after the book had appeared. "Jack was downstairs with a whole pile of these books. . . . It was just a wonderful disarray of papers, letters from Prime Ministers and congressmen and people you've heard about, some under wet bathing suits and some under the bed." When Spalding asked how the book was selling, "[Jack's] eyes lit up and he said, 'Oh, very well. I'm seeing to that.' He was seeing that the books were handed out and he was really moving the books. . . . It was just a sort of amusing pragmatism that he hadn't just written the book and then he was going to just disappear. He was going to see that it got sold. He was just laughing at his own success. . . . He was doing everything he could to promote it. And he was good at that. . . . The interviews, radio programs, answering letters, autographing copies, sending them out, checking bookstores."

IN THE SUMMER OF 1940, aside from promoting his book, Jack was at loss for what to do next. He had thoughts of attending Yale Law School, but health problems persuaded him to temporarily abandon such plans. In addition, he had doubts about a law career. It would mean not only competing with brother Joe, who was enrolled at Harvard, but also abandoning what Lem Billings called his intellectual interests. "I don't think there was any question but that he was thinking he would go into journalism and teaching." But like millions of other young Americans in 1940, the state of world affairs made private decisions hostage to public developments. "There was an awful vacuum there in 1940," Lem remembered, "a very uncomfortable period for a guy who was graduating from school. I mean, what to do? We were so damn close to going to war. . . . You didn't know what you were going to do[,] so what was the point of getting into any lifelong thing?" Everybody "was just sort of marking time." The passage of a bill in September 1940 authorizing the first peacetime draft had put the country's young men on notice that military service might take precedence over personal plans.

And so Jack went to Stanford in September to nurse himself back to health in the warm California sun. His graduate work, which lasted only one quarter, to December 1940, was supposed to focus on business studies, but his courses and interests remained in political science and international relations. A young woman he dated while in California remembered his attentiveness to contemporary events. "He was fascinated with the news. He always turned it on in the car, on the radio. . . . He was intrigued by what was going on in the world." Another Stanford contemporary recalled Jack's conversations with Stanford's student body president about the nature of effective government leadership — he pointed to FDR as a model of how to make big changes without overturning traditional institutions. This student also remembered Jack's telling him and other "remote westerners . . . that there was a war on, that it had been on for a year, and that we were going to get into it." In December, he attended an Institute of World Affairs conference in Riverside, California, on current international problems, where he acted as a "rapporteur" for four of the sessions: "War and the Future World Economy," "The Americas: Problems of Hemispheric Defense & Security," "War and the Preservation of European Civilization," and "Proposed Plans for Peace."

His interest in overseas affairs was more than academic. When Joe resigned his ambassadorship in December 1940, Jack counseled him on what to say to insulate him from charges of appeasement and identification with Chamberlain's failed policies. More important, he now convinced his father not to take issue with the Lend-Lease bill FDR proposed as a means to help Britain defeat Germany. If we failed to give this aid now and Britain were defeated, Jack argued, it would cost the United States much more later and might force us into a war with Hitler, which Joe, above all, wished to avoid. Under pressure from Roosevelt as well, Joe publicly accepted his son's reasoning.

Jack's term at Stanford was an interlude of no lasting consequence. His unresolved health difficulties drew him back to the East Coast at the start of 1941, where he busied himself for the first three

months of the year with finding a ghostwriter for his father's memoirs and thinking about renewing his application to Yale Law School.
But when his mother and sister Eunice went to Latin America in the
spring, Jack decided to join them and then travel on his own. He visited Argentina, Brazil, and Chile, with brief stops in Uruguay, Peru,
Ecuador, Colombia, and Panama.

Although the trip was valuable, upon his return the direction
of Jack's life still remained unclear. There was, however, little question that it would sooner or later take a serious turn. However self-
indulgent, Jack had no intention of becoming a career playboy trading
on his father's fame and influence. And Joe and Rose believed it
inconceivable for any of their children to settle for a sybaritic life.
The material benefits of their wealth were all too obvious, from the
opulent houses to the cars, clothing, jewelry, foreign travel, lavish
vacations, and parties at home and abroad with all the social lions
of their time. But a life without ambition, without some larger purpose than one's own needs and satisfaction, was never part of the
Kennedy ethos. It is one of the great ironies of this family's saga that
however frivolous any of its members might be at one time or
another, it was impermissible to make frivolity a way of life.

At the age of twenty-three, Jack understood that he needed a life-
work; just as important, he had considerable confidence that he
would succeed. His background and experience had created a belief
in himself as someone special, as standing apart from the many
other talented, promising young men he had met at home and
abroad. His privileged life had opened the way for his success, but
it was hardly the full measure of what would make for an uncommon life.

CHAPTER 3

The Terrors of Life

Great men, great nations, have not been boasters and buffoons, but perceivers of the terror of life, and have manned themselves to face it.

— Ralph Waldo Emerson

DESPITE THE FAMILY'S WEALTH and palatial houses, Jack had never seemed to feel as if he had a home, or at least a special place in one of the houses that was exclusively his. A young woman who went with Jack to Hyannis Port when the rest of the family was in Palm Beach "was surprised to see him go through the empty house like an intruder, peeking into his father's room and looking in his dresser draw[er]s, and picking up objects on all the surfaces as if he hadn't seen them before."

Part of the reason had to do with his mother. Rose's absences had always made Jack unhappy. In 1923, when he was almost six and Rose was about to depart on a six-week trip to California, Jack exclaimed, "Gee, you're a great mother to go away and leave your children all alone." Jack, who had been apart from his parents earlier for an extended hospital stay, saw any separation as a return of that unhappy experience. And while he seemed able to tolerate his father's business trips, with his mother it was different. He told LeMoyne Billings that whenever Rose announced another trip, he openly cried, which greatly irritated her and made her more distant than ever from her anxious son. Jack learned, as he told Billings, to act stoically in the face of her departures. "Better to take it in stride," he said.

That said, her presence wasn't necessarily an improvement. Rose's insistence on rigid rules of behavior upset and angered Jack.

One commentator has said: "[She] organized and supervised the large family with the institutional efficiency she had learned from the Ursuline nuns of Sacred Heart Academy. She insisted on strict adherence to domestic routines and an idealistic dedication to the doctrines of the Roman Catholic Church." Lem Billings remembered her as "a tough, constant, minute disciplinarian with a fetish for neatness and order and decorum." She discouraged any excessive emotional display. Touching, personal warmth, sensuality of any kind, was frowned on. "She was terribly religious. She was a little removed," Jack said as an adult. In private, he complained that Rose never told him that she loved him. Jack's friend Charles Spalding, who saw the family up close, described Rose as "so cold, so distant from the whole thing . . . I doubt if she ever rumpled the kid's hair in his whole life. . . . It just didn't exist: the business of letting your son know you're close, that she's there. She wasn't." Jacqueline Bouvier Kennedy told the journalist Theodore White that "history made him [Jack] what he was . . . this lonely sick boy. His mother really didn't love him. . . . She likes to go around talking about being the daughter of the Mayor of Boston, or how she was an ambassador's wife. . . . She didn't love him. . . . History made him what he was."

In response, Jack staged minor rebellions. He refused to toe the line on her religious concerns or follow her household rules. Once when she instructed the children on a Good Friday to wish for a happy death, Jack said he wanted to wish for two dogs. He occasionally interrupted Rose's recitations of Bible stories with impious questions. What happened to the donkey Jesus had ridden into Jerusalem on the way to his crucifixion? Jack asked. Who attended to the donkey after Jesus was gone? Jack also expressed his antagonism to Rose by keeping a messy room, dressing sloppily, and arriving to meals tardy.

His annoyance with her compulsive demands poked through a letter he wrote in response to a round-robin note she sent to all the children in 1941, when he was twenty-four. "I enjoy your round robin letters," he answered. "I'm saving them to publish — that style of yours will net us millions. With all this talk of inflation and where is our money going — when I think of your potential earning power . . . it's enough to make a man get down on his knees and thank God for the Dorchester High Latin School [sic] which gave you that very sound grammatical basis which shines through every slightly mixed metaphor and each somewhat split infinitive."

If Jack and the other children had their tensions with Rose, they were not the product of the child-rearing habits of a thoughtless, selfish mother. On the contrary, Rose saw her maternal duties as a high calling requiring considered and devoted action. "I looked on child rearing not only as a work of love and duty," she said, "but as a profession that was fully as interesting and challenging as any honorable profession in the world, and one that demanded the best I could bring to it." There was in fact a professionalism to Rose's organization of her large family that rested on the conventional wisdom of the day: Dr. L. Emmett Holt's widely read book, *The Care and Feeding of Children: A Catechism for the Use of Mothers and Children's Nurses* (1934). Holt was the Dr. Benjamin Spock of the first half of the twentieth century, and Rose closely followed his rules, which included the need for a daily bath, regular outdoor activity, strict discipline — "spare the rod and spoil the child" — and limited displays of affection. As Holt recommended, Rose kept file cards on her children's illnesses and made neatness and order a high priority, though to little avail in Jack's case.

It is also essential to remember that she was burdened with a retarded daughter who consumed a large part of her energy and reduced her freedom to attend to and practice a more joyful give-and-take with her other children. Rosemary, the third child, had been born in the midst of the flu epidemic of 1918. Whether the contagion or some genetic quirk or brain damage from inexpertly used forceps during her delivery was the cause of her disability is impossible to know. By the time she was five, however, it was clear that her physical and mental development was dramatically abnormal. She could not feed or dress herself, had limited verbal skills, and could not keep up with the physical activities of her siblings or her classmates at school. Determined not to send her to an institution, as was accepted practice at the time for "feebleminded" children, Joe and Rose committed themselves to keeping her at home under Rose's supervision, helped by a special governess and several tutors.

Rose gave the child unqualified love and attention. Eunice remembered the many hours Rose spent playing tennis with Rosemary, even though she never played with the other children. Moreover, Rose and Joe required everyone in the family to treat Rosemary as an equal as much as possible. The other children responded with an attentiveness and kindness that speaks well of all their characters and the strength of shared family purpose. To Rose,

Rosemary's disability was a kind of gift from God, reminding the most fortunate that they must give as well as receive. She also believed that Rosemary's difficulties sensitized her other children to the meaning of daily hardship and suffering, which was the lot not just of the poor and underprivileged.

Certainly for Jack, Rosemary's retardation gave him an uncommon compassion for human failings. One friend recalled that he had "a marvelous capacity for projecting himself into other people's shoes. That was one of the great keys to his whole personality. He could become a little old lady who was being embarrassed by her husband's conduct. I saw it happen so many times." The friend recounted an episode in a New York restaurant when a drunk at a nearby table began verbally assaulting Jack, who was by then a well-known public figure. The friend suggested that they leave, but Jack, who sat stoically through the abuse, said, "Would you look at that guy's wife and what she's going through?" The woman looked as if she were "about to die. She was purple with embarrassment. . . . Eventually the wife did take over and get him out of there. And," Jack's friend said, "I thought that was so humane. There were loads of things like that."

Jack himself was as generous toward his sister as any of the children and undoubtedly felt as much remorse as others at her deterioration in 1939–41 when she reached physical maturity. After years of effort that had produced small gains in her ability to deal with adult matters, Rosemary turned violent at the age of twenty-one, throwing tantrums and raging at caretakers who tried to control her. In response, Joe, without Rose's knowledge, arranged for Rosemary to have a prefrontal lobotomy, which contemporary medical understanding recommended as the best means for alleviating her agitation and promising a more placid life. The surgery, however, proved to be a disaster, and Joe felt compelled to institutionalize Rosemary in a Wisconsin nunnery, where she would spend the rest of her life.

Part of the family's impulse in dealing with Rosemary as they did was to hide the truth about her condition. In the twenties and thirties, mental disabilities were seen as a mark of inferiority and an embarrassment best left undisclosed. Rosemary's difficulties were especially hard to bear for a family as preoccupied with its glowing image as the Kennedys. It was one thing for them to acknowledge limitations among themselves, but to give outsiders access to such information or put personal weaknesses on display was to open the family to possible ridicule or attack from people all too eager to knock down Kennedy claims to superiority. Hiding family problems, particularly medical concerns, later became a defense against jeopardizing election to public office.

Yet there was a benefit to keeping quiet about family suffering that served Jack in particular. The corollary to not speaking openly about family problems was bearing individual suffering stoically. The Kennedys believed that people as fortunate as they were should be uncomplaining about adversity. A visitor to the Hyannis Port home remembered how one Kennedy child, seeking sympathy for an injury suffered while playing, fell to the floor in front of Rose and began to whine. "'On your feet,' Rose ordered. The child promptly rose and practically stood at attention. 'Now you know how to behave,' she added. 'Go out there and behave as you know you should.'" The premium placed on strength and courage as answers to personal burdens would serve Jack well through a lifetime of medical problems and physical suffering.

BACK IN JUNE 1934, as Jack's junior year at Choate ended and he began feeling ill again, Joe had sent him to the famous Mayo brothers' clinic in Rochester, Minnesota. He spent a miserable month there. "The Goddamnest hole I've ever seen. I wish I was back at school," he wrote Lem Billings. By himself at the Mayo and then nearby St. Mary's Hospital, where he was transferred after two weeks, he kept his sanity and his hopes for a return to friends and family through a series of letters to Lem. We can only imagine how endless, painful, intrusive, and embarrassing the tests he was subjected to by strangers must have seemed to a seventeen-year-old wrestling with normal adolescent concerns about sex and his body. But having learned from his parents, Jack was stoic and uncomplaining about his difficulties. Lem Billings later told an interviewer, "We used to joke about the fact that if I ever wrote a biography, I would call it 'John F. Kennedy: A Medical History.' [Yet] I seldom ever heard him complain." Trying to be optimistic that the doctors would figure out his problem and restore him to health, Jack told Billings that during a telephone conversation with his father, "he was trying to find out what was wrong with me and for 20 minutes we were trying to hedge around the fact that we didn't know."

Judging from his letters describing the medical tests administered to him and later medical records, Jack had "spastic colitis," which the doctors initially thought might be peptic ulcer disease. They began by prescribing a diet of rice and potatoes preparatory to tests Jack hoped would be over in a few days. But the exams lasted much longer than he had anticipated. "I am suffering terribly out here," he wrote Billings on June 19. "I now have a gut ache all the time. I'm still eating peas and corn for my food and I had an enema." He expected to be there for at least another twelve days. By then, "I'll be dipped in shit. . . . My bowels have utterly ceased to be of service and so the only way that I am able to unload is for them to blow me out from the top down or from the bottom up."

Two days later he told Billings: "God what a beating I'm taking. I've lost 8 lbs. And still going down. . . . I'm showing them a thing or two. Nobody able to figure what's wrong with me. All they do is talk about what an interesting case. It would be funny," he declared wishfully, "if there was nothing wrong with me. I'm commencing to stay awake nights on that. Still don't know when I'll get home. My last eight meals have been peas, corn, prunes. Pul l l lently [sic] appetizing."

Six days later he gave another graphic description of his ordeal. He had heard that he might have to stay in the hospital until July 4. "Shit!! I've got something wrong with my intestines. In other words I shit blood." He feared he might be dying: "My virility is being sapped. I'm just a shell of the former man and my penis looks as if it has been through a wringer." The doctors were still trying to determine the cause of his illness: "I've had 18 enemas in 3 days!!!! I'm clean as a whistle. They give me enemas till it comes out like drinking water which," he said in an expression of rage toward his caretakers, "they all take a sip of. Yesterday I went through the most harassing experience of my life. First, they gave me 5 enemas until I was white as snow inside. Then they put me in a thing like a barber's chair. Instead of sitting in the chair I kneeled . . . with my head where the seat is. They (a blonde) took my pants down!! Then they tipped the chair over. Then surrounded by nurses the doctor first stuck his finger up my ass. I just blushed because you know how it is. He wiggled it suggestively and I rolled them in the aisles by saying 'you have a good motion.' He then withdrew his finger and then, the shmuck, stuck an iron tube 12 inches long and 1 inch in diameter up my ass. They had a flashlight inside it and they looked around. Then they blew a lot of air in me to pump up my bowels. I was certainly feeling great as I know you would having a lot of strangers looking up my asshole. Of course, when the pretty nurses did it I was given a cheap thrill. I was a bit glad when they had their fill of that. My poor bedraggled rectum is looking at me very reproachfully these days. . . . The reason I'm here is that they may have to cut out my stomach — the latest news."

On June 30, he was "still in this God-damned furnace and it looks like a week more." He had become "the pet of the hospital." It was testimony to his extraordinary stoicism and good humor that he had managed to charm the staff despite his ongoing ordeal. "I only had two enemas today so I feel kind of full," he told Billings. "They have found something wrong with me at last. I don't know what but it's probably something revolting like piles or a disease of my vital organ. What will I say when someone asks me what I got?" His question was not posed hypothetically. As with Rosemary, Jack and the family were determined to hide the seriousness of his medical problems. Nothing good could come from revealing that Jack might have some debilitating long-term illness that could play havoc with his future.

All the gastrointestinal tests indicated that Jack had colitis and digestive problems, which made it difficult for him to gain weight and threatened worse consequences if the colon became ulcerated or bled. In July 1944, Dr. Sara Jordan, a gastroenterologist at Boston's Lahey Clinic, would note that Jack's diagnosis at the Mayo Clinic and then at Lahey was "diffuse duodenitis and severe spastic colitis," intestinal and colonic inflammations that could become life-threatening diseases. The premium was not only on finding a better diet for him but also on relieving emotional stress, which in those days was assumed to be a major contributor to ulcers and colitis.

Judging from accounts of colitis therapy published in the January 1934 and December 1936 Mayo Clinic journal, *Proceedings*, the treatment given to Jack was a combination of restricted diet and injection or subcutaneous implant of a serum obtained from horses. Although the clinic claimed a measure of success with this treatment, it was clearly no cure-all. Indeed, in November 1935, the *American Journal of Medical Sciences* recommended a "calcium and parathyroid" therapy. The use of parathyroid extract (parathormone) paralleled the development of adrenal-hormone extracts, which the Mayo Clinic, along with other research centers, was then testing. These extracts held promise in the treatment of a variety of illnesses, including chronic spastic and ulcerated colitis. Obtaining these extracts was then very costly. "We always had adrenal extract for those who could afford it," Dr. George Thorn, an expert at Harvard and Boston's Peter Bent Brigham Hospital, said in 1991. There seems no doubt that Joe was able to pay for the medication.

There are intriguing questions about Jack's medical history that remain difficult, if not impossible, to resolve. In 1937, the first clinical use of adrenal extracts — corticosteroids, or anti-inflammatory agents — became possible with the preparation of DOCA (desoxycorticosterone acetate). This drug was administered in the form of pellets implanted under the skin. It is now well known that Jack was treated with DOCA in 1947 after his "official" diagnosis of Addison's disease (a disease of the adrenal glands characterized by a deficiency of the hormones needed to regulate blood sugar, sodium and potassium, and the response to stress; it is named after the nineteenth-century English physician Thomas Addison). But there are earlier references to Jack implanting pellets. Early in 1937, in a handwritten note to Joe, Jack worried about getting his prescription — probably the parathyroid extract, or DOCA — filled in Cambridge. "Ordering stuff here very [illegible word]," he wrote his father. "I would be sure you get the prescription. Some of that stuff as it is very potent and he [Jack's doctor] seems to be keeping it pretty quiet." Nine years later, in 1946, Paul Fay, one of Jack's friends, watched him implant a pellet in his leg. He remembers Jack using "a little knife . . . [to] just barely cut the surface of the skin, try not to get blood, and then get underneath and put this tablet underneath the skin, and then put a bandage over it. And then hopefully this tablet would dissolve by the heat of the body and be absorbed by the bloodstream." Thus, before the diagnosis of Addison's, Jack may have been on steroids — still in an experimental stage, with great uncertainty as to dosage — which may have been successfully treating his colitis, but at the possible price of stomach, back, and adrenal problems.

Physicians in the 1930s and 1940s did not realize what today is common medical knowledge: namely, that adrenal extracts are effective in treating acute ulcerative colitis but can have deleterious long-term chronic effects, including osteoporosis with vertebral column deterioration and peptic ulcers. In addition, chronic use of corticosteroids can lead to the suppression of normal adrenal function and may have caused or contributed to Jack's Addison's disease.

It is also possible that the DOCA had little impact on Jack's back or adrenal ailments. Unlike synthetic corticosteroids, which did not become available until 1949, the initial DOCA compounds did not have the sort of noxious side effects associated with the later compounds. Nevertheless, by 1942, twenty-eight varieties of DOCA or adrenal extracts had become available, and since no one can say which of these Jack may have been using or exactly what was in them, it remains conceivable that the medicine was doing him more harm than good.

Jack could also have been suffering from celiac sprue, an immune disease common to people of Irish ancestry and characterized by "intolerance to gluten, a complex mixture of nutritionally important proteins found in common . . . food grains such as wheat, rye, and barley." Although Jack would manifest several symptoms associated with the disease — chronic diarrhea, osteoporosis, and Addison's — other indications of celiac sprue — stunted growth in children, iron deficiency anemia, and family history — were absent. The presence of persistent, severe spastic colitis (now described as irritable bowel syndrome) and the possibility that he had Crohn's disease (an illness marked by intestinal inflammation and bleeding as well as back and adrenal problems) also diminish, though do not eliminate, the likelihood that Jack had celiac sprue, a disease of the small intestine, not the colon. Moreover, despite many hospitalizations at some of the country's leading medical centers after 1950, when celiac sprue was first identified, none of his doctors suggested such a diagnosis. However, the fact that physicians in the fifties and sixties did not readily recognize the disease in adults leaves such a diagnosis as a possibility.

From September 1934 to June 1935, Jack's senior year, the Choate infirmary had kept close watch on Jack's blood count. In turn, Joe passed the results on to the Mayo doctors. At that time, there was also concern that Jack might be suffering from leukemia, a fatal disease resulting from uncontrolled proliferation of the white blood cells. With the benefit of current knowledge, it seems likely that the changes in Jack's blood counts were a reaction to the drugs he was taking. When he fell ill the following year, Dr. William Murphy of Harvard advised that Jack had agranulocytosis, a drug-induced decrease of granular white blood corpuscles, which made him more susceptible to infections.

Some of Jack's hospitalizations were brief. Except for his short stay in the infirmary in April 1935, he enjoyed good health during his final year at Choate. While in London in October for his post-Choate courses at the London School of Economics, he had to be hospitalized, but a quick recovery allowed his enrollment at Princeton for the fall term. Jack's relapse probably resulted from an inconsistent use of the medicines or a reduction of dosage when his health showed improvement.

But sometimes Jack's visits were lengthy. When he had to withdraw from Princeton to enter Peter Bent Brigham in Boston, he spent most of the next two months there. Uncertain as to whether they were dealing strictly with colitis or a combination of colitis and ulcers and worried that his medicines were playing havoc with his white blood cell count, his doctors performed additional tests. Jack told Billings it was "the most harrowing experience of all my storm-tossed career. They came in this morning with a gigantic rubber tube. Old stuff I said, and rolled over thinking naturally that it would [be] stuffed up my arse. Instead they grabbed me and shoved it up my nose and down into my stomach. They then poured alchohol [sic] down the tube. . . . They were doing this to test my acidosis. . . . They had the thing up my nose for 2 hours." The test measured Jack's acid levels to see if he was prone to stomach ulcers. The doctors were concerned anew about his blood count. According to what Jack wrote Billings, it was 6,000 when he entered the hospital and three weeks later it was down to 3,500. "At 1500 you die," Jack joked. "They call me '2000 to go Kennedy.'"

By the end of January, he was more worried than ever about his health, though he continued with more biting humor to defend himself against thoughts of dying. "Took a peak [sic] at my chart yesterday and could see that they were mentally measuring me for a coffin. Eat drink & make Olive [his current girlfriend], as tomorrow or next week we attend my funeral. I think the Rockefeller Institute may take my case. . . . Flash — they are going to stick that tube up my ass again as they did at Mayo." His frustration with and anger at medical experts who seemed better able to inflict painful and humiliating tests on him than explain and cure what he had was evident when he wrote Billings: "All I can say is it's bully of them or more power to my smelly farts."

And yet behind the jokes was Jack's fear that he was slated for an early demise, making him almost manic about packing as much pleasure into his life as he could in the possibly short time remaining to him. His letters to Billings are full of frenetic talk about partying and having sex. He was frustrated at having to stay in Boston, even though he left the hospital on weekends to socialize. He heard that there were "'millions of beautiful young misses arriving in Palm Beach daily,' so am getting rather fed up with the meat up here, if you know what I mean," he wrote Billings. He gave him a scorecard of his actions: "Got the hottest neck out of Hansen Saturday night. She is pretty good so am looking forward to bigger and better ones. Also got a good one last night from J. so am doing you proud." "Flash —," he added in another letter, "B.D. came to see me today in the hospital and I laid her in the bath-tub." As for another date, he declared: "The next time I take her out she is going to be presented with a great hunk of raw beef, if you know what I mean."

Jack's seeming indifference to the young women he was using for his sexual pleasures was not entirely due to his sense of urgency. It was also a measure of the times in which Jack came to manhood. In the thirties and forties, Jack's "catting about" was accepted practice among well-off college boys "sowing wild oats." What became anathema in the last third of the twentieth century with the rise of women's liberation and the change in social mores was little frowned upon by men in that bygone era. Jack certainly had genuine regard for his sisters Rosemary and Kathleen. He treated Rosemary with great sensitivity and had only respect for Kathleen, who, like Jack and unlike elder brother Joe, had a rebellious streak. She was the sibling he felt closest to. But under the influence of his father's example, contemporary male behavior, and the appeal of hedonism to a teenager facing a possibly abbreviated life, glaring contradictions toward women became a mainstay of his early and later years.

In preparation for attending Harvard in the fall of 1936, Jack had spent that spring recuperating in Arizona, where he enjoyed improved health. But he remained worried that it would not last. "Plunked myself down for an injection after reading of Irving Carters' [sic] death from the same thing I have, to the Dr.'s office," he wrote Billings in May. "This morning I awoke with a hacking cough which Smokey [James "Smokey Joe" Wilde, a Choate friend with him in Arizona] assures me is T.B. in the more advanced stage. It will be the fucking last straw if I come down with T.B." He did not, and the rest of his stay in the desert and then at Cape Cod in the summer gave him a renewed sense of well-being. During his first year at Harvard there were no serious medical crises, which allowed him to compete on the freshman football and swimming teams. In the summer of 1937, however, during his trip to Europe, he was stricken by swelling, hives, and a reduced blood count. Billings, who was with him, said later, "Jack broke out in the most terrible rash, and his face blew up, and we didn't know anybody and had an awful time getting a doctor." Exactly what accounted for his symptoms is unknown, but at least one doctor suspected an allergic reaction to something Jack ate, although the reduced blood count suggests continuing agranulocytosis.

Whatever he had cleared up quickly, but it did not signal an end to his medical problems. On the contrary, from the beginning of 1938 to the end of 1940, stomach and colon problems continued to plague him. In February 1938, he had gone back to the Mayo Clinic for more study. The Mayo treatment for ulcerated colitis now consisted of blood transfusions, liver extract, nicotinic acid, thiamine chloride, and Neoprontosil, a sulphur drug, but the clinic itself acknowledged that its therapy was of limited value. At the end of the month, Jack found himself in the Harvard infirmary suffering from grippe, and at the beginning of March he had "an intestinal type infection" that lasted two weeks and forced him to enter New England Baptist Hospital. Though he was able to return to school to finish out the term, he spent another two weeks in New England Baptist in June for the same complaints.

By October he was still "in rotten shape," but he refused to reenter the hospital for what now seemed like additional pointless tests. At the end of his fall term in February 1939, however, he gave in and went back to the Mayo Clinic. It was the same old routine: a diet of rice and potatoes three times a day and another inspection of his colon and digestive system. By November, under the care of Dr. William Murphy of Harvard, the Nobel laureate who co-discovered the treatment of pernicious anemia and had an uncommon faith in the healing power of liver extracts, Jack recorded that he was going to "take my first liver injection today and I hope they work." It did not. A year later, he was still wrestling with abdominal pain, a spastic colon, and low weight. If the adrenal extracts were limiting the effects of his colitis — and it is not clear that they were — it certainly was worsening his stomach problems. Nevertheless, it did not stop him from attending to the crisis that had engulfed the world. "For a man with a weak stomach," his father wrote him in September 1940, "these last three days [the Battle of Britain] have proven very conclusively that you can worry about much more important things than whether you are going to have an ulcer or not." In fact, whatever the effects of the parathyroid hormone and then adrenal extracts on his colitis, they were almost certainly contributing to the onset of a duodenal ulcer. Though such a condition remained undiagnosed until November 1943, when "an x-ray examination reported an early duodenal ulcer," current medical knowledge suggests that the extracts were a prime cause of this condition. In 1944, a gastroenterologist concluded that Jack was still suffering from a spastic colon. Moreover, there was evidence of "spasm and irritability of the duodenum [or small intestine] . . . which was suggestive of a duodenal ulcer scar." But there would be no public acknowledgment of any of this, nor any privately evident self-pity. Stoically refusing to let health concerns stop him became a pattern that would allow Jack to pursue a political career.

The onset of serious back problems in 1940 added to Jack's miseries. In 1938 he had begun to have "an occasional pain in his right sacro-iliac joint. It apparently grew worse but at times he was completely free from symptoms," a medical history made in December 1944 recorded. "In the later part of 1940 while playing tennis he experienced a sudden pain in his lower right back — it seemed to him that 'something had slipped.' He was hospitalized at the Lahey Clinic . . . for ten days. A low back support was applied and he was comfortable. Since that time he has had periodic attacks of a similar nature." Although he had suffered football injuries and other mishaps that could help account for his emerging back pain, the onset of his back problem could have been related to his reliance on adrenal extracts and/or parathyroid hormone to control his colitis; they may have caused osteoporosis and deterioration in his lumbar spine. Back surgery in 1944 showed clear evidence of this condition. During the surgery "some abnormally soft disc interspace material was removed and . . . very little protrusion of the ruptured cartilage present" was noted, which would make him vulnerable to progressive back injury. It was, as it had long been with Jack, one thing after another.

IN THE FALL OF 1940, Jack, at age twenty-three, was among the first slated for induction into the U.S. Army. Because he was enrolled at Stanford for 1940–41, he was not to be called until the end of the academic year. His colon, stomach, and back problems, however, promised to give him an easy out. "The only humorous thing in my life to date," a Harvard friend at law school wrote Jack in the fall of 1940, "has been you getting drafted. I swear to God Jack I thought I'd die of exhaustion from laughing. . . . Christ of all the guys in the world. . . . It's a lucky thing you've got your stomach."

But Jack wanted to serve. "This draft has caused me a bit of concern," he wrote Billings. "They will never take me into the army — and yet if I don't [serve], it will look quite bad." He wanted to keep his medical problems as quiet as possible, and failing to qualify for service would subject his difficulties to public discussion. In addition, it would add to the criticism already leveled against his father for being adamantly opposed to American involvement in the war. There was also the fact that he remained uncertain about a career. Thoughts of attending law school did not excite him. A stint in the military seemed like a challenging alternative, especially alongside a desire not to let Joe Jr., who was becoming a navy pilot, outshine him.

Yet none of these reasons seem sufficient to explain his readiness to enter the military in spite of his medical difficulties. It was an impressive act of courage. His intestinal and back problems would make a military regimen a constant struggle and seemed likely to further undermine his health. When, in 1941, Jack failed the physical exams for admission to first the army's and then the navy's officer candidate schools, he turned to his father to pull strings on his behalf. Although he followed an exercise routine all summer to prepare himself for another physical, no program of calisthenics was going to bring him up to the standards required for induction into either service. Only a denial of his medical history would allow him to pass muster, and he was able to ensure this through Captain Alan Kirk, his father's former naval attaché at the American embassy in London and current head of the Office of Naval Intelligence (ONI) in Washington, D.C. Kirk had arranged for Joe Jr. to enter the navy as an officer in the spring of 1941, and now at Joe Sr.'s request he did the same for Jack that summer. "I am having Jack see a medical friend of yours in Boston tomorrow for physical examination and then I hope he'll become associated with you in Naval Intelligence," Joe wrote Kirk in August.

One month later, the board of medical examiners miraculously gave Jack a clean bill of health. Reading the report of his exam, one would think he never had a serious physical problem in his life. The doctors listed the "usual childhood diseases" and noted that he had been on a "restricted . . . diet of no fried food or roughage," but they claimed that he had "no ulcers," and declared him "physically qualified for appointment" as an officer in the naval reserve. It was a complete whitewash that would never have been possible without his father's help. The Office of Naval Intelligence was delighted to accept this "exceptionally brilliant student, [who] has unusual qualities and a definite future in whatever he undertakes." True, being in intelligence made it unlikely that he would be exposed to physical danger, but once in the service almost anything could happen.

Jack entered the navy in October 1941 as an ensign and immediately went to the Foreign Intelligence Branch of the ONI in Washington. He became a paper-pusher, collating and summarizing reports from overseas stations for distribution in ONI bulletins. It was uninteresting work. One of six officers assigned to a plain room with metal desks and typewriters, Jack spent his days "writing, condensing, editing" news of international developments. But his humdrum nine-to-five, six-day-a-week job changed with Japan's December 7 attack on Pearl Harbor. Jack's office then went to a round-the-clock schedule. He drew the night shift, working seven nights a week from 10:00 P.M. to 7 A.M., an exhausting cycle. "Isn't this a dull letter," he wrote Billings on December 12, "but I'm not sleeping much nights."

In contrast with his navy job, Jack enjoyed a rich social life in Washington. His sister Kathleen, who was a reporter for the conservative *Times-Herald*, gave him instant access to a social whirl in which groups of young men and women spent evenings together eating, attending movies, playing party games, exchanging gossip, and romancing one another. Through her, Jack met Inga Arvad, a blond, blue-eyed Dane who "exuded sexuality" and was described as "a perfect example of Nordic beauty." *New York Times* columnist Arthur Krock, who had helped Inga get a job at the *Times-Herald*, was "stupefied" by her beauty. Four years older than Jack, twice married, and worldly-wise, Inga Binga (as Jack fondly called her) was a daily columnist. "She couldn't write anything extended at all," her editor said later, "but she had a good intuitive style of writing about people." Her interviews under the title "Did You Happen to See?" engaged a faithful audience as much by her personality as by her subjects. A column she did on Jack provided an amusing portrait of "a boy with a future" who did not like to be called "Young Kennedy" lest he be seen as in his father's shadow and short on accomplishments.

The column was a small window on Jack and Inga's relationship. She liked Jack, Inga told a fellow reporter. She thought him "refreshing" because "he knows what he wants. He's not confused about motives." As Inga was still married to her second husband, from whom she was separated, they began with an understanding that theirs was no more than a passing affair. "I wouldn't trust him as a long term companion, obviously," she added. "And he's very honest about that. He doesn't pretend that this is forever. So, he's got a lot to learn and I'll be happy to teach him."

Jack and Inga kept up a pretense of not being lovers by double-dating with Kathleen and her current beau, John White, a feature writer at the *Times-Herald*, but despite the modest attempts to hide his involvement with Inga, Jack's affair was an open secret. Joe, who kept tabs on everything the children were doing, was certainly well informed, and he did not object to Jack's involvement with a twice-married woman as long as it was nothing more than a fling.

In spite of his intentions to keep the romance from becoming serious, Jack found himself smitten by Inga, and she reciprocated the affection. "He had the charm that makes birds come out of their trees," she said later. "When he walked into a room you knew he was there, not pushing, not domineering but exuding animal magnetism." But their growing attachment became a source of unhappiness for both of them. A non-Catholic divorcée was hardly what Joe and Rose would find acceptable as a mate for any of their sons. And if that were not enough to sabotage the romance, revelations that Inga had been given privileged access to Nazi higher-ups, including Hitler, during a journalistic stint in Germany raised suspicions that she was a spy. The FBI had begun tracking her movements in the middle of 1941 after she had come to the United States to earn a journalism degree at Columbia University. Her affair with Jack fanned Bureau suspicions. It also worried the ONI, which now saw Jack as a potential weak link in naval security. Consequently, in January 1942, when nationally syndicated columnist Walter Winchell revealed that Jack was having an affair with Inga, it raised the possibility that he might be forced out of the service. Instead, the navy transferred him to a desk job at the Charleston Navy Yard in South Carolina. Jack later told a reporter, "They shagged my ass down to South Carolina because I was going around with a Scandinavian blonde, and they thought she was a spy!"

For almost two months after going to Charleston, Jack clung to the relationship. He was unhappy about being sent into exile, disliked his work, and greatly missed Inga. "Jack finds his present post rather irksome," Rose said in a round-robin letter to her children in February, "as he does not seem to have enough to do and I think will be glad of a transfer." His desk job in Charleston "just seemed to him a waste of time," Billings recalled. "He was very frustrated and unhappy."

Without work to absorb him, Jack was easily preoccupied with Inga. They exchanged love letters, spoke on the phone, and spent long weekends together in Charleston, where she went to visit him a few times. But their relationship grew stormy. FBI wiretaps on their telephone calls and conversations in a hotel room during her visits to South Carolina make clear the growing divide between them. She was worried about being pregnant and "accused Jack of 'taking every pleasure of youth but not the responsibility.'" When she "spoke of the possibility of getting her marriage annulled," Jack "had very little comment to make on the subject." It was clear to Inga that he would never be able to wed her. "We are so well matched," Inga told him. "Only because I have done some foolish things must I say to myself 'NO.' At last I realize that it is true. We pay for everything in life."

In fact, it is doubtful that Jack would have agreed to marry Inga, but any thoughts he might have had along those lines were largely squelched by his father, who warned Jack that he would be ruining his career and hurting the whole family. In early March 1942, Jack, with Inga's assent, ended the romance. "There is one thing I don't want to do," Inga told him, "and that is harm you. You belong so wholeheartedly to the Kennedy-clan, and I don't want you ever to get into an argument with your father on account of me. . . . If I were but 18 summers, I would fight like a tigress for her young, in order to get you and keep you. Today I am wiser." And possibly richer: Inga's ready acquiescence in the breakup raises the possibility that Joe paid her off to end the romance quietly. Joe had made such arrangements for himself. Although their intimacy ended, Jack and Inga kept up a correspondence and a friendly relationship that lasted for three more years.

The recurrence of Jack's back problems in March and April added to his miseries. Since the treatment at the Lahey Clinic in 1940 for back pain, Jack had suffered "periodic attacks of a similar nature." After he entered the navy, his spasms had become "more severe." Moreover, in March 1942 he told Billings that he had thrown out his back while doing calisthenics. His stomach was also acting up again. He went to Palm Beach to talk to Joe, who advised him to consult Dr. Lahey in Boston again.

By April his backache had become so severe that he sought medical attention from the local navy doctor, who declared him unfit for duty and noted that the Mayo Clinic had "advised that a fusion operation was indicated." The navy physician diagnosed the problem as a chronic, recurrent dislocation of the right sacroiliac joint and set it down to a "weak back." By May, with no change in Jack's condition, he was authorized to go to the naval hospital in Chelsea, Massachusetts, for further evaluation and treatment. He was then also able to consult his doctors at the Lahey Clinic about possible back surgery. Since such an operation might end his naval career, Jack and the doctors were reluctant to do it. Besides, the navy physicians at Chelsea concluded that it was unnecessary. They saw no ruptured disk, and now advised that "tight muscles in his legs and abnormal posture consequent thereto" were causing Jack's back pain. By late June his doctors (perhaps with prodding of navy brass by Joe) changed Jack's diagnosis from a dislocation to a "strain, muscular, lower back," which was described as "probably secondary to arthritic changes due to unusual strain from the tenseness of his leg muscles." The recommended course of action was no more than massage and exercise.

There is no hint in these navy medical records of any treatment for his colitis. It may be assumed that Jack and Joe agreed that he should continue to hide the severity of his intestinal problems and say nothing to the navy about any treatment he was receiving. According to the notation in the Chelsea Naval Hospital record, Jack's "general health has always been good. Appendectomy in 1932. No serious illnesses." It is unlikely that any of Jack's navy doctors would have picked up on the possibility that steroids might be causing the "arthritic changes" or deterioration of bone in his lower back. When Rose saw him in September, Jack's stomach, colon, and back problems went unremarked. "You can't believe how well he looks," she told Joe Jr. "You can really see that his face has filled out. Instead of it being lean, it has now become fat." (This was a likely consequence of steroid therapy.) By late June, Jack's doctors declared him fit for duty.

At this time, Jack considered renouncing Catholicism as a kind of retaliation against his parents for their pressure on him to drop Inga. But Jack's ties to Joe and Rose and the Church were stronger than his rebellious inclinations. His iconoclasm went no further than threats to teach a Bible class, which he thought would be seen as "un-Catholic." "I have a feeling that dogma might say it was," he wrote his mother, "but don't good works come under our obligations to the Catholic Church. We're not a completely ritualistic, formalistic, hierarchical structure in which the Word, the truth, must only come down from the very top — a structure that allows for no individual interpretation — or are we?"

His impulse to challenge authority also extended to the medical experts, who seemed unable to solve his health problems. In the midst of the war, however, Jack deferred his inclination to defy conventional wisdom and instead applied for sea duty, which would allow him to get out of the United States and away from his parents and Inga. But, as he would quickly find, life on the front lines provided no escape from his tensions with authority. Instead of unpalatable parental and religious constraints, he found himself frustrated by military directives and actions that seemed to serve little purpose.

IN JULY 1942, the navy granted Jack's request for sea duty and instructed him to attend midshipman's school at a branch of Northwestern University in Chicago. There, he underwent the training that was producing the "sixty-day wonders," the junior naval officers slated for combat. Jack found the demands of the program tiresome and less than convincing as a training ground for sea duty. "This goddamn place is worse than Choate," he wrote Billings. "But as F.D.R. always says, this thing is bigger than you or I — it's global — so I'll string along."

Jack's ambition was to command a motor torpedo boat, one of the PTs (for "patrol-torpedo"), as they were popularly known. The papers were full of stories about the heroic work of these small craft and their foremost spokesman, Lieutenant Commander John Bulkeley, who had won a Congressional Medal of Honor for transporting General Douglas MacArthur from the Philippines through five hundred miles of enemy-controlled waters to Australia. Bulkeley was a great promoter of these craft and had convinced President Roosevelt of their worth. In fact, in his drive to attract aggressive young officers to join his service, Bulkeley had vastly exaggerated the importance and success of the PTs. While Jack's natural skepticism made him suspicious of Bulkeley's claims about all the damage his boats were inflicting on the Japanese, the glamour of the PTs and, most of all, the chance to have his own command and escape the tedium of office work and navy bureaucracy made Bulkeley's appeal compelling.

The competition to become a PT commander was so keen and Jack's back problems so pronounced that he saw little likelihood of being accepted by Bulkeley. But against his better judgment, Joe intervened on Jack's behalf. The positive publicity likely to be generated by having the former ambassador's son in his command and the very positive impression Jack made in an interview persuaded Bulkeley to give Jack one of 50 places applied for by 1,024 volunteers. Once accepted, though, Jack worried about surviving the physical training required for assignment to a boat. Riding in a PT, one expert said, was like staying upright on a bucking bronco. At full speed it cut through the water at more than forty knots and gave its crew a tremendous pounding. In September, while on leave, Jack went to see Joe at the Cape. "Jack came home," Joe wrote his eldest son, "and between you and me is having terrific trouble with his back. . . . I don't see how he can last a week in that tough grind of Torpedo Boats and what he wants to do of course, is to be operated on and then have me fix it so he can get back in that service when he gets better."

Since he wasn't about to have an operation and since the navy was not objecting to his service in the PTs, he decided to test the limits of his endurance. The almost daily exercises at sea put additional strain on his back. "He was in pain," a bunkmate of Jack's during training in Melville, Rhode Island, recalled, "he was in a lot of pain, he slept on that damn plywood board all the time and I don't remember when he wasn't in pain." But he loved the training in gunnery and torpedoes, and particularly handling the boats, which his years of sailing off Cape Cod made familiar and even enjoyable work. "This job on these boats is really the great spot of the Navy," he wrote Billings, "you are your own boss, and it's like sailing around as in the old days." Rose told her other children that Jack's presence at Melville had changed "his whole attitude about the war. . . . He is quite ready to die for the U.S.A. in order to keep the Japanese and the Germans from becoming the dominant people on their respective continents. . . . He also thinks it would be good for Joe [Jr.]'s political career if he [Jack] died for the grand old flag, although I don't believe he feels that is absolutely necessary."

Rose and Joe were relieved that he didn't think it "absolutely necessary" to give his life, but they found nothing funny in Jack's flippant remark about sacrificing himself for his brother's ambitions. Jack's decision to enter combat in the PTs was "causing his mother and me plenty of anxiety," Joe told a priest. He was proud of his sons for entering the most hazardous branches of the service, but it was also causing their parents "quite a measure of grief."

Joe's anxiety about seeing Jack enter combat as a PT commander may have been the determining influence behind a decision to keep Jack in Rhode Island for six months to a year as a torpedo boat instructor. A few of the best students in the program were routinely made instructors, Jack's commander said later. But a fitness report on him, which described Jack as "conscientious, willing and dependable" and of "excellent personal and military character," also considered him "relatively inexperienced in PT boat operations" and in need of "more experience" to become "a highly capable officer." Why someone as inexperienced as Jack was made a training officer is difficult to understand unless some special pressure had been brought to bear.

Jack certainly saw behind-the-scenes manipulation at work, and he moved to alter his orders. He went directly to Lieutenant Commander John Harllee, the senior instructor at Melville. "Kennedy was extremely unhappy at being selected as a member of the training squadron," Harllee recalled, "because he yearned with great zeal to get out to the war zone. . . . As a matter of fact, he and I had some very hard words about this assignment." But Harllee insisted that Jack stay.

It was not for long, however. Jack, distrusting his father's willingness to help, went to his grandfather, Honey Fitz, who arranged a meeting with Massachusetts senator David Walsh, the chairman of the Naval Affairs Committee. Walsh, who was very favorably impressed with Jack, wrote a letter to the Navy Department urging his transfer to a war zone. In January 1943, Jack was detached from his training duties and instructed to take four boats to Jacksonville, Florida, where he would be given reassignment.

Though he thought he was on his "way to war," as he wrote his brother Bobby, who was finishing prep school, he was not there yet. During the thousand-mile voyage, he became ill with something doctors at the naval station in Morehead City, North Carolina, diagnosed as "gastro-enteritis." Since he recovered in two days and rejoined the squadron on its way to Jacksonville, he probably had an intestinal virus or food poisoning rather than a flare-up of his colitis. It was a signal nonetheless that his health remained precarious and that he was a wounded warrior heading into combat. "Re my gut and back," he soon wrote Billings, "it is still not hooray — but I think it will hold out." Upon his arrival in Jacksonville, his new orders assigned him to patrol duty at the Panama Canal. Unwilling to "be stuck in Panama for the rest of the war," he immediately requested transfer to the South Pacific and prevailed upon Senator Walsh to arrange it. By the beginning of March, he was on his way to the Solomon Islands, where Japanese and U.S. naval forces were locked in fierce combat. After U.S. victories in the Coral Sea and at Midway in the spring of 1942, both sides had suffered thousands of casualties and lost dozens of ships in battles for control of New Guinea and the Solomons.

Jack's eagerness to put himself at risk cries out for explanation. Was it because he felt invincible, as the young often do, especially the privileged? This seems doubtful. The reality of war casualties had already registered on him. "Your friend Jock Pitney," he wrote Lem on January 30, 1943, "I saw the other day is reported missing and a class-mate of mine, Dunc Curtis . . . was killed on Christmas day." Was Jack then hoping for a war record he could use later in politics? Almost certainly not. In 1943, Joe Jr. was the heir apparent to a political career, not his younger brother. Instead, his compelling impulse was similar to that of millions of other Americans who believed in the war as an essential crusade against evil, an apocalyptic struggle to preserve American values against totalitarianism. One wartime slogan said it best: "We can win; we must win; we will win." Small wonder, then, that Jack applauded Lem's success in getting himself close to combat in North Africa by becoming an ambulance driver in the American Field Service. "You have seen more war than any of us as yet," he told Billings, who had failed his army physical, "and I certainly think it was an excellent idea to go." Jack also admired their friend Rip Horton for thinking about transferring from the Quartermaster Corps to the "Paratroopers — as he figured if my stomach could stand that [the PTs] he could stand the other. He'll be alright if his glasses don't fall off."

The seventeen months Jack would spend in the Pacific dramatically changed his outlook on war and the military. "I'm extremely glad I came," Jack wrote Inga, "I wouldn't miss it for the world, but I will be extremely glad to get back. . . . A number of my illusions have been shattered."

Among them were assumptions about surviving the war. The combat he witnessed in March 1943, on his first day in the Solomons, quickly sobered him. As his transport ship approached Guadalcanal, a Japanese air raid killed the captain of his ship and brought the crew face to face with a downed Japanese pilot, who rather than be rescued by his enemy began firing a revolver at the bridge of the U.S. ship. "That slowed me a bit," Jack wrote Billings, "the thought of him sitting in the water — battling an entire ship." An "old soldier" standing next to Jack blew the top of the pilot's head off after the rest of the ship's crew, which was "too surprised to shoot straight," filled the water with machine-gun fire. "It brought home very strongly how long it's going to take to finish the war."

It also made the perils of combat clearer to Jack. His Harvard friend Torbert Macdonald described a letter Jack wrote the next day, telling Macdonald "to watch out and really get trained, because I didn't know as much about boats as he [Jack] did, and he said I should know what the hell I was doing because it's different out in the war zone." A visit to the grave of George Mead, a Cape Cod friend who had been killed in the Guadalcanal fighting, underscored the grim realities of the war for Jack. It was "among the gloomier events," he told Inga. "He is buried near the beach where they first landed." It was "a very simple grave" marked by "an aluminum plate, cut out of mess gear . . . and on it crudely carved 'Lt. George Mead USMC. Died Aug. 20. A great leader of men — God Bless Him.' The whole thing was about the saddest experience I've ever had and enough to make you cry." When Rose told Jack that "all the nuns and priests along the Atlantic Coast" were "putting in a lot of praying time" on his behalf, he declared it comforting. But he hoped "it won't be taken as a sign of lack of confidence in you all or the Church if I continue to duck."

What impressed Jack now was not the eagerness of the men in the war zone for heroic combat — that was romantic stuff dispelled by battlefield losses — but their focus on getting home alive. He told Inga that the "picture that I had in the back of my greatly illusioned mind about spending the war sitting on some cool Pacific Beach with a warm Pacific maiden stroking me gently" had disappeared. What "the boys at the front" talked about was "first and foremost . . . exactly when they were going to get home." He wrote his parents: "When I was speaking about the people who would just as soon be home, I didn't mean to use 'They' — I meant 'We.'" He urged them to tell brother Joe not to rush to join him in the Pacific, as "he will want to be back the day after [he] arrives, if he runs true to the form of everyone else." When Billings told Jack that he was considering a transfer to Southeast Asia to fight with the British, Jack expressed delight that he was "still in one piece," noting that "you have certainly had your share of thrills," and advised him to "return safely to the U.S. and join the Quartermaster Corps + sit on your fat ass for awhile. . . . I myself hope perhaps to get home by Christmas, as they have been good about relieving us — as the work is fairly tough out here."

Jack's letters make clear that he was particularly cynical about commentators back home pontificating on the war from the safety and comfort of their offices and pleasure palaces. "It's not bad here at all," Jack wrote Billings, "but everyone wants to get the hell back home — the only people who want to be out here are the people back in the states — and particularly those in the Stork Club." He made a similar point to Inga: "It's one of the interesting things about this war that everyone in the States, with the exception of that gallant armed guard on the good ship U.S.S. Stork Club — Lt. Commander Walter Winchell — wants to be out here killing Japs, while everyone out here wants to be back at the Stork Club. It seems to me that someone with enterprise could work out some sort of exchange, but as I hear you saying, I asked for it honey and I'm getting it." "I always like to check from where he [the columnist] is talking," he wrote his parents, "it's seldom out here." All the talk about "billions of dollars and millions of soldiers" made "thousands of dead" sound "like drops in the bucket. But if those thousands want to live as much as the ten I saw [on my boat] — they should measure their words with great, great care."

Jack admired the courage and commitment to duty he saw among the officers and men serving on the PTs, but he also sympathized with their fear of dying and saw no virtue in false heroics. When one of the sailors under his command, a father of three children, became unnerved by an attack on their PT, Jack found his reaction understandable and tried to arrange shore duty for him. After the man was killed in another attack on Jack's boat, he wrote his parents: "He never said anything about being put ashore — he didn't want to — but the next time we came down the line — I was going to let him work on the base force. When a fellow gets the feeling that he's in for it — the only thing to do is to let him get off the boat — because strangely enough they always seem to be the ones that do get it."

Jack reserved his harshest criticism for the high military officers he saw "leading" the men in his war zone. General Douglas MacArthur, commander of all U.S. Army forces in the Pacific, was no hero to him. Jack thought MacArthur's island-to-island strategy was a poor idea. "If they do that," he wrote his parents, "the motto out here 'The Golden Gate by 48' won't even come true." Jack reported that MacArthur enjoyed little or no support among the men he spoke to. The general "is in fact, very, very unpopular. His nick-name is 'Dug-out-Doug,'" reflecting his refusal to send in army troops to relieve the marines fighting for Guadalcanal and to emerge from his "dug-out in Australia."

The commanders whom Jack saw up close impressed him as no better. "Have been ferrying quite a lot of generals around," he wrote Inga, "as the word has gotten around evidently since MacArthur's escape that the place to be seen for swift and sure advancement if you're a general is in a PT boat." His description to Inga of a visit to their base by an admiral is priceless. "Just had an inspection by an Admiral. He must have weighed over three hundred, and came bursting through our hut like a bull coming out of chute three. . . . 'And what do we have here?'" he asked about a machine shop. When told what it was, he wanted to know what "you keep in it, harrumph ah . . . MACHINERY?" Told yes, he wrote it "down on the special pad he kept for such special bits of information which can only be found 'if you get right up to the front and see for yourself.'" After additional inane remarks about building a dock in a distant bay, he "toddled off to stoke his furnace at the luncheon table. . . . That, Binga, is total war at its totalest."

Worse than the posturing of these officers was the damage Jack saw some of them inflicting on the war effort. As far as he was concerned, many of them were little more than inept bureaucrats. "A great hold-up seems to be the lackadaisical way they handle the unloading of ships," he wrote his parents a month after arriving in the Solomons. "They sit in ports out here weeks at a time while they try to get enough Higgins boats to unload them. . . . They're losing ships, in effect, by what seems from the outside to be just inertia up high. . . . They have brought back a lot of old Captains and Commanders from retirement and stuck them in as heads of these ports and they give the impression of their brains being in their tails, as Honey Fitz would say. The ship I arrived on — no one in the port had the slightest idea it was coming. It had hundreds of men and it sat in the harbor for two weeks while signals were being exchanged." Jack was pleased to note, however, that everyone had confidence in the top man, Admiral William "Bull" Halsey. But he was especially doubtful about the academy officers he met. Now Rear Admiral John Harllee recalled Kennedy's feeling in 1947 that "many Annapolis and West Point graduates were not as good material as the country could have selected. . . . He felt, for example, that some of the senior officers with whom he had had contact in the Navy left something to be desired in their leadership qualities." Somewhat ironically, given his own convoluted path into military service, Jack saw political influence on admitting candidates to the academies as the root of the problem. The resulting unqualified officers were a significant part of what he called "this heaving puffing war machine of ours." He lamented the "super-human ability of the Navy to screw up everything they touch."

Another difficulty Jack and others saw was the overestimation of the PTs' ability to make a substantial contribution to the fighting. Despite wartime claims that just one PT squadron alone had sunk a Japanese cruiser, six destroyers, and a number of other ships in the fighting around Guadalcanal, a later official history disclosed that in four months of combat in the Solomons, all the PT squadrons combined had sunk only one Japanese destroyer and one submarine. One PT commander later said, "Let me be honest. Motor torpedo boats were no good. You couldn't get close to anything without being spotted. . . . Whether we sunk anything is questionable. . . . The PT brass were the greatest con artists of all times. They got everything they wanted — the cream of everything, especially personnel. But the only thing PTs were really effective at was raising War Bonds." Jack himself wrote to his sister Kathleen: "The glamor of PTs just isn't except to the outsider. It's just a matter of night after night patrols at low speed in rough water — two hours on — then sacking out and going on again for another two hours." The boats were poorly armed with inadequate guns and unreliable World War I torpedoes, had defective engines and highly imperfect VHF (very high frequency) radios that kept conking out, lacked armor plating, and turned into floating infernos when hit.

Jack's doubts about local commanders and the PTs as an effective fighting force extended to the crews manning the boats. In May he told his parents, "When the showdown comes, I'd like to be confident they [his crew] knew the difference between firing a gun and winding their watch." By September, he declared that he "had become somewhat cynical about the American as a fighting man. I had seen too much bellyaching and laying off."

During his initial service in the Solomons in April and May 1943, Jack had seen limited action. The United States had won control of Guadalcanal by then, and Kennedy arrived during a lull in the fighting. Nevertheless, the island-hopping campaign against the Japanese was not close to being over. In anticipation of another U.S.

offensive and to reinforce garrisons southeast of their principal base at Rabaul on New Britain Island, the capital of the Australian-mandated territory of New Guinea, the Japanese launched continual air and naval raids. In June, when U.S. forces began a campaign to capture the New Georgia Islands and ultimately oust the Japanese from New Guinea, the PTs took on what U.S. military chiefs in the region called the "Tokyo Express": Japanese destroyers escorting rein-forcements for New Georgia through "the Slot," the waters in New Georgia Sound southeast of Bougainville Strait and between Choiseul Island and the islands of Vella Lavella, Kolombangara, and New Georgia itself.

Jack's boat was sent to the Russell Islands southeast of New Georgia in June and then in July to Lumbari Island in the heart of the combat zone west of New Georgia. On August 1, his boat — PT 109 — was one of fifteen PTs sent to Blackett Strait southwest of Kolombangara to intercept a Japanese convoy that had escaped detection by six U.S. destroyers posted north of the island. The fif-teen were the largest concentration of PTs to that point in the Solomons campaign. It also proved to be, in the words of the navy's official history, "the most confused and least effective action the PT's had been in." In a 1976 authoritative account, Joan and Clay Blair Jr. describe the results of the battle as "a personal and professional dis-aster" for PT commander Thomas G. Warfield. He blamed the defeat on the boats' captains: "There wasn't much discipline in those boats," he said after the war. "There really wasn't any way to control them very well. . . . Some of them stayed in position. Some of them got bugged and didn't fire when they should have. One turned around and ran all the way out of the strait."

The attack by the boats against the superior Japanese force failed. Broken communications between the PTs produced uncoor-dinated, futile action; only half the boats fired torpedoes — thirty-two out of the sixty available — and did so without causing any damage. Worse yet, Jack's boat was sliced in half by one of the Japan-ese destroyers, killing two of the crew members and casting the other eleven, including Jack, adrift.

Since the speedy PTs were fast enough to avoid being run over by a large destroyer and since Jack's boat was the only PT ever rammed in the entire war, questions were raised about his performance in battle. "He [Kennedy] wasn't a particularly good boat commander," Warfield said later. Other PT captains were critical of him for sit-ting in the middle of Blackett Strait with only one engine running, which reduced the amount of churning water that could be seen (and likelihood of being spotted and bombed by Japanese planes) but decreased the boat's chances of making a quick escape from an onrushing destroyer.

In fact, the failure lay not with Jack but with the tactics followed by all PT boat captains and circumstances beyond Kennedy's control. Since only four of the fifteen boats had radar and since it was a pitch-black night, it was impossible for the other eleven PTs to either follow the leaders with radar or spot the Japanese destroyers. After the radar-equipped boats fired their torpedoes, they returned to base and left the other PTs largely blind. "Abandoned by their leaders and enjoined to radio silence, the remaining PT boats had no real chance, in pitch dark, of ambushing the Japanese destroyers," one of the boat commanders said later.

The ramming of Jack's PT was more a freak accident than a " 'stupid mistake' " on Jack's part, as Warfield's successor described it. With no radar and only one of his three engines in gear, Jack could not turn the PT 109 away from the onrushing destroyer in the ten to fifteen seconds between the time it was spotted and the collision.

With six crew members, including Jack, clinging to the hull of the boat, which had remained afloat, Kennedy and two other crewmen swam out to lead the other five survivors back to the floating wreck. One of the men in the water, the boat's engineer, Pat "Pappy" McMahon, was seriously burned and Jack had to tow him against a powerful current. He then dove into the water again to bring two other men to the comparative safety of the listing hull. Two of the crew were missing, apparently killed instantly in the collision. They were never found, and Jack remembered their loss as a "terrible thing." One, who had feared that his number was up, had been part of Jack's original crew; the other had just come aboard and was only nineteen years old.

At 2:00 P.M., after nine hours of clinging to the hull, which was now close to sinking, Kennedy organized the ten other survivors into two support groups for a swim to a seventy-yard-wide deserted speck of land, variously known as Bird or Plum Pudding Island. Jack, swimming on his stomach, towed his wounded crewman by clenching the ties of his life jacket in his mouth while "Pappy" McMahon floated on his back. The swim took five grueling hours. Because the island was south of Ferguson Passage, a southern route into Blackett Strait normally traveled by the PTs, Kennedy decided to swim out into the passage to flag a boat. Although he had not slept in thirty-six hours, was exhausted, and would face treacherous currents, he insisted on going at once. An hour's swim brought him into position to signal a passing PT with a lantern, but no boats showed up that night; believing that no one on the *PT 109* had survived the collision, the commanders had shifted their patrol to the northeast in the Vella Gulf. Bouts of unconsciousness marked Jack's return swim to his crew, who had given him up for lost until he returned at noon. Too exhausted to try another swim to the passage on the night of August 3, he sent another crew member, who returned on the fourth with no better result.

That day, the party swam to the larger nearby Olasana Island, where they found no drinking water to relieve their increasing thirst except for some rain they caught in their mouths during a storm. On the fifth, Kennedy and Barney Ross, another officer who had come on the boat just for the August 1 patrol, swam to Cross Island, which was closer to Ferguson Passage. There they found a one-man canoe, a fifty-five-gallon drum of fresh water, and some crackers and candy. Jack carried the water and food in the canoe back to Olasana, where the men, who had been surviving on coconuts, had been discovered and were being attended to by two native islanders. The next day, after Jack returned to Cross Island, where Ross had remained, he scratched a message on a coconut with a jackknife, which the natives agreed to take to Rendova, the PT's main base. NATIVE KNOWS POSIT HE CAN PILOT 11 ALIVE NEED SMALL BOAT KENNEDY. The next day, four islanders appeared at Cross with a letter from a New Zealand infantry lieutenant operating in conjunction with U.S. Army troops on New Georgia: "I strongly advise that you come with these natives to me. Meanwhile, I shall be in radio communication with your authorities at Rendova and we can finalize plans to collect balance of your party." On the following day, Saturday, the seventh day of the survivors' ordeal, the natives brought Jack to the New Zealander's camp. Within twenty-four hours, all were aboard a PT, being transported back to Rendova for medical attention.

"In human affairs," President Franklin Roosevelt had told the uncooperative Free French leader Charles de Gaulle at the Casablanca Conference the previous January, "the public must be offered a drama." Particularly in time of war, he might have added.

Jack Kennedy was now to serve this purpose. Correspondents for the Associated Press and the United Press covering the Solomons campaign immediately saw front-page news in *PT 109*'s ordeal and rescue. Journalists were already on one of the two PTs that went behind enemy lines to pick up the survivors. In their interviews with the crew and base commanders, they heard only praise for Jack's courage and determination to ensure the survival and deliverance of his men. Consequently, when Navy Department censors cleared the story for publication, Jack became headline news: KENNEDY'S SON IS HERO IN PACIFIC AS DESTROYER SPLITS HIS PT BOAT, the *New York Times* disclosed. KENNEDY'S SON SAVES 10 IN PACIFIC; KENNEDY'S SON IS HERO IN THE PACIFIC, the *Boston Globe* announced with local pride.

Jack became the center of the journalists' accounts, though not simply because he was a hero — there were many other stories of individual heroism that did not resonate as strongly as Jack's. Nor was his family's prominence entirely responsible for the newspaper headlines. Instead, Jack's heroism spoke to larger national mores: he was a unifying example of American egalitarianism. His presence in the war zone and behavior told the country that it was not only ordinary G.I.s from local byways risking their lives for national survival and values but also the privileged son of a wealthy, influential father who had voluntarily placed himself in harm's way and did the country proud. Joe Kennedy, ever attentive to advancing the reputation of his family, began making the same point. "It certainly should occur to a great many people," he declared, "that although a boy is brought up in our present economic system with all the advantages that opportunity and wealth can give, the initiative that America instills in its people is always there. And to take that away from us means there is really nothing left to live for."

Jack himself viewed his emergence as an American hero with wry humor and becoming modesty. He never saw his behavior as extraordinary. "None of that hero stuff about me," he wrote Inga. "The real heroes are not the men who return, but those who stay out there, like plenty of them do, two of my men included." Asked later by a young skeptic how he became a hero, he said, "It was easy. They cut my PT boat in half." He understood that his heroism was, in a way, less about him than about the needs of others — individuals and the country as a whole. Later, during a political campaign, he told one of the officers who had rescued him, "Lieb, if I get all the votes from the people who claim to have been on your boat the night of the pickup, I'll win easily!" When *The New Yorker* and *Reader's Digest* ran articles about him and *PT 109*, he enjoyed the renown but had no illusions about military heroes and worried about their influence on national affairs. "God save this country of ours from those patriots whose war cry is 'what this country needs is to be run with military efficiency,'" he wrote a friend. When Hollywood later made a film about *PT 109*, which served his political image and ambitions, he was happy to go along. But at a special White House showing, he made light of the occasion. "I'd like you to meet the lookout on *PT 109*," he jokingly introduced Barney Ross. In his chuckle was an acknowledgment of an absurdity that had lasted.

In fact, for all the accuracy of the popular accounts praising Jack's undaunted valor, the full story of his courage was not being told. Everything he did in the normal course of commanding his boat and then his extraordinary physical exertion during the week after the sinking was never discussed in the context of his medical problems, particularly his back. Lennie Thom, Jack's executive officer on *PT 109*, was writing letters home at the time discussing Kennedy's back problem and his refusal to "report to sick bay. . . . Jack feigned being *well*, but . . . he knew he was always working under duress." Jack acknowledged to his parents that life on the boats was not "exactly what the Dr. (Jordan) ordered. If she could have put in the last week with me, she would have had that bed turned down for me at the [New England] Baptist [Hospital]." Yet Jack did not let on to his crew or commanding officer that he was ill or in pain. And except for his chronic back ailment, which he simply could not hide and which he seemed to take care of by wearing a "corset-type thing" and sleeping with a plywood board under his mattress, his men on *PT 109* saw no health problems. Joe Kennedy knew better, writing son Joe after news of Jack's rescue that he was trying to arrange Jack's return to the States, because "I imagine he's pretty well shot to pieces by now." Joe Sr. told a friend, "I'm sure if he were John Doake's son or Harry Hopkins' son he'd be home long before this."

But even if the navy were willing to send him home, Jack was not ready to go. He wanted some measure of revenge for the losses he and his crew had suffered. He felt humiliated by the sinking of his boat. According to Inga: "It was a question of whether they were going to give him a medal or throw him out." Jack's commanding officer remembered that "he wanted to pay the Japanese back. I think he wanted to recover his own self-esteem — he wanted to get over this feeling of guilt which you would have if you were sitting there and had a destroyer cut you in two." He took ten days to recuperate from the "symptoms of fatigue and many deep abrasions and lacerations of the entire body, especially the feet," noted by the medical officer attending him. On August 16, he returned to duty "very much improved."

The PTs were now in bad standing, but there were so many of them that the navy needed to put them to some good purpose. Consequently, the brass was receptive to converting some PTs into more heavily armed gunships. Jack's boat — which he helped design — was the first of these to enter combat, in early October. And for the next six weeks he got in a lot of fighting and, to his satisfaction, inflicted some damage on the enemy.

By the late fall, however, he was weary of the war and ready to go home. He wrote Inga that the areas over which they were battling were "just God damned hot stinking corners of small islands in a group of islands in a part of the ocean we all hope never to see again." And the war itself now seemed "so stupid, that while it has a sickening fascination for some of us, myself included, I want to leave it far behind me when I go."

EVEN MORE IMPORTANT than the war-weariness stimulating Jack's desire to go home were his continuing health problems. He now had almost constant back pain and stomachaches, which added to his normal fatigue from riding the boat at nights and struggling to sleep in the heat of the day. But unless he brought his medical difficulties to the attention of the navy doctors, he doubted that they would send him back to the States. "I just took the physical examination for promotion to full Looie," he wrote his brother Bobby. "I coughed hollowly, rolled my eyes, croaked a couple of times, but all to no avail. Out here, if you can breathe, you're one A and 'good for active duty anywhere' and by anywhere, they don't mean the El Morocco or the Bath and Tennis Club, they mean right where you are." He wrote Billings: "I looked as bad as I could look, which is ne plus ultra, wheezed badly, peed on his [the doctor's] hand when he checked me for a rupture to show I had no control, all to no avail. I passed with flying colors, ready 'for active duty ashore or at sea' anywhere, and by anywhere they mean no place else but here. . . . Everyone is in such lousy shape here that the only way they can tell if he is fit to fight is to see if he can breathe. That's about the only grounds on which I can pass these days."

By November 23, however, his stomach pain had become so severe that he had to go to the navy hospital at Tulagi in the Solomons for an examination. X rays showed "a definite ulcer crater," which indicated "an early duodenal ulcer." It was enough to compel Jack's return to the States. On December 14, his commander detached him from the PT squadron and ordered his return to the Melville, Rhode Island, PT training center by the first available air transport. Once back in the States, where he didn't arrive until January, he was entitled to thirty days' leave before reporting for duty.

He went first to Los Angeles to visit Inga, who saw him as "definitely not in good shape," and then to the Mayo Clinic for an examination. Joe Sr. joined Jack in Rochester and thought he was "in reasonably good shape, but the doctors at Mayo's don't entirely agree with me on this diagnosis." The doctors suggested that he consider having surgery to relieve the constant pain in his lower back, but, Joe wrote Rose, "Jack is insistent that he wants to get going again, so he left here Saturday to go and see his brothers and sisters and then report for duty." Before heading to Rhode Island, however, he visited Palm Beach and New York for some R and R. "He is just the same," Rose wrote his siblings, "wears his oldest clothes, still late for meals, still no money. He has even overflowed the bathtub, as was his boyhood custom." The rest did not ease his ills, which now compelled him to take additional leave from duty for further medical evaluation in Boston's New England Baptist Hospital. There, in February, the doctors also recommended back surgery.

But Jack was in no hurry to have an operation. He delayed, perhaps in the hope that the problem would let up or that it could wait until the war ended and he got out of the navy. His reluctance rested partly on the concern that it might raise questions about his failure to disclose his pre-service back, stomach, and colon problems and lead to a medical discharge under a cloud. In the meantime, the navy had reassigned him to a PT base in Miami, Florida, where he did nothing of consequence. "Once you get your feet upon the desk in the morning," he told John Hersey, who was writing *The New Yorker* article on *PT 109*, "the heavy work of the day is done." With no work of importance and his pain too great to delay further treatment, however, he agreed in May to have surgery. Occasional high fevers, coupled with a yellow-brown complexion — which was later diagnosed as malaria — underscored his need for medical attention. He joked that he would get through the war "with nothing more than a shattered constitution." The navy now gave him permission for back surgery at New England Baptist by a Lahey Clinic doctor.

He entered the Chelsea Naval Hospital on June 11 and was diagnosed as having a ruptured disk. On June 22, he was transferred to

New England Baptist, where the following day a Lahey surgeon operated on him. The surgery disclosed not a herniated or ruptured disk
but "abnormally soft" cartilage, which was removed. A subsequent
"microscopic report showed fibrocartilage with degeneration."

Jack did well for the first two weeks after the operation, but
when he began walking, he suffered severe muscle spasms in his
lower back that "necessitated fairly large doses of narcotics to keep
him comfortable." The surgeon noted that only nine other patients
out of more than five hundred had exhibited similar symptoms. Jack
continued to have considerable pain when standing, and the physician predicted that it would be at least six months before he could
return to active duty.

It was an overly optimistic prognosis. When Jack transferred
back to the Chelsea Naval Hospital in August, a neurosurgeon described the case as "an interesting complication of disc surgery where
the surgeon at the Lahey Clinic may well have failed to get to the
bottom of the situation. . . . The pathology seen at operation was
not evidently a clear cut disc." Jack was "obviously incapacitated,"
and the navy physician had no answer to his problem, as he believed "there is some other cause for his neuritis."

Jack's back difficulties were only one of several medical problems afflicting him. He was also described as having "a definite
doudenal ulcer which recently was healed by x-ray, but he now has
symptoms of an irritable colon." Sara Jordan, the leading gastroenterologist at Lahey, told the navy doctors that Jack had "diffuse duodenitis and severe spastic colitis." Though prior to entering the navy
he had suffered "abdominal pain, sometimes of a dull nature and
sometimes acute," he had been in "good condition for some time,
having had no abdominal symptoms, but using considerable discretion in his diet and some times resorting to antispasmodic medication." He told Dr. Jordan that his current distress had begun after his
ordeal in the Solomons. Jordan's report said nothing about the
extensive Mayo Clinic workup and treatment ten years earlier. By the
middle of July, Jack had almost constant abdominal pain that only
codeine could relieve.

During September and October, his back symptoms eased up,
but the intestinal troubles continued. "The main difficulty," the navy
doctors noted on November 6, "is now failure to gain weight and
strength with continuation of spasmodic pain" in the left side of his
abdomen. Since Jack's recovery was going to take "an indefinite
amount of time," his surgeon declared him "unfit for service." The

doctors now changed his diagnosis from "hernia, intervertebral disc" to "colitis, chronic." By the end of November, the medical team at Chelsea Naval Hospital declared him permanently unfit for service and recommended that he appear before a retirement board.

Jack was now at the end of his patience with doctors and their treatments. In August, after eight weeks of hospitalization, he wrote a friend: "In regard to the fascinating subject of my operation, I . . . will confine myself to saying that I think the doc should have read just one more book before picking up the saw." In November, he wrote Lem: "Am still in that god damned hospital — have had two ops. and Handsome Hensen, who is now in charge of my case, wants to get cutting again. He is the stupidest son of a bitch that ever drew breath. . . . He's a mad man with a knife."

The chief of the navy's medical bureau, a Dr. B. H. Adams, now also temporarily frustrated Jack by raising questions about the origins of his disability. Jack's restricted diet before he entered the navy seemed to "clearly indicate that the subject officer suffered some type of gastro-intestinal disease prior to his appointment in the U.S. Naval Reserve." Adams disputed the conclusion that "'the background of his present physical status is an exhausting combat experience . . . .' This opinion would appear to be not supported by the past history as set forth above." Prior to Jack's appearance before a retiring board, Adams wanted "the history relating to the gastro-intestinal disease . . . clarified." But other medical officers overruled Adams, declaring that Kennedy's "present abdominal symptoms started" after "he spent over 50 hours in the water and went without food or drinking water for one week." They took at face value Jack's statement that "his present abdominal discomfort is different than that noted previous to enlistment." After interviewing Jack on December 27, the retiring board concluded that his incapacity for naval service was permanent and was "the result of an incident of the service . . . suffered in [the] line of duty." He was placed on the navy's retirement list as of March 1, 1945.

Perhaps Jack experienced a different type of abdominal pain from what had plagued him before entering the navy, but his difficulties were all of one piece. The colitis had been afflicting him since at least 1934, when he was only seventeen, and his back problems had begun in 1938 and had been a constant source of difficulty since 1941. The steroid treatment for the colitis, which apparently began in 1937, may have been the principal contributor to his back trouble and ulcer without curing his "spastic colitis." Because they could not identify the origins of his back miseries, the doctors now called it an "unstable back."

The available evidence suggests that adrenal extracts in the form of implanted pellets used to control his colitis may have been the basis of his stomach ulceration and back difficulties. Jack apparently used these drugs episodically, relying on them when his colon disease flared up and stopping when he felt better. No doubt circumstances — the difficulty of consistently having so new a drug available during his nine months in the Pacific, for example — also made his use of them erratic. One expert on steroids says that regulating dosages was initially a serious problem, especially as DOCA was given intramuscularly or inserted under the skin with the expectation that it would be effective for a period of eight to ten months. Considerable uncertainty as to how much or how little was appropriate for a patient suggests that even under the best of circumstances Jack's use of them was uneven.

What makes assertions that Jack's stop-and-start use of steroids was a source of his stomach and lumbar diseases more convincing is the events in his medical history between 1945 and 1947. At the beginning of 1945, Jack went to Castle Hot Springs, Arizona, to recover his health. It was an elusive quest. Although Jack refused to complain to his father about his continuing maladies, Dr. Lahey saw him in Phoenix and reported to Joe that he was not "getting along well at all." His back remained a source of almost constant pain and he had trouble digesting his food. A companion in Arizona remembered that "he looked jaundiced — yellow as saffron and as thin as a rake." After a month in the desert, he told Billings that his back was "so bad that I am going to Mayo's about the first of April unless it gets a little better."

It did not, and so in mid-April he went back to Rochester, Minnesota. Since his doctors had nothing new to recommend, he decided against additional medical workups. Instead, in May, as the war ended in Europe, he went to work as a correspondent for the Hearst newspapers covering the United Nations conference in San Francisco and then the British elections and the Potsdam Conference in Germany. When friends saw him in San Francisco, he looked sickly and spent a lot of time in bed resting his back. In July he was down with a fever in London, and then in August, after returning to London from Germany, he became terribly ill with a high fever, nausea, vomiting, "vague abdominal discomfort," and "loose stool." Doctors at the U.S. Navy Dispensary in London noted "a similar episode in 1942" and a previous history of malaria in 1944, but recorded his current illness as "gastro-enteritis, acute." In June 1946, after marching in a parade in Boston on a blistering hot day, he collapsed. One witness to the onset remembered that he "turned very yellow and blue" and looked like someone having a heart attack.

Dr. Elmer C. Bartels, an endocrinologist at the Lahey Clinic who subsequently treated him for his Addison's, recalled that Jack was negligent about taking his medicine with him on trips. During his 1947 visit with Kathleen in Ireland, Jack became ill and cabled home asking that prescriptions be filled and sent with either his younger sister Patricia or a friend sailing to England. Before his sister or friend arrived with the medication, however, he became very ill in London. Seen at Claridge's Hotel by Dr. Sir Daniel Davis, a prominent physician, Jack was immediately hospitalized at the London Clinic, where he was diagnosed with Addison's. His nausea, vomiting, fever, fatigue, inability to gain weight, and brownish yellow color were all classic symptoms of the disease. (Because malaria had similar symptoms and because Jack's long history of stomach and colon problems suggested that his difficulties were related to an ulcer or colitis, his previous doctors had not diagnosed the Addison's.) Jack's failure to take his medicine probably triggered this Addisonian crisis.

Kennedy's Addison's disease, like the ulcer and osteoporosis and degeneration of his lumbar spine, was likely the result of the supplemental hormones he had apparently been taking on and off since the 1930s. It is now also understood that sustained treatment with steroids can cause the adrenal glands to shrivel and die. Doctors who had treated Jack's Addison's or read closely about his condition have concluded that he had a secondary form of the disease, or a "slow atrophy of the adrenal glands," rather than a rapid primary destruction. Because his sister Eunice also suffered from Addison's, it is nevertheless possible that the disease had an inherited component.

Yet whatever the etiology of the problem, it was yet another potentially life-threatening disorder for Jack. An insufficient supply of cortisone reduces the body's capacity to resist infection and makes people ill with Addison's disease susceptible to medical crises from any sort of surgery, even the extraction of a tooth. By the time Jack was diagnosed with Addison's, however, medical science had developed hormone replacements that, if given in proper doses, could ensure a normal life span. But it was hard, even given the Kennedy family confidence, not to fear that Jack's days were numbered.

* * *

JACK'S MEDICAL ORDEAL paralleled family suffering that, added to his experience in the war, made him intensely conscious of the precariousness of life. In 1944, his brother Joe had been flying antisubmarine patrols in the English Channel. Although he had been entitled to return home after thirty missions, he insisted on remaining through at least the D-Day invasion to help guard the amphibious Allied forces against possible German U-boat attacks. But even after contributing to the success of the June 6 landing by providing air cover against submarines, Joe Jr. was not content to go home. Part of his eagerness to stay in the war zone was a competitive urge to outdo Jack. On August 10, Joe wrote him that he had read Hersey's *New Yorker* article and was "much impressed with your intestinal fortitude." But he could not resist asking: "Where the hell were you when the destroyer hove into sight, and exactly what were your moves, and where the hell was your radar." The underlying message was: Some hero to have let your boat been sunk. Joe was also intensely conscious of who got what awards. "My congrats on the [navy and marine] medal," he wrote Jack. "To get anything out of the Navy is deserving of a campaign medal in itself. It looks like I shall return home with the European campaign medal if I'm lucky."

But it was not enough. In August, Joe volunteered for a terribly dangerous mission flying a navy PB4Y Liberator bomber loaded with 22,000 pounds of explosives, the highest concentration of dynamite packed into a plane up to that point in the war. The objective was for Joe and his copilot to fly the plane toward the principal German launch site on the Belgian coast of the V-1s, which were then terrifying London with their distinctive buzzing sound before impact and destruction of lives and property. The two pilots were to parachute out after activating remote-control guidance and arming systems, turning the plane into a drone controlled by a second trailing bomber. Although Joe assured Jack in his letter of August 10 that he was not "intending to risk my fine neck . . . in any crazy venture," he knew that he had taken on what might well be a suicide mission. Several earlier attempts to strike the V-1s in this way had failed with casualties to the pilots, who had to bail out at dangerously high speeds and low altitudes. "If I don't come back," Joe told a friend shortly before taking off, "tell my dad . . . that I love him very much."

The mission on August 12 ended in disaster when Joe's plane exploded in the air before reaching the English Channel coast. An

American electronics officer had warned Joe before he took off that the remote-controlled arming system on the plane was faulty and that a number of things — "radio static, a jamming signal, excessive vibration, excessive turbulence, an enemy radio signal" — could prematurely trigger the explosives. Joe waved off the warning, assured by Headquarters Squadron that tests with 63,000 pounds of sand, substituting for the cargo of explosives, had produced "excellent" flight results and a "perfect" performance by the equipment.

An air force report on August 14 assessing the causes of the explosion speculated that it could have resulted from any one of seven possibilities, including "static — electrical explosion" or "electric heating of Mark 143 electric fuse from unknown source." The analyst believed "a static electric explosion . . . highly improbable." Because "the explosion was of a high order," he suspected "a possible electrical detonation . . . by a friendly or enemy stray or freak radio frequency signal."

U.S. military authorities never established a clear cause of the premature explosion. In 2001, however, a veteran of the British Royal Electrical and Mechanical Engineers serving as a telecommunications mechanic in Suffolk, England, where the Kennedy plane exploded, came forward with an explanation. "The Americans, based all over the South [of England], had turned off their radars," he explained, "so as not to interfere with their flying armada. Unfortunately, they did not warn their British Allies of the exploit, so that it came under the scrutiny of a large number of powerful and less-powerful ground-based radars. Their pulses upset the delicate radio controls of the two Liberator bombers, leading to gigantic aerial explosions and the total destruction of the air armada." It was a crucial, and fatal, error of omission by the U.S. air command.

Joe's death devastated his father, who told a friend, "You know how much I had tied my whole life up to his and what great things I saw in the future for him." To another friend, he explained that he needed to interest himself in something new, or he would go mad, "because all my plans for my own future were all tied up with young Joe and that has gone to smash." Joe's death also confirmed his father's worst fear that U.S. involvement in the war would cost his family dearly, deepening his antagonism to American involvements abroad for the rest of his life.

His brother's death also evoked a terrible sense of loss in Jack. He eased his grief partly by conceiving the idea for a book of personal reminiscences about Joe by family and friends. *As We Remember Joe* was not only a tribute to him but a kind of lament for all the fine young men who had perished in the war and would never realize their promise.

His heroic death left Jack with unresolved feelings toward his brother and father. His competition with Joe had "defined his own identity," he told Lem Billings. Now there was no elder brother to compete against, and Joe Jr.'s death sealed his superiority "forever in his father's heart." "I'm shadowboxing in a match the shadow is always going to win," Jack said.

Less than a month later, the family suffered another blow when Kathleen's English husband, William Hartington, was also killed in combat by a German sniper in Belgium. "The pattern of life for me has been destroyed," Kathleen wrote Jack in October. "At the moment I don't fit into any design." Four months later, in February 1945, when Kick, as the family affectionately called her, heard news of two other friends killed in the fighting, she wrote from England: "The news of Bill Coleman really upset me because I know how much he meant to Jack and how Jack always said that he would do better than anyone else he knew, and then Bob MacDonald lost in a submarine. Where will it all end?"

"Luckily I am a Kennedy," Kathleen told Lem Billings. "I have a very strong feeling that makes a big difference about how to take things. I saw Daddy and Mother about Joe and I know that we've all got the ability to not be got down. There are lots of years ahead and lots of happiness left in the world though sometimes nowadays that's hard to believe."

Jack shared Kathleen's resiliency. He also saw valuable lessons in human suffering and tragedy. As he later said of the poet Robert Frost, "His sense of the human tragedy fortified him against self-deception and easy consolation." Having been spared in the war, enjoying so much God-given talent, Jack was determined to make a mark on the world. But how? It was a question he had been struggling to answer for a number of years. Now, at long last, he would begin to answer it.

PART TWO

Public Service

They are wrong who think that politics is like an ocean voyage or a military campaign, something to be done with some particular end in view, something which leaves off as soon as that end is reached. It is not a public chore, to be got over with. It is a way of life.

— Plutarch

There is no cause half so sacred as the cause of a people. There is no idea so uplifting as the idea of service to humanity.

— Woodrow Wilson, October 31, 1912

CHAPTER 4

Choosing Politics

*I saw how ideally politics filled the Greek definition
of happiness — "a full use of your powers along lines
of excellence in a life-affording scope."*

— John F. Kennedy (1960)

SIGMUND FREUD BELIEVED that a well-spent life rests on successful engagement with *Arbeit* and *Liebe* — work and love. Both require difficult choices, and neither is made easier by the abundance of possibilities open to the offspring of society's most comfortable families.

For Jack Kennedy, finding a life's vocation was a crucial matter of his early adulthood, but especially after he returned from the war and turned twenty-eight in 1945. Some useful — indeed, vital — occupation was the only acceptable goal for the Kennedy children (except Rosemary). But the boys carried the family name and were explicitly responsible for upholding its public reputation, and for Joe Kennedy, the family's reputation was a consuming concern. "The desire to enhance the Kennedy image was a driving force in this complicated man," one biographer wrote, "and the skill he evinced at creating just the right image was phenomenal."

From early on, Joe ruled out a business career for his sons as likely to be more a source of frustration than satisfaction. He had been highly successful at making money, and he did not want them to stand in his shadow. Moreover, adding to a multimillion-dollar fortune seemed pointless. Joe had made all the money the family would ever need. Some other productive calling made more sense.

A logical alternative was politics. The careers of Honey Fitz and P. J. Kennedy were local examples, but Joe was thinking on a grander scale. He believed that the Depression marked a sea change in American life, from a country dominated by business to one controlled by government. In 1930, Joe declared that "in the next generation the people who run the government would be the biggest people in America." High public office, which FDR's administration opened to Catholics and Jews, had replaced accumulating money as the greater social good and a worthy aspiration for second- and third-generation immigrants reaching for higher social status. Joe himself had crossed over from business titan to FDR partisan and head of the Securities and Exchange Commission and the Maritime Commission, then ambassador to Britain; and as he did so, Joe Jr. and Jack became increasingly attentive to public affairs.

Although Jack's navy service had put his career plans on hold, he spent the war thinking about politics and international relations. In the fall of 1941, while serving in the ONI in Washington, he had begun gathering material for a book on the isolationist-internationalist split in the United States. Put off by strict ideological advocates, he prided himself on his realism and pragmatism. Before Pearl Harbor, he noted in a memo to himself that "for people to take a die-hard position on the war is wrong. Our policy must be flexible, fluid, if it is to stay abreast of the changing conditions of the world." In the winter of 1942, from his exile in Charleston, he had fretted over reverses in the Pacific and worried about isolationist impediments to American willingness to make necessary sacrifices in the fighting. "I never thought in my gloomiest day that there was any chance of our being defeated," he wrote Lem Billings in February. But American reluctance to look at widespread "examples of inefficiency that may lick us" greatly troubled him. "It seems a rather strange commentary that it will take death in large quantities to wake us up. . . . I don't think anyone really realizes that nothing stands between us and the defeat of our Christian crusade against Paganism except a lot of Chinks who never heard of God and a lot of Russians who have heard about him but don't want Him."

Jack's qualified pessimism lasted as long as he remained sidelined in Charleston. Once he got to the South Pacific and began to take part in the fighting, he became more hopeful; his activism relieved much of the feeling of defeatism that ran through his commentaries in early 1942. The American naval victories in the Coral Sea and at Midway in May and June of 1942, respectively, were also salutary in changing his perspective.

What remained the same, however, was an intense interest in the political questions that would need attention as postwar challenges replaced military exigencies. During his almost nine months in the war zone, while many of his fellow officers diverted themselves with card games, Jack, according to his commander in the Solomons, "spent most of his time looking for officers who weren't in any game, as he did with me. We'd sit in a corner and I'd recall all the political problems in New Jersey and Long Island where I come from. He did that with everybody — discussed politics." One of Jack's navy friends in the Pacific recalled: "Oh, yeah, he had politics in his blood. . . . We used to kid Jack all the time. I'd say, after the war is over, Jack, I'm gonna work like hell and we're going to carry Louisiana for you." Another of Jack's pals, who remembered spending "a lot of time, every single day practically, with him" just before Jack returned to the States, said, "He made us all very conscious of the fact that we'd better . . . be concerned about why the hell we're out here, or else what's the purpose of having the conflict, if you're going to come out here and fight and let the people that got us here get us back into it again. . . . He made us all very aware of our obligations as citizens of the United States to do something, to be involved in the process."

In the winter of 1944–45, as he left the navy and settled outside of Phoenix to recuperate from back surgery, Jack wrote an article, "Let's Try an Experiment for Peace," which he hoped might contribute to postwar stability. The essay formed a sharp departure from the argument in *Why England Slept*. Whereas he had previously pressed the case for a U.S. arms buildup in response to German and Japanese aggression, he now warned against a postwar arms race that could precipitate another conflict and cripple American democracy. He predicted that an American effort to outbuild a big-power rival such as Russia would lead Moscow to match U.S. military might and would provoke smaller states to form alliances against the United States. As bad, such an American buildup would divert resources from productive domestic enterprise and the creation of jobs for returning veterans. Jack feared that an effort "to compete with a dictatorship like Russia in maintaining large armies for an indefinite period" would destroy the U.S. economy and democracy. "Democracy sleeps fitfully in an armed camp," he concluded. Jack underestimated the economic benefits to the nation from continuing defense production; ultimately, it was, of course, the Soviet Union that could not bear the cost of the arms race. Nevertheless, he accurately foresaw that an international struggle like the Cold War would put a debilitating strain on America's democratic institutions just as earlier isolationists had warned.

Although Jack saw his essay as innovative, editors at *Life, Reader's Digest,* and the *Atlantic Monthly* all rejected it. *Reader's Digest* thought the piece too "exhortative." The *Atlantic* editor dismissed the article as "an oversimplification of a very complicated subject. Some profounder thinking is needed here and conclusions not based on cliches," he said. There was some merit in this dismissal: Jack's argument was in fact not much more than a statement of liberal orthodoxy in 1945 America. Arms limitation, disarmament, and world government were progressive prescriptions for postwar peace; even future conservatives such as Ronald Reagan considered them viable alternatives at the time.

If Jack lacked originality in addressing postwar armament and peace, at least he was well informed about foreign affairs; the same was not true of domestic issues. Yet he worked hard to round himself out. During his stay in Arizona, he became friends with Pat Lannan, a Chicago millionaire who was also nursing himself back to health. Lannan explained that "labor was going to be a very important force in the country." "Jack," Lannan told him, "you don't know the difference between an automatic screw machine and a lathe and a punch press and you ought to!" Jack took Lannan's words as a challenge and asked his father to send him a crateful of books on labor and labor law. Lannan remembered that Jack, with whom he shared a cottage, "sat up to one or two in the morning reading those books until he finished the whole crate." The episode speaks volumes about Jack's combination of intense curiosity, ambition, and competitiveness.

IN APRIL 1945, shortly before the war ended in Europe, in response to a suggestion from Joe, the Hearst *Chicago Herald-American* invited Jack to cover the United Nations conference in San Francisco. He jumped at the chance, perhaps seeing his work in journalism as a prelude to a political career — a career whose scope might be hinted at by the fact that writing for Hearst newspapers in Chicago and New York (the *Journal-American*) was not an especially effective way to win political standing in Massachusetts. In addition, in May 1945, when Joe wrote daughter Kathleen about a possible appointment in the new Truman administration, he said, "But if he's going to give me a job, I'd rather have him give it to Jack and maybe make him minister to some country or Assistant Secretary of State or Assistant Secretary of the Navy." That said, neither father nor son saw Jack running for office.

In sending Jack to San Francisco, the newspapers were not doing the Kennedys a favor. They received good value for the $250 a dispatch they paid Jack. As the author of a successful book on foreign affairs, someone with access to significant American and British officials — including the ambassador to Moscow, Averell Harriman; Soviet expert Charles E. Bohlen; and British foreign secretary Anthony Eden — and a navy hero who could speak "from a serviceman's point of view," Jack had credibility with his editors and reading audience as an expert on postwar international affairs.

However, just how hard he worked is debatable. Arthur Krock described Jack in his room at San Francisco's Palace Hotel, "dressed for a black-tie evening, with the exception of his pumps and evening coat . . . lying on his bed, propped up by three pillows, a highball in one hand and the telephone receiver in the other. To the operator he said, 'I want to speak to the editor of the *Chicago Herald American*.' (After a long pause:) 'Not in? Well, put someone on to take a message.' Another pause. 'Good. Will you see that the boss gets this message as soon as you can reach him? Thank you. Here's the message: Kennedy will not be filing tonight.'"

But however much of a social lion he may have been in San Francisco, Jack did manage to file seventeen 300-word stories between April 28 and May 28, principally reporting tensions with the Soviets and emphasizing a need for realism about what the new world organization could achieve. Jack explained that Soviet foreign minister Vyacheslav Molotov had shocked and frustrated the American and British delegations by his overbearing manner and insistent demands to ensure his country's national security. Jack warned against expecting good relations with the USSR: Twenty-five years of distrust between Russia and the West "cannot be overcome completely for a good many years," he accurately predicted. Yet the fact that the Soviets were participating in the conference and were interested in creating a world organization was a hopeful sign.

But in the end, the conference eroded Jack's optimism. By the close of the meeting, he saw a war between Russia and the West as a distinct possibility and the U.N. as an ineffective peacemaker. He thought that the new world body would be little more than "a skeleton. Its powers will be limited. It will reflect the fact that there are deep disagreements among its members. . . . It is unfortunate that more cannot be accomplished here. It is unfortunate that unity for war against a common aggressor is far easier to obtain than unity for peace." Jack feared that "the world organization that will come out of San Francisco will be the product of the same passions and self-ishness that produced the Treaty of Versailles in 1919."

Privately, Jack expanded on his views in a letter to a PT boat shipmate. "Things cannot be forced from the top," he said. "The international relinquishing of sovereignty would have to spring from the people," but they were not yet ready for world government. "We must face the truth that the people have not been horrified by war to a sufficient extent to force them to go to any extent rather than have another war. . . . War will exist until that distant day when the conscientious objector enjoys the same reputation and prestige that the warrior does today."

With the close of the San Francisco Conference, Jack's thoughts turned to political developments in Europe, where the British were about to hold an election and the victorious powers were planning a summit meeting in Potsdam, Germany. His U.N. articles persuaded the Hearst editors to send him to England and Germany to cover what they hoped would be the next big international stories.

After a month in England following Churchill's campaign around the country, Jack reluctantly concluded that despite his indomitable war leadership, Churchill and his Conservative party faced a left-wing tide that seemed likely to sweep them away. Perhaps blinded by admiration for the man he saw as the most extraordinary leader on the world scene, Jack could not bring himself to accept Chur-chill's probable defeat, and as the campaign came to a close, he fore-cast a narrow Conservative victory, although he did not think it would last long. It was only "a question of time before Labor gets an opportunity to form the government," Jack told American readers. Labour's triumph came sooner than Jack anticipated: The July elec-tions replaced Churchill and gave Labour a landslide majority.

The conclusion of the British elections freed Jack to travel to the Continent as a guest of U.S. navy secretary James Forrestal. The sec-retary, who knew Joe well and was greatly impressed by his twenty-eight-year-old son, wanted Jack to join his staff in the Navy Department. But first he invited Jack to go with him to Potsdam and then around Germany for a look at the destruction of its cities and factories from five years of bombing, and assess the challenges posed by rehabilitating a country divided into Russian and Western sectors. In the course of their travels, Jack met or at least saw up close many of the most important leaders of the day: President Harry Truman; General Dwight D. Eisenhower; Britain's new Labour leaders, Prime Minister Clement Attlee and Foreign Secretary Ernest Bevin; and Soviet foreign minister Molotov and Ambassador Andrey Gromyko. When Forrestal's plane landed in Frankfurt, a journalist recalled, "the plane doors opened, and out came Forrestal. Then, to my amazement, Jack Kennedy. Ike was meeting Forrestal. So Jack met Ike."

Watching all these influential but fallible men in action stirred feelings in Jack that he could do as well. His assumption came not from arrogance or a belief in his own infallibility or even a conviction that he could necessarily outdo the current crop of high government officials but from the sort of self-confidence that sometimes attaches itself to people reared among power brokers and encouraged to think of themselves as natural leaders. Aside from perhaps Churchill, he believed that his ideas were a match for the officials — East and West — he saw in action. The issue was to how make his voice heard.

ENTERING POLITICS or taking on public obligations did not intimidate Jack. But it was nothing he had seriously thought to do as long as his brother Joe was alive. As he explained later, "I never thought at school or college that I would ever run for office myself. One politician was enough in the family, and my brother Joe was obviously going to be that politician. I hadn't considered myself a political type, and he filled all the requirements for political success. When he was twenty-four, he was elected as a delegate to the Democratic Convention in 1940, and I think his political success would have been assured. . . . My brother Joe was killed in Europe as a flier in August 1944 and that ended our hopes for him. But I didn't even start to think about a political profession for more than a year later."

In fact, discussions with his father and others about a political career had begun earlier than Jack retrospectively claimed. There is evidence that Joe raised the matter of a political career with his son in December 1944, only a few months after Joe Jr.'s death, at Palm Beach. Paul "Red" Fay, a navy friend from the Pacific, who spent the Christmas holiday with Jack in Florida, recalled Jack telling him, "When the war is over and you are out there in sunny California . . . I'll be back here with Dad trying to parlay a lost PT boat and a bad back into a political advantage." In August 1957, Joe told a reporter, "I got Jack into politics. I was the one. I told him Joe was dead and that it was therefore his responsibility to run for Congress." At the same time, Jack himself told another reporter, "It was like being drafted. My father wanted his eldest son in politics. 'Wanted' isn't the right word. He *demanded* it. You know my father."

But nothing was settled that December. Jack still had not been released from the navy, and his health was too precarious for any firm planning. He was also reluctant to commit himself to a political career. As he told Fay, "Dad is ready right now and can't understand why Johnny boy isn't 'all engines ahead full.'" One day in Palm Beach, as he watched his father cross the lawn, he said to Fay, "God! There goes the old man! There he goes figuring out the next step. I'm in it now, you know. It's my turn. I've got to perform." Arthur Krock was asked later whether he fully subscribed to the theory that Jack was filling Joe's shoes when he entered politics. He answered, "Yes. In fact, I knew it. It was almost a physical event: now it's *your* turn." And Jack "wasn't very happy. It wasn't his preference." Joe himself recalled in the 1957 interview that Jack "didn't want to [do it]. He felt he didn't have ability. . . . But I told him he had to."

Still, despite his father's wishes, Jack hesitated throughout 1945. When Jack spoke to Lannan in Arizona about future plans early in 1945, "[he] said he thought he'd go into 'public service.' It was the first time I'd ever heard that term," Lannan recalled. "I said, 'You mean politics?' He wouldn't say 'politics' to save his life. It was 'public service.'" Such a phrase covered a multitude of possibilities. "I take it that you definitely have your hat in the ring for a political career," Billings wrote him in January 1946. But in February, Jack told Lem, "I am returning to Law School at Harvard . . . in the fall — and then if something good turns up while I am there I will run for it. I have my eye on something pretty good now if it comes through." Exactly what Jack had in mind remained unsaid, but it was clearly no more than a contingency.

If Jack was a reluctant candidate, he found compelling reasons to try his hand at electoral politics. As his former headmaster George St. John perceptively wrote Rose that August: "I am certain he [Jack] never forgets he must live Joe's life as well as his own." Joe Sr. hoped St. John was right. "Jack arrived home," Joe wrote an English friend on August 22, "and is very thin, but is becoming quite active in the political life of Massachusetts. It wouldn't surprise me to see him go into public life to take Joe's place."

For someone who prided himself on his independence — whose sense of self rested partly on questioning authority, on making up his own mind about public issues and private standards — taking on his elder brother's identity was not Jack's idea of coming into his own. Indeed, if a political career were strictly a case of satisfying his father's ambitions and honoring his brother's memory by fulfilling his life plan, it is more than doubtful that he would have taken on the assignment. To be sure, he felt, as he wrote Lem Billings, "terribly exposed and vulnerable" after his brother's death. Joe's passing burdened him with an "unnamed responsibility" to his whole family — to its desire to expand upon the public distinction established by Joe Sr. and to fulfill Joe Jr.'s intention to reach for the highest office.

Nor was his father completely confident that Jack was well suited for the job. As Joe said later, his eldest son "used to talk about being President some day, and a lot of smart people thought he would make it. He was altogether different from Jack — more dynamic, more sociable and easy going. Jack in those days back there when he was getting out of college was rather shy, withdrawn and quiet. His mother and I couldn't picture him as a politician. We were sure he'd be a teacher or a writer." Mark Dalton, a politician close to the Kennedys in 1945, remembered Jack as far from a natural. He did not seem "to be built for politics in the sense of being the easygoing affable person. He was extremely drawn and thin. . . . He was always shy. He drove himself into this. . . . It must have been a tremendous effort of will." Nor was he comfortable with public speaking, impressing one of his navy friends as unpolished: "He spoke very fast, very rapidly, and seemed to be just a trifle embarrassed on stage."

Yet not everyone agreed. Lem Billings thought that politics was Jack's natural calling. "A lot of people say that if Joe hadn't died, that Jack might never have gone into politics," Lem said much later. "I don't believe this. Nothing could have kept Jack out of politics: I think this is what he had in him, and it just would have come out, no matter what." Lem echoed the point in another interview: "Knowing his abilities, interests and background, I firmly believe that he would have entered politics even had he had three older brothers like Joe." Barbara Ward, an English friend of Jack's sister Kathleen, remembered meeting Jack during his visit to England in 1945. "He asked every sort of question of what were the pressures, what were the forces at work, who supported what . . . and you could see already that this young lieutenant [sic] was political to his fingertips. . . . He seemed so young — but with an extraordinarily . . . well-informed interest in the political situation he was seeing."

Jack himself was not as sure as Billings about the direction his professional life would have taken had Joe lived. Political curiosity and "well-informed interest" don't automatically translate into political ambition. But Jack did recall that his attraction to politics rested on much more than family pressure or faithfulness to his brother's memory. He remembered that the responsibilities of power — "decisions of war and peace, prosperity and recession" — were a magnet. "Everything now depends upon what the government decides," he said in 1960. "Therefore, if you are interested, if you want to participate, if you feel strongly about any public question, whether it's labor, what happens in India, the future of American agriculture, whatever it may be, it seems to me that governmental service is the way to translate this interest into action." If this sounds similar to what his father had said in 1930 about how "the people who run the government would be the biggest people in America," it is not only because the son had been influenced by the father but because the father had been correct.

Comparisons with other professions made politics especially appealing to Jack. Alongside the drudgery of working in a law firm, writing "legislation on foreign policy or on the relationship between labor and management" seemed much more attractive. "How can you compare an interest in [fighting an antitrust suit] with a life in Congress where you are able to participate to some degree in determining which direction the nation will go?" Nor did he see journalism as a more interesting profession. "A reporter is *reporting* what happened. He is not *making* it happen. . . . It isn't participating. . . . I saw how ideally politics filled the Greek definition of happiness — 'a full use of your powers along lines of excellence in a life-affording scope.'" Two of Jack's closest aides later said that Jack "was drawn into politics by the same motive that drew Dwight Eisenhower and other World War II veterans, with somewhat the same reluctance, into the political arena — the realization that whether you really liked it or not, this was the place where you personally could do the most to prevent another war." "Few other professions are so demanding," Jack said later, "but few, I must add, are so satisfying to the heart and soul." In 1960, he told an interviewer, "The price of politics is high, but think of all those people living normal average lives who never touch the excitement of it."

A strong family interest, great family wealth, and a personal belief in the "necessity for adequate leadership in our political life, whether in the active field of politics or in the field of public service," had all given him the incentive to seek elective office. Encouragement from professional politicians also persuaded him to run. He remembered how after he gave a public address in the fall of 1945 to help raise money for the Greater Boston Community Fund charity, "a politician came up to me and said that I should go into politics, that I might be governor of Massachusetts in ten years." Joe Kane, a Kennedy cousin and highly regarded Boston pol, a man described as "smart and cunning, with the composure of a sphinx and ever present fedora pulled down over one eye in the manner of [then popular movie actor] Edward G. Robinson," encouraged Jack by telling Joe, "There is something original about your young daredevil. He has poise, a fine Celtic map. A most engaging smile." In a dinner speech, "he spoke with perfect ease and fluency but quietly, deliberately and with complete self-control, always on the happiest terms with his audience. He was the master, not the servant of his oratorical power. He received an ovation and endeared himself to all by his modesty and gentlemanly manner." From what we know about Jack's less-than-perfect public speaking abilities in 1945, Kane was ingratiating himself with Joe. Nevertheless, he was among the first to see the qualities that would ultimately make Jack such an attractive national public figure.

WHILE JACK WAS MAKING UP his mind, Joe was setting the stage for Jack's political career. Asked later what he did for Jack, Joe denied playing any part; he was eager to ensure that, as Rose wrote Kathleen, "whatever success there is will be due entirely to Jack and the younger group." When pressed by the interviewer, who said, "But a father who loves his son as you so obviously do is bound to help his son," Joe replied, "I just called people. I got in touch with people I knew. I have a lot of contacts. I've been in politics in Massachusetts since I was ten." Two of JFK's later aides, Kenneth P. O'Donnell, a college friend of Jack's brother Bobby, and David F. Powers, a Boston Irish politician Jack recruited for his 1946 campaign, downplayed Joe's part. They said that "his reputation as a prewar isolationist and his falling out with the New Deal might do Jack some harm," so Joe stayed behind the scenes. But even there he confined himself to "fretting over small details, worrying whether Jack's unpolitician-like style of campaigning was wrong for the Boston scene." When JFK biographer Herbert Parmet interviewed O'Donnell in 1976 about Joe's part in the events of 1945–46 that brought Jack into politics, he "became heated at suggestions that the Ambassador had played a prominent role. . . . He scoffed at stories about Joe Kennedy's expertise and . . . pointed out that the Ambassador had been 'out of touch' with Boston politics for a long time. 'He no longer knew a goddamn thing about what was going on in Massachusetts.'"

The record says otherwise. In the spring and summer of 1945, Joe made a special effort to renew the Kennedy presence in Massachusetts. If memories of his ambassadorship did not serve him in most parts of the country, his home state was more forgiving. In April, Joe made the front page of the *Boston Globe* when he lunched with Governor Maurice J. Tobin, gave a speech urging postwar reliance on the city's air and sea ports to expand its economy, announced a half-million-dollar investment in the state, and agreed to become the chairman of a commission planning the state's economic future. The chairmanship assignment allowed Joe to spend much of the summer crisscrossing Massachusetts to speak with business, labor, and government leaders. "When he took the economic survey job for Tobin," a Boston politician stated, "it was to scout the state politically for Jack." In July, Joe added to the family's public visibility with a ship-launching ceremony for the USS *Joseph P. Kennedy,* which reminded people that two of his sons were war heroes. There were also discussions with Tobin about Jack's becoming his running mate in 1946 as a candidate for lieutenant governor.

But Joe and Jack preferred a congressional campaign that could send Jack to Washington, where he could have national visibility. There was one problem, however: Which district? To this end, Joe secretly persuaded James Michael Curley to leave his Eleventh Congressional District seat for another run as Boston's mayor. A fraud conviction and additional legal actions had put Curley in substantial debt, and he welcomed Joe's hush-hush proposal to help him pay off what he owed and to finance his mayoral campaign.

The Eleventh District included Cambridge, with 30 percent of the registered voters, where former Cambridge mayor and state legislator Mike Neville was well entrenched; parts of Brighton, with 22,000 uncommitted Democrats; three Somerville wards, distinguished by warehouses, factories, and a large rail center that employed many of the area's residents; one Charlestown ward populated by Irish Catholic stevedores who worked at the nearby docks and supported John

Cotter, well known in the Eleventh as the long-serving secretary to the district's congressmen; Boston's North End, where Italian immigrants had largely replaced the Irish; and East Boston's Ward One, another Italian American working-class enclave, which, like the North End, seemed warmly disposed to Joseph Russo, who had represented them on the Boston City Council for almost eight years. It was by no means a shoo-in for Jack.

Despite his father's help — or perhaps because of it — Jack continued to have great doubts about whether he was making the right decision. He could not shake the feeling that he was essentially a stand-in for Joe Jr. When he spoke with *Look* magazine, which published an article about his campaign, he said that he was only doing "the job Joe would have done." Privately he told friends, "I'm just filling Joe's shoes. If he were alive, I'd never be in this." He later told a reporter, "If Joe had lived, I probably would have gone to law school in 1946." He disliked the inevitable comparisons between him and his brother, in which he seemed all too likely to come off second-best, but it seemed impossible to shake them.

Jack's poor health also gave him pause. One returning war veteran who knew Jack in 1946 said, "I was as thin as I could be at that time, but Jack was even thinner. He was actually like a skeleton, thin and drawn." Despite the steroids he was apparently taking, he continued to have abdominal pain and problems gaining weight. Backaches were a constant problem. Because hot baths gave him temporary relief, he spent some time every day soaking in a tub. But it was no cure-all, and considerable discomfort was the price of a physically demanding campaign. He also had occasional burning when urinating, which was the result of a nonspecific urethritis dating from 1940 and a possible sexual encounter in college, which when left untreated became a chronic condition. He was later diagnosed as having "a mild, chronic, non-specific prostatitis" that sulfa drugs temporarily suppressed. Moreover, a strenuous daily routine intensified the symptoms — fatigue, nausea, and vomiting — of the Addison's disease that would not be diagnosed until 1947. A more sedate lifestyle must have seemed awfully attractive when compared with the long hours of walking and standing demanded of anyone trying to win the support of thousands of voters scattered across a large district.

Jack also felt temperamentally unsuited to an old-fashioned Boston-style campaign. False camaraderie was alien to his nature. He was a charmer but not an easygoing, affable character like his grandfather Honey Fitz, who loved mingling with people. Drinking in bars with strangers with whom he swapped stories and jokes was not a part of JFK's disposition. "As far as backslapping with the politicians," he said, "I think I'd rather go somewhere with my familiars or sit alone somewhere and read a book."

One local pol who met Jack in 1946 "didn't think he [Jack] had much on the ball at all. He was very retiring. You had to lead him by the hand. You had to push him into the pool rooms, taverns, clubs, and organizations." He would give a speech at a luncheon and try to escape as quickly as possible afterward without trying to win over members of the audience. "He wasn't a mingler," one campaign volunteer recalled. "He didn't mingle in the crowd and go up to people and say, 'I'm Jack Kennedy.'" The volunteer remembered how Jack had snubbed him and his wife one afternoon when he saw them on the street walking their baby in a carriage. "Sometimes," the volunteer said, "I used to feel that ice water rolled in his veins. . . . I don't know if he was shy or a snob. All I'm getting at is that he was very unpolitical for a man who was going to run for Congress." Jack himself said, "I think it's more of a personal reserve than a coldness, although it may seem like coldness to some people."

Jack also doubted that he could bring many voters to his side with his oratory. He accurately thought of himself as a pretty dull public speaker at the time. *Stiff* and *wooden* were the words most often used to describe his delivery. One observer said that Jack spoke "in a voice somewhat scratchy and tensely high-pitched," projecting "a quality of grave seriousness that masked his discomfiture. No trace of humor leavened his talk. Hardly diverging from his prepared text, he stood as if before a blackboard, addressing a classroom full of pupils who could be expected at any moment to become unruly."

Family members tried to help him become a more effective speaker. At one gathering, his sister Eunice noticeably mouthed his words as he spoke. Afterward, Jack told her, "Eunice, you made me very very nervous. Don't ever do that to me again." And Eunice said, "Jack, I thought you were going to forget your speech."

Joe was more subtle and successful in boosting him. Eunice recalled that "many a night when he'd come over to see Daddy after a speech, he'd be feeling rather down, admitting that the speech hadn't really gone very well or believing that his delivery had put people in the front row fast asleep. 'What do you mean,' Father would immediately ask. 'Why, I talked to Mr. X and Mrs. Y on the phone right after they got home and they told me they were sitting right in the front row and that it was a fine speech. And then I talked with so-and-so and he said last year's speaker at the same event had forty in the audience while you had ninety.' And then, and this was the key, Father would go on to elicit from Jack what *he* thought he could change to make it better the next time. I can still see the two of them sitting together, analyzing the entire speech and talking about the pace of delivery to see where it worked and where it had gone wrong."

Jack also had to worry about disciplining himself sufficiently to keep to a schedule. Even before he announced his candidacy, a friendly critic warned him that he needed to rein himself in. "You must organize yourself first and your campaign second," Drew Porter, a bank official, wrote him. "You cannot run a campaign for Congress on a Fraternity brotherhood basis. It must be on a strict, hard boiled, cut throat, business basis. I was shocked this A.M. when you answered the phone. Our original meeting was for 10 o'clock and you moved it up to 11 o'clock. OK. At 11:45, I called you. In business and politics, we have to break many dates, but we always promptly call and say we cannot be on time or we cannot keep the appointment. In this case, it was not important, but in others, you will lose contact and friends."

The advice only partly registered on Jack. Dave Powers, who became a principal aide in the campaign and a friend with whom Kennedy could find welcome relaxation from the daily political grind, remembered that "Jack had a funny sense of time and distance. . . . I've been with him in his apartment in the middle of Boston and he's soaking in the tub at quarter of eight, and we're due in Worcester at eight, and he'd say, 'Dave, how far is it to Worcester?' And I'd say, 'Well, if we're driving, we're late already.' It would go like that."

Jack also justifiably worried that political opponents would attack him as an outsider with no real roots in the Eleventh Congressional District. In fact, newspaper stories and private speculation that he would run brought out just such antagonism. Before he entered the race, an encounter with Dan O'Brien, a Cambridge undertaker with political clout and a Neville supporter, confirmed Jack's worst fears. In a meeting at O'Brien's funeral parlor on a snowy night in January, Jack looked to O'Brien "like a boy just out of school who had no experience politically, and . . . I don't think he even knew where the district was." O'Brien told him scornfully, "You're not going to win this fight. You're a carpetbagger. You don't belong here. I'll tell you what I'll do — if you pull out of the fight and let Neville go to Washington, I guarantee you I'll get you the job down there as Neville's secretary." As Jack left, he vented his annoyance with the sort of wry humor that became a trademark of his political career, mentioning that he "would rather not have O'Brien handle his funeral arrangements." O'Brien and Neville went to see Joe before Jack announced his candidacy: They said that if Jack did not run, they would give him "a shot later on. And he [Joe] coldly sat back in his chair and he said, 'Why[,] you fellows are crazy. My son will be President in 1960.'"

The private show of antagonism to Jack's candidacy became a drumbeat in the speeches and newspaper columns of opponents. One of Jack's competitors for the congressional seat said in a radio talk, "We have a very young boy, a college graduate, whose family boasts of great wealth. It is said they are worth thirty million dollars. This candidate has never held public office." He did not even have a residence in the district. "He is registered at the Hotel Bellevue in Boston, and I daresay that he has never slept there. He comes from New York. His father is a resident of Florida and because of his money is favored by the newspapers of Boston. . . . Insofar as certain responsibilities are concerned, this candidate does not live in the district . . . and knows nothing about the problems of its people."

One newspaper, the *East Boston Leader*, was furious at Jack's "unmerited" candidacy. They parodied his campaign by announcing: "Congress seat for sale — No experience necessary — Applicant must live in New York or Florida — Only millionaires need apply." A *Leader* columnist belittled Jack as "Jawn" Kennedy, the rich kid who was "[ever] so British. . . . In my opinion, Kennedy's candidacy is the nerviest thing ever pulled in local politics. He moves in and establishes a phoney residence in a hotel and solely on the strength of his family connections announces that he is undecided whether to become lieutenant governor or a congressman. . . . What has he, himself, ever done to merit your vote?"

Personal limitations and the prospect of ad hominem attacks certainly discouraged Jack, but the challenge of mastering a demanding political campaign was more an inducement to run than to back away. Nor did he see harsh personal attacks as a reason to stand aside; he did not need to be a politician to understand that politics was a tough game in which competitors went all-out to win. For him, on one level politics was another form of the competitive sports like football or boat racing that excited his lifelong drive to be the best. Indeed, the fight *was* the fun. "The fascination about politics," he told a reporter in 1960, "is that it's so competitive. There's always that exciting challenge of competition."

Of greater concern to him were practical questions about how to defeat better-known local rivals for the Eleventh District seat by winning enough blue-collar ethnic — mainly Irish and Italian — votes in an area that extended across Boston and some of its suburbs. It was no small challenge. When Dave Powers first met Jack, he privately echoed Jack's own concerns. "Here's a millionaire's son from Harvard trying to come into an area that is longshoremen, waitresses, truck drivers, and so forth," Powers remembered. "I said, 'To start with, I'd get somebody on the waterfront for sure, somebody tied up with the labor unions and all that.' And he's writing this stuff down, and I'm thinking to myself, 'It won't do him any good. A millionaire's son from Harvard, they're going to laugh at him down there.'"

The challenge as Jack saw it was not only to create some sort of connection to the working-class folks living in the district but also to overcome the apathy that marked a primary campaign in which no more than 20 to 25 percent of voters usually went to the polls. How could he convince people that a vote for Jack Kennedy might make a difference in their lives? He had every confidence that his war record and seriousness of purpose would make voters see him as a deserving young man. But would that be enough?

Curley, whose well-funded mayoral campaign was successful, said, "With those two names, Kennedy and Fitzgerald, how could he lose?" Jack, too, understood that his family ties would give him visibility in the campaign from the moment he announced his candidacy. He also appreciated that his background made him "a new kind of Democrat in town, a sort of aristocrat of the masses, at once engagingly modest yet quick of mind, well-read and self-confident." One of Jack's backers said, "Compared to the Boston Irish politicians we grew up with, Jack Kennedy was like a breath of spring. He never said to anybody, 'How's Mother? Tell her I said hello.' He never even went to a wake unless he knew the deceased personally." Seeing Jack's amateur status as a distinct asset, especially after a poll Joe commissioned revealed greater interest in Jack as a war hero than as a politician, the campaign gave high visibility to returning veterans working on Jack's behalf, men such as Ted Reardon, Joe Jr.'s Harvard classmate, and Tony Galluccio, Jack's college friend. The emphasis was on public-spirited young men who had done their war service and now intended to set things right at home.

Yet none of these advantages would be sufficient to win an election. Jack needed to get out on the hustings and impress himself on voters as someone who understood their needs and problems. Despite his misgivings, he began going into saloons and barbershops and pool halls and restaurants to talk to the men and women who controlled his fate: the letter carriers, cabdrivers, waitresses, and stevedores. He went to factories and the docks, where he stood on street corners introducing himself and asking for votes. One day when Joe saw Jack across a street shaking hands with longshoremen, he said to his companion, "I would have given odds of five thousand to one that this thing we [are] seeing could never have happened. I never thought Jack had it in him."

Gradually, he learned to give expression to his natural charm and sincerity. At a forum with several other candidates, all of whom made much of their humble backgrounds, Jack disarmingly declared, "I seem to be the only person here tonight who didn't come up the hard way." The audience loved his candor. At an American Legion hall, where he spoke to gold star mothers (women who had lost a son in the war), Jack honored the memories of the fallen men by discussing the sacrifices in war that promised a better, more peaceful future, adding, "I think I know how all you mothers feel because my mother is a Gold Star mother, too." The reaction to his talk, Dave Powers recalled, was unlike anything he had ever seen: an outpouring of warmth and affection that seemed to ensure the support of everyone in the audience.

And there was the hard work of campaigning. Out of bed by 6:15–6:30 in the morning, Jack would be on the street by 7:00 — in time to stand at the factory gates and docks for an hour or more to shake hands with arriving workers. After a quick breakfast, he would start pounding the pavement, knocking on every door in neighborhoods with triple-decker houses. It made a strong impression on startled housewives, who had never had that sort of contact with a political candidate before. After lunch, he and his aides would "hit the barber shops, the neighborhood candy or variety stores and the taverns, the fire stations and the police stations. At four o'clock, back at the Navy Yard, catching the workers coming out of a different gate from the one where we worked that morning," Dave Powers recalled. They would ride the trolley cars from Park Street to Harvard Square, with Jack walking the aisles, shaking hands, and introducing himself, "Hello, I'm Jack Kennedy."

In the evenings, Jack would make the rounds of three to six house parties organized by his sisters Eunice and Pat. They included anywhere from fifteen to seventy-five young women — schoolteachers, nurses, telephone operators — who would be served tea or coffee with cookies and would listen to an introductory spiel, more an entertainment than a political appeal, followed by Jack's arrival, a brief comment from him, and a question-and-answer session. Jack was at his best with these small groups, flashing his disarming smile, answering questions with a leg draped over an armchair, combining serious discussion with boyish informality. Within days, the campaign would issue invitations to all the young women to become volunteers for Kennedy. The technique created a corps of workers who expanded Jack's ability to reach out to hundreds and possibly thousands of other voters.

Jack paid a heavy price in physical exhaustion. The people around him noticed his bulging eyes, jaundiced complexion, and a limp caused by unremitting back pain. They marveled at his stamina and refusal to complain. But he saw no alternative: The demanding schedule was indispensable not just in making contacts but in destroying the claims by his opponents that he was simply a spoiled rich man's son who never had to work for a living.

But all the hard work would not have paid off in votes if he did not have something meaningful to say, something that made ordinary people feel he was a worthy young man who understood their personal concerns. In a stroke of genius, Joe Kane captured Jack's appeal as a new kind of Irish politician who reflected the past and the future by coining a compelling campaign slogan: "The New Generation Offers a Leader."

Kane and Jack's other advisers did not have to talk Jack into emphasizing his war record as a way to reach voters. Patriotism remained a strong suit in 1945–46 and a war hero commanded unqualified public approval. Although Jack was not comfortable selling himself in this role, he accepted it as an essential starting point of his campaign. Thus, in January 1946, he helped set up the Joseph P. Kennedy Jr. Veterans of Foreign Wars post in the Eleventh District with himself as post commander; agreed to preside over a national VFW convention; and joined the American Legion. He also crafted a speech that described the sinking of PT 109, downplaying his part in the rescue operation while praising the heroism of his men. The speech also recounted the special camaraderie among combat troops and called on his audiences to work together in a similar fashion to secure the country's future. His father financed the distribution throughout the district of 100,000 copies of "Survival," a Reader's Digest summary of John Hersey's New Yorker article about PT 109.

However strong the appeal of his war record, district voters were also keenly interested in securing their economic future. Mindful of the need to address their domestic concerns, Jack spoke repeatedly during the campaign about the bread-and-butter issues that mattered most to working-class voters. He promised to fight to make housing available for returning veterans and to create more and better-paying jobs. There was no specific agenda of just how he would accomplish any of this, but when the League of Women Voters asked him to describe the most important postwar issues facing the country, he listed housing, military strength to ensure the national security, expanded Social Security benefits, raising the minimum wage to 65 cents an hour, and modernizing Congress.

As important as what he advocated was the means he used to get his name, war record, and message before the public. And here he had the advantage of Joe's wealth. Joe may have spent between $250,000 and $300,000 on the campaign, though the precise amount will never be known since so much of it was handed out in cash by Eddie Moore, Joe's principal aide. (A frequent location for Kennedy campaign financial exchanges was in pay toilets. "You can never be too careful in politics about handing over money," Moore said.) It was "a staggering sum" for a congressional race in 1946, Joe Kane remembered. "It was the equivalent of an elephant squashing a peanut," two political journalists wrote later. Joe himself is supposed to have said, "With what I'm spending I could elect my chauffeur." It was, for example, six times the amount Tip O'Neill would spend six years later to win Jack's open seat. As Kane told the two reporters, "[Everything Joe] got, he bought and paid for. And politics is like war. It takes three things to win. The first is money and the second is money and the third is money." Jesse Unruh, Speaker of the California State Assembly in the 1960s, echoed the point: "Money is the mother's milk of politics."

Joe's money allowed the campaign to hire a public relations firm, which then saturated the district with billboard, subway, newspaper, and radio ads and direct mailings. The visual displays were headed "Kennedy for Congress" and contained a picture of Jack with a war vet's father pointing at Jack and saying, "There's our man, son." Joe's spending also paid for polls that persuaded the campaign to stress Jack's war service and for locally managed campaign headquarters in every section of the district. With only a single office in their home neighborhoods, Jack's opponents could not match the aggressive promotion of his candidacy. Mike Neville, Jack's principal opponent, complained to a companion as they walked past a craps game, "Only way I'll break into the newspapers will be if I join that game and get pinched by the cops."

The money also permitted the campaign to stage an elaborate event at the Hotel Commander in Cambridge, a fancy establishment to which most of the invited guests had never been. The mainly Irish ladies who received engraved, hand-addressed invitations to attend a reception to meet the entire Kennedy family turned out in formal gowns — many of them rented — to shake hands with these new Boston Brahmins and bask in the glow of their success. Joe, in white tie and tails, and Rose, dressed in the latest Paris fashion, greeted almost 1,500 delighted guests. The event created a traffic jam in Harvard Square, and the newspapers carried prominently placed stories about the "tea." One reporter said it was "a demonstration unparalleled in the history of Congressional fights in this district." Coming three days before the primary, one old Boston pol predicted, "This kid will walk in."

The evening house parties and hotel reception also allowed Jack to reconnect with his sisters Eunice, Pat, and Jean, four, seven, and eleven years, respectively, his junior. Away at Choate, Harvard, and then the navy while they were growing up, Jack was not as close to them as he had been to Joe Jr. and Kathleen. The same was true of the twenty-year-old Bobby and the fourteen-year-old Ted. The campaign became an exercise in family togetherness that pleased Joe and Rose and deepened Jack's affection for his siblings.

All the hard work and family commitment to the campaign paid off in a decisive primary victory. Jack won 22,183 votes to Mike Neville's 11,341, John Cotter's 6,671, and Joe Russo's 5,661. Two other candidates split 5,000 votes, another came in below 2,000, and four others scored in the hundreds. Jack's share of the ballots was a solid 40.5 percent, but the turnout of only 30 percent of potential voters meant that Jack had won the nomination with only 12 percent of the district's Democratic voters. It was hardly a ringing endorsement or a demonstration that a compelling young politician with a golden future had come on the scene. One of Jack's backers recalled that "it was very, very quiet at campaign headquarters. . . . We were happy that Jack had won, but there certainly was no tremendous victory celebration that night."

There was never any question about Jack's defeating a Republican who commanded only 30 percent of the district's registered voters. But a weak showing in November would not bode well for Jack's future as a Democrat in a largely Democratic state and country. Nor was it reassuring that the Republicans seemed likely to score impressive gains in Congress and recapture control of the House and Senate for the first time since 1930. Jack's frustration at the low voter turnout in his district found expression in a talk at Choate in September: "In Brookline, a very well-to-do community, only twenty percent of the people voted in the primary," he said. "We must recognize that if we do not take an interest in our political life we can easily lose at home what so many young men so bloodily won abroad."

To meet the task of establishing himself more strongly in the district as a good party man, Jack gave a speech titled "Why I Am a Democrat." It sounded the Roosevelt/New Deal themes that had made the Democrats the majority party in the country. He was not a Democrat simply because his family was tied to the party, he said. Rather it was because the Democrats for decades, and especially under FDR's leadership after 1932, had met the test of seeing to the national well-being at home and abroad. In the spirit of the New Deal, Jack urged delegates to the Veterans of Foreign Wars convention in September to pass a resolution approving the Wagner-Ellender-Taft Bill providing for low-cost public housing to help veterans find affordable places to live.

However, with inflation, strikes by union labor, postwar scarcity of consumer goods, and fears of communist aggression abroad and subversion at home dogging Harry Truman's administration and congressional Democrats, Jack saw party identity as insufficient. The Republican refrain carried a compelling message: "Had enough shortages? Had enough inflation? Had enough strikes? Had enough Communism?" Jack joined in. "The time has come when we must speak plainly on the great issue facing the world today. The issue is Soviet Russia," which he described as "a slave state of the worst sort." Moreover, it had "embarked upon a program of world aggression" and unless the "freedom-loving countries of the world" stopped Russia now, they would "be destroyed." The Soviet threat represented both a "moral and physical" crisis. This speech, delivered over the radio in Boston in October and repeated several times in the closing days of the campaign, struck a resonant chord with thousands of Jack's constituents.

The November 5 vote produced a national and statewide Republican tidal wave. In Massachusetts, the Democrats lost a U.S. Senate seat and the governorship; nationally, the Democrats lost control of both houses of Congress for the first time since 1930. Jack, however, did just fine. Lester Bowen, his Republican opponent, managed only 26,007 votes to Jack's 69,093. It was a decisive victory for a twenty-nine-year-old political novice and launched a House career that held out promise of greater future victories.

CHAPTER 5

The Congressman

*Congress is so strange. A man gets up to speak and says
nothing. Nobody listens — and then everybody disagrees.*

— Senator Alexander Wiley quoting a Russian observer (1947)

JACK'S ARRIVAL in Washington in January 1947 coincided with a
dramatic turnabout in Democratic party fortunes and mounting
national concern about the communist threat. With numerous labor
walkouts over insufficient wage hikes to meet a 6.5 percent inflation
rate in 1946 and growing fears of communist subversion and expansion, the country had rewarded the Republicans with a fifty-eight-
seat majority in the House and a four-seat advantage in the Senate.

Harry Truman took the brunt of the public beating. In his
twenty-one months in office his approval ratings had fallen a staggering 55 points, from 87 percent to 32 percent. Republicans joked
that the president woke up feeling stiff most mornings because of
trying to put his foot in his mouth. They wondered how Roosevelt
would have handled the country's problems, and asked, "I wonder
what Truman would do if he were alive." Members of Truman's party
offered little comfort. Arkansas congressman J. William Fulbright
suggested that the president appoint Republican senator Arthur Vandenberg secretary of state and then resign so that, in the absence of
a vice president, Vandenberg could replace him. Truman privately
responded that Fulbright should be known as "Halfbright."

Rising Soviet-American tensions over Eastern Europe, Greece,
Turkey, and Iran — all of which Moscow seemed intent on dominating — aroused fears of another war. And though an American
monopoly of atomic weapons gave the United States a considerable
advantage, the American public shuddered at the possibility of killing

millions of Soviet citizens. A civil war in China between Chiang Kai-shek's nationalists and Mao Tse-tung's communists aroused additional fears that U.S. armed forces might have to intervene in Asia. Columnist Walter Lippmann wondered how a president who had lost the support of the country could possibly deal effectively with these foreign threats. As troubling, alleged communist infiltration of the government seemed to threaten the country's traditional way of life. In 1946, news of a Soviet spy ring in Canada and accusations of "communist sympathizers," or even party members, in the government agitated the public. Massachusetts' own Joseph Martin, the new House Speaker, declared that there was "no room in the government of the United States for any who prefer the Communistic system."

NO SPECIAL CEREMONY among the Kennedys marked Jack's entrance into Congress. The family, especially Joe, saw it as little more than a first step. John Galvin, the 1946 campaign's public relations director, recalled that the Kennedys were "*always* running for the next job." (Years later Arthur Schlesinger Jr., Jack and Bobby's friend and associate, was asked whether Maryland lieutenant governor Kathleen Kennedy Townsend, Bobby's eldest child, was interested in a higher office. "Is she a Kennedy?" he replied.)

For freshman House Democrats eager to make their mark, the next two years under Republican control promised little personal gain. A system that favored the most senior members of the majority party meant that newcomers such as Jack would do well to establish themselves as strong voices for local constituents and temporarily give up any idea of leading significant legislation through Congress. But Jack's agenda did not include some major legislative triumph. He was less interested in what he could accomplish in the House, which he never saw as providing much opportunity for significant national leadership, than in using the office as a political launching pad.

"I think from the time he was elected to Congress, he had no thought but to go to the Senate as fast as he could," Arthur Krock said. "He wanted scope, which a freshman in the House cannot have, and very few actually of the seniors; so that I think the House was just a way-station." Kennedy campaign biographer James Mac-Gregor Burns agreed: "The life of the House did not excite him. It is doubtful that he spent ten minutes considering the possibility of the speakership."

This is not to suggest that Jack had little regard for the leaders of the Eightieth Congress. Speaker Martin and majority leader Charles A. Halleck of Indiana commanded his respect, as did veteran Democrats Sam Rayburn of Texas, whose service in the House dated from 1912 and included fourteen years as Speaker, and John W. McCormack of Massachusetts, the party's second-most-powerful House member. But most of the leadership (the Republican chairmen and ranking minority members of the chamber's principal committees) impressed the twenty-nine-year-old Jack Kennedy as being gray and stodgy — as indeed they were. Ranging in age from sixty-eight to eighty-three, the dominant figures on the Appropriations, Ways and Means, Rules, Banking and Currency, and Foreign Affairs Committees were all conservative men who worshiped at the altar of party regularity and, in the words of one observer, looked like legislators — "industrious, important, responsible, high-minded, and — however deceptively in certain cases — sober." As for many other members of the House, Jack seemed to share Mark Twain's view: "Suppose you were an idiot. And suppose you were a member of Congress. But I repeat myself."

Though in theory Jack liked the idea of being one of only 435 congressmen in a country of 150 million people, he had certainly felt a greater sense of accomplishment and satisfaction from the publication of his book and the wartime heroics that had given him national attention. His friend Chuck Spalding said that "the job as a congressman after he had it for a little while began to look like a [Triple A] League job to a major-league player." One House colleague watched Jack saunter into the chamber with his hands in his pockets and an attitude that said "Well, I guess if you don't want to work for a living, this is as good a job as any." Jack said of another Massachusetts representative, "I never felt he did much in the Congress, but I never held that against him because I don't think I did much. I mean you can't do much as a Congressman." Jack was often so downcast about the day's work in the office or on the House floor that he practiced swinging a golf club in his inner office to relieve the tedium.

"We were just worms in the House — nobody paid much attention to us nationally," Jack said. "Congressmen get built up in their districts as if they were extraordinary," he declared in 1959. "Most other Congressmen and most other people outside the district don't know them." Lem Billings recalled that Jack "found most of his fellow congressmen boring, preoccupied as they all seemed to be with their narrow political concerns. And then, too, he had terrible problems with all the arcane rules and customs which prevented you from moving legislation quickly and forced you to jump a thousand hurdles before you could accomplish anything. All his life he had had troubles with rules externally imposed and now here he was, back once again in an institutional setting."

Jack's advance had to be carefully orchestrated. Running too soon for the governorship or a Senate seat could work against him, his reach for higher office taking on the appearance of self-serving ambition devoid of serious interest in public service. And that would have been misleading, because genuine idealism and a core concern with the national well-being were central to his eagerness for political advancement. He also needed to learn some things before taking the next step. "I wasn't equipped for the job. I didn't plan to get into it, and when I started out as a Congressman, there were lots of things I didn't know, a lot of mistakes I made, maybe some votes that should have been different," he recalled. One of them was supporting Republican attacks on Roosevelt, particularly his "concessions" to Stalin at Yalta, which became synonymous with wartime appeasement of Russia.

Since so few congressmen ever end up with memorable legislative records, election to higher office can be a useful yardstick of performance in the Lower House. For most, however, the House is as high as they get. Indeed, of the thousands and thousands of men and women who served in the House between 1789 and 1952, when Jack would try for the Senate, only 544 won seats in the Upper House. But being a Kennedy was about changing the odds.

BECAUSE NO ONE could be sure when Jack would undertake a statewide campaign, first he had to secure a hold on his congressional district. To this end, he and Joe hired reliable aides to staff Washington and Boston offices that could respond effectively to constituent demands. At the same time, convinced that it was never too soon to begin reaching for higher office, Joe began using his money and connections to build Jack's public image, both in Massachusetts and beyond. The objective was to identify Jack with as many major national issues as possible: It would help make him less cynical about being a junior congressman with no influence and would make it more likely that voters would see him as a worthy representative trying to do right by both the Eleventh District and the national interest.

In Washington, Jack occupied room 322 in the Old House Office Building, a two-room suite in "freshman row," where all the new-comers were housed. It was "about as far from the Capitol . . . as you could get," one of Jack's aides said. Ted Reardon headed the staff. Though bright, talented, handsome, and athletic, Reardon was a passive character who was content to be a man Friday. He "had a brain but unfortunately he didn't use it that much," one of his office mates recalled. "I used to get annoyed with him. He just wouldn't apply himself. Much of the time, he wasn't in the office."

The other Washington staffer who came down from Boston was Billy Sutton, "the court jester," as Jack and the rest of the staff called him. Sutton was Mr. Personality, buzzing around the Capitol, quickly getting to know everybody who was anyone. "It was good," the office secretary said, "because if you needed anything, Billy always knew somebody." Jack saw Sutton's gift for mimicry and affinity for practical jokes as a valuable asset, especially when set alongside daily office chores. Billy was a perfect intermediary. Jack once encouraged him to get on the phone and imitate radical congressman Vito Marcantonio of the American Labor party. At Jack's urging, Billy called fashion designer Oleg Cassini's wife and in a heavily accented voice asked her to speak at a rally for Progressive party candidate Henry Wallace. Jack dined out for days afterward on her "speechless indignation." More important, Jack did not like greeting constituents — pressing the flesh, as his fellow congressman from Texas Lyndon Johnson described it — and was especially put off by tales of woe from constituents looking for help. "I can't do it," he told his Boston staff after listening to just a few of the many favor seekers scheduled to see him. "You'll have to call them off." Sutton, with his gift of gab, was able to satisfy most constituent complaints on his own.

The mainstay of the Washington office was Mary Davis. A year younger than Jack, she joined his staff after eight years as a secretary to other congressmen. She was a pro who managed everything. "Mary Davis was unbelievable," Billy Sutton said. "She could answer the phone, type a letter, and eat a chocolate bar all at once. She was the complete political machine, knew everybody, how to get anything done. . . . When Mary came in, you could have let twelve people go." Jack "never did involve himself in the workings of the office," Mary herself said. "He wasn't a methodical person. Everything that came into the office was handed to me. I took care of everything. If I had any questions, I'd take them in to him at a specific time and say, 'Here, what do you want me to say about that?' Nothing would land on his desk. I'd pin him down on the spot, get his decision, then do it." Davis was paid sixty dollars a week, but wanted more, citing her experience, background, and talent, and mindful of the family wealth — $40 million, if *Fortune* magazine was to be believed. Jack would not budge, promising only to "talk about it one of these days."

The Boston office served Jack equally well. Frank Morrissey, an attorney who was Joe's eyes and ears, oversaw the staff, which worked on the seventeenth floor of the federal building downtown. Morrissey, who spent most of his time practicing law or taking care of errands for Joe, left the daily work in the hands of Joe Rosetti, a war veteran attending night classes on hotel management at Northeastern University. Rosetti worked hard but did not like politics. "No matter how many good things you did for Jack's constituents, the only thing they remembered is what you *couldn't* do for them. That irritated me a great deal," Rosetti recalled.

The principal work of the Boston office fell to Grace Burke, an unmarried fifty-year-old lady who, like Mary Davis, was the soul of efficiency and devoted to serving Jack. "She was very dedicated," Rosetti said. "She would not allow anything to take place in that office that was going to be detrimental to Jack. She kept her three-by-five cards, her filing system, had her own personal contacts at City Hall and the State House. She was on top of everything."

The effectiveness of Jack's two offices rested partly on Joe's commitment to pay the costs of hiring more staff than any other congressman. Mary Davis said that "in those days Congressmen made twelve thousand dollars a year, plus a small expense allowance and they didn't have as many fringe benefits. So I was told that any expenses for Jack or the office were to be sent to Paul Murphy in New York. He had full charge of issuing checks and, of course, seldom questioned anything. Jack wasn't an extravagant guy."

Joe also put his money and influence to work crafting Jack's public reputation. In January 1947, the U.S. Junior Chamber of Commerce named Jack one of the ten outstanding young men of 1946. Joe helped arrange the selection through Steve Hannagan, a prominent New York publicist (or "press agent," as such operators were then known). Hannagan enlisted the backing of the nationally famous singer Morton Downey and Union Pacific Railroad president William M. Jeffers, a selection committee judge, to promote Jack's candidacy. Joe was "more than delighted" at Jack's number one ranking among the ten, with the boxer Joe Louis number seven, the Pulitzer Prize–winning historian Arthur Schlesinger Jr. ninth, and Bill Mauldin, the creator of the famous wartime "Willie and Joe" cartoons on life in the U.S. Army, tenth.

In subsequent months, a stream of favorable newspaper and radio stories Joe helped generate in the *New York Times, Boston Globe,* and other outlets served Jack's image as a rising political star. "GALAHAD IN THE HOUSE," Paul F. Healy, a Jack booster, declared in a Massachusetts Catholic paper. "In a poll of the Congressional Press Gallery he would be picked as one of the five young congressmen most likely to succeed," Healy wrote in July 1950. "As a former author, newspaperman, embassy attaché, and war hero, Kennedy takes his legislative responsibilities extremely seriously. He is one of a small group of World War II veterans who have done much to raise the moral and intellectual tone of the House. Lacking the seniority that wields so much power in Congress, these men have exerted influence by sheer intelligence and integrity."

JOE'S HELP CAME at a price: Jack often felt compromised or too much under his father's control. In February 1947, when he gave an interview to a Washington journalist who said "that it was nice to meet Kathleen's brother," Jack replied, "For a long time I was Joseph P. Kennedy's son, then I was Kathleen's brother, then Eunice's brother. Some day I hope to be able to stand on my own feet."

No sophisticated psychological understanding is required to see that a largely unspoken but omnipresent concern for Jack as he turned thirty was to separate himself from Joe and establish a more autonomous sense of self. At a cocktail party shortly after Jack entered the House, Joe turned to Kay Halle, a family friend, and said, "I wish you would tell Jack that he's going to vote the wrong way. . . . I think Jack is making a terrible mistake." Jack bristled: "Now, look here, Dad, you have your political views and I have mine. I'm going to vote exactly the way I feel I must vote on this. I've got great respect for you but when it comes to voting, I'm voting my way." Joe smiled and said, "Well, Kay, that's why I settled a million dollars on each of them, so they could spit in my eye if they wished." "I guess Dad has decided that he's going to be the ventriloquist," Jack told Lem, "so I guess that leaves me the role of dummy."

Joe's intrusiveness was nothing the Kennedys wished to advertise; indeed, Joe and Jack may have staged the exchange in front of Halle as a way to publicize Jack's independence. Their intense concern with public image, especially now that Jack was a congressman, certainly makes it conceivable. His father's reputation as an appeaser, isolationist, and anti-Semite — or at least someone ready to accommodate himself to Nazi domination of Europe — seemed certain to hurt Jack's political standing if it were known that Joe had a big part in what Jack did. And so the objective was to keep as quiet as possible about Joe's behind-the-scenes political machinations.

Jack, however, appreciated that Joe's assertiveness and connections gave him considerable advantages. For example, his father was instrumental in arranging Jack's appointment to the House Education and Labor Committee, where he could have a say in major battles that were looming over labor unions and federal aid to education. Jack said later that he did not remember how he came by the selection, but it seems transparent that John McCormack, in response to Kennedy pressure, agreed to give Jack the assignment. (The Republican leadership bestowed the same award on Richard Nixon, a promising California freshman they wanted to help after he had won an upset victory over prominent liberal Democrat Jerry Voorhis.) Jack also gained appointment to the Veterans' Affairs Committee and membership on a special subcommittee on veterans' housing, another issue certain to command national attention in the coming session.

Jack was grateful for his father's and McCormack's help in giving him a part in public discussions about education, housing, and labor. But he was also eager to demonstrate his independence from them. Billy Sutton remembered Jack's arrival at Washington's Statler Hilton on the morning of January 3, 1947: "His hair was tousled, he was completely tanned [from a vacation in West Palm Beach]; black cashmere coat and a grey suit over his arm." Sutton and Ted Reardon reported several calls from McCormack's office asking for Jack's attendance at a Democratic caucus. "We should be in a hurry now, Jack, make it snappy. . . . You have a caucus meeting. You've got two pretty good committees: Labor and Education, District of Columbia." "Well," Jack replied, "I'd like a couple of eggs." As Jack ate breakfast, Billy and Ted kept pressuring him to get a move on: "Mr.

McCormack is quite anxious that you get up there," Billy said. Jack asked, "How long would you say Mr. McCormack was here?" When Billy answered twenty-six years, Jack responded, "Well, I don't think Mr. McCormack would mind waiting another ten minutes."

COMMITTEE ASSIGNMENTS and self-education or not, Jack's congressional work was a source of constant frustration to him. He was a fiscal conservative who often felt out of sync with the demands of constituents eager for federal largesse. He also had little patience with the resistance to legislation he saw as essential to the national well-being; it reminded him of the adage "with what little wisdom the world is governed." Nor did he have much, if any, regard for doctrinaire politicians on the left and the right — congressmen who seemed to put wrongheaded principles above compromise and good sense.

He was never happy with having to slavishly support constituent demands, but he understood that accommodating himself to this political reality was essential if he hoped to be reelected. In the first two months of his term, he considered proposing that the 1948 Democratic National Convention be held in Boston. "An excellent political manoeuvre [sic]," one adviser told him. It seemed certain to impress local businessmen, who would profit from such a development, and would create feelings of pride among Eleventh District voters that Jack was establishing himself as a party leader. But he seemed less in tune with the eagerness of his many relatively poor, working-class constituents for expanded government programs or more New Deal "liberalism." "In 1946 I really knew nothing about these things," Jack said ten years later. "I had no background particularly; in my family we were interested not so much in the ideas of politics as in the mechanics of the whole process. Then I found myself in Congress representing the poorest district in Massachusetts. Naturally, the interests of my constituents led me to take the liberal line; all the pressures converged toward that end."

Jack's fiscal conservatism could be seen in his antagonism to unbalanced budgets, which he believed a threat to the national economy. In 1947, he openly opposed a Republican proposed tax cut, which he attacked as not only unfair to lower-income citizens but also a menace to economic stability. In 1950, he spoke out against Democratic-sponsored spending plans on social programs that could lead to a "dangerous" $6 billion deficit; he instead suggested a 10 percent across-the-board cut in appropriations. "I do not see how we can go on carrying a deficit every year," he declared on the House floor. "Does not the gentleman think that a very important item in the cold war is the economic stability of the country so that we have resources in case of war?"

Roosevelt's New Deal had put in place Social Security, unemployment insurance, and public housing, which Jack saw as being sacrosanct among his constituents and impossible for an Eleventh District congressman to oppose without committing political suicide. But privately he had substantial concerns about some of them. "The scarlet thread that runs throughout the world — is one of resignation of major problems into the all absorbing hands of the great Leviathan — the state," he declared in a poorly crafted 1950 speech at the University of Notre Dame. He warned against the "ever expanding power of the Federal government" and asserted that "control over local affairs was the essence of liberty." His conservatism partly found expression in a vote with the Republican majority for the Twenty-second Amendment to the Constitution (limiting presidents to two terms). The act of revenge against Franklin Roosevelt, as it was known, had much appeal to Jack as an indirect way to retrospectively censure FDR for having fostered "socialist" measures, run for a fourth term as a sick and dying man, and "appeased" Stalin at Yalta.

At the same time, however, Jack had genuine compassion for the needs of the blue-collar workers dependent on government to ease their lives. The failure of Congress to act on some social welfare measures he considered transparently vital to the well-being of deserving citizens frustrated him and added to his discontent about serving in the House. In particular, Congress's failure in 1945–46 to enact housing legislation impressed him as a dereliction of duty to veterans. Federal remedies for the country's housing shortage, which affected thousands of returning veterans in Boston and around the country, commanded his full support. The absence of wartime construction and the rapid growth of postwar families made this a compelling concern. In February 1947, he told a Boston radio audience of his high hopes for passage of the Wagner-Ellender-Taft Bill, which he described as "desperately needed."

But he was disappointed, despite outspoken demands on his part for congressional action. He could not understand why some members of the House would not rise above their political self-interest and false assumptions about free enterprise for the sake of larger national needs. "The only time that private enterprise alone any-where near met the demand for houses was in 1925," he told his colleagues in April. By July, his frustration at House inaction boiled over in an attack on the Republican majority, which, he said, was willing to help big-business interests, but the veterans' "drastic" need of affordable dwellings would have to wait on "an investigation of the housing shortage." Since the facts were already known, Jack declared on the House floor, "this gesture by the Republican party is a fraud. . . . They have always been receptive to the best interests of the real estate and building association, but when it came to spend-ing money to secure homes for the people of this country, they just were not interested."

Jack's strong advocacy of federally financed housing won him warm praise in his district. One supporter sent a letter to all the Boston newspapers, lauding Jack's "moral courage." And although the personal political benefit of supporting veterans' housing was not lost on Jack, the selfishness of the realty interests and the short-sightedness of conservative VFW and American Legion leaders (who had aligned themselves with those interests) legitimately upset him. Quoting a Catholic newspaper, Jack called the American Legion a "legislative drummer boy for the real estate lobby." In response, a Legion spokesman belittled Jack as an uninformed "embryo" con-gressman. When the Legion then supported what Jack saw as a fiscally irresponsible bonus bill for veterans while continuing its opposition to the housing measure, Jack told the House that "the leadership of the American Legion had not had a constructive thought for the benefit of this country since 1918!" After this out-burst, Jack, who believed it "terribly important" to his political future to be seen as "rational" and "thoughtful," worried that he had gone too far. "Well, Ted," he told Reardon when he got back to the office, "I guess we're gone. That finishes us down here." But his prin-cipled stand redounded to his benefit: public reaction was strongly in his favor, especially from veterans, whose letters backed him ten to one.

It was an important lesson. A humane government looking out for the powerless or less powerful was a necessary counter to busi-ness interests that thought primarily about the bottom line. In 1947, Jack did not think of himself as a New Deal liberal, but the housing fight was a first step in that direction. Additional steps were some-times small, as the struggles over the power of labor unions, which became the major issue before Congress during 1947, reveal. As a representative of a working-class district, he felt duty-bound to speak and vote for the interests of the unions, which were under sharp attack for putting their own needs above the national good. Jack was mindful of the long struggle for labor rights stretching back into the nineteenth century and culminating in the victories of the 1930s that legalized collective bargaining and secured the right to strike. But he saw the unions as fiercely self-serving and no more ready than corporate America to put the needs of the country above their own interest. Communist infiltration of the unions, which allegedly made them vulnerable to manipulation by Soviet agents putting Moscow's needs before those of the United States, especially troubled him. In subcommittee hearings in 1947 on communist subversion of the United Electrical Workers and the United Auto Workers, Jack hammered away at witnesses suspected of communist sympathies and, in the case of the UAW, of impeding American industrial mobilization in 1941 when Soviet Russia was allied with Nazi Germany. A motion to bring perjury charges against union leaders whom Jack believed part of a communist conspiracy gave him standing as a tough-minded anticommunist intent on ferreting out and prosecuting subversives.

Nevertheless, he opposed measures that would make labor again vulnerable to management's arbitrary control over wages and working conditions. When the House considered the excessively harsh Hartley Bill in April 1947, which would have substantially reined in labor's right to strike, Jack called instead for a balanced law as a way to head off labor-industry strife destructive to the nation. He acknowledged that the unions "in their irresponsibility have been guilty of excesses that have caused this country great discomfort and concern." But while the bill before the House had attractive features, it would "so strangle collective bargaining with restraints and limitations as to make it ineffectual." It would "bring not peace but labor war — a war bitter and dangerous. This bill in its present form plays into the hands of the radicals in our unions, who preach the doctrine of class struggle." A vote for the Hartley Bill, he said, would be a vote for industrial warfare.

Jack's dissent put him in company with 106 other House opponents of the bill, who were swamped by 308 Republicans and conservative Democrats ready to risk industrial strife. When the more moderate Taft-Hartley version emerged from a conference committee in June, Jack briefly considered voting for it. But the interests of his district, the conviction that such a vote would end his House career, and the defects in a bill he saw as still too draconian toward unions persuaded him to join 78 congressmen in opposing 320 supporters. After Truman vetoed Taft-Hartley, the House and Senate, with Jack voting to sustain the president, overrode the veto.

By the end of 1947, Jack's voting record on supporting the unions received a perfect score from the Congress of Industrial Organizations (CIO): eleven out of eleven correct votes. Given Jack's district, the votes are not surprising, but they little reflect the ambivalence Jack felt on labor issues.

Jack was no more comfortable with battles over federal aid to education. As a Catholic representing a heavily Catholic district, he became an immediate exponent of helping parochial schools. The anti-Catholic bias on the issue angered and frustrated him. In 1947, a representative of the Freemasons testifying at a subcommittee hearing on educational aid sounded familiar clichés about Catholic loyalty to Church over country. "Now you don't mean the Catholics in America are legal subjects of the Pope?" Kennedy sharply asked the witness. "I am not a legal subject of the Pope." When the man cited canon law overriding all secular rules, Kennedy replied, "There is an old saying in Boston that we get our religion from Rome and our politics from home."

The willingness of the committee to hear from such a witness speaks volumes about the outlook of many in the Congress and the country toward helping Catholic schools with public funds. In 1947, twenty-eight states had laws against "acting as a trustee for the disbursement of federal funds to non-public schools," and the U.S. Senate Education and Labor Committee had reported out a bill that "would make it impossible for the states to use any of the federal funds for parochial schools." A Gallup poll found that 49 percent of Americans favored giving federal aid entirely to public schools, while 41 percent wanted part of it to go to parochial institutions; the division between Protestants (against) and Catholics (for) on the issue seemed unbridgeable.

Jack shared the view of most American Catholics that legislation forbidding any aid to religious schools was discriminatory and unconstitutional. In this, he was in harmony with the Supreme Court, which had ruled in a 1947 New Jersey case, *Everson v. Board of Education*, that public monies could be used to reimburse private-school students for bus transportation. By its 5–4 decision, the Court had declared direct aid to pupils, regardless of where they attended school, no violation of First Amendment restrictions on making laws "respecting an establishment of religion." Kennedy took this to mean that noneducational services such as bus rides, health examinations, and lunches could be freely provided to students in public and private, including religious, schools. But although Jack would consistently support this sort of federal aid, he was not without reservations about the whole idea of federal financing for schools, which states and counties had traditionally paid for. He was concerned that "present federal educational activities are tremendously costly" and might impose a "staggering" burden on taxpayers. To rein in what he feared could become runaway costs, he urged that such aid to education be given only when there was a demonstrable need. In addition, he called for federal requirements that states make greater efforts "through properly balanced taxation and efficiency of operation" to improve their own educational systems.

Jack was also unhappy with being identified as a Catholic congressman promoting parochial interests. It is true that public stands for equal federal treatment of public and parochial schools won him high praise from Catholic Church and lay leaders. (One Catholic newspaper called him "a white knight" committed to "courageous representation of his constituency.") But he was uncomfortable with the perception that he was a spokesman of the Catholic Church and a captive of his Catholic constituents. He wished to be known as a public servant whose judgment rested not on narrow ideological or personal prejudices, and little mattered to him more during his term in the House than making clear that he operated primarily in the service of national rather than more limited group interests.

A controversy concerning Boston mayor Curley demonstrates Kennedy's eagerness to create some distance between himself and the ruling Catholic clique in Boston. After his return to the mayor's office in 1946, Curley had been indicted for fraudulent use of the mail to solicit war contracts for bogus companies. The following year he was convicted and sent to the federal penitentiary in Danbury, Connecticut, to serve a six-to-eighteen-month term. Seventy-two years old, suffering from diabetes and high blood pressure, Curley asked the court for clemency, citing a physician's prediction that his imprisonment would be a death sentence. When the judge refused his plea, 172,000 of Curley's supporters, about a quarter of

Boston's population, petitioned President Truman to commute the sentence. John McCormack asked New England congressmen to support the request.

All the Massachusetts representatives followed McCormack's lead except for Jack. When McCormack approached him about signing, Kennedy asked whether the president had been consulted. McCormack said no and, irritated with the young man's implied defiance, declared, "If you don't want to sign, don't sign it." Having learned from the surgeon general that Curley's imprisonment was not life-threatening and that he would receive proper care in the prison hospital, Jack refused to sign. Because his district was a Curley stronghold, Jack worried that he might now be "politically dead, finished," as he told Ted Reardon.

At the same time, however, Jack saw good political reasons to resist. He was not beholden to district party regulars; his election had been more the result of building a personal organization than of getting help from the traditional pols. Moreover, it defined Jack as a new kind of Boston politician, a member of a younger generation with broader experience and a wider view of the world. It also allowed Jack to please Honey Fitz, who despised Curley for having cut short his political career. More important to Jack, though, was the injustice of giving Curley something he had denied other constituents: backing for an undeserved pardon. When Curley was released after five months and returned to the mayor's office with declarations that he felt better than he had in years, Jack gained in standing as a politician who thought for himself.

Though Jack was feeling his way on domestic issues, tacking between political expediency and moral conviction, he felt more comfortable in dealing with major foreign policy questions. His book, wartime experience, and newspaper articles about postwar peacemaking gave him a surer sense of what needed to be done.

In March 1947, after the president announced the Truman Doctrine proposing aid to Greece and Turkey as a deterrent to Soviet expansion in the Near East, Jack spoke at the University of North Carolina in support of the president's plan. He believed it essential to national security to prevent Europe's domination by any single power. To those who warned that aiding Greece and Turkey would provoke Moscow and possibly lead to another global conflict, he invoked the failure at Munich to stand up to Hitler as a miscalculation that had led to the Second World War. A firm policy now against Soviet imperialism would discourage Moscow from dangerous adventures in the future, he predicted. To those who believed that America should rely on the United Nations to preserve the independence of Greece and Turkey, Kennedy cautioned that it lacked the wherewithal to meet the challenge. America's aim was "not to dominate by dollar imperialism the Governments of Greece and Turkey, but rather it is to assist them to live in freedom." The president's policy was "the only path by which we will reach security and peace." Jack was equally enthusiastic and outspoken about the Marshall Plan to restore economic health and stability to Western Europe with loans and grants of up to $17 billion.

Of course, while Kennedy's stand for an internationalist policy rested on the belief that Truman was right, it also sprang from a concern to separate himself from his father. Recently, Joe had publicly complained that the United States lacked the financial means to meet its obligations at home and send hundreds of millions of dollars abroad to combat communism. His solution was to let the communists take over Greece and Turkey and other nations, predicting that these communist regimes would collapse after proving to be unworkable. An isolationist, prosperous United States would then become a model for both industrial and emerging nations, in which we could comfortably invest. Joe's shortsightedness was evident to foreign policy realists, who warned that allowing Soviet expansion to go unchecked would be a disaster for all the democracies, including the United States. Joe's bad judgment irritated Jack, who understood that it was more the product of personal concerns about family losses than reasoned analysis of the national interest. But Joe's misjudgments made Jack more confident about a public career: On foreign affairs, he correctly believed that he was much more realistic than his "old man."

NO ONE IN 1947 would have described Jack as ready for a leading role in national affairs. His first term in the House was a kind of half-life in which he divided his time between the public and the private. He was never indifferent about the major issues besetting the country; housing, labor unions, education, and particularly the communist challenge to U.S. national security received close attention between 1947 and 1949. But he was a quick study, and as only one of 435 voices in the House — and a junior one in the minority party at that — he found himself with ample time to enjoy a social life, especially since his large, able office staff took care of constituent demands. An English friend who lived around the corner from him in Georgetown remembered Jack as "a mixture of gaiety and thought. . . . He seemed quite serious, and then suddenly, he'd break away from reading and start to make jokes, and sing a song. But I think he did appear to be quite a serious thinker and always probing into things — literature, politics, etc."

Though having turned thirty in May 1947, his boyish good looks and demeanor bespoke not ambition and seriousness of purpose but casualness, ease, and enjoyment. Rumpled jackets, wrinkled shirts, spotted ties, khaki pants, loose-fitting sweaters, and sneakers were his clothes of choice; the expensive tailored suits he wore only out of deference to the customs of the House — and even then, perhaps not as often as he should have.

A rented three-story town house at 1528 Thirty-first Street in Georgetown, which Jack shared with Billy Sutton; his twenty-six-year-old sister Eunice, who worked at the Justice Department for a juvenile delinquency committee; and Margaret Ambrose, a family cook, had the feel of a noisy, busy fraternity that reflected casual living. Despite the presence of George Thomas, a black valet, who struggled to keep a rein on Jack's sloppiness, clothes were draped over chairs and sofas, with remnants of half-eaten meals left in unlikely places. Billy Sutton recalled how people were always "coming and going, like a Hollywood hotel. The Ambassador, Rose, Lem Billings, Torby, anybody who came to Washington. You never knew who the hell was going to be there but you got used to it."

Jack's idea of a good time was an unplanned evening with a friend. One young woman, who resisted any romantic involvement, recalled how "he would come by, in typical fashion, honk his horn underneath my garage window and call out, 'Can you go to the movies?' or 'Can you come down to dinner?' He was not much for planning ahead. Sometimes I'd go down for dinner and he'd be having dinner on a tray in his bedroom and I'd have my dinner on a tray in his bedroom. He was resting, you see? The back brace and different things would be hanging around. Then he'd find out what was at the movies and he'd get dressed and we'd go to the movies. And I'd pay for it because he never had any money." When he stayed home, he could be found sprawled in a chair, reading. Or as a reporter said, "Kennedy never sits in a chair; he bivouacs in it."

Jack still took special pleasure in athletics, reportedly making a habit of pickup football, basketball, or softball games with local teenagers. An Associated Press reporter described Jack in full uniform at a high school football practice. The team's star halfback, who thought Jack was a new recruit, gave him a workout, catching and throwing passes, running down punts, and tackling. "How's the Congressman doing?" the coach asked the unsuspecting halfback. "Is that what they call him?" he replied. "He needs a lot of work, Coach." (Given Jack's health problems, was the A.P. story a puff piece?)

For all Jack's devotion to his social life, he had few close friends. Not that he couldn't have drawn other congressmen, journalists, and Washington celebrities into close ties. His charm, intelligence, and wit made him highly attractive to almost everyone he met. But he felt little need for what current parlance would describe as male bonding. His strong family connections and frenetic womanizing gave him all the companionship he seemed to need.

He quickly developed a reputation as quite a ladies' man. "Jack liked girls," recalled fellow congressman George Smathers. Smathers, thirty-three and the son of a prominent Miami attorney and judge, shared a privileged background and affinity for self-indulgence that made him one of Jack's few good friends. "He came by it naturally. His daddy liked girls. He was a great chaser. Jack liked girls and girls liked him. He had just a great way with women. He was such a warm, lovable guy himself. He was a sweet fella, a really sweet fella." A contemporary gossip columnist for a New York newspaper supported Smathers's recollections. "Palm Beach's cottage colony wants to give the son of Joseph P. Kennedy its annual Oscar for achievement in the field of romance. The committee says that young Mister Kennedy splashed through a sea of flaming early season divorcees to rescue its sinking faith in the romantic powers of Florida." Supreme Court justice William O. Douglas remembered Jack as a "playboy," and New Jersey congressman Frank Thompson Jr., another of Jack's friends in the 1950s, said that "the girls just went crazy about him"; he had "a smorgasbord of women" to choose from.

Most of these women were one-night stands — airline stewardesses and secretaries. "He was not a cozy, touching sort of man," one woman said. Another woman described Jack as "nice — considerate in his own way, witty and fun. But he gave off light instead of heat. Sex was something to *have done, not to be doing*. He wasn't in it for the cuddling."

He wanted no part of marriage at this time. His friend Rip Horton remembered going to his Georgetown house for dinner. "A lovely-looking blonde from West Palm Beach joined us to go to a movie. After the movie we went back to the house and I remember Jack saying something like 'Well, I want to shake this one. She has ideas.' Shortly thereafter, another girl walked in. Ted Reardon was there, so he went home and I went to bed figuring this was the girl for the night. The next morning a completely different girl came wandering down for breakfast. They were a dime a dozen."

Several of Jack's contemporaries and biographers have concluded that he was a neurotic womanizer fulfilling some unconscious need for unlimited conquests. Priscilla Johnson, an attractive young woman who worked on political and foreign issues for Jack in the fifties, concluded that "he was a very naughty boy." (She rejected invitations from him to go to his hotel suite at the Waldorf-Astoria when they were in New York.) Kennedy family biographers Peter Collier and David Horowitz have described his affairs as "less a self-assertion than a search for self — an existential pinch on the arm to prove that he was there." This is shorthand for the view that Jack was a narcissist whose sexual escapades combated feelings of emptiness bred by a cold, detached mother and a self-absorbed, largely absent father. They quote Johnson: "I was one of the few he could really talk to. Like Freud, he wanted to know what women really wanted, that sort of thing; but he also wanted to know the more mundane details — what gave a woman pleasure, what women hoped for in marriage, how they liked to be courted. During one of these conversations I once asked him why he was doing it — why he was acting like his father, why he was avoiding real relationships, why he was taking a chance on getting caught in a scandal at the same time he was trying to make his career take off. He took a while trying to formulate an answer. Finally he shrugged and said, 'I don't know really. I guess I just can't help it.' He had this sad expression on his face. He looked like a little boy about to cry."

Johnson and others thought it was as much the chase as anything that excited Jack. "The whole thing with him was pursuit," she said. "I think he was secretly disappointed when a woman gave in. It meant that the low esteem in which he held women was once again validated. It meant also that he'd have to start chasing someone else." Like Johnson, Doris Kearns Goodwin sees more at work here than simply "a liking for women. So driven was the pace of his sex life, and so discardable his conquests, that they suggest a deep difficulty with intimacy."

A sense of his mortality may also have continued to drive Jack's incessant skirt-chasing. The discovery of his Addison's disease, his adrenal insufficiency, in the fall of 1947 put a punctuation point on the medical problems that had afflicted him since childhood. Although the availability of DOCA made his problems treatable by the late 1940s, no one could be certain that the disease would not cut short Jack's life. His English physician, who diagnosed the Addison's disease during Jack's 1947 trip to Ireland, told Pamela Churchill, "That young American friend of yours, he hasn't got a year to live." Jack was not told this, but his cumulative experience with doctors had made him skeptical about their ability to mend his ills. Moreover, when he came home from London in September 1947, he was so ill that a priest came aboard the *Queen Mary* to give him extreme unction (last rites) before he was carried off the ship on a stretcher. In the following year, when bad weather made a plane trip "iffy," he told Ted Reardon, "It's okay for someone with my life expectancy," but he suggested that his sister Kathleen and Reardon go by train. "His continual, almost heroic sexual performance," Garry Wills said, was a "cackling at the gods of bodily disability who plagued him." Charles Spalding believed that Jack identified with Lord Byron, about whom Jack read everything he could find. Byron also had physical disabilities, saw himself dying young, and hungered for women. Jack loved — perhaps too much — Lady Caroline Lamb's description of Byron as "mad, bad, and dangerous to know."

Events affecting Jack's sister Kathleen deepened his feelings about the tenuousness of life. Jack and Kathleen, as their letters to each other testify, had a warm, affectionate relationship. Jack was closer to her than to any of his other siblings. They shared an attraction to rebelliousness or at least to departing from the confining rules of their Church and mother. Jack had supported Kick in a decision to marry Billy Hartington, outside of her faith. Billy's death in the war had brought her closer than ever to Jack. Each had a mutual sense of life's precariousness, which made them both a little cynical and resistant to social mores. And so in the summer of 1947, during his visit to Lismore Castle in Ireland, Jack was pleased to learn that Kathleen had fallen deeply in love with Peter Fitzwilliam, another wealthy English aristocrat and much-decorated war hero. A breeder of racehorses and a man of exceptional charm, with a reputation for womanizing despite being married to a beautiful English heiress, Fitzwilliam reminded some people of Joe Kennedy — "older, sophisticated, quite the rogue male." Jack saw Kathleen's determination to marry Fitzwilliam — who would have to divorce his current wife first — despite Rose's warnings that she and Joe would disown her, as a demonstration of independence and risk taking that he admired. Before any final decision was reached, however, a tragic accident burdened the Kennedys with a far greater trauma. In May 1948, while on an ill-advised flight in stormy weather to the south of France, Kathleen and Fitzwilliam were killed when their private plane crashed into the side of a mountain in the Rhône Valley.

Jack found it impossible to make sense of Kathleen's death. When it was confirmed by a phone call from Ted Reardon, Jack was at home listening to a recording of Ella Logan singing the lead song from *Finian's Rainbow,* "How Are Things in Glocca Morra?" She has a sweet voice, Jack said to Billy Sutton. Then he turned away and began to cry. "How can there possibly be any purpose in her death?" Jack repeatedly asked Lem Billings. He later told campaign biographer James MacGregor Burns, "The thing about Kathleen and Joe was their tremendous vitality. Everything was moving in their direction — that's what made it so unfortunate. If something happens to you or somebody in your family who is miserable anyway, whose health is bad, or who has a chronic disease or something, that's one thing. But, for someone who is living at their peak, then to get cut off — that's the shock."

Kathleen's death depressed Jack and made him more conscious than ever of his own mortality. He told the columnist Joseph Alsop that he did not expect to live more than another ten years, or beyond the age of forty-five, "but there was no use thinking about it . . . and he was going to do the best he could and enjoy himself as much as he could in the time that was given him." He queried Ted Reardon and George Smathers about the best way to die: in war, freezing, drowning, getting shot, poisoning? (War and poisoning were his choices.) "The point is," he said to Smathers, "that you've got to live every day like it's your last day on earth. That's what I'm doing." Chuck Spalding remembered that "he always heard the footsteps. . . . Death was there. It had taken Joe and Kick and it was waiting for him. So, whenever he was in a situation, he tried to burn bright; he tried to wring as much out of things as he could. After a while he didn't have to try. He had something nobody else did. It was just a heightened sense of being; there's no other way to describe it."

Spalding's recollections are not a sentimental exaggeration about Kennedy or the influences that played on him. Kathleen's death seemed to heighten not only his determination to live life to the fullest but also his ambition for a notable public career. It is clear that the initial shock of Kick's death greatly distracted him. Billings said that "he was in terrible pain. . . . He couldn't get through the days without thinking of Kathleen at the most inappropriate times. He'd be sitting at a congressional hearing and he'd find his mind drifting uncontrollably back to all the things he and Kathleen had done together and all the friends they had in common." He had trouble sleeping through the night, repeatedly awakened by images of Kathleen and him sitting and talking together.

AFTER KATHLEEN'S DEATH, stoicism about accepting the uncontrollable joined a healthy determination to go forward and build a successful political career. During his first year and a half in Congress, Jack had already considered running for a statewide office. He wanted to get to the Senate, but if he won the nomination in 1948, it would mean challenging incumbent Republican Leverett Saltonstall. Since early polls showed New York Republican governor Thomas Dewey taking the presidency from Truman that year, and since Saltonstall, a popular moderate, would be difficult to beat, Jack backed away from challenging him. He focused, instead, on the possibility of running for governor. As a prelude, he began spending three or four days a week in Massachusetts speaking before civic groups — less to make clear where he stood on public questions than to get himself known by as many attentive citizens as possible. He largely stuck to safe issues such as the communist danger, at home and abroad, veterans' benefits, a balanced approach to labor unions, and the need to increase New England's economic competitiveness.

The most striking feature of his travels around the state is the energy it required and how forcefully it demonstrates his determination to advance to higher political office. The trips from Washington to Boston by plane and back to D.C. by train in an uncomfortable sleeping-car berth that left him bleary-eyed the next day were reason enough not to take on the job. Visits to the 39 cities and 312 towns in Massachusetts by car were an additional argument against launching a statewide campaign he might not win. He followed a grueling schedule, often attending twelve or more events a day, speaking at Communion breakfasts, church socials, Elks clubs, fraternal groups, Holy Name Societies, PTAs, VFW or American Legion chapters, volunteer fire departments, and women's organizations. To reach as many towns as possible, Jack, his driver (an ex-prizefighter), and two or three of his supporters usually began the day at dawn and ended at midnight, eating cheeseburgers and drinking milkshakes along the way. John Galvin, who accompanied Kennedy on many of these weekends, remembered that with no state expressways and few nice motels, "we usually ended up sleeping in a crummy small-town hotel with a single electric lightbulb hanging from the ceiling over the bed and a questionable bathtub down at the far end of the hall."

Jack suffered almost constant lower back pain and spasms in spite of his 1944 surgery. And no wonder: X rays of his back showed that by 1950, the fourth lumbar vertebra had narrowed from 1.5 cm to 1.1 cm, indicating further collapse in the bones supporting his spinal column. By March 1951, there would be clear compression fractures in his lower spine. At his age, this may have been another indication of the price paid for his steroid therapy. At the end of each day on the road, Jack would climb into the backseat of the car, where, as his friend and expert on state politics Dave Powers recalled, "he would lean back . . . and close his eyes in pain." At the hotel, he would use crutches to help himself up stairs and then soak in a hot bath for an hour before going to bed. "The pain," Powers added, "often made him tense and irritable with his fellow travelers."

Like a general fighting a war, Powers had tacked a state map to the wall of Jack's Boston apartment on Bowdoin Street and began using colored pins to show where they had been. Jack pressed Powers to fill the gaps with dates in the neglected cities and towns. "When we've got this map completely covered with pins," Jack would say, "that's when I'll announce that I'm going to run for statewide office."

Jack was away from Washington so much that veteran Mississippi congressman John Rankin told him and Smathers, who was spending a lot of time in Florida preparing for a 1950 Senate campaign, "You young boys go home too much. . . . I've got my people convinced that the Congress of the United States can't run without me. I don't go home during the Session because I don't want them to find out any different. . . . You fellows are home every week — you're never around here. . . . And your people are finally going to realize the Congress can run just as good without you as with you. And then you're in trouble."

By the fall of 1947, Massachusetts' newspapers had begun speculating that Jack was a possible candidate for the Senate or governorship. And by 1948, Henry Wallace's Progressive party backers in the state declared themselves ready to support him for governor. Since he seemed to be a strong labor advocate and his anticommunism would have little impact on foreign policy as governor, he was more acceptable to Progressives than his rivals for the nomination, traditional Democrats former governor Maurice Tobin and Paul Dever, the front-runner. Progressives also considered Kennedy much preferable to incumbent Republican governor Robert F. Bradford.

But a private Roper poll in June 1948 persuaded Jack not to run. The survey showed Jack losing to Bradford, 43.3 to 39.8 percent. Neither this small margin nor a straw poll of Democrats that put Jack and Tobin in a dead heat and Jack ahead of Dever by almost two to one was enough to convince him otherwise. More important was evidence that only five months before the election, he had made little impression on Massachusetts voters as a potential governor and officeholder: 85 percent of the Roper survey said they knew too little about Kennedy to predict whether he would be a good governor, while 64 percent said they did not have enough information to cite anything about him or his policies that they particularly liked. So it was time to wait. In the meantime, reelection to the House was assured. With no challenger in the primary or the general election, Jack received 94,764 votes, over 25,000 more than in his first race.

Jack had no illusions about winning higher office: As he knew from the history of Massachusetts politics, money and a winning strategy were essential for success. His father's wealth relieved him of fund-raising concerns. And so in January 1949, he began focusing on the issues that he believed could carry him to the State House or the Senate in 1952.

If Jack needed additional inducement to bear the burdens of a statewide campaign, he found it in the public response in 1950 to a family tragedy suffered by Mayor James Curley and the passing of his grandfather, Honey Fitz. Early in the year, the deaths of two of Curley's four surviving children — five others and his wife had already passed away — stunned Boston. Curley's forty-one-year-old daughter Mary died unexpectedly from a cerebral hemorrhage and her thirty-six-year-old brother succumbed the same day in the same way. Eight months later Honey Fitz, at age eighty-seven, died of old age. Curley's tragedy had brought over 50,000 people from around the state to his home to pay their respects. Likewise, more than 3,500 people attended the church service to mark Honey Fitz's passing. To Jack, it was more than a demonstration of affection for two legendary public figures; "it made him realize" more fully than before, Billings said, "the extraordinary impact a politician can have on the emotions of ordinary people" — indeed, on the substance of their lives. This was something good and powerful, and it stirred not only Jack's heart but his ego.

In laying the groundwork for a 1952 campaign, Jack could have chosen to emphasize domestic matters such as education, veterans' housing, unemployment, union rights, rent control, health care and insurance, reduced government spending, and lower taxes — all of which he addressed repeatedly during his first two House terms. But he did not see these as stirring the kind of public passion that he hoped to summon in a statewide race. The key, he believed, to commanding broad and favorable attention was a focus on foreign policy, anticommunism in particular. As he would say in a speech in 1951, "Foreign policy today, irrespective of what we might wish, in its impact on our daily lives, overshadows everything else. Expenditures, taxation, domestic prosperity, the extent of social services — all hinge on the basic issue of war or peace."

IN CONSISTENTLY SEIZING upon foreign affairs and anticommunism as his campaign themes, Jack identified himself not with one party or the other but with the national interest. When it suited him, he could be highly partisan. During the 1948 presidential campaign, for example, he aggressively attacked the Grand Old Party for its support of special interests and "perpetual, unending war on all fronts against the rights and aspirations of American workers." He called the Republicans "vicious" and complained that "they follow the Hitler line — no matter how big the lie; repeat it often enough and the masses will regard it as truth." Once he launched his own campaign in 1949, however, he aimed to win voter backing by espousing "Americanism." (Jack may have remembered the observation of Pennsylvania Republican boss Boise Penrose in 1920 when asked for the meaning of "Americanism," which Warren G. Harding was advocating in the presidential race. "Damned if I know," Penrose disarmingly replied. "But you can be sure it will get a lot of votes.")

"Americanism" for Jack mostly meant anticommunism, and his political timing was astute. In January 1949, American anxiety over the communist threat was reaching fever pitch. Between 1946 and 1949, warnings of communist infiltration of U.S. government agencies — especially the State Department — had filled the air. FBI director J. Edgar Hoover had said that no less than 100,000 communists were at work in America trying to overthrow the government. Cardinal Spellman of New York warned that America was in imminent danger of a communist takeover. Under what Secretary of State Dean Acheson later described as "the incendiary influence" of the House Un-American Activities Committee, the Truman administration felt compelled to set up the Federal Employees Loyalty and Security Program. In January 1949, 72 percent of Americans did not believe that Russia genuinely wanted peace. A like number later in the year said that Moscow wanted to rule the world.

Events abroad gave resonance to these concerns. In 1948, a successful communist coup in Czechoslovakia had solidified Soviet control of Eastern Europe; Western Europe, despite the Marshall Plan, was still far from a postwar economic recovery and seemed vulnerable to communist political subversion and military attack; and the civil war in China between the nationalists and communists had just turned decisively in Mao's favor with the planned retreat of Chiang's forces to Formosa.

Jack began using foreign policy issues for a statewide campaign as early as the fall of 1947. In an endorsement of a $227 million aid request to defend Italy from "the onslaught of the communist minority," Jack depicted the country "as the initial battleground in the communist drive to capture western Europe." Jack's strongly worded appeal reflected his genuine concern about the Soviet threat to Europe and America, but he also knew that it was excellent politics in a state with a significant Italian voting bloc. Nor did he overlook the political advantage (from Massachusetts' Jewish and Polish minorities) of urging an end to a Palestine arms embargo, which deprived Jews of "the opportunity to defend themselves and carve out their partition," and the admission to the United States of eighteen thousand displaced Polish soldiers, which was a small atonement for "the betrayal of their native country" by FDR at the Yalta Conference. Jack made no mention of Roosevelt's limited options in helping Poland as the war was ending or of his father's readiness to sacrifice Poland to Hitler's ambitions five years before.

The common thread running through these pronouncements was the defense of the West against a communist advance. At times, however, overreaction to communist dangers and political cynicism skewed Jack's judgment on international affairs. Chiang's defeat in 1949, for example, provoked Kennedy into the least-astute foreign policy pronouncement of his young political career. "The failure of our foreign policy in the Far East," he announced on the House floor and then in a speech in Salem, Massachusetts, "rests squarely with the White House and the Department of State." America's refusal to provide military aid unless there was a coalition government in China had crippled Chiang's nationalists. "So concerned were our diplomats and their advisers, the [Owen] Lattimores and the [John K.] Fairbanks, with the imperfections of the democratic system in China after twenty years of war, and the tales of corruption in high places, that they lost sight of our tremendous stake in a noncommunist China. . . . What our young men had saved [in World War II], our diplomats and our president have frittered away." His conviction that American actions were more responsible for events in China than what the Chinese themselves did helped agitate unrealistic judgments on the power of the United States to shape political developments everywhere in the world. Kennedy's comments also encouraged right-wing complaints that the Truman administration had "lost" China and helped destroy the credibility of the State Department's experts on Asia.

Coming so soon after Truman had won a stunning upset victory in the 1948 campaign, which made him a dominant political force, Jack's attack on the White House indicates how strongly he felt about the communist danger. Yet he also knew that it was very good politics: What better way to command the attention of Massachusetts voters than to take issue with the head of his own party on a matter most people in the state saw as he did? In 1949, anticommunism was a surefire issue for any aspiring national politician: 83 percent of Americans favored registration of communists with the Justice Department; 87 percent thought it wise to remove communists from jobs in defense industries; and 80 percent supported the signing of loyalty oaths by union leaders.

Playing this card meant sometimes playing rough, but Jack was getting more used to that, too. He admired George Smathers's 1950 Senate nomination campaign against incumbent Democrat Claude Pepper, in which Smathers successfully exploited Pepper's reputation as a doctrinaire New Dealer and forceful advocate of the welfare state, which opened him to attacks as a Soviet sympathizer and "Stalin's mouthpiece in the Senate," or "Red" Pepper, as unscrupulous opponents called him. Whimsically taking advantage of the climate of suspicion and the extraordinary ignorance of his audience,

Smathers shamelessly described Pepper in a speech as an "extrovert," who practiced "nepotism" with his sister-in-law and "celibacy" before his marriage, and had a sister who was a Greenwich Village "thespian."

Nevertheless, in 1949–50, despite his hyperbole about China and uncritical support of Smathers, Jack was relatively restrained in his attacks on Truman's national security and foreign policies. He did focus on "the lack of adequate national planning for civil defense in case of a national emergency," complaining that only one man was working full-time on the matter of "wartime civil disaster relief. . . . It is amazing to learn, particularly in view of the President's recent disclosure of Russia's Atomic Bomb, that at this late date no further progress has been made in setting up an adequate and organized system of Civil Defense." Jack's office informed forty-five newspaper editors in Massachusetts about a letter he had sent to Truman regarding the problem. Kennedy worried that in case of an atomic attack no one would have a clear idea of how to respond. By July, with the United States now fighting in Korea and the administration giving little heed to Jack's warnings, he decried the "inexcusable delay" in the failure to set up an adequate program to cope with a surprise attack. When ten thousand copies of a government manual on how to protect oneself from atomic radiation "sold like hot cakes," Jack saw it as a kind of vindication.

But nothing provoked Jack's criticism of the administration more than initial U.S. defeats in Korea. He said that the reverses in the fighting in the summer of 1950 forcefully demonstrated "the inadequate state of our defense preparations. Our military arms and our military manpower have been proven by the Korean incident to have been dangerously below par." He had already taken the administration to task on preparedness in February, when he had inserted a column by Joseph and Stewart Alsop in the *Congressional Record* attacking Defense Secretary Louis A. Johnson for failing to tell the public about U.S. military weakness. Jack now also attacked Truman for failing to prepare the country to defend its interests in Europe as well as in Asia. He believed that the United States had insufficient forces to fight in Korea and hold the line in Western Europe, where he said the Soviets had eighty divisions to the new North Atlantic Treaty Organization's twelve.

Jack's criticism reflected popular feeling: Whereas a majority of Americans consistently approved of Truman's leadership in 1949 and initially rallied around him after the outbreak of the Korean War in June 1950, only 37 to 43 percent thought he was doing a good job after that. By November 1950, Americans were more critical than approving of the administration's Korean policy. After driving North Korean forces back above the Thirty-eighth Parallel in September and then crossing into North Korea in hopes of unifying the peninsula under a pro-Western government in Seoul, the United States found itself in a wider war with China, which had entered the fighting in November. A Chinese offensive that pushed U.S. forces back below the Thirty-eighth Parallel — arousing fears of an extended, costly war — convinced 71 percent of Americans that the administration's management of the conflict was only fair or poor.

In November 1950, in a seminar at the Harvard Graduate School of Public Administration, Jack spoke candidly about many of the key issues and personalities of the times. In contrast with Truman, who had vetoed the McCarran Act, which required the registration of communists and communist-front organizations and provided for their internment during a national emergency, Jack said that he had voted for it and complained that not enough was being done to combat communists in the U.S. government. He also said that he had little regard for the foreign policy leadership of the president or Secretary of State Dean Acheson.

As for Republican senator Joseph McCarthy of Wisconsin, who early in 1950 had begun stirring sharp debate with unproved accusations about widespread subversion among government officials under FDR and Truman, Jack had little quarrel with him, saying, "He may have something." It was not simply that his father, sister Eunice, and he were personally acquainted with McCarthy; Jack valued his anticommunism, even if it were overdrawn, as well as his "energy, intelligence, and political skill in abundant qualities." At a Harvard Spee Club dinner in February 1952, when a speaker praised the university for never having produced an Alger Hiss, a former State Department official under suspicion of spying for Moscow, or a Joe McCarthy, Jack uncharacteristically made a public scene, angrily saying, "How dare you couple the name of a great American patriot with that of a traitor!" Jack was just as sympathetic to Richard Nixon, with whom he had established a measure of personal rapport during their service in the House. He openly declared himself pleased that Nixon, a tough anticommunist, had beaten liberal Democrat Helen Gahagan Douglas in a 1950 California Senate race, and he had no complaints about Nixon's depiction of Douglas as a "fellow traveler" or the "Pink Lady."

Like so many others in the country, Jack was partly blind to the political misjudgments and moral failings generated by the anticommunism of the time. Fearful that America was losing the Cold War, supposedly because of disloyal U.S. officials, and that McCarthy was correct in trying to root out government subversives, millions of Americans uncritically accepted unproved allegations that abused the civil liberties of loyal citizens. Unlike Truman, who in March 1950 called McCarthy "a ballyhoo artist" making "wild charges," Jack was all too ready to take McCarthy's accusations about government spies at face value. Overreacting to the events of 1949–50, Jack saw the dangers of communist success compelling the sacrifice of some traditional freedoms. He was ready to place limits on dissent as a way to give it freer rein at some future time. Less than two years later and forever thereafter, Jack tried to deny the generally accurate portrayal in a *New Republic* article of what he had said at the Harvard seminar.

Unlike Joe McCarthy, Kennedy never engaged in systematic red-baiting or the repeated use of innuendo to destroy anyone's reputation. And by the end of 1951, he publicly declared that the issue of communists in the executive branch was no longer of importance and that accusations of communists in the Foreign Service were "irrational." Yet there is no question that he had taken advantage of the anticommunist mood to advance his political standing in Massachusetts by voicing policy differences with Truman and his administration, though, unlike McCarthy, Kennedy's opposition rested principally on matters of substantive concern that had some merit.

The issue of how to defend Western Europe with limited resources in the midst of the Korean fighting is a case in point. Jack believed that Europe was America's first and most important line of defense against a Soviet advance in the Cold War. To better inform himself about European defense needs, he spent five weeks in January and February 1951 traveling from England to Yugoslavia. On his return, Jack gave a nationwide radio talk carried by 540 stations of the Mutual Broadcasting Company on "Issues in the Defense of Western Europe." Sixteen days later he testified before the Senate Foreign Relations and Armed Services Committees. His balanced, sensible analysis of European dangers was in striking contrast to some of his earlier overdrawn rhetoric about foreign affairs and won bipartisan approval. His conversations with U.S. representatives and high government officials in England, France, Italy, West Germany, Yugoslavia, and Spain, he said, made clear that the Soviets would not invade Western Europe in the coming year. Since "the Russians had not attacked before, why should they now when the bomb is still as much a deterrent as it was before?" An additional restraint on Soviet aggression was the "tremendous" problem Moscow would face of feeding Western Europe following any conquest. More important, Jack wondered why they would "take the risk of starting a war, when the best that they could get would be a stalemate, during which they would be subjected to atomic bombing? Why should they throw everything into the game, why should they take risks that they don't have to — especially when things are going well in the Far East? In addition, Stalin is an old man, and old men are traditionally cautious."

Because "a series of chain events as in the first war" might produce a conflict anyway, Kennedy continued to urge a military buildup. He was against strict reliance on U.S. forces, however, instead encouraging a ratio system in which the Europeans would match each American division with six of their own, warning that without such a commitment from its allies, the United States would find itself burdened with a disproportionate responsibility for Europe's defense. Because the White House opposed a ratio system and seemed unlikely to enforce it, Jack also urged that the Congress monitor any commitments the Europeans made to the buildup. This was not a backhanded proposal for pulling out of Europe; rather, he wanted to protect the American economy from excessive burdens by getting the Europeans to do their share.

In his testimony, Jack had the added satisfaction of directly separating himself from his father's continuing advocacy of isolationism. Georgia senator Walter George asked him to comment on a speech Joe gave in December 1950 urging withdrawal from Europe. Joe's speech was another demonstration of his inability to translate his realistic prognostications on the domestic economy into wise assessments of international affairs. "The truth," Joe said, "is that our only real hope is to keep Russia, if she chooses to march, on the other side of the Atlantic. It may be that Europe for a decade or a generation or more will turn communistic." In contrast, Jack testified that losing the "productive facilities" of Western Europe would make matters much more difficult for the United States in the Cold War and thought "we should do our utmost within reason to save it." Jack's differences with his father on foreign affairs were no bar to the great family enterprise of advancing Jack's political career: Joe promptly paid for the printing and distribution of ten thousand copies of Jack's testimony.

Jack's conviction about the importance of foreign affairs to the nation's future and, more narrowly, to his 1952 political campaign moved him to focus his attention on more than Western Europe. In April 1951, he spoke to a Massachusetts Taxpayers Foundation meeting in Boston about Middle Eastern and Asian problems susceptible to Soviet exploitation. In Morocco, Iran, Egypt, Indochina, Malaya, Burma, India, and Pakistan, Jack said, the "nationalistic passions . . . directed primarily against the Colonial policies of the West" were of great consequence to America. To combat Soviet efforts to take control in these countries, Kennedy wanted the United States to develop nonmilitary techniques of resistance that would not create suspicions of neo-imperialism or add to the country's financial burden. The problem, as Jack saw it, was not simply to be anticommunist but to stand for something that these emerging nations would find appealing. Communism was spreading because the democracies had failed, especially in Asia, to explain themselves effectively to the masses or to make the potential ameliorating effects of democracy on their lives apparent. Too many subjects of Western colonial rule remembered the cruelty of their masters to accept their systems of self-government as transparently superior to communism.

To learn more, Jack — accompanied by his brother Robert and sister Pat — made a seven-week, 25,000-mile trip that fall to Israel, Iran, Pakistan, India, Singapore, Thailand, French Indochina, Korea, and Japan. "I was anxious to get some first-hand knowledge of the effectiveness or ineffectiveness of our policies in the Middle East and in the Far East," he told a nationwide radio audience on his return. He had wanted to learn "how those peoples regarded us and our policies, and what you and I might do in our respective capacities to further the cause of peace." Along the way he met with U.S. and foreign military chiefs as well as prime ministers, ambassadors, ministers, consuls, businessmen, and ordinary citizens willing to speak spontaneously about current and future international relations.

The journey became a chance for Jack not only to educate himself about regions, countries, and peoples with which he had small acquaintance but also to get to know his twenty-six-year-old younger brother, Robert, better. The eight-year gap in their ages had made them almost distant relatives, separated by the different rhythms of their lives. Robert, who had briefly worked in Jack's 1946 campaign after returning from navy service, had graduated from Harvard in 1948, where he had majored in "football" and earned poor grades. He was reluctantly accepted by the University of Virginia's law school, where his diligence carried him through to an L.L.B. and a respectable grade point average that placed him in the upper half of his class.

Unlike Jack, who found much attraction in iconoclasm, Robert was a conformist who courted Rose and Joe by being as devout as his mother and a faithful reflector of his father's views and wishes. Bobby, as his siblings and friends called him, was the first of the Kennedy children to have a profession, get married, and have children. In 1950, at the age of twenty-five, he wed Ethel Skakel, the next-to-youngest of seven children of a wealthy Chicago Catholic family that shared the Kennedys' conservative values.

Only after prodding from Joe had Jack taken Bobby with him on his Middle Eastern and Asian trip. Jack feared that his often moody, taciturn, brusque, and combative brother would be "a pain in the ass." But Bobby's lighter, less apparent side as a relentless teaser endeared him to Jack. There was more at work than shared humor. Because both brothers, as historian Ronald Steel believes, "shunned open displays of emotion as a sign of weakness, the preferred mode of discourse was kidding. This permitted familiarity without the danger of vulnerability or sentiment." As important, Bobby's determined efforts to make objective sense of what they were finding and his unblinking realism deepened Jack's respect for him. Bobby's emphasis on "the importance of associating ourselves with the people rather than just the governments, which might be transitional, transitory; the mistake of the [French] war in Indochina; . . . [and] the failure of the United States to back the people" echoed Jack's thinking. He began to see Bobby as an asset in future political contests and challenges.

Kennedy believed it imperative for the United States to align itself with the emerging nations. But he acknowledged this as no easy task. Because of its wartime and post-1945 policies, America was "definitely classed with the imperialist powers of Western Europe." "We are more and more becoming colonialists in the minds of the people," he noted in a trip diary. "Because everyone

believes that we control the U.N. — because our wealth is supposedly inexhaustible, we will be damned if we don't do what they [the
emerging nations] want done." America needed to throw off the
image of a great Western power filling the vacuum left by British and
French decline and to demonstrate that its enemy was not just communism but "poverty and want," "sickness and disease," "injustice
and inequality," which were the daily fare of millions of Arabs and
Asians. "It is tragic to report," he said in his radio address, "that not
only have we made no new friends, but we have lost old ones." U.S.
military strength was only part of the equation. "If one thing was
bored into me as a result of my experience in the Middle as well as
the Far East," he said, "it is that Communism cannot be met effectively by merely the force of arms. The central core of our Middle
Eastern policy," Jack asserted, "is [or should be] not the export of
arms or the show of armed might but the export of ideas, of techniques, and the rebirth of our traditional sympathy for and understanding of the desires of men to be free."

The U.S. dilemma was most pronounced in Indochina, where
America had "allied ourselves to the desperate effort of a French
regime to hang on to the remnants of empire. . . . To check the
southern drive of Communism makes sense," Jack also said prophet-
ically, "but not only through reliance on the force of arms. The task
is rather to build strong native non-Communist sentiment within
these areas and rely on that as a spearhead of defense rather than
upon the [French] legions. . . . And to do this apart from and in defiance of innately nationalistic aims spells foredoomed failure."

For Jack and Bobby the trip evoked a mutual affinity for noblesse
oblige — the family's moral imperative, bound up with Rosemary's
disability, to emphasize the obligations of the advantaged to the disadvantaged, the need of the rich and powerful few to help the less
fortunate many. Joe had always had an evangelical streak that made
him such an outspoken isolationist, and he had clearly instilled
in his children an affinity for crusading fervor. Now his sons had
together found a cause worth fighting for.

Yet Jack's enthusiasm was largely self-generated; back home and
among Americans abroad, his journey of discovery evoked more indifference and hostility than encouragement or praise. In the Middle
East, he crossed paths with Franklin D. Roosevelt Jr., who told an
Arab leader urging U.S. sympathy for nationalistic revolutions that
the really important issue was the U.S.-Soviet struggle. FDR Jr. had

"simply, completely missed the whole point of the nationalist revolution that is sweeping Asia," Bobby wrote his father. Bobby personally did not think there was a chance of changing anything unless the whole State Department crowd was swept aside.

In India, where they dined with Nehru, the prime minister seemed bored, looking at the ceiling and speaking only occasionally to Pat Kennedy, Bobby and Jack's attractive twenty-seven-year-old sister. When Jack asked Nehru about Vietnam, he condescendingly dismissed the French war as an example of doomed colonialism with U.S. aid being poured down a "bottomless hole." Like a schoolmaster lecturing mediocre students, Nehru explained that communism had offered "something to die for" and the West proposed nothing but the status quo. French officials in Saigon, who were more in need of Nehru's lecture than Jack and Bobby, complained to the State Department that the Kennedys were trying to undermine their policy. Nor did most U.S. diplomats see Jack's criticism as helpful.

Jack's call for a change in perspective and policy did not alter his father's thinking, either. He followed Jack's radio address with one of his own, urging not an effort to align ourselves with the struggling masses but to shun additional alliances that could further undermine our autonomy in dealing with international affairs. "Perhaps our next effort will be to ally to ourselves the Eskimos of the North Pole and the Penguins of the Antarctic," he sarcastically announced.

IN SEPTEMBER 1951, Jack asked his sister Pat, who was working in television in New York, to arrange a weekly "public service type" telecast of ten or fifteen minutes, "with me interviewing important people down in Washington about their jobs, etc., and about problems of the day." The idea was to get it shown throughout Massachusetts.

More important than immediate efforts to expand Jack's visibility in the state was the decision on whether to run for governor or senator. Jack much preferred to be a senator than be the chief executive of Massachusetts. He thought of the latter as a job "handing out sewer contracts." The office had limited powers: The mayor of Boston had greater control over patronage than the governor, and any Democrat in the State House would likely have to deal with a Republican-controlled legislature, with all that meant for making much of a record as chief executive. To get anything done, Jack believed he would have "to be on the take," as he put it, or bypass the legislature and the politicians in the State House by going to the people, and since he would have entered office with "no standing," it seemed unlikely that he would accomplish much.

Jack's interest in foreign affairs also made the Senate more attractive, as did his father's unqualified preference for a Senate bid. Joe predicted that Jack "would murder [incumbent Henry Cabot] Lodge," but because sophisticated political observers told Joe that the chances against Lodge were only fifty-fifty and Joe did not want anyone to be overconfident, he also declared that "the campaign against Lodge would be the toughest fight he could think of, but there was no question that Lodge could be beaten, and if that should come to pass Jack would be nominated and elected President of the United States." Frank Morrissey, who ran Jack's Boston office, remembered Joe, "in that clear and commanding voice of his," saying to Jack, " 'I will work out the plans to elect you President. It will not be any more difficult for you to be elected President than it will be to win the Lodge fight.' " Chuck Spalding recalled that Jack saw the Senate race as a bigger challenge than the governor's chair, but that "if he was going to get anywhere . . . he'd have to be able to beat somebody like Lodge. . . . So I think he made the decision, 'I've been long enough in the House, it's time for me to move ahead. If I'm going to do it I've got to take this much of a chance.' " Jack talked to Justice William O. Douglas, who encouraged him to run for the Senate seat. In December 1951, during an appearance on NBC's *Meet the Press*, Jack said he was "definitely interested in going to the Senate" and was considering running next year.

Only incumbent governor Paul Dever stood in the way. After winning the State House twice in 1948 and 1950, Dever was interested in running for the Senate. But he was uncertain of beating Lodge, whose famous name and three terms in the Upper House made him something of a Massachusetts icon. For his part, Jack saw a fight with Dever as hurting his chances of defeating Lodge. Nevertheless, Jack was confident that Dever's own assessments would discourage him from taking on Lodge, and thus Kennedy. Jack decided to wait on an announcement until Dever made up his mind. He also approached Dever with an offer. Jack told him early in 1952, "If you want to run for the United States Senate, I'll run for governor. If you want to run for governor, then I'll run for the United States Senate. Will you please make up your mind and let me know?" This may have been more than a bit of a ploy. William O. Douglas remembered that when he and Kennedy spoke, Jack only casually mentioned the governorship. "By the time that he was talking to me, I think he had discarded that [a run for governor] essentially and had decided to run for the Senate." In any case, Dever was so slow in deciding that Jack prepared a statement announcing his Senate candidacy. Fortunately, before he acted on it, Dever called to say that he would seek reelection as governor. Jack was relieved and happy, telling an aide, "We got the race we wanted."

According to daughter Eunice, Joe "had thought and questioned and planned for two years," and he now made Jack's election his full-time concern. One campaign insider said that Joe, as in 1946, "was the distinct boss in every way. He dominated everything." He took a comfortable apartment at 84 Beacon Street, near Jack's place on Bowdoin Street, where he supervised campaign expenditures, publicity, the preparation of speeches, and policy statements. "The Ambassador worked around the clock," a speechwriter Joe brought up from New York said. "He was always consulting people, getting reports, looking into problems. Should Jack go on TV with this issue? What kind of an ad should he run on something else? He'd call in experts, get opinions, have ideas worked up."

To make Lodge seem overconfident, Joe leaked the story to the press that Lodge had sent him word not to waste his money. In a race against Jack, he expected to win by 300,000 votes. Lodge later denied that he ever predicted an easy victory — to Joe or anyone else. On the contrary, he saw the contest as "much harder" than his three previous races. "All along," he said, "I always knew if there came a man with an honest, clean record who was also of Irish descent, he'd be almost impossible to beat."

Joe's fierce commitment to winning sometimes made him abusive to campaign workers and ready to cut corners. During the campaign, Jack enlisted Gardner Jackson, a liberal with strong ties to Americans for Democratic Action (ADA) and labor unions, to help him win support from liberal Democrats. Jackson persuaded the ADA to back Jack. But to solidify his hold on liberals, he wanted Kennedy to sign a newspaper ad declaring "Communism and McCarthyism: Both Wrong." Since ninety-nine Notre Dame faculty members and John McCormack agreed to sign, Jack did, too, but he asked Jackson to read the statement to his father and some of his aides. Jack, who no doubt knew what his father's reaction would be, left for early-morning campaign business before Jackson began. Almost immediately, Joe jumped up, tilting the card table they were sitting around against the others and began to shout, "You and your sheeny friends are trying to ruin Jack." Joe's tirade attacking liberals, labor unions, Jews, and Adlai Stevenson (the Democratic presidential nominee) concluded with the promise that the statement would never be published, which it was not. Though Jack rationalized his father's behavior by telling Jackson that Joe was acting out of "love of his family," he also conceded that "sometimes I think it's really pride." But whatever Joe's motive, Jack was not averse to squelching the ad; it was poor politics. McCarthy remained very popular with the state's 750,000 Irish Catholics. Indeed, before Adlai Stevenson made a September trip to Boston, he was advised by a member of Jack's campaign staff not to attack McCarthy. "He is very popular with people of both parties."

As in 1946, Joe supported Jack with large infusions of money. The campaign finance laws were an invitation to break the rules. Although the candidate himself could spend only $20,000 and individuals were limited to $1,000 contributions, there was no bar to indirectly using state party funds to boost a nominee; nor was there any limitation on giving $1,000 to any and all political committees that might be set up on a candidate's behalf. Joe organized four thinly disguised committees — in addition to Citizens for Kennedy, there was a More Prosperous Massachusetts committee and three "improvement" committees, supposedly working to advance the shoe, fish, and textile industries. Joe may have put several million dollars into the campaign, which more than matched the $1 million the state Republican party spent to support Lodge. The Kennedy money paid for billboard, newspaper, radio, and television ads; financed Jack's trips around the state; and paid for the many local campaign offices, postage for mailings, telephone banks, receptions, and famous Kennedy teas that attracted thousands of women. A person "could live the rest of [their] lives on [his] billboard budget alone," one commentator asserted. "Cabot was simply overwhelmed by money," Dwight Eisenhower later said. Lodge agreed, saying that he lacked the financial wherewithal to keep up with the Kennedy spending machine.

The single most telling expenditure Joe made in the campaign was a loan of $500,000 to John J. Fox, the owner of the *Boston Post*, who after he bought the paper for $4 million in June 1952 faced a financial crisis. The paper was losing half a million dollars a year and needed to replace an antiquated physical plant and introduce a home-delivery system to return to profitability. In the fall of 1952, Joe helped rescue the paper from bankruptcy with his loan. Although there is no hard evidence of a quid pro quo, Jack did get a *Post* endorsement on October 25, less than two weeks before the election. Because the *Post*'s backing was believed to be worth forty thousand votes and because five other newspapers with a combined circulation 20 percent greater than the *Post*'s were supporting Lodge, the Kennedys had been particularly eager for the *Post*'s endorsement. (The *Globe*, then the second-most-read paper in Boston, with half the *Post*'s circulation, held to its tradition of not endorsing candidates.) Lodge claimed that Fox had promised to back him. "I've never doubted for a moment that Joe Kennedy was the one who turned Fox around," Lodge said later, "though I imagine he handled it pretty subtly, with all sorts of veiled promises and hints rather than an outright deal." In 1960, when the journalist Fletcher Knebel asked Jack about the loan, he said, "'Listen that was an absolutely straight business transaction; I think you ought to get my father's side of the story.'" But as he got up to leave, Knebel said that Jack added, "'You know we had to buy that fucking paper.' As if he just had to level." Knebel never published Jack's last remark.

Joe also made his mark by driving out Mark Dalton as campaign manager. Jack asked Dalton, who had headed his congressional race in 1946, to run the 1952 Senate contest. Dalton put aside a thriving law practice to take on the assignment. But he quickly ran afoul of Joe, who did not think he was aggressive or savvy enough. Two months into the campaign, Joe humiliated Dalton by accusing him of spending funds with no good results. He also blocked an official announcement naming Dalton as campaign manager. Dalton, who took it as "a very grave blow" when Jack would not reverse his father's decision, resigned.

Robert Kennedy, who was working as an attorney at the Justice Department, was reluctantly persuaded to take over managing the campaign. "I'll just screw it up," he told Kenneth O'Donnell, who was one of Jack's inner-circle advisers, objecting that he knew nothing about electoral politics. But he agreed to take on the job when O'Donnell warned that without him the campaign was headed for "absolute catastrophic disaster." Bobby worked eighteen-hour days, driving himself so hard that he lost twelve pounds off a spare frame.

He put in place a Kennedy organization that reached into every part of the state and stirred teams of supporters to work almost as hard as he did. In addition, he took on difficult, unpleasant jobs Jack shunned. When he found professional politicians hanging around the Boston headquarters, he threw them out. "Politicians do nothing but hold meetings," he complained. "You can't get any work out of a politician." When Paul Dever's organization, which began to falter in the governor's race, tried to join forces with Kennedy's more effective campaign, Bobby shut them off. "Don't give in to them," Jack told his brother, "but don't get me involved in it." Bobby had a bitter exchange with Dever, who complained to Joe about his abrasive son, with whom he refused to deal in the future.

Journalists Ralph Martin and Ed Plaut later concluded that Bobby Kennedy gave the campaign "organization, organization, and more organization." The result was "the most methodical, the most scientific, the most thoroughly detailed, the most intricate, the most disciplined and smoothly working state-wide campaign in Massachusetts history — and possibly anywhere else." "In each community," Dave Powers noted, the campaign set up "a political organization totally apart from the local party organization. . . . Kennedy volunteers delivered 1,200,000 brochures to every home in Massachusetts." It was an unprecedented effort to reach voters.

With Bobby running the day-to-day operation, Jack was free to concentrate on the issues — anticommunism, Taft-Hartley and labor unions, the Massachusetts and New England economies, civil rights, government spending, and which of the two candidates had performed more effectively in addressing these matters. Ted Reardon prepared a "Black Book" of "Lodge's Dodges," emphasizing the extent to which Lodge had been on all sides of all issues. The campaign also put out comparative charts on what the candidates "Said and Did From 1947–1951" about major public policies of greatest concern to voters.

Yet in spite of the great energy the campaign — and Jack in particular — put into focusing on issues, they were of relatively little importance in determining the vote. On all major policy matters, the two candidates largely resembled each other. They were both internationalist supporters of containment as well as conservatives with occasional bows to liberalism; they both favored sustaining labor unions, less government intervention in domestic affairs, and balanced federal budgets. Lodge, who spearheaded Eisenhower's drive for the presidency against the candidacy of Ohio senator Robert Taft, had his problems with conservative Republicans, some of whom turned to Kennedy as a more reliable anticommunist and some of whom voted for neither candidate, which cost Lodge more than it did Jack. At the same time, however, Jack could hardly trumpet his six years in the House as a model of legislative achievement. To be sure, his constituents had few complaints about his service to the district; but if he were asking voters to make him a senator because he had been an innovative legislator or a House leader, he would have been hard-pressed to make an effective case. If his political career had come to an end in 1952, he would have joined the ranks of the thousands of other nameless representatives who left no memorable mark on the country's history.

Most observers — then and later — agreed that the election turned more on personality than on issues. Kennedy aides O'Donnell and Powers believed that "voters in that election were not interested in issues. Kennedy won on his personality — apparently he was the new kind of political figure that the people were looking for that year, dignified and gentlemanly and well-educated and intelligent, without the air of superior condescension that other cultured politicians, such as Lodge and Adlai Stevenson, too often displayed before audiences." A former mayor of Pittsfield, Massachusetts, said in 1960, "There's something about Jack — and I don't know quite what it is — that makes people want to believe in him. Conservatives and liberals both tell you that he's with them, because they want to believe that he is, and they want to be with him. They want to identify their views with him."

Jack's narrow margin of victory over Lodge — 70,737 votes out of 2,353,231 cast, 51.5 percent to 48.5 percent — was impressive in light of a 208,800-vote advantage for Eisenhower over Stevenson in the state and Dever's loss of the governorship to Christian Herter by 14,000 votes. The outcome surprised some people, including Lodge, who had an unbeaten string of electoral victories dating from 1932 and had the benefit of an Eisenhower visit to Massachusetts on the final day of the campaign. "I felt rather like a man who has just been hit by a truck," Lodge said. The fact that only six other congressmen who served with Jack — Nixon, Smathers and LBJ (the only two Democrats), Jacob Javits and Kenneth Keating of New York, and Thruston Morton of Kentucky — made it to the Senate speaks forcefully about Kennedy's achievement.

Electorally, he certainly had commanded the support of the Irish, Italians, Jews, French Canadians, Poles, Slovaks, Greeks, Albanians, Portuguese, Latvians, Finnish, Estonians, and Scandinavians. Torby Macdonald, who was now also a Massachusetts congressman, had it right when he told Jack on election night that he would win despite Ike's certain victory in the state. When Jack asked him why, Macdonald replied, "I think that you represent the best of the new generation. Not generation in age but minorities, really. The newer arrived people. And Lodge represents the best of the old-line Yankees. I think there are more of the newly arrived people than there are of the old-line Yankees." To this, Macdonald might have added women as a group that would help Jack get to the Senate.

Indeed, the campaign had made special efforts to attract ethnic and female voters. The evening teas for thirty to forty women at private homes ultimately attracted as many as 70,000 voters, most of whom cast their ballots for Jack. Jewish voters were also given special attention because Jack had to overcome allegations that his father had been anti-Semitic and even pro-Nazi and that he was less sympathetic to Israel than was Lodge. Several appearances before Jewish organizations and outspoken support from Eleanor Roosevelt, Franklin D. Roosevelt Jr., and John W. McCormack, as well as several nationally prominent Jews such as Senator Herbert Lehman and current or former congressmen Emanuel Celler, Abraham Ribicoff, and Sidney Yates, brought the great majority of Jewish voters into Jack's camp. Jack's charm and his request to one Jewish audience, "Remember, I'm running for the Senate and not my father," were indispensable in helping swing Jews to his side.

The statistics on ethnic voting for Jack are striking. In 1952, 91 percent of Massachusetts voters went to the polls, an increase of more than 17 percent from the Senate contest in 1946, with most of the greater voting occurring in ethnic districts. In the Catholic precincts of Boston, for example, where Lodge had won respectable backing in 1946 of between 41 and 45 percent, his support now dropped to between 19 and 25 percent. The shift was even more pronounced in Boston's Jewish districts. Where Lodge had won between 60 and 66 percent of the vote against incumbent Catholic senator David I. Walsh in 1946, his support slipped to below 40 percent in 1952.

Jack's success rested on something more than being the "First Irish Brahmin"; he was the first American Brahmin elevated from the ranks of the millions and millions of European immigrants who had flooded into the United States in the nineteenth and twentieth centuries. The beneficiary of his father's fabulous wealth, a Harvard education, and a heroic career in the military fighting to preserve American values, Jack Kennedy was a model of what every immigrant family aspired to for themselves and their children. And even if they could never literally match what the Kennedys had achieved in wealth and prominence, they took vicarious satisfaction from Jack's identification as an accepted member of the American elite. Many of those voting for him could remember the 1920s and 1930s, when being a first- or second-generation minority made your standing as an American suspect. In voting for Jack, the minorities were not simply putting one of their own in the high reaches of government — they had been doing that for a number of years — but were saying that he and they had arrived at the center of American life and no longer had to feel self-conscious about their status as citizens of the Great Republic. Jack's election to the Senate opened the way to a romance between Jack Kennedy and millions of Americans. It would be one of the great American love affairs, and in his election day grin, it was just possible to imagine that Jack himself knew the match had been made.

CHAPTER 6

The Senator

We have not fully recognized the difficulty facing a politician conscientiously desiring, in [Daniel] Webster's words, "to push [his] skiff from the shore alone" into a hostile and turbulent sea.

— John F. Kennedy, *Profiles in Courage* (1956)

AS ONE OF ONLY NINETY-SIX senators, Jack Kennedy hoped to have an impact on domestic and foreign affairs surpassing anything he possibly could have done in the Lower House. He knew that some of the country's most memorable politicians — John C. Calhoun, Henry Clay, Stephen A. Douglas, the "fighting" Bob La Follettes, Sr. and Jr., George Norris, Charles Sumner, and Daniel Webster — had made their mark in the Senate. But he had no illusions that membership in America's most exclusive club conferred automatic distinction; the great majority of senators — past and present — were unexceptional. In 1935, Senator J. Hamilton Lewis told Harry Truman after Truman became a Missouri senator that initially, "you will wonder how the hell you got here, and after that you will wonder how the hell the rest of us got here." If Jack did not know this quote before his election, he certainly came to agree with it once he took up residence on the Senate floor. His fellow senators were cautious, self-serving, and unheroic, more often than not the captive of one special interest or another. Just three months into his term, Jack told a journalist, "I've often thought that the country might be better off if we Senators and Pages traded jobs." In 1954, after a year in the Senate, when someone asked Jack, "What's it like to be a United States senator?" he said after a moment, "It's the most corrupting job in the world." He saw senators as all too ready to cut deals and court campaign contributors to ensure their political futures. Jack also enjoyed the famous comment of Senate Chaplain Edward Everett Hale: "Do you pray for the senators, Dr. Hale?" "No," he replied, "I look at the senators and I pray for the country."

First as a congressman and then, even more so, as a senator, Jack disliked the pressure to obscure and compromise strongly held beliefs in the service of political survival. During his first months as a senator, he received a number of letters chiding him for not being a "true liberal." "I'd be very happy to tell them that I am not a liberal at all," Jack told a reporter. "I'm a realist."

But as much as he disliked compromise, Jack was never indifferent to the vital role that accommodation played in a democracy: Politics, he said in 1956, was "the fine art of conciliating, balancing and interpreting the forces and factions of public opinion." He did see limits to this process: Jack also believed that a man of conscience "realizes that once he begins to weigh each issue in terms of his chances for reelection, once he begins to compromise away his principles on one issue after another for fear that to do otherwise would halt his career and prevent future fights for principle, then he has lost the very freedom of conscience which justifies his continuance in office. But to decide at which point and on which issue he will risk his career is a difficult and soul-searching decision." As his later actions demonstrated, Kennedy had an imperfect record in meeting his own standard; holding, and then moving beyond, his Senate seat took precedence over political principles more than once in the next eight years.

In 1953, at the start of Jack's Senate service, international perils made philosophical questions about a senator's behavior abstractions of secondary concern. The Soviet detonation of an atomic bomb in 1949, the U.S. explosion of a 150-times-more-powerful hydrogen bomb in October 1952, a Chinese communist regime since 1949 leading a chorus of Third World opposition to U.S. imperialism, and the continuing conflict in Korea made questions of war and peace central concerns of the new Eisenhower administration and the Eighty-third Congress. During Eisenhower's and Kennedy's first six months in office, ending the Korean fighting and responding to a Soviet "peace offensive" after Stalin died in March were continually in the headlines. The question of how to rein in Joe McCarthy, whose incessant reckless accusations about communists in high places had undermined civil liberties and divided the nation, was another topic of constant discussion on Capitol Hill.

Although these matters of state held Jack's interest, they initially commanded less of his attention than practical questions about his Senate influence and even more mundane ones about organizing his Senate office. Republican control of the Upper House by a two-seat margin — 49 to 47 — meant that Kennedy, a freshman member of the minority, would be one of the least-influential members of the Senate. Like the House, the Senate placed greater value on membership in the majority and seniority than on a new senator's abilities, however impressive they might be.

But even if circumstances were different, Jack's top priority had to be setting up an office that met the needs of his home state. He relied on the same devoted and effective assistants that had helped him in the House. Ted Reardon became his D.C. administrative assistant, and Frank Morrissey continued to head the Boston office. To meet his larger responsibilities as a senator, Jack hired two native Nebraskans, Evelyn Lincoln as his personal secretary and Theodore C. Sorensen as his number two legislative assistant.

Mrs. Lincoln, as Jack always addressed her, was born Evelyn Maurine Norton in the hamlet of Polk, Nebraska. Her father, a farmer and devoted Democrat, served two terms in the U.S. House of Representatives in the late 1920s and early 1930s. As a resident of the capital, Evelyn Norton earned a degree from George Washington University. After marrying Harold Lincoln, a political scientist, Mrs. Lincoln worked on Capitol Hill from 1950 to 1953, where she became acquainted with Congressman Kennedy and worked in his 1952 Senate campaign. "A pleasant brunet with a ready twinkle," the forty-year-old Mrs. Lincoln impressed Jack as certain to be a devoted aide who would patiently meet every request. He was not disappointed. As he later told Sorensen, "If I had said just now, 'Mrs. Lincoln, I have cut off Jackie's head, would you please send over a box?' she still would have replied, 'That's wonderful. I'll send it right away. Did you get your nap?'"

Sorensen was another exceptional find for a new ambitious senator. Jack hired him after two five-minute interviews; but he had ample information about the twenty-four-year-old lawyer from Lincoln, Nebraska, who had been "a lowly attorney" at the Federal Security Agency and then counsel to the Temporary Committee of the Congress on Railroad Retirement Legislation. Sorensen came from a progressive Republican family with a father who had been a crusading Nebraska attorney general and ally of Senator George W. Norris. Sorensen's mother, Annis Chaikin, was the offspring of Russian

Jews and, like her husband, a social activist committed to women's suffrage and other progressive causes. Kennedy also knew that Sorensen was his parents' child — a civil rights activist, an avowed pacifist, and an outspoken member of Americans for Democratic Action (ADA), an organization supporting reform candidates and causes.

Sorensen was an unlikely choice. In fact, before he went to his first interview, a knowledgeable D.C. attorney told him, "Jack Kennedy wouldn't hire anyone Joe Kennedy wouldn't tell him to hire — and, with the exception of Jim Landis [a former dean of the Harvard Law School and Kennedy family lawyer], Joe Kennedy hasn't hired a non-Catholic in fifty years!" But Jack needed a stronger liberal voice in his circle than his own if he were to advance his political career, and Sorensen was the sort of cerebral, realistic liberal Jack felt comfortable with. Sorensen saw himself as someone moved more by "intellectual than emotional persuasion. I am personally convinced," he said, "that the liberal who is rationally committed is more reliable than the liberal who is emotionally committed." When Joe Kennedy first met Sorensen eight or nine months after Jack hired him, Joe told him, "You couldn't write speeches for me. You're too much of a liberal. But writing for Jack is different."

Despite agreeing to work for Kennedy, Sorensen had doubts about the senator's willingness to fight the good fight. He wrote later that he immediately liked Kennedy, "impressed by his 'ordinary' demeanor. He spoke easily but almost shyly, without the customary verbosity and pomposity. The tailor-made suit that clothed a tall, lean frame was quietly stylish. A thatch of chestnut hair was not as bushy as cartoonists had portrayed it. He did not try to impress me, as officeholders so often do on first meetings, with the strength of his handshake, or with the importance of his office, or with the sound of his voice. Except for the Palm Beach tan on a handsome, youthful face, I saw few signs of glamour and glitter in the Senator-elect that winter." But Sorensen felt that if he "were going to throw in with him, there were certain things [I] wanted to know. I didn't want us to be too far apart on basic policy and so I asked the questions — about his father, Joe McCarthy, the Catholic Church." Jack was self-effacing and ready to tell Sorensen what he wanted to hear. Blessed with the instincts of the politician who can read an audience or intuit how to put himself in line with a listener's concerns, Kennedy described himself as more liberal than his House record suggested. "You've got to remember," he said, "that I entered Congress just out of my father's house," that is, still partly under his conservative influence.

Lincoln, Reardon, and Sorensen set to work in room 362, a four-room suite, in the Old Senate Office Building. In time, the middle room, where the door was always open during work hours, became a hive of activity, crowded with desks, filing cabinets, ringing telephones, clattering typewriters, and a constant stream of visitors. Mrs. Lincoln presided over this domain, while two small offices to the left housed Reardon and Sorensen, who in time were joined by several other aides providing expertise on domestic and foreign issues. To the right was Jack's spacious inner office with a large glass-faced bookcase topped by models of World War II ships and a stuffed nine-foot sailfish Jack caught off Acapulco in 1953. The wall in the far right corner of the room displayed old prints and inscribed framed photos of political friends. The senator sat at a large desk set in the center of the room before a green marble fireplace. Books, reports, and souvenirs, including the coconut shell Kennedy had used to arrange the rescue of his *PT 109* crew, covered his desk. "An air of intense informality hung over the office," making it, at times, seem "like a five-ring circus, as Kennedy simultaneously performed as senator, committee member, Massachusetts politician, author, and presidential candidate." Sorensen in particular unstintingly put his exceptional talent as an analyst and writer in the service of his new boss: He was "devoted, loyal, and dedicated to the Senator in every way possible," Evelyn Lincoln would say later. "Time meant nothing to him — he gave it all to the Senator."

The first task Jack set himself and the staff was fulfilling the promise of his campaign to do more for Massachusetts than his predecessor. Asked on *Meet the Press* shortly after his election what accounted for his victory over Lodge, Jack pointed to the decline of the state's economy "in the last six years with its competition with the South and its loss of industry. The feeling of the people of the state was that our interests had been neglected."

Sorensen, Harvard economist Seymour Harris, and three members of Joe's New York staff developed forty proposals for New England economic expansion. Jack described them in three carefully crafted Senate speeches in the spring of 1953. "The Economic Problems of New England — A Program for Congressional Action" argued that what was good for New England was good for America. "This Nation's challenge to meet the needs of defense mobilization and to achieve national and international economic stability and development," Jack asserted, "cannot be fully met if any part of the country is unproductive and unstable economically." The program urged help for various Massachusetts industries, including fishing, textiles, and shipbuilding, as well as for the Boston seaport. Kennedy's suggestions for stimulating the region's economy appealed to Democrats and Republicans alike by offering benefits to business and labor and promising to serve the national defense. The Congress would eventually enact most of the program, though slowly and with little fanfare.

Congress's tortoiselike pace meant that, as Ted Reardon told a supporter, "no great fireworks . . . resulted" from Jack's initiative. Since the object of the exercise was not only to help New England but also to publicize Jack's fulfillment of 1952 campaign promises, the office blitzed the media with publicity. Reardon distributed 30,000 copies of the program to special interest groups throughout New England, and Jack and Sorensen collaborated on articles about it in *American Magazine,* the *Atlantic Monthly,* the *New Republic,* and the *New York Times Magazine.*

The aggressive promotion of Jack's achievements and reputation included blunting attacks on him in the state. When Elmer C. Nelson, the chairman of the Republican State Committee, "made some slurring remarks about Jack," describing him as a "young Democratic fellow with a whirlygig in his hair" who went around serving tea to ladies to get elected, Jack sent word that if Nelson continued to refer to him that way, he would "take actions which he thinks are called for." Nelson did not test Jack's resolve.

THE POSSIBILITY OF BECOMING the first Catholic president intrigued Jack from the start of his political career. To advance his national visibility, he staked out a controversial position on the St. Lawrence Seaway, a proposed river transit system between northern Canada and the Great Lakes. Although advocates of the project argued its value to the national economy in general and the Midwest in particular, concerns that it would crimp the economic life of Boston's port had kept Massachusetts senators and representatives from casting a single vote for the project on the six occasions over the twenty years it had been before Congress. Jack wrestled with the issue for months before deciding to speak for the bill's passage in January 1954.

Few issues had troubled him as much during his years in Congress, he declared at the start of his speech. But several considerations had persuaded him to break with prevailing opinion in his state and support U.S. participation in building and managing the Seaway. First, if necessary, Canada would build the waterway without the United States. Second, a joint effort would give America part owner-ship and control of a vital strategic international artery, which would facilitate the shipment of high-grade iron ore the United States might need for national defense. Third, he believed there would ulti-mately be little, if any, damage to Boston's port, where 75 percent of traffic was "coastwise, intraport and local, which no one has claimed would be affected by the Seaway." Fourth, though he saw no reason to think that the city and state would benefit directly from the proj-ect, he believed that it would provide indirect economic gains. Finally, to oppose the Seaway would be to take "a narrow view of my functions as a U.S. Senator." Quoting Daniel Webster, Kennedy con-cluded, "Our aim should not be 'States dissevered, discordant [or] belligerent'; but 'one country, one constitution, one destiny.'"

Although the *Boston Post* asserted that he was "ruining New En-gland," Jack won more than he lost from what some described as a courageous stand for the national interest. At least one Massachu-setts newspaper came to his defense and two members of the state's congressional delegation, persuaded by Jack's arguments, voted with him for the Seaway. More important from Jack's perspective, his out-spoken backing of the St. Lawrence project won him attention. In February 1954, when he appeared on NBC's *Meet the Press,* the host described him as only the third Democrat in Massachusetts history to win a U.S. Senate seat. "His sensational victory [had] created international interest. He is in the news again because of his posi-tion on the St. Lawrence Seaway." His stand on the St. Lawrence project, Ted Sorensen said later, "certainly had the effect of making him a national figure."

So did his pronouncements on defense and foreign policy. Even after Eisenhower arranged a Korean truce in July, three of the four most worrisome issues to people were ousting communists from government, preventing another war, and formulating a clear foreign policy. In April 1954, 56 percent of Americans remained primarily concerned about threats of war, communist subversion, and national defense. By June, despite strong confidence in Eisenhower's leader-ship, the number of citizens troubled by these issues had risen to 67 percent. When asked directly about the possibility of a war in the next five years, between 40 and 64 percent of Americans saw a conflict as likely. A majority of the country expected atomic and hydrogen bombs to be used against the United States.

Kennedy's readiness to speak out on such questions was partly a case of cynical showboating. He understood that, as a journalist friend told him, his pronouncements on foreign affairs put his "eager boyish puss and ingratiating tones . . . all over the place." If he was going to run for president, establishing himself as a Senate leader on foreign affairs seemed like an essential prerequisite. But foreign policy was also his long-standing area of expertise, and joining a debate on vital matters of national security appealed to him as the highest duty of a senator.

It was, of course, rather courageous of a retired navy lieutenant and junior senator to take on a popular president whose credentials as a successful World War II and NATO military chief had carried him to the White House. But Jack believed that the Eisenhower-Dulles policy of reduced defense spending to balance the federal budget and reliance on massive retaliation or nuclear weapons rather than more conventional ones was an inadequate response to the communist menace. His recollections of misguided naval actions initiated by high-ranking officers in World War II encouraged his outspokenness.

In a Jefferson Jackson Day speech in May 1953, Kennedy said that it may be that Moscow will continue to rely "on the weapons of subversion, economic disintegration and guerilla warfare to accomplish our destruction, rather than upon the direct assault of an all-out war. But we cannot count on it." The Soviets and their satellites were devoting a large percentage of their national production to war preparations. Their large land armies supported by air and sea forces exceeding those in the West put America's national security in peril, especially when one considered the military budget cuts proposed for 1954 by the Eisenhower administration. Kennedy could "not see how the Western Alliance with a productive potential substantially larger than that of the Communist bloc, can be satisfied with anything less than a maximum effort, one that has some relation to the unrelenting efforts of the Soviets to build irresistible military strength." This was not an issue "on which the Democrats can win elections, for only disaster can prove us correct." Rather, it was a matter of serving the cause of peace and national well-being, or so he believed.

Kennedy had little impact on the Eisenhower defense budgets, and his fears of an all-out war were a misreading of Soviet intentions. As George Kennan, the architect of containment, understood at the time, the Soviets viewed their buildup as defensive, a response to Western plans for the destruction of communism. Their goal was to defeat the West not with a full-scale war, which they saw themselves losing, but by political subversion. Kennedy's defense proposals, however, were an improvement on Eisenhower's policy of massive retaliation, which provided "more bang for the buck," as the administration advertised, while reducing America's capability to fight a limited or non-nuclear war. Nevertheless, the increased defense spending Kennedy favored threatened to expand the arms race and bring the two sides closer to an all-out conflict. Kennedy's proposals were less an imaginative way to ease tensions with Moscow than a variation on what Kennan described as "the militarization of the Cold War."

KENNEDY'S EFFORTS to alter the American response to France's struggle in Indochina were wiser than his pronouncements on defense budgets. As France's hold on the region became increasingly tenuous, Jack's concern to find an effective means of addressing the crisis was amplified. He asked Priscilla Johnson, a foreign-policy specialist on his staff, to calculate the extent of French spending on Indochina's economic welfare and to suggest reforms that would spur the anticommunist war effort. Johnson replied that the proportion of French spending on welfare was very small compared with military aid. She added that the French had given limited control of affairs to citizens of Cambodia, Laos, and Vietnam — the three Associated States, as they were called; it was difficult to suggest reforms, Johnson reported, "since the problem is not that of changing existing institutions, which are being maladministered, but of introducing institutions which so far do not exist at all."

In May 1953, Jack privately told Secretary of State John Foster Dulles that increasing aid would give the United States the right to insist on changes that would give "the native populations . . . the feeling that they have not been given the shadow of independence but its substance. The American people want in exchange for their assistance the establishment of conditions that will make success a prospect and not defeat inevitable." The State Department agreed that a transfer of authority to the Associated States was desirable but saw no way to make this more than a "gradual" process.

In response, Kennedy put his case before the Congress and the public. In the summer of 1953, he urged the Senate to make U.S. aid to the French in Indochina contingent on policies promoting freedom and independence for Cambodia, Laos, and Vietnam. He believed that French resistance to reform was retarding the war effort. Jack acknowledged that these were "harsh words to say about an ancient friend and ally," but he spoke them in the belief that America's financial share of the fighting, which was at 40 percent and rising, entitled the United States to recommend changes that held out greater hope of success than the stumbling French policy followed since 1946. He was reluctant, however, to give the French an ultimatum, as Arizona's Republican senator Barry Goldwater urged; withholding aid unless France initiated democratic reforms in the Associated States seemed likely to force Paris to abandon the war in Indochina and open all of Southeast Asia to communism. Jack proposed instead that American aid "be administered in such a way as to encourage through all available means the freedom and independence desired by the peoples of the Associated States."

As French military failure grew more likely in the winter of 1953–54, Jack pressed the case for a French commitment to end its colonial rule. He also asked the White House to explain how massive retaliation could save Indochina and the rest of Southeast Asia from communist control. He wondered "how the new Dulles policy and its dependence upon the threat of atomic retaliation will fare in these areas of guerilla warfare. . . . Of what value would atomic retaliation be in opposing Communist advance which rested not upon military invasion but upon local insurrection and political deterioration?"

On *Meet the Press* in February 1954, Kennedy was asked if he was suggesting that the United States replace France in Indochina. No, he answered, because without commitments to independence for these French colonies, the United States would be facing a hopeless task. Since he was on record as saying that to lose Indochina was to lose all of Asia, didn't he believe it essential for the United States to fight? No, he said, because he saw no prospect of victory, "and therefore it would be a mistake for us to go in." However, he still had hope that the French could alter matters by promising independence and bringing educated local leaders and enough manpower to their side to reverse the tide of battle. But U.S. military involvement without this promise would be doomed to failure: "No amount of American military assistance in Indochina," he told the Senate, "can conquer an enemy which is everywhere and at the same time nowhere, 'an enemy of the people' which has the sympathy and covert support of the people." The only path to victory was through the creation of a "native army" that expected sacrifices in blood and treasure to bring self-determination.

Kennedy's assessment of French policy received strong support in the United States. But it meant nothing to the outcome in Southeast Asia, where French resistance collapsed in May 1954 with the defeat at the fortress of Dien Bien Phu in the Vietnamese highlands. As agreed to by China, France, the United States, and the Soviet Union at a Geneva conference later that year, the country was split in two at the Seventeenth Parallel — a North Vietnam under a communist government in Hanoi led by Ho Chi Minh and a South Vietnam under a pro-Western regime in Saigon led by Ngo Dinh Diem, a Catholic backed by promises of U.S. economic and military aid. Determined to supplant French influence in the south, Washington engineered Diem's replacement of Bao Dai, the ruling emperor, who had been a figurehead chief beholden to French power.

Kennedy was now more emphatic than ever that U.S. military involvement would be a mistake. In a TV appearance in May, he emphasized the pointlessness of committing U.S. forces, which echoed what the White House was saying. He feared that Indochina "is lost, and I don't think there is much we can do about it. . . . There is no outright military intervention that the United States could take in Indo-China which I believe would be successful." Indeed, U.S. intervention seemed certain to provoke a Chinese reaction, and "we'd find ourselves in a much worse situation than we found ourselves in Korea."

Kennedy's response to the crisis won him substantial attention and considerable praise in the press for sensible realism. His disagreements with earlier predictions by Eisenhower officials that "the French are going to win" moved commentators to describe Kennedy as an astute foreign policy analyst with a bright political future. No one noted, however, that Kennedy had exaggerated hopes for what could be expected of a so-called autonomous Vietnam — a country that would be dependent on American money and supplies in any further struggle against communist insurgents. This imperfect judgment would become apparent to Kennedy himself and others only in time.

KENNEDY'S POLITICAL FUTURE partly depended on finding ways to avoid alienating antagonistic factions debating McCarthy's anticommunist crusade. Because McCarthy had little proof to back up his charges and kept changing the number of subversive government officials, opponents labeled him a reckless demagogue. Yet others saw the loss of China, the Soviet detonation of an atomic bomb, and the convictions of Julius and Ethel Rosenberg for atomic spying and of Alger Hiss, a once respected State Department official, for falsely denying that he had passed secrets to the Soviet Union as giving the ring of truth to McCarthy's accusations.

In spite of increasing doubts about McCarthy's reliability, in November 1953, 46 percent of those surveyed said it was a good idea for the Republicans to raise fresh questions about communists in government during the FDR-Truman years. The following month, the public listed getting rid of communists in government as the country's number one problem, and 50 percent approved of McCarthy's commitment to do so.

But they did not like his methods. In the first months of 1954, 47 percent of Americans disapproved of his behavior, and when he launched an investigation of subversion in the U.S. Army in the spring, it further undermined confidence in his tactics. In May, 87 percent of Americans knew about the McCarthy hearings, but a majority thought they would do more harm than good. By the summer, 51 percent of those with an opinion were opposed to McCarthy.

His intemperateness had largely contributed to his decline. He had called President Truman "a son of a bitch" counseled by men drunk on "bourbon and Benedictine," and he had attacked General George C. Marshall, a World War II hero, as the architect of "a conspiracy so immense and an infamy so black as to dwarf any previous such venture in the history of man." When he also accused Protestant clergymen and U.S. Army officers of, respectively, supporting and shielding communists, it increased public doubts about his rational good sense.

Democrats, led by Senate majority leader Lyndon B. Johnson, now saw an opportunity to break his hold on the country. McCarthy is "the sorriest senator up here," LBJ had told Senate secretary Bobby Baker. "Can't tie his goddamn shoes. But he's riding high now, he's got people scared to death some Communist will strangle 'em in their sleep, and anybody who takes him on before the fevers cool — well, you don't get in a pissin' contest with a polecat." Understanding how daily exposure would go far to defeat him, Johnson arranged to have McCarthy's army hearings televised. Thirty-six days of TV coverage between April and June 1954 allowed people, in

Johnson's words, to "see what the bastard was up to." McCarthy's physical features — his unshaved appearance and nasal monotone — joined with evidence of his casualness about the truth to ruin him. In September, after nine days of hearings orchestrated by LBJ, a special Senate committee recommended that McCarthy be "condemned" for breaking Senate rules and abusing an army general. In December, after the congressional elections, the Senate voted condemnation by a count of 67 to 22.

The only Senate Democrat not to vote against McCarthy — or more precisely, *not* vote on the issue — was Kennedy. Jack had no illusions about the man's ruthlessness and unreliability. In 1953, when a reporter asked what he thought of Joe, he replied, "Not very much. But I get along with him. When I was in the House, I used to get along with [Vito] Marcantonio and [John] Rankin," demeaning McCarthy by lumping him with extremists on the left and the right. In January 1953, when Jack heard that his father had arranged for Bobby to be appointed as counsel to McCarthy's subcommittee on investigations, he regretted what his father had done. "Oh, hell, you can't fight the old man," he said in disgust. Jack was especially critical of the false charges McCarthy brought against foreign service officers for the "loss" of China. He dismissed as "irrational" allegations of communists in the diplomatic corps. In February 1954, he publicly complained of McCarthy's "excesses." "You reach the point of diminishing returns in all of these extreme charges and counter-charges," he added.

Jack also differed with McCarthy on a number of appointments needing Senate confirmation. In 1953, Jack voted in support of Charles Bohlen as ambassador to Russia and in 1954 for James Conant as ambassador to West Germany, despite McCarthy's attacks on both men as insufficiently anticommunist. These votes, however, required no direct confrontation with McCarthy. Neither did Jack's support of a ban on speeches by former McCarthy aide Scott McLeod, who, as a State Department employee, was violating civil service rules against political activities. But Jack's successful opposition to appointing former senator Owen Brewster, a McCarthy friend, as counsel to the investigations committee, and Robert Lee, another McCarthy friend, to the Federal Communications Commission incensed McCarthy. "Now wait until you try to get some special legislation for Massachusetts," McCarthy threatened Jack. "He was really furious," Jack said. "After that, it was just 'Hello Jack' when we passed in the hall, but he never really talked to me again after that."

Kenneth Birkhead, who was assistant to the Senate Democratic whip and the party's expert on McCarthy, later recalled that Kennedy was in constant touch with him about McCarthy's background and current accusations. "I don't think there was any other member of the Senate," Birkhead said, "who spent as much time contacting me about McCarthy as did the then Senator Kennedy." In July 1954, at the close of the army hearings, when the Senate initially considered censuring McCarthy, Jack was ready to vote against him. Sorensen prepared a speech that Kennedy never delivered, because of a decision to delay consideration of the charges against McCarthy until after formal hearings and the November elections. In July, however, Jack was prepared to say that the issue of McCarthy's censure "is of such importance that it is difficult for any member not to set forth clearly his position on this matter." Though the speech was hedged with numerous qualifiers, it defended the "dignity and honor" of the Senate by censuring McCarthy's conduct — or more precisely, the conduct of two of his aides for whom he was responsible.

Why then did Jack fail to vote for condemnation, a lesser charge than censure, at the end of 1954? After all, by then McCarthy had been largely repudiated. Historian and Kennedy supporter Arthur Schlesinger Jr. later said that an unequivocal stand against McCarthy might have antagonized some Massachusetts Catholics, but it would have improved Jack's standing with millions of others in the state. Connecticut senator Brien McMahon, from a state with a similar percentage of Catholics to that of Massachusetts, had openly opposed McCarthy, and Schlesinger said that "it didn't hurt him." But not everyone concurred. One Massachusetts newspaper may have accurately described the current mood in the state when it said: "[It was] certainly futile to expect any candidate running for Massachusetts statewide political office with any chance of winning to criticize Senator McCarthy. Adherents of both parties are evidently scared to death of offending the Boston electorate." Ex-governor Paul Dever said, "Joe McCarthy is the only man I know who could beat Archbishop Cushing in a two-man election fight in South Boston." Most important, Kennedy's gut told him that his constituents would punish him if he acted against McCarthy. Reflecting on these judgments, Jack told one critic of his failure to take a stand, "What was I supposed to do, commit hara-kiri?"

Jack came to regret his decision. His failure to join all his fellow Democrats and a majority of the Senate in condemning McCarthy's disgraceful behavior became an enduring political problem. Jack gave a number of unconvincing explanations for his non-vote. "I never said I was perfect," he began one defense of himself in 1960. "I've made the usual quota of mistakes. The Joe McCarthy thing? I was caught in a bad situation. My brother was working for Joe. I was against it, I didn't want him to work for Joe, but he wanted to. And how the hell could I get up there and denounce Joe McCarthy when my own brother was working for him? So it wasn't so much a thing of political liability as it was a personal problem." It was a weak and, if believed, selfish excuse.

His father, Kennedy also claimed, exerted pressure. "He liked McCarthy," Jack said in the same interview. "He still has a good word to say for McCarthy if you were sitting around with him in the evening. Contribute money to support McCarthy? I wouldn't doubt it for a minute."

In addition, Jack's non-vote rested on a detached view of the people McCarthy attacked. "I had never known the sort of people who were called before the McCarthy committee," Jack later told a journalist. "I agree that many of them were seriously manhandled, but they all represented a different world to me. What I mean is, I did not identify with them, and so I did not get as worked up as other liberals did." Unquestionably, former Communist Party members, 1930s radicals hoping Marxism might rescue America from the Depression, were not part of any circle Jack frequented. But intellectuals and foreign service officers? They were objects of McCarthy's public attacks as well, and Jack knew and admired some of these people.

In the final analysis, Jack offered a legalistic explanation for his non-vote. Reminding critics that he was in the hospital for back surgery during the Senate's final deliberations on McCarthy, Jack said he was like an absent member of a jury who had not heard all the evidence and was not entitled to vote. This is, to say the least, not very convincing. The matter was more a moral issue than a legal or technical one, and it had not come out of the blue but after years of McCarthy's misbehavior. Jack may have been more candid when he told a journalist in 1960, "I went into the hospital and I heard nothing about it and cared less and I didn't have any contact with anyone at my office and maybe Ted [Sorensen] should have paired me [i.e., joined someone with an opposite vote in abstaining], but at the time I didn't care about the thing. I couldn't care less. I was in bad shape and I had other things on my mind." His preoccupation with his health is no doubt true. Yet it seems inconceivable that Joe, Bobby, and others attentive to Jack's political future would have let the vote on McCarthy slide by without a decision on what he should do. For someone who admired courage of any kind — physical, emotional, political — Kennedy failed the test by ducking the vote, avoiding taking a stand for reasons of political expediency, and short-term political expediency at that.

Jack's inaction would have negative political consequences for the next six years. He repeatedly had to explain his non-vote to political opponents. His caution also bothered his conscience and made him more attentive to matters of political independence and courage. The best one can say about his passive response to the Senate's vote on McCarthy is that he subsequently questioned his own decision and publicly celebrated past examples of senators who had shown more political courage than he had.

PRIVATE CONCERNS PREOCCUPIED Kennedy during the debate on condemning McCarthy's behavior. In 1953, he had reluctantly decided to marry. Up till that time, he had seemed perfectly content to be the "Gay Young Bachelor," as a *Saturday Evening Post* article then described him: a handsome, casual millionaire who dashed about Washington in "his long convertible, hatless, with the car's top down," and had the pick of the most beautiful, glamorous women in and out of town. But Jacqueline Bouvier, a beautiful twenty-two-year-old socialite, had entered his life, and political necessities dictated that he end his career as the "'Senate's Confirmed Bachelor.'" One close Kennedy friend doubted that Jack would have married if he had lost the senate race in 1952, but a wife was essential for a young senator intent on higher office.

This is not to suggest that he was marrying strictly for reasons of political expediency; he had, in fact, fallen in love with Jackie. In 1951, after they met at a dinner party given by their journalist friend Charlie Bartlett, they began a two-year courtship. From the first, Jackie seemed like an ideal mate, or as close to it as Jack was likely to find: physically attractive, bright and thoughtful, shy but charming, and from a prominent Catholic *Social Register* family. Jackie also added to Jack's public aura, which partly satisfied the political side of the marriage. She helped legitimize Jack's standing as an American Brahmin — a royal marrying another member of the country's aristocracy.

They shared backgrounds of personal suffering. Jackie's parents, John Vernou Bouvier III, a New York Stock Exchange member, and Janet Lee Bouvier, had divorced when Jackie was nine. Tensions with her mother and an absent father, whose drinking and womanizing further separated him from his family, had made Jackie distrustful of people and something of a loner. By contrast, Jack had countered his anguish about his health and parental strains by constant engagement with friends. Though outwardly opposites in their detachment from and affinity for people, beneath the skin they were not so different.

"He saw her as a kindred spirit," Lem Billings said. "I think he understood that the two of them were alike. They had both taken circumstances that weren't the best in the world when they were younger and," Billings emphasized, "learned to *make themselves up* as they went along. . . . They were so much alike. Even the names — Jack and Jackie: two halves of a single whole. They were both actors and I think they appreciated each other's performances. It was unbelievable to watch them work a party. . . . Both of them had the ability to make you feel that there was no place on earth you'd rather be than sitting there in intimate conversation with them." Chuck Spalding said that "Jack appreciated her. He really brightened when she appeared. You could see it in his eyes; he'd follow her around the room watching to see what she'd do next. Jackie *interested* him, which was not true of many women."

But there were also frictions that threatened the potential union. Joe Kennedy worried that Jack might not want to give up his freedom. "I am a bit concerned that he may get restless about the prospect of getting married," Joe wrote Jack's friend Torb Macdonald six weeks before the wedding. "Most people do and he is more likely to do so than others."

Jack's reluctance expressed itself in a "spasmodic courtship" that bothered Jackie. She was in Europe for a while after they began dating, and when she returned, Jack's campaign for the Senate took priority over the courtship. After that, Jack was often in Massachusetts, where he would call her "from some oyster bar . . . with a great clinking of coins, to ask me out to the movies the following Wednesday in Washington." Possibly more threatening to the relationship were rumors of Jack's womanizing. But this, in fact, actually seemed to make him more attractive to Jackie. Chuck Spalding believed that "she wasn't sexually attracted to men unless they were dangerous like old Black Jack [Bouvier]," her father, whose philandering had destroyed his marriage to Jackie's mother. "It was one of those terribly obvious Freudian situations," Spalding said. "We all talked about it — even Jack, who didn't particularly go for Freud, but said that Jackie had a 'father crush.' What was so surprising was that Jackie, who was so intelligent in other things, didn't seem to have a clue about this one."

They married at Jackie's stepfather's estate in Newport, Rhode Island, on September 12, 1953. It was a celebrity affair attended by the rich and famous and numerous members of the press, who described it as the social event of the year — the marriage of "Queen Deb" to America's most eligible bachelor. "At last I know the true meaning of rapture," Jack wired his parents during his honeymoon in Acapulco. "Jackie is enshrined forever in my heart. Thanks mom and dad for making me worthy of her."

This devotion did not last long. The first fifteen months of their marriage produced tensions that were some of the "other things" that were on Jack's mind during McCarthy's condemnation. Jackie was unhappy with the priority Jack gave his work over her; even when he was at home, she said, he seemed so preoccupied that she might "as well be in Alaska." "I was alone almost every weekend," she recalled. "It was all wrong. Politics was sort of my enemy and we had no home life whatsoever." Jack complained that she spent money like water and redecorated their various residences so often that he felt "like a transient." He tried to rein her in. "[Jack] insists that Jackie either travel or eat well," Rose wrote daughter Pat, "so the week ends she spends money on traveling she has to practically starve at home."

Since they had not lived together before marrying, Jackie was unprepared for what she called Jack's "violent" independence — by which she meant not just his habit of going off with his male friends but, more important, his thinly disguised promiscuity. In theory, she may have been drawn to her husband's bad side, but the practical result was painful. She was not, Lem Billings recalled, "prepared for the humiliation she would suffer when she found herself stranded at parties while Jack would suddenly disappear with some pretty young girl." Jackie rationalized Jack's behavior by saying, "I don't think there are any men who are faithful to their wives. Men are such a combination of good and evil." But one of Jack's friends recalled that "after the first year they were together, Jackie was wandering around looking like the survivor of an airplane crash."

Jackie's unhappiness was no inducement to Jack to restrain himself. In the summer of 1956, while she was in the late stages of a pregnancy that ended in a miscarriage, Jack went on a yachting trip with George Smathers in the Mediterranean, where he enjoyed "a bacchanal, with several young women getting on and off the boat at its ports of call." He was especially drawn to "a stunning but not particularly intelligent blonde who . . . referred to herself as 'Pooh.'" Even after getting the news that Jackie had lost their child, Jack did not decide to go home until Smathers warned him that a divorce would play havoc with his presidential ambitions. In 1958, when younger brother Ted got married, Jack was caught on tape whispering to him "that being married didn't really mean that you had to be faithful to your wife."

Health problems compounded Jack's marital tensions. After the diagnosis of his Addison's disease in September 1947, he continued to struggle with medical concerns. Over the next six years, headaches, upper respiratory infections, stomachaches, urinary tract discomfort, and almost constant back pain plagued him. He consulted an ear, nose, and throat specialist about his headaches, took medication and applied heat fifteen minutes a day to ease his stomach troubles, consulted urologists about his bladder and prostate discomfort, had DOCA pellets implanted and took daily oral doses of cortisone to control his Addison's disease, and struggled unsuccessfully to find relief from his back miseries. "Senator Kennedy has been a patient of the Lahey Clinic at intervals since 1936, and has had quite a variety of conditions," a Lahey Clinic urologist summed up Jack's problems in March 1953. The physician described him as "doing well" in regard to his Addison's disease. In 1951, however, while in Japan during his Far East trip, he had suffered a severe Addisonian crisis. He ran a temperature of 106 degrees and the doctors feared for his life. The episode convinced him to be more fastidious about taking his medicine, and over the next two years his back problems became his principal complaint.

In July 1953, Kennedy entered George Washington University Hospital for back treatment. By the following January, with no relief in sight, he consulted a specialist at New York Hospital, and then in

April he entered the Lahey Clinic for further consultations. The pain had become almost unbearable. X rays showed that the fifth lumbar vertebra had collapsed, most likely a consequence of the cortico-steroids he was taking for the Addison's disease. He could not bend down to pull a sock on his left foot and he had to climb and descend stairs moving sideways. Beginning in May, he had to rely on crutches to get around, and his walks to the Senate from his office on hard marble floors for quorum and roll calls became daily ordeals. His discomfort made him so short-tempered that Evelyn Lincoln considered leaving her job. A brief stay in the Bethesda Naval Hospital in July provided no remedy. In August, a team of Lahey physicians visited him at the Cape, where they described a complicated surgery to achieve spinal and sacroiliac fusions. They explained that without the operation he might lose his ability to walk, but they warned that so difficult a surgery on someone with Addison's disease posed a grave risk of a fatal infection.

Rose Kennedy said later, "Jack was determined to have the opera-tion. He told his father that even if the risks were fifty-fifty, he would rather be dead than spend the rest of his life hobbling on crutches and paralyzed by pain." Joe tried to dissuade Jack from chancing the surgery, reminding him of FDR's extraordinary achievements despite being confined to a wheelchair. But Jack assured him, "'Don't worry, Dad, I'll make it through.'" After he entered New York's Hospital for Special Surgery on October 10, the team of endocrinologists and surgeons postponed the operation three times until October 21 to ensure an "extended metabolic work-up prior to, during, and after surgery."

The more-than-three-hour operation was a limited success. A metal plate was inserted to stabilize the lumbar spine. Afterward a urinary tract infection put Jack's life in jeopardy. (Steroids are also immunosuppressives and make infection more likely and more seri-ous.) He went into a coma, and a priest was called to administer the last rites. Fearful of losing his second son, Joe wept openly before Arthur Krock. "His entire body shook with anger and sorrow," Rose recalled. But by December, Jack had shaken the infection and recov-ered sufficiently to be moved to the family's Palm Beach home. It was clear, however, that he remained far from well; his doctors could not promise that he would ever walk again. Moreover, there was rea-son to believe that the plate itself was infected. Consequently, in February, another operation was performed at the same New York hospital to remove the plate. Extracting it meant removing three screws that had been drilled into the bone and replacing shattered cartilage with a bone graft. After another three months recuperating in Florida, Jack returned in May to Washington, where he received a warm welcome from Senate colleagues who admired his determination to maintain his career in the face of such debilitating medical problems.

Because his absence from Washington over so long a period could not be hidden, the Kennedys had no choice but to acknowledge his illness. Public knowledge of Jack's surgery and slow recovery, however, benefited rather than undermined his image. Jack came through this medical ordeal looking courageous — not weak and possibly unfit for higher office, as his family had feared. Nevertheless, the Kennedys did not trust that coming clean about Jack's health problems in the future would generate a similar result.

Throughout it all, Jack worried that his non-vote on McCarthy's censure had been politically unwise and morally indefensible. In December, as he was about to be carried on a stretcher from the hospital for his trip to Florida, Chuck Spalding, who was in his room, recalls him saying, "'You know, when I get downstairs I know exactly what's going to happen. Those reporters are going to lean over my stretcher. There's going to be about ninety-five faces bent over me with great concern, and every one of those guys is going to say, 'Now, Senator, what about McCarthy?'" And he said, "'Do you know what I'm going to do? I'm going to reach back for my back and I'm just going to yell, Oow, and then I'm going to pull the sheet over my head and hope we can get out of there.'"

INCREASINGLY FASCINATED with the issue of moral and political courage — "at which point and on which issue he [a politician] will risk his career" — Kennedy now began thinking about writing a book on the subject. This was partly a retrospective coming to terms with his moral lapse on McCarthy, but it was also more: He had been interested in the subject for a long time, going back to at least the failure of British political leaders in the thirties to oppose popular resistance to rearming. And his election to the House and the Senate gave him added reason to think about the proper role of an elected legislator in dealing with conflicting pressures every time he had to vote. Where is the line between satisfying local demands and sometimes defying them for the sake of larger national needs? Early in 1954, after reading in Herbert Agar's *Price of Union* about the independence demonstrated by John Quincy Adams, Kennedy asked Ted Sorensen to find other examples of senators "defying constituent pressures." Feelings about conforming to his father's wishes and acting on his own judgment were surely also part of the interest that drew Kennedy to the problem.

Kennedy understood that there were varieties of courage. He had firsthand knowledge of the bravery men showed in war and competitive sports. There was also self-mastery of the sort Franklin Roosevelt had shown in overcoming private suffering to pursue a successful public career. Jack quoted Eleanor Roosevelt's description of her husband's polio attack as a "turning point" that "proved a blessing in disguise; for it gave him strength and courage he had not had before." Jack's colitis, Addison's disease, and back miseries had provided him with a similar, if not as large, challenge. In a 1956 magazine article about his back surgery, "What My Illness Taught Me," Jack described a letter he had received from a ninety-year-old lady when he was flat on his back in the hospital and feeling glum. Though she was bedridden, she was "full of hope and good humor." She had never voted for a Democrat and wanted the chance to vote for at least one before she died. She thought it "might stand me in good stead up above. So I want you to be up to running in 1958. Don't waste away feeling sorry for yourself," she advised. "Keep busy. Do all the things you never had time to do." Jack said the letter was "a tonic for my spirits," and if he had not received it, he might "never have got around to writing my book." Whether the lady's advice was quite as important as Jack represented it to be is beside the point; his illness gave him additional inspiration to write what would eventually be called *Profiles in Courage*.

The book recounts the careers of eight senators — John Quincy Adams, Daniel Webster, Thomas Hart Benton, Sam Houston, Edmund G. Ross, Lucius Lamar, George W. Norris, and Robert Taft — all of whom had shown uncommon courage in risking their political careers by taking unpopular stands that put them at odds with majorities in their parties, states, and regions. It was a celebration in a time of uncertain prospects for democracy in its competition with communism, and a healthy antidote to the periodic cynicism that besets Americans about politicians and the country's system of self-rule.

Published in 1956, the book became a national bestseller and added to Jack's prominence, but it also raised questions. Where did a busy U.S. senator sidelined by serious medical problems find the wherewithal to write so successful a book? According to one earlier biographer, interviews and research into contemporary papers, including those of Ted Sorensen, who helped Jack with the book, prove "Jack Kennedy's involvement: from start to finish, the responsibility was clearly his. . . . Personalities to be included were suggested by several people; the Preface acknowledges many debts, but the choices, message, and tone of the volume are unmistakably Kennedy's." Sorensen and Professor Jules Davids of Georgetown University, with whom Jackie had taken courses, gathered materials for the book and drafted chapters, but the final product was essentially Jack's. He edited what Sorensen and Davids gave him and then dictated final chapter drafts for a secretary to type. The tapes of these dictations, which are available at the John F. Kennedy Library, provide conclusive evidence of Jack's involvement. Jack did more on the book than some later critics believed, but less than the term *author* normally connotes. *Profiles in Courage* was more the work of a "committee" than of any one person.

As interesting as the debate about Jack's authorship were his private and public reactions to questions that were raised about it. Suggestions that the book was not his idea or the product of his work incensed him. In 1956, when a Harvard classmate and radio journalist ribbed Jack about the allegations, he became furious. Jack normally loved that kind of repartee with old friends, but questions about his authorship were different; they touched something in him that left no room for humor. When *New York Times* editor John Oakes privately passed along the rumor that Jack was not the author, Jack confronted him with "evidence" to the contrary. ("I sure wasn't convinced by this," Oakes said. "Undoubtedly Ted [Sorensen] or someone else wrote it.") When columnist Drew Pearson asserted in a television interview that the book was "ghostwritten," Jack asked prominent Washington attorney Clark Clifford to compel a retraction, which Pearson reluctantly gave.

Jack certainly hoped that *Profiles* would identify him with uncompromising political responses to national dangers. He yearned for a challenge that would give him an opportunity to act like a political hero. The best he could find was a congressional proposal to reform the electoral system. Jack took up the cudgels against what he described as "one of the most far-reaching — and I believe mistaken — schemes ever proposed to alter the American constitutional system. No one knows with any certainty what will happen if our electoral system is totally revamped as proposed." Jack emphasized how well the existing electoral system had worked to ensure the influence of the popular vote, the two-party system, and "the large-State-small-State checks-and-balances system." The proposed amendment, which he feared could destabilize American politics at a time of grave foreign challenges, was nothing voters had demanded or even knew about. Although Jack gave a lengthy, authoritative Senate speech that contributed to the defeat of the amendment, his opposition hardly registered on the press or the public; reform of the electoral college was an invisible controversy.

OTHER THAN THE MCCARTHY CONTROVERSY, the most significant political challenges Kennedy faced between 1954 and 1956 centered on the Massachusetts Democratic party — a venue not for heroics but for self-serving, brass-knuckle politics disconnected from any larger public good. In 1954, Kennedy found himself in a battle with Foster Furcolo, a Yale-trained Italian American attorney who had served as a Massachusetts congressman and state treasurer and was a Democratic candidate for Republican Leverett Saltonstall's U.S. Senate seat. In 1952, Furcolo, looking ahead to a Senate race and the need for independent and Republican votes, gave Jack cautious support against Lodge. In response to this tepid endorsement, Jack, who had an excellent working relationship with Saltonstall and a high personal regard for him, was reluctant to back Furcolo. And like Furcolo two years before, Jack did not want to antagonize non-Democrats who had supported him and might vote for him again in 1958. Nor was Jack eager to help someone he saw as an ambitious rival for statewide influence and possible national power.

Jack's tensions with Furcolo came to a head in October 1954, just before he entered the hospital for surgery. In a joint television appearance with Robert Murphy, the party's gubernatorial candidate, and Furcolo, Jack showed himself to be visibly more sympathetic to Murphy than to Furcolo. He also ignored Furcolo's demand that he directly attack Saltonstall. At one point, before the program began, Jack, who was on crutches and in a great deal of pain, stormed out of the studio, saying to Frank Morrissey, "That goddamn guinea." After Morrissey told a journalist that Jack did not want Furcolo elected, Kennedy's office refused further comment on the clash. But it was an open secret, and in the view of Kennedy aides Ken O'Donnell and Dave Powers, "the only wrong political move Jack Kennedy ever made."

More constructive was an eighteen-month battle for statewide control of the Democratic party. Jack had initially been reluctant to get into an intraparty conflict he associated with traditional Boston politics, and his father urged against it as well: "Leave it alone and don't get into the gutter with those bums up there in Boston," Joe told him. But O'Donnell and another Kennedy aide, Larry O'Brien, advised otherwise. Speculation that Jack might be Adlai Stevenson's running mate in 1956 convinced them that Jack's selection and political future now turned on delivering the Massachusetts delegation to Stevenson at the party's nominating convention. Consequently, they urged Jack to wrest control of the state party committee from John McCormack and his ally William H. ("Onions") Burke, the chairman of the Democratic State Committee, who intended to back New York governor Averell Harriman for the presidential nomination. Massachusetts congressman Philip Philbin also urged Jack to take on McCormack and Burke. "There is a great 'hassle' going on in the erudite Massachusetts Democracy," he sarcastically told Jack in March 1955. "Various learned 'savants' and 'intellectuals' who shape the upper crust of our party organization are conducting a campaign for control, perhaps I should say a campaign to insure our defeat at the next election." Kennedy and his team needed, Philbin said, to clean "up this deplorable situation."

With Jack still recuperating from his surgery in Florida, he was not ready to act. He praised O'Brien and O'Donnell for their analysis of the situation but deferred a decision until he could return to Massachusetts for discussions. In the meantime, he asked them "to study proposed courses of action." They began doing more than that, pressuring Democratic state bosses to accept Jack as their leader. And Jack, who shared their conviction that a fight for party control, however unpalatable, was vital to his future, soon threw himself into the battle with characteristic determination. Pointing to polls demonstrating his popularity and threatening to put himself forward as a favorite-son presidential candidate, Jack persuaded McCormack and Burke to give him an equal say in choosing the party's 1956 delegation to the national convention. At the same time, however, he instructed O'Brien and O'Donnell to work secretly to oust Burke and his allies from the state committee. "So we can't let Burke or McCormack know that we're trying to get our people on the state committee," he told his aides. "At least, not for the time being. Keep working on it, but don't let Burke know about it, and don't mention my name to anybody."

Since Jack's opposition to Burke was well known, Burke took precautions to counter Kennedy's attack. In March and April 1956, while Jack helped organize a write-in vote for Stevenson in the state's Democratic presidential primary, Burke countered with a favorite-son campaign for John McCormack. With support from *Boston Post* publisher John Fox, a staunch McCarthy backer and all-out opponent of Stevenson, the Burke forces gave McCormack a 10,000-vote victory over Adlai.

Jack now saw no alternative to an open fight with Burke. Although the Burke machine had the advantage of incumbency in a May 19 election for the party's eighty committee seats, Jack moved quickly to exploit Burke's unsavory image and unpopularity around the state. A short, rotund, balding onion farmer from the Berkshires, Burke had limited appeal to Boston Democrats. More important, a propensity for riding roughshod over opponents had created many enemies, who were all too happy to join Jack's campaign. Sensing Burke's vulnerability when contrasted with himself, Jack let it be known that he had given Burke an ultimatum — resign or be ousted. He issued a judicious statement of intent that further contrasted him favorably with Burke. "I do not relish being involved in this dispute," he said, but he saw no other way "to restore our party to dignity and respect." When Burke associated Stevenson supporters with communist sympathizers and falsely accused Jack of trying to bribe him with a promise of appointment as Democratic national committeeman, it incensed Democrats and added to the feeling that Burke was unworthy of high public influence.

The struggle turned into a no-holds-barred contest. Jack wrote, called, and met with committee candidates to ask for their support in overthrowing Burke. Needing to suggest a replacement, he reluctantly picked John "Pat" Lynch, the longtime mayor of Somerville. Lynch was a surprising choice; he was one of the old pols Jack seemed determined to defeat. Indeed, when O'Donnell brought Lynch in to see Jack, he "saw the shock on Jack's face." The small, bald-headed fifty-five-year-old "leprechaun," as O'Donnell described him, dressed in a wide-brimmed hat and velvet-collared coat typical of Boston's Irish politicians was no one Jack wanted to identify with. But when the Dever Democrats made clear that it would be Lynch or Burke, Jack endorsed Lynch. Even then, threatened fistfights and mayhem marked a three-hour committee meeting that produced a 47–31 vote for Lynch and Jack's undisputed control of the state party.

It had been the first time Jack had been "caught in a mud-slinging Boston Irish political brawl. We never saw him so angry and frustrated," O'Donnell and Powers wrote. During and after the fight, Kennedy took pains to divorce himself publicly from "gutter" politics. In an article published in the April *Vogue* and a June commencement address at Harvard, when the university gave him an honorary degree, he decried the current antagonism between intellectuals and politicians and reminded readers and listeners that the two were not mutually exclusive. Recalling the careers of Jefferson, Madison, Hamilton, Franklin, and the Adamses, he said "[The] nation's first great politicians . . . included among their ranks most of the nation's first great writers and scholars." Recounting an anecdote about an English mother who urged her son's Harrow instructors not to distract him from a Parliamentary career by teaching him poetry, Jack declared, "If more politicians knew poetry and more poets knew politics, I am convinced that the world would be a little better place to live."

The speech partly eased Jack's discomfort with the ugly fight he had just passed through, and it may also have been aimed at Adlai Stevenson, who shared Jack's affinity for a union of poetry and power. But more important, it expressed his genuine idealism about what he wished to see in American political life. Seven years later, at the height of his public influence, he repeated the value he placed on those committed to the life of the mind. In an October 1963 speech at Amherst College, he would say, "The men who create power make an indispensable contribution to the nation's greatness, but the men who question power make a contribution just as indispensable, especially when that questioning is disinterested, for they determine whether we use power or power uses us."

IN 1956, JACK thought less about the uses of power than about its acquisition — specifically, how to gain the vice presidency. In September 1955, after Eisenhower suffered a heart attack and speculation arose that he might not run again, Democratic party prospects in 1956 brightened. A vice presidential nomination for Jack could be the prelude to an eight-year term as VP, followed by a run for the White House in 1964, when he would be only forty-seven years old.

For the Democrats to win the White House, however, Joe and Jack thought that the party would have to find a nominee other than Adlai Stevenson. They preferred Lyndon Johnson. Although no southern Democrat had won the presidency or even been nominated in the twentieth century (Woodrow Wilson, a Virginian by birth, ran as governor of New Jersey), Johnson seemed a reasonable bet to break that tradition. A dominant figure in the Senate and the party, with credentials as a moderate who could appeal to all regions of the country, Johnson was keenly interested in running.

In October 1955, Joe asked Tommy Corcoran, a prominent Washington "fixer" and friend of LBJ's from the New Deal days, to carry a message to Johnson. If Lyndon would declare for the presidency and privately promise to take Jack as his running mate, Joe would arrange financing for the campaign. Because raising enough money would not be easy for any Democrat in 1956 and because Jack would bring a number of attributes to the ticket, Joe believed his offer would get serious consideration. But LBJ immediately rejected it. Reluctant to declare before he was sure that Eisenhower would not run and fearful that an announcement would encourage other candidates to join a "stop Lyndon" movement, Johnson simply said he was not running. According to Corcoran, Johnson's response "infuriated" Bobby Kennedy, who declared it "unforgivably discourteous to turn down his father's generous offer." In a conversation between Jack and Corcoran in Jack's Senate office, Kennedy said, "'Listen, Tommy, we made an honest offer to Lyndon through you. He turned us down. Can you tell us this: Is Lyndon running without us? . . . Is he running?'" Corcoran answered, "Of course he is. He may not think he is. And certainly he's saying he isn't. But I know God damned well he is." Joe Kennedy called Lyndon directly, but the answer was still no.

Johnson's rejection did not deter Jack from putting himself forward as a potential running mate. In January 1956, when a Massachusetts state senator advised Jack that he wanted to start such a campaign, Jack agreed to talk with him but cautioned against an overt effort; he preferred to keep a low profile until he had convinced Democrats, especially Stevenson, that he would be a strong addition to the ticket. Part of this quiet strategy entailed controlling the Massachusetts delegation to the party's national convention. It also meant getting sympathetic journalists to talk up Jack's candidacy. In February 1956, Fletcher Knebel, a *Look* writer, described Jack as on everyone's list of possible Stevenson running mates. Jack had "all the necessary Democratic assets": youth, good looks, liberal views, a record of military bravery, and proven vote-getting ability.

Moreover, his religion, which would have been a bar to nomination in the past, was described as no longer a problem. On the contrary, Knebel cited a document Ted Sorensen had prepared arguing that a Catholic on the ticket in 1956 would be a distinct asset in northern states with large Catholic populations. In June, Knebel addressed the issue directly in an article, "Can a Catholic Become Vice President?"

Sorensen also prepared a comparative study of twenty-one potential Stevenson running mates, analyzing their attributes in twelve categories: availability, compatibility, political outlook, public reputation, marital condition, officeholding or political experience, age and health, military record, voter appeal, TV personality, and wealth. On Sorensen's chart, not surprisingly, only Jack received a positive mark in every category. (Sorensen apparently did not know the full story of Jack's various health problems.) In August, shortly before the convention met, Sorensen put the case for Jack before Stevenson through an aide. Despite a growing list of public endorsements, led by New England governors and Tennessee senator Albert Gore Sr., Stevenson — who saw Kennedy's Catholicism as an insurmountable obstacle — was not convinced. Jim Farley, FDR's Catholic postmaster general and Democratic party "wheel horse," concurred, telling Adlai that "America is not ready for a Catholic yet." House Speaker Sam Rayburn weighed in against Jack as well. "Well, if we have to have a Catholic," he said, "I hope we don't have to take that little piss-ant Kennedy. How about John McCormack?"

And if Stevenson was the nominee, Joe remained convinced that Jack should not run. Eisenhower's recovery from his heart attack and decision to stand again made it unlikely that Stevenson could win. A straw poll in June 1956 showed the president with a 62 to 35 percent lead over Adlai. Moreover, Joe feared that a Democratic defeat would be blamed on Jack's Catholicism and would undermine his chances for the presidency.

But Jack was not convinced. He continued to press the case for his nomination, telling Joe that "while I think the prospects are rather limited, it does seem of some use to have all of this churning up." In July, Sargent Shriver, Eunice Kennedy's husband and director of Kennedy enterprises at the Merchandise Mart in Chicago, directly urged Jack's candidacy on Stevenson during a plane trip from Cape Cod to Chicago. Shriver made clear to Adlai that despite Joe Kennedy's publicly stated misgivings, he would be "100% behind Jack" and described Joe as ready to return from his summer vacation in

France in twenty minutes if Jack wanted him. Eunice wrote her father in August that without a vice presidential nomination and campaign, which would make him "better known," Jack did not think the party would "select him as a presidential candidate any . . . time in the future."

Stevenson was not swayed. He believed he needed a southerner, or at least a border state senator. Moreover, with a number of candidates actively seeking the nomination, he hoped to avoid alienating any of them by letting the convention choose for him. It was a thin tightrope to walk. Stevenson was eager to maintain good relations with Joe Kennedy, who was a promising source of campaign funds in what "looked like a thin year for the Democrats." But Adlai's refusal to follow tradition by picking a running mate angered the Kennedys, who saw it as a way to avoid taking Jack.

Although Stevenson's decision made it extremely difficult for Jack to win the nomination, he did have several things working in his favor. On Monday, August 13, the first night of the Chicago convention, he was the narrator of a film celebrating the Democratic party and its recent heroes such as Roosevelt and Truman. The *New York Times* compared his appearance to that of a "movie star" whose personality and good looks made him an instant celebrity. And before the convention even met, Kennedy supporters had set up a headquarters in the Palmer House hotel to promote Jack's candidacy.

On Wednesday, ostensibly to give Jack greater visibility and prominence but largely as a way to blunt Jack's drive for the second spot, Stevenson asked him to put his name in nomination for the presidency. Jack complied, and although Stevenson denied it, Kennedy accurately saw Stevenson's request as a compensatory gesture for being denied the vice presidency. And indeed, Stevenson's decision to leave the VP choice to the convention had placed significant obstacles in Kennedy's way. Instead of having only to convince Stevenson and his advisers to put him on the ticket, Jack now had to bring a majority of the convention delegates to his side. In a competition with Tennessee senator Estes Kefauver, who had a large base of delegate support, Jack had little chance to win.

But Jack was determined to push ahead. Jack instructed Bobby to call their father on the Riviera to tell him about Stevenson's maneuver, to say that Jack was running, and to ask Joe to press Jack's case over the telephone with as many influential Democrats as he could reach. Joe Kennedy thought his son was making a terrible mistake.

According to Rose Kennedy and Kenny O'Donnell, Joe exploded in anger. He "denounced Jack as an idiot who was ruining his political career." "Whew! Is he mad!" Bobby said after the phone connection was lost. Anticipating Joe's reaction, Jack had left the room; deciding to run was an act of defiance against his father, and it was easier to let Bobby take the heat. (Lem Billings recalled that Jack had initially experienced "a sudden warmth" after deciding to ignore Joe's advice — as if he had drunk "an entire bottle of wine." But Jack suffered a "momentary paralysis" after hearing Joe's reaction.) True, once Jack had made up his mind to run, Joe did everything in his power to help. But it was no small act of personal courage for Jack to make so big a political decision without his father's initial approval.

Kennedy's backers entered the fight with a "realistic sense of futility." Led by Jack and Bobby, they spent the night after Stevenson announced the open VP contest arranging for the banners, buttons, leaflets, placards, and noisemakers needed for a winning effort. They also ran from one convention hotel to another, asking, begging, cajoling, flattering, and pressuring delegates to join the swelling ranks of a man they described as a likely future president who would remember their support in his hour of need.

Kefauver retained a significant lead. His unsuccessful competition with Stevenson for the presidential nomination had nevertheless left him with a large number of delegates — 483½ — who were ready to back his vice presidential candidacy, despite having no mandated obligation to do so. This was, however, 203 short of selection, and Jack's first ballot total of 304 turned the nomination into a real contest. Because Kefauver was unpopular in the South, where his support of civil rights had made him a renegade and because Stevenson had broken precedent by allowing the convention to choose his running mate, the nomination was genuinely up for grabs. With support from anti-Kefauver southerners led by the Texas delegation — "Texas proudly casts its fifty-six votes for the fighting sailor who wears the scars of battle," LBJ announced — Jack surged ahead of Kefauver on the second ballot by 648 to 551½, just 38 short of nomination. But Kefauver's backers promptly persuaded several state delegations, led by Tennessee, Oklahoma, and Missouri, to switch and shift the momentum back to him. A vote of 755½ to Jack's 589 gave Kefauver the victory and the nomination.

Bobby Kennedy would later remember that "we lost because we weren't properly organized. If the delegates had known when

Tennessee had switched that we were only thirty-eight votes from a majority, there wouldn't have been all those switches to get on the Kefauver bandwagon. They didn't realize we were that close." But other things worked against Jack as well. Liberals, led by Eleanor Roosevelt, who had resisted Jack's request for her support by complaining that he had not actively opposed McCarthy, were generally unenthusiastic about putting Kennedy on the ticket. In addition, a lot of Democrats, including many Catholics, believed that a Catholic running mate would undermine chances of beating Eisenhower and of holding the Congress. Ike's illness had forcefully reminded voters that a VP was "only a heartbeat away from the Oval Office." Kefauver's runner-up status for the presidential nomination, however circumscribed by the limited number of primaries (he had won 39 percent of Democratic primary votes to Stevenson's 52 percent), had also made it difficult for the party to deny him second place.

Although the defeat stung Jack, most commentators agreed that his candidacy had been a net gain. An appearance before the convention to ask unanimous backing for Kefauver was a triumph of public relations, as was the impression he made throughout the proceedings. Despite his defeat, Jack "probably rates as the one real victor of the entire convention," a Boston journalist wrote. "He was the one new face that actually shone. His charisma, his dignity, his intellectuality, and, in the end, his gracious sportsmanship . . . are undoubtedly what those delegates will remember. So will those who watched it and heard it via TV and radio." Joe agreed: He thought that Jack had come "out of the convention so much better than anyone could have hoped. . . . His time is surely coming!" Arthur Schlesinger Jr. wrote Jack that "you clearly emerged as the man who gained most during the Convention. . . . Your general demeanor and effectiveness made you in a single week a national political figure. . . . The campaign provides a further opportunity to consolidate this impression."

Jack's upward trajectory continued into the fall as he campaigned for Stevenson. Though Stevenson's aides wanted him to concentrate on Massachusetts and a few other swing states with a big Catholic vote, Kennedy organized an itinerary that gave him much wider exposure and promised to do more for his political future than for Stevenson's candidacy. Whatever discomfort he might have felt at putting his interests ahead of the candidate was eased by the realistic assessment that Stevenson's campaign was a losing effort from the start. Running against a popular incumbent, whose four-year term included an end to the Korean War; economic expansion; and a deft handling of difficulties with Communist China over the offshore islands of Quemoy and Matsu, the Hungarian uprising against Soviet rule (which the administration used to blacken Moscow's international reputation in the Third World), and the Suez crisis, Stevenson never had a chance.

Whatever hope Stevenson may have had evaporated in a campaign Bobby Kennedy described as "the most disastrous operation" he had ever seen. Bobby, who traveled with Stevenson at the candidate's request, thought he did almost everything wrong. He read speeches where he should have spoken them to create some sense of spontaneity; he focused on arcane matters that resonated little with voters; he wasted time on organizational questions he should have delegated to aides; and he showed indecision on all manner of things. "Stevenson was just not a man of action at all," Bobby concluded at the time.

Meanwhile, Jack seemed to be everywhere, exuding charm, offering sensible pronouncements, and muting his competitiveness and ambition for greater national recognition with self-deprecating humor. He crisscrossed twenty-four states, giving more than 150 speeches that endeared him to audiences. The lesson of running a national political campaign, he told a Boston group, is to "be prepared. Be prepared to travel day and night, east and west, in an overheated limousine in ninety-three-degree weather in Fort Lauderdale, Florida, and in an open-car motorcade in raw thirty-degree temperature in Bellows Falls, Vermont, and in Twin Falls, Idaho." (Twin Falls was "one of the most important metropolises I visited in my search for Democratic voters," he declared to the amusement of his audience. "Despite the ill effects of that freezing ride on my health and morale, there was at least no danger to my person in that Republican stronghold, for there were more of us in the motorcade than there were on the streets to greet us.") He reminded his listeners that for "one brief moment of glory" he had been a candidate for VP. "Socrates once said that it was the duty of a man of real principle to avoid high national office, and evidently the delegates at Chicago recognized my principles even before I did."

Kennedy balanced his public effectiveness by shrewd private judgments. He said to Rose that if brother Joe had lived, he would have entered politics and been elected to the House and the Senate.

"And, like me, he would have gone for the vice-presidential nomination at the 1956 Convention, but unlike me, he wouldn't have been beaten. Joe would have won the nomination. And then he and Stevenson would have been beaten by Eisenhower, and today Joe's political career would have been in shambles."

JACK UNDERSTOOD that his defeat in Chicago had been a stroke of luck. And a Pulitzer Prize, which was awarded him in April 1957 for *Profiles in Courage*, was another piece of good fortune. Though the Pulitzer jurors had put five distinguished works of biography ahead of his, the board had decided to give his book the prize as "a distinguished American biography . . . teaching patriotic and unselfish service to the people." Recognizing that Jack's prize was an extraordinary event, Torby Macdonald sent him a telegram jesting that he had probably also won the Irish Sweepstakes and received land grant deeds naming him the rightful owner of Texas and California.

Indeed, the Pulitzer seemed more than a bit unlikely, and there is some evidence that Arthur Krock may have personally lobbied the board for Jack. On Christmas Eve 1955, Jack called Evan Thomas Sr., his editor at Harper & Brothers, to ask that publication be moved up from January to December. "Why is that?" Thomas asked. "Well," he said, "I've just been talking to Arthur Krock and I understand it would win the Pulitzer Prize this year." Thomas refused Jack's request, but the book won anyway.

The Pulitzer was largely a case of good timing: In a period of national challenge and peril, when self-indulgence was a national watchword, Jack's book was seen as a rallying cry to put public needs above private concerns. But Jack understood how useful the prize was to his ambition. At the age of thirty-nine, he feared being seen as too young and untested for heavy responsibilities better suited to older, more experienced men such as Eisenhower. The Pulitzer gave him the stamp of seriousness and even wisdom that Americans saw as invaluable in meeting difficulties abroad and at home. It also carried perils. The Pulitzer sparked predictable envy: New rumors circulated that he had not written the book. It was also alleged that sales figures were doctored to get and keep the book on the bestseller list. If the rumors proved to be true, an FBI report stated, "then the charge of fraud will be made on the awarding of the Pulitzer Prize." But since no one could prove the accusations, they came to nothing.

* * *

EVEN WITHOUT UGLY CHARGES about the book, Jack believed that his youth, Catholicism, limited support from party leaders, and questionable health made him far from a sure bet for president in 1960. He was right. In fact, it was an act of unprecedented political nerve for Kennedy to think that he could win a presidential nomination that year. Although a handful of candidates had won the White House when they were in their late forties, no forty-three-year-old had ever made it to the presidency. Theodore Roosevelt was forty-two when McKinley's assassination put him in the office, but when he ran in 1904, he was forty-six. More important, only one Catholic had run for president, Al Smith in 1928, and Herbert Hoover had decisively defeated him.

In a conversation with his father on Thanksgiving Day 1956, Jack discussed the conditions working against his candidacy. But Joe, with his extraordinary feel for the direction of national events, asked Jack to remember that "this country is not a private preserve for Protestants. There's a whole new generation out there and it's filled with the sons and daughters of immigrants from all over the world and those people are going to be mighty proud that one of their own was running for President. And that pride will be your spur."

Jack did not need much persuading. His own ambition for the highest office, his self-confidence that he could win, and his understanding that he already enjoyed the support of millions of Americans (including, of course, his father, who would help finance the campaign) made him hopeful of success. "Well, Dad," he replied, "I guess there's only one question left. When do we start?"

Jack muted any doubts about whether he was healthy enough to bear the rigors of a campaign and the burdens of office. The daily use of cortisone gave him confidence that his Addison's disease would not deter him from being president. Moreover, he did not think that his other ailments would be an impediment to serving in the office. In 1960, he told Kenny O'Donnell, "I'm forty-three years old, and I'm the healthiest candidate for President in the United States. You've traveled with me enough to know that. I'm not going to die in office."

Yet however confident Kennedy was about taking on the job, he understood that public knowledge of his many chronic health problems would likely sink his candidacy. Consequently, the state of his health was a closely guarded secret. Apparently, only Jackie, Bobby,

Joe, and Jack's several doctors knew the full extent of his difficulties. Evelyn Lincoln was responsible for ensuring that Jack took his medications on schedule, but it is doubtful that she had a substantial knowledge of why he needed them. The medical records collected by his physician Janet Travell show that Kennedy's health was even more problematic than previously understood. Between May 1955 and October 1957, while he was launching his vice presidential and presidential bids, he was secretly hospitalized nine times for a total of forty-four days, including two weeklong stays and one nineteen-day stretch.

All these confinements were at New York Hospital except for one day in July 1955 at New England Baptist. Terrible back pain triggered a weeklong hospitalization beginning May 26, 1955. A general workup noted continuing back miseries with a chronic abscess at the site of his 1954–55 surgeries; repeated bouts of colitis with abdominal pain, diarrhea, and dehydration; and prostatitis marked by pain when urinating and ejaculating as well as urinary tract infections. On July 3, he spent one day at New England Baptist being treated for severe diarrhea caused by colitis. Eleven days later, he entered New York Hospital for a week to relieve his back pain and treat another attack of diarrhea. After six relatively healthy months, on January 11, he returned for three days to New York Hospital, where he received large doses of antibiotics to counter respiratory and urinary tract infections. To learn more about his prostate troubles, his doctors performed a cystoscopy under anesthesia. When nausea, vomiting, dehydration, and continuing urinary discomfort occurred at the end of the month, he spent two more days in the hospital. Another six-month respite ended on July 18, when he spent forty-eight hours at New York Hospital for abdominal cramps. Fevers of unknown origin, severe abdominal discomfort, weight loss, throat and urinary infections, a recurrence of his back abscess (which was surgically drained), and his all-too-familiar acute back pain and spasms resulted in three hospitalizations for a total of twenty-two miserable days in September and October.

During 1955, Kennedy had consulted Travell, a specialist in musculoskeletal pain, about the muscle spasms in his lower left back that radiated to his left leg and made him unable to "put weight on it without intense pain." He asked her repeatedly about the origins of his back troubles, but she found it impossible "to reconstruct by hindsight what might have happened to him over the years." It was clear to her, however, that Kennedy "resented" the back surgeries, which had given him no relief and "seemed to only make him worse." He might have done better, of course, to blame the physicians who had prescribed the steroids that weakened his bones, but he had no idea that this was the root of his back problems.

The medical records from this time describe Kennedy as having zero flexion and extension of his back, with difficulty reaching his left foot to pull up a sock, turn over in bed, or sit in a low chair. He also had problems bending his right knee and could raise his left leg to only 25 percent of what was considered normal. There was "exquisite tenderness" in his back, and he was suffering from arthritis.

The treatments for his various ailments included oral and implanted cortisone for the Addison's and massive doses of penicillin and other antibiotics to combat the prostatitis and abscess. He also received anesthetic injections of procaine at trigger points to relieve back pain, antispasmodics — principally, Lomotil and trasentine — to control the colitis, testosterone to bulk him up or keep up his weight (which fell with each bout of colitis and diarrhea), and Nembutal to help him sleep. He had terribly elevated cholesterol — 410, in one testing — apparently caused by the testosterone, which also may have heightened his libido and added to his stomach and prostate problems.

Kennedy's collective health problems were not enough to deter him from running. Though they were an inconvenience, none of them was life-threatening. Nor did he believe that the many medications he took would reduce his ability to work effectively; on the contrary, he saw them as ensuring his competence to deal with the day-to-day rigors of public responsibility. And apparently none of his many doctors — the endocrinologists, neurologists, surgeons, gastroenterologists, or urologists — told him that were he elevated to the presidency, his health problems (or the treatments for them) could pose a danger to the country.

Seeing no compelling reason to stand aside, by the end of 1956 Kennedy had begun campaigning for the Democratic nomination. After the defeat in Chicago, Jack told Kenny O'Donnell and Dave Powers, "I've learned that you don't get far in politics until you become a total politician. That means you've got to deal with the party leaders as well as the voters. From now on, I'm going to be a total politician." This meant courting all possible factions. After the 1956 convention, where Democratic members of Congress publicly complained that Kennedy's voting record or erratic support of party positions made him a liability in a national campaign, Jack privately wrote Democratic leaders to "set the record straight." He had "actively opposed" Taft-Hartley, he claimed, and had supported Truman's veto. He had opposed legislation giving the Atomic Energy Commission the authority to make contracts with private companies to replace public power generated by the TVA. True, on farm legislation he had opposed guaranteed government payments providing a kind of welfare for all farm families. However, he pointed out, he was "the only New England Senator to support the [Senator Hubert] Humphrey amendment, which would have provided 'payments' for small family farmers, flexible support for medium-sized farmers and no aid to wealthy farmers. . . . In view of the very vigorous opposition of New England farmers to the entire farm program," he told Missouri representative Leonor Sullivan, "I believe I have gone more than halfway in recognizing the needs in other sections of the country." And in the fall of 1956, when some Mississippi newspapers reported that an "'anti-Southern' attitude and legislative record" had made southern support of Jack's vice presidential candidacy unwise, he wrote the state's governor to convince him otherwise; he had "never been 'anti-Southern' in any sense of the word," he told James Coleman. Although he acknowledged that his support of Massachusetts' interests sometimes clashed with those of Mississippi, he had principally devoted himself to the national interest and looked forward to serving the needs of both their regions in the future.

BUT WINNING SOUTHERN SUPPORT for the 1960 nomination was much more complicated than writing a letter. Since 1955 the Democrats had been in control of the Senate, where Lyndon Johnson had become majority leader and Mississippi's James Eastland chaired the Judiciary Committee, which had blocked civil rights legislation from reaching the floor. In 1957, it was clear to congressional leaders, including Johnson and other southerners, that pressure from southern blacks led by Martin Luther King Jr. and the Southern Christian Leadership Conference (SCLC), coupled with Supreme Court decisions mandating desegregation of public schools and integration of the Columbia, South Carolina, and Montgomery, Alabama, municipal bus systems, made changes in race relations across the South inevitable, including possible passage of a civil rights law. The only question was how fast and far-reaching these changes would be.

Johnson, who was also planning on running for president, under-stood that he could never win the White House unless he estab-lished himself as a national leader supportive of reforms giving African Americans full constitutional rights. James Rowe, LBJ's old New Deal friend, urged him to lead a civil rights bill through Con-gress that would give him "all the credit for . . . a compromise . . . with the emphasis in the South on compromise, and emphasis in the North on getting a bill."

Both Johnson and Kennedy saw such a political strategy as the best way to advance their presidential ambitions. For his part, Jack's interest in civil rights was more political than moral. The only blacks he knew were chauffeurs, valets, or domestics, with whom he had minimal contact. He was not insensitive to the human and legal abuses of segregation, but as Sorensen wrote later, in the fifties he was "shaped primarily by political expedience instead of basic human principles." He could not empathize, and only faintly sympathize, with the pains felt by African Americans. He did not even consider an aggressive challenge to deeply ingrained southern racial attitudes, and he was far from alone. No one could imagine southerners again rising up in armed rebellion, but threats to the traditional mores seemed certain to provoke enough rage to discourage most white Americans from wanting to combat southern racism. Unlike Hubert Humphrey, another rival for the White House, who had a long-standing, visceral commitment to ending segregation, or even LBJ, whose political actions masked a sincere opposition to segregation, Jack Kennedy's response to the great civil rights debates of 1957–60 was largely motivated by self-serving political considerations.

In 1956–57, Jack mapped out a strategy for accommodating all factions of the Democratic party on civil rights, including black voters, who were seen in the late fifties as holding "the balance of power in the big states where elections are won or lost." Yet his con-cern with political expediency sometimes resulted in contradictions and tangles. During an October 1956 *Meet the Press* interview, when the host asked Jack why African American voters should want to see Democratic congressional majorities, which would lead in turn to southern committee chairmen blocking civil rights legislation, Jack replied that Congress could bypass an obstructionist committee and that his party's record of favoring economic and social reforms bene-ficial to low-income Americans gave it a claim on black voters. But in 1957, when a civil rights bill came to the Senate from the House,

Jack opposed bypassing the Judiciary Committee, where Eastland was certain to table it. Jack said his opposition to invoking Rule XIV, a little-used device for bringing a bill directly to the Senate floor, rested on the belief that this was a "highly questionable legislative course" that would give up "one of our maximum protections" against arbitrary action. It was a "dangerous precedent," he told NAACP Executive Secretary Roy Wilkins, "which can be used against our causes and other liberal issues in the future." Instead, he favored the conventional but more difficult use of a discharge petition to bring the bill to the Senate floor. Knowing that civil rights advocates would win the discharge petition fight, which they did by a 45–39 vote, Jack felt free to side with the southerners. And because four liberal western Democrats joined the minority (trading their votes for southern support of the Hells Canyon Dam on the Snake River in Idaho, a controversial public power project), it gave Jack some cover with liberals.

Not surprisingly, civil rights proponents began attacking Kennedy for having sided with the South. In response, he leapt into a Senate debate about Titles III and IV of the House bill, which gave the attorney general broad powers. Southerners complained that the Title III provision would allow "the reimposition of post–Civil War Reconstruction," specifically military intervention to enforce school desegregation. They also objected to Title IV, which sanctioned trials by federal judges without juries to punish defiance of the law. Aware that Title III was too radical to win a Senate majority, Jack felt free to favor it publicly. Thus, when a southern-moderate coalition eliminated the provision by a vote of 52–38, Jack reestablished his credibility with liberals while losing little ground with southern conservatives, who read his vote as a bow to northern interests essential to his political future — again, hardly a profile in political courage.

Elimination of Title III turned the bill into a voting rights act, and the issue that now divided supporters and opponents was whether violators of someone's right to vote should be entitled to a jury trial. Advocates of the bill had no confidence that southern white juries would convict registrars barring blacks from the polls. In order to assuage liberals, Johnson agreed to omit jury trials in civil contempt cases while insisting that it apply to criminal proceedings. He also agreed to an amendment guaranteeing "the right of *all* Americans to serve on [federal] juries, regardless of race, creed, or color."

The battle over the jury trial amendment drew considerable attention and put Jack in a difficult position. Only after consulting several legal experts and the addition of the amendment promising interracial juries did Jack declare his support of jury trials, which he saw as the only way to enact the civil rights bill: A vote against jury trials, he said, would have provoked a filibuster that would have been "impossible" to defeat with cloture (the two-thirds vote needed for ending a filibuster). A majority of his Senate colleagues, who approved the jury trial amendment by a vote of 51–42, agreed.

Not surprisingly, enactment of the law brought an outpouring of criticism from civil rights advocates. The bill was a "mere fakery," a policeman's gun without bullets, and "like soup made from the shadow of a crow which had starved to death." They were right: two years later, not a single southern black had been added to the voting rolls and nothing had been accomplished for other civil rights. Yet some civil rights proponents saw reason for optimism. The law marked the first time since Reconstruction that Congress had acted to protect civil rights. Bayard Rustin saw the measure as establishing "a very important precedent." And George Reedy, LBJ's Senate aide, said the act was "a watershed. . . . A major branch of the American government that had been closed to minority members of the population seeking redress for wrongs was suddenly open. The civil rights battle could now be fought out legislatively in an arena that previously had provided nothing but a sounding board for speeches."

Kennedy himself received a lot of criticism. ("Why not show a little less profile and a little more courage?" one Senate colleague asked.) Although his vote allowed him, in the view of one journalist, to maintain a "stout" bridge to the South and border states, it opened him to additional attacks from liberals. Roy Wilkins publicly berated Jack for "rubbing political elbows" with southern segregationists, and in private exchanges initiated by Jack, he continued to criticize him for his jury trial vote. Jack told Wilkins that he could not understand why he was being singled out from the nearly three dozen non-southerner senators who voted for jury trials. The answer was simple and could hardly have escaped Jack's notice: None of the others was running for president, and given Kennedy's southern ties, no black leader had much confidence that a Kennedy presidency would produce significant advances against segregation.

To Jack's satisfaction, events in September muted the criticism. When Arkansas governor Orval Faubus used the National Guard to prevent integration of Little Rock's Central High School and Eisenhower had to federalize the Arkansas Guard to keep the peace and enforce Court injunctions, it made Johnson and Kennedy seem like sensible moderates trying to advance equal treatment of blacks and national harmony through the rule of law. Jack reinforced his image as a centrist during a speaking engagement in Mississippi in October. At the end of a speech urging moderation and national unity, he responded to a query published in the press from the state Republican chairman about Kennedy's vote for Title III. Jack said, "I think most of us agree on the necessity to uphold law and order in every part of the land. Now I invite the Republican chairman to tell us his views and those of President Eisenhower and Vice President Nixon." The audience cheered him.

IN DECEMBER 1956, Bobby Kennedy, who was serving as counsel for the Senate Permanent Subcommittee on Investigations, agreed to look into labor racketeering, particularly among the Teamsters. During the family's Christmas get-together in Hyannis Port, Joe attacked Bobby for jeopardizing Jack's labor support in 1960. The "father and son had an unprecedentedly furious argument." But Bobby would not budge. And after Joe's urging, William O. Douglas failed to dissuade Bobby as well, telling his wife that Bobby "feels it is too great an opportunity."

For Bobby, an intensely moralistic man with an "exacting sense of individual responsibility," the investigation was a chance to eliminate some of the rampant corruption that had taken hold in unions. No small part of his commitment was to the rank and file being cheated and abused by crooked and violent labor bosses. But these noble ends might produce restrictive legislation that could turn unions against his brother. "If the investigation flops," Bobby told Kenny O'Donnell, "it will hurt Jack in 1958 and in 1960, too. . . . A lot of people think he's the Kennedy running the investigation, not me. As far as the public is concerned, one Kennedy is the same as another Kennedy."

Yet Jack's vulnerability came more from his own doing than from anything Bobby did. Lyndon Johnson, Bobby recalled, had warned Jack against taking on labor if he was serious about running in 1960. But Jack decided to accept assignment as a member of the joint investigations and labor subcommittee probing the unions. Jack claimed he did so at his brother's urging, to preserve its balance between conservatives and moderates — hardly a compelling reason to risk his chances in 1960.

Yet Jack and Bobby believed that their involvement in the investigation promised greater political gains than losses. They were right. For one, it would keep Jack's name before the public and, regardless of the outcome, identify him with a good cause. The Kennedys also remembered that Senate committee investigations of war profiteering and organized crime had made Harry Truman and Estes Kefauver, respectively, nationally known political figures. Moreover, in the 1950s, labor unions, which were identified with unsavory characters such as Dave Beck and Jimmy Hoffa of the Teamsters, were an inviting target for an aspiring politician. Indeed, the contrast between Jack and Bobby on one side and Beck and Hoffa on the other was a political bonanza. When Beck was convicted of stealing almost $500,000 from union coffers, including money taken "from a trust fund set up for a friend's widow," the Kennedys were in turn identified with union honesty. Hoffa, who escaped going to jail in the fifties, was a more elusive target. But his public image as a ruthless bully more interested in maintaining control than in representing rank-and-file opinion made him a perfect foil for Jack and Bobby. (In the summer of 1959, a seven-part series in the *Saturday Evening Post*, "The Struggle to Get Hoffa," burnished Jack's and Bobby's image as union reformers.) Even if the unions saw themselves as injured by an investigation Jack supported, he was able to win wider public approval as a senator who, like the heroes of his book, put the country above personal political gain. The brothers had correctly perceived that LBJ's advice was largely self-serving. As a rival for the Democratic presidential nomination in 1960, Johnson was less concerned with protecting Jack from losing labor support than with deterring him from being identified as a successful union critic.

The prospect of enacting a Kennedy labor reform bill also drew Jack and Bobby to the controversy. After five years in the Senate, Jack had not attached his name to any major piece of legislation. But partisan politics blunted Jack and Bobby's efforts to advance labor reform. In March 1958, after months of hearings by the McClellan Committee and extensive consultations with leading university experts on labor relations, Jack introduced a bill to prevent the expenditure of union dues for improper purposes or private gain; to forbid loans from union funds for illicit transactions; and to compel audits of unions, which would ensure against false financial reports. Initially,

George Meany, president of the AFL-CIO, objected to the bill as singling out unions for regulations that could also be applied to government officials and corporate chiefs. (When Jack gave Meany the names of the experts who had helped him draft the legislation, Meany replied, "God save us from our friends.") Amendments to the legislation and public assurances from Jack that he wished to strengthen unions largely eliminated differences with Meany, but the bill failed anyway. Opposed by the National Association of Manufacturers and Eisenhower's labor secretary, James P. Mitchell, as too pro-labor, and the Teamsters and United Mine Workers as too draconian, Kennedy-Ives (Jack's New York Republican cosponsor) passed the Senate but was shelved in the House. "Jimmy Hoffa can rejoice at his continued good luck," Kennedy announced. "Honest union members and the general public can only regard it as a tragedy that politics has prevented the recommendations of the McClellan committee from being carried out this year."

Although another Kennedy labor bill would win Senate approval in 1959, the Senate decision to instead agree on the House's more restrictive Landrum-Griffin Act deprived Kennedy of any significant political gain in the labor wars. More disappointing, Bobby and Jack found "appalling public apathy" generating "the merest lip-service" to reform. Yet Jack's image as an honest crusader had been promoted. But even if the public agreed with the Kennedys, when it came to promoting actual legislation, the eyes of the voters glazed over. They paid more attention in 1960, however, when Bobby published *The Enemy Within*, describing the Kennedy crusade to overcome union corruption and break up the Mafia or Italian crime families Bobby had also investigated in 1958–59.

OF COURSE, JACK had never seen intervention in domestic issues as the primary means of advancing his presidential ambitions. On the contrary, they were a political minefield in which a presidential aspirant could alienate more voters than he might attract. Although promises of prosperity had been an essential ingredient of every successful twentieth-century presidential campaign, national security often ran a close second, and in 1952 and 1956 it commanded more voter attention than the economy.

Standing up for the nation, rather than self-serving factions, and arguing in favor of overseas actions that could affect the lives of all Americans and millions of others abroad appealed to Jack's idealism. He was not dogmatic and understood that no one had a monopoly of wisdom on the best means for dealing with external events. But he had a degree of self-confidence about foreign affairs that he rarely displayed in addressing domestic ones. Back in 1953, he had asked Ted Sorensen which cabinet posts would interest him most if he ever had a choice. "Justice, Labor and Health-Education-Welfare," Sorensen replied. "I wouldn't have any interest in any of those," Kennedy said emphatically, "only Secretary of State or Defense."

A focus on foreign policy also helped Jack refute assertions that his interest in the presidency was largely inspired by his father. During a 1953 meeting of Joe and Jack with some Hearst editors, Joe dominated the conversation with pronouncements on how to meet Cold War challenges. Jack abruptly left the room. "Jesus, Jack, what's happening?" his friend Paul Fay, who followed him into another room, asked. "Why did you do that?" Jack responded, "Listen, I've only got three choices. I can sit there and keep my mouth shut, which will be taken as a sign that I agree with him. I can have a fight with him in front of the press. Or I can get up and leave." In 1960, he told a journalist, "My father is conservative. We disagree on many things. He's an isolationist and I'm an internationalist. . . . I've given up arguing with him. But I make up my own mind and my own decisions."

Jack's appointment to the Senate Foreign Relations Committee in January 1957 helped his standing as a party spokesman on foreign affairs. To join the committee, Kennedy needed Johnson's support. Jack's rival for the assignment was Kefauver, whose four-year seniority to Jack gave him a stronger claim. But "I have never had the particular feeling that when I called up my first team and the chips were down that Kefauver felt he ought to be . . . on that team," LBJ bluntly told Kefauver in January 1955. In contrast, Jack had been cooperative with Lyndon during his four years in the Senate and had been rewarded with Johnson's support for the VP nomination. And appointing Jack to Foreign Relations meant that if Jack's presidential campaign faltered, Lyndon could count on Joe and Jack for their support. According to LBJ, Joe "bombarded me with phone calls, presents and little notes telling me what a great guy I was. . . . One day he came right out and pleaded with me to put Jack on the Foreign Relations Committee, telling me that if I did, he'd never forget the favor for the rest of his life. Now, I knew Kefauver wanted the seat bad and I knew he had four years' seniority on Kennedy. . . . But I kept picturing old Joe Kennedy sitting there with all that power and wealth feeling indebted to me for the rest of his life, and I sure liked that picture."

Jack used his committee membership to encourage public discussion of wiser overseas actions and to build his reputation as a foreign policy expert. He had no illusion that anything he said would necessarily alter America's response to the world or reach great numbers of voters. But he believed it useful to speak out anyway: A national debate on foreign policy was essential in the midst of the Cold War, and his contribution to such a discussion could encourage intellectuals and party leaders to take his presidential candidacy more seriously.

An Algerian crisis — the struggle of a French North African colony to gain independence — became an opportunity for Kennedy to restate anticolonial ideas voiced in 1954 over Vietnam. "The most powerful single force in the world today," he declared in a Senate speech in July 1957, "is neither communism nor capitalism, neither the H-bomb nor the guided missile — it is man's eternal desire to be free and independent." And "the single most important test of American foreign policy today is how we meet the challenge of imperialism. . . . On this test more than any other, this Nation shall be critically judged by the uncommitted millions in Asia and Africa." Neither foreign aid nor a greater military arsenal nor "new pacts or doctrines or high-level conferences" could substitute for an effective response to anticolonialism. More specifically, he urged U.S. backing for Algerian self-determination through a mediated settlement. If, however, the French refused to negotiate, he favored outright U.S. support of independence.

Kennedy's bold proposal did not sit well with either the French government or the Eisenhower administration, which disputed the wisdom of his recommendations. And though he responded to his critics by restating his firm belief in his proposal, he told his father that perhaps he had made a mistake. Joe assured him otherwise: "You lucky mush," Joe said. "You don't know it and neither does anyone else, but within a few months everyone is going to know just how right you were on Algeria."

Taking heart from his father's prediction, Jack restated the need to rethink American foreign policy in an article in the October 1957 issue of *Foreign Affairs*. "A Democrat Looks at Foreign Policy" left no doubt that he was offering a partisan alternative to Republican thinking about world politics. Nevertheless, the article was more an exercise in analysis than a polemical attack. Kennedy began by urging that America not see the world strictly through "the prisms of our own historic experience." The country needed to understand that we lived not simply in a bipolar world of Soviet-American rivalry but a global environment in which smaller powers were charting an independent course. America needed not only to oppose communism but also to help emerging nations regardless of their attitude toward the Cold War.

Kennedy described "two central weaknesses in our current foreign policy: first, a failure to appreciate how the forces of nationalism are rewriting the geopolitical map of the world . . . and second, a lack of decision and conviction in our leadership . . . which seeks too often to substitute slogans for solutions." Jack's proposals for change, however, suffered from some of the same limitations as Eisenhower's. He urged policy makers to replace "apocalyptic solutions" with something he called "a new realism," which was to substitute economic aid for military exports and to work against "the prolongation of Western colonialism." But how? The "new realism" was as much a political slogan as a genuine departure from current thinking about overseas affairs

In private, Jack was also critical of his Democratic colleagues. Early in 1958, he told economist John Kenneth Galbraith that "the Democratic party has tended to magnify the military challenge to the point where equally legitimate economic and political programs have been obscured. . . . It is clear also that, however tempting a target, the attacks on Mr. Dulles [for brinksmanship and insensitivity to the Third World] have been taken too often as a sum total of an alternative foreign policy — a new kind of devil theory of failure." To counter this, he stated his intention "to give special attention this year to developing some new policy toward the underdeveloped areas."

Yet at the same time as he was discussing alternative Cold War actions, Kennedy could not ignore the military competition with Moscow. Fears that the Soviet Union was surpassing the United States in missile technology and would soon be able to deliver a devastating attack on North America made defense policy a centerpiece of all discussions on foreign affairs. In October 1957, the Soviets successfully launched *Sputnik I*, a space satellite that orbited the earth. The accomplishment shocked Americans and produced an outcry for a vast expansion of U.S. defense spending. A government-sponsored committee headed by H. Rowan Gaither, chairman of the board of the Ford Foundation, advised Eisenhower that American defenses against Moscow were inadequate, that there was a missile gap favoring the Soviets, and that unless the United States began an immediate buildup, it would face defeat in a nuclear war. Three members of Gaither's committee urged a preventive war before it was too late.

Like Eisenhower, who refused to give in to the country's overreaction and launch an arms race, Kennedy urged a balance among military strength, economic aid, and considered diplomacy. In a *New York Times* interview in December 1957, he warned against neglecting economic aid programs and disarmament talks in a rush to outdo the Soviet arms buildup. In June 1958, he spoke on the Senate floor against shifting control over foreign economic assistance from the State Department to the Defense Department. He feared weakening the power of the secretary of state and a greater militarization of the Cold War.

Yet the opportunity to take political advantage of what seemed like a major failing on the part of the Eisenhower administration was irresistible. In August 1958, Jack spoke in the Senate about a fast-approaching "dangerous period" when we would suffer a "gap" or a "missile-lag period" — a time "in which our own offensive and defensive missile capabilities will lag so far behind those of the Soviets as to place us in a position of grave peril." The gap was the result of a "complacency" that put "fiscal security ahead of national security."

By criticizing White House defense policy, Jack hoped both to serve the nation's security and score political points. But although his speech enhanced his party standing as a serious analyst of foreign and defense issues, it added little to his hold on the public and did nothing to convince the administration that it needed to substantially alter defense planning. Only a small minority of Americans shared his fears of a missile gap: in October 1957, just 13 percent of a Gallup poll thought that defense preparedness or Sputnik "missiles" was the most important problem facing the country. People were instead far more concerned about racial segregation and finding ways to reach accommodations with Russia that could reduce the likelihood of a nuclear war.

But Jack's growing public appeal — and it was clearly growing — rested on more than his policy pronouncements. During 1957–58 he became emblematic of a new breed of celebrity politician, as notable for his good looks, infectious smile, charm, and wit as for his thoughtful pronouncements on weighty public questions. "Seldom in the annals of this political capital," one journalist noted in May 1957, "has anyone risen as rapidly as Senator John F. Kennedy." Popular and news magazines — *Look, Time, Life,* the *Saturday Evening Post, McCall's, Redbook, U.S. News & World Report, Parade,* the *American Mercury,* and the *Catholic Digest* — regularly published feature stories about Jack and his extraordinary family. ("Senator Kennedy, do you have an 'in' with *Life,*" a high school newspaper editor asked him. "No," he replied, "I just have a beautiful wife.") One critical journalist wrote: "This man seeks the highest elective office in the world not primarily as a politician, but as a celebrity. He's the only politician a woman would read about while sitting under the hair dryer, the subject of more human-interest articles than all his rivals combined." But in the words of another, he had become the "perfect politician" with a beautiful wife and, in November 1957, a daughter, Caroline Bouvier Kennedy.

By the fall of 1959, Joe Kennedy was able to tell reporters that "Jack is the greatest attraction in the country today. I'll tell you how to sell more copies of a book. Put his picture on the cover. Why is it that when his picture is on the cover of *Life* or *Redbook* that they sell a record number of copies? You advertise that he will be at a dinner and you will break all records for attendance. He can draw more people to a fund-raising dinner than Cary Grant or Jimmy Stewart. Why is that? He has more universal appeal."

Jack's 1958 Senate reelection campaign had borne out his extraordinary political attractiveness. With no Republican of any stature willing to run against him, Jack was able to coast to a record-breaking victory. Despite a campaign designed by Larry O'Brien and Kenny O'Donnell to keep Jack's "direct and personal participation to an absolute minimum," he won 874,608 votes out of 1.32 million cast, 73.6 percent, the largest popular margin ever received by a candidate in Massachusetts and the second-largest margin tallied by any U.S. Senate candidate that year. The numbers seemed to support the predictions of Kennedy admirers that the country was witnessing "the flowering of another great political family, such as the Adamses, the Lodges, and the La Follettes." "They confidently look forward to the day," a friendly journalist wrote months before Kennedy's 1958 victory, "when Jack will be in the White House, Bobby will serve in the Cabinet as Attorney General, and Teddy will be the Senator from Massachusetts."

JACK'S SIX YEARS in the Senate had schooled him in the major domestic, defense, and foreign policy issues. His education was essential preparation for a presidential campaign and, more important, service in the White House. To be sure, his Senate career had produced no major legislation that contributed substantially to the national well-being. But it had strengthened his resolve to reach for executive powers that promised greater freedom to implement ideas that could improve the state of the world. In a 1960 tape recording, explaining why he was running for president, he stated that the life of a legislator was much less satisfying than that of a chief executive. Senators and congressmen could work on something for two years and have it turned aside by a president in one day and one stroke of the pen. Jack believed that effective leadership came largely from the top. Being president provided opportunities to make a difference no senator could ever hope to achieve. The time had come.

PART THREE

Can a Catholic Become President?

I am not the Catholic candidate for President. I am the Democratic party's candidate for President, who happens also to be a Catholic.

— John F. Kennedy, September 12, 1960

CHAPTER 7

Nomination

No, sir, th' dimmycratic party ain't on speakin' terms with itsilf. Whin ye see two men with white neckties go into a sthreet car an' set in opposite corners while wan mutthers "Traiter" an' th' other hisses "Miscreent" ye can bet they're two dimmycratic leaders thryin' to reunite th' gran' ol' party.

— Finley Peter Dunne, *Mr. Dooley's Opinions*, 1901

JACK KENNEDY'S REELECTION VICTORY in Massachusetts and his growing national visibility since the 1956 Democratic convention put him on everyone's list of possible candidates for the presidency in 1960. He was an appealing alternative to Eisenhower. Ike was much admired, even loved, by millions of Americans, but alongside Kennedy, the sixty-nine-year-old president, who was in declining health and had become the oldest man ever to serve in the office, seemed stodgy. Kennedy's vigor ("vigah," Jack pronounced it, in the New England way) was seen as a potential asset in dealing with Soviet challenges, a sluggish economy, racial divisions, and what the literary critic Dwight Macdonald described as the "terrible shapelessness of American life."

In 1957, more than 2,500 speaking invitations from all over the country testified to Kennedy's appeal. Seizing upon the opportunity to reach influential audiences, he agreed to give 144 talks, nearly one every other day, in 47 states. By early 1958, he was receiving a hundred requests a week to speak. Some Massachusetts newspapers, eager to boost a native son, already pegged him as the Democratic nominee. Numerous party leaders agreed. A majority of the party's forty-eight state chairmen described him as the likely choice, and 409 of the 1,220 delegates to the 1956 Democratic convention declared their preference for Kennedy in 1960. Although Democratic governors did not foresee a first-ballot victory, they thought that Jack would certainly lead in the early balloting.

Kennedy backers took additional satisfaction from polls in 1959 depicting him in the most flattering terms. Even Republicans conceded that he was "very smart . . . nice-looking . . . likeable . . . [and] knowledgeable about politics." Although some in the GOP set him down as a "smart-alec . . . millionaire . . . headline hunter," others wished that he were a member of their party. Democrats had only nice things to say about Jack, describing him with words and phrases like "truthful," "not afraid to express himself," "family man," "nice-looking," "vigorous," "personable," "intelligent," and "level-headed." Some independents thought he was "too outspoken," but the great majority described him in extremely favorable terms. Sixty-four percent of all potential voters with an opinion about Kennedy believed that he had "the background and experience to be President."

Despite this widespread esteem, knowledgeable political observers, including many in the Kennedy camp, saw formidable obstacles to Kennedy's nomination and election. His positive image, however useful, allowed critics to describe him as more the product of a public relations campaign funded by his family's fortune than the result of political accomplishments. William Shannon, a well-known columnist for the New York Post, wrote: "Month after month, from the glossy pages of Life to the multicolored cover of Redbook, Jack and Jackie smile out at millions of readers; he with his tousled hair and winning smile, she with her dark eyes and beautiful face. We hear of her pregnancy, of his wartime heroism, of their fondness for sailing. But what has all this to do with statesmanship?" New York Times columnist James Reston complained that "[Kennedy's] clothes and hair-do are a masterpiece of contrived casualness." Reston worried that there had been too much emphasis "on how to win the presidency rather than on how to run it." Chicago Daily News reporter Peter Lisagor and other journalists met with Jack in 1958: They "looked at him walking out of the room, thin, slender, almost boyish really," and one of them said, "'Can you imagine that young fellow thinking he could be President of the United States any time soon?' I must say the thought occurred to me, too," Lisagor recalled.

Polls assessing Kennedy's candidacy in a national campaign echoed Lisagor's doubts. They foresaw a close contest with Vice President Richard M. Nixon, whose eight years under Eisenhower gave him a commanding lead for the Republican nomination. Moreover, a vigorous campaign for Nixon by Ike, whose approval ratings in the next-to-last year of his presidency ranged between 57 percent and 66 percent, seemed to promise a third consecutive Republican term. But no sitting vice president had gained the White House since Martin Van Buren in 1836, and several straw polls matching Adlai Stevenson and Kennedy against Nixon and New York governor Nelson Rockefeller, or Kennedy directly against Nixon, gave the Democrats a slight edge. Nothing in the surveys, however, suggested that Kennedy and the Democrats could take anything for granted.

The criticism and doubts bothered Jack, but he blunted them with humor. At the 1958 Gridiron dinner, an annual Washington ritual in which the press and politicians engaged in humorous exchanges, Jack poked fun at his father's free spending in support of his political ambitions. He had "just received the following wire from my generous daddy," JFK said. "'Dear Jack — Don't buy a single vote more than is necessary — I'll be damned if I'm going to pay for a landslide.'" To answer predictions that a Catholic president would have divided loyalties, Jack promised to make Methodist bishop G. Bromley Oxnam, an outspoken opponent of electing a Catholic, his personal envoy to the Vatican. To counter Oxnam's complaint that a Catholic in the White House would be in constant touch with the pope, Jack declared his intention to have Oxnam "open negotiations for that Trans-Atlantic Tunnel immediately." The Republicans did not escape his barbs: A 1958 recession had moved President Eisenhower to declare that, in Jack's version, "we're now at the end of the beginning of the upturn of the downturn." He added, "Every bright spot the White House finds in the economy is like the policeman bending over the body in the alley who says cheerfully, 'Two of his wounds are fatal — but the other one's not so bad.'"

Jack's wit scored points with journalists but had limited impact on Democratic voters and party officials, who would have the initial say about his candidacy. In 1959, Democrats were evenly divided between Kennedy and Stevenson. Each of them was the choice of between 25 percent and 30 percent of party members. Less encouraging, congressional Democrats put Kennedy fourth behind Lyndon Johnson, Stevenson, and Missouri senator Stuart Symington for the nomination. They thought that the forty-two-year-old Kennedy was too young to be president and preferred to see him run as vice president.

But Jack had no patience with being second. "We've always been competitive in our family," he explained. "My father has been

competitive all his life, that's how he got where he is." When Newton Minow, a Stevenson law partner, told Kennedy in 1957 that he
could probably have the vice presidential nomination in 1960, Jack
said: "'I'm not interested in running for vice president. I'm interested in running for president.' 'You're out of your mind,'" Minow
replied. "'You're only thirty-nine years old, you haven't got a chance
to run for President.' 'No, Newt,'" Jack answered, "'if I'm ever going
to make it I'm going to make it in 1960.'" Sensible political calculations were shaping his decision. "If I don't make it this time, and a
Democrat makes it," he told a reporter, "then it may [be] for eight
years and there will be fresher faces coming along and I'll get shoved
in the background." Besides, the vice presidency was "a dead job."
Nor did he think he could work with Stevenson, who "is a fuss-
budget about a lot of things and we might not get along." Settling
for second place was tantamount to defeat.

The greatest impediments to Jack's nomination seemed to be liberal antagonism and doubts that a Catholic could or should win a
general election. The two were not mutually exclusive. "Catholic-
baiting is the anti-Semitism of the liberals," one conservative declared. The Church frightened progressive Democrats, who regarded
it as an authoritarian institution intolerant of ideas at odds with its
teachings. Suspicion of divided Catholic loyalties between church
and state was as old as the American Republic itself, and since the
1830s, when a mass migration of Catholics to America had begun,
Protestants had warned against the Catholic threat to individual
freedoms. In May 1959, 24 percent of voters said that they would
not cast their ballots for a Catholic, even if he seemed to be well
qualified for the presidency.

Most liberals subscribed to the view of Kennedy as an ambitious
but superficial playboy with little more to recommend him than
his good looks and charm. On none of the issues most important
to them — McCarthyism, civil rights, and labor unions — had Jack
been an outspoken advocate. As Arthur Schlesinger Jr. said later of
liberal antagonism to Jack, "Kennedy seemed too cool and ambitious, too bored by the conditional reflexes of stereotyped liberalism,
too much a young man in a hurry. He did not respond in anticipated
ways and phrases and wore no liberal heart on his sleeve." Joe
Kennedy's reputation as a robber baron and prewar appeaser of Nazi
Germany also troubled liberals. And, despite numerous examples of
political divergence between father and son, they saw Jack as little

more than a surrogate for Joe, whom they believed to have been planning to buy the White House for one of his children since at least 1940.

Kennedy's threat to a third Stevenson campaign was an additional source of liberal antagonism. Liberals hoped that despite Stevenson's two defeats by Eisenhower, he might be able to win against Nixon in 1960. Some journalists shared this belief. (James Reston privately lamented "the effects upon this country of the advertising profession, the continual deterioration of our citizens, the lulling of their consciences, the degradation of their morals, and Adlai seems to me to be the only one that can raise our sights. He is the only one who speaks with the voice of a philosopher, of a poet, of a true leader.") Journalist Theodore White wrote that California, Illinois, New York, Oregon, and Wisconsin "youngsters Stevenson had summoned to politics with high morality in 1952 had now matured and were unwilling in their maturity to forsake him."

To discourage a stop-Kennedy drive, Jack publicly denied that he was a candidate. In 1958, he said that his campaign for reelection to the Senate required all his attention and that he needed to "take care of that matter before doing anything else." When a journalist pointed out that he was giving speeches in five western and midwestern states in just one month, Jack explained that he was "interested in the Democratic party nationally" and was "delighted to go where I am asked." In 1959, a reporter asked when Jack was "going to drop this public pretense of non-candidacy." The time to declare his future intentions would be in 1960, he replied.

Early in 1958, as Jack's presidential candidacy was gaining momentum, Eleanor Roosevelt published a magazine article in which she repeated her complaint that he had "dodged the McCarthy issue in 1954." In May 1958, she made a more direct attack on Jack's candidacy, telling an AP reporter that the country was ready to elect a Catholic to the presidency if he could separate the church from the state, but that she was "not sure Kennedy could do this." In December, she stepped up her opposition to Jack in a television appearance, expressing doubts about his readiness for the presidency and noting his failure to demonstrate the kind of independence and courage he had celebrated in his book.

Jack avoided any public fight with her, answering her opposition in a private letter. He challenged her to support an allegation made during her TV appearance that his "father has been spending oodles of money all over the country and probably has a paid representative in every state by now. . . . I am certain you are the victim of misinformation," Jack wrote, and asked her to have her "informant back up the charge with evidence." She replied that if her comment was untrue, she would "gladly so state," but she cited his father's declaration that "he would spend any money to make his son the first Catholic President of this country, and many people as I travel about tell me of money spent by him on your behalf." In response, Jack expressed disappointment that she would "accept the view that simply because a rumor or allegation is repeated it becomes commonly accepted as a fact." He asked her to "correct the record in a fair and gracious manner." When she published a newspaper column quoting Jack's letter, he pressed her for a fuller retraction. When she agreed to write another column if Kennedy insisted, Jack told her not to bother, saying, "We can let it stand for the present." Jack's suggestion that they "get together sometime in the future to discuss other matters" provoked a snide telegram: "MY DEAR BOY I ONLY SAY THESE THINGS FOR YOUR OWN GOOD. I HAVE FOUND IN [A] LIFETIME OF ADVERSITY THAT WHEN BLOWS ARE RAINED ON ONE, IT IS ADVISABLE TO TURN THE OTHER PROFILE."

MRS. ROOSEVELT'S REPRIMAND stemmed partly from a conviction that Jack's denials about his father were misleading. She had no direct evidence of Joe's spending in his son's behalf, but she believed that all the rumors were more than idle gossip. And of course she was right. Joe had financed all Jack's campaigns, including the 1958 romp, when he spent an estimated $1.5 million to ensure the landslide that would help launch Jack's presidential bid.

As important, between 1958 and 1960, Joe became the campaign's principal behind-the-scenes operator in the nomination fight. "You do what you think is right," Joe told Jack after he was elected to the Senate, "and we'll take care of the politicians." And anything else that needs to be done, he might have added. When Jack wanted prominent civil rights advocate Harris Wofford to join his campaign, Joe pressed Father John Cavanaugh, Notre Dame University's former president, to get sitting president Father Theodore Hesburgh to release Wofford from teaching duties at the law school. When Wofford told Sargent Shriver about Joe's intervention, Shriver replied, "'Don't ever underestimate Mr. Kennedy.' This was the only time I personally saw the long hand of Joe Kennedy," Wofford wrote, "but if he would intervene so vigorously on such a small matter, I could imagine what he was like when he dealt with Mayor Daley for delegates. 'And that is exactly who did deal with Daley most of the time,' said Shriver." Although Jack would pay ceremonial visits to Daley, "the long, tough talks were between the mayor and Joe Kennedy. Shriver said this was true of the negotiations with the Philadelphia leader, Congressman William Green, and with other Irish-Americans of the old school who were in key positions in a number of city and state Democratic organizations, including California and New York."

"[Joe] knew instinctively who the important people were, who the bosses behind the scenes were," New York congressman Eugene Keogh said. "From 1958 on he was in contact with them constantly by phone, presenting Jack's case, explaining and interpreting his son, working these bosses." Tip O'Neill remembered that when Joe learned that Joe Clark, a Pennsylvania state official, was the power behind Congressman Bill Green, he flew Clark to New York for a meeting in his suite at the Waldorf-Astoria. Joe also went to see Pennsylvania governor David Lawrence. During a secret meeting at a Harrisburg hotel, Joe was, as Lawrence remembers, "very vigorous." When Lawrence asserted that a Catholic could not win the White House, Joe recounted a story about a New York bank president who said the same thing. "I was so goddamn mad at that fella," Joe added. "I had nine million dollars in that bank and I felt like I'd pull out of that bank that day."

New York party leader Mike Prendergast recalled how Joe "sent a lot of people in to donate money to the state organization, which we used for Jack's election." In July 1959, syndicated columnist Marquis Childs asserted that Joe had already spent one million dollars on Jack's campaign and was the brains behind the whole operation. Jack's acquisition of a plane leased to him by a Kennedy family corporation belied Kennedy denials that Joe had anything to do with the campaign. Harry Truman echoed the concerns about Joe when he told friends, "It's not the Pope I'm afraid of, it's the pop." Jack knew this was the perception, but there seemed no other route to the presidency but along this tightrope.

THE 1958 CONGRESSIONAL ELECTIONS had given the Democratic party a decidedly liberal tilt. A recession producing higher unemployment nationwide and farm failures in the Midwest, Republican support of integration in the South and anti-union right-to-work laws in industrial states, and the "missile gap" — fears that America was losing the arms race to Russia — had translated into nearly two-to-one Democratic margins in both houses; their twenty-eight-seat gain in the Upper House was the most one-sided party victory in Senate history. Of the fifteen new Democratic senators, five were liberals and ten were moderates.

Because liberals would thus have a major say in who became the Democratic nominee, Jack had attempted to win Adlai Stevenson's support. But Stevenson was uncooperative. After 1956, he had consistently denied any interest in another campaign, but when one of his law partners privately confided his own intention to back Kennedy, Stevenson predicted that "the Catholic issue is going to be badly against him, and, after all, Nixon must be beaten." The partner took this to mean: "I want to be urged to run, and I want to be nominated." Stevenson also told Newton Minow that Kennedy was too young and inexperienced to handle the job. Stevenson confided his doubts to *Time* reporter John Steele as well, setting Jack down as too ambitious and maybe even a little foolish, a young man reaching too quickly for the coveted prize. He was even more blunt with the British economist Barbara Ward Jackson. "I don't think he'd be a good president," Stevenson said. "I do not feel that he's the right man for the job; I think he's too young; I don't think he fully understands the dimensions of the foreign affairs dilemmas that are coming up."

With Stevenson refusing to help, Jack explored other means of bringing liberals to his side. In March 1958, when a TV interviewer asked him, "Do you think that the candidate in the Democratic party would have to be definitely associated with the liberal wing of the party in 1960?" Jack replied, "I do." "Do you believe that you are in that wing?" the reporter continued. "I do," Jack answered. "Do you count yourself as a liberal?" the reporter persisted. "I do," Jack responded unequivocally.

His answers were part of a larger campaign to convince party liberals that he was one of them, or at the very least would be responsive to their concerns. But he also felt that liberals were uninformed about his record on civil liberties, civil rights, and labor. Consequently, between 1957 and 1960, he publicly emphasized that he had established his "independence from the Democratic party," but that this was "essentially an independence from party organization rather than from its credo." He believed that his votes on progressive issues compared favorably with those cast by congressional liberals. His speeches from this period are replete with references to his support of advanced progressive ideas. Liberals nevertheless remained reluctant to embrace him as a reasonable alternative to Stevenson, and this frustrated and angered him, partially because he believed it unrealistic of liberals to hope that Stevenson could be an effective candidate. In 1960, during a conversation with Peter Lisagor, who predicted that Stevenson would be the nominee, Kennedy "leaned forward — I remember this so vividly," Lisagor said. It was "almost the only time I ever saw him angry . . . and he said, 'Why, that's impossible. Adlai Stevenson is a bitter man. He's a bitter, deeply disillusioned, deeply hurt man.'" As Jack told another journalist regarding Stevenson, "People who want to be deluded are going to be deluded no matter what they are told." In September, after economist John Kenneth Galbraith publicly supported Kennedy's candidacy, Jack wrote him, "I rather imagine your voice will be drowned out by the antiphonal choruses of support for [California governor] Pat Brown, [Michigan governor] Soapy Williams and [New York mayor] Bob Wagner!" — all more acceptable liberals.

The gulf between Kennedy and party liberals came partly from an unbridgeable difference in perspective. New Deal–Fair Deal Democrats thought in terms of traditional welfare state concerns — economic security, social programs, racial equality. But as Jack told Harris Wofford, "The key thing for the country is a new foreign policy that will break out of the confines of the cold war. Then we can build a decent relationship with developing nations and begin to respond to their needs. We can stop the vicious circle of the arms race and promote diversity and peaceful change within the Soviet bloc. We can get this country moving again on its domestic problems." He conceded that "Stevenson may see this, but he's a two-time loser and has no real chance; nor has [Chester] Bowles or Humphrey, with whom I agree even more. The most likely alternatives are Johnson or Symington, but if either of them is nominated we might as well elect Dulles or Acheson; it would be the same cold-war foreign policy all over again." (This was certainly prophetic about the Johnson presidency.)

Kennedy also gave voice to his thinking through James MacGregor Burns, who was writing Kennedy's campaign biography, chiefly from interviews. Kennedy's "mixed voting record" and resistance to being labeled as a New Dealer or a Fair Dealer made people question his liberal credentials, Burns wrote in his book. But Kennedy was a new kind of liberal, Burns asserted. Because the New Deal and the Fair Deal had "become properly entrenched in our way of life, and hence [were] no longer a disputed political issue," Kennedy believed that "liberalism must be rethought and renewed." As for foreign policy, a series of questions Burns posed to him made it clear that Kennedy was trying to craft fresh ways of thinking about the Cold War. In particular, Jack cautioned against overblown hopes: "It takes two to make peace," he said. "I think it would be misleading to suggest that there are some magic formulas hitherto untried which would ease the relations between the free world and the communistic world, or which would shift the balance of power in our favor."

He hoped nevertheless that "paramount" military power might "encourage the Russians and the Chinese to say a farewell to arms," which could produce a competitive shift "to nonmilitary spheres." Kennedy then foresaw "a struggle between the two systems . . . a test as to which system travels better, which system of political, economic, and social organization can more effectively transform the lives of the people in the newly emerging countries."

Schlesinger signed on to Kennedy's campaign principally because he saw him as a more realistic liberal than Stevenson, and it was Schlesinger who helped Jack find a distinctive liberal outlook. Eager to give "his campaign identity — to distinguish his appeal from that of his rivals and suggest that he could bring the country something no one else could," Kennedy seized upon a memorandum Schlesinger wrote arguing that "the Eisenhower epoch, the period of passivity and acquiescence in our national life, was drawing to its natural end, and that a new time — a time of affirmation, progressivism and forward movement — impended."

Schlesinger noted in his journal at the time: "This, I suppose, is the real irony. I have come, I think, to the private conclusion that I would rather have K as President than S. S is a much richer, more thoughtful, more creative person; but he has been away from power too long; he gives me an odd sense of unreality. . . . In contrast K gives a sense of cool, measured, intelligent concern with action and power. I feel that his administration would be less encumbered than S's with commitments to past ideas or sentimentalities; that he would be more radical; and, though he is less creative personally, he might be more so politically."

A lack of clear definition, however, made Kennedy's "new" liberalism suspect. Indeed, the details of his domestic program sounded much like the old liberalism or little different from what progressive Democrats were advocating in 1960: "comprehensive housing legislation . . . a ten-point 'bill of rights' for improved living standards for older people . . . [a] bill to outlaw the bombing of homes, churches, schools, and community centers"; antilynching and anti–poll tax bills; a higher minimum wage; and an end to loyalty oaths. On foreign and defense policies as well, Kennedy seemed to be treading on familiar ground. True, he called for fresh thinking about Africa, Latin America, Asia, and the Middle East, emphasizing economic assistance, but a focus on military strength and the "'magic power' on our side [of] the desire of every person to be free, of every nation to be independent" gave little indication of just how he might turn the Cold War in a new direction.

BECAUSE THERE WERE only sixteen state primaries, the road to the nomination in 1960 principally involved winning over state party leaders. Direct contacts between Jack and prominent Democrats across the country seemed essential. Beyond wooing local party leaders, however, no one around Kennedy at the end of 1958 had a clear conception of how to proceed. O'Donnell and Powers thought the nomination fight would be a larger version of Kennedy's 1952 and 1958 Senate races. As in Massachusetts, where they had largely shunned party chiefs, they initially thought in terms of a 1960 grass roots campaign. Bobby Kennedy agreed, telling a reporter that they could not rely on "the politicians" who controlled the big state delegations to the convention. "We have to get organized in those states," he said, "and have secretaries in every major city." The secretaries were to set up Kennedy clubs, or "citizen organizations," mounting a "grass roots appeal over the party regulars." The Republican nominations of Wendell Willkie in 1940, Tom Dewey in 1944, and Eisenhower in 1952 were models of how to wrest the nomination from the "bosses."

By the beginning of 1959, however, as Jack, Bobby, and the rest of the Kennedy team thought about the challenge before them, they concluded that shunning party leaders was a prescription for defeat; with only sixteen primaries, they would need the backing of party "bosses" as well as rank-and-file Democrats to have any realistic hope of being nominated. Implementing this strategy meant creating more formal organization than had existed so far. To this end, they installed Steve Smith, who was married to Jack's sister Jean, in a nine-room office in the Washington, D.C., Esso building on Constitution Avenue near the Capitol. Because they were eager to keep the operation quiet, the building directory and office door listed only "Stephen E. Smith." The thirty-two-year-old Smith, the son of a wealthy New York shipping family with some business experience, was asked to manage four secretaries corresponding with Democratic governors and state chairmen and local and grass root supporters around the country. Smith and his staff set up a card file of backers and potential allies and rated their loyalty on a one-to-ten scale. Detailed wall maps identifying areas of strength and weakness across the country gave the operation, which took the form of letters and telephone calls to any and all likely convention delegates, the feel of a military campaign.

But even with the Smith office in place, more questions than answers remained about winning the nomination. On April 1, Jack, Joe, and Bobby met at Joe's house in Palm Beach with Smith, pollster Lou Harris, and Jack's Senate staff: O'Brien, O'Donnell, and Sorensen. They reviewed each state in detail, asking: "Where do we stand?" Who are the "key figures" that will "influence the delegation? . . . Should JFK be scheduled there this fall or earlier? Should Bobby be scheduled to speak there this spring or summer? Should a poll be taken — and when?" Which state primaries should they enter? "What kind of organization do we need within the state? Should we be lining up our own delegate slate?"

Although Smith's office and the April meeting provided no definitive answers to their questions, by the fall the campaign had made some significant gains. In October, when Gallup asked 1,454 Democratic county chairmen, "Regardless of whom you personally prefer, what is your best guess . . . as to who will get the Democratic nomination for President in 1960?" 32 percent chose Kennedy, 27 percent said Symington, 18 percent picked Stevenson, 9 percent selected Johnson, and 3 percent named Humphrey; 11 percent refused to say.

IF JACK COULD begin to feel somewhat optimistic about his chances for the nomination, he was discouraged by Gallup's finding that 61 percent of Democratic and Republican county chairmen thought that Nixon would beat Kennedy in the 1960 campaign; only 34 percent thought that Jack could defeat someone as well-known and experienced in national politics as the vice president. Fifty-five percent of the county chairmen believed that New York governor Nelson Rockefeller could also beat Kennedy. These surveys were in sharp contrast to polls showing Democrats favored over Republicans in the 1960 congressional elections by 57 to 43 percent and on party registration by 55 to 37 percent.

The disappointing numbers underscored the need for Kennedy to launch an all-out campaign that demonstrated his national appeal to voters. And so by the autumn of 1959, despite still not having announced his candidacy, he had settled into an exhausting routine that took him to every part of the country. In October and November, he spent four days in Indiana, one day each in West Virginia, New York, and Nebraska, two days in Louisiana, made a stopover in Milwaukee on the way to Oregon, flew back to New York, followed by three- and four-day stays in Illinois, California, and Oregon, and briefer visits to Oklahoma, Delaware, Kansas, and Colorado. He addressed audiences of every size on street corners, at airports, on fairgrounds, and in theaters, armories, high schools, state capitols, restaurants, gambling casinos, hotels, and pool, union, lodge, and convention halls. The groups he addressed were as varied as the venues — farmers, labor unions, chambers of commerce, bar associations, ethnic societies, state legislatures, college and university students and faculties, and civic organizations.

As he traveled, he learned how to pace his talks and strike responsive chords with audiences. When Katie Louchheim, the vice chairman of the Democratic National Committee, heard him speak at a party meeting in July 1959, she described him as "certainly brilliant, his choice of topics, words, his fluency, all excellent. But his delivery took the cream off his own milk. He fairly rushes along, almost breathless, and his smiles are merely indicated, not given." It was a familiar and long-standing criticism of Kennedy's public speaking, and during the fall tour he made conscious efforts to improve. "I'm getting a lot better on speeches," he told an interviewer, concluding that "at least now I've got a control over the subject matter and a confidence so that I can speak more and more off the cuff, and I know that the off the cuff is much better than the prepared speech. Perhaps when I get enough control, I can have more confidence about making them less declaratory and more emotional." He also improved his technique of working a crowd. During this time, Sorensen wrote later, "he learned the art of swiftly getting down from the speaker's stand into a crowd for handshaking instead of being trapped by a few eager voters behind the head table." In short, he was becoming a master campaigner.

But it was difficult, sometimes demoralizing work carried out despite continuing back pain and spasm, which he eased with early-morning and late-night hot baths. A journalist who followed him around said, "The tone was tiredness, drained tiredness of one hotel room after another hotel room," nonstop speech-making, "people pulling you this way and that . . . smiling and smiling until your mouth is so dehydrated it doesn't seem to belong to you any more . . . more hands than you can shake, more names than you can remember, [and] more promises than you can keep." Through it all, Jack could never escape the thought that it might be in vain — a marathon run that tested the limits of his physical and psychological resilience and then ended in possible defeat. He countered such thoughts by remembering the potential payoff. There seemed no other justification imaginable.

To improve Jack's chances of winning, Bobby gave up his Senate staff job to become campaign manager. He immediately convened a meeting of seventeen principal people at his house in Hyannis Port at the end of October. Bobby was all business. "Jack," he said in a staccato voice, "what has been done about the campaign, what planning has been done?" Before Jack could answer, Bobby asked: "Jack, how do you expect to run a successful campaign if you don't get started? A day lost now can't be picked up at the other end. It's ridiculous that more work hasn't been done already." Jack, mimicking his brother's delivery, said to no one in particular, "How would you like looking forward to that voice blasting in your ear for the next six months?"

The group began by discussing a six-page summary of Jack's political standing. It was decidedly upbeat, noting that Kennedy was "well on his way" to getting the nomination and winning the White House. His appeal to "rank-and-file voters" indicated that he was "the only Democrat who can beat either Nixon or Rockefeller." But, refusing to take anything for granted, the report also acknowledged "handicaps of age, religion and a[n imperfect liberal] Senate voting record." The conclusion: Jack would have to work hard for the nomination by entering the primaries and staking out controversial positions. Another, more recent analysis in October cited widespread doubts among Democrats about Jack's seriousness, maturity, and credentials as a bona fide liberal.

Jack believed it essential to show both close advisers and the larger public that he was not a stand-in for his father or under the control of his family but an independent leader who was passionate about using politics to advance the national well-being. So he used the October meeting to demonstrate his knowledge about vital issues. He also wanted to remind everyone — including his brother — who was ultimately in charge. For example, after he agreed to Bobby's suggestion that the thirty-three-year-old journalist Pierre Salinger run campaign press operations, Jack took Salinger to task for issuing a statement on Bobby's say-so. "Check those things with me," he told Salinger. "You're working for me, not for Bob now."

The meeting was an opportunity not for "hard-and-fast, dramatic, black-and-white decisions," Sorensen said later, but for Jack to prove to his team that a forty-three-year-old Catholic senator with no executive experience deserved to be president. Dressed casually in "slacks and loafers, looking thoroughly boyish," Kennedy "amaze[d] them all by a performance that remains in the memory of all those who listened. . . . For three hours, broken only occasionally by a bit of information he might request of the staff, he proceeded, occasionally sitting, sometimes standing, to survey the entire country without map or notes. It was a tour of America region by region, state by state," and a demonstration that "he knew all the [party] factions and the key people in all the factions," and where he needed to go.

There was some strategizing, too. Minutes of the meeting show a concern with bringing former Connecticut governor and congressman Chester Bowles into the campaign — not because he was a leading progressive voice on foreign affairs and close to Kennedy's thinking, as Jack later emphasized to him, but because he was so closely identified with party liberals. Nevertheless, rumors that Bowles might become secretary of state were to be encouraged. A discussion of winning southern support included somewhat cynical suggestions that liberal labor opposition to Jack be publicized as widely as possible in the region, where anti-union sentiment was prevalent.

On Saturday, January 2, 1960, Kennedy formally announced his candidacy before an audience of three hundred supporters in the Senate Caucus Room. In choosing a slow news day after the New Year's holiday, he assured himself extensive press coverage. His terse two-page statement sounded the themes he believed could carry him to the nomination and the White House. He wanted to become president, he said, to ensure "a more vital life for our people" and freedom for peoples everywhere. Specifically, he wished to end or alter the burdensome arms race, support freedom and order in the newly emerging nations, "rebuild the stature of American science and education . . . prevent the collapse of our farm economy and the decay of our cities," rekindle economic growth, and give fresh direction to "our traditional moral purpose." He had toured every continental state in the Union during the previous forty months and would now "submit to the voters his views, record and competence in a series of primary contests." To answer objections that so young and inexperienced a senator would be a risky nominee, he emphasized his eighteen years of service to the country as a naval officer and member of Congress, and the extensive foreign travels that had taken him to "nearly every continent and country."

Reflecting skepticism about his candidacy, reporters asked if he would "refuse the vice presidential nomination under any circumstance." His answer was unequivocal: "I will not be a candidate for Vice President under any circumstances and that is not subject to change." As for the likely debate to erupt over his religion, he also gave an unqualified response. He acknowledged that it would be a matter of substantial discussion. But he saw only one concern for voters: "Does a candidate believe in the Constitution, does he believe in the First Amendment, does he believe in the separation of church and state." Having said that, he dismissed the issue as one that had been settled 160 years ago and concluded that he saw "no value in discussing a matter which is that ancient, when there are so many issues in 1960 which are going to be important."

Despite everything he had said that day, few political commentators and activists thought Kennedy could get the nomination. House Democrats and party state chairmen now predicted Symington's nomination; Democratic senators and southern leaders expected Johnson to get the top spot; most Democratic governors, editors, and "influential intellectuals" picked Stevenson or Humphrey, his stand-in, as the ultimate winner. Jack shrugged off their predictions.

Kennedy saw Humphrey as the least likely to beat him. True, party liberals loved Humphrey: He had been fighting for civil rights and New Deal social programs since he had come to the Senate from Minnesota in 1949. When he spoke at a July 1959 party meeting in Washington, he outdid Kennedy and Symington. Katie Louchheim said that Jack "scored 100 — but then so did Stuart, in his calm, dignified, statesmanlike brief speech. But it was Hubert who got the hand, was interrupted many times with applause. He shook 'em, he impassioned on their 'topic,' and yet he said nothing the others hadn't said." After Humphrey, with Jack's encouragement, had spoken at the University of Virginia law school, where Jack's brother Ted was a student, Kennedy asked his brother, "How did Hubert do down there?" Ted replied that he "had never heard anyone speak like Hubert Humphrey. He had a packed student audience, they were crawling all over the roof, and he just got standing ovation after standing ovation. That wasn't quite the answer [Jack] wanted to hear," Ted Kennedy recalled.

But as a practical matter, Jack saw Humphrey as too liberal and unable to muster the 761 delegates needed to nominate him. He was "unpopular in some sectors," like the business community, where people objected to his "extremism," Jack told Lisagor. Jack told another journalist in the fall of 1959, "I don't have to worry with Humphrey. . . . [He] is dead. . . . Whether or not he knows it, he is just a stalking horse for Stevenson and Symington."

As for Johnson, Jack, Bobby, and Ted believed that "no Southerner can be nominated by a Democratic convention" — and this included "the able majority leader, Lyndon Johnson. . . . Even if he were . . . conceded every Southern state, every border state and most of the moderate Eastern and Western states . . . there is still too large a bloc of states with liberal and minority votes that he cannot touch." Joe Kennedy was more concerned about Johnson than Jack was, but Jack saw him as an outsize personality, "a 'riverboat gambler,'" who was omnipotent in the Senate "but had no popularity in the country." The fact, Jack said, that he had had a heart attack in 1955, which everyone knew about, and that he was someone "who has no very firm principles and does not believe in anything very deeply" would also work against him.

Symington worried Kennedy as a potential compromise candidate. A former air force secretary with strong liberal credentials and Harry Truman's support, Symington was acceptable to all wings of the party. Should the convention reach a deadlock over the nomination, Jack thought that Symington could emerge as the party's choice. He told his father and brothers: "[Symington] comes from the right state, the right background, the right religion, age and appearance, with a noncontroversial voting record and speaking largely on matters of defense which offend no one. His appeal is largely to the older-line professional politicians, rallying under former President Truman . . . and their hope is that the convention will find objections with each of the other candidates and agree on Symington."

Jack also feared that the other candidates would bloody one another in the primaries while Symington stood on the sidelines. "I wish I could get Stu into a primary," Jack privately told a reporter, "any primary, anywhere." Barring that, the best strategy against Symington was to win the nomination on the first ballot or before a standoff could make him a viable choice. In the meantime, however, Joe Kennedy tried to find dirt on Symington. In particular, he asked investigators to look into why President Roosevelt had asked Harry Truman to find out whether the Emerson Electric Company, which Symington had headed in the forties, had shortchanged the war effort.

But it was Stevenson's "sleeping candidacy" that impressed Kennedy as his greatest threat. Jack never trusted his avowed noncandidacy. He accepted that Stevenson disliked the thought of another campaign and would not go after the nomination directly. "But he still has powerful friends — so his name belongs on the list of candidates," the Kennedys concluded. Joe, however, was less worried about Stevenson than Jack was. "He is not a threat," Joe told a journalist. "The Democratic party is through in the East if he is nominated. The leaders realize that it would be disastrous. . . . To elect their State ticket they need Jack. . . . The nomination is a cinch. I'm not a bit worried about the nomination."

Joe's remarks were a brave show of public confidence, which was a good campaign tactic. But at the start of 1960, Jack knew that nothing was settled. "Look," he told a reporter, "when someone says to you, 'You're doing fine,' it doesn't mean a thing, and when someone says, 'Just call any time you need anything,' that doesn't mean a thing, and when someone says, 'You've got a lot of friends out here,' that doesn't mean a thing . . . but when they say, 'I'm for you,' that is the only thing that means something."

Most discouraging to Jack was the persistence of the country's irrational anti-Catholicism. Fourteen years had passed since he entered politics, and still Jack was being asked the same offensive questions. Antagonism to the Church and fear of its influence over him were discussed openly. Katie Louchheim's friends and relatives, for example, who were "definitely and categorically anti," told her, "After all, this is still a Protestant country." One of them said, "How would you like it if the country were run the way the Catholics run Conn[ecticut] and Mass[achusetts]?" When Schlesinger saw Jack on the evening of January 2, Kennedy "conveyed an intangible feeling of depression. I had the sense that he feels himself increasingly hemmed in as a result of a circumstance over which he has no control — his religion; and he inevitably tends toward gloom and irritation when he considers how the circumstance may deny him what he thinks his talent and efforts have earned."

THE FIRST PRIMARY contest in New Hampshire on March 6 would be a chance to show that Kennedy could attract a decisive number of Protestant votes, but New Hampshire was not seen as a significant test of Jack's national appeal, since as a New England native son with no other serious contender, he seemed certain to win. To assure as big a margin as possible, however, the campaign sent Rose and Jack to speak across the state, which both did with great effectiveness. The outcome — 85 percent of the vote against a smattering of write-ins for Stevenson and Symington — was all the Kennedys could have hoped for.

Kennedy's unopposed candidacy in Indiana and Nebraska would give him those states' delegates. Polls in California had showed that Jack could beat Governor Pat Brown in a primary, and as a trade-off for not running, Jack got a promise from Brown that if he won primaries in New Hampshire, Wisconsin, and West Virginia, ran second behind Senator Wayne Morse in Oregon, and was leading for the nomination in the Gallup polls, Brown would support him at the convention.

Ohio required some especially tough negotiations with Governor Mike DiSalle, who wanted to run as a favorite son and then barter his state's delegates at the convention. But the Kennedys, threatening to back Cleveland Democratic leader Ray Miller, DiSalle's chief rival, as the head of the Ohio delegation, forced Disalle into a public endorsement of Kennedy in January. At a meeting between Jack and DiSalle in an airport motel in Pittsburgh, Jack told him, "Mike, it's time to shit or get off the pot. . . . You're either going to come out for me or we are going to run a delegation against you in Ohio and we'll beat you." When Jack's threat did not settle matters, Bobby Kennedy, accompanied by party chairman John Bailey, went to Ohio to force the issue. Bailey, "a veteran politician who does not shock easily," told Ken O'Donnell later that "he was startled by the going-over that Bobby had given DiSalle." The conversation added to Bobby's growing reputation as Jack's hatchet man, but it forced DiSalle into a commitment like Brown's that gave Jack valuable momentum.

Deals and promises were not enough, though. Jack had to win a truly contested primary to show that it wasn't all back-room dealings that qualified him for the nomination. (He thought that Johnson and Symington were making a serious mistake by staying out of all the primaries. Indeed, the day after announcing his candidacy, Kennedy had said that any aspiring nominee who avoided these contests did not deserve to have his candidacy taken seriously.) To meet the challenge, he reluctantly decided to run against Humphrey in Wisconsin. It meant risking the nomination. Wisconsin had a large Protestant population, so a defeat by Humphrey would increase doubts about a Catholic nominee. Joe Kennedy wrote a friend in Italy, "If we do not do very well there . . . we should get out of the fight." He believed Wisconsin was "the crisis of the campaign."

In addition to the possible religious split, Humphrey had the advantage of being a next-door neighbor — the "third senator from Wisconsin," as supporters called him. His rapport with Wisconsin farmers and liberals clustered in the university community in Madison made him a formidable opponent. Moreover, because Wisconsin was essential to his hopes of a nomination, Hubert seemed certain to make an all-out fight for a majority of the popular vote and the state's thirty-one delegates.

Yet Jack had some reason for optimism. Between May 1958 and November 1959, he had laid the groundwork for a possible statewide campaign. He had spent sixteen days in Wisconsin giving speeches and meeting Democrats in cities and towns he had never heard of before — Appleton, Ashland, Darlington, La Crosse, Lancaster, Platteville, Rhinelander, Rice Lake, Sparta, and Viroqua joined Green Bay, Milwaukee, and Sheboygan as vital to his political future. Leaving nothing to chance, he also chose a "full-time advance man and organizer of Kennedy clubs," and enlisted the support of Pat Lucey, the state's party chairman, and Ivan Nestingen, the mayor of Madison, both of whom were now convinced of Kennedy's liberal credentials. Private polls in January 1960 showing Kennedy ahead of Humphrey helped ease the difficult but, in Jack's mind, unavoidable decision to make the race.

The six-week Wisconsin campaign running from mid-February to early April tested Jack's endurance and commitment to winning the presidency. O'Donnell and Powers remembered it as a "winter of cold winds, cold towns and many cold people. Campaigning in rural areas of the state where nobody seemed to care about the presidential election was a strange and frustrating experience." In a tavern, where Jack introduced himself to a couple of beer drinkers, saying, "I'm John Kennedy and I'm running for President," one of them asked, "President of what?" On a freezing cold morning, as Jack stood for hours in the dark shaking hands with workers arriving at a meat packing plant, Powers whispered to O'Donnell, "God, if I had his money, I'd be down there on the patio at Palm Beach." Powers might have added, "God, if I had his medical problems and all the physical discomfort campaigning added to them . . ." But Jack was determined to see his commitment through. When an elderly woman stopped him on the street to say, "You're too soon, my boy, too soon," Jack replied, "No, this is my time. My time is now." Despite his youthful and robust appearance, he knew that in eight years — assuming the victor would serve two terms — his deteriorating back and chronic colitis might make running even more of a problem than it was in 1960.

The battle was against more than wind chill and back pain. The abuse leveled at him by Humphrey's campaign and a hostile press were enough alone to discourage him from competing. Sorensen said later that "vicious falsehoods were whispered about Kennedy's father, Kennedy's religion and Kennedy's personal life." Humphrey pilloried him as a Democratic Nixon who had recently joined the liberal ranks to win the nomination. Appealing to populist antagonism to Kennedy's wealth, Humphrey declared, "Thank God, thank God" for his own "disorderly" campaign. "Beware of these orderly campaigns. They are ordered, bought and paid for. We are not selling corn flakes or some Hollywood production." Voters had to make their choice, the balding Humphrey said, "on more than . . . how we cut our hair or how we look." He complained of a Republican-inspired press buildup for Kennedy as a way to run Nixon against a weak opponent. Echoing the charge that Jack had "little emotional commitment to liberalism," Humphrey said, "You have to learn to have the emotions of a human being when you are charged with the responsibilities of leadership." Humphrey also attacked Jack as a recent convert to helping farmers, echoed criticism of Kennedy's cautious response to Joe McCarthy, and before a Milwaukee Jewish audience implicitly compared Kennedy's "organized campaign" to Nazi Germany, "one of the best-organized societies of our time."

Humphrey saw his attacks as a response to "an element of ruthlessness and toughness" in Kennedy's campaign. Though he couldn't prove it, he believed that Bobby Kennedy had started and helped circulate a rumor that the corrupt Teamsters union was working for Humphrey's election. Moreover, he thought that the Kennedys were stimulating Catholics to vote for Jack by sending anonymous anti-Catholic materials to Catholic households.

Kennedy largely ignored Humphrey's assaults. James Reston noted that Jack "remained remarkably self-possessed. . . . He has shown not the slightest trace of anger. He has made no claims of victory. He has made no charges against Humphrey on the local shows or from the stump." Instead, he ran a largely positive campaign, giving full rein to his charm and intelligence. Riding in a car with Kennedy for an appearance at a shopping center, Peter Lisagor asked, "'Do you like these crowds and this sort of thing?' [Kennedy] turned back and said, 'I hate it.'" But the moment he stepped out of the car, "he lit up and smiled. He signed autographs on the brown shopping bags of these ladies who came pouring to him. . . . He went along as if he'd been doing this all of his life and loved it."

The Kennedy campaign was, for a very large part, Pat Lucey said, "just an effective presentation of a celebrity. . . . The family was an asset . . . genuinely glamorous as well as glamorized, so the people were anxious to meet them wherever they went." As a result, Humphrey felt like a "corner grocer running against a chain store." With Jack, Bobby, Rose, and the Kennedy sisters all campaigning in Wisconsin, Humphrey was outmanned. The Kennedys are "all over the state," he complained, "and they look alike and sound alike. Teddy or Eunice talks to a crowd, wearing a raccoon coat and a stocking cap, and people think they're listening to Jack. I get reports that Jack is appearing in three or four different places at the same time."

On April 5, Kennedy won a substantial victory, taking 56.5 percent of the vote. The 476,024 Kennedy ballots were the most votes ever received by a candidate in the fifty-seven-year history of Wisconsin primaries, and Kennedy's majorities in six out of ten districts entitled him to 60 percent of the state's convention delegates. But Jack saw his success as raising more questions about his candidacy than it answered. Because the six districts he won included large numbers of Catholic voters and Humphrey's districts were principally Protestant enclaves, including Madison, the center of liberal sentiment, Kennedy could not convince party chiefs that he would command broad backing in a national election. When Ted Sorensen heard the first returns showing Humphrey ahead in the western, rural areas of the state, he turned "ashen." These numbers made him "mighty uneasy." Dave Powers tried to put a positive face on the result: "A shift of . . . less than 3/10 of 1% of the vote . . . would have given Kennedy 8 districts to 2." Powers also listed thirteen counties where 70 percent or more of non-Catholic votes were for Jack and six with substantial numbers of Catholics he lost. None of this, however, could change the initial perception of Kennedy as a candidate whose religion made a difference. When Jack heard the returns, he jumped from his seat and paced the room, muttering, "Damn religious thing."

Noticing the glum expression on Jack's face as he studied the returns, Eunice Kennedy asked him, "What does it all mean?" He replied, "It means that we've got to go to West Virginia in the morning and do it all over again. And then we've got to go on to Maryland and Indiana and Oregon and win all of them." Only then might the press stop publishing photos of Kennedy shaking hands with nuns and church officials and continually referring to Jack's Catholicism. Kennedy kept track of how often newspaper accounts mentioned his religion, and he had not missed the fact that two days before the primary, the *Milwaukee Journal* had listed the number of voters in each county under three headings: Democrats, Republicans, and Catholics. "The religious issue became prominent because the newspapers said it was prominent," Lucey asserted. When CBS newsman Walter Cronkite asked Jack after his Wisconsin victory whether being a Catholic had hurt him, Jack's annoyance with Cronkite was unmistakable. Afterward, Bobby exploded at Cronkite and his staff, shouting that they had violated an agreement not to ask about religion and that his brother would never give them another interview. Cronkite was unaware of such a promise, and there would be many future interviews with both brothers. But Bobby's outburst illustrated how angry he and Jack were at the implicit questions being raised about their loyalty to the country.

If Wisconsin left the overall situation unsettled, Jack's victory did accomplish something real and important. The outcome in Wisconsin essentially ended Humphrey's bid for the nomination. If he could not win in a neighboring state with so many Protestants, farmers, and liberals, he was unlikely to win anywhere. But, stung by his defeat and confident that he could beat Jack in West Virginia, a state only 4 percent Catholic, Humphrey decided to continue his campaign. A Harris poll showed Jack ahead of Humphrey in West Virginia by 70 to 30 percent, but even if Humphrey closed some of that gap, Harris predicted, Jack would have "a comfortable margin of victory." Harris saw West Virginia as "a powerful weapon against those who raise the 'Catholic can't win' bit."

After Wisconsin, however, Jack and his advisers were not so sure. The Wisconsin race had made West Virginia voters more aware of Kennedy's religion, and his lead over Humphrey disappeared. A poll of Kanawha county, the seat of the state capital, Charleston, showed Humphrey with 60 percent to Kennedy's 40 percent. A report coming in to Dave Powers in April concluded that "public opinion had shifted and [Kennedy] would be lucky to get 40 per cent of the vote." On April 6, the day after Wisconsin, Bobby, O'Donnell, and O'Brien went to Charleston, where they met with Kennedy organizers. "Well, what are our problems?" Bobby asked the gathering in a crowded hotel room. "There's only one problem," one man shouted. "He's a Catholic. That's our God-damned problem!" A Kennedy supporter in the state wrote Franklin D. Roosevelt Jr. that "[U.S. Senator] Bob Byrd is getting out his Bible and fiddle to make the rounds of the country churches. These people weren't thinking much of the religious issue, one way or another. But now every hate-monger, radio preacher and backwoods evangelist is being stirred up for an assault which will make 1928 look pale by comparison."

The state's labor unions would also be a problem for Kennedy. A member of the United Steel Workers reported that Kennedy had been relying on "the reactionary element of the Democratic party . . . to head his state organization. He would be weak in . . . the Democratic stronghold in southern W. Va. In a race between Kennedy and Humphrey, we believe that Humphrey would win, even though the Kennedy forces would be better financed."

Though some of Jack's advisers suggested that he skip West Virginia and concentrate instead on Indiana, Nebraska, and Maryland, he felt compelled to take up Humphrey's challenge and show that a Catholic could win in a Protestant state. Robert McDonough, who ran Jack's West Virginia office, believed that a victory there might allow Kennedy to "bury the religious issue." At a planning meeting on April 8, Bobby stated their intention "to meet the religious issue head on." The goal was to give rational answers to questions about Jack's Catholicism and then move on to "something more important to those people." Bobby consulted with Frank Fischer, West Virginia's Junior Chamber of Commerce president, who knew the state as well as anyone. Fischer urged Bobby to talk about the "Four F's . . . food, Franklin [Roosevelt], family, and the flag."

Jack set this strategy in motion on the first day of his West Virginia campaign. Before a crowd of three or four hundred people gathered on the steps of the Charleston post office, Jack, microphone in hand, aggressively fielded a question about his religion, "I am a Catholic, but the fact that I was born a Catholic, does that mean that I can't be the President of the United States? I'm able to serve in Congress, and my brother was able to give his life, but we can't be president?" McDonough "could just feel the crowd respond to and accept his answer." With Humphrey making his campaign theme song "Give Me That Old Time Religion" and Baptists warning that a Catholic would owe allegiance to the pope, Jack continuously reminded voters that he had risked his life for the country. "Nobody asked me if I was a Catholic when I joined the United States Navy," he declared. "Nobody asked my brother if he was a Catholic or Protestant before he climbed into an American bomber plane to fly his last mission." The message was clear: How can you doubt my primary loyalty to America?

Kennedy spent two intense weeks in the state between April 5 and May 10. "He was the most attractive candidate imaginable," Bob McDonough said. "He just went up every valley in the state, down every road, and over every hill, and he shook hands by the thousands." "I am the only Presidential candidate since 1924, when a West Virginian ran for the presidency," Kennedy told audiences, "who knows where Slab Fork is and has been there." He spoke so often and so loudly that he lost his voice and had to have his brother Ted and Sorensen speak for him. "Over and over again," journalist Theodore White recorded, "there was the handsome, open-faced candidate on the TV screen, showing himself, proving that a Catholic wears no horns." As important, a skillfully crafted TV documentary, which the campaign put on local stations around the state, displayed his winning manner and his achievements as a war hero, a Pulitzer Prize–winning author, and the father of a beautiful two-year-old daughter. A compelling sincerity about his devotion to American freedoms dissolved most objections to his Catholicism.

Jackie Kennedy, despite concern among Jack's advisers that her stylish dress and manners might alienate voters, effectively connected with audiences in West Virginia. Word of her considerateness spread after "a nice old man said he would love to meet Jackie but could not leave his invalid wife." After Jackie visited their home, the man said, "Now I believe in Santa Claus. She looks like a real queen." She endeared herself to audiences when introducing Jack.

"I have to confess, I was born a Republican," she said, "but you have to have been a Republican to realize how nice it is to be a Democrat." Her two-year-old daughter Caroline's vocabulary was increasing with each primary, she reported. Her "first words were 'plane,' 'goodbye,' and 'New Hampshire,' and just this morning she said 'Wisconsin' and 'West Virginia.'" Already a month pregnant in April, Jackie, at risk of another miscarriage, would largely disappear from the rest of the 1960 campaign, but in West Virginia she worked aggressively on behalf of her husband.

She was not alone. Understanding how crucial the state was to his chances, Kennedy enlisted all his relatives and friends in the campaign. "The Senator is still in West Virginia," Evelyn Lincoln recorded on April 26. "Things do not look very good for him. . . . The Senator has brought all the people he can think of into the campaign. He has Lem Billings, Chuck Spalding, Ben Smith, Grant Stockdale, Bob Troutman, Sarge Shriver and many others down there working for him. Bobby is going all over making speeches and Teddy is too. Larry O'Brien is in charge of the organization and Kenny O'Donnell arranges his speaking schedule. Ralph Dungan is handling the labor setup. Chuck Roche and Pierre Salinger handle the press releases, TV, etc. Ted Reardon is in Wheeling."

Winning votes for Jack also meant taking them from Humphrey by neutralizing his advantage as a passionate advocate of liberal programs. If this began as cynical campaign politics, Kennedy's visits to the state transformed it into a genuine concern. "Kennedy's shock at the suffering he saw in West Virginia was so fresh," Teddy White thought, "that it communicated itself with the emotion of original discovery." Ted Sorensen remembered how appalled Kennedy was "by the pitiful conditions he saw, by the children of poverty, by the families living on surplus lard and cornmeal, by the waste of human resources." He gained a fuller understanding of the unemployed workers, the pensioners, and the relief recipients demoralized by their poverty but eager for a chance to improve their lives. "I assure you that after five weeks living among you here in West Virginia," Kennedy declared, "I shall never forget what I have seen. I have seen men, proud men, looking for work who cannot find it. I have seen people over 40 who are told that their services are no longer needed — too old. I have seen young people who want to live in the state, forced to leave the state for opportunities elsewhere. . . . I have seen older people who seek medical care that is too expensive for them to afford. I have seen unemployed miners and their families eating a diet of dry rations." Attacking the indifference of the Eisenhower administration, Jack laid out a ten-point program to relieve suffering and expand economic opportunity. He promised to increase unemployment benefits, modernize Social Security, expand food distribution, establish a national fuels program, stimulate the coal industry, and increase defense spending in the state. "Much more can and should be done," he announced in a letter to fellow Democrats. "That is why West Virginia will be on the top of my agenda at the White House."

On April 12, the fifteenth anniversary of Franklin Roosevelt's death, Kennedy reminded an audience that Roosevelt had accomplished more in a hundred days than Eisenhower and Nixon had in eight years. "And now it is time for another 'New Deal' — a New Deal for West Virginia," Jack declared. To hammer home the point, Joe Kennedy suggested that they ask FDR Jr., a Kennedy supporter, to join the campaign, which he did with great success, drawing worshipful crowds wherever he went. A West Virginia journalist said it was like "God's son coming down and saying it was all right to vote for this Catholic, it was permissible, it wasn't something terrible to do." Joe also shrewdly convinced FDR Jr. to send letters praising Jack from Hyde Park, New York, the site of FDR's home and resting place, to West Virginia Democrats.

To undercut Humphrey's stronger liberal identification, the Kennedys argued that a vote for Humphrey, who could not possibly get the nomination, would destroy prospects for the welfare reforms Jack proposed. Jack also described Humphrey as the tool of a "stop-Kennedy gang-up" backed by Lyndon Johnson and Stuart Symington. Senator Byrd publicly acknowledged the accuracy of Jack's assertion. "If you are for Adlai Stevenson, Senator Stuart Symington, Senator Johnson or John Doe, this primary may be your last chance to stop Kennedy," he declared. Seizing on Byrd's candid statement, Jack responded: "Hubert Humphrey has no chance to win the Democratic nomination for President, and he knows it, so why is he running against me in this primary? To stop me and give the nomination to Johnson or Stevenson or Symington. If Johnson and the other candidates want your vote in the November election, why don't they have enough respect for you to come here and ask for your vote in the primary?" It was a compelling argument that appealed to the self-interest and sense of fair play of West Virginia

Democrats. At the same time Kennedy challenged Johnson publicly, he confronted him privately, complaining that Johnson was using Humphrey as a stalking-horse. According to Johnson, when he denied he was running, Jack pressured him to "get Senator Byrd 'out of West Virginia.'" Johnson defended himself by telling Kennedy that he could not get Byrd out of his own state and reminded Jack that he had supported his vice presidential bid in 1956 and given him choice committee assignments.

With so much at stake in the election, the contest turned ugly. Humphrey attacked his "rivals" for the nomination as "millionaire 'money' candidates backed by political machines." Specifically, he went after Kennedy's free spending: "I don't think elections should be bought. . . . American politics are far too important to belong to the money men. . . . Kennedy is the spoiled candidate and he and that young, emotional, juvenile Bobby are spending with wild aban-don. . . . Anyone who gets in the way of papa's pet is going to be destroyed. . . . I don't seem to recall anybody giving the Kennedy family — father, mother, sons or daughters — the privilege of decid-ing who should . . . be our party's nominee."

When Kennedy complained about the "personal abuse" and "gutter politics," Humphrey shot back, "Poor little Jack. That is a shame. And you can quote me on that." Humphrey also ridiculed his complaint of an anti-Kennedy coalition: "I wish he would grow up and stop acting like a boy. What does he want, all the votes?" Humphrey asserted that Kennedy was "attempting to set up an alibi should he lose."

Although Humphrey was never proud of his negative attacks, which did more to hurt him than Kennedy, he had reason for com-plaint. "I would suggest that brother Bobby examine his own con-science about innuendoes and smears," he said. "If he has trouble knowing what I mean, I can refresh his memory very easily." An FDR Jr. assertion that Humphrey had been a draft dodger, which Humphrey believed was approved by Bobby, if not Jack, particularly incensed him. In possession of information that Humphrey may have sought military deferments during World War II, Bobby had pressed Roosevelt to use this in retaliation for Humphrey's harsh words. In fact, having tried and failed to get into the service because of physical disabilities, Humphrey corrected the record with the Ken-nedys. "They believed me," he wrote later, "but never shut F.D.R. Jr., up, as they easily could have." Jack publicly announced, "Any discus-sion of the war record of Senator Humphrey was done without my knowledge and consent, as I strongly disagree with the injection of this issue into the campaign." His statement, however, did not challenge the accuracy of what Roosevelt had said. Having addressed issues of food, Franklin, and family in the campaign, the Kennedys were now taking care of the flag.

But it was Kennedy spending that Humphrey knew was his biggest problem. In West Virginia politics, money was king. "As I told you last time you were down here," a state political veteran wrote FDR Jr. in April, "most of these coal-field counties are for sale. It is a matter of who gets there first with the most money." Teddy White wrote, "Politics in West Virginia involves money — hot money, under-the-table money, open money."

The payoffs involved a system of slating, which was a form of legalized bribery. To sort through dense ballots with long lists of names, voters relied on "slates" given to them by county political bosses, usually the county sheriff. Voters would then vote for those candidates on the slate. It was all very simple: The candidate who paid the most to the county Democratic boss (under the conceit of subsidizing "printing" costs) would have his list of backers identified as the "approved slate." When one county sheriff told a Humphrey campaign organizer what each name on a slate would cost in his county and the man passed the word to Humphrey, the response was, "We would pay it, but we don't have the money." Where Humphrey's total expenditures on the campaign amounted to $25,000, the Kennedys spent $34,000 on TV programming alone. With the Kennedys' approval, Larry O'Brien independently negotiated the payments for the slates. "Our highest possible contribution was peanuts compared to what they [county leaders] had received from the Kennedy organization," Humphrey complained. Such payments did not, O'Donnell noted, bother "the earthy and realistic people of West Virginia, who were accustomed to seeing the local candidate for sheriff carrying a little black bag that contained something other than a few bottles of Bourbon whiskey."

On May 10, Kennedy won a landslide, 60.8 to 39.2 percent. As Joe Tumulty, Woodrow Wilson's secretary, said of the 1920 Harding victory, "It wasn't a landslide, it was an earthquake." It did not matter that the vote was not binding on the state's twenty-five convention delegates. Kennedy had proved that he could amass a big majority among Protestants. Kennedy opponents tried to downplay the result with accusations of vote buying. An investigation by Eisenhower's attorney general William P. Rogers turned up no significant wrongdoing. The editor of the *Charleston Gazette* "sent two of our best men out. They spent three to four weeks checking. Kennedy did not buy that election," he concluded. "He sold himself to the voters." It was a fair assessment. The Kennedy expenditures financing the slates were technically legal. The combination of Jack's personal appeal, lavish Kennedy campaign spending, an emphasis on economic uplift, assurances about Jack's commitment to separation of church and state, and Humphrey's pointless candidacy after Wisconsin gave Jack the decisive victory. When *Newsweek* quoted Humphrey as believing that the election was stolen from him, he wrote the editor, "I have no complaints about the election — Senator Kennedy won it and I lost it."

Within ten days after West Virginia, Jack had beaten Wayne Morse in Maryland by 70 to 17 percent and then defeated him in Oregon, his home state, by 51 to 32 percent. It was Kennedy's seventh straight primary victory and convinced Jack's advisers that he was on his way to the nomination.

THERE WERE OTHER HURDLES to be cleared, however. Because many liberals still had hopes of nominating Stevenson, the Kennedys tried to weaken him by getting Humphrey to support Jack. After Humphrey conceded defeat in West Virginia, he sent word to Bobby Kennedy that he was dropping out of the race. Bobby immediately went to see him at his hotel in Charleston. He was not a welcome guest. In the words of liberal attorney Joe Rauh, Bobby was "the devil as far as this camp [was] concerned. . . . He was the one whom all our people were so bitter about." The defeat had humiliated Humphrey; Rauh remembered his appearance at his campaign headquarters as "the saddest sight I've ever seen. . . . Humphrey stood all alone in the middle of this big room . . . and looked at the blackboard, and almost was speechless. The banjo player had started to cry, and Hubert had to comfort him." Humphrey's wife, Muriel, was furious. "She did not want to see any Kennedy, much less be touched by one," Humphrey recalled. "When Bob arrived in our room, he moved quickly to her and kissed her on the cheek. Muriel stiffened, stared, and turned in silent hostility, walking away from him, fighting tears and angry words." Bobby's gesture was not enough to bring Humphrey to Jack's side.

It was more important for Stevenson to back Kennedy at the convention; this would make Jack's nomination a near certainty.

Believing he was between eighty and one hundred votes short of the goal, Jack thought "it would be most helpful if Adlai could throw his votes . . . [my] way at the proper moment. If he hangs on to his votes," Jack told Schlesinger through an intermediary, "it will only mean that either Symington or Johnson will benefit."

Although Jack had little hope that Stevenson could be persuaded to support him, he was determined to try. Months before, he had sent word to Stevenson through Connecticut governor Abe Ribicoff that if he could not get the nomination, he would publicly announce his wish to run as Stevenson's VP, "which would nail down the Catholic vote" for Stevenson. "If he comes out for me and I've got the nomination and I win," he had also asked Ribicoff to tell Stevenson, "I'll make him Secretary of State." Stevenson would not agree. In May 1960, Jack approached Stevenson again. On his way back from a trip to the West Coast, Jack stopped at his home in Libertyville, Illinois. Stevenson refused to make any promises except not to join a "stop-Kennedy movement" or to encourage any draft of himself. Kennedy was disappointed. "God, why won't he be satisfied with Secretary of State?" he said to Stevenson's law firm partner Bill Blair. "I guess there's nothing I can do," he added, "except go out and collect as many votes as possible and hope that Stevenson will come along." As he got on a plane to fly to Boston, Jack added, "Guess who the next person I see will be — the person who will say about Adlai, 'I told you that son-of-a-bitch has been running for President every moment since 1956'?" Blair replied: "Daddy."

Jack shared his father's view and was furious with Stevenson for standing in his way. Jack believed that Stevenson had an overblown reputation as an intellectual. As the author of two books, Kennedy thought that he deserved to be seen as more cerebral than Stevenson, and told friends that he read more books in a week than Stevenson did in a year. He referred to Stevenson as a "switcher," or bisexual, and wondered what women, who were his strongest supporters, saw in him. When Jack asked Stevenson's friend Clayton Fritchey to explain the attraction, Fritchey replied, "He likes women, he likes to talk to them, to be around them. Do you like them?" Fritchey asked, twitting Jack for his reputation as a philanderer. "I wouldn't go that far," Jack answered. Kennedy preferred columnist Joe Alsop's description of him as "a Stevenson with balls."

Kennedy was even more angry at Johnson. After West Virginia, LBJ began saying that Kennedy had bought the election there and that the country would not want to nominate a president based on what four or five or even eight states did in primaries with limited voter participation. Johnson also told columnist Drew Pearson that "none of these big-city leaders in New York, New Jersey, or Illinois want Kennedy. Most of them are Catholics and they don't want a Catholic heading up the ticket." Johnson also went to see Stevenson. "Now, listen, Adlai, you just hang loose here," he said. "Don't make any commitments. You may still get it. Don't help that kid, Kennedy. You just stay neutral."

In May, after the Soviets shot down an American U-2 spy plane and Moscow canceled a summit meeting between Eisenhower and Khrushchev, Kennedy criticized the administration's failure to suspend such flights before the summit and refusal to acknowledge that it had spied. Johnson, seeing an opportunity to illustrate Jack's inexperience in foreign affairs, declared, "I am not prepared to apologize to Mr. Khrushchev." He then excluded Kennedy from a telegram he, Stevenson, Rayburn, and Fulbright sent the Soviet leader asking him to hold the summit conference with the president.

Even Truman joined the anti-Kennedy chorus, calling at a televised press conference for an open convention — not a "prearranged . . . mockery . . . controlled by one . . . candidate" — and declaring that the world crisis required someone "with the greatest possible maturity and experience." Jack publicly replied that "Mr. Truman regards an open convention as one which studies all the candidates, reviews their records, and then takes his advice." Jack also said that Truman's maturity test "would have kept Jefferson from writing the Declaration of Independence, Washington from commanding the Continental Army, [and] Madison from fathering the Constitution."

Despite Stevenson's refusal to bow out and Johnson's belated effort to become the nominee, the smart money was still on Kennedy. At the end of May, Bobby calculated that Jack had 577 delegates and could pick up the additional 184 needed for nomination from seven other states. Joe wrote an English friend, "If we can get a break at all in Pennsylvania and a reasonable break in California, we're home." In June, after Jack told his father that the Pennsylvania delegation was now solidly behind him, Joe declared, "Well, that's it. We've got a solid majority." Johnson conceded privately that "those wanting to bet the favorite had better put their money on Jack."

Events in the days before the convention opened in Los Angeles on Monday, July 11, however, persuaded the Kennedys to take nothing for granted. Johnson announced his candidacy on July 5, and began publicly attacking Jack. LBJ's backers reminded journalists and delegates of Kennedy's response to Joe McCarthy, quoted Eleanor Roosevelt's criticism of Kennedy, publicized Jack's absenteeism as a senator ("Where was Jack?" an LBJ flyer asked), and, most troubling to the Kennedys, publicly asked for an evaluation of Jack's health, explaining that he had Addison's disease, which raised questions about his capacity to serve as president. Johnson called Dr. Gerald Labiner, an internist in Los Angeles who had been a fellow at the Lahey Clinic and knew Kennedy's medical history, to ask if Jack had Addison's disease. Although it was an open secret among Jack's physicians, Labiner refused to confirm Johnson's assumption.

In private, Johnson was more scathing, especially about Jack's age and well-being. "Did you hear the news?" Johnson asked Minnesota congressman Walter Judd. "What news?" Judd replied. "Jack's pediatricians have just given him a clean bill of health!" Johnson described Kennedy to Lisagor as "a little scrawny fellow with rickets. Have you ever seen his ankles?" Johnson asked. "'They're about so round,' and he traced a minute circle with his finger." If Johnson had known the full story of Jack's poor health, he would undoubtedly have leaked it to the press. But the Kennedys had managed largely to keep Jack's health problems a secret. Johnson also predicted that if Jack became president, Joe would run the country and Bobby would become secretary of labor.

The evening before Johnson and Rayburn flew to Los Angeles, they met with Eisenhower at the White House. Ike later told journalist Earl Mazo that they regarded Kennedy "as a mediocrity in the Senate, as a nobody who had a rich father. . . . And they'd tell some of the God-damndest stories." They went on for two hours telling Eisenhower, "Ike, for the good of the country, you cannot let that man become elected President. Now, he might get the nomination out there, he probably will, but he's a dangerous man." They repeated the phrase several times. They obviously wanted Eisenhower to say something publicly that would help them block Kennedy's nomination. But Ike did no more than assure them that if Kennedy were the candidate, Dick Nixon would beat him.

Some of Johnson's remarks got back to Bobby. "I knew he hated Jack. But I didn't think he hated him that much," Bobby said to Lisagor. When Bobby Baker, LBJ's Senate aide, complained to Bobby Kennedy that brother Ted was putting out stories about Johnson's heart condition, Bobby angrily replied: "You've got your nerve. Lyndon

Johnson has compared my father to the Nazis, and [Texas governor] John Connally . . . lied by saying that my brother was dying of Addison's disease. You Johnson people are running a stinking damned campaign and you'll get yours when the time comes."

Calling Johnson's tactics "despicable," the Kennedys released statements denying that Jack had "an ailment classically described as Addison's Disease" and describing Jack's health as "excellent." The statements more than shaded the truth: While Jack might not have had classical or primary Addison's, at a minimum, he had a secondary form of the ailment. The Kennedys had never allowed Eugene Cohen, Jack's endocrinologist, "the opportunity to carry out the necessary tests that would have been required to establish the diagnosis," Cohen told Dr. Seymour Reichlin, another endocrinologist. "Thus, [Cohen] could never say definitively that Kennedy had the disease." If it were known, however, that he also suffered from colitis, compression fractures of his spine, which forced him to take a variety of pain medications, and chronic prostatitis, it could have raised substantial doubts about his fitness for the presidency. Kennedy's friend Bill Walton said later that during the campaign an aide followed Jack everywhere with a special little bag containing the medical support needed all the time. When the medical bag was misplaced during a campaign trip to Connecticut, Kennedy called up Abe Ribicoff and said, "There's a medical bag floating around and it can't get in anybody's hands. . . . You have to find that bag. It would be murder" if the wrong people got hold of it and revealed its contents, which would have shown Jack's reliance on so many drugs. (The bag was recovered.)

All the political churning in the run-up to the convention made the Kennedys apprehensive. They expected to win. But history had demonstrated that conventions were volatile and could produce unpredictable results. Two Democratic front-runners earlier in the century — Champ Clark in 1912 and William G. McAdoo in 1924 — had found themselves upended by events beyond their control. Arthur Schlesinger Jr. counseled against assuming anything. He described a convention as "far too fluid and hysterical a phenomenon for exact history. Everything happens at once and everywhere, and everything changes too quickly. People talk too much, smoke too much, rush too much and sleep too little. Fatigue tightens nerves and produces susceptibility to rumor and panic. No one can see a convention whole. . . . At the time it is all a confusion; in retrospect it is all a blur."

During a July 10 interview on *Meet the Press,* Jack was asked if he thought the convention was "wrapped up." "No, I don't," he replied. "No convention is." While he predicted a victory, he would not say on which ballot. Nor would he acknowledge his concern that a failure to win on the first ballot could lead to disaster. When Bobby was asked later why they had not given much initial thought to who would be vice president, he answered: "We wanted to just try to get the nomination. . . . We were counting votes. We had to win on the first ballot. We only won by fifteen votes. . . . I think in North Dakota and South Dakota we won it by half a vote. California was falling apart. . . . [New York's] Carmine De Sapio came to me and said what we'd like to do is make a deal — 30 votes will go to Lyndon Johnson and then you'll get them all back on the second ballot. I said to hell with that; we're going to win it on the first ballot. So you know, it was all that kind of business. There wasn't any place that was stable." They were worried that support in a number of states, especially Minnesota, New Jersey, and Pennsylvania, might erode on second and third ballots and open the way for LBJ to win the nomination. Jack told Sorensen that if they did not win by the second ballot, it would be "never." Joe Kennedy stopped in Las Vegas on his way to Los Angeles to place a substantial bet on Jack's nomination. He was less interested in winning money than in encouraging a bandwagon psychology by reducing the odds on Jack's success.

Although Stevenson had too few delegates to be nominated, his backers were so vocal, so intense, that they sustained illusions of a possible victory. When Harris Wofford arrived at the convention, he "found thousands of supporters marching and chanting, 'We want Stevenson.' Inside, other thousands in the galleries were continuing the cry at each opportunity. The next afternoon, when Stevenson himself entered to sit in the Illinois delegation, he received a huge ovation and was almost carried to the platform in a sea of enthusiasm." "This was more than a demonstration," Teddy White wrote later, "it was an explosion."

Stevenson, swept up in the outpouring of emotion, lost perspective and tried to engineer a last-minute coup on his own behalf. He asked Richard Daley, who had announced the Illinois delegation for Kennedy, to switch on the first ballot. According to Bobby Kennedy, Stevenson told Daley, " 'We've got to have a favorite son and I come from Illinois, and you've got to be with me because it would be embarrassing if I don't have Illinois.' And Dick Daley almost threw him out of the office. He said Illinois had met their responsibilities to Adlai Stevenson and that they had pledged to Jack Kennedy and that's the way they were going. . . . It seemed to us to be the actions of an old woman." Daley recalled telling Stevenson that he had no support in the delegation and was lucky to have the two votes he got out of sixty-eight.

Nothing was left to chance. When Johnson took a fresh swipe at Kennedy on foreign affairs, declaring that "the forces of evil . . . will have no mercy for innocence, no gallantry for inexperience," they prepared a fact sheet on Lyndon Johnson's limited understanding of foreign affairs compared to Kennedy's travels, knowledge, and experience. Kennedy volunteers took up a vigil over each of the fifty-four delegations. They ate, drank, and all but lived with them, reporting on their "moods, questions, and trends, and, above all . . . their votes." Bobby insisted on practically having the name, address, and telephone number of every half vote. "I don't want generalities or guesses," he said. "There's no point in our fooling ourselves. I want the cold facts." When one volunteer complained at being asked to appear at 8:00 A.M. the next morning after three nights with almost no sleep, Bobby sharply responded, "Look, nobody asked you here. . . . If this is too tough for you, let us know and we'll get somebody else."

The Kennedy organization orchestrated Jack's every move. Dave Powers found Jack a three-bedroom "hideaway" penthouse apartment on North Rossmore Avenue, a fifteen-minute drive from the downtown Biltmore Hotel, where Bobby set up campaign headquarters in an eighth-floor triple suite from which he exercised "precise, taut, disciplined" control. A floor above, Jack had a private suite adjacent to a press room from which Salinger turned out a daily four-page paper, the "Kennedy Convention News," that was delivered to every delegate's room. A band playing "High Hopes" and dancing girls dressed in "colorful candy-striped outfits" were part of a crowd of five thousand people meeting Jack at L.A.'s airport on Saturday, July 9. Another well-planned demonstration greeted Jack's arrival at the Biltmore, where he worked his way through crowds of well-wishers at a Kennedy hospitality suite. In his ninth-floor sitting room, he studied the latest delegate counts and conferred with former New York governor Averell Harriman, George Meany, Jim Farley, and Mike Prendergast. After an NBC-TV interview, he joined Pennsylvania governor Dave Lawrence, who briefed him on conversations with several other big-city and state party leaders.

Jack spent Sunday, July 10, seeing several governors, attending a brunch for the California delegation, greeting twenty-five hundred convention delegates at a reception in the Biltmore ballroom, speaking to an NAACP conference at the Shrine Auditorium, attending a black-tie Democratic National Committee dinner at the Beverly Hilton Hotel, and appearing on TV network news programs. The pace picked up on Monday and Tuesday, when Jack, in a white air-conditioned Cadillac equipped with a telephone (a rarity in 1960), sped from one state caucus to another, shaking hands, making brief remarks, and answering questions. Inviting media coverage and arranging a Kennedy press conference with 750 journalists, the campaign added to the picture of an energetic, healthy, smiling candidate moving confidently toward an inevitable victory.

Despite all the outward signs of optimism, developments on Tuesday increased apprehensions among Kennedy supporters. In response to the passionate demonstrations for Stevenson, the California delegation shifted from Kennedy to an even split between Kennedy and Stevenson. The Kansas and Iowa caucuses defied their respective governors, who had promised their delegations to Jack, by agreeing to cast first-ballot votes for favorite sons.

Simultaneously, Johnson kept up his attacks. Before the Washington state delegation he pilloried Joe Kennedy as a Nazi appeaser: "I wasn't any Chamberlain — umbrella policy man," he declared. "I never thought Hitler was right." Privately, Johnson's supporters asked whether a Catholic could put the interests of the country ahead of those of his church. On Tuesday afternoon, Johnson challenged Jack to a debate before the Massachusetts and Texas delegations. When Kennedy accepted, Johnson assailed his voting record on farm legislation and civil rights, and his absenteeism. Jack deftly turned aside the criticism by saying he saw no need for a debate with Johnson "because I don't think that Senator Johnson and I disagree on the great issues that face us." Jack then praised LBJ's record as majority leader and drew laughter by promising to support him for another term.

The excitement at the convention increased on Wednesday with the formal nominations of Johnson, Kennedy, and Stevenson. (Recognizing the hopelessness of his candidacy, Symington had dropped out.) The explosion of enthusiasm for Stevenson exceeded anything seen at a Democratic convention since William Jennings Bryan had gained the nomination on an emotional tide of protest in 1896. A brilliantly cadenced speech by Minnesota senator Eugene McCarthy ignited the demonstration. "Do not reject this man," McCarthy pleaded. "Do not reject this man who has made us all proud to be Democrats. Do not leave this prophet without honor in his own party." Having filled the floor and packed the galleries with their supporters, Stevenson's backers cheered, shouted, sang, chanted, marched, and snake-danced their way around the hall, shouting, "We want Stevenson." Only after party officials had turned out the lights could they restore order. Watching the spectacle on television at his father's rented Beverly Hills estate, Jack said, "Don't worry, Dad. Stevenson has everything but delegates." Joe was not so sure. The night before at a dinner party, he had been scathing about Stevenson's refusal to step aside: "Your man must be out of his mind," Joe said to Bill Blair. When Blair replied that he was for Jack, Joe "shook his fist at me and said, 'You've got 24 hours.'"

Jack was right about Stevenson's delegate support. But Bobby refused to take the nomination for granted. Earlier in the day, he had told organizers, "We can't miss a trick in the next twelve hours. If we don't win tonight, we're dead." Although they gained twice as many delegates as Johnson on the first ballot, they did not clinch the victory until the end of the roll call, when Wyoming's fifteen votes gave them 763 delegates, two more than the required majority. At the convention hall, where Jack and Bobby had a private moment together after the nomination, Jack could be seen smiling and Bobby, with his customary intensity and head bowed, repeatedly hitting the open palm of his left hand with the fist of his right hand. The next day, when Dick Daley tried to sell Jack on a vice presidential candidate with a reminder of how much he had done to help him get the nomination, Kennedy responded, "Not you nor anybody else nominated us. We did it ourselves."

CHAPTER 8

Election

I know nothing grander, better exercise, better digestion,
more positive proof of the past, the triumphant result of
faith in human kind, than a well-contested American
national election.

— Walt Whitman, "Democratic Vistas"

BECAUSE VICE PRESIDENTS traditionally counted for little after assuming office, presidential nominees thought almost exclusively about how their choice would affect the coming election. Indifference to qualifications had been so pronounced that in 1908, William Jennings Bryan had chosen an unknown wealthy eighty-four-year-old who would help finance his campaign. Woodrow Wilson had commented on the office, "In saying how little there is to be said about it, one has evidently said all there is to say." Despite seven presidential deaths elevating vice presidents, presidential candidates' thinking about possible successors remained largely the same. As recently as 1945, after making Truman his VP, Roosevelt had failed to inform him about the atomic bomb. The onset of the Cold War and Nixon's rise to political prominence, however, had made the vice presidency a more important office. And though Kennedy at age forty-three saw no reason to worry about dying, at least not since he had begun using replacement cortisone in 1947, he wanted someone who could help in a close election and have indisputable competence as a possible successor.

A rich field of candidates to choose from complicated Kennedy's decision. Humphrey, Johnson, and Symington were obvious front-runners, because of their rival candidacies and their standing as experienced congressional leaders. Senator Henry "Scoop" Jackson of Washington, an expert on defense issues, and even Stevenson were other possibilities.

Why and how Kennedy made his decision seems beyond precise recounting. We know that he had been thinking about the question for some time before the convention. On June 29, Sorensen had given him a list of twenty-one possibilities. According to Sorensen, Kennedy consulted other party leaders, who put Humphrey, Stevenson, Johnson, Symington, Minnesota liberal Orville Freeman, and Jackson at the top of their lists. Believing that it was an effective means to discourage bitter-end opposition from rivals for the presidency who were also interested in the second spot, Kennedy gave no clear indication of whom he would choose.

Liberal opposition to Kennedy before and during the convention reduced the likelihood that he would select someone from that camp. Stevenson's refusal to step aside and Humphrey's continuing resistance to Jack's nomination pushed them outside the circle. On July 14, the day after Jack's selection, when news commentator Edward Morgan privately asked him if he would give the vice presidency to Humphrey, Kennedy replied, "No, absolutely not. The credibility of that camp has been destroyed." As Stevenson, Humphrey, and Freeman urged party unity at the convention before Jack gave his acceptance speech, Joe, watching the proceedings at Time-Life publisher Henry Luce's house, made snide remarks about each of them. "There was no respect for any of these liberals," Luce said. "He just thought they were all fools on whom he had played this giant trick."

To be sure, in a race against Nixon, liberal support of the party's nominee was a given, but Kennedy's past problems with liberals and an aftermath of anger at him over Stevenson's defeat gave him reason to worry that some of them might stay away from the polls. He had tried to accommodate them by backing the strongest possible civil rights plank in the party's platform and telling Martin Luther King Jr. privately and the NAACP publicly that he wanted "no compromise of basic principles — no evasion of basic controversies — and no second-class citizenship for any American anywhere in this country." In his speech to the NAACP a few days before his nomination, he said it was not enough to fight segregation only in the South; he intended to combat "the more subtle but equally vicious forms of discrimination that are found in the clubs and churches and neighborhoods of the rest of the country." He also planned to use the "immense moral authority of the White House . . . to offer leadership and inspiration. . . . And the immense legal authority of the White House" to protect voting rights, end school segregation, and assure equal opportunity in federally funded jobs and housing.

Kennedy himself, at the end of June and again at the convention, had told Clark Clifford that he favored Symington. Labor leaders were partial to him, and his candidacy might help in the Midwest, where Jack did not think he would do well. The journalist John Seigenthaler of the *Nashville Tennessean* cited Robert Kennedy as also saying that Symington was Kennedy's choice. But, in fact, Symington was no more than a stalking-horse. Truman's backing for Symington was more a minus than a plus: Richard Daley's assertion that Symington's appeal downstate could make the difference in Illinois and Sorensen's prediction that he could help with farmers were insufficient to counter his youth. He was "too much like JFK (We don't want the ticket referred to as 'the whiz kids')," Sorensen told Kennedy.

The logical choice seemed to be Lyndon Johnson. At a personal level, the Kennedys were not well-disposed toward him. He had said harsh things about Jack and Joe and antagonized Bobby by rejecting his father's suggestion of an LBJ-JFK ticket in 1956. In November 1959, when Jack had sent Bobby to see Johnson at his Texas ranch to ask if he was running, Johnson, in some peculiar test of manhood or as a way of one-upping the Kennedys, insisted that he and Bobby hunt deer. When Bobby was knocked to the ground and cut above the eye by the recoil of a shotgun Johnson had lent him, Johnson exclaimed, "Son, you've got to learn to handle a gun like a man." It was an indication of his low regard for the whole Kennedy clan.

But with so much at stake, Jack put aside personal feelings about Johnson. Annoyance at Johnson for his attacks on Joe and Jack did not diminish the belief that he was well qualified to be president, if it ever came to that. In 1958, Kennedy had told MIT economist Walt W. Rostow that "the Democratic party owes Johnson the nomination. He's earned it. He wants the same things for the country that I do. But it's too close to Appomattox for Johnson to be nominated and elected. So, therefore, I feel free to run."

Politically, Johnson seemed the most likely of all to help win crucial states. The traditionally solid Democratic South promised to be a sharply contested battleground. An overtly liberal running mate wouldn't net any additional Kennedy votes in that region. In addition, reluctance among southern Protestants to vote for a Catholic worried Jack and encouraged him to seek an advantage in Texas and across the South by taking Johnson.

On Monday, July 11, when columnist Joe Alsop and *Washington Post* publisher Phil Graham urged Kennedy to pick Johnson, he "immediately agreed, so immediately as to leave me doubting the easy triumph," Graham recalled, "and I therefore restated the matter, urging him not to count on Johnson's turning it down but to offer the Vpship so persuasively as to win Johnson over. Kennedy was decisive in saying that was his intention, pointing out that Johnson would help the ticket not only in the South but in important segments of the Party all over the country." Johnson responded skeptically to the news, saying "he supposed the same message was going out to all the candidates."

Kennedy doubted that Johnson would accept an invitation to join the ticket. Johnson had declared, "I wouldn't want to trade a vote for a gavel, and I certainly wouldn't want to trade the active position of leadership of the greatest deliberative body in the world for the part-time job of presiding." On July 12, when Tommy Corcoran told Jack that asking Johnson was the best way to win in November and avoid a defeat that could discourage another Catholic from running "for generations," Kennedy had replied, "Stop kidding, Tommy, Johnson will turn me down." Kennedy found it difficult to imagine that as dominating a personality as LBJ would be willing to take a backseat to someone who had deprived him of the presidency, especially someone he viewed as less qualified and less deserving of the job.

In fact, Johnson wanted the vice presidency. By 1960, his control of the Senate as majority leader had begun to wane; the election of several liberals in 1958 had undercut his dominance. He also assumed that if Kennedy won the presidency without him, the White House would set the legislative agenda and he would be little more than the president's man in the Senate. Moreover, if Nixon became president, he would have to deal with a Republican chief who would be less accommodating than Eisenhower and less inclined to allow Johnson to exercise effective leadership. Running for vice president would not only free him from future problems as majority leader but also might give him significant benefits. If Kennedy lost, he would nevertheless have a claim on the Democratic nomination in 1964. And if Kennedy won, Johnson hoped to use his political talent, which had made him an exceptional majority leader, to expand the influence of the vice president's office as a prelude to running for president in 1968. The vice presidency is "my only chance ever to be President," Johnson told Clare Booth Luce, Henry Luce's wife and Eisenhower's ambassador to Italy. He also saw running with Kennedy as a way to elevate the role of his native region. As a congressman and a senator, he had devoted himself to bringing the South back into the mainstream of the country's economic and political life. An effective southern VP could influence policy making and open the way to the first southern president since the Civil War.

For all Jack's doubts about the majority leader's willingness to join him, Johnson had actually sent clear signals to Jack that he was interested in second place. Indeed, one month before the convention, in June, when Bobby Baker and Ted Sorensen had discussed the possibility, Baker had "cautioned" Sorensen "not to be so certain that his boss would reject a Kennedy-Johnson ticket." The day before Kennedy's nomination, Sam Rayburn told John McCormack and Tip O'Neill that "if Kennedy wants Johnson for Vice President . . . then he has nothing else he can do but to be on the ticket." Rayburn also said that if Jack called him with an offer for Johnson, he would insist that Johnson take it. When O'Neill gave Kennedy the message, Jack responded, "Of course I want Lyndon Johnson. . . . The only thing is, I would never want to offer it and have him turn me down; I would be terrifically embarrassed. He's the natural. If I can ever get him on the ticket, no way we can lose." Kennedy promised to call Rayburn that night. Immediately after Jack won the nomination, Johnson sent him a warm telegram of congratulations with the sentence, "LBJ now means Let's Back Jack."

The telegram solidified Kennedy's decision. At about 2 A.M. Powers called Johnson's hotel room so that Jack could speak with him. When an aide said that Johnson was asleep, Kennedy asked Evelyn Lincoln to arrange a meeting with Johnson at ten in the morning. At 8:00 A.M. Jack met privately with Bobby in his Biltmore suite. As they came out of the room where they had been talking, Powers heard Bobby say, "If you are sure it's what you want to do, go ahead and see him." Bobby returned to his room for a bath. When O'Donnell entered Bob's suite, Salinger greeted him with the news that Bobby had just asked him "to add up the electoral votes in the states we're sure of and to add Texas." O'Donnell, who, with Kennedy's approval, had promised labor leaders and civil rights groups that they would never take LBJ, was furious. In the bathroom of Jack's suite, the only place O'Donnell and Kennedy could find for a private discussion, O'Donnell told him, "This is the worst mistake you ever made." It meant going "against all the people who supported you." He warned that they would have to spend the campaign apologizing for having Johnson on the ticket and "trying to explain why he voted against everything you ever stood for."

Kennedy turned pale with anger. He was "so upset and hurt that it took him a while before he was able to collect himself." He explained that he was less concerned with southern votes than with getting Johnson out of the Senate, where he could play havoc with a Kennedy administration legislative agenda. With Johnson gone, "I'll have [Montana senator] Mike Mansfield as the leader . . . " Kennedy said, "somebody I can trust and depend on." He urged O'Donnell to carry this message to labor leaders and liberals more generally, who were as exercised by the news as O'Donnell was.

But the liberals were not so easily appeased. When a labor group went to Kennedy's suite at eleven o'clock, Bobby "was very distressed, Ken O'Donnell looked like a ghost, and Jack Kennedy was very nervous." Jack justified his decision by saying that Johnson "would be so mean as Majority Leader — that it was much better having him as Vice President where you could control him." Kennedy also tried to leave the question open by saying that he could not "see any reason in the world why [Johnson] would want it." One of the labor leaders warned, "If you do this, you're going to fuck everything up." They threatened to block Johnson's nomination with a floor fight.

Jack and Bobby spent the afternoon trying to resolve the dilemma. Bobby went to see Johnson at about 2 P.M. to describe the opposition and suggest that he might want to be Democratic national chairman instead of vice president. When Johnson refused to see Bobby, he gave the message to Sam Rayburn, who fixed Bobby with "a long look and responded simply, 'Shit.'" Phil Graham then called Jack to say that Johnson would only take the nomination if Kennedy "drafted" him. Jack replied that "he was in a general mess because some liberals were against LBJ." Kennedy asked Graham to call back in three minutes, when he would finish a meeting and have a decision. During their next conversation, Kennedy told Graham, "It's all set. . . . Tell Lyndon I want him."

But Jack remained unsure. He sent word to Johnson through Rayburn that he would call him directly at about 3 P.M. When no call came, Graham called Jack at 3:30. Though Kennedy promised to call Johnson at once, "he then again mentioned opposition to LBJ and asked for my judgment." Graham predicted that southern gains would surpass liberal losses and urged against any change in plans. Shortly after 4:00 P.M., Johnson summoned Graham, who reported that Bobby had just been back and urged him to "withdraw for the sake of the party." As Bobby remembered it, he told Johnson that there was a lot of opposition and that his brother "didn't think he wanted to go through that kind of unpleasant fight." Instead, Jack wanted him to run the party, and he could put his people in control as a prelude to running for president in eight years. Bobby recalled that Johnson looked like "he'd burst into tears. I didn't know if it was just an act or anything. But he just shook and tears came into his eyes, and he said, 'I want to be Vice President, and if the President will have me, I'll join with him in making a fight for it.'" Bobby then reversed course and responded, "Well, then, that's fine. He wants you to be Vice President if you want to be Vice President."

Amid the confusion, Graham now called Jack again. Kennedy, to hide his own ambivalence and reassure Johnson, told Graham, "Bobby's been out of touch and doesn't know what's been happening." Graham believed that Bobby had acted on his own in trying to bar Johnson from the ticket. Bobby disputed this: "With the close relationship between my brother and me, I wasn't going down to see if he would withdraw just as a lark on my own." His explanation rings true. Jack *was* trying to avoid a fight with liberals, but ultimately he was less concerned about offending them than with the price of forcing Johnson off the ticket and then seeing him do nothing for, or even quietly oppose, his election in the South.

Kennedy was not alone in his calculations. More realistic liberals saw Johnson as adding strength to the ticket and had no interest in dividing the party and helping to elect Nixon. Realizing this, and because Johnson promised to support the party's civil rights plank, they backed away from a floor fight. The Kennedys further finessed the issue at the convention by suspending the rules and asking for a voice ballot just before the voting reached Michigan, the delegation most likely to oppose Johnson. Although the shouted "ayes" and "nays" seemed about evenly divided, Governor LeRoy Collins of Florida, the convention chairman, declared that two thirds of the delegates had concurred and announced Johnson's nomination by acclamation. Eisenhower, who remembered Johnson's warnings about Kennedy, told journalist Earl Mazo, "I turned on the television and there was that son of a bitch becoming a vice-presidential candidate with this 'dangerous man.'"

HAVING SECURED THE NOMINATION through an exhausting campaign and settled the vice presidential dispute without serious political damage, Kennedy confronted the election battle with relief and excitement. He saw much work to be done and numerous political shoals to be navigated, but he was clear on the central theme or principal direction of his campaign. He shared a belief with most commentators and analysts that America had lost its sense of national purpose, that the material well-being of the 1950s had translated into a "bland, vapid, self-satisfied, banal" society lacking the moral resolve to meet domestic and world problems. "The prosperity of the Eisenhower age is a deceptive sign of vigor and health," *Commentary* editor Norman Podhoretz declared. He complained of the "boredom one senses on all sides, the torpor, the anxiety, the listlessness." Literary critic Dwight Macdonald described Americans as "an unhappy people, a people without style, without a sense of what is humanly satisfying." Adlai Stevenson feared that the fifties would end up like the twenties, when private gain had eclipsed public concern and then ended in disaster. Stevenson asked, "With the supermarket as our temple and the singing commercial as our litany, are we likely to fire the world with an irresistible vision of America's exalted purposes and inspiring way of life?"

Kennedy also saw the need to reestablish a sense of shared purpose, of inspirational goals, at the center of his campaign. Could an America that had become the richest, most comfortable society in world history stand up to the communist challenge? Were we as ready to make the kind of sacrifices the ideologues in Moscow and Peking urged upon their peoples in the long struggle they foresaw with the United States? Could we be as fired as the revolutionaries in Cuba, Laos, Vietnam, and Africa?

In an early-evening acceptance speech at the Los Angeles Coliseum before eighty thousand people and a television audience of millions, Kennedy sounded his theme. Close observers agreed that his speech was imperfectly delivered: Kennedy was exhausted by the exertions of the last few days and partly blinded by the setting sun.

(His disappointing performance convinced him in the future to increase the amounts of steroids he normally took whenever he faced the stress of giving a major speech or press conference.) Although the speech, to which a number of writers, including Ted Sorensen, made contributions, was a familiar recitation of campaign themes, it nevertheless was a memorable appeal to the country to renew its commitment to larger goals than personal, self-serving ones.

Early on he addressed the opportunity Americans had to overcome an unspoken religious test for election to the highest office: "The Democratic Party, by nominating someone of my faith, has taken on . . . a new and hazardous risk," he said. The answer to anyone who believed that his religion would hinder him as president was his record of rejecting "any kind of religious pressure or obligation that might directly or indirectly interfere with my conduct of the Presidency in the national interest. . . . I am telling you now what you are entitled to know: that my decisions on every public policy will be my own — as an American, a Democrat and a free man."

More important than this parochial issue were the larger problems of war and peace, of economic and social justice, and of the willingness of Americans to commit themselves to these noble ends. "Today our concern must be with the future," Kennedy announced. "For the world is changing. The old era is ending. The old ways will not do. Abroad, the balance of power is shifting. There are new and more terrible weapons — new and uncertain nations — new pressures of population and deprivation. . . . The world has been close to war before — but now man, who has survived all previous threats to his existence, has taken into his mortal hands the power to exterminate the entire species some seven times over. Here at home, the changing face of the future is equally revolutionary. The New Deal and the Fair Deal were bold measures for their generations — but this is a new generation. . . .

"Too many Americans have lost their way, their will and their sense of historic purpose," Kennedy asserted. "It is a time, in short, for a new generation of leadership — new men to cope with new problems and new opportunities. . . . I stand tonight facing west on what was once the last frontier," Kennedy said with evident passion and conviction. "From the lands that stretch three thousand miles behind me, the pioneers of old gave up their safety, their comfort and sometimes their lives to build a new world here in the West. They were not the captives of their own doubts, the prisoners of their own price tags. Their motto was not 'every man for himself' — but 'all for the common cause.' . . . We stand today on the edge of a New Frontier — the frontier of the 1960s — a frontier of unknown opportunities and perils — a frontier of unfulfilled hopes and threats."

Kennedy had little use for slogans. But he understood that to mobilize Americans, he needed a captivating image, and the New Frontier was Kennedy's way of communicating the challenge, the country's fresh rendezvous with greatness. "The New Frontier of which I speak," he explained, "is not a set of promises — it is a set of challenges. It sums up not what I intend to *offer* the American people, but what I intend to *ask* of them. . . . Can a nation organized and governed such as ours endure? That is the real question. Have we the nerve and the will? . . . Are we up to the task — are we equal to the challenge? . . . That is the question of the New Frontier. That is the choice our nation must make — a choice . . . between the public interest and the private comfort — between national greatness and national decline. . . . All mankind waits upon our decision. A whole world looks to see what we will do. We cannot fail their trust, we cannot fail to try."

THE JULY DAYS after the convention were a heady time for Jack and his whole family. He had gained the second most coveted prize in American politics — a presidential nomination — and now stood only one campaign away from becoming the thirty-fourth American ever to reach the White House. Initial polls following the Democratic convention gave Jack a 17 to 22 percent lead in the five biggest states — California, Illinois, New York, Pennsylvania, and Texas.

A prominent member of a famous family, Kennedy had long known what it was like to be under public scrutiny. But the attention accorded him and his family after the nomination surpassed anything he or his famous father had ever experienced. To recuperate from the months of traveling and the pressures of the convention, Jack flew from Los Angeles to Hyannis Port to rest, swim, cruise on the family yacht, sun himself with Bobby and others on lawn chairs, and talk about the coming campaign. Jackie, who was five months pregnant, was to take almost no part in the general election.

Arthur Schlesinger Jr. remembers a visit to the Kennedy compound on a "shining summer Saturday. . . . The once placid Cape Cod village had lost its wistful tranquillity. It looked more like a town under military occupation, or a place where dangerous criminals or wild beasts were at large. Everywhere were roadblocks, cordons of policemen, photographers with cameras slung over their shoulders . . . tourists in flashy shirts and shorts waiting expectantly as if for a revelation. The atmosphere of a carnival or a hanging prevailed. . . . A stockade now half surrounded the Kennedy compound, and the approach was like crossing a frontier, with documents demanded every ten feet."

Schlesinger "had never seen Kennedy in better form — more relaxed, funny and free." The afternoon was spent cruising serenely for several hours off the Cape, with Martha's Vineyard dimly outlined in the distance. Swimming, cocktails, luncheon, and conversation filled a perfect day. But politics remained near to hand. Jack, Bobby, O'Brien, O'Donnell, Powers, Salinger, Sorensen, and Joe were all churning in anticipation of launching the fight for the greatest prize, and after only two days of rest at the Cape, Jack and Bobby plunged into a series of planning meetings, strategy sessions, and unity discussions with party rivals. Bobby summed up their outlook: "run and fight and scramble for ten weeks all the way."

Bobby gave new meaning to the term "hardball": There was nothing subtle about his approach. "Gentlemen," he told a group of New York reform Democrats, "I don't give a damn if the state and county organizations survive after November, and I don't give a damn if *you* survive. I want to elect John F. Kennedy." The campaign's Florida coordinator said Bobby was "absolutely strong, steel-willed. . . . He just was blunt and hard and tough and was of course a magnificent campaign manager." Party workers who displeased him complained, "Little Brother Is Watching You." Adlai Stevenson dubbed him the "Black Prince," and Eisenhower, who called Jack "Little Boy Blue," referred to Bobby as "that little shit." Bobby was mindful of all the hard feelings but not apologetic: "I'm not running a popularity contest," he told Hugh Sidey. "It doesn't matter if they like me or not. . . . If people are not getting off their behinds and working enough, how do you say that nicely? Every time you make a decision in this business you make somebody mad."

If Bobby was the taskmaster, the relentless overseer demanding superhuman efforts from everyone, Jack was the conciliator, the candidate eager to bring everyone to his side in the service of progressive goals. "This was a politician who knew what his duties were and he accepted them not without relish," Henry Brandon, the Washington correspondent for the London *Sunday Times*, noted in a memo to himself after a conversation with Jack in June. "He is a child of his times. He instinctively knows how to use all the techniques of the modern mass media to his best advantage. . . . He may lack warmth, he may be cold and calculating, but those eager to work for him suspect or at least hope that he would follow up ideas with action." By contrast with Bobby, for example, whose visceral dislike of LBJ clouded his political judgment, Jack let practical electoral calculations be his guide.

Similarly, despite his personal antagonism toward Stevenson, Jack met with him at the Cape at the end of July to ask for his help with New York liberals. When Stevenson suggested the creation of a foreign policy task force to prepare for a possible transition to the presidency, Jack immediately agreed and asked him to head it. In early August, Jack went to Independence, Missouri, to seek Harry Truman's support. Campaign imperatives dissolved his anger toward Truman for having been against his nomination. Truman, who despised Nixon, was receptive to Jack's appeal. He told Abe Ribicoff, "I never liked Kennedy. I hate his father. Kennedy wasn't so great as a Senator. . . . However, that no good son-of-a-bitch Dick Nixon called me a Communist and I'll do anything to beat him." Asked by reporters how he could see Kennedy as now ready for the presidency after having described him in July as too young and inexperienced, Truman replied with a grin, "When the Democratic convention decided to nominate him, that's when I decided."

Kennedy then traveled to Hyde Park, New York, to enlist Eleanor Roosevelt in his cause. Like Truman, the onetime antagonist was now eager to help. Jack gave her "the distinct feeling that he is planning to work closely with Adlai. I also had the feeling," she wrote a friend, "that here was a man who could learn. I liked him better than I ever had before because he seemed so little cock-sure, and I think he has a mind that is open to new ideas. . . . My final judgement is that here is a man who wants to leave a record (perhaps for ambitious personal reasons, as people say), but I rather think because he really is interested in helping the people of his own country and mankind in general. I will be surer of this as time goes on, but I think I am not mistaken in feeling that he would make a good President if elected."

Kennedy's success with Truman, Stevenson, and Eleanor Roosevelt did not translate into grass roots enthusiasm for his candidacy among liberals. Although Kennedy had voiced his support for pro-

Boston mayor John F. "Honey Fitz" Fitzgerald, JFK's maternal grandfather; he launched the family political dynasty. JOHN F. KENNEDY LIBRARY

JFK's middle-class childhood home in Brookline, Massachusetts, before the Kennedys became one of the country's richest families. JOHN F. KENNEDY LIBRARY

Rose Kennedy in 1922 with her five children: Eunice, Kathleen, Rosemary, John, and Joseph Jr. (Another four would be born between 1924 and 1932.)
BACHRACH STUDIOS

The ten-year-old John F. Kennedy in 1927; his mother remembered him as a boy with his own ideas.
JOHN F. KENNEDY LIBRARY

The already storied Kennedy family in September 1931: Joe, Rose, and eight children. (Ted would be born in 1932.) JOHN F. KENNEDY LIBRARY

We're puttin' on our top hat,
Tyin' up our white tie,
Brushin' off our tails,

In order to
Wish you

A Merry Christmas

Rip.   Leem.   Ken.

JFK in November 1935 with Ralph "Rip" Horton and LeMoyne Billings. Classmates at Choate, they enjoyed breaking school rules and became lifelong friends. JOHN F. KENNEDY LIBRARY

JFK enjoying himself in Nuremberg, Germany, in August 1937, on his first visit to Europe, where international tensions sparked his interest in public affairs. JOHN F. KENNEDY LIBRARY

Joe Jr., Joe, and Jack aboard ship after Joe had become FDR's ambassador to Britain in 1938. JOHN F. KENNEDY LIBRARY

America's most prominent Catholic family: Joe, Rose, and all the children except Joe Jr. at Pope Pius XII's investiture, 1939. JOHN F. KENNEDY LIBRARY

JFK, who became a serious student in his final two years of college, at his Harvard graduation, June 1940.
JOHN F. KENNEDY LIBRARY

Jack in 1943 in the Solomon Islands, where he saw extensive combat.
JOHN F. KENNEDY LIBRARY

Jack commanded *PT 109*, which was cut in half by a Japanese destroyer in 1943, killing two of the crew and leading to Jack's prominence as a hero who rescued the rest of his men. JOHN F. KENNEDY LIBRARY

JFK and Lem Billings in wartime uniforms, 1944. Despite medical conditions that exempted them, both chose to serve. JOHN F. KENNEDY LIBRARY

Jack speaking on Memorial Day, May 30, 1946, during his first congressional campaign. His decision to enter politics came after Joe Jr.'s death in the war but reflected a lifelong fascination with shaping public affairs. JOHN F. KENNEDY LIBRARY

Jack voting in the primary with his grandparents, June 1946. Mayor Fitzgerald's prominence in Boston helped Jack defeat more experienced political rivals. JOHN F. KENNEDY LIBRARY

Joe and Rose in 1948 at Hyannis Port, the family's Massachusetts home, with six of the children. Joe and Kathleen had died, and Rosemary had been institutionalized after an unsuccessful lobotomy to ease physical and emotional problems dating from her birth. JOHN F. KENNEDY LIBRARY

Jack (in background) as a congressman, during a 1951 visit to Vietnam, where the French were struggling to hang on to their colony. JOHN F. KENNEDY LIBRARY

JFK, whose lifelong medical problems included osteoporosis of the lumbar spine and almost constant pain, on crutches, circa 1952. JOHN F. KENNEDY LIBRARY

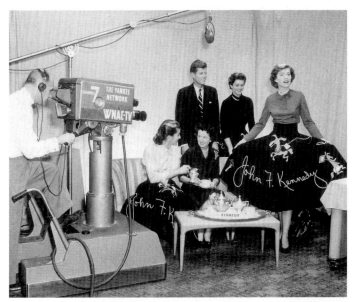

Jack with his mother and sisters Eunice, Pat, and Jean, who hosted teas during his 1952 Senate campaign against incumbent Henry Cabot Lodge Jr. JOHN F. KENNEDY LIBRARY

Jack with campaign workers in Fall River, Massachusetts. By 1952 he had become a skillful campaigner. JOHN F. KENNEDY LIBRARY

Best of luck to John Kennedy
Oct. 17, 1952
Harry Truman

President Harry S
Truman helping Jack
in the 1952 campaign.
JOHN F. KENNEDY
LIBRARY

Jack with Lodge, November 10, 1952, a few days after scoring an upset victory
over him. JOHN F. KENNEDY LIBRARY

Jack and Jackie at their wedding party, September 12, 1953, at her stepfather's Rhode Island estate. Theirs was described as the "celebrity marriage of the year." JOHN F. KENNEDY LIBRARY

Jack and Jackie with a secretary in Jack's Senate office. The prominent and highly attractive couple had private tensions over Jack's undiminished affinity for womanizing. JOHN F. KENNEDY LIBRARY

Jack with brother Bobby, his closest friend and political collaborator, at a Senate hearing on labor corruption in May 1957. JOHN F. KENNEDY LIBRARY

Support for Jack by ethnic voters helped him win the Wisconsin Democratic primary in April 1960. JOHN F. KENNEDY LIBRARY

JFK and Nixon during the first of four televised debates, September 26, 1960, that helped Kennedy defeat Nixon by a paper-thin margin. AP/WIDE WORLD PHOTOS

Jack with his family meeting the press at the Hyannis Port Armory after Nixon had conceded the election, November 9, 1960. ©NEW BEDFORD STANDARD-TIMES

gressive legislation during a special August congressional session, liberal interest in his campaign remained flat. Part of the reason was a lack of liberal positions on the Kennedy platform. After Stevenson saw Jack at the Cape, he had written Mrs. Roosevelt that Kennedy's "interest and concentration seemed to be on organization not ideas at this stage." Schlesinger, who doubted the wisdom of giving highest priority to building a campaign organization, as Jack and Bobby planned, told Jack at the end of August, "Organization has an important role to play, of course; but to suppose that organization *per se* will win New York or California is nonsense." Jack needed "to elicit the all-out support of the kind of people who have traditionally provided the spark in Democratic campaigns. . . . The liberals, the reformers, the intellectuals . . . people who have entered politics, not because it is their livelihood, but because they care deeply about issues and principles. . . . Once the issue-minded Democrats catch fire, then the campaign will gather steam." Harvard professor Henry Kissinger, "who hardly qualifies as a bleeding heart," Schlesinger wrote a few days later, ". . . said to me, 'We need someone who will take a big jump — not just improve on existing trends but produce a new frame of mind, a new national atmosphere. If Kennedy debates Nixon on who can best manage the status quo, he is lost. The issue is not one technical program or another. The issue is a new epoch.'"

Kennedy was receptive to Schlesinger's prodding. "I don't mind criticism at this point," he told him. "I would rather have you tell me now than to wait until November." In the middle of September, Kennedy met the problem head-on with a strong speech before the Liberal party in New York, where he sounded familiar liberal themes, which began to evoke the sort of excitement Schlesinger saw as essential to a winning campaign.

IT WAS APPARENT by September that much more than liberal enthusiasm was essential if Jack was going to beat Nixon. The Republican convention at the end of July — a coronation of sorts for Nixon and running mate Henry Cabot Lodge, featuring effective speeches about the Soviet challenge and the nominees' superior capacity to enhance national security — boosted Republican poll numbers. Gallup trial heats showed Nixon ahead by 53 to 47 percent in one survey and 50 to 44 percent in another. As troubling, 31 percent of Nixon-Lodge supporters said they were "very strongly" committed to their candidates, while only 22 percent of Kennedy-Johnson backers expressed the same intensity. Happily, from Kennedy's viewpoint, 60 percent of Americans said that they had paid little or no attention to the presidential race so far.

The Kennedys expected Nixon to fight hard and dirty. During four years together in the House, Kennedy and Nixon had enjoyed a civil relationship. During the fifties, however, Nixon's campaign tactics and harsh attacks on the Democrats, which echoed some of McCarthy's excesses, had diminished Kennedy's regard for him. To be behind in the polls before Nixon unleashed any trademark kidney punches was discouraging.

By the end of August, a new poll showed Nixon and Kennedy locked in a dead heat. Neither man had convinced a majority of voters that he was better qualified to be president. Nixon's reputation for excessive partisanship and Kennedy's youth and Catholicism dulled public enthusiasm for seeing one or the other in the White House.

Despite the improvement in Jack's public standing, the Kennedys were still distressed. While Nixon moved freely about the country in August, emphasizing his fitness for the highest office, the special congressional session kept Jack tied down in Washington. Teddy White saw a firsthand demonstration of the Kennedy frustration during a visit to Jack's campaign headquarters. While he sat chatting with two Kennedy staffers, Bobby emerged from an inner office and began to shout: " 'What are you doing?! What are we all doing? Let's get on the road! Let's get on the road tomorrow! I want us all on the road tomorrow!' And without waiting for a reply, he clapped the door shut and disappeared."

Fueling Bobby's explosion were emerging attacks on Jack's character and record that put him on the defensive and distracted him from an affirmative appeal to voters. In response, the campaign produced a "Counterattack Sourcebook" for use in answering derogatory assertions about Kennedy's religion, health, inexperience, profligate campaign spending, voting record on labor, civil liberties, and civil rights, opposition to southern interests, Senate attendance, response to McCarthyism, and opposition to France's repressive Algerian policy.

Warnings that Kennedy's Catholicism and youth made him unfit for the White House worried Jack and Bobby the most. "Senator Kennedy is an attractive young man, but he is untrained for the job of President," Republicans asserted. He had never held an executive position or had any experience in strategic military planning or in dealing with the communists. At the age of forty-three, "he would be the youngest man ever elected to the White House," and at the age of thirty-one, his "wife is too young to be First Lady." John Kenneth Galbraith told the brothers that after speaking with more than "a hundred journalists, farm leaders, dirt farmers and Democratic professionals," he had concluded that "religion in the rural corn belt, Great Plains and down into rural Texas has become an issue greater than either income or peace. . . . In the absence of a clear view of what either candidate stands for or can do about these issues, religion is entering as a deciding factor." And the complaints came from both sides: Some prominent Catholics were unhappy with Jack's opposition to "the Catholic position on many public issues."

A more muted concern was gossip about Jack's womanizing. In June 1959, the FBI had received letters and a photograph "containing allegations regarding personal immorality on the part of Jack Kennedy. Apparently," the FBI's memo noted, "this data has received widespread distribution — correspondent allegedly sent copies to 'about thirty-five reporters.'" The memo also noted that "some months ago," the Bureau "had received from a reliable source information . . . on Senator Kennedy's sex life. You will also recall that we have detailed substantial information in Bu[reau] files reflecting that Kennedy carried on an illicit relationship with another man's wife during World War II." In March 1960, the agent in charge of the New Orleans Bureau office reported that members of the mob, in conjunction with Frank Sinatra, were financially supporting Kennedy's campaign. The agent also related "a conversation which indicated that Senator Kennedy had been compromised with a woman in Las Vegas, Nevada." There were also reports that an airline hostess in Miami had been "sent to visit Sen. Kennedy." In May, the Bureau received a photo published in a right-wing newspaper of Jack "leaving his girlfriend's house at 1 o'clock in the morning. She is a glamour employee of his."

Rumors about Kennedy's philandering were so common that Henry Van Dusen of the Union Theological Seminary in New York asked Adlai Stevenson "to sit down with . . . some . . . friends who would like to silence the stories about Senator Kennedy." But Stevenson, who knew "nothing himself first hand," was unwilling to give credence to the gossip. He believed that Kennedy "may have been overactive in that direction prior to 1955," when acute back problems had put his survival in doubt. But after a series of operations gave him "a normal expectancy he seems to have settled down to preparing himself for his ambition — the Presidency." Stevenson found confirmation for this conclusion in the fact that "most of the stories about his private life seem to date from 1955 and before. My view, therefore, is that such rumors are out of date and largely unsubstantiated. And I must add even if they were true they would hardly seem to be crucial when the alternative is Nixon! Having been the victim of ugly rumors myself, I find this whole business distasteful in the extreme!"

Stevenson was not the only one who saw public discussion of an elected official's sex life as out of bounds. William Randolph Hearst, the great press baron who was "a pioneer of slash-and-burn assaults on public figures," drew the line at probing into private lives, and Hearst — vulnerable himself to charges of being a libertine — was quite representative of media mores in the 1950s and early 1960s. Humphrey, Johnson, Nixon, and even Jimmy Hoffa, who despised the Kennedys and would have done almost anything to beat Jack, said many unflattering things about him, but, in a universe of harsh assaults on political enemies, discussions of sexual escapades crossed the line. The thirty-five reporters mentioned in the FBI memo, for example, never used the information in a story. It may be that they could not find sufficient confirmation of the rumors. Or, in Nixon's case, like Hearst, he may have feared attacks on himself as a hypocrite. Congressman Richard Bolling had heard stories about Nixon's having a girlfriend, and Bolling learned that Joe Kennedy was ready to unleash an airing of such if Nixon made an issue of Jack's philandering. But the standards of the time made such a tit for tat almost impossible to imagine, and Jack did not worry that his womanizing would play any significant part in the campaign, unlike attacks on his religion and youth.

Religion remained an obstacle. On September 7, the *New York Times* carried a front-page article about the ironically named National Conference of Citizens for Religious Freedom, an organization of 150 Protestant ministers led by Dr. Norman Vincent Peale; they said that the Roman Catholic Church, with its dual role as both a church and a temporal state, made Kennedy's faith a legitimate issue in the campaign. Like Khrushchev, one member declared, Kennedy was "a captive of a system." Although the clergymen were all conservative Republicans eager for Nixon's election (and were guilty of transparent hypocrisy in doing what they said Kennedy's church would do — interfere in secular politics), their political machinations did not cancel out the effects of their warnings.

Estimates suggested that unless this propaganda was countered and the anti-Catholic bias overcome, Kennedy's religion might cost him as many as 1.5 million votes. The Kennedy campaign quickly organized a Community Relations division to meet the religious problem head-on. James Wine, a staff member at the National Council of Churches, headed the operation. Wine was as busy as any member of Jack's campaign team, answering between six hundred and a thousand letters a week and urging lay and clerical Protestants to combat the explicit and implicit anti-Catholicism in so much of the anti-Kennedy rhetoric.

A highly effective and much publicized appearance Kennedy made before a group of Protestant ministers in Houston, Texas, on September 12 helped. Bobby, Jack's campaign staff, Johnson, and Rayburn all advised against the appearance. "They're mostly Republicans and they're out to get you," Rayburn told Kennedy. But Kennedy believed he had to confront the issue sometime, and he wanted to do it early in the campaign so that he could move on to more constructive matters. "I'm getting tired of these people who think I want to replace the gold at Fort Knox with a supply of holy water," he told O'Donnell and Powers. In fact, his knowledge of Church doctrine and ties to the Church were so limited that he brought in John Cogley, a Catholic scholar, to coach him in preparation for his appearance.

Although he saw his speech and response to audience questions, which were to follow his remarks, as a crucial moment in the campaign, Kennedy went before the audience of three hundred in Houston's Rice Hotel Crystal ballroom (and the millions of television viewers around the country) with no hesitation or obvious sign of nervousness. The sincerity of what he had to say armed him against his adversaries and conveyed a degree of inner surety that converted a few opponents and persuaded some undecided voters that he had the maturity and balance to become a fine president.

He began his speech by emphasizing that although the religious question was the one before them tonight, he saw "far more critical issues in the 1960 election . . . for war and hunger and ignorance and despair know no religious barrier." But his religion was the immediate concern, and he stated his views and intentions without equivocation. He declared his belief in "an America where the separation of church and state is absolute. . . . I believe in a President whose views on religion are his own private affair, neither imposed on him by the nation or imposed by the nation upon him as a condition to holding that office. . . . I am not the Catholic candidate for President," he declared. "I am the Democratic Party's candidate for President, who happens also to be a Catholic. I do not speak for my church on public matters — and the church does not speak for me. . . . If the time should ever come . . . when my office would require me to either violate my conscience, or violate the national interest, then I would resign the office, and I would hope that any other conscientious public servant would do likewise." He ended with a plea for religious tolerance that would serve the national well-being. "If this election is decided on the basis that 40,000,000 Americans lost their chance of being President on the day they were baptized, then it is the whole nation that will be the loser in the eyes of Catholics and non-Catholics around the world, in the eyes of history, and in the eyes of our people."

Although some of the questions that followed showed an indifference to his pledges, he responded with such poise and restraint that the ministers stood and applauded at the close of the meeting, and some came forward to shake his hand and wish him well in the campaign. Rayburn, who watched the speech on television, shouted, "By God, look at him — and listen to him! He's eating them blood raw. This young feller will be a great President!"

THE HOUSTON APPEARANCE temporarily muted the religious issue and allowed Kennedy to concentrate on convincing voters that he was not too young or inexperienced to be president. The surest way to counter these assertions was to compete directly with Nixon in a debate. Eisenhower advised Nixon against accepting the unprecedented challenge of a televised confrontation: He was much better known than Kennedy, had eight years of executive experience as vice president, and had established himself as an effective spokesman and defender of the national interest by standing up to a stone-throwing mob in Caracas, Venezuela, in 1958 and to Khrushchev in the Moscow "kitchen debate" in 1959. But Nixon relished confrontations with adversaries and, remembering his successful appearance before the TV cameras in the 1952 campaign (his Checkers speech — a response to allegations of accepting illegal gifts — was the most successful use of television by an American politician to that date), he agreed to four debates. He also believed that saying no to a debate could cost him politically in the new TV age.

Kennedy was as confident, especially after his Houston appearance, that he could establish himself as more worthy of the White House by besting or even just holding his own against Nixon before the press and millions of TV viewers. Either outcome would refute assertions about his being too immature to merit election.

Consequently, on the evening of September 26, in Chicago's CBS studio, the two candidates joined Howard K. Smith, the moderator, and a four-member panel of television reporters to discuss campaign issues before some seventy million Americans, nearly two thirds of the country's adult population. Kennedy had spent most of the day preparing responses to possible questions. As campaign historian Theodore White described him, Kennedy lay on his bed in the Ambassador East Hotel dressed in a white, V-neck T-shirt and khaki pants and holding a pack of "fact cards" prepared by aides; he reviewed a variety of topics, tossing each card onto the floor as he finished a subject. Suggestions from his speechwriters for an eight-minute opening statement did not satisfy him, and he dictated his own version to a secretary.

Although he and Nixon spent a great part of the contest arguing over specific issues, Kennedy gained an early advantage by addressing his opening statement directly to the American people. He did the same in his closing statement. By contrast, Nixon used his introduction and summary to draw contrasts between himself and Kennedy. The difference was telling: Kennedy came across as a leader who intended to deal with the nation's greatest problems; Nixon registered on voters as someone trying to gain an advantage over an adversary. Nixon's language was restrained, but in comparison to Kennedy he came off as unstatesmanlike, confirming the negative impression many had of him from earlier House, Senate, and vice presidential campaigns. Henry Cabot Lodge, his running mate, who had urged Nixon not to be abrasive, said as the debate ended, "That son of a bitch just lost the election."

Kennedy, as was universally agreed, also got the better of Nixon because he looked more relaxed, more in command of himself, or, as Theodore White wrote, "calm and nerveless. . . . The Vice-President, by contrast, was tense, almost frightened, at turns glowering and, occasionally, haggard-looking to the point of sickness." The camera showed Nixon "half slouched, his 'Lazy Shave' powder faintly streaked with sweat, his eyes exaggerated hollows of blackness, his jaws, jowls, and face drooping with strain." ("My God!" Mayor Daley said, "They've embalmed him before he even died.") In addition, against the light gray stage backdrop, Nixon, dressed in a light gray suit, "faded into a fuzzed outline, while Kennedy in his dark suit had the crisp picture edge of contrast." Not yet fully recovered from a recent hospitalization to care for an infected knee injured in an accident, and exhausted by intense campaigning, Nixon appeared scrawny and listless. Ironically, Kennedy, whose medical problems greatly exceeded anything Nixon had, appeared to be the picture of robust good health.* Kennedy further seized the advantage during the debate when he looked bored or amused as Nixon spoke, as if he were thinking, "How silly."

At the end of the debate, as they stood on stage exchanging pleasantries, Nixon, watching photographers out of the corner of his eye, "put a stern expression on his face and started jabbing his finger into my chest, so he would look as if he were laying down the law to me about foreign policy or Communism," Kennedy said. Again, the image was not one of command but of a schoolyard bully.

ALTHOUGH POLLS and larger, more enthusiastic crowds encouraged the belief that Kennedy had won the first debate, he knew it would be folly to take a lead for granted. And by contrast with TV viewers, the radio audience thought that Nixon had defeated Kennedy, demonstrating how important the contrasting visual images were before the cameras. Kennedy saw the race as still too close to call, and as likely to turn on voter feelings about past and current Republican failings. Attacks on the GOP, however, needed to

---

*Somebody in the Nixon campaign might have thought otherwise: Attempts to steal records from two of Kennedy's doctors' New York offices may have been the work of Nixon aides trying to build on Johnson's accusations, which, according to *New York Times* columnist William Safire, had been passed along to them by a "disgruntled" LBJ supporter unhappy with JFK's nomination. Although forty-two years later, participants in the Nixon campaign and others sympathetic to Nixon emphatically denied the allegation, the episodes certainly can be read as preludes to Watergate and a break-in at Daniel Ellsberg's psychiatrist's office in Beverly Hills. Moreover, John Ehrlichman, an advance man in the 1960 campaign, acknowledged "dirty tricks" on both sides. None of this is a clear demonstration that a Nixon operative tried to steal Kennedy's medical records, but it is plausible. Who else but the Nixon campaign would have benefited from obtaining them?

exclude mention of Eisenhower, who remained popular. Journalist John Bartlow Martin, who had written speeches for Stevenson and was now doing the same for Kennedy, urged Jack to answer complaints that improper makeup had hurt Nixon in the debate by saying, "No matter how many makeup experts they bring into the television studio, it's still the same old Richard Nixon and it's still the same old Republican party." The way to capture "the large body of independents," a document on "Campaign Reflections" stated, was by highlighting "the *demerits of Mr. Nixon*." The staff put together "a nearly exhaustive volume of Nixon quotes" containing "an up-to-date analysis of contradictions and inconsistencies in Nixon statements over the years." Kennedy portrayed Nixon as a conventional reactionary. "I stand today where Woodrow Wilson stood, and Franklin Roosevelt and Harry Truman stood," Jack said. "Dick Nixon stands where McKinley stood, where Harding and Coolidge and Landon stood, where Dewey stood. Where do they get those candidates?"

Eisenhower helped. Ike had long been sensitive to suggestions that he had "reigned rather than ruled," and he personally resented suggestions by Nixon that the vice president had been running the government. When a journalist asked the president to name a single major idea of the vice president's that he had adopted, he replied, "If you give me a week, I might think of one. I don't remember."

Yet however assailable Nixon was as a contradictory figure and an abrasive personality — Ike's secretary described him as someone who was "acting like a nice man rather than being one" — it was his identification with recent economic and foreign policy stumbles that made him most vulnerable to defeat. And those were the issues, under the heading "Let's Get the Country Moving Again," on which Kennedy criticized him most effectively in the last weeks of the campaign.

Although Kennedy had no well-developed economic program to put before voters, he was able to point to a number of problems that had bedeviled Eisenhower and Nixon. Between 1953 and 1959, economic growth had averaged only 2.4 percent a year, compared with 5.8 percent since 1939 under the Democrats; the industrialized economies of Western Europe and Japan were expanding faster than America's, while, according to CIA estimates, recent Soviet increases were more than 7 percent a year. The fifties had also seen two recessions, joblessness and underemployment at 7 percent, rising inflation, and a gold drain produced by an unfavorable balance of payments. Another economic downturn beginning in April 1960 and lasting through the campaign gave resonance to Kennedy's complaints. When Nixon asserted that unemployment would not be a significant issue unless it exceeded 4.5 million, Kennedy replied, "I . . . think it would become a significant issue to the 4,499,000 . . . unemployed."

"Foreign policy for the first time in many years will be the great issue, as Mr. Nixon has so often told us," Kennedy wrote former secretary of state Dean Acheson, and despite Nixon's credentials as an anticommunist, Kennedy believed that his own travels, writings, public addresses, and service on the Foreign Relations Committee made him more than a match for the vice president. Kennedy's 1958 *Foreign Affairs* article, "A Democrat Looks at Foreign Policy," and a 225-page book published in 1960, *The Strategy of Peace*, a compilation of his recent speeches on international affairs and national security, were meant to show that he had prepared himself to manage the great overseas challenges certain to confront the next president.

In July 1960, Gallup reported that "the overwhelming majority of those interviewed regard relations with Russia and the rest of the world as being the primary problem facing the nation today." Fidel Castro's pro-Soviet regime in Cuba, coupled with Khrushchev's warnings that Moscow was grinding out missiles like sausages and that communism would bury capitalism, stirred fears of attack against which the United States had no apparent defense. When people in cities around the world were asked if U.S. prestige had increased or decreased in the last year, 45 percent said it had decreased and only 22 percent believed it had increased.

Kennedy saw clear political advantages in emphasizing international dangers to the United States. In August 1958, he had given his notable Senate speech on the missile gap. Warning that America was about to lose its advantage over the Soviet Union in nuclear weapons, he quoted army general James Gavin, who saw "our own offensive and defensive Missile capabilities" lagging "so far behind those of the Soviets as to place us in a position of great peril." Kennedy asserted that the Soviet combination of intercontinental and intermediate-range missiles, "history's largest fleet of submarines," and long-range supersonic jet bombers might give them the ability to "destroy 85 percent of our industry, 43 of our 50 largest cities, and most of the Nation's population." He added, "We tailored our strategy and military requirements to fit our budget" — instead of the other way around. Over the next two years, Kennedy repeatedly came back to this problem in his public pronouncements, so much so that in September 1960, John Kenneth Galbraith complained to Lou Harris, "J.F.K. has made the point that he isn't soft. Henceforth he can only frighten."

In August 1960, when the public gave higher marks to the Republicans than the Democrats as the party best able to manage world peace, Kennedy intensified his efforts to publicize the Eisenhower-Nixon shortcomings on defense. But his focus on relative U.S. military weakness was not strictly motivated by politics. He had genuine concerns that America was facing a crisis that demanded new thinking and initiatives. In this, he was following the lead of many defense experts who warned that the United States was falling behind the Soviets. In addition to Gavin, H. Rowan Gaither Jr., of the Ford Foundation, who had chaired a committee studying national security in the atomic age, concluded that "our active defenses are not adequate" and our passive or civilian defenses "insignificant." "Gaither practically predicted the end of Western civilization," one historian said. Gaither also described the Soviets as having a more expansive economy than the United States, as spending more on defense, and as out-building the U.S. in nuclear weapons, ICBMs, IRBMs, submarines, and air defenses, not to mention space technology.

Whether the gap existed was, even at the time, debatable. Eisenhower had solid evidence from U-2 spy planes that there was no missile gap, and he instructed his military chiefs to persuade Kennedy of this, but Eisenhower's fear of leaks and his conviction that Kennedy would lose made him reluctant to share his sources. He also believed that authoritative denials of a gap would agitate the Soviets into a buildup; as long as the public record suggested that Moscow was getting ahead of the United States, Ike assumed that Khrushchev would hold back from investing in a large, costly expansion of ICBMs. But the administration's reluctance to give Kennedy fuller information persuaded Jack that Eisenhower did not want to acknowledge a failing that could cost Nixon the election. Kennedy was in possession of numbers showing frightening and growing gaps between Soviet and American military strength. When he asked CIA director Allen Dulles about the missile gap, Dulles replied that only the Pentagon could properly answer the question. It was a signal to Kennedy that Dulles did not have enough information to rule out the possibility of a significant Soviet advantage.

Other Democrats warned Kennedy that Nixon would not only deny the reality of our defense problem but, if this did not work, would then try to blame the country's vulnerability on the Democrats. Indeed, Nixon hoped to scare voters into thinking that Kennedy would either risk war with an unnecessary buildup or continue his party's alleged policies of failing to invest enough in defense. Kennedy may have known about a Nixon memo to Attorney General William Rogers asking him to supply information for speeches showing that JFK "would be a very dangerous President, dangerous to the cause of peace and dangerous from the standpoint of surrender." But it was a tactical blunder: The missile gap was an easy issue to explain to voters, and it was hard for Nixon to escape the box Eisenhower and Kennedy had put him in.

While Kennedy truly cared about the possibility of a missile gap, political opportunism was more at work in his response to Castro's Cuba. Frustration at the rise of a communist regime "ninety miles from America's shore" was an irresistible campaign issue, especially in Florida, an electoral battleground. To be sure, Kennedy was sincerely concerned about the potential dangers to the United States from a communist regime in Latin America. "What are the Soviets' eventual intentions?" a prescient staff memo written early in the campaign asked. "Do they intend to use Cuba as a center for Communist expansion in Latin America, or as a missile base to offset ours in other countries?" Dean Acheson counseled Kennedy to "stop talking about Cuba — I didn't think this was getting anywhere. . . . He was likely to get himself hooked into positions which would be difficult afterwards," Acheson remembered later. He urged Kennedy to focus instead on broad foreign policy questions. But the political advantage in emphasizing that Castro's ascent had come on the Eisenhower-Nixon watch was too inviting to ignore. The potency of the issue led to overreach: In October the campaign issued a statement that suggested Kennedy favored unilateral intervention in Cuba. The outcry from liberals, who warned against ignoring Latin American sensibilities, and from Nixon, who favored intervention but cynically condemned Kennedy's statement as a dangerous challenge to Moscow, forced Jack to amend the statement and take Acheson's advice about dropping Cuba as a fit topic of discussion.

Civil rights was an even more difficult issue to manage in the campaign. The conflict between pressures for economic, political, and social justice for black Americans and southern determination to maintain the system of de jure and de facto segregation presented Kennedy with no good political options. He was mindful of the political advantages to himself from a large black turnout, and of the transparent moral claims to equal treatment under the law for an abused and disadvantaged minority. But he was also greatly concerned with the counterpressure from white southerners who were antagonistic to the Democratic party's advanced position on civil rights. Virginia senator A. Willis Robertson reflected the division in the party in a letter to Kennedy saying he would support the entire party ticket in November but refused to "endorse and support the civil rights plank that was written into our Party platform over the protests of the delegates from Virginia and other Southern States." LBJ's vice presidential nomination had been, as intended, some solace to southerners, but not enough to counter Kennedy's aggressive commitment to civil rights.

Once again, political imperatives determined Kennedy's course of action. Liberals were already angry at Johnson's selection, and if Kennedy gave in to southern pressure on civil rights, it would mean losing their support (not to mention black votes). Kennedy signaled his intentions by writing Robertson, "I understand the problem the platform presents to you," but he offered nothing more than the "hope [that] it will be possible for us to work together in the fall."

Kennedy was not happy about having to choose between the party's competing factions, but once he chose, he moved forward. When he saw civil rights advocate Harris Wofford in August, he said, "Now in five minutes, tick off the ten things a President ought to do to clean up this goddamn civil rights mess." Although he was uncomfortable adopting an aggressive civil rights agenda, he nevertheless followed all of Wofford's suggestions: They set up a civil rights section in the campaign and appointed Marjorie Lawson, a black woman, and William Dawson of Chicago, the senior black congressman, to head the division; chose Frank Reeves, who had NAACP contacts all over the country, to travel with Kennedy; enlisted the help of Louis Martin, a black publisher, to handle a variety of media assignments; paid $50,000 to New York congressman Adam Clayton Powell, who enjoyed "wide popular appeal among blacks," to give ten speeches; and encouraged the Reverend Joseph

Jackson of Chicago to organize a National Fellowship of Ministers and Laymen to lead a nationwide voter registration drive among blacks. By the end of a special congressional session in August, it had become clear to Senator Richard Russell of Georgia that "Kennedy will implement the Democratic platform and advocate civil rights legislation beyond what is contained in the platform."

Kennedy agreed to speak before several black conventions, praised peaceful sit-ins at segregated public facilities across the South, criticized Eisenhower for failing to integrate public housing "with one stroke of the pen," and sponsored a national advisory conference on civil rights. In a speech, he described civil rights as a "moral question" and promised not only to support legislation but also to take executive action "on a bold and large scale." And the more he said, the more he felt. By the close of the campaign, he had warmed to the issue and spoke with indignation about American racism. After Henry Cabot Lodge announced that Nixon would appoint a black to his cabinet — which angered Nixon — Kennedy declared on *Meet the Press* that jobs in government should go to the best-qualified people, regardless of race or ethnicity. But he emphasized the need to bring blacks into the higher reaches of government. "There are no Federal District Judges — there are 200-odd of them; not a one is a Negro," he said. "We have about 26 Negroes in the entire Foreign Service of 6,000, so that particularly now with the importance of Africa, Asia and all the rest, I do believe we should make a greater effort to encourage fuller participation on all levels, of all the talent we can get — Negro, white, of any race."

Nothing tested Kennedy's support of black rights during the campaign more than the jailing of Martin Luther King. Arrested for trying to integrate a restaurant in an Atlanta department store and then sentenced to a four-month prison term at hard labor for violating his probation on a minor, trumped-up traffic violation, King was sent to a rural Georgia prison. His wife, who was five months pregnant, feared for his life. In October, two weeks before the election, she called Wofford to ask his help in arranging King's release. The desperation in her voice moved Wofford to call Sargent Shriver and ask for Kennedy's moral support. After O'Donnell, Salinger, and Sorensen — who, fearful of losing southern votes, seemed certain to object — had left the room, Shriver urged Jack to call Mrs. King. Kennedy, partly out of political calculation and partly from sympathy for the Kings, made the call at once. Jack expressed concern for King's well-being and offered to help in any way he could.

When Bobby Kennedy learned of the call, he upbraided the instigators for risking Jack's defeat in three southern states that might decide the election. Still, Bobby was personally outraged at the injustice of the sentence and the embarrassment to the country from the actions of a judge he privately called a "bastard" and "a son of a bitch." With the story in the news, he decided to phone the judge, who had promised Georgia's governor, Ernest Vandiver, that he would release King if he got political cover for himself — namely a phone call from Jack or Bobby. Bobby's call freed King. The Kennedy phone calls and Nixon's failure to do anything gave Jack a big advantage among blacks and may have helped swing five states — Delaware, Illinois, Michigan, New Jersey, and South Carolina — to his side.

And as election day results showed, every vote and every state mattered. By the middle of October, Kennedy had surged to a 51 to 45 percent lead. On October 20, veteran Democrat Jim Farley believed that "the situation looks marvelous" and predicted that Kennedy would not lose many states. But with Eisenhower agreeing to put aside health concerns and campaign in late October, and with the public possibly having second thoughts about giving the White House to so untested a young man, whose religion also continued to leave doubts, Nixon closed the gap. The final Gallup poll, three days before the election, showed a dead heat: Kennedy-Johnson, 50.5 percent, to Nixon-Lodge, 49.5 percent.

But Kennedy held an edge in a different way. At the start of the campaign, newspaper columnist Eric Sevareid had complained that Kennedy and Nixon were the same: tidy, buttoned-down junior executives on the make. He saw no political passion in either man; they were both part of the Fraternity Row crowd, "wearing the proper clothes, thinking the proper thoughts, cultivating the proper people." It seemed to some that the choice was between "the lesser of two evils." By November, however, observers saw a striking change in the two men. Nixon, who had started out projecting "an image of calm, of maturity, the dignity of the experienced statesman," had become angry and grim. A posture of indignation had replaced the earlier "quiet, chatty manner." Harrison Salisbury of the *New York Times* said, "The crowds tensed him up. I watched him ball his fists, set his jaw, hurl himself stiff-legged to the barriers at the airports and begin shaking hands. He was wound up like a watch spring. . . . No ease."

By contrast, CBS commentator Charles Kuralt said, "the change in Kennedy has been the reverse of the change in Nixon. It is hard to recognize in the relaxed, smiling, and confident Kennedy . . . the serious man who . . . in July . . . seemed all cold efficiency, all business." Eleanor Roosevelt believed, as she told Arthur Schlesinger Jr., that no one "in our politics since Franklin has had the same vital relationship with crowds." It was as if running against someone as humorless and possibly ruthless as Nixon strengthened Kennedy's faith in himself — in the conviction not only that he would be a better president but that the energy to get the job done could come not just from within, and not just from family dynamics, but from the sea of American faces that smiled when he stepped toward them.

Yet for all this, Kennedy himself might have thought that Roosevelt's view was a little too romantic. He had no illusion that his positive impact on voters was as strong as she believed. On election night, as he watched the returns at the family's Hyannis Port compound, the results illustrated his marginal hold on the electorate. When he went to bed at 3:30 in the morning, the election still hung in the balance. He was reasonably sure he had won, but with Pennsylvania, Missouri, Illinois, Minnesota, Michigan, and California too close to call definitively, he refused to assume a victory. Despite the uncertainty, he was so exhausted he slept for almost six hours. When he awoke at about nine, Ted Sorensen gave him the news in his upstairs bedroom: He had carried all six states. In fact, California was still a toss-up and ultimately went for Nixon, but it didn't matter; the other five states were enough to ensure Kennedy's election. But even then, it was not until noon, when final returns came in, that they knew with any certainty that he had won. Only when Nixon's press secretary issued a concession statement a little after that did Kennedy agree to appear before the press in the Hyannis Port armory as the president-elect. There, Joe Kennedy, more elated than Jack or Bobby at winning a prize he had long hoped for, appeared in public with Jack for the first time since the start of the campaign.

Although Jack ended up with 303 electoral votes to Nixon's 219, his popular margin was a scant 118,574 out of 68,837,000 votes cast. True, he and Nixon had generated enough interest to bring 64.5 percent of the electorate to the polls, one of the highest turnouts in recent history. But he had won the presidency with only 49.72 percent of the popular vote. (Senator Harry F. Byrd of Virginia, running as a segregationist, siphoned off 500,000 votes.) Although Kennedy joined a long line of minority presidents, including Woodrow Wilson, who had gained the White House in the three-way 1912 election with barely 42 percent popular backing, it was small comfort. Kennedy's margin was the smallest since Grover Cleveland's 23,000-vote advantage over James G. Blaine in 1884, and Benjamin Harrison had turned back Cleveland's bid for a second term with 65 more electoral votes but 100,456 fewer popular votes.

Any number of things explain Kennedy's victory: the faltering economy in an election year; anxiety about the nation's apparently diminished capacity to meet the Soviet threat; Kennedy's decidedly greater personal charm alongside Nixon's abrasiveness before the TV cameras and on the stump; Lyndon Johnson's help in winning seven southern states (Alabama, Arkansas, Georgia, Louisiana, North Carolina, South Carolina, and Texas); an effective get-out-the-vote campaign among Democrats, who, despite Eisenhower's two elections, remained the majority party; the black vote for Kennedy; and the backing of ethnic voters, including but much broader than just Catholics, in big cities like New York, Buffalo, Chicago, Newark, Philadelphia, and Pittsburgh. Kennedy's margins in Detroit, Minneapolis–Saint Paul, and Kansas City helped give him 50.9, 50.6, and 50.3 percent majorities in Michigan, Minnesota, and Missouri, respectively. Contributing to Kennedy's win was an unwise Nixon promise to visit all fifty states, which had diverted him from concentrating on crucial swing areas toward the end of the campaign. Ike's blunder in dismissing Nixon's claims of executive leadership and his failure, because of health concerns, to take a larger role in his vice president's campaign may also have been decisive factors in holding down Nixon's late surge.

Almost immediately, Nixon supporters complained that fraudulent voting in Illinois and Texas (where Kennedy won by 8,800 and 46,000 votes, respectively) had given Kennedy the election, but the accusations were impossible to prove. Daley's machine probably stole Illinois from Nixon (before the final tally was in, he reported Illinois for Kennedy), but Jack would have won even without Illinois. As for Texas, 46,000 fraudulent votes would have been more than the most skilled manipulator of returns could have hidden. Although Nixon publicly took the high ground by refusing to challenge the outcome, Senator Thruston B. Morton, Republican National Committee chairman, urged state and local Republican officials in eleven states "to take legal action on the alleged vote fraud." But no one could demonstrate significant fraud anywhere. Recounts in Illinois and New Jersey, for example, made no change in the final vote, and in other states, judges found insufficient evidence to order recounts. However close, Kennedy's victory represented the will of the electorate.

In the final analysis, the most important question is not why Kennedy won but why his victory was so narrow. Harry Truman was amazed at the closeness of the race. "Why, even our friend Adlai would have had a landslide running against Nixon," he told Senator William Benton of Connecticut. Given the majority status of the Democrats, the discontent over the state of the economy and international affairs, and Kennedy's superior campaign and campaigning, he should have gained at least 52 or 53 percent of the popular vote. Everyone on his staff had predicted a victory of between 53 and 57 percent. The small margin shocked them. What they missed was the unyielding fear of having a Catholic in the White House. Although about 46 percent of Protestants voted for Kennedy, millions of them in Ohio, Wisconsin, and across the South made his religion a decisive consideration. It was the first time a candidate had won the presidency with a minority of Protestant voters.

Forty-three years after the election of 1960, it is difficult to imagine the importance of something that no longer seems significant in discussions about suitability for the White House. Whatever gains and losses John Kennedy's presidency might have brought to the country and the world, his election in 1960 marked a great leap forward in religious tolerance that has served the nation well ever since.

PART FOUR

The President

Most of us enjoy preaching, and I've got such a bully pulpit!

— Theodore Roosevelt, 1905

The Presidency is not merely an administrative office.
That's the least of it. It is more than an engineering job,
efficient or inefficient. It is pre-eminently a place of moral
leadership. All our great Presidents were leaders of thought
at times when certain historic ideas in the life of the nation
had to be clarified.

— Franklin D. Roosevelt, September 11, 1932

On my desk I have a motto which says "The buck stops
here."

— Harry S Truman, December 19, 1952

CHAPTER 9

The Torch Is Passed

I am an idealist without illusions.

— attributed to John F. Kennedy by
Arthur Schlesinger Jr., c. 1953

JACK KENNEDY'S ELECTION to the presidency by the narrowest of margins frustrated and exhilarated him. He was "more perplexed than bothered by the narrowness of his victory," Arthur Schlesinger Jr. recalled. Kennedy was clearly "jubilant" and "deeply touched" at becoming only the thirty-fourth American to become president. But after seeing him, journalist Henry Brandon thought that the result had actually somewhat "hurt his self-confidence and pride." Kennedy himself asked Kenny O'Donnell, "How did I manage to beat a guy like this by only a hundred thousand votes?"

But Kennedy had little time to savor or question his victory; the transition from candidate to president-elect confronted him with immediate new pressures. The problems he had complained of during the campaign — an uncertain public lacking inspired leadership in the Cold War, the missile gap, a nuclear arms race, Cuba, communism's appeal to developing nations, a stagnant economy, and racial injustices — were now his responsibility.

In the seventy-two days before he took office, he had first to overcome campaign exhaustion. The day after the election, during the press conference at the Hyannis Port Armory, his hands, although out of camera range, trembled. One reporter, responding to Kennedy's appearance the following day, asked whether rumors about his health problems were true. Two weeks after the election, when Ted Sorensen visited him at his father's vacation retreat in Palm Beach, he had not fully recovered. His mind was neither "keen" nor "clear," Sorensen recalls, and he "still seemed tired then and reluctant to face up to the details of personnel and program selection." As he and his father drove to a Palm Beach golf course, Jack complained, "Jesus Christ, this one wants that, that one wants this. Goddamn it, you can't satisfy any of these people. I don't know what I'm going to do about it all." Joe responded, "Jack, if you don't want the job, you don't have to take it. They're still counting votes up in Cook County."

Kennedy knew he could not afford to show any signs of flagging in public. How could he get the country moving again or create the sense of hope, the belief in a better national future that had been so central to his campaign if he gave any indication of physical or psychological fatigue? Thus, in response to the reporter's question about his health, he declared himself in "excellent" shape and dismissed rumors of Addison's disease as false. "I have been through a long campaign and my health is very good today," he said. An article based largely on information supplied by Bobby Kennedy echoed Jack's assertions. Published in *Today's Health*, an American Medical Association journal, and summarized in the *New York Times*, the article described Jack as in "superb physical condition." Though it reported some adrenal insufficiency, which a daily oral medication neutralized, the journal assured readers that Jack would have no problem handling the demands of the presidency.

The reality was, of course, different. Kennedy's health remained as uncertain as ever. Having gone from one medical problem to another throughout his life, he believed his ongoing conditions were no cause to think that he could not be president. But whether someone with adrenal, back, colon-stomach, and prostate difficulties could function with high effectiveness under the sort of pressures a president faced was a question that remained to be answered. True, FDR had functioned brilliantly despite his paralysis, but he was never on a combination of medicines like the one Kennedy relied on to get through the day. When he ran for and won the presidency, Kennedy was gambling that his health problems would not prevent him from handling the job. By hiding the extent of his ailments, he had denied voters the chance to decide whether they wanted to join him in this bet.

Kennedy's hope was to return the center of decision to the Oval Office, rather than let it remain in the hands of the subordinates who were supposedly running Eisenhower's government. But obviously he needed a cabinet, and selecting it was not simple. Appointing prominent older men could revive campaign charges that Kennedy was too young to take charge and needed experienced advisers to run his administration. At the same time, however, Kennedy did not want to create the impression that he would surround himself with pushovers and ciphers who would not threaten his authority. He wanted the most talented and accomplished people he could find, and he was confident that he could make them serve his purposes.

He also understood that his thin margin of victory gave him less a mandate for fresh actions than a need to demonstrate lines of continuity with Eisenhower's presidency. The margin convinced him that it was essential to conciliate Republicans and indicate that as president he would put the national interest above partisan politics.

Indeed, Kennedy's announcement of appointments two days after the election suggested not new departures but consistency with the past. At a dinner with liberal friends the day after the election, Kennedy's mention of the CIA and the FBI had brought pleas for new directors and novel ways of thinking about Cold War dangers. To his friends' surprise, the next morning he announced that Allen Dulles and J. Edgar Hoover would continue to head the CIA and the FBI, respectively. Kennedy hoped this would put Democrats on notice that he would not be beholden to any party faction and would make up his own mind about what would best serve the country and his administration. (He may also have been guarding against damaging leaks from Hoover about his private life. As Lyndon Johnson would later put it, better to keep Hoover inside the tent pissing out than outside pissing in.)

Four days later, Kennedy flew in a helicopter to Key Biscayne to meet Nixon. When O'Donnell asked him what he would say to Nixon, he replied, "I haven't the slightest idea. Maybe I'll ask him how he won in Ohio." The meeting had its intended symbolic value, showing Kennedy as a statesman above the country's political wars. The *New York Times* reported Kennedy's determination not to exclude the Republicans from constructive contributions to his administration, though Nixon himself would not be offered any formal role. Nevertheless, Kennedy could not ignore their political differences. O'Donnell recalled the conversation between Kennedy and Nixon as neither interesting nor amusing. Nixon did most of the talking. "It was just as well for all of us that he didn't quite make it," Kennedy told O'Donnell on the return ride to Palm Beach. Nixon did not reveal his Ohio strategy, Kennedy said later.

In any case, the outgoing vice president was basically irrelevant; relations with Eisenhower, however, were crucial to the transition and coming assumption of power. Though election as the youngest president and service as the oldest separated Kennedy and Eisenhower, the two were among the most attractive personalities ever to occupy the White House. Ike's famous grin and reassuring manner and JFK's charm and wit made them almost universally likable. The "almost" certainly applied here: The two men did not have high regard for each other. Kennedy viewed Ike as something of an old fuddy-duddy, a sort of seventy-year-old fossil who was a "non-president" more interested in running the White House by organizational charts than by using executive powers. In private, he was not above making fun of Ike, mimicking him and calling him "that old asshole." Eisenhower privately reciprocated the contempt, sometimes intentionally mispronouncing Kennedy's name and referring to the forty-three-year-old as "Little Boy Blue" and "that young whipper-snapper." Ike saw the Kennedys as arrivistes and Jack as more celebrity than serious public servant, someone who had done little more than spend his father's money to win political office, where, in the House and Senate, he had served without distinction.

Truman and Ike, whose differences in the 1952 campaign had carried over into the postelection transfer of power, had only one twenty-minute meeting at the White House, which was formal and unfriendly. Kennedy was eager to avoid a comparable exchange, so he seized upon an invitation to consult with Eisenhower at the White House in December. "I was anxious to see E[isenhower]," Kennedy recorded. "Because it would serve a specific purpose in reassuring the public as to the harmony of the transition. Therefore strengthening our hands."

At an initial meeting on December 6, Kennedy wanted to discuss organizational matters, "the present national security setup, organization within the White House . . . [and] Pentagon organization." Kennedy also listed as topics for discussion: "Berlin — Far East (Communist China, Formosa) — Cuba, [and] De Gaulle, Adenauer and MacMillan: President Eisenhower's opinion and evaluation of these men." Above all, Kennedy wanted "to avoid direct involvement in action taken by the outgoing Administration." Yet despite his reluctance to enter into policy discussions, he prepared for the meeting by reading extensively on seven foreign policy issues Ike had suggested they review: "NATO Nuclear Sharing, Laos, The Congo, Algeria,

Disarmament [and] Nuclear test suspension negotiations, Cuba and Latin America, U.S. balance of payments and the gold outflow." Only one domestic topic made Eisenhower's list: "The need for a balanced budget."

The meeting began with an outward display of cordiality by both men at the north portico of the White House, where the president greeted his successor before press photographers and the marine band played "The Stars and Stripes Forever." Kennedy, eager to use his youth and vigor to rekindle public hope, stepped from his car before it had come to a full stop and rushed forward alone to shake hands before the president could remove his hat or extend his hand. It perfectly symbolized the changing of the guard.

During the meeting, which lasted over an hour, longer than anticipated, Eisenhower did most of the talking. It was by far the most time Kennedy had ever spent with Eisenhower. Jack found much of Ike's discourse unenlightening, later describing the president to Bobby as ponderous and poorly informed about subjects he should have mastered. He did not appreciate Ike's advice that he "avoid any reorganization before he himself could become well acquainted with the problem." But he also came away from the meeting with a heightened appreciation of Ike's appeal and a more intimate realization that Eisenhower's political success rested on the force and effectiveness of his personality.

Eisenhower was more impressed with Kennedy. He saw greater substance to the man than he had formerly. Kennedy convinced him that he was "a serious, earnest seeker for information and the implication was that he will give full consideration to the facts and suggestions we presented." (Jack had obviously done an effective job of masking his limited regard for the president's presentation of issues.) Eisenhower had some reservations: He believed that Kennedy was a bit naive in thinking that he could master issues by simply putting the right men in place around him. Despite this concern, Ike sent word to Washington attorney Clark Clifford, the head of Kennedy's transition team, that he had been "misinformed and mistaken about this young man. He's one of the ablest, brightest minds I've ever come across."

Ten weeks after his election, Kennedy had a clearer idea of priorities, and he requested another meeting with Eisenhower. His principal worries, he said, in order of importance, were Laos, the Congo, Cuba and the Dominican Republic, Berlin, nuclear test talks and disarmament, Algeria, "an appraisal of limited war requirements vs. limited war capabilities," and "basic economic, fiscal, and monetary policies." Eisenhower declared himself ready to discuss any of these topics in a "larger meeting," but he wanted to talk with Kennedy alone about presidential actions in a defense emergency, particularly authorization of the use of atomic weapons, and covert or "special operations, including intelligence activities."

In their private meeting, which lasted forty-five minutes, Ike, who looked "very fit, pink cheeked," and seemed "unharassed," reviewed the emergency procedures for response to "an immediate attack." It was one expression of current fears about a Soviet nuclear assault, even if, as Eisenhower knew, Moscow lacked the where-withal to strike successfully against the United States. The prevailing wisdom, after the horrors of World War II and Soviet repression in the USSR and Eastern Europe, was that fanatical communists were capable of terrifying acts, especially against Western Europe, which Western political leaders would be irresponsible to ignore.

Kennedy marveled at Eisenhower's sangfroid in discussing nuclear conflict. Ike assured Kennedy that the United States enjoyed an invulnerable advantage over Moscow in nuclear submarines armed with Polaris missiles, which could reach the Soviet Union from undetectable positions in various oceans. He seemed to take special pleasure in showing Kennedy how quickly a helicopter could whisk him to safety from the White House in case of a nuclear attack. With evident glee at a president's military mastery, Ike said, "Watch this," and instructed a military aide on the telephone: "Opal Drill Three." The marine helicopter that landed almost at once on the White House lawn brought a smile of approval to JFK's face as well.

But Kennedy's main focus remained on Laos. A three-sided civil war between Pathet Lao communists, pro-Western royalists, and neutralists presented the possibility of communist control in Laos and, by extension, the loss of all Southeast Asia. As Kennedy noted in a later memo, "I was anxious to get some commitment from the outgoing administration as to how they would deal with Laos, which they were handing to us. I thought particularly it would be helpful to have some idea as to how prepared they were for military intervention."

Speaking for the president, Eisenhower's secretaries of state and defense urged a commitment to block communist control of Laos. They saw the Soviet bloc testing the unity and strength of Western intentions. They believed that the communists would avoid a major war in the region but that they would "continue to make trouble right up to that point." They described Laos as "the cork in the bottle. If Laos fell, then Thailand, the Philippines," and even Chiang Kai-shek's Nationalist regime on Formosa would go. Eisenhower himself favored unilateral intervention if America's allies would not follow its lead, predicting that Cambodia and South Vietnam would also be victims unless the United States countered communist aggression in Southeast Asia. He also advised against a coalition government in Laos: "Any time you permit Communists to have a part in the government of such a nation, they end up in control." Kennedy was not happy at the prospect of having to send American forces into Laos as the first major action of his term. "Whatever's going to happen in Laos," he had said to Sorensen before the January meeting, "an American invasion, a Communist victory or whatever, I wish it would happen before we take over and get blamed for it." Despite his bold talk, Eisenhower was reluctant to intervene, and there was no chance he would act in the closing days of his term.

By contrast with Laos, Cuba barely registered as an immediate worry. Eisenhower advised Kennedy that he was helping anti-Castro guerrilla forces to the utmost and that the United States was currently training such a group in Guatemala. "In the long run the United States cannot allow the Castro Government to continue to exist in Cuba," Eisenhower said. None of this, however, was news to Kennedy. Bobby Kennedy had received a memo as early as August 1960, which Jack's friend Florida senator George Smathers warmly endorsed, recommending that the U.S. government encourage formation of "a respectable government-in-exile" to replace Castro. Moreover, by October, Bobby knew that Cuban exiles in Miami were describing "an invasion fever in Guatemala" but that they felt themselves "being rushed into it and that they are not yet equipped for it." Bobby was also advised that "this invasion story is in the open." The fact, however, that no action seemed imminent put the Castro problem lower on Kennedy's list of worries than Laos, and in his memo of the conversation with the president, Jack made no mention of Cuba.

In preparing for power, Kennedy wanted to ensure that he not be the captive of any group or individual. As the youngest man ever elected to the presidency, he anticipated dealing with more experienced Washington hands who would see his youth as a reason to assert their authority over him. He did not view potential appointees and advisers as intent on maliciously weakening his control but as forceful men accustomed to leading and eager to help an untested Chief Executive burdened with unprecedented responsibilities. His concern to ensure his authority registered clearly on Schlesinger, to whom he spoke repeatedly about Franklin Roosevelt's "capacity to dominate a sprawling government filled with strong men eager to go into business on their own."

Kennedy's determination to maintain control of organizational, procedural, and substantive matters was evident even before he was elected. In August, he had asked Clark Clifford to prepare transition briefs. "If I am elected," he said, "I don't want to wake up on the morning of November 9 and have to ask myself, 'What in the world do I do now?'"

Clifford was the consummate Washington insider. Tall, handsome, silver haired, he looked more like a matinee idol than a savvy attorney who had learned the inner workings of the White House as an aide to Truman. Clifford had made political control into a fine art: He greeted visitors to his office with a minute of silence and seeming indifference to their presence while he searched through papers on his desk. The visitor's relief at being recognized gave Clifford the upper hand he considered useful in a world of power brokers intent on gaining any and every edge. For all his usefulness to Kennedy as someone who could instruct the president-elect about the executive bureaucracy and how to prepare for the takeover, Clifford also posed a threat as someone who might leak stories to the press about his dominant role in shaping the new administration. Jack joked that Clifford wanted nothing for his services "except the right to advertise the Clifford law firm on the back of the one-dollar bill." Clifford did, however, blunt some of Kennedy's concerns by declaring himself unavailable for any appointment in the administration.

At the same time Kennedy invited Clifford to set an agenda for the transition, he asked Richard Neustadt, a Columbia political scientist who had recently published a widely praised book on presidential power, to take on the same assignment. On September 15, when Neustadt presented Kennedy with his memo on "Organizing the Transition," Jack took an instant liking to the tone and substance of Neustadt's advice: He counseled Kennedy against trying to repeat FDR's Hundred Days, which had little parallel with the circumstances of 1961, and to settle instead on a presidential style that suited his particular needs. Kennedy disliked Clifford's recommendation that he "see Congressmen all day long. 'I can't stand that,'" he told Neustadt. "Do I have to do that? What a waste of time." Neustadt replied: "'Now, look, you cannot start off with the feeling that the job must run you; that you have to do it this way because this is the way Truman did it. We'll just have to think of devices to spare you as much of this as you don't like. . . . We'll just have to use our ingenuity.' He seemed relieved to be told what I am sure he hoped to hear," Neustadt recalled. Kennedy asked him to elaborate in additional memos on a list of problems Neustadt expected to arise during the transition. Kennedy instructed him "'to get the material directly back to me. I don't want you to send it to anybody else.' 'How do you want me to relate to Clark Clifford?'" Neustadt asked. "I don't want you to relate to Clark Clifford," Kennedy answered. "I can't afford to confine myself to one set of advisers. If I did that, I would be on *their* leading strings."

BECAUSE KENNEDY THOUGHT in terms of people rather than structure or organization, his highest priority during the transition was to find the right men — no women were considered for top positions — to join his administration. Selecting a White House staff was little problem. Since he intended to be his own chief of staff who issued marching orders to subordinates, this eliminated the issue of elevating one close aide over others and making some of them unhappy. It was obvious to Kennedy that the men who had worked with him so long and so hard to build his Senate career and make him president — Sorensen, O'Brien, O'Donnell, Powers, and Salinger — were to become the White House insiders. Their occupancy of West Wing offices near the president's Oval Office and their access to Kennedy without formal appointments signaled their importance in the administration. "The President was remarkably accessible," Sorensen recalls. "O'Donnell and Salinger — and usually [McGeorge] Bundy [special assistant to the president for national security affairs], O'Brien and myself were in and out of the Oval Office several times a day." Each member of the Kennedy team had particular responsibilities — O'Brien as legislative liaison, O'Donnell as appointments secretary, Powers as a political man Friday, Salinger as press secretary, and Sorensen as special assistant for programs and policies — but none operated within narrow bounds, working instead on anything and everything.

Choosing other officials was much more difficult. "Jack has asked me to organize [a] talent search for the top jobs," Sargent Shriver told Harris Wofford two days after the election. "The Cabinet, regulatory agencies, ambassadors, everything. We're going to comb the universities and professions, the civil rights movement, business, labor, foundations and everywhere, to find the brightest and best people possible." Kennedy relished the idea of "appointing outstanding men to top posts in the government." But it was not easy to identify and convince the seventy-five or so individuals needed for the cabinet and subcabinet to serve. As Jack told O'Donnell and Powers, "For the last four years I spent so much time getting to know people who could help me get elected President that I didn't have any time to get to know people who could help me, after I was elected, to be a good President." In addition, some talented people were not keen to interrupt successful careers to take on burdens that might injure their reputations. And Kennedy saw some of those eager for jobs as too self-serving or too ambitious to accept a role as a team player devoted to an administration's larger goals. Kennedy also believed that his narrow electoral victory required him to make other nonpartisan appointments like those of Dulles and Hoover.

During the course of discussions with potential cabinet appointees who modestly explained that they had no experience in the office the president-elect wanted them to fill, Kennedy invariably replied that he had no experience being president either. They would, he explained with some levity, all learn on the job. His response was partly meant to reassure future officials that he had enough confidence in their native talents and past performance to believe that they would serve his administration with distinction. But he was also signaling his intention to keep policy commitments to a minimum until he could assess immediate realities. Arthur Schlesinger Jr. recalled that after Bobby had asked if he would like to be an ambassador and Schlesinger replied that he would prefer to be at the White House, Jack said to him: "'So, Arthur, I hear you are coming to the White House.' 'I am,'" Schlesinger replied. "'What will I be doing there?' 'I don't know,'" Kennedy answered. "But you can bet we will both be busy more than eight hours a day." And Schlesinger would be. He operated from the East Wing, which, except for Schlesinger, was filled with peripheral administration officials who, in Sorensen's words, "were regarded almost as inhabitants of another world." Schlesinger, who would usually see the president two or three times a week, would be the administration's spokesman to liberals at home and abroad as well as "a source of innovation, ideas and occasional speeches on all topics."

Kennedy, remembering the wartime service of Republicans Henry Stimson and Frank Knox in FDR's cabinet, made clear to O'Donnell that he would do something similar. "If I string along exclusively with Galbraith and Arthur Schlesinger and Seymour Harris and those other Harvard liberals, they'll fill Washington with wild-eyed ADA people," he said. "And if I listen to you and Powers and [John] Bailey and [Dick] Maguire [at the DNC], we'll have so many Irish Catholics that we'll have to organize a White House Knights of Columbus Council. I can use a few smart Republicans. Anyway, we need a Secretary of the Treasury who can call a few of those people on Wall Street by their first names."

For Kennedy, the two most important cabinet appointments were Treasury and Defense. Since he intended to keep tight control over foreign policy, finding a secretary of state was a lower priority. Help in managing the domestic economy and national security came first. He wanted moderate Republicans for both posts who could give him some political cover for the hard decisions a minority president would need to make to expand the economy and bolster the national defense.

Although Kennedy felt more comfortable addressing defense and foreign policy issues, he knew that reinvigorating a sluggish economy was essential to a successful administration. The country's substantial economic growth between 1946 and 1957 had ground to a halt with a nine-month recession in 1957–58, when unemployment had increased to 7.5 percent, the highest level since the Great Depression. Another economic downturn in 1960 had followed a relatively weak recovery in 1958–59. As one economist explained the problem, the backlogged demands of the war years had been largely sated and the nation now faced a period of excess capacity and higher unemployment. On top of these difficulties, an international balance-of-payment deficit causing a "gold drain" had raised questions about the soundness of the dollar. In these circumstances, winning the confidence of businessmen, especially in the financial community; labor unions; and middle-class consumers would be something of a high-wire act that no one was sure the new, untested president could perform.

As a Democrat who could count on traditional backing from labor and consumers, Kennedy felt compelled to pay special attention to skeptical bankers and business chiefs. But how was he to quiet predictable liberal antagonism to a prominent representative of Wall Street, who seemed likely to favor tax and monetary policies serving big business rather than working-class citizens, in the Treasury Department? Giving a Republican so much influence over economic policy seemed certain to touch off an internal battle and produce even greater damage to the administration's standing in the business community than the initial choice of a Democrat.

Kennedy hoped to solve this problem by making Republican Robert Lovett secretary of the treasury. A pillar of the New York banking establishment, Lovett had intermittently served as a high government official since World War II. His worldliness and track record of putting country above partisanship moved Kennedy to offer him State, Defense, or Treasury. But failing health, caused by a bleeding ulcer, decided Lovett against accepting any office, and Kennedy turned instead to C. Douglas Dillon. Dillon was an even more imposing establishment figure: His father had founded the Wall Street banking firm of Dillon, Read & Company. A privileged child, Dillon had graduated from Groton, FDR's alma mater, and Harvard, and, with family apartments and homes in New York, New Jersey, Washington, D.C., Maine, Florida, and France, he enjoyed connections with America's wealthiest, most influential people. During World War II, he had served in the southwest Pacific, where he had won medals as a navy aviator. After the war, he had become chairman of Dillon, Read and of the New Jersey State Republican committee. His early support of Eisenhower had led to his appointment as ambassador to France, where his effective service had persuaded Ike to make him undersecretary of state for economic affairs and then the undersecretary, the second-highest State Department official. Dillon impressed populists like Tennessee senator Albert Gore as an enemy of the people, but in fact he was an open-minded moderate, a liberal Republican whom Kennedy believed he could trust.

Dillon had to be persuaded to accept. Eisenhower warned him against taking the job, urging a written commitment to a free hand lest Kennedy give him no more than symbolic authority. But although Kennedy promised to do nothing affecting the economy without Dillon's recommendation, he refused to give him any written pledge, saying, "A President can't enter into treaties with cabinet members." Kennedy extracted a commitment from Dillon, however, that if he resigned, it would be "in a peaceful, happy fashion and wouldn't indicate directly or indirectly that he was disturbed about what President Kennedy and the administration were doing."

For both economic and political considerations, Kennedy felt he had to balance Dillon's appointment with a Council of Economic Advisers (CEA) made up of innovative liberal Keynesians who would favor bold proposals for stimulating the economy and would convince Democrats that he was not partial to Eisenhower's cautious policies. Although he told Dillon that he was appointing the Keynesians for strictly political reasons, Kennedy truly wanted them as a prod to more advanced thinking and a way to educate the public and himself. As he freely admitted, he was unschooled in economics, telling everyone that he had received a C in freshman economics at Harvard (in fact, it was a B) and could not remember much, if anything, from the course.

Walter Heller was a University of Minnesota economics professor whom Kennedy had met during the campaign through Hubert Humphrey. At his first session with Heller, Kennedy asked him four questions: Could government action achieve a 5 percent growth rate? Was accelerated depreciation likely to increase investment? Why had high interest rates not inhibited German economic expansion? And could a tax cut be an important economic stimulus? Heller's replies were so succinct and literate that Kennedy decided to make him chairman of the CEA. During a December meeting, Kennedy told Heller, "I need you as a counterweight to Dillon. He will have conservative leanings, and I know that you are a liberal." Heller wanted to know if Kennedy would ask for a tax cut and whether he would have carte blanche to choose his CEA colleagues. Not now, Kennedy said of the tax reduction, explaining he could not ask the country for sacrifice at the same time he proposed lower taxes. The answer to the second question was yes. Heller also had the advantage of not being from the Ivy League or the Northeast, as James Tobin and Kermit Gordon, the other economists Heller asked to have as council colleagues, were. Kennedy was not well schooled in economics and found much of the theory mystifying, but he had a keen feel for who had the essential combination of economic knowledge and political common sense vital to successful management of the economy.

Finding a defense secretary who could ease the political and national security concerns of Democrats and Republicans was a bit easier than assembling an economic team. Liberals were not as worried about the impact of a defense chief as they were about a treasury secretary. Besides, with the deepening of the Cold War, when the Soviet Union seemed to pose so grave a threat to the nation's future, partisanship had become less of a problem. Still, Kennedy remembered the political pummeling the Democrats had taken in the late forties and fifties over Yalta, China, and Korea, and he knew that any misstep on defense could quickly become a political liability. After all, he had made effective use of the missile gap in his campaign and understood that if the opportunity presented itself in the next four years, the Republicans would not hesitate to use a defense failure against his reelection. He briefly considered reappointing the incumbent Thomas Gates, but concluded that it would open him to charges of political cynicism for having been so critical of the administration's defense policies during the campaign.

A number of names came before him, but none as repeatedly as that of Ford Motor Company president Robert S. McNamara, a nominal Republican with impeccable credentials as a businessman and service as an air force officer during World War II, when he had increased the effectiveness of air power by applying a system of statistical control. McNamara seemed to be on everybody's list of candidates for the job. Michigan Democrats, including United Auto Workers officials, and principal members of the New York and Washington establishments described him as an exceptionally intelligent man with the independence, tough-mindedness, and, above all, managerial skills to make the unwieldy Defense Department more effective in serving the national security. "The talent scouts," McNamara biographer Deborah Shapley writes, "were delighted to find a Republican businessman who had risen meteorically at Ford and who was, at forty-four, only a year older than the president-elect. . . . That a young Republican businessman could also be well thought of by labor, be Harvard-trained, support the ACLU, and read Teilhard de Chardin were all bonuses."

Without ever having met McNamara, Kennedy authorized Sargent Shriver to offer him an appointment as secretary of the treasury or secretary of defense. (Dillon had not yet been offered the Treasury job.) When McNamara got a message that Shriver had called, he asked his secretary who he was. (McNamara or his secretary, having never heard of Shriver, wrote him on the calendar as "Mr. Shriber.") The offer of the Treasury job stunned McNamara, who turned it down as something he wasn't qualified to handle. He said the same about the Defense post but had enough interest to agree to come to Washington to meet with Kennedy on the following day. McNamara and Kennedy made positive impressions on each other. Nevertheless, McNamara continued to declare himself unqualified to head the Defense Department. Kennedy countered with the assertion that there was no school for defense secretaries or presidents.

McNamara refused to commit himself at the first meeting but promised to come back for a second conversation in a few days. When he did, he gave Kennedy a letter asking assurances that he could run his own department; could choose his subordinates, meaning he would not have to agree to political appointees; and would not have to participate in the capital's social life. Bobby, who sat in on the second meeting, said McNamara's letter made it clear that he "was going to run the Defense Department, that he was going to be in charge; and although he'd clear things with the President, that political interests or favors couldn't play a role." He recalled that his brother "was so impressed with the fact that [McNamara] was so tough about it — and strong and stalwart. He impressed him." McNamara's letter, Bobby felt, flabbergasted his brother, but because Kennedy saw McNamara as so suited for the job, he accepted his conditions. To pressure McNamara into officially accepting, Kennedy leaked his selection to the *Washington Post*, which ran a front-page story. ("The Ship of State is the only ship that often leaks at the top," a Kennedy aide later said.) After McNamara had accepted the appointment, he told Kennedy that after talking over the job with Tom Gates, he believed he could handle it. Kennedy teasingly responded in echo, "I talked over the presidency with Eisenhower, and after hearing what it's all about, I'm convinced I can handle it."

After JFK's election, many assumed that Kennedy would have to choose Adlai Stevenson as his secretary of state. Stevenson remained the party's senior statesman and had established himself as an expert on foreign policy. Although in January 1960, Kennedy had promised to make Stevenson secretary of state if he supported his candidacy, Stevenson's failure to do so had nullified the proposal. After Kennedy got the nomination, however, he encouraged Stevenson's ambition for the job by asking him to prepare a report on foreign policy problems. This had some practical reasoning behind it — Stevenson was, after all, experienced and knowledgeable about a great deal — but was also somewhat petty and personal. Jack had absolutely no intention of appointing Stevenson. "Fuck him," Kennedy said to Abe Ribicoff after the election. "I'm not going to give him anything." Kennedy remained angry at Stevenson for failing to support his nomination, believed he was too equivocal to help make tough foreign policy decisions, and worried that he "might forget who's the President and who's the Secretary of State." Kennedy wanted no part of the arrangement that seemed to have made John Foster Dulles the most important foreign policy decision maker in Eisenhower's administration.

Liberal pressure to give Stevenson something, however, pushed Kennedy to offer him a choice of three jobs: ambassador to Britain, attorney general, or ambassador to the United Nations. Stevenson did not want to go to the U.K. or head the Justice Department, and he felt humiliated at the idea of accepting the U.N., a post with no real policy making authority, telling Bill Blair, "I will never be ambassador to the U.N."

In deciding on a secretary of state, Kennedy wanted to ensure that the State Department would be under his control. He asked John Sharon, who had worked with Stevenson on the foreign policy report, for "'a shit list' — that was his word," Sharon said, "— of people in the state department who ought to be fired." But before he could get rid of department bureaucrats who might obstruct his policies, he needed to decide on a cooperative secretary. Chester Bowles, Harvard University dean McGeorge Bundy, and diplomat David Bruce all received brief consideration, but Bowles was too idealistic, Bundy too young and inexperienced, and Bruce too old for the assignment.

William Fulbright, the chairman of the Foreign Relations Committee, received more serious consideration. Kennedy knew Fulbright from their work together in the Senate and admired his handling of the Foreign Relations Committee. Kennedy "thought he had some brains and some sense and some judgment," as Bobby put it. "He was really rather taken with him." But Bobby and their father talked Jack out of choosing him. As a southern senator "who had been tied up in all the segregation votes" and had signed a southern manifesto opposing the Supreme Court's school desegregation orders, Fulbright seemed certain to stir antagonism among Third World countries, especially in Africa, a sharply contested region of the world in the East-West struggle. Fulbright also had enemies in the Jewish community, where he had aroused hostility with pro-

Arab pronouncements. Seeing the international opposition as too great for him to serve successfully and uncertain that he wanted to trade his Senate seat for the administration of an unwieldy bureaucracy, Fulbright asked Kennedy not to make the offer.

By process of elimination, and determined to run foreign policy from the White House, Kennedy came to Dean Rusk, the president of the Rockefeller Foundation. Rusk was an acceptable last choice, with the right credentials and the right backers. A Rhodes scholar, a college professor, a World War II officer, an assistant secretary of state for the Far East under Truman, a liberal Georgian sympathetic to integration, and a consistent Stevenson supporter, Rusk offended no one. The foreign policy establishment — Acheson, Lovett, liberals Bowles and Stevenson, and the *New York Times* — all sang his praises. But most of all, it was clear to Kennedy from their one meeting in December 1960 that Rusk would be a sort of faceless, faithful bureaucrat who would serve rather than attempt to lead. "It is the President alone who must make the major decisions of our foreign policy," Kennedy had publicly announced the previous January. He called the office "the vital center of action in our whole scheme of government" and declared his belief that a president must "be prepared to exercise the fullest powers of his office — all that are specified and some that are not." It was an open secret that Jack intended to be his own secretary of state. Journalists, congressmen, and Kennedy intimates saw Rusk's selection as confirmation of this assumption and as the principal reason behind the attempt to consign Stevenson to a second-line diplomatic post.

According to Rusk, an exploratory meeting with Kennedy at his Georgetown home did not go well. He told Bowles, "Kennedy and I could not communicate. If the idea of making me Secretary ever actually entered his mind, I am sure it is now dead." But Rusk had misread Kennedy's intentions. He was as close to what Kennedy wanted as he seemed likely to find. His diffidence was transparent. He set no conditions for taking the job; in making no demands about freedom to choose subordinates, he persuaded Kennedy that he would reflect the president's opinions rather than try to determine them. The Kennedys made much of the idea that people who came into the administration needed to be tough. When Bobby told Ken O'Donnell to check on someone as a possible secretary of the army, he described him as a "hard-working tough guy." And one of Jack's initial inquiries about Rusk was whether he was "tough-fibered." But with Jack and Bobby there to take a strong line on foreign affairs and a tough-minded Bob McNamara at Defense, they could afford to have a pliable secretary of state. It was clear to Kennedy that Rusk would be passive in future policy debates: After he had served as secretary for a while, Kennedy said that when they were alone, Rusk would whisper that there were still too many others present.

Now Kennedy came back to Stevenson, who badly wanted to serve in some major foreign policy capacity and announced he could work well with Rusk. Still, Stevenson equivocated, and Kennedy came close to withdrawing the U.N. offer. Finally, despite his earlier pronouncements, and the likelihood that he would have little influence on policy, Stevenson agreed.

If Bobby was genuinely torn about a postelection career choice, his indecision did not last long. His first priority had to have been helping his brother succeed as president. It was inconceivable that after all the hard work to put his brother in the White House, Bobby would now walk away from the tough fights Jack faced as president. As Ribicoff told the president-elect, "I have now watched you Kennedy brothers for five solid years and I notice that every time you face a crisis, you automatically turn to Bobby. You're out of the same womb. There's an empathy. You understand one another. You're not going to be able to be President without using Bobby all the time." Jack agreed. He told Acheson that "he did not know and would not know most of the people who would be around him in high cabinet positions — and he just felt that he had to have someone whom he knew very well and trusted completely with whom he could just sort of put his feet up and talk things over."

The principal question for Jack about Bobby was where he would serve in the administration. At first, there were thoughts of making him an undersecretary of defense or an assistant secretary of state. But on reflection, this seemed like a poor idea. As Dean Acheson told him, it would "be a great mistake. . . . It would be wholly impossible for any cabinet officer to have the President's brother as second in command. . . . This would not be fair to anybody — and, therefore, if he were to be brought in at all, he ought to be given complete responsibility for a department of government, or be brought to the White House and be close to the President himself." Bobby, however, wanted no part of a White House appointment working directly under his brother. "That would be impossible,"

Bobby told Schlesinger. "I had to do something on my own, or have my own area of responsibility. . . . I had to be apart from what he was doing so I wasn't working directly for him and getting orders from him as to what I should do that day. That wouldn't be possible. So I never considered working at the White House." Even if he had, Jack's promise during the campaign that he "would not appoint any relative to the White House staff" ruled out giving Bobby such an assignment.

Jack had actually asked Bobby about heading the Justice Department before he turned to Ribicoff and Stevenson, but Bobby had worried about charges of nepotism. Bobby also expected an attorney general to provoke so much antagonism over civil rights that it would undermine Jack's political standing for him to take the position. "It would be the 'Kennedy brothers' by the time a year was up," Bobby said, "and the President would be blamed for everything we had to do in civil rights; and it was an unnecessary burden to undertake." Others reinforced Bobby's concerns. Dean Acheson, Clark Clifford, Drew Pearson, and Sam Rayburn all warned against the repercussions of having Bobby at the Justice Department. And the *New York Times*, to which Jack leaked the idea of his brother's appointment, opposed it as politicizing an office that should be strictly nonpartisan and as a gift to someone lacking enough legal experience. But after Ribicoff and Stevenson had rejected offers to become attorney general, Kennedy decided that his brother should take the job, despite Bobby's doubts.

Bobby was particularly sensitive to complaints that he had not practiced law or sat on the bench. When Jack joked with friends that he "just wanted to give him a little legal practice before he becomes a lawyer," Bobby upbraided his brother: "Jack, you shouldn't have said that about me." "Bobby, you don't understand," Jack replied. "You've got to make fun of it, you've got to make fun of yourself in politics." Bobby answered, "You weren't making fun of yourself. You were making fun of me."

Once Jack had decided to appoint Bobby to the Justice Department, he tried to minimize the political damage. So Jack, Bobby, and their father encouraged the belief that Joe had forced Bobby and Jack into doing it. Jack told Clark Clifford that his father was insisting on Bobby's appointment against their wishes. Clifford listened with "amazement" to Kennedy's description of the family argument and thought it "truly a strange assignment" when Jack asked him to talk his father out of the idea. Clifford went to New York to make the case to Joe, but to no avail. Looking Clifford straight in the eye, Joe said, *"Bobby is going to be Attorney General.* All of us have worked our tails off for Jack, and now that we have succeeded, I am going to see to it that Bobby gets the same chance that we gave to Jack."

As Bobby later described events, he had decided in December not to take the job. He recalled how he called Jack up to say he didn't want the job and then told a friend, "This will kill my father." Jack had refused to talk about it on the phone, and insisted that they discuss it over breakfast the next morning. Bobby and John Seigenthaler, a reporter from the *Nashville Tennessean,* whom Bobby brought with him, described Jack as determined to appoint Bobby. They recounted Jack's concern to have a cabinet member who would tell him "the unvarnished truth, no matter what," when problems arose. "He thought it would be important to him and that he needed some people around that he could talk to so I decided to accept it," Bobby said later. Remembering Jack's advice to inject some humor into the account, Bobby also described how Jack then said, "So that's it, General. Let's grab our balls and go" talk to the press. But before they did, Jack told him to go upstairs and comb his hair. As they went outside, Jack counseled him, "Don't smile too much or they'll think we're happy about the appointment." (Bobby remembered Jack telling Ben Bradlee of *Newsweek* that he had actually wanted to announce the appointment some morning at about 2 A.M. He would open the front door of his house, look up and down the street, and if no one was there, he would whisper, "It's Bobby.")

The story of Bobby's reluctance, Joe's insistence, and Jack's need for an intimate in court was a useful means of muting criticism. But the written record shows it was mostly fiction. A letter Bobby wrote to Drew Pearson on December 15, the day before Jack supposedly talked him into taking the job and they announced Bobby's appointment, makes clear that the story of Bobby's reluctance was meant to disarm critics. "I made up my mind today and Jack and I take the plunge tomorrow," Bobby told Pearson. "For many reasons I believe it was the only thing I could do — I shall do my best and hope that it turns out well." Seigenthaler's presence at the morning meeting during which Bobby and Jack pretended to be debating Bobby's possible appointment guaranteed public knowledge of the invented account.

Evelyn Lincoln, Jack's secretary, was given the same false view of Bobby's appointment as Seigenthaler. In a diary entry on December 15, at the same time Bobby was telling Pearson of his decision to accept the appointment, Lincoln recorded that Bobby called Jack, who "tried to persuade him to take the Attorney Generalship, if not that Senator from Massachusetts, if not that then perhaps be Under Secretary of State for Latin Affairs. Bobby said he wasn't interested in any of them — would rather write a book." That Jack and Bobby were hiding their true intentions to quiet objections was without question. When Ethel Kennedy greeted her husband at the West Palm Beach airport after Jack and Bobby had disclosed the appointment, "she flashed a big smile and shouted, 'We did it.'"

The Kennedys believed that Bobby's expected effectiveness as attorney general and the success of the administration ultimately would make misgivings about the appointment disappear. But Bobby's selection generated sharp criticism despite the Kennedys' manufactured story. Journalists and legal experts complained that Bobby's background gave him no claim on the office. Political insiders were no less skeptical. "Dick Russell," Lyndon Johnson told Senate secretary Bobby Baker, "is absolutely shittin' a squealin' worm. He thinks it's a disgrace for a kid who's never practiced law to be appointed. . . . I agree with him." But Johnson did not believe that Bobby's influence as attorney general would be very great. He also told Baker, "I don't think Jack Kennedy's gonna let a little fart like Bobby lead him around by the nose." Johnson made the same point to his former Senate colleagues, who needed to rationalize voting for Bobby's appointment. Johnson also appealed to his friends on personal grounds, telling Baker, "I'm gonna put it on the line and tell 'em it's a matter of my personal survival." Reluctant to challenge the new administration on a matter of executive privilege — the freedom of a president to choose his cabinet — senators repressed their doubts and confirmed Bobby's nomination.

Other cabinet and subcabinet appointments came together almost randomly. Kennedy emphasized his eagerness for high-quality people rather than representatives of particular groups or factions. "Kennedy wanted a ministry of talent," Sorensen said, but he was under constant pressure from private groups advocating one candidate or another. Governor Luther Hodges of North Carolina became secretary of commerce not only because he had proven his effectiveness as a public official but also because his reputation as a moderate would appeal to southerners and the business community. Arthur Goldberg and Stewart Udall were appointed labor secretary and interior secretary, respectively, not only because of their competence and ties to Kennedy but also because they satisfied special interest groups in the Democratic party like labor unions and conservationists.

Personal predilections also came into play. Ribicoff turned down Kennedy's offer of the Justice Department out of concern that civil rights disputes would antagonize southerners, who would ultimately bar him from a high-court appointment. In addition, he did not think it a good idea for a Jewish attorney general to be forcing racial integration on white Protestants at the direction of a Catholic president. Ribicoff preferred and received appointment as secretary of health, education, and welfare, which meant that former governor G. Mennen Williams of Michigan, who wanted HEW, would have to become an assistant secretary of state for Africa. When Schlesinger advised Kennedy that liberals were discontented with their limited representation in the cabinet, he replied that the program was more important than the men. "We are going down the line on the program," he said. Schlesinger interpreted this to mean that it would be an administration of "conservative men and liberal measures." JFK agreed: "We'll have to go along with this for a year or so. Then I would like to bring in some new people." But then "he paused and added reflectively, 'I suppose it may be hard to get rid of these people once they are in.'"

Still, Kennedy believed that a strong president with clear ideas of what he wanted to accomplish would be more important than the men who served under him or their cabinet discussions. One of the things that sold him on Dillon was his almost contemptuous description of Eisenhower's cabinet meetings, with their "opening prayers, visual aids, and rehearsed presentations." Although Kennedy invested considerable energy in finding the right people for his administration and even told Sorensen that their decisions on appointments "could make or break us all," he had a healthy skepticism about whether people he brought into the government would have much impact on the issues he saw as of greatest importance. When he interviewed someone for Agriculture, for example, a department that was never at the forefront of his concerns, he found the man and the discussion so boring that he fell asleep. It was an indication of how little Kennedy intended to rely on cabinet meetings for important administration decisions.

Nevertheless, the cabinet was reflective of the tone and direction the new administration seemed likely to take. Just as Eisenhower's selection of so many businessmen proved to be a clear signal of policies favoring less government regulation and influence, so Kennedy's choice of so many highly intelligent, broad-minded men indicated that his presidency would be open to new ideas and inclined to break with conventional wisdom in search of more effective actions at home and abroad. It also promised to embody noblesse oblige — well-off Americans responsive to the suffering of the less fortunate in the United States and around the globe. Kennedy's presidency, of course, would never be a perfect expression of these values, but if there was an indication of the New Frontier's distinctive contours, it could be found in the men Kennedy appointed to his government's highest positions.

Kennedy believed that what he said and the impression he made on the country at the start of his term were more important than who made temporary headlines as cabinet members. Nevertheless, he made every cabinet selection the occasion for a press conference at which he not only emphasized the virtues of the appointee but also his own attentiveness to and knowledge of the major issues facing them. He used the press in other ways, too. Having asked groups of experts to provide task force analyses on everything from relations with Africa to domestic taxes, Kennedy converted the reports during the transition into press releases on current understanding of how to meet various difficulties. The resulting image was one of vigorous engagement, somewhat in contrast to Kennedy's less than daring cabinet selections. "There is no evidence in Palm Beach," journalist Charles Bartlett told his readers at the end of November, "that the New Frontiersmen are being moved to temper their objectives for the nation by the close election. The objectives which the candidate enunciated in his campaign were measured statements of intent." "Reporters are not your friends," Joe had told his sons. But Jack, like every skillful politician since Theodore Roosevelt, saw how useful they could be in advancing his political goals.

KENNEDY BELIEVED that no single element was more important in launching his administration than a compelling inaugural address. Remembering how brilliantly Franklin Roosevelt's inaugural speech had initiated his presidency, Kennedy wished to use his address to inspire renewed national confidence and hope. True, the current challenge was not as great as that FDR had faced, but fears that communist aggression might force the U.S. into a nuclear war generated considerable anxiety. Pollster Lou Harris, who gave Kennedy periodic soundings on public mood, advised him to concentrate on two major themes rather than on "a plethora of specifics . . . : The spirit of inspired realism that will be the mood of this new Administration; [and] the nature of the challenge and the broad approaches that can bring about national fulfillment and peace for all peoples everywhere." Kennedy wished to draw the strongest possible contrast between the "drift" of his predecessor and the promise of renewed mastery.

As one symbol of the change in Washington, Kennedy decreed that top hats were required dress at the Inauguration, a shift from the black homburgs Eisenhower had made part of the 1952 dress code. (When Kennedy spotted a newsman in a homburg outside his Georgetown home, he asked in mock horror, "Didn't you get the word? Top hats are the rule this year.") Yet during Inauguration Day, the *New York Times* reported, "Kennedy, who is usually hatless, seemed self-consciously uncomfortable in his topper. He wore it as briefly as possible in the trips back and forth from the White House to Capitol Hill." Despite "a Siberian wind knifing down Pennsylvania Avenue . . . [that] turned majorettes' legs blue, froze baton twirlers' fingers and drove beauty queens to flannels and overcoats," Kennedy stood bareheaded and without his overcoat while taking the oath, giving his address, and watching the three-and-a-half-hour inaugural parade along Pennsylvania Avenue. His only concession to the cold was an occasional sip of soup or coffee.

Nothing worried Kennedy more about his appearance than the effects of the cortisone he took to control his Addison's disease. He was reluctant to take his pills, which made him look puffy faced and overweight. Evelyn Lincoln took responsibility for making sure that he adhered to the regime prescribed by his doctors, keeping daily account of whether he had taken his medicine. She recalled that on January 16, as he dictated a letter and paced the floor of his bedroom, he caught a view of himself in a mirror. "My God," he said, "'look at that fat face, if I don't lose five pounds this week we might have to call off the Inauguration.' I was so full of laughter I could hardly contain myself," Lincoln recorded. Kennedy's humor masked a concern that nothing detract from the view of him as in picture-perfect health. When newsmen asked about his medical condition two hours before his swearing in, two physicians announced that an examination earlier in January had shown the president-elect to be in continuing "excellent" health.

He need not have worried. His seeming imperviousness to the cold coupled with his bronzed appearance — attributed to his pre-inaugural holiday in the Florida sun — and his neatly brushed thick brown hair made him seem "the picture of health." Despite only four hours of sleep following an inaugural concert and gala the previous night, Kennedy "seemed unaffected and unfrightened as he approached the responsibilities of leadership." "He looked like such a new, fresh man," Lincoln said, "someone in whom we could have confidence." One Washington columnist compared him to a Hemingway hero who exhibits "grace under pressure. . . . He is one of the handsomest men in American political life," she wrote without fear of exaggeration. "He was born rich and he has been lucky. He has conquered serious illness. He is as graceful as a greyhound and can be as beguiling as a sunny day."

Using the Inauguration to help rebuild national hope required other symbols. His large family, including Jackie, who was still recovering from a difficult childbirth in November, joined him on the platform. To contrast Eisenhower's inertia on civil rights and encourage liberals to see him as ready to move forward on equality for African Americans, he asked Marian Anderson to sing "The Star-Spangled Banner." He also invited Robert Frost to read a poem at the Inauguration as a symbol of renewed regard for men of thought and imagination — another perceived deficiency of Eisenhower's presidency. When Stewart Udall, a friend of Frost's, had suggested the poet have a role, "Kennedy's eyes brightened in approval, but he had quick second thoughts. 'A great idea,'" he said, "but let's not set up a situation like Lincoln had with Edward Everett in Gettysburg," referring to the two-hour oration that initially put Lincoln's brief address in its shadow. "Frost is a master with words," Kennedy continued. "His remarks will detract from my inaugural address if we're not careful. Why not have him read a poem — something that won't put him in competition with me?"

Kennedy assumed that Frost would read the sixteen lines of his "national poem," "The Gift Outright." But, eager to celebrate the new generation's rise to national leadership, Frost composed a new poem for the occasion, titled "Dedication," in which he announced "The glory of a next Augustan age." When he stepped to the podium, however, the bright sunlight and wind conspired to rob the eighty-six-year-old Frost of his sight, and despite Lyndon Johnson's effort to shield the paper from the blinding sun with his top hat, Frost had to abandon his surprise poem and recite "The Gift Outright" from memory.

Jack had started thinking about his inaugural speech immediately after his election, and he had asked Sorensen to gather suggestions from everyone. He also asked Sorensen, the principal draftsman, to make the address as brief as possible and to focus it on foreign affairs. He believed that a laundry list of domestic goals would sound too much like a continuation of the campaign and would make the speech too long. "I don't want people to think I'm a windbag," he said. He also made it clear that he did not want partisan complaints about the immediate past or Cold War clichés about the communist menace that would add to Soviet-American tensions. Above all, he wanted language that would inspire hopes for peace and set an optimistic tone for a new era under a new generation of leaders.

Suggestions of what to say came from many sources and took many forms: "Pages, paragraphs and complete drafts had poured in," Sorensen says, "solicited from [journalist Joseph] Kraft, Galbraith, Stevenson, Bowles and others, unsolicited from newsmen, friends and total strangers." Clergymen provided lists of biblical quotes. Sorensen searched all past inaugural speeches for clues to what worked best and, at Kennedy's suggestion, he studied "the secret of Lincoln's Gettysburg Address." Sorensen found that some of the "best eloquence" in past inaugurals had come from some of our worst presidents, and that the key to Lincoln's Gettysburg Address was its brevity and use of as few multisyllable words as possible.

Yet for all the advice and numerous drafts produced by others, the final version came from Kennedy's hand. He was tireless in working to make it an eloquent expression of his intentions, as well as the shortest twentieth-century inaugural speech. Though ultimately he could not be more concise than FDR, whose 1944 address was about half the length of Kennedy's 1,355 words, compared with the previous forty-four inaugurals, which averaged 2,599 words, Kennedy's was a model of succinctness. But it was not just the prose and length that concerned him; it was also his delivery: In the twenty-four hours before he gave the speech, he kept a reading copy next to him, so that "any spare moment could be used to familiarize himself with it." On Inauguration morning, he sat in the bathtub reading his speech aloud, and at the breakfast table he kept "going over and over it" until he had gotten every word and inflection to his liking.

The speech itself was one of the two most memorable inaugurals of the twentieth century and was an indication of the premium Kennedy put on formal addresses to lead the nation. (There would be two other landmark speeches in the next thousand days.) Kennedy's inaugural stands with Franklin Roosevelt's great first address as an exemplar of inspirational language and a call to civic duty. It began, as Thomas Jefferson's had in 1801, during the first transfer of power from one party to another, with a reminder of shared national values rather than partisanship. "We are all Federalists. We are all Republicans," Jefferson had said. "We observe today not a victory of party but a celebration of freedom," Kennedy declared. Though the world was now vastly different — "man holds in his mortal hands the power to abolish all forms of human poverty and all forms of human life" — Kennedy asserted that the "same revolutionary beliefs for which our forebears fought are still at issue around the globe. . . . Let every nation know, whether it wishes us well or ill, that we shall pay any price, bear any burden, meet any hardship, support any friend, oppose any foe to assure the survival and success of liberty."

To the Third World, the developing nations "struggling to break the bonds of mass misery," he pledged "our best efforts to help them help themselves . . . not because the communists may be doing it . . . but because it is right. If a free society cannot help the many who are poor, it cannot save the few who are rich." And "to our sister republics south of our border, we offer a special pledge — to convert our good words into good deeds — in a new alliance for progress." Lest anyone believe that he was a sentimental crusader oblivious to the harsh realities of international competition, Kennedy laid down a warning to Castro's Cuba and its Soviet ally: "Let all our neighbors know that we shall join with them to oppose aggression or subversion anywhere in the Americas. And let every other power know that this Hemisphere intends to remain the master of its own house."

Kennedy did not want Moscow to see his administration as intent on an apocalyptic showdown between East and West. To the contrary, much of the rest of his speech was an invitation to find common ground against a devastating nuclear war. He would not tempt America's adversaries with weakness, he said, "For only when our arms are sufficient beyond doubt can we be certain beyond doubt that they will never be employed. . . . Let us never negotiate out of fear," he advised. "But let us never fear to negotiate. . . . And if a beachhead of cooperation may push back the jungle of suspicion, let both sides join in creating a new endeavor, not a new balance of power, but a new world of law, where the strong are just and the weak secure and the peace preserved."

Concerned not to appear naive or overly optimistic about negotiations, and eager to separate himself from FDR and excessive expectations of quick advance, Kennedy predicted, "All this will not be finished in the first one hundred days. Nor will it be finished in the first one thousand days, nor in the life of this Administration, nor even perhaps in our lifetime on this planet. But let us begin."

The closing paragraphs were a call to national commitment and sacrifice. "Now the trumpet summons us again — not as a call to bear arms, though arms we need — not as a call to battle, though embattled we are — but a call to bear the burden of a long twilight struggle, year in and year out . . . a struggle against the common enemies of man: tyranny, poverty, disease and war itself. . . . And so, my fellow Americans: ask not what your country can do for you — ask what you can do for your country." The sentence joined FDR's "nothing to fear but fear itself" as the most remembered language in any twentieth-century inaugural.

Kennedy's rhetoric thrilled the crowd of twenty thousand dignitaries and ordinary citizens gathered in twenty-degree temperature in temporary wooden grandstands on the east front of the Capitol. President Eisenhower declared the speech "fine, very fine," and Republican minority leader Senator Everett Dirksen called it "inspiring, a very compact message of hope." Eisenhower's speechwriter Emmet John Hughes told Kennedy, "You have truly inspired the excitement of the people. . . . You have struck sparks with splendid swiftness." Democratic senator Mike Monroney of Oklahoma was as effusive, describing the address as the best of the twelve inaugurals he had heard, starting with Woodrow Wilson's second in 1917. Stevenson saw it as "eloquent, inspiring — a great speech," and Truman believed, "It was just what the people should hear and live up to." Arthur Krock told Kennedy over dinner the night of the Inauguration that the address was the best political speech anyone had given in America since Wilson. (Eager to encourage views of a new administration likely to rival the best in the country's history, Kennedy hoped Krock would make his judgment of the speech public, which he did.) But while the positive response to his speech delighted Kennedy, it was not enough to quiet his inner doubts about its quality and effectiveness. A critical editorial by Max Ascoli of *The Reporter*, who said that he was neither "impressed [n]or stirred by it," "disturbed" the new president. Kennedy told Jackie that he did not think his speech was as good as Jefferson's.

Jefferson and his unmatched brilliance were indeed the mark against which Kennedy intended to measure himself. When James MacGregor Burns told Jack during the interregnum that he hoped he would be the Jefferson of the twentieth century, Kennedy, who was preceding him down the stairs of his Georgetown house, turned and looked at him with a smile that suggested both skepticism and satisfaction. During a dinner for Nobel Laureates at the White House, Kennedy told them that this was the greatest array of brainpower assembled in the mansion since Jefferson had dined there alone. He then quoted the description of Jefferson as "a gentleman of thirty-two who could calculate an eclipse, survey an estate, tie an artery, plan an edifice, try a cause, break a horse, dance a minuet, and play the violin."

After Kennedy's speech, almost three quarters of Americans approved of their new president. The numbers indicated that Kennedy had effectively managed the transition. But he had no illusion that he could maintain public support for long without following through on the commitment to get the country moving again. The problems of leading the nation onto higher ground, however, were more daunting than he ever imagined.

CHAPTER 10

The Schooling of a President

I claim not to have controlled events, but confess plainly that events have controlled me.

— Abraham Lincoln, April 4, 1864

Though the President is Commander-in-Chief, Congress is his commander.

— Thaddeus Stevens, January 3, 1867

ALTHOUGH KENNEDY DISCOURAGED the belief that his first hundred days would produce major achievements, he understood that to sustain the momentum created by his inaugural he would need quickly to demonstrate a mastery of some issues. He doubted that he could do it in domestic affairs. At his first press conference five days after becoming president, a reporter asked him why his inaugural speech had dealt only with international problems. "Well," Kennedy replied, "because the issue of war and peace is involved, and the survival of perhaps the planet, possibly our system." He also explained that the views of his administration on domestic affairs were already well known to the American people and would become better known in the next month. By contrast, he said, "we are new . . . on the world scene, and therefore I felt there would be some use in informing countries around the world of our general view on the questions which . . . divide the world."

Fourteen years in Washington had taught Kennedy that presidents had greater control over foreign than domestic policy and had a better chance of promoting national unity with foreign initiatives than domestic ones, which were certain to provoke acrimonious political divisions. Yet he also understood that he could not shelve domestic issues, despite a conviction that Congress would not agree to bold reforms. The House promised to be a particular problem. Although the Democrats held an 89-seat advantage, 262 to 173, 101 of the Democrats were from the Old South, and a majority of them seemed certain to side with conservative Republicans on domestic issues. Worse, conservative southerners Howard Smith of Virginia and William Colmer of Mississippi dominated the twelve-member House Rules Committee, which decided whether a bill would reach the House floor for a vote. Smith and Colmer invariably joined the four Republicans on the committee in turning back reform proposals. To give his administration a better chance of eventually winning House support for economic, education, health, and civil rights reforms, and to signal his determination to fight for these gains, Kennedy joined Speaker Sam Rayburn in trying to expand the committee to fifteen members, including two more progressive Democrats.

The fight on the Rules Committee was a formidable first test of Kennedy's political skills. When a reporter asked him at his January 25 news conference whether he was living up to his commitment to be in the thick of the political battle, Kennedy voiced his support for Rayburn's proposed change, saying that the whole House should have the opportunity to vote on the many controversial measures that his administration would present and that a small group of men should not prevent the majority of members from "letting their judgments be known." At the same time, however, he declared his commitment to allowing the House "to settle this matter in its own way" and pledged not to "infringe upon that responsibility. I merely give my view as an interested citizen," he concluded with a broad smile and to the amusement of the press corps, which erupted in laughter. The fight, which lasted eleven days, was touch and go, and moved Bobby at one uncertain moment to phone Richard Bolling of Missouri, who was a leading reform advocate, to complain that he was destroying his brother by getting him into a battle he was going to lose. "Bullshit, buddy," Bolling told him. "It's a tough fight and we're going to win it." Which they did, on January 31, by a 217 to 212 vote.

Bolling acknowledged later that the victory over Smith and the other conservatives on the Rules Committee actually guaranteed nothing, since the composition of the House made it difficult for Kennedy to exploit the change in the committee. Because Kennedy anticipated such a problem and because he wished to create some sense of forward movement on domestic problems, he began his administration with executive actions that signaled his determination to get things done with or without the Congress.

As one of his first Executive Orders, Kennedy directed the Agriculture Department to increase food distributions to the unemployed, which would ensure that they received a more varied diet. The press wanted to know how Kennedy could do something that Ezra Taft Benson, Eisenhower's agriculture secretary, said he lacked legislative authority for. Kennedy refused to comment on Benson's inaction, but assured the journalists that he had the power to act and emphasized instead that the diet provided to the unemployed was "still inadequate." It was smart politics and bolstered him with liberals: Let's not quibble over fine points of the law, he was saying, when the fundamental right to an adequate diet is at stake.

Civil rights reform was more difficult to manage. Kennedy's only mention of racial justice in his inaugural address was a sentence describing America as committed to human rights at home and around the world. He understood that a southern-dominated Congress was unlikely to advance black equality by legislative action, despite passage in 1957 of the first civil rights law since 1875. To win approval of more progressive measures would have meant investing much of his political capital in a potentially losing fight. Consequently, he intended to rely on executive authority in behalf of racial equality to satisfy liberals and encourage blacks to expect more and bolder steps in the future.

As an opening move, Kennedy appointed Robert C. Weaver, a black expert on housing, as administrator of the Housing and Home Finance Agency (HHFA). In a meeting with JFK, Weaver asked for assurances that Kennedy would make him secretary of a housing and urban affairs department, should Congress create one, but Kennedy would not commit himself; persuading Alabama, Mississippi, and Virginia senators to confirm Weaver as head of HHFA was challenge enough. Although complaining that Weaver was "pro-Communist," southern Democrats, reluctant to undermine their party's new president, grudgingly agreed to accept Kennedy's recommendation.

Kennedy also established a Committee on Equal Employment Opportunity (CEEO) to eliminate discrimination in hiring federal employees, help expand the number of black government workers, and deny federal contracts to businesses refusing equal opportunity to blacks. Kennedy asked Lyndon Johnson to chair the committee. Johnson was reluctant to take on an assignment that could antagonize southern congressmen and senators and undermine his chances of ever running for president. But Kennedy, who believed that Johnson could help blunt southern opposition to civil rights advances, was insistent, and Johnson, who had led the 1957 civil rights bill through Congress and sincerely believed in equal justice, accepted the challenge.

Kennedy's strategy on civil rights became public immediately after he took office. As he watched coast guard marchers troop by during the inaugural parade, he noted the absence of blacks in their ranks and instructed his treasury secretary, who had jurisdiction over the coast guard, to bring them into that branch of the service. Similarly, at his first cabinet meeting, he asked each cabinet secretary to expand opportunities for blacks in his department. He took special note of the foreign service, where he felt an absence of blacks hurt America's image abroad. He appointed Clifford R. Wharton as ambassador to Norway, the first African American to become the top U.S. diplomat in a predominantly white country.

By the middle of February, Kennedy's dealings with the Congress had confirmed his judgment that he could not secure passage of a significant civil rights bill in the current session. Winning a cloture vote to halt a filibuster by southerners was clearly out of reach. But he did not want anyone to think that he was abandoning civil rights reform. On February 16, he told White House aide Mike Feldman to maintain close contact with Pennsylvania senator Joe Clark and Brooklyn congressman Emanuel Celler, whom he had asked to implement the civil rights commitments of the platform. "It may be proper for them to hold hearings this year on various legislative proposals and then have the fight next year," Kennedy wrote Feldman, "but I don't want statements to be issued that we have withdrawn our support of this matter." The announcement on April 7, 1961, that pursuant to Executive Order 10925, issued by Kennedy on March 6, the CEEO would begin its work heartened some of those disappointed at the new administration's failure to ask Congress for a major civil rights law guaranteeing equal treatment in places of public accommodation and the right to vote.

Kennedy gained additional standing with civil rights advocates by opposing the slated expiration in the fall of the Civil Rights

Commission, a six-member agency mandated to keep watch on the state of civil rights around the country. As a signal that he would not let the commission die, Kennedy asked sitting commissioners John Hannah and Father Theodore Hesburgh to continue to serve. Although willing, they doubted that Kennedy would take bold initiatives. When Hesburgh emphasized the urgency of action by citing statistics about the absence of blacks in southern state universities and in the Alabama National Guard, Kennedy replied, "Look, Father, I may have to send the Alabama National Guard to Berlin tomorrow and I don't want to do it in the middle of a revolution at home." It was a clear signal of Kennedy's priorities.

Understanding the constraints on Kennedy, Hannah and Hesburgh wanted the commission to exert counterpressure by having special access to the White House through a liaison. Kennedy said that Harris Wofford, whom he had made a full-time special assistant on civil rights, was already on the job, which was false. But Hannah and Hesburgh responded that Wofford was taking an office at the administration's new Peace Corps. Kennedy replied, "That's only temporary." As soon as they had left, a Kennedy aide called Wofford to come to the White House at once. There, "a solemn-looking man in a dark suit, carrying a book," approached Wofford. The man said that the president had ordered him to swear Wofford in, although neither he nor Wofford knew to what position. Wofford swore to uphold the Constitution and then was ushered into the Oval Office. Kennedy made it clear that Wofford would become a special assistant to the president on civil rights and would devote himself to making sure that civil rights advocates were "not too unhappy, and beyond that [Kennedy] wanted to make substantial headway against what he considered the nonsense of racial discrimination." The strategy for 1961, he told Wofford, was "minimum civil rights legislation, maximum executive action." In March, when two conservative Civil Rights Commission members resigned, Kennedy appointed antisegregationists, who won Senate approval over the objections of southerners. At the same time, however, Kennedy hesitated to make a direct request to Congress to extend the life of the commission. Reluctant to risk losing ground on civil rights by a possible negative vote in Congress, he kept the agency alive by executive action.

In the first hundred days, the economy was Kennedy's biggest domestic worry. The 1960 recession that had helped elect him continued into 1961. In his State of the Union Message on January 30, he made economic expansion his primary domestic goal. "We take office," he declared, "in the wake of seven months of recession, three and one half years of slack, seven years of diminished economic growth, and nine years of falling farm income." With five and a half million unemployed — nearly 7 percent of the workforce — and business bankruptcies at their highest level since the Great Depression, Kennedy justifiably described the economy as "in trouble. The most resourceful industrialized country on earth ranks among the last in the rate of economic growth," he said.

But, as with civil rights, Kennedy felt he had limited capacity to force immediate change. He had already ruled out a tax cut as politically unacceptable when he was asking people to sacrifice for the good of the country. Nor did he believe that he could force a big economic program through Congress that included spending a lot of money on public works programs. When one liberal economist proposed a 60 percent increase in the federal deficit in order to help with unemployment, Kennedy told him: "With the seven percent unemployment we have now, ninety-three percent of the people in the country are employed. That other seven percent isn't going to get enough political support to do it. I don't believe that, right or wrong, there's any possibility of doing the kind of all-out economic operation that you want." Nor was he inclined to talk conservative Federal Reserve chairman William McChesney Martin into reducing interest rates, another means liberals saw for stimulating a recovery. He thought a rate reduction would antagonize bankers, as would replacing Martin, and would worsen the country's balance of payments by discouraging foreign investments in U.S. Treasury bonds.

So once again, he relied on executive action. A special message to Congress on February 2 cautioned against expecting "to make good in a day or even a year the accumulated deficiencies of several years." It was better to be "realistic" about what they could achieve in 1961: reverse the downward trend, narrow the gap of unused potential, "abate the waste and misery of unemployment," and maintain reasonable price stability. Then, in 1962–63, they could hope to expand "American productive capacity at a rate that shows the world the vigor and vitality of a free economy." Kennedy announced more rapid federal spending on building highways and post offices; speedier payment of tax refunds, veteran benefits, and farm subsidies; and stepped-up efforts to implement urban renewal programs. Wherever possible, federal purchasing would be channeled into areas of high unemployment. State and local governments were also urged to spend federal allocations for public programs as fast as possible. Recognizing that these proposals might not promptly "restore momentum to the American economy," Kennedy promised that "if these measures prove to be inadequate to the task, I shall submit further proposals to the Congress within the next 75 days."

After only six weeks, however, with evidence that the economy was getting weaker rather than stronger, CEA chairman Walter Heller had prepared a "second-stage recovery program." As Kennedy joked at the press's annual Gridiron dinner in early March, "The Secretary of Treasury reported that the worst of the recession was not yet spent — but everything else was."

Heller may have had "profiles in courage" in mind as he urged Kennedy to do the right thing for the economy — a tax cut, lower interest rates, and deficit spending — without regard for political constraints. But liberal economists Paul Samuelson and Leon Keyserling had little confidence that Kennedy would respond positively to such an appeal. Keyserling, who was particularly cynical about Kennedy, said, "Kennedy never thought of anything except in terms of how it will affect [him] in reelection four years from now." Keyserling was being far too critical. The political consequences of a failed economic initiative with Congress and the Federal Reserve were unquestionable constraints on Kennedy, but he nevertheless asked the CEA to develop "bold" proposals for implementation should the economy continue a slow recovery from its latest decline.

Happily for Kennedy, an upturn that became evident in early April freed him from having to make immediate hard choices about the economy. "The financial program of the Administration is now beginning to show impressive results," the CEA told him. At the end of May, Heller reported a likely $9 billion rise in GNP from the first to the second quarter, with an additional $50 billion expansion forecast over the next fifteen months. Although Heller did not expect this economic growth to reduce unemployment much below 6 percent, it further eased Kennedy's need to invest political capital in bold economic measures to get the country moving again.

As it was, he could take comfort from the fact that administration proposals being enacted by Congress — an Area Redevelopment Act aimed at depressed regions, a twenty-five-cent rise in the minimum wage to $1.25, expanded Social Security benefits, and a nearly $5 billion low-and-middle-income-housing bill — were promising to provide enough economic stimulation to make Americans more hopeful about the future. In early March, 35 percent of Americans had expressed the belief that more people in their community would be out of work in the next six months, but by late April, only 18 percent said this. In the same two polls, the number of optimists about the economy increased from 34 to 58 percent.

Judging from a series of other opinion surveys from March and April, the public was warmly disposed toward Kennedy's presidency. On March 13, *Newsweek* reported that the "new, young, and untried President . . . now had the great part of the American people behind him." Lou Harris told JFK that his approval rating was at 92 percent, and Gallup put it at a still-impressive 72 percent. Kennedy understood that more than economic steps and hopes were generating public goodwill. Even before his inauguration, columnist Joe Alsop thought Kennedy had changed the public mood. "I don't think you've put a foot wrong since election day," Alsop told him. "It's been an astonishing performance. . . . I can all but see my friends, including a most surprising number of Republican friends, breathing in new hope, and . . . getting ready to move forward in the rough times that lie ahead." One Kennedy aide ascribed the shift to "the simple fact that an active, do-something administration has now replaced a passive, do-nothing administration."

Kennedy himself believed that weekly press conferences, which were broadcast live on television and radio for the first time in American history, were making a difference. Apprehensions that live appearances with occasional inadvertent statements might have "grave consequences" did not deter him. Columnist James Reston, warning that the format could lead to a catastrophe, characterized it as "the goofiest idea since the hula hoop." But convinced that such fears were overdrawn and that direct communication with the public made the small risk of misstatements worth taking, Kennedy dismissed the concerns as unwarranted.

He also knew that news conferences allowed him to put his intelligence and wit on display. Schlesinger remembered the conferences as "a superb show, always gay, often exciting, relished by the reporters and by the television audience. . . . The conferences," he added, "offered a showcase for a number of [Kennedy's] most characteristic qualities — the intellectual speed and vivacity, the remarkable mastery of the data of government, the terse self-mocking wit, the exhilarating personal command." Some of his funniest responses, which he gave at breakfast prep sessions, were too barbed for public consumption. Still, he thought of these conferences as "The 6 O'Clock Comedy Hour."

His quick mastery of the press interviews before TV cameras and microphones persuaded Kennedy that "we couldn't survive without TV." It allowed him not only to charm the public, but also to reach people directly without the editorializing of the news media through interpretation or omission. Perhaps most important, whether on television or in person, Kennedy came across to the public as believable. Unlike Nixon, who never overcame a reputation for deceitfulness, Kennedy's manner — his whole way of speaking, choice of words, inflection, and steady gaze — persuaded listeners to take him at his word. And the public loved it. By April 1962, a Gallup poll would show that nearly three out of every four adults in the country had seen or heard one or more of the president's news conferences. Ninety-one percent of them had a favorable impression of his performance; only 4 percent were negative. In addition, by a 61 to 32 percent margin, Americans favored the spontaneous TV format.

ENCOURAGING DEVELOPMENTS in relations with the Soviet Union from the first week of Kennedy's presidency also contributed to his high approval ratings. Back in July 1960, a U.S. patrol plane had been lost while flying a mission over the Barents Sea north of Russia. Ten days later, Moscow had announced that the plane had invaded its air space and been shot down but that two crew members had survived and were in Soviet custody. During the next six months — the remainder of Eisenhower's term — the two governments argued about the appropriateness of the Soviet attack. After Kennedy's inauguration, Khrushchev had announced that "step by step, it will be possible to remove existing suspicion and distrust and cultivate seeds of friendship and practical cooperation." Kennedy's noncommittal response that his government stood ready "to cooperate with all who are prepared to join in genuine dedication to the assurance of a peaceful and a more fruitful life for all mankind" suggested that the new administration would measure Khrushchev's words by future deeds.

At his first press conference, on January 25, Kennedy announced that the Soviets had released the two fliers. Khrushchev privately revealed that just before the election, Ambassador Llewellyn Thompson had told him that if he released the fliers, "he would set himself in right with Mr. Nixon." But Nixon's reputation as an anti-communist ideologue and Khrushchev's falling-out with Eisenhower over the U-2 incident had made Moscow partial to a more flexible Democrat like Kennedy. The Soviet decision to release the fliers after January 20 was a gift to the new president that gave Kennedy instant credibility as a foreign policy leader. In response, Kennedy declared that Moscow had "removed a serious obstacle to harmonious relations."

Kennedy's responses to unauthorized public statements by U.S. military chiefs demonstrated that he intended to assert the closest possible control over the making of foreign policy, particularly toward Moscow. His critical view of some World War II navy chiefs, skepticism about investing so much in defense at the expense of foreign economic aid, and a January 17, 1961, Eisenhower farewell speech warning against "unwarranted influence . . . by the military-industrial complex" had increased Kennedy's sensitivity to what Ike described as "the potential for the disastrous rise of misplaced power."

Speeches by Admiral Arleigh Burke, chief of naval operations, on the U.S.-Soviet rivalry particularly impressed Kennedy as destructive to potential initiatives for easing tensions. Arthur Sylvester, McNamara's press officer, remembers that he "hardly had been in the damn job, didn't even know where the men's room was," when the navy chief of information brought him a speech in which "this stupid Burke was going to . . . [attack] the Soviet Union from hell to breakfast not knowing all the facts." Sylvester took the speech to the White House, where Kennedy ordered Burke to rein in his rhetoric. "You old son-of-a-bitch," Burke told Sylvester, "I'll write a new speech." Burke apparently leaked the story to the *New York Times,* which brought charges of muzzling from senators on the Armed Services Committee. But seeing limits on the military as essential to gains in Soviet-American relations, Kennedy told Sylvester, "Arthur, the greatest thing that's happened in the first three months of my administration was your stopping the Burke speech." To prevent Burke and other military chiefs from publicly challenging Kennedy's freedom to make conciliatory gestures toward Moscow, the administration announced in January that all officers on active duty would have to clear public statements with the White House.

The clash with Burke, followed by a McNamara revelation in February that there was no missile gap, encouraged public faith in

Kennedy's foreign policy leadership. Initially, the missile gap revelation threatened to embarrass the president by suggesting that he had used national defense for cynical purposes during the campaign. And indeed, when McNamara told reporters in a background briefing that the United States had more operational missiles than the Soviets, it provoked a furor in the press. Kennedy refused to confirm McNamara's assertion, saying at a news conference that a study was under way to determine the facts and that it was "premature to reach a judgment as to whether there is a gap or not a gap."

But to Kennedy's surprise, the issue did not resonate with the public. On the contrary, it seemed to care much less about who had said what about the missile gap than about America's advantage over Moscow. It was as if Kennedy's presence in the White House had magically granted the United States military superiority over the Soviet Union. In April 1960, 50 percent of the country had believed it a good idea to raise taxes to help eliminate the missile gap. A few days after the press reported McNamara's comment, 49 percent of Americans accepted that the United States was stronger than Russia, while only 30 percent continued to think that it was the reverse. By June, despite little additional press discussion of the issue, 54 percent of Americans believed that the United States led Moscow in long-range missiles and rockets, with only 20 percent seeing the Soviets as ahead. The public was more concerned that the Soviets seemed to be eclipsing the United States in a global contest for hearts and minds. Sixty-six percent wanted to equal Moscow's public relations budget to tell "our side of the story to Europe and the world."

Kennedy partly satisfied the national yearning to outdo Moscow in the promotion of national values by setting up the Peace Corps. The proposal had originated with Hubert Humphrey. Kennedy had been considering the idea for a number of months, having discussed it during a late-night campaign stop at the University of Michigan. On March 1, he issued an Executive Order authorizing the dispatch of American men and women "to help foreign countries meet their urgent needs for skilled manpower." The corps was not to be "an instrument of diplomacy or propaganda or ideological conflict." Instead, it would allow "our people to exercise more fully their responsibilities in the great common cause of world development." And life in the corps would "not be easy." Volunteers would receive "no salary and allowances will be at a level sufficient only to maintain health and meet basic needs. Men and women will be expected to work and live alongside the nationals of the country in which they are stationed — doing the same work, eating the same food, talking the same language." Kennedy hoped that service in the corps would be "a source of satisfaction to Americans and a contribution to world peace."

The response in the United States to the proposal was all Kennedy hoped it would be. Seventy-one percent of Americans declared themselves in favor of such a program, and thousands of young Americans volunteered to share in the adventure of helping less-advantaged peoples around the world. Over the next two years, the program maintained a high profile among Americans and overseas, with 74 percent of the American public well-disposed toward the work of the corps.

One measure of the program's success was the antagonism it generated in Moscow and among some Third World citizens. They complained that the Peace Corps was nothing more than a propaganda trick that would also allow the CIA to plant agents in African, Asian, and Latin American countries. Critics dubbed the corps "Kennedy's Kiddie Korps," "a lot of kids bouncing around the world in Bermuda shorts." But Kennedy understood that the corps would help combat Soviet depictions of the United States as a typical capitalist country, entirely self-interested and only too willing to take advantage of weaker, dependent nations. He knew that American self-interest and idealism were not mutually exclusive; indeed, one was as much a part of the national tradition as the other. And he believed that Peace Corps workers would make a genuine contribution not only to the well-being of the peoples they served but also to U.S. national security by encouraging emerging nations to take the United States rather than Soviet Russia as their model.

To underscore the Peace Corps' commitment to idealistic aims, Kennedy appointed Sargent Shriver as director. Shriver later joked that JFK chose him because no one thought it could succeed, "and it would be easier to fire a relative than a political friend." But, in fact, Kennedy picked him because he was a recognized idealist who believed that "if you do good, you'll do well" and wished to do his "best for folks who couldn't do theirs." Shriver was known for the motivating mottoes on his office walls. "There is no place in this club for good losers," one said. "Bring me only bad news; good news weakens me," another declared. He was also a man of unquestioned integrity and boundless energy. He directed that no member of the corps was to engage in any diplomatic activities or intelligence gathering. "Their only job was to help people help themselves," he told them. He was indefatigable, working sometimes until three or four o'clock in the morning. He wanted only devoted evangelists around him, telling the chairman of AT&T that he wished there were a telephone system that "had us all plugged in like an umbilical cord so we could never get away."

The Peace Corps proved to be one of the enduring legacies of Kennedy's presidency. As with some American domestic institutions like Social Security and Medicare, the Peace Corps became a fixture that Democratic and Republican administrations alike would continue to finance for over forty years. It made far more friends than enemies and, as Kennedy had hoped, convinced millions of people abroad that the United States was eager to help developing nations raise standards of living.

In no region of the world was Kennedy more determined to encourage a positive image of the United States than in Latin America. Fidel Castro's summons to peoples of the Western Hemisphere to throw off the yoke of U.S. domination challenged Kennedy to offer a competing message of hope that countered convictions about Yankee imperialism. Khrushchev deepened Kennedy's concern in January 1961, when he publicly declared Moscow on the side of "wars of national liberation." Kennedy believed that Khrushchev's speech "made clear the pattern of military and paramilitary infiltration and subversion which could be expected under the guise of 'wars of liberation.'" Kennedy told his ambassador to Peru that "Latin America required our best efforts and attention." This was not simply rhetoric on Kennedy's part: His presidency generated more documents and files on Cuba than on the USSR and Vietnam combined.

Part of Kennedy's response to the communist challenge in Latin America was the Alliance for Progress. He believed it essential for the United States to put itself on the side of social change in the hemisphere. He understood, said Schlesinger, whose White House work included Alliance projects, "that, with all its pretensions to realism, the militant anti-revolutionary line represented the policy most likely to strengthen the communists and lose the hemisphere. He believed that, to maintain contact with a continent seized by the course of revolutionary change, a policy of social idealism was the only true realism for the United States." Though Kennedy would not be able to resist pressures for old-fashioned interventionism, and though he worried that the problems of the southern republics might prove more intractable than he imagined, he nevertheless enthusiastically proposed an alliance between the United States and Latin America to advance economic development, democratic institutions, and social justice. He believed that the contest with communism and old-fashioned American idealism dictated nothing less.

On March 13, in a speech before congressional leaders and hemisphere ambassadors in the East Room of the White House, Kennedy spoke passionately about the opportunity to realize the dream articulated by Simón Bolívar 139 years before of making the Americas into the greatest region in the world. "Never in the long history of our hemisphere has this dream been nearer to fulfillment, and never has it been in greater danger," Kennedy said. Science had provided the tools "to strike off the remaining bonds of poverty and ignorance. Yet at this very moment of maximum opportunity, we confront the same forces which have imperiled America throughout its history — the alien forces which once again seek to impose the despotisms of the Old World on the people of the New. . . . Let me be the first to admit," Kennedy disarmingly acknowledged, "that we North Americans have not always grasped the significance of this common mission, just as it is also true that many in your own countries have not fully understood the urgency of the need to lift people from poverty and ignorance and despair." He then called on "all people of the hemisphere to join in a new Alliance for Progress — *Alianza para Progreso* — a vast cooperative effort, unparalleled in magnitude and nobility of purpose, to satisfy the basic needs of the American people for homes, work and land, health and schools — *techo, trabajo y tierra, salud y escuela.*"

Kennedy, who had little facility for foreign languages or much talent for pronouncing them (his struggles with high school Latin and French are well documented), had spent part of the afternoon before giving his speech practicing his Spanish. Speechwriter Richard Goodwin, who had drafted the address, tried to help him, but it was pretty useless. Amused at his own imperfect pronunciations, Kennedy asked Goodwin later, "How was my Spanish?" "Perfect," Goodwin lied. "I thought you'd say that," Kennedy said with a grin.

Although everyone in the room understood that Kennedy was launching a memorable program and that he sincerely wanted to achieve a dramatic change in relations with the southern republics and in their national lives, the president's rhetoric did not dispel all doubts. One speech, however sincerely delivered, was not enough to convince the audience that traditional U.S. neglect of the region — the conviction, as Henry Kissinger later facetiously put it, that Latin America is a dagger pointing at the heart of Antarctica — was at an end. Latin American representatives to the United States also believed that American idealism was little more than a tool for combating the communist challenge. Some derisively called the Alliance for Progress the Fidel Castro Plan.

There was some justification in the Latin American dismissal of the Alliance. Kennedy and the great majority of Americans could not ignore Soviet rhetoric and actions, which demonstrated a determination to undermine U.S. power and influence by propaganda, subversion, and communist revolutions in Africa, Asia, Latin America, and the Middle East. True, Khrushchev ruled out a nuclear war as madness, a prescription for destroying hundreds of millions of lives and civilization. But his assertions about Soviet missile superiority and predictions that communism would win control of Third World countries made it impossible for Kennedy or any American president to set Khrushchev's challenge aside.

In private, Kennedy was never a knee-jerk anticommunist. In a meeting with a group of Soviet experts on February 11, he displayed "a mentality extraordinarily free of preconceived prejudices, inherited or otherwise . . . almost as though he had thrown aside the normal prejudices that beset human mentality," State Department Soviet expert Charles Bohlen said. "He saw Russia as a great and powerful country, and it seemed to him there must be some basis upon which the two countries could live without blowing each other up."

Kennedy friend and British economist Lady Barbara Ward Jackson urged Kennedy to mount "a sustained offensive on current clichés" in a speech she proposed he give before the United Nations General Assembly. "The animosities, the festering fears of the Cold War so cloud our minds and our actions that we no longer see reality save through the distorting mirrors of malevolent ill-will." She paraphrased W. H. Auden, "We must love each other or/ We must die." Kennedy, who had promised to "pay any price, bear any burden, meet any hardship," was sympathetic to Jackson's appeal. But he saw no way to go before the U.N., or, more to the point, before the country's many cold warriors, and quote Auden about the choice between love and death. Perhaps he might eventually "find another forum," he told Jackson, "in which to present your thoughts, which are important."

NUCLEAR WAR was Kennedy's "greatest nightmare," Walt W. Rostow, his head of the State Department's Policy Planning Council, said. In March 1960, Kennedy had privately written Eisenhower, "I have been greatly disturbed by the possibility that our current nuclear test ban negotiations might be jeopardized by the approach of a presidential election." He had assured Ike that he would support and sustain any agreement he might reach, and said that he hoped his pledge would "help you to proceed — unhindered by thoughts of the coming election — with your efforts to bring about agreement on this vital matter, and thus bring us one step closer to world peace."

Once in office, Kennedy made clear to his subordinates that he was eager to sign a test ban treaty. He saw it as "in the overall interest of the national security of the United States to make a renewed and vigorous attempt to negotiate a test ban agreement." But the Soviets, whose nuclear inferiority to the United States made them reluctant to conclude a treaty, showed little inclination in talks at Geneva to sustain a current informal ban on testing. The Soviet "stand at Geneva," Kennedy told British prime minister Harold Macmillan in April, "raises the question of whether to break off the talks and under what conditions. There is a great deal of pressure here to renew tests," Kennedy added. Deputy Defense Secretary Roswell Gilpatric remembers that "every approach toward arms control" agitated opposition among some in the White House, the State Department, and especially the military. "They felt this was as much of a foe or a threat as the Soviet Union or Red China. They had just a built-in, negative . . . knee-jerk reaction to anything like this." If it became necessary for the United States to resume testing, JFK told West German chancellor Konrad Adenauer, it must be clear to the world that this was done "only in the light of our national responsibility."

However strong his determination to avoid a nuclear conflict with the Soviet Union, Kennedy could not rule out the possibility. The Soviet acquisition of a nuclear arsenal had provoked American military planners into advocacy of a massive first-strike stockpile, or what they called "a war-fighting capability over a finite deterrent [or] (retaliatory) posture." They believed that the more pronounced the

United States' nuclear advantage over Moscow was, the more likely it would be "to stem Soviet cold war advances." But such a strategy would also mean an arms race, which seemed likely to heighten the danger of a war. It was a miserable contradiction from which Kennedy was never able entirely to escape.

The possibility, under "command control" rules he had inherited from Eisenhower, that "a subordinate commander faced with a substantial Russian military action could start the thermonuclear holocaust on his own initiative" added to JFK's worries about the inadvertent outbreak of a nuclear conflict. When Henry Brandon asked Strategic Air commander General Thomas Powers "whether he was not worried by the fearful power he had at his fingertips, he said he was more worried by the civilian control over him and equally frightened by both." Gilpatric said later, "We became increasingly horrified over how little positive control the President really had over the use of this great arsenal of [thousands of] nuclear weapons." A February 15 report from a subcommittee of the Atomic Energy Commission reviewing NATO procedures deepened Kennedy's concern that accidental use of a nuclear weapon "might trigger a world war." In response, Kennedy tried to guard against a mishap and to assure himself of exclusive control over the nuclear option. But even with this greater authority, the conviction of the military chiefs that in any Soviet-American war we would have to resort to nuclear force made Kennedy feel that he might be pressured into using these weapons against his better judgment.

Perhaps not surprisingly, from the start of his term, Kennedy felt little rapport with the military chiefs. His World War II memories of uninspiring commanders with poor judgment, military miscalculations in the Korean fighting, and the Eisenhower policy of massive retaliation made him distrustful of the U.S. defense establishment. Specifically, neither Kennedy nor McNamara saw Lyman Lemnitzer, the army chief of staff and chairman of the Joint Chiefs of Staff, taking "the lead in bringing the military along to a new doctrine such as flexible response," the freedom to choose from a wider array of military responses in a conflict with the Soviet Union. And of course Burke had already fallen out of favor.

Kennedy's greatest tensions, however, were with NATO commander General Lauris Norstad and air force chief of staff General Curtis LeMay. Harvard's dean of faculty McGeorge Bundy, whom Kennedy had brought to Washington as national security adviser, told the president that Norstad "is a nuclear war man," meaning that he believed any war with the Soviet Union would quickly escalate into a nuclear exchange if the United States were to have any hope of emerging victorious. Bundy urged Kennedy to make clear to Norstad that "*you* are in charge and that your views will govern. . . . If Norstad sets a very different weight on the uses of nuclear war from your own, you need to know it and you need to make him know who is boss."

LeMay was even more of a problem. In charge of firebombings on Japan during World War II and the Berlin airlift in 1948–49, he enjoyed widespread public support. A gruff, cigar-chewing, outspoken advocate of air power who wanted to bomb enemies back to the Stone Age and complained of America's phobia about nuclear weapons, he became the model for the air force general Jack D. Ripper in the 1963 movie *Dr. Strangelove*. After McNamara opposed some of his demands for additional air forces, LeMay privately complained, "Would things be much worse if Khrushchev were Secretary of Defense?" Gilpatric described LeMay as "unreconstructable." Every time the president "had to see LeMay," Gilpatric said, "he ended up in a fit. I mean he just would be frantic at the end of a session with LeMay because, you know, LeMay couldn't listen or wouldn't take in, and he would make what Kennedy considered . . . outrageous proposals that bore no relation to the state of affairs in the 1960s. And the president never saw him unless at some ceremonial affair, or where he felt he had to make a record of having listened to LeMay. . . . And he had to sit there. I saw the president right afterwards. He was just choleric. He was just beside himself, as close as he ever got . . . " Gilpatric said without concluding the sentence.

Paul Nitze, who had worked with Acheson at the State Department on defense issues and had become McNamara's assistant secretary of defense for international security affairs, believed that Kennedy "was always troubled with . . . how do you obtain military advice; how do you check into it; how do you have an independent view as to its accuracy and relevance?" Kennedy saw the decision to make the "transition from the use of conventional weapons to nuclear weapons" in a conflict as his responsibility, not that of the Joint Chiefs of Staff. "I don't think he ever really satisfied himself that he had found a way to get the best possible military help on such matters," Nitze said.

"The plan that he inherited," Rostow said, "was, 'Mr. President, you just tell us to go to nuclear war, and we'll deal with the rest.' And the plan called for devastating, indiscriminately, China, Russia,

Eastern Europe — it was an orgiastic, Wagnerian plan, and he was determined, from that moment, to get the plan changed so he would have total control of it." It was clear to Kennedy that an all-out nuclear conflict would be "a truly monstrous event in the U.S. — let alone in world history." Despite the understanding that the United States had a large advantage over the Soviets in nuclear weapons and the capacity to deliver them, it was assumed that a nuclear exchange would bring "virtual incineration" to all of Europe and the United States. Kennedy staff members attending the briefing by the Joint Chiefs remembered how tense the president was listening to Lemnitzer, who used thirty-eight flip charts sitting on easels to describe targets, the deployment of forces, and the number of weapons available to strike the enemy. There could be no half measures once the war plan was set in motion, Lemnitzer explained. Even if the United States faced altered conditions than those anticipated, he warned that any "rapid rework of the plan" would entail "grave risks." Kennedy sat tapping his front teeth with his thumb and running his hand through his hair, indications to those who knew him well of his irritation with what was being said. Lemnitzer's performance made him "furious." As he left the room, he said to Dean Rusk, "And we call ourselves the human race."

The pressure wasn't just from the Pentagon; America's European allies also expected Kennedy to answer a Soviet attack with nuclear weapons. But the president preferred a strategy of "flexible response" to the current plan of "massive retaliation." He told Adenauer that he was "not so happy . . . with having ballistic missiles driven all over Europe. Too many hazards were involved in this enterprise and this aspect therefore required careful examination." In order to raise "the threshold for the use of atomic weapons," Kennedy proposed that the United States and NATO increase their conventional armies to levels that could "stop Soviet forces now stationed in Eastern Germany." Because the West Germans feared that "these plans might lessen the prospects for the use of atomic weapons in defense of Western Germany," Kennedy "made it clear" that the United States was as much committed to their use as before. Kennedy would have been happier if he could have disavowed a first-strike strategy, Nitze said, but without a continuing commitment to "first strike," Washington feared Franco-German abandonment of NATO, a negotiated compromise with the Soviet Union, and the neutralization of Europe, which would "have left the United States alone to face the whole communist problem." Nevertheless, Kennedy urged McNamara publicly to "'repeat to the point of boredom' that we would use nuclear weapons only in response to a major attack against the U.S. or the allies; that we were not contemplating preventive war; and the Europeans should not believe that by firing off their own nuclear weapons they would drag the United States into a war, that we would withdraw our commitment to NATO first."

For all his anxiety about nuclear war, Kennedy, supported by McNamara, kept LeMay in place. It would be good to have a Curtis LeMay commanding U.S. air forces if the country ever went to war, Kennedy explained. And the reality of Soviet weakness, which became increasingly clear to Kennedy and American military planners in the first months of 1961, did not deter the president and the Pentagon from an expansion of nuclear weapons. Instead, Kennedy feared that Khrushchev still might push the United States into an all-out conflict and he saw no alternative to expanded preparedness. "That son of a bitch Khrushchev," he told Rostow, "he won't stop until we actually take a step that might lead to nuclear war. . . . There's no way you can talk that fella into stopping, until you take some really credible step, which opens up that range of possibilities" for improved relations. A meeting with Khrushchev in June only confirmed JFK's view that he might have to fight a nuclear war and that the United States had no choice but to continue building its arsenal and even consider a first strike as an option against an aggressive Soviet Union. "I never met a man like this," Kennedy told Hugh Sidey. "[I] talked about how a nuclear exchange would kill seventy million people in ten minutes and he just looked at me as if to say, 'So what?' My impression was that he just didn't give a damn if it came to that."

At the end of March 1961, Kennedy announced increases in the defense budget that would expand the number of invulnerable Polaris submarines from 6 to 29 and their nuclear-tipped missiles aimed at Soviet targets from 96 to 464. He also ordered a doubling of total Minutemen intercontinental ballistic missiles from 300 to 600 and a 50 percent increase in B-52 strategic bombers on fifteen-minute ground alert.

In Kennedy's judgment, there was nothing strictly rational about the expansion of forces. Would it deter the Soviet Union from aggression? How much of a buildup was necessary to keep Moscow in check? Could Khrushchev's aggressive Cold War rhetoric be ignored or discounted? Could the Soviets, despite their inferiority to the United States in missile, bomber, and submarine forces, get some of their nuclear bombs past U.S. defenses? How much of a defense expansion would be enough to satisfy the Congress, the public, and the press that America was safe from a devastating attack? When a reporter at a news conference repeated "charges that we have not adequately maintained the strength or credibility of our nuclear deterrent and that we also have not fully convinced the leaders of the Soviet Union that we are determined to meet force with force," Kennedy systematically described his administration's defense increases. Afterward, his frustration with the pressure to meet the Soviet threat with ever stronger words and actions registered on Pierre Salinger. "They don't get it," Kennedy said to him about critics of his defense policies. Khrushchev's bluster combined with U.S. fears left Kennedy unable to stand down from the maddening arms race.

Kennedy biographer Herbert S. Parmet said that JFK "would have been profoundly disturbed to know that so many historians would later stress that his contribution to human existence was the extension of the cold war and the escalation of the arms race." Such distress would have been understandable. Despite irresistible pressures to add to American military power and overreact to communist "dangers," Kennedy ensured that a decision for nuclear war would be his alone, which meant that he could avert an unprecedented disaster for all humankind — which he did. His management of one international crisis after another to avert what he described as "the ultimate failure" was the greatest overall achievement of his presidency.

AS A SENATOR who had seen Africa as a major potential Cold War battleground, Kennedy had come to the White House eager to guard against Soviet advances on the continent. The focus of his concern immediately became the Congo, which, as he pointed out in his January 30 State of the Union Message, was "brutally torn by civil strife, political unrest and public disorder." Independence from Belgium in 1960 had produced violent divisions, with Katanga, the country's richest province, declaring its independence from Leopoldville. The assassination of former prime minister Patrice Lumumba in January, in which the Soviets alleged a United Nations peacekeeping force was involved, undermined U.N. influence and moved Moscow to assert its own influence by sending technicians and arms to back

Lumumba's followers. Kennedy had responded to the Soviet threat by stating at a news conference in mid-February, "I find it difficult to believe that any government is really planning to take so dangerous and irresponsible a step." He felt "it important that there be no misunderstanding of the position of the United States in such an eventuality." He made clear that he supported the U.N. presence in the Congo and that it was the only alternative to a U.S.-Soviet confrontation there. The U.N., he told reporters, was a bar to "massive unilateral intervention by great powers with all the risks of war that might bring." As he said repeatedly in private, "The U.N. could not bring the great powers together in the Congo, but at least it could keep them apart."

At every turn, Kennedy emphasized American backing for the U.N. as the only appropriate agency for ending the civil strife, and he sent messages to Khrushchev urging that the Congo not become an obstacle to improved Soviet-American relations. But a conversation between Ambassador Llewellyn Thompson and Khrushchev in March gave little hope that Moscow would show any give on the Congo. Khrushchev claimed that U.N. secretary-general Dag Hammarskjöld had connived to kill Lumumba, and that the U.N. was being "used to oppress peoples and help colonialists retain colonies." Thompson's reply that it would be "wise to keep [the] cold war out of Africa" moved Khrushchev to ask "how socialist states could support a policy of assistance to those who betray their own people." He promised that the Soviet Union "would struggle against this policy with all its means."

Although, as events made clear in the coming months, Khrushchev was more interested in scoring propaganda points with Africans than in risking a Soviet-American confrontation, Kennedy, taking Khrushchev at his word, sent Johnson to Africa to counter Soviet initiatives. Johnson left a strong impression on everyone he met in Senegal, an East-West battleground. He insisted that a seven-foot bed, a special showerhead that emitted a needlepoint spray, cases of Cutty Sark, and boxes of ballpoint pens and cigarette lighters with L.B.J. inscribed on them accompany him to Dakar. Against the advice of the ambassador, who urged him to shun contact with villagers he described as dirty and diseased, Johnson visited a fishing village, where he handed out pens and lighters, shook hands with everyone, including some fingerless lepers, and urged the uncomprehending natives to be like Texans, who had increased their annual income tenfold in forty years. The contrast with what Johnson called "Cadillac diplomacy," the failure of U.S. representatives to get out of their limos and meet the people, was, however much professional foreign service officers saw it as cornball diplomacy, just what Kennedy wanted from his vice president.

Kennedy had seen the Khrushchev speech in January promising to support "wars of liberation or popular uprisings" of "colonial peoples against their oppressors" as a direct challenge to Western influence in developing areas. Kennedy, who took the speech "as an authoritative exposition of Soviet intentions," read it "time and again — in his office, at Cabinet meetings, at dinners with friends, alone. At times he read it aloud and urged his colleagues to comment." Perhaps with the speech in mind, he ordered the Defense Department to place "more emphasis on the development of counter-guerrilla forces." Because this was not a high priority with the army and because he believed it would encourage views of his administration as receptive to fresh thinking about military threats, he suggested that a paper by General Edward Lansdale on special forces be converted into a popular magazine article. Lansdale's reputation for successful counterinsurgency in the Philippines against communist subversion seemed likely to excite public interest in antiguerrilla warfare. But Kennedy saw more at work here than good public relations. He believed that training and deploying such forces would prove to be a valuable tool in "the subterranean" or "twilight" war with communism. He instructed the National Security Council to distribute Lansdale's study to the CIA and to U.S. ambassadors in Africa and Asia. He also endorsed a $19 million allocation to support a three-thousand-man special forces group, which promised to give the United States "a counter-guerrilla capability" in meeting insurgencies in future limited wars. The Green Berets, a name and appearance that set these special forces apart from regular army troops, would become a receptacle for fantasies and illusions about America's ability to overcome threats in physically and politically inhospitable places around the world. Although Kennedy assumed that the effectiveness of these units would largely depend on joining their military actions to backing for indigenous progressive reforms, he could not entirely rein in wishful thinking about how much counterinsurgency units or "freedom fighters" alone could achieve at relatively small cost in blood and treasure.

The first test in the contest for the "periphery," as Kennedy had feared, came in Laos. He was not happy about it. No foreign policy issue commanded as much attention during the first two months of his presidency as this tiny, impoverished, landlocked country's civil war. "It is, I think, important for all Americans to understand this difficult and potentially dangerous problem," he declared at a March 23 news conference. He explained that during his conversation with Eisenhower on January 19, "we spent more time on this hard matter than on any other thing." A constant stream of questions about Laos had come up at press conferences, and numerous private discussions with American military and diplomatic officials paralleled exchanges with British and French leaders about how to prevent a communist takeover, which could make the country a staging ground for assaults on South Vietnam and Thailand. On March 21, the *New York Times* carried a front-page story based on conversations with high government officials about the administration's determination to keep Laos out of the Soviet orbit. But as Kennedy told Kenny O'Donnell, "I don't think there are probably 25 people [in the United States] other than us in the room who know where it is. And for me to explain how in my first month in office that I'm embarked on a military venture" would jeopardize the future of the administration.

Winthrop Brown, the U.S. ambassador to Laos, told Kennedy during a meeting at the White House on February 3 that it was unrealistic to expect that "any satisfactory solution of the problem in the country could be found by purely military means." Brown believed that "Laos was hopeless . . . a classic example of a political and economic vacuum. It had no national identity. It was just a series of lines drawn on a map." The people were "charming, indolent, enchanting . . . but they're just not very vigorous, nor are they very numerous, nor are they very well organized." Galbraith, who had become JFK's ambassador to India and was helping to bring the Indians into a diplomatic solution to the Laos conflict, wrote from New Delhi, "These jungle regimes, where the writ of government runs only as far as the airport, are going to be a hideous problem for us in the months ahead. . . . The rulers do not control or particularly influence their own people. . . . As a military ally the entire Laos nation is clearly inferior to a battalion of conscientious objectors from World War I." Assistant Secretary of State for Far Eastern Affairs Averell Harriman told Brown, "We must never face the President with the choice of abandoning Laos or sending in troops."

Publicly Kennedy made loud noises about preserving Laos's independence. He stated at the March 23 news conference, "Laos is far away from America, but the world is small. . . . The security of all

Southeast Asia will be endangered if Laos loses its neutral independence. Its own safety runs with the safety of us all." Shortly after, he
privately told Chalmers Roberts of the *Washington Post* that military
intervention in Laos was a realistic option. He "said that if he had to
go in and if it meant he would be around only one term, nonetheless he would do it. All that was said in a highly convincing manner." At the end of March, Kennedy sent five hundred U.S. Marines
to the Thai-Lao border and others were deployed aboard ships in the
South China Sea. Llewellyn Thompson advised Khrushchev that "the
United States as a great power could not stand by if forces hostile to
the United States sought to take over the country by military means."

It was all a bluff. At the same time Kennedy was talking a hard
line, he asked Harold Macmillan to convince Eisenhower that military intervention in Laos was a poor idea. Eisenhower's opinion
would be influential in how the public gauged Kennedy's Laos policy, and Macmillan was happy to help. We all feel strongly about
keeping Laos out of communist hands, Macmillan wrote Ike. "But I
need not tell you what a bad country this is for military operations. . . . President Kennedy is under considerable pressure about
'appeasement' in Laos." Macmillan said that he understood the
impulse not to forget the lessons of history, but he believed it a poor
idea to "become involved in an open-ended commitment on this
dangerous and unprofitable terrain. So I would hope that in anything which you felt it necessary to say about Laos you would not
encourage those who think that a military solution in Laos is the
only way of stopping the Communists in that area."

Happily for Kennedy, neither Eisenhower nor the Russians saw
fighting in Laos as a good idea. Despite urging Kennedy in their second transition meeting not to let Laos fall under communist control,
Ike told journalist Earl Mazo after JFK's March press conference,
"That boy doesn't know what the hell he's doing. He doesn't even
know where Laos is. You mean have Americans fight in that god-
damned place?" The Soviets, likewise, had no appetite for a punish-
ing conflict in so remote a place, especially since it might provoke
Chinese intervention and a wider conflict between the United States
and China.

But the Russians had little control over events, as renewed fighting at the end of April in a civil war demonstrated. On April 26,
Ambassador Brown reported the likelihood that communist forces
would gain control in Laos unless the president authorized the use

of U.S. air and land forces. At a National Security Council meeting the next day, members of the Joint Chiefs urged just that. Kennedy wanted to know what they intended if such an operation failed. They answered, "You start using atomic weapons!" Lemnitzer promised that "if we are given the right to use nuclear weapons, we can guarantee victory." Someone suggested that the president might want to ask the general "what he means by victory." Kennedy, who had been "glumly rubbing his upper molar, only grunted and ended the meeting." He saw Lemnitzer's guarantee as absurd: "Since he couldn't think of any further escalation, he would have to promise us victory," Kennedy said.

Kennedy, his principal advisers, and congressional leaders vetoed the military's recommendations. Although he left open the possibility that he might later use force in Laos, Kennedy accepted the "general agreement among his advisers that such a conflict would be unjustified, even if the loss of Laos must be accepted." Democratic and Republican congressional leaders unanimously confirmed the feeling that despite concern about the rest of Southeast Asia, it would be unwise to become a party to the Laotian civil war. When Kennedy visited Douglas MacArthur at the Waldorf-Astoria in New York the weekend of this crisis, the general told him, "It would be a mistake to fight in Laos. It would suit the Chinese Communists."

The Laotian crisis extended into the fall of 1961, when the exhausted opponents agreed to establish a neutral coalition government. Although critics complained about Kennedy's irresolute response to a communist threat, more compelling concerns pushed Laos aside and the issue temporarily "dribbled to a conclusion." One of these more urgent concerns was South Vietnam. In the early fifties, Kennedy had seen the area as a testing ground for innovative U.S. policies toward a colony struggling to establish autonomy without communist control. By the late fifties, however, he had shifted his attention to Algeria as the latest Soviet-American battleground for Third World influence. But South Vietnam, where an insurgency supported by North Vietnam's communist regime threatened Diem's pro-Western government, reclaimed Kennedy's attention after he became president.

In January, Lansdale, who had made a fact-finding mission to Vietnam for the Pentagon, described the country as in "critical condition and . . . a combat area of the cold war . . . needing emergency treatment." In a meeting with Lansdale and other national security advisers, Kennedy told the general that his report "for the first time, gave him a sense of the danger and urgency of the problem." It is "the worst one we've got," Kennedy told Rostow about Vietnam. Commitments by Eisenhower of military supplies, financial aid, and some six hundred military advisers had made the United States an interested party in Vietnam's six-year-old civil war. To deal with the mounting danger, Kennedy authorized funding for an increase of twenty thousand additional South Vietnamese troops and the creation of a task force to help avert a South Vietnamese collapse.

The Laotian crisis added to worries about Vietnam. A possible communist victory in Laos threatened cross-border attacks on "the entire western flank of South Vietnam." To bolster the South Vietnamese, Kennedy decided to send Johnson on "a special fact-finding mission to Asia." When asked whether he was "prepared to send American forces into South Viet-Nam if that became necessary to prevent Communist domination," Kennedy evaded the question. Sending troops, he said, "is a matter still under consideration." Although he had great doubts about making such a commitment, it made sense to keep the communists guessing as to what the United States might do if Vietnam seemed about to collapse. In the meantime, as he had done in Africa, Johnson could show the flag and quiet fears that Kennedy's refusal to send troops into Laos implied that he was abandoning Southeast Asia.

Johnson's trip was an exercise in high-visibility diplomacy. (After his Asian swing, one U.S. diplomat said, "Saigon, Manila, Taipei, and Bangkok will never be the same.") The six-foot-three-and-a-half-inch Texan, who had made a reputation as a larger-than-life figure in the Senate, was perfectly suited to the job. On his way into Saigon from the airport, he stopped the motorcade several times to shake hands with people in the crowds lining the roads. As in Africa, he handed out pens, cigarette lighters, and gold-and-white passes to the U.S. Senate gallery. "Get your mamma and daddy to bring you to the Senate and Congress to see how the government works," he told bewildered children. Trying to draw connections to British resistance to Nazi tyranny in World War II, Johnson made an arm-waving speech in downtown Saigon comparing South Vietnamese president Diem to Winston Churchill. The campaign continued the next day, when Johnson staged a photo op by chasing a bunch of Texas steer around a ranch. He then carried American informality to something of a new high — or low — by changing clothes before a group of foreign correspondents invited to a press conference in his hotel room.

Part of Johnson's mission was to get out and meet the people and sell them on the virtues of American democracy and free enterprise. But there was also the more important business of bolstering a shaky South Vietnamese government. A letter Johnson carried from Kennedy to Diem promised funds for an additional twenty thousand troops the South Vietnamese army wanted and proposed collaboration in "a series of joint, mutually supporting actions in the military, political, economic and other fields" to counter communist aggression. Johnson's visit reassured him, Diem wrote Kennedy, that America would continue to support Vietnam, and he expressed particular pleasure at being asked by the vice president for ideas on how to meet the crisis. "We have not become accustomed to being asked for our own views as to our needs," Diem wrote.

Diem's satisfaction with Johnson's visit partly rested on his understanding that he had won a convert to his cause. "I cannot stress too strongly the extreme importance of following up this mission with other measures, other actions, and other efforts," LBJ told Kennedy on his return. "The battle against Communism must be joined in Southeast Asia with strength and determination," Johnson advised, ". . . or the United States, inevitably, must surrender the Pacific and take up our defenses on our own shores." Though Johnson did not urge the dispatch of combat troops, only military advisers, his rhetoric was apocalyptic: "The basic decision in Southeast Asia is here. We must decide whether to help these countries to the best of our ability or throw in the towel in the area and pull back our defenses to San Francisco and a 'Fortress America' concept."

Kennedy had other advice that challenged Johnson's evangelism and encouraged skepticism about larger commitments to a repressive Saigon government and a region of questionable importance to U.S. national security. From India, Galbraith, echoing his comments about Laos, warned JFK that spending "our billions in these distant jungles" would be of no value to the United States and of no harm to the Soviets. He wondered "what is so important about this real estate in the space age" and urged any kind of political settlement as preferable to military involvement. He conceded that this was a choice between "the disastrous and the unpalatable." But he wondered "if those who talk in terms of a ten-year war really know what they are saying in terms of American attitudes."

* * *

IN THE FIRST MONTHS of his term, Kennedy's focus on Laos, Vietnam, and the Congo paled alongside that on Cuba. *Look* journalist Laura Berquist Knebel observed that, whenever she saw Kennedy, he "nearly always" wanted to discuss Cuba, "his 'albatross,' as he used to call it." During the 1960 campaign, he had already learned how frustrating Cuba could be as an issue. In 1958–59, he had been sympathetic to Castro's revolution against the corrupt and repressive Batista regime. By 1960, however, he shared the growing perception in the United States that Castro, who may have begun as a "utopian socialist," had abandoned his romantic idealism for an alliance with Cuban communists who were likely to help solidify his hold on power. The new regime in Havana seemed hell-bent on making the U.S. into a whipping boy and using widespread anti-American sentiment in Cuba to tie itself to Moscow and Peking. After facing attacks by liberals and Nixon during the presidential campaign for favoring an invasion by Cuban exiles, Kennedy had accepted Acheson's advice and conspicuously avoided further comments on Cuba.

In early January 1961, Kennedy tried to stay above the battle, refusing to comment "either way" on Eisenhower's decision to break relations with Cuba. He did not want to rule out the possibility of "a rapprochement" with Castro. He asked John Sharon, a Stevenson adviser on foreign policy, what he thought of the idea. He also questioned him about the Eisenhower economic sanctions: Were they working? Would the United States gain any advantage by ending them? A week before he took office, Kennedy had received a report Adlai Stevenson passed along from Chicago union leader Sidney Lens, who had just returned from Cuba. It confirmed the loss of freedoms under Castro but emphasized that the country largely supported him and that reporting by American journalists there was unreliable: They were "culling the negative and not reporting the positive." In addition, Lens said that the U.S. embargo was not effective because other countries were filling the vacuum. Lens also warned that Castro spies had infiltrated the anti-Castro groups in America and were informing Castro about "their plans and conspiracies." At the same time, Allen Dulles briefed the president-elect on a CIA plan to use Cuban exiles being trained in Guatemala to infiltrate Cuba and topple Castro. Without endorsing anything, Kennedy instructed Dulles to go ahead with the planning.

Two days after he became president, the CIA had begun urging Kennedy to move against Cuba. At a January 22 meeting of Rusk,

McNamara, Bobby Kennedy, Lemnitzer, Dulles, and other national security and foreign policy experts, Dulles emphasized that the U.S. had only two months "before something would have to be done about" the Cubans being trained in Guatemala. The urgency rested partly on the belief that Castro had plans to promote communism in Latin America, and that he "already had power among the people in the Caribbean countries and elsewhere, particularly in Venezuela and Colombia." Because the CIA planners were now considering direct U.S. intervention, Rusk "commented on the enormous implications of putting U.S. forces ashore in Cuba and said we should consider everything short of this, including rough stuff." He feared "we might be confronted by serious uprisings all over Latin America if U.S. forces were to go in." He also worried that such a move might trigger "Soviet and Chi[nese] Com[munist] moves in other parts of the world." The meeting ended with admonitions to consider "the so-called 'shelf-life' of the Cuban unit in Guatemala . . . [and] the question of how overtly the United States was prepared to show its hand."

During the last week in January, Kennedy held two White House meetings on Cuba in which Lemnitzer and CIA planners emphasized that time was working against the United States. Castro was tightening his hold on the island and seemed likely to make Cuba a permanent member of the communist bloc, "with disastrous consequences to the security of the Western Hemisphere." They proposed overthrowing Castro's government by secretly supporting an invasion and establishing a provisional government, which the United States and the Organization of American States (OAS) could support. In response, Kennedy authorized continuing covert CIA operations, a revised CIA invasion plan, a prompt diplomatic initiative to isolate Castro, and a strenuous effort to keep these discussions secret. He also tried to ensure that no decision would be taken without his authority. "Have we determined what we are going to do about Cuba?" he asked McGeorge Bundy on February 6. "If there is a difference of opinion between the agencies I think they should be brought to my attention."

Differences among his advisers about the results of an invasion did not give Kennedy much assurance. Bundy told him on February 8 that Defense and the CIA were much more optimistic than State about the outcome of an invasion. The military foresaw an invasion touching off "a full-fledged civil war in which we could then back the anti-Castro forces openly." And should there be no immediate uprising, the invaders could take refuge in the surrounding mountains and work toward the day when a critical mass of Cubans joined their cause. By contrast, State anticipated "very grave" political consequences in the United Nations and Latin America. Troubled by State's predictions, Kennedy pressed advisers later that day "for alternatives to a full-fledged 'invasion,' supported by U.S. planes, ships and supplies."

Kennedy now faced two unhappy choices. If he decided against an invasion, he would have to disarm the Cubans in Guatemala and risk public attacks from them for failing to implement Eisenhower's plans to combat communism in the hemisphere. The CIA offered Kennedy no alternative: They "doubted that other really satisfactory uses of the troops in Guatemala could be found." As O'Donnell later put it, a decision to scrap the invasion would then make Kennedy look like an "appeaser of Castro. Eisenhower made a decision to overthrow Castro and you dropped it." Kennedy would have been faced with "a major political blowup."

But an invasion might also produce an international disaster. "However well disguised any action might be," Schlesinger told Kennedy, "it will be ascribed to the United States. The result would be a wave of massive protest, agitation and sabotage throughout Latin America, Europe, Asia and Africa (not to speak of Canada and of certain quarters in the United States). Worst of all, this would be your first dramatic foreign policy initiative. At one stroke, it would dissipate all the extraordinary good will which has been rising toward the new Administration through the world. It would fix a malevolent image of the new Administration in the minds of millions."

Kennedy shared Schlesinger's concern. He remembered his own rhetoric about liberty, justice, and self-determination, and understood that a visible U.S. role in an invasion would justifiably be seen as a betrayal of the progressive principles to which he was supposedly committed. But he was also attracted to the idea of toppling a Castro government that seemed to have little regard for the democratic freedoms promised by the Cuban revolution or for the autonomy of other Latin countries, which Castro hoped to destabilize and bring into the communist orbit. During the February 8 meeting, Kennedy asked CIA planners if the Cuban brigade could "be landed gradually and quietly and make its first major military efforts from the mountains — then taking shape as a Cuban force within Cuba, not as an invasion force sent by the Yankees."

The CIA and the military gave him assurances that the Cuban exiles could succeed without the participation of U.S. forces. On March 10, the Joint Chiefs told McNamara that "the small invasion force" of some twelve to fifteen hundred men "could be expected to achieve initial success. Ultimate success will depend on the extent to which the initial assault serves as a catalyst for further action on the part of anti-Castro elements throughout Cuba." The Chiefs also predicted that the invading brigade "will have a good chance of sustaining itself indefinitely."

In turn, the CIA endorsed and went beyond the Chiefs' recommendations. At a meeting with JFK on the eleventh, Dulles and Richard Bissell, the agency's deputy director of plans, predicted that Castro would not fall without outside intervention and that within a matter of months his military power would reduce the likelihood of a successful invasion. "The Cuban paramilitary force if effectively used [in the next month] has a good chance of overthrowing Castro, or of causing a damaging civil war, without the necessity for the United States to commit itself to overt action against Cuba." Kennedy declared himself "willing to take the chance of going ahead; [but] . . . he could not endorse a plan that put us in so openly, in view of the world situation. He directed the development of a plan where US assistance would be less obvious."

The CIA now assured the president that an invasion at Cuba's Bay of Pigs in the Zapata region some hundred miles west of Trinidad, the original site for the attack, would look less like a "small-scale World War II amphibious assault" and more like "an infiltration of guerrillas in support of an internal revolution." Although Dulles and Bissell warned that communist accusations of U.S. involvement were inevitable, they thought it preferable to the "certain risks" of demobilizing the Cuban exiles and returning them to the United States, where they seemed bound to launch ugly political attacks on the administration for losing its nerve.

Schlesinger urged Kennedy not to let the threat of political attacks push him into a questionable military operation. He saw "a slight danger of our being rushed into something because CIA has on its hands a band of people it doesn't quite know what to do with." Allen Dulles worried that if the CIA scotched the invasion and transferred the exiles from Guatemala to the United States, they would wander "'around the country telling everyone what they have been doing.' Obviously," Schlesinger concluded, "this is a genuine problem, but it can't be permitted to govern US policy."

CIA revisions of the invasion plan muted Schlesinger's warning. The CIA, Bundy told the president on March 15, "[has] done a remarkable job of reframing the landing plan so as to make it unspectacular and quiet, and plausibly Cuban in its essentials. . . . I have been a skeptic about Bissell's operation, but now I think we are on the edge of a good answer."

Kennedy was still not so sure. At a meeting that day, he seemed to accept the essentials of the new plan but objected to a dawn landing, suggesting instead that "in order to make this appear as an inside guerrilla-type operation, the ships should be clear of the area by dawn." Though the CIA returned the next day with the requested changes, which Kennedy approved, he "reserved the right to call off the plan even up to 24 hours prior to the landing."

Although planning went forward for an early-April invasion, Kennedy remained hesitant, and even a little distraught about what to do. Admiral Burke deepened Kennedy's concerns on March 17, when he told him that "the plan was dependent on a general uprising in Cuba, and that the entire operation would fail without such an uprising." On March 28, Schlesinger asked JFK, "What do you think about this damned invasion?" Kennedy replied, "I think about it as little as possible," implying that it was too painful a subject with too many uncertainties for him to dwell on it. But of course it was at the center of his concerns. At yet other meetings about Cuba on March 28 and 29, Kennedy instructed the CIA to inform Cuban Brigade leaders that "U.S. strike forces would not be allowed to participate in or support the invasion in any way." Kennedy also wanted to know whether the Cubans thought the invasion could succeed without U.S. military intervention and whether they wished to proceed under the limitations he had described. Brigade leaders responded that despite Kennedy's restrictions, they wished to go ahead.

The willingness of the Cubans, the CIA, and the U.S. military to proceed partly rested on their assumption that once the invasion began, Kennedy would have to use American forces if the attack seemed about to fail. One of the invaders remembers being told, "If you fail we will go in." The pressure for U.S. intervention was evident to Undersecretary of State Chester Bowles, who opposed the plan. On March 31, he told Rusk, "If the operation appears to be a failure in its early stages, the pressure on us to scrap our self-imposed restriction on direct American involvement will be difficult to resist." The danger, Bowles added, is that a failure would "greatly enhance Castro's prestige and strength." And Bowles saw the odds of a failure as two to one. He believed it better to scrap the invasion and live with Castro's regime. The United States could then blockade any Soviet attempt to provide Cuba with large amounts of arms and use force, with likely OAS backing, against any overt Castro aggression in Latin America.

"No one," Schlesinger said later, "expected the invasion to galvanize the unarmed and the unorganized into rising against Castro at the moment of disembarkation. But the invasion plan, as understood by the President and the Joint Chiefs, did assume that the successful occupation of an enlarged beachhead area would rather soon incite organized uprisings by armed members of the Cuban resistance." Dulles and Bissell, Schlesinger also pointed out, "reinforced this impression" by claiming "that over 2,500 persons presently belonged to resistance organizations, that 20,000 more were sympathizers, and the Brigade, once established on the island, could expect the active support of, at the very least, a quarter of the Cuban people." A CIA paper of April 12 on "The Cuban Operation" estimated that "there are 7,000 insurgents responsive to some degree of control through agents with whom communications are currently active." The paper conceded that the individual groups were "small and very inadequately armed," but after the invasion the Agency hoped to supply them with air drops and make "every effort . . . to coordinate their operations with those of the landing parties."

In the days leading up to the attack on April 17, Kennedy continued to hear dissenting voices. At the end of March, he asked Dean Acheson what he thought of the proposal to invade Cuba. Acheson did not know there was one, and when Kennedy described it to him, Acheson voiced his skepticism in the form of a question: "Are you serious?" Kennedy replied, "I don't know if I'm serious or just . . . I'm giving it serious thought." When Acheson asked how many men Castro could put on the beach to meet the nearly 1,500 invaders and Kennedy answered 25,000, Acheson declared, "It doesn't take Price-Waterhouse to figure out that fifteen hundred aren't as good as twenty-five thousand." Schlesinger peppered JFK with memos and private words about the injury to U.S. prestige and his presidency; Rusk lodged muted protests; and Fulbright, who as chairman of the Foreign Relations Committee had been briefed about the plan, spoke forcefully against U.S. hypocrisy in denouncing Soviet indifference to self-determination and planning an invasion of a country that was more a thorn in the flesh than a dagger in the heart.

These warnings reinforced Kennedy's own considerable doubts about so uncertain an operation. Allen Dulles countered them by saying, "Mr. President, I know you're doubtful about this. But I stood at this very desk and said to President Eisenhower about a similar operation in Guatemala, 'I believe it will work.' And I say to you now, Mr. President, that the prospects for this plan are even better than our prospects were in Guatemala." Dulles emphasized that there was small risk of failure and no risk of U.S. involvement that would sacrifice American credibility when it came to professing regard for self-determination. Dulles clearly could not foresee later critical assessments by historians complaining that CIA operations overturning a popular government in Guatemala City solidified America's reputation as an imperial power hypocritically ignoring commitments to democracy for all peoples. Or, if he did foresee this, he found it easy enough to ignore when pressing the president about Cuba.

Other subtle psychological impulses were at work in persuading Kennedy to approve the invasion plan. One element was Kennedy's conception of military action. The possibility of a nuclear war was abhorrent to him, but the idea of patriotic men prepared to sacrifice their lives for the freedom of their country was an entirely different matter. He saw no higher recommendation for someone than patriotic courage. Schlesinger remembered how much the commitment of the Cuban Brigade moved Kennedy. The invasion also had a romantic appeal for him, the quality of an adventure like that which had drawn Kennedy to command a PT boat. He and Bobby shared an affinity for Ian Fleming's James Bond novels and their urbane hero. Bissell, who did so much to sell Kennedy on the Bay of Pigs, seemed to be something of a real-life Bond himself — an Ivy League graduate, socially sophisticated, tall and handsome, "civilized, responsible," "a man of high character and remarkable intellectual gifts." His description of himself as "a man-eating shark" delighted the Kennedys.

Despite Dulles's assurances, the operation had the code name "Bumpy Road." Moreover, because Kennedy did not entirely trust Dulles's predictions, he kept emphasizing in the two weeks before the invasion that it needed to "appear as an internal uprising" and that "the United States would not become overtly engaged with Castro's armed forces." At a meeting on April 6, he insisted on "everything possible to make it appear to be a Cuban operation partly from within Cuba, but supported from without Cuba, the objective being to make it more plausible for US denial of association with the operation, although recognizing that we would be accused."

Newspaper stories about anti-Castro forces being trained by Americans made it all the harder to deny U.S. involvement. Castro "doesn't need agents over here," Kennedy said privately. "All he has to do is read our papers." At a news conference on April 12, with press stories predicting an imminent invasion, Kennedy was asked how far the United States would go "in helping an anti-Castro uprising or invasion of Cuba." He replied, "There will not be, under any conditions, an intervention in Cuba by the United States Armed Forces. This Government will do everything it can . . . to make sure that there are no Americans involved in any actions inside Cuba." Two days later, Kennedy ordered Bissell to "play down the magnitude of the invasion" and to reduce an initial air strike by Cuban pilots flying from outside Cuba from sixteen to eight planes.

On Saturday, April 15, eight B-26s flying from Puerto Cabezas, Nicaragua, bombed three Cuban airfields. It was the beginning of what historian Theodore Draper later called "one of those rare events in history — a perfect failure." The bombers destroyed only five of Castro's three dozen combat planes and left the invaders, traveling by boats from Nicaragua, vulnerable to air attacks before and after landing on the beaches. To give credence to a CIA cover story, the Agency arranged to have a ninth bomber with Cuban air force markings and bullet holes fly from Nicaragua to Miami, where it made an "emergency" landing and the CIA-trained pilot declared himself a defector who had flown from Cuba.

Adlai Stevenson, who was not among those the White House believed needed to know the truth, sincerely denied U.S. involvement before a U.N. General Assembly committee considering charges of United States "imperialist aggression" against Cuba. When the implausibility of the CIA cover plot quickly became evident, an outraged Stevenson complained to Rusk and Dulles on April 16, "I do not understand how we could let such an attack take place two days before debate on the Cuban issue in GA." Nor could he understand "why I could not have been warned and provided pre-prepared material with which to defend us." He saw the "gravest risk of another U-2 disaster in such uncoordinated action."

A second planned air strike in support of the invasion on the morning of April 17 became a casualty of the CIA's unraveling ruse. Until the brigade could establish a beachhead and make a plausible case for the fiction that their B-26s were taking off from and landing on the beach, Kennedy, who was keeping a low profile at his retreat in Glen Ora, Virginia, grounded the exiles' sixteen planes. After giving the order by phone to Rusk, Kennedy paced "the room in evident concern," worried now that the whole operation might prove to be a fiasco. "Those with him at Glen Ora," Schlesinger recorded, "had rarely seen him so low." When Bundy passed Kennedy's order along to Dulles's two principal deputies, they warned that "failure to make air strikes in the immediate beachhead area the first thing in the morning (D-Day) would clearly be disastrous." When informed of the president's decision, other CIA planners concluded that "it would probably mean the failure of the mission."

The failure, which became evident by Tuesday afternoon, April 18, resulted less from any decision about air attacks than from the flawed conception of the plan — illusions about an internal uprising and 1,400-plus invaders defeating Castro's much larger force. By noon of April 18, Mac Bundy told Kennedy that "the situation in Cuba is not a bit good. The Cuban armed forces are stronger, the popular response is weaker, and our tactical position is feebler than we had hoped. Tanks have done in one beachhead, and the position is precarious at the others. . . . The real question is whether to reopen the possibility of further intervention and support or to accept the high probability that our people, at best, will go into the mountains in defeat." Kennedy had no intention of sending in a U.S. rescue mission, however bad the situation might be.

Kennedy's poise in the face of the Bay of Pigs defeat began to crumble during the afternoon and evening of April 18. Admiral Burke recalled that at an hour-and-a-half White House meeting with the president and his principal advisers, "nobody knew what to do. . . . They are in a real bad hole," Burke recorded, "because they had the hell cut out of them. . . . I kept quiet because I didn't know the general score." Because Burke had been less demonstrative than Lemnitzer in his support of the invasion, Bobby Kennedy called him after the meeting to say that the president needed his advice and intended to bypass "the usual channels of responsibility in the management of the crisis." Burke had no answers, and Kennedy reconvened his advisers around midnight in the Cabinet Room. Coming from a White House reception for Congress dressed in white tie and tails, Kennedy reviewed the deteriorating situation for four hours without success. Bissell and Burke pressed for the use of carrier planes to shoot down Castro's aircraft and for a destroyer to shell Castro's tanks. But Kennedy stuck to his resolve not to intervene directly with U.S. forces. He later told Dave Powers that the Chiefs and the CIA "were sure I'd give in to them. . . . They couldn't believe that a new President like me wouldn't panic and try to save his own face. Well, they had me figured all wrong."

On Tuesday morning, Castro's air force had sunk the brigade's principal supply ship with ten days' ammunition and most of its communication equipment. By late that afternoon, Castro had pinned down the invaders with a force of twenty thousand men and Soviet tanks, while his arrest of twenty thousand potential opponents had guarded against the CIA-predicted internal uprising. As for plans of escape to the Escambray Mountains, an eighty-mile stretch of swampland between the beach and the mountains made this impossible. The outgunned and outmanned invaders faced dying on the beaches in a hopeless fight or surrender. Almost 1,200 of the 1,400-plus attackers gave up.

Kennedy at first tried to put the best possible face on the failed invasion, which was obviously a U.S.-sponsored operation. During lunch on Tuesday with Schlesinger and James Reston, he described the defeat as "an incident, not a disaster." When asked about the blow to American prestige, he responded philosophically: "What is prestige? Is it the shadow of power or the substance of power? We are going to work on the substance of power. No doubt we will be kicked in the can for the next couple of weeks, but that won't affect the main business." He felt he had made a mistake in keeping Dulles at the CIA. He did not know him and had been unable to assess his advice wisely. He saw the necessity for someone in the Agency "with whom I can be in complete and intimate contact — someone from whom I know I will be getting the exact pitch." He believed he would be better off with brother Bobby as director. "It is a hell of a way to learn things," he said, "but I have learned one thing from this business — that is, that we will have to deal with CIA."

A six-month secret review by Lyman Kirkpatrick, the Agency's inspector general, blamed the Bay of Pigs failure largely on the CIA and confirmed Kennedy's conviction that both Dulles and Bissell would have to resign. "Under a parliamentary system of government it is I who would be leaving office," Kennedy told Dulles. "But under our system it is you who must go." Although Dulles and Bissell blamed the canceled air strikes for the defeat, Kirkpatrick concluded that this was not "the chief cause of failure"; a better-conceived plan would never have confronted Kennedy with such a decision. Kirkpatrick saw the root cause in the CIA's poor "planning, organization, staffing and management." More specifically, he blamed the false assumption that "the invasion would, like a *deus ex machina*, produce a shock . . . and trigger an uprising," and the "multiple security leaks" that alerted Castro to the attack and allowed him to respond effectively. CIA officials "should have gone to the President and said frankly: 'Here are the facts. The operation should be halted.' . . . The Agency became so wrapped up in the military operation that it failed to appraise the chances of success realistically."

Although the invasion had become a fiasco that cost more than a hundred lives and deeply embarrassed Kennedy and the United States, the president was determined not to compound his problems by publicly denying a U.S. role. But while he responded philosophically to the defeat in public, he was anything but composed in private. On April 19, Jackie told Rose that Jack "was so upset all day & had practically been in tears. . . . She had never seen him so depressed except once at the time of his operation." Dave Powers recalled that "within the privacy of his office, he made no effort to hide the distress and guilt he felt." At the end of the late-night meeting on April 18, he went into the Oval Office with Salinger and O'Donnell, where in the middle of a sentence he broke off the conversation and walked out into the Rose Garden. He stayed there for almost an hour, walking on the wet grass and keeping his grief to himself. The next morning, Salinger found him crying in his bedroom. At a meeting shortly after with Albert Gore, Kennedy, with messed hair and tie askew, seemed "extremely bitter" about the defeat.

Wire service journalist Henry Raymont, who had been in Cuba during the invasion, had similar recollections of Kennedy's distress. When Raymont returned to the United States after several days in a Cuban jail on charges of being a CIA agent before being expelled from the country, Kennedy invited him to the White House. Raymont was eager for the chance to chide the president for being so foolish as to think that an uprising would greet the invasion. Any high school student in Cuba or any diplomat in Havana could have told you otherwise, Raymont planned to tell Kennedy. But when he got into the Oval Office, he found the president so full of self-recrimination and so dejected at his short-sightedness that Raymont only gently reinforced what Kennedy already understood about the reasons for the failure.

Ill-timed health problems further rattled Kennedy. Immediately prior to and during the invasion on April 17 and 18, he struggled with "constant," "acute diarrhea" and a urinary tract infection. His doctors treated him with increased amounts of antispasmodics, a puree diet, and penicillin, and scheduled him for a sigmoidoscopy.

For days after the defeat, Kennedy's anguish and dejection were evident to people around him. At a cabinet meeting on April 20, Chester Bowles saw him as "quite shattered." He would talk to himself and interrupt conversations with the non sequitur "How could I have been so stupid?" He felt responsible for the deaths of the valiant Cubans on the beaches. The episode even seemed to revive memories of his brother's death in World War II. When he met at the White House to console the six-member Cuban Revolutionary Council, three of whom had lost sons in the invasion, Kennedy produced a photograph of Joe and explained, "I lost a brother and a brother-in-law in the war." Kennedy described the meeting and the Bay of Pigs episode as "the worst experience of my life." Weeks after the invasion, he told an aide one morning that he had not slept all night. "I was thinking about those poor guys in prison down in Cuba."

Kennedy was not only angry at himself for having signed on to what in retrospect seemed like such an unworkable plan but also at the CIA and the Chiefs for having misled him. When newspapers began publishing stories blaming different officials except the Joint Chiefs for the debacle, Kennedy took note of the omission and told his aides that none of the decision makers was free of blame. He named Fulbright as the only one in the clear but thought that he also would have backed the operation if he had been subjected to the same barrage of misleading information about "discontent in Cuba, morale of the free Cubans, rainy season, Russian MIGs and destroyers, impregnable beachhead, easy escape into the Escambray, [and] what else to do with these people."

To Kennedy's credit, he had no intention of publicly blaming anyone but himself. He authorized a White House statement saying, "President Kennedy has stated from the beginning that as President he bears sole responsibility. . . . The President is strongly opposed to anyone within or without the administration attempting to shift the responsibility." He understood the impulse of some to shun their role in a failed operation. He quoted "an old saying that victory has a hundred fathers and defeat is an orphan." This was his defeat: "I'm the responsible officer of the Government," he told the press.

Later that year, when *Time* began trying to use the Cuban disaster against the administration to help Republicans in 1962, Kennedy wrote publisher Henry Luce that "the testimony of the participants in an ill-fated failure should be taken with a good deal of caution." If *Time* aimed "to clear the Defense Department and the CIA from all responsibility," Kennedy declared an article it had published "a success." The same was true if *Time* intended to demonstrate "the incompetence of the men who played a part in this venture." But if the article hoped "to set the record straight," Kennedy sardonically described its success as "more limited." For the time being, he believed it not a good idea to rehash the Bay of Pigs failure. "I have felt from the beginning," he told Luce, "that it would not be in the public interest for the United States to take formal responsibility for the Cuban matter other than the personal responsibility which I have earlier assumed."

He was more interested in understanding why he had allowed so unsuccessful an operation to go forward than in assessing blame. True, he had some impulse to think, "They made me do it": The false hopes pressed on him by the CIA and the Chiefs had led him astray. But "How could I have been so stupid?" was his way of asking why he had been so gullible. He puzzled over the fact that he had not asked harder questions and had allowed the so-called collective wisdom of all these experienced national security officials to persuade him to go ahead. He had assumed, he later told Schlesinger, that "the military and intelligence people have some secret skill not available to ordinary mortals." The experience taught him "never to rely on the experts." He told Ben Bradlee: "The first advice I'm going to give my successor is to watch the generals and to avoid feeling that just because they were military men their opinions on military matters were worth a damn."

More immediate concerns than understanding what had gone wrong were repairing the damage to Kennedy's prestige and deciding what to do next about Cuba. Initially, the Bay of Pigs seemed like a terrible blow to Kennedy's reputation. When journalist Henry Brandon told Kennedy that Peter Lisagor had suggested he make fun of Castro, JFK replied, "Well, for the time being, they're making fun of me." The hope and excitement of the first ninety days had turned to cynical complaint, especially in western Europe, about an administration whose progressive, inspiring rhetoric seemed nothing more than a cover for old-fashioned imperialism. Worse yet, the fiasco raised Moscow's standing in the Third World, strengthened Castro in Cuba, and increased his appeal across Latin America. There was also the concern that political opponents would use the failure to score points against the administration. "Not much time remains for the education of John F. Kennedy," one hostile southern newspaper declared. "In his first great crisis, he bungled horribly." Nixon and Republican congressional leaders privately agreed to hold their fire only until the crisis had passed, but the Republican Congressional Committee's newsletter said, "It is doubtful if any President had gotten the United States in so much trouble in so short a time."

The setback infuriated Jack and Bobby. Losing or even second best was not in their vocabulary, and except for the sinking of PT-109 and the vice presidential contest in 1956, Kennedy had (publicly) nothing but a string of high-profile victories. Even the loss of his boat had been less a defeat than an opportunity to become a hero who had rescued his crew.

Now, in response to the Bay of Pigs, no one was allowed to seem wiser than Kennedy or to overshadow him. When Mac Bundy told Kennedy that, like Fulbright, Schlesinger had been prescient, Kennedy not only played down Fulbright's wisdom, he also dismissed Schlesinger's advice as calculated to make him "look pretty good when he gets around to writing his book on my administration. Only he better not publish that memorandum while I'm still alive." Bowles, whose warnings against the operation were leaked to the press, also earned the Kennedys' wrath. "When he disagreed with the President," Bobby said later, "he talked to the press. He was rather a weeper. He came up in a rather whiny voice and said that he wanted to make sure that everybody understood that he was against the Bay of Pigs." Such self-righteousness was "resented." When Bowles, substituting for Rusk, presented some State Department reflections at White House and National Security Council meetings on the impossibility of doing anything about Castro without another ill-advised U.S. invasion, Bobby, who had written his brother a memo urging decisive action on Cuba, "savagely" and "brutally" tore into Bowles. "That's the most meaningless, worthless thing I've ever heard," Bobby shouted. "You people are so anxious to protect your own asses that you're afraid to do anything. All you want to do is dump the whole thing on the President. We'd be better off if you just quit and left foreign policy to someone else." Richard Goodwin, who watched JFK calmly tapping his teeth with a pencil, suddenly realized that "Bobby's harsh polemic reflected the president's own concealed emotions, privately communicated in some earlier, intimate conversation. I knew, even then, there was an inner hardness, often volatile anger, beneath the outwardly amiable, thoughtful, carefully controlled demeanor of John Kennedy."

But worries about Kennedy's loss of political clout in the United States evaporated quickly, in part because he personally appealed to Nixon's vanity and Eisenhower's patriotism. He called Nixon, whose daughter told him, "I knew it! It wouldn't be long before he would get into trouble and have to call on you for help." Although Kennedy rejected Nixon's suggestion of direct intervention in Cuba, he flattered him by speaking candidly about politics and their shared interest in international relations. "It really is true that foreign affairs is the only important issue for a President to handle, isn't it?" Kennedy asked, knowing that Nixon agreed. "I mean, who gives a shit if the minimum wage is $1.15 or $1.25, in comparison to something like this?" Nixon promised to support him to the hilt if Kennedy attacked Cuba.

With Eisenhower, whom he invited to lunch at Camp David, the presidential retreat in Maryland's Catoctin Mountains, Kennedy played the student being lectured by the master teacher gently reprimanding him on a poor performance. "There is only one thing to do when you get into this kind of thing," Eisenhower told him. "It must be a success." Kennedy replied, "Well, I assure you that, hereafter, if we get into anything like this, it is going to be a success." Eisenhower said that he was "glad to hear that." Before the press, Eisenhower declared, "I am all in favor of the United States supporting the man who has to carry the responsibility for our foreign affairs."

With Nixon, Eisenhower, and most other public officials backing Kennedy, a Gallup poll at the end of April showed him with an 83 percent approval rating. As reassuring, 61 percent of the public supported Kennedy's "handling [of] the situation in Cuba," and 65 percent specifically opposed sending "our armed forces into Cuba to help overthrow Castro." But Kennedy could not put the failure aside. He dismissed the polls, saying, "It's just like Eisenhower. The worse I do, the more popular I get."

Because he believed that Castro now more than ever represented a threat to U.S. interests in the hemisphere, and because defeat at the Bay of Pigs gave an added incentive to topple Castro's regime, Kennedy gave a high priority to finding an effective policy for dealing with the Cuban problem. On April 21, he set up a task force to study "military and paramilitary, guerrilla and anti-guerrilla activities which fall short of outright war." The task force chairman was General Maxwell Taylor, a World War II hero whose 1959 book, *The Uncertain Trumpet*, had "reoriented our whole strategic thinking," Bobby said. Taylor's book affirmed JFK's opposition to massive retaliation with nuclear weapons and support for counterinsurgency forces designed to fight guerrilla wars. Bobby, Burke, and Dulles (who did not leave office until later in the year) served with Taylor and agreed to "give special attention to the lessons that can be learned from recent events in Cuba."

Though ostensibly a study group to work against a replay of the Bay of Pigs fiasco, the committee quickly became a vehicle for suggesting ways to overturn Castro. At a National Security Council meeting on May 4, Kennedy and his advisers "agreed that U.S. policy toward Cuba should aim at the downfall of Castro," but that neither a blockade nor direct military action should be the means for doing it, though U.S. intervention should remain a possibility. The study group's report of June 13 concluded, "There can be no long-term living with Castro as a neighbor." He constituted "a real menace capable of eventually overthrowing the elected governments in any one or more of weak Latin American republics." But action against him needed to rest on a wide range of international and domestic considerations. With only 44 percent of the American public favoring aid to anti-Castro forces and 41 percent opposed, a program of clandestine subversion seemed the best of the planners' options. Decisions on exactly how to proceed were left for the future.

Despite his high approval ratings, Kennedy was disappointed with the results of his first hundred days. To be sure, he had established himself as an attractive and even inspirational leader, but rising tensions with Castro and ongoing communist insurgencies in Southeast Asia and Africa joined with a sluggish economy and civil rights divisions at home to shake Kennedy's confidence in mastering the challenges of his presidency. The May 5 edition of *Time* declared,

"Last week, as John Kennedy closed out the first 100 days of his administration, the U.S. suffered a month-long series of setbacks rare in the history of the Republic." Asked how he liked being president, Kennedy replied that he liked it better before the Bay of Pigs. He also described himself as "always on the edge of irritability." "Sons of bitches," Kennedy said after reading *Time*'s critical assessment of his first hundred days. "If they want this job they can have it tomorrow."

Yet however frustrated he was by events and his own stumbles, Kennedy was determined to use the problems of his first months as object lessons in how to be more effective. His resolve stood him in good stead: He managed coming crises with greater skill and a growing conviction that he might be an above average and maybe even a memorable president after all.

CHAPTER 11

A World of Troubles

We face a relentless struggle in every corner of the globe.
— John F. Kennedy, April 20, 1961

IN THE FIFTEEN YEARS since the onset of the Cold War, Americans had struggled with their fears. The long tradition of "free security," weak neighbors, and vast oceans, which had insulated the country from foreign dangers, had done little to prepare it for a drawn-out contest with a hostile superpower convinced that its ideology and that of the United States could not coexist. The tensions over the East-West divide and America's apparently unprecedented vulnerability to attack tested the country's self-confidence.

In the aftermath of the Bay of Pigs, Kennedy mirrored this national anxiety. In a speech to the American Society of Newspaper Editors on April 20, he spoke apocalyptically about the Cold War. "If the self-discipline of the free cannot match the iron discipline of the mailed fist — in economic, political, [and] scientific . . . struggles as well as the military — then the peril to freedom will continue to rise," he predicted. Cuba was a case in point. "The evidence is clear — and the hour is late," he said. "We and our Latin friends will have to face the fact that we cannot postpone any longer the real issue of survival of freedom in this hemisphere itself." It was "clearer than ever that we face a relentless struggle in every corner of the globe that goes beyond the clash of armies or even nuclear weapons. . . . We dare not fail to see the insidious nature of this new and deeper struggle . . . [which] is taking place every day, without fanfare, in thousands of villages and markets — day and night — and in classrooms all over the globe." The message underlying this clash was that "the complacent, the self-indulgent, the soft societies are about to be swept away with the debris of history. Only the strong, only the industrious, only the determined, only the courageous, only the visionary who determine the real nature of our struggle can survive." It sounded like Theodore Roosevelt and what Kennedy himself had said in the forties in response to earlier foreign threats.

In the spring of 1961, Labor Secretary Arthur Goldberg reported that Soviet steel production had equaled that of the United States in the fourth quarter of 1960. As more thoughtful observers understood then and as we know now, Soviet competitiveness, except in armaments, was illusory. Back in 1958, Willard Mathias in the Office of National Estimates had predicted that communism's inability to produce sufficient consumer goods and resistance to sharing power with a growing middle class of Soviet professionals and technocrats would ultimately destroy the party's power. (Six years later, Mathias would describe this "evolution" as "probably irreversible.") In June 1961, Walter Heller told JFK that "the Soviets have no reasonable hope of outproducing us in the next 10–25 years unless the U.S. economy slows down miserably. . . . On a *per capita* basis, the Soviet GNP in 1959 was only 39% of ours." The Soviets could not equal U.S. output until 1990, Heller said — and that was in the unlikely event they maintained a 6 percent annual growth rate; it would probably not be until 2010 that the Soviets caught up to the United States, if even then. But such assessments of Soviet weakness were frowned upon in the fifties and sixties. An American army general told Mathias that he was "suspected of being a communist agent because [he had] not been tough enough on the Russians." And for the moment, Kennedy was as much in the grip of conventional Cold War thinking as most other Americans. The keen analytic powers and wise judgments displayed in his pre-presidential views on colonialism temporarily deserted him.

Convinced that the Bay of Pigs failure could be attributed partly to press stories that had alerted Castro to an invasion, Kennedy used an April address to the American Newspaper Publishers Association to urge the country to sacrifice some of its traditional freedoms. Kennedy twitted the largely Republican audience by suggesting that his talk might better be called "The President Versus the Press" rather than "The President and the Press." He denied an intention to impose any form of censorship or to establish an "official secrets act," as Allen Dulles suggested, or to control the flow of information through an office of war information, but he urged the publishers to ask themselves if what they printed was not only news but "in the interest of national security." Seeing Kennedy's remarks as an implicit threat, several editors and publishers requested a meeting at the White House. Kennedy agreed, and at the meeting they pressed him to cite examples of irresponsible reporting. Kennedy singled out the *New York Times* and revelations about the Cuban invasion. At the close of the meeting, however, in an aside to *Times* editor Turner Catledge, Kennedy acknowledged the essential role of a critical free press: "Maybe if you had printed more about the operation," he said, "you would have saved us from a colossal mistake."

KENNEDY'S TENSIONS with the press extended to worries about invasions of his privacy. In his address to the publishers, he denied that his remarks were "intended to examine the proper degree of privacy which the press should allow to any President and his family." He wryly observed that the attendance of reporters and photographers at weekly church services had "surely done them no harm." He was unapologetic about breaking with Eisenhower's practice of letting journalists attend his golf games. But then, Kennedy noted with charming self-deprecation, Ike's golfing accomplishments did not include the beaning of a Secret Service agent.

But Kennedy's concern was not with the usual press aggressiveness in covering a president's family and recreational activities. Rather, he was increasingly worried about disclosures detailing his much-rumored womanizing. Almost everyone in the press corps knew about or at least suspected his philandering, columnist Bob Novak later said. From the start of his presidency, some ultra-right-wing papers and what one historian called the "underground market" were swamped with exposés about JFK's hidden, illicit romances. But the mainstream press resisted such scandal mongering. Lyndon Johnson's hideaway office on Capitol Hill, for example, where he indulged in recreational sex, was an open secret during his vice presidency; reporters privately joked about LBJ's "nooky room." Yet nobody in the mainstream press thought it was worth writing about.

The fact that such gossip was confined to a fringe media, which earned a living from unsubstantiated rumors, made Kennedy himself largely indifferent to these articles at the start of his presidency. The fact that the gossip, much of which was true, might trouble Jackie was not enough to rein him in. Indeed, such talk, which added to a romantic, macho image that contrasted sharply with that of his stodgy predecessor, may even have appealed to JFK. Nevertheless, despite the press restraint, people around the president worried about his vulnerability to enemies who might try to break tradition and embarrass him with published accounts of his affairs. Ten days after Kennedy became president, J. Edgar Hoover passed along a report from a field agent about a woman who claimed to be JFK's lover. "Once every two or three months, similar missives would arrive in Bobby's office from the director, not-so-subtle signals that Hoover was keeping, and regularly updating, a file on the president. Blackmail," Bobby Kennedy biographer Evan Thomas concluded, "was an efficient means towards Hoover's true end, the preservation of his own power." It was also Hoover's way of ingratiating himself with Bobby, his immediate boss, and the president. His reports were meant to say, I am your protector, keeping you up-to-date on allegations and dangers you might want to preempt.

THERE IS NO EVIDENCE that rumors about Kennedy's sex life or, for that matter, the escapades themselves distracted him from important business in the first months of his term. Between November and February he had exchanged conciliatory messages with Khrushchev, and on February 22, he expressed the hope that they might be able to meet soon "for an informal exchange of views," which could contribute to "a more harmonious relationship between our two countries." But the Bay of Pigs invasion undermined whatever goodwill the initial Kennedy-Khrushchev exchanges had generated. Seeing Kennedy as thrown on the defensive by his embarrassing failure, Khrushchev went on the attack. "It is a secret to no one," he wrote Kennedy, "that the armed bands invading" Cuba "were trained, equipped and armed in the United States of America." He promised to give Cuba "all necessary help to repel armed attack" and warned that "conflagration in one region could endanger settlements elsewhere."

Kennedy manfully responded that the invasion was a demonstration of brave patriots determined to restore freedom to Cuba. He emphasized that the United States intended no military intervention on the island but was obliged "to protect this hemisphere against external aggression." Kennedy also warned against using Cuba as a pretext for inflaming other areas of the world, which would endanger the general peace. He asked Khrushchev to "recognize that free people in all parts of the world do not accept the claim of historical inevitability for Communist revolution. What your government believes is its own business; what it does in the world is the world's business. The great revolution in the history of man, past, present, and future, is the revolution of those determined to be free."

Kennedy's greatest fear was that Moscow might use Cuba as an excuse to close off West Berlin, to which many educated East Germans and other East Europeans were fleeing from communism. When Nixon had urged JFK to find an excuse for invading Cuba, Kennedy had replied that an invasion would risk a war with Russia over Berlin and his priority had to be world peace. If there was to be a next world war, Berlin, Kennedy believed, would be where it began.

Khrushchev answered Kennedy with a fifteen-page letter reiterating his accusations about U.S. interference in Cuba and restating his warnings that this was no way to ease Soviet-American tensions. Kennedy wisely left Khrushchev's letter unanswered. Still, because Khrushchev was as intent as Kennedy on avoiding a nuclear conflict, the Soviet leader seized upon the president's February proposal for a meeting in Vienna on June 3 to 4. Although Khrushchev did not say so, it was clear to Kennedy that Berlin, which Khrushchev described as "a dangerous source of tension in the very heart of Europe," was also his greatest concern.

KENNEDY'S FIRST THREE MONTHS in office had confirmed his belief that overseas perils should take priority over economic and social reforms, but because he believed that an effective foreign policy partly depended on a strong economy and social cohesion at home, he felt compelled to strike a balance between external and internal initiatives. His dilemma, as he saw it, was that domestic proposals could do more to divide than unite the country.

On April 18, in the midst of the Bay of Pigs crisis, he asked Congress to create a new cabinet department of urban affairs and housing as a way to halt "the appalling deterioration of many of our country's urban areas," rehabilitate the nation's cities, where 70 percent of Americans lived, and ensure "adequate housing for all segments of our population." It seemed like an apple pie and motherhood proposal, but it quickly ran into opposition from southern senators and congressmen representing rural areas and small cities. A greater emphasis in a revised bill on small communities promised to neutralize the latter, but southern opposition to an act that could primarily serve inner-city blacks and make Housing and Home Finance Agency administrator Robert Weaver the first African American cabinet secretary was unyielding. The bill was also held hostage to budget constraints imposed by the improving but still sluggish economy and increasing defense expenditures. Kennedy's reluctance to fight for something he saw as a secondary priority was as much a drag on aggressive action as the economy and southern opposition.

Consequently, in May, Kennedy proposed legislation that would stimulate the economy with limited tax reductions tied to revenue gains. He described his proposal as "a first though urgent step along the road to constructive reform." He said he planned to send a more comprehensive tax reform program to the Congress in 1962 that would stimulate "a higher rate of economic growth, [and create] a more equitable tax structure, and a simpler tax law." In the meantime, he proposed a tax incentive to businesses in the form of a credit for modernization and expansion of plant and equipment. To make up for lost income here, he proposed the end of tax exemptions for Americans earning incomes abroad in economically advanced countries and for estate taxes on overseas properties, withholding taxes on interest and dividend payments, the continuation of corporate and excise taxes scheduled to be reduced or ended in July, and a tax on civil aviation providers to help pay for the operation and improvement of the federal airways system.

Business leaders, who preferred liberalized depreciation allowances to tax credits for new plant and equipment costs, successfully blocked Kennedy's bill, demonstrating both their power as a lobby and White House inattentiveness or carelessness. Fearful of sharing the spotlight and thus diminishing JFK's standing as a domestic leader, the White House had barred Lyndon Johnson, the most skilled legislator in the administration, from a meaningful role in dealing with Congress. Instead, Kennedy, who had never shown an affinity for the sort of cooperative endeavor needed to enact major bills, relied on inexperienced aides to advance his legislative agenda. Complaining that his contacts on the Hill were not being used, Johnson said, "You know, they never once asked me about that!" The result, predictably, was a stumbling Kennedy legislative effort.

Despite his defeats on creating a housing department and tax reform, Kennedy could point to some gains in domestic affairs. The Congress agreed to an Area Redevelopment Act that fulfilled his campaign promise to help ease chronic unemployment in West Virginia and nine other states. In addition, the Congress gave Kennedy significant additions to several existing programs: expanded unemployment benefits, a higher minimum wage that included 3.6 million uncovered workers, increases in Social Security, aid to cities to improve housing and transportation, a water pollution control act to protect the country's rivers and streams, funds to continue the building of a national highway system begun under Eisenhower, and an agriculture act to raise farmers' incomes and perpetuate "a most outstanding accomplishment of our civilization . . . to produce more food with less people than any country on earth."

Despite these advances, the administration could not take much satisfaction from its initial domestic record. Aside from area redevelopment, the White House had no major legislative achievements. Kennedy's "highest-priority items," tax reform, federal aid to elementary and secondary education, college scholarships, and health insurance for the aged, never got out of congressional committees. Historian Irving Bernstein, who closely studied the struggles over the education and health bills, described them as political snake pits. Federal involvement in education was anathema to conservatives, who wished to preserve local control. Emotional arguments about public funding for parochial schools opened an unbridgeable gap between Catholics and Protestants. Determined to keep his campaign pledges on separation of church and state, Kennedy provoked unyielding opposition from Catholics for refusing to support direct aid to parochial schools. While some critics of his stand on education protested his adherence to traditional thinking, his advocacy of health insurance for the elderly under Social Security provoked the opposite response — warnings against administration plans to imitate communist countries by socializing medicine. Nor could a health insurance bill win approval from the House Ways and Means Committee, whose chairman, Wilbur Mills of Arkansas, would endorse only bills with clear majorities.

Supporters of the education and health bills blamed Kennedy for not providing stronger leadership. He had in fact spoken forcefully for both measures during the presidential campaign, describing them as legislative priorities. But Richard Neustadt's recent book *Presidential Power* had deepened Kennedy's understanding of a president's limited personal influence and the folly of fighting for lost causes in a Congress dominated by conservative southern Democrats allied with Republicans. The almost certain defeat of these bills in the first session of the 87th Congress made him reluctant to spend much political capital on them.

Because Kennedy had been so cautious in backing the school and health bills, pollster Lou Harris urged him to understand the need for a more substantial domestic record. "Phase Two" of Kennedy's administration "is now beginning and it is time for a new upbeat," Harris wrote him in June. "The President needs some major and specific score-throughs. While the foreign policy crisis has dominated . . . [your] time and energies, the quickest, most easily understood, and most dramatic gains are likely to be on domestic issues." Harris counseled him to make a September back-to-school fight for an education bill. It should become "a new number one domestic priority." After an education bill passed, Harris urged him to announce "Medical Care for the Aged by '62." He suggested a three-pronged attack: "A frontal assault on the AMA as an obstructive lobby holding back progress," a "grass roots" movement by "older people . . . who could make the Kennedy bill their rallying point," and a direct appeal to a national audience "through three separate television shows." Given the makeup of Congress in 1961, Harris's advice was less a demonstration of smart politics than an expression of frustration, shared by Kennedy, at the president's inability to make headway on two of the country's most compelling social needs and on issues that could give the Democrats a significant advantage in the 1962 congressional campaigns. Although unwilling to bring either bill up again in the fall, Kennedy vowed another effort the next year.

NOWHERE, HOWEVER, was Kennedy's frustration more evident than on civil rights. Throughout the 1960 campaign and most of his presidency he felt underappreciated by civil rights activists. After watching Kennedy's performance in the opening months of his term, Martin Luther King predicted that the new administration would do no more than reach "aggressively" for "the limited goal of token integration." He told Harris Wofford, "In the election, when I gave my testimony for Kennedy, my impression then was that he had the intelligence and the skill and the moral fervor to give the leadership we've been waiting for and do what no President has ever done. Now," after watching him in office, "I'm convinced that he has the understanding and the political skill but so far I'm afraid that the moral passion is missing." James Forman of the Student Nonviolent Coordinating Committee (SNCC) was less convinced of the president's good intentions, describing Kennedy on civil rights as nothing more than "quick-talking [and] double-dealing." Bayard Rustin, a founder of the Congress of Racial Equality (CORE), believed Kennedy was "the smartest politician we have had in a long time." At one minute, according to Rustin, he called black leaders together and promised to help them get money for voter registration. The next he cozied up to "the Dixiecrats and gives them Southern racist judges who make certain that the money the Negro gets will not achieve its purpose." Rustin added: "This is the way all presidents behave. They give you as little as they can. And one of the reasons for that is they're president of all the people and they have to accommodate all segments. . . . So they are constantly weighing where is the weight of the problem for me if I don't act?" Rustin believed that "anything we got out of Kennedy came out of the objective situation and the political necessity, and not out of the spirit of John Kennedy. He was a reactor."

Much of the resentment during the first six months of Kennedy's term concerned the fact that he would neither sign a promised Executive Order desegregating federally financed housing nor ask Congress for a civil rights law. He saw either action as certain to anger southerners and lose any chance of support for other reforms. Having criticized Eisenhower's refusal to act on housing by emphasizing that it required only a stroke of the pen, Kennedy began receiving pens in the mail as a reminder of his words during the campaign. In response, Kennedy "kept muttering and kidding about how in the world he had ever come to promise that one stroke of the pen."

In May, the African American deputy DNC director, Louis Martin, wrote Ted Sorensen to say that the president's silence on the issue showed the administration as "timid and reluctant to put its full weight behind Civil Rights legislation. . . . His enemies are now being given an opportunity to charge him with inaction in a very vital area." The criticism angered the president and Bobby. They believed that they were doing as much as possible for civil rights under current constraints. True, when a Gallup poll in January asked people in the South whether the day would ever come when blacks and whites would share the same public accommodations, 76 percent said yes. But all the other polling data suggested that neither the North nor the South had a majority ready to see this happen soon. If there were federal aid to education, should money go to all public schools, including those practicing racial segregation? Gallup asked. Almost seven years after the Supreme Court declared "separate but equal" schools unconstitutional and two thirds of the country said it supported desegregation in public schools and all forms of public transportation, 68 percent of Americans answered yes. In May and June, when asked if integration should be brought about by every means in the near future, only 23 percent agreed; 61 percent preferred gradual change. The Kennedys shared majority sentiment that peaceful demonstrations challenging southern segregation laws would do more to hurt than help bring about integration.

But it was not simply public opinion that restrained them. The Kennedy lawyers in the Justice Department believed that there were distinct limits to what the White House could do about racial injustices. Burke Marshall, the head of the department's Civil Rights Division, told Martin Luther King that constitutional federalism placed severe restrictions on the government's power to intervene in school desegregation or police brutality cases. The only substantial latitude the Justice Department had was to protect voting rights, and even there they had to struggle against the resistance of local southern officials to enfranchising blacks.

In March and April, a controversy erupted over hotel accommodations in Charleston, South Carolina, for a black member of the National Civil War Commission planning to attend the commemoration of the battle of Fort Sumter. When Kennedy wrote a letter to General Ulysses S. Grant III, the head of the commission, urging equal treatment for all commission members, southern delegates to the ceremony decried Kennedy's unauthorized intrusion into the actions of a privately owned hotel. Grant's response that the commission had no business interfering in "racial matters," Kennedy's inability to persuade any Charleston hotel to satisfy his request, and a decision to move the commemoration dinner to a nearby U.S. naval base that segregated its personnel embarrassed Kennedy and reinforced his determination to shun "racial politics."

Kennedy's relationship with Martin Luther King in 1961 reflected the administration's eagerness to avoid too much entanglement in civil rights struggles. King was not invited to the Inauguration nor to a meeting of civil rights leaders on March 6 in Bobby's office. As King biographer Taylor Branch said, "King's name was too sensitive at the time, too associated with ongoing demonstrations that were vexing politicians in the South." In late March, after King asked for a private appointment with Kennedy, O'Donnell told King that the "present international situation" — Laos, Africa, Cuba, and Soviet difficulties — made it impossible for the president to find time for a meeting. Only at the end of April did the White House agree to a secret, off-the-record discussion in a private dining room at Washington's Mayflower Hotel between King, Bobby, Louis Martin, and several Justice Department officials. King was so self-effacing and agreeable during the meeting that he got a few minutes with Kennedy at the White House afterward, and Bobby gave him the private phone numbers of Justice Department officials John Seigenthaler and Burke Marshall with instructions to call them any time voter registration workers in trouble could not get through to the FBI.

The gestures were of a piece with other administration actions the Kennedys believed gave them a claim on the appreciation of civil rights leaders. A White House "Summary of Civil Rights Progress for the Nine Months — January 20 Through October 1961" stated the Kennedy case. It described the president's Executive Order establishing a "Committee on Equal Employment Opportunity with far greater power of enforcement than held by any predecessor agencies" and its record of having persuaded "about half of the fifty largest government contractors to undertake specific 'plans for progress' involving recruitment, training, hiring and upgrading of Negro employees." The committee hoped to enlist all fifty contractors in this program of "affirmative action" by the end of the year. More than "fifty outstanding Negroes" had already been appointed to high-level policy-making jobs in the administration, and government agencies were actively recruiting "qualified Negroes for federal service in the U.S. and overseas." The Justice Department had filed twelve voting rights suits and intended to "support in every appropriate way efforts of Negroes to . . . register and vote." The administration had taken legal action and given moral and political backing to implement school desegregation across the South. And the president had set up a subcabinet group on civil rights to coordinate all federal civil rights actions. Finally, the administration stated its intention to end segregation and other forms of discrimination in interstate bus, train, and plane travel everywhere in the country within a year.

The claim about desegregating interstate transportation was a good example of why the Kennedys had limited credibility with civil rights leaders. The administration had been reluctantly drawn into the controversy. In early May, thirteen black and white members of CORE boarded Greyhound and Trailway buses in Washington, D.C., to travel to New Orleans through Virginia, the Carolinas, Georgia, and Alabama. The goal was to reach New Orleans by May 17, the seventh anniversary of the Supreme Court's school desegregation ruling. Although CORE had notified the Justice Department of its actions and a reporter had told Bobby, the White House itself had no advance warning of the trip. On May 15, newspaper stories about violence in Alabama against the Freedom Riders caught the Kennedys by surprise. Kennedy, who was scheduled to go to Canada in two days, saw the headlines as another blow to America's international prestige. "Can't you get your goddamned friends off those buses?" he asked Harris Wofford. "Tell them to call it off! Stop them!" When the Freedom Riders, several of whom had been badly beaten, abandoned the bus trip to fly from Birmingham to New Orleans and found themselves trapped in the Birmingham airport by bomb threats, Bobby asked Seigenthaler to go help them. "What sort of help do they need?" Seigenthaler asked. Bobby, who a week before at the University of Georgia had made a forceful statement of the administration's determination to enforce civil rights laws as a way to assist the fight against international communism, replied, "I think they primarily need somebody along just to hold their hand and let them know that we care."

The Kennedys believed that Bobby's Georgia speech, which had won praise from blacks and whites, and Seigenthaler's presence in Birmingham, where he helped get the Freedom Riders to New Orleans, were ample demonstrations of their commitment to civil rights and entitled them to cooperation and support from activists. A Gallup poll showing that only 24 percent of the country approved of what the Freedom Riders were doing and that 64 percent disapproved added to the Kennedys' conviction that their actions showed political courage.

Rights leaders, however, believed that the administration was doing as little as it could and much less than needed to be done. Consequently, a group of Nashville students, despite warnings that they might be killed and counterpressure from Seigenthaler, decided to go to Birmingham and then complete the bus trip to New Orleans. On their arrival, they were arrested and imprisoned by local police for violating segregation laws. The activists, held illegally in "protective custody," demanded immediate release to resume their trip. To keep the president clear of "racial politics," Bobby told the press that only he and his deputies were discussing how to proceed. But Kennedy met with this team in his bedroom, where he sat in pajamas before an uneaten breakfast. All agreed that they needed a plan for direct intervention. They ruled out federalizing the Alabama National Guard, which would add to the sense of crisis and engage the president beyond what they wanted. Instead, the president called Alabama governor John Patterson, his most reliable southern ally during the 1960 campaign. Patterson, who had no intention of falling on his sword for the Kennedys, replied through a State House operator that he was fishing in the Gulf of Mexico and was unreachable. When another call to Patterson from Kennedy brought a more direct refusal to talk, Bobby told the governor's aides that the president would be compelled to send in federal forces unless Patterson agreed to protect the Freedom Riders. Grudging agreement from Patterson to act and pressure from Bobby on Greyhound to find a driver who would risk driving an integrated bus finally got the protesters on their way to Montgomery.

In order to get Greyhound on board, Bobby had been forced to threaten a company supervisor in Birmingham. "Do you know how to drive a bus?" Bobby had asked with controlled rage. When the man said no, Bobby exploded: "Well, surely somebody in the damn bus company can drive a bus, can't they? . . . I think you . . . had better be getting in touch with Mr. Greyhound or whoever Greyhound is, and somebody better give us an answer to this question. I am — the Government is — going to be very much upset if this group does not get to continue their trip." Eavesdroppers on Bobby's telephone conversation leaked it to the press, which ran front-page stories across the South charging that Bobby was backing and abetting the Freedom Riders. In addition to the bad publicity in the South, the reports gave the Kennedys little credit with civil rights backers, who saw Bobby as reacting rather than leading on an important issue. And they undermined the administration's political influence with southern congressmen and senators, who now seemed certain to make life more difficult than ever for Kennedy on the Hill. "I never recovered from it," Bobby later said of the newspaper allegations.

The ordeal of the activists and the administration's struggle to protect them resumed in Montgomery, where a white mob carrying ax handles, baseball bats, chains, and lead pipes assaulted the Freedom Riders at the bus terminal. In the absence of city policemen, who shared local antagonism to the riders, the unrestrained mob beat the activists, reporters, photographers, and Seigenthaler, who tried to protect two women being pummeled. John Doar, a Justice Department attorney on assignment in Montgomery, was watching from a federal building window. He described the melee to Burke Marshall on the telephone in Washington. "Oh, there are fists, punching!" he shouted into the phone. "There are no cops. It's terrible! It's terrible! There's not a cop in sight. People are yelling, 'There those niggers are! Get 'em, get 'em!' It's awful." Rioters with pipes clubbed Seigenthaler to the ground, where he lay unconscious for half an hour before being taken to a hospital.

Patterson refused to discuss the latest riot with Bobby, and after a conversation with Jack, who was away for the weekend in Middleburg, Virginia, Bobby decided to send federal marshals to Montgomery to protect the "interstate travelers." News that King was also heading for Montgomery, to preach to the Freedom Riders at black minister Ralph Abernathy's First Baptist Church, upset Bobby, who unsuccessfully tried to dissuade King from putting himself in harm's way and adding to the local tensions. To guarantee King's safety, fifty U.S. marshals met him at the airport and escorted him to Abernathy's home. After Byron White, Kennedy's old friend and a deputy U.S. attorney general, met with Governor Patterson, who demanded withdrawal of the U.S. marshals, White called the president to recommend just that. But Kennedy, who had issued a statement after the riot at the Montgomery bus terminal saying that the U.S. government would meet its responsibility to maintain public calm, rejected White's suggestion.

Except for his statement issued from the White House press office, Kennedy remained out of sight, though Bobby consulted with him constantly during the weekend. On Sunday, May 21, a new violent confrontation erupted between the marshals and a white mob surrounding Abernathy's church, where fifteen hundred supporters of the Freedom Riders had gathered to hear King speak. To continue insulating the president from the crisis, Bobby took the lead in deploying the marshals and negotiating with local law enforcement to keep the peace. During repeated mob assaults on the church, which the marshals repelled with tear gas, King and Bobby clashed on the telephone. While King and his audience waited for more marshals to arrive, he told Bobby, "If they don't get here immediately, we're going to have a bloody confrontation." After Alabama National Guardsmen replaced the marshals and intimidated people inside the church by refusing to let them leave, King upbraided Bobby for having abandoned the congregation to the control of Patterson's hostile guardsmen. "Now, Reverend," Bobby replied impatiently, "you know just as well as I do that if it hadn't been for the U.S. marshals you'd be dead as Kelsey's nuts right now." Bobby's reference did not amuse King, who had never heard the Irish expression describing impotence. "Who's Kelsey?" he asked some aides. "That ended the conversation," Wofford says, "but there were harder words to come."

Although the people in the church were allowed to depart before dawn and the administration had a sense of triumph at having preserved law and order, the gulf between the Kennedys and civil rights advocates deepened. When Patterson had complained that the presence of U.S. marshals in Alabama was "destroying us politically," Bobby replied, "John, it's more important that these people in the church survive physically than for us to survive politically." But on Monday, after the all-night crisis at the church, Bobby wanted the Freedom Riders to call off their campaign. "They had made their point," he told Wofford. Publicly, Bobby called for a "cooling-off" period. James Farmer of CORE responded sharply. "Negroes have been cooling off for a hundred years," he said, and would be "in a deep freeze if they cooled any further." For his part, King told *Time* magazine, "Wait, means 'Never.'" When a reporter asked Ralph Abernathy if he was concerned about embarrassing the president, Abernathy answered, "Man, we've been embarrassed all our lives." King told some of his associates after rejecting Bobby's request, "You know, they don't understand the social revolution going on in the world, and therefore they don't understand what we're doing."

After he had issued his public statement on the disorders in Alabama, Kennedy met with a group of liberals, including the actor Harry Belafonte and Eugene Rostow, the dean of the Yale School and W. W. Rostow's brother. Belafonte respectfully asked if the president "could say something a little more about the Freedom Riders." No less respectfully, but more forcefully, Rostow urged "the need for moral leadership on the substantive issue of equal access to public facilities." After they left, Kennedy asked Wofford, "What in the world does [Rostow] think I should do? Doesn't he know I've done more for civil rights than any President in American history? How could any man have done more than I've done?" There was something to be said for Kennedy's point, but not as much as he thought. He had gone beyond other presidents, but it was not enough to keep up with the determined efforts of African Americans to end two centuries of oppression.

When the Freedom Riders returned to Washington after serving time in a Jackson, Mississippi, jail, Kennedy refused to see them at the White House. Nor would he follow Wofford's suggestion that he issue a statement, which "Eisenhower never did . . . to give clear moral expression to the issues involved. The only effective time for such moral leadership is during an occasion of moral crisis," Wofford asserted. "This is the time when your words would mean most." Black leaders and newspaper editorials were complaining that "despite your criticism of Eisenhower on this score, you have not chosen yet to say anything about the right of Americans to travel without discrimination." Because making the moral case for a statement seemed unlikely to persuade Kennedy, Wofford also emphasized its impact on foreign affairs. "Some such vigorous statement and public appeal, on top of the effective actions of the Attorney General, past and planned, should have a good effect abroad. I note from reading the foreign press that some strong Presidential statement is awaited."

Kennedy's refusal to follow Wofford's suggestion rested on his conviction that he had done as much as he could. He understood the sense of injustice that blacks felt toward a system of apartheid in a country priding itself on traditions of freedom and equal opportunity. Southern abuse of blacks, including physical intimidation of courageous men and women practicing nonviolent protest, was not lost on him. He knew this was not simply a five-or-ten-cent increase in the minimum wage but an issue that contradicted the country's credo. Nonetheless, he gave it a lower priority than the danger of a nuclear war in which tens of millions of people could be killed and the planet suffer damages that would jeopardize human survival. He seemed to operate on the false assumption that openly and aggressively committing himself to equal rights for black Americans would somehow undermine his pursuit of world peace. Many civil rights activists justifiably concluded that Kennedy simply did not have the moral commitment to their cause, that his background as a rich man insulated from contacts with African Americans and their plight made him more an interested observer than a visceral proponent, like Hubert Humphrey, of using federal power to cure the country's greatest social ill.

FROM MAY 16 to 18, in the midst of the strife in Alabama, Kennedy made his first trip as president abroad, to Canada. Although he knew that the timing of his visit might anger civil rights activists, he saw conversations in Ottawa as too important to be deferred. Prime Minister John Diefenbaker, who wished to separate Canada from U.S. Cold War policies, opposed Washington's pressure for Canadian membership in the Organization of American States and requests to deploy nuclear weapons on Canadian soil. Because Kennedy had no hope of changing Diefenbaker's mind through private conversations, he used a speech before Parliament to plead the case for U.S. policies. He described America's historic friendship with Canada as the "unity of equal and independent nations," and urged Canadians to join the OAS as one way to make "this entire area more secure against aggression of all kinds." He emphasized how heartened the OAS would be by Canada's participation. As important, he urged the deployment of nuclear weapons for the defense of all NATO areas, meaning Canada as well as Europe, and warned, "Our opponents are watching to see if we in the West are divided. They take courage when we are."

Diefenbaker resented Kennedy's attempt to force him into unwanted actions, and after Kennedy returned to the United States, the prime minister threatened him with the publication of a memo in which Kennedy allegedly described Diefenbaker as an S.O.B. Ted Sorensen claimed that the handwritten note included an illegible reference to the OAS and nothing about Diefenbaker. After the memo incident, Bobby recalled that his brother "hated . . . Diefenbaker — had contempt for him." In a private, candid response to the flap over the memo, Kennedy said, "I didn't think Diefenbaker was a son of a bitch, I thought he was a prick." ("I couldn't have called him an S.O.B.," Kennedy joked. "I didn't know he was one — at that time.") Personal animus aside, the visit to Canada added to Kennedy's foreign policy worries. Like Churchill during World War II, he could complain that the only thing worse than having allies was not having them.

The trip to Canada and a special message to Congress on May 25, a week after his return from Ottawa, reflected Kennedy's ongoing concern to restore confidence in his foreign policy leadership after the Bay of Pigs failure. Normally, he explained, a president spoke only annually on the state of the union, but these were "extraordinary times" confronting Americans with an "extraordinary challenge." Delivering his speech from the well of the House before a joint session, Kennedy solemnly reminded the Congress that the U.S. had become the world's "leader in freedom's cause. . . . The great battleground for the defense and expansion of freedom today," he said, "is the whole southern half of the globe — Asia, Latin America, Africa, and the Middle East — the lands of the rising peoples." The adversaries of freedom were working to capture this revolution and turn it to their advantage. And although they possessed "a powerful intercontinental striking force, [and] large forces for conventional war," their "aggression is more often concealed than open."

Since America's advantage in numbers of nuclear weapons and capacity to deliver them was secondary in this "battle for minds and souls," Kennedy omitted mention of it. Nor did he feel compelled to include the civil rights movement across the South as part of the struggle of oppressed peoples against "injustice, tyranny, and exploitation." It would be no selling point to southern congressmen and senators, whose votes were essential to increase appropriations for national defense.

The nation's security, he explained, depended first on a stronger American economy. And this meant reducing unemployment through a Manpower Development and Training program that would give hundreds of thousands of workers displaced by technological changes new job skills. Second, business and labor needed to improve America's balance of payments at the same time they held down prices and wages. He also proposed a new Act for International Development that could raise living standards in developing countries and make them less vulnerable to communist subversion. An increase in funding for the United States Information Agency would also combat communism in the propaganda wars being waged on radio and television in Latin America and Asia.

Expanded military assistance programs for Southeast Asian, Latin American, and African countries were no less important. In addition, spending on new kinds of forces and weapons would give the United States greater flexibility to fight either a traditional ground war or an unconventional guerrilla conflict. This was not a recommendation for diminished nuclear fighting capacity; Kennedy believed it essential to maintain the country's nuclear arsenal at the highest level as well. Improved intelligence, especially after the Bay of Pigs, was yet another priority. It was "both legitimate and necessary as a means of self-defense in an age of hidden perils."

Halfway through his speech, Kennedy came to even bigger ticket items. He wanted to triple spending on civil defense, with additional large increases in the future. "Apathy, indifference, and skepticism" had greeted past suggestions for a national civil defense policy,

Kennedy declared. Indeed, comedians had ridiculed arguments that a "well-designed" program could save millions of American lives, facetiously instructing students during a nuclear attack to "move away from windows, crouch under desks, put your head between your legs, and kiss your ass good-bye." As for survival in a nuclear war, 83 percent of people polled saw their chances as poor or no more than fifty-fifty. Ninety-five percent of the public had made no plans to prepare their homes for a nuclear conflict. A majority was more receptive to building community fallout shelters, but overcoming national skepticism about an effective civil defense program was a hard sell. Soviet citizens were no less cynical about civil defense. "What should I do if a nuclear bomb falls?" a Moscow joke went. "Cover yourself with a sheet and crawl slowly to the nearest cemetery. Why slowly? To avoid panic."

Initially, Kennedy himself had been skeptical of investing in a costly fallout shelter program. In early May, when he met with several governors urging an expanded program, he had doubts that a more extensive civil defense plan would "really do the job." Marcus Raskin, an aide at the NSC, reinforced Kennedy's skepticism. Raskin expressed "great fears for this civil defense program," which he did not think would "decrease the probabilities of war" and might even increase them. Moreover, any proposal seemed likely to intensify an unresolvable argument over whether blast or fallout shelters would save more lives.

But shelter advocates gave Kennedy two reasons for going ahead. Publicizing a shelter program "would show the world that the U.S . . . is really prepared to suffer the consequences" of a war and "would thus strengthen our negotiating position" and allied confidence in America's willingness to protect them against Soviet aggression. Second, an expanded civil defense program would put additional strains on the Soviet economy by forcing them to spend more on nuclear arms — in retrospect, an amazing, even nutty, prescription for protecting Americans from a potential nuclear attack.

There was more. Kennedy described the program as an insurance policy, "which we could never forgive ourselves for forgoing in the event of catastrophe." The slightest possibility that millions of lives could be saved was enough to convince any president that he needed to make it part of the country's national defense. Criticism from New York governor Nelson Rockefeller, a likely Republican opponent in 1964, of the administration's "complacency" on the issue was not lost on Kennedy. Indeed, Rockefeller's political challenge was more important than any real hope that the so-called shelters could save millions of Americans from an initial nuclear blast or the subsequent radiation fallout.

Kennedy's other major initiative in his speech was a declaration of intent to land a man on the moon and return him to earth before the end of the decade. Such a mission, he believed, would be of compelling value in the contest with the Soviets for international prestige, as well as a way to convince allies and neutral Third World nations of American superiority. Because he saw such a commitment as certain to divert resources from other essential needs for years to come, he believed Americans would be reluctant to embrace the idea. Indeed, Sorensen noted that the only time Kennedy ever departed extensively from a prepared text in speaking to Congress was in emphasizing the pointlessness of going ahead with a manned moon landing unless the country was willing to make the necessary sacrifices. "There is no sense in agreeing or desiring that the United States take an affirmative position in outer space, unless we are prepared to do the work and bear the burdens," he said. And, as he anticipated, Kennedy faced substantial opposition — both among the general public and within the government. A panel of scientists Eisenhower had asked to evaluate a moon flight had believed it worth doing, but Eisenhower saw a manned moon landing as a "stunt" and said privately that he "couldn't care less whether a man ever reached the moon." Kennedy's science advisers conceded that successful space probes could advance America's international prestige, but they doubted that the U.S. could beat the Russians to the moon and warned that such a project could be prohibitively expensive. David Bell, Kennedy's budget director, wondered whether the benefits of manned space flights would exceed the costs and said that the administration could find better and cheaper means of raising America's international standing. A majority of Americans agreed: 58 percent of the public thought it a poor idea to spend an estimated $40 billion — roughly $225 per person — on something the Soviets might beat them at.

But Kennedy refused to accept what he saw as a timid approach to space exploration. Acknowledging in his speech that the Soviets had a lead on the United States and that no one could guarantee "that we shall one day be first," he did "guarantee that any failure to make this effort will make us last." Psychologically, the challenge of putting a man on the moon and beating the Russians in the effort to do it resonated with Kennedy's affinity for heroic causes and the whole spirit of the New Frontier. For Kennedy, it was "clearly one of the great human adventures of modern history." As he said in a later speech, "But why, some say, the moon? . . . And they may well ask, why climb the highest mountain? Why, thirty-five years ago, fly the Atlantic? . . . We choose to go to the moon in this decade, and do the other things, not because they are easy, but because they are hard; because that goal will serve to organize and measure the best of our energies and skills."

Other considerations were at work in shaping Kennedy's decision. He shared with James Webb, the head of NASA, and Johnson, the chairman of Kennedy's National Space Council, the conviction that a manned mission would yield technological, economic, and political advantages. The thirty to forty billion dollars the government seemed likely to spend on the project promised to advance America's ability to predict the weather and achieve high-speed electronic communications with satellites. Space spending would also provide jobs, and the political gains in the South and West, where NASA would primarily spend its funds, were not lost on savvy politicians like Kennedy and Johnson.

More important to Kennedy, however, than any tangible benefit was the potential boost to America's world image. In April, after Soviet cosmonaut Yury Gagarin had orbited the earth and the Bay of Pigs had humiliated the administration, Kennedy had asked Johnson to make "an overall survey of where we stand in space. Do we have a chance of beating the Soviets by putting a laboratory in space, or by a trip around the moon, or by a rocket to land on the moon, or by a rocket to go to the moon and back with a man? Is there any other space program that promises dramatic results in which we could win?" Johnson had confirmed Kennedy's supposition that a strong effort was needed at once to catch and surpass the Soviets if the United States wanted to win "control over . . . men's minds through space accomplishments." Landing a man on the moon would have "great propaganda value. The real 'competition' in outer space," Johnson had added, was between the communist and U.S. social systems. Control of outer space would "determine which system of society and government [would] dominate the future. . . . In the eyes of the world, first in space means first, period; second in space is second in everything." When people complained about the costs of the moon mission, Johnson replied, "Now, would you rather have us be a second-rate nation or should we spend a little money?" The president obviously agreed.

Kennedy's concern about the impact of space travel on the country's morale and its hold on world opinion registered clearly before NASA's first manned mission. Prior to Commander Alan Shepard's brief but successful space flight on May 5, Kennedy talked to Rusk and Webb about the risks of television coverage. The president "is afraid of the reaction of the public in case there is a mishap in the firing," Evelyn Lincoln noted in her diary on May 1. Webb told Kennedy that "he had tried to keep the press away from this and likewise the TV but they had been given the go sign long before he took over. In fact, the previous administration had sold rights to *Life* magazine on reports of this launching." Kennedy, Lincoln added, had tried unsuccessfully to reach the network executive in charge of the TV coverage "to play down the publicity and this venture as much as possible." A Pierre Salinger follow-up call had had no better result.

By contrast with civil defense, which in time proved to be a wasteful, foolish idea, a manned moon mission amounted to a highly constructive program with benefits much beyond the boost to America's international prestige. When the Shepard mission was a success, the television and magazine coverage was greatly appreciated by the administration, which realized that similar reporting could galvanize public support for the moon program.

In June, as Johnson rode in a car with the president, FCC director Newton Minow, and Shepard to a National Convention of Broadcasters, Kennedy poked the vice president and said, "You know, Lyndon, nobody knows that the Vice President is the Chairman of the Space Council. But if that flight had been a flop, I guarantee you that everybody would have known that you were the Chairman." Everyone laughed except Johnson, who looked glum and angry, especially after Minow chimed in, "Mr. President, if the flight would have been a flop, the Vice President would have been the next astronaut."

KENNEDY'S MAY 25 ADDRESS was also a forum for justifying a trip to Europe to meet with de Gaulle in Paris and Khrushchev in Vienna. He described discussions with de Gaulle as "permitting the kind of close and ranging consultation that will strengthen both our countries." Left unsaid were differences with the French that — like those with Canada — seemed harmful to U.S. national security. Kennedy hinted at the problems, saying in his May 25 speech, "Such serious conversations do not require a pale unanimity — they are rather the instruments of trust and understanding over a long road."

De Gaulle was an inherited problem. Although the French leader liked to quote Sophocles' belief that "one must wait until the evening to see how splendid the day was," de Gaulle understood that he had become a legend in his own lifetime — "a great captain of the Western World," Kennedy called him. His leadership of the Free French in World War II and his restoration of French influence after 1945 had established him as one of the twentieth century's greats, but his determination to reestablish France as a European and world power had also brought him into conflict with every president from FDR to JFK. At six-foot-three-and-a-half-inches, his physical stature complemented an imperiousness that had angered previous American presidents. Roosevelt had compared the temperamental de Gaulle to Joan of Arc and Clemenceau. He irritated Eisenhower no less. Indeed, in their January 19 meeting, Eisenhower had told Kennedy that de Gaulle's attitude jeopardized the entire Western alliance.

But Kennedy had genuine regard for de Gaulle. He admired his courage in supporting unpopular causes and shared his conviction that only through difficulty could a leader realize his potential and that "small men cannot handle great events." Specifically, Kennedy agreed with de Gaulle's conviction that the West had to resist compromises with the Soviets over Berlin; needed to back self-determination in Africa, especially in Algeria, where de Gaulle was finally accepting an end to French control; and should integrate European economies as a way to avoid resurgent German nationalism. These common beliefs encouraged Kennedy's hopes for Franco-American cooperation.

Yet Kennedy also knew that differences over nuclear weapons, NATO, and Southeast Asia put considerable strain on America's relations with France. De Gaulle, who did not trust American commitments to defend Europe with nuclear weapons, wanted the United States to share nuclear secrets to help France build an independent deterrent. American proposals to provide "enough conventional strength in Europe to stay below the nuclear threshold" heightened de Gaulle's suspicion that the U.S. would not fight a nuclear war to preserve Europe from Soviet communism. De Gaulle also objected to American control over NATO's freedom to respond to a Soviet offensive. He was unwilling to commit France to a larger role in defending Southeast Asia against communist subversion. He dismissed Laos as a "peripheral area that can be abandoned with impunity" and warned about the difficulties of fighting in Vietnam.

De Gaulle, Kennedy believed, "seemed to prefer tension instead of intimacy in his relations with the United States as a matter of pride and independence." Harvard political scientist Nicholas Wahl, who had met de Gaulle several times, counseled the White House, "Even when there is a dialogue, one usually emerges with the impression that it has all been carefully 'managed' by de Gaulle from the beginning. . . . He often uses the third person to refer to himself, which is more his own historian speaking than the megalomaniac, the latter not being completely absent." Still, Kennedy hoped that his discussions with de Gaulle would at least create the appearance of Franco-American unity. Such an appearance could serve him well in his subsequent discussions with Khrushchev and help reestablish some of his lost credibility at home and abroad after the Bay of Pigs. It was a shrewd assessment of what he could gain from the visit to France: The public ceremonies were much more helpful to Kennedy than the private discussions. In preparation for their meeting, Kennedy read de Gaulle's war memoirs. De Gaulle's recollection that "behind his patrician mask of courtesy Roosevelt regarded me without benevolence," but that "for the sake of the future, we each had much to gain by getting along together" convinced Kennedy that de Gaulle would be publicly accommodating to him as well.

The only topic for discussion de Gaulle had agreed to in advance was Berlin. Since he had no hope that Kennedy would agree to tripartite (the U.S., France, and the U.K.) consultations about Europe or to share nuclear secrets, de Gaulle wanted no discussion of these subjects. De Gaulle, who understood perfectly what Kennedy hoped to gain from seeing him, may have had some expectation that he could bend the inexperienced young president to his purposes, something he hadn't been able to do with Eisenhower. But his willingness to help Kennedy make the most of his Paris visit partly rested on concrete self-interest. Aside from possible improvements in France's world position, positive newspaper articles and huge crowds lining procession routes eager for a glimpse persuaded de Gaulle that he would gain politically from Kennedy's visit. De Gaulle, who almost never greeted English-speaking visitors in anything but French, asked Kennedy on his arrival, "Have you made a good aerial voyage?" The trip from Orly Airport to the center of Paris in an open limousine, with the two seated side by side and escorted by fifty motorcycle policemen decked out in special uniforms, demonstrated de Gaulle's regard for his visitor. At a formal dinner that night, de Gaulle praised Kennedy for his "energy and drive," and his "intelligence and courage." Although de Gaulle privately regarded Kennedy as "suffering the drawbacks of a novice," he said before the dinner audience, "Already we have discerned in you the philosophy of the true statesman, who . . . looks to no easy formula or expedient to lighten the responsibility which is his burden and his honor."

Berlin, NATO, Laos, and Vietnam received their share of attention during three days of talks, but no minds were changed or major decisions made. Kennedy used the talks to flatter de Gaulle, showing him the sort of deference the seventy-year-old expected from the young, inexperienced American who had proved, in de Gaulle's words, "somewhat fumbling and over eager" after the Bay of Pigs. Kennedy had memorized quotes from de Gaulle's memoirs and gave him an original letter from Washington to Lafayette, which de Gaulle considered a thoughtful, tasteful gift. "You've studied being head of a country for fifty years," JFK said to him. "Have you found out anything I should know?" De Gaulle advised him to hear the advice of others but to decide matters for himself and live by his own counsel. When de Gaulle told him that intervention in Southeast Asia would be "a bottomless military and political quagmire," Kennedy expressed the hope that "you will not say that in public." De Gaulle replied, "Of course not. I never speak to the press. Never." Kennedy was indeed grateful that de Gaulle gave no public indication of their differences over Europe and Asia. He also listened respectfully to everything de Gaulle told him, though after their talks, Kennedy told an English friend that de Gaulle cared for nothing except the "selfish" interests of his country.

So the conference was a case study in symbol over substance. Photographs and television pictures of the two standing together were by themselves a boost to Kennedy's prestige. The legendary de Gaulle treating JFK as an equal immediately raised Kennedy to the level of a world statesman. His was an image of vibrancy, competence, and strength.

The greatest enemy of this image was Kennedy's health. During his visit to Canada, while turning over a spadeful of earth at a tree-planting ceremony at Government House in Ottawa, Kennedy had aggravated his chronic back problem; he had triggered painful spasms by forgetting to bend his knees, but this was an injury waiting to happen. The bone loss and destruction in his lower back from steroids had been the source of back pain since at least 1940. And while the 1954 surgery that his Addison's disease had made so risky had given him some limited relief, he continued to live with almost constant discomfort. As president, he sometimes took five hot showers a day to ease his pain. A rocking chair, which put less pressure on the muscles and nerves in his lower back than a conventional chair or sofa with soft cushions, gave him additional relief. Procaine, a variation of novocaine, injected into his lower back since 1951, also eased his pain. (During periods of travel, when he had less access to the hydrotherapy and the rocking chair, he relied more on the procaine.) During the campaign in 1960, he had begun seeing Dr. Max Jacobson, the New York physician who had made a reputation for treating celebrities with "pep pills," or amphetamines, that helped combat depression and fatigue. Jacobson, whom patients called "Dr. Feelgood," administered back injections of painkillers and amphetamines that allowed Kennedy to stay off crutches, which he believed essential to project a picture of robust good health. All of this was kept secret. When he went to France to meet de Gaulle, his longstanding physician Dr. Janet Travell, and Dr. George G. Burkley, an admiral and member of the White House medical staff, accompanied JFK on *Air Force One*. Unknown to Travell and Burkley, Jacobson flew on a chartered jet to Paris, where he continued giving the president back injections.

Biographers have speculated on whether Kennedy's medical treatments, including daily cortisone for Addison's and back injections, affected his performance as president. Previously secret medical records gathered by Janet Travell give us a more authoritative answer to the question. During the first six months of his presidency, stomach/colon and prostate problems, high fevers, occasional dehydration, abscesses, sleeplessness, and high cholesterol accompanied Kennedy's back and adrenal ailments. Medical attention was a fixed part of his routine. His physicians administered large doses of so many drugs that they kept an ongoing "Medicine Administration Record" (MAR), cataloging injected and oral corticosteroids for his adrenal insufficiency; procaine shots to painful "trigger points," ultrasound treatments, and hot packs for his back; Lomotil, Metamucil, paregoric, Phenobarbital, testosterone, and Transentine to control his diarrhea, abdominal discomfort, and weight loss; penicillin and other antibiotics for his urinary infections and abscesses; and Tuinal to help him sleep.

Though the treatments occasionally made him feel groggy and tired, Kennedy did not see them as a problem. He dismissed questions about Jacobson's treatment, saying famously about the injections, "I don't care if it's horse piss. It works." When he felt especially tired a few days before a press conference, he wanted additional cortisone to help buoy him up. Moreover, Kennedy did not concern himself with having a single physician oversee his medical care. There was no one, historian Michael Beschloss pointed out, who "was in overall charge to anticipate or deal with the danger that an interaction of cortisone, procaine, amphetamines, or whatever else Jacobson had in his syringe could cause the President to behave in Vienna in a way that could have had dire consequences." Presidential biographer Richard Reeves said that "doctors came and went around Kennedy. In a lifetime of medical torment, Kennedy was more promiscuous with physicians and drugs than he was with women." Though Kennedy's doctors would eventually address this issue, in June 1961, it was unresolved. But if the combination of drugs was having a destructive impact on Kennedy's ability to function effectively, it did not manifest itself in Paris.

The president was not the only White House resident treated by Dr. Feelgood. In May, after deciding to go to Europe, Kennedy had asked Dr. Jacobson to treat Jackie for the headaches and depression she was suffering after the birth of John F. Kennedy Jr. in November 1960. Kennedy wanted Jackie, who had met and impressed de Gaulle during his visit to the United States in 1960, to come with him to Paris. Jacobson administered a series of injections to Jackie that gave her the wherewithal to make the trip.

Kennedy's instinct to bring his wife was a good one. Her command of the French language and expressions of regard for French culture and taste made her an instant hit with the French, who lined up by the thousands to catch a glimpse of her passing automobile or arrivals at and departures from well-publicized ceremonies. Dazzled by her beauty and knowledge of French history and art, de Gaulle publicly spoke of Jackie's "charm." The French press, thrilled by her appearance in a white silk Givenchy gown, anointed her "a queen" and described the Kennedy–de Gaulle dinner as an "Apotheosis at Versailles." Kennedy delighted French and American journalists with

opening remarks at a Paris press luncheon: "I do not think it altogether inappropriate to introduce myself to this audience. I am the
man who accompanied Jacqueline Kennedy to Paris, and I have
enjoyed it." When the journalist Marianne Means later interviewed
Kennedy for a book on First Ladies, it was clear to her that he had
actually resented Jackie's spectacular emergence from his shadow.
But public images were much more important to Kennedy in Paris
than any personal feelings, and his joke struck a perfect ending to a
highly successful visit. A column in the *International Herald Tribune*
reflected the renewed confidence in his leadership: Kennedy, journalist Marguerite Higgins declared, "intends to act not only as his
own foreign minister but as his own Soviet expert, French expert,
Berlin expert, Laotian expert, nuclear test ban expert, etc."

THE BACKGROUND MUSIC was less harmonious. On May 31, during
his first day in Paris, Kennedy received word of the assassination of
General Rafael Trujillo, the Dominican Republic's long-standing dic-
tator. The failed Cuban invasion had triggered fears of a communist
coup in the Republic and Haiti, and the White House saw the two
countries as the "most vulnerable to a Castro takeover." In April and
May, Kennedy had directed that the NSC develop emergency plans
for intervention by U.S. troops to maintain order and preclude communist control. At the same time, however, he wanted no direct
U.S. involvement in rumored plots to topple Trujillo. On May 24,
Kennedy had received a State Department report of an imminent
"attempt [by political opponents] to assassinate Trujillo." Consequently, when Pierre Salinger, unaware that news of Trujillo's death
was still a secret, revealed the assassination to the press at a news
conference in Paris, Kennedy was furious. The administration's early
knowledge of the plot and Trujillo's death suggested that it might
have been in on the killing, which it was not.

Kennedy's bigger problem was whether to send in the marines.
Although there was no clear evidence that Joaquin Balaguer, Trujillo's likely successor, would tilt to the left, White House officials,
led by Bobby, urged U.S. intervention. Bowles, who was heading the
department while Rusk was in Paris, opposed an action that could
"throw us into a war in the most casual fashion." Although Bowles
agreed to the deployment of forces outlined in contingency plans,
he emphasized the need to keep it as low-key as possible. But Bobby,
who Bowles believed "was clearly looking for an excuse to move in

on the island," raised a ruckus. Convinced that the new Dominican government "might team up with Castro," Bobby, supported by McNamara, Goodwin, and Schlesinger, wanted to take what Bowles accurately called "half-cocked action" or "action for action's sake." For starters, Bobby suggested that they consider blowing up the American consulate to provide the rationale for an invasion. When Bowles resisted, Bobby, whom Bowles described as "aggressive, dogmatic, and vicious," and ready to destroy the new government — "with an excuse if possible, without one if necessary" — attacked him as a "gutless bastard." Bowles reported the disagreement to Kennedy, and the president sided with him. "Well, I'm glad to hear it," Bowles replied, "and in that case would you clarify who's in charge here?" "You are," Kennedy answered. "Good," Bowles exclaimed. "Would you mind explaining it to your brother?"

The excessive fears about communist control of hemisphere countries extended to British Guiana, a small outpost of empire with a population of less than 600,000 — one half East Indian, one third African, and the rest British, Portuguese, native Indian, and Chinese. The British hoped to give the colony independence after elections in August 1961. Cheddi Jagan, the head of the colony's People's Progressive party, a man with strong leftist leanings, seemed likely to become head of government. Although British authorities "tended to minimize, if not discount, the view that Jagan was a communist," and a CIA report concluded that "neither the Communist bloc nor Castro has made any vigorous effort to exploit the British Guiana situation" and that Jagan seemed unlikely "to establish an avowed Communist regime," Kennedy and the NSC unsuccessfully pressed the British to prevent or allow the U.S. to stop Jagan's election in August. It was a secret demonstration of limited regard for democratic elections, which, if known, would have deepened hemisphere skepticism about America's genuine commitment to an alliance for progress. For Kennedy, democracy in Latin America could never be put ahead of perceived threats to U.S. national security, even if those dangers might turn out to be more illusory than real.

IT WAS AGAINST THIS BACKDROP of anxiety about the communist menace in Latin America, Asia, Africa, and above all central Europe, where Moscow seemed determined to alter the status of East Germany and Berlin, that Kennedy met Khrushchev in Vienna. Kennedy had come armed with advice from America's leading Soviet experts —

Charles Bohlen, George Kennan, and Llewellyn Thompson — and de Gaulle on what to expect. Averell Harriman, who had represented Roosevelt and Truman in dealings with Moscow and was negotiating with the Russians about Laos, insisted on seeing Kennedy in Paris to give him his opinion. "I hear there is something you want to say to me," Kennedy told him at de Gaulle's state dinner, which Harriman had arranged to attend. "Go to Vienna," the seventy-year-old confidently advised the president. "Don't be too serious, have some fun, get to know him a little, don't let him rattle you; he'll try to rattle you and frighten you, but don't pay any attention to that. Turn him aside, gently. And don't try for too much. Remember that he's just as scared as you are . . . he is very aware of his peasant origins, of the contrast between Mrs. Khrushchev and Jackie. . . . His style will be to attack and then see if he can get away with it. Laugh about it, don't get into a fight. Rise above it. Have some fun."

Kennedy had asked de Gaulle for his views on Moscow's policy toward Berlin, the most contentious East-West issue since 1945. At the end of World War II, Germany had been divided into British, French, and U.S. zones in the west and a Soviet area of occupation in the east. Berlin, which was 110 miles inside the Soviet zone, was also divided into four parts. The Soviets had agreed to guarantees of Western access to Berlin through their zone. A reunified and rearmed Germany allied with the West was Moscow's constant fear. Consequently, a separate East German state had been central to Moscow's German policy throughout the fifties. By 1961, the embarrassing exodus of East Germans and other east Europeans to the west through Berlin provoked the Soviets into warnings that they would sign a peace treaty with East Germany, creating an independent state that could then choose to end allied rights in Berlin by integrating the city under its control. Such a treaty promised to reduce chances of a unified Germany posing renewed threats to Moscow.

Kennedy's chief worry about Khrushchev was that after the Bay of Pigs, he would not believe JFK's resolve on Berlin or anything else. De Gaulle had urged Kennedy to be firm but to understand that the Soviet leader had no intention of going to war over the status of the city: "Khrushchev has been saying and repeating that his prestige is engaged in the Berlin question and that he will have to have a solution of it in six months, and then again in six months and then still in six months. This seems to indicate that Mr. Khrushchev does not want war. If he had wanted war about Berlin he would have acted already." De Gaulle further said that when he asked Khrushchev if he wanted war, he had replied no. "In that case," de Gaulle had told him, "do nothing that can bring it about."

"For domestic political reasons," Kennedy had wanted to announce specific subjects on which he and Khrushchev would confer and make progress. Although the Soviets resisted this request, Kennedy decided to go ahead anyway, believing that a summit could reduce differences and help avoid a nuclear war. The State Department encouraged Kennedy's hopes: "Khrushchev would prefer that the talks end on a note of accord, and may make some conciliatory gestures for this reason," a background paper advised the president. Ambassador Thompson in Moscow echoed the point: "Believe Khrushchev will wish meeting with President to be pleasant one and that he will desire if possible to make some proposal or take position on some problem which would have effect of improving atmosphere and relations." Even the Soviets had told him that there was no "unbridgeable gulf" between them.

George Kennan was less sure. He saw the Soviets in conjunction with the Chinese as primarily intent on shattering America's "world position and influence" and undermining NATO by a "series of sharp indirect political pressures, ruthless exploitation of colonial issue, and all-out propaganda attack." Kennan urged Kennedy to tell Khrushchev that "a political program founded on such calculation is not only wholly inconsistent with any attempt to improve international atmosphere" but seemed certain at some point to create a military confrontation beyond anyone's control. Such an approach represented "a grievous disservice to any efforts to improve world situation" and played into the hands of those who opposed any improvement in Soviet-American relations.

Initially, Kennedy's arrival in Vienna and first exchanges with Khrushchev promised to make the summit another public relations triumph for JFK. A tepid turnout for Khrushchev on the afternoon of June 2 as he rode in an open car from the Vienna railway station to the Soviet embassy contrasted with the excited crowds greeting Kennedy the next morning on his route from the airport to the U.S. embassy. Kennedy's pleasure at the reception registered on Rusk, who sat beside him in the car. "You make a hell of a substitute for Jackie," the president joked. The placard-waving crowd at the airport gave the feel of a political campaign rally for JFK: "Give 'em hell, Jack," "Lift the Iron Curtain," "Innocents Abroad Say Howdy."

The first encounter between the two leaders also favored Kennedy. Bounding down the steps of the American embassy, where the first meeting occurred at 12:45 P.M. on June 3, the youthful Kennedy towered over the short, squat sixty-seven-year-old Khrushchev. When photographers asked for more shots of the two shaking hands as they turned to go inside, Kennedy seized the initiative: "Tell the Chairman," he said to his interpreter, "that it's all right with me if it's all right with him." The smiling Khrushchev agreed. As they were led into the embassy's music room, where the two seated themselves on a rose-colored sofa, Khrushchev bantered with the president, who, as the morning's host, expressed pleasure at seeing the chairman and recalled a 1959 meeting of the Senate Foreign Relations Committee where they had met. Kennedy expressed the hope that a better understanding of the problems confronting the two nations would emerge from the meeting. Khrushchev also "wished the conversation to be useful," but he picked up on Kennedy's recollection of their first meeting to score a point against the president: Khrushchev remembered him as "a young and promising man in politics." Eager to mute the differences between them in age and experience, JFK replied, "He must have aged since then." Reflecting on how the young want to look older and older people want to look younger, Khrushchev said that "he would be happy to share his years with the President or change places with him."

Moving to a large table for their more formal conversation, Khrushchev turned what Kennedy had hoped might be a discussion of current issues into a philosophical debate about the virtues of their respective systems. Kennedy began the exchange by suggesting that they needed to find "ways and means of not permitting situations where the two countries would be committed to actions involving their security or endangering peace." In response, Khrushchev seized on Kennedy's friendly, essentially innocuous opening to begin a hectoring attack on America's past failures to advance Soviet-American friendship, emphasizing that the United States wanted to reach agreements with Moscow that would be "at the expense of other peoples." He would not agree to this, Khrushchev said. He also emphasized that there was no inherent conflict of economic interests between the U.S. and the USSR, and though the Soviet Union intended to eclipse America economically, it had no intention of standing "in the way of U.S. economic development." Kennedy, who had not yet realized the extent to which Khrushchev was intent on beating up on him, answered Khrushchev's insupportable claims by remarking how the Soviet growth rate had impressed him and "that this was surely a source of satisfaction to Mr. Khrushchev, as it was to us."

Khrushchev ignored Kennedy's polite affirmation of what JFK knew were false assertions to complain about America's anti-Soviet policies. He asserted that Eisenhower secretary of state John Foster Dulles had aimed to liquidate communism and that good relations between the two countries depended on a mutual acceptance of each other's systems. Kennedy, now rising to the challenge, declared that it was not the United States that was unsettling the global balance of power or seeking to overturn existing spheres of control but the Soviet Union. "This is a matter of very serious concern to us," Kennedy said. Kennedy's rejoinder seemed to incense Khrushchev or give him an excuse to follow through with his planned assault on the president. He disputed the assertion that Moscow aimed to impose its will on any country. Communism would triumph, he said, because history was on its side. Kennedy retorted that Americans did not share the chairman's view of an inevitable communist victory. But, trying to move the discussion back to current realities, Kennedy said that the problem was to find means of averting conflict in areas where the two sides had clashing interests.

Khrushchev acknowledged JFK's point but reverted to arguing that they faced a contest of ideas that communism would win. When Kennedy tried to restate the point that the clash of ideas should not produce a conflict of interests that could lead to a military confrontation, Khrushchev asked him if he was suggesting that any expansion of communist influence would be seen as a reason for Soviet-American conflict. Before Kennedy could answer, Khrushchev dismissed the president's view that the spread of communist ideology would threaten the peace. When Kennedy again tried to divert Khrushchev from his philosophical ruminations to worries he had about international "miscalculations," the chairman contemptuously dismissed the talk of "miscalculation" as an excuse for getting the "USSR to sit like a schoolboy with his hands on his desk." Talk of "miscalculation" was a means of trying to intimidate the Soviet Union and inhibit it from freely voicing ideas that would outstrip those advocated by the United States. After Kennedy countered by giving an example of miscalculation — the U.S. failure to anticipate Chinese intervention in the Korean war — Khrushchev conceded that their purpose was not to worsen but to improve relations.

The atmosphere eased a bit at lunch. When Kennedy asked about two medals on Khrushchev's jacket, he described them as Lenin Peace Prizes. "I hope you get to keep them," Kennedy answered. Khrushchev joined in the laughter, and Salinger had the sort of delightful anecdote for the press that added to the Paris image of the president as poised and quick-witted.

During the meal, Khrushchev alternated between being pleasant and combative, purposely encouraging impressions of himself as erratic and maybe dangerous — the leader of a country convinced it could outdo the United States in peace and war, if necessary. Exchanges about Soviet space gains brought a Kennedy suggestion that they might go to the moon together. Caught off guard, Khrushchev commented on the military advantages attached to space travel and then added weakly, "All right, why not?" Khrushchev advised Kennedy that he had voted for him by not releasing the RB-47 fliers until after the election and made fun of Nixon, bringing smiles to everyone's face when he declared that a lot of people thought that the dour-looking Andrey Gromyko resembled the former vice president. Khrushchev followed a brief, gracious Kennedy toast with a rambling performance marked by professions of Soviet desire for peace, expressions of regard for Eisenhower, Kennedy, and the American people, additional harsh words about Nixon, denials that Moscow was responsible for communist insurgencies in other countries, and assertions of his readiness for a continuing competition with the much younger American president.

During a stroll in the garden after lunch, Kennedy tried to establish greater rapport with Khrushchev. But the Soviet premier was unrelenting. O'Donnell and Powers watched them from an upstairs embassy window: "Khrushchev was carrying on a heated argument, circling around Kennedy and snapping at him like a terrier and shaking his finger." Later, while an exhausted Kennedy soaked in a tub, Powers said, "You seemed pretty calm while he was giving you a hard time out there." They had been arguing over Germany and Berlin. "What did you expect me to do?" Kennedy said with some exasperation. "Take off one of my shoes and hit him over the head with it?" Eager to end their stroll on a more positive note, Kennedy asked how the chairman found time to hold prolonged, uninterrupted meetings with American visitors. Khrushchev, still looking to score points, described a system of shared power that freed him from distractions. When Kennedy complained that the American governmental system imposed on him a "time-consuming process," Khrushchev shot back: "Well, why don't you switch to our system?"

The afternoon's formal conversations produced more sparring and antagonism. Kennedy began the second round of talks by coming back to his concern that the present competition between the U.S. and the USSR not lead to war. He tried to clarify what he meant by "miscalculation." He had made a "misjudgment" over Cuba, he acknowledged. It was essential that their discussions "introduce greater precision in these judgments so that our two countries could survive this period of competition without endangering their national security." Although Khrushchev agreed that this was a good idea, he seized upon Kennedy's admission of a mistake as an expression of weakness. He attacked the United States for seeing people's revolutions as communist plots. This was dangerous, he said, because the Soviets were on the side of anticolonialism not for self-serving reasons but out of an understanding that these were "holy wars." The United States, which had once sided with democratic revolutions, now favored the status quo and mistakenly, as in Cuba, tried to suppress the aspirations of the people and threaten Moscow with war when it objected to U.S. imperialism. Moscow, by contrast, Khrushchev asserted, wanted only to keep the peace. Kennedy replied that America ruled out war for the simple reason that the current balance of military power between East and West meant that both sides would be losers in a nuclear conflict.

Kennedy's admission of Soviet strength equal to that of the United States exhilarated Khrushchev, who took it as another reason to press the case for superior Soviet morality in international affairs and greater devotion to democratic hopes and world peace. After the afternoon meeting ended, Khrushchev told his comrades about JFK: "He's very young . . . not strong enough. Too intelligent and too weak." Khrushchev's gamble — that he should take advantage of the USSR's current prestige (the result of its perceived missile superiority, the rise of procommunist insurgencies in Asia and Africa, Kennedy's Bay of Pigs failure, and the success of the Soviet space program) and attack his American counterpart — seemed to be paying off. Khrushchev believed that if he bested JFK at the Vienna summit, it would undermine U.S. political standing. He had not come to negotiate. He had come to compete.

The afternoon meeting had ended on an ominous note. When Kennedy suggested that they discuss nuclear tests, disarmament, and Germany later that evening over dinner or the next day, Khrushchev said that he intended "to connect the questions of nuclear tests and disarmament." The main problem with Germany was the need for a peace treaty, which he hoped both countries could sign. "This would improve relations. But if the United States refuses to sign a peace treaty, the Soviet Union will do so and nothing will stop it."

Khrushchev's behavior irritated and frustrated Kennedy. A British journalist who saw him as he escorted Khrushchev to his car thought he looked "dazed." Pacing the floor of his bedroom in the embassy, he exclaimed, "He treated me like a little boy, like a little boy." He asked Llewellyn Thompson, "Is it always like this?" The ambassador replied, "Par for the course." Bohlen thought that the president was "a little depressed." And though he tried to comfort him by declaring that "the Soviets always talk tough," he believed that Kennedy had gotten "a little bit out of his depth" by being drawn into an ideological debate. Kennan thought that Khrushchev had tied the president in knots and that Kennedy appeared hesitant and overwhelmed. Kennedy himself may have wondered what Harriman could possibly have meant when he used the word *fun*.

A long day under much tension certainly accounts for most of Kennedy's weariness by the early evening, but we cannot discount the impact of the Jacobson chemicals on him as well. As the day wore on and an injection Jacobson had given him just before he met Khrushchev in the early afternoon wore off, Kennedy may have lost the emotional and physical edge initially provided by the shot. But more important than Kennedy's energy level was the fundamental difference in approach that each leader brought to the summit. Kennedy's eagerness to be reasonable and encourage understanding was no match for Khrushchev's determination to debate and out-argue the less experienced president.

In any case, it was clear that Khrushchev had won the first day's debate. But to what end? It was absurd for Khrushchev to believe that scoring points against his younger opponent would do anything but stiffen Kennedy's resolve to meet the communist challenge. Khrushchev may have believed his own rhetoric about Soviet ascendancy over the United States and been unable to resist bragging about it. In response to pressure from comrades in the Kremlin and Chinese efforts to supplant Moscow as the leader of international communism, Khrushchev felt compelled to act more like an aggressive advocate than a conciliator. As Kennan had accurately foreseen, a principal object of the summit for Khrushchev was to sustain Moscow's momentum at the expense of the United States without driving Washington into a war. But Khrushchev's actions were miserably shortsighted.

Today, perhaps, we can have some sympathy for Khrushchev's dilemma. He presided over an ineffective economic system that had shown little room for improvement. In the long run, there was no escape from accepting the failings of Soviet communism, as Mikhail Gorbachev would understand thirty years later. But in 1961, Khrushchev could not see that far ahead; nor could he discount the possibility that a tough approach to the Americans might intimidate them into selling out Germany and even Western Europe, as de Gaulle feared, to save the United States and the world from nuclear destruction.

Although Khrushchev was principally responsible for the abrasive tone of the proceedings, no one should see Kennedy as blameless. True, he struck several conciliatory notes in the talks, admitting mistakes in Cuban and Asian policies and placating Soviet amour propre by conceding the equality of their armed might. But he was as intent on the competition for international prestige as the Soviets. It was common knowledge that the president regularly monitored United States Information Agency (USIA) polls on international opinion toward the U.S. and the USSR. His rhetoric at his Inauguration and in his May address to Congress left no doubt that the new president, if anything, would be more aggressive about asserting U.S. global influence and power than the more mature and secure Eisenhower had been. But however one distributes blame for the harsh Khrushchev-Kennedy exchanges, they marked an unwise escalation in the Cold War, which the talks had been meant to ease.

Concerned not to impress himself on the Americans and international opinion as simply a scold defending national and ideological interests, Khrushchev tried to produce a charm offensive during a formal dinner party at the Schönbrunn Palace, a seventeenth-century country estate built by the Hapsburgs. But he only went so far: Refusing to wear black tie, Khrushchev and his entourage thumbed their noses at Western imperial decadence by dressing in business suits. Nina Petrovna, Khrushchev's wife, a matronly woman wearing no makeup, impressed Rose Kennedy, who attended the dinner, as someone who could serve in an American household as an entirely reliable baby-sitter. Sitting next to Jacqueline Kennedy, Khrushchev regaled her with gags and stories that made her feel as if she were watching an Abbott and Costello movie. When Khrushchev, turning serious, tried to educate her on the greater number of teachers per capita currently in the Ukraine than in the tsar's time, Jacqueline admonished him, "'Oh, Mr. Chairman, don't bore me with statistics' — and he suddenly laughed and became for a moment almost cozy."

The distinguishing feature of the second day of the summit, which took place at the Soviet embassy, was a focus on Germany, but not before Kennedy turned aside fresh attempts by Khrushchev to provoke a renewed ideological debate. When Kennedy began by asking the chairman what part of the USSR he was from, Khrushchev answered, in the vicinity of Kursk, near the Ukrainian border, where thirty billion tons of iron ore had been found, six times the amount in the entire United States. Kennedy did not take the bait. A discussion of Laos brought the renewed complaint that "the United States is so rich and powerful that it believes it has special rights and can afford not to recognize the rights of others." Moscow could not accept this, Khrushchev said, and intended to help subject peoples seeking freedom. "Look, Mr. Chairman," Kennedy countered, "you aren't going to make a communist out of me and I don't expect to make a capitalist out of you, so let's get down to business."

The principal "business" of Khrushchev was to attack U.S. proposals for a nuclear test ban and disarmament, and American resistance to a Soviet peace settlement with Germany. Unwilling to stop testing, which Moscow believed essential if it was going to achieve nuclear parity with the United States, Khrushchev objected to on-site United Nations inspections to prevent underground testing as "tantamount to espionage, which the Soviet Union cannot accept." The U.N.'s behavior in the Congo, Khrushchev claimed, demonstrated that Moscow could not trust Dag Hammarskjöld, whom it accused of complicity in Lumumba's assassination. Three inspections would be possible, but they would have to be done by a three-member commission consisting of an American, a Soviet, and a truly neutral representative. Moreover, Khrushchev argued, a test ban would be superfluous if the United States agreed to "general and complete" disarmament.

Kennedy agreed that a test ban would not inhibit arms production by the U.S. or the USSR but pointed out that it would make the development of nuclear weapons by other countries less likely. Without a test ban, the number of nuclear powers could multiply to ten or fifteen in a few years. Kennedy urged Khrushchev to balance the risk of espionage with the peril from nuclear proliferation, which "is bound to affect the national security of our two countries, and increase the danger of major conflicts." A test ban could be a first step, since it would take a very long time to reach agreement on general disarmament. When Khrushchev repeated his arguments about giving general disarmament priority over a test ban, an exasperated Kennedy declared that "the conversation was back where it had started."

The discussion of Berlin was even more frustrating to Kennedy. Whereas the failure of test ban talks would present long-term dangers, Berlin loomed as an immediate crisis. Khrushchev spoke with considerable passion; conditions in central Europe were clearly his greatest concern, and everything that had occurred in the first day and a half of the summit had been a prelude, a run-up to the real business of the conference — ensuring that a reunited Germany would be incapable of inflicting fresh suffering on Russia and closing off Berlin as an escape hatch for those oppressed by communist rule.

Khrushchev reminded Kennedy that the USSR had lost twenty million people in World War II and that Germany, the architect of that conflict, had regained the kind of military strength that opened the way to a third, even more devastating world war. The USSR intended to sign a peace treaty with both Germanys, if possible, or at least with East Germany, to guard against a united nation. Such a treaty, Khrushchev explained, would invalidate all post-1945 arrangements, including the West's access by road and air to Berlin through East Germany. If the U.S. signed a peace agreement, Berlin could remain a "free" city, but a refusal to sign would end all rights of Western access to Berlin.

Kennedy left no doubt that the United States would not be bullied into an agreement. "Here we are not talking about Laos," JFK said. "This matter is of greatest concern to the US. We are in Berlin not because of someone's sufferance. We fought our way there. . . . If we were expelled from that area and if we accepted the loss of our rights no one would have any confidence in US commitments and pledges." He urged Khrushchev not to threaten the existing balance of power in Europe and provoke a response from the United States.

But Khrushchev was unrelenting. "No force in the world would prevent the USSR from signing a peace treaty," he said. Khrushchev's only concession to Kennedy's strong response was a pledge not to sign the treaty until December. He declared that America would be responsible for any war fought over Berlin, and only a "madman, who . . . should be put in a straightjacket" would want such a conflict. Kennedy's counter that Moscow's assault on the existing power balance would be the cause of any war seemed to make no impression. Khrushchev ended the discussion by saying that Moscow had prepared an aide-mémoire on Berlin that would allow the U.S. to "return to this question at a later date, if it wished to do so."

Exchanges over lunch offered no respite from Khrushchev's hostility. He raised the subject of nuclear weapons and noted that, like the United States, the Soviet Union had nuclear-armed submarines, that it had short-range, medium-range, and intercontinental missiles in production, and that renewed Soviet nuclear tests would only occur if the U.S. resumed testing. The USSR would not try to reach the moon ahead of the United States, he said, because it would weaken Moscow's defense buildup. Indeed, the president's message on defense spending had led him to consider increasing Soviet land forces and artillery.

Kennedy refused to give ground. He acknowledged the Soviet Union as a great power with weapons of mass destruction comparable to those held by the United States. It was essential, therefore, he said, that both countries act in responsible ways to avoid war. Germany was a case in point: "Each side should recognize the interests and responsibilities of the other side. . . . This goal can be achieved only if each is wise and stays in his own area." Hoping to flatter Khrushchev, who had told Kennedy that at age forty-four he had been chairman of the Moscow Planning Commission, Kennedy said that when he reached the chairman's age of sixty-seven, he would like to be head of the Boston Planning Commission and perhaps chairman of the Democratic National Committee. But smarting from JFK's refusal to bend on Germany, Khrushchev "interjected that perhaps the President would like to become head of the Planning Commission of the whole world."

Khrushchev's unrelenting belligerence agitated Kennedy into asking him to meet privately for a brief review of issues. "I can't leave here without giving it one more try," Kennedy said to an aide. "I'm not going to leave until I know more." As he went back upstairs to the conference room, he told Rusk, "This is the nut-cutter." Kennedy began the final meeting by saying that he hoped Khrushchev would not confront the United States with an issue such as Berlin that "so deeply" involved its national interest. He also asked Khrushchev to see the difference between signing a peace treaty and challenging America's rights of access to Berlin. Khrushchev showed no give: The U.S., he said, was trying to humiliate the USSR, and Kennedy needed to understand that Moscow intended to counter any U.S. aggression against East Germany with force. Kennedy "then said that either Mr. Khrushchev did not believe that the US was serious or the situation in that area was so unsatisfactory to the Soviet Union that it had to take this drastic action." He regretted leaving Vienna with the impression that the U.S. and the USSR were heading toward a confrontation. Khrushchev replied that it was the United States that was threatening to impose the calamity of war on the world, not the USSR. "It is up to the US to decide whether there will be war or peace," he said. Kennedy somberly answered, "Then, Mr. Chairman, there will be war. It will be a cold winter."

Kennedy could not hide his distress over the harsh exchanges, which promised worse future relations. Before cameras, as the two men left the Soviet embassy, Khrushchev put on a show of merriment, but Kennedy was grim, unsmiling. In a conversation afterward with James Reston at the U.S. embassy, JFK came across as "very gloomy." He sank onto a couch, pushed a "hat over his eyes like a beaten man, and breathed a great sigh. 'Pretty rough?' Reston asked. 'Roughest thing in my life,' the President answered." Kennedy also told Reston that he had two problems: figuring out what accounted for Khrushchev's behavior, and figuring out how to respond. He believed that Khrushchev had "just beat [the] hell out of me" because of his weak showing over the Bay of Pigs. He now needed to convince Khrushchev that he could not be pushed around, and the best place currently to make U.S. power credible seemed to be in Vietnam. On *Air Force One* going to London, where he was to see Macmillan, Kennedy continued to stew over Khrushchev's nastiness. He called O'Donnell to his stateroom and vented his anger for over an hour about the conference and the dangers he would be facing in the coming months of a possible war with Russia. He characterized the atmosphere in Vienna to reporters in the plane press pool as "somber" and repeated his description of the exchanges as "rough."

His own performance especially troubled Kennedy. His anger and frustration were as much with himself as Khrushchev. For the second time in three months, he believed he had acted unwisely —

first in approving the Bay of Pigs attack, and now in thinking that he could reduce differences with Khrushchev by rational explanation. Instead of being responsive to Kennedy's expressions of regard for Soviet power and appeals to reason over Berlin, Khrushchev had become more assertive and unbending. Kennedy was angry with himself for not having shown a tougher side from the beginning of the talks. He believed that his behavior had strengthened Khrushchev's conviction after the Bay of Pigs that he was an inexperienced and irresolute president who could be bullied into concessions on Germany and Berlin. Worst of all, he feared that his performance at the meeting had increased rather than diminished the chances of an East-West war.

On one hand, he could not imagine that Khrushchev actually meant to go to war over Berlin. He told O'Donnell shortly after he left the last meeting, "As De Gaulle says, Khrushchev is bluffing and he'll never sign that treaty. Anybody who talks the way he did today, and really means it, would be crazy, and I'm sure he's not crazy." Fighting a war that would kill millions of people over access rights to Berlin or because the Germans wanted to reunify their country impressed him as "particularly stupid. . . . If I'm going to threaten Russia with a nuclear war, it will have to be for much bigger and more important reasons than that."

Yet he also understood that smaller issues than those at stake over Berlin had sparked past wars, including World War I. And so he was "shaken" by and "angry" at Khrushchev's rhetoric and behavior. It was the first time he had ever met "somebody with whom he couldn't exchange ideas in a meaningful way," Bobby Kennedy said later. "I think it was a shock to him that somebody would be as harsh and definitive" — as "unrelenting" and "uncompromising" — as Khrushchev was in Vienna. However difficult and frustrating the meeting had been, Kennedy understood that the greatest challenges to him as president now lay ahead.

CHAPTER 12

Crisis Manager

When I ran for the Presidency of the United States, I knew that this country faced serious challenges, but I could not realize — nor could any man realize who does not bear the burdens of this office — how heavy and constant would be those burdens.

— John F. Kennedy, Report to the American People
   on the Berlin Crisis, July 25, 1961

LONDON WAS A WELCOME RESPITE from the tension of Vienna. Although Macmillan had initially been "appalled" that someone so young was president and had feared that Kennedy would see him as "so old that he wasn't worthwhile talking to," they had established an excellent rapport at two meetings in Washington during Kennedy's first months in office. Macmillan's intelligence and dry, quick wit had delighted the president. Going to see the prime minister was like being "in the bosom of the family," Kennedy told Henry Brandon. "I am lucky to have a man to deal with with whom I have such a close understanding." "It was the gay things that linked us together," Macmillan told Schlesinger, "and made it possible for us to talk about the terrible things."

Kennedy's meeting with Khrushchev, Macmillan thought, had left JFK stunned. "For the first time in his life Kennedy met a man who was impervious to his charm." The chairman was "much more of a barbarian" than he had anticipated. Because Kennedy seemed so tired, Macmillan suggested that they meet without Foreign Office officials — "a peaceful drink and chat by ourselves." Kennedy was pleased at the suggestion, but their discussion was anything but relaxing. Khrushchev's threats were impossible to ignore, and for the better part of an hour the two allies explored ideas on a formal response. They believed it essential to stand by what Kennedy had told Khrushchev: The Russians could do what they liked about a peace treaty with the DDR, but "the West stood on their rights and would meet any attack on these with all the force at their command."

Kennedy returned to Washington on the morning of June 6. He met with congressional leaders that afternoon and spoke to the American people from the Oval Office at 7:00 P.M. He gave the sixteen Senate and House leaders a candid assessment of the talks, reading some excerpts from minutes of the meetings rather than simply giving them his gloss on what had occurred. He had no intention, he told the leaders, of saying anything "that would seem to put Khrushchev in a corner where he must fight back." But he also wanted them to understand that the United States was competing with an adversary intent on world dominance. Kennedy believed the test ban talks were now pointless and hoped to end them while making Soviet responsibility for the failure clear. On Berlin, Kennedy said that the U.S. would not cede its rights of access. "The Soviets feel that our edge is gone on the nuclear side," he added, meaning not that Moscow had greater nuclear might than the United States but that it doubted U.S. resolve to fight a nuclear war.

Kennedy's evening TV address struck a balance between signaling emerging dangers and avoiding rhetoric that could provoke a crisis. To mute the difficulties with Russia, he partly spoke about his successful meetings with de Gaulle and Macmillan. But, as with the congressional leaders, he left no doubt that the United States faced a tough challenge from the Soviet Union. "It was a very sober two days" in Vienna, he said. To be sure, although the gap between the two countries had not been materially reduced, "the channels of communication were opened more fully." Yet no one should ignore the fact "that the Soviets and ourselves give wholly different meanings to the same words — war, peace, democracy, and popular will. We have wholly different views of right and wrong." Yet both sides realized that they had the capacity to inflict enormous damage on each other and the world. Consequently, they owed "it to all mankind to make every possible effort" to avoid an armed clash.

Kennedy was not optimistic that Moscow would act sensibly. The Soviets had no desire to provoke a direct conflict with the United States and its allies, but it was clear that the contest between East and West would now spread to developing countries where

Moscow gained a foothold. America, Kennedy said, needed to resist such communist advances with economic and military assistance programs to emerging nations struggling to remain free. And though he hid his private anxieties about a possible war over Berlin, his closing words left no doubt about the difficulties ahead: "We must be patient. We must be determined. We must be courageous. We must accept both risks and burdens."

Renewed public and private expressions of doubt about Kennedy's performance in Vienna made his sensible statesmanship all the more difficult. After the meeting, *Time* reported "a widespread feeling that the Administration has not yet provided ample leadership in guiding the U.S. along the dangerous paths of the cold war." Privately, Macmillan shared this concern: "I 'feel in my bones' that President Kennedy is going to fail to produce any real leadership. The American press and public are beginning to feel the same." Mac Bundy told Kennedy that he and columnists Joe Alsop and Walter Lippmann believed that "this problem of Berlin is one which you will have to master and manage, under your own personal leadership and authority." He would need to be "in immediate, personal, and continuous command of this enormous question." And he would have to do better than he had been doing so far.

Kennedy now worried that a defeat over Berlin or in Vietnam, where the Saigon government remained in jeopardy, could be a decisive blow to his presidency. He told Galbraith, "There are limits to the number of defeats I can defend in one twelve-month period. I've had the Bay of Pigs, and pulling out of Laos [or refusing to fight there], and I can't accept a third."

Kennedy had enough detachment about himself and the magnitude of the problems he confronted not to let criticism or negative perceptions control his public actions toward the USSR. The personal concerns underlying his father's unwise isolationism remained an object lesson in how not to make foreign policy. He was determined to shape an image of himself as clear and firm about international affairs, but not at the risk of being reckless or allowing considerations other than avoiding a nuclear war to shape what he said and did. Where Bobby would explode in anger toward someone like Chester Bowles for seeming to criticize his brother, JFK was much more restrained. Being president, of course, was vastly different from being attorney general. The reflective temperament that set Kennedy apart from his father, Bobby, Acheson, and most American military chiefs served him well in a job one shudders to imagine in any of their hands in 1961.

THE BERLIN CRISIS as it evolved during the summer of 1961 was arguably the most dangerous moment for a nuclear conflict since the onset of the Cold War. It tested Kennedy's ability to strike an effective balance between intimidating the Soviets and giving them a way out of their dilemma. How could Moscow halt the migration from East to West, which threatened the collapse of East Germany, without altering existing U.S. treaty rights of unfettered access to Berlin and pushing Washington toward war? Khrushchev had some hope that a Soviet–East German peace treaty might not cause the United States to fight. The Western press, which repeatedly described him as not believing that JFK would pull the nuclear trigger, encouraged the chairman to accept these reports as evidence that Kennedy would not act. But he could not be sure.

On June 10, six days after he left Vienna, Khrushchev publicly released the aide-mémoire he had given Kennedy insisting on a German peace treaty that he hoped could be used to alter Western rights of unfettered access to Berlin through East Germany. Two days later, the Soviet delegate at the Geneva test ban talks "dropped all pretense of serious interest in concluding an agreement." Khrushchev had "no further interest in keeping the test talks alive as a means of promoting an accommodation with Washington," the CIA concluded. On June 15, Khrushchev spoke to his people on television about the urgency of concluding a peace treaty and changing the status of Berlin. East Germany's head of government, Walter Ulbricht, added to the sense of crisis by threatening to shut off Western access to Berlin, including the city's Tempelhof Airport.

Kennedy's initial public response was muted. In the three weeks after Moscow released the aide-mémoire, he said nothing directly about Berlin. Instead of making him look responsible, Kennedy's silence made him seem like an indecisive leader or perhaps a politician seeking a middle ground. International relations expert Hans J. Morgenthau complained that Kennedy's response to Khrushchev's threat to Berlin was reminiscent of the failed "half-measures" he had used during the Cuban invasion.

But behind the scenes, Berlin was Kennedy's greatest daily concern. "He's imprisoned by Berlin, that's all he thinks about," cabinet members complained. It was the highest priority for almost everybody around the president. National security advisers, academic experts, journalists close to the administration, and even Acheson were asked for their input on how to discourage Soviet implementation of the aide-mémoire and what to do if Khrushchev went ahead.

Much of the argument now revolved around "the need for re-establishing the credibility of the nuclear deterrent." Acheson pressed for acceptance of a formal proposition that the U.S. might have to resort to nuclear war. A failure to defend Western rights in Berlin, he argued, would destroy international confidence in the United States. "The whole position of the United States is in the balance," Acheson said. The Soviets might make nuclear war unavoidable, but in the meantime Kennedy needed "to increase the nuclear deterrent to the greatest extent we can devise. This . . . offers the best hope of avoiding war short of submitting to Moscow's demands."

By the end of June, Kennedy was under irresistible pressure to speak publicly again on Berlin. Stories in *Time* and *Newsweek* that made him seem well behind the public and the Pentagon in determination to face down the Soviets in Germany incensed him. "Look at this shit. This shit has got to stop," he told Salinger. A Nixon dig that "never in American history has a man talked so big and acted so little" was an additional incentive to speak out.

When Kennedy finally did say something at a press conference on June 28, his remarks were measured, calculated to restrain Moscow without deepening the crisis. The Soviet insistence on signing a peace treaty was "to make permanent the partition of Germany" and close off allied access to West Berlin. "No one can fail to appreciate the gravity of this threat," Kennedy said. "It involves the peace and security of the Western world." Kennedy also complained of Moscow's refusal to negotiate a test ban and warned that the United States would respond to renewed Soviet nuclear testing with tests of its own. He then turned Khrushchev's claim that the USSR would outproduce the United States by 1970 into a call for peaceful competition. He predicted that the Soviet Union, whose GNP was 39 percent of America's, would not outproduce the United States in the twentieth century. But he encouraged Moscow to try; it "could only result in a better living standard for both of our people."

When reporters tried to draw Kennedy into more concrete statements about the gravity of the "crisis" or U.S. intentions, he refused. He denied that any proposal for a partial mobilization to meet the Berlin threat had come before him, "though of course we will be considering a whole variety of measures"; defended the value of the Vienna meeting, which had added to his store of information about the Soviets, though no plans for another meeting were in the works; denied any evidence of renewed Soviet nuclear testing; and declared that decisions on measures to counter the Soviet threat to Berlin were under consideration and that public discussion of a matter of such "extreme seriousness" should wait until the administration's deliberations were complete. Kennedy's remarks struck an effective balance between firmness and restraint, and contrasted Soviet belligerence with American interest in peaceful economic competition.

Behind the scenes, however, a vigorous argument had begun to rage over what all agreed was now a full-blown crisis. On one side stood advocates led by Acheson, the Joint Chiefs, Allen Dulles, and some State and Defense Department officials urging an overt military buildup to intimidate Moscow, and on the other, Rusk, Stevenson, Bowles, Harriman, Schlesinger, and Sorensen arguing for a more flexible response that included possible negotiations coupled with military preparations.

Kennedy refused to choose openly between the two alternatives, nor would he move precipitously. Above all, he was determined to control the decision making. On June 28, he told the Joint Chiefs that they were his principal advisers on all military matters, but that he also regarded them as "more than military men and expected their help in fitting military requirements into the over-all context of any situation, recognizing that the most difficult problem in Government is to combine all assets in a unified, effective pattern." The message was clear enough: The military needed to understand that it was part of a larger process in which the president would set military considerations alongside other factors before deciding what best served the national interest.

In a meeting with Acheson and national security officials the next day, Kennedy, who said little, nevertheless made clear that he would not foreclose additional discussions with Khrushchev about Berlin. Although Acheson believed that "no negotiation can accomplish more than to cover with face-saving devices submission to Soviet demands," Kennedy asked him what would be "the right answer" if the chairman proposed a summit that summer. Acheson suggested that talks could begin at "a lower level. . . . There were plenty of 'elderly unemployed' people like himself who could be sent to interminable meetings" and "could converse indefinitely without negotiating at all." Kennedy's preference for talks had registered three days before when he met with three Soviet journalists. Most of the discussion was about Berlin: He explained that the American people would impeach him if he gave up U.S. rights in Berlin, urged against a showdown over the city, and predicted that a Soviet-American war would "leave everything to the rest of the world — including the Chinese," a prediction Kennedy understood would not be lost on the Russians, who were growing increasingly apprehensive about their competition with Peking.

During the first week of July, *Newsweek* boosted Soviet-American tensions over Berlin by reporting a leak about Pentagon planning that included a declaration of limited national emergency, the removal of U.S. military dependents from West Germany and France, the reinforcement and increase of American divisions in Germany, and "some demonstration of U.S. intent to employ nuclear weapons," either by a resumption of testing or by moving atomic weapons in the NATO stockpile "to advanced 'ready' positions." Kennedy may have authorized the leak to send Khrushchev an unmistakable message. In response, Khrushchev gave private and public indications that Moscow was both ready for and horrified at the prospect of a nuclear fight. "Why should two hundred million people die for two million Berliners?" he asked the British ambassador. Upping the ante on his side, on July 8, Khrushchev publicly canceled plans to reduce Soviet forces by more than a million men, announcing instead a one-third increase in the defense budget.

Kennedy now pressed advisers for political alternatives to the potential military confrontation. He complained to Schlesinger that Acheson was "far too narrowly" focused on military solutions and asked him to bring Berlin planning "back into balance." Kennedy, who was leaving that afternoon for a weekend in Hyannis Port, where he was to meet with Rusk, McNamara, and General Maxwell Taylor, instructed Schlesinger to write a paper on the unexplored Berlin political issues. Working furiously for two hours with State Department counselor Abram Chayes and Harvard professor Henry Kissinger, Schlesinger delivered a memo as Kennedy was about to leave in a helicopter from the White House south lawn. The memo concluded that Kennedy should ask Rusk "to explore negotiating alternatives, and ask Acheson to supply the missing political dimension in his argument."

Kennedy's determination to give himself more than the nuclear option in the growing crisis registered forcefully on his three weekend companions. While they cruised off Cape Cod, Kennedy peppered

Rusk, inappropriately dressed in a business suit (which perfectly symbolized his and the State Department's unhelpful formality and inability to think imaginatively), McNamara, and Taylor with questions about diplomatic initiatives and military alternatives that might deter Moscow from a nuclear attack.

Determined not to find himself confronting inadequate military options, as he had during the Bay of Pigs, and to rein in public pressure for overt military preparations, which might prove wasteful and dangerous, Kennedy asked McNamara and Bundy to extract concrete explanations from the Pentagon on anticipated Berlin outcomes. At the same time, he directed Pentagon press officer Arthur Sylvester to write William Randolph Hearst Jr., providing a catalogue of actions refuting complaints in his newspapers about insufficient military preparedness. Sylvester hoped that Hearst would "give these additional facts . . . the same prominence that you gave your earlier report."

During July, as planning proceeded on how to respond to the Soviet threat, Kennedy sought the greatest possible flexibility. He wanted no part of a Pentagon plan that saw a ground war with Soviet forces as hopeless and favored a quick resort to nuclear weapons. Nor did he want pseudonegotiations that would make the United States look weak and ready to yield before Soviet pressure. He believed that "the only alternatives were authentic negotiation or mutual annihilation." As he told *New York Post* editor James Wechsler, "If Khrushchev wants to rub my nose in the dirt, it's all over."

To make his intentions clear to Moscow and reassure Americans and European allies, Kennedy scheduled a highly publicized television address on July 25. As a run-up to the speech, he used a July 19 press conference to urge Moscow "to return to the path of constructive cooperation," looking toward "a just and enduring settlement of issues remaining from" World War II. He also outlined the themes of his forthcoming speech, promising a discussion of responsibilities and hazards as well as a statement of "what we must do and what our allies must do to move through not merely the present difficulties" but also the many challenges ahead.

As Sorensen and several other aides helped Kennedy draft his television address, the president continued to worry about perceptions that he lacked the guts to fight an all-out war. Bobby heard from a Soviet embassy source that Moscow's ambassador Mikhail Menshikov was privately telling Khrushchev that JFK "didn't amount to very much, didn't have much courage." Bobby dismissed this as Menshikov "telling Khrushchev what he'd like to hear," but American press reports (probably leaked by Pentagon sources eager to pressure the White House) of Menshikov's opinion added to Kennedy's problem over Berlin.

Acheson privately shared Menshikov's assessment. After Kennedy made clear in the July meetings that he would not strictly follow Acheson's advice, the former secretary of state said to a small working group, "Gentlemen, you might as well face it. This nation is without leadership." Mac Bundy believed it essential for the president to counter these impressions.

Given all this, Kennedy's speech on the twenty-fifth was the most difficult moment for him since the Bay of Pigs. Speaking from the Oval Office, crowded with TV cameras and klieg lights that added to the heat of the summer night, Kennedy struggled not to appear uncomfortable. Additional steroids helped ease the tensions of the moment, but he suffered physical discomfort nevertheless, which added to the pressure of speaking to hundreds of millions of people around the world seeking reassurance that the young American president would fend off a disastrous conflict. Too little emphasis on military planning and too much on negotiations seemed certain to bring cries of appeasement; too much talk of readiness to fight and too little on possible discussions or interest in another summit would provoke shouts of warmonger.

But the speech struck a masterful balance between the competing options, effectively blaming the crisis on Moscow. More important, Kennedy made it clear that he would not permit the Soviets to overturn America's legal rights in West Berlin or its promise "to make good on our commitment to the two million free people of that city." Using a map, he illustrated the Soviet–East German ability to close off Western access to the city. But it would be a mistake, he said, for Moscow to look upon Berlin as "a tempting target" because of its location. It had "now become — as never before — the great testing place of Western courage and will. . . . We cannot and will not permit the Communists to drive us out of Berlin, either gradually or by force. . . . We will at all times be ready to talk, if talk will help. But we must also be ready to resist with force, if force is used upon us." And to make sure that the United States had "a wider choice than humiliation or all-out nuclear action," Kennedy declared his intention to ask Congress for an additional $3.25 billion appropriation for defense, an increase in army strength from 875,000 to one million men, with smaller increases in navy and air force personnel, a doubling and then tripling of draft quotas, a call-up of reserves to meet manpower needs, and expanded funding for greater civil defense planning.

The choice, however, was "not merely between resistance and retreat, between atomic holocaust and surrender. . . . Our response to the Berlin crisis will not be merely military or negative," Kennedy declared. "We do not intend to abandon our duty to mankind to seek a peaceful solution." He was ready to talk with other nations if they had constructive proposals and if they sought "genuine understanding — not concession of our rights." He expressed sympathy for Moscow's security concerns "after a series of ravaging invasions," but not at the expense of Berlin's freedom or Western treaty rights. "To sum it all up: we seek peace — but we shall not surrender."

The response to Kennedy's speech pleased and partly surprised the White House. Predictably, it created a "rally" effect, with Americans and West Europeans approving of the president's "determination and firmness." Majorities in the United States and the Western European countries backed Kennedy's intention to defend American rights in Berlin and supported the right of Berliners to self-determination. What startled Kennedy and others in the administration was the public's lack of support for negotiations. And reactions in the press and Congress and from Nixon reflected the current national view that an unbridgeable divide between the U.S. and the USSR would end in a nuclear war. Sixty percent of Americans believed that Soviet insistence on control of Berlin would mean a war, and 55 percent thought that chances were either nil or poor that Moscow would give in. The press, which always found conflict more interesting than diplomacy, saw the U.S. military buildup as the headline in Kennedy's speech, even though the White House leaked suggestions that the president might be ready to accept alterations in East Germany's boundary or a nonaggression pact with Moscow guaranteeing Russian safety from a German attack. As a result, Congress rushed to approve funding not only for Kennedy's defense requests but also for arms that the administration believed unnecessary.

Despite public and press militancy, Kennedy was not about to be stampeded into military action. And though Khrushchev was unhappy with Kennedy's speech, he also deciphered Kennedy's restraint. Khrushchev publicly emphasized his determination not to be intimidated and predicted that Soviet nuclear superiority could make Kennedy America's last president, but he also declared his continuing faith in Kennedy's reason and said that "after thunderstorms people cool off, think problems over and resume human shape, casting away threats."

During the next two weeks, Khrushchev publicly mixed harsh warnings with invitations to negotiate. It was what a State Department analyst called the "twin tactics" of "maintaining, even stepping up his threats . . . and at the same time, gradually broadening the possible terms of negotiation." It was more stick than carrot, but it allowed Khrushchev to save face while Moscow laid plans to extricate itself from a confrontation in which it was increasingly clear Kennedy would not give ground.

EARLY SUNDAY MORNING, August 13, while Kennedy was in Hyannis Port, East German security forces threw up barriers that blocked access from East to West Berlin. There had been some talk in Washington about such a development. In a television interview on July 30, Senator William Fulbright had wondered "why the East Germans didn't close their border, because I think they have a right to close it." Five days later, during a stroll in the White House Rose Garden with Walt Rostow, Kennedy, reflecting on how unbearable Khrushchev's refugee problem was, said, "East Germany is hemorrhaging to death. The entire East bloc is in danger. He has to do something to stop this. Perhaps a wall. And there's not a damn thing we can do about it." Kennedy also said: "I can get the alliance to move if he tries to do anything about West Berlin but not if he just does something about East Berlin."

But this was all conjecture; Kennedy had no advance knowledge of Khrushchev's plan, and the administration's failure to anticipate the development left him frustrated and angry. Moreover, there is no indication that he saw the border closing as ending the Berlin crisis; quite the opposite: "With this weekend's occurrences in Berlin there will be more and more pressure for us to adopt a harder military posture," he told McNamara. "I do not think we can leave unused any of the men or money that were offered by the Congress with the exception perhaps of the bomber money." At the same time, Kennedy asked Rusk, "What steps will we take this week to exploit politically propagandawise the Soviet–East German cut-off of the border? This seems to me to show how hollow is the phrase 'free city' and how despised is the East German government, which the Soviet Union tries to make respectable. The question we must decide is how far we should push this. It offers us a very good propaganda stick."

Kennedy responded to the border closing with studied caution. He stayed at the Cape until his scheduled return Monday morning and confined the administration's initial response to a State Department statement declaring the action without impact on the "Allied position in West Berlin or access thereto." Nevertheless, the department noted "violations of existing agreements" that would be "the subject of vigorous protests through appropriate channels."

The restrained response reflected Kennedy's realization that the Berlin Wall, as the thirteen-foot-high barrier came to be known, was something of a godsend. "Why would Khrushchev put up a wall if he really intended to seize West Berlin?" Kennedy asked O'Donnell. "There wouldn't be any need of a wall if he occupied the whole city. This is his way out of his predicament. It's not a very nice solution, but a wall is a hell of a lot better than a war."

With the wall, Kennedy's problem was in fact more with his allies — the West Germans in particular — than with the Soviets. On August 16, Edward R. Murrow, USIA director, who had been visiting Berlin when the wall went up, cabled Washington that conversations with West Berlin's mayor, Willy Brandt, and newspaper, radio, and TV journalists had indicated a degree of demoralization that "can and should be corrected." The absence of any "sharp and definite follow up" to Washington's response had produced a "letdown" that amounted to "a crisis of confidence." At a public rally, Brandt asked Kennedy to demonstrate his commitment to Berlin by reinforcing the U.S. garrison stationed in the city. Embarrassed by the appeal, which Kennedy believed a campaign tactic to help Brandt win election to the chancellorship, JFK bristled: "Look at this! Who does he think he is?" But the pressure to do something was irresistible. At a meeting on August 17 with national security officials, Kennedy cautioned them against considering the issue of the wall itself — "our writ does not run in East Berlin" — and asked them to address instead the question of West Berlin morale. The discussion persuaded him to send additional troops to Berlin along with a letter delivered publicly to Brandt by Johnson, who had played almost no part to that point in the Berlin crisis, and General Lucius D. Clay, the architect of the 1948 Berlin airlift that had saved the Western sector from a Soviet blockade. As Kennedy told Brandt in the letter, he appreciated that these actions were more symbolic than substantive, but not entirely. (The troop reinforcement underlined the U.S. rejection of Soviet demands for "the removal of Allied protection from West Berlin.") More important, Kennedy promised to continue the buildup of military forces in Europe to counter the Soviet threat to Berlin.

Johnson thought the trip a poor idea, less because he feared for his safety — as Kenny O'Donnell later suggested — than because he believed it would intensify the crisis. When Johnson heard that he would be expected to greet the American troops traveling through the Eastern Zone to West Berlin, he predicted, "There'll be a lot of shooting, and I'll be in the middle of it. Why me?" General Norstad also believed it a mistake to send the vice president: It "would run the risk of exciting great expectations in West Berlin and possibly also among the unhappy East Germans," he cabled the Joint Chiefs from Paris.

Kennedy, however, believing that Johnson's mission would send just the right message to Khrushchev, the West Germans, and the allies, ordered LBJ and Clay to fly to Bonn on August 18. Johnson threw himself into the assignment with characteristic energy, staying awake on the overnight transatlantic flight to work on his speeches. At the Bonn airport, he told a waiting crowd that America was "determined to fulfill all our obligations and to honor all our commitments." Chancellor Konrad Adenauer assured LBJ that his presence was a refutation to an old woman in the crowd waving a sign that said "Action, Not Words." Flying on to West Berlin, Johnson rode to the city center in an open car cheered by 100,000 spectators lining the roads. Stopping the car repeatedly, he plunged into the appreciative crowds, shaking hands, distributing ballpoint pens, and responding with visible emotion to the displays of enthusiasm. At city hall, he told 300,000 cheering Berliners to maintain faith in themselves and "in your allies, everywhere throughout the world. This island does not stand alone."

The next day, Sunday, at 9:00 A.M., Johnson and Clay awaited the arrival at the Helmstedt entrance to West Berlin of sixteen hundred U.S. Army troops crossing the 110-mile stretch of autobahn separating the city from West Germany. Kennedy, who normally spent summer weekends in Hyannis Port, stayed in Washington to monitor the progress of the convoy; he intended to control the response to any possible confrontation with Soviet troops at East

German military checkpoints along the road. For more than twelve hours from Saturday night to Sunday afternoon in Washington, Kennedy's military aide reported to the president every fifteen minutes on the progress of the column. Berliners greeted the arrival at 10:00 A.M. of the first elements of the convoy with shouts, tears, and flowers. The U.S. commander described the event as "the most exciting and impressive thing I've ever seen in my life, with the possible exception of the liberation of Paris."

No one in the Western camp saw Johnson's trip as more than a temporary morale booster; it offered no formula for ending the confrontation. Kennedy wanted to issue an invitation before September 1 to Moscow to begin talks and to make "plain to our three Allies that this is what we mean to do and that they must come along or stay behind." But he also wanted fresh proposals to work with. He suggested that the allies "examine all of Khrushchev's statements for pegs on which to hang our position. He has thrown out quite a few assurances and hints . . . and I believe they should be exploited." When no one came up with anything that seemed likely to advance negotiations, hopes for meaningful talks remained no more than that. In these circumstances, de Gaulle warned the president, negotiations "would be considered immediately as a prelude to the abandonment, at least gradually, of Berlin and as a sort of notice of our surrender." Discussions now "would be a very grave blow to our Atlantic Alliance." Reported "trends towards neutralism" in Europe, new Soviet threats to civil air and road access to West Berlin, and Moscow's resumption of nuclear testing on August 30 led Max Taylor to tell Kennedy that "Khrushchev intends using military force, or the threat thereof, to gain his ends in Berlin." It all further diminished Kennedy's hopes of early productive talks.

Nevertheless, since the alternative to diplomacy might be a nuclear war, Kennedy saw the continuing search for a negotiating formula as imperative. So did Khrushchev, who invited columnist Drew Pearson during a visit to Russia to come to his summer retreat on the Black Sea for an interview. During their talk, he emphasized that "there isn't going to be a war." Consequently, when George Kennan reported from Belgrade, where he was serving as ambassador, that his Soviet counterpart, under instructions from Khrushchev, wanted to discuss Germany and Berlin, Washington agreed.

Throughout, Kennedy tried to placate Adenauer, who, like Acheson, believed that only military steps would restrain the Soviets. Kennedy endorsed the chancellor's "estimate of the severity of the crisis . . . and of the likelihood that worse is yet to come." Yet Kennedy disputed Adenauer's contention that negotiations "might be misinterpreted as a sign of weakness on our part." Khrushchev had no reason for illusions about Western firmness. And Kennedy believed that the sheer "logic of a thermonuclear war demands that we exhaust every effort to find a peaceful solution consistent with the preservation of our vital interests." Little Soviet interest in negotiations did not discourage Kennedy. "It isn't time yet," he told Rusk. "It's too early. They are bent on scaring the world to death before they begin negotiating, and they haven't quite brought the pot to boil. Not enough people are frightened."

Publicly, Kennedy demonstrated only determination to face down Khrushchev. On August 30, he announced the appointment of General Clay as his personal representative in Berlin and described renewed Soviet nuclear testing as a demonstration of "utter disregard of the desire of mankind for a decrease in the arms race . . . [and] a threat to the entire world by increasing the dangers of a thermonuclear holocaust." (Privately, he had been furious with the report that the Soviets had resumed testing: "Fucked again," he told the national security official who brought him the news. "The bastards. That fucking liar," he said of Khrushchev.) Declaring the Soviet announcement "a form of atomic blackmail, designed to substitute terror for reason in the present international scene," Kennedy invited the USSR to join the U.S. and Britain in banning atmospheric nuclear tests producing radioactive fallout. In addition, he ordered the resumption of underground explosions as a response to ten Soviet tests but said the United States remained eager for "a controlled test ban agreement of the widest possible scope."

Although Khrushchev privately described the resumption of tests as essential to build Russia's nuclear strength, Soviet scientist Andrei Sakharov believed otherwise. Soviet testing, Sakharov predicted, would simply provoke U.S. testing and a further lead for the United States in the arms race. When Sakharov confronted Khrushchev with this reality, the chairman, playing to hard-line critics in the Kremlin, publicly reprimanded Sakharov for not understanding politics. The Americans, Khrushchev lectured, did not understand any other language than displays of military strength. And Kennedy, Khrushchev felt, was of no help in reaching useful agreements. "We helped elect Kennedy last year," Khrushchev told a Soviet lunch group. "Then we met with him in Vienna, a meeting that could have been a turning point. But what does he say? 'Don't ask for too much. . . . If I make too many concessions, I'll be turned out of office.' Quite a guy! He comes to a meeting but can't perform. What the hell do we need a guy like that for?"

However poor prospects for productive talks seemed, Kennedy pressed aides, allies, and Moscow to find a negotiated solution to Berlin. In a conversation on September 5 with Rusk, Stevenson, and other White House officials, he described several plausible elements of a negotiating strategy. He also instructed Ambassador Thompson to discuss a possible basis for negotiations with Foreign Minister Gromyko. Meanwhile, Kennedy sent Khrushchev conciliatory messages through the American press: On September 6, James Reston quoted the president as ready for an "honorable accommodation." Two weeks later, James Wechsler of the New York Post described Kennedy as believing that nothing was nonnegotiable "except the dignity of free men."

Never forgetting how devastating a nuclear exchange with the United States would be for the Soviet Union, and relieved of his émigré problem through Berlin, Khrushchev began a slow but unmistakable shift away from threats and toward talks. Worried that a peace treaty with East Germany would "spark a Western economic embargo against the socialist bloc," which would destabilize Moscow's Eastern European satellites, he had ample reason to maintain the status quo with Germany. But after repeatedly threatening to sign a treaty, Khrushchev needed a graceful means of retreat.

Khrushchev sent a message to the president, carried by Cyrus Sulzberger of the New York Times, that he was not "loath to establishing some sort of informal contact with him to find a means of settling the crisis without damaging the prestige of the United States — but on the basis of a German peace treaty and a Free City of West Berlin." A preliminary discussion between Rusk and Gromyko in September signaled further Soviet interest in an accommodation. Khrushchev then sent Kennedy a message through Soviet press spokesman Mikhail Kharmalov. At a dinner with Salinger at the Carlyle Hotel in New York on September 24, the night before Kennedy was to mark the opening of the U.N.'s annual session with a speech before the General Assembly, Kharmalov said, "The storm in Berlin is over." Kharmalov also described the chairman as ready for a summit discussion that could head off a Soviet-American conflict, and relayed Khrushchev's hope that Kennedy's upcoming U.N. address would "not be another warlike ultimatum like the one on July 25. He didn't like that at all." Salinger delivered the message to the president, who was dressed in pajamas and chewing on an unlit cigar, in his hotel suite at one o'clock in the morning. Kennedy commented, "He's not going to recognize the Ulbricht regime — not this year, at least — and that's good news."

To encourage Khrushchev's interest in talks, Kennedy's speech the next day mixed condemnation with conciliation. He denounced renewed Soviet nuclear testing and seeming indifference to the horrors of a conflict — "Mankind must put an end to war — or war will put an end to mankind," Kennedy declared in a memorable line. "This is not the time or the place for immoderate tones," he added. Although he left no doubt that Moscow was responsible for the current confrontation, he declared the crisis unnecessary and himself willing to talk. "We are committed to no rigid formula," he explained. "We see no perfect solution. . . . But we believe a peaceful agreement is possible. . . . There is no need for a crisis over Berlin, threatening the peace — and if those who created this crisis desire peace, there will be peace and freedom in Berlin." At the same time, he instructed Bobby to give interviews that emphasized the dangers to peace from Soviet threats. "The United States and the Soviet Union," Bobby told Knight journalists, "are on a collision course. Unless the situation changes, we will run into one another in a short period of time. I don't think that there is any problem that even comes close to this. . . . On this question really rests the future not just of the country but of the world."

Three days after Kennedy spoke, Khrushchev sent him a back-channel twenty-six-page letter delivered by Kharmalov to Salinger. The letter flattered the president as someone who "prepossessed" people with his "informality, modesty and frankness, which are not to be found very often in men who occupy such a high position." It also struck warm, folksy notes, describing the chairman's retreat into tranquility on the Black Sea, where he enjoyed the sun, bathing, and the "grandeur of the Caucasian Mountains." In this setting, Khrushchev found it "hard to believe that there still exist problems in the world which . . . cast a sinister shadow on peaceful life, on the future of millions of people." His letter was meant to be an informal and personal approach to their mutual problems — "Only in confidential correspondence can you say what you think without a backward glance at the press."

Most important, Khrushchev mirrored Kennedy's concern not to bring the world to disaster through rash actions provoking a nuclear war. He sounded positive notes about shared interest in "striving towards that noble goal" of disarmament and in finding a solution to their German problem. With the Berlin Wall easing Soviet embarrassment, Khrushchev focused on his other concern, keeping Germany divided. Khrushchev now proposed private talks about Germany between personal representatives as a prelude to a summit meeting between Kennedy and himself. "We can argue, we can disagree with one another," Khrushchev concluded, "but weapons must not be brought into play."

A week after Kennedy received Khrushchev's letter, Gromyko asked to see him at the White House. "This is really the first time since Vienna that they've wanted to talk," the president told O'Donnell and Powers. "It looks like a thaw." Kennedy greeted Gromyko with expressions of satisfaction at the recent exchanges between him and Rusk and suggested that Ambassador Thompson continue the discussions in Moscow. Tediously reading from a prepared text for an hour, Gromyko, whose wooden, formal demeanor irritated the president, said nothing that Kennedy had not heard before, except that Khrushchev no longer saw a "fatal date," meaning that a year-end treaty signing no longer applied. Kennedy answered Gromyko that current Soviet proposals on Germany and Berlin "meant [their] trading an apple for an orchard. It would result in a decline of our position in West Berlin and would require our acceptance of other changes which are in the interest of the U.S.S.R." It amounted to "not a compromise but a [U.S.] retreat." Nevertheless, Kennedy stressed American willingness to continue discussions in Moscow and expressed the determination not to protract them month after month.

On October 17, before Khrushchev received a firm but cordial written reply to his letter, in which Kennedy agreed to the likely benefit of "wholly private" exchanges, Khrushchev publicly announced his satisfaction with indications of Western interest in a solution to the German and West Berlin problems and the diminished need to sign a peace treaty by the close of the year.

The "thaw," however, did not end American planning for a possible confrontation. After Khrushchev's false private assurances on renewing nuclear tests, Kennedy remained distrustful of Soviet professions of peace and good intentions on Germany. In addition, Franco-German opposition to negotiations made a Berlin settlement unlikely, and at home Kennedy faced considerable pressure from mindless right-wingers all too ready to fight a nuclear war. During a White House luncheon, E. M. Dealey, the publisher of the *Dallas*

Morning News, verbally assaulted the president for heading an administration of "weak sisters." Dealey believed that the United States needed "a man on horseback" to deal with the Soviet threat. "Many people in Texas and the Southwest think that you are riding Caroline's tricycle," Dealey commented. Kennedy, with evident but controlled anger, replied, "Wars are easier to talk about than they are to fight. I'm just as tough as you are — and I didn't get elected President by arriving at soft judgments."

Kennedy signaled his determination to keep his military guard up in an October 20 letter to General Norstad. The president authorized a continuation of the contingency planning and buildup in NATO military strength. But he also wanted to be sure that in a new Berlin crisis his wishes for a controlled escalation would be clear to U.S. commanders and would be closely followed. He told the general that military moves would only come after diplomacy had failed; current planning was only meant to assure against any "half-cocked" action. Nor would he take the country into a nuclear war until he had exhausted every diplomatic and more traditional military step in defense of the United States and Western Europe.

Yet Kennedy's cautious approach was tempered by both international and domestic constraints that dictated he exert continuing pressure on Moscow to stand down more definitively. Consequently, on October 21, Kennedy had Deputy Defense Secretary Roswell Gilpatric publicly describe U.S. nuclear superiority to the Soviet Union. Despite concerns that the speech might propel the Soviets into greater efforts to achieve missile parity, Kennedy believed it would reduce the risk of war over Berlin and fears in the West that he still lacked the toughness to deter communist aggression. According to Gilpatric, the speech, given before a business council meeting in Hot Springs, Virginia, aimed to convince Moscow of America's readiness to meet any threat to Berlin and to persuade America's allies that increasing conventional forces did not preclude fighting a nuclear war. Rather, conventional forces were a form of insurance against a hasty, and possibly unnecessary, escalation to the ultimate weapons.

The Soviets responded to Gilpatric's speech with mixed signals. Two days later, on October 23, the Soviets detonated a thirty-megaton nuclear bomb; Soviet Defense minister Rodion Malinovsky, speaking to the Twenty-second Communist Party Congress, declared his country unintimidated by Gilpatric's threatening words; and Russian officers provoked a temporary confrontation between Soviet and American tanks at a checkpoint between East and West Berlin. On November 9, Khrushchev followed these actions with another long letter to Kennedy about Soviet-American differences over Germany. He returned to his complaints about the emergence of West German militarism and insisted on the continuation of two German states. "Any other approach would inevitably lead us to collision, to war." He also complained about the dearth of fresh proposals on Berlin and warned of the "extremely sad" consequences for both the United States and the Soviet Union that could flow from "unreasonable decisions."

At the same time, however, the Soviets struck several conciliatory notes. Little was said at the annual party congress about Berlin, Khrushchev told reporters on November 7 that "for the time being, it was not good for Russia and the United States to push each other"; urged the West German ambassador to believe that rapprochement between their two countries was his highest priority; and, in his latest letter to Kennedy, emphasized Soviet devotion to "the principles of peaceful co-existence" and his belief that reconciliation between them was not only possible but essential.

All this back and forth left official Washington uncertain and on edge. Bundy called it "a time of sustained and draining anxiety." In a circular cable to all diplomatic posts in November, Rusk interpreted the Soviet party Congress as signaling an avoidance of a "serious risk of nuclear war" balanced by vigorous Soviet action to establish communist regimes in developing nations. Rusk thought it evident that the Soviets were as determined as ever to win the Cold War. "Unity, preparedness, and firmness of purpose" remained essential in blunting threats to Germany and Berlin.

In a conversation at the end of the month with Aleksei Adzhubei, Khrushchev's son-in-law and *Izvestia* editor, Kennedy, speaking on the record, echoed Rusk's concerns. He bluntly told Adzhubei that international difficulties were the result of Soviet efforts "to communize, in a sense, the entire world. . . . It is this effort to push outward the communist system, on to country after country, that represents, I think, the great threat to peace." In a private conversation with Adlai Stevenson, who had objected to the American resumption of nuclear tests, Kennedy said, "What choice did we have? They had spit in our eye three times. We couldn't possibly sit back and do nothing at all. . . . All this makes Khrushchev look pretty tough. He has had a succession of apparent victories — space,

Cuba, the Wall. He wants to give out the feeling that he has us on the run."

But by November 1961, Kennedy could take satisfaction from the fact that his successful handling of the Berlin problem had forced Khrushchev to retreat. Kennedy's measured, firm response to Khrushchev's threats had preserved West Berlin from communist control. True, Moscow had brought an end to the talent drain from East to West by erecting the wall, but the barrier dividing Berlin became an instant potent symbol of East European discontent with communism. Of course, Kennedy took no pleasure in the continuing plight of the millions of Europeans trapped behind the Iron Curtain, no matter the propaganda advantage. But Khrushchev's backtrack restored Kennedy's faith in his foreign policy leadership, and Berlin could now be considered his first presidential victory in the Cold War.

DESPITE HIS SUCCESS, Kennedy had no illusion that reduced tensions over Germany promised a grand rapprochement in East-West relations or an easing of the Soviet-American contest for global influence. Russia might not force America out of Berlin or into the permanent partition of Germany, but if it established communist governments across Latin America, Africa, and Asia, it would leave the United States and its allies surrounded by hostile regimes. Any sign of weakness or hesitation to answer the communist threat in these regions would encourage Soviet hopes that America lacked the resolve to stand up for itself and its allies in new direct challenges to the United States.

Kennedy had hoped that the Alliance for Progress could help meet the communist threat in Latin America. But domestic and foreign constraints quickly demonstrated that the Alliance was no immediate or possibly even long-term answer to hemisphere problems. Kennedy began by setting a ten-year time frame for the plan and asking Adolf A. Berle, an assistant secretary of state under FDR, to head a Latin American task force. In June, however, Schlesinger told the president that the State Department's Latin American experts "keenly resent the intervention of 'outsiders'" and were "predominantly out of sympathy with the *Alianza.*" These men formed "a sullen knot of resistance to fresh approaches." The administration would need to break their grip on policy if there were to be anything resembling "a new look in Latin America."

Resistance to reform in Latin America itself was an even greater obstacle. Kennedy's idealistic rhetoric about transforming the region had not persuaded entrenched interests across the hemisphere. "The governments of most Latin American countries have not yet grasped what this program calls for in the way of economic and social change, nor do the economically privileged groups understand the sacrifices which will be required of them," Ambassador Thomas Mann in Mexico told Rusk in October. "The obstacles to change vary from country to country but they are all deep-seated and each will be extremely difficult to remove." Bowles agreed. He doubted that the administration had considered how much a successful Alliance required revolutionary change. "What we are asking is that the philosophy of Jefferson and the social reforms of F.D.R. be telescoped into a few years in Latin America. And these steps will have to be taken against the wills of the rich and influential Latin Americans and the people in power. . . . The reforms we want them to make appear very radical to them. We take progressive income tax for granted, but this is shockingly radical to those countries."

If cautious firmness was the formula for dealing with Khrushchev in Europe, where a major miscalculation could provoke the ultimate conflict, Kennedy embraced largely covert but determined anticommunist efforts in Latin America. However undemocratic such actions might have been, Kennedy believed that he had no choice but to make sure that American surrogates got what they needed to combat Moscow-supported threats.

To facilitate counterinsurgency struggles in developing regions generally and Latin America in particular, Kennedy felt compelled to remove Bowles from the number two job in the State Department. Kennedy saw several reasons to replace him; one was his inability to reform the department's bureaucracy, which JFK saw as miserably ineffective in acting imaginatively or promptly in responding to crises like Cuba and Berlin. Bowles's tensions with Bobby and other advocates of practical — as opposed to what they called "fanciful" — answers to hard foreign policy questions also played a part. Bowles's antagonism to administration hard-liners was an open secret. "The question that concerns me most about this new Administration," Bowles wrote privately after the Bay of Pigs, "is whether it lacks a genuine sense of conviction about what is right and what is wrong. . . . The Cuban fiasco demonstrates how far astray a man as brilliant and well intentioned as Kennedy can go who lacks a basic moral reference point." As for Bobby, Bowles thought he demonstrated the perils of a newcomer to foreign policy who, "confronted by the nuances of international questions . . . becomes an easy target for the military-CIA-paramilitary-type answers which can be added, subtracted, multiplied or divided." Bowles certainly had it right about Bobby. Moreover, he was one of the few high officials — Schlesinger was another — who wisely raised moral questions about administration foreign policies and the negative consequences to the country in letting apparent national security imperatives eclipse ethical concerns. For the long run, however, he misjudged how much the Cuban failure would cause JFK to share Bowles's doubts about facile military answers to foreign challenges.

Bowles's conflicts with the administration's hard-liners had registered most clearly over Cuba and the Dominican Republic. By July, this infighting had joined with his failings as an administrator to convince Kennedy to shift him from the State Department to an embassy. But Bowles refused to accept a posting to Brazil, and when press accounts appeared about the president's decision to oust him, Kennedy, concerned about alienating liberals, felt compelled to back away — but not for long. In the fall, Bowles and the Kennedys clashed over the value of counterinsurgency forces fighting Third World communism. Bobby, "a true believer in counterinsurgency," which he called "social reform under pressure," envisioned special forces training guerrilla fighters to combat communist subversion and helping the downtrodden build hospitals, roads, and schools. Bobby and the president also wanted to train Third World police forces to counter clandestine infiltration and communist-inspired mob violence. In September, Kennedy issued a National Security Action Memo (NSAM) instructing McNamara to establish police academies to train the Latin American military in these techniques. When Bowles wisely opposed this as a poor substitute for aid programs that directly met the needs of peasants in rural poverty, it convinced the president and Bobby that Bowles had to go. In November, during Thanksgiving weekend, Kennedy announced a reorganization of the State Department that made Bowles a roving ambassador and replaced him with George Ball, another Stevensonian in whom Kennedy had more confidence.

Pushing Bowles aside was part of Kennedy's renewed determination to do something about Cuba. For six months after the Bay of Pigs failure, the administration had reached no decision on how to deal with Castro. Kennedy had approved the creation of a Special Group to discuss counterinsurgency in Cuba, but it provided no effective plan. "The Cuba matter is being allowed to slide," Bobby noted in a memo on June 1. "Mostly because nobody really has the answer to Castro. Not many are really prepared to send American troops in there at the present time but maybe that is the answer. Only time will tell." In July, discussions of CIA support for an underground movement foundered on the realization that no group in Cuba had sufficient political appeal to overturn Castro. Would the United States have to invade Cuba to get rid of him? JFK asked Admiral Burke at the end of the month. Burke believed that although "all hell would break loose . . . some day we would have to do it." In September, Kennedy told Dick Goodwin that he wanted "'to play it very quiet' with Castro because he did not want to give Castro the opportunity to blame the United States for his troubles." Publicly ignoring Castro and avoiding even indirect action that could encourage comparisons to David and Goliath seemed like the best temporary policy.

During the summer, at a conference in Montevideo, Che Guevara, Castro's close associate, who was representing Cuba, spoke with Goodwin. "Che was wearing green fatigues, and his usual overgrown and scraggly beard," Goodwin told the president. "Behind the beard his features are quite soft, almost feminine, and his manner is intense. He has a good sense of humor, and there was considerable joking back and forth during the meeting." Che "wanted to thank us very much for the invasion — that it had been a great political victory for them — enabled them to consolidate — and transformed them from an aggrieved little country to an equal." Goodwin said, "You're welcome. Now maybe you'll invade Guantanamo." "Never," Che responded with a laugh. He also suggested the possibility of talks looking toward a rapprochement. But fearful that it would be seen as a victory for Castro and would stir sharp political protest in the United States, Kennedy expressed no interest in the idea.

By October, with the Berlin crisis winding down and the growing conviction that the Soviet-American struggle would shift to the Third World, Kennedy exhibited renewed concern about removing Castro "in some way or other . . . from the Cuban scene." Although this was not "a crash program . . . it should proceed with reasonable speed," Bundy told State Department officials charged with the assignment. On November 3, after Goodwin urged Kennedy to make Bobby the commander of an anti-Castro operation, the president authorized Operation Mongoose, "the development of a new program designed to undermine the Castro government." As Bobby, whom Kennedy directed to run the operation, noted, "My idea is to stir things up on the island with espionage, sabotage, general disorder, run & operated by Cubans themselves with every group but Batistaites & Communists. Do not know if we will be successful in overthrowing Castro but we have nothing to lose in my estimate." At a November 21 meeting attended by Kennedy, Bobby, General Edward Lansdale (whom Bobby had made chief of operations), and Goodwin, Bobby, speaking for the president, "expressed grave concern over Cuba, [and] the necessity for immediate dynamic action," including "a variety of covert operations, propaganda" discrediting Castro, and "political action" supported by the OAS.

The CIA had been plotting Castro's assassination during the closing months of Eisenhower's administration, so it was not unprepared for this not-so-new assignment. Senator Frank Church's Select Committee investigating alleged assassination plots in 1975 turned up eight schemes to kill Castro hatched between 1960 and 1965, including a contract with mobsters eager to reestablish lost business interests in Cuba. Kennedy himself discussed assassinating Castro. In March 1961, he had asked George Smathers whether "people would be gratified" if Castro were killed. In 1988, Smathers recalled Kennedy telling him that the CIA had encouraged him to believe that Castro would be "knocked off" at the start of the Bay of Pigs attack. There are additional indications that the president and Bobby talked in the fall of 1961 about killing the Cuban leader. Bobby Kennedy's biographer Evan Thomas pointed out that "on the very same day that the Attorney General — for the first time in four months — asked about a case that risked exposing CIA plotting against Castro, the administration requested a study on the likely effect of removing Castro — and further ordered that the President's interest in this subject be kept quiet. . . . There can be little doubt," Thomas concluded, "that they discussed assassination as at least an option, however sordid." "We were hysterical about Castro at the time of the Bay of Pigs and thereafter," McNamara said later. In a conversation on November 9 with *New York Times* reporter Tad Szulc, Kennedy asked, "What would you think if I ordered Castro to be assassinated?" When Szulc denounced it as immoral and impractical, Kennedy entirely agreed with him. Szulc also recalled the president saying that he had raised the question because "he was under terrific pressure from his advisers." (Szulc thought Kennedy was talking about Bobby, whom CIA officials remember pressing them at this time to use any means to "get rid" of Castro.)

Bobby was not advancing an assassination plot against his brother's wishes. No secrets on foreign policy existed between them. Assassination was undoubtedly a topic of discussion and something the emotional, messianic Bobby may have seen as a necessary evil. But his more dispassionate brother seems to have resisted the suggestion, not necessarily as immoral, but as impractical and counterproductive. Kennedy realized that Castro's death seemed likely to strengthen rather than eliminate communist control in Cuba, where the leader's brother Raul and Che Guevara could convert his death into an emotional plea vindicating his life and beliefs. Poor planning at the Bay of Pigs had ended in disaster. By contrast, careful, modulated responses to Khrushchev's pressure over Germany and Berlin had produced at least a temporary stand-down. The two episodes had strengthened Kennedy's instinctual caution about any response to international dangers that could lead to war. Although the CIA continued to see assassination as a possible response to pressure to remove Castro, there is no evidence that the White House, perhaps after briefly entertaining it, saw it as anything more than a bad idea. Nevertheless, as with the Bay of Pigs fiasco, Kennedy was the accountable party for his administration's actions. Hidden acts of aggression against Third World countries by overzealous agencies were the president's responsibility.

Kennedy's caution in the fall regarding the advancement of American interests in the hemisphere also revealed itself in his dealings with British Guiana. There can be no question that he saw a communist takeover in the British colony as impermissible. Like Castro, Cheddi Jagan claimed to be an anticommunist social democrat, but the experience with Castro had made Washington wary. British reassurances that Jagan could be kept in the Anglo-American camp gave Kennedy only minor reason to hope that Guiana would not turn into another Cuba. In addition to his own worries about a second communist enclave in the hemisphere, which would jeopardize U.S. security and deal his administration another serious blow, he was under pressure from Senator Thomas Dodd of Connecticut, who was denouncing Jagan as a communist agent.

Jagan's selection as prime minister in September, after his party won majority control of a legislative council, gave Kennedy little choice but to try to work with him. In late October, he agreed to receive Jagan at the White House during a trip to America to ask economic assistance. Though Jagan struck a number of responsive chords with Kennedy, he came across as an unreliable romantic who Kennedy believed would eventually suspend constitutional democracy and "cut his opposition off at the knees." Kennedy refused to give him a relatively large aid package but did agree to some help in the belief that support would reduce the chances of his going communist from 90 percent to 50 percent. To guard against that eventuality, Kennedy approved a covert program aimed at destroying communist influence in the country. But the watchword was caution: The covert program was to "be handled with the utmost discretion and probably confined at the start to intelligence collection." A wait-and-see attitude would parallel efforts to work "against pro-Communist developments by building up anti-Communist clandestine capabilities." It was, considering the pressure Kennedy was under, a restrained effort, and would remain so. That would not be the case — tragically — in the next place to which Kennedy turned his attention. That place had only a limited hold on the public's imagination in 1961, but before long millions of Americans would know about South Vietnam.

Reluctant Warrior

*Let us pray . . . that there will be no veterans of any further
war — not because all shall have perished but because all
shall have learned to live together in peace.*

— John F. Kennedy, Remarks at Arlington National Cemetery,
    November 11, 1961

IN 1961, it was unimaginable to Kennedy that within a decade and a
half Vietnam would become the locale where more American troops
died than in any other foreign conflict except World War II. Nor
could he have dreamed that U.S. air forces would drop more than
twice the tonnage of bombs used between 1941 and 1945 against
Germany, Italy, and Japan in the struggle to contain communist expansion in Southeast Asia.

If South Vietnam, with its apparently cooperative government,
seemed to offer an opportunity to defeat communism in developing
nations, it also, as Ros Gilpatric recalled, was a blank slate on which
America could write anything it liked. In the many hours of discussion about Vietnam, there would be ample emphasis on South Vietnamese failings, limited U.S. resources in a world crying out for
American commitments, and U.S. public reluctance to sacrifice
blood and treasure in a place of questionable value to the national
security. Some asked: Were not worries about Europe, Latin America,
and Africa enough without making Southeast Asia a high priority?
But the principal planners assigned to consider the problem of Laos
and Vietnam — General Maxwell Taylor, Walt W. Rostow, Robert
Komer, and U. Alexis Johnson — were "tasked," in the language of
the day, to come up with a workable design to save Southeast Asia
from communism. Confessions of inadequacy, declarations of inca-

pacity to meet the challenge, were simply not acceptable responses. Public servants of the most powerful country in history, men speaking for a nation with almost unimaginable resources, were never going to conclude that this was too complicated or too demanding a job to get done.

It was as if Vietnam had no past to provide a cautionary tale for any nation trying to shape its destiny. But of course there was a history, a story of unrelenting struggle against centuries of Chinese control, followed by a hundred years of French rule dating from the 1860s and a period of Japanese occupation during World War II. A fight for independence led by Ho Chi Minh beginning in 1946 had culminated in the 1954 victory at Dien Bien Phu over the French and the north-south division. American assumptions that the United States would do better than the French in defeating Vietnamese aspirations for a unified independent country rested on the arrogance of a modern superpower battling a so-called backward people. Henry Kissinger had it right, but late, when in 1979 he puzzled over the succession of outsiders (including himself) who had mistakenly entered "that distant monochromatic land" in the name of some principle or other "only to recede in disillusion."

Despite Kennedy's publicly expressed doubts in the 1950s about Western efforts to thwart Vietnamese self-determination, Cold War imperatives, including an Eisenhower domino theory predicting communist control of all Southeast Asia following a South Vietnamese collapse, moved him to continue Eisenhower's policy of trying to defeat a North Vietnamese takeover of the South. Kennedy had instructed Gilpatric to draft a plan for Saigon's survival and sent Johnson to bolster South Vietnamese president Diem's morale and promise more aid. Although there was some discussion of sending U.S. troops to prevent a communist victory, no one, including Johnson, Rusk, and the National Security Council officials responsible for Vietnam planning, recommended it in 1961. Ted Sorensen came closest to Kennedy's thinking in an April 28 memo declaring, "There is no clearer example of a country that cannot be saved unless it saves itself — through increased popular support; governmental, economic and military reforms and reorganizations; and the encouragement of new political leaders."

It was also crystal clear that Kennedy had no immediate intention to allow the country or the region to become an acknowledged battleground for American forces. *Acknowledged* was key: In March

1961, U.S. war planes were ordered to destroy "hostile aircraft" over South Vietnam, but any such action was to be held as a closely guarded secret. (In the event of U.S. aircraft losses, the U.S. Military Assistance Advisory Group [MAAG] in Saigon planned to describe them as the result of an accident during a "routine operational flight.") Kennedy wanted to keep such U.S. military actions secret to avoid complaints both that Washington was violating international agreements and that it was provoking expanded communist aid to the Viet Cong. But at the end of May, Rostow, speaking for the State Department's policy planning council, warned Kennedy that conditions in Vietnam were endangering world peace and that the administration needed to publicly deflate the crisis. "If it comes to an open battle," Rostow predicted, "the inhibitions on our going in will be less than in Laos; but the challenge to Russia and China will be even greater."

Rostow had hoped that the president would speak with Khrushchev in Vienna about Vietnam as another of the trouble spots that could trigger a Soviet-American confrontation. But Kennedy had scarcely mentioned Vietnam to Khrushchev in Vienna. It was not that he was indifferent to America's stake in Vietnam: Indeed, he was eager to honor promises of increased aid, and before going to Europe he had assured Saigon's foreign minister that he intended to increase the size of MAAG, even though this meant violating the 1954 Geneva Accords. However, limited appropriations for foreign military aid and Diem's resistance to pressure for economic and political reforms had sidetracked these commitments.

Nevertheless, throughout the summer of 1961, while the Berlin crisis commanded most of the president's attention, planning for increased aid to Vietnam went forward. Kennedy authorized a Special Financial Group under the direction of Eugene A. Staley, a Stanford economist, to work with Saigon in developing means to fund South Vietnamese military, social, and economic programs.

Kennedy was reluctant to go beyond economic aid. In a White House meeting on Southeast Asia at the end of July, he responded skeptically to proposals for U.S. military intervention in southern Laos. He "emphasized the reluctance of the American people and of many distinguished military leaders to see any direct involvement of U.S. troops in that part of the world." Some of Kennedy's advisers "urged that with a proper plan, with outside support, and above all with a clear and open American commitment, the results would be very different from anything that had happened before. But the President remarked that General de Gaulle, out of painful French experience, had spoken with feeling of the difficulty of fighting in that part of the world."

After the meeting, Rostow sent Kennedy a memo summarizing his and General Taylor's understanding that "you would wish to see every avenue of diplomacy exhausted before we accept the necessity for either positioning U.S. forces on the Southeast Asian mainland or fighting there; you would wish to see the possibilities of economic assistance fully exploited to strengthen the Southeast Asian position; you would wish to see indigenous forces used to the maximum if fighting should occur; and that, should we have to fight, we should use air and sea power to the maximum and engage minimum U.S. forces on the Southeast Asian mainland." As a prelude to any direct involvement in Vietnam, Kennedy wanted to focus world attention on North Vietnamese aggression against Laos and Saigon. Still smarting over the embarrassment to Washington from the Bay of Pigs invasion, Kennedy believed it essential to prepare public opinion to accept possible U.S. intervention — "otherwise any military action we might take against Northern Vietnam will seem like aggression on our part." Kennedy's basic message to his advisers was that U.S. military involvement was to be a last resort.

In early August, Kennedy sent Diem a letter largely agreeing to the program of support worked out between Staley and the South Vietnamese. He promised to finance the expansion of Diem's army from 170,000 to 200,000 men, but only on the condition that Saigon had an effective plan for fighting Viet Cong subversion. Kennedy emphasized that U.S. aid was "specifically conditioned upon Vietnamese performance with respect to particular needed reforms." Indeed, most of Kennedy's letter focused not on U.S. military aid but on Vietnamese financial and social reforms that "will be most effective to strengthen the vital ties of loyalty between the people of Free Viet-Nam and their government." In this, he was returning to the argument he had made to the French in the fifties: Stable Vietnamese ties to the West depended on popular self-government. But Diem was proving as resistant to the argument as Paris had been. The South Vietnamese ruler felt that repression of dissenting opinion would save his political future better than democratization. In sticking with Diem, the administration was implicitly admitting that it saw no viable alternative.

The receding problems over Berlin, joined to the conviction that Laos — headed by an even less reliable ally than Diem — would be a poor place to take a military stand against communist aggression, had moved Kennedy to give Vietnam greater attention. And so, in his U.N. speech at the end of September, when he had reported to the assembly "on two threats to peace," Vietnam had come first and Germany and Berlin second. "The first threat on which I wish to report," he said, "is widely misunderstood: the smoldering coals of war in Southeast Asia." These were not "wars of liberation" but acts of aggression against "free countries living under their own governments."

Kennedy's remarks at the U.N. had been a response to reports that the end of the rainy season in October would bring a major assault on South Vietnam by communist infiltrators from the North. On September 15, Rostow had advised Kennedy of Diem's belief that Hanoi was about to shift from guerrilla attacks to "open warfare." Three days later, in response to a query from Kennedy about "guerrilla infiltration routes through Laos into South Vietnam," Taylor had reported a two-year increase in Viet Cong forces from twenty-five hundred to fifteen thousand, most of which had come from outside the country. In his U.N. address, Kennedy had asked "whether measures can be devised to protect the small and the weak from such tactics. For if they are successful in Laos and South Viet Nam," he declared, "the gates will be opened wide."

The pressure on Kennedy to do something about Vietnam now reached new levels. Before his Bobby-engineered ouster, Bowles had told Rusk on October 5 that an agreement on Laos would not reverse America's steadily more precarious position throughout Southeast Asia, where it faced "a deteriorating military situation in Vietnam and a highly volatile political position in Thailand." Diem's government, which lacked "an effective political base," was growing weaker, putting the communists "in a position to rapidly increase their military pressure with every prospect for success." Was the answer U.S. military intervention? Not surprisingly, Bowles had thought not: "A direct military response to increased Communist pressure," he had said, "has the supreme disadvantage of involving our prestige and power in a remote area under the most adverse circumstances."

The journalist Theodore White, whose skeptical writings about Chiang Kai-shek and the Chinese Nationalists during and after

World War II had made him famous, sent the president a similar message. On October 11, after returning from a trip to Asia, he wrote Kennedy that "any investment of our troops in the paddies of the [South Vietnamese] delta will, I believe, be useless — or worse. The presence of white American troops will feed the race hatred of the Viet-Namese." He thought the U.S. would be forced into a guerrilla war that could not be won. "This South Viet-Nam thing is a real bastard to solve — either we have to let the younger military officers knock off Diem in a coup and take our chances on a military regime . . . or else we have to give it up. To commit troops there is unwise — for the problem is political and doctrinal."

But most of Kennedy's advisers thought otherwise. In a paper titled "Concept for Intervention in Viet-Nam," U.S. military and State Department officials recommended "the use of SEATO [Southeast Asia Treaty Organization] (primarily U.S.) Forces 'to arrest and hopefully to reverse the deteriorating situation' in Vietnam." A force of between 22,800 and 40,000 men would be needed, it said, and if the North Vietnamese and Chinese intervened, that might have to increase to four divisions.

Although he did not openly dismiss the proposal, Kennedy was quite skeptical of military commitments that could become open-ended. At a White House meeting on October 11, he instructed Taylor, Rostow, Lansdale, and several other military and diplomatic officials to visit Vietnam. Kennedy made clear to Taylor that he preferred alternatives to sending American forces. He was willing to send a token contingent that would establish "a U.S. 'Presence' in Vietnam," but he wanted discussions in Saigon to focus on providing more assistance rather than U.S. combat troops. To reduce press speculation that the mission was a prelude to committing American forces, Kennedy considered announcing it as an "economic survey." At a press conference later that day, Kennedy described the mission as seeking "ways in which we can perhaps better assist the Government of Viet-Nam in meeting this threat to its independence." But despite his hopes, the press now speculated that Kennedy was preparing to send U.S. troops to Vietnam, Thailand, or Laos.

Though he did not characterize the mission as limited to economic concerns, Kennedy responded to press reports of possible U.S. military intervention by telling the New York Times off the record that American military chiefs were reluctant to send U.S. troops and that they intended instead to rely on local forces assisted by U.S. advisers. At the same time, Rusk told Budget Director Dave Bell that "Vietnam can be critical and we would like to throw in resources rather than people if we can." General Lyman Lemnitzer cabled Admiral Harry Felt, the commander of U.S. Pacific forces, that the increase in press reports about sending combat troops was troubling the president; he wanted the Saigon discussions to consider the use of American forces, but only if it were "absolutely essential." Felt agreed: The introduction of U.S. troops into Vietnam, he said, could identify America with neocolonialism, provoke a communist reaction, and involve it in extended combat.

The Taylor-Rostow mission, which lasted from October 17 to November 2, produced a blizzard of paper on Vietnam. With rumors flying about what Taylor would recommend, Kennedy instructed him not to discuss his conclusions, "especially those relating to U.S. forces." Kennedy was eager to prevent leaks about military actions that he did not want to take.

TAYLOR'S FIFTY-FIVE-PAGE REPORT to the president, which represented the collective judgment of mission members from the State and Defense Departments, the Joint Chiefs, the CIA, and the intelligence division of the International Cooperation Administration (ICA), emphasized the need for an emergency program promptly implemented, including retaliation against North Vietnam if it refused to halt its aggression against the South. Taylor and his colleagues believed that more was at stake here than Vietnam — namely, the larger question of "Khrushchev's 'wars of liberation'," or "para-wars of guerrilla aggression. This is a new and dangerous Communist technique which bypasses our traditional political and military responses," Taylor said. But the U.S. was anything but helpless in the face of this new kind of warfare. "We have many assets in this part of the world," Taylor declared, "which, if properly combined and appropriately supported, offer high odds for ultimate success."

The Taylor group recommended that the United States expand its role in Vietnam from advisory to a "limited partnership." U.S. representatives needed to "participate actively" in Saigon's economic, political, and military operations. "Only the Vietnamese could defeat the Viet Cong; but at all levels Americans must, as friends and partners — not as arm's-length advisors — show them how the job might be done — not tell them or do it for them." Most telling, Taylor's report recommended introducing a military task force of six to eight thousand men, split between combat and logistical troops operating under U.S. control, in order to raise South Vietnamese morale, give logistical support to South Vietnamese forces, "conduct such combat operations as are necessary for self-defense," and "provide an emergency reserve to back up the Armed forces of the GVN [Government of Vietnam] in the case of a heightened military crisis." The American troops could be dispatched under the fiction of helping the Vietnamese recover from a massive flood in the Mekong Delta.

The planners also considered the possibility of ousting Diem in a South Vietnamese military coup. His regime was a cauldron of intrigue, nepotism, and corruption joined to administrative paralysis and steady deterioration. "Persons long loyal to Diem and included in his official family now believe that South Viet Nam can get out of the present morass only if there is early and drastic revision at the top." But the planners uniformly recommended against overthrowing the existing government. It would be dangerous, "since it is by no means certain that we could control its consequences and potentialities for Communist exploitation." It seemed better to force "a series of de facto administrative changes via persuasion at high levels, using the U.S. presence . . . to force the Vietnamese to get their house in order in one area after another." In any case, the U.S. could not afford to abandon Vietnam: It would mean losing "not merely a crucial piece of real estate, but the faith that the U.S. has the will and the capacity to deal with the Communist offensive in that area."

McNamara, Gilpatric, and the Joint Chiefs now weighed in with recommendations for military steps that went beyond Taylor's. They agreed that the fall of South Vietnam would represent a sharp blow to the United States in Southeast Asia and around the world, and they felt that the likelihood of stopping the communists in Vietnam without the introduction of U.S. forces seemed small. "A US force of the magnitude of an initial 8–10,000 men — whether in a flood control context or otherwise — will be of great help to Diem. However, it will not convince the other side (whether the shots are called from Moscow, Peiping, or Hanoi) that we mean business." They urged the president to face "the ultimate possible extent of our military commitment": A prolonged struggle requiring six U.S. divisions — a force of about 205,000 men — to counter North Vietnamese and potential Chinese intervention.

Rusk and the State Department were less confident that sending in a massive or even limited number of U.S. combat troops made sense. In a memo to the president on November 8, Rusk, McNamara, and the Joint Chiefs recommended a compromise between the competing Taylor, Defense, and State policy recommendations. They agreed that Vietnam's collapse would represent a disaster for the United States, "particularly in the Orient," but also at home, where the "loss of South Vietnam would stimulate bitter domestic controversies in the United States and would be seized upon by extreme elements to divide the country and harass the Administration." They also described the chances of preventing Vietnam's collapse without direct U.S. military support as distinctly limited; for the immediate future, however, they were content to endorse Taylor's proposals for a "limited partnership," including the reorganization and expansion of MAAG to ensure the fulfillment of cooperative military and political goals.

Despite considerable concern about losing Vietnam, Kennedy was determined to resist the mounting pressure for an overt American military response. In October, he had told *New York Times* columnist Arthur Krock that "United States troops should not be involved on the Asian mainland. . . . The United States can't interfere in civil disturbances, and it is hard to prove that this wasn't largely the situation in Vietnam." He told Schlesinger much the same thing. "They want a force of American troops," Kennedy said. "They say it's necessary in order to restore confidence and maintain morale. But it will be just like Berlin. The troops will march in; the bands will play; the crowds will cheer; and in four days everyone will have forgotten. Then we will be told we have to send in more troops. It's like taking a drink. The effect wears off, and you have to take another." He believed that if the conflict in Vietnam "were ever converted into a white man's war, we would lose the way the French had lost a decade earlier."

After a private meeting at the White House with the president on November 5, Taylor recorded that Kennedy "had many questions. He is instinctively against introduction of U.S. forces." At a "high-level meeting" scheduled for November 7, Kennedy wanted advisers to assess the quality of the proposed program, say how it would be implemented, and describe its likely results. He did not ask for a discussion of sending U.S. troops to Vietnam. Indeed, to counter pressure for a substantial military commitment, Kennedy mobilized opposing opinion. Rusk, who faithfully reflected the president's views, responded to the Taylor-JCS proposals for military deployments by favoring more help to the Vietnamese to do their own fighting.

During the first two weeks of November, while Taylor and others argued the case for military commitments, Mike Mansfield, the Senate majority leader and an expert on Asia, Galbraith, George Ball, and Averell Harriman opposed the suggestion in letters and an oral presentation to the president. All four agreed that sending U.S. combat forces to Vietnam carried grave risks. Although they offered no uniform or convincing alternatives for saving Vietnam from communist control, they shared the conviction that putting in American combat units would be a serious error. Mansfield saw "four possible adverse results: A fanfare and then a retreat; an indecisive and costly conflict along the Korean lines; a major war with China while Russia stands aside; [or] a total world conflict." At the very least, "involvement on the mainland of Asia would . . . weaken our military capability in Berlin and Germany and . . . leave the Russians uncommitted."

Ball was as emphatic. At a meeting with McNamara and Gilpatric on November 4, he told them how appalled he was at Taylor's proposal for sending U.S. forces to South Vietnam. His two colleagues had no sympathy for his view. Instead, they were "preoccupied with the single question, How can the United States stop South Vietnam from a Viet Cong takeover? . . . The 'falling domino' theory . . . was a brooding omnipresence." During a conversation with the president three days later, Ball told Kennedy that committing American forces to Vietnam would be "a tragic error." Like Mansfield, who had wondered where "an involvement of this kind" would conclude — "in the environs of Saigon? At the 17th parallel? At Hanoi? At Canton? At Peking?" — Ball predicted that "within five years we'll have three hundred thousand men in the paddies and jungles and never find them again. That was the French experience," he reminded Kennedy. "Vietnam is the worst possible terrain both from a physical and political point of view."

Kennedy agreed, dismissing such involvement as out of the question. "To my surprise," Ball remembered, "the President seemed quite unwilling to discuss the matter, responding with an overtone of asperity: 'George, you're crazier than hell. It isn't going to happen.'" Ball later wondered whether Kennedy meant that events would so evolve as not to require escalation or that "he was determined not to permit such escalation to occur." Judging from his conversations and actions, Kennedy doubted the wisdom of sending combat troops to fight openly in Vietnam and seemed determined to fend off such a commitment. Avoiding a large conflict on the

Asian mainland was a firmly held conviction from which he never departed. Yet at the same time, his compulsion to send in advisers complicated the escalation question.

In preparation for a White House meeting on November 11, Kennedy armed himself with eight questions for his advisers. The first five addressed the central issues under consideration: "Will this [Taylor's] program be effective without including the introduction of a U.S. troop task force? What reasons shall we give Diem for not acceding to his request for U.S. troops? Under what circumstances would we reconsider our decision on troops? . . . Is the U.S. commitment to prevent the fall of South Vietnam to Communism to be a public act or an internal policy decision of the U.S. Government? [And] to what extent is our offer of help to Diem contingent upon his prior implementation of the reform measures which we are proposing to him?"

After the meeting with Taylor, Rostow, Rusk, McNamara, Lemnitzer, Bobby, and others on the eleventh, Lemnitzer summarized Kennedy's remarks: "Troops are a last resort. Should be SEATO forces. Will create a tough domestic problem. Would like to avoid statements like Laos & Berlin" that could provoke a confrontation with Moscow. To underscore the president's wishes, Bobby said that a presidential statement on Taylor's report should say, "We are not sending combat troops. [We are] not committing ourselves to combat troops. Make it [any statement about sending troops] [as] much SEATO as possible." The coalition aspect to any military intervention was crucial: Kennedy felt the exclusive use of American troops would arouse a public outcry in the United States.

William Bundy, Mac's older brother, who was assistant secretary of state for East Asia and was at the meeting, believed "the thrust of the President's thinking was clear — sending organized forces was a step so grave that it should be avoided if this was humanly possible." Kennedy also resisted making a categorical commitment to saving South Vietnam. The president saw an outright pledge to keep Vietnam out of the communist orbit as unrealistic without a collateral promise to use American military power. So the best course of action seemed to be to make noise about using U.S. military might and even send advisers, but to hold back from assuming principal responsibility for South Vietnam's national security.

Consequently, Kennedy now approved a recommendation that the military prepare contingency plans for the use of U.S. forces "to signify United States determination to defend South Viet-Nam," to assist in fighting the Viet Cong and Hanoi without direct participation in combat, and to join the fighting "if there is organized Communist military intervention." Kennedy, however, remained reluctant to actually initiate any of these plans. In a memo to Rusk and McNamara in preparation for a meeting on November 15, he asked that Taylor's nonmilitary proposals be made more precise and that Harriman's suggestion of negotiations with Moscow on Vietnam be further explored.

At the NSC meeting on the fifteenth, Kennedy "expressed the fear of becoming involved simultaneously on two fronts on opposite sides of the world. He questioned the wisdom of involvement in Viet Nam since the basis thereof is not completely clear." Comparing the war in Korea with the conflict in Vietnam, he saw the first as a case of clear aggression and the latter as "more obscure and less flagrant." He believed that any unilateral commitment on the part of the United States would produce "sharp domestic partisan criticism as well as strong objections from other nations." By contrast with Berlin, Vietnam seemed like an obscure cause that "could even make leading Democrats wary of proposed activities in the Far East."

When Lemnitzer warned that a communist victory in Vietnam "would deal a severe blow to freedom and extend Communism to a great portion of the world," Kennedy "asked how he could justify the proposed courses of action in Viet Nam while at the same time ignoring Cuba." Lemnitzer urged simultaneous steps against Cuba. Kennedy restated doubts about having congressional or public support for U.S. combat troops in Vietnam and concluded the meeting by postponing action until he had spoken with Vice President Johnson and received "directed studies" from the State Department.

FOR ALL KENNEDY'S RELUCTANCE, international and domestic pressures persuaded him to commit new U.S. resources to Vietnam. Everything he said about Vietnam during the first ten months in office made clear that he doubted the wisdom of expanded involvements in the fighting. But after the defeat at the Bay of Pigs, Khrushchev's uncompromising rhetoric in Vienna, the refusal to fight in Laos, construction of the Berlin Wall, and Soviet resumption of nuclear tests, Kennedy believed that allowing Vietnam to collapse was too politically injurious to America's international standing and too likely to provoke destructive domestic opposition like that over China after Chiang's defeat in 1949.

Taylor's report had emphasized that the United States could not act too soon to prevent a Vietnamese collapse. He described his recommendations as an "emergency program which we feel our Government should implement without delay." Walt Rostow also warned that any delay in helping Saigon would produce "a major crisis of nerve in Viet-Nam and throughout Southeast Asia. The image of U.S. unwillingness to confront Communism . . . will be regarded as definitively confirmed. [Without it,] there will be real panic and disarray." When Ambassador Frederick Nolting asked permission on November 12 to come home for consultations, Rusk replied, "We cannot afford inevitable delay" in implementing Taylor's program, which Nolting's absence from Saigon would bring. In the existing circumstances time was a "crucial factor." The sense of urgency about saving Vietnam with a demonstration of greater U.S. support became a pattern by which Washington, with too little thought to what lay ahead, incrementally increased its commitments until the conflict had become a major American war.

Although Kennedy would not yet agree to send combat troops to fight Saigon's war, he sent Diem a message on November 15 declaring U.S. readiness "to join . . . in a sharply increased joint effort to avoid a further deterioration in the situation." He intended to provide additional military equipment and to more than double the twelve hundred American military personnel assisting the Vietnamese in training and using their armed forces. To rationalize not committing U.S. troops to combat, Kennedy told Diem that "the mission[s] being undertaken by our forces . . . are more suitable for white foreign troops than garrison duty or missions involving the seeking out of Viet Cong personnel submerged in the Viet-Nam population." It was Kennedy's way of saying, We don't want to fight an Asian land war or to be accused of reestablishing colonial control over Vietnam.

But even without a direct part in the fighting, the stepped-up U.S. program meant acting as much more than an adviser. "We would expect to share in the decision-making process in the political, economic and military fields as they affected the military situation," Kennedy wrote Diem. Specifically, Kennedy proposed to "provide individual administrators and advisers for the Governmental machinery of South Viet-Nam," as well as "personnel for a joint survey with the GVN of conditions in each of the provinces to assess the social, political, intelligence and military factors bearing on the prosecution of the counter-insurgency program."

As a condition of American help, Kennedy insisted that Diem put his "nation on a wartime footing to mobilize its entire resources" and "overhaul" his military command "to create an effective military organization for the prosecution of the war." Simultaneous with Kennedy's marching orders to Diem, the White House drafted a letter to Kennedy to be published under Diem's name. It was a demonstration of how little the White House trusted Diem to meet American demands and how eager Kennedy was to convince people at home and abroad of the justification for this deepening U.S. involvement in Vietnam's civil war. Diem's ghosted letter, which the White House published in December, said the North Vietnamese were relying on "terror . . . to subvert our people, destroy our government, and impose a communist regime upon us." The nation, it said, faced the "gravest crisis" in its history. Diem's letter promised a full mobilization of national resources but asked for further assistance to ensure a victory over the communist aggressors. His subsequent actions would give the lie to what Kennedy had committed him to in the letter.

AFTER HIS NOVEMBER 15 DECISIONS on Vietnam, Kennedy braced himself for protests from the domestic left and right. In speeches shortly afterward, he focused on their unrealistic views of foreign affairs. Though he never mentioned Vietnam, he had it in mind when he criticized liberals "who cannot bear the burden of a long twilight struggle." They were impatient for "some quick and easy and final and cheap solution [to the communist threat] — now." Nor, he said, were they correct in seeing U.S. involvement in Southeast Asia as neocolonialism or a defense of the international status quo. Kennedy saw the right's criticism of Vietnam policy as even more skewed. Their depiction of limited intervention as "appeasement," or a failure to use America's military muscle to decisively defeat communism, was part of a campaign of suspicion and fear that undermined rational responses to foreign problems.

During the winter of 1961–62, as the U.S. government implemented Kennedy's directives on Vietnam, further obstacles were thrown up by Saigon. Diem, who accurately saw the U.S. program turning his government and country into a protectorate of

Washington, resisted ceding too much control. His opposition partly took the form of Vietnamese press criticism of U.S. diplomats and military officers. The Vietnamese complained that Americans lacked a proper understanding of an underdeveloped country's problems in becoming a Western-style democracy.

But democracy and democratization seemed far from Diem's mind, and from India, Galbraith recommended that the U.S. rid itself of him. "He has run his course," Galbraith told Kennedy. "He cannot be rehabilitated." Since he did not think that Diem could or would "implement in any real way the reforms Washington has requested, we should make it quietly clear that we are withdrawing our support from him as an individual. His day would then I believe be over." Galbraith thought it a cliché that there was no alternative to Diem. A better rule was that "nothing succeeds like successors."

Kennedy's problems with implementing Taylor's limited program matched his difficulties with Diem. Kennedy did not trust either the State or the Defense Department to carry out his wishes. "I've told the Secretary frankly," Bundy advised Kennedy of a conversation with Rusk, "that you feel [the] need to have someone on this job that is wholly responsive to your [Vietnam] policy, and that you really do not get that sense from most of us." Similarly, Kennedy worried about the reliability of both the embassy and the MAAG in Saigon. At Kennedy's request, Taylor entered into "considerable discussion . . . over the kind of organization required in South Vietnam to administer the accelerated U.S. program." Taylor's advice was to stick with the organization already in place in Saigon until it proved inadequate. But Kennedy thought this was already the case.

Whatever the pace and whatever the organization, despite Kennedy's refusal to have Americans become full combatants, "advisers" were inevitably drawn into firefights with the Viet Cong. Instructing Saigon's forces on antiguerrilla tactics meant accompanying them on field missions and involvement in the fighting. In addition, because the South Vietnamese lacked the training to fly some of the newest airplanes and helicopters, the MAAG assigned U.S. pilots to fly them and pretended they were under Vietnamese command by assigning one Vietnamese airman to every attack mission. To give the president "plausible deniability" on air combat, the State Department euphemistically described "combined crew operations" in aircraft bearing SVN markings. It was "an agreed approach" sanctioned by the White House and State "to avoid pinning down the President."

* * *

KENNEDY KNEW THAT PUBLICITY about America's combat role would result in unwanted international and domestic repercussions. American involvement in the fighting was a clear violation of the 1954 Geneva Accords and made U.S. complaints about North Vietnamese and Chinese support of the Viet Cong appear hypocritical. More important, an avowal of American military operations would increase tensions with Hanoi, Peking, and Moscow, and difficulties with the USSR in reaching agreements on Southeast Asia, Germany, and arms control. It would be especially embarrassing to Moscow, which had promised to support wars of national liberation in Asia and Africa against former colonial masters and neo-imperialists in Washington. On November 28, before expanded operations began, Rusk cabled the Saigon embassy, "Do not give other than routine cooperation to correspondents on coverage current military activities in Vietnam. No comment at all on classified activities."

Kennedy also saw public disclosure of American involvement as touching off domestic demands for military commitments that could guarantee victory, even at the risk of nuclear war. If the struggle against the Viet Cong and Hanoi now became a losing cause, full knowledge of the South Vietnamese–American failure would stimulate an outcry for the United States to do more. Kennedy hoped that the current U.S. effort could be enough to shore up Saigon and force the communists into negotiations that would preserve an independent South Vietnam tied to the West. At the very least, he hoped that U.S. support would keep South Vietnam free of communist control for the foreseeable future. Ideally, U.S. help would give the Vietnamese the wherewithal to stand on their own and free American troops to go home. But if Vietnam was about to fall, he did not want to identify the United States too closely with its defeat.

By the middle of January 1962, two months after the Taylor program had been set in motion, reporters began to ask hard questions. Although only one American had been killed, restrictions on press freedom to cover combat missions aroused understandable suspicions that Washington and Saigon were hiding the truth about U.S. military operations in Vietnam. On January 15, when a reporter asked Kennedy at a news conference, "Are American troops now in combat in Vietnam?" he answered, "No."

The press was justifiably not convinced. The presence of nearly thirty-five hundred U.S. military "advisers" in Vietnam encouraged the belief that they were actively engaged in the fighting. By the middle of February, the State Department's public affairs officer warned that "we seem headed for a major domestic furor over the 'undeclared' war in South Viet-Nam and [over] US imposed 'secrecy regulations' that prevent American newsmen from telling our people the truth about US involvement in that war." Although reporters had ferreted out enough information to describe the United States as "now involved in an undeclared war in South Vietnam," the White House refused to ease its press restrictions. Pierre Salinger recalled that Kennedy was "particularly sensitive" about press accounts of U.S. involvement in combat. He "pushed hard for us to tighten the rules there under which correspondents would observe field operations in person."

The State Department now instructed the embassy in Saigon to follow a policy of "maximum feasible cooperation, guidance and appeal to good faith of correspondents." But the department laid down guidelines that tightened rather than eased restrictions: Reporters were told that critical stories about Diem "only make our task more difficult."

At a February 14 press conference, a reporter asked Kennedy about his response to a Republican National Committee complaint that "you have been less than candid with the American people as to how deeply we are involved in Viet-Nam." Kennedy's answer, like the restrictions on the journalists in Saigon, was meant to obscure the truth. "We have increased our assistance to the government — its logistics; we have not sent combat troops there, although the training missions that we have there have been instructed if they are fired upon to — they would of course fire back, to protect themselves. But we have not sent combat troops in the generally understood sense of the word. We have increased our training mission, and we've increased our logistic support. . . . I feel that we are being as frank as we can be."

Unconvinced by Kennedy's explanation, the press continued to report on America's growing involvement in the conflict. Relying on U.S. military and South Vietnamese government sources, NBC and *Time* correspondents learned about the combat operations of American air forces. The embassy believed that it would be increasingly difficult to keep such information under wraps. (Diem wanted to try by proposing to expel *Newsweek* and *New York Times* correspondents, but the U.S. embassy convinced him that it would do more harm than good.)

Two conditions made problems with the press irreducible. First, and most obvious, the U.S. role in the fighting was simply more than Kennedy was willing to admit. But second, and less clear, was the fact that U.S. personnel in Saigon were exceeding what Kennedy wanted them to do. On April 4, Harriman, who had become assistant secretary of state for Far Eastern affairs, cabled the Saigon embassy that press critics in Vietnam were describing the conflict as more of a U.S. than a Vietnamese war. The names of combat operations like "Sunrise" and "Farmgate" suggested "U.S. rather than GVN planning," and Americans were making themselves too conspicuous in their advisory activities. Reports of a large group of American colonels and civilians inspecting a stockade in Operation Sunrise was a case in point. "Why do large groups of Americans inspect anything?" Harriman asked. Moreover, why were American officers talking so freely about their role in planning operations? "It cannot be over stressed," Harriman declared, "that the conduct and utterances public and private of all U.S. personnel must reflect the basic policy of this government that we are in full support of Viet-Nam but we do not assume responsibility for Viet-Nam's war with the Viet Cong."

A week later, Rusk cabled Saigon reinforcing the need for U.S. personnel to adhere to America's limited role in the fighting. The press was getting an "erroneous impression" that was "factually wrong and lacking perspective." He urged all posts to make clear that "U.S. personnel are not participating directly in war nor are they directing war. Major U.S. effort is to train instructors rather than troops. However, given the fluidity and ubiquity of guerrilla warfare, necessarily Americans suffer occasional casualties in carrying out their training and logistical functions — e.g., taking part in training patrol exercises."

Kennedy's desire to limit U.S. involvement in the conflict by keeping it off the front pages made a certain amount of sense, since the aim was as much, if not more, to limit America's part in the fighting as to maintain Saigon's autonomy. But would it not have been better for the administration to acknowledge its ambivalence about involving U.S. ground forces in Vietnam and encourage public debate? Assertions that such a debate would have demoralized the Vietnamese are unpersuasive. As U.S. policy makers understood, if the Vietnamese were going to save themselves from a communist takeover, they would have to take prime responsibility for their fate. And as Kennedy knew from World Wars I and II and Korea, fighting a costly foreign war required steady public commitments that could only follow a national debate educating Americans about the country's vital stake in the conflict. By obscuring America's role and future choices in the conflict, Kennedy was making it impossible to fight in Vietnam — if that is what the country chose to do — with the backing necessary for a supportable war effort.

ALL THE ADMINISTRATION'S PRONOUNCEMENTS and directives could not alter the reality of direct American involvement in the conflict. Kennedy understood that he could only deny this fact for so long, that as Saigon's military failings increased pressure for more "advisers" and American casualties rose, public demands for an accounting would mount. Consequently, when Galbraith returned to Washington in early April to testify on India before the House Foreign Affairs Committee, Kennedy welcomed a memo from him on how to escape the Vietnam trap. Galbraith's advice was simple. He warned that the United States was in danger of becoming the new colonial force in the area and then bleeding as the French did. The U.S. should help forge a neutral coalition government in South Vietnam and then perhaps leave. He urged, above all, against combat commitments. "Americans in their various roles should be as invisible as the situation permits."

On April 6, Kennedy discussed Vietnam with Harriman. He showed him Galbraith's memo, then asked that it be forwarded to McNamara and that Galbraith be instructed to ask the Indian government to approach Hanoi about holding peace talks. "The President observed generally that he wished us to be prepared to seize upon any favorable moment to reduce our involvement, recognizing that the moment might yet be some time away."

Indeed, Kennedy had no illusion that an end to the Vietnam conflict was in sight or that American involvement would not grow. In March, when asked by a reporter to assess "the subterranean war" in Vietnam, he replied, "I don't think you can make a judgment of the situation. It's very much up and down, as you know, from day to day, and week to week, so it's impossible to draw any long-range conclusions." Mindful, however, of the dangers Galbraith had described, he was eager for the earliest possible withdrawal. True, he had approved a declaration by Bobby during a visit to Saigon in February that "we are going to win in Vietnam. We will remain here until we do win." But that was more an attempt to bolster Diem's morale and discourage the communists than a reliable commitment to an unconditional policy. For the time being, Kennedy wished to impress Hanoi, Peking, and Moscow with his determination to save Vietnam, and most everyone else with the belief that he would keep Vietnam from turning into a draining land war. If a limited U.S. commitment could maintain South Vietnam's independence for the immediate future, Hanoi might agree to a temporary settlement, which would allow an honorable exit for American troops. For all the reasons that had drawn him more fully into the conflict in November, Kennedy remained eager to preserve South Vietnam's autonomy. But his higher priority was to avoid leading the United States into a Southeast Asian disaster that would weaken its international standing and play havoc with his domestic political power.

During a May 1 conversation at the White House, Kennedy asked Harriman and Roger Hilsman, State's chief intelligence officer, if there was "any merit in J. K. Galbraith's suggestion of negotiating a neutralized coalition government." When the two "vigorously opposed this recommendation," Kennedy decided against trying it. He was not about to weaken the impression that he intended to save Saigon from a communist takeover by proposing unrealizable talks. But his query revealed his ongoing reluctance to deepen U.S. involvement in a possibly unwinnable war that could undermine U.S. prestige and freedom of maneuver abroad and political stability at home.

BETWEEN THE FALL OF 1961 and the spring of 1962, Vietnam was only one of Kennedy's burdens. Questions about whether and when to resume nuclear tests also caused him no small amount of anguish. In the run-up to the Vienna meeting with Khrushchev, Kennedy had struggled to find ways to convince Moscow of the need for a test ban treaty, looked for ways to "increase public awareness of Soviet intransigence" on the issue, and wondered whether U.S. national security made new tests essential. But the meeting with Khrushchev in June had forced Kennedy's hand. Khrushchev's uncompromising response to negotiating proposals on weapons control had convinced Kennedy that the United States would have to resume testing, however repugnant it was to him. Added to this was the Soviet announcement at the end of August that they were resuming tests. "Of all the Soviet provocations" in 1961 and 1962, Mac Bundy wrote, "it was the resumption of testing that disappointed Kennedy most."

In November, after the Soviets had exploded a fifty-megaton bomb and conducted fifty atmospheric tests in sixty days, Kennedy felt compelled to make additional test preparations. At a National Security Council meeting on November 2, Kennedy's science advisers told him that "if we test only underground and the Soviets tested in the atmosphere, they would surely pass us in nuclear technology." In response, the president announced that the United States would now prepare atmospheric tests. But he also declared that America would only test if "effective progress were not possible without such tests." Even then, it would be done in a manner to restrict the fallout "to an absolute minimum."

Kennedy was so conflicted over the consequences of new atmospheric tests that, in Atomic Energy Commission head Glenn Seaborg's words, "we now entered a prolonged period of uncertainty regarding preparations for atmospheric testing. A decision would seem to be made one day and withdrawn the next. Kennedy wanted to take a firm stand and be ready; yet he wanted to keep his options open: he was reluctant to take steps that might bar the way to a test ban."

Kennedy's ambivalence was on display during a two-day meeting with Macmillan in Bermuda in December. The British wanted to continue negotiating with the Russians for a test ban and a comprehensive arms control agreement, however unrealizable these seemed. Macmillan believed that Khrushchev was as eager as they were to avoid a nuclear holocaust. (When Macmillan asked him what would happen if all the bombs in the world exploded, Khrushchev responded, "There would be nobody left but the Chinese and the Africans.") Kennedy was sympathetic to British concerns, but he emphasized how untrustworthy Moscow had been in recent arms talks. They had prepared their latest tests while negotiating insincerely in Geneva. "We could not get taken twice," he said. He described himself as a "great antitester" but said he felt compelled to prepare to test and then only do so if it were absolutely essential. Kennedy accurately forecast that "before long the nuclear arms race would come to a standoff where neither side could use these weapons because it would be destroyed if it did."

Seaborg came away from the Bermuda talks, where he was a "spectator," with the distinct impression that in private Kennedy was "considerably more in favor of accepting risks and making compromises in order to achieve a test ban than either he or U.S. negotiators ever allowed themselves to be in public." The realities of American politics, especially Senate skepticism about a test ban agreement, constrained them.

As Ted Sorensen put it to Seaborg: "Kennedy was a multi-faceted individual. By that I don't mean that he was all things to all men. I simply mean that he had a way of engaging the other person, of building bridges to him, of keeping his interest and sympathy without committing himself to the other's view until he had weighed all the options. . . . Kennedy was determined not to permit himself to buy a test ban agreement which the Senate would reject because he felt that would be a disastrous setback to the whole movement in which he believed so strongly."

At the close of the conference, Kennedy and Macmillan announced their determination, "as a matter of prudent planning," to prepare atmospheric tests. However, the final decision would depend on future arms talks, which they pledged to continue with full understanding that an agreement was the only way to break out of the current dangerous arms race

Over the next two months, while chances for a test ban agreement slipped away, Kennedy repeatedly sought assurances from his advisers that a decision to resume testing was essential. On January 15, when asked at a news conference about the most rewarding and disappointing events during his first year in office, he began with his greatest disappointment: "Our failure to get an agreement on the cessation of nuclear testing, because . . . that might have been a very important step in easing the tension and preventing a proliferation of [nuclear] weapons." The most heartening thing he could cite was a "greater surge for unity in the Western nations, and in our relations with Latin America." No wonder that when Sorensen told him that reporters were considering writing books on the Year of the New Frontier, Kennedy looked at him quizzically and said, "Who would want to read a book on disasters?"

Kennedy agreed to atmospheric tests at the end of April but directed that they be done on Christmas Island, a British possession in the Pacific, rather than at a Nevada test site. He feared the domestic reaction to newspaper pictures of a mushroom cloud over the United States. Still, because he felt so strongly about the issue and the need to explain it fully to peoples everywhere, Kennedy gave a lengthy (forty-five-minute) prime-time televised address from the Oval Office. His distress at having to announce atmospheric tests was evident in his grim demeanor and words. By unleashing the power of the atom, he said, mankind had taken "into his mortal hands the power of self-extinction. . . . For of all the awesome responsibilities entrusted to this office, none is more somber to contemplate than the special statutory authority to employ nuclear arms in defense of our people and freedom." The ongoing threat to America's survival dictated that it maintain a sufficient deterrent force — a nuclear arsenal that could survive any surprise attack and devastate the attacker. Kennedy then recounted the history of the moratorium on testing dating from 1958 and the callous Soviet decision to resume mostly atmospheric tests the previous fall. Saying that "no single decision of this Administration has been more thoroughly or more thoughtfully weighed," Kennedy announced the need to conduct atmospheric tests in the Pacific at the end of April. Assuring viewers that the tests would present no significant health hazard to the world, and certainly "far less than the contamination created by last fall's Soviet series," he nevertheless regretted "that even one additional individual's health may be risked in the foreseeable future" by testing.

The rest of his speech was chiefly an explanation of U.S. technical gains from the explosions and the impact they might have on relations with Moscow, and an expression of his continuing hopes for an end to tests and the arms race. Most important, Kennedy believed that a resumption of U.S. nuclear tests would be not only a deterrent to war but also a demonstration that Moscow could not achieve nuclear superiority and would do better to negotiate a test ban than to continue tests that would injure its international prestige, pollute the world's atmosphere, and increase tensions with the West. "It is our hope and prayer," Kennedy concluded, "that these . . . deadly weapons will never have to be fired — and that our preparations for war will bring about the preservation of peace."

THE BERLIN CRISIS in the summer and fall of 1961 had made civil defense a more compelling security and political priority, and between the spring of 1961 and the summer of 1962, civil defense preparations became another administration headache. In his July address on Berlin, Kennedy had announced that the secretary of defense would now take responsibility for a fallout shelter program and that he would ask Congress to triple the appropriation for civil defense from $104 to $311 million. In August, he had instructed

McNamara to move "as quickly as possible on Civil Defense." He wanted weekly reports on the progress of the program and wondered whether "it would be useful for me to write a letter to every homeowner in the United States giving them instructions as to what can be done on their own to provide greater security for their family." In September, Kennedy provided a letter to *Life* magazine urging readers to consider seriously the contents of an article entitled "You Could Be Among the 97% to Survive If You Follow Advice in These Pages." Realistically, Kennedy did not share this illusion; his science adviser Jerome Wiesner characterized the article as "grossly misleading." Nevertheless, Kennedy still believed — or said he believed — in civil defense as "an insurance policy" that could save some lives. The political dangers to a president choosing to ignore the issue or honestly debunk shelters as a false defense against civilian casualties were enough to force Kennedy into outspoken support.

In October, Kennedy commended the nation's governors for their attentiveness to civil defense and told a press conference that it was wise to do everything possible to increase the chances of protecting families from the dangers of a nuclear war. At the same time, the Pentagon completed a draft of a survival pamphlet slated for distribution to every household in America. Marc Raskin and other skeptics at the NSC and the White House made fun of it as potentially "the most widely distributed piece of literature in man's history outside of the Bible." (They also ridiculed the booklet's simplistic recommendations on how to protect yourself from a nuclear attack by referring to it as "Fallout Is Good for You.") A chain reaction of additional concerns soon ensued. Stories about suburbanites in New Jersey and California arming themselves with weapons to fend off migrants from New York and Los Angeles seeking refuge in their shelters created additional antipathy for the program. A church official's assurance to parishioners that it was permissible to shoot neighbors trying to break into their shelters moved *Newsweek* to compare such citizens to prehistoric cavemen. In November, Galbraith, Schlesinger, and Sorensen weighed in with letters to the president complaining of a program that seemed calculated "to save the better elements of the population" and write off the less affluent, who lacked the means to build fallout shelters. Schlesinger saw the program as generating "an alarming amount of bewilderment, confusion and, in some cases, (both pro and con) of near hysteria." People were beginning to have "a false sense of security — a belief that . . . a nuclear war will be no worse than a bad cold." This would encourage pressure for militancy over negotiation. By contrast, he said, pacifists panicked by thoughts of war would demand unilateral disarmament and would ask Americans, Wouldn't you be "better red than dead"? Sorensen told Kennedy, "Civil defense is rapidly blossoming into our number one political headache, alienating those who believe we're doing too much or too little." Sorensen also doubted that the fallout program would significantly reduce casualties in a nuclear war. It would do nothing to discourage an attack and might "only spur the enemy into developing even more destructive weapons."

Nothing may have done more to rein in Kennedy's enthusiasm for the shelter program than a discussion with nuclear scientist Edward Teller, a leading exponent of nuclear weapons and a warm advocate of civil defense. During discussions with the president, Wiesner, and Mac Bundy at the White House, Teller shocked them with appeals for a three-pronged program of fallout, blast, and fire shelters, and plans to dig deeper shelters if the Russians built bigger bombs. Afterward, Bundy told the president, "I am horrified by the thought of digging deeper as the megatonnage gets bigger, which is the notion of civil defense that Dr. Teller spelled out to me after your meeting with him. . . . This is a position from which you will wish to be disassociated."

Kennedy, regretting that he had ever fixed so much attention on civil defense and encouraged such false hopes, now pushed the program to the side with benign neglect. He insisted on a revised booklet making more modest claims, dropped plans to give a televised address when it appeared, and decided on much more restricted distribution for it. In July 1962, after Congress had reduced a December 1961 request for civil defense from $695 million to $80 million, a reporter asked Kennedy whether he intended to prod the Congress into holding hearings on fallout shelters and to renew his appeal for the program. Kennedy said no, and justified his restraint by saying that he was following the advice of responsible administration officials.

AND STILL there was Latin America. On December 1, 1961, when Castro told the Cuban people that he was a dedicated Marxist-Leninist and would be for the rest of his life, the Kennedy administration urged the OAS to defend the hemisphere from "any extension of the treachery of Fidelismo." Castro's statement also spurred Kennedy's Special Group on Cuba to intensify their planning "to help Cuba overthrow the Communist regime." The scheme was to build "a nucleus of anti-Castro Cubans" in Cuba and follow it with "a number of collateral supporting actions." Lansdale characterized the project as "long-term" and "difficult" and as more political than economic or paramilitary.

During the first half of 1962, the Special Group laid plans to oust Castro by the fall of that year, but CIA director John McCone believed it would "be extremely difficult to accomplish," because they lacked the backing in Cuba for such a result. Kennedy agreed, but ending Castro's rule remained "the top priority in the United States Government — all else is secondary," Bobby told national security officials. Bobby reported the president as saying, "The final chapter on Cuba has not been written," and, Bobby added, "It's got to be done and will be done."

Because the likelihood of an internal revolt seemed so small, the planners began discussing a pretext for a direct U.S. invasion. But Kennedy remained skeptical that circumstances favoring U.S. military intervention would arise. Although contingency planning would proceed, "it was clearly understood [that] no decision was expressed or implied approving the use of such forces." By the spring, however, there was growing optimism that as soon as August the planners could begin preparations for "an organized revolt of substantial proportions" in Cuba. As with the Bay of Pigs, there was more wishful thinking here than reliable evidence or good sense. Mary Hemingway, Ernest's widow, may have "irked" Kennedy during an April 1962 White House dinner when she told him that his Cuban policy was "stupid, unrealistic and, worse, ineffective," but her point was not entirely lost on him.

Because Kennedy saw Castro's assassination or an invasion of the island as counterproductive in aligning the hemisphere with the United States in the anticommunist struggle, he hoped that clandestine actions might shield him from additional embarrassments over Cuba. At the same time, he remained eager to advance the Alliance for Progress as serving U.S. national security interests in the hemisphere. But ensuring stable democratic governments intent on greater economic and social justice seemed nearly impossible. Moreover, honoring promises of noninterference or a revival of Franklin Roosevelt's Good Neighbor policy proved impossible.

The Dominican Republic was another source of frustration. Instability in Santo Domingo had followed Trujillo's assassination in 1961, and although preferring a government broadly acceptable to the Dominican people, Washington was ready to support a friendly military dictatorship rather than have a pro-Castro administration. Consequently, it made undisguised efforts to support the elected president, Joaquin Balaguer, against Trujillo's brothers, who seemed ready to seize power in November. The appearance of U.S. naval forces off Santo Domingo and a message from Kennedy to the Trujillos to leave the island or risk U.S. intervention forced the brothers to flee and gave Balaguer control. U.S.-brokered negotiations between the Dominican government and opposition parties led to the creation of a council of state that lasted only until mid-January, when a military-civilian junta seized power. The "successful" management of the Dominican problem — preserving the country from a civil war — gave the administration some hope of making other gains in Latin America.

In July, after Kennedy had decided not to attend a Montevideo conference because of the Berlin crisis, Latin American ambassadors had been openly critical. A December trip to Venezuela and Colombia was partly an attempt to repair the damage. In speeches in Caracas and Bogotá, and in discussions with Venezuelan president Romulo Betancourt and Colombian president Alberto Lleras Camargo, Kennedy identified himself with FDR's Good Neighbor policy and described the Alliance for Progress as a substantive commitment to raise living standards across the hemisphere. "We in the United States have made many mistakes in our relations with Latin America," Kennedy said in an after-dinner talk at the Bogotá embassy. "We have not always understood the magnitude of your problems, or accepted our share of responsibility for the welfare of the hemisphere. But we are committed in the United States — our will and our energy — to an untiring pursuit of that welfare and I have come to this country to reaffirm that dedication." He called on Latin America's industrialists and landowners "to admit past mistakes and accept new responsibilities." Without a willingness on their part to accept basic land and tax reforms, he predicted that hopes for progress would "be consumed in a few months of violence."

Remembering the hostility to Nixon during a 1958 trip, U.S. State Department and security officials had doubted the wisdom of Kennedy's journey. Although Kennedy had shrugged off their warnings, he also had doubts. But indisputable enthusiasm for the U.S. president and his message from cheering crowds in Venezuela and Colombia heartened Kennedy. "I too found the warmth with which we were received extremely gratifying," Kennedy wrote FDR's postmaster general, Jim Farley. "I think we are beginning to make real strides in Latin America." Kennedy's youth, his Catholicism, his stylish wife (who accompanied him), and, most of all, his transparent wish to improve people's lives made for a genuine outpouring of approval and even affection. "Do you know why those workers and *campesinos* are cheering you like that?" Lleras Camargo asked him. "It's because they believe you are on their side." But although the uncommon expression of genuine affection for an American president by Latin Americans would endure, Kennedy's problems with hemisphere neighbors were far from over.

CHAPTER 14

The Limits of Power

All the President is, is a glorified public relations man who spends his time flattering, kissing and kicking people to get them to do what they are supposed to do anyway.

— Harry S Truman, November 14, 1947

AFTER A YEAR in the presidency, it was easy for Kennedy to think of himself as a crisis manager — a Chief Executive trying to keep problems with the Soviets, Cuba, Laos, and Vietnam from turning into catastrophes, and difficulties with the economy and civil rights from destabilizing the country and embarrassing it overseas. But in the midst of all his difficulties — "the fix that he was in as President of the United States," as Sorensen described it — Kennedy maintained his objectivity and sense of humor. His ability to detach himself and avoid turning a dilemma into a strictly personal challenge was a singularly useful attribute in dealing with awesome burdens. He also took comfort in his faith. During the flight home from Europe in June 1961, where discussions with Khrushchev made a nuclear war seem all too possible, Evelyn Lincoln, while clearing the president's desk of papers, found a note written in Kennedy's hand. It recalled Abraham Lincoln's reassurance to himself on the eve of the Civil War: "I know that there is a God and I see a storm coming. If he has a place for me I am ready."

No rational person faced with possible responsibility for a nuclear war, in which tens of millions of people would die, could live without substantial tension. Yet that tension was never evident from what Kennedy said to friends, all of whom, with the exception of Bobby, he kept at arms' length. There was no one who could readily describe himself as a close Kennedy friend — not any of the

White House insiders, not Sorensen or Schlesinger, nor any of the three members of the Irish mafia, O'Brien, O'Donnell, and Powers. "He and I continued to be close in a peculiarly impersonal way," Sorensen said later. And pre-presidential friends like Billings, Paul Fay, Torby Macdonald, Smathers, and Walton were less close than before.

Although he kept his counsel about his innermost feelings, people around the president detected signs of stress. "He was tired and a little cranky," Evelyn Lincoln recorded in a diary entry describing one instance of the president's response to his burdens. "So much depends on my actions, so I am seeing fewer people, simplifying my life, organizing it so that I am not always on the edge of irritability," he told Dave Powers. In the summer of 1961, after a meeting with the president, Averell Harriman thought Kennedy was "less tense than when I saw him last, but his hands are still constantly in motion." In October 1961, when reporters asked Bobby, "Do you think your brother can handle the Presidency without harming his health?" he replied that the demands on him were no greater than what he had faced during the presidential campaign. But he acknowledged that "the responsibilities are so great and weigh so heavily that it is bound" to have an impact.

Personal problems added to the strains of office, testing Kennedy's physical and emotional endurance. His health troubles were a constant strain on his ability to meet presidential responsibilities. The records of his maladies for August 1961 provide a window into his struggle to remain effectively attentive to the public's business. His stomach and urinary ailments were a daily distraction. On August 9, for example, he complained of "gut" problems, "loose stool," and "cramps." On the morning of the eleventh, he woke up at 5:00 A.M. with abdominal discomfort. On August 23, tests showed an "E. coli" urinary tract infection at the same time he was suffering "acute diarrhea" and the usual back miseries. Codeine sulfate and procaine injections for his pain, penicillin for his infection, cortisone for his Addison's, Bentyl, Lomotil, Transentine, and paregoric for his colitis, testosterone to counter weight loss, and Ritalin for night rest gave him some relief, but they caused him to complain of feeling "tired," "groggy," and "sleepy." "He was being treated with narcotics all the time," Dr. Jeffrey Kelman, a physician who reviewed JFK's medical records said. "He was tired because he was being doped up."

Kennedy's back pain was his greatest physical distraction, not simply because it made it harder to focus his attention but because it was more difficult to hide from a public that thought of him as athletic and robust. Something as simple as bending over a lectern to read a speech caused him terrible pain. Out of sight of the press, he went up and down helicopter stairs one step at a time. Janet Travell worked with engineers to design a reading stand that would reduce the strain, but solving the lectern problem was no cure-all. (His friend Charlie Bartlett thought that diet was at the root of JFK's difficulties. Bartlett saw the richness of the White House food and all that wine and "those damned daiquiris" he was consuming as the culprits.) In June 1961, after the administration's food for peace program director George McGovern had expressed sympathy to Bobby about JFK's suffering, Bobby acknowledged the seriousness of the difficulty. If it were not for Travell's care during the last several years, Bobby wrote, his brother "would not presently be President of the United States." To relieve his suffering, which in the spring and summer of 1961 had become almost unbearable, Travell injected him with procaine two or three times a day. On August 27 she noted in her records that Kennedy's cries of pain in response to the injections brought Jackie in from another room to see what was wrong. Travell's shots were in addition to the concoction of painkillers and amphetamines that Max Jacobson was administering.

White House physician Admiral George Burkley believed that the injections as well as the back braces and positioning devices that immobilized Kennedy were doing more harm than good. Burkley and some Secret Service men who observed the president's difficulties getting up from a chair and his reliance on crutches feared that he would soon be unable to walk and might end up in a wheelchair. During Kennedy's meeting with Harold Macmillan in Bermuda in December, the prime minister recorded that, "in health, I thought the President *not* in good shape. His back is hurting. He cannot sit long without pain." Burkley now insisted that Dr. Hans Kraus, a New York orthopedic surgeon, be consulted. Eugene Cohen, an endocrinologist who had been treating Kennedy's Addison's disease, directly urged him not to rely on Travell for the treatment of his back problems but instead to follow Burkley's recommendations. When Travell resisted Burkley's suggestion that they consult Kraus, Burkley threatened to go to the president.

Kraus confirmed Burkley's worst concerns. A brusque Austrian émigré, Kraus told Kennedy that if he continued the injections and did not begin regular exercise therapy to strengthen his back and abdominal muscles, he would become a cripple. Fearful that Kraus's visits to the White House might trigger press inquiries and unwanted speculation about his health, Kennedy was reluctant to accept his recommendation. The lost medical kit and apparent attempts to steal his medical records during the 1960 campaign had put Kennedy on edge about the potential political harm from opponents armed with information about his health problems.

Kennedy's ailments were not life threatening, unlike those faced by several earlier presidents, principally Cleveland, Wilson, and Franklin Roosevelt. But because ignoring Kraus's advice might have eventually confined him to a wheelchair, Kennedy accepted that something had to be done. He and Kraus agreed to describe the therapy as exercises improving the president's condition from very good to excellent. He began a regimen of three exercise sessions a week in a small White House gymnasium next to the basement swimming pool. Barring Travell from treating Kennedy, Burkley and Kraus used exercises, massages, and heat therapy to ease his back spasms. A telephone in Kraus's car gave the president immediate access to him. Becoming part of Kennedy's daily routine, the exercises reduced his pain and increased his mobility. Performed against a backdrop of his favorite country-and-western and show tunes, the exercise therapy became a pleasant respite from the pressures of daily meetings and demands that crowded Kennedy's schedule. By January 1962, Burkley and Kraus saw him having a better month than at any time in 1961. At the end of February, they described the past four weeks, "medically speaking," as the "most uneventful month since the inauguration; since the 1960 campaign, for that matter." And in April they pronounced his "general condition excellent." Nevertheless, Kennedy remained so concerned to hide the truth about his health that on April 10 O'Donnell ordered Travell and Burkley to "have all medical records, including all notes relating to the health of the President . . . stored in the vault maintained by Mrs. Lincoln."

Jacqueline Kennedy both eased and added to her husband's burdens. Her distaste for politics and the obligations of being First Lady irritated Kennedy. During the presidential campaign, she told Johnson's secretary that she felt "so totally inadequate, so totally at a loss, and I'm pregnant; and I don't know how to do anything." Early in the presidency, Kennedy asked Angier Biddle Duke, White House chief of protocol, to discuss the First Lady's role with Jackie. When Duke explained the usual ceremonial duties of the job and asked her what else she might like to do, she replied, "As little as possible. I'm a mother. I'm a wife. I'm not a public official." Cass Canfield, the editor of *Harper's*, recalled a visit with Jackie at the White House: "I don't think she enjoyed political life much, although she forced herself to become accustomed to it. . . . It was perfectly evident to me that Jackie K was looking forward to a long weekend in Middleburg [Virginia, at the Kennedy's Glen Ora estate] and was more interested in what she was doing there than in the White House." A Secret Service agent, who spoke to journalist Seymour Hersh about his two-year assignment at the Kennedy White House, recalled feeling "sorry for Jackie. She was real lonesome. She seemed sad — just a sad lady."

There is testimony from Jackie's own hand of her initial unhappiness as First Lady. In a June 1962 eleven-page letter to Bill Walton, she asked him to become head of her Fine Arts Commission. She acknowledged that "it would be cruel to put all the ritual and paperwork into your life — Like me — you hate it and 9/10 of it is unnecessary. . . . Before you cringe completely from what looks like a big headache — just let me tell you what I did — I was tired — and I wanted to see my children — so I just told Tish [Baldrige, the White House social secretary] — who nearly died from the shock — that I would NEVER go out — lunches, teas, degrees, speeches, etc. For 2 months it was a flap. Now it is a precedent established. . . . I have learned one thing — and now my life here which I dreaded — and which at first overwhelmed me — is now all under control and the happiest time I have ever known — not for the position — but for the closeness of one's family — the last thing I expected to find in the W. House. . . . And now my life is the way I want it — though deadly little details always do crop up."

One of those "little details" that incensed JFK was Jackie's extravagance. She spent without regard for cost, and Kennedy complained that she was reducing his capital. The official White House entertainment budget could not begin to cover her outlays, which Kennedy then had to pay himself. The overruns bothered him so much that he asked a prominent accountant to help rein in Jackie's spending on ceremonial functions. According to one historian, Jackie's personal expenses in 1961 and 1962 exceeded her husband's annual $100,000 salary; nearly half went for clothing. One day, when a congressman entered the Oval Office for a meeting, an agitated Kennedy showed him $40,000 worth of bills for Jackie's clothes. "What would you do if your wife did that?" JFK asked. That evening Kennedy confronted Jackie in front of Ben Bradlee and his wife. "What about this?" he asked. Jackie lamely countered that she knew nothing about it. After all, she said, it was not as if she had bought a sable coat or anything like it.

Far more distressing, in December 1961 Joe Kennedy suffered a stroke. Although urged by doctors to counter warning signs of such an event by taking anticoagulants, Joe, who disliked being out of control and refused to acknowledge any vulnerability, had rejected the advice. While playing golf at his Palm Beach club during Christmas week 1961, he became ill and was rushed to a local hospital, where a priest administered last rites. When informed that a life-threatening stroke had felled his father, Kennedy flew to his bedside. Although conscious, Joe could not recognize his son for two days. The stroke left Joe paralyzed on his right side and unable to speak clearly. For the remaining eight years of his life, he struggled to talk and walk. His immobility was complicated by two later heart attacks. One can only imagine how much Joe's impaired, barely coherent speech and loss of physical vigor upset his son. A family premium on athleticism, physical beauty, and self-control must have made Joe's dependency on others for his most basic human needs a painful reminder to JFK of his own vulnerability.

One response to all the difficulties crowding in on Kennedy was a more frenetic pace of womanizing than ever. The sources of his pre-presidential affinity for philandering — the examples set by the English aristocrats he admired, like Lord Melbourne, and his father, together with his sense of mortality engendered by health problems and the premature deaths of his brother and sister — still shaped his behavior. His knowledge of how close the world might be to a nuclear war only heightened Kennedy's impulse to live life to the fullest — or with as much private self-indulgence as possible. Truman and Eisenhower, of course, shouldered the same burden without this sort of behavior. But with Kennedy's womanizing an already well-developed habit, the doomsday prospect may have added to his rationalization for what he probably would have been doing anyway.

Kennedy's womanizing had, of course, always been a form of amusement, but it now also gave him a release from unprecedented daily tensions. Kennedy had affairs with several women, including Pamela Turnure, Jackie's press secretary; Mary Pinchot Meyer, Ben

Bradlee's sister-in-law; two White House secretaries playfully dubbed Fiddle and Faddle; Judith Campbell Exner, whose connections to mob figures like Sam Giancana made her the object of FBI scrutiny; and Mimi Beardsley, a "tall, slender, beautiful" nineteen-year-old college sophomore and White House intern, who worked in the press office during two summers. (She "had no skills," a member of the press staff recalled. "She couldn't type.") There were also Hollywood stars and starlets and call girls paid by Dave Powers, the court jester and facilitator of Kennedy's indulgences, who arranged trysts in hotels and swimming pools in California, Florida, and at the White House.

There was something almost madcap about Kennedy's behavior. He told Harold Macmillan during their Bermuda meeting in December 1961 that if he did not have a woman every three days, he would have a terrible headache. But sometimes his trysts involved more than sex. Tensions in his marriage and his public position, which barred a divorce, may have made his affair with Mary Meyer understandable. Meyer was a beautiful, intelligent, and sophisticated woman from the politically prominent Pinchot family. More important, she was a source of comfort to him. "He could enjoy life with her," JFK biographer Herbert Parmet has written. "He could talk in ways she understood, and their trust was mutual. . . . She was an important support. She understood all about the pompous asses he had to put up with. When he was with her, the rest of the world could go to hell. He could laugh with her at the absurdity of the things he saw all around his center of power." Meyer believed that Kennedy loved her and that were it not for uncontrollable circumstances they would have been permanently together. Kennedy apparently thought otherwise, saying more than once to Ben Bradlee, "Mary would be rough to live with." But there was no doubt that Meyer meant something more to him than many of the other women did.

Kennedy also must have taken comfort from the fact that he was able to hide his affair with Mary Meyer from Ben Bradlee. Bradlee said that he had "heard stories about how he had slept around in his bachelor days. . . . I heard people described as 'one of Jack's girlfriends' from time to time. It was never topic A among my reporter friends, while he was a candidate. . . . In those days reporters did not feel compelled to conduct full FBI field investigations about a politician friend. My friends have always had trouble believing my innocence of his activities, especially after it was revealed that . . . Mary

Meyer had been one of Kennedy's girlfriends. So be it. I can only repeat my ignorance of Kennedy's sex life, and state that I am appalled by the details that have emerged, appalled by the recklessness, by the subterfuge that must have been involved."

If Kennedy had concerns about Jackie's feelings, she helped him minimize them by discreetly avoiding a head-on clash with him over his womanizing. But she had no illusions about her husband's behavior. At the end of their visit to Canada in 1961, while the president and Jackie were saying good-bye to people in a receiving line that included a "blonde bimbo," as JFK's military aide General Godfrey McHugh described her, Jackie "wheeled around in fury" and said in French to McHugh and Dave Powers standing behind her, "Isn't it bad enough that you solicit this woman for my husband, but then you insult me by asking me to shake her hand!" One day, as she escorted a Paris journalist around the White House, she said to him in French, as they walked past "Fiddle," "This is the girl who supposedly is sleeping with my husband." Jackie seemed to have assumed that her remark would not shock a sophisticated Frenchman, but he said to one of Salinger's aides, "What is going on here?"

Jackie's pattern was similar to Rose's denial of Joe's affairs and her refusal to confront him. Jackie made a point of keeping Kennedy's staff informed about her absences from and returns to the White House so that, as one naval aide put it, the president could get his "friends" out of the way. This is not to say that Jackie approved of her husband's infidelity. It obviously made her angry and unhappy, but she chose to live with it.

Did potential whistle-blowers in the press put Kennedy in political jeopardy? He did not think so. In 1962, he continued to assume that while fringe newspapers and magazines might pick up on gossip about his sex life, the mainstream press would hold to traditional limits when discussing a president's private behavior. He received some reassurance from a case involving one of his principal aides, a married man whose girlfriend had become pregnant. The press office received word that a reporter was going to ask Kennedy about the affair at a news conference. Kennedy took special care that day to call on only journalists he trusted, and the threat never materialized. Besides, as Salinger aide Barbara Gamarekian concluded, so many people in the press were sleeping around that for them to have gone after Kennedy would have been an act of embarrassing hypocrisy.

Kennedy also sent signals that the press should be careful. In February 1962 *Time* did an article that referred to a *Gentlemen's Quarterly* cover story about the president. Kennedy called *Time* correspondent Hugh Sidey to the White House. "I never posed for any picture," he berated Sidey. "Any President who would pose for *GQ* [a magazine allegedly with special appeal to homosexuals] would be out of his mind. . . . I'm not kidding," Kennedy said menacingly. "I'm goddamn sick and tired of it. This is all a lie. . . . What are you trying to do to me? What do you think you're doing?" Kennedy intimidated Sidey into promising a retraction.

Similarly, in May 1962, after a well-publicized forty-fifth-birthday party for JFK at Madison Square Garden, during which movie actress Marilyn Monroe entertained the president in a skin-tight, silver-sequined dress with a breathless rendering of "Happy Birthday," rumors of a Kennedy-Monroe affair threatened to become an embarrassment to the White House. Kennedy enlisted a former New York reporter who was a member of his administration in a campaign to squelch the talk. He asked his aide to tell editors that he was speaking for the president and that stories about him and Marilyn simply were not true.

Kennedy also believed that reporters liked him and would be reluctant to embarrass him by publishing stories about his sex life. Of course, he understood that a president's relations with the press are always to some degree adversarial. But throughout his political career and even more so when he began running for president, he made himself available to the press, and by so doing created subtle ties that reporters were loathe to undermine. At the 1956 convention, when Kennedy, in T-shirt and undershorts, began to leave his hotel bedroom to take a phone call in the sitting room, an aide said, "You can't go out there in your shorts, there are reporters and photographers there." "I know these fellows," Kennedy replied loudly enough for them to hear. "They're not going to take advantage of me."

Kennedy's wit and articulateness especially endeared him to those journalists who had soldiered through the Eisenhower years with a president who often left the press puzzling over what he had actually said or meant to say. Two taped TV specials on President's Day that gave Americans an unprecedented view of Kennedy at work, and a February 1962 guided tour by Jackie of the executive mansion that described the restoration of the White House heightened media regard for the Kennedys and made it unlikely that reporters would debunk JFK's attractive image as a family man.

Kennedy's popularity with the press and public also partly rested on the glamour he and Jackie brought to the White House. Though most Americans did not think of themselves as connoisseurs of highbrow culture, they saw the president and First Lady as American aristocrats. Their stylish White House soirees — the president in white tie and tails and Mrs. Kennedy in the most fashionable of gowns — interest in the arts, and association with the best and the brightest at home and abroad made the country feel good about itself. To millions of Americans, under JFK the United States was reestablishing itself not only as the world's premier power but also as the new center of progressive good taste, a nation with not only the highest standard of living but also a president and First Lady who compared favorably with sophisticated European aristocrats. However overdrawn some of this may have been, it was excellent politics for a Kennedy White House working to maintain its hold on the public imagination.

By contrast with the press and public, Kennedy was not so sure he could control the FBI. After Hoover made clear to Kennedy in March 1962 that he had information about Judith Campbell Exner's ties to mob figures, Kennedy stopped seeing her. Nor apparently would he take her phone calls. Hoover did not, as Johnson told some reporters, have "Jack Kennedy by the balls." Hoover was past retirement age, and his continuation in office depended on Kennedy's goodwill. Still, Kennedy might have assumed that if Hoover was ready to call it quits, he would try to take him down before leaving.

Did Kennedy's compulsive womanizing distract him from public business? Some historians think so, especially when it comes to Vietnam. Kennedy's reluctance, however, to focus the sort of attention on Vietnam he gave to Berlin or other foreign and domestic concerns is not evidence of a distracted president, but of a determination to keep Vietnam from becoming more important to his administration than he wished it to be. Certainly, when one reviews Kennedy's White House schedules, he does not seem to have been derelict about anything he considered a major problem. One can certainly argue that his judgment was imperfect about what should have been his highest priorities. A number of domestic matters received relatively less attention than foreign policy issues. But the supposition that he was too busy chasing women or satisfying his sexual passions to attend to important presidential business is not borne out by the record of his daily activities. And according to

Richard Reeves, another Kennedy historian, the womanizing generally "took less time than tennis." By the spring of 1962, after fifteen months in the White House, Kennedy had little reason to believe that his philandering was an impediment to his ability to govern and lead.

BY AUGUST 1961, Heller and Federal Reserve chairman Martin had told Kennedy that the economy was in a vigorous recovery like those that had followed the two previous recessions in the fifties. Martin believed that the economy was in better shape than it had been for a long time and that the country could look forward to "a non-inflationary period of expansion and growth." Holding down deficits and inflation now replaced talk of tax cuts as higher priorities.

Corporate views of Kennedy as a traditional "tax and spend" Democrat had made him eager to convince the business community that his administration was not "engaged upon a reckless program of [defense] spending beyond control and of artificially easy money." In September 1961, he instructed Heller, budget director David Bell, and White House aide Fred Dutton to describe expanded spending on defense as fueling the recovery. He also asked them to rebut articles in *Reader's Digest* and *Life* describing a large increase in welfare programs. The *Digest's* assertion that his programs would cost taxpayers "18 billion dollars annually in a few years," was, he stated, "wholly untrue and we ought to make him [the article's author] eat it."

Kennedy's courting of business partly rested on doubts that the economy would hold up through the next presidential election. "On a number of occasions . . . you have expressed concern about the *duration* of the current business upswing," the CEA told him in September. Kennedy wanted assurances that the economy would be "on the upgrade in the summer and fall of 1964." Heller responded that to ensure against a recession then "would require action in 1962." He saw the need for a bill promoting capital or infrastructure improvements and "a flexible tax proposal" triggering tax cuts. "Lord, that's a tough one," Kennedy replied. Kennedy feared that legislation requiring tax cuts in response to economic slowing would be seen as restricting congressional control over the economy or trampling on Congress's "fiscal prerogatives." Moreover, in the fall of 1961, Kennedy continued to worry that tax cuts would increase deficits and mark him out as a liberal Keynesian at odds with balanced budgets and fiscal conservatives.

Kennedy's two greatest economic worries between September 1961 and June 1962 were the country's balance-of-payment problems, which reduced the strength of the dollar, and inflation. With inflation running at only a little over 1 percent a year since 1958, most commentators were hard-pressed to understand Kennedy's concern. But his worry, which the CEA shared, rested largely on the conviction that any sign of "upward price movements would tilt the Fed, the Treasury, and the conservatives in Congress against an expansionary fiscal policy and the reduction of unemployment." As for balance-of-payment issues, the fear was that foreign holders of dollars might exercise their right to convert them into gold, causing a destabilizing drain on U.S. gold reserves and diminished confidence in the greenback. Sorensen recalled Kennedy's near obsession with the issue: " 'I know everyone thinks I worry about this too much,' he said to me one day as we pored over what seemed like the millionth report on the subject. 'But if there is ever a run on the bank, and I have to devalue the dollar or bring home our troops, as the British did, I'm the one who will take the heat. Besides it's a club that de Gaulle and all the others hang over my head. Any time there's a crisis or a quarrel, they can cash in all their dollars and where are we?' "

Kennedy's balance-of-payments concern was a case study in applying a lesson of the past inappropriately to a present dilemma. And the conviction that something had to be done about the problem presented, in Heller's words, "a cruel dilemma." Domestic economic expansion would increase imports and temporarily worsen the balance of payments. But checking the outflow of dollars by raising interest rates and taxes and cutting government expenditures would impede or stop the domestic recovery and increase unemployment. "The pressures to grasp the second horn of the dilemma," Heller warned, "are going to be very strong. But we [at the CEA] urge you to resist them. We believe that it would be shortsighted folly to sacrifice the domestic economy for quick improvement in the balance of payments."

Nevertheless, demands for action on the problem continued from Federal Reserve chairman Martin, Treasury officials, and Kennedy himself. At a meeting in late August, Martin described the balance of payments as the economic "cloud on the horizon," and Dillon "agreed with Martin that we must be very careful to present a posture of responsibility in fiscal and financial affairs in order to keep our European friends from becoming jittery about the dollar."

It was apparent to those at this meeting that Kennedy was "greatly concerned about the future of the balance of payments and that this was the main economic problem that was really worrying both Dillon and the President."

But despite his constant attention to the difficulty, requesting regular reports on estimated gold losses and discussing draconian reforms, Kennedy would not sacrifice domestic recovery for greater dollar stability. He signed on to several stopgap measures — increased foreign buying of military equipment, reduced reliance of U.S. agencies on overseas offices, mandatory use of American goods for foreign aid, more tourism to the United States, and systematic expansion of foreign trade — that helped reduce the loss of U.S. gold reserves from $1.977 billion to $459 million in the ten months after January 1961. But beyond joking that he might reduce the outflow of gold to France by keeping his father at home and encouraging his wife to see America first, that was all Kennedy would do until a more effective solution to the difficulty arrived with the Trade Expansion Act he put before Congress in his January 1962 State of the Union Message.

WHEN KENNEDY ASKED CONGRESS in July 1961 for increased defense outlays to meet the Berlin crisis, he had announced a potential tax increase in January 1962 if it were needed to maintain a balanced budget and low inflation. He gave especially close attention to steel prices, which he saw as the major threat to price stability. The industry bulked so large "in the manufacturing sector of the economy" that it could "upset the price applecart all by itself," Heller told him. Between 1947 and 1958, Heller added, "forty percent of the rise in the Wholesale Price Index was due to the fact that steel prices *rose* more than the average of all other prices."

Armed with statistics from the CEA, Kennedy began "jawboning" the steel industry not to raise prices after a scheduled October 1, 1961, increase. In September, he sent letters to the CEOs of the twelve largest steel companies and to the Steelworkers Union urging responsible price and wage actions in negotiations that were about to begin for a new contract. When the steel companies agreed not to increase their prices in the last quarter of 1961, Kennedy hoped that both sides in the negotiations would follow his lead on holding down inflation.

But reactions from labor and corporate chiefs to Kennedy's pressure were more antagonistic than cooperative. When Arthur Goldberg lectured delegates at an AFL-CIO convention in December on the need for wage restraints and nonstrike settlements, they booed him publicly and privately warned him not to interfere in union negotiations with industry. Similarly, business chiefs applauded the administration's pressure on labor but rejected any government say in determining prices in 1962.

Despite business-labor resistance, Kennedy refused to back off. If the steelworkers struck, half a million workers would be idle, plus thousands more in mining and transportation. Besides, Kennedy believed he could effectively press the case for a settlement. In December 1961, Goldberg met with Dave McDonald, the head of the steelworkers, and R. Conrad Cooper, U.S. Steel Corporation's vice president for industrial relations. He urged a settlement as being in the national interest and warned that obstructionism by either side would antagonize the administration. At the same time, Kennedy addressed the AFL-CIO's annual convention in Miami. Putting aside his text to speak more informally and passionately, he emphasized "the heavy responsibility" labor shouldered for the country's well-being in this "most critical time" of global challenges. His praise for America's free labor movement found a warm reception. "After your speech," Arthur Goldberg told Kennedy, "President Meany stated: '. . . We are delighted that we have a Chief Executive in the White House who understands the ideals and the aspirations of our people . . . and merely say to you, Don't worry about us. We will cooperate 1,000 percent.'"

In January 1962, Kennedy met secretly with Roger Blough, chairman of U.S. Steel's board, McDonald, and Goldberg at the White House. He persuaded the two sides to enter into early negotiations to work out a noninflationary agreement. The discussions from the middle of February to the beginning of April produced a contract with a ten-cent-an-hour boost in pension contributions and steps to reduce unemployment among steelworkers but no wage increase.

Kennedy, Goldberg, and Heller were "jubilant." The president publicly congratulated both sides for "the early and responsible settlement," calling their contract "a document of high industrial statesmanship." They had fully justified his belief that they would put the national interest ahead of any selfish interest. He also said that the agreement was "obviously non-inflationary and should provide a solid base for continued price stability."

But on April 10, the steel companies broke faith with Kennedy by announcing a 3.5 percent price hike. Blough, who received an appointment to see Kennedy that afternoon, brought a copy of a statement on the increases that was being released as they met. Kennedy was understandably furious. "You have made a terrible mistake," he told Blough. "You double-crossed me." (Kennedy told Kenny O'Donnell that talking to Blough was like interacting with "a wet fish," nothing but silence and formal responses.) The country now seemed likely to suffer inflation and an economic slowdown. In addition, the unions felt deceived and betrayed, and Kennedy looked weak and ineffective. Having worked so hard to repair the damage to his standing after the Bay of Pigs and the difficult exchanges with Khrushchev at Vienna, he found himself once more on the defensive — a Chief Executive unable to bend a formidable adversary to his will.

At a meeting of White House aides, Bobby, and the CEA following Blough's departure, the president was seething. Those present had never seen him so angry. O'Donnell remembered Kennedy as "livid with rage — white with anger." He let off steam by almost furious motion in his rocking chair, pacing the room, and scathing remarks about Blough and other steel executives who were falling into line with U.S. Steel's increases. "He fucked me. They fucked us and we've got to try to fuck them," he exclaimed. Steel had "made a fool of him." "My father told me businessmen were all pricks, but I didn't really believe he was right until now. . . . God, I hate the bastards." He told Dave McDonald, "You've been screwed and I've been screwed." He suspected a conspiracy with Nixon. Steel had promised Nixon "not to raise prices until after the election," he told Ben Bradlee. "Then came the recession, and they didn't want to raise prices. Then when we pulled out of the recession they said, 'Let Kennedy squeeze the unions first, before we raise prices. So I squeezed McDonald. . . . And they kicked us right in the balls. . . . The question really is: are we supposed to sit there and take a cold deliberate fucking?" Goldberg was "terribly depressed," and told Kennedy, "Shit, I might as well quit. There's nothing I can do now."

But their anger was a source of energy, too. "This is war," Goldberg said. And Kennedy began plotting the campaign to force capitulation. The White House leaked Kennedy's remarks about businessmen, but cleaned up the language a bit by calling them "sons of bitches" rather than pricks. (Kennedy himself never remembered whether he called them "sons of bitches, or bastards, or pricks.") The next day Kennedy used a press conference to denounce the companies. He was determined first to bring public opinion to his side. His remarks were caustic. The price rise was "a wholly un-justifiable and irresponsible defiance of the public interest," he said. Citing statistics to demonstrate that there was "no justification for an increase in steel prices," he denounced steel's "ruthless disregard of their public responsibilities." The steel companies were not only playing fast and loose with the country's economic health, they were also jeopardizing its national security.

"In this serious hour in our Nation's history," Kennedy declared, "when we are confronted with grave crises in Berlin and Southeast Asia, when we are devoting our energies to economic recovery and stability, when we are asking reservists to leave their homes and fam-ilies for months on end and servicemen to risk their lives — and four were killed in the last two days in Vietnam — and asking union members to hold down their wage requests at a time when restraint and sacrifice are being asked of every citizen, the American people will find it hard, as I do, to accept a situation in which a tiny hand-ful of steel executives whose pursuit of private power and profit exceeds their sense of public responsibility can show such utter con-tempt for the interests of 185 million Americans."

The public left no doubt where it stood. By a 58 to 22 percent margin, it approved of the president's pressure to force the steel companies to reverse course. Not surprisingly, two-thirds of the nation's blue-collar workers backed Kennedy. And even business and professional people came down on his side by 45 to 34 percent. His general approval rating stood at 73 percent. If Kennedy were running against Nixon now, Gallup asked, whom would you favor? Two-thirds of the respondents chose Kennedy.

Kennedy was not confident he could force a price rollback, but he felt compelled to try. "I can't go make a speech like that . . . and then go sit on my ass," he told Bradlee. Bobby agreed, seeing inac-tion as "bad for the country — it would have been bad internally — and it would have been bad all around the world, because it would have indicated that the country was run by a few manufacturers. I don't think we would ever have reestablished ourselves." Kennedy ordered Bobby to have his antitrust division investigate possible steel collusion, urged Congress to conduct its own investigation, and directed Solicitor General Archibald Cox to draft legislation requir-ing a rollback. Anyone in the administration acquainted with a steel executive was directed to pressure him. The Defense Department

began shifting contracts to smaller steel companies that were holding the price line. Bobby turned loose the FBI to speak to steel executives and reporters about price-fixing. An FBI agent phoned an A.P.
journalist at 3:00 A.M. and insisted on interviewing him an hour
later at his house about a story he had written on the steel companies. Bobby later described how they went for broke in investigating
the steel executives: "Their expense accounts and where they'd been
and what they were doing. I picked up all their records and told the
FBI to interview them all — march into their offices the next day. We
weren't going to go slowly. . . . All of them were hit with meetings
the next morning by agents. All of them were subpoenaed for their
personal records. All of them were subpoenaed for their company
records. . . . It was a tough way to operate. But under the circumstances, we couldn't afford to lose."

Kennedy also enlisted Clark Clifford in the campaign. "Can't
you just see Clifford outlining the possible courses of action the
Government can take if they showed signs of not moving?" Kennedy
asked navy undersecretary Paul "Red" Fay. "Do you know what
you're doing when you start bucking the power of the President of
the United States? I don't think U.S. Steel or any other of the major
steel companies wants to have Internal Revenue agents checking all
the expense accounts of their top executives. . . . Too many hotel
bills and night club expenses would be hard to get by the weekly
wives' bridge group out at the Country Club."

Convinced that they were acting in the national interest and
knowing the public was decisively on their side, the Kennedys felt
free to pressure the steel executives by all possible means — even if
it meant crossing legal boundaries. Since they believed that Blough
and his collaborators had acted ruthlessly, they saw no reason to
worry about legal niceties or be less than ruthless in return. Besides,
as Kennedy's jocular comments on Bobby's actions demonstrated,
he and his brother enjoyed the forceful response they gave the steel
men. It was all reminiscent of their college sporting contests in
which the toughest competitor won. And they had won.

The pressure was more than the steel industry could bear. Inland
Steel, the most productive and profitable of all the companies, led
by Joseph Block, a Blough adversary and a Kennedy admirer,
declared that it felt very strongly about holding down prices. When
Kaiser and Armco agreed, and Bethlehem, the second-largest company, fearing losses to competitors with lower prices, announced a

change of policy, all the other offenders gave in. Blough tried to save face and profits by asking how Kennedy would respond to a 50 percent reduction in the price hike, but Kennedy insisted on a full rollback. He instructed his aides to guard against any public gloating. He would have enough difficulties with the hard feelings bound to surface in the business community and among conservatives over his take-no-prisoners approach to the steel executives. But in private, he could not resist some mirth over his victory. When Schlesinger asked him how a White House meeting with Blough on April 17, four days after the reversal, had gone, Kennedy, remembering Grant and Lee at Appomattox, joked, "I told him that his men could keep their horses for the spring plowing." And at a private White House dinner with family members and close friends, Kennedy offered a toast to Bobby. He reported a conversation with Republic Steel president Jim Patton: "I was telling Patton what a son of a bitch he was," Kennedy said to much laughter, "and he was proving it. Patton asked me, 'Why is it that all the telephone calls of all the steel executives in all the country are being tapped?' And I told him that . . . he was being wholly unfair to the attorney general and that I was sure that it wasn't true. And he asked me, 'Why is it that all the income tax returns of all the steel executives in all the country are being scrutinized?' And I told him that, too, was wholly unfair, that the attorney general wouldn't do any such thing," Kennedy said with mock horror. "And then I called the attorney general and asked him why he was tapping the telephones of all the steel executives and examining all [their] tax returns . . . and the attorney general told me that was wholly untrue and unfair. And of course, Patton was right." To the further amusement of the guests, Bobby interrupted to explain, "They were mean to my brother. They can't do that to my brother."

In public, Kennedy tried to ease tensions with the country's business leaders. At an April 18 press conference, he announced that the administration "harbors no ill will against any individual, any industry, corporation, or segment of the American economy." He decried feelings of hostility or vindictiveness as destructive to economic growth and price stability. "When a mistake has been retracted and the public interest preserved, nothing is to be gained from further public recrimination. . . . And we agree on the necessity of preserving the Nation's confidence in free, private, collective bargaining and price decisions, holding the role of Government to the minimum level needed to protect the public interest." In a speech to the chamber of commerce at the end of the month, he discussed present and future government relations with business and tried to clear away "the dust of controversy that occasionally rises to obscure the basic issues and the basic relationships." He assured his audience that he did not wish to add decisions about prices for particular goods to the burdens he confronted as president. He also assured them that no administration could survive if it were anti-business and anti-growth. Quoting the Bible, he described "'a time for every purpose under the heaven . . . a time to cast away stones and a time to gather stones together.' And ladies and gentlemen, I believe it is time for us all to gather stones together to build this country as it must be built in the coming years."

But businessmen and conservative publications were unforgiving. They complained of price-fixing by the White House and the administration's police state tactics. They compared Kennedy to Mussolini, called his actions "quasi-Fascist" and better suited to the Soviet Union than a free enterprise America. Conservative Arizona senator Barry Goldwater described the president as trying to "socialize the business of the country." Businessmen proudly wore buttons identifying them as members of the "S.O.B. Club." Bumper stickers announced: "Help Kennedy Stamp Out Free Enterprise," and "I Miss Ike — Hell, I Even Miss Harry." On May 28, when the Dow Jones Industrial Average fell almost 6.5 percent, the greatest one-day decline since the market collapse on October 28, 1929, investors blamed it on the administration's "anti-business" views and the steel rollback in particular. Wall Street joked that the drop caused Joe to speak for the first time since his stroke: "To think I voted for that son-of-a-bitch."

When the White House rashly canceled its subscription to the *New York Herald Tribune* in anger over stories that Kennedy saw as "patently false articles" — including an accusation that his steel actions would win Khrushchev's approval — he gracefully acknowledged his mistake to the press. "Well, I am reading more and enjoying it less," he told a May news conference. The press was "doing their task, as a critical branch, the fourth estate. And I am attempting to do mine. And we are going to live together for a period, and then go our separate ways," he said to the amusement of the reporters. Kennedy also had to defend the FBI's "nocturnal activities" or post-midnight interviews with reporters about their sources for stories on price-fixing.

Whatever Kennedy's overreach in pressuring steel into a stand-down, it would have all but crippled his presidency to have passively accepted a price increase that could have deepened the country's economic problems. And regardless of what it did to the economy, accepting the increase would have made him look weak, and, in the eyes of many abroad, like a cipher who took his marching orders from business moguls. Worse, it would have added to the feeling in Moscow that he could be had — that, as Theodore Roosevelt said of McKinley, he had the backbone of a chocolate éclair. Meeting the challenge from the steel executives head-on was possibly even more essential for the success of Kennedy's foreign policy than for the management of his many problems at home, a classic example of a challenge in one sphere whose ultimate effects are felt in another.

AT THE END OF 1961, Richard Neustadt gave the White House a one-year assessment of Kennedy's presidential leadership. The president had established himself as an impressive leader, Neustadt asserted. His high Gallup approval ratings were "no accident," but the product of smart politics, which was "an enormous asset for the President *and* for our government." Part of Kennedy's success resulted from his sensible efforts "to scale down public expectations of the future, to promote realism about our situation in the world, our power and our prospects. For the first time since World War II," Neustadt wrote, "we've been offered no 'light at the end of the tunnel,' no assurance that this *next* effort . . . will turn the tide or do the trick. Instead, the theme has been cool, relatively unimpassioned: if we persevere we *may* end neither red nor dead. . . . From what I can observe of his sense of timing, Cuba aside, Kennedy strikes me more than ever as the ablest politician who has emerged in our age-group, very conceivably the ablest since FDR."

Neustadt's analysis gratified Kennedy, but at the start of 1962, he understood that he was a long way from significant presidential achievements. And before he could lay claim to noteworthy gains, he would have to hold the Congress for his party, and — more important but less likely — help elect additional cooperative congress-men and senators. History made it seem like a nearly impossible task: Only once in the last hundred years — 1934 — had a president managed to strengthen his hold on Congress in midterm elections. To have any chance, Kennedy believed that he would have to shift ground from his first year and give higher priority to domestic issues than to foreign affairs and convince Americans that effective reforms depended on their giving him a more supportive Congress.

Kennedy's State of the Union Message on January 11 reflected his eagerness for domestic advance. "Our overriding obligation in the months ahead," he declared, "is to fulfill the world's hopes by fulfilling our own faith." Unless we could achieve our national ideals, others around the globe would see no reason to follow our lead. During the past year, the economy had left "the valley of recession" for "the high road of recovery and growth." America's economy, which Khrushchev had called a "stumbling horse," was "racing to new records in consumer spending, labor income, and industrial production." Yet unemployment remained at over 6 percent, and legislation to train people for a changed job market coupled with an 8 percent investment tax credit to spur greater productivity were essential to additional economic expansion. And to bar against another recession, Kennedy asked for standby authority to reduce taxes and speed up federally aided capital-improvement programs, and for permanent higher unemployment benefits. Kennedy also asked for help in achieving a balanced budget, urban renewal, and a new comprehensive farm program to sustain production and conservation. These measures would show the world that "a free economy need not be an unstable economy," but the most productive and "most stable form of organization yet fashioned by man."

Civil rights, health and welfare, and education reforms were necessary complements to economic advance. Full and equal rights — to vote, to travel without hindrance across state lines, and to have access to free public education — required fresh actions by the executive, the courts, and the Congress. The acts of every branch of government, Kennedy said, should make the hundredth anniversary in January 1963 of Lincoln's Emancipation Proclamation a demonstration that "righteousness does exalt a nation." Help to the indigent, stressing "services instead of support, rehabilitation instead of relief, and training for useful work instead of prolonged dependency," would mark America out as a compassionate nation. So would improvements in the country's health care system, including the creation of National Institutes of Health to expand research, a mass immunization program to stamp out polio, diphtheria, whooping cough, and tetanus among children, improved food and drug regulation, and, most of all, health insurance for the aged. Education was no less important. Kennedy declared his intention to press the case for a program to overcome illiteracy of eight million Americans and to renew his call for federal aid to elementary, secondary, and higher education. "Civilization," Kennedy said, quoting H. G. Wells, "is a race between education and catastrophe. It is up to you in this Congress to determine the winner of that race."

In the following week, Kennedy held two White House meetings with congressional Democrats to arm them for the 1962 elections and encourage their cooperation with his agenda in the coming congressional session. He pointed to favorable Gallup polls: a 77 percent approval rating; 56 percent who believed that they had an improved standard of living; and millions of Americans who supported welfare reforms, health insurance for the elderly, and federal aid to education. An opinion survey that indicated a 60 to 40 percent split favoring Democratic control of Congress gave Kennedy additional ammunition to press for greater cooperation than in the previous year.

In a document (stamped "Propaganda") describing the challenge in the House and the Senate to win majority votes and the first session's major accomplishments, Kennedy emphasized the difficulties of overcoming a southern Democratic–Republican coalition, and the administration's considerable success in passing thirty-three major bills, compared with eleven during FDR's 1933 session and twelve in Ike's 1953 session. Journalists made privy to the administration's argument responded skeptically, pointing out that Kennedy had lost his aid to education and Medicare fights and that many of the Kennedy laws were not New Frontier measures but extensions of earlier programs. Nevertheless, Kennedy put a briefing paper before the legislators making the case for his successes: No one could attack his government for communist subversion, corruption, inflation, or appeasement; he expected to balance the budget in fiscal 1963; he had avoided a Korea-type war; defense appropriations were up 15 percent; the religion and youth arguments against him had all but disappeared; prosperity was increasing; and farmers were less discontented.

For all Kennedy's efforts to talk up his legislative accomplishments, a defensive tone revealed his own doubts and his limited interest in domestic affairs. And despite leading his State of the Union Message with a discussion of domestic issues, he focused nearly 60 percent of the address on international affairs: national security, the U.N., Latin America, new and developing nations, the Atlantic community, the balance of payments, and trade.

The discrepancy was further reflected in Kennedy's limited domestic accomplishments during the first half of 1962. His strong remarks about civil rights in his State of the Union speech did not translate into significant gains between January and July. Limited public support for aggressive actions made the White House reluctant to ask for a civil rights bill or to step up the use of Executive Orders. In April, when Gallup asked, "What do you think is the most important problem facing the country?" only 6 percent said racial problems or segregation, compared with 63 percent who answered, "War, peace, international tension." In May, 67 percent of an opinion survey thought that the administration was pushing integration either enough or too fast; only 11 percent believed it was not fast enough. Kennedy was too much of a politician to challenge such numbers, however sad was the nation's seeming indifference to the moral imperative of ending segregation.

The Kennedys remained sensitive to black complaints about ongoing racial bias, but they continued to hope that executive action would be sufficient. Although Johnson and the CEEO had managed to get a majority of the government's largest contractors to sign up for the Plans for Progress program, by the fall of 1961, the *New York Times* reported that solid gains in black employment were not evident. One CEEO staff member described company commitments to more jobs for blacks as not "worth the paper they were written on, they were just absolutely meaningless documents." Kennedy himself worried that Plans would "turn out to be a fraud or a delusion or an illusion, that there were a lot of plans signed and then no Negroes would be hired." A staff shake-up in the program and a shift from voluntary to compulsory compliance made for some advances in black hiring but hardly enough to make a dent in the double-digit unemployment of African Americans, twice that of whites.

Although the bad news overshadowed the modest gains in the program, it was the first time any White House had made a serious effort to compel integration by companies on government contracts. Moreover, Plans for Progress heightened public consciousness of racial bias, which excluded blacks from jobs or kept them in the lowest ranks of company employees. The administration also prided itself on other substantive and symbolic civil rights initiatives: an advisory committee on integration in the armed forces; Justice Department suits in behalf of school integration in seven southern states; investigations and suits in seventy-five southern counties over excluding blacks from the polls; and a successful appeal to use the 1957 Civil Rights Act against arbitrary state prosecutions of blacks. At the same time, the Kennedys resigned their memberships in the Metropolitan and Cosmos clubs in Washington, D.C., in protest against a whites-only policy and pressured restaurant owners along Highway 40 in Maryland north of Baltimore, the most traveled route by African diplomats between Washington and the United Nations, to serve customers without regard for race.

At the same time, however, the White House continued to be less than forthcoming in fulfilling its promise to integrate federally financed housing. In the fall of 1961, Wofford told Kennedy that his housing pledge was his most specific commitment on civil rights and "certainly the best remembered by Negroes." A failure to issue an Executive Order "would seriously jeopardize all our gains to date." But in January 1962, when a reporter asked Kennedy why he intended to postpone this integration order "for some time," he answered defensively that his administration had "made more progress in the field of civil rights on a whole variety of fronts than were made in the last 8 years." He added that he would meet his responsibilities on the housing matter when he believed it would be in the public interest. In April, he publicly welcomed a Civil Rights Commission inquiry into equal opportunity in housing in Washington, D.C., but continued to resist pressure for an Executive Order. In August, when a White House counsel prepared an Executive Order, the president asked that the document remain confidential; he continued to believe that it would undermine his 1962 legislative program and weaken Democratic chances in November by antagonizing southern congressmen and voters. Allowing politics to trump a transparently moral commitment served neither JFK's legislative agenda nor his reputation for acting in behalf of social arrangements that did the nation's democratic traditions proud.

Civil rights advocates were also ambivalent about the administration's record on judicial appointments. During the first eighteen months of his term, the president nominated Thurgood Marshall to join William H. Hastie as the only blacks ever chosen for appointment to the U.S. Circuit Court of Appeals. Moreover, in the spring of 1962, when Kennedy had the chance to make his first Supreme Court selection, he considered nominating Hastie, but Chief Justice Earl Warren and Associate Justice William O. Douglas opposed him on the grounds that Hastie was insufficiently liberal. Kennedy then turned to Deputy Attorney General Byron White, but told Schle-singer, "I figure that I will have several more appointments before I am through, and I mean to appoint [Paul] Freund [at the Harvard Law School], Arthur Goldberg and Bill Hastie."

Limited actions and hopes to expand the number of African Americans on the bench, however, could not balance the five south-ern racists Kennedy appointed to federal judgeships: Clarence All-good and Walter Gewin of Alabama, Robert Elliott of Georgia, E. Gordon West of Louisiana, and William Harold Cox of Missis-sippi. During their tenure, they did all in their power to obstruct school integration and deny voting rights to blacks. West dismissed the Supreme Court's 1954 *Brown* v. *Board of Education* ruling as "one of the truly regrettable decisions of all time." Cox, whose opinions were often reversed by higher courts, was an even more outspoken opponent of civil rights. His injudiciousness was stunning. In open court, he shouted at black plaintiffs that they were "a bunch of nig-gers . . . acting like a bunch of chimpanzees."

None of this should have surprised the president and attorney general. Early on, NAACP executive secretary Roy Wilkins had wired the president about Cox: On the bench, he would stand for "the mores of 1861. For 986,000 Negro Mississippians Judge Cox will be another strand in their barbed wire fence, another cross over their weary shoulders and another rock in the road up which their young people must struggle." Furthermore, Bobby had interviewed Cox at the Justice Department. "We sat on my couch in my office, and I talked to him. And I said that the great reservation that I had was whether he'd enforce the law and live up to the Constitution. . . . He assured me that he would. He was really, I think, the only judge whom I've ever had that kind of conversation with. He was very gra-cious. He said that there wouldn't be any problem. . . . I was con-vinced that he was honest with me and he wasn't."

There was much more at work here than Bobby's naïveté. The tradition of deferring to Senate prerogative and assuring cooperation on a legislative program were more compelling than anything Cox told him. Cox was a good friend of Mississippi's Senator James East-land, actually his college roommate, and Eastland's power as chair-man of the Judiciary Committee was enough to produce the deference Eastland expected for his choice. Though Bobby denied discussing Cox with Eastland, he later told an interviewer, "The Pres-ident of the United States is attempting to obtain the passage of important legislation in many, many fields, and the appointment of a judge who is recommended by the chairman of a committee or a key figure on a committee can make the whole difference on his legislative program."

Though Wilkins told Kennedy that he had not "gained anything [in 1961] by refusing to put a civil rights bill before" Congress, Kennedy hoped that his restraint might pay off in the Eighty-seventh Congress's second session. "He wasn't a man to give up easily," Wilkins admitted, though it was more than stubbornness motivating Kennedy. In fact, Kennedy had few hopes his patience would now result in less legislative friction over civil rights. Instead, he felt that his deference to the southerners on civil rights might get them to act on education or Medicare, issues that politically would be much more advantageous for him.

But it was a hope misplaced. In October 1961, HEW secretary Abe Ribicoff had told him that "the passage of any broad-scale education legislation will be a most difficult task." A personal survey of congressional and public sentiment had convinced Ribicoff not to expect any affirmative action. "A broad program of grants to States for public school construction and teacher's salaries is virtually impossible to pass. There is substantial Southern opposition to any bill for elementary and secondary schools. . . . Republican opposition to any general aid bill is strong, and is overwhelming against teachers' salaries." Ribicoff saw three principal impediments to reform: southern determination to preserve segregated schools, opposition to eroding local control over education, and resistance to providing aid to private or religion-based schools. Although he suggested a piecemeal approach in the coming session as an alternative to the failed comprehensive one in 1961, Ribicoff also believed that another unsuccessful effort at a more comprehensive bill might turn out to be useful in the upcoming elections.

Kennedy agreed, which is not to suggest that he saw education as principally a political tool. He strongly believed in the need for federal aid to education at all levels as essential to progress at home and abroad. But taking a bold stand on education, despite its poor legislative prospects, seemed a good way to counter liberal complaints about his timidity on civil rights and win Democratic backing in 1962.

It was much the same with medical insurance for the elderly. In February 1962, Kennedy reintroduced his bill to provide health coverage for the aged under Social Security. He encouraged public rallies to pressure Congress, publicly thanked a group of physicians favoring his program, spoke passionately in support of his bill before twenty thousand people at Madison Square Garden, and took on the American Medical Association for opposing Social Security and calling his proposal "a cruel hoax." But Kennedy's passion (and that of organized labor and senior citizens) was insufficient to identify a formula that would disarm conservative opponents and satisfy a majority of liberal advocates. In July, the administration's medical insurance bill failed in the Senate, where it fell short by 52 to 48. One newspaper summarized the defeat as "Kennedy's Blackest Week with Congress." Kennedy himself called the vote "a most serious defeat for every American family." Once again, the only good news here was the political advantage it seemed to give Kennedy in pressing his party's case for more congressional seats. (When asked if the fact that twenty-one Senate Democrats voted against him on the insurance plan would tend "to inhibit [him] in setting this forth as an issue," Kennedy replied that it would not: "The fact of the matter is this administration is for Medicare and two-thirds of the Democrats are for Medicare and seven-eighths of the Republicans are against it. And that seems to me to be the issue.")

Other domestic problems dogged him during the first half of 1962. In April, he sent Congress a special message on the nation's transportation system, which he described as vital to domestic growth and productivity and the ability to compete abroad. "A chaotic patchwork of inconsistent and often obsolete legislation and regulation" burdened the country's movement by air, ground, rail, and water. "Fundamental and far-reaching" changes in federal policies were essential to ensure the national well-being. And while he went on to describe in detail the many difficulties besetting everything from interstate highways to international aviation and inner-city traffic, he acknowledged that he had no clear answers and that Congress would need to "devote considerable time and effort" to identifying means to fend off "permanent loss of essential services," which would then compel "even more difficult and costly solutions in the not-too-distant future."

POLITICS WAS ANOTHER CHALLENGE. After Kennedy's election as president, the family had decided to run brother Edward — Ted, as he was called — for Jack's vacant Senate seat. But Ted could not hold the office until 1962, when he would turn thirty, the minimum age required by the Constitution. In December 1961, Jack tested the waters with a rumor published in the *Boston Globe* about Ted's candidacy. When House majority leader John W. McCormack called the president to propose his own nephew, Massachusetts attorney general Edward McCormack, as an interim appointment, Kennedy had replied, "I'm putting someone in. I want to save that seat for my brother."

Though the governor of Massachusetts technically held the appointment power, the selection was Kennedy's call. The interim appointee was Benjamin A. Smith, Kennedy's college friend, who was to stand aside for Ted in two years. Assumptions that Bobby was in line for the seat and that a likely political backlash against Kennedy nepotism would derail the plan both proved false. With regard to the former, Bobby's collaboration with his brother inside the administration made him too valuable to send to the Senate. Besides, Ted was eager to run, and Joe insisted on it. Bobby remembered Joe as the moving force behind the decision. "He just felt that Teddy had worked all this time during the campaign and sacrificed himself for his older brother," Bobby said, "that we had our positions, and so he should have the right to run."

But Kennedy himself had doubts. Teddy was twenty-nine in 1961, with no credentials to speak of other than having worked on his brother's 1958 and 1960 campaigns. He told Ted to test the waters in Massachusetts by speaking around the state. "I'll hear whether you are really making a mark up there," Kennedy told him. "I will tell you whether this is something that you ought to seriously consider." But Joe saw no need for an apprenticeship or any test. "He felt that it was a mistake to run for any position lower than [U.S. senator]," Bobby remembered. "Certainly, he was as qualified as Eddie McCormack to run for the Senate or anybody else who was being mentioned in Massachusetts, [people] who were perhaps older but weren't particularly outstanding figures."

Kennedy remained uncertain nevertheless. In January 1962, a reporter asked the president, "Your brother, Teddy, in Massachusetts, seems to be running for something but none of us are very certain just what it is. Could you tell us if you have had an opportunity to discuss this with him and whether you can tell us the secret?" Kennedy replied, "Well, I think he's the man . . . who's running and he's the man to discuss it with." In March, when Ted announced his candidacy, he stated his opposition to his brother's involvement in his campaign. It was a strategy for reducing the president's political liability. "Well, in part, I am aware of the campaign," Kennedy told the press, "but my brother is carrying this campaign on his own and will conduct it in that way." In May, when a reporter asked the president about reports of "administration aid and comfort to [Ted's] senatorial campaign," Kennedy reiterated his distance from the primary contest. "What about your associates, sir?" a reporter probed further. "No member of the White House staff is planning to go to the [state] convention, nor will be, to the best of my knowledge, in Massachusetts between now and the convention."

But of course, JFK, Bobby, and the White House were deeply involved. For starters, they schooled Ted to talk of a Kennedy dynasty with good-natured humor. When Kennedy biographer James MacGregor Burns told JFK of his interest in the seat and declared, "I'm sure I'm about number 99 on your list," Jack graciously, but evasively, replied, "Oh, no, Jim, you're number two or three." When a reporter complained of "too many Kennedys," Ted joked, "You should have taken that up with my mother and father." Reluctant to step on Ted's line, Kennedy responded to the same complaint with the deadpan observation, as "my brother pointed out, there are nine members of my family. It is a big family. They are all interested in public life." And the great issues were, after all, centered in the nation's capital.

According to Adam Clymer, Ted's biographer, Kennedy "made it clear that a defeat would be not just Ted's loss, but his own, too, and would not be tolerated." In March, as Ted prepared to go on *Meet the Press*, Kennedy brought him into the Oval Office, sat him down behind his desk, and questioned him like a prosecuting attorney. (Kennedy ultimately was too nervous to watch his brother's performance, which was more than adequate.) At a secret White House meeting of Massachusetts politicians in April, some of whom flew in from Boston under assumed names, the president pressured everyone to advance Ted's candidacy. He "suggested discreetly using patronage." And though few jobs were apparently delivered, "the hope of them was certainly dangled before a lot of ambitious politicians." Ted Sorensen provided quotes for speeches and one administration aide took a leave of absence to work directly on Teddy's campaign.

Kennedy himself dealt with the most potentially explosive issue jeopardizing Ted's candidacy. In 1951, during Ted's freshman year at

Harvard, the university expelled him for having a classmate take his final exam in Spanish. After almost two years in the army, he returned to Harvard, in September 1953. He graduated in 1956 and went on to the University of Virginia Law School. Fearful that the cheating scandal would become a prominent story in the *Boston Globe*, the Kennedys decided to keep control of the issue by revealing it themselves. The president invited a *Globe* reporter to the White House, where he offered to provide Ted's Harvard file if the reporter would mute the incident by including it in a biographical profile. Though the *Globe* insisted on making the profile a front-page story, it buried the details of the scandal in the fifth paragraph of an account innocuously headlined "Ted Kennedy Tells About Harvard Examination Incident." Other papers featured the story the next day, but they were no more than echoes of the *Globe*'s report. And with the *Globe*, now the state's leading newspaper, downplaying the incident, Ted's vulnerability was greatly reduced. It was an emphatic demonstration of shrewd politics and the press's friendly attitude toward a president they liked and were reluctant to undermine.

Kennedy worried nevertheless that the scandal would hurt Ted's chances of election. "It won't go over with the WASPs," he told Ben Bradlee. "They take a very dim view of looking over your shoulder at someone else's exam paper. They go in more for stealing from stockholders and bankers." The president urged Bradlee to have *Newsweek* look into the record of Eddie McCormack, Ted's likely primary opponent. "I asked him what he meant," Bradlee recalled, "and [he] told me that McCormack had resigned his commission in the Navy on the day he graduated from Annapolis on a medical disability. 'Half of it was nerves and half of it was a bad back,'" Kennedy explained, "'and he's been drawing a 60 percent disability ever since up until six months ago.'" It was a perfect example of Kennedy hardball politics. Bradlee never investigated the allegation, but it put him in mind of the maxim "Don't get mad, get even."

In June, after Ted won a majority of delegates at the state convention and Edward McCormack decided to contest his nomination in a September primary, a wave of criticism threatened to make Ted's candidacy an issue in the fall elections. Did the president think Ted was up to the job? a reporter asked, and would his candidacy have some negative fallout in November? The voters of Massachusetts would decide the matter, Kennedy answered diplomatically, but he could not resist making the case for his brother. Ted had managed his successful reelection campaign in 1958 and managed the pre-convention fight for western state delegates and then the presidential contest in the same states. "I have confidence in his ability," Kennedy declared.

BECAUSE THE TRUMAN and Eisenhower presidencies had suffered from embarrassing scandals that had undermined their credibility, Kennedy was determined to ensure against any wrongdoing that would weaken his ability to govern or lead. Thus, a scandal involving Billy Sol Estes, a Texas businessman, and the administration's Agriculture Department was more worrisome to the president than his brother's Senate campaign. When information emerged in March about Estes's payoffs to four Agriculture Department officials to obtain grain and cotton storage contracts, the White House assigned seventy-five FBI agents to the case, and the Justice Department made certain that Agriculture secretary Orville Freeman and undersecretary Charles Murphy were untainted. Kennedy assured the press that his administration had given Justice and the IRS carte blanche to ferret out improper actions and that no guilty official would go unpunished.

Nevertheless, the political heat was intense. Eisenhower publicly suggested that because all the investigative agencies in the administration and the Congress were under Democratic control, some Republicans ought to be brought into the process. At the same time, the New York Herald Tribune began describing the case as another Teapot Dome and predicting that Secretary Freeman would have to resign. The Tribune also printed a picture of Kennedy's Inaugural Address signed by him to Estes. Kennedy's explanation that the DNC had distributed sixty thousand copies of the photo with machine-signed signatures without his knowledge of the recipients insulated him from charges of any direct involvement with Estes, but the death of Henry H. Marshall, an Agriculture Department official investigating the Estes case, raised additional questions. Although Marshall had bruises on his hands, arms, and face and had been shot five times with a bolt-action rifle that had to be pumped each time to eject a shell, a Texas grand jury ruled the death a suicide. Reports in the Dallas Morning News that the president had taken a personal interest in the Marshall case and that the attorney general had repeatedly called the judge presiding over the grand jury embarrassed the White House. A Newsweek report that Marshall's death was the result of "an extra-curricular romance," relieved Kennedy and Bobby, who told Ben Bradlee, "That explains it perfectly, and to think those bastards on the *Herald Tribune* must have known this and were still writing it as Billy Sol Estes." The fact that the *Tribune* had given less coverage to a comparable scandal involving George M. Humphrey, Eisenhower's secretary of the treasury, particularly incensed the Kennedys, who attributed the paper's emphasis to a Republican bias.

Throughout the uproar, the president and Bobby were less worried about their involvement than Johnson's. His reputation as a fabulous wheeler-dealer who had won a Senate seat with tainted ballots in 1948 and had accumulated a $15-million fortune in radio, television, real estate, and bank holdings with influence peddling had made him an object of press speculation. Estes was, after all, his fellow Texan, and rumors abounded about joint business ventures, lobbying at agriculture in Estes's behalf, gifts — including an airplane used to fly to the 414-acre Johnson ranch with a sixty-three-hundred-foot landing strip — and efforts to impede the FBI's investigation. Kennedy and Bobby kept close tabs on these allegations, especially one, that a Republican congressman was preparing impeachment proceedings against the vice president. Although Johnson and his staff dismissed the charges as baseless, Bobby insisted on a thorough FBI investigation of the stories. It turned up nothing, and though some later historians of the FBI speculated that Hoover might have suppressed information tying Johnson to Estes's crimes or that Johnson arranged to have incriminating files destroyed, a reading of FBI materials obtained through a Freedom of Information request demonstrates that the Bureau indeed made a rigorous effort to find the truth. As Johnson said later, "The damn press always accused me of things I didn't do. They never once found out about the things I did do."

Worries about Johnson extended to his management of the space program. Despite the success of Alan Shepard's suborbital flight in May 1961, by February 1962 NASA had still not matched cosmonaut Yuri Gagarin's orbital success the previous April. Bad weather and technical problems had aborted ten televised U.S. planned launchings between May and February. But on February 20, John Glenn's spaceship orbited the earth three times in just under five hours before a pinpoint landing in the Atlantic near Bermuda, where helicopters from a nearby U.S. cruiser waited to lift Glenn and his capsule from the ocean. The White House was jubilant, especially because it knew that problems with the capsule's heat shield had brought the mission close to disaster. Another successful flight by Scott Carpenter in May gave Kennedy — in contrast with the steel price conflict, stock market downturn, and Estes scandal — something to cheer about. (If only Glenn "were a Negro," Johnson told Kennedy, who laughed at what became his favorite example of Lyndon's constant preoccupation with political calculations.)

Glenn's successful mission allowed Kennedy to encourage common actions with Moscow in space exploration. He publicly suggested a joint weather-satellite system, "operational tracking services from each other's territories," cooperative efforts to map the earth's magnetic field from space, joint communications satellites, and shared information on space medicine as preludes to wider cooperation in unmanned lunar exploration and possible manned flights to Mars or Venus. But fearing that any such commitment would reveal the limits of the Soviet Union's military rockets and space programs and would burden already strained defense budgets, Khrushchev turned aside the president's suggestions by insisting that a general and complete disarmament agreement had to precede cooperative space exploration.

Public gains from the orbital missions counteracted behind-the-scenes worries that NASA contracts might open the administration to charges of sweetheart deals arranged by Johnson. With plans in tow to shift half of NASA's operations from Florida's Cape Canaveral to a command center in Houston, Johnson came under attack for serving his own and his state's special interests. In 1962, lobbyists and congressmen from outside the South began complaining about a southwestern monopoly on NASA contracts. Johnson, Bobby said later, was "awarding these contracts badly, and they were getting in the wrong hands." Ohio, Michigan, and Pennsylvania representatives objected to a loss of contracts, and reporters pressed the president for an explanation. He answered that they were looking to see if "the distribution of contracts is as equitable as it can be." Nixon, who, in 1962, was running for governor of California, attacked the Kennedy administration for "injecting politics in the allocation of defense contracts." Because defense expenditures in California were higher than they had been under Eisenhower and Nixon, Kennedy did not think "that that was a fuse sufficient to light off Mr. Nixon." But politics was politics, and to rein in Johnson's influence, Kennedy made congressional staffer Richard Callaghan an aide to NASA chief James Webb. Callaghan was instructed to ensure a more geographically diverse distribution of contracts and to find out whether Johnson was pulling any strings at NASA for his supporters. Callaghan told *Time-Life* reporter Robert Sherrod that Kenny O'Donnell, Kennedy's liaison to Congress, "wasn't only interested in getting the contractors [and congressmen] off his back." He wanted to know about Johnson's "influence on the Space Agency." O'Donnell later told Sherrod that they had found no wrongdoing. Consequently, in May, when a reporter asked the president about rumors that Johnson would be dropped from the ticket in 1964, Kennedy emphatically denied them, describing Johnson as "invaluable" to the administration.

In March 1962, after Teddy announced his Senate candidacy, a journalist told Kennedy that Teddy had said on television that "after seeing the cares of office on you, he wasn't sure he'd ever be interested in being the President. I wonder if you could tell us whether if you had it to do over again, you would work for the presidency and whether you can recommend the job to others." Kennedy replied, "Well, the answer is — to the first is 'yes' and the second is 'no.' I don't recommend it to others — [laughter] — at least for a while."

CHAPTER 15

Frustrations and "Botches"

What is there in this place that a man should ever want to
get into it?

— President James A. Garfield, 1881

IN THE SPRING of 1962, a reporter asked the president about the frustration mobilized reservists were feeling at being held in the service while other young men enjoyed a "normal life." Kennedy praised the reservists' contribution to the nation's security and sympathized with their complaints. "There is always inequity in life," he observed. "Some men are killed in war and some men are wounded, and some men never leave the country, and some men are stationed in the Antarctic and some are stationed in San Francisco. It's very hard in military or in personal life to assure complete equality. Life is unfair. Some people are sick and others are well."

His observation was grounded in his own life experience. His good fortune in being a privileged American, his health problems (which his family's wealth and status could not prevent or master), his brother Joe's and sister Kathleen's accidental deaths, his sister Rosemary's retardation, his brush with death during the war, and the circumstances that had elevated him to the presidency by the narrowest of margins had made Kennedy philosophical about the uncertainties affecting everyone's life.

He saw his time in office as partly a case study in the fortuitous — a coming together of uncontrollable events challenging his judgment and resiliency. Nothing had been easy. Despite an eighty-eight-seat margin in the House and a twenty-nine-seat advantage in the Senate, the Congress had bottled up his principal legislative initiatives. Rhetorical and administrative expressions of support for civil rights had won little appreciation from liberals and angered many in the South. In response to continuing economic sluggishness, tensions with business chiefs, and talk of a recession in 1964, critics complained that he was an ineffective domestic leader. The Bay of Pigs failure, the acrimonious exchanges with Khrushchev in Vienna, the crisis over Berlin, the collapse of arms control talks and the resumption of nuclear testing, Western European questions about U.S. commitments to the region's defense, doubts about the Alliance for Progress, the uncertain settlement in Laos, and the continuing crisis in South Vietnam had raised questions about his mastery of foreign affairs also.

All these difficulties made Kennedy think that he might be a one-term president. He intended to fight as hard as he could for reelection and hoped that events might favor him in the next two and a half years, but he knew how quickly public sentiment could change. Though he still enjoyed solid backing from the public, by the summer of 1962 his approval ratings had dropped from the 70s into the 60s.

As a realist, someone who prided himself on not blinking away unpleasant facts about his political fortunes, Kennedy began to think about his legacy, or the way in which historians would view his presidency. He was eager to ensure that they saw all its complexities and gave a sympathetic hearing to the many challenges he or any other president would have faced in the 1960s. As an amateur historian with two books to his credit, he knew how important a detailed contemporary record was to an accurate reconstruction of the past. After reading Barbara Tuchman's bestselling 1962 book, *The Guns of August*, a recounting of the miscalculations that drove the great powers into World War I, Kennedy focused on a 1914 conversation between two German leaders. "How did it all happen?" one asked. "Ah," the other replied, "if only one knew." Kennedy told White House staff members, "If this planet is ever ravaged by nuclear war — and if the survivors of that devastation can then endure the fire, poison, chaos and catastrophe — I do not want one of those survivors to ask another, 'How did it all happen?' and to receive the incredible reply: 'Ah, if only one knew.'"

With this in mind, in July 1962, Kennedy installed taping systems in the White House. Kennedy instructed a secret service agent to install recording devices in the Cabinet Room, Oval Office, and the library of the executive mansion. The agent placed reel-to-reel tape recorders in a basement room of the West Wing and connected them by wires to microphones hidden behind wall drapes in the Cabinet Room and under the president's desk and a coffee table in the Oval Office. Inconspicuous buttons at the Cabinet Room table and the president's desk allowed Kennedy to record conversations as he chose. A Dictaphone connected to an Oval Office telephone allowed him to record phone conversations as well. Initially, only two secret service agents and Evelyn Lincoln knew about the tapes, though by 1963 Bobby and his secretary, Angie Novello, also knew. The 260 hours of recordings — 248 hours of meetings and 12 hours of telephone conversations — provide an important window on Kennedy's decision making over the next sixteen months. The tapes demonstrate more clearly than any other source can the daunting domestic and foreign problems that threatened to unhinge the economy, provoke civil strife, and, worst of all, trigger a nuclear war.

Kennedy was not simply self-serving in deciding what to tape. He wanted a realistic record of what shaped events. If he hoped to demonstrate the inhibitions placed on presidential achievements, he could not solely tape flattering depictions of his effectiveness. The tapes certainly include discussions that little serve his historical reputation. Nor did he use the tapes to make speeches that would impress future listeners. As scholars Philip Zelikow and Ernest May have pointed out, he "could hardly have known just what statements or positions would look good to posterity, for neither he nor his colleagues could know how the stories would turn out."

That said, holes remain. Three tapes, Zelikow and May add, may have been "cut and spliced, for two of these tapes . . . concerned intelligence issues and may have involved discussion of covert efforts to assassinate Castro." It is also possible that embarrassing passages involving Marilyn Monroe and Judith Campbell Exner were removed. In addition, a small number of tapes may have been destroyed or lost. There are, for example, unopened transcripts at the Kennedy Library for four missing tapes, which may contain embarrassing revelations or national security secrets. By and large, however, the tapes seem to provide a faithful record of some of the most important events in Kennedy's presidency, and of the constant burdens of a working president.

MAINTAINING ECONOMIC GROWTH and lowering the unemployment rate were constant, daunting concerns in 1962. The stock market tumble on May 28 sent a wave of fear through the White House.

Memos flew back and forth on how to bolster business and consumer confidence. Should the president make a statement? Kennedy's advisers opposed the idea as likely to do more harm than
good. Instead, Kennedy asked Congress to cut taxes.

From the perspective of forty years later, after Richard Nixon's
announcement in 1971 that "we are all Keynesians now," and Republican advocacy under Reagan and both George Bushes of lower
taxes, it is difficult to recapture the boldness attached to Kennedy's
requests in June 1962 for an immediate 40 percent reduction in
corporate tax rates and comprehensive tax reform beginning in
January 1963. Kennedy was convinced that America's tax system was
a drag on the economy, and he looked particularly to Western
Europe, where tax rates were lower and growth double that of the
United States. Heller concurred. Though Kennedy was not ready to
provide details on "the range of the net tax cut," it was clear that he
would ask for a substantial reduction in the 50 percent rate that
Americans in the $32,000 to $36,000 income bracket were paying
and a cut in the 91 percent assessment on marginal income over
$400,000.

In a national culture that put a high premium on frugality and
balanced budgets, Kennedy faced considerable hostility from an
orthodoxy preaching the economic and moral dangers of deficits
and debt. A Gallup poll asking whether people favored a tax cut if
it increased government debt showed 72 percent opposed and only
19 percent in favor. To contain public concern that he might be
jeopardizing the nation's future by risking unbalanced budgets,
Kennedy described the tax reductions in terms of millions rather
than billions: business was to get a $1,300 million tax credit rather
than a $1.3 billion reduction; the potential budget surplus of $8,000
million, however, was stated as $8 billion, and the increase in the
gross national product was also described as in the billions.

Opposition to tax cuts was not just on the conservative side. Ken
Galbraith warned the president that "a very large part of American
conservative and business opinion" would "argue with great enthusiasm for a tax reduction. . . . Of course, after the taxes are reduced,
these people will . . . attack you for an unbalanced budget." Galbraith saw "a nasty congressional brawl with a disagreeable aftermath.
What will satisfy the liberals will outrage the rich and vice-versa.
Both, in the end, will be angry at the Administration." When JFK
lectured Galbraith on the virtues of Keynesianism, Galbraith acknowledged his standing as "a charter member of the worshipful

following," but observed that "the orthodoxy is always one step behind the problem. And so it is now that Keynes is official." Instead of a tax cut, Galbraith wanted an attack on "the infinity of problems that beset a growing population and an increasingly complex society in an increasingly competitive world. To do this well," Galbraith advised, "costs the money that the reducers would deny."

But Kennedy saw Galbraith's iconoclasm as less convincing than Heller's. The great economic challenge for Americans, Kennedy believed, was to abandon outworn clichés about deficits. In a commencement address at Yale in June, he asserted that "the great enemy of the truth is very often not the lie . . . but the myth," the dogged attachment "to the clichés of our forebears . . . the comfort of opinion without the discomfort of thought." And the myths about fiscal policy, he said, "are legion and the truth hard to find." The experience of the last fifteen years demonstrated that old slogans about deficits creating inflation and surpluses preventing it were out of date. Public and private debt could fuel expansion and strength.

Kennedy's sense of urgency about the tax cut increased at the end of June when Heller recounted the "storm signals . . . rolling in at a rapid rate. . . . A dozen top economists — of varying political and methodological hues — agreed that there was little hope for a spontaneous revival in the months ahead." Moreover, in July, Heller worried that the "millions of stockholders who have recently taken a drubbing feel the Administration is rather detached and inert about the whole thing." Toward the end of the month, it was clear that the economy remained sluggish. Although consumer purchasing had remained steady and some corporate profits were better than expected, business investment, on which economic expansion and lower unemployment depended, remained below expectations.

Yet the Congress was not ready, one opposing congressman even charging that the president had used "rigged data" to support a tax reduction. "It is clear," Ted Sorensen told the president on August 9, "on the basis of the hearings now completed that neither this committee nor the Congress would approve an immediate tax cut before adjourning next month."

Despite a jump in unemployment from 5.3 to 5.8 percent in August, and gloomy September estimates on the economy, Kennedy decided that political resistance made an immediate tax cut impossible. Believing it essential for the next year, however, he began trying to convert Wilbur Mills, the chairman of the Ways and Means

Committee, to the idea. In two White House conversations in August, they agreed that the economy remained sluggish and would not expand as fast as they had hoped. But unless Congress saw the country as at least in a recession, Mills said, it would be reluctant to follow Kennedy's lead. Kennedy conceded that a proposal would complicate the political lives of Democrats running for reelection in November. "If I go up and ask for a tax cut now," he told Mills, it might suggest that the economy was troubled, that "the Democrats have failed to bring the economy back," and that "they're fiscally irresponsible. And a lot of bastards then come out and say they're not for a tax cut, and . . . [they] will break with me. And in other words, it will make our problem almost impossible come November."

With additional evidence in September and October that the economic expansion of 1961–62 was "running out of gas," and that the AFL-CIO was increasingly unhappy with an administration that promised more than it delivered, Kennedy stiffened his resolve to press Congress to enact a landmark tax bill in 1963. But for now, he expected nothing.

In July, the White House had begun a series of meetings — luncheons, dinners, discussions — with business leaders and the business press. The president, the CEA, and cabinet officials briefed corporate chiefs on the state of the economy and the need for a tax cut to fuel expansion. Kennedy believed that the meetings were doing some good. After one July luncheon of businessmen at the White House, Thomas Lamont of IBM told the president that he seemed to be "fully aware of the important role which business plays in our national economy" and that his detailed knowledge of the problems businessmen faced had impressed his guests. In addition, his appeal to them for modern policies that left outdated economic thinking behind had had some effect.

Nevertheless Kennedy resented having to cultivate educated and generally sophisticated executives, many of whom seemed blinded by bias and self-doubt. The business community had lost confidence in itself, Kennedy told Schlesinger. "Whenever I say anything that upsets them, businessmen just die. I have to spend time and energy trying to prop them up." A Gallup poll showing that only one in five businessmen labeled Kennedy as "anti-business" failed to convince the president that he could take them for granted.

The only unqualified point of agreement Kennedy had with his business antagonists was the need to reduce the unfavorable balance of payments. He still shared corporate fears of a gold drain that could force devaluation of the dollar and bring on economic disaster. His answer to the problem was the Trade Expansion bill he had put before Congress in January 1962, which would allow him to negotiate lower tariffs with Europe's Common Market countries and increase U.S. exports. Seven months later, the bill still not passed, Kennedy called it "the most important measure to be considered by many a Congress . . . vital to the future of this country. . . . If we cannot make new trade bargains with the Common Market in the coming year," he said, "our export surplus will decline, more plants will move to Europe, and the flow of gold away from these shores will become more intensified." Kennedy predicted that expanded trade arising from passage of his bill would boost employment in the United States as well as bring the balance of payments under control.

Some opponents worried that the law would give the Japanese and Europeans trade advantages harmful to a variety of industries in the United States. But supporters of the bill invested it with miraculous powers. One distinguished columnist with a reputation for detached analysis saw the bill as "the unifying intellectual principle of the New Frontier." Its failure would cause the United States "to default on power [and] resign from history." Evangelists for the law like George Ball made a point of wearing "a suit made in Britain, shoes manufactured in Hong Kong, and a silk tie made in France."

If Kennedy's support did not run to that extreme, he nevertheless saw the bill as easing some of his difficulties with the U.S. business community as well as serving the national well-being. After the bill passed Congress by lopsided margins in October, he called it "the most important international piece of legislation . . . affecting economics since the Marshall Plan. It marks a decisive point for the future of our economy, for our relations with our friends and allies, and for the prospects of free institutions and free societies everywhere." Yet as the coming year would demonstrate, the bill was no nostrum for the balance of payments, the U.S. economy, or the progress of freedom around the globe. Myth and illusion were not the exclusive preserve of the country's business community or Americans wedded to balanced budgets.

THROUGHOUT 1962, civil rights remained a distinctly secondary concern alongside domestic worries about the economy and the gold drain. In the first two months after he began taping important conversations, for example, Kennedy recorded numerous discussions about international affairs and domestic economic problems but absolutely nothing about civil rights, except for one brief discussion with Johnson about the CEEO. At the end of March, an unsigned White House memo pointed out that "the proper groundwork has not been laid for [civil rights] legislation in Congress. Negroes are not convinced that the Administration is *really* on their side. Southern whites still believe that the turmoil is a combination of 'ward politics' and 'outside agitators.' . . . If legislation is submitted to Congress before the moral issue is clearly drawn, the result will be disaster. The country will be exposed to several weeks of divisive and inflammatory debate. The debate is likely to come to no conclusion — thus disillusioning the Negroes and strengthening the bigots in their conclusion that the country is 'really with' them. The Republicans will have a field day. And in addition to the civil rights cause, the President's whole program will go down the drain."

The burden was on Kennedy, who needed to "make the kind of moral commitment" that would "rescue the situation and restore unity," the memo advised. He should ask the three former presidents, Hoover, Eisenhower, and Truman, and Republican congressional leaders for help and to make clear to blacks that "he is on their side because they are right." He also needed to make the moral case for civil rights in a nationwide TV speech and to hold face-to-face conversations with people across the South — "not as their antagonist, but as their President" — to educate them about "the simple rights and wrongs of the situation."

It is not clear that Kennedy ever saw this memo, but he felt the heat anyway from civil rights advocates pressing for bolder action. The Civil Rights Commission urged him to support a voting rights law, but the president and Bobby were committed to a less comprehensive strategy — lawsuits against the worst offending southern counties. Seeing this as a form of incrementalism producing uncertain results, the commission planned to hold hearings in Louisiana and Mississippi, where the most pronounced abuses existed, to underscore the need for legislation. Afraid that the commission's presence in the Deep South would touch off "large scale" violence, Kennedy's Justice Department resisted.

By 1962, Father Hesburgh and Bobby were locked in a bureaucratic conflict that stunned Harris Wofford and provoked the president's intervention. Bobby called the commissioners a bunch of "second-guessers" and complained that they were making it more difficult for him to accomplish what needed to be done. "I didn't have any great feeling that they were accomplishing anything of a positive nature," Bobby recalled. "It was almost like the House Un-American Activities Committee investigating Communism. They were investigating violations of civil rights in areas in which we were making investigations. I thought that they could do more in the North." "It's easy to play Jesus and it's fun to get into bed with the civil rights movement," a Justice Department attorney said, "but all of the noise they make doesn't do as much good as one case." But Hesburgh, who saw the commission as a "burr under the saddle of the administration," refused to back off.

Although Bobby was able to delay commission hearings in Louisiana and Mississippi for a while, he lacked authority to stop them. The hearings, which refused to shade the truth and mute tensions between the administration and the white South, described Mississippi as using terror tactics against aspiring black voters. Kennedy himself lobbied against publication of the commission's report, which recommended withholding federal funds from the state until it demonstrated its "compliance with the Constitution and laws of the United States." "You're making my life difficult," he told two commissioners. When he heard that the commission, including Harvard Law School dean Erwin Griswold, was unanimous in its determination to go ahead, Kennedy asked, "Who the hell appointed Griswold?" "You did," the commission's chairman replied. "Probably on the recommendation of Harris Wofford," Kennedy said, acknowledging his inattentiveness to the commission's operations.

In July 1962, Martin Luther King Jr. added to Kennedy's difficulties with a public statement that the president "could do more in the area of moral persuasion by occasionally speaking out against segregation and counseling the Nation on the moral aspects of this problem." Kennedy answered cryptically that his commitment to full constitutional rights for all Americans had been made very clear and that his administration had "taken a whole variety of very effective steps to improve the equal opportunities for all Americans and would continue to do so." But the president's words did little to advance the cause of civil rights or ease the tensions that were erupting in sporadic violence.

Kennedy's frustration at the impasse between the growing movement of black activists practicing nonviolent opposition and defenders of segregation registered clearly in his response to clashes in the southwest Georgia city of Albany, where blacks had launched the "Albany Movement" to challenge the city's segregation laws. On August 1, when Kennedy was asked his reaction to a Justice Department report on conditions in Albany, he explained that he had "been in constant touch with the Attorney General," who had "been in daily touch with the authorities in Albany in an attempt to provide a solution." He all but acknowledged a sense of powerlessness. "I find it wholly inexplicable," he told reporters, "why the City Council of Albany will not sit down with the citizens of Albany, who may be Negroes, and attempt to secure them, in a peaceful way, their rights. The United States Government is involved in sitting down at Geneva with the Soviet Union. I can't understand why the government of Albany . . . cannot do the same for American citizens."

Bureaucratic infighting and limited advances added to Kennedy's sense of frustration. By August, conflicts between Johnson and Robert Troutman, Kennedy's Georgia friend who had originated Plans for Progress, and complaints of too few gains forced Troutman's resignation from the CEEO. Although the president lauded the "immediate and dramatic results" of Troutman's efforts, it was an open secret that he was leaving because he and the vice president were at odds over the CEEO's poor performance. With Troutman going, Kennedy agreed to make Hobart Taylor Jr., a black attorney from Michigan with roots in Texas, where Johnson had known him, CEEO executive vice chairman. To draw attention away from the fact that he was replacing a white southerner with an African American, Kennedy delayed announcing Taylor's appointment for several days.

But an appointment was far from enough. As Arthur Schlesinger Jr. later said, "The Kennedy civil rights strategy, however appropriate to the congressional mood of 1961, miscalculated the dynamism of a revolutionary movement." It was clear to King and other civil rights activists that the president remained reluctant to take significant political risks for the sake of black equality. King released a telegram to Kennedy "asking for Federal action against anti-Negro terrorism in the South," and one civil rights group threatened to picket the White House unless the president did more to protect blacks. In September, when reporters pressed him to say what he was doing about King's demand for protective action, Kennedy's frustration with the situation and southern resistance to black complaints of inequality and abuse was palpable. "I don't know any more outrageous action which I have seen occur in this country for a good many months or years than the burning of a church — two churches — because of the effort made by Negroes to vote," he told a news conference. "To shoot, as we saw in the case of Mississippi, two young people who were involved in an effort to register people, to burn churches as a reprisal" for asking for voting rights was "both cowardly as well as outrageous." He promised that FBI agents would bring the perpetrators to justice and said that "all of our talk about freedom [was] hollow" unless we could assure citizens the right to vote. The rhetoric was all civil rights advocates and anyone devoted to the rule of law could ask. But conditions in the South cried out not for prose but for action, and action now.

IN SEPTEMBER, James Meredith, a black Mississippian, tried to break the color line at the state's lily-white university in Oxford. Meredith, a twenty-eight-year-old air force veteran with a sense of divine mission to overturn segregation, had been fighting since January 1961 to gain admission to Ole Miss. Supported by the NAACP in a series of court contests, Meredith won an appeal to the U.S. Supreme Court on September 10, 1962, ordering the university to end its "calculated campaign of delay, harassment, and masterly inactivity," and admit him.

Three days later, Mississippi governor Ross Barnett, a devoted segregationist, whom Bobby later described as "an agreeable rogue and weak," spoke on statewide television. Denouncing the federal government's assault on Mississippi's freedom to choose its way of life, the governor invoked the repudiated pre–Civil War doctrine of interposition, the right of a state to interpose itself between the U.S. government and the citizens of a state. Emotionally promising not to "surrender to the evil and illegal forces of tyranny," he theatrically declared, "we must either submit to the unlawful dictates of the federal government or stand up like men and tell them 'NEVER.'"

The governor's defiance, supported by the state legislature with resolutions blocking Meredith's registration, forced the White House to enter the conflict. In twenty conversations with Barnett between September 15 and 28, Bobby expressed sympathy for Barnett's political problem and raised no moral questions about the transparent unfairness of unequal treatment of blacks. Instead, he emphasized the need to obey the law and made clear that the president intended to enforce the court's directives. Barnett shared an interest with the

Kennedys in getting Meredith enrolled without violence. But his strategy — which he did not share with the Kennedys — was to submit to federal authority with a show of cynical resistance that would enhance his popularity in Mississippi. Barnett and the White House thus struggled for political advantage. Neither side doubted that federal authority would ultimately prevail, but how it occurred had large consequences.

Former Mississippi governor James Coleman, a moderate, urged Bobby not to use troops, which would be "fatal," or to make Barnett a martyr by jailing him, but to cut off all federal aid to the state, including old age assistance. Because Mississippi received $668 million in federal monies — some $300 million more than it sent to Washington in taxes — a reduction in federal largesse was one means to force Barnett's hand. Ted Sorensen counseled the president to threaten the businessmen backing the governor by holding up NASA, defense, and other federal contracts. The possible suspension of accreditation, disruption of the university's football schedule, and loss of postseason eligibility for bowl games seemed like promising means to dampen student enthusiasm for mob opposition to federal authority.

But the threat of reduced federal outlays in the state was insufficient to bring Barnett into line. "I won't agree to let that boy get to Ole Miss," Barnett told Bobby on September 25. "I will never agree to that. I would rather spend the rest of my life in a penitentiary than do that." The same day, Barnett, who was more interested in scoring political points than ensuring law and order, personally blocked Meredith's registration in a confrontation at the trustee's room in a state office building in Jackson, the capital. On the twenty-sixth, Lieutenant Governor Paul Johnson, supported by state police and county sheriffs, stopped Meredith and federal marshals accompanying him from reaching the Oxford campus. On the twenty-seventh, a crowd of two thousand protesters blocked marshals, forcing Barnett to abandon a cynical plan to allow Meredith to register if it was done before cameras showing federal marshals with drawn pistols. By this means, Barnett had hoped to avoid violence, which would further blight Mississippi's good name, and also obtain political cover with segregationists, who would see him and his state as the victims of superior federal power.

Believing that Barnett's "defiance should be against the majesty of the United States" rather than against John Kennedy, the president had left private and public discussions of the issues to the attorney general. By September 29, however, he felt compelled to pressure Barnett directly. Despite coming across in telephone conversations as "a soft pillow" who would ultimately agree to Meredith's registration, Barnett gave no guarantee that it would be done peacefully. Kennedy wired Barnett, citing the "breakdown of law and order in Mississippi" and asking if he intended to keep the peace when court directives were executed. Unsatisfied with Barnett's responses, late that night Kennedy signed an order federalizing units of the Mississippi National Guard. After discussing the document with Norbert Schlei, a White House legal counsel, who assured him that it was like one Eisenhower had signed in the Little Rock crisis of 1957, Kennedy tapped the table they had been sitting at and said, "That's General Grant's table." Eager as much as possible to soften the use of his authority against a southern state, he told Schlei not to tell waiting reporters anything about the furniture.

The next morning Bobby told Barnett that the president would speak to the nation that evening and say that he had called up the guard because the governor had reneged on an agreement to let Meredith register. Barnett promised to cooperate if Kennedy did not mention their agreement. Kennedy thus believed he had assurances that Meredith would be able to register without incident. Consequently, on the evening of September 30, he told the nation that court orders "are beginning to be carried out" and that "Meredith is now in residence on the campus of the University." This had been accomplished without the use of the National Guard, and he hoped that the combination of state law enforcement officials and U.S. marshals would be able to keep the future peace. His address celebrated American reliance on the rule of law and praised Mississippi for its contributions to the national good ahead of the sectional good. He saw "no reason why the books on this case cannot now be quickly and quietly closed."

Kennedy's speech demonstrated his limited feel for the passion and volatility surrounding race relations across the South. It was a mistake to trust Barnett's promises, for one thing. In fact, the night of the speech, as soon as a mob showed up, Barnett withdrew the state's highway patrol officers who were supposed to assist in the protection of Meredith. Left behind were the five hundred marshals, no match for a mob of between two thousand and four thousand people. Kennedy sent in regular army troops, but it took several hours to get to Oxford from Memphis, where most of them were quartered. Before they arrived, a local resident of Oxford and a foreign journalist had been killed and 160 marshals had been injured, including 27 with gunshot wounds.

Kennedy was furious at the army's ineptitude in getting the troops to Oxford promptly. Bobby later recalled that "President Kennedy had one of the worst and harshest conversations with [Secretary of the Army] Cy Vance and with the general [in command] that I think I've ever heard." The incident immediately intensified Kennedy's distrust of the military, which kept saying the troops were on the way when they had not even left their bases, and reminded Bobby of the poor advice the chiefs had given the president about Laos. Kennedy himself said, "They always give you their bullshit about their instant reaction and their split-second timing, but it never works out. No wonder it's so hard to win a war." When he heard that retired general Edwin Walker, a right-wing extremist, was in Oxford encouraging people to oppose desegregation, the president said, "Imagine that son of a bitch having been a commander of a division up till last year. And the Army promoting him."

"I haven't had such an interesting time since the Bay of Pigs," Kennedy added with evident irony during a vigil lasting until 5:30 in the morning. Said Bobby, "We are going to have a hell of a problem about why we didn't handle the situation better. . . . We are going to have to figure out what we are going to say. . . . We are going to take a lot of knocks because of people getting killed, the fact that I didn't get the people up there in time." Bobby later remembered how concerned they were about explaining "this whole thing, because it looked like it was one of the big botches."

In fact, Kennedy escaped from the clash with relatively little political damage. True, some newspapers criticized his handling of Oxford. The press also described the vice president as unhappy with Kennedy's failure to consult him. But the good news was that the administration got Meredith enrolled. "Forget the Monday morning quarterbacks and the myopic few among the journalists," Phil Graham told Bobby. "Accept instead the feeling of a wide majority of thoughtful men: That the President and you deserve well of the Republic." Johnson, who was out of the country, sent word to the president that "the situation in Mississippi had been handled better than he could ever have thought of handling it." Polls of northern industrial states showed the president enjoying between 4–1 and

3–1 backing on Mississippi. Pollster Lou Harris advised him that every Democrat outside the South who was "running for major office should put front and center that this country needs firm and resolute leadership such as the President demonstrated in the Mississippi case." Foreign press opinion showed a "startling similarity." Whether in Africa, Latin America, the Far East, Middle East, South Asia, or Western Europe, the media cited the administration's "firmness and determination . . . in enforcing law and order," while also finding it difficult to understand how "racial tension could persist in an advanced country like the U.S."

However the press and public saw the crisis, the loss of life and rioting over Meredith's enrollment were partly the consequence of Kennedy's misreading of southern racism. He knew that most southern whites had an irrational contempt for blacks. But he could not quite understand how educated southern leaders could be so impractical as to believe that they could permanently maintain their outmoded system of apartheid. He had contempt for the unreasonable attitude southern whites had toward African Americans. They seemed incapable of practical good sense in their dealings with blacks. He puzzled over their intransigence in denying the franchise to blacks. Could they not see that if they conceded the vote and accepted desegregated schools, they would probably be able to extend the life of segregation in other walks of life? Kennedy saw this as a viable compromise. But it was certainly not an accommodation African Americans would any longer accept.

Kennedy had a highly imperfect understanding of African American impatience with racial divides. He understood the black fight against segregation as a well-justified struggle for self-interest. He also admired the courage shown by black demonstrators against superior state-controlled force. But he believed that national security and domestic reforms advancing prosperity, education, and health care for all trumped the needs and wishes of blacks. To some extent, his response to civil rights upheavals was a shortsighted curse on both houses. With so much else at stake, especially overseas, he felt compelled to make civil rights a secondary concern. But even if international dangers had not preoccupied Kennedy, it is doubtful that he would have acted more aggressively in support of black rights in 1962. Fears of civil strife across the South, with negative political repercussions for North and South, were enough to make Kennedy a temporizer on an issue he wished to keep as quiet as possible.

* * *

As THE SOUTH HEATED UP, Kennedy saw no easing of the international problems that had confronted him in the first fifteen months of his term. If anything, they were even more troubling than before. In March the journalist William Haddad, who had joined the United States Information Agency, told Kennedy that he doubted if the United States "[could] ever have a 'policy'" for Latin America. "At best," he said, "we will have a country-by-country, crisis-by-crisis standard." An Inter-American Development Bank official advised Kennedy that without "a massive information program" to mobilize Latin American public opinion, the president would never reach his goals. Despite spending a billion dollars in a year, "not a single Latin American nation is embarked on a development program under the Alliance for Progress." As to why not, the explanation was "the political instability of Latin American countries, their inability to concentrate on development, [and] their ingrained cynicism about the U.S. . . . But even within these very real and important political limitations things have not gone as well as they should."

That instability was far from hidden. At the end of March, a military coup against Argentina's President Arturo Frondizi was a serious setback to democratic hopes in the hemisphere, and it caused discouraging speculation that a Washington-sponsored austerity program to stabilize the economy had helped provoke the military's action. "The International Monetary Fund has had a complete lack of success in stabilizing economies in Latin America without the Government falling from power," Schlesinger told the NSC on April 2. In May, Teodoro Moscoso, an Agency for International Development official and Alliance coordinator, advised the president that the Alliance was "facing stormy weather." Latin leaders simply saw the program as "a money-lending operation. . . . And no money-lender in history has ever evoked great enthusiasm." Moreover, the Alliance had in no way been wedded to Latin American nationalism; it looked "'foreign' and 'imported' . . . a 'Made in the U.S.A.' product."

In public, Kennedy continued to speak hopefully about the Alliance, but privately he doubted that it could generate enough progress in the near term to sustain congressional commitments to "necessary funds." In July, the Peruvian military added to Kennedy's skepticism by overturning an election it described as fraudulent and arresting President Manuel Prado. Although Kennedy withheld recognition of the junta for a month, he eventually accepted its promises of future free elections and a return to constitutional government as reason for the resumption of diplomatic relations. But publicly describing the coup as "a grave setback to the principles agreed to under the Alliance for Progress," the administration delayed the reinstatement of full military assistance to Lima until a crisis with Cuba in October compelled a need for hemisphere "solidarity."

British Guiana remained another troubling problem. By February 1962, the state department was expressing doubts that "a working relationship [could] be established with Jagan which would prevent the emergence of a communist or Castro-type state in South America." In March, Schlesinger told Kennedy that both the State Department and the CIA were "under the impression that a firm decision has been taken to get rid of the Jagan government. . . . British Guiana has 600,000 inhabitants. Jagan would no doubt be gratified to know that the American and British governments are spending more man-hours per capita on British Guiana than on any other current problem!" Although London did not see any "communist threat to British Guiana," the administration persisted in believing that after independence it "would go the way of Castro" and that the United States needed to support "a policy of getting rid of Jagan." In the summer of 1962, the CIA was hard at work on covert plans to oust him from power. Because chances of carrying out "a really covert operation" seemed so small, however, the administration discouraged the British government from giving Guiana independence until Kennedy and Prime Minister Macmillan could further discuss the issue in 1963. Despite any certainty as to Jagan's course, exaggerated fears of what another radical regime in Latin America — however limited its reach — might mean led Kennedy to favor a policy of ousting Jagan, ignoring all the administration's professions of regard for national self-determination throughout the hemisphere.

But it was Brazil, potentially the most important Latin member of the Alliance, that concerned Kennedy more than any other hemisphere country aside from Cuba. In 1961, Brazilian president Juscelino Kubitschek described his country as "the playboy of economic development." Impressive increases in national output were accompanied by destabilizing graft and inflation. Jânio Quadros, who replaced Kubitschek as president in 1961, promised more measured expansion, but he disappointed such hopes by resigning in August in a ploy to extract greater executive authority from the Brazilian

Congress. Instead, the Congress accepted Vice President João Goulart, a member of Brazil's Labor party, as the new president. The Brazilian military saw Goulart as a dangerous leftist and refused to sanction his succession. Despite his own doubts about Goulart, Kennedy announced that this was "a matter which should be left to the people of Brazil. It is their country, their constitution, their decisions, and their government." Brazil's Congress resolved the crisis with a constitutional amendment creating a parliamentary system that included both a president and a strong prime minister. The compromise allowed Goulart to assume the presidency, and Tancredo Neves, a fiscal conservative, to become prime minister.

By November 1961, American defense officials warned of a distinct leftward shift in Rio. A shake-up in the Brazilian military, which had replaced anticommunist officers with men "suspected of being Communist sympathizers or even secret agents," paralleled the "infiltration of the civilian branches of the government" with possible pro-communist officials. These developments foretold a possible "foreign policy oriented increasingly toward the Soviet bloc in world affairs and toward the Castro regime in inter-American affairs." The expropriation in February 1962 of American-owned International Telephone & Telegraph (IT&T) property by the state of Rio Grande do Sul strengthened the conviction that Brazil was drifting to the left and would be unreceptive to better relations with the United States and a principal role in the Alliance. In April, however, despite misgivings, Kennedy agreed to release $129 million in funding for a Brazilian stabilization program that he hoped could increase U.S. influence over Brazil's domestic politics.

During the summer and fall of 1962, White House concerns that Goulart was trying to subvert Brazil's parliamentary system and use October elections to expand his power provoked covert intervention. At a July 30 meeting with Kennedy, U.S. ambassador to Brazil Lincoln Gordon described Goulart's reach for greater control through an anti-American and anti-Alliance strategy. Because "the elections really could be a turning point," Kennedy agreed to have the CIA spend "$5 million funding the campaigns of anti-Goulart candidates for 15 federal seats, 8 state governorships, 250 federal deputy seats, and some 600 seats for state legislatures." He was also receptive to letting the Brazilian military know that the administration would support a coup against Goulart if it were clear that he was "giving the damn country away to the — Communists." Although he believed that Goulart was more of a populist dictator and an opportunist than a communist, Kennedy saw him as a menace to stability in the hemisphere and an imperfect partner in trying to advance the Alliance.

Cuban efforts to export communism to other hemisphere countries gave further urgency to problems with Brazil. Cuban intelligence officers under the direct supervision of Castro were providing three- to five-day courses on subversion to radicals from Venezuela, Guatemala, the Dominican Republic, Ecuador, Peru, Bolivia, Paraguay, Panama, Honduras, and Nicaragua. The objective was "to train a large number of guerrillas in a hurry." Concerned that Soviet military representatives in Cuba would try to restrain Havana from a program that could further unsettle relations with the United States, Castro hid as much of this operation as possible from Moscow.

In December 1962, Kennedy told President Jorge Alessandri of Chile that some people think "the Alliance for Progress has not been successful . . . that the problems in Latin America have become more serious, that the standard of living of the people has not risen." Kennedy publicly acknowledged hemisphere problems as "staggering." But he waxed optimistic about the future, urging against "impatience with failure" and seeing no reason to "desist because we've not solved all the problems overnight."

Privately he knew better. An August 1962 State Department survey of American business communities in Latin America had revealed that "virtually nothing is being done in the name of the Alliance for Progress." Moreover, how could he have much hope for hemisphere democracy when military chiefs in Argentina and Peru had taken the rule of law into their hands and leaders like Quadros and Goulart refused to respect Brazil's constitution? And how could he square professions of self-determination — a central principle of the Alliance — with the reality of secret American interventions in Cuba, Brazil, British Guiana, Peru, Haiti, the Dominican Republic, and every country that seemed vulnerable to left-wing subversion? (And that was just the beginning: A June National Security directive approved by the president had listed four additional Latin American countries "sufficiently threatened by Communist-inspired insurgency" — Ecuador, Colombia, Guatemala, and Venezuela — as requiring the attention of the "Special Group" responsible for counterinsurgency.) In its brief eighteen-month life, the Alliance had become an imperfect cover for traditional actions serving perceived U.S. national security.

* * *

THE NOVEMBER 1961 NEUTRALITY AGREEMENT on Laos, which required a coalition government to become effective, fell apart in the winter of 1961–62. General Nosavan Phoumi, America's client in the struggle between the pro-communist Pathet Lao and centrist Prince Souvanna Phouma, resisted sharing power with his two rivals. Despite threats of reduced U.S. aid, Phoumi, who believed that Washington would not abandon him, provoked a battle with Pathet Lao forces at Nam Tha, near the border with Thailand. There he was completely routed. The U.S. adviser on the ground, putting the best possible face on the defeat, advised Washington, "The morale of my battalion is substantially better than in our last engagement. The last time, they dropped their weapons and ran. This time, they took their weapons with them."

Although U.S. officials believed that Phoumi might have contrived his retreat as a way to increase American involvement, the White House did not believe it could abandon Phoumi or simply leave Laos to the communists. Kennedy agreed that a failure to do anything would encourage the Pathet Lao, but he insisted that U.S. action not "provoke the Viet Minh or the Chinese into large-scale counter-action, but rather . . . suggest to them that we [are] prepared to resist encroachments beyond the cease-fire line."

Possible public pressure from Eisenhower to intervene especially worried Kennedy. Eisenhower had said in April that "he might make a public statement under some conditions. If it is so, we will be in a tough position," Kennedy told George Ball. Kennedy told other advisers that an Eisenhower statement would put domestic pressure on him for military action leading to a possible war, or, if he resisted sending troops and Laos fell, it would politically embarrass him. A conversation between Eisenhower and CIA director John McCone added to Kennedy's concern. Eisenhower said that if the United States sent troops to Laos, it needed to follow up "with whatever support was necessary to achieve the objectives of their mission, including — if necessary — the use of tactical nuclear weapons."

In response, the president sent McCone, McNamara, and Lemnitzer to see Eisenhower. They informed him that Kennedy was ordering units of the Seventh Fleet into the South China Sea toward the Gulf of Siam and would deploy some eighteen hundred men plus two air squadrons in Thailand on the border with Laos. Eisenhower, who believed the loss of Laos jeopardized South Vietnam and Thailand, "indicated both his support of a dynamic effort and a willingness to try to influence [the] political leadership of his party from entering into public debate on the question." He also promised that "he would not at this time privately or publicly urge moving U.S. combat troops into Laos."

Eisenhower thus under wraps, Kennedy now encouraged press and public uncertainty about U.S. intentions toward Laos. He wanted "to maintain vis-a-vis the Communist bloc an attitude of 'veiled ambiguity,'" he told his advisers. He also wanted Phoumi to understand that the administration had no confidence in him and would not intervene in Laos on his behalf. "All United States moves," Kennedy said, "should be designed (a) to bring Phoumi to the conference table, and (b) to have the desired effect on the Soviets and on the Chinese." But he wanted no irreversible commitments that might drag the country into an unwanted war. He "wished to retain the element of reversibility in all military actions. He wanted no public announcement of landings until after he had ordered such landings. Furthermore, he wanted it again made clear to the Lao that we were undertaking no new commitments toward them." Compared to Latin America, where fears of Cuban subversion throughout the hemisphere had agitated Kennedy into anticommunist excesses, policy toward Laos was a model of sensible restraint.

U.S. military threats produced a quick response. Since Moscow and Peking had no intention of risking a wider war for control of Laos, the Pathet Lao responded to American troop movements by immediately resuming negotiations. On June 12, after the Laotian factions agreed to form a coalition government under Souvanna Phouma, Khrushchev wired Kennedy: "Good news has come from Laos." The political accommodation seemed likely to serve both the Laotian people and peace in Southeast Asia. The result also strengthened the conviction that other unresolved international problems might yield to reasonable exchange. Kennedy answered Khrushchev: The Laotian solution "will surely have a significant and positive effect far beyond the borders of Laos."

Khrushchev reiterated his enthusiasm for the settlement in a message through Georgi Bolshakov, the ostensible Soviet embassy press officer in Washington. To take advantage of JFK's wish to bypass his own national security bureaucracy, Khrushchev used Bolshakov, really a high-ranking military intelligence agent, to speak to the president through Bobby Kennedy, with whom Bolshakov met every couple of weeks. A report in the *Times* of London that the CIA was "actively opposing US policy in Laos and working against a neutral government" may have moved Khrushchev to tell Kennedy that "the settlement in Laos was an extremely important step forward in the relationship of the Soviet Union and the United States." JFK valued Khrushchev's message, which he hoped signaled an interest in other agreements. The *Times* account of CIA opposition worried him. When Pierre Salinger told him of his intention to deny the *Times* story as "preposterous and untrue," Kennedy replied, "The story I assume is untrue — Do they offer evidence?" Kennedy had learned the hard way that the CIA could not always be trusted, and he now wondered if the *Times* might be onto something.

AFTER THE LAOTIANS SIGNED a neutrality declaration in July, Kennedy instructed Harriman to explore the possibility of negotiations with the North Vietnamese. He hoped that Hanoi and Moscow, especially after Khrushchev's comments, might be willing to neutralize all of Indochina as a way to limit Chinese control in the region. But at a secret meeting with North Vietnam's foreign minister in a Geneva hotel suite, Harriman and William Sullivan, his deputy, hit a stone wall. "We got absolutely nowhere," Sullivan said.

The alternative was to continue helping Saigon. Reports from American military and civilian officials there in the spring of 1962 that U.S. aid was turning the tide in South Vietnam made this acceptable, and even appealing. McNamara told a House committee that the administration was hoping to clean up the conflict in Vietnam by "terminating subversion, covert aggression, and combat operations." He saw no need for U.S. combat troops. In May, at the end of a two-day trip to Vietnam, his first, McNamara, unshaven and dressed in rumpled khaki shirt and trousers and hiking boots dusty from his travels in the countryside, carried data-filled notebooks into a press conference at the ambassador's residence. "I've seen nothing but progress and hopeful indications of further progress," he declared. Pressed by reporters to move beyond declarations of good news boosting Saigon's morale, McNamara, UPI's Neil Sheehan recorded, was "a Gibraltar of optimism." Following him out to his car, Sheehan asked the secretary to speak the truth off the record. Fixing Sheehan with a cold stare, McNamara replied, "Every quantitative measurement we have shows we're winning this war." By July, reinforced by a military briefing in Honolulu that predicted a U.S. military exit one year after South Vietnamese forces had become "fully operational" in 1964, McNamara could see "tremendous progress to date."

In September 1962, after his first visit to Vietnam since the fall of 1961, Max Taylor also reported that "much progress has been accomplished. . . . The most notable perhaps is the snowballing of the strategic hamlet program which has resulted in some 5,000 hamlets being fortified or in process of fortification." Dating from February 1962, the hamlets were supposedly winning the support of Vietnamese farmers by creating allegedly safe havens against the Viet Cong with South Vietnamese forces. Conversations with junior U.S. officers attached to South Vietnamese units led Taylor to tell Kennedy, "You have to be on the ground to sense a lift in the national morale. . . . I'm sure you would get a great deal of encouragement out of hearing these young officers." U.S. embassy officials in Saigon confirmed Taylor's impressions, reporting in September that they were "tremendously encouraged. . . . The military progress had been little short of sensational. . . . The strategic hamlet program had transformed the countryside and . . . the Viet Cong could not now destroy the program." After receiving these reports, Kennedy told Nguyen Dinh Thuan, Diem's cabinet secretary, who was visiting Washington, that recent reports from Saigon were encouraging. The president expressed "admiration for the progress being made in Viet-Nam against the Communists."

Optimism — or wishful thinking — was so strong now that Kennedy ordered McNamara to begin planning a U.S. military exit from Vietnam. According to Deputy Defense Secretary Gilpatric, the president "made clear to McNamara and me that he wanted to not only hold the level of U.S. military presence in Vietnam down, but he wanted to reverse the flow." To that end, McNamara drew up a three-year plan for the reduction of U.S. forces in Vietnam. U.S. military planners told him that "advisers" could leave by 1965, but McNamara extended the date to 1968. By then, he hoped to withdraw the last fifteen hundred U.S. troops and reduce military assistance payments to $40.8 million, less than a quarter of 1962 layouts. McNamara rationalized the plan by saying that "it might be difficult to retain public support for U.S. operations in Vietnam indefinitely. Political pressures would build up as losses continued. Therefore . . . planning must be undertaken now and a program devised to phase out U.S. military involvement."

There is no direct record of Kennedy's agreement with McNamara's plan, but it is difficult to believe that McNamara did not have the president's approval. They were close, very close, or as close as anyone in the administration was to the president, aside from Bobby. McNamara was Kennedy's idea of a first-rate deputy. The president "thought very highly of Bob McNamara," Bobby recalled, "very highly of him. . . . He was head and shoulders above everybody else. . . . In the area of foreign policy or defense," Bobby added, "obviously, it was Bob McNamara, not Dean Rusk." With his affinity for numbers, for unsentimental calculation, McNamara "symbolized the idea that [the administration] could manage and control events, in an intelligent, rational way. . . . He was so impressive and loyal," David Halberstam wrote later, "that it was hard to believe, in the halcyon days of 1963 when his reputation was at its height, that anything he took command of could go wrong." Kennedy himself said, McNamara would "come in with his twenty options and then say, 'Mr. President, I think we should do this.' I like that. Makes the job easier."

McNamara was one of only two members of the cabinet — the other being Douglas Dillon — who enjoyed a consistent social relationship with the Kennedys. Charming, gay, gregarious, a sort of modern Renaissance man with a capacity to discuss the arts and literature, he became a favorite of Jacqueline Kennedy's. "Men can't understand his sex appeal," Jackie said. "Why is it," Bobby wondered, "that they call him 'the computer' and yet he's the one all my sisters want to sit next to at dinner?"

In proposing to get out of Vietnam before it turned into a political liability in the United States, McNamara reflected the president's thinking. Kennedy wanted the lowest possible profile for U.S. involvement in the conflict. In May, he instructed that there be no "unnecessary trips to Vietnam, especially by high ranking officers," who might draw more attention to America's role in the fighting. In a meeting with congressional leaders, Kennedy made it clear that he did not want to announce increases in U.S. troops. The objective for JFK, Fulbright said, was to keep the United States from becoming "formally involved." The increase in advisers was less important than keeping things "on an informal basis, because . . . we couldn't withdraw if it gets too formal." In October, Kennedy reluctantly agreed to let the military destroy crops in Viet Cong–controlled areas. It was a small concession to the Joint Chiefs, who were pressing him to use more muscle in Vietnam. "His main train of thinking," an NSC member told Bundy, "was that you cannot say no to your military advisers all the time." But he wanted to be sure that crop destruction did not become an embarrassment to the administration. "What can we do about keeping it from becoming an American enterprise which would be surfaced with [or described as] poisoning food?" Kennedy asked his advisers.

Knowing nothing of the Kennedy-McNamara plan to reduce military commitments to Vietnam, American correspondents in Saigon remained highly critical of administration policy. Seeing U.S. officials as misled by the Vietnamese and their own illusions, reporters disputed Diem-embassy assertions of steady progress in the conflict. In October 1962, Halberstam, speaking for many of his colleagues, said, "The closer one gets to the actual contact level of the war, the further one gets from official optimism." By protecting Diem from criticism, Halberstam added, the U.S. embassy was turning into "the adjunct of a dictatorship," and if reporters accepted the official line on Diem and the war, they would "become the adjuncts of a tyranny."

The press, an embassy official reported in September, "believes that the situation in Viet Nam is going to pieces and that we have been unable to convince them otherwise." Taylor said that American journalists in Saigon "remained uninformed and often belligerently adverse to the programs of the U.S. and SVN Governments." His observations and discussions in Vietnam told him that press reports of difficulties between U.S. military advisers and South Vietnamese officers were false. The administration needed to push publishers into "responsible reporting," he said. In his conversation with Thuan, Kennedy urged "the GVN not to be too concerned by press reports. He assured Mr. Thuan that the U.S. government did not accept everything the correspondents wrote even if it appeared in the *New York Times*. He emphasized that if the Vietnamese government was successful, the public image would take care of itself." The president added that "inaccurate press reporting . . . occurred every day in Washington."

This last statement was said with real conviction. Kennedy was not as tolerant of the press as he seemed. He believed that its affinity for the sensational and its instinctive impulse to be critical of the White House had repeatedly produced unfair attacks on his administration. *Time* magazine's coverage of his presidency particularly irritated him. He viewed it as inconsistent and much more friendly to his predecessor. Complaints to *Time* publisher Henry Luce evoked a strong defense of the magazine's performance but left Kennedy unconvinced.

Kennedy sympathized with the belief in Saigon that American reporters were opportunists trying to build reputations with controversial stories belittling Diem and progress in the war. This allowed him to rationalize new October directives to the State and Defense departments about press interviews. In response to national security leaks, including those involving Vietnam, Kennedy ordered officials not to hold one-on-one meetings with reporters, and if they did, "to report promptly and in writing on any conversation with 'news media' representatives." A leak to *New York Times* military correspondent Hanson Baldwin, which seemed to compromise U.S. satellite intelligence on Soviet ICBM installations, especially upset the president. He saw the press and the *New York Times* in particular as "the most privileged group," who regarded any attempt to rein them in "as a limitation on their civil rights. And they are not very used to it." Joe Alsop called the restrictions on interviews "news-control devices" that threatened healthy democratic debate about vital issues. But Kennedy refused to back down. The restrictions were "aimed at the protection of genuinely sensitive information," he told Alsop through Bundy. Nor would the directives prevent "responsible reporters from doing their job." The president's order "was so rarely and humorously observed," Sorensen remembered, "that it soon fell into disuse." Nevertheless, the directives undermined Kennedy's generally good relations with the press and made reporters more distrustful of White House pronouncements on everything.

Kennedy believed that newspaper stories from Saigon, whatever their accuracy, made it difficult for him to follow a cautious policy of limited involvement. If people believed that we were losing the conflict, it would create additional pressure to expand U.S. commitments. His political strategy was to keep the war off the front pages of America's newspapers. Press accounts arousing controversy drew more attention to Vietnam than he wanted, and an inflamed public debate would make it difficult to hold down commitments and maintain his freedom to withdraw when he saw fit. As with Laos, and, again, unlike with Latin America, Kennedy maintained a good sense of proportion about the limits of Vietnam's importance in the overall scheme of U.S. national security. But his good sense of proportion could not withstand other pressures.

As KENNEDY BEGAN to pay more attention to Vietnam, he could not neglect larger threats. After announcing plans to resume atmospheric tests at the end of April, he made last-ditch efforts to halt the slide into an escalating arms race. On March 5, he thanked Khrushchev for agreeing to have their foreign ministers open a new round of disarmament talks in Geneva on March 14. He also urged against additional "sterile exchanges of propaganda." He proposed, "Let us, instead, join in giving our close personal support and direction to the work of our representatives, and let us join in working for their success."

But Kennedy could not persuade the Soviets that international verification was essential to a comprehensive test ban treaty. The sticking point in Soviet-American discussions was on-site investigation of seismic shocks. The Americans insisted that only direct observation could establish the difference between an earthquake and a nuclear explosion, "a natural and an artificial seismic event." The Soviets rejected the distinction as an American espionage ploy. Gromyko privately told Rusk that "even one foreigner loose in the Soviet Union could find things out that could be most damaging to the USSR." Although it was possible to ascribe Soviet suspicion to paranoid fears of foreigners, Macmillan saw more rational calculation at work. Convinced that on-site investigations would reveal nuclear inferiority to the West and eager to use American tests as an excuse for additional tests of their own, the Soviets were resigned to pushing the United States into atmospheric explosions. (Much later, Khrushchev admitted as much.)

The administration suffered a public relations setback after the Defense Department released preliminary results of a seismic research study concluding that international detection stations in the Soviet Union might not be essential to monitor underground nuclear explosions. When Arthur Dean, U.S. ambassador to the disarmament talks, publicly acknowledged this as a possibility, it gave the Soviets a propaganda bonanza. In fact, although the seismic study weakened the case for on-site inspection stations, the Pentagon maintained that they were still essential to prevent Soviet cheating. But that now seemed like a secondary detail, and because Moscow continued to reject inspections, prospects for a comprehensive test ban largely disappeared. At a July 27 White House meeting on arms control, Kennedy vented his irritation at the premature release of the report. "We had messed up the handling of the new data," he said. "Information about it was all over town before we had decided what effect it would have on our policy."

Kennedy's frustration with professional diplomats and military officers who, in addition to Dean, had undermined America's position in the test ban talks was part of a larger concern. On July 30, three days after complaining about the Pentagon's misstep, he expressed his low opinion of America's professional diplomats and military chiefs. In a taped conversation with Rusk, Bundy, and Ball, Kennedy described U.S. career envoys as weak or spineless: "I just see an awful lot of fellows who . . . don't seem to have *cojones*." By contrast, "the Defense Department looks as if that's all they've got. They haven't any brains. . . . You get all this sort of virility . . . at the Pentagon and you get a lot of Arleigh Burkes: admirable nice figure without any brains."

In fact, the Pentagon's premature release of a report undermining a White House policy was partly the consequence of bureaucratic chaos. The *New York Times*, in particular, had frequently complained about the hit-or-miss procedures of a government poorly coordinated by the White House. Kennedy was not unsympathetic to the *Times'* argument. He had already expended more energy than he cared to on trying to bring greater order to his foreign policy agencies — defense, state, and the CIA. Predictably, domestic red tape bothered him less than poorly functioning foreign policy machinery; he was fond of saying, "Domestic policy can only defeat us; foreign policy can kill us." But there seemed only so much that could be done. Certainly, Kennedy was temperamentally uncomfortable with managing everything from the White House. Why had he surrounded himself with so many talented people if he were going to oversee every agency? And perhaps some disorder was even a good thing. "Creative governments will always be 'out of channels,'" Schlesinger told *Times* publisher Orvil Dryfoos. "[They] will always present aspects of 'confusion' and 'meddling'; [they] will always discomfit officials whose routine is being disturbed or whose security is being threatened. But all this is inseparable from the process by which new ideas and new institutions enable government to meet new challenges. Orderly governments are very rarely creative; and creative governments are almost never orderly." The balance between constructive chaos and bureaucratic mess seemed hard to maintain, however.

In September, the Soviets rejected U.S. proposals for both comprehensive and limited test bans, proposing instead a nonbinding ban on atmospheric explosions and a moratorium on underground detonations, both to begin on January 1, 1963. Kennedy accepted the cutoff date, but insisted at an August 29 press conference that it should rest on "workable international agreements; gentlemen's agreements and moratoria do not provide the types of guarantees that are necessary. . . . This is the lesson of the Soviet government's tragic decision to renew testing just a year ago." On September 7, when the Geneva talks recessed to make way for the U.N. General Assembly session in New York, a reliable test ban agreement of any kind remained an uncertain hope.

INTO 1962 KENNEDY STRUGGLED to find some formula for accommodation with Moscow over Germany and Berlin. In November 1961, the president suggested the creation of an International Access Authority made up of NATO, Warsaw Pact, and neutral representatives to eliminate the possibility of confrontations over Allied movements in and out of Berlin. Although the East Germans promptly rejected this plan as colonialist, Kennedy expanded the idea to include flights, over which East Germany had no control. Seeing the suggestion as a way to block productive talks, the Soviets began harassing civil aircraft flying in the Berlin air corridors.

Despite mutual recognition of the importance of Berlin to improved Soviet-American relations, both sides doggedly stuck to their positions: The United States would not give up access to Berlin or concede to a permanent division of Germany, both changes Moscow believed essential to its future national security. Although Kennedy persuaded Khrushchev to end the buzzing of air traffic, they could not break the impasse. By June, Kennedy saw no point in continuing the exchange of private messages on Germany. "Matters relating to Berlin are currently being discussed in careful detail by Secretary Rusk and Ambassador Dobrynin," he wrote Khrushchev, "and I think it may be best to leave the discussion in their capable hands at this time." In July, when Khrushchev answered with a stale proposal for the replacement of western occupation forces with U.N. troops, Kennedy dismissed the suggestion as an extension of Moscow's "consistent failure . . . to take any real account of what we have made clear are the vital interests of the United States and its Allies."

An incident at the Berlin Wall, in which East German security guards killed a defector, together with Khrushchev's fears of a U.S. first strike against the Soviet Union, heightened tensions between Moscow and Washington in the summer. In March, Adenauer had told Bobby that Khrushchev told him that he genuinely believed that "the United States wants to destroy the Soviet Union." In an interview with journalist Stewart Alsop, Kennedy said that, "in some circumstances we must be prepared to use the nuclear weapon at the start, come what may — a clear attack on Western Europe, for example." Khrushchev told Salinger that this "new doctrine" was "a very bad mistake for which [the President] will have to pay!" Although Kennedy's full statement left little doubt that his concern was with avoiding nuclear war, Khrushchev ordered a special military alert in response to the article.

In June, Bolshakov reported a conversation with Bobby Kennedy that renewed Khrushchev's worries about a U.S. nuclear attack. Do war hawks enjoy special influence in the United States? Bolshakov had asked Bobby. "In the government, no," he had replied, "[b]ut among the generals in the Pentagon . . . there are such people. Recently," Bobby had added, "the [Joint] Chiefs [of Staff] offered the President a report in which they confirmed that the United States is currently ahead of the Soviet Union in military power and that *in extremis* it would be possible to probe the forces of the Soviet Union."

Although Bobby Kennedy assured Bolshakov that the president "had decisively rejected any attempt by zealous advocates of a clash between the United States and the Soviet Union . . . to [get him to] accept their point of view," the conversation upset Khrushchev. If Bobby's "candor" was aimed at encouraging Khrushchev to reach agreements on Berlin and test bans, it backfired. Khrushchev sent back a message through Bolshakov restating his determination to sign a peace treaty with East Germany that would liquidate "war remnants . . . and on this basis the situation in West Berlin — a free demilitarized city — would be normalized." To underscore Soviet determination not to be intimidated by U.S. military might, Khrushchev told Interior Secretary Stewart Udall during a September visit to Russia that if "any lunatics in your country want war, Western Europe will hold them back. War in this day and age means no Paris and no France, all in the space of an hour. It's been a long time since you could spank us like a little boy — now we can swat your ass."

Nevertheless, because Khrushchev was eager to help the president in the congressional elections, he sent a message asking if Kennedy preferred that he wait on a Berlin treaty until after November 6. After Sorensen told Dobrynin that the president "could not possibly lay himself open to Republican charges of appeasement in his response to any buildup in Berlin pressures between now and

November 6," Khrushchev promised not to "hurt [his] chances in the November elections." Khrushchev said that he intended to give Kennedy a choice after the elections: "go to war, or sign a peace treaty. We will not allow your troops to be in Berlin. We will permit access to West Berlin for economic or commercial purposes, but not for military purposes. Everybody is saying nowadays that there will be a war. I don't agree. Sensible people won't start a war. What is Berlin to the United States? . . . Do you need Berlin? Like hell you need it. Nor do we need it."

It was not clear to Kennedy why Khrushchev had reverted to such belligerence. He concluded that Khrushchev was an unstable personality, an irresponsible character carried away by delusions. He was wildly erratic and unpredictable, friendly one day and unfriendly the next. He was "like the gangsters both of us had dealt with," Bobby said. "Khrushchev's kind of action — what he did and how he acted — was how an immoral gangster would act and not . . . a statesman, not as a person with a sense of responsibility." Khrushchev, Kennedy told Cyrus Sulzberger of the *New York Times*, reminded him of Joe McCarthy and Jimmy Hoffa — rough, tough characters who could disarm people with their politeness. Llewellyn Thompson shared Kennedy's view. There was "a kind of hypocrisy" to the man, Thompson told Kennedy during a conversation about Khrushchev in August. "It's like dealing with a bunch of bootleggers or gangsters." Yet Kennedy also knew that Khrushchev was a shrewd, calculating politician who never acted without some self-serving purpose. Events in October 1962 would reveal what Khrushchev was trying to achieve.

CHAPTER 16

To the Brink — And Back

When at some future date the high court of history sits in judgment on each of us, it will ask: "Were we truly men of courage — with the courage to stand up to one's enemies — and the courage to stand up, when necessary, to one's associates?"

— John F. Kennedy, address to the Massachusetts Legislature, January 9, 1961

IN THE SPRING AND SUMMER OF 1962, Khrushchev's renewed threats against Germany and Berlin were tied to his belief that Washington was planning an invasion to topple Castro. He was wrong. In March, when Cuban exile leader José Miró Cardona asked Bundy for help with an invasion, he refused. "Decisive action [cannot] be accomplished without the open involvement of U.S. armed forces," Bundy said. "This would mean open war against Cuba which in the U.S. judgment [is] not advisable in the present international situation." The following month Kennedy told Cardona the same thing. But even if the United States had no immediate invasion plan, Khrushchev felt that Castro's support of subversion would eventually persuade Kennedy to act against him. In addition, concern that Castro was moving closer to communist China gave Khrushchev another reason to strengthen Soviet-Cuban relations.

To do this, he decided to turn Cuba into a missile base from which he could more directly threaten the United States. In May and June, Khrushchev and Soviet military and political chiefs agreed to deploy on the island twenty-four medium-range R-12 missiles, which could travel 1,050 miles, and sixteen intermediate R-14 missiles, with a range of 2,100 miles. The forty missiles would double the number in the Soviet arsenal that could reach the continental United States. The plan also called for approximately forty-four thousand support troops and thirteen hundred civilian construction workers, as well as a Soviet naval base housing surface ships and "nuclear-missile equipped submarines."

Khrushchev saw multiple benefits from the deployment of Soviet missiles abroad. It would deter a U.S. attack on Cuba, keep the island in Moscow's orbit, and give him greater leverage in bargaining with Washington over Berlin. Yet such a substantial change in the balance of power seemed likely to provoke a crisis and possibly a war with the United States. Khrushchev convinced himself, however, that the "intelligent" Kennedy "would not set off a thermonuclear war if there were our warheads there, just as they put their warheads on missiles in Turkey." These fifteen intermediate-range Jupiter missiles under U.S. command, which became operational in 1962, had indeed frightened Moscow, but Khrushchev did not anticipate using his missiles. "Every idiot can start a war," Khrushchev told Kremlin associates, "but it is impossible to win this war. . . . Therefore the missiles have one purpose — to scare them, to restrain them . . . to give them back some of their own medicine." The deployment would equalize "what the West likes to call 'the balance of power.' The Americans had surrounded our country with military bases and threatened us with nuclear weapons, and now they would learn just what it feels like to have enemy missiles pointing at [them]."

Khrushchev's Cuban plan also rested on a hope of regaining political influence lost because of domestic and foreign setbacks. He had failed to achieve predicted levels of food production, which had forced increases in consumer prices. Also, he had made no appreciable headway in forcing a final Berlin settlement, or in ensuring Castro's safety from an outside attack, or in squelching a Chinese challenge to Moscow's leadership of world communism. Most important, he had failed to close the missile gap between Russia and the United States.

Khrushchev's aim was to hide the buildup in Cuba until after the American elections, when he planned to attend the U.N. General Assembly and see Kennedy. He would then reveal the existence of the Cuban missile base and extract concessions from the president over Berlin and Cuba. As historians Aleksandr Fursenko and Timothy Naftali concluded, borrowing from JFK, it was "one hell of a gamble."

Not the least of the risk was hiding from America's sophisticated intelligence apparatus the movement of men and equipment to Cuba. As was eventually learned from Soviet documents released in 1999, the Soviets had deployed nuclear missiles in East Germany in 1959 and managed to remove them later that year without apparent discovery by the West. Although Western intelligence agencies detected the Soviet deployment, the information apparently did not reach "top-level policymakers in the U.S. until late 1960." Nor did any Western intelligence agency give any indication to the Soviets that they knew of Moscow's unprecedented missile deployment. Although transporting missiles from Russia to Cuba was more difficult to hide than placing them in East Germany, Khrushchev believed that the Americans still assumed that he would never send weapons of mass destruction abroad. He acknowledged that the Americans would notice the increased shipments of men and arms to Cuba but believed that they would see them as no more than a strengthening of Cuban defenses against another invasion. By the time the Americans woke up to what was happening, the missiles would be in place.

His reasoning had some merit. In August 1962, U.S. intelligence reported increased Soviet military equipment going to Cuba, where it was transported to the interior of the island under Soviet guards. U.S. national security officials concluded that the Soviets were installing SA-2 missiles, a modern anti-aircraft weapon with a thirty-mile range. The report noted that the SA-2s could be fit with nuclear warheads, "but there is no evidence that the Soviet government has ever provided nuclear warheads to any other state, on any terms. It seems unlikely that such a move is currently planned — but," the analysts warned, "there is also little reason to suppose that the Soviets would refuse to introduce such weapons if the move could be controlled in the Soviet interest."

Soviet private and public statements also gave Kennedy assurances that the military buildup represented a change in degree but not in kind. In April 1961, after the Bay of Pigs invasion, Khrushchev had told Kennedy, "We have no bases in Cuba, and do not intend to establish any." On July 30, 1962, in order to reduce the likelihood of exposure, Khrushchev asked Kennedy, "for the sake of better relations," to stop reconnaissance flights over Soviet ships in the Caribbean. Eager to avoid any international crisis during the election campaign, Kennedy ostensibly agreed, on the condition that Moscow put the Berlin question "on ice." Though Khrushchev wanted to know what the president meant by "on ice," he agreed to Kennedy's request. In early September, he sent word to Kennedy through Ambassador Anatoly Dobrynin, promising, "Nothing will be undertaken before the American congressional elections that could complicate the international situation or aggravate the tension in the relations between our two countries." At the same time, he had Georgi Bolshakov tell Bobby that the Soviet Union was placing no more than defensive weapons in Cuba.

Khrushchev gave Interior Secretary Stewart Udall the same message. During their September 6 conversations, Khrushchev said, "Now, as to Cuba — here is an area that could really lead to some unexpected consequences. I have been reading what some irresponsible Senators have been saying on this. A lot of people are making a big fuss because we are giving aid to Cuba. But you are giving aid to Japan. Just recently I was reading that you have placed atomic warheads on Japanese territory, and surely this is not something the Japanese need. So when Castro comes to us for aid, we give him what he needs for defense. He hasn't much military equipment, so he asked us to supply some. But only for defense."

However much Kennedy wished to believe the Soviet professions of restraint, he could not take their assurances at face value; their deviousness in secretly preparing renewed nuclear tests had made him suspicious of anything they said. Besides, McCone and Bobby were asserting that the "defensive" buildup might presage offensive missile deployments, and even if not, they saw the expanding Soviet presence in Cuba as reason to topple Castro's regime as quickly as possible. Complaints from Republicans about timid responses to the Cuban danger joined with the McCone-Bobby warnings to heighten Kennedy's concerns. On August 31, New York Republican senator Kenneth Keating complained in a floor speech that the administration had no effective response to the installation of Soviet rockets in Cuba under the control of twelve hundred Soviet troops; nor, Keating added, did the administration seem prepared to deal with the troubling construction of other missile bases.

At the beginning of September, Kennedy, trying to strike a balance between competing pressures, privately promised congressional leaders to take action against Cuba if Khrushchev was deploying surface-to-surface nuclear missiles. Therefore, it seemed prudent to issue a forceful warning to Moscow. Such a public statement would have the added benefit of blunting potential Republican political gains from assertions about White House inattentiveness to a crucial national security problem.

ON SEPTEMBER 4, Kennedy and his advisers spent several hours preparing a statement about Soviet missiles in Cuba. To be as clear as possible, Kennedy expanded an admonition about "offensive weapons" to include a warning against "ground-to-ground missiles." He also eliminated any mention of the Monroe Doctrine and kept references to Cuba to a minimum. He wanted the statement to focus on Soviet aggression and not on U.S. power in the Western Hemisphere or on the administration's eagerness to topple Castro's regime. "The major danger is the Soviet Union with missiles and nuclear warheads, not Cuba," he said in a taped conversation.

At six in the evening, Pierre Salinger read Kennedy's statement to the press. He cited evidence of anti-aircraft missiles with a twenty-five-mile range and torpedo boats equipped with ship-to-ship guided missiles. He also pointed to some thirty-five hundred Soviet support technicians in Cuba or en route there to facilitate the use of these weapons. He emphasized, however, that allegations of organized Soviet combat forces were unconfirmed, as were assertions that the Soviets had introduced weapons with an offensive capability, such as ground-to-ground missiles. "Were it to be otherwise," Kennedy declared, "the gravest issues would arise." Castro's regime would "not be allowed to export its aggressive purposes by force or the threat of force. It will be prevented by whatever means may be necessary from taking action against any part of the Western Hemisphere." On September 7, Kennedy also revealed that he was calling 150,000 army reserves to active duty for twelve months.

Kennedy balanced his public statement cautioning the Soviets with private resistance to congressional pressure for prompt action against Havana. "What is our policy in relation to Cuba?" Wisconsin Republican senator Alexander Wiley asked. "I'm just back from the hinterland and everybody is inquiring about it . . . .[Is it] just to sit still and let Cuba carry on?" Kennedy promised that any use of Cuba's new weapons against a neighboring country would bring a U.S. intervention. But a U.S. attack on Cuba now "would be a mistake. . . . We have to keep some proportion," Kennedy said. "We're talking about 60 MiGs, we're talking about some ground-to-air missiles . . . which do not threaten the United States. We are not talking about nuclear warheads. We've got a very difficult situation in Berlin.

We've got a difficult situation in Southeast Asia and a lot of other places." Wiley, who had been calling publicly for a blockade of Cuba, asked Kennedy about this possibility. "It's an act of war," Kennedy replied, and would likely produce a retaliatory blockade of Berlin. The danger from Cuba was "by subversion and example. There's obviously no military threat, as yet, to the United States. . . . Even though I know a lot of people want to invade Cuba," Kennedy added, "I would be opposed to it today."

Kennedy's counsels of restraint could not inhibit Republicans fearful of Khrushchev's intentions and eager to exploit a political advantage from urging military action against Castro. But the Republicans were not the only ones pressing for a stronger White House response. The press chimed in with dire warnings. And the eighty-eight-year-old poet Robert Frost, after meeting Khrushchev in Russia, told a press conference in New York on September 9 that Khrushchev thought Americans were "too liberal to fight." The comment angered Kennedy, who felt it added to the pressure on him to get tough with Castro and Khrushchev. "Why did Frost say that?" Kennedy asked Udall, who had been with the poet in Russia. Udall responded that it was Frost's way of paraphrasing Khrushchev's assertion that America and the West were in decline. (Khrushchev had reminded Frost of Tolstoy's famous comment to Maxim Gorky about sex and old age: "The desire is the same, it's the performance that's different.") But the damage was done.

Democratic senators at risk in the November elections also pressed the president for stronger action. They sent word through majority leader Mike Mansfield that they might "have to leave [him] on this matter" unless there were "at least a 'do-something' gesture of militancy." They urged Kennedy to consider everything from "a Congressional resolution to a 'quarantine' of Cuba (short of blockade) to all out war, at least with Cuba and perhaps with Russia as well."

The hysteria chilled Kennedy, who tried "to set the matter in perspective" at a September 13 news conference. Castro's charges of an imminent American invasion, he said, were an attempt to divert attention from self-inflicted economic problems and to justify increased Soviet military aid. Loose talk of an invasion by some in the United States served "to give a thin color of legitimacy to the Communist pretense that such a threat exists." Unilateral U.S. intervention, he argued, was neither required nor justified. Castro posed no direct military threat to the United States or to any of his neighbors. If any of this should change, however, the United States would not hesitate to protect its interests. He hoped that the American people would "in this nuclear age . . . keep both their nerve and their head."

The CIA reinforced Kennedy's counsels of caution. On September 19, the Agency, in an updated assessment of the Cuban buildup, reiterated that deploying ballistic missiles or building a submarine base would give the Soviets considerable military advantages, but, they noted, "[It] would be incompatible with Soviet practice to date and with Soviet policy as we presently estimate it. It would indicate a far greater willingness to increase the level of risk in US-Soviet relations than the USSR has displayed thus far."

On September 28, Khrushchev encouraged Kennedy's caution. In a long letter about nuclear tests and Soviet-American relations more generally, he emphasized his determination to settle the German/Berlin problem by signing a peace treaty. As Kennedy had requested, he had been willing to put the issue "on ice" until after the November elections. But the call-up of 150,000 reservists and U.S. threats to invade Cuba were forcing his hand, and Khrushchev wished the United States to be under no illusion: An American attack on Cuba would bring retaliatory action against Berlin.

The CIA assessment and Khrushchev's warnings outweighed arguments for direct action against Havana, but public assurances that the United States was under no new threat and private warnings to Moscow not to create one did not mute the congressional and public outcry over Cuba. On September 20, the Senate passed a resolution by 86 to 1 authorizing the president "to prevent the creation or use of an externally supported offensive military capability endangering the security of the United States." Schlesinger urged that Rusk call in Dobrynin and tell him that persistence in arming Cuba would "preclude the resolution of any outstanding disagreement" between them, force an increase in the U.S. defense budget, and possibly compel action "to eliminate Castro and his regime." One National Security Council member echoed Schlesinger's point: "The question is no longer whether we should 'do something about Cuba,'" William Jordan told Walt Rostow, "but rather what we should do, how, when, and where. There is urgent need for a program of action that will address itself to such things as: the great and growing sense of deep frustration on the part of millions of Americans as regards Cuban developments."

But as long as the Cuban buildup seemed to be defensive, Kennedy refused to go beyond warning Moscow and indirect intimidation. Secretly he ordered McNamara to put plans for military operations against Cuba into motion. There were also large-scale maneuvers, which were held on October 22 along the southern Atlantic coast and around Puerto Rico. The exercise — pointedly and obviously code-named "Ortsac" (Castro spelled backwards) — involved seventy-five hundred marines in a mock invasion of Puerto Rican beaches. Seventy thousand servicemen participated in air force maneuvers. Everything about the maneuvers seemed calculated to send Moscow signals of U.S. readiness to take military action.

Kennedy further instructed Bobby to step up the activities of the Special Group responsible for Mongoose operations to topple Castro. A Group meeting on October 4 produced "a sharp exchange" between Bobby and McCone. Bobby reported the president's dissatisfaction with Mongoose — "nothing was moving forward" — and yelled at General Lansdale for failing to attempt any acts of sabotage. McCone attributed this failure to the administration's reluctance to have anything blamed on Washington. Bobby denied that was the case and emphasized the need to throw aside worries about risks. Lansdale was instructed "to give consideration to new and more dynamic approaches," including sabotage, mining of harbors to impede Soviet military deliveries, and possible capture of Cuban officers for interrogation. But Bobby's abrasive comments were less a spur to "more dynamic approaches" than an admission of Mongoose's incapacity to shake Castro's popularity and firm hold on power.

Fearful that implementation of plans for a naval base would be quickly detected by U.S. intelligence and would stimulate a military response, Khrushchev canceled the deployment of surface ships and nuclear-armed submarines to Cuba. Instead, he approved the transit by ship of a squadron of light bombers and six short-range Luna missiles with their nuclear bombs. He also authorized a draft order to his Cuban commander to decide whether to use nuclear weapons in response to a U.S. invasion if communications with Moscow were lost. Khrushchev did not sign the order, however, but he kept it ready for possible future implementation.

On October 1, McNamara and the Joint Chiefs received disturbing information about offensive weapons in Cuba. On September 21, the Defense Intelligence Agency had learned of "a first-hand sighting on September 12 of a truck convoy of 20 objects 65 to 70 feet long which resembled large missiles." The convoy had "turned into an airport on the southwest edge of Havana." Because early reports of a similar nature had proved false, the DIA described the information as only "potentially significant." However, photographs received in the last week of September and reports of surface-to-air missile (SAM) sites produced "a hypothesis that MRBM [medium-range ballistic missile] sites were under preparation in Pinar del Rio province."

High-altitude U-2 reconnaissance flights were essential to confirm the report. But concern that Soviet SA-2 anti-aircraft missiles might shoot down a U-2 made such surveillance risky. Detection on August 30 of a U-2 over Soviet airspace and the loss of a Taiwanese U-2 on September 8 to a Chinese missile had produced a temporary suspension of such flights over Cuba. But the CIA warned that the SA-2s might be guarding other missile installations in western Cuba and argued that whatever the risks, U-2 flights were called for. "Don't you ever let . . . up?" Rusk asked the CIA's representative at a September 10 White House meeting. "How do you expect me to negotiate on Berlin with all these incidents?" But Bobby believed that the stakes were too high for them to avoid the risk. "What's the matter, Dean," he asked, "no guts?"

On October 5, Bundy and McCone argued for U-2 flights directly over Cuba. McCone believed that the existence of Soviet offensive missiles in Cuba was "a probability rather than a mere possibility," but Bundy held to the conviction that "the Soviets would not go that far." The same day, Bolshakov carried another message to Bobby from Khrushchev: "The weapons that the USSR is sending to Cuba will only be of a defensive character."

But the reported possible MRBM sites at San Cristobal in Pinar del Río settled the argument. On October 9, Kennedy approved a U-2 mission to take place as soon as weather permitted. Clear visibility up to seventy-four thousand feet, the U-2's altitude, did not occur until October 14. In the meantime, on October 10, Keating publicly announced that he had evidence of six IRBM (intermediate-range ballistic missile) sites in Cuba. The IRBMs, which could reach targets twenty-one hundred miles away, had twice the range of MRBMs. On the thirteenth, in a conversation with Chet Bowles, who had been a roving ambassador since November 1961, Dobrynin had "expressed worry and surprise at the intensity of U.S. public reaction" over Cuba. He gave Bowles fresh assurances that "in spite of [their] worries, the U.S.S.R. was not shipping offensive weapons and well understood the dangers of doing so."

If Keating, whom Kennedy referred to as a "nut," was posturing for political gain in the rapidly approaching elections, the White House had to have a more effective refutation than Khrushchev's word or the likelihood that Moscow would not be so rash. To blunt Republican accusations of a passive White House, the administration leaked details of Operation Mongoose to James Reston, which he used in a column. But on the off chance that missile sites were going up and that Keating was right, the administration needed to face hard choices on how to eliminate them.

To Kennedy's distress, the October 14 U-2 flight over the island, which lasted six minutes and produced 928 photographs, revealed conclusive evidence of offensive weapons: three medium-range ballistic missile sites under construction; one additional MRBM site discovered at San Cristobal; and two IRBM sites at Guanajay. The photos also revealed twenty-one crated IL-28 medium-range bombers capable of delivering nuclear bombs. The CIA's report on the discoveries reached Bundy on the evening of October 15, but he decided to wait until morning to present this "very big news" to the president, when enlargements of the photographs would be available. Besides, it seemed to him that a late-night meeting, which might attract attention, would be a bad idea. "It was a hell of a secret," and it needed to remain such until the president could consider how to deal with it. Also, a rested president, who was returning from a strenuous week of campaigning for congressional Democrats, would be better prepared to confront the crisis than an exhausted one. Nevertheless, Bundy shared the news, which CIA chiefs already had, with Rusk and McNamara and a few of their deputies on the evening of the fifteenth.

At 8:45 on the morning of the sixteenth, Bundy brought the bad news to Kennedy in his bedroom. The president ordered Bundy to set up a White House meeting in the Cabinet Room before noon and ticked off the names of the national security officials he wanted there. He then called Bobby, who had been first on his list. "We have some big trouble. I want you over here," the president told him. Determined not to create a public crisis and demands for press comments before he had had a chance to consider his options, Kennedy kept his early-morning appointments.

After twenty-one months in the White House, the Kennedys were not strangers to "big trouble." The Bay of Pigs, Berlin, Laos, Vietnam, the Congo, the Freedom Riders, the clash with big steel, Soviet nuclear tests, and, most recently, the September crisis in Mississippi had schooled them in the strains of holding power. But this was worse than anything they had seen before. Indeed, no president or administration had confronted so much danger to the national survival since Roosevelt had led the country through the Second World War. True, Truman and Eisenhower had shouldered Cold War burdens in every corner of the globe, and Truman had presided over a frustrating conflict in Korea, which had cost some twenty-five thousand American lives. But Soviet missiles in Cuba were an unprecedented provocation — a challenge to American national security that threatened to bring on a nuclear war. And on a more trivial but still potent note, if Kennedy failed to remove them by negotiation or force, he assumed that a successor would come to power on the promise that he would.

Although the Kennedys did not have the luxury to reflect on how they had come to this confrontation with Moscow, the question could not have been far from their minds. Obviously Castro deserved some of the blame. His determination to train Latin American radicals committed to subverting as many hemisphere governments as possible provoked the Kennedy White House into counteractions. This ongoing crisis in U.S.-Cuban relations presented Khrushchev with an irresistible opportunity. By putting missiles on the island, he could achieve several objectives: reduce the Soviet missile gap with the United States; possibly compel a German settlement more compatible with Moscow's security needs than just a wall ending the embarrassing flight of refugees from East to West; outshine China in competition for Third World hearts and minds; and boost his standing at home, where his state-managed economy had failed to deliver the goods. Of course, the Kennedys could not dismiss an American share of responsibility for the crisis. The Bay of Pigs fiasco, Operation Mongoose, and exaggerated fears of communist takeovers in Latin America, which, for all the rhetoric of good intentions, made the United States more an advocate of the status quo than a supporter of democratic change, had all contributed to the hemisphere tensions that drove Castro firmly into the Soviet camp.

THE FIRST ORDER OF BUSINESS was not to assign blame for the Soviet-American confrontation but to find some way to eliminate the missiles and avert a nuclear war. At 11:45 A.M., thirteen men joined the president in the Cabinet Room for an hour-and-ten-minute discussion. The group came to be called Ex Comm, the Executive Committee of the National Security Council. Kennedy sat in the center of an oblong table, with Rusk, Ball, and Deputy Undersecretary of State U. Alexis Johnson to his immediate right and McNamara, Gilpatric, Joint Chiefs chairman Maxwell Taylor, and acting CIA director Marshall Carter (McCone was at a family funeral) to his immediate left. Bundy, Dillon, Bobby, and Johnson sat across from the president. Two experts on aerial photography, Arthur Lundahl and Sidney Graybeal, briefed the group on the U-2 photos, which were propped on easels. Though Ex Comm would create the impression that Kennedy governed by committee, it was in fact the exception. Though he had appointed the most talented people he could find to his cabinet, for example, he had made almost no use of cabinet meetings in deciding major questions. Instead, consultations with a variety of individuals, including cabinet officers, before initiating policy had been his modus operandi. Regular formal cabinet discussions were never a significant part of his decision-making process.

As the Ex Comm discussion began, Kennedy activated the Cabinet Room tape recorder. After the experts presented the evidence of medium-range ballistic missile sites, Kennedy wanted to know if the missiles were ready to be launched. When told no, he asked how long before they could be fired. No one could be sure, but, McNamara said, "there is some reason to believe that the warheads aren't present and hence they are not ready to fire." The question of "readiness to fire" is "highly critical in forming our plans," McNamara added. Consequently, Kennedy agreed that additional U-2 flights were essential to discover where nuclear warheads might be stored and when the Soviets might be able to use them.

Kennedy wanted his advisers to explain, if they could, why Khrushchev was doing this. Perhaps it would give him a better idea of how to respond. "What is the advantage?" Kennedy asked. "Must be some major reason for the Soviets to set this up." He answered his own question: "Must be that they're not satisfied with their ICBMs." Taylor echoed the president's view: "What it'd give them is, primarily . . . [a] launching base for short-range missiles against the United States to supplement their rather defective ICBM system. . . . That's one reason." Citing McCone, Rusk said that Khrushchev might be animated by concerns about our nuclear superiority. Rusk also believed that "Berlin is very much involved in this." Khrushchev may be hoping to "bargain Berlin and Cuba against each other," he said, or use a U.S. attack on Cuba as an excuse to act against Berlin.

The principal focus of the meeting was on how to eliminate the missiles from Cuba. Rusk thought that they could do it by a "sudden, unannounced strike of some sort," or by a political track in which they built up the crisis "to the point where the other side has to consider very seriously about giving in." Perhaps they could talk sense to Castro through an intermediary, Rusk suggested. "It ought to be said to Castro that this kind of a base is intolerable. . . . The time has now come when he must, in the interests of the Cuban people . . . break cleanly with the Soviet Union and prevent this missile base from becoming operational." The alternative to the quick strike, Rusk said, was "to alert our allies and Mr. Khrushchev that there is an utterly serious crisis in the making here. . . . We'll be facing a situation that could well lead to a general war. . . . We have an obligation to do what has to be done, but to do it in a way that gives everybody a chance to pull away from it before it gets too hard."

For the moment, Kennedy was not thinking about any political or diplomatic solution; his focus was on military options and how to mute the crisis until they had some clear idea of what to do. He saw four possible military actions: an air strike against the missile installations; a more general air attack against a wide array of targets; a blockade; and an invasion. He wanted preparations for the second, third, and fourth possibilities, decisions on which could come later. But "we're certainly going to do number one," he said. "We're going to take out these missiles." Just when, he did not say, but he wanted knowledge of the missiles limited to as few officials as possible. He believed that the news would leak anyway in two or three days. But even when it became known, he wanted policy decisions to remain secret. "Otherwise," he said, "we bitch it up."

He scheduled another Ex Comm meeting for 6:30 that evening. Again to avoid any hint of crisis, he followed his prearranged afternoon schedule. The only public indication of his concern came in ad lib remarks to journalists attending a State Department conference. "The United States, and the world, is now passing through one of its most critical periods," he said. "Our major problem over all, is the survival of our country . . . without the beginning of the third and perhaps the last war." He reflected his sense of burden and irritation with people in the press and Congress who were second-guessing him by reciting a verse: "Bullfight critics row on row/Crowd the enormous plaza full/But only one is there who knows/And he is the one who fights the bull."

The evening meeting included the morning's participants as well as Sorensen and Edwin Martin, a State Department expert on Latin America. Kennedy came back to his puzzlement over Khrushchev's actions. Khrushchev had, all things considered, been cautious over Berlin, so how did the Russian experts explain his willingness to risk a war by putting nuclear missiles in Cuba, especially if, as some believed, it did not reduce America's military advantage over the USSR? "Well, it's a goddamn mystery to me," Kennedy admitted. "I don't know enough about the Soviet Union, but if anybody can tell me any other time since the Berlin blockade where the Russians have given so clear a provocation, I don't know when it's been, because they've been awfully cautious, really."

Ball, Bundy, and Alex Johnson saw the Soviets as trying to expand their strategic capabilities. But McNamara was not so sure. The Joint Chiefs thought the Soviet missile deployments "substantially" changed the strategic balance, but McNamara believed it made no difference. Taylor acknowledged that the missiles in Cuba meant "just a few more missiles targeted on the United States," but he considered them "a very, a rather important, adjunct and reinforcement" to Moscow's "strike capability."

Kennedy saw other reasons for eliminating them. If the United States left them in place, it would be an inducement for the Soviets to add ever greater strength to their forces in Cuba. In addition, it would make the Cubans, he added, "look like they're coequal with us." Besides, he said, "We weren't going to [allow it]. Last month I should have said that we don't care. But when we said we're not going to [allow it], and then they go ahead and do it, and then we do nothing, then I would think that our risks increase. . . . What difference does it make? They've got enough to blow us up now anyway." But more was at stake here than matters of strategic balance. "After all, this is a political struggle as much as military," he said.

THE QUESTION THAT REMAINED, then, was how to remove the missiles without a full-scale war. Despite his earlier certainty, Kennedy had begun to have doubts about a surprise air strike and may already have ruled this out as a sensible option. When he asked at the morning meeting, "How effective can the take-out be?" Taylor had answered, "It'll never be 100 percent, Mr. President, we know.

We hope to take out the vast majority in the first strike, but this is not just one thing — one strike, one day — but continuous air attack for whenever necessary, whenever we discover a target." Kennedy picked up on the uncertain results of such an operation: "Well, let's say we just take out the missile bases," he said. "Then they have some more there. Obviously they can get them in by submarine and so on. I don't know whether you just keep high strikes on."

Bobby, who had been so eager for clandestine action, doubted the wisdom of air attacks, which he had described in the morning discussion as likely "to kill an awful lot of people." It was one thing to have professional spies and devoted Cuban opponents risk their lives to topple a communist regime in Cuba. But killing possibly hundreds, maybe thousands, of people, including surely some innocent civilians, chilled him. At the evening meeting, he passed a note to Sorensen: "I now know how Tojo felt when he was planning Pearl Harbor."

It seems possible, even likely, that Bobby was reflecting his brother's views. Bobby was not given to freelancing; he was his brother's spokesman on most matters. In this early stage of the discussions about what to do, it would have made Kennedy seem weak to shy away openly from air raids for fear they might not work well or would claim some innocent victims. He surely had not ruled out the possibility, and absent another good solution he could imagine using air power to eliminate the missile sites. However, he was reluctant to follow that option. (When Soviet expert Charles Bohlen, who was leaving for Paris to become ambassador, wrote a memo advocating an ultimatum before any air strikes, Kennedy asked him to stay in Washington to participate in the deliberations. But concern that a delayed departure might alert the press to the crisis persuaded JFK to let him go.) Kennedy may also have tipped his bias against a quick air attack by telling Acheson that a U.S. bombing raid would be "Pearl Harbor in reverse." (Refusing to compare air raids on the missile sites to an unprovoked sneak attack, Acheson told the president, "It is unworthy of you to speak that way.")

The only new idea put forth at the evening meeting came from McNamara. He suggested a middle ground between the military and political courses they had been discussing. He proposed a "declaration of open surveillance: a statement that we would immediately impose a blockade against offensive weapons entering Cuba in the future, and an indication that, with our open surveillance reconnaissance, which we would plan to maintain indefinitely for the future, we would be prepared to immediately attack the Soviet Union in the event that Cuba made any offensive move against this country."

After a long day of discussions, Kennedy was no closer to a firm decision on how to proceed. On Wednesday, the seventeenth, while he continued to hide the crisis from public view by meeting with West Germany's foreign minister, eating lunch with Libya's crown prince, and flying to Connecticut to campaign for Democratic candidates, his advisers held nonstop meetings. But first he saw McCone, who had returned to Washington, at 9:30 in the morning. The CIA director gained the impression that Kennedy was "inclined to act promptly if at all, without warning, targeting on MRBMs and possible airfields." McCone may have been hearing what he wanted to hear, or, more likely, Kennedy created this impression by inviting McCone to make the case for prompt air strikes.

As part of his balancing act, Kennedy invited Adlai Stevenson into the discussion. After learning about the crisis from the president, who showed him the missile photos on the afternoon of the sixteenth, Stevenson predictably urged Kennedy not to rush into military action. When Kennedy said, "I suppose the alternatives are to go in by air and wipe them out, or to take other steps to render the weapons inoperable," Stevenson replied, "Let's not go into an air strike until we have explored the possibilities of a peaceful solution."

The next day, before he returned to the U.N. in New York, Stevenson wrote a letter urging the president to send personal emissaries to see Castro and Khrushchev. He predicted that an attack would bring Soviet reprisals in Turkey or Berlin and would "risk starting a nuclear war [which] is bound to be divisive at best and the judgments of history seldom coincide with the tempers of the moment." Stevenson's appeal to take the long view was not lost on Kennedy, who understood that his actions could permanently alter the course of human affairs. To underscore his point, Stevenson added: "I know your dilemma is to strike before the sites are operational or to risk waiting until a proper groundwork of justification can be prepared. The national security must come first. *But the means adopted have such incalculable consequences that I feel you should have made it clear that the existence of nuclear missile bases anywhere is negotiable before we start anything.*" This was not a counsel of defeat, Stevenson concluded. The Soviets needed to be told "that it is they who have upset the precarious balance in the world in arrogant disregard of your warnings — by threats against Berlin and now from Cuba — and that we have no choice except to restore the balance, i.e., blackmail and intimidation *never*, negotiation and sanity *always*."

The differences between McCone and Stevenson were repeated in various forms during discussions among Kennedy's advisers on the seventeenth. At midnight, after three long meetings, Bobby summarized five options that advisers were putting before the president: (1) on October 24, after a week's military preparation and notification to Western European and some Latin American leaders, bomb the MRBMs and send Khrushchev a message of explanation — Rusk opposed this plan; (2) attack the MRBMs after notifying Khrushchev — defense chiefs opposed this proposal; (3) inform Moscow about our knowledge of the missiles and our determination to block additional ones from entering Cuba, declare war, and prepare an invasion — Rusk and Ball favored this option but wanted it preceded by surveillance without air strikes; (4) engage in "political preliminaries" followed by extensive air attacks with preparations for an invasion; and (5) the "same as 4, but omit the political preliminaries."

When Ex Comm met again on Thursday morning, October 18, additional reconnaissance photos revealed construction of IRBM launching pads. They had now discovered five different missile sites. McCone reported that the Soviets could have between sixteen and thirty-two missiles ready to fire "within a week or slightly more." Concerned about convincing the world of the accuracy of their information, Kennedy wanted to know if an untrained observer would see what the experts saw in the photos. Lundahl doubted it. "I think the uninitiated would like to see the missile, in the tube," he said.

Sensing the president's hesitancy about quick action without clear evidence to convince the world of its necessity, Rusk asked whether the group thought it "necessary to take action." He believed it essential. The Soviets were turning Cuba into "a powerful military problem" for the United States, he said, and a failure to respond would "undermine our alliances all over the world." Inaction would also encourage Moscow to feel free to intervene wherever they liked and would create an unmanageable problem in sustaining domestic support for the country's foreign policy commitments. Rusk then read a letter from Bohlen urging diplomatic action as a prelude to military steps. An attack on Cuba without a prior effort at diplomatic pressure to remove the missiles, Bohlen said, would alienate all America's allies, give Moscow credibility for a response against Berlin, and "greatly increase the probability of general war."

Bohlen's argument echoed Kennedy's thinking. People saw the United States as "slightly demented" about Cuba, the president said. "No matter how good our films are . . . a lot of people would regard this [military action] as a mad act by the United States." They would see it as "a loss of nerve because they will argue that taken at its worst, the presence of those missiles really doesn't change the [military] balance."

But the evidence of additional missile sites had convinced the Joint Chiefs to urge a full-scale invasion of Cuba. Kennedy stubbornly resisted. "Nobody knows what kind of success we're going to have with this invasion," he said. "Invasions are tough, hazardous. We've got a lot of equipment, a lot of — thousands of — Americans get killed in Cuba, and I think you're in much more of a mess than you are if you take out these . . . bases." And if Bobby's opinion remained a reflection of his brother's thinking, Kennedy also opposed unannounced air strikes. Ball made what Bobby called "a hell of a good point." "If we act without warning," Ball said, "without giving Khrushchev some way out . . . that's like Pearl Harbor. It's the kind of conduct that one might expect of the Soviet Union. It is not conduct that one expects of the United States." The way we act, Bobby asserted, speaks to "the whole question of . . . what kind of a country we are." Ball saw surprise air strikes as comparable to "carrying the mark of Cain on your brow for the rest of your life." Bobby echoed the point: "We've fought for 15 years with Russia to prevent a first strike against us. Now . . . we do that to a small country. I think it is a hell of a burden to carry."

KENNEDY HAD NOT RULED OUT military action, but his remarks at the meetings on October 18 revealed a preference for a blockade and negotiations. He wanted to know what would be the best way to open talks with Khrushchev — through a cable, a personal envoy? He also asked, if we established a blockade of Cuba, what would we do about the missiles already there, and would we need to declare war on Havana? Llewellyn Thompson, who had joined the Thursday morning discussion, addressed Kennedy's first concern by suggesting Kennedy press Khrushchev to dismantle the existing missile sites and warn him that if they were armed, our constant surveillance would alert us, and we would eliminate them. As for a declaration of war, Kennedy thought it would be unwise: "It seems to me that with a declaration of war our objective would be an invasion."

To keep up the facade of normality, Kennedy followed his regular schedule for the rest of the day, including a two-hour meeting with Soviet foreign minister Andrey Gromyko. Nothing was said about the offensive missiles by Gromyko or Kennedy. But they gave each other indirect messages. Gromyko ploddingly read a prepared statement. He emphasized that they were giving Cuba "armaments which were only defensive — and he wished to stress the word defensive — in character." After the meeting, Kennedy told Bob Lovett about Gromyko, "who, in this very room not over ten minutes ago, told more barefaced lies than I have ever heard in so short a time. All during his denial that the Russians had any missiles or weapons, or anything else, in Cuba, I had the . . . pictures in the center drawer of my desk, and it was an enormous temptation to show them to him." Instead, Kennedy told Gromyko that the Soviet arms shipments had created "the most dangerous situation since the end of the war."

Whatever hints Kennedy offered, Gromyko missed them. He noticed that Rusk was red "like a crab" and unusually emotional, and Kennedy was more deliberate than usual. Eager to believe that they were outwitting Kennedy, Gromyko advised Khrushchev that "the situation is in general wholly satisfactory."

Lovett's advice to Kennedy was similar to McNamara's: Establish a blockade around Cuba. If it failed, air strikes and an invasion could follow, but a blockade might persuade the Russians to withdraw the missiles and avoid bloodshed. It would also insulate the United States from charges of being "trigger-happy." When Bobby entered the room, the president asked Lovett to repeat what he was saying. When he did, Bobby agreed with the wisdom of "taking a less violent step at the outset, because, as he said, we could always blow the place up if necessary, but that might be unnecessary, and then we would be in the position of having used too much force."

Kennedy reconvened his advisers at a secret late-night meeting on the second floor of the executive mansion. He wanted to hear the results of the day's deliberations. Bundy now argued the case for doing nothing. He believed that any kind of action would bring a reprisal against Berlin, which would divide the NATO alliance. But Kennedy thought it was impossible to sit still. As he had said earlier in the day, "Somehow we've got to take some action. . . . Now, the question really is . . . what action we take which lessens the chances of a nuclear exchange, which obviously is the final failure." They agreed that a blockade against Soviet shipments of additional offensive weapons would be the best starting point. Instead of air strikes or an invasion, which was tantamount to a state of war, they would try to resolve the crisis with "a limited blockade for a limited purpose."

On Friday, October 19, Kennedy kept his campaign schedule, which took him to Cleveland and Springfield, Illinois, and Chicago. He considered canceling the trip, but when he asked Kenny O'Donnell, who knew about the crisis, if he had called it off, O'Donnell replied, "I didn't call off anything. I don't want to be the one who has to tell Dick Daley that you're not going out there."

In the morning, however, he held a secret forty-five-minute meeting with the Joint Chiefs. The discussion was as much an exercise in political hand-holding as in advancing a solution to the crisis. Kennedy knew that the Chiefs favored a massive air strike and were divided on whether to follow it with an invasion. He saw their counsel as predictable and not especially helpful. His memories of the navy brass in World War II, the apparent readiness of the Chiefs to risk nuclear war in Europe and their unhelpful advice before the Bay of Pigs, and the army's stumbling performance just a few weeks before in Mississippi deepened his distrust of their promised results.

Nevertheless, Kennedy candidly discussed his concerns with the Chiefs. An attack on Cuba would provoke the Soviets into blockading or taking Berlin, he said. And our allies would complain that "we let Berlin go because we didn't have the guts to endure a situation in Cuba." Moreover, we might eliminate the danger in Cuba, but the Berlin crisis would likely touch off a nuclear war.

Taylor respectfully acknowledged the president's dilemma but asserted the need for military action. Without it, we would lose our credibility, he said, and "our strength anyplace in the world is the credibility of our response. . . . And if we don't respond here in Cuba, we think the credibility is sacrificed."

Curtis LeMay was even more emphatic. He did not share the president's view "that if we knock off Cuba, they're going to knock off Berlin." Kennedy asked, "What do you think their reply would be?" LeMay did not think there would be one. He saw military intervention as the only solution. "This blockade and political action," he predicted, "I see leading into war. I don't see any other solution.

It will lead right into war. This is almost as bad as the appeasement at Munich." LeMay indirectly threatened Kennedy with making his dissent public. "I think that a blockade, and political talk, would be considered by a lot of our friends and neutrals as being a pretty weak response to this. And I'm sure a lot of our own citizens would feel that way, too. In other words, you're in a pretty bad fix at the present time."

LeMay's response irritated Kennedy, who asked, "What did you say?" LeMay repeated himself: "You're in a pretty bad fix." Kennedy responded with a hollow laugh, "You're in there with me." After the meeting, referring to LeMay's assertion about a Soviet nonresponse, Kennedy asked O'Donnell, "Can you imagine LeMay saying a thing like that? These brass hats have one great advantage in their favor. If we listen to them, and do what they want us to do, none of us will be alive later to tell them that they were wrong."

The Chiefs were angry, too. After Kennedy left the room, marine commandant David Shoup said to LeMay, "You, you pulled the rug right out from under him." LeMay replied, "Jesus Christ. What the hell do you mean?" Shoup replied that he agreed with LeMay "a hundred percent" and added, "If somebody could keep them from doing the goddamn thing piecemeal. That's our problem. You go in there and friggin' around with the missiles. You're screwed. . . . You can't fiddle around with hitting the missile sites and then hitting the SAM sites. You got to go in and take out the goddamn thing that's going to stop you from doing your job." Earle Wheeler, the army's representative on the Joint Chiefs, thought that Kennedy was set against military moves: "It was very apparent to me, though, from his [Kennedy's] earlier remarks, that the political action of a blockade is really what he's [after]."

As he left Washington, Kennedy told Bundy to keep the possibility of air strikes alive until he returned. His request may have partly resulted from Bundy's advice that a blockade alone would not get the missiles out. Having changed his mind, Bundy now urged an air strike as a "quick . . . and a clean surgical operation." At the same time, Kennedy, who impressed Sorensen as "impatient and discouraged" by his meeting with the Chiefs, told Bobby and Sorensen "to pull the group together quickly — otherwise more delays and dissension would plague whatever decision he took."

At a late-morning gathering of the Ex Comm, Acheson, Bundy, Dillon, and McCone lined up with the Chiefs in favor of an air strike. McNamara, undoubtedly alerted to the president's preference, favored a blockade over air action. Bobby, grinning, said that he had spoken with the president that morning and thought "it would be very, very difficult indeed for the President if the decision were to be for an air strike, with all the memory of Pearl Harbor. . . . A sneak attack was not in our traditions. Thousands of Cubans would be killed without warning, and a lot of Russians too." The president supported a blockade, which would "allow the Soviets some room for maneuver to pull back from their over-extended position in Cuba."

Following an afternoon break, during which advocates of an air strike and a blockade formed themselves into committees to develop their respective arguments, the whole group reconvened for further discussion. After two and a half hours, they seemed to agree that a blockade should be a first step with air strikes to follow if the Soviets did not remove the missiles. But worried that support for a blockade remained shaky, Bobby urged the president to pretend he was ill with a cold and return to Washington to forge a clearer consensus.

For two hours and forty minutes, beginning at 2:30 P.M., on Saturday, October 20, Kennedy and the National Security Council reviewed their options. None impressed him as just right, but under the president's prodding the group agreed to a blockade or, rather, a "quarantine," which could more readily be described as less than an act of war and seemed less likely to draw comparisons to the Soviets' 1948 Berlin blockade. The announcement of the quarantine was to coincide with a demand for removal of the offensive missiles from Cuba and preparations for an air strike should Moscow not comply. Kennedy was willing to discuss the removal of U.S. missiles from Turkey or Italy in exchange, but only if the Soviets raised the issue. Should the United States make this concession, he intended to assure the Turks and Italians that Polaris submarines would become their defense shield.

Managing domestic opinion was another Kennedy concern. He planned to reveal the crisis to the public and announce the quarantine in a televised speech on Monday evening, October 22, in which he intended to state clearly "that we would accept nothing less than the ending of the missile capability now in Cuba." To mute the crisis until then, he asked the New York Times and Washington Post, which had learned of the crisis from Pentagon leaks, to hold off publishing emerging details of the danger.

Kennedy spent Monday working to create a national and international consensus for the blockade. Remembering LeMay's implicit threat to reveal Kennedy's reluctance to use air power as the Chiefs wanted, he told Taylor, "I know you and your colleagues are unhappy with this decision, but I trust that you will support me." Kennedy telephoned former presidents Hoover, Truman, and Eisenhower and consulted advisers about messages to foreign heads of state and his planned evening address. At an afternoon National Security Council meeting he "outlined the manner in which he expected Council Members to deal with the domestic aspects of the current situation. He said everyone should sing one song in order to make clear that there were now no differences among his advisers as to the proper course to follow." Kennedy feared that domestic dissent might encourage Moscow to defy the blockade or strike at Berlin in the belief that the president would lack national support for a military response. He also believed that domestic divisions could weaken the Democrats in the November elections.

A meeting with congressional leaders for an hour before he spoke to the nation heightened his doubts about being able to generate the strong support he felt essential in the crisis. Their opposition to a blockade was as intense as that voiced by the Chiefs and seemed more likely to become public; unlike the military, congressional barons were not under presidential command. Senator Richard Russell saw a blockade as a weak response to the Soviet action. "It seems to me that we are at a crossroads," he said. "We're either a first-class power or we're not." Since Russell believed that a war with Russia was "coming someday," he thought that the time to fight was now. William Fulbright also favored an invasion. He saw a blockade as the worst possible policy; by contrast, an invasion of Cuba would "not actually [be] an affront to Russia." Seizing or sinking a Russian ship was an act of war. "It is not an act of war against Russia to attack Cuba," he said.

As they left the meeting, Kennedy joked with Hubert Humphrey: "If I'd known the job was this tough, I wouldn't have beaten you in West Virginia." "I knew, and that's why I let you beat me," Humphrey answered. Facing the possibility of an imminent nuclear war, the pressure on Kennedy was unimaginable. It was one reason for his calls to the three ex-presidents. He thought they were the only ones who could imagine his burden. "No one," Kennedy told historian David Herbert Donald in February 1962, "has a right to grade a

President — not even poor James Buchanan — who has not sat in his chair, examined the mail and information that came across his desk, and learned why he made decisions." Eisenhower was particularly helpful to Kennedy: "No matter what you're trying to do," he said, ". . . I'll be doing my best to support it."

Kennedy later described his session with the congressional leaders as "the most difficult meeting. . . . It was a tremendous strain," he told Bobby, who had been absent. Kennedy understood their outrage at Khrushchev's recklessness; it mirrored his own anger when he first heard about the missiles and Khrushchev's deception in putting them in Cuba. But unlike the congressmen, he could not allow his anger or any sense of personal slight to cloud his judgment. As for Russell and Fulbright, he banked on their patriotism and party ties to ensure their support. He also expected the public to rally behind him, which would discourage military and political opponents of the blockade from taking issue with his policy.

KENNEDY SAW HIS SPEECH to the country and the world explaining the crisis and his choice of a blockade as crucial not only in bringing Americans together but also in pressuring Khrushchev to accede to his demands. He also sent Khrushchev a letter, which Dobrynin received at the State Department an hour before Kennedy spoke. He had an ongoing concern, Kennedy wrote, that "your Government would not correctly understand the will and determination of the United States in any given situation." He feared a Soviet miscalculation, "since I have not assumed that you or any other sane man would, in this nuclear age, plunge the world into war which it is crystal clear no country could win and which could only result in catastrophic consequences to the whole world, including the aggressor." He reminded Khrushchev that "certain developments" in Cuba would force the United States to "do whatever must be done to protect its own security and that of its allies." He insisted that Khrushchev remove the missile bases and other offensive weapons in Cuba that were threatening Western Hemisphere nations.

Kennedy's seventeen-minute speech Monday night reached one hundred million Americans, who had been alerted to the crisis by the media; it was the largest audience ever up to that point for a presidential address. The president's words matched his grim demeanor. Looking drawn and tired, he spoke more deliberately than usual, making clear the gravity of what the United States and USSR, and, indeed, the whole world faced. Moscow had created a "nuclear strike capability" in Cuba. The missiles could hit Washington, D.C., or any other city in the southeastern United States. IRBMs, when installed, could strike most of the major cities in the Western Hemisphere. Kennedy bluntly condemned the Soviets for lying: The deployment represented a total breach of faith with repeated Soviet promises to supply Cuba with only defensive weapons. The United States, Kennedy announced, could not tolerate this threat to its security and would henceforth quarantine Cuba to block all offensive weapons from reaching the island. A Soviet failure to stop its buildup would justify additional U.S. action. Any use of the missiles already in Cuba would bring retaliatory attacks against the Soviet Union. Kennedy demanded prompt dismantling and withdrawal of all offensive weapons in Cuba under U.N. supervision. He also promised to counter any threat to America's allies, including "the brave people of West Berlin."

With no response yet from Khrushchev on Tuesday morning, the country and the world feared the worse. Rusk woke George Ball, who was sleeping on a couch in his State Department office, with some graveyard humor: "We have won a considerable victory," he said. "You and I are still alive." The two needed to prepare for a 10:00 A.M. Ex Comm meeting at the White House. Kennedy had issued a National Security Action Memorandum giving formal status to the group, which was to meet every morning in the Cabinet Room for the duration of the "current crisis."

Ex Comm's first priority Tuesday was to ensure domestic support by convincing people in the Congress and the press that the administration had not been dilatory in identifying the offensive threat in Cuba. The president and Bobby agreed that McCone should brief skeptics about the timeliness of their actions. Kennedy also wanted the public to understand that the only way the United States could have stopped the Soviet deployment was through an invasion of Cuba in the previous two years, but, he reminded his advisers, "there wasn't anybody suggesting an invasion of Cuba at a time when they necessarily could have stopped these things coming onto the island." The committee endorsed Stevenson's use at the U.N. of reconnaissance photos to combat Soviet charges that a crisis was being manufactured as a pretext for invading Cuba. The discussion also produced an agreement that if a U-2 reconnaissance plane were lost, the United States would destroy a SAM site.

A reply from Khrushchev, which reached the president by noon, gave little hope of a peaceful settlement. Khrushchev complained that Kennedy's speech and letter to him represented a "serious threat to peace." A U.S. quarantine would be a "gross violation of . . . international norms." Khrushchev reaffirmed that the weapons going to Cuba were defensive and urged Kennedy to "renounce actions pursued by you, which could lead to catastrophic consequences." Kennedy read Khrushchev's letter on the phone to Lucius Clay, who had ended his service as Kennedy's special representative in Berlin in the spring of 1962. The president asked Clay to make himself available for consultations and predicted that they were going to face "difficulties in Berlin as well as other places."

By late afternoon, after Rusk, in what some called his finest hour, had persuaded the Organization of American States to give unanimous approval to Kennedy's announced plan, Kennedy ordered a quarantine to begin the next morning. At an evening meeting, Ex Comm discussed how to enforce the blockade against twenty-seven Soviet and Eastern-bloc ships heading for Cuba. To avoid unnecessary tensions, they agreed not to stop and search ships that reversed course. They also agreed to answer Khrushchev's letter with a reaffirmation of their view that the Soviets had caused the current crisis by "secretly furnishing offensive weapons to Cuba." Kennedy's reply restated his intention to enforce the quarantine and asked that they both "show prudence and do nothing . . . to make the situation more difficult to control."

At the close of the evening meeting, Kennedy recorded a candid conversation with his brother. "How does it look?" Bobby asked. "Ah, looks like hell — looks real mean, doesn't it?" Kennedy responded rhetorically. He nevertheless felt that they had done the right thing. "If they get this mean on this one, it's just a question of where they go about it next. No choice," Kennedy said. "I don't think there was a choice." Bobby confirmed his brother's conclusion: "Well, there isn't any choice. . . . You would have been impeached," he said. "That's what I think," Kennedy declared. "I would have been impeached."

In his eagerness to find a way out of the crisis, Bobby had asked journalists Frank Holeman and Charles Bartlett to tell Bolshakov that the White House might be receptive to dismantling Jupiter missiles in Turkey if the Soviets removed the missiles in Cuba. But the American move could come only after the Soviets had acted — "in a time of quiet and not when there is the threat of war." When Bobby reported to Kennedy, the president suggested that his brother directly approach Dobrynin, which he did that evening. Telling the ambassador that he was there on his own, without instructions from the president, Bobby angrily accused him and Khrushchev of "hypocritical, misleading and false" actions. Bobby asked "if the ships were going to go through to Cuba." Dobrynin believed they would. As he left, Bobby declared, "I don't know how all this will end, but we intend to stop your ships."

At the morning Ex Comm meeting on the twenty-fourth, the group feared that they were on the brink of an unavoidable disaster. The Soviets were making "rapid progress" in the completion of their missile sites and bringing their military forces "into a complete state of readiness." In fact, by the morning of the twenty-fourth, all of the Soviet MRBMs and their warheads were in Cuba and close to operational. In addition, Soviet ships were continuing on course, and two of them, which seemed to be carrying "offensive weapons," would approach the quarantine line by about noon, or in two hours. The presence of Soviet submarines screening the ships made it "a very dangerous situation." U.S. forces had increased their state of readiness from Defense Condition 3 to DEFCON 2, only one level below readiness for a general war. Soviet military intelligence had intercepted an order from the Pentagon to the Strategic Air Command to begin a nuclear alert.

The president's tension was reflected in his appearance and physical movements. "This was the moment . . . which we hoped would never come," Bobby wrote later. "The danger and concern that we all felt hung like a cloud over us all. . . . These few minutes were the time of greatest worry by the President. His hand went up to his face & covered his mouth and he closed his fist. His eyes were tense, almost gray, and we just stared at each other across the table. Was the world on the brink of a holocaust and had we done something wrong? . . . I felt we were on the edge of a precipice and it was as if there were no way off."

Only a State Department intelligence report gave a glimmer of hope. Khrushchev's "public line," the analysts advised — which continued to be that Moscow had no offensive weapons in Cuba — "seems designed to leave him with some option to back off, if he chooses." A written report handed to McCone during the meeting suggested that Khrushchev might be doing just that. "Mr. President,"

McCone interrupted McNamara, who was explaining how the navy would deal with the Soviet subs, "I have a note just handed to me. . . . It says we've just received information through ONI [Office of Naval Intelligence] that all six Soviet ships currently identified in Cuban waters — and I don't know what that means — have either stopped or reversed course." McCone left the room to ask for clarification on what "Cuban waters" meant: Were these ships approaching or leaving Cuba? The good news that it was indeed ships heading toward Cuba momentarily broke the mood of dire concern. "We're eyeball to eyeball," Rusk whispered to Bundy, "and I think the other fellow just blinked." But no one saw this as an end to the crisis. There were serious concerns that a U.S. naval vessel might deepen the crisis by unauthorized actions. Did our navy know that it was not supposed to pursue the retreating ships? Rusk asked. Kennedy worried that a destroyer might sink a ship that had turned around.

His concern was warranted. In the afternoon, McNamara went to the navy's command center in the Pentagon, a secure room under constant marine guard. McNamara learned that it had taken hours for some of the information on Soviet ship movements to reach the White House. He began chiding the duty officers for the delay, when Admiral George Anderson, the navy's representative on the Joint Chiefs, entered. Mindful of the president's concern about unauthorized navy action, McNamara began interrogating Anderson about procedures for dealing with the Soviet ships. Anderson saw the president's instructions as an unwarranted interference in the navy's freedom to do its job. Anderson told McNamara that his local commanders would decide on the details of how to deal with Soviet ships crossing the quarantine line, and said, "We've been doing this ever since the days of John Paul Jones." He waved the navy regulations manual at McNamara, saying, "It's all in there." McNamara heatedly replied, "I don't give a damn what John Paul Jones would have done. I want to know what you are going to do, now." The objective was to deter Khrushchev and avert a nuclear war, McNamara explained. Anderson answered that they would shoot across the bow, and if the ship did not stop, they would disable its rudder. Anderson defiantly added, "Now, Mr. Secretary, if you and your deputy will go back to your offices, the navy will run the blockade." McNamara ordered him not to fire at anything without his permission and left. "That's the end of Anderson," the secretary told

Gilpatric, who had witnessed the exchange. "He's lost my confidence." (In 1963, Kennedy made him ambassador to Portugal.)

At a late-afternoon meeting with congressional leaders, Kennedy reported some hopeful signs. Some of the ships headed for Cuba had changed course, and Khrushchev had sent British pacifist Bertrand Russell a telegram promising no rash actions or response to American provocations. He intended to do everything possible to avoid war, he said, including a meeting with Kennedy. Nevertheless, Kennedy emphasized that they would not know for twenty-four hours whether the Soviets would still try to cross the quarantine line, and they still had the problem of getting the missiles removed from Cuba. "If they respect the quarantine," Kennedy told Harold Macmillan on the telephone that evening, "then we get the second stage of this problem, and work continues on the missiles. Do we then tell them that if they don't get the missiles out, that we're going to invade Cuba? He will then say that if we invade Cuba that there's going to be a general nuclear assault, and he will in any case grab Berlin. Or do we just let the nuclear work go on, figuring he won't ever dare fire them, and when he tries to grab Berlin, we then go into Cuba?"

Khrushchev put a fresh damper on hopes that Moscow would not challenge the quarantine, with a letter arriving on the night of the twenty-fourth. His language was harsh and uncompromising. He objected to the U.S. "ultimatum" and threat of "force," described U.S. actions toward Cuba as "the folly of degenerate imperialism," and refused to submit to the blockade. We intend "to protect our rights," he wrote, and ominously declared, "We have everything necessary to do so."

At the same time, however, Khrushchev invited William E. Knox, the head of Westinghouse International, who was in Moscow on business, to meet with him at the Kremlin. During a three-and-a-quarter-hour conversation in which Khrushchev was "calm, friendly and frank," he acknowledged that he had ballistic missiles with both conventional and thermonuclear warheads in Cuba, and that if the U.S. government "really wanted to learn what kind of weapons were available for the defense of Cuba . . . all it had to do was to attack Cuba and Americans would find out very quickly. He then said he was not interested in the destruction of the world, but if we all wanted to meet in Hell, it was up to us." He declared himself "anxious to have a meeting with President Kennedy; that he would be glad to receive him in Moscow . . . [or] to visit him in Washington; they both could embark on naval vessels and rendezvous at sea; or they could meet at some neutral place where, without fanfare, some of the major problems between our two great countries could be resolved."

An unyielding reply from Kennedy to Khrushchev's letter, which reached Moscow on the morning of the twenty-fifth, plus indications that the Americans might invade Cuba, convinced Khrushchev it was time to negotiate an end to the crisis. More than anything else, it was Khrushchev's concern with Soviet military inferiority that compelled him to back down. "He could not go to war in the Caribbean with any hope of prevailing," Fursenko and Naftali write.

During a midday Kremlin meeting, Khrushchev stated his eagerness for a resolution of the U.S.-Soviet missile crisis. Additional caustic exchanges with Kennedy would be unproductive, he said. Instead, he proposed that four transports carrying missiles to Cuba now turn back and a new means be found to protect Cuba or make it into "a zone of peace." His solution was for the United States to pledge not to invade Cuba in return for dismantling the missiles, which the U.N. could verify.

Kennedy spent the twenty-fifth temporizing. Since a dozen Soviet ships had turned away from the quarantine line, the White House had some time to consider which remaining Cuba-bound ships to stop and inspect. Kennedy told the morning Ex Comm meeting that he did not want "a sense of euphoria to get around. That [October 24] message of Khrushchev is much tougher than that." At the same time, however, a proposal from U.N. secretary general U Thant for a cooling-off period, during which Moscow and Washington would avoid tests of the quarantine, persuaded Kennedy to temporarily suspend a decision to board a Soviet ship. Kennedy told U Thant that the solution to the crisis was Soviet removal of offensive weapons from Cuba. Kennedy now also told Macmillan, "I don't want to have a fight with a Russian ship tomorrow morning, and a search of it at a time when it appears that U Thant has got the Russians to agree not to continue."

Yet Kennedy was doubtful that U Thant's initiative would come to much. On the afternoon of the twenty-fifth, he watched a televised confrontation at the U.N. between Stevenson and Soviet ambassador Valerian Zorin. When Stevenson pressed Zorin to say whether the Soviets had put offensive missiles in Cuba, he replied, "I am not in an American courtroom, and therefore I do not wish to answer a question that is put to me in the fashion in which a prosecutor puts questions." Stevenson would not let him evade the question. "You are in the courtroom of world opinion right now, and you can answer yes or no," Stevenson shot back. "You will have your answer in due course," Zorin answered. "I am prepared to wait for my answer until hell freezes over," Stevenson said. He then embarrassed the Russians by putting U-2 photos of the missiles before the Security Council. "I never knew Adlai had it in him," Kennedy said of his performance. "Too bad he didn't show some of this steam in the 1956 campaign."

To make clear that he was not backing away from the quarantine while they waited for Khrushchev's answer to U Thant, Kennedy authorized the boarding of a Soviet-chartered Lebanese ship on the morning of October 26. Since it was not a Soviet ship per se and since the boarding went off without incident, the White House had not jeopardized U Thant's proposal. But Kennedy had sent a message.

At the Ex Comm meeting at 10:00 A.M. on the twenty-sixth, it was clear that the quarantine was no longer the central issue. There were no ships close to the quarantine line; nor did they expect any "quarantine activity with respect to Soviet ships . . . in the next few days." The concern now was the continuing missile buildup in Cuba. "Even if the quarantine's 100 percent effective," Kennedy said, "it isn't any good because the missile sites go on being constructed." And time was running out on a peaceful solution to that problem: "We can't screw around for two weeks and wait for them [the Soviets] to finish these [missile bases]," he declared. Moreover, he saw only "two ways of removing the weapons. One is to negotiate them out. Or the other is to go in and take them out. I don't see any other way you're going to get the weapons out." Nor was he convinced that negotiations would work. He anticipated using an air strike followed by an invasion, which would risk Soviet use of the missiles against U.S. territory. He told Macmillan that evening, "If at the end of 48 hours we are getting no place, and the missile sites continue to be constructed, then we are going to be faced with some hard decisions."

But Kennedy did not have to wait two days. Within two hours after talking to Macmillan, he received a long, rambling letter from Khrushchev, which Llewellyn Thompson, who was with the president when he read it, believed Khrushchev had written in a state of near panic without consultation. It was an unmistakable plea for a settlement. He justified Soviet help to Cuba as preserving its right of self-determination against U.S. aggression, and he continued to dispute Kennedy's characterization of the missiles as offensive weapons, but declared, "Let us not quarrel now. It is apparent that I will not be able to convince you of this." He had no interest in mutual destruction. It was time for "good sense." To that end, he proposed an exchange: If the United States promised not to invade or support an invasion of Cuba and would recall its fleet, the Soviet Union would no longer see a need for armaments on the island — "the presence of our military specialists in Cuba would disappear." He urged Kennedy to avoid the catastrophe of a nuclear war, but warned, should there be one, "We are ready for this."

Because he could not bring himself to say directly that he would remove the missiles from Cuba — to acknowledge his defeat and humiliation — Khrushchev spoke more clearly through a subordinate. On the afternoon of the twenty-sixth, Aleksandr Feklisov, who was officially known as Aleksandr Fomin, the KGB station chief in Washington, ostensibly a Soviet embassy counsel, asked John Scali, an ABC television journalist, to meet him. Scali, who had had occasional meetings with Fomin for ten months, suggested lunch at the Occidental restaurant in downtown Washington. Fomin made a startling proposal. Scali should transmit to the State Department a three-point proposal for ending the Cuban crisis. In return for a promise not to invade Cuba, Moscow would dismantle its missile bases on the island, and Castro would pledge never to accept offensive weapons of any kind.

But fresh evidence of Soviet progress on the missile sites, coupled with reports that six Soviet and three satellite ships remained on course toward the quarantine line, put a damper on Khrushchev's negotiating proposal. "We cannot permit ourselves to be impaled on a long negotiating hook while the work goes on on these bases," Kennedy told the Ex Comm at the October 27 morning meeting. They feared that Khrushchev's letter might be a ploy for engaging them in drawn-out talks that would allow Soviet completion of the missile sites.

A new initiative from Moscow, which reached Kennedy during the morning Ex Comm discussions, deepened their suspicions. The Kremlin had released a more polished version of Khrushchev's October 26 letter to the press. It now included a proposal that the United

JFK with Lyndon B. Johnson at the inauguration, January 20, 1961. JOHN F. KENNEDY LIBRARY

JFK conferring with his vice president, February 7, 1961. LBJ helped win crucial southern states but hated being second in command. Kennedy tried to give him a greater sense of importance in what the first vice president, John Adams, called "the most insignificant office that ever the invention of man contrived." JOHN F. KENNEDY LIBRARY

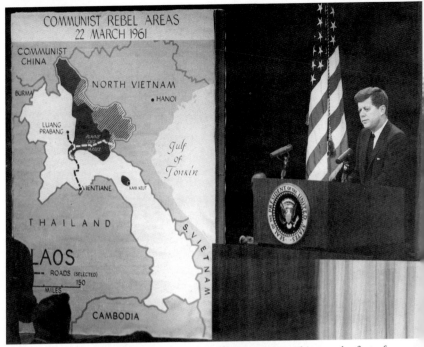

JFK explaining the civil war in Laos, March 23, 1961. This was the first of many foreign policy crises in Asia and Europe that dominated his administration. JOHN F. KENNEDY LIBRARY

JFK with former president Eisenhower, April 22, 1961, after the Bay of Pigs fiasco. Kennedy successfully enlisted Ike's backing in overseas challenges. JOHN F. KENNEDY LIBRARY

LBJ, Arthur Schlesinger Jr. (special assistant to the president), Admiral Arleigh Burke, JFK, and Jackie watching the liftoff of Commander Alan Shepard into space, May 5, 1961. JFK subsequently committed the United States to land a man on the moon by the end of the decade. JOHN F. KENNEDY LIBRARY

JFK at the Vienna summit meeting with Nikita Khrushchev, June 4, 1961. Instead of settling differences, the conference increased tensions over the future of Berlin. JOHN F. KENNEDY LIBRARY

Mimi Beardsley, intern in the Kennedy White House. CNN

JFK's back problems were exacerbated by turning over a shovelful of dirt during a visit to Canada in May 1961. He is seen here on crutches, June 16, 1961. JOHN F. KENNEDY LIBRARY

Admiral George Burkley, one of Kennedy's White House physicians. The president hid most of his ailments and treatments from the public. JOHN F. KENNEDY LIBRARY

Dr. Janet Travell, the White House physician who had been treating Kennedy's back problems since the early 1950s, at a press conference. She and Burkley battled over how best to treat the president. JOHN F. KENNEDY LIBRARY

JFK with Secretary of the Treasury C. Douglas Dillon, one of several Republicans Kennedy brought into his administration to foster bipartisanship. Dillon had just returned from Latin America, July 21, 1961. It was a region of special concern to Kennedy in the Cold War. JOHN F. KENNEDY LIBRARY

JFK speaks to the nation about the crisis with Moscow over Berlin, July 25, 1961, trying to discourage Khrushchev from doing anything precipitous and to assert effective foreign policy leadership after stumbles at the Bay of Pigs and Vienna. JOHN F. KENNEDY LIBRARY

JFK with his children, John Jr. and Caroline, June 22, 1962. He was a doting father. JOHN F. KENNEDY LIBRARY

With the children at play in the Oval Office, October 10, 1962. JOHN F. KENNEDY LIBRARY

JFK and Bobby conferring at the White House, October 3, 1962. Bobby was the president's most trusted adviser on civil rights and international affairs. JOHN F. KENNEDY LIBRARY

JFK with the Ex Comm during the Cuban missile crisis, the most dangerous moment in the forty-five-year Cold War, October 29, 1962. JOHN F. KENNEDY LIBRARY

JFK meeting with Secretary of Defense Robert McNamara and Secretary of State Dean Rusk, December 10, 1962. Kennedy saw McNamara as an exceptionally bright and effective colleague trying to rein in his department, and Rusk as a passive bureaucrat who left foreign policy making to the president. JOHN F. KENNEDY LIBRARY

JFK with special counsel Ted Sorensen, March 12, 1963. Kennedy surrounded himself with brilliant men who served him loyally. JOHN F. KENNEDY LIBRARY

JFK speaks to a quarter of a million cheering West Berliners, June 26, 1963. Kennedy was exhilarated by the warmth of his reception. JOHN F. KENNEDY LIBRARY

JFK, LBJ, and leaders of the March on Washington, August 28, 1963. It was a notable moment in the black struggle for equal rights, highlighted by Martin Luther King Jr.'s stirring "I Have a Dream" speech. JOHN F. KENNEDY LIBRARY

JFK, Jackie, and the children observing the Black Watch Tattoo from a White House balcony, November 13, 1963. JOHN F. KENNEDY LIBRARY

JFK's casket in the Capitol Rotunda, November 24, 1963. The president's death badly shook the nation and stirred a controversy about who killed him that remains to this day. JOHN F. KENNEDY LIBRARY

John F. Kennedy's grave in Arlington National Cemetery with the Eternal Flame. The 1994 photograph by Joseph R. Connors is the National Park Service's most heavily purchased photograph.
COURTESY OF JOSEPH R. CONNORS

States remove its Jupiter missiles from Turkey in return for the dismantling of what "you regard as offensive weapons" in Cuba. The revised letter also maintained the demand for a pledge against invading Cuba and reliance on the U.N. as an intermediary.

The altered proposal created consternation among the Ex Comm members. It impressed them as the work of the Politburo eager to gain more advantages than Khrushchev had originally demanded. Could they, then, simply ignore the addition of Turkey to the exchange of pledges and respond only to Khrushchev's first proposal? "Well now, that's just what we ought to be thinking about," Kennedy said. But it would put the United States "in an unsupportable position" because "to any man at the United Nations or any other rational man, it [the Turkey-Cuba swap] will look like a very fair trade." Bundy disagreed, arguing that such a trade-off would not sit well with our European allies, who would see us as "trying to sell our allies for our interests." To buy time, the group released an interim press statement. "Several inconsistent and conflicting proposals have been made by the U.S.S.R. within the last 24 hours," the White House announcement said. "The proposal broadcast this morning involves the security of nations outside the Western Hemisphere. But it is the Western Hemisphere countries and they alone that are subject to the threat that has produced the current crisis." Only after this threat had ended would the United States take up proposals concerning the security of nations elsewhere.

For almost four hours beginning at 4:00 P.M. on Saturday the twenty-seventh, the Ex Comm agonized over Khrushchev's Cuba-for-Turkey missile swap. With the Cuban missile sites nearing completion and reports that a SAM had shot down a U-2 flying over Cuba and killed its pilot, the Joint Chiefs were pressing for a massive air strike no later than Monday morning, the twenty-ninth, to be followed by an invasion in seven days. Kennedy and his advisers saw Khrushchev's proposal as possibly the last chance to reach a settlement and avoid military action that could lead to a nuclear exchange.

Everyone agreed that trading the Jupiters in Turkey for the missiles in Cuba would undermine the NATO alliance and weaken faith in U.S. willingness to take risks for the defense of its allies. Llewellyn Thompson also believed that it was unnecessary to include the Turkish missiles in the deal; Khrushchev would be able to boast of saving Cuba from a U.S. invasion, and he did not need to remove the Jupiters to end the crisis.

But Kennedy was not so sure. He was eager to do everything possible to avoid military action and the "ultimate failure," a nuclear war. He wanted to promise to discuss the Jupiters in Turkey if Khrushchev would suspend work on the missile sites and "disarm these weapons." If we keep the missiles in Turkey, Kennedy believed, "we are either going to have to invade or have a massive strike on Cuba which may lose Berlin. That's what concerns me," he said. He thought that once the bloodletting began, the NATO countries would look back and say the Turkish deal "was a pretty good proposition."

Nevertheless, Kennedy's advisers convinced him to omit any mention of Turkey in his written reply to Khrushchev — in other words, to answer the first letter and largely ignore the second. He told Khrushchev that he first had to stop work on offensive missile bases in Cuba, make all offensive weapons systems there "inoperable," and halt the further introduction of such weapons. All of it was to be done under U.N. supervision. In return, the United States would end the quarantine and give assurances against an invasion of Cuba. Such a settlement "would enable us to work toward a more general arrangement regarding 'other armaments,' as proposed in your second letter which you made public. . . . The continuation of this threat, or a prolonging of this discussion concerning Cuba by linking these problems to the broader questions of European and world security, would surely lead to an intensification of the Cuban crisis and a grave risk to the peace of the world."

At the same time Kennedy cabled his letter to Moscow, he had Bobby hand deliver it to Dobrynin. By using his brother as the messenger, Kennedy was indicating that this was no committee or bureaucratic response but a statement of his personal eagerness to end the crisis on the terms described in the letter. Bobby's mission was also meant to signal the urgency of a positive response from Khrushchev to relieve Pentagon pressure on the president for military action. As is clear from a memo Bobby subsequently made of his conversation with Dobrynin, he left no question that a failure to agree to the proposed exchange would have disastrous consequences. Bobby told him that the attack on the U-2 and death of the pilot compelled the administration "to make certain decisions within the next 12 or possibly 24 hours. There was very little time left. If the Cubans were shooting at our planes, then we were going to shoot back." Bobby told Dobrynin "that he had better understand the situation and he had better communicate that understanding to

Mr. Khrushchev. . . . We had to have a commitment by at least tomorrow that those bases would be removed. This was not an ultimatum, I said, but just a statement of fact. He should understand that if they did not remove those bases then we would remove them. His country might take retaliatory action but he should understand that before this was over, while there might be dead Americans there would also be dead Russians." Bobby warned that "drastic consequences" would come from a failure to accept the president's proposal by the next day.

When Dobrynin asked about Khrushchev's proposal on Turkey, Bobby was ready with an answer. At a meeting with the president and several of his advisers just before he met with the ambassador, Bobby was instructed by Kennedy and Rusk to say that "while there could be no deal over the Turkish missiles, the President was determined to get them out and would do so once the Cuban crisis was resolved." The group agreed that knowledge of this commitment would be a closely guarded secret, since "this unilateral private assurance might appear to betray an ally." Bobby was also told to make plain to Dobrynin that if Moscow revealed this pledge, it would become null and void. On October 27, Kennedy secretly instructed Rusk to telephone Andrew Cordier, a Columbia University dean, who had served under U Thant at the U.N., and ask him to be prepared to give the secretary general a statement proposing the simultaneous removal of the missiles in Turkey and Cuba. Although this contingency plan was never activated and Rusk did not reveal its existence until 1987, it leaves no doubt that the president would have publicly given up the Jupiters for an end to the crisis.

No one involved in the October 27 discussions could have doubted that the United States was on the brink of military action against Cuba, which seemed likely to lead to a crisis in Europe and a possible war with the Soviet Union. Kenny O'Donnell remembered an Ex Comm evening meeting as "the most depressing hour that any of us spent in the White House during the President's time there." A State Department cable to the U.S. NATO mission said it all: Khrushchev's second, public, letter had "diminished" hope for a settlement. The situation "is increasingly serious and time is growing shorter." Recounting the loss of the U-2 and continuing Soviet ship movements toward the quarantine line, despite promises to the contrary, the cable advised that the United States "may find it necessary within a very short time in its own interest and that of its fellow nations in the Western Hemisphere to take whatever military action may be necessary to remove this growing threat to the Hemisphere."

At ten in the evening, after the Ex Comm had reviewed the gloomy prospects if Khrushchev rejected the president's offer, Bobby asked McNamara, "How are you doing, Bob?" "Well. How about yourself?" McNamara replied. "All right," Bobby said. "You got any doubts?" McNamara asked. "No," Bobby answered, "I think that we're doing the only thing we can." McNamara wanted to be sure that Moscow did not misread U.S. intentions. "I think the one thing, Bobby . . . we ought to seriously do before we attack them, you've got to be *damned sure they understand it's coming.*"

They did. At a meeting of the entire Soviet presidium in a Moscow suburb, Khrushchev declared the need for a "retreat" in order to save Soviet power and the world from a nuclear catastrophe. As a prelude to a discussion on how to respond to Kennedy's offer, the presidium authorized Soviet forces to repel a U.S. attack on Cuba if there were no settlement. During the presidium discussion, the arrival of Dobrynin's report on his meeting with Bobby created a sense of urgency about ending the crisis. Khrushchev immediately dictated a letter accepting Kennedy's terms and instructed that it be broadcast on the radio to ensure its prompt receipt in Washington before some incident triggered military action. At the same time, Khrushchev sent the president a secret communication expressing satisfaction at Kennedy's promise to remove the Jupiters from Turkey in four or five months and promised to hold this agreement in confidence.

The Soviet broadcast, which was heard in Washington at 9:00 A.M. Sunday morning, lifted a pall of apprehension from Kennedy and his Ex Comm advisers. Only the Joint Chiefs refused to take Khrushchev's "surrender" at face value. Led by LeMay, they sent the president a letter recommending execution of the planned air strikes on Monday followed by the invasion unless there were "irrefutable evidence" of immediate Soviet action to remove the missile sites. They cautioned against a Soviet delaying tactic while they finished their missile buildup in preparation for "diplomatic blackmail." A few days later, when Kennedy met with the Chiefs to thank them for their counsel and help during this most difficult period, they were not mollified. Admiral Anderson told the president, "We have been had!" LeMay called the settlement "the greatest defeat in our history," and urged a prompt invasion. McNamara remembered Kennedy as "absolutely shocked" and "stuttering in reply."

Kennedy told his advisers that the quarantine would continue until they could be sure that the terms of the agreement were met. He would remain uncomfortable with the continued presence of Soviet IL-28 bombers in Cuba, which had been omitted from the required elimination of offensive weapons. He also anticipated no end to communist subversion in the hemisphere and expected the two sides would be "toe to toe on Berlin" by the end of November. But for the moment, the danger of a Soviet-American war had receded. Kennedy urged everyone to be reserved and to avoid gloating, which would humiliate Khrushchev and only add to future difficulties between the United States and the USSR.

KHRUSHCHEV'S PROMISE to remove the missiles from Cuba ended the immediate danger of a military clash, but Kennedy could not assume that the crisis was concluded. Although he was confident that Khrushchev had backed down rather than risk a nuclear war, he could not afford to take anything for granted. Khrushchev's initial lies about the presence of offensive weapons made Kennedy unwilling to take him at his word. Bob Komer of the National Security Council encouraged the president's suspicions: "We've given K. a bloody nose in a way very hard for USSR to take without attempting in some way to recoup. [The] whole image of Soviet 'invincibility' will be eroded if K. doesn't do something." Kennedy shared Komer's concern: "We must operate on the presumption that the Russians may try again," he told McNamara on November 5. "I am sure that we are watching for any developments by the Soviet Union of a submarine base in Cuba," he wrote John McCone in December. "Will you keep me informed periodically as to whether or not anything of a suspicious nature has turned up in this regard?"

In refusing to declare the crisis at an end, Kennedy wished to avoid an embarrassing possible reversal, which would be a political disaster and an irresistible prod to military action. He planned to officially end the quarantine after the Soviets dismantled the launching sites and shipped the missiles back to Russia. He also wanted the IL-28 bombers removed. Three weeks of negotiation and continued flights over Cuba produced a mutually agreeable formula. At a news conference on November 20, Kennedy announced that Khrushchev would remove all the IL-28 aircraft from Cuba within thirty days and would allow U.S. observation of the procedure. He also reported that "all known offensive missile sites in Cuba have been dismantled," that the Soviets had loaded the missiles on departing ships, and that inspection at sea had confirmed their departure. A naval quarantine was no longer necessary. He was thankful that the crisis had concluded peacefully and hoped that the outcome "might well open the door to the solution of other outstanding problems."

Though the missiles were gone, because Castro rejected U.N. inspection of Cuba Kennedy would not abandon schemes to oust him from power. He declared at his news conference that to protect the hemisphere from offensive weapons, the United States would "pursue its own means of checking on military activities in Cuba." The continuing presence of Soviet ground combat units made ongoing vigilance essential. Moreover, he promised that if Cuba was "not used for the export of aggressive Communist purposes, there will be peace in the Caribbean." But he described efforts to halt subversion and encourage the establishment of freedom in Cuba as "very different from any intent to launch a military invasion of the island." As he told McNamara in a memo of November 5, he still believed an invasion of Cuba carried huge military risks: "Considering the size of the problem, the equipment that is involved on the other side, the Nationalists['] fervor which may be engendered, it seems to me we could end up bogged down. I think we should keep constantly in mind the British in the Boer War, the Russians in the last war with the Finnish and our own experience with the North Koreans." At the same time, Kennedy told Schlesinger, "An invasion would have been a mistake — a wrong use of our power. But the military are mad. They wanted to do this." Kennedy had little attraction to a direct American assault on Cuba, especially after McNamara gave him estimated casualties of between forty and fifty thousand. If they were to bring down Castro's regime, it would have to be by covert subversion, which the administration continued to support in the coming months.

Kennedy received justifiable plaudits for resolving the crisis. Yet he had no illusion that his response was the principal reason for success. Rather, America's local military superiority, Moscow's limited national security stake in keeping missiles in Cuba, and the Soviets' difficulty justifying to world opinion a possible nuclear conflict over Cuba were of greater importance in persuading Khrushchev to back down. Still, Kennedy's resistance to pressure from military chiefs for air attacks and an invasion, and his understanding that patient diplomacy and measured pressure could persuade the Soviets to remove the missiles were essential contributions to the peaceful outcome of the crisis.

Of course, Kennedy's problem with Cuba was not strictly of his making, but partly the consequence of an "unimaginative and sterile" policy in 1959–1960. "Probably no United States policy could have prevented Castro's movement into the Soviet orbit," Schlesinger wrote Kennedy in November 1962, but "a more imaginative U.S. policy could have made it much harder for Castro to join the Soviet bloc." Indeed, a greater measure of sympathy for a government striving to right the many wrongs visited on Cuba by a U.S.-backed Batista regime was a regrettable Eisenhower omission. And indeed, some historians believe that Kennedy's role in provoking the confrontation makes him less than heroic in resolving it. As Barton J. Bernstein has said, "a different president than Kennedy might well have chosen not to launch the Bay of Pigs venture, not to pursue clandestine activities against Cuba and Castro, not to build up the American nuclear arsenal well beyond the size of the Soviets', and not to place the Jupiters in Turkey." Bernstein believes that these actions, but especially plotting against Castro and indications of a possible invasion, provoked Khrushchev into his Cuban missile adventure.

Bernstein's argument has merit. Without Kennedy's Cuban provocations, Khrushchev would have been hard-pressed to justify placing missiles on the island. The administration's anti-Castro actions gave Moscow an inviting opportunity to use Cuba to reduce America's nuclear advantage over the USSR and/or force a favorable resolution of the Berlin problem. Yet, as Ernest May and Philip Zelikow have pointed out, Khrushchev probably acted "more from instinct than from calculation. Whether Berlin or the strategic balance or concern about Cuba was uppermost in his mind at the time he ordered the missiles sent to Cuba, he himself could probably not have said." Khrushchev, in the view of two close aides, was a "reckless" gambler or "hothead," who made a big bet in hopes of getting a huge payoff. Having stumbled badly in advancing his country's economic well-being and believing that Kennedy would wilt in a confrontation rather than go to war, Khrushchev sent the missiles to Cuba hoping to win a big foreign policy victory that could secure his political fortunes. He was wrong, and the consequences of his error were nearly fatal. But his ultimate good sense joined with Kennedy's wise judgment to avert a disaster that the president believed would have been described as the "final human failure."

Forty years after the crisis, historians almost uniformly agree that this was the most dangerous moment in the forty-five-year Cold War. Moreover, despite his part in provoking the crisis, they generally have high praise for Kennedy's performance. His restraint in resisting a military solution that would almost certainly have triggered a nuclear exchange makes him a model of wise statesmanship in a dire situation. One need only compare his performance with that of Europe's heads of government before World War I — a disaster that cost millions of lives and wasted unprecedented sums of wealth — to understand how important effective leadership can be in times of international strife. October 1962 was not only Kennedy's finest hour in the White House; it was also an imperishable example of how one man prevented a catastrophe that may yet afflict the world.

CHAPTER 17

New Departures:
Domestic Affairs

*The winds of change appear to be blowing more strongly
than ever, in the world of communism as well as our own.
For 175 years we have sailed with those winds at our
back. . . . Today we still welcome those winds of change —
and we have every reason to believe that our tide is
running strong.*

— John F. Kennedy, State of the Union Message,
January 14, 1963

KENNEDY'S HIGHEST PRIORITIES during the missile crisis had been
to rid Cuba of Soviet missiles without a nuclear war and to ensure
against a future confrontation by convincing Khrushchev that there
could be no payoff from attempted nuclear blackmail. At the same
time, however, he was mindful of the political consequences to his
administration. With midterm congressional elections only a week
away when Khrushchev pledged to remove the missiles, Kennedy
appreciated that a failure to deal effectively with the crisis would
have been a terrible blow to the future of his presidency.

Kennedy's successful diplomacy gave the Democrats an advantage in the November elections that he was happy to exploit. The
White House welcomed descriptions by Acheson, Bundy, Harriman,
Norman Cousins of *The Saturday Review,* and General Norstad of a
president who had been "extraordinarily skillful," "firm," "reasonable," and "calm." It also took satisfaction from *Newsweek*'s assertion
that Kennedy "had given Americans a sense of deep confidence in
their President and the team he had working with him."

The public had only a limited understanding of how resolute Kennedy had been. Health problems continued to dog him during the crisis. He took his usual doses of antispasmodics to control his colitis; antibiotics for a flareup of his urinary tract problem and a bout of sinusitis; and increased amounts of hydrocortisone and testosterone as well as salt tablets to control his Addison's disease and increase his energy. Judging from the tape recordings of conversations made during the crisis, the medications were no impediment to long days and lucid thought; to the contrary, Kennedy would have been significantly less effective without them and might not even have been able to function. But the medicines were only one element in helping him focus on the crisis; his strength of will was indispensable. With so much at stake in the Soviet-American confrontation, he was not about to let personal pain or physical problems deter him from the most important business of his presidency. He undoubtedly had his own experience in mind when he wrote in an article on physical fitness for *Look* magazine in 1963, "Whether it is the astronaut exploring the boundaries of space, or the overworked civil servant laboring into the night to keep a Government program going, the effectiveness and creativity of the individual must rest, in large measure, on his physical fitness and vitality."

This is not to suggest that Kennedy was superhuman or to exaggerate his invulnerability to physical and emotional ills. On November 2, he took 10 additional milligrams of hydrocortisone and 10 grains of salt to boost him before giving a brief report to the American people on the dismantling of the Soviet missile bases in Cuba. In December, Jackie asked the president's gastroenterologist, Dr. Russell Boles, to eliminate antihistamines for food allergies. She described them as having a "depressing action" on the president and asked Boles to prescribe something that would ensure "mood elevation without irritation to the gastrointestinal tract." Boles prescribed 1 milligram twice a day of Stelazine, an antipsychotic that was also used as an anti-anxiety medication. When Kennedy showed marked improvement in two days, they removed the Stelazine from his daily medications.

Kennedy burnished his image as the principal architect of Soviet defeat by allowing journalists to draw comparisons with Adlai Stevenson. In December, when Stewart Alsop and Charles Bartlett published a *Saturday Evening Post* article on the crisis, which Kennedy had seen in draft form, they contrasted Kennedy's firmness with

Stevenson's soft approach; Stevenson wanted "a Munich," they said. It is true that Stevenson exceeded Kennedy's readiness to make concessions, including especially a willingness to close the U.S. military base at Guantanamo. But in fact he had been in sync with the president on avoiding an air strike or a premature invasion and was an early supporter of the quarantine idea. When the press interpreted the Alsop-Bartlett article as an indirect request from the president for Stevenson's resignation, Kennedy emphatically denied it, but he left the charges of softness unanswered by refusing to comment on Ex Comm discussions. To boost Stevenson, who was demoralized by the flap, Kennedy released a letter to him praising his contribution at the U.N. Nevertheless, the public depiction of Stevenson as an appeaser strengthened the view of Kennedy as a tough-minded leader comparable to America's best past and present defenders of the national interest. It increased his freedom to negotiate an arms control agreement and weakened the capacity of conservative critics to press him into more forceful military action in Vietnam. Petty revenge for old slights cannot be ruled out as another motive.

Kennedy understood that a strong showing in the November elections could make Congress more receptive to his major domestic proposals. Although his administration publicly made much of its legislative record, privately it was unhappy. The president had won between 81 and 85 percent of the roll call votes on domestic proposals in 1961 and 1962. And on roll calls involving foreign policy, he had received 96.5 percent backing. But his overall record was much less noteworthy. Many of the bills Congress passed were relatively minor reforms, like temporarily reducing duty exemptions on Americans returning from abroad, authorizing an additional assistant secretary of labor, extending the Sugar Act of 1948, or reorganizing the Federal Home Loan Bank Board. Most of his legislative requests — 56 percent in 1962, to be exact — had never emerged from House and Senate committees, where conservative chairmen bottled them up.

Johnson and Hubert Humphrey were so concerned about Kennedy's ineffective congressional leadership that in August 1962 they suggested ways to improve it. They wanted him to make his presence and influence more visible on the Hill. "[Both men] were talking quite honestly about the problem of getting effective results," Bundy told the president. "I did not detect any personal soreness in either of them, and both spoke in the framework of great commitment to your program and to you." So did Truman, who wrote Kennedy at the same time: "The President is just as great as the Congress — and really greater — when he exercises his Constitutional Prerogatives. You are going through the same situations and troubles that Franklin Roosevelt, Abraham Lincoln and I had to meet. Don't like to put myself in that high class — but I had a hell of a time. You meet 'em, cuss 'em & give 'em hell and you'll win in 1964."

Kennedy saw no point in risking prestige or expending political capital by openly campaigning for particular candidates. Instead, he worked behind the scenes to advance the political fortunes of vulnerable Democrats. Moreover, Kennedy took Lou Harris's advice that his best means of influencing the electorate was to speak "over and over again" about the measures needed to get the country moving forward. Harris was convinced that the people were eager to be led and that once "aroused and mobilized, Congress, business, and all groups will respond as a man to the reverberating chorus."

During the summer and fall, Kennedy crisscrossed the country in support of a Democratic Congress. He said that the nation's well-being — its future prosperity and social advance — depended on electing more House and Senate Democrats who would vote for his programs. Since 1938, the Congress had been more or less deadlocked in its consideration of new progressive measures. He described himself as fighting the same battles Wilson, FDR, and Truman had faced "to provide progress for our people." "I believe we should have the opportunity and not have the kind of balance in the Congress which will mean two . . . more years of inertia and inaction. That's why this is an important election. Five, ten seats one way or the other can vitally affect the balance of power in the Congress and vitally affect our future. . . . So this is not an off-year, it is an important year." Kennedy catalogued his legislative victories and defeats, pointing out, "We have won fights by 3 or 4 votes in the House of Representatives, and we have lost fights by 3 or 4 votes." Ignoring the opposition to his proposals of conservative southern Democrats, he blamed Republicans for his problems: 75 percent of them had voted against his higher education bill; 84 percent of Republican senators had opposed extended unemployment benefits; 81 percent and 95 percent of House Republicans had voted against his area redevelopment and public housing bills, respectively; and 80 percent of House Republicans had resisted increasing the minimum wage to $1.25. "On a bill to provide medical care for our older citizens . . . seven-eighths of the Republican Members of the Senate voted 'no,' just as their fathers before them had voted 90 percent against the social security [bill] in the 1930's." As he came closer to the election, Kennedy acknowledged that conservative Democrats were also a problem. If liberal Democrats failed to vote, he told an audience in Pittsburgh on October 12, every proposal that we bring before the Eighty-eighth Congress in January 1963, "will be in the control of a dominant Republican–Conservative Democratic coalition that will defeat progress on every single one of these measures."

Despite not risking his presidential standing by investing excessively in any single congressional race, Kennedy's general endorsement of Democrats sympathetic to his legislative agenda tested his personal influence. He approached the campaign confident that his presidential performance had given him a stronger hold on the electorate than he had had in 1960. He understood that, whatever the appeal of his message, the public liked him. His good looks, intelligence, wit, and charm, which were so regularly and exuberantly on display at press conferences, now drew large audiences to hear him on the campaign trail. Some inside the administration could see Kennedy's obvious imperfections — the insatiable sexual appetite contradicting the picture of the ideal family man married to a perfect wife; the manipulation of image to hide missteps; the fierce competitiveness to win, which made him and Bobby all too willing to exploit friends; and the private physical suffering, which occasionally made him glum and cranky. Yet no one could doubt that Kennedy's two years in the White House had created an imperishable view of him as a significant American president worthy of the office.

Still, the reality was that Kennedy had no real hope of breaking the congressional deadlock. Though preelection polls showed 56 percent of voters favoring Democrats over Republicans, a significant part of this support was for southern members of the party, who were unsympathetic to progressive measures. So, despite a satisfying gain of four Democratic seats in the Senate and the loss of only four seats in the House, which made this, except for FDR's, the best midterm showing for any incumbent president in the twentieth century, Kennedy acknowledged that "we'll probably be in a position somewhat comparable to what we were in for the last two years." If they could maintain the unity of congressional Democrats and win some support from moderate Republicans, he foresaw legislative gains. But he believed it more likely that they would struggle, as they had during his first two years, with narrow margins of victory and defeat. He was gratified that brother Ted had won his Senate race in Massachusetts, which he had helped, or at least hoped would help, by appointing Cleveland mayor Anthony Celebrezze as HEW secretary, a choice that appealed to Italian American voters in Massachusetts. But beyond Ted's victory, Kennedy saw little to cheer about.

There was other bad news. Despite a 12-point jump in his approval rating to 74 percent and what was being hailed as "your excellent showing in congressional races and your net pick-up in the Senate," urban areas in "pivotal industrial states" had, according to Lou Harris, shown some "big Democratic slippage over 1960" among Catholic and Jewish voters. To some extent, Kennedy's abnormally high Catholic vote in 1960 made a decline among this bloc predictable. More troubling was the fact that Irish Catholics were becoming more conservative, or Republican, in their voting, while Polish and Italian Catholics, unhappy with recent Democratic failures to provide greater economic benefits, were simply voting in smaller numbers for the party. Moreover, Kennedy's perceived sympathy for disadvantaged blacks, who were in growing competition with big-city ethnics for jobs and housing, antagonized blue-collar Catholics. In reaction to civil rights pressures, the traditional Democratic South was becoming more Republican.

DESPITE THE TRENDS, and possibly because of them, Kennedy could not ignore black claims on equal treatment under the law; African American voters remained the Democratic party's most reliable supporters. For both political and moral reasons, then, on November 20, Kennedy finally announced his decision to sign an Executive Order integrating federally supported public housing.

While he waited for any backlash that might accompany his signing of the Executive Order, Kennedy worried about increasing negative revelations about his personal life and how they might jeopardize his presidency. He remained confident that the mainstream press would not publicize his womanizing. But when rumors of a Marilyn Monroe–JFK affair began appearing in gossip columns, Kennedy made a concerted effort to squelch them. He asked former journalist and inspector general of the Peace Corps William Haddad to "see the editors. Tell them you are speaking for me and that it's just not true," Kennedy said. Haddad later told Richard Reeves, "He lied to me. He used my credibility with people I knew." Haddad obviously came to believe the many stories circulated about JFK and Marilyn. Almost as much ink has been spilled over their alleged relationship and one between Bobby and Marilyn as over the Cuban missile crisis. Peter Lawford, the actor and Kennedy brother-in-law, dismissed these speculations as "garbage." But numerous phone calls listed in White House logs from Monroe to Kennedy suggest something more than a casual acquaintance. Whatever the truth, Kennedy obviously understood that no good could come to his presidency from gossip about an affair with someone as famously promiscuous and troubled as Monroe.

Kennedy's worries about his public image extended to medical matters. Because he believed that revelations about his health problems were more likely (and more likely to be damaging) than about his sexual escapades, he became more cautious about publicizing his interactions with his many physicians. According to George Burkley, Kennedy was so concerned about not giving the impression that he was "physically impaired . . . and required the constant supervision of a physician" that he shunned having "a medical man in near proximity to him at all times."

Kennedy especially felt compelled to quell private concerns about the injections Travell and Jacobson were giving him. Hans Kraus told him in December 1962 "that if I ever heard he took another shot, I'd make sure it was known. No President with his finger on the red button has any business taking stuff like that." In addition, Kraus told Evelyn Lincoln "that if Dr. Travell was going to continue making suggestions and innuendos concerning the President's health he was going to get out of the picture. He said it had to be 'Yes' or 'No' — that he was not interested in half way tactics." Eugene Cohen also warned Kennedy that Travell was a "potential threat to your well-being." Kennedy agreed to take control of his back treatments away from Travell and turn it entirely over to Burkley and Kraus. To ensure against alienating Travell, however, and risking leaks from her to the press about his condition, Kennedy kept her on as White House physician and continued to identify her as the principal doctor in charge of his health care. In fact, however, beginning in June 1963, she could not order medical services at Walter Reed Army Medical Center for anyone at the White House without Burkley's approval.

Nevertheless, though Jacobson and Travell played diminished roles in Kennedy's treatment, neither of them was without some continuing part in his care. Through much of 1962, Jacobson made occasional professional visits to the White House. It is well known that in June Bobby instructed an FBI laboratory to analyze the substance Jacobson was injecting into his brother's back. Bobby was concerned that the president might become addicted to the amphetamines Jacobson was using. Inconclusive lab tests, however, allowed Jacobson to continue treating Kennedy through at least the fall of 1962.

Similarly, for all the limitations Burkley, Cohen, and Kraus imposed on Travell, she remained more than a presence at the White House, though in a diminished capacity, something she complained about to Jackie. Her records indicate that she kept close track of the president's condition and use of medicines and may have had an ongoing part in medicating him. But according to Dr. James M. Young, a thirty-three-year-old navy captain who became the White House physician in June 1963, Travell was without a say in managing Kennedy's health care during the five months after he came to the White House; she was never at twice-a-month medical evaluation meetings Young attended with Kennedy. But Young acknowledged that her records suggest that she may have had a behind-the-scenes role.

Young's meetings with Kennedy convinced him that the president was in "robust health having no difficulty with his chronic back problems. He was well-controlled on his other medications — even so much as to say finitely controlled," Young remembered. This is difficult to square with Travell's records, which describe substantial ongoing problems. Was Kennedy setting Young up for a part in the 1964 campaign, when he might want a medical authority to testify to his physical capacity to remain as president? Kennedy's attentiveness to managing his image as someone in excellent health makes such a manipulation plausible.

KENNEDY KNEW that shielding himself from bad publicity to maintain his personal public standing would not give his administration the sort of momentum he hoped to bring to a reelection campaign. The perception of a vigorous president was important, but it was no substitute for a healthy economy and a record of social advancements.

"The Congress looks more powerful sitting here than it did when I was there in the Congress," Kennedy told some journalists in

December 1962. If a president puts forward a significant program, he told them, it will affect powerful interests and produce a fight in which "the President is never wholly successful." With this understanding, he had to decide whether to focus exclusively on the tax cut or to supplement it with renewed requests for education and health insurance reforms and an Urban Affairs Department. Walter Heller also asked him to consider proposing new laws affecting farm programs, immigration, presidential campaign finance, the Taft-Hartley Labor Act, and consumer protections.

Economic advance had to come first. As Phil Graham told him, "The economic conditions of the Western World are not good. And a sudden shock could lead to a very serious panic. . . . The greatest force the Communists ever had working for them — greater even than the Red Army — was the terrible depression of the 1930's. The military power of Communism is blocked today. We must not allow them to advance by reason of the chaos and despair of a major depression."

Whether Graham, who would take his life in the coming year, accurately reflected the state of western economies or his own despair, Kennedy felt he could not ignore the warning. Any sign of a recession or economic slowdown evoked memories for millions of Americans of 1930s breadlines. In the closing weeks of 1962, Kennedy made boosting the economy his highest priority. More than ever, he believed that long-term growth required a tax cut and tax reforms. In December 1962, Kennedy took up the cause of tax reform in another public address, which he compared with his appearance before the Houston Protestant ministers' conference during the presidential campaign: He saw a national commitment to a tax cut that increased federal deficits as comparable to convincing voters that a Catholic could be a good president.

In an attempt to exploit Cold War fears, Kennedy described the country's national security as directly bound up with its economic performance. Addressing familiar concerns that tax cuts would lead to larger deficits and runaway inflation, Kennedy said, "The lesson of the last decade is that budget deficits are not caused by wild-eyed spenders but by slow economic growth and periodic recessions. . . . In short, it is a paradoxical truth that tax rates are too high today and tax revenues are too low and the soundest way to raise the revenues in the long run is to cut rates now." He said that "the hope of all free nations" was riding on the tax cut; America's safety and that of the free world depended on the United States' continuing capacity to outproduce the Soviet Union.

Nevertheless, a request to Congress for these measures in January 1963 seemed certain to arouse renewed skepticism and opposition. Wilbur Mills in the House and Albert Gore in the Senate, key Democratic figures in the looming battle over the tax legislation, remained unsympathetic to prompt action. Mills saw no need for a tax bill as long as the economy was not in a recession or slowing down and substantial federal budget deficits continued to threaten confidence in the "fiscal responsibility of the government." He was willing to support changes in individual and corporate tax rates as a way to promote long-term economic expansion but not before January 1964 and not unless reductions in nondefense spending matched tax cuts. Gore warned the president that "a reduction in revenue will set off a howling campaign for reduction in expenditures and your administration will be put in an economic straight jacket. The ax would most likely fall heaviest on foreign aid and on programs that may be needed to stimulate the economy, such as public works." Gore also feared that tax reform would favor the rich and shortchange the poor. "People with large incomes would have their take-home pay (income after taxes) increased 50%, 100% and, in some instances even 200%, while the average tax payer would have an increase of less than 10%, most of them only 3% to 5%. This simply cannot be justified — socially, economically or politically. And I hold these sentiments passionately! This is something that no Republican administration has dared do; it is something you must not do."

By late December, it was clear to Kennedy that a tax cut and a bold reform agenda would have little chance of enactment in 1963. Bobby Baker, the secretary to Senate majority leader Mike Mansfield, who kept close tabs on sentiment in the Upper House, predicted that "we are in serious danger of being unable to pass" the tax cut. Nor did Baker see more than a 50–50 chance of creating an Urban Affairs Department, and even if the Senate approved it, it seemed unlikely to pass the House. Likewise, the House would be the problem in passing medical insurance and aid to elementary and secondary education. Any attempt to create a domestic peace corps would "cause considerable strain and possibly affect the present Peace Corps. . . . Temporary Unemployment Compensation will have rough sledding in both Houses." Baker saw brighter prospects for a mass transportation law, a higher education bill, aid to medical research, and conservation measures, but, overall, it did not seem like a promising year for presidential reform initiatives.

Nevertheless, Kennedy refused to give in to counsels of caution. A failure to present a bold domestic program would make him look timid and resigned to conservative influence. Besides, if Congress rejected his proposals, it would more clearly set him apart from conservative opponents in a 1964 campaign.

Kennedy also hoped that appeals to the national well-being might sway congressional majorities to support a tax cut and other reforms. In his January 1963 State of the Union Message, he announced a program of changes, which he described as essential to the nation's future. Although the most recent recession was over, with a million more people working than two years before, this was no time to relax: "The mere absence of recession is not growth," he said. To achieve greater expansion, "one step, above all, is essential — the enactment this year of a substantial reduction and revision in Federal income taxes. . . . It is increasingly clear . . . that our obsolete tax system exerts too heavy a drag on private purchasing power, profits and employment." He proposed to lower tax liabilities by $13.5 billion, $11 billion on individuals and $2.5 billion on corporations. Individual tax rates were to drop from between 20 and 91 percent "to a more sensible range of 14 to 65 percent." The corporate rate would drop 5 points from 52 to 47 percent. To combat the temporary deficits anticipated from the cuts, Kennedy proposed phasing them in over three years and holding expenditures, except for defense and space, below current levels.

IN OCTOBER 1962, when he prepared his 1963 budget, he privately acknowledged that education reforms, which would increase the annual deficit, were "not going to pass." We should "just . . . start off with that realization," he told budget director Dave Bell. No one could doubt his eagerness for federal support of elementary, secondary, and higher education. During 1963, he repeatedly quoted Jefferson: "If a nation expects to be ignorant and free, . . . it expects what never was and never will be." In a seventy-five-hundred-word message to Congress, he described education as "the keystone in the arch of freedom and progress." He believed that federal monies could improve the "quality of instruction" and reduce "alarming" dropout rates. Federal dollars were also needed to help colleges meet a 100 percent increase in enrollments by 1970, and secondary schools a 50 percent rise in students attending. "Soviet institutions of higher education are graduating 3 times as many engineers and 4 times as many physicians as the United States," Kennedy said. "While trailing behind this country in aggregate annual numbers of higher education graduates, the Soviets are maintaining an annual flow of scientific and technical professional manpower more than twice as large as our own." Yet for all his outspokenness on the importance of education, Kennedy made it a lower budget priority in 1963 than defense and space, and continuing political tensions over aid to parochial schools and racial integration discouraged the president from stronger support of congressional action.

Medicare presented similar dilemmas. Although he spoke out forcefully at the beginning of 1963 for health reform legislation and health insurance for seniors in particular, the familiar litany of national needs could not break resistance in the House and the Senate to initiating new and potentially costly welfare programs. Special messages to the Congress in February on improving the nation's health and the needs of the nation's senior citizens did no more than put Kennedy back on record as favoring help for America's seventeen and a half million elderly. There was no shortage of talk and goodwill in Congress toward seniors, including thirty-six bills proposing ways to insure everyone over sixty-five. But a focus on Kennedy's suggested tax cut and increased deficits pushed health proposals aside. The House Ways and Means Committee did not agree even to hold hearings on health insurance until November.

By the spring of 1963, Kennedy had accepted the political realities working against legislative health reforms. Between April and October, aside from brief remarks in the White House Rose Garden to the National Council of Senior Citizens urging a congressional vote on medical care for the aged under Social Security, he said nothing in public and put no pressure on Congress to act. In May, he told HEW secretary Anthony Celebrezze, "There seems to be some speculation that we have abandoned health insurance for this year. While it may be that events will not permit legislative action in 1963, I believe we should proceed on the assumption that we are attempting to secure it. The failure then will not be ours." In November, when a reporter asked if he would press Mills to send Medicare to the House floor for a vote, Kennedy replied, "I think we are going to get that bill out of committee — not this year, but next year — and I think we will have a vote on it and I think it will pass." Believing that congressmen and senators would court the elderly in 1964 by backing health reforms, Kennedy predicted that "this is going to be an 18-month delivery!"

By contrast with education and Medicare, which Kennedy believed would have improved chances of congressional action in the next year, he doubted that a tax cut would gain any legislative momentum in the coming months. There were, granted, some glimmers of hope. The president's appearances in support of tax reform were paying dividends, Heller advised. He said he saw "a lot of willingness to help put the tax program through. . . . To mobilize this aid and convert it into votes in Congress should be a major part of our tax offensive." He also reported that a survey of consumers showed 63 percent in favor of a tax cut. Dillon advised Kennedy that concerns about the cut disproportionately favoring the rich were unfounded. But throughout 1963, conventional thinking about the danger of increased deficits from a tax reduction sustained conservative opposition to Kennedy's tax proposals. We "favor . . . a reduction in both individual and corporate tax rates," Republican legislators declared. "However, we believe that a tax cut of more than $11 billion, with no hope of a balanced budget for the foreseeable future, is both morally and fiscally wrong." The prospect of larger deficits so bothered Eisenhower that he joined the chorus of opposition. He declared a tax cut "highly desirable but only if the persistent and frightening increase in Federal expenditures is halted in its tracks." Mills's Ways and Means Committee would not budge on the tax bill unless the White House made clear how it intended to reduce federal spending over the next several years.

The strength of the economy in 1963 also worked against prompt action on Kennedy's tax bill. Steady GNP expansion between 1961 and 1963 and stable unemployment at 5.7 percent had convinced congressional majorities that any additional economic stimulus was unnecessary. Kennedy himself acknowledged that over the last two years the GNP had expanded by 20 percent, industrial production was up 22 percent, and personal income had risen 15 percent. Nevertheless, he believed it shortsighted to assume that strong growth could be sustained without lower taxes. Business cycles in the past decade had produced three recessions, and he expected another downturn by the middle of 1964 unless Congress cut taxes.

In August, when Ways and Means finally voted out of committee a tax bill, Kennedy thanked it for a measure that would "provide much needed jobs for our economy, increase our rate of economic growth, promote balance in our international payments and benefit the individual and corporate tax payer." The long-range result of their action would be "a balanced budget in a balanced full-employment economy. It is clear that this goal cannot be achieved without a substantial tax reduction and the greater national income it will produce. . . . Let me stress once again that the surest way to alter the pattern of deficits which has characterized seven of the last ten years is to enact at this session an effective tax reduction program."

Kennedy was no less emphatic in private, telling Congresswoman Martha W. Griffiths of Michigan, "We've got the best means of insuring that 1964 isn't a recession year. That's why I'm hanging on." Despite the likelihood that some corporation presidents favored the tax cut in order "to use the money to try to [beat] us," Kennedy did not "mind that," he told Griffiths, because he believed the bill would be "a terrific asset to us [the Democrats]." He urged Heller to pressure labor economists to lobby Congress and "get us some votes for Christ sakes." The oil and gas lobbyists, who were fighting a reduction in their industry's depletion allowance, which would increase federal revenues and lower the deficit, particularly angered him. "Those robbing bastards," he told Heller. "The day's gonna come when we're gonna have the Congress and the President financed by the government" rather than corporations like the oil companies, Kennedy told Mills. "And it'll be the best thing that ever happened. God, you know those oil companies. . . . I don't mind anybody getting away with some, but what they get away with."

Despite repeated public appeals by Kennedy for prompt action and support from a Business Committee for Tax Reduction organized by the administration and including prominent businessmen like Henry Ford II and David Rockefeller, Kennedy could not get his bill passed. A tax cut won a House vote on September 25, but it had been stripped of the reform features that promised to close loopholes and generate $4.5 billion in additional revenues. The likelihood that the deficit would now be that much higher brought Senate approval into doubt. Albert Gore remained a particular problem. He wanted to slow things down by holding extended hearings, and his opposition enraged Kennedy, who repeatedly called him "a son of a bitch" in a meeting with economic advisers on September 30. "If we get a good recession next summer, it's not going to do him much good, is it?" Kennedy said. By the third week in November, the Senate Finance Committee had still not concluded its hearings, and prospects for passage of a bill in 1963 seemed dim. In a conversation with Dillon and Fowler, Kennedy lamented: "If we don't get that tax bill, [the country] will pay a hell of a price for it."

BY CONTRAST WITH HIS BUOYANT PUSH for the tax bill, during the first five and a half months of 1963, Kennedy maintained a cautious approach to civil rights. After issuing the limited housing order in November 1962, he refused to initiate a more comprehensive civil rights program, especially a major legislative attack on segregation, which he continued to believe would make passage of his tax, education, and medical reform bills impossible by antagonizing southern Democrats. Though the same earlier strategy had failed to advance these measures, he still assumed that avoiding a head-on congressional clash over civil rights would at least preserve some chance of getting his other reforms approved. Besides, he continued to believe that executive initiatives could be an effective, if temporary, substitute for congressional action on advancing equal rights for blacks.

If he was legislatively passive, he was at least rhetorically aggressive. In his State of the Union Message, Kennedy urged that "the most precious and powerful right in the world, the right to vote . . . not be denied to any citizen on grounds of his race or color. . . . In this centennial year of Emancipation all those who are willing to vote should always be permitted." In his January economic message to Congress, he tied "an end to racial and religious discrimination" to economic growth. The development and effective use of "our human resources" was vital to the national well-being. In February, after receiving a Civil Rights Commission report on a hundred years of racial discrimination, he praised the courage of black citizens fighting to throw off "legal, economic, and social bonds — bonds which, in holding back part of our Nation, have compromised the conscience and haltered the power of all the Nation. In freeing themselves, the Negroes have enlarged the freedoms of all Americans . . . . [Yet] too many of the bonds of restriction still exist. The distance still to be traveled one hundred years after the signing of the Emancipation Proclamation is at once a reproach and a challenge." America must not rest "until the promise of equal rights for all has been fulfilled."

At the end of February, Kennedy called upon Congress to eliminate abuses of black rights. The catalogue of wrongs was transparent: Black children were about half as likely to complete high school as whites and had one-third as much chance of earning a college degree or of becoming a professional. They had about twice as much chance of becoming unemployed, with only half the earning power and seven fewer years of life than whites. Discrimination reduced economic growth, hampered our world leadership by contradicting our message of freedom, marred "the atmosphere of a united and classless society," and increased "the costs of public welfare, crime, delinquency and disorder." But "above all," Kennedy said, "it is wrong. . . . It is not merely because of the Cold War, and not merely because of the economic waste of discrimination, that we are committed to achieving true equality of opportunity. The basic reason is because it is right."

He described denial of the franchise as especially egregious. Five southern states had "over 200 counties in which fewer than 15% of the Negroes of voting age are registered to vote. This cannot continue," Kennedy declared. "I am, therefore, recommending legislation to deal with the problem." He also urged the fulfillment of the Supreme Court's nine-year-old decision on desegregation of public schools, the enforcement of fair hiring and other labor practices, and the end to racial segregation in all places of public accommodation — hotels, restaurants, theaters, recreational facilities, airports, rail and bus stations, and all means of public transportation. "Surely there could be no more meaningful observance of the centennial [of Lincoln's Proclamation]" Kennedy concluded, "than the enactment of effective civil rights legislation and the continuation of effective executive action."

Yet, since he was still thinking of the consequences for his overall agenda, Kennedy's actions did not match his words. It was still only in the realm of voting rights that Kennedy actually offered legislation. He refused to risk his 1963 congressional program by supporting reform of Rule XXII, which would reduce the votes needed to end a filibuster from two-thirds to three-fifths — relevant since a filibuster seemed likely in the case of civil rights but not in response to his other reform proposals. Nor did he follow his February message to Congress with specific recommendations for ending southern segregation.

In March, a reporter asked Kennedy to comment on Governor Rockefeller's assertion that he had been "appointing 'segregationist judges' to the Federal bench in the South." The reporter also pointed out that "that had blunted [to] a certain amount the aggressive stand that the executive branch had taken against segregation." Kennedy responded defensively: "No. I think that some of the judges may not have ruled as I would have ruled in their cases. In those cases there is always the possibility for an appeal." Overall, he said, the southern judges appointed by him and Eisenhower had a "very creditable record." In a telephone conversation the next day with Deputy Attorney General Nicholas Katzenbach, Kennedy and Katzenbach were more candid, naming several judges who were problematic. But instead of trying to do something about it, they thought of short-term political equations. Katzenbach pointed out that they had "as much trouble from Republican appointees down there as . . . from the Democrats." Kennedy said he wanted the Justice Department "to get up a memo on . . . the Republicans and Democrats 'cause . . . this might get to be one of those issues they keep talking about. So I'll be able to talk about [the Republican segregationist judges] in case it comes up again." The strategy was to mask his administration's shortcomings on judicial appointments by demonstrating that Eisenhower's were even worse or, at least, no better.

At the end of April, Kennedy was on the defensive again about his refusal to accept a Civil Rights Commission recommendation that the federal government cut off funds to Mississippi until it complied with court orders protecting blacks from violence and discrimination. Since Kennedy would not follow the commission's recommendation, a reporter asked, "Could you discuss with us what alternative steps the Federal Government might be able to take to bring some of these [southern] States into line with the law of the land?" Kennedy replied that his administration had instituted lawsuits to remedy the problems. But he accurately described it as "very difficult," because "we do not have direct jurisdiction." He said that "a blanket withdrawal of Federal expenditures from a State" was beyond his powers, but he was using every "legislative and legal tool at our command to insure protection for the rights of our citizens."

By the spring of 1963, Kennedy's frustration over civil rights was greater than ever. He felt he had exercised stronger executive leadership in support of equal racial opportunity than any administration in U.S. history. His Justice Department had filed forty-two lawsuits in support of black voting rights. He had fought the battle of Mississippi to enroll Meredith in the university. He had appointed forty blacks to important administration posts and elevated Thurgood Marshall to the federal Circuit Court of Appeals in New York. Though belatedly, he had signed the Executive Order barring discrimination in federally financed public housing. He had also recommended a voting rights law, but public and congressional apathy had stalled it in committee. But his failure to request a ban on segregation in places of public accommodation had been glaring and evoked continuing complaints that he was too timid and that only a bold proposal for change could end the injustices of discrimination and produce real progress for African Americans.

Tensions in the administration over how to handle civil rights problems produced a running battle between Bobby and Johnson. Bobby was convinced that unless the administration delivered on greater equality for blacks, it would miss a chance to advance simple justice for an oppressed minority, lose liberal support, and alienate millions of voters by appearing ineffective and weak. Fearful that his brother could lose the 1964 election over a failure to produce enough gains on civil rights, Bobby pressed everyone in the administration to do their utmost. Burke Marshall recalls that Bobby "fussed and interfered . . . with almost every other department of the government in 1963 . . . on their employment policies, and on whether or not Negroes were allowed to participate in federally financed programs." As head of the Committee on Equal Employment Opportunity, Johnson became a principal target of Bobby's prodding. Johnson was proud of the committee's record in 1962 after Troutman had resigned and Hobart Taylor, Johnson's appointee, had replaced him. The committee had increased black job holding in the federal government that year by 17 percent and doubled the number of remedial actions taken by private contractors in response to complaints from black employees. Johnson also took pride in public statements echoing the president's call for an end to segregation and racism. Yet Johnson's rhetoric, like Kennedy's, was an inadequate substitute for effective action. The gains made by the CEEO resulted in no more than an upward blip in black employment. Moreover, newspaper stories during the first half of 1963 describing the CEEO's Plans for Progress as "largely meaningless" persuaded Bobby that Johnson's committee was "mostly a public relations operation" and that Taylor was "an Uncle Tom." Bobby worried not only about the limited gains in black employment but also about the committee's impact on the 1964 campaign. "I could just see going into the election of 1964," he said later, "and eventually these statistics or figures would get out. There would just be a public scandal." Bobby also recalled that when he spoke to the president about the problem, he "almost had a fit."

At CEEO meetings in May and July, after police attacks on black demonstrators in Birmingham, Alabama, had put civil rights back in the headlines, Bobby gave clear expression to White House dis-satisfaction with the committee's performance. According to one observer, he treated Johnson "in a most vicious manner. He'd ridicule him, imply he was insincere." In May Bobby "asked a lot of questions that were impatient, very impatient," Burke Marshall said. "It made the Vice President mad." Bobby blamed Johnson and Taylor for the 1 percent black federal employment in Birmingham, a city with a 37 percent black population. "I was humiliated," Johnson said afterward. At the July meeting, Bobby made NASA's James Webb the target of his complaints. Webb, who was working closely with Johnson on space plans, had no information on black employment at NASA, and Bobby castigated him for neglecting the issue. "It was a pretty brutal performance, very sharp," one participant recalled. "It brought tensions between Johnson and Kennedy right out on the table and very hard. Everybody was sweating under the armpits. . . . And then finally, after completely humiliating Webb and making the Vice President look like a fraud and shutting Hobart Taylor up completely, he got up. He walked around the table . . . shook my hand . . . and then he went on out."

The clashes between Bobby and Johnson were partly personal. "No affection contaminated the relationship between the Vice President and the Attorney General," Schlesinger remembered. "It was a pure case of mutual dislike." Seventeen years, six inches in height, and "southwestern exaggeration against Yankee understatement" separated them. "Robert Kennedy, in the New England manner, liked people to keep their physical distance. Johnson, in the Texas manner, was all over everybody — always the grip on the shoulder, tug at the lapel, nudge in the ribs, squeeze of the knee."

Both men were powerful, at times overbearing, tyrannical characters who did not treat opponents kindly. They were tough alley fighters, hell-bent on winning at almost any cost. Intimidation and hard bargains were weapons they carried into their political campaigns for high office and legislative gains. They also shared bold, indeed, noble dreams for the country of better race relations, less poverty, and security from foreign threats. They held a common regard for the national system that had allowed them both to gain prominence and power. But each self-righteously saw the other as less capable of achieving the great ends bringing them together in the same party and the same administration. Although the president kept his distance from the Bobby-Johnson tensions and had little taste for the personal abuse Bobby used against adversaries, he seems to have accepted his brother's harsh treatment of Johnson as a necessary prod to making him a more effective member of the administration.

IN APRIL, MARTIN LUTHER KING and the Alabama Southern Christian Leadership Conference launched a campaign in Birmingham to challenge the city's segregated facilities and employment practices. TCI, the Tennessee Coal, Iron & Railroad Company, the city's leading employer, had only eight black white-collar employees out of a workforce of twelve hundred. Most black men in Birmingham worked in the least desirable blue-collar jobs, while those black women who worked usually served as domestics. The city administration had no black policemen, firemen, or elected representatives. Because it was one of the most racist communities in the South, any sort of victory for equal treatment would represent an opening wedge in the struggle to change the mores of the whole region. And because Eugene "Bull" Connor, the city's police commissioner, seemed certain to reply with repressive tactics likely to make the national news and draw the Kennedy administration into the struggle, the city became the ideal target for a renewed attack on southern racism.

Connor and the city fathers did not disappoint King and SCLC protesters. On May 3 and 4, when black demonstrators, including many high school and some elementary schoolchildren, marched in defiance of a city ban, the police and firemen attacked the marchers with police dogs that bit several demonstrators, and high-pressure fire hoses that knocked marchers down and tore off their clothes. The TV images, broadcast across the country and around the world, graphically showed out-of-control racists abusing innocent, young advocates of equal rights. Kennedy, looking at a picture on the front page of the *New York Times* and TV news coverage of a dog lunging to bite a teenager on the stomach, said that the photo made him "sick."

Still, Kennedy's initial response to the crisis was a moderate urge to compromise. For the sake of civic peace, America's international reputation, and King's public influence, Kennedy wanted to negotiate a quick halt to the Birmingham strife.

He viewed Birmingham's power brokers as unreasonable reflectors of outdated social mores whose unyielding racism threatened their city's civic peace and prosperity. He also saw an end to racial strife in the South as essential to America's international standing in its competition with Moscow for influence in Third World countries. But at the same time, while he sympathized with the crusade against southern racism, Kennedy also saw King as self-serving and possibly under the influence of communists trying to embarrass the United States. J. Edgar Hoover fanned the flames of suspicion about King or, more to the point, about two of King's associates, Stanley Levison and Hunter Pitts O'Dell, whom he accused of being communists. (Although Levison had ended his ties with the Communist Party in 1956, his history made him vulnerable to Hoover's accusations. And because Hoover was so emphatic about Levison's ongoing radicalism, and because the FBI had a reputation for successfully identifying subversives, Bobby and Burke Marshall found it difficult to ignore their warnings.) A drawn-out crisis in Birmingham might persuade Hoover to leak stories to the media that communist subversives were manipulating King in Alabama.

At a press conference on May 8, Kennedy declared that in the absence of violations of federal civil rights or other statutes, he was working to bring "both sides together to settle in a peaceful fashion the very real abuses too long inflicted on the Negro citizens of that community." He intended to halt "a spectacle which was seriously damaging the reputation of both Birmingham and the country." A reporter wanted to know if "a fireside chat on civil rights would serve a constructive purpose." "If I thought it would I would give one," Kennedy replied. But he had his doubts. "I made a speech the night of Mississippi — at Oxford — to the citizens of Mississippi and others," he said. "That did not seem to do much good." Afterward, Civil Rights commissioner Erwin Griswold publicly complained, "It seems clear to me that he hasn't even started to use the powers that are available to him." An angry Kennedy said privately, "That son of a bitch. Let him try."

Finding a middle ground between the segregationists and the SCLC seemed like an insurmountable challenge. Understanding that King was intent on full integration, in all the city's public facilities, including its retail businesses, Birmingham's white leaders viewed any compromises as opening the way to a social revolution repugnant to most whites in the city, state, and region.

Nevertheless, Kennedy sent Burke Marshall to Birmingham to work out a settlement. King believed that the administration wanted him to suspend demonstrations until the Alabama Supreme Court had ruled on the legitimacy of a more moderate city government battling Connor for control of city hall. But King saw delay as defeat. In a famous letter to white clergymen written from the Birmingham jail, where he had been imprisoned after an April demonstration, King expressed disappointment at their opposition to civil disobedience and their counsels of patience. He wrote: "'Wait' has almost always meant 'Never.' . . . When you are forever fighting a degenerating sense of 'nobodiness' — then you will understand why we find it difficult to wait."

King reserved his strongest complaints for white moderates, among whom he included the Kennedys. "I have almost reached the regrettable conclusion that the Negro's great stumbling block in his stride toward freedom is not the White Citizen's Councilor or the Ku Klux Klanner, but the white moderate, who is more devoted to 'order' than to justice, who . . . constantly says, 'I agree with you in the goal you seek, but I cannot agree with your methods of direct action,' who paternalistically believes he can set the timetable for another man's freedom." King publicly took issue with Kennedy's assertion that "there were no federal statutes involved in most aspects of this struggle. . . . I feel that there have been blatant violations of basic constitutional principles."

During a week of tedious negotiations, Marshall convinced both sides to compromise: The SCLC won agreements to desegregate department store fitting rooms, downtown lunch counters, washrooms, rest rooms, and drinking fountains. Blacks were to fill a small number of white-collar jobs, and a committee would be formed to discuss future racial problems and employment. Under direct pressure from cabinet secretaries Dillon, McNamara, Hodges, and W. Willard Wirtz, and U.S. Steel president Roger Blough, who called Birmingham business chiefs as a way to get back in Kennedy's good graces, the white power structure agreed to the changes, which promised an end to demonstrations and a return to normal business activity.

But the compromise agitated diehard segregationists. They could not abide a King declaration that the concessions were a great civil rights victory opening the way to the end of discrimination in Birmingham, or Bobby's description of the agreement as "a tremendous step forward for Birmingham, for Alabama, and for the South generally." Birmingham's new moderate mayor, Albert Boutwell, announced that he would not be bound by the settlement, and, as King anticipated, Alabama's segregationist press dismissed the agreement as a defeat for the SCLC. On Saturday, May 11, Alabama and

Georgia Klansmen staged a rally in a suburban Birmingham park, and that night bombs exploded at the home of the Reverend A. D. King, Martin Luther King's brother, and at the black-owned Gaston Motel, where King stayed during his visits to Birmingham. Blacks responded with attacks on police and firemen, which brought state troopers and city anti-riot forces to the scene. A four-hour rampage by local residents left a nine-block area of the black ghetto a smoldering shambles. The explosion of violence by southern blacks against white oppression was unprecedented in the twentieth century. "The passivity and nonviolence of American Negroes could never again be taken for granted," two experts on southern race relations said. "The 'rules of the game' in race relations were permanently changed in Birmingham."

Now Kennedy was forced toward a fresh response to the civil rights crisis. His first concern was to stem the violence, which threatened to destroy the compromise agreement. He knew that he could not rely on Alabama governor George Wallace to help. Wallace had begun his political career in the fifties as a moderate and promptly lost a gubernatorial campaign to an out-and-out racist who had openly courted the Klan. Determined not to let any political opponent ever again outdo him as a segregationist (to be "out-niggered again," Wallace said), he had won the governorship in 1962 by infamously promising segregation now, segregation tomorrow, segregation forever. He also personally pledged to stand in the schoolhouse door to block any "illegal" federal court order mandating integration. It was clear that if Wallace controlled the state's National Guard, they were likely, Kennedy thought, to be "sticking bayonets in people and hitting people with clubs, guns, et cetera." And this seemed certain to destroy black adherence to the Birmingham compromise, as Wallace hoped. Kennedy feared the result would be "rallies all over the country . . . with people calling on the President to take forceful action."

If the White House decided to federalize the Alabama National Guard and send troops to Birmingham, it seemed certain to antagonize just about everyone. The guard, after all, would be deployed to counter not white rioters, as in Mississippi in 1962, but the rampaging blacks, who might return to the streets on Sunday night. Yet despite being sent to curb black violence, federal troops would remind southerners of military reconstruction and could undermine Birmingham's white moderates, who had agreed to the settlement and were already under attack for having allied themselves with the SCLC. "If that agreement blows up," Burke Marshall told the president, "the Negroes will be —" Kennedy finished his thought: "Uncontrollable." Marshall added: "And I think not only in Birmingham."

King now emerged as a crucial, if unacknowledged, ally, in trying to save the Birmingham settlement. Kennedy asked Marshall to find out what King intended. Marshall reported back to Kennedy that King, indeed, hoped to control "his people" and believed he could if there were no other incidents. Kennedy wanted to know if King had said anything about troops, which he had not.

Although he did not underestimate the dangers Birmingham posed to civic peace across the South and to the future of his presidency, Kennedy's success in managing the Cuban missile problem had given him confidence that he could find a satisfactory solution to the current crisis. He was also confident that the American people would back appeals to equal treatment under the law. He instructed McNamara, Marshall, Katzenbach, and Edwin Guthman, Bobby's public affairs spokesman at the Justice Department, to draft a declaration promising a restoration of public order and constitutional rights for blacks. Although Kennedy eventually complained that their statement "leaned too much on the side of the Negroes," his announcement left no doubt that he wished to preserve the gains made in the Birmingham agreement. In a televised Oval Office speech to the country on Sunday night, May 12, he praised it as "a fair and just accord," which "recognized the fundamental right of all citizens to be accorded equal treatment and opportunity." He promised that the federal government would not permit "a few extremists" on each side to sabotage the settlement. To facilitate these goals, Kennedy announced the return of Burke Marshall to Birmingham for additional consultations, the dispatch of riot control forces to military bases near the city, and steps to federalize the Alabama National Guard, should they be needed to keep the peace. The next day the White House released a telegram to Wallace describing the basis for presidential authority to suppress domestic violence and the preparations for such possible action.

The combination of King's appeals to the black community for quiet and Kennedy's determination to maintain order and support the Birmingham settlement disposed of the immediate crisis. But Kennedy did not believe that the Birmingham agreement ensured future improvements in race relations or an end to civil rights conflicts across the South. A survey Bobby made of southern cities suggested that as many as thirty of them might explode in violence during the summer.

Events in Alabama and Mississippi during the next two weeks confirmed their fears. On May 22, Wallace, who had pledged to go to jail rather than allow integration of the University of Alabama, the last remaining segregated state university in the nation, responded to a May 21 federal district court order by restating his determination to resist the enrollment of black students. Privately he rejected Bobby's overtures to talk, telling his state attorney general, "Dammit, send the Justice Department word, I ain't compromising with anybody. I'm gonna *make 'em* bring troops into this state." When Bobby persisted, Wallace agreed to see him in Montgomery if the attorney general requested the meeting in writing.

On April 25, after Bobby had sent a telegram asking to see him, Wallace met with him in the governor's office. On the ride to the state capitol, observing pickets carrying inflammatory signs, Bobby told Burke Marshall, "It's like a foreign country." As he walked up the steps of the capitol, Bobby saw state troopers with Confederate flags painted on steel helmets. A crowd of onlookers was friendly and eagerly shook Bobby's hand, but the troopers were overtly hostile. The head of the protective detail turned his back when Bobby extended his hand, and one of the troopers put his nightstick against Bobby's stomach and shoved him back as he attempted to approach some excited young women trying to greet him. The only ground for agreement Bobby could find with Wallace in their eighty-minute conversation was that the governor would greet the president when he paid a visit to Muscle Shoals, Alabama, on May 18 to mark the thirtieth anniversary of the Tennessee Valley Authority.

That encounter between the president and Wallace gave Kennedy no hope that Wallace would desist from his bitter-end segregationist views. Though he would deny it later, during a fifty-minute helicopter ride from Muscle Shoals to the Redstone Arsenal at Huntsville, Wallace replied to Kennedy's questions about black employment in Birmingham department stores by denouncing King and other black activists as self-indulgent, cigar-smoking womanizers who drove around in big Cadillacs and lusted after black, "white and red women too." Not amused, Kennedy made it clear at Redstone that he did not wish to be photographed with Wallace.

The prospect of race wars across the South convinced Kennedy that he had to take bolder action to address the problem. Burke Marshall recalled that the president now saw Birmingham as a pattern that "would recur in many other places." Bobby told his brother, "There must be a dozen places where we're having major problems today." JFK, Marshall said, "wanted to know what he should do — not to deal with Birmingham, but to deal with what was clearly an explosion in the racial problem that could not, would not, go away, that he had not only to face up to himself, but somehow to bring the country to face up to and resolve."

At meetings on May 20 and 21, Bobby and his civil rights and political advisers recommended personal appeals by the president to southern white officeholders and businessmen to meet with blacks to discuss opening places of public accommodation and jobs to them. But Kennedy saw the southerners as "hopeless, they'll never reform." He added, "The people in the South haven't done anything about integration for a hundred years, and when an outsider intervenes, they tell him to get out; they'll take care of it themselves, which they won't." It was time, he declared, to be less concerned about southern feelings.

KENNEDY BELIEVED that he would now have to ask Congress for a major civil rights bill that would offer a comprehensive response to the problem. "These people who object to mob action, unreasonable demonstrations and so on [don't get it]," Kennedy told aides. "The problem is [that] there is no other remedy for them [the black rioters]. This will give another remedy in law. Therefore, this is the right message. It will remove the [incentive] to mob action." Kennedy was uncertain about what exactly to include in such a bill. Nevertheless, on May 22, when a reporter asked him if he was considering asking for new civil rights legislation as a result of the recent developments down South, he answered: "Yes . . . we are considering whether any additional proposals will be made to the Congress. And the final decision should be made in the next few days."

Kennedy's sense of urgency about a new legislative initiative increased in the next three weeks. On May 24, Bobby met in the Kennedys' New York family apartment on Central Park South with an elite group of black activists. James Baldwin, the author of a disturbing November 1962 *New Yorker* article on the condition of black men in America, organized the meeting at Bobby's request. Jerome Smith, a black radical, dominated the discussion, describing himself as nauseated by the necessity of being in the same room with the attorney general. The fact that he had to explain the personal abuse inflicted on him in the South showed, he said, what little progress had been made in race relations, and he doubted that he could follow King's prescription of nonviolence much longer. Indeed, he didn't even feel he could fight for America were he ever asked to do so. Bobby's evident anger at Smith moved the playwright Lorraine Hansberry to say, "Look, if you can't understand what this young man is saying, then we are without hope at all because you and your brother are representatives of the best that a white America can offer; and if you are insensitive to this, then there's no alternative to our going in the streets . . . and chaos." When Schlesinger listened to a stunned Bobby describe his distress over the encounter, he feared that Bobby's "final reaction would be a sense of futility rather than of the urgency of trying to bridge the gap."

Schlesinger need not have worried. However strong Bobby's initial indignation, he shortly asked the Senate Judiciary Committee, "How long can we say to a Negro in Jackson, 'When war comes you will be an American citizen, but in the meantime you're a citizen of Mississippi — and we can't help you'?" An outburst of violence in Jackson at the end of May against protesters trying to desegregate a Woolworth's lunch counter, combined with demonstrations over integrating Baton Rouge, Louisiana, schools, strengthened the Kennedys' resolve to ask Congress for comprehensive civil rights legislation. And while Kennedy remained relatively dispassionate, there was a mounting sense of urgency. On June 3, when Louisiana governor Jimmie Davis told the president, "Either we have federal orders to stop some of these demonstrations, marches . . . [or] it is going to spread," Kennedy replied, "It's going to be up North. . . . This isn't any more just a southern matter. . . . It's Philadelphia and it's going to be Washington, D.C., this summer, and we're trying to figure out what we can do to put this stuff in the courts and get it off the street because somebody's going to get killed."

Conversations with Louisiana's Davis and Mayor Allen Thompson of Jackson, Mississippi, provided Kennedy with evidence that southern moderates wanted to reach an accommodation giving African Americans a greater sense of equality and economic opportunity. Thompson, who had been critical of Kennedy's civil rights actions, urged the president to ignore what he said about him in public: "I really think the world of you," Thompson told him. "I know you're a marvelous man and have a terrible job, an impossible job." "I give you full permission to denounce me in public," Kennedy joked, "as long as you don't in private." More important, Thompson's amazement "at the fine Negro leaders who have called

602 ★ ROBERT DALLEK

me" and his conviction that "people are sick and tired" of the agitation troubling their communities helped give Kennedy hope for a reasoned outcome to southern racial strife.

On June 3, newspapers reported that Kennedy would ask Congress for a major civil rights law. The vice president, who prided himself on his mastery as a legislator and doubted that the administration had made adequate preparations to get a bill passed, told Ted Sorensen, "I don't know who drafted it [the bill]. I've never seen it. Hell, if the Vice President doesn't know what's in it, how do you expect the others to know what's in it? I got it from the *New York Times.*" Johnson counseled greater preparation before sending up a bill. Johnson also advised Kennedy to travel through the South. "If he goes down there and looks them in the eye," Johnson said, "and states the moral issue and the Christian issue, and he does it face to face, these southerners at least respect his courage." Kennedy would next have to invite in black leaders and persuade them that he was genuinely on their side. "The Negroes feel and they're suspicious that we're just doing what we got to," Johnson said. "Until that's laid to rest I don't think you're going to have much of a solution." Kennedy accepted Johnson's advice as "very wise" and delayed sending his bill to Congress for more than a week.

In the meantime, he looked for ways to make the moral case to the nation. The situation at the University of Alabama offered Kennedy a moral high ground. On June 2, after Wallace repeated his promise on *Meet the Press* to block two black students from enrolling at the University of Alabama on June 11, the Justice Department obtained a court order prohibiting Wallace's interference, though he was not barred from appearing on campus. Neither the administration nor Wallace wanted their differences to erupt in violence or for Wallace to go to jail over defiance of the court order, which seemed likely to deepen the crisis and increase the chances of disorder. In response to a request from Bobby, Averell Harriman asked business leaders with Alabama interests to pressure Wallace to restrain himself. Wallace, who was primarily interested in presenting himself as an opponent of federal intrusion in state affairs rather than as a martyr to a lost cause, was happy to comply. Remembering the difficulties in Mississippi in 1962, the Kennedys decided to federalize the Alabama National Guard to ensure against violence.

On June 10, one of Bobby's deputies representing the Justice Department tried to convince a friendly journalist to publish a story about a "nervous disability" Wallace had suffered during World War II service in the air force. The objective was to demonstrate Wallace's instability and suggest that segregationists like Wallace were unworthy of public support. The tactic failed when Wallace acknowledged his nervous condition and the reporter's editors at *Newsday*, nevertheless fearing a libel suit, refused to run anything about it. The administration found other ways to put Wallace in a bad light and advance the argument for a civil rights bill. The White House agreed to allow a documentary filmmaker to record Bobby and the president conferring during the crisis. Wallace also agreed to let a film crew follow him around, but the advantage in this pictorial competition went to the Kennedys, who appeared sure of themselves, compared with Wallace, who seemed nervous, as if he were "on amphetamines." This was the intent all along: Bobby had instructed Nick Katzenbach, who was sent to the campus to demand that Wallace step aside and allow the black students to enroll, "Make him look ridiculous. That's what the President wants you to do." And though Katzenbach looked frazzled in the summer heat, and though the five-foot seven-inch Wallace, standing atop a wooden box, measured up to the taller Katzenbach's height and refused to step aside until ordered to do so by the general commanding the federalized Alabama Guard, what the camera crews ultimately recorded was clearly a Kennedy victory. Furthermore, when the university was integrated without violence, Wallace's opposition registered on the country as pointless posturing.

Seizing upon their success in facing down Wallace, Kennedy decided to give a televised evening speech announcing his decision to ask Congress for a civil rights law. Except for Bobby, Kennedy's advisers opposed the idea; he might, they worried, be investing too much of his personal standing in a measure likely to fail. But Kennedy believed that larger national needs required it. With only six hours to prepare, it was uncertain whether Sorensen would be able to deliver a polished speech in time. The president and Bobby talked about what he should say in an extemporaneous talk should no text be ready. Five minutes before Kennedy went on television, Sorensen gave him a final draft, which Kennedy spent about three minutes reviewing.

Though Kennedy delivered part of the talk extemporaneously, it was one of his best speeches — a heartfelt appeal in behalf of a moral cause. It included several memorable lines calling upon the country to honor its finest traditions: "We are confronted primarily with a moral issue," he said. "It is as old as the scriptures and is as clear as the American Constitution. The heart of the question is whether all Americans are to be afforded equal rights and equal opportunities. . . . One hundred years of delay have passed since President Lincoln freed the slaves, yet their heirs, their grandsons, are not fully free. They are not yet freed from the bonds of injustice. They are not yet freed from social and economic oppression. And this Nation, for all its hopes and all its boasts, will not be fully free until all its citizens are free. . . . Now the time has come for this Nation to fulfill its promise. . . . The fires of frustration and discord are burning in every city, North and South, where legal remedies are not at hand. . . . A great change is at hand, and our task, our obligation, is to make that revolution, that change, peaceful and constructive for all. . . . Next week I shall ask the Congress of the United States to act, to make a commitment it has not fully made in this century to the proposition that race has no place in American life or law."

The following week, on June 19, Kennedy asked for the enactment of the most far-reaching civil rights bill in the country's history. He presented it against the backdrop of the murder of Medgar Evers, a leading black activist in Mississippi and veteran of the D-Day invasion, assassinated a day after the president's speech by a rifle shot in the back at the door to his house in front of his wife and children.

The proposed law would ensure any citizen with a sixth-grade education the right to vote, and would eliminate discrimination in all places of public accommodation — hotels, restaurants, amusement facilities, and retail establishments. Kennedy described the basis for such legislation as clearly consistent with the Fourteenth Amendment's equal protection clause, the Fifteenth Amendment's right of citizens to vote regardless of race or color, and federal control of interstate commerce. He also asked for expanded powers for the attorney general to enforce court-ordered school desegregation; bring an end to job discrimination and expand funds for job training, which could help African Americans better compete for good jobs; and create a federal community relations service, which could work to improve race relations.

Because bipartisan support was essential to overcome southern Democratic opposition, Kennedy met with Republican House and

Senate leaders and Eisenhower to enlist their backing. He asked every member of Congress to put aside sectional and political ties for the sake of the national well-being.

In asking Congress to put civil rights at the center of its deliberations, Kennedy believed that he was also putting his presidency at risk. "He always felt that maybe this was going to be his political swan song," Bobby said. "He would ask me every four days, 'Do you think we did the right thing by sending the legislation up? Look at the trouble it got us in.'" The "trouble" Kennedy saw came from southern Democrats. After he sent up the civil rights bill, Kennedy said in a telephone conversation with Congressman Carl Albert of Oklahoma, "I suppose that civil rights thing has just got 'em all excited." In explaining why a public works bill had failed, Albert replied, "We lost some of the southern boys that we would otherwise have had." Albert thought that civil rights was "overwhelming the whole, the whole program." He saw it "affecting mass transit and killing Kennedy's farm bills." "Civil rights did it," Kennedy concluded.

Regardless of the legislative consequences, Kennedy felt that he had to act. As Everett Dirksen, quoting Victor Hugo, said in the following year, "Stronger than all the armies is an idea whose time has come. The time has come for equality . . . in education and in employment. It will not be stayed or denied. It is here." Remembering *Profiles in Courage*, Kennedy told Luther Hodges, his southern commerce secretary, "There comes a time when a man has to take a stand and history will record that he has to meet these tough situations and ultimately make a decision."

But more than moral considerations were at work in Kennedy's decision. Bobby and the president understood that unless they now acted boldly, African Americans would lose hope that the government would ever fully support their claims to equality and would increasingly engage in violent protest. The alternative to civil rights legislation was civil strife, which would injure the national well-being, embarrass the country before the world, and jeopardize the Kennedy presidency. And since the South seemed likely to vote Republican in the next election, a show of political courage made good political sense and would probably gain him more than he would lose. "Kennedy will lose the segregationist vote," a reporter for the *Chattanooga Times* said in May. "But he'll get 110% of the Negro vote no matter how much Martin Luther King and others criticize him for doing less than the maximum for civil rights. In a close election in Tennessee, the Negroes hold the balance." The journalist had it right, except for the part about King, who himself led a chorus of praise for Kennedy's bill. King called Kennedy's civil rights proposals "the most sweeping and forthright ever presented by an American president," and predicted that they would "take the Nation a long, long way toward the realization of the ideals of freedom and justice for all people." Yet the fight had only begun. If the White House were going to defeat a southern filibuster, Kennedy would have to go beyond earlier rhetorical appeals and fully assert his political influence before the end of the 1963 congressional session.

CHAPTER 18

New Departures: Foreign Affairs

While maintaining our readiness for war, let us exhaust every avenue for peace.

— John F. Kennedy, October 1963

KENNEDY UNDERSTOOD that advances at home alone were insufficient to ensure America's overseas success. Managing the Cold War remained as great a challenge as ever. And Kennedy left no doubt that this was still his highest priority. In a December 17, 1962, TV and radio interview with William Lawrence of ABC and George Herman of CBS, he spent most of the hour-long discussion on foreign affairs. Kennedy described the missile crisis as a turning point that had opened a new era in history. "Cuba was the first time," he said, "that the Soviet Union and the United States directly faced each other with the prospect of the use of military forces . . . which could possibly have escalated into a nuclear struggle." Its successful resolution now allowed him to set a more rational agenda on nuclear weapons and to encourage possibilities of Soviet-American détente, which would in turn free him to give more attention to other world problems threatening America's long-term national interest.

Kennedy believed it essential to rein in the nuclear arms race. "There is just a limit to how much we need," he told the newsmen. "[We have] submarines in the ocean, we have Minutemen on the ground, we have B-52 planes, we still have some B-47's, we have the tactical forces in Europe. I would say when we start to talk about the megatonnage we could bring into a nuclear war, we are talking about annihilation. How many times do you have to hit a target with nuclear weapons?" He found it inconceivable that anyone could speak casually about a nuclear war, which some of the military and far-right politicians did. A massive nuclear exchange would bring 150 million fatalities in the first eighteen hours in Western Europe, the Soviet Union, and the United States. And displaying a greater confidence than ever to take on the U.S. military and the defense industry, Kennedy described the B-70 bomber as "a weapon that isn't worth the money we would have to put into it," and stated that, congressional pressure notwithstanding, spending $10 to $15 billion on an airplane that added nothing to U.S. security made no sense. Nor did he think it currently worth billions of dollars to build a Nike Zeus antimissile system until tests proved that it worked. And Polaris submarine and Minuteman ground-to-ground missiles made a Skybolt air-to-surface missile project obsolete, so building it would waste $2.5 billion.

Kennedy did not discount the continuing importance of East Germany to the Soviets in sustaining their hold on Eastern Europe, but he was hopeful that Khrushchev realized "the care with which he must proceed now, as do we." (Khrushchev did. Within days after the missile crisis, Yuri Zhukov, *Pravda*'s foreign editor, told Salinger that Khrushchev would not renew difficulties over Berlin.) Although Berlin would remain a source of tension in Soviet-American relations, it did not seem likely to become a major point of contention again anytime soon — and indeed, for the rest of the Cold War it would remain a back-burner issue. Khrushchev believed that "the socialist countries have gained more in Berlin from the wall than they would have gained by a peace treaty, which would have provided that no wall could be built."

Kennedy hoped that the Soviet-American thaw might encourage more sophisticated thinking in the United States about world affairs. "I do think we have a tendency to think of the world as Communist and free," Kennedy mused at the end of 1962, "as if it were two units. The fact of the matter is our world is so divided, so poverty stricken, so desperate in many conditions, that we have a full-time job just strengthening the section of the world which is not Communist, all of Africa, newly independent and poverty stricken." Latin America, where people lived on $100 a year, was another tempting ground for communist subversion. If the United States could raise standards of living in these Third World areas, he said, "then I think we can be successful."

Attention to problems with European allies, however, had to precede détente with the Soviets and greater attention to the Third World. In the winter of 1962–63, difficulties with Britain, Germany, and France crowded out bold initiatives elsewhere. Seeing unity with Europe as essential to other advances overseas, and remembering that the history of any alliance is the history of mutual recrimination, Kennedy worked to ease tensions.

Kennedy's decision to drop Skybolt had greatly upset the British, who had had the wherewithal to build nuclear warheads but not the missiles to which they were attached. Macmillan had staked British prestige on having an independent nuclear deterrent, which the air-to-ground missile — Eisenhower had promised to supply — was supposed to give them. Kennedy's policy reversal threatened to topple Macmillan's government and leave his successor skeptical of any future U.S. commitment. Some in Britain now echoed Chamberlain's observation in the thirties that it was best not to rely on the Americans for anything.

Kennedy felt compelled to bail Macmillan out. Leaving him without some fallback would have not only betrayed his closest European ally but added to feelings in France and Germany that Washington was insensitive to the political and security needs of its friends. When he met Macmillan at a conference in Bermuda on December 18 and 19, Kennedy offered to continue Skybolt's development if the British agreed to share the building costs. But Macmillan no longer saw the missile as being of any use. Not only had the political damage been done, but in the interim the Skybolt had failed during routine testing. ("The Lady had been violated in public," Macmillan said with reference to reports of failed Skybolt tests and Kennedy's public comments.) With Macmillan now predicting a rift with the United States unless some new agreement were reached at once, Kennedy found a formula that satisfied British amour propre: The United States would scrap Skybolt and instead with Britain jointly build nuclear submarines armed with Polaris missiles. The weapons would technically be part of a multilateral NATO force, but an agreement to let London use them unilaterally in time of "supreme peril" would preserve the fiction of an independent British nuclear deterrent.

The British now satisfied, Kennedy rested assured that Skybolt was dead. But just three days after the Bermuda meeting, while Kennedy was vacationing in Palm Beach, he received word that there had been a successful Skybolt test. He was mystified that McNamara had approved the test after he had decided to scrap the missile. Evelyn Lincoln remembers Kennedy sitting by the pool getting a manicure and trying to get hold of McNamara, who was on his way to Aspen, Colorado. Instead, he reached Gilpatric, to whom he read "the riot act. . . . I can't understand McNamara doing this," Kennedy said to Lincoln. "He is generally so good on everything." But Kennedy, despite believing otherwise, had failed to make his intent clear to his defense secretary. Kennedy felt compelled to discount the importance of the test to the press, and to emphasize U.S. commitment to the Nassau Agreement, as the Bermuda understanding was called. A highly visible misstep like this injured the administration's recently established reputation for foreign policy mastery. Kennedy was so annoyed by the incident that in March 1963, he asked Richard Neustadt to review the episode and explain to him what had gone wrong. How could he have gotten at cross-purposes with his closest ally and its prime minister, whom he held in higher regard than any other foreign leader? Why were the British so surprised by the Skybolt decision? Hadn't we given them ample notice? Was there a failure of communication? And if so, by whom and for what reasons? Neustadt concluded that there had indeed been a failure of communication between both sides at the highest levels of government.

The Nassau Agreement made for additional difficulties. To appease French sensibilities, which would also have been offended by a follow-through on Skybolt, Kennedy offered de Gaulle the same deal he had made with London. But de Gaulle wanted no part of it. Unlike the British, the French still lacked the ability to make nuclear warheads, though successful nuclear detonations convinced de Gaulle that it was only a matter of time. De Gaulle still did not trust Washington to defend Europe with nuclear weapons, believing that the administration would rather let Western Europe fall under communist control than risk a Soviet nuclear attack on American cities. De Gaulle intended to build an independent nuclear arm that would be immune from any American coordination or restriction. He also wanted to keep the British, whom he saw as ciphers of the Americans, at a distance. To drive this point home, on January 14, 1963, in a well-prepared performance at a semi-annual press conference, de Gaulle announced a French veto of British membership in the European Economic Community (EEC). Less than two decades after World War II, he now saw Germany as a more reliable French ally.

Not surprisingly, the Germans were receptive to his overtures. Adenauer, like de Gaulle, distrusted U.S. determination to stand up to the Soviets in a European crisis and correctly understood that Washington might ultimately recognize East Germany and resist German reunification. In February 1963, Bonn signed a mutual defense pact with Paris that implied diminished Franco-German reliance on NATO and American power. De Gaulle was receptive to having Germany follow him into the family of nuclear nations, and Adenauer was interested, having long resented a Kennedy public declaration to the Russians in November 1961 that "if Germany developed an atomic capability of its own, if it developed many missiles, or a strong national army that threatened war, then I would understand your concern, and I would share it."

Kennedy feared that Adenauer and de Gaulle were putting NATO at risk and making Europe less, rather then more, secure. "What is your judgment about the course of events?" Kennedy asked Macmillan in a January telephone conversation. "I think this man's gone crazy," Macmillan replied. "Absolutely crazy." Macmillan added that de Gaulle wanted to be "the cock on a small dung hill instead of having two cocks on a larger one." Crazy or not, de Gaulle had to be dealt with. Franco-German independence defied Kennedy's plans for continuing American leadership of Europe's defense, which he considered essential to deter Soviet aggression on the continent. "There is always the argument in Europe that the United States might leave Europe, which is, of course, in my opinion, fallacious, because the United States can never leave Europe," he said at an off-the-record press conference on December 31. "We are too much bound together. If we left Europe, Europe would be more exposed to the Communists."

In January 1963, Kennedy decided that he would make a mid-year visit to rally the allies. He told ambassador to France James M. Gavin, "Well, I am going to see the General in the next few months, and I think that we will be able to get something done together." Kennedy shared Acheson's conviction that it was "not possible to persuade, bribe, or coerce General de Gaulle from following a course upon which he is set. But he can and does in time recognize the inevitable and adjust his conduct to it, as in Algeria. Years ago I asked Justice Brandeis whether a certain man was intelligent," Acheson related. "'Yes,' he said. 'He has the sort of intelligence which leads a man not to stand in front of a locomotive.'" Acheson believed that de Gaulle would come to his senses when he understood that France simply could not afford the cost of developing its own nuclear deterrent.

Sufficiently strong ties between Paris, Berlin, and Washington encouraged hopes that better relations were not out of reach. In early January, when André Malraux, French minister of cultural affairs, brought the *Mona Lisa* to Washington for an exhibition at the National Gallery of Art, he graciously marked the occasion by recalling the contribution of American fighting men to French victory and liberation in the two world wars. "[This] is a painting," Malraux said, "which he [the American soldier] has saved." Despite Kennedy's unhappiness with de Gaulle, who, he said privately, "relies on our power to protect him while he launches his policies based solely on the self-interest of France," he responded with good humor. "I want to make it clear that grateful as we are for this painting," he told Malraux, "we will continue to press ahead with the effort to develop an independent artistic force and power of our own."

KENNEDY'S RESPONSE to European crosscurrents demonstrated his growing mastery of foreign affairs. He realized that America's European allies could not be taken for granted and that by traveling to Europe in 1963 he could sustain ties essential to future Western security. But more specifically, he saw the road to peace not through hectoring France and Germany into agreements they were resisting, but through broader arrangements on nuclear weapons and better relations with Moscow, which could make NATO less important. While the French and Germans busied themselves pointing fingers, he would leapfrog them and take care of the real business at hand.

That said, the United States had no intention of reducing its defense spending or determination to develop more effective weapons systems, Kennedy said in his State of the Union Message. But, he stated, "our commitment to national safety is not a commitment to expand our military establishment indefinitely." The fact that the British, French, and Germans devoted about 28 or 29 percent of their respective annual budgets to defense, which was about half the percentage spent by the United States, including space costs, frustrated him. Public and congressional resistance to providing foreign aid also troubled him. Like Eisenhower, who had won appropriations for language and regional studies programs in universities by including them in a bill titled the National Defense Education Act, Kennedy urged his budget director to rename foreign aid "international security." Appropriations to "strengthen the security of the free world" or to combat communism would find greater receptivity than anything that seemed like a giveaway to dependent developing nations asking for American help.

In hopes of reducing America's heavy defense burdens and the unfavorable balance of payments roiling the dollar, Kennedy saw disarmament as something more than "an idle dream." He firmly believed that a test ban could significantly slow, if not halt, proliferation of nuclear weapons. His advisers had told him that continued U.S. and Soviet testing would make it cheaper and easier to produce bombs. "It might go down by a factor as large as ten or a hundred," Kennedy was told, "so that it will cost very little to produce nuclear weapons. . . . And furthermore, the diffusion of nuclear technology is to be anticipated if both of us test this knowledge. . . . This does seep out." In twenty-five years, "in the absence of a test ban, the risk of diffusion would be very great indeed."

Khrushchev shared Kennedy's concern to find some way out of the escalating arms race. Because the Soviets were so far behind the United States in the development and building of intercontinental ballistic missiles, they intended to work toward parity as soon as possible, especially after the failure to reduce the missile gap by placing IRBMs and MRBMs in Cuba. But they hoped to slow the U.S. pace of building and possibly prevent Chinese advances by reaching a ban of some kind on nuclear tests. In a message to Kennedy on November 12, 1962, Khrushchev stated his belief that "conditions are emerging now for reaching an agreement on the prohibition of nuclear weapons, [and the] cessation of all types of nuclear weapons tests." Khrushchev also believed that such agreements could rein in Chinese development of nuclear arms, the prospect of which alarmed him as much as Russia's military inferiority to the United States. On December 19, he expressed a sense of urgency about ending nuclear tests "once and for all." The end of the Cuban crisis had "untied our hands to engage closely in other urgent international matters and, in particular, in such a problem which has been ripe for so long as cessation of nuclear tests."

Kennedy was eager for negotiations. A test ban could possibly inhibit France, Germany, China, and Israel from building bombs that seemed likely to increase the risks of a nuclear war. In addition, Kennedy was uncertain that the latest round of U.S. tests had contributed much, if anything, to America's strategic advantage over the

Soviets. While the tests, Glenn Seaborg told the president, "achieved much in improving our weapons capability," their impact on the Soviet-American military balance was less certain. In November 1962, Kennedy instructed national security officials and science advisers to report to him on this matter. And when an assessment of the tests became available in December, it confirmed Kennedy's suspicions that they were of little value to America's national defense.

After announcing the Polaris agreement with Macmillan, Kennedy promptly assured Khrushchev that this was not a step on the road to proliferation; to the contrary, it was a way to inhibit it. He sent Khrushchev a message through Dobrynin that the British Polaris missiles "assigned to NATO" would not become operational until 1969 or 1970. His objective "in making these missiles available was to prevent, or at least delay, the development of national nuclear capabilities." Without this commitment, the British would try "to create their own missile, not tied into NATO controls," and they might then cooperate with the French and the Germans in helping them build nuclear arsenals. The commitment to London, he said, was "[keeping] open the possibility of agreement on the non-proliferation of nuclear weapons and has gained time for our further efforts in the field of disarmament." Kennedy assured Khrushchev that any disarmament pact "would take priority over any such arrangements which were made in the absence of a disarmament agreement."

Despite these expressions of goodwill, differences between the two sides on banning nuclear tests seemed too great to bridge. Khrushchev complained that while Kennedy might see the Polaris arrangement with Britain as a bar to greater proliferation, he could only view it as an expansion of nuclear armaments that would intensify rather than diminish the arms race. At the same time, they could not agree on the number and location of on-site inspections, which Washington still insisted be part of any test ban treaty. Khrushchev was under the impression that Kennedy would settle for three or four inspections a year as opposed to the twelve to twenty he had been asking for. In fact, Kennedy explained, he was ready to accept between eight and ten inspections, but three were too few.

Although Khrushchev agreed to talks in New York between Soviet and U.S. representatives to take place in the first four months of 1963, the discussions produced little progress. In late March, when a reporter asked Kennedy if he still had any hope of achieving a test ban agreement, he answered, "Well, my hopes are somewhat dimmed, but nevertheless, I still hope. . . . Now, the reason why we keep moving and working on this question . . . is because personally I am haunted by the feeling that by 1970, unless we are successful, there may be 10 nuclear powers instead of 4, and by 1975, 15 or 20. . . . I regard that as the greatest possible danger and hazard."

Khrushchev shared Kennedy's concern, but his own political pressures kept him from reaching any agreement. During a meeting in Moscow with *Saturday Review* editor Norman Cousins in April, he claimed that false American promises to reduce the number of on-site inspections had embarrassed him and stalled the talks. He said that he had convinced his council of ministers to accept three on-site inspections as the price of a treaty and that Kennedy had then upped the ante to eight. "And so once again I was made to look foolish," Khrushchev said. "But I can tell you this: it won't happen again."

In addition to this "misunderstanding" over on-site inspections, two other differences undermined the talks. Kennedy believed that a principal value of a test ban treaty could be its inhibition of Chinese nuclear development. "Any negotiations that can hold back the Chinese Communists are most important," he said [at an NSC meeting in January], "because they loom as our major antagonists of the late 60's and beyond." But because the Chinese understood that a treaty would be directed partly against them, they pressured Moscow to resist Washington's overtures. Though Khrushchev shared American hopes of inhibiting Peking's acquisition of nuclear weapons, he was also reluctant to open himself to Chinese attacks for signing a treaty that "betrayed" a communist comrade. On the American side, Senate opposition, fueled by warnings from the hawkish U.S. Joint Chiefs, to anything but an airtight agreement with Moscow on verification made it impossible for Kennedy to accept Soviet proposals that could be seen as giving them even the smallest leeway to cheat.

On April 1, Dobrynin handed Bobby a twenty-five-page message from his government that seemed to signal a collapse of hopes for a test ban agreement or accommodation on anything else. Bobby looked it over and returned it without passing it on to Kennedy. As he summed it up for his brother, the U.S. insistence on more than two or three inspections showed U.S. contempt for Moscow: "Who did we think we were in the United States trying to dictate to the Soviet Union?" the message said. "The United States had better learn that the Soviet Union was as strong as the United States and did not enjoy being treated as a second-class power." As he returned the document to Dobrynin, Bobby told him that Dobrynin "had never talked like this before." He considered the paper "so insulting and rude to the President of the United States that I would never accept it nor transmit its message."

Yet Kennedy, who was determined to do all he could to salvage the test ban talks, saw some indications of Soviet receptivity to additional negotiations. At the end of 1962, the American physicist Leo Szilard received encouragement from Khrushchev to hold "an unofficial Soviet-American meeting at a non-governmental level to exchange views and examine the possibility of coming to an agreement on disarmament." In addition, Macmillan urged Kennedy not to give up on test ban talks, describing himself in a long letter to the president in March as having a "very deep personal obligation" to ban nuclear explosions "before it is too late." Kennedy also took hope from Khrushchev's statement through Dobrynin that past confidential exchanges with the president "had been helpful," and he would be glad to reopen "this area of contact." He also obliquely suggested that another summit meeting "might be helpful." In addition, Kennedy saw something positive in Soviet acceptance on April 5 of discussions to create a Teletype "hot line" between Moscow and Washington for use during a crisis.

Taking Khrushchev at his word and seizing upon a suggestion from Macmillan that they jointly propose additional negotiations, Kennedy wrote Khrushchev on April 11 apologizing for any misunderstanding on the number of on-site inspections, promising to offer new suggestions on the matter from himself and Macmillan in the near future, and emphasizing how eager he and the prime minister were to head off "the spread of national nuclear forces." Kennedy also followed a Macmillan suggestion that he ask whether Khrushchev would be interested in "a fully frank, informal exchange of views" with a Kennedy personal representative. Following up on April 15 with another letter, Kennedy and Macmillan suggested that there be private tripartite discussions either at Geneva or between their representatives meeting in Moscow. If these negotiations came close to an agreement, the three of them could meet to conclude a treaty.

Kennedy and Macmillan's renewed efforts at negotiations — a tedious, stubborn slog of requests and oblique promises — brought only grudging acknowledgment from Khrushchev of the need for further talks. When the new U.S. ambassador, Foy Kohler, and British ambassador Sir Humphrey Trevelyan gave Khrushchev the JFK-Macmillan letter, Khrushchev's reaction was "almost entirely negative." His attitude "was almost one of disinterest," and after reading the letter, he dismissed it as containing "nothing . . . positive or constructive." He saw "no basis for agreement." Kohler and Trevelyan could not budge him with oral arguments. Instead, resurrecting differences over Germany, Khrushchev emphasized them as the "key to everything," and said that the nuclear test ban "really had no importance." It would be of no benefit to either the U.S. or USSR; nor would it "deter others from testing and developing nuclear capabilities and would not relieve tensions."

Khrushchev gave formal response to the Kennedy-Macmillan letter in lengthy written replies on April 29 and May 8. With the United States apparently intent on allowing other NATO states to acquire nuclear weapons and still insistent on inspections, which he continued to describe as an espionage cover, Khrushchev saw little reason to hope for a breakthrough in test ban talks. However, he did announce that he was willing nevertheless to receive Kennedy's personal envoy, who would be given a full and respectful hearing. Kennedy replied that he took little encouragement from Khrushchev's messages, which continued to demonstrate "the gaps which separate us on these problems." In another follow-up letter from him and Macmillan, they confirmed their eagerness to send personal envoys for discussions during the summer but emphasized that they disagreed with Khrushchev's assessment of the need for on-site inspections and their purpose, which they categorically and honestly affirmed had no hidden espionage design.

It is indeed difficult to believe that Khrushchev saw espionage as the prime motive behind the U.S. insistence on inspections. Instead, it was a convenient excuse to hold up any sort of agreement. Llewellyn Thompson saw Khrushchev's resistance to a test ban treaty as principally motivated by an eagerness to buy time for additional nuclear tests that could make Soviet nuclear forces more competitive with the United States'. Khrushchev's "quarrel with the ChiComs," Thompson said, was also apparently "taking precedence at the present time over other issues. . . . It is important to him at this juncture not to do anything which exposes him to further Chinese attack, both for internal reasons and in connection with the struggle for control of other communist parties." Averell Harriman, who spent three days in Moscow at the end of April, underscored Khrushchev's difficulties with Peking. "This challenge by the ChiComs of Kremlin leadership of the Communist International is causing the gravest concern."

KENNEDY SAW LITTLE HOPE for a breakthrough unless there were some new departure or fresh impetus to get the genie back in the bottle, as he put it at two May press conferences. He still believed that a failure to ban nuclear testing "would be a great disaster for the interests of all concerned," and promised to push "very hard in May and June and July in every forum to see if we can get an agreement."

Kennedy now decided to embrace a suggestion Norman Cousins had made to him on April 22 after returning from his meeting with Khrushchev in Moscow. When Cousins told the president that Khrushchev was under pressure from others in his government to take a hard line, Kennedy responded that he and Khrushchev "occupy approximately the same political positions inside our governments. He would like to prevent a nuclear war but is under severe pressure from his hard-line crowd." Kennedy said he had "similar problems. . . . The hard-liners in the Soviet Union and the United States feed on one another, each using the actions of the other to justify his own position." Cousins urged the president to overcome both groups of militants by a "breathtaking new approach toward the Russian people, calling for an end to the cold war and a fresh start in American-Russian relations." In a follow-up letter on April 30, Cousins pressed Kennedy to make "the most important speech of your presidency . . . [including] breathtaking proposals for genuine peace . . . [a] tone of friendliness for the Soviet people and . . . [an] understanding of their ordeal during the last war."

Kennedy saw risks in publicly urging a transformation in Soviet-American relations and pressing Moscow for a test ban agreement. He would almost certainly confront forceful opposition from his military chiefs and national security advisers, who would see him as letting idealism eclipse sensible realism. There was some logic, at least some political logic, to this. When Cousins told Kennedy that Americans wanted the nuclear powers to stop poisoning the atmosphere with nuclear tests, Kennedy pointed out that in fact the public did not seem to care; recent White House mail had shown more interest in daughter Caroline's horse than in negotiating a treaty. And those who wrote about nuclear testing were fifteen to one against a ban.

But Kennedy saw more reasons to try a speech than not. Most important, he believed a plea for better Soviet-American relations and a test ban treaty was right. With his credibility as a foreign policy leader at new highs, he believed that a forceful speech could have an impact on American public opinion and might persuade Khrushchev to take negotiations for a ban more seriously. Kennedy also had an encouraging report from Glenn Seaborg, who had spent two weeks at the end of May in Russia leading a delegation of U.S. scientists in discussing peaceful uses of atomic energy with their Soviet counterparts. Seaborg described a meeting with Soviet president Leonid Brezhnev in which Brezhnev had said that Khrushchev was genuinely interested in peaceful coexistence: "'This is not propaganda,' Brezhnev had added. 'It is the sincere desire of our government, of our people, and of our party, which leads the country. I can't say more than that.'"

In May, Kennedy decided to turn a June 10 commencement address at American University in Washington into a "peace speech" arguing the case to Americans and Soviets for a test ban treaty. The June date reflected a concern that the speech precede a Sino-Soviet meeting in Moscow in July; Kennedy hoped his remarks could be a counterweight to whatever pressure Peking would put on Khrushchev to avoid any agreement with Washington. Because he wanted to avoid counterpressures from Defense and State Department officials and hackneyed "threats of destruction, boasts of nuclear stockpiles and lectures on Soviet treachery," Kennedy confined his preparation of the speech to an inner circle of White House advisers — Sorensen, Bundy, Schlesinger, Rostow, Bundy's deputy, Carl Kaysen, and Thomas Sorensen, Ted's brother, who was a deputy director at the United States Information Agency. McNamara, Rusk, and Taylor were not told of the speech until June 8, after the president had already left on a speaking tour that would last until the morning of the tenth.

The speech was one of the great state papers of any twentieth-century American presidency. Kennedy's topic was the "most important . . . on earth: world peace. What kind of peace do I mean? What kind of peace do we seek? Not a *Pax Americana* enforced on the world by American weapons of war," he said, with the Soviets and China particularly in mind. "Not the peace of the grave or the security of the slave." In that one brief sentence, he dismissed both the kind of peace that would follow a cataclysmic nuclear war, which "hard-liners" in Moscow, Peking, and Washington seemed ready to fight, and the sort of peace a generation reared on memories of appeasement feared might come out of negotiations limiting American armaments. This was to be "not merely peace for Americans but peace for all men and women — not merely peace in our time but peace for all time" — the realization of Woodrow Wilson's ideal, announced in response to the century's first great war.

To fulfill so bold a vision, it would not be enough for the Soviet Union to adopt a more enlightened attitude. It was also essential that "[we] reexamine our own attitude — as individuals and as a Nation — for our attitude is as essential as theirs." There was too much defeatism about peace in the United States, too much inclination to see war as inevitable and mankind as doomed. "We need not accept that view," Kennedy asserted. "Our problems are manmade — therefore, they can be solved by man." This would not require a change in human nature, only a change in outlook that leads to "a series of concrete actions and effective agreements which are in the interest of all concerned." The goal was not a world without tensions but a kind of community peace in which "mutual tolerance" eased quarrels and conflicting interests.

Specifically, Kennedy urged a reexamination of our attitude toward the Soviet Union. "As Americans, we find communism profoundly repugnant as a negation of personal freedom and dignity. But we can still hail the Russian people for their many achievements — in science and space, in economic and industrial growth, in culture and in acts of courage." Americans needed to remember the terrible suffering of the Russian people in World War II and understand that a Soviet-American conflict would within twenty-four hours destroy "all we have built [and] all we have worked for."

To avert such a disaster, it seemed essential to improve communications and understanding between Moscow and Washington. One step toward that end was the creation of a "hot line"; another was mutual commitments to arms control, and a test ban in particular, which could discourage the spread of nuclear weapons. An agreement was in sight, but a fresh start was badly needed, Kennedy said. To this end, he announced the agreement to begin high-level talks in Moscow and a pledge not to resume "nuclear tests in the atmosphere so long as other states do not do so." With an eye on the U.S. Senate, which would have to ratify any treaty, Kennedy declared that no agreement could "provide absolute security against the risks of deception and evasion. But it can — if it is sufficiently effective in its enforcement and if it is sufficiently in the interests of its signers — offer far more security and far fewer risks than an unabated, uncontrolled, unpredictable arms race."

Like Lincoln's Gettysburg Address, Kennedy's peace speech did not have much initial resonance. As historian Lawrence Freedman has pointed out, Kennedy's bold address "hardly electrified the American people. It received barely a mention in the press, and the White House mailbag failed to bulge." In the seventeen days after June 10, Kennedy received 1,677 letters about the speech; only 30 of them were negative. But at the same time, almost 52,000 letters flooded in about a freight rate bill. Disgusted, Kennedy said, "That is why I tell people in Congress that they're crazy if they take their mail seriously." Predictably, unbending congressional Republicans denounced the speech as "a soft line that can accomplish nothing . . . a shot from the hip . . . a dreadful mistake."

The Soviet reaction was much more encouraging. The Soviet press published uncensored copies of the speech, and the government broke precedent by allowing the Voice of America to broadcast the speech in Russian with only one paragraph deleted, and in its entirety in a rebroadcast. The Soviets then suspended all jamming of the VOA, which the State Department believed showed their desire for "an atmosphere of détente with the West in order to deal as effectively as possible with pressing intra-bloc problems and Chinese rivalry in the international communist movement." Khrushchev initially told British Labour Party leader Harold Wilson that Kennedy's willingness to say what he had in public deeply impressed him. Later in the summer, Khrushchev described the speech to Harriman as "the best statement made by any President since Roosevelt." Glenn Seaborg said, "It was as though Khrushchev had been looking for a weapon to use against Chinese criticism of his policies toward the United States and Kennedy had provided it."

Though the peaceful end of the Cold War makes it difficult to understand now, public cant about communist dangers in the fifties and sixties made it almost impossible for an American politician to make the sort of speech Kennedy gave. It was a tremendously bold address that carried substantial risks. By taking advantage of his recent success in facing down Khrushchev in Cuba, Kennedy gave voice to his own and the country's best hopes for rational exchange between adversaries that could turn the East-West competition away from the growing arms race.

On June 20, Moscow gave Kennedy additional reason to believe that something might now come of test ban talks. The Soviets signed an agreement in Geneva establishing "a direct communications link between their respective capitals. . . . Both Governments," the White House announced, "have taken a first step to help reduce the risk of war . . . by accident or miscalculation. . . . We hope agreement on other more encompassing measures will follow. We shall bend every effort to go on from this first step." An American test message — "The quick brown fox jumps over the lazy dog" — puzzled Kremlin recipients, who must have wondered whether the device would increase or reduce misunderstanding between the two sides.

During June and early July, the administration struggled to produce a realistic agenda for the talks. Before the White House could even settle on a set of instructions, it had to ensure that the Joint Chiefs, who were scheduled to testify in July before the Senate Armed Services Committee, would not foreclose approval in the Upper House if and when an agreement arrived there. "I regard the Chiefs as key to this thing," Kennedy told Mike Mansfield. "If we don't get the Chiefs just right, we can . . . get blown." The Chiefs have "always been our problem," Kennedy added. The Chiefs did in fact oppose both a comprehensive and a more limited test ban. In their view, a prohibition on all testing without sufficient surveillance would allow the Soviets to cheat and work toward parity with America's nuclear arsenal. They further believed that a more limited agreement, which did not bar underground tests, would still permit Moscow to gain ground on the United States. To head off any discussion of divisions within the administration, which could become a rallying cry for treaty opponents, Kennedy instructed McNamara not to ask the Chiefs for their collective judgment or for a formal statement of their position. In addition, he excluded any military officers from the American delegation to the talks and made sure that cables coming from Moscow describing the progress of the negotiations did not go to the Defense Department.

Warnings that a limited ban would produce public pressure for a moratorium on underground tests did not dissuade Kennedy from the attractions of a limited treaty. Nor did he believe that Soviet underground testing would bring them up to par with the United States as a nuclear power or change the existing strategic balance. When Khrushchev announced on July 2 that he preferred a comprehensive treaty without inspections — Moscow would not "open its doors to NATO spies" — but would agree to more limited test bans above ground and underwater, Kennedy instructed Harriman — whom he had chosen, despite objections from the State Department, to be the leader of the negotiating team — to accept such a proposal.

Kennedy also directed Harriman to seek an agreement with Khrushchev on inhibiting Chinese testing and development of a nuclear arsenal. Although Harriman doubted that Khrushchev would be willing to talk about joint pressure on China, Kennedy was eager for him to pursue the matter nevertheless. At the start of the talks, after Khrushchev confirmed this prediction, the president cabled Harriman: "I remain convinced that Chinese problem is more serious than Khrushchev comments in first meeting suggest, and believe you should press question in private meeting with him. . . . Relatively small forces in hands of Chicoms could be very dangerous to us all. . . . You should try to elicit Khrushchev's view of means of limiting or preventing Chinese nuclear development and his willingness either to take Soviet action or to accept US action aimed in this direction." Kennedy did not make clear what "US action" meant — a preemptive strike against Chinese nuclear facilities, diplomatic pressure, or an exchange of prohibitions on German and Chinese nuclear arms.

BEFORE HARRIMAN WENT to Moscow, Kennedy followed through on his promise to visit Europe to build support for the negotiations and provide reassurance of U.S. determination to defend NATO allies against Soviet aggression. A Soviet proposal to make a non-aggression pact between Eastern- and Western-bloc countries part of a test ban treaty had further chilled the West Germans, who saw it as consolidating existing European boundaries and conditions. The White House viewed the trip partly as a chance to have the president bypass or speak over the heads of state and reach out to ordinary Europeans, many of whom seemed to share Kennedy's preference for nonproliferation over Franco-German acquisition of nuclear arms.

The trip from June 23 to July 2 was a grand triumph of public diplomacy. Pointedly avoiding a visit to Paris and de Gaulle and stopping for only one day in England (in Sussex, at the prime minister's country home, rather than in London, where a sex scandal had put Macmillan's government in jeopardy and might tarnish Kennedy), JFK spent four days each in Germany and Ireland and two in Italy. Though the visits to Ireland and Italy deepened impressions of Kennedy as an exceptionally popular world leader who inspired worshipful support for himself and American values, it was in Germany that he received his greatest ovations and effectively demonstrated that no German government could tie itself too closely to France at the expense of good relations with Washington.

Kennedy assured a Bonn audience that just as Germany had freed itself from "the forces of tyranny and aggression," so the United States had freed itself from "the long process of isolation. . . . The United States is here on this continent to stay. So long as our presence is desired and required, our forces and commitments will remain." Americans, he said, did not see their part "in the great fight for freedom all around the globe . . . as a burden. They regard it as a privilege to play their part in these great days." In fact, Kennedy had privately complained that "Europe is getting a 'free ride' and that on both the political and defense side, this situation with our NATO allies had to be changed this year." As he had told the Joint Chiefs, his administration had "put more money in defense in the past two years than any other previous Administration. . . . We had gone from $44 billion up to $49 billion and . . . are now at $52 billion." In urging Europe's full partnership in the alliance, Kennedy was thinking not only of its independence but also of its contributions that could reduce U.S. budget and balance-of-payment deficits.

At a press conference in Bonn, Kennedy was asked if he saw "any chance of overcoming the division of Germany." Although he could not mark out a date when this might happen, he replied that it was very likely and urged Germans not to despair. He denied that any consideration was being given to an exchange of nonaggression statements with Moscow, which would amount to recognition of East Germany. As the negotiations in Moscow would shortly demonstrate, however, Kennedy had not ruled out this concession to Khrushchev as a way to advance détente with the Soviets.

In Berlin, where three-fifths of the city turned out to greet him, "clapping, waving, crying, cheering, as if it were the second coming," Schlesinger recalled, Kennedy gave his most heartfelt statements of support. After visiting the Berlin Wall, which "shocked and appalled" him, he spoke to a million people gathered in front of the city hall, "a sea of human faces," Sorensen remembers, "chanting 'Kenne-dy,' 'Kenne-dy.'" His speech was an uncharacteristically passionate recitation that stirred the crowd to something resembling the communal outbursts at Nazi rallies. (The crowd's vigorous response was so extreme as to upset Adenauer, who said to Rusk, "Does this mean Germany can one day have another Hitler?" It also troubled

Kennedy, who said to his military aide General McHugh, "If I told them to go tear down the Berlin Wall, they would do it.")

"Two thousand years ago," Kennedy proclaimed, "the proudest boast was *'civis Romanus sum.'* Today, in the world of freedom, the proudest boast is *'Ich bin ein Berliner.'* . . . There are many people in the world who really don't understand, or say they don't, what is the great issue between the free world and the communist world. Let them come to Berlin. There are some who say that communism is the wave of the future. Let them come to Berlin. And there are some who say in Europe and elsewhere we can work with the Communists. Let them come to Berlin. And there are even a few who say that it is true that communism is an evil system, but it permits us to make economic progress. *Lass' sie nach Berlin kommen.* Let them come to Berlin." In the midst of so tumultuous a reception, no one was ready to complain that Kennedy should have said, *"Ich bin Berliner"* instead of *"ein Berliner,"* which was colloquial German for a jelly doughnut. Nor did anyone compare his American University appeal for rational exchange with Moscow to his dismissive "some who say . . . we can work with the Communists." (Later that day, in more measured remarks at the Free University of Berlin, he declared that "when the possibilities of reconciliation appear, we in the West will make it clear that we are not hostile to any people or system providing they choose their own destiny without interfering with the free choice of others.") Instead, the crowd roared in approval.

Kennedy departed Germany with a sense of exhilaration. He told the crowd bidding him farewell at Berlin's Tegel Airport that he planned "to leave a note for my successor which would say, 'To be opened at a time of some discouragement,' and in it would be written three words: 'Go to Germany.' I may open that note myself someday." On the plane flying to Dublin, he told Sorensen, who had crafted most of the words he had spoken to the Germans, "We'll never have another day like this one as long as we live."

The visit to Ireland was supposedly a vacation that Kennedy had insisted on. Kenny O'Donnell told him, "It would be a waste of time. It wouldn't do you much good politically. You've got all the Irish votes in this country that you'll ever get. If you go to Ireland, people will say it's just a pleasure trip." But a "pleasure trip" was just what Kennedy wanted.

Still, the stop in Ireland was more than a sentimental journey to the land of his origins. It also allowed him to emphasize the inter-connectedness of all peoples and the importance of small nations in holding to ideals that influenced the entire world. In a brilliant speech full of literary references before the Irish Parliament, he declared, "Modern economics, weaponry and communications have made us realize more than ever that we are one human family and this one planet is our home." Kennedy quoted George Bernard Shaw on the influence of the Irish: "Speaking as an Irishman, [Shaw] summed up an approach to life: Other people . . . 'see things and . . . say: Why? . . . But I dream things that never were — and I say: Why not?'" A small nation like Ireland, Kennedy said, would continue to play a significant part in advancing the cause of liberty around the globe.

KENNEDY'S TRIUMPHANT TOUR of Europe increased his freedom to have Harriman negotiate a test ban treaty. The opening conversations in Moscow made clear to the U.S. delegation that the Soviets were eager for an agreement. Khrushchev's remarks to Harriman and Lord Hailsham, his British counterpart, "on desirability of relaxation of tensions and protection against risk of nuclear war" was only one signal of Soviet receptivity. In a discussion between lower-level officials about forthcoming negotiations on cultural exchanges, the Soviet representative suggested that the United States "make a 'big thing' out of them." He explained that after both sides had felt "the breath of death" in the missile crisis, it was time for them to cooperate. "He was particularly hopeful that a test ban would be reached."

Khrushchev still considered inspections unacceptable, which precluded U.S. acceptance of a ban on underground tests, but he was ready to embrace a limited agreement covering the atmosphere, outer space, and underwater. He wished to tie such a treaty to a nonaggression pact, but — believing it would be a long time before Peking could build nuclear weapons and before Paris could accumulate stockpiles comparable to those of the U.S. and USSR — saw no need to include France and China in the arms control agreement. He also expected a treaty would isolate China and put it under pressure from developing countries to sign a test ban. Harriman declared a U.S. preference for a comprehensive treaty and for excluding non-aggression clauses from any test ban accord but stated American willingness to accept limited bans and to leave talks on nonaggression arrangements for a later time. One essential ingredient Kennedy saw in an agreement was a clause allowing the United States to escape from the treaty if a nonsignatory exploded a nuclear weapon that seemed to jeopardize American national security. The provision was a prerequisite for getting a test ban through the U.S. Senate.

As Harriman anticipated, negotiations "[ran] into heavy weather in attempting to get reasonable treaty language," but Khrushchev's desire for a U.S.-Soviet accommodation made him willing to sign a limited test ban agreement "without commitment on other subjects." Reciprocal American eagerness for a treaty led to completion of a test ban pact only ten days after Harriman went to Moscow.

Thoughts of an agreement with the United States, which would improve relations with Washington and Europe and free Moscow to focus more on an emerging threat from Peking, exhilarated Khrushchev. As Harriman reported to Kennedy, Khrushchev was jovial in his exchanges. At a large reception on July twentieth attended by the diplomatic corps and numerous Soviet officials, Khrushchev asked where Harriman was. When he appeared, Khrushchev said he was "glad to see the 'imperialist.'" Harriman replied, "When you came to my house in New York you called me a capitalist. Is this a promotion or a demotion — or did we have to consult the protocol officer?" "No," he said, "it must be a promotion because there are many capitalists who only deal with matters in their own country, whereas an imperialist is a capitalist who interferes in other countries, for example, as you are in South Viet-Nam." Harriman, amid much laughter, said he "was very much flattered" at the promotion. After Harriman explained that he was going to a track meet, Khrushchev exclaimed, "It is better to have this kind of race than the arms race."

After the treaty — which outlawed atmospheric but not underground testing of nuclear weapons — was initialed, Khrushchev and Harriman walked across Cathedral Square on their way to dinner in Catherine the Great's palace. Khrushchev stopped to chat with a crowd of people who applauded him. He introduced Harriman as "Gospodin Garriman," saying, "He has just signed a test ban treaty and I am going to take him to dinner. Do you think he deserves dinner?" The crowd responded enthusiastically. Harriman, who had clear memories of Stalin during World War II, saw a "fantastic contrast [in Khrushchev] to the way Stalin used to behave. Stalin never appeared in public. He lived in the Kremlin where no one was allowed to enter. When he went to his dacha from the Kremlin, he traveled at high speeds . . . with the blinds of his car windows drawn." Whatever the consequences for the arms race and long-term

U.S.-Soviet relations, the agreement was a public relations triumph for Khrushchev, who seemed to be giving socialism a human face.

Kennedy was happy, too, but there was still much to be done. Remembering Woodrow Wilson's League of Nations defeat at the hands of the Senate and fearful that a coalition of southern conservative Democrats and Republicans would find the thirty-four votes needed to block the treaty, he mounted a determined campaign to ensure approval. During the negotiations, he had kept all senators abreast of developments and asked five of them — three Democrats and two Republicans — to attend a treaty-signing ceremony in Moscow. The reluctance of any Republican senator to accept, joined by private expressions of doubts by the Joint Chiefs and public warnings by conservatives and newspapers that the United States might be courting disaster, deepened the president's concern about ratification.

As he had done so well before, Kennedy decided to play to his greatest strengths: He would speak directly to the country in behalf of the treaty. His speech on July 26 avoided any suggestion that he was trying to dodge the concerns of skeptical military chiefs and senators. But his address presented an apocalyptic vision of a world teetering on the brink of universal disaster. In the eighteen years since World War II, he said, the United States and USSR had talked past each other, producing "only darkness, discord, or disillusion." This fog of gloom threatened to turn into a conflict unlike any before in history — a war that, in less than sixty minutes, "could wipe out more than 300 million Americans, Europeans, and Russians, as well as untold numbers elsewhere. And the survivors, as Chairman Khrushchev warned the Communist Chinese, 'the survivors would envy the dead.'" But now, he said, "a shaft of light [has] cut into the darkness. . . . For the first time, an agreement has been reached on bringing the forces of nuclear destruction under international control." The test ban agreement was no panacea, Kennedy conceded, but it was a step away from war: It reduced world tensions; limited the dangers from radioactive fallout; raised the likelihood of nuclear nonproliferation; and promised to rein in the arms race between East and West.

Kennedy worked hard behind the scenes, too. The military and senators were told that this was not a "ban the bomb" treaty; it would in no way inhibit the United States from using nuclear weapons in a war, and it allowed the United States to withdraw from the treaty if national safety dictated. They were also assured that the United States would be free to hold underground tests, maintain laboratories for upgrading nuclear weapons, and design plans for renewed atmospheric testing if it seemed essential. Assertions that a treaty served the United States by driving a wedge between Russia and China scored additional points with skeptics.

Ultimately, Kennedy's fear that the Senate would reject the treaty and repudiate his administration was overdrawn. His courting of clear opponents as well as potential supporters had obviously helped. But the treaty was so transparently a step in the direction of better Soviet-American relations and away from the brinksmanship of the Cuban missile crisis that it is difficult to imagine the public and the Senate turning it aside. "Maybe we can save a total war" with the agreement, Truman told Kennedy. Fulbright had worried that the physicist Edward Teller, the architect of the hydrogen bomb and an anti-Soviet evangelist, might weaken support for the agreement, but he could not believe that "these fellows [a majority of senators] [would be] so stupid as to vote against this treaty." A Harris poll published on September 1 showed 81 percent approval for the pact. Moreover, as one Republican senator predicting Senate approval candidly told *Newsweek* in August, "I don't see any political mileage in opposing the treaty." He predicted Senate approval. He was right. On September 24, the Upper House overwhelmingly endorsed the agreement by an 80 to 19 vote.

Of course, there would be second-guessing. Could Kennedy have had a more comprehensive ban if he had agreed to the limit of three annual inspections Khrushchev had proposed? Perhaps, though Khrushchev's determination to use underground testing to catch up with the United States probably put a broader agreement out of reach. And the conviction in the United States that three inspections would be an insufficient bar to Soviet cheating made Kennedy's reluctance to accept Moscow's limit understandable. Did the treaty inhibit proliferation and slow the arms race? Clearly not. The agreement did not deter China, France, India, Israel, or Pakistan from developing nuclear weapons. Nor did it prevent the building of additional and more devastating nuclear bombs and delivery systems. Yet Kennedy, Macmillan, and Khrushchev took great and understandable satisfaction from the treaty. The agreement, as millions of people appreciated, marked a pause in Cold War tensions that, in the early sixties, seemed to make a global conflict all too likely.

In March 1963, 60 percent of a poll expected the Soviets to use a hydrogen bomb against the United States in a war. In June, before the completion of the test ban treaty, 37 percent of Americans believed it "impossible to reach a peaceful settlement of differences with Russia." In September, after the successful negotiations for a ban, only 25 percent of a survey saw a threat of war as the greatest problem facing the country. The *Bulletin of the Atomic Scientists*, which features a doomsday clock on its cover, moved the clock back from seven minutes before midnight to twelve minutes before midnight.

The treaty, as Kennedy publicly acknowledged, "will not resolve all conflicts, or cause the Communists to forego their ambitions, or eliminate the dangers of war. It will not reduce our need for arms or allies. . . . But it is an important first step — a step towards peace — a step towards reason — a step away from war." In this, he was correct. The treaty — the first significant arms control agreement between the United States and USSR — was a milestone in the successful forty-five-year struggle to prevent the Cold War from turning into an all-out conflict that would have devastated the planet. It raised the possibility of détente, of a belief that Moscow and Washington were not strictly in the grip of militant cold warriors who saw safety only in the ability of their military establishments to outbuild their adversaries. And it gave hope to millions of people who believed, with Kennedy, that mankind must do away with nuclear war or war would do away with mankind. The treaty, which was universally recognized as Kennedy's handiwork, created an imperishable conviction that he might bring the Cold War to a peaceful conclusion.

CHAPTER 19

An Unfinished Presidency

Countless individuals have noted that the President's death affected them even more deeply than the death of their own parents. The reason, I believe, is that the latter situation most often represented a loss of the past — while the assassination of President Kennedy represented an incalculable loss of the future.

— Theodore C. Sorensen, December 1963

BY 1963 IT WAS CLEAR to all who saw him in the White House that Kennedy enjoyed being president. One of the first things visitors to the Oval Office noticed was how much he had put his stamp on the decor; a naval motif expressed his love of the sea, and his desk, which had belonged to President Hayes, was constructed from timbers of the H.M.S. *Resolute*. Aside from an alligator desk set, a gift from de Gaulle, naval artifacts covered the desk: the coconut shell with the message that helped rescue the PT-109 crew, two whale teeth engraved with sailing ships and a third with the presidential seal, a ten-inch glass ornament etched with a likeness of PT-109, and bookends with replicas of brass cannons on the U.S.S. *Constitution*. The walls flanking the fireplace held pictures of the famous naval engagement in 1812 between the *Constitution* and the British frigate *Guerriere*. Above the mantel was a picture of the September 1779 engagement between the *Bonhomme Richard* and the British ships *Serapis* and *Countess of Scarborough*. The sword of naval hero John Barry, crossed with a boarding saber, hung on another wall.

Kennedy "loved being President," Schlesinger said, "and at times he could hardly remember that he had ever been anything else. He never complained about the 'terrible loneliness' of the office or its 'awesome burdens.'" Dave Powers echoed Schlesinger's recollection: "John F. Kennedy enjoyed being President. He loved being where the action was. He was always at his best under pressure. He became more determined after each disappointment." This attitude partly explains why Kennedy saw his health problems not as a deterrent to becoming president but as a challenge he enjoyed overcoming.

Yet, not everything was dandy. In July 1963, O'Donnell and Powers recalled that Kennedy was frustrated over the tax cut, civil rights, and problems with Vietnam. His inability to win congressional approval for education and Medicare bills also troubled him. "We will probably get our jocks knocked off on this aid to education," he told Sorensen earlier in the year. Nor did he always find the compulsory socializing at the White House appealing. One evening in January, when Jackie and her sister, Lee Radziwill, had arranged a dinner party with several Hollywood entertainers, Kennedy asked, "Are they all coming to dinner?" When told yes, he said, "You girls must be crazy, but I guess there isn't anything I can do now." Yet in spite of these occasional annoyances, O'Donnell and Powers remember Kennedy at this time as "more forceful and sure of himself, and more relaxed and happier than we had ever seen him."

In April 1963, when Newsweek journalist James M. Cannon interviewed the president for an article about his brother Joe, Cannon "was struck first by the serenity of the [Oval Office] surroundings and the self-possession of the principal." Cannon recorded in some notes he made on the meeting, "In this man, at this moment, there was no evidence that he was worn with the cares of office. He was casual. He was affable. He was unhurried, unbadgered . . . .'How are you doing?' I said. 'I must say you look fine. From all appearances, the job seems to be agreeing with you.' 'Well,' he said, with a big smile, 'I think it's going well. As you know we do have our ups and downs, the tides ebb and flow. . . . [But] in general, I think things are going well.'"

Kennedy's self-assurance registered not only on White House insiders and Americans more generally but also on Western Europeans. His popularity with them, Time magazine journalist John Steele privately told the White House, was "at an exceedingly high, really inspired level." The British were ready to consider Kennedy the initiator of a family dynasty: They expected the president to have a second term, followed by the attorney general for eight years and then the senator from Massachusetts. ("Whatever other deficiencies the family may have, it is abundantly supplied with heirs," one English writer observed.) Pressed to provide some philosophical wisdom about the position, Kennedy joked, "I have a nice home, the office is close by and the pay is good." His quick wit about his family and politics was on display at a 1963 gala: "I was proud of the Attorney General's first appearance before the Supreme Court yesterday," he solemnly declared. "He did a very good job, according to everyone I talked to: Ethel, Jackie, Teddy." Bobby's performance showed that "he does have broader interests — that he isn't limited to the slogan: 'Stop the world — I want to get Hoffa.'" Kennedy also made light of the resistance to his legislative proposals: "With all our contacts in show business and culture," he said, "the Democrats should make some progress. I'm trying to get [television series doctors] Dr. Kildare and Ben Casey to support my Medicare bill. And Kirk Douglas said he would support my proposals to strengthen the nation's economy with a tax cut. In fact, he said he's willing to go all the way and pay no taxes at all." During a presidential briefing breakfast with economic advisers, Kennedy turned aside criticism with good humor. When a favorable review for right-wing columnist Victor Lasky's book *JFK: The Man and the Myth* came up, the president recalled the only time he had been at the reviewer's home, where he had been served "some kind of orange pop, and people sat stiffly around." Kennedy jokingly added, "Never trust a man who serves only soft drinks."

By October 1963, Kennedy had established the sort of rapport with the public that had made Theodore Roosevelt, FDR, Truman in 1948, and Ike so popular. The death in August 1963 of Patrick Bouvier Kennedy, a baby born five weeks before term, only deepened the public's ties to the president and Jackie. The loss registered on millions of Americans, who sympathized with the Kennedys and identified with their vulnerability to human suffering. Picking up on an item in the *New York Times* — "As they walked out of the Presidential office, Mr. Kennedy took a white handkerchief from his pocket and wiped the boy's nose" — *New Yorker* editor E. B. White composed an affectionate poem about JFK:

> A President's work is never done,
> His burdens press from sun to sun:
> A Berlin wall, a racial brew,
> A tax cut bill, a Madame Nhu.
> One crisis ebbs, another flows —
> And here comes John with a runny nose:

A President must rise and dress,
See senators, and meet the press,
Be always bold, be sometimes wary,
Be kind to foreign dignitary,
And while he's fending off our foes
  Bend down and wipe a little boy's nose.

BUT FOR ALL his occasional insouciance, Kennedy never lost sight of the limitations and frustrations all presidents face. "Every President," he wrote in 1963, "must endure a gap between what he would like and what is possible." He was also fond of FDR's observation that "Lincoln was a sad man because he couldn't get it all at once. And nobody can." When James Reston pressed him to say what he hoped to achieve by the end of his term, Kennedy, Reston said, "looked at me as if I were a dreaming child. I tried again: Did he not feel the need of some goal to help guide his day-to-day decisions and priorities? Again a ghastly pause. It was only when I turned the question to immediate, tangible problems that he seized the point and rolled off a torrent of statistics." It was not that Kennedy was without larger hopes and goals — better race relations and less poverty in America and improved East-West relations, with diminished likelihood of nuclear war, were never far from his mind. But it was the practical daily challenges standing in the way of larger designs that held his attention and seemed to him the principal stuff of being president.

By 1963 Kennedy had few doubts about his suitability for the presidency. But his self-confidence did not include the conviction that he was politically invulnerable. He understood that his political fortunes could change overnight — that unanticipated events could suddenly undermine his popularity and make him vulnerable to defeat in 1964. And the source of his eclipse could come from revelations about private behavior as well as from a downturn in public affairs or a stumble in handling a domestic or foreign crisis.

In March, when Schlesinger returned from a trip to England, he had given the president news of an emerging embarrassment involving John Profumo, Macmillan's war minister, who had been having an extramarital affair with Christine Keeler, a twenty-one-year-old call girl who was also the mistress of a Soviet deputy naval attaché. Even though no one could prove that Profumo had given away state secrets, his indiscretion made Macmillan's government vulnerable to collapse. A Gallup poll Schlesinger brought to Kennedy's attention in June showed 71 percent of British voters favoring either Macmillan's resignation or dissolution of parliament and a test of his popularity in a general election.

Kennedy's interest in the scandal had been evident to Ben Bradlee, who later described the president as having "devoured every word about the Profumo case; it combined so many of the things that interested him: low doings in high places, the British nobility, sex and spying." After someone in the state department sent Kennedy a cable from U.S. ambassador David Bruce recounting the details of the case, Kennedy "ordered all further cables from Bruce on that subject sent to him immediately." And it was concern about Profumo fallout that led Kennedy to visit Macmillan in Sussex instead of London.

Kennedy saw the Profumo scandal as a cautionary tale. In June, when he discussed civil rights with Martin Luther King at the White House, he took King for a walk in the Rose Garden, where he warned him to disassociate himself from Levison and O'Dell. "You've read about Profumo in the newspapers?" the president asked King. "That was an example of friendship and loyalty carried too far. Macmillan is likely to lose his government because he has been loyal to his friend. You must take care not to lose your cause for the same reason." King replied that the accusations against Levison could not be true. (King remembered that Kennedy "turned red and shook." But understanding that continuing ties to O'Dell would strain relations with Kennedy and might weaken administration support for reform legislation, King put O'Dell on notice that he would have to quit the SCLC. Because Kennedy wanted O'Dell fired immediately, the White House leaked a story to the *Birmingham News* about his communist ties that forced King to act at once. Similarly, the Kennedys brought additional pressure to bear on King to distance himself from Levison. When King tried to finesse the issue by proposing to communicate with Levison only through a mutual friend, Bobby ordered FBI wiretaps on the friend. Levison himself solved the problem by volunteering to break off all communications with King.)

Kennedy also worried that the Profumo scandal might directly embarrass him. On June 29, a week after he had spoken with King, the *New York Journal-American* published a front-page story about a "high elected American official" and Suzy Chang, a New York prostitute, who was living in England and was part of the Keeler vice or

"V-girl" ring. Chang privately claimed that she had slept with Kennedy and eaten dinner with him at the "21" club in New York when he was a senator. To head off potential damage to his brother, on July 1 Bobby asked the two *Journal-American* reporters who had published the story to meet with him at the Justice Department. They claimed that the "high official" was the president of the United States. Bobby chided them for publishing a story "without any further check to get to the truth of the matter." One of the reporters said "he had other sources of a confidential nature." An FBI agent, who sat in on the meeting, reported to Hoover that Bobby "treated the newspaper representatives at arms' length and the conference ended most coolly and, in fact, there was almost an air of hostility between the Attorney General and the reporters." According to Seymour Hersh, Bobby used his considerable influence with the Hearst family, who owned the *Journal-American*, to squelch the story.

Yet Bobby and his brother understood, as their friend Charlie Bartlett pointed out in a 1963 syndicated column, that no president has an iron-clad hold on the press: "Gratitude stirred by favors has an immensely transient quality, particularly among newsmen whose attentions must shift rapidly, and the solid ingratiation of a vast press corps with an independent tradition would be an enterprise beyond the capacities of any set of officials."

Two days after Bobby saw the *Journal-American* reporters, he confronted another potential scandal that seemed even more threatening to the president's political future. On July 3, Hoover advised Bobby of accusations that Kennedy had been involved with a German-born twenty-seven-year-old call girl, Ellen Rometsch, who might be an East German spy. Rometsch had grown up in East Germany, where she had belonged to communist youth groups and allegedly worked as a secretary for Walter Ulbricht, the head of the DDR, before fleeing to the West. A dark-haired beauty described as an Elizabeth Taylor lookalike, Rometsch was introduced to Kennedy by Senate secretary Bobby Baker, who had long made call girls available to senators and other high-government officials. In the spring and summer of 1963, Rometsch apparently made repeated visits to the White House, where she attended naked pool parties and had sex with Kennedy.

The danger from any revelations about the president's involvement with Rometsch was not lost on Bobby. Though he told Hoover's assistant Courtney Evans, who briefed Bobby on the rumors, that unfounded allegations about prominent people were common, Evans recorded that the attorney general "made particular note of Rometsch's name." Bobby also expressed appreciation for Hoover's discretion in privately informing him of the stories. While the FBI investigated the accusations, Bobby ensured that Rometsch herself would not embarrass the president with leaks to the press about their trysts. On August 21, he arranged to have her deported to West Germany. Her escort on the flight to Europe was LaVern Duffy, an old Bobby associate on the Senate Rackets Committee in the fifties, who had been seeing Rometsch romantically for months and now became the conduit for Kennedy money buying her silence.

But Rometsch's distance from potentially inquisitive American reporters and an agreement not to discuss her relations with Kennedy did not eliminate the possibility of a public scandal. In September 1963, Republicans on the Senate Rules Committee began looking into allegations that Bobby Baker had engaged in influence peddling and other ethical violations. On October 7, Baker gave up his Senate position and devoted himself to combating the investigation. Understanding that the White House and Senate Democrats could squelch the probe, Baker tried to enlist Bobby's support. The unspoken understanding between them was that Bobby — who disliked Baker and his strongest ally, Johnson — would not encourage the Senate inquiry, and in turn, Baker would sit on information about the president and Rometsch. But with evidence of Baker's wrongdoing mounting, no one could hold back an investigation.

Moreover, a story on October 26 in the *Des Moines Register* by the well-regarded investigative reporter Clark Mollenhoff brought the Rometsch scandal to public attention. Mollenhoff raised questions about Rometsch's deportation and cited allegations of associations between the "party girl" and "several high executive branch officials" described as "prominent New Frontiersmen from the executive branch of government." The story more than caught Kennedy's attention. "The President came in all excited about the news reports concerning the German woman & other prostitutes getting mixed up with government officials, Congressmen, etc.," Evelyn Lincoln noted in her diary on Monday, October 28. "He called Mike Mansfield to come to the office to discuss the playing down of this news report." Mollenhoff's story said nothing about Rometsch's possible East German ties, which would have made his revelations as sensational as those about Profumo and would have made Kennedy as vulnerable as Macmillan, who lost power in October 1963. The president instructed O'Donnell to get every White House aide on record as having had nothing to do with any Baker call girls.

Bobby became the point man in heading off possible damage to his brother and others at the White House. He sent word to Hoover asking him to discourage any Senate investigation of the Rometsch allegations. Bobby said he was "greatly concerned, as was the President, with the possible harm which will come to the United States if irresponsible action is taken on the Hill in connection with the Ellen Rometsch allegations." Hoover suggested that they stop Rometsch from getting a visa to return to the United States, so that it would be difficult for the Senate to probe her White House involvements. Bobby, speaking for the president, asked Hoover to meet with Senate leaders, which he did. In a conversation with Mansfield and Everett Dirksen at Mansfield's apartment in northwest Washington, Hoover assured them that an FBI investigation had turned up no evidence that Rometsch was a spy or a visitor to the White House. He did have, however, plenty of evidence that Baker's call girls had serviced various senators. Not surprisingly, Hoover's initiative convinced the Senate to stay away entirely from Baker's call girls. To further discourage any investigation, JFK told Ben Bradlee that Hoover had lots of "dirt" on senators, which Kennedy implied Bradlee might want to uncover if they began looking into anyone else's sexual misdeeds.

The Baker probe also raised concerns at the White House. Johnson had not only been Baker's mentor in the fifties, when Lyndon had been majority leader, he had also publicly attended the opening of a luxury motel in Ocean City, Maryland, in 1962, where Baker, a part owner, entertained "the advise-and-consent set." Allegations of corrupt dealings by Baker put Johnson under suspicion of unethical behavior. The president had a "keen interest" in the Baker case, and Bobby monitored the probe for evidence of any wrongdoing by the vice president. Johnson believed that Bobby, who obviously disliked him, saw him as of little help to the administration and had instigated the Baker investigation in order to throw him off the ticket in 1964.

In fact, Johnson's suspicions were largely unfounded, but once the stories about Baker became public, the Kennedys shrewdly encouraged rumors that LBJ would be dropped in the following year. The simultaneous leaks and reassurances were smart politics. If Johnson were implicated in any of Baker's misdeeds, the Kennedys could follow through on the rumors and rid themselves of a political liability. If the talk of Johnson's wrongdoing proved false, which it did, the White House could simply echo earlier reassurances about keeping him as the ideal running mate.

IN PREPARATION FOR THE 1964 ELECTIONS, the Senate Democratic policy committee and the White House began discussions of how to deal with the country's concerns and turn them into political advantages over the GOP. Specifically, the administration complained about the "stubborn and destructive obstructionism" of congressional Republicans to tax reforms that could expand the economy, inhibit inflation, and reduce unemployment. Opinion polls in the spring of 1963 had revealed that national defense, nuclear war, communist subversion, education, inflation, unemployment, and racial tensions were principal public worries.

Kennedy believed that the upcoming campaign would largely be about his record. He had every confidence that he would win, especially if the Republicans made conservative senator Barry Goldwater their nominee. But nothing could be taken for granted about the economy, civil rights, space exploration, Cuba, and Vietnam, which impressed him as the problems that needed the greatest attention in the next year and a half. He did not expect to resolve these difficulties in the near term. Instead, he would be content to keep them under control or frame them as challenges that might be effectively addressed in the future. His immediate goal, then, was to put conditions in place that would advance his administration toward a greater mastery of the country's most compelling dilemmas in a second term.

By the fall of 1963, the president remained focused on the economy and how it would fare in the coming year without tax reform, which was on indefinite hold in Congress. Economic growth in the first quarter of the year had exceeded expectations, making a recession and a tax reduction unlikely. CEA predictions in the summer and fall that the first half of 1964 would see a significant slowdown unless there were a tax cut had no significant impact on Congress. Senators in particular were determined to resist reductions in tax revenues without assurances of a balanced budget. Ten of seventeen senators on the Finance Committee, for example, supported chairman Robert Byrd's determination to hold up the bill until he had such a commitment from the White House. And even if the administration could promise this unlikely result, there seemed little chance of winning major tax revisions in an election year without a recession.

Since Kennedy believed that a slowdown would occur, if not in 1964 then certainly in his second term, he was confident that he could eventually win his tax cut. He intended to couple it with an attack on poverty. John Kenneth Galbraith's assertion in his 1958 book, *The Affluent Society,* that the country had a permanent class of impoverished citizens had brought the issue to Kennedy's attention. But it was Michael Harrington's compelling book, *The Other America,* describing the suffering of forty to sixty million Americans, coupled with Dwight Macdonald's fifty-page *New Yorker* essay-review on the invisible poor, that stirred Kennedy to plan a post-'64 election campaign to break the cycle of poverty in which so many elderly and minority Americans lived.

In October 1963, Kennedy discussed the issue with Walter Heller. A *New York Times* story on Kentucky underscored for Kennedy that "there was [a] tremendous problem to be met." He wanted to make "a two- or three-day trip to some of the key poverty-stricken areas to focus the spotlight and arouse the American conscience on this problem from which we are so often shielded. It's perfectly clear," Heller said in a note to himself, "that he is aroused about this and if we could really produce a program to fill the bill, he would be inclined to run with it." When they revisited the subject in November, Kennedy said he remained "very much in favor of doing something," but he wanted Heller to "make clear that we're doing something for the middle-income man in the suburbs as well." Kennedy understood that the success of any big social program like Social Security partly depended on including the middle class as well as the poor.

CIVIL RIGHTS, which had become a more compelling issue in May and June, now stood at the center of domestic affairs. The chances of passing Kennedy's civil rights bill, however, were poor. Getting a strong bill through the House seemed possible: Northern Democrats would likely join with moderate Republicans to outvote southern Democrats; they might even be able to end discrimination in places of public accommodation and re-create a Fair Employment Practices Commission (FEPC), the two most controversial civil rights reforms. But the twenty-two southern senators from the old Confederacy were confident of finding twelve conservative allies to defeat Kennedy's bill. In addition, the Senate had never been able to muster the two-thirds-plus-one vote to stop a civil rights filibuster. If the White House agreed to quietly abandon the issue of segregation in public accommodations, Mansfield believed that they might bring enough Republicans along to win a limited civil rights law. "The assumption is that it is better to secure passage of as much of the Administration's legislative proposals on civil rights as is possible," Mansfield told the president, "rather than to run the very real risk of losing all in an effort to obtain all."

The White House had some small hope that it might convince "a leading southern Senator . . . to play the role that [Michigan senator] Arthur Vandenberg [had] played in the isolationist fight" at the start of the Cold War. Eventually, some southerner was going to say that "the world had changed, that the struggle for equal rights was irresistible and that the South, instead of wasting its energies in vain recrimination and resistance," needed to accept "a constructive resolution" to a problem that undermined the country's domestic and international well-being. Lister Hill of Alabama, a New Dealer, who did not have to run again until 1968, when he would be seventy-four and might not stand for reelection anyway, seemed a good choice. But Hill, like his fellow southerners in both Houses, would not break a commitment to the region's mores.

It was clear to Kennedy that getting any kind of civil rights law would require an all-out lobbying effort. He needed to enlist as many groups as possible in bringing pressure to bear on uncommitted congressmen and senators. As Johnson had pointed out to civil rights leaders in June, the administration began with about two-to-one support in the Senate for a bill, but what he meant was that there were only fifty votes for and twenty-two against. The remaining twenty-eight uncommitted senators would decide the issue, which meant selling civil rights to them and their constituents during the few months left in the congressional session. Educators, women, and labor and religious leaders who were already sympathetic to legislative action were asked at White House meetings to educate others about the destructive effects of discrimination and personally do all they could to advance social justice. Businessmen, especially those most affected by the law's provision that would end segregation in places of public accommodation, were urged to understand the national need for such a reform.

Yet Kennedy remained uncertain that he could sway Congress, and he worried that failure might be disastrous for his administration. In a White House meeting with civil rights leaders on June 22, he predicted a hard struggle that might cost him dearly. "The Vice President and I know what it will mean if we fail," Kennedy said. "I have just seen a new poll — national approval of the administration has fallen from 60 to 47 percent." (No one ever located the poll Kennedy cited; his Gallup approval rating at the time was, in fact, 61 percent.) "A good many programs I care about may go down the drain as a result of this," he said, "so we are putting a lot on the line." He added, "I may lose the next election because of this." On August 1, a reporter at a news conference asked Kennedy to comment on "indications lately that your policies on civil rights are costing you heavily in political prestige and popularity." The reporter asked Kennedy to say "whether civil rights are worth an election." Kennedy replied "[I] assume what you say is probably right." But because civil rights currently represented "a national crisis of great proportions," he believed that "whoever was President would meet his responsibilities" by advancing the rights of all citizens to equal opportunity.

Kennedy's dire predictions were partly aimed at convincing civil rights advocates to accept a compromise bill, which was the only sort of measure he believed could pass. "The worst trouble of all would be to lose the fight in the Congress," he asserted. He wanted to discourage the gathering on the twenty-second of rights activists King, James Farmer, A. Philip Randolph, Joe Rauh, Walter Reuther, Bayard Rustin, Roy Wilkins, and Whitney Young from doing anything that jeopardized passage of even a watered-down law.

Kennedy was especially negative about a march on the Capitol. White House press leaks were already discouraging the idea when the Urban League's Whitney Young asked him at the meeting whether newspaper reports about the president's opposition were accurate. Kennedy responded, "We want success in the Congress, not a big show on the Capitol." He acknowledged that civil rights demonstrations had pushed the administration and Congress into consideration of a major reform bill, "but now we are in a new phase," he said, "the legislative phase, and results are essential. The wrong kind of demonstration at the wrong time will give those fellows [on the Hill] a chance to say that they have to prove their courage by voting against us. To get the votes we need we have, first, to oppose demonstrations which lead to violence, and, second, give Congress a fair chance to work its will."

Randolph, King, and others defended the idea of a march and said they could not stop it. "There *will* be a march," Randolph declared; the principal question was whether it would be violent or nonviolent. King argued the case for a march as good politics. It could dramatize the issue and "[mobilize] support in parts of the country that don't know about the problem firsthand. I think it will serve a purpose. It may seem ill-timed. Frankly, I have never engaged in a direct-action movement that did not seem ill-timed. Some people thought Birmingham was ill-timed," King said. "Including the Attorney General," Kennedy interjected, acknowledging that his administration had a less than perfect record in the fight for civil rights.

Also present was Johnson, who invoked his authority as a past majority leader and explained that Kennedy was taking the right approach to Congress. He would move them by arm twisting, deal making, and corridor politics, where the president could call on them to think of the larger picture and do right by the country. Publicly challenging the Congress on moral grounds had its limits, but a president who knew each member's personal wants and could make arrangements with them privately, quietly, would achieve more than a crowd of marchers flaunting their sense of moral indignation at lawmakers refusing to act.

When others at the meeting explained that resistance on their part to a march would alienate them from the membership of their organizations, Kennedy said, "Well, we all have our problems. You have your problems. I have my problems," mentioning Congress, the Soviets, NATO, and de Gaulle. As he left for a briefing on what to expect in Europe during his upcoming trip, he concluded by saying that they should work together and stay in touch. Though they would disagree from time to time on tactics, their strength was in unity of purpose.

Since it was now clear that they would be unable to stop the August 28 march, the Kennedys tried to ensure its success. Worried about an all-black demonstration, which would encourage assertions that whites had no serious interest in a comprehensive reform law, Kennedy asked Walter Reuther, head of the Automobile Workers union, to arrange substantial white participation by church and labor union members. Kennedy also worried that a small turnout would defeat march purposes, but black and white organizers answered this concern by mobilizing over 250,000 demonstrators. To ensure that as little as possible went wrong, Bobby directed his Civil Division assistant attorney general to devote himself full-time for five weeks to guarding against potential mishaps, like insufficient food and toilet facilities or the presence of police dogs, which would draw comparisons to Bull Connor in Birmingham. Moreover, winning agreement to a route running from the Washington Monument to the Lincoln Memorial precluded the demonstration at the Capitol that the president feared would antagonize the Congress.

The march marked a memorable moment in a century-long crusade for black equality, its distinctive features not violence or narrow partisanship on behalf of one group's special interest but a dignified display of faith on the part of blacks and whites that America remained the world's last best hope of freedom and equality for all: that the fundamental promise of American life — the triumph of individualism over collectivism or racial or group identity — might yet be fulfilled.

Nothing caught the spirit of the moment better, or did more to advance it, than Martin Luther King's concluding speech in the shadow of Lincoln's memorial. In his remarks to the massive audience, which was nearly exhausted by the long afternoon of oratory, King had spoken for five minutes from his prepared text when he extemporaneously began to preach in the familiar cadence that had helped make him so effective a voice in the movement: "I have a dream that one day on the red hills of Georgia the sons of former slaves and the sons of former slave-owners will be able to sit together at the table of brotherhood. . . . I have a dream that one day every valley shall be exalted, every hill and mountain shall be made low, the rough places will be made plain and the crooked places will be made straight, and the glory of the Lord shall be revealed and all flesh shall see it together. . . . And when this happens . . . we will be able to speed up that day when all of God's children, black men and white men, Jews and Gentiles, Protestants and Catholics, will be able to join hands and sing in the words of the old Negro spiritual, 'Free at last! Free at last! Thank God Almighty, we are free at last!'"

As the marchers dispersed, many walked hand in hand singing the movement's anthem:

> We shall overcome, we shall overcome,
> We shall overcome, some day.
> Oh, deep in my heart, I do believe,
> We shall overcome some day.

Despite the success of the march, which received broad network TV coverage, Kennedy remained uncertain about prospects for a bill of any kind. But he was genuinely impressed and moved by King's speech. "I have a dream," he greeted King at a White House meeting with march organizers that evening. (When King asked if the president had heard Walter Reuther's excellent speech, which had indirectly chided Kennedy for doing more to defend freedom in Berlin than Birmingham, Kennedy replied, "Oh, I've heard him plenty of times.")

Almost euphoric over the size of the turnout and the well-behaved, dignified demeanor of the marchers, Wilkins, Randolph, and Reuther expressed confidence that the House would pass a far-reaching bill, which would put unprecedented pressure on the Senate to act. Kennedy offered a two-pronged defense of continuing caution. First, he said, though "this doesn't have anything to do with what we have been talking about," the group should exercise their substantial influence in the Negro community by doing something that "the Jewish community has done," putting an emphasis on "educating their children, on making them study, making them stay in school and all the rest." The looks of uncertainty, if not disbelief, on the faces of the civil rights leaders toward a proposal that, at best, would take a generation to implement moved Kennedy to follow on with a practical explanation for restraint in dealing with Congress. He read from a list prepared by special assistant for congressional relations Larry O'Brien of likely votes in the House and Senate. The dominance of negative congressmen blunted suggestions that Kennedy could win passage of anything more than a limited measure, and even that was in doubt.

Kennedy's analysis of congressional resistance moved Randolph to ask the president to mount "a crusade" by going directly to the country for support. Kennedy countered by suggesting that rights leaders pressure the Republican party to back the fight for equal rights. He believed that the Republicans would turn a crusade by the administration into a political liability for the Democrats among white voters. And certainly bipartisan consensus would better serve a push for civil rights than a one-sided campaign by liberal Democrats. King asked if an appeal to Eisenhower might help enlist Republican backing generally and the support of House minority leader Charlie Halleck in particular. Kennedy did not think that an appeal to Eisenhower would have any impact on Halleck, but he liked the idea of sending a secret delegation made up of religious clerics and businessmen to see the former president. (Signaling his unaltered conviction that the "bomb throwers" — as Johnson called uncompromising liberals — would do more to retard than advance a civil rights bill, Kennedy jokingly advised against including Walter Reuther in the delegation seeing Ike.) In the end, Kennedy concluded the one-hour-and-ten-minute meeting by promising nothing more than reports on likely votes in the House and the Senate. It was transparent to more than the civil rights leaders that Kennedy saw a compromise or bipartisan civil rights measure as his only chance for success.

On September 2, when he gave CBS anchor Walter Cronkite an interview at Hyannis Port, Kennedy did not blink at the likelihood that his support of major reforms, especially civil rights, would hurt him in the South. But he tried to blunt potential Republican gains and advance the civil rights bill by asking Republicans to "commit themselves to the same objective of equality of opportunity. I would be surprised," he said, "if the Republican Party, which, after all, is the party of Lincoln and is proud of that fact, as it should be . . . if they did not also support the right of every citizen to have equal opportunities, equal chance under the Constitution."

A bombing at a church in Birmingham on September 15, which killed four young black girls, made the sense of urgency greater than ever. On the nineteenth, King and a group of black Birmingham leaders met with Kennedy at the White House to discuss ways to avert further violence against blacks and preserve the city's tranquillity. King described the situation in Birmingham as so serious that it not only threatened the stability of the city "and Alabama but of the whole nation. . . . More bombings of churches and homes have taken place in Birmingham than any city in the United States and not a one of these bombings over the last fifteen to twenty years has been solved," King told the president. "The Negro community is about to reach a breaking point. . . . There is a feeling of being alone and not being protected. . . . If something isn't done to give the Negro a new sense of hope and a sense of protection," King warned, ". . . then we will have the worst race rioting we have ever seen in this country." The presence of state troopers was no help. To the contrary, "their methods," King said, were "just unbelievable and barbaric. . . . We feel that these troopers should be removed, and be replaced with federal troops, to protect the people." Second, King urged the cancellation of federal government contracts with Birmingham businesses that continued to discriminate against blacks.

Kennedy resisted both suggestions. If conditions in Birmingham continued to deteriorate, he promised to consider dispatching troops, but he believed that once he sent in federal forces, he would have "an awful time getting them out" (as he feared would be the case in Vietnam). He thought it essential for the black community to avoid violence. "If the Negroes begin to respond, shoot at whites, you lose," he said. "Because when everybody starts going for guns, they'll shoot some innocent people, and they'll be white and then that will just wipe away" any white goodwill toward blacks. "I can't do very much," Kennedy added. "Congress can't do very much unless we keep the support of the white community throughout the country." If that disappears, "then we're pretty much down to a racial struggle, so that I think we've just got to tell the Negro community that this is a very hard price they have to pay to get this job done." All Kennedy would commit to was sending former Secretary of the Army Kenneth Royall and former West Point football coach Colonel Earl Blaik to mediate the crisis. Kennedy saw their national status as so high that they would be able to draw Birmingham's white moderates into some kind of agreement with the city's black leaders, which Governor Wallace would find difficult to challenge. He also met with Birmingham officials at the White House. He had no illusion, he told them, that the desire for segregation would disappear, and he predicted that a city with a 40 or 45 percent black population could not cling to traditional habits without increasing tensions and racial violence. He urged the hiring of some Negro policeman and clerks in department stores as a useful way to head off further agitation. The alternative was a city that would likely disintegrate as a viable community.

When the city fathers complained that these steps would probably lead to integration in places of public accommodation, Kennedy encouraged them to develop a sense of proportion about what they faced. Integrating the police force and department stores or even public accommodations like hotels and motels would be relatively painless, he said. There would be few black policemen and clerks; nor, he said with a slight condescending twinge, would many blacks have the financial wherewithal to stay at hotels and motels. The greatest difficulty he saw would be in integrating elementary and secondary schools, where classes would be almost evenly divided between blacks and whites. When the city fathers complained that outside agitators like King, Fred Shuttlesworth, and Young were a principal source of their problem, Kennedy replied that even without black activists from outside the state, Birmingham's problem would not go away. In addition, if moderates like King stood aside, more radical groups like SNCC would take their place, and "they're sons of bitches," Kennedy emphasized. He ended by asking his visitors to support the Royall-Blaik initiative, which would allow the federal government to stay out of Birmingham and create some sense of progress and provide a breathing spell from more violence. As newcomers to the city's government, the city officials pleaded for time to establish their administration before addressing so controversial an issue as civil rights .

Kennedy knew that it would take years and years to resolve race relations in the South, but he still believed that passage of a limited civil rights bill would be "very helpful" in buying time for the country to advance toward a peaceful solution to its greatest domestic social problem. But it was not to be. Between the end of September and the third week in November, House Democrats and Republicans — liberals and conservatives — entered into self-interested maneuvering over the administration's civil rights proposals. A lot of "these fellas would rather have an issue than a bill," Kennedy said about liberals and conservatives. He was so discouraged by late October over the "bad news" coming out of the House that he told Evelyn Lincoln, "he felt like packing his bags and leaving." He also complained that the Republicans were tempted "to think that they're never going to get very far with the Negroes anyway — so they might as well play the white game in the South." Still, because he believed that it would be "a great disaster for us to be beaten in the House," he made a substantial effort to arrange a legislative bargain. Kennedy's intervention in a meeting with Democratic and Republican House leaders on October 23 produced a compromise bill that passed the Judiciary Committee by 20 to 14 on November 20. But the Rules Committee remained a problem. Larry O'Brien and Ted Sorensen asked the president how they could possibly get the bill past Committee chairman Howard Smith, the Virginia segregationist, who was determined to stop it from getting to the House floor in the 1963 session. Kennedy left for a political trip to Dallas on November 21 without an answer to their question. If, as seemed most likely, Smith could keep the bill bottled up in his committee for just one month, it would go over to the 1964 session, when so controversial a measure would have little chance of surviving in an election year.

Yet the news on civil rights was not all bad for Kennedy. After a visit to Arkansas in October, where he spoke about the state, the South, and the country, the *Arkansas Gazette* declared his visit a "solid success," that "suggests that the Republicans may be counting prematurely in adding up all those electoral votes for 1964 from a Solid Republican South." The paper acknowledged that the president was "probably . . . beyond help in Mississippi and Alabama, but then Mississippi and Alabama weren't even with him the last time around." Southern moderates saw Kennedy as a voice of reason in the shrill debate over civil rights. The president "came to Arkansas as a friend and not to do battle with anyone," the *Gazette* declared. "He said the state and national governments should be partners, not antagonists. His good humor was evident, along with a flashing wit, and his habit of mixing with the crowds stands him in good stead. There is not much question that the President, as they say, did himself some good on this venture into the South."

If Kennedy's political problems in the South were less than he feared, the racial divide in the region remained a problem that seemed certain to dog the country and his administration for the foreseeable future. Even in the unlikely event that the administration's November 20 bill won House and Senate approval, it would not have satisfied civil rights advocates for long. The bill had eliminated retail stores and personal services from the public accommodations section, included no Fair Employment Practices Commission, sharply restricted EEOC enforcement powers and federally assisted programs that had to meet desegregation standards, and limited voting rights to federal elections. Constrained by fear of white resistance, including possible violence, to a comprehensive civil rights statute and by concerns about southern support in 1964, Kennedy had reached for compromise solutions that could buy time and allow him to address the issue again in a second term.

In doing so, Kennedy misread the situation, as he had in dealing with southern congressional Democrats in the Eighty-seventh and Eighty-eighth Congresses between 1961 and 1963. His hope that avoiding a confrontation with southern congressmen and senators over civil rights might help win passage of other administration priorities, like a tax cut, Medicare, and federal aid to education, proved false. Would a strong appeal for civil rights legislation from the first have better served Kennedy's legislative agenda? Almost certainly not, but given congressional resistance to his initiatives, it wouldn't have hurt it, either. And it would have put the administration in a stronger position to win passage of a comprehensive civil rights bill in 1963. If Kennedy had urged such a law from the start of his presidency, he could then have argued that his bill would have prevented the racial strife in Mississippi and Alabama in 1962 and 1963. It would have been a forceful justification for enactment of civil rights legislation in the summer of 1963.

Kennedy also failed to see that even the most committed segregationist senators and congressmen and the great majority of southern whites would accept a congressionally mandated civil rights bill. In August 1963, no less than Bonnie Faubus Salcido wrote him "to give you hope in the fight for civil rights. I want you to know there are many in the South who are for you tho [sic] are afraid to speak out. I am the sister of [Orval Faubus] the Governor of Arkansas. . . . Five of my brothers and sisters are for you also." Having fought and lost the civil war over slavery and states rights, most southerners were not about to urge another secession crisis in response to federal imposition of the Constitution's equal protection clauses. Except for a tiny minority of racist extremists, they could imagine nothing less than a unified nation in the face of an international communist threat.

Moreover, Kennedy did not fully understand what Johnson was telling him about the importance of taking a moral stand on civil rights and leading a crusade for something that could be defined as fundamental American values. To be sure, Kennedy's June appeals for civil rights legislation rested on forceful statements of this kind. But his willingness to reach compromises with various congressional groups undermined his ability to press the issue. It did not need to be so. As Kennedy himself said in one of his conversations in October, while polls showed that most Americans were not ready to have Negroes living next door to them, they did support a defense of constitutional rights. With majority sentiment thus favoring congressional action if couched correctly, Kennedy could have taken the moral high ground and invoked the dangers to the national well-being from a failure to enact a bill that could largely ensure equal treatment under the law. His attempt to find a middle ground made him less effective in a fight that required unqualified expressions of faith in the righteousness of the cause. Since civil rights — more so than any other national issue confronting him — raised fundamental ethical questions, he certainly could have made it the one great domestic moral cause of his presidency.

* * *

BY CONTRAST WITH his uncertain handling of civil rights, Kennedy had no doubts about the wisdom of landing a man on the moon by the end of the decade. Budget deficits and demands for greater spending on domestic programs could not deter him from a commitment he believed essential to America's international prestige. In June 1962, after the successful orbital flights by Alan Shepard and John Glenn, Kennedy told a press conference that he had no intention of diverting money from space programs. "I do not think the United States can afford to become second in space because I think that space has too many implications militarily, politically, psychologically, and all the rest." He cited a survey of French students, two-thirds of whom regarded the Soviet Union as being first in science and technology. "I think the fact that the Soviet Union was . . . first in space in the fifties had a tremendous impact upon a good many people who were attempting to make a determination as to whether they could meet their economic problems without engaging in a Marxist form of government. I think the United States cannot permit the Soviet Union to become dominant in the sea of space." Kennedy partly justified the lunar program's costs by citing its "many industrial benefits." "No one can tell me that the United States cannot afford to do what the Soviet Union has done so successfully with a national income of less than half of ours," he said.

In 1962, a double orbit by two Soviet cosmonauts and continuing advantages in the "size and total of weights placed in orbit, in the thrust of their operational rocket engines, and in the development of" space rendezvousing techniques strengthened Kennedy's commitment to the Apollo program. Surveys of West European opinion on the Soviet-American space competition showed a growing regard for U.S. capabilities, further bolstering Kennedy's determination to advance the lunar landing. In August, to counter allegations that Apollo primarily aimed to give the United States a military advantage in space, Kennedy directed the National Security Council to encourage public understanding of America's peaceful intentions. (The NSC was a peculiar choice as spokesman for the administration's opposition to militarizing space.)

Kennedy also urged NASA officials to consider accelerating the manned lunar mission by diverting monies from other space projects. At a meeting with budget advisers in November, he clashed with NASA head Jim Webb, who opposed putting more money into the lunar program to advance the landing date. A forceful, overbearing character who did not like being contradicted, Webb bristled at Kennedy's policy directives, interrupting and speaking over the president. Webb urged a balanced program of space exploration that did not overemphasize the lunar probes. He described the moon walk as just one of several space priorities and invoked the authority of scientists, who "think the highest priority is to understand the environment of space."

Believing that public support for his space program would weaken without clearly tying it to the Soviet-American competition for space dominance, Kennedy rejected Webb's advice. While only 33 percent of the public endorsed the expenditure of $40 billion on the manned moon mission, Kennedy saw a well-defined and dramatic achievement as essential to sustain national backing. And he saw that backing as vital to a larger national security goal. "Everything we do ought to really be tied in to getting on to the moon ahead of the Russians," he told Webb. "Otherwise we shouldn't be spending that kind of money, because I'm not interested in space. . . . [The costs] wreck our budget on all these other domestic programs, and the only justification for it . . . is because we hope to beat them to demonstrate that instead of being behind by a couple of years, by God we passed them." .

"Do you still have the same enthusiasm and high hopes for the results of the vast outlays we have undertaken in the space projects . . . [as] when you first started into these?" a reporter asked Kennedy in December 1962. He acknowledged that $5 billion in the coming year was a lot to spend on the program but pointed to the "tremendous effect" that *Sputnik* had in the fifties. It made people everywhere believe that Moscow had "the secret of the organization of society." He also urged the reporters to keep in mind that space expenditures translated into new industries and new technical skills.

Kennedy's commitment to the moon landing did not insulate the administration from growing complaints about the "moon-doggle," as critics began calling it. U.S. scientists were among the most outspoken critics. They asserted that "large-scale applied research ought to concentrate on problems 'here on earth': Medicine, Third World development, urban renewal" were all more worthy of investment and study than the moon program. Liberals joined the attack by pointing out that space spending could be funding valuable social programs. On the other side of the fence, Republicans, led by Eisenhower, weighed in with complaints that Kennedy's moon project was too focused on America's international prestige and too little on gaining military advantages in space. Eisenhower said that spending a total of $40 billion to reach the moon was "just nuts."

In the spring of 1963, Kennedy launched an aggressive response to his critics. In April, he asked Johnson to tell him what technical and scientific accomplishments might result from space exploration. At the same time, Kennedy told the press that nothing had changed his mind about "the desirability of continuing this program. Now, some people say that we should take the money we are putting into space and put it into housing or education," but, Kennedy asserted, if they "cut the space program . . . you would not get additional funds for education." Instead, the Congress would use the monies to balance budgets. Slowing or eliminating the manned moon mission would only produce later recriminations over our failure to keep up with the Soviets.

At the end of July, to blunt continuing attacks on Apollo, Kennedy wanted Johnson to tell him whether the Eisenhower administration had ever had a moon program, what its time schedule was, and how much they had planned to spend on it. He also asked Johnson to report on how much of the space program was militarily useful. The vice president replied that Eisenhower had no moon program and that it was impossible "to ascribe a quantitative measure to the military spin-offs from the non-military portion of the space program." However, Johnson confidently asserted that everything they were doing in space was both directly and indirectly of military value, concluding that the "space program is expensive, but it can be justified as a solid investment which will give ample returns in security, prestige, knowledge, and material benefits."

When reports about Soviet second thoughts on a manned moon mission surfaced in the summer, Kennedy came under additional pressure to reconsider the U.S. program. He refused. He continued to see substantial Soviet gains in prestige from space exploration. According to a USIA worldwide opinion survey asking which country was "ahead in space developments," people everywhere believed the Soviets had the advantage. In Japan, 69 percent of the poll saw Moscow in the lead, while only 6 percent said the United States; in Britain, the split was 59 to 13, and in France, opinion ran 68 percent to 5 percent against the U.S.; in Argentina, Brazil, and Venezuela, only 10 to 18 percent believed that the United States was winning the space race. "Are we going to divert ourselves from our effort in an area where the Soviet Union has a lead, is making every effort to maintain that lead, in an area which could affect our national security as well as great peaceful development?" Kennedy rhetorically asked reporters in July.

To increase public support for Apollo, Kennedy emphasized the idealistic as well as the practical advantages of his policy. In particular, he publicly urged Soviet-American cooperation in outer space. In a September 20, 1963, speech before the United Nations General Assembly, he underscored the rising hopes for peace resulting from reduced tensions over Berlin, Laos, and the Congo and the test ban treaty. "In a field where the United States and Soviet Union have a special capacity — in the field of space — there is room for new cooperation," Kennedy declared, "for further joint efforts in the regulation and exploration of space. I include among these possibilities a joint expedition to the moon. . . . Why . . . should man's first flight to the moon be a matter of national competition?" There was no need for the immense duplication of research, construction, and expenditure. "Surely we should explore whether the scientists and astronauts of our two countries — indeed of all the world — cannot work together in the conquest of space, sending some day in this decade to the moon not the representatives of a single nation, but the representatives of all of our countries." Though Khrushchev gave no response to Kennedy's proposal, in November, JFK instructed Webb personally to assume responsibility for exploring possibilities of Soviet-American cooperation and to report back to him on "the progress of our planning by December 15."

At the end of October, when Khrushchev told journalists that they were "not at present planning flight by cosmonauts to the moon," American newspapers gave his remarks front-page coverage. (Khrushchev reflected Soviet ambivalence about a manned moon mission; it was not until 1964 that Russian leaders formally committed themselves to enter this competition.) But Kennedy refused to take Khrushchev's statement as an excuse to quit the moon race. "I would not make any bets at all upon Soviet intentions," he told the press. When Khrushchev confirmed to reporters that Moscow had not dropped out of the moon race, Kennedy accepted it as vindication of his policy. "An energetic continuation of our strong space effort is essential," Kennedy told Congressman Albert Thomas. "In the larger sense, this is not merely an effort to put a man on the moon; it is a means and a stimulus for all the advances in technology, in understanding and in experience, which can move us forward toward man's mastery of space."

As demonstrated by a 1965 survey showing 58 percent of Americans endorsing the country's moon mission, Kennedy accurately assessed a shift toward increased public backing for the expensive space effort. As important, the success of the manned moon landing program by 1969 — the end of the decade, as Kennedy had promised — ensured an enduring U.S. commitment to space exploration. He had indeed helped open a new frontier.

IN 1963, along with the battle to keep the moon mission on track, Kennedy struggled to find answers to continuing difficulties with Cuba and South Vietnam. At the center of his policies toward both countries was a search for effective compromises that would free his administration to focus on bigger challenges from Moscow and at home, where a presidential campaign was certain to consume considerable energy, and his plans for a tax cut, civil rights, Medicare, and aid to education had been stalled.

Cuba, which had been a constant concern since January 1961, seemed especially in need of some fresh thinking. Kennedy's eagerness to settle the Cuban problem without overt military action had been evident since the Bay of Pigs and was as apparent during the missile crisis. His affinity for finding compromises on Cuba surfaced again in November 1962, when he agreed to give up on-site inspections in return for removal of the IL-28s.

But tensions remained. Khrushchev wanted an unqualified non-invasion pledge, but the best he could get, Kennedy told him on November 21, was that "there need be no fear of any invasion of Cuba while matters take their present favorable course." In response, Khrushchev asked Kennedy to "clearly confirm . . . the pledge of non-invasion of Cuba by the United States and your allies." Kennedy replied on December 14 that "it is clearly in the interest of both sides that we reach agreement on how finally to dispose of the Cuban crisis. . . . We have never wanted to be driven by the acts of others into war in Cuba. The other side of the coin, however, is that we do need to have adequate assurances that all offensive weapons are removed from Cuba and are not reintroduced, and that Cuba itself commits no aggressive acts against any of the nations of the Western Hemisphere."

Through the fall of 1963, Kennedy remained open to the possibility that Cuban aggression or developments on the island could compel U.S. military action. At a Palm Beach conference with defense and military chiefs in December 1962, he told them that despite the lull in Cuban difficulties, "we must assume that someday we may have to go into Cuba, and when it happens, we must be prepared to do it as quickly as possible." He asked them to plan an invasion "one, two, three, or four years ahead." On February 28, when the Chiefs advised him that it would take almost three weeks to launch an attack, he wanted suggestions on how to get "some troops quickly into Cuba in the event of a general uprising." At the end of April, he asked McNamara, "Are we keeping our Cuban contingency invasion plans up to date?" In October 1963, he told McNamara that "the situation could develop in the Caribbean which would require active United States military intervention." He doubted that the United States was "prepared for this satisfactorily," and he asked McNamara to give such plans "the highest priority." The 150,000 Cuban exiles in Florida also pressed Kennedy to act against Castro or at least to allow them to act on their own. (Kennedy made futile efforts to persuade the exiles to settle in other states, which would blunt their political influence in a presidential contest for Florida's votes.)

In a speech in Miami's Orange Bowl to welcome members of the Cuban brigade, whom Castro had released after twenty months of imprisonment, Kennedy celebrated their courage and devotion to Cuba's freedom. Few of the forty thousand Cuban exiles listening to the president's speech could imagine that he had anything in mind for Cuba other than its eventual liberation from Castro's rule. Presented with the brigade's flag for safekeeping until it could be returned to Havana, Kennedy in emotional, unrehearsed remarks declared, "I can assure you that this flag will be returned to this brigade in a free Havana." The president's speech triggered shouts from the crowd of *"Guerra! Guerra!"*

The presence of thousands of Soviet troops in Cuba gave Castro's elimination an enduring appeal, but subversion remained a greater concern. At a post–missile crisis meeting on November 3, when Rusk cited sabotage in Venezuela that was "instigated by a pro-Castro group of Cubans," Kennedy responded, "We should be as tough as we can in dealing with such situations." To reduce Cuban influence all over the hemisphere, Kennedy asked U.S. national security officials to pressure Latin governments into lessening, and possibly eliminating, "the flow of students, labor leaders, etc., who go to Cuba for training and indoctrination and then go back to their own country as possible communist organizers."

In January 1963, an Interdepartmental Coordinating Committee on Cuban Affairs had been set up to replace the failed Mongoose. The unauthorized decision of William Harvey, CIA Mongoose coordinator, to send reconnaissance teams into Cuba during the missile crisis had provoked a Harvey-Bobby shouting match, which, following a blowup between them in September over other Cuban missteps, spelled the end of Mongoose. The new ICC was "to work out an improved arrangement for our handling of Cuban policy and action," including the creation of a subcommittee on Cuban subversion. It was to gather information on the dissemination of communist propaganda, arms shipments, and transfers of funds to other Latin American countries. In September 1963, Llewellyn Thompson, relying on the subcommittee's findings, told Dobrynin that Cuban-trained guerrillas were engaged in "terroristic activities" all over the hemisphere; that Cuba was "furnishing funds to revolutionary groups"; and that Castro and other Cuban leaders were publicly exhorting revolutionaries "to resort to sabotage, terrorism and guerrilla action."

Yet despite continuing interest in ousting Castro, renewed discussions yielded no better plans than in the previous two years. The ICC wished to encourage "developments within Cuba that offer the possibility of divorcing the Cuban government from its support of Sino-Soviet Communist purposes." But how? The ICC could only suggest applying "increasing degrees of political, economic, psychological and military pressures . . . until the Castro/Communist regime is overthrown." It offered no explanation of just how this would be done or why it would work. And though the CIA had resumed covert activities, including new assassination plots against Castro, they were as ineffective as before. Indeed, their schemes were often ludicrous. In 1962, for example, McCone suggested they could acquire a Soviet fighter plane through defection, purchase, or U.S. manufacture. The plane could then be used "in a provocation operation in which Soviet aircraft would appear to attack U.S. or friendly installations in order to provide an excuse for U.S. intervention." Although McCone made no mention of Cuba in his memo, the U.S. base at Guantanamo was a perfect fit for his idea. The White House ignored the proposal.

According to Lawrence Freedman, "Kennedy was maintaining his military options [against Cuba] for no better reason than his preference for never closing any options off, just in case circumstances changed." JFK's affinity for competing rapprochement proposals makes Freedman's assertion convincing. In November, as the Cuban missile crisis ended, Castro's anger at Khrushchev for giving in to U.S. pressure and agreeing to on-site inspections raised the possibility that Castro might actually welcome a rapprochement with the United States. In fact, Castro announced himself ready for an agreement with Washington, but his conditions for an accommodation — an end to Washington's economic embargo, subversion, exile raids, U-2 overflights, and control of Guantanamo — were more than any American government could accept, especially if it hoped to avoid a firestorm of criticism from Cuban exiles and their American allies.

Castro's demands did not kill Kennedy's interest in reducing Cuban-American tensions. In February, after an NSC staffer urged him to talk publicly about isolating Cuba from the Soviet bloc and not other hemisphere countries, Kennedy told newsmen that the communist threat in the hemisphere did not emanate "primarily" from Cuba. Instead, it fed on economic "hardships" suffered by Latin American peoples. If Cuban subversion disappeared, a communist threat would still exist. A few days later, when a Cuban MIG fighter fired at an American shrimp boat in the Caribbean, the administration's measured protest and a "soft" Cuban reply avoided an escalation in Cuban-American tensions, and, as the *New York Times* reported, became instead an opportunity for the two sides to discuss their overall differences.

Bobby remained the principal voice in the administration for anti-Castro action, and the failure of Mongoose and the CIA to propose practical means of ousting Castro moved him to look to Cuban exiles to rescue their country. In March 1963, when McCone told an NSC meeting that an internal military coup in Cuba was more likely than a civil uprising facilitated from the outside and predicted that congressional pressure over Cuba would ease, Bobby disputed his analysis. He also took exception to Rusk's advice against giving the Cuban exiles false hopes. The next day, he sent his brother a memo urging "periodic meetings of half a dozen or so top officials of the Government to consider Cuba and Latin America." He felt that the NSC meeting showed an insufficient commitment to new anti-Castro actions. They needed to "come up with a plan for a future Cuba." "I would not like it said a year from now," he explained, "that we could have had this internal breakup in Cuba but we just did not set the stage for it."

When the President ignored Bobby's recommendations, Bobby wrote his brother: "Do you think there was any merit to my last memo? . . . In any case, is there anything else on this matter?" Another Bobby suggestion in early April that the administration support a five-hundred-man raiding party also received no reply.

Kennedy was in no mood to exacerbate tensions with Cuba. In March, after Cuban exiles attacked Soviets ships and installations in Cuba, Kennedy expressed concern at the potential damage to Soviet-American relations and the need to prevent further assaults. He told an NSC meeting that "these in-and-out raids were probably exciting and rather pleasant for those who engage in them. They were in danger for less than an hour. This exciting activity was more fun than living in the hills of Escambray, pursued by Castro's military forces." McCone warned against openly cutting off the commandos; it would produce "intense public and press criticism" as well as congressional complaints. And while he acknowledged that the raids would probably increase difficulties with Castro and the Soviets, he also saw potential benefits, including a Soviet reappraisal of their Cuban commitment, which might cause them "to open a discussion of their presence [in Cuba] with the United States." Kennedy was not convinced. Although he was willing to consider encouraging the raiders to strike only at Cuban targets, this was as much to give himself political cover as to promote Castro's demise. Negotiations with Castro for the release of twenty-two American citizens held in Cuban prisons as CIA agents were one reason for discouraging exile attacks. James B. Donovan, a New York lawyer who had negotiated the release of the nearly twelve hundred exile Cubans captured at the Bay of Pigs in exchange for $53 million worth of medicines, had Kennedy's approval for these additional talks. In April, Kennedy privately made clear to the exiles that for the time being he wanted no more attacks. By May, the CIA described the exile groups as "puzzled with regard to the American policy toward Cuba and the exile community." Exile leaders, the CIA also reported, saw "[no] real reason for unity because obviously there is no moral or financial support forthcoming from the U.S. government and without this support there is no point to unity."

Though Donovan was careful to emphasize his status as a private citizen during his April visit, Castro and Kennedy saw him as an intermediary who might help initiate better Cuban-American relations. During his five days in Cuba, Donovan spent more than twenty-four hours in conversations with Castro. A first meeting on Sunday, April 7, lasted from 1:00 A.M. to 6:30 A.M. Castro asked Donovan for suggestions on "how relationships could be established

with the United States." When Donovan replied that American public sentiment toward Castro might be changing, as White House limits on the exiles and majority opinion against a war with Cuba
demonstrated, Castro declared that a future "ideal" Cuban government "was not to be Soviet oriented. . . . There was absolutely no
chance that Cuba would become a Soviet satellite." He also stated
that "Cuba was not exporting subversion to other Latin American
countries." He pressed Donovan to say how Havana and Washington could achieve better political relations and raised the possibility
that Donovan be given some official status that would allow him to
continue these discussions in Havana. Castro saw official relations
with the United States as a "necessity," but explained that "certain
Cuban Government officials, communists," currently limited what
he could do. A report from Donovan greatly interested Kennedy,
especially the part about Castro's eagerness for better relations and
his description of communist constraints.

In May, when Castro visited Moscow for a month, the CIA,
White House, and State Department tried to decipher the consequences for Cuban-American relations. Was Castro's visit meant to
remind the United States that no attack on Cuba would be tolerated? Was it an effort to reduce Soviet-Cuban tensions and head
off a U.S.-Cuban accommodation? Or was it a demonstration of
Khrushchev's conviction that a Cuban "rapprochement with the U.S.
[was] a necessity" and that Castro needed "indoctrination to this
end"? Although the State Department acknowledged that the visit
might signal the start of a campaign to improve Cuban-American
relations, it argued against a rapprochement: An agreement with
Castro would be destructive to the development of democracy in
Latin America and would touch off a firestorm of domestic political
opposition. Yet Kennedy did not want to close off the possibility of
reaching an accommodation with Castro. As the NSC conceded at
the end of May, all of the existing courses of action proposed for
toppling Castro "were singularly unpromising." Bundy was even
more emphatic: The anti-Castro measures being considered "will not
result in his overthrow."

Pessimism about U.S. capacity to alter conditions in Cuba, however, did not deter the administration from agreeing to renewed
raids and sabotage. The political consequences of open efforts at rapprochement were more than Kennedy felt he could risk a year before
his reelection campaign. Though raids and sabotage would not

unseat Castro, they would meet continuing domestic pressures for action and encourage the belief that he was vulnerable to defeat. In September and October, respectively, when Dobrynin and Foreign Minister Andrey Gromyko told Kennedy of Khrushchev's unhappiness with these raids, Kennedy conceded that they were serving "no useful purpose."

Consequently, albeit secretly, Kennedy agreed to further explore the possibility of improved relations. The principal advocate of change was William Attwood, a former *Look* magazine editor, who had interviewed Castro and had served from March 1961 to May 1963 as ambassador to Guinea, where he had helped bring a government friendly to Moscow into the Western camp. Appointed an adviser to the United States Mission to the U.N. in the summer of 1963, Attwood listened attentively to "neutral diplomats," who suggested "a course of action which, if successful, could remove the Cuban issue from the 1964 campaign." Stripping the Republicans of the Cuban matter by "neutralizing Cuba on our terms" had considerable appeal to Kennedy. It would also eliminate international embarrassment over the image of a superpower America bullying a weak island country. If rapprochement included the removal of all Soviet forces from Cuba, an end to Cuba's hemisphere subversion, and Havana's commitment to nonalignment in the Cold War, Kennedy believed he could sell it to the American public.

With Adlai Stevenson's support and the president's approval, Attwood secretly discussed the possibility of a Cuban-American dialogue with Carlos Lechuga, Cuba's U.N. ambassador. Lechuga urged that someone travel to Havana for an initial talk with Castro. Attwood was not hopeful. Lechuga and Castro might be interested, but they were "too well boxed in by such hardliners as Guevara to be able to maneuver much." But Attwood, who believed that he could handle the assignment in secret, was eager to try. After a meeting with Bobby about possible negotiations, Attwood suggested to Lechuga that they hold secret talks at the U.N. "The ball is in Cuban hands and the door is ajar," Attwood told Bundy in October.

Kennedy's receptivity to a possible accommodation with Castro registered forcefully on Jean Daniel, a French journalist on his way to Havana at the end of October. Agreeing to a meeting with Daniel at Ben Bradlee's urging, Kennedy did not want to talk about Vietnam or say much about de Gaulle. "I'd like to talk to you about Cuba," Kennedy said. He began by acknowledging U.S. responsibility for

Cuban miseries perpetrated by Batista. "I believe that we created, built and manufactured the Castro movement out of whole cloth and without realizing it," he declared. Batista was "the incarnation of a number of sins on the part of the United States." All this, which Kennedy assumed would be repeated to Castro, was meant to suggest that he had genuine concern for Cuba's well-being. Castro's willingness to act as an agent of Soviet communism in Cuba and the hemisphere, Kennedy added, had put them at odds; indeed, Castro had brought the world to the brink of a nuclear war. Kennedy did not know whether Castro understood this or even cared. Kennedy stood up at this point to signal an end to the conversation, but Daniel asked him about the economic blockade of Cuba. The end of subversive activities in the hemisphere could bring an end to the blockade, Kennedy replied. Kennedy asked Daniel to see him again after returning from Cuba. "Castro's reactions interest me," he said.

Castro surprised the Americans by sending word that he "would very much like to talk," but that it would have to be in Cuba, not at the U.N. He "appreciated the importance of discretion" and offered to send a plane to Mexico or Key West to fly an American official to Cuba, where they could meet in a secret airfield near Havana. Castro did not wish to be seen as in any way soliciting U.S. friendship. As a Greek intermediary told Attwood, "Castro would welcome a normalization of relations with the United States if he could do so without losing too much face." Similarly, Bobby told Attwood that the administration could not risk accusations that it was "trying to make a deal with Castro."

On November 12, Bundy advised Attwood that the president saw the visit of any U.S. official to Cuba now as impractical. Instead, he, as Bobby had before him, suggested that Castro send his personal envoy to see Attwood in New York. Kennedy wanted Castro to say first whether there was any prospect of Cuban independence from Moscow and an end to hemisphere subversion. "Without an indication of readiness to move in these directions, it is hard for us to see what could be accomplished by a visit to Cuba." Bundy advised Attwood to make clear to the Cubans "that we were not suppliants in this matter and the initiative for exploratory conversations was coming from the Cubans." On the eighteenth, Castro sent word to Attwood that the invitation to come to Cuba remained open and that the security of the visit was guaranteed. When Attwood said that a preliminary meeting "was essential to make sure there was something useful to talk about," Castro's emissary promised to send an "agenda" for discussion between Attwood and Lechuga as a prelude to a future meeting with Castro.

On the same day, Kennedy spoke in Miami before the Inter-American Press Association. His speech included veiled references to an altered relationship with Cuba. Latin America's problems would "not be solved simply by complaining about Castro, by blaming all problems on communism, or generals or nationalism," he said. He declared it "important to restate what now divides Cuba from my country and from the other countries of this hemisphere. It is the fact that a small band of conspirators has stripped the Cuban people of their freedom and handed over the independence and sovereignty of the Cuban nation to forces beyond the hemisphere. They have made Cuba . . . a weapon in an effort dictated by external powers to subvert the other American Republics. This, and this alone, divides us. As long as this is true, nothing is possible. Without it, everything is possible. Once this barrier is removed, we will be ready and anxious to work with the Cuban people in pursuit of those progressive goals which a few short years ago stirred their hopes and the sympathy of many people throughout the hemisphere."

The Cuban community in Florida did not miss the president's implied receptivity to a fresh start in relations with Cuba. In general, the exiles saw the speech as "expressions of willingness to accept 'Fidelismo sin Fidel.'" This did not please the substantial number of conservatives in the community. If they had known about the Attwood initiative and the Daniel conversation, they would have been up in arms.

There was still intense pressure for covert action. On October 1, Desmond Fitzgerald, the CIA's director of planning and new head of secret operations, described a 5 to 7 percent decline in Cuban production, with a 20 percent drop in the sugar harvest, which had caused a deterioration in living conditions and undermined Castro's popularity. The fact that the economic downturn had not yet affected the Cuban military made it difficult to foresee a coup. But when the decline continued into November, "causing increasing hardships to the civilian population," U.S. analysts thought that Castro's "grip [was] weakening." Since U.S.-sponsored sabotage seemed likely to further weaken the economy and Castro's popularity, McCone urged a continuation of such harassment.

Kennedy, however, had heard too much optimistic talk about bringing down Castro to trust current assessments and predictions. At a November 12 meeting on Cuba, he asked whether the sabotage program "was worthwhile and whether it would accomplish our purpose." Nevertheless, his unresolved problems with Cuba and continuing worries about threats to the hemisphere and his own reelection made him reluctantly receptive to continuing subversion. Indeed, no one listening to his Inter-American Press Association speech on the eighteenth could have doubted that overturning Castro's government remained an active option.

Kennedy's dual-track Cuban policy in 1963 did not, however, include assassinating Castro. A CIA scheme (or, more precisely, a Desmond Fitzgerald scheme) set in motion on November 22, to have Rolando Cubela Secades, an anti-Castro member of the Cuban government, kill Castro with an injection from a hypodermic needle hidden in a ballpoint pen, was directly at odds with Kennedy's policies. It was one thing to hope that hit-and-run raids and economic sanctions could provoke an internal uprising, but assassinating Castro seemed certain to make things worse. The devoted communists, who were allegedly holding Castro back from a rapprochement, seemed likely to react to a martyred Castro by ending any chance of accommodation.

No one knows what the future of Cuban-American relations would have been after November 22 or during a second Kennedy term, when he would not have had to answer to American voters again. The great likelihood that Castro was going to outlast U.S. plotting against him made it almost certain that Kennedy would have had to deal with him during that second term. And given the growing interest in moving beyond the stale conflict of the previous five years, who can doubt that a Cuban-American accommodation might have been an achievement of Kennedy's second four years? Whatever the uncertainties in November 1963 about future Castro-Kennedy dealings, it is clear that they signaled a mutual interest in finding a way through their antagonisms, which were doing neither of them any good.

UNCERTAINTIES OVER CUBA were matched by those on Vietnam. Back in February 1962, after the administration announced the creation of Military Assistance Command, Vietnam (MACV), and an anonymous official told the press that the United States was determined "to win" the war, a reporter had pressed the president to answer a Republican charge that he had been less than candid with the public about U.S. involvement. Kennedy had reviewed the "long history" of U.S. commitment, urged a continuation of the "very strong bipartisan consensus," and described U.S. assistance as logistics and "training missions," not combat. In March and April, reporters had only three brief questions about Vietnam: How was the war going? Would he ask Congress for approval before sending combat troops? And what did he intend to do about American soldiers being killed? Kennedy's assurances that the South Vietnamese were holding their own, that he did not plan to send combat troops, and that the handful of losses were regrettable accidents of war had satisfied the press, which asked nothing more about the war in the President's twice monthly news conferences during the rest of the year.

The lull in discussion about Vietnam, however, ended in November and December 1962 when conflicting reports about progress in the strategic hamlet program reached Washington and then leaked to the press. Indications that Diem saw the program more as a way to control rural areas than to ensure their security, coupled with a paucity of hard information from the hamlets themselves, provoked questions in the executive branch about the program's effectiveness. In early November, Mike Forrestal, the State Department's official most responsible for Vietnam, told Bobby that "Averell and I feel that the war is not going as well out there as one might be led to believe. . . . The political problem is growing relatively worse. . . . The major fault lies with the GVN." To get a clearer picture of developments, Kennedy asked Mike Mansfield, who enjoyed a reputation as an Asian expert, to visit Vietnam.

On December 18, Kennedy received two conflicting reports on Vietnamese conditions and prospects. Theodore Heaver, the State Department's Vietnam specialist, who had spent March and April in the country and then another forty days visiting seventeen provinces in the fall of 1962, acknowledged that "fact is not always easy to come by in Viet-Nam." He had concluded nevertheless that a standoff in the war was now more likely than Saigon's defeat. "But the tide has not turned. The VC are still very strong, and our key programs are still in many respects experimental." If they worked, he foresaw a GVN standing on its own "with greatly reduced US military assistance."

Mike Mansfield had been less confident. He said, "[It distresses me] to hear the situation described in much the same terms as on my last visit, although it is seven years and billions of dollars later.

In short, it would be well to face the fact that we are once again at the beginning of the beginning." He certainly had heard "extremely optimistic" evaluations of the strategic hamlet program, which Vietnamese and Americans in Saigon predicted would solve the insurgency problem in a year or two. But having heard optimistic talk like this from the French in the early 1950s, he doubted the wisdom of uncritically accepting such current hopes. The "real tests [of strategic hamlets] are yet to come." They involved "an immense job of social engineering, dependent on great outlays of aid on our part for many years and a most responsive, alert and enlightened leadership in the government of Vietnam." If current remedies failed, Mansfield foresaw "a truly massive commitment of American military personnel and other resources — in short, going to war fully ourselves against the guerrillas — and the establishment of some form of neocolonial rule in South Vietnam. That is an alternative which I most emphatically do not recommend," he had told Kennedy. "Our role is and must remain secondary. . . . It is their country, their future which is most at stake, not ours." The alternative to being trapped in unwanted commitments in Vietnam was to press for negotiations that could neutralize all of Southeast Asia.

At a December 1962 news conference, Kennedy took a wait-and-see attitude. "As you know, we have about 10 or 11 times as many men there as we had a year ago. We've had a number of casualties. We put in an awful lot of equipment. We are going ahead with the strategic hamlet proposal." But he acknowledged "the great difficulty . . . in fighting a guerrilla war . . . especially in terrain as difficult as South Viet-Nam. So we don't see the end of the tunnel, but I must say I don't think it is darker than it was a year ago, and in some ways lighter." Privately, Kennedy was less sanguine. He had angrily told Mansfield during a meeting in Palm Beach that his advisers were giving him more optimistic assessments of what to expect in Vietnam. "I got angry with Mike for disagreeing with our policy so completely," Kennedy later told O'Donnell, "and I got angry with myself because I found myself agreeing with him." Kennedy's public conformity with optimistic estimates, however, served a useful political purpose: If he was going to get out of Vietnam, it was essential to encourage the idea that there was progress in the war and that the United States could soon reduce its role in the fighting. As Defense Department public affairs officer Arthur Sylvester famously said, "It's inherent in [the] government's right, if necessary, to lie to save itself."

On February 1, Kennedy met with army Chief of Staff General Wheeler, who had assessed conditions in Vietnam during a January visit. Wheeler frustrated and irritated Kennedy with a report Forrestal described as "rosy euphoria" and "a complete waste of . . . time." Wheeler also was no help in suggesting how to bring the GVN more closely into line with "U.S. views on fighting the war and on foreign policy," or how to "develop gradually a more independent posture for the U.S. in South Vietnam and very carefully dissociate ourselves from those policies and practices of the GVN of which we disapprove."

Troubled by the different assessments of South Vietnamese effectiveness, Kennedy sent Roger Hilsman, still the head of the State Department's intelligence division, and Forrestal to Vietnam to give him their appraisal of the war. Although they believed that things were "going much better than they were a year ago," they did not see them "going nearly so well as the people here in Saigon both military and civilian think they are." The Viet Cong were "being hurt," but "the negative side of the ledger" was "still awesome." Their overall judgment was that the United States was "probably winning, but certainly more slowly than we had hoped," and they expected the war to "last longer than we would like, cost more in terms of both lives and money than we anticipated, and prolong the period in which a sudden and dramatic event would upset the gains already made." The CIA, which weighed in with a report now as well, said "the war remains a slowly escalating stalemate."

While Kennedy announced in the opening paragraphs of his January 1963 State of the Union Message that "the spearpoint of aggression has been blunted in Viet-Nam," he also publicly conceded that Vietnam, along with Berlin, the Congo, Cuba, Laos, and the Middle East, remained "points of uncertainty." He could not see how South Vietnam would survive without substantial U.S. economic and military aid. "I think that unless you want to withdraw from the field and decide that it is in the national interest to permit that area to collapse," he told a news conference on March 6, the United States had to continue providing support. In an April 2 special message to Congress on economic and military aid to nations battling communist subversion, Kennedy said that assistance to beleaguered countries like Vietnam should not be reduced, however strong the desire to help balance the U.S. budget by cutting foreign aid. Of course he was eager to protect Vietnam from a communist takeover. But by 1963 he was more skeptical than ever about putting in ground forces, which would suffer losses and increase pressure on him to commit additional men to the fighting. He wished to mute America's role in the conflict and leave himself free to withdraw sixteen thousand U.S. military "advisers" now on the ground (about twenty times the number that had been there at the start of 1961), some of whom, he publicly acknowledged, were being killed in combat. At the end of January, Kennedy instructed Harriman to clear all visits to Vietnam. According to Hilsman, the president called him to complain about "press reports of unscheduled visits by senior U.S. officials to Vietnam." The stories appeared to increase the U.S. commitment in Vietnam. "That is exactly what I don't want to do," he told Hilsman.

A *Washington Post* interview published on May 12 with Ngo Dinh Nhu, Diem's brother and director of the strategic hamlet program, increased Kennedy's interest in withdrawal. Nhu complained that there were too many U.S. military advisers in Vietnam and that at least half could be safely withdrawn. At a news conference on the twenty-second, when asked to comment on Nhu's remarks, Kennedy testily declared the United States ready to withdraw "any number of troops, any time the Government of South Vietnam would suggest it. The day after it was suggested, we would have some troops on their way home."

That month, Kennedy began planning the withdrawal of U.S. military advisers. But a plan was not a commitment. O'Donnell remembered a conversation between the president and Mansfield that month in which Kennedy said that he "now agreed with the Senator's thinking on the need for a complete withdrawal from Vietnam. 'But I can't do it until 1965 — after I'm reelected.'" A withdrawal in 1963 or 1964, Kennedy feared, would jeopardize his chances for a second term. After Mansfield left, according to O'Donnell, Kennedy told him, "If I tried to pull out completely now from Vietnam, we would have another Joe McCarthy scare on our hands, but I can do it after I'm reelected. So we had better make damned sure that I am reelected." In the 1970s, Mansfield confirmed that Kennedy had told him of his interest in withdrawing military advisers. He "felt that even then with 16,000 troops we were in too deep."

However calculating Kennedy was about politics — and he and Bobby did not hesitate to cut lots of corners — it is hard to credit his willingness to let boys die in Vietnam for the sake of his reelection. What seems more plausible is that Kennedy never forgot that politics and policy making were the art of the possible. He had no intention of being drawn into an expansion of American ground forces in Vietnam and the possibility of an open-ended war. At the same time, however, he was not ready to say just when he would reduce U.S. forces and ultimately bring them all home. There was always the chance that if his actions backfired politically and he was voted out, the next president would send even more troops. Barry Goldwater had certainly given no sign of desiring any sort of Vietnam pullback.

Diem undermined Kennedy's political strategy by provoking a crisis with his country's Buddhist majority. Between May and July, Buddhist demonstrations, including self-immolations by monks, against repressive government policies embarrassed Washington. The abuse of a religious majority by Diem's Catholic minority regime particularly discomfited Kennedy. On July 17, a reporter asked the president whether the conflict between Diem's government and the Buddhists, which had stirred "a good deal of public concern" in the United States, had become "an impediment to the effectiveness of American aid in the war against the Viet Cong?" Kennedy thought it had and regretted the conflict at a time when the military effort had begun to show progress.

During the summer of 1963, Kennedy largely left management of U.S.-Vietnamese relations to subordinates. The civil rights crisis, his trip to Europe, the tax cut, negotiation of the test ban treaty, and the campaign to ensure its Senate approval claimed most of his attention. Experience had taught him that appearing indecisive was better than rushing into a policy that ended up failing and having ongoing negative consequences, like the Bay of Pigs. In the six months between May 22 and November 22, for example, none of the 115 telephone conversations he chose to record was about Vietnam. Of the 107 taped meetings the Kennedy Library has for this period, only 14 include discussions about Vietnam, and all but one of these were in the three months between August and November, when problems with Diem reached a breaking point. In June, after the State Department warned Diem that unless he worked out an accommodation with the Buddhists, the United States would "have to re-examine our entire relationship with his regime," Kennedy temporarily reclaimed control of Vietnam policy by embargoing any further warnings or ultimatums to Diem without his clearance. On July 3, Max Frankel of the *New York Times* described Kennedy's concern to keep uncertainties about Vietnam as quiet as possible. "Once in a while," he wrote, "Washington remembers that there is a war on in Vietnam. . . . But for long stretches, the war against communist-led guerrillas in Vietnam fades from memory here, not because no one cares, but because the men who care most decided long ago to discuss it as little as possible."

Kennedy's hesitancy over what to do about Vietnam registered strongly with his advisers in conversations between June and October. Or, more to the point, his uncertainty about how to lead Vietnam toward greater stability and freedom from communist control without a significant increase in U.S. aid, especially American combat troops, was evident to aides battling to push him in one direction or another. His indecisiveness was partly the result of an argument among his advisers about what would work. A few even thought there was nothing that could be done. Like Kennedy, Paul Kattenburg, a State Department Asian expert and chairman of an interdepartmental working group on Vietnam, listened to the debate with mounting doubts that anyone in Washington or Saigon had a solution to the Vietnam problem. Neither supporters of Diem and strategic hamlets nor advocates of a new government led by a military chief who would follow a more aggressive counterinsurgency plan convinced him that they knew how to save South Vietnam from communism. He urged withdrawal.

Kennedy decided to make Henry Cabot Lodge ambassador to Saigon. He saw the appointment as good politics and a boost for effective policy. Possibly remembering FDR's selection of Herbert Hoover's secretary of war Patrick J. Hurley as ambassador to China in 1944 to negotiate a coalition between the nationalists and the communists, Kennedy understood that sending a prominent Republican to Saigon would give him some political cover should Vietnam collapse. A fresh ambassador would also allow the U.S. embassy to renew efforts to bend Diem to Washington's will and control American correspondents in Saigon, whose front-page reports on the Buddhist crisis were undermining Kennedy's efforts to mute Vietnam as a compelling issue in the United States. Diem certainly saw Lodge's selection as evidence that Kennedy intended to control or unseat him. "They can send ten Lodges," Diem said defiantly, "but I will not permit myself or my country to be humiliated."

At a July 4 meeting with Bundy, Harriman, Ball, Hilsman, and Forrestal, Kennedy had heard mostly bad news. Diem's uncompromising antagonism to the Buddhists might force the United States "publicly to disassociate itself from the GVN's Buddhist policy." Forcing Diem's brother and sister-in-law, the Nhus, out of the government seemed like a good but undoable proposal. Coup attempts over the next several months with unpredictable results seemed likely. In keeping with his reluctance to decide anything about Vietnam or to wait on events before acting, Kennedy's only response was to get Lodge to Saigon as soon as possible, though he told Hilsman to work out the actual timing. Moreover, on July 8, when Kennedy met with outgoing ambassador Fred Nolting, he decided against sending Diem a personal message pressing him to initiate reforms (despite a *New York Times* report to the contrary). He also ignored the urging of State Department officials during the next month to pressure journalists to accept the "official" view of "the Vietnamese situation" and to encourage greater aggressiveness by U.S. officials pushing Diem to accept a policy of conciliation with the Buddhists.

His unresponsiveness reflected not indifference but a continuing sense of limitations. With Diem's government apparently self-destructing, Kennedy wanted to keep his distance from any direct involvement in the growing crisis. Compared to the many lengthy meetings he had on Cuba and other foreign and domestic matters, a thirty-five-minute discussion with an ambassador heading into a firestorm without any but the most general presidential directive speaks loudly about Kennedy's intentions. He remained uncertain about what to do and worried about being trapped in an unwinnable war.

A *New York Times* David Halberstam story saying things were going badly in the fighting heightened Kennedy's concern about the war effort, as demonstrated by a request on August 15 to McNamara and Rusk for an update on the effectiveness of "military operations in Vietnam." The following day marine corps general Victor Krulak told McNamara that Halberstam's article not only suffered from "factual and statistical weaknesses" but also exhibited "a lack of understanding of our entire Vietnam strategy." Halberstam, Krulak said, missed the fact that we were "driving the Viet Cong southward — away from their sources of strength and compressing them in the southernmost area of the peninsula." The hope was to trap and let them "rot there. If Halberstam understood clearly this strategy, he might not have undertaken to write his disingenuous article." Krulak repeated his optimistic assessment of conditions in Vietnam in a meeting with the president on August 21.

At the same time, Mansfield weighed in with renewed warnings to Kennedy that regardless of whether "[we dealt] with the present government or with a replacement — we are in for a very long haul to develop even a modicum of stability in Viet Nam. And, in the end, the costs in men and money could go at least as high as those in Korea." Mansfield urged Kennedy to ask himself "the fundamental question: Is South Viet Nam as important to us as the premise on which we are now apparently operating indicates?" Mansfield advised the president to begin stressing "the relatively limited importance of the area in terms of specific U.S. interests" and consider withdrawing 10 percent of our advisers from Vietnam as a "symbolic gesture" and indication that under certain circumstances we would end our commitment to Vietnam.

No direct record exists of what Kennedy thought about Krulak's assessment or Mansfield's recommendations. But a White House memo on August 20 from Max Taylor to McNamara reflected both contradictory analyses. As a follow-up to Kennedy's May directive on U.S. troop strength in Vietnam, Taylor outlined a plan for the withdrawal of one thousand advisers by the end of 1963. Though the final decision to implement the plan was to be withheld until late October, the pullback was to be well publicized in order "to produce the desired psychological impact, both domestic and foreign." The plan fit perfectly with Kennedy's apparent eagerness either to seize upon battlefield gains to announce reduced U.S. commitments or to declare an American withdrawal in response to Saigon's political instability and failure to fight effectively.

When Lodge arrived in Saigon on August 22, the prospect of a South Vietnamese collapse seemed more likely than a victory. On the twenty-first, despite promises to Nolting that he would be conciliatory toward the Buddhists and would expel Madame Nhu (who had applauded Buddhist immolations and openly advocated uncompromising repression of dissident monks), Diem had unleashed a nationwide attack on pagodas to crush Buddhist opposition. Kennedy now felt compelled to instruct Lodge to inform Diem that he must rid himself of the Nhus' influence; should he refuse, Lodge was to tell Vietnamese military chiefs that we could no longer support Diem. Lodge was to "examine all possible alternative leadership and make detailed plans as to how we might bring about Diem's replacement if this should become necessary." Kennedy directed that Lodge and General Paul Harkins, the head of MACV, have the freedom to implement the department's instructions by whatever means they believed wise. When Lodge responded that chances of persuading Diem to act against the Nhus were nil and asked permission to go directly to the generals, Kennedy agreed.

Almost at once, however, Kennedy began to have second thoughts. He felt pressured by Halberstam's stories that were critical of Diem and by State Department advocates who saw no alternative to dumping Diem. "Diem and his brother, however repugnant in some respects, have done a great deal along the lines that we desire," Kennedy said, "and when we move to eliminate this government, it should not be a result of *New York Times* pressure." (At a meeting on August 26, Kennedy told state and defense officials that "we [should] not permit Halberstam unduly to influence our actions.") Again recalling the Bay of Pigs failure, Kennedy worried that he was being drawn into a similar misstep in Vietnam. Kennedy wanted to know what chance of succeeding a coup had, and he wanted to ensure that whatever the United States did would remain hidden from public view. Kennedy also asked "what would happen if we find we are faced with having to live with Diem and Nhu." Hilsman said it would be "horrible," and Rusk advised that unless there were a major change in GVN policy, the United States would either have to leave or send in combat troops.

At another meeting the next day, Kennedy peppered his aides with questions about prospects for a successful coup. Nolting doubted the likelihood of a "clean coup" and dismissed the Vietnamese generals as lacking "the guts of Diem or Nhu." Krulak assured the president that the current civil disturbances were having no significant impact on the military campaign against the communists. Kennedy responded that he saw "no point in trying a coup unless there was a chance of its success." Moreover, unpersuaded by Krulak's assurance, he thought that it was possible to delay a coup and wait to see if internal divisions were undermining the war effort. Kennedy ended the meeting by repeating Nolting's doubts about the ability of the Vietnamese generals to replace Diem, emphasizing the need to hide any U.S. role in a coup, and directing that Lodge and Harkins be asked for their opinions on "whether we should proceed with the generals or wait."

But despite Kennedy's doubts, the pressure to support a coup was now too great to reverse. The CIA analysts in Saigon warned that if Diem and the Nhus continued in power, "they and Vietnam [would] stagger on to final defeat at the hands of their own people and the VC" and "American public opinion and Congress, as well as world opinion, would force withdrawal or reduction of American support for VN." Lodge and Harkins also recommended a coup, and at a meeting on the twenty-eighth, George Ball said that it would be "difficult if not impossible" for the United States to live with the existing government in Saigon. He added that as for a coup, the administration was already "beyond the point of no return." Kennedy disagreed, and Nolting opposed a coup as a breach of faith with Diem. But Ball objected that it was Diem, not the United States, that had broken promises. Harriman was even more emphatic, giving Nolting a tongue-lashing that embarrassed everyone in the room. Diem had double-crossed us, Harriman snapped, and without a successful coup we would face defeat in Vietnam. Nevertheless, Max Taylor, McNamara, McCone, and Johnson shared Nolting's doubts. "The government split in two," Bobby said. "It was the only time really, in three years, the government was broken in two." The debate over what to do became so heated that Kennedy told Charlie Bartlett, "My God! My government's coming apart!"

The passions reflected memories and assessments of the recent past. If only the United States had found a reliable replacement for Chiang Kai-shek, the logic went, it might have saved China from communist control. However costly American losses in Korea, U.S. intervention had certainly rescued Seoul from Pyongyang. And coup advocates saw little resemblance between Cuba and South Vietnam, where the United States could act decisively with generals ready to follow our lead.

After hearing Lodge argue that "any course is risky, and no action at all is perhaps the riskiest of all," and "we are launched on a course from which there is no respectable turning back: The overthrow of the Diem government," Kennedy agreed to a U.S.-backed coup. As with the Bay of Pigs, however, he wished to mute America's role as much as possible. To ensure against another embarrassing defeat, Kennedy sent Lodge a top secret or strictly personal cable marked "no Department or other distribution whatever." "Until the very moment of the go signal for the operation by the Generals," Kennedy wrote, "I must reserve a contingent right to change course and reverse previous instructions. While fully aware of your assessment of the consequences of such a reversal, I know from experience that failure is more destructive than an appearance of indecision. . . .

When we go, we must go to win, but it will be better to change our minds than fail. And if our national interest should require a change of mind, we must not be afraid of it." Lodge did not dispute the president's authority, but he warned that the coup would have to be "a Vietnamese affair with a momentum of its own. Should this happen you may not be able to control it, i.e. the 'go signal' may be given by the Generals."

The accuracy of Lodge's analysis became apparent the next day. By the afternoon of August 30, U.S. officials agreed that "the Generals were either backing off or were wallowing," and that prospects for a change of government were "very thin." On the thirty-first, the CIA station in Saigon reported that "this particular coup is finished." The Vietnamese told Harkin that they "did not feel ready and did not have sufficient balance of forces." Lodge cabled the State Department that evening: "There is neither the will nor the organization among the generals to accomplish anything." Rusk now felt that they were back to where they had been on August 21, and that they needed to reopen communications with Diem. He also stated, "We, first, should decide that we will not pull out of Viet-Nam and, second, that the US is not going to operate a coup d'etat itself." McNamara, Taylor, and LBJ agreed. Johnson thought it would be a disaster to pull out or stage a coup. Instead of "playing cops and robbers," he said, we should get on with winning the war.

Only Paul Kattenburg dissented. He thought the advisers around Kennedy were "hopeless. . . . There was not a single person there that knew what he was talking about. . . . They didn't know Vietnam. They didn't know the past. . . . The more this meeting went on, the more I sat there and thought, 'God, we're walking into a major disaster.'" Unable to contain himself, Kattenburg declared that he had known Diem for ten years, and the South Vietnamese leader was incapable of change. He predicted steady deterioration in Saigon and advised a dignified withdrawal.

In CBS and NBC interviews during the first two weeks of September, Kennedy tried to pressure Saigon into establishing greater popular control and to remind the American people why we were involved in Southeast Asia: "I don't think . . . unless a greater effort is made by the Government to win popular support that the war can be won out there. In the final analysis, it is their war. They are the ones who have to win it or lose it. We can help them, we can give them equipment, we can send our men out there as advisers, but they have to win it, the people of Viet-Nam against the Communists. . . . But I don't agree with those who say we should withdraw. That would be a great mistake. . . . This is a very important struggle even though it is far away. We . . . made this effort to defend Europe. Now Europe is quite secure. We also have to participate — we may not like it — in the defense of Asia." Did he believe in the "domino theory"? Chet Huntley asked him. "I believe [in] it," Kennedy declared. The loss of Vietnam would "[give] the impression that the wave of the future in southeast Asia was China and the Communists." The interviews not only signaled Diem that Washington insisted on greater popular rule and encouraged Americans to back a limited war effort but also implied, despite Kennedy's denials and domino theory conceits, that he would consider withdrawing unless the South Vietnamese effectively met the communist threat.

Having used his television appearances to prod Diem and suggest future U.S. options, Kennedy now wanted to get Vietnam off the front pages. Its continued presence seemed likely to undermine relations with Saigon and provoke a public debate between those advocating a greater military effort and those eager to abandon a repressive regime fighting an unsuccessful civil war. A public argument over what to do about Vietnam seemed certain to increase Kennedy's problems. Consequently, on September 3, Kennedy told State Department public affairs officer Robert Manning that it would be a good idea to avoid press interviews and television appearances on Vietnam. When Manning reported that "Hilsman had been turning down press calls and TV requests, the President agreed that was wise."

Privately, Kennedy simultaneously pursued two options. He increased pressure on Diem to reform his government while also signaling the Vietnamese generals that the United States remained interested in a coup. "We should wait for the generals to contact us," he said in a meeting on September 3. "When they come to us we will talk to them. [But] we should avoid letting the generals think that the U.S. [has] backed off."

In the meantime, he tried again to persuade Diem to abandon repressive, anti-Buddhist policies. At a White House meeting on September 6, Bobby said, "We have to be tough. . . . Lodge has to do more than say our President is unhappy. We have to tell Diem that he must do the things we demand or we will have to cut down our effort as forced by the U.S. public." The president was particularly concerned about "shutting up" Madame Nhu, "if only for the public relations problem here in this country." Madame Nhu had publicly claimed that the CIA was planning a coup and that Lodge was trying to remove her from Vietnam or even have her "murdered." (Told of Madame Nhu's actions, Kennedy facetiously suggested a publicity release pointing out that in one week Madame Nhu, Castro, Governor George Wallace, and Mao Tse-tung had all attacked him.) The CIA also reported that Nhu had "ordered Vietnamese soldiers to open fire on Americans or foreigners involved in acts hostile to the GVN." The State Department now cabled Lodge that "from the viewpoint of Vietnamese solidarity and world and domestic US opinion, it is important that Nhu not have a key role."

Conflicting assessments of the war made Kennedy's decisions on Vietnam as difficult as ever. Reports from Krulak and Harkins on Krulak's visit to interview U.S. military advisers could not have been more upbeat. They described the Vietnamese military as "attentive to fighting the war, certain that steady progress is being made, convinced that present thrust will ultimately bring victory, [and] assured that their units are worrying about the Viet Cong and not about politics or religion." If there had been any change in the war effort, it was "small." Krulak predicted that "the Viet Cong war will be won if the current U.S. military and sociological programs are pursued, irrespective of the grave defects in the ruling regime."

But Hilsman and Harriman were "sore as hell" over these reports that said "everything's wonderful in Vietnam." Joseph Mendenhall, another Asian expert in the State Department, who visited Vietnam with Krulak, disputed the general's assessment. He saw "a virtual breakdown of the civil government in Saigon as well as a pervasive atmosphere of fear and hate arising from the police reign of terror and the arrests of students. The war against the Viet Cong has become secondary to the 'war' against the regime." Mendenhall concluded that "the war against the Viet Cong could not be won if Nhu remains in Vietnam." Referring to Krulak and Mendenhall, Kennedy asked, "The two of you did visit the same country, didn't you?"

Kennedy's frustration was reflected in his comments and questions to advisers at a September 10 meeting. He "recalled that he had made a number of public statements condemning the Vietnamese Government's actions but this has ignited nothing." When Rufus Phillips, a director of rural operations in Vietnam, suggested cuts in U.S. aid, Kennedy asked, "What about the possibility that Nhu's response would be to withdraw funds from the war and field to Saigon — retreating to Saigon and charging publicly that the US was causing them to lose the war?" He also wanted to know how

Krulak's differences with Mendenhall and Phillips could be explained. Krulak responded that "the battle was not being lost in a purely military sense." Phillips countered that "this was not a military war but a political war. It was a war for men's minds more than battles against the Viet Cong."

The only immediate effective step Kennedy saw was to rein in the American press war over differences in U.S. policy toward Vietnam. He declared himself "disturbed at the tendency both in Washington and Saigon to fight our own battles via the newspapers. . . . He said he wanted these different views fought out at this table and not indirectly through the newspapers." He saw only negative results from this bad publicity — pressure to escalate our commitments without sufficient consideration of consequences or to withdraw support before it seemed wise to do so.

Kennedy continued to temporize for the next several weeks. With his advisers remaining sharply divided and CIA reports of new plans to oust Diem and Nhu and, if necessary, assassinate them, Kennedy believed it best to wait on developments, so he sent McNamara and Taylor to Saigon on yet another fact-finding mission. Lodge believed it a poor idea. It would "be taken here as [a] sign that we have decided to forgive and forget and will be regarded as marking the end of our period of disapproval of the oppressive measures. . . . It would certainly put a wet blanket on those working for a change of government." Lodge also feared that it would take the pressure off Diem to respond to his push for reforms. Kennedy, however, believed that they could "stage manage" the mission so as not to give Diem any comfort or undercut Lodge.

On October 2, in a report to Kennedy on their trip, McNamara and Taylor cited "great progress" in the military campaign, acknowledged "serious political tensions in Saigon," and saw small likelihood of a successful coup, although assassination of Diem or Nhu was "always a possibility." They had little hope that American pressure would "move Diem and Nhu toward moderation," but without such pressure they seemed "certain to continue past patterns of behavior." McNamara and Taylor suggested the suspension of some economic aid to deter Diem from further political repression but recommended waiting two to four months to see his response before considering more drastic action. They also counseled against actively encouraging a change in government, though building contacts with "an alternative leadership" seemed like a good idea on the off chance that unforeseen factors might precipitate a coup.

As for the U.S. role in the war, McNamara and Taylor recommended stepped-up training "so that essential functions now performed by U.S. military personnel can be carried out by Vietnamese by the end of 1965. It should be possible to withdraw the bulk of U.S. personnel by that time." In accordance with this program, "the Defense Department should announce in the very near future . . . plans to withdraw 1000 U.S. military personnel by the end of 1963." The publication of this plan should be "explained in low key [terms] as an initial step in a long-term program to replace U.S. personnel with Vietnamese without impairment of the war effort."

The report was hardly a vote of confidence in Diem's regime — it was more a confession of bankruptcy than a viable statement of how to compel reform in Saigon and preserve South Vietnam's autonomy. Asked at an October 9 news conference how U.S. policy was progressing in Vietnam, Kennedy frankly stated, "I don't think that there have been changes in the situation in the last month. I think we are still dealing with the same problems."

Unable to compel changes in Vietnam, Kennedy focused instead on getting the U.S. government to speak with one voice and ensure that U.S. newspaper reports did not generate pressure on him to take unwise steps. Bundy directed state, CIA, DOD, USIA, and JCS to clear with the White House all cabled instructions to "the field." Bundy did not underestimate the resentment such an order might generate from officials convinced they had a "right" not to be monitored so closely from above. "But," Bundy told Kennedy, "your interest is not served by the uncritical acceptance of that right."

At the same time, Kennedy tried to curtail critical press reports coming from Saigon. In September, when Halberstam reported a split between U.S. military advisers and the Vietnamese on the strategic hamlet program, Kennedy had asked McNamara to assess the accuracy of the story. McNamara's reply that the article was inaccurate and that Halberstam's objectivity was open to question heightened Kennedy's irritation with a press corps that he believed demonstrated an excessively "zealous spirit of criticism and complaint." On October 21, during a lunch with Arthur "Punch" Sulzberger, the new publisher of the *New York Times*, Kennedy urged him to get Halberstam out of Vietnam. Sulzberger refused, and Kennedy was left to worry all the more.

Kennedy worried that publicly promising to withdraw one thousand troops by the end of the year might undermine larger withdrawal plans if conditions made it unwise. Should the United States have to back away from an announced withdrawal, it seemed likely to encourage press discussion of the need for an expanded U.S. effort. But McNamara's argument that an announcement had "great value" as a way to answer complaints that we were becoming "bogged down forever in Vietnam" persuaded Kennedy to go ahead as planned. Kennedy did not dispute McNamara's additional statement at an October 2 meeting: "We need a way to get out of Vietnam, and this is a way of doing it."

At the close of the meeting, Pierre Salinger publicly announced the president's endorsement of the McNamara-Taylor recommendations. He accepted "their judgment that the major part of the U.S. military task can be completed by the end of 1965. . . . They reported that by the end of this year, the U.S. program for training Vietnamese should have progressed to the point where 1,000 U.S. military personnel assigned to South Viet Nam can be withdrawn." Kennedy had not wanted Diem to see the announcement as part of the pressure on him to abandon political repression, which is exactly what some Kennedy advisers hoped it might do. (Max Taylor said, "Well, goddammit, we've got to make these people put their noses to the wheel — or the grindstone or whatever. If we don't give them some indication that we're going to get out sometime, they're just going to be leaning on us forever.") Thus, Kennedy instructed that the decision to remove advisers "not be raised formally with Diem. Instead, the action should be carried out routinely as part of our general posture of withdrawing people when they are no longer needed." This would also free him to alter the end-of-year timetable without a press flap about progress in the war.

The decisions on troop withdrawals were given official expression in a National Security Action Memorandum on October 11 with the proviso that "no formal announcement be made of the implementation of plans to withdraw 1,000 U.S. military personnel by the end of 1963." News of Defense Department steps to bring U.S. troops out of Vietnam was to be done by a "leak to the press." But on October 31, during a news conference, Kennedy himself acknowledged the plan to remove one thousand troops from Vietnam before the end of the year. "If we are able to do that," he said, "that would be our schedule."

Kennedy's announcement was a public confirmation of a private conclusion. It had become crystal clear to him after hearing from McNamara and Taylor on October 2, if not before, that Diem's regime was incapable of winning the war. Major General Duong Van Minh ("Big Minh") told Taylor, "[My country is] in chains with no way to shake them off." On October 5, Minh asked Lieutenant Colonel Lucien Conein, a CIA contact in Saigon, to see him at his headquarters. After getting Lodge's approval, Conein and Minh met alone for over an hour. During their conversation, Minh declared the need for a prompt statement of Washington's attitude toward a change of government in the "very near future." Minh predicted that without action soon, the war would be lost to the Viet Cong. He wanted assurances "that the USG will not attempt to thwart this plan." Conein promised nothing, but agreed to report back on his government's attitude. Lodge urged conformity with Minh's request for assurances and a promise to Minh of continued U.S. military support for a new government devoted to defeating the communists. After discussion with Kennedy, McCone advised Lodge that they did not wish "to stimulate [a] coup," but they would not thwart one or deny support to a new, more effective regime. "We certainly would not favor assassination of Diem," McCone added, but "we are in no way responsible for stopping every such threat of which we might receive even partial knowledge." As always, Kennedy saw "deniability" of direct U.S. involvement as of utmost importance should a coup occur.

As more information came in during the next two weeks, the White House became concerned that a coup, for which the United States would be held responsible, might fail and embarrass the administration. "We are particularly concerned about hazard that an unsuccessful coup . . . will be laid at our door by public opinion almost everywhere," Bundy cabled Lodge on October 25. "Therefore, while sharing your view that we should not be in position of thwarting coup, we would like to have option of judging and warning on any plan with poor prospects of success. We recognize that this is a large order, but President wants you to know of our concern."

Lodge believed that the White House was asking for something beyond the embassy's control. He cabled Rusk on October 29, "It would appear that a coup attempt by the Generals' group is imminent; that whether this coup fails or succeeds, the USG must be prepared to accept the fact that we will be blamed, however unjustifiably; and finally, that no positive action by the USG can prevent a coup attempt." Since the plotters promised to give Lodge only four hours notice, he saw no way that the United States could "significantly influence [the] course of events."

Still, Kennedy wanted him to try. If the coup failed, Bobby predicted, "Diem will throw us out." Rusk countered that if the United States opposed the uprising, "the coup-minded military leaders will turn against us and the war effort will drop off rapidly." Taylor and McCone thought that a failed revolt would be "a disaster and a successful coup would have a harmful effect on the war effort." Harriman disagreed, arguing that Diem could not win the war. With pro- and anti-Diem forces in Vietnam so equally divided, Kennedy thought a coup "silly," and wanted Lodge to discourage an uprising. "If we miscalculated," Kennedy said, "we could lose our entire position in Southeast Asia overnight." But it was too late. Despite additional appeals to Lodge over the next forty-eight hours to restrain the generals, the coup was launched at 1:45 P.M. on November 1. And once it began, as Bundy had cabled Lodge on the thirtieth, it was "in the interest of the U.S. Government that it should succeed." At a meeting following news of the coup, Kennedy emphasized "the importance of making clear publicly that this was not a U.S. coup." Contrary reports about who at any given moment held the upper hand in Saigon made this even more complicated. When Diem called Lodge at 4:30 P.M. to ask, "What is the attitude of the United States?" he replied evasively, "I do not feel well enough informed to be able to tell you. . . . It is 4:30 A.M. in Washington and U.S. Government cannot possibly have a view." Lodge added, "I am worried about your physical safety," and offered to help get him out of the country if Diem asked. Rusk at once counseled Lodge against premature recognition lest the coup be described as "American-inspired and manipulated."

On the morning of November 2, Diem and Nhu, who had taken refuge in a private residence in suburban Saigon, offered to surrender to the generals if they guaranteed them safe conduct out of the country. When the generals made no firm promise of safe passage and troops tried to seize them, Diem and Nhu took refuge in a Catholic church, where they were arrested and placed in an armored personnel carrier. Early on the morning of the second, Conein received a call from Minh asking him to provide a plane for Diem's exile. Still reluctant to give any indications of U.S. involvement, CIA operatives falsely answered that no aircraft with sufficient range to fly Diem to an asylum country was available for at least twenty-four hours. Before any plane became accessible, Diem and Nhu were assassinated in the personnel carrier. Even had a plane been available, it is doubtful that the generals would have allowed Diem or the Nhus to leave the country and set up a government in exile.

The news of their deaths reached Kennedy during a morning meeting with the National Security Council. According to Taylor, the president at once "leaped to his feet and rushed from the room with a look of shock and dismay on his face," which Taylor had never seen before. Taylor attributed Kennedy's reaction to his having been led to believe or having persuaded himself that a change in government could be carried out without bloodshed. Schlesinger, who saw the president shortly after, found him "somber and shaken." He had "not seen him so depressed since the Bay of Pigs." Kennedy refused to believe that Diem and Nhu, devout Catholics, would have killed themselves, as the Vietnamese generals were claiming. "He said that Diem had fought for his country for twenty years and that it should not have ended like this." The fact that Diem had a million dollars in large denominations in a briefcase when he died added to Kennedy's skepticism about the generals' suicide account. So large a sum of money suggested that Diem intended to make himself comfortable in exile. Indeed, it was possible that the CIA had given him the money as an inducement to leave the country.

Kennedy tried to assuage his guilt about the assassinations by taping a statement in the Oval Office that future historians could consult. "Monday, November 4, 1963," he began. "Over the weekend, the coup in Saigon took place. It culminated three months of conversations about a coup, conversations that divided the government here and in Saigon." He listed Washington opponents as Taylor, his brother, McNamara ("to a somewhat lesser degree"), and McCone — "partly because of an old hostility to Lodge," whose judgment he distrusted. The advocates were at state, "led by Averell Harriman, George Ball, Roger Hilsman, supported by Mike Forrestal at the White House."

Kennedy did not spare himself from blame: "I feel that we [at the White House] must bear a good deal of responsibility for it, beginning with our cable of early August in which we suggested the coup. In my judgment that wire was badly drafted. It should never have been sent on a Saturday. I should not have given my consent to it without a roundtable conference at which McNamara and Taylor could have presented their views. While we did redress that balance in later wires, that first wire encouraged Lodge along a course to which he was in any case inclined. Harkins continued to oppose the coup on the ground that the military effort was doing well. . . . Politically the situation was deteriorating, militarily it had not had its effect. There was a feeling, however, that it would."

Kennedy then turned to the assassinations: "I was shocked by the death of Diem and Nhu. I'd met Diem with Justice Douglas many years ago. He was an extraordinary character. While he became increasingly difficult in the last months, nevertheless over a ten-year period, he'd held his country together, maintained its independence under very adverse conditions. The way he was killed made it particularly abhorrent. The question now is whether the generals can stay together and build a stable government or whether Saigon will begin — whether public opinion in Saigon, the intellectuals, students, etc. — will turn on this government as repressive and undemocratic in the not too distant future." Kennedy then matter-of-factly turned away from Vietnam to discuss other current events.

His truncated discussion was a sign that he had made up his mind. The lesson Kennedy seemed to take from all this was that U.S. involvement in so unstable a country was a poor idea. He was immediately dismissive of the new government and its prospects for survival. And having been so concerned, as he had told McNamara on November 5, not to get "bogged down" in Cuba as the British, the Russians, and the Americans had in South Africa, Finland, and North Korea, respectively, it was hardly conceivable that Kennedy would have sent tens of thousands more Americans to fight in so inhospitable a place as Vietnam. Reduced commitments, especially of military personnel, during a second Kennedy term were a more likely development. The failed coup had — just as the Bay of Pigs had in Cuba — pushed Kennedy further away from direct engagement.

Kennedy's official and public statements about Vietnam were predictably upbeat. On November 6, he cabled Lodge, "Now that there is a new Government, which we are about to recognize, we must all intensify our efforts to help it deal with its many hard problems." The fact that the administration had encouraged a change of government created a responsibility for it "to help this new government to be effective in every way that we can." The goal was to concentrate on "effectiveness rather than upon external appearances." The new regime needed to "limit confusion and intrigue among its members, and concentrate its energies upon the real problems of winning the contest against the Communists." If it could do this, "it would have met and passed a severe test."

At a press conference on November 14, two days after the State Department announced a Honolulu conference of U.S. officials on Vietnam, Kennedy offered an "appraisal of the situation in South Viet-Nam" and the goals of the Hawaii meeting scheduled for November 20. The Honolulu conference would be an "attempt to assess the situation: what American policy should be, and what our aid policy should be, how we can intensify the struggle, how we can bring Americans out of there. Now, that is our objective," he emphasized, "to bring Americans home, permit the South Vietnamese to maintain themselves as a free and independent country, and permit democratic forces within the country to operate."

Bundy returned from Honolulu with the impression that "the course the US country team will chart in Vietnam is by no means decided upon. . . . Briefings of McNamara tend[ed] to be sessions where people [tried] to fool him, and he tried to convince them they cannot." As for the new regime, Bundy said, "it was too early to see what course it might follow, but it was clear that the coalition of generals might not last." Were it not for the fact that influential defense, state, national security, and military officials remained determined to continue the fight, newspaper editorials advocating negotiations with North Vietnam aimed at neutralization might have convinced Kennedy. But the likely internal and congressional hullabaloo over such a strategy, the hope that the new government might fight the war more effectively, and the indifference of most Americans to our involvement made such a policy difficult to embrace just yet.

Nevertheless, somebody in the administration took seriously Kennedy's apparent interest in eliminating U.S. military commitments in South Vietnam. In an undated, unsigned memo in the president's office files from the late summer or fall of 1963, possibly even after November 1, the writer provided "Observations on Vietnam and Cuba." Since the Soviets seemed to feel trapped in Cuba and the United States in Vietnam, might it not make sense to invite de Gaulle to propose a swap with the Soviets of neutralization for both countries? Whether Kennedy ever saw this memo or what reaction he might have had to it is unknown. Nonetheless, it is clear that by late November 1963, Kennedy welcomed suggestions for easing difficulties with Cuba and Vietnam as alternatives to the policies that, to date, had had such limited success. On November 21, the day he was leaving for Texas, Kennedy told Mike Forrestal that at the start of 1964 he wanted him "to organize an in-depth study of every possible option we've got in Vietnam, including how to get out of there. We have to review this whole thing from the bottom to the top," Kennedy said.

THE PROBLEMS WITH VIETNAM, as with Cuba and domestic affairs, did not seem to undermine Kennedy's reelection chances in 1964. Most soundings on national politics encouraged optimism about the president's prospects in the next campaign. At the end of 1962, Americans listed Kennedy as the world public figure they most admired, ahead of Eisenhower, Winston Churchill, Albert Schweitzer, Douglas MacArthur, Harry Truman, and the Reverend Billy Graham. No other officeholder or active politician, including Nixon, made the top ten. Although Kennedy's approval ratings fell between January and November 1963 from 76 percent to 59 percent and his disapproval numbers went up from 13 percent to 28 percent, he took comfort in the consistently high public affirmation of his presidential performance. In March 1963, 74 percent of Americans thought that he would be reelected. Moreover, when Gallup ran trial heats pitting him against Goldwater, Rockefeller, Michigan governor George Romney, or Nixon, Kennedy consistently had double-digit leads over all of them.

In-depth state surveys of North Dakota and Pennsylvania added to the optimism. North Dakota had been a reliable Republican state, with Kennedy winning less than 45 percent of the popular vote in 1960. But the election of a Democrat to a U.S. Senate seat in 1960 and the reelection of the senior senator, another Democrat, in 1962 — albeit by the narrowest of margins in both contests — encouraged some hope that the president might win the state in 1964. In an April 1963 survey of North Dakota voters, Kennedy had an astonishing 77 percent approval rating. In statewide straw polls against four potential Republican nominees, Kennedy beat all of them except for Romney, who had only a slight 51 percent to 49 percent lead. Pollsters concluded that "from the loss of the State with a bare 44.5% of the total vote, the President has soared to a situation in which he might beat any Republican presidential candidate."

The news from Pennsylvania was even better. In 1960, Kennedy had won the state by 117,000 votes, or 51.2 percent, to Nixon's 48.8 percent. By the spring of 1963, his popularity had "increased significantly." Rockefeller was Kennedy's strongest opponent in straw polls, but he was "not running anywhere near as strong as Nixon did against Kennedy" in 1960, while other potential Republican nominees "might have difficulty defeating Kennedy among Republicans, let alone Democrats."

Journalists echoed the polling results. Charlie Bartlett quoted a current jingle: "Never wait for an uptown car on the downtown side of the street." Top administration officials "feel strongly now that they are waiting on the right side of the street for events that are moving in a favorable direction." In May, a *Chattanooga Times* reporter predicted a Kennedy victory in Tennessee, where Negroes, who "hold the balance," would back him "110%. . . . About the worst thing that could happen to Kennedy," the reporter said, ". . . would be the death of John XXIII and the election of an austere, reactionary Pope. John is very popular with many Protestants and this, combined with Kennedy's own careful handling of the religious problem, has done much to water down the church issue in the South." A Rochester, New York, newsman saw Kennedy "holding fast" to 1960 voters and winning over about one in ten Nixon supporters. " 'I voted for Nixon, but Kennedy seems to be doing a good job' " was the standard comment of these crossover voters. Kennedy's Catholicism and "inexperience" had largely disappeared as issues, and a feeling that he was going to win anyway was creating a bandwagon effect.

Yet like any savvy American politician, Kennedy knew better than to take voters for granted. So much could happen in 1964 that might weaken his hold on the electorate and force him into a close election. "I suppose . . . we're going to get a very tough fight," he told a British visitor in October 1963. The chairman of the Westchester County, New York, Democratic Committee predicted in November that "if civil rights and tax cut legislation [are] on the books and off television by January, we will do better than '60. If not, we will just have to work harder." Kennedy saw little reason to think that either bill would gain passage by then and assumed that they would indeed have to "work harder." Whenever he spoke to O'Donnell and Powers about '64, he "[made] a point of saying it is going to be another tough campaign." He would remind people that the Democrats had won only 52.8 percent of the congressional vote in 1962, and that since 1884, except for FDR, the Democrats had never won a majority of the popular vote for president. When he assessed recent voting patterns of "swing groups" likely to tip the election one way or another, the numbers confirmed his expectations of a very close contest. His gains in the East and the West and among women were "soft," while Republicans had a "slight gain among men" and a "solid gain" in the South, where Kennedy did not think enough blacks would switch to him and the Democrats in 1964 to make a significant difference.

By November 1963, the campaign had already begun. During the last week in September, Kennedy made a trip through several western states that was billed as a "conservation tour" but was more an attempt to improve his political image in a region where he had done poorly in 1960. The Republicans had also launched their campaign, with attacks on the administration's economic policies. In response, Kennedy was "hell-bent to talk about our faster growth rates than the European rates" in 1962–63. When Walter Heller told him that this was more a case of "expansion" — an upsurge from a recession — than "growth," Kennedy responded that "in light of what the opposition was saying, one had to sometimes bypass these fine distinctions." Heller agreed, "so long as we don't fool ourselves," and underestimate the importance of the tax cut and economic growth.

Kennedy was also worried about the negative impact of his civil rights proposals on voters. In New Jersey, where he had won by only twenty-two thousand votes in 1960, "the weakening of the Democratic political machine, plus the frightening backlash flowing from the whole civil rights issue" convinced the White House that they would have to do a great deal of work to win the state again. "To put it another way," a New Jersey member of the Interior Department told O'Donnell, "we have to win in Arizona, Colorado, Nevada and New Mexico to offset a loss in New Jersey."

Kennedy's greatest worry was losing the South. He had acknowledged to Walter Cronkite during a September 2, 1963, interview the importance of civil rights as an issue working against him in the region. He granted that he would again lose some southern states, but he refused to concede the Old Confederacy to the Republicans. Lou Harris had urged him to ignore the accepted wisdom about the area. The common assumptions that "the main stream of southern politics today is segregationist, states rights, and right wing conservatism," Harris advised, were "superficial shibboleths of the noisiest, not most representative elements in the region. . . . The outstanding developments in the South today do not directly concern the race question. Foremost is the industrial explosion that is taking place . . .

accompanied by a comparable educational awakening." A New South was in the making by moderate governors and businessmen, who were boosters of southern development councils. "You can well go into the South throughout 1964," Harris told him, "not to lay down the gauntlet on civil rights, but rather to describe and encourage the new industrial and educational explosion in the region." The votes Kennedy will lose in the South on civil rights, former FDR political adviser Jim Farley predicted, would be offset by gains on other issues.

Kennedy also saw the hard right as a threat to his reelection. In August 1963, he asked White House counsel Myer Feldman to assess the influence of right-wing organizations. Feldman's survey distinguished between conservatives and the radical right, which he described as a formidable force in American political life. Well funded by "70 foundations, 113 business firms and corporations, 25 electric light, gas and power companies, and 250 identifiable individuals," these organizations and men saw "the Nation as imperiled on every front by a pro-Communist conspiracy," which was softening the country up for an imminent takeover. Most troubling, they had been politically more successful than realized: They had managed to elect 74 percent of their over 150 congressional candidates. Broadcasting a fifteen-minute radio program on three hundred radio stations 343 times a day and mailing eighty thousand copies a week of their newspaper, *Human Events,* "the radical right-wing," Feldman told Kennedy, "constitutes a formidable force in American life today."

Yet Kennedy saw the ultraright more as a political gift than a danger. He did not discount their ability to heighten the public's fears of communist subversion or to put pressure on him to be more militant toward communist threats abroad. But he also understood that middle America and more traditional conservatives regarded these extremists as a threat to popular government programs like Social Security and unemployment insurance and as too rash in foreign affairs, where they could not be trusted with nuclear weapons.

Consequently, Kennedy wanted to run against Goldwater, the favorite candidate of the country's most conservative elements; the Arizona senator's denunciations of New Deal social programs and glib talk about "lobbing one into the men's room of the Kremlin" made him appear to be an easy mark. When Salinger showed Kennedy a poll indicating that the Republicans would make the wild westerner their nominee, Kennedy said, "Dave Powers could beat

Goldwater," and quipped that a race against Goldwater would allow "all of us . . . [to] get to bed much earlier on election night than we did in 1960." At a press conference on October 31, when a reporter asked him to comment on Goldwater's charge that the administration was falsifying the news to keep him in office, Kennedy gleefully replied, "I think it would be unwise at this time to answer . . . Senator Goldwater. I am confident that he will be making many charges even more serious than this one in the coming months. And, in addition, he himself has had a busy week selling TVA and giving permission to or suggesting that military commanders overseas be permitted to use nuclear weapons, and attacking the President of Bolivia while he was here in the United States, and involving himself in the Greek election. So I thought it really would not be fair for me this week to reply to him."

More worrisome as a candidate until the middle of 1963 was New York governor Nelson Rockefeller. Kennedy thought that Rockefeller would have beaten him in 1960, but he was confident that as president he would have the advantage over him in 1964. Nevertheless, he took nothing for granted and made a systematic effort to learn everything he could about Rockefeller. Kennedy made Ros Gilpatric, who had worked with Rockefeller, a sort of go-between. Whenever Rockefeller was in Washington, Kennedy wanted to see him. "I never saw more concentrated attention given to any political subject, from the time I got to know the President well," Gilpatric recalls. But in the summer of 1963 Rockefeller married a divorcée with four children; his poll numbers plunged and Goldwater emerged as the new front-runner for the nomination.

Rockefeller's fading candidacy was a relief to Kennedy, though he worried that Romney, a moderate like Rockefeller, might fill the vacuum and take the nomination away from Goldwater. At a November 13 staff meeting with Bobby, Sorensen, O'Donnell, O'Brien, brother-in-law Steve Smith, John Bailey and Dick Maguire from the DNC, and Richard Scammon, the director of the Census Bureau and a demographer, Kennedy discussed campaign plans for three hours. A successful businessman and devout Mormon who neither smoked nor drank and was awaiting a message from God on whether to run, Romney impressed Bobby as someone who could win both moderate and conservative votes. "People buy that God and country stuff," Kennedy observed. "Give me Barry," he pleaded half jokingly. "I won't even have to leave the Oval Office."

"As usual, the campaign will be run right from here," Kennedy told the group. And the first step in that direction would be to give Steve Smith control at the DNC. Bailey, who was seen as "rather weak," would become a figurehead, though no one, of course, said so at the meeting. Kennedy, borrowing from Wilson in 1916, described his campaign theme as "peace and prosperity." He planned to underscore the administration's commitment to economic uplift for all Americans by promising a war on poverty in eastern Kentucky, "the most severely distressed area in the country." It was also a way to encourage the impression that he was compassionate and to make people feel more "personally involved with him." Scammon, however, cautioned against investing too much in appeals to the poor. "You can't get a single vote more by doing anything for poor people," Scammon advised. "Those who vote are already for you."

Instead, Scammon wanted the campaign to focus on the new suburbanites — the upwardly mobile families who might be lost to the Republicans. His analysis fascinated Kennedy, who wanted to know at what point in their upward economic and social climb Democrats became Republicans. Scammon promised to see if he could find out. Kennedy, mindful of the growing importance of television, which would broadcast the conventions in 1964, wanted to make the Democratic meeting more entertaining for the mass audience, which might tune in, at least for a while. "For once in my life, I'd like to hear a good keynote speech," Kennedy said.

AS PART OF THE EMERGING CAMPAIGN, Kennedy planned trips to Florida and Texas in November. Convinced that his stand on civil rights would make it difficult to win most southern states, he intended to make special efforts to hold on to Florida and Texas. On November 18, he visited Tampa and Miami, where he spoke to politicians, labor leaders, and the Inter-American Press Association about the domestic economy and foreign affairs, particularly relations with Latin America.

During the trip to Texas, he hoped to raise campaign funds and mend political fences. Kennedy had been pressing Governor John Connally for months to arrange a dinner with rich Texas donors. But Connally, who was up for reelection in 1964, was not eager to identify himself with a president whose civil rights record had alienated many Texas voters. Nor was Johnson keen on the trip. He did not think that Kennedy could do much to heal a breach in the Texas

Democratic party between Connally conservatives and liberals led by Senator Ralph Yarborough. Johnson feared that a visit would only exacerbate tensions and underscore his own ineffectiveness in controlling the state party. None of the Texas political crosscurrents, however, deterred Kennedy. He intended to tell Texas party leaders that they needed to improve on his forty-six-thousand-vote margin in 1960 if they expected him to provide the kind of federal largesse he could favor them with in a second term. "He was doing the thing he liked even better than being President," recalled O'Donnell and Powers, "getting away from Washington to start his campaign for reelection in a dubious and important state, with twenty-five electoral votes, where he was sure he could win the people even though many of the bosses and most of the big money were against him. It was a tough political challenge that he relished with much more enjoyment than he found in his executive duties in the White House." Bobby agreed: When the president "was in Washington, it depressed him a little bit. Not depressed him — that's too strong a word. But you read all those columns, and none of them were very enthusiastic for him. . . . Everybody was, you know, sort of finding fault with him . . . that's why he loved it [campaigning] so much. Every time he came back, he said, 'It's a different country.' . . . The people in Washington really missed the depth of his popularity."

On the morning of November 21, as Kennedy prepared to leave for Texas, Dave Powers conferred with him in the Oval Office. Powers remembered that "he looked taller than his six feet standing there on the gray-green carpet with the American eagle woven in its center. . . . Although he was still plagued by his aching back, he was the picture of health" — 172½ pounds with "the build of a light heavyweight boxer." His routine of calisthenics and swimming in the heated White House pool, with its backdrop of colorful seascape murals, had eased his back problems, though the pain was always with him, increasing and decreasing in response to his activities.

The day's schedule was a typical twenty-four hours in the life of a traveling president. A three-and-one-half-hour flight from Andrews Air Force Base to San Antonio was followed by forty-five-minute flights to Houston and then Fort Worth. Greeting hundreds of people at the three airports and riding for two and a half hours in motorcades waving to crowds was exhilarating and exhausting. The dedication of an aerospace medical facility in San Antonio and remarks in Houston to the League of Latin American Citizens and at a dinner honoring Congressman Albert Thomas, a Kennedy ally who had helped win appropriations for the space program, were satisfying but unexceptional events. Jackie's presence on the trip gave the crowds and press something to talk about. And the open hostility between Connally and Yarborough, punctuated by news accounts of Yarborough's refusal to ride in a car with Johnson, Connally's ally, generated additional local interest in the president's visit.

The possibility of overt right-wing demonstrations against Kennedy had raised doubts about the wisdom of visiting Texas. After a crowd of ultraconservatives had jeered and physically threatened Adlai Stevenson during a United Nations Day visit to Dallas on October 24, some of the president's friends wondered whether he should risk going to the city. On November 4, Texas Democratic National Committeeman Byron Skelton sent Bobby a newspaper story about retired general Edwin Walker, a supporter of the radical-right John Birch Society, who said that "'Kennedy is a liability to the free world.' A man who would make that kind of statement is capable of doing harm to the President," Skelton advised. "I would feel better if the President's itinerary did not include Dallas. Please give this your earnest consideration." Bobby had passed the letter along to O'Donnell, who had concluded that "showing the letter to the President would have been a waste of his time." Kennedy would have dismissed him as mad if he had suggested "cutting such a large and important city as Dallas from the itinerary because of Skelton's letter."

A John Birch Society ad in the *Dallas Morning News* on November 22 gave resonance to the concern. It accused Kennedy of being soft on communism, while allowing his brother to prosecute loyal Americans who criticized the administration. The ad implied that the Kennedys were pro-communist. When he showed the black-bordered ad to Jackie, the president said, "We're heading into nut country today. But, Jackie, if somebody wants to shoot me from a window with a rifle, nobody can stop it, so why worry about it?"

Of course, there were security precautions that could be taken, but in protecting the president from potential threats during his trip to Texas, and Dallas in particular, the Secret Service and FBI worried too much about the ultraright and too little about a possible assassin from the radical left. Consequently, neither agency picked up on the fact that Lee Harvey Oswald, an unstable ne'er-do-well who had lived in Russia for almost three years, openly identified himself with

Castro's Cuba, and unsuccessfully tried to breach a State Department ban on visiting the island, might be a threat to the president. If they had been attentive to Oswald's movements, they would have noted his presence in Dallas, where he worked in the downtown Dealey Plaza building of the Texas School Book Depository, which overlooked Kennedy's motorcade route. If he had been an object of clear concern, they would have taken notice of the mail-order Italian rifle he purchased shortly after the president's visit was announced.

Unimpeded by any law enforcement agency and animated by possibly nothing more than resentment against a symbol of the authority, success, and fame he craved and could never hope to achieve, Oswald fired three shots from the sixth-floor window of the Depository building at the president riding directly below in an open car. The second bullet struck Kennedy in the back of the neck. Were it not for a back brace, which held him erect, a third and fatal shot to the back of the head would not have found its mark. At 1:00 P.M. central time, half an hour after the attack, doctors at Dallas's Parkland Memorial Hospital told Mrs. Kennedy that the president was dead.

KENNEDY'S DEATH SHOCKED the country more than any other event since the December 1941 attack on Pearl Harbor. The assassination produced an outpouring of grief that exceeded that felt by Americans over the killings of Lincoln, James A. Garfield, and William McKinley, or over FDR's sudden death in April 1945. However traumatic Lincoln's assassination, the four years of Civil War bloodletting, which took 620,000 lives, somewhat muted the horror of losing the nation's leader. It was as if Lincoln's demise was foreordained — the culmination of a four-year catastrophe that tested the nation's capacity to survive. The Garfield and McKinley assassinations were assaults on presidents serving in a politically diminished office and on men who enjoyed a lesser hold on the country's imagination than FDR or JFK did. The approaching victory in World War II made Roosevelt's passing less traumatic than if it had come in the midst of the conflict, when the loss of his leadership would have seemed more difficult for the nation to surmount.

By contrast, Kennedy's sudden violent death seemed to deprive the country and the world of a better future. Despite initial glaring misjudgments about civil rights, Cuba, and Soviet Russia, Kennedy's subsequent performance had raised global expectations that he could improve the state of world affairs. His transparent eagerness for better relations between the United States and the USSR and for higher standards of living everywhere had impressed people as not simply the usual peace and prosperity rhetoric promised by all politicians but the product of thoughtful conviction. When he called for tax cuts and legislation guaranteeing the equal treatment promised in the Constitution, it seemed fresh and bold and likely to advance the national well-being. When he urged nuclear arms limitations, he seemed to be not only a defender of the national interest but also a humanist arguing the case for a rational world struggling against the age-old blights of fear, hatred, and war.

The British philosopher and historian Isaiah Berlin reflected feeling abroad when he wrote Schlesinger, "I do not wish to exaggerate: perhaps it is not at all similar to what men may have felt when Alexander the Great died; but the suddenness and the sense of something of exceptional hope for a large number of people suddenly cut off in mid-air is, I think, unique in our lifetime — it is as if Roosevelt had been murdered in 1935, with Hitler and Mussolini and everybody else still about and a lot of [Neville] Chamberlains and [Edouard] Daladiers knocking about too."

In the United States, the theologian Reinhold Niebuhr lamented, "I never knew how his brief and brilliant leadership had touched the imagination and the hearts of the common people until this terrible deed ended his career." Chief Justice Earl Warren undoubtedly spoke for millions of Americans when he wrote Jackie, "America now has a higher duty to undertake — completion of the unfinished work of your beloved husband. No American during my rather long life ever set his sights higher for a better America or centered his attack more accurately on the evils and shortcomings of our society than did he. It was God's will that he should not remain with us to complete his self-prescribed task, but I have the faith to believe it was also God's will that we who survive him should use this adversity to memorialize his farsightedness and humanitarianism. That memorial should be the consummation of his ideal for our nation. I feel confident that there are many millions of Americans, of whom I am one, who will consider this to be their solemn duty."

IN THE FORTY YEARS since Kennedy's assassination, family, friends and the whole country have struggled to come to terms with his senseless murder. What could possibly explain the sudden violent end to the life of someone as young, attractive, and politically powerful as John F. Kennedy? Is there some way to give constructive meaning to his death?

Jacqueline Kennedy, the most directly affected by JFK's death, struggled to maintain her rationality. White House physician Dr. James M. Young, who saw her in Washington and Hyannis Port two or three times a day during the ten days after the assassination, remembers her as "emotionally distraught" but generally composed and self-contained. She "did not break down and cry," and with the help of sleeping medication "she did well." There were occasional expressions of anger at the failings of the Secret Service and at Kennedy's doctors. She called Janet Travell a "Madame Nhu," George Burkley, who would pass patients off to other physicians, a "communist," and Eugene Cohen, who was at odds with Travell, a "psychopath."

Her husband's tragic death seemed to have dissolved her anger toward him for his womanizing. At least she said nothing to Dr. Young about the problem, but to the contrary, spoke only lovingly of Jack, remembering the scars on his back as a symbol of his fortitude in dealing with his physical pain, the hard mattress he needed, and the pleasure of being with him in bed.

She seemed to find purpose and solace in preserving JFK's memory. Only thirty-four years old, deprived of decades of life with her husband, faced with raising her six-year-old and three-year-old children without their father — whom they would never know — Jackie kept her balance — indeed sanity — by focusing on Kennedy's legacy. She understood that no one was going to forget him; rather, her concern was how the world would remember him.

She began with his funeral. Although some members of the family wished to bury the president in Brookline, Massachusetts, JFK's birthplace, Jackie insisted on Arlington Cemetery. An eternal flame, like one in Paris at the Tomb of the Unknown Soldier built after World War I at the base of the Arc de Triomphe, was to mark the grave. She also asked that the ceremony resemble Lincoln's, the most revered of the country's martyred presidents. A procession from the White House to the Roman Catholic St. Matthew's Cathedral, eight blocks away, consisted of Jackie, Bobby, Ted, President and Mrs. Johnson, principal Kennedy associates, and representatives of ninety-two nations, including de Gaulle and Anastas Mikoyan, Khrushchev's first deputy. The international contingent and fears that assassins associated with Oswald or incited by his example might try to kill some of the dignitaries made the ceremony a more portentous occasion than that of Franklin Roosevelt's passing.

It may be that Jackie, as one writer said, "needed the myth of her fallen husband to secure her own brittle identity," but a more generous analysis should admit that her effort to lionize Kennedy must have provided a therapeutic shield against immobilizing grief. A few days after his funeral, she granted an interview to Theodore White, whose book on the 1960 election had drawn a flattering portrait of her husband. Describing Kennedy's death as marking the end of Camelot, a romanticized association with King Arthur's court that White faithfully recorded in a *Life* magazine article on December 6, Jackie helped create an idyllic portrait that Schlesinger has said "would have provoked John Kennedy to profane disclaimer."

Their son's death staggered Joe and Rose. Still immobilized by his 1961 stroke, Joe did not attend the funeral. He was either too incapacitated or too shocked to comprehend the awful news. The family shielded him from the reports on television until the next morning, when Teddy and Eunice told him. Rose could not bear to be in the room when they did. "We have told him, but we don't think that he understands it," Rose said.

The news temporarily shook Rose's faith. She "walked and walked and walked" in the yard of the Hyannis Port house and on the beach and "prayed and prayed and prayed, and wondered why it happened to Jack. He had everything to live for. . . . Everything — the culmination of all his efforts, abilities, dedication to good and to the future — lay boundlessly before him. Everything was gone and I wondered why." Rose was so upset that she could not walk with the procession to the cathedral for fear that she might collapse.

But no one among the Kennedys suffered more acutely than Bobby. Though a man of unquestioning faith, he could not find any sense or meaning in his brother's death. "Why, God?" he asked as he sobbed in the privacy of the Lincoln bedroom the night of November 22. "The innocent suffer — how can that be possible and God be just?" he asked himself in the days after the assassination. LeMoyne Billings remembered him as devastated. He had so fully devoted himself to his brother's career that the president's death left him bewildered. "He didn't know where he was. . . . Everything was just pulled out from under him." In the weeks and months after the tragedy, Bobby took to reading Greek classics by Aeschylus,

Euripides, Herodotus, and Sophocles and works by the modern existentialists, especially Albert Camus, to help understand the agony and suffering in every life. They gave him the solace needed to sustain a public career, now more than ever in behalf of those most vulnerable to personal and social problems.

The depths of Bobby's anguish may partly have sprung from guilt. John McCone believed that Bobby was either directly or indirectly involved in Castro assassination plots, which Bobby suspected had led Castro agents to kill his brother. Biographer Evan Thomas concluded that Bobby "gave lip service to the single-gunman explanation" in the government's official report on the assassination, but "he never quieted his own doubts." Bobby, according to Thomas, thought the killing might have been the work of the CIA or mobster Sam Giancana or Castro or Jimmy Hoffa or the Cuban exiles.

Lyndon Johnson shared the conviction that an undetected conspiracy was behind Kennedy's assassination. He initially believed that the president's death was in revenge for Diem's killing. In time, he concluded that Castro supporters were responsible. "President Kennedy tried to get Castro, but Castro got Kennedy first," he told Joseph Califano, his domestic affairs chief. Kennedy's death came a year after Castro's government foiled a CIA-assassination plot in Havana. "We had been operating a damned Murder Inc. in the Caribbean," Johnson told a journalist.

Johnson saw the country's initial reaction to the assassination as "troubled, puzzled, and outraged." But after Jack Ruby, an unsavory Dallas nightclub operator, killed Lee Harvey Oswald, the prime suspect in the assassination, in the garage of a Dallas police station on his way to a court hearing, the country concluded that Kennedy's death was the work of more than just one man. Although the Warren Commission, the government's inquiry into the assassination headed by Chief Justice Earl Warren, described Oswald in its September 1964 report as the lone killer, a majority of Americans never accepted that conclusion. To be sure, the commission's failure to ferret out and disclose CIA assassination plots against Castro or to reveal and condemn the FBI for inattentiveness to Oswald raised questions later about the reliability of its evidence and judgment. But in December 1963, even before the commission published its findings, 52 percent of the country saw "some group or element" behind the assassination. By January 1967, the belief in a conspiracy had risen to 64 percent.

Despite an authoritative 1993 book, *Case Closed*, by attorney Gerald Posner refuting numerous conspiracy theories, the public, inflamed by a popular 1991 Oliver Stone film, *JFK*, believed otherwise. In 1992, fewer than one-third of Americans accepted the Warren Commission's findings as persuasive. In February of that year, the *New York Times Book Review* listed as bestsellers one hardcover and three paperback books describing Kennedy assassination theories. To this day, a substantial majority in America assumes that an aggrieved group rather than just Oswald was behind Kennedy's killing. The prime suspects are pro- or anti-Castro Cubans, Vietnamese retaliating for Diem's death, "the mob" or labor bosses hurt by Kennedy, and the CIA, military chiefs, and Lyndon Johnson opposed to détente with Moscow.

The fact that none of the conspiracy theorists have been able to offer convincing evidence of their suspicions does not seem to trouble many people. The plausibility of a conspiracy is less important to them than the implausibility of someone as inconsequential as Oswald having the wherewithal to kill someone as consequential — as powerful and well guarded — as Kennedy. To accept that an act of random violence by an obscure malcontent could bring down a president of the United States is to acknowledge a chaotic, disorderly world that frightens most Americans. Believing that Oswald killed Kennedy is to concede, as *New York Times* columnist Anthony Lewis said, "that in this life there is often tragedy without reason."

Despite his own suspicions of a conspiracy, Johnson was eager to reassure the country that only Oswald was involved. He feared that speculation about Cuban or Soviet responsibility might provoke a nuclear war. As he told Earl Warren when convincing him to head the commission, rumors that either Castro or Khrushchev was part of a conspiracy "might even catapult us into a nuclear war if it got a head start." To overcome Georgia senator Richard Russell's resistance to joining the commission, Johnson warned him that forty million Americans might lose their lives in a nuclear conflict if accusations about Castro and Khrushchev were not refuted.

Kennedy's assassination provoked not only conspiracy theories but also an extraordinary public attachment to his memory. Forty years after his death, Americans consistently rate Kennedy as one of the five greatest presidents in U.S. history. Fifty-two percent of respondents in a 1975 Gallup poll ranking presidents put Kennedy first, ahead of Lincoln and FDR; ten years later, he remained number one, with 56 percent backing. A poll released on Presidents Day in February 1999 declared Lincoln the greatest of our presidents, with Washington, JFK, Ronald Reagan, and Bill Clinton tied for second. In 2000, Kennedy topped the list, followed by Lincoln, FDR, and Reagan. Stories about Reagan's ninetieth birthday in 2001 propelled him to the top spot, with Kennedy second and Lincoln third.

How can one explain Kennedy's enduring hold on the public's imagination? His thousand-day presidency — the sixth-briefest in the country's history — hardly measures up to the administrations of Washington, Lincoln, and FDR, our most notable presidents. Nor are professional historians persuaded that Kennedy deserves such high standing. The want of landmark legislation, an overly cautious response to black pressure for equal treatment under the law, and a mixed record in foreign affairs, where success in the missile crisis and with the test ban treaty are balanced against unresolved Cuban problems and deeper involvement in Vietnam, have persuaded scholars that Kennedy was not a truly distinguished president.

Moreover, revelations about Kennedy's womanizing and health have raised questions about whether he could have made it through a second term. In his 1991 book, A Question of Character, historian Thomas C. Reeves concluded, "Had Kennedy lived to see a second term, the realities of his lechery and dealings with [mobster] Sam Giancana might have leaked out while he was still in office, gravely damaging the presidency. . . . Impeachment might well have followed such public disclosure." In his 1997 book, The Dark Side of Camelot, Seymour Hersh asserted that JFK's tawdry behavior during his presidency put him "just one news story away from cataclysmic political scandal."

In 1982, two thousand scholars asked to categorize American presidents as great, near great, above average, average, below average, and failure, ranked Kennedy as number thirteen, in the middle of the above-average group. In 1988, seventy-five historians and journalists described JFK as "the most overrated public figure in American history." An October 2000 survey of seventy-eight scholars in history, politics, and law, which gave considerable weight to length of presidential service, ranked Kennedy number eighteen, at the bottom of the above-average category.

But the public has other yardsticks for measuring presidential greatness. The muckraking about Kennedy's private life has had no significant impact on public admiration for his presidential record. Most Americans set his health problems, sexual escapades, and dealings with Giancana down as unproven gossip that had no demonstrable effect on his official duties. Despite a voyeuristic interest that makes bestsellers out of books offering sensational revelations, Kennedy's personal magnetism has had more enduring appeal than allegations of deceitfulness and immoral behavior. Substantial public interest in White House tapes and a Hollywood film demonstrating Kennedy's effectiveness during the missile crisis, as well as long lines of people in New York, Boston, and Washington eager to view an exhibit of Jackie Kennedy's personal wardrobe and effects as First Lady, are fresh demonstrations of the Kennedys' continuing popularity.

The assassination and Kennedy's martyrdom no doubt remain the most important factors in perpetuating high public regard for his leadership and importance as a president. But this alone cannot explain his popularity. In 1941, forty years after William McKinley, who had been among the small number of presidents elected twice, was assassinated, he was an all but forgotten chief. The advent of television, which captured Kennedy's youthful appearance, good looks, charm, wit, and rhetorical idealism and hope, also contributed to his ongoing appeal. The public's faith in Kennedy's sincerity is an additional element in his continuing hold on the country. In an era of public cynicism about politicians as poseurs who are stage-managed and often insincere, Kennedy's remembered forthrightness strengthens his current appeal. These attributes have encouraged a belief that had he lived, the United States would have avoided many of the problems it suffered under Johnson and Nixon during the 1960s and 1970s.

Public attachment to Kennedy also rests on the conviction that his election reduced religious and ethnic tests for the presidency. True, no other Catholic has become president since Kennedy, but Ronald Reagan, though not a practicing Catholic, had a Catholic father. Moreover, the vice presidential candidacies of Geraldine Ferraro, a Catholic, in 1984, and of Joseph Lieberman, a Jew, in 2000, demonstrate that JFK's presidency significantly reduced religion as a barrier to the White House. It also helped make the election of a woman to the presidency conceivable. For millions of ethnic Americans, Kennedy remains more than a bright, promising young president whose life and time in office were prematurely snuffed out. He is an enduring demonstration that ethnics and minorities, who, despite rhetoric to the contrary, did not feel fully accepted in America before 1960, have come into their own as first-class citizens. Kennedy's identification with a rich and famous family, Harvard degree, heroism in World War II, and election to the House, Senate, and White House have been enough to make him a great president in the eyes of hyphenated Americans. Then and now, they share dreams realized by the Kennedys of becoming American aristocrats.

KENNEDY'S DEATH WAS initially a triumph of the worst in human relations over the promise of better times. But, as Warren anticipated, the grief over his loss became a compelling drive for the enactment of legislative and international gains that remain living memorials to his vision of a fairer, more prosperous, and peaceful world. The "idealist without illusions," as Kennedy described himself, would have taken satisfaction from the advances that his senseless death helped bring to life. But it was limited compensation to those who believed that another five years in the White House and a postpresidential career might have allowed Kennedy to shield the country from losses and defeats, avoiding the doubts and cynicism flowing from the assassination and the Vietnam War and bringing benefits that would have served countless millions at home and abroad.

Epilogue

ALL THE MYTHMAKING — positive and negative — about Kennedy would not have interested him as much as a fair-minded assessment of his public career. He would probably have been less than happy that biographers had unearthed so much of the truth about his private life. Nor would he have had any illusions that historians would be of one mind about his policies and actions. He understood that history, as the great Dutch historian Pieter Geyl asserted, is an argument without end. (In October 1961, he told scholars editing the John Adams papers "how difficult it ever is to [get] to the 'bone' of truth on any great historical controversy.") All the debate generated by his congressional and especially presidential careers would not have surprised him. But he also understood that opposing judgments on his life and times did not preclude balanced appraisals, and forty years after his death — with the consequences of his actions reasonably clear and the documents to assess his achievements and failings for the most part available — such an analysis seems within reach.

If Kennedy had never become president, it is doubtful that biographers, historians, and the mass public would have had a lot of interest in him. His famous father, heroism in World War II, elections to the House and Senate, publication of a Pulitzer Prize–winning book on political courage, failed bid for the vice presidential nomination in 1956, and presidential nomination in 1960 as only the second Catholic to hold that distinction would have made him an object of some curiosity. But his career probably would have generated little more than the limited interest most losing contenders for the presidency receive. Some defeated presidential candidates like Henry Clay, Daniel Webster, Stephen A. Douglas, William Jennings Bryan, Charles Evans Hughes, Robert M. La Follette, Henry A. Wallace, and Barry Goldwater are remembered for their associations with larger political developments or other public service. But Kennedy's pre-presidential career as a relatively minor political figure would have made him less interesting to historians. He left no especially notable marks as a congressman or a senator.

As matters now stand, however, no detail about the Kennedys escapes scrutiny. Jack and Jackie, Joe, Rose, and Bobby have been the particular focus of public attention, but the other members of the family are also ongoing projects for numerous journalists, biographers, and historians in America and abroad. Would Robert Kennedy's three years as attorney general, fewer than four years as a New York senator, and assassination as a presidential candidate have netted him so much biographical and historical attention were he not a Kennedy? Would John Kennedy Jr.'s tragic death in 1999 have received such worldwide news coverage if he had not been JFK's son? The Kennedys, with all their strengths and weaknesses, seem to fulfill an American longing for a royal family — perhaps like the one in Britain, which is the object of both reverence and criticism.

No Kennedy life has been more thoroughly probed than JFK's. His medical history has received justifiable investigation. Since the president controls nuclear weapons and so much else, his physical and mental health have become compelling concerns. A disabled president like Wilson in 1919–20 or even one with the less severe medical ailments of an Eisenhower has become unacceptable in a post-1945 era of nuclear weapons and world power. (The Twenty-fifth Amendment, stating the means for replacing a disabled president, was added to the Constitution in 1967.) As we know now, Kennedy feared that his Addison's disease, colitis, back troubles, and prostatitis would be used against him in the 1960 campaign. More to the point, he worried that disclosure of his repeated hospitalizations in the 1950s and his reliance on steroids to combat the debilitating effects of Addison's disease and on antispasmodics, painkillers, testosterone, antibiotics, and sleeping pills to help him cope with collateral problems would almost certainly block him from becoming president.

Consequently, Kennedy was less than open about his medical history. And this deception continued after his death: At Bobby's request, autopsy notes were destroyed; Dr. William Herbst, a urologist who treated JFK in the fifties, burned his files in a basement furnace after informing Bobby that the FBI had asked for them; and, James Young believes, Bobby persuaded Burkley to destroy his records. The deception was calculated to preserve JFK's and Bobby's reputations for honest dealings with the public. The ruse, like that practiced by Wilson about his medical condition, certainly undermines Kennedy's historical standing as a democratic leader. Yet unlike Wilson, Kennedy successfully bet that he could function effectively as president. My reading of the most extensive collection of medical records ever available to a Kennedy biographer, combined with close study of his day-to-day performance, demonstrates that he was right. Despite almost constant stress generated by international and domestic crises, he survived a presidency that was more burdened with difficulties than most. Prescribed medicines and a program of exercises begun in the fall of 1961, combined with his intelligence, knowledge of history, and determination to manage presidential challenges, allowed him to sensibly address potentially disastrous problems. His opposition to excessive reliance on nuclear weapons and to international proliferation, his decision not to use American military power to save the invaders at the Bay of Pigs, his restrained dealings with Khrushchev over Berlin and particularly Cuba, his reluctance to expand the fighting in Vietnam, and his eventual understanding that civil rights reform had to come to the top of the domestic agenda demonstrate the rational judgments of someone undistracted by health problems. It seems fair to say that Kennedy courageously surmounted his physical suffering: His medical difficulties did not significantly undermine his performance as president on any major question.

Looking backwards from today, we can conclude that full disclosure of Kennedy's ailments would, as he believed, have barred him from the White House. In holding back this information, Kennedy was saying to the country, "Trust me to perform effectively as president. Though I will be younger than anyone else ever elected to the office and though my religious faith is different from that of most voters and would make me the only Catholic ever to become president, a vote for me is an expression of confidence in my promise to serve the nation effectively and of the country's genuine commitment to judging someone by their personal attributes rather than their religion, race or ethnicity." (He would surely have come to include gender in this measuring rod.) His appeal convinced enough Americans to give the office to him rather than to Richard Nixon. It is difficult to believe that voters would want to gamble again on someone with the sort of severe health problems Kennedy suffered. But given the way Nixon performed in the White House, how many people would retrospectively offer him their vote for 1960, even knowing of Kennedy's health problems?

One cannot speak as confidently about Kennedy's reckless womanizing. Up to a point, Kennedy had justifiable confidence that the mainstream media was not going to publicize his affairs, as with a Mary Meyer, or more scandalous sex parties with call girls in the White House. But as the Profumo scandal in Britain made clear, trysts with women like Judith Campbell Exner and Ellen Rometsch, which made Kennedy vulnerable to charges of mob influence and national security breaches, were a dangerous indulgence. Bobby's protective actions and J. Edgar Hoover's cooperation in hiding the president's behavior were not guarantees against a public scandal jeopardizing his presidency. Kennedy certainly could have spent eight years in office without public discussion of his philandering. It is also conceivable that he could have survived a scandal by effectively denying it. But the more important questions biographers confront are, Why was he so incautious? Why did he not get caught? and Did his sexual escapades affect his presidency?

The answer to the first requires speculation about personal motives that are never easy to discern. I have suggested that his father's behavior, difficulties with his mother, anxiety about a truncated life, which Joe Jr.'s and Kathleen's early deaths and his health concerns made all too real, and the prevailing mores of his class, time, and place helped make him a compulsive womanizer. Kennedy himself, who could not explain his need for sex with so many women, probably rationalized his behavior as a diversion comparable with what British aristocrats did, or with the golf, sailing, and fishing presidents traditionally used to ease tensions. Bruce Grant, an Australian writer who read *Profiles in Courage* after meeting Kennedy in 1960, noted that the men Jack wrote about were less "lustrous heroes" than "complex, even enigmatic American politicians. It was obvious from the tone and the content of this prize-winning book that the author was himself, not darkly troubled perhaps but full of complexities, inconsistencies and doubts." The answer to the second question — his success in hiding his philandering — seems easier to explain; a journalistic taboo on violating a president's privacy largely shielded Kennedy from public discussions of his sex life that could have played havoc with his presidency. And as for the third question, as far as I can tell, Kennedy's dalliances were no impediment to his being an effective president.

The sum of Kennedy's actions in domestic and foreign affairs should be central to any assessment of his abbreviated presidency; the overheated discussions of his private life have told us little, if anything, about his presidential performance. Most historians are willing to acknowledge that Kennedy was at the very least an above-average president. Decisive moments in the struggle over civil rights and in the Cold War gave his presidency a greater importance than that of many longer administrations. But no president can lay claim to high ratings merely for having served two terms or for having faced seminal events. Otherwise, failed presidents like James Buchanan and Herbert Hoover would stand in the front ranks of chief executives. Such rankings, as Kennedy himself complained, are a poor substitute for measuring the complexities of a presidential term. Kennedy's presidency is better understood as a patchwork of stumbles and significant achievements.

The domestic record of Kennedy's thousand days was distinctly limited. On civil rights, the greatest domestic issue of the early 1960s, he was a cautious leader. Despite Executive Orders and federal lawsuits opposing southern segregation, he was slow to recognize the extent of the social revolution fostered by Martin Luther King and African Americans, and he repeatedly deferred to southern sensitivities on racial matters, including appointments of segregationist judges in southern federal districts. It took crises in Mississippi and particularly in Alabama to persuade him to put a landmark civil rights bill before Congress in June 1963, and even then he was willing to weaken its provisions to win approval from an unreceptive Congress.

Kennedy's appointment of Byron White as an associate justice of the Supreme Court in April 1962 tellingly demonstrates his mixed record on civil rights. White, who went to the Court after fifteen months as deputy attorney general and with a record of support for desegregating schools, was a less reliable voice on the Court for equal rights. Though he supported busing and a court-ordered tax increase to pay for a desegregation plan, he was the architect of an opinion requiring proponents of affirmative action to show that government policies that produced discriminatory results were intentional rather than random. His majority opinion was seen as a distinct setback for black rights.

None of Kennedy's major reform initiatives — the tax cut, federal aid to education, Medicare, and civil rights — became law during his time in office. Yet all his significant reform proposals, including plans for a housing department and a major assault on poverty, which he had discussed in 1961 and 1963, respectively, came to fruition under Lyndon Johnson. Johnson, of course, deserves considerable credit for these reforms. Relying on the skills he had mastered as a congressman and senator, and especially as senate majority leader, he won passage of the tax cut and civil rights bills in 1964, the antipoverty, federal aid to education, Medicare, and voting rights laws in 1965, and statutes creating cabinet-level transportation and housing and urban development departments in 1966. Most of these measures came after Johnson had won his landslide victory over Barry Goldwater and two-thirds majorities in both houses of Congress in the 1964 presidential and congressional elections.

Johnson's enactment of Kennedy's reform agenda testifies to their shared wisdom about the national well-being. Part of Kennedy's legacy should be an understanding that he proposed major domestic reforms that have had an enduring constructive impact on the country. No one should deny Johnson credit in winning passage of so many Great Society bills, as he called his reform program. Nor should anyone discount the importance of his unprecedented margins in the 1964 campaign as opening the way to his legislative advances. Nevertheless, it is arguable that Kennedy would have made similar gains in a second term. If Kennedy had been running against Goldwater in 1964, which is more than likely, he would also have won a big victory and carried large numbers of liberal Democrats into the House and Senate with him. He would then have enjoyed the same success as Johnson in passing the major bills that were on his administration's legislative agenda at his death in November 1963. It is doubtful that Kennedy would have been as aggressive as Johnson in expanding the reform program set before Congress in 1965 and 1966, but the major bills pending from Kennedy's first term would all have found their way into the law books. The most important of the Great Society measures deserve to be described as Kennedy-Johnson achievements.

Foreign affairs, as Kennedy himself would have argued, were the principal concerns of his presidency. The Peace Corps, the Alliance for Progress, and Apollo are significant measures of his foreign policy performance. The Peace Corps and his commitment to land a man on the moon were great successes; the Alliance was an exercise in unrealized hopes. All three programs initially generated great enthusiasm, at home and abroad, where they were seen as representative of America at its best — a generous, advanced nation promoting a better life for less fortunate peoples around the globe and greater scientific understanding. The Peace Corps rose to the challenge and continues to provide a helping hand to developing countries. The moon walk, though coming after Kennedy's presidency, will stand as a landmark in the history of space exploration. By contrast, the plan for Latin America fell victim to international conditions and traditional U.S. paternalism toward the southern republics, which Kennedy found more difficult to abandon than he had anticipated at the start of his term.

Kennedy's focus on Cuba, relations with Soviet Russia, and actions in Vietnam are additional telling measures of his presidential effectiveness. The Bay of Pigs failure followed by repeated discussions of how to topple Castro show Kennedy at his worst — inexperienced and driven by Cold War imperatives that helped bring the world to the edge of a disastrous nuclear war. But the almost universal praise for his restraint and accommodation in the missile crisis followed by secret explorations of détente with Havana more than make up for his initial errors of judgment. Indeed, a second Kennedy term might have brought a resolution to unproductive tensions with Castro and foreclosed more than forty years of Cuban-American antagonism.

Vietnam, which became America's worst foreign policy nightmare in the twelve years after Kennedy's death, is a source of sharp debate between critics and admirers of Kennedy's leadership. His increase in military advisers from hundreds to over sixteen thousand and his agreement to the Vietnamese coup, which led to Diem's unsanctioned assassination, are described as setting the course for America's later large-scale involvement in the Vietnam War. Johnson continually justified his escalation of America's role in the conflict by emphasizing that he was simply following Kennedy's lead.

A close reading of the record suggests that Kennedy had every wish to keep Vietnam out of the Soviet-Chinese communist orbit. But he was unwilling to pay any price or bear any burden for the freedom of Saigon from communist control. His skepticism about South Vietnam's commitment to preserving its freedom by rallying the country around popular policies and leaders fueled his reluctance to involve the United States more deeply in the conflict. His fears of turning the war into a struggle on a scale with the Korean fighting and of getting trapped in a war that demanded ever more U.S. resources became reasons in 1963 for him to plan reductions of U.S. military personnel in South Vietnam. His eagerness to mute press criticism of America's failure to defeat communism in Southeast Asia also rested on his resistance to escalating U.S. involvement in the struggle. Press attacks on administration policies seemed likely to produce not demands for an American retreat from the fighting but rather pressure for escalation, which would lead, at a minimum, to political problems in a 1964 presidential campaign against a militant Republican like Goldwater.

No one can prove, of course, what Kennedy would have done about Vietnam between 1964 and 1968. His actions and statements, however, are suggestive of a carefully managed stand-down from the sort of involvement that occurred under LBJ. Johnson's decision to launch "Rolling Thunder" in March 1965, the sustained bombing campaign against North Vietnam, was nothing Kennedy had signed on to. Nor did Kennedy ever consent to sending one hundred thousand combat troops to Vietnam, as Johnson did in July. With no presidential track record to speak of in foreign affairs during 1964–1965, Johnson had a more difficult time limiting U.S. involvement in a tottering Vietnam than Kennedy would have had. By November 1963, Kennedy had established himself as a strong foreign policy leader. After facing down Khrushchev in the missile crisis and overcoming Soviet and U.S. military and Senate resistance to a test ban treaty, Kennedy had much greater credibility as a defender of the national security than Johnson had. It gave Kennedy more freedom to convince people at home and abroad that staying clear of large-scale military intervention in Vietnam was in the best interests of the United States.

Kennedy's greatest achievements as president were his management of Soviet-American relations and his effectiveness in discouraging a U.S. military mind-set that accepted the possibility — indeed, even likelihood — of a nuclear war with Moscow. Kennedy came to the presidency after his experiences in World War II with a negative bias toward the military that was only strengthened by Eisenhower's

January 17, 1961, warning about "the military-industrial complex" and his own experiences with Laos, the Bay of Pigs, the Cuban missile crisis, and Vietnam. Kennedy's abiding conviction that a nuclear war was a last, horrible resort made him an effective partner in negotiations with Khrushchev and the Soviets, who feared the consequences of a nuclear exchange as much as, if not even more than, Kennedy. The crises over Berlin and Cuba tested the resolve of both sides to avoid a nuclear holocaust. As important, they opened the way to a notable test ban treaty that reduced dangerous radiation fallout and increased confidence in the possibility of a Soviet-American détente. As with Cuba and Vietnam, no one can say with any certainty that two full Kennedy terms would have eased the Cold War between the United States and the USSR. But it is certainly imaginable.

The sudden end to Kennedy's life and presidency has left us with tantalizing "might have been's." Yet even setting these aside and acknowledging some missed opportunities and false steps, it must be acknowledged that the Kennedy thousand days spoke to the country's better angels, inspired visions of a less divisive nation and world, and demonstrated that America was still the last best hope of mankind.

Epilogue for the 2013 Edition

A FEW YEARS AGO, Gallup pollsters asked Americans to assess the last nine presidents from John F. Kennedy to George W. Bush. Kennedy came out on top, with an 85 percent approval rating. The only one close to him was Ronald Reagan, with a 74 percent endorsement. The poll was not an aberration. Ever since his assassination in 1963, surveys have elevated Kennedy to a place alongside Washington, Lincoln, and Franklin Roosevelt as one of the truly notable presidents in the country's history. At various times in the 1970s and 1980s and again in 2000, a majority of Americans ranked him as the country's foremost president, Founding Fathers and Honest Abe included.

It is a puzzling result. Kennedy, after all, was president for only a thousand days — one of the shortest Oval Office tenures in U.S. history. Moreover, as this book demonstrates, his record of achievement in domestic affairs was pretty barren. None of the four major initiatives Kennedy put before Congress — the $11 billion tax cut to expand the economy, which had been in recession under President Eisenhower; Medicare, providing health insurance to seniors sixty-five and older; federal aid to improve U.S. schools, which lagged behind the Soviet Union in producing engineers and scientists; and civil rights legislation to rectify historic wrongs across the South, where segregation denied African Americans equal opportunity and representative government — won approval during his time in office. I remain convinced, as I said in the first edition of this book, that Kennedy deserves some credit for laying the groundwork for Johnson's passage of these measures. But Kennedy's contribution to these landmark laws is hardly enough to elevate him to the front rank of presidents.

In foreign affairs as well it still seems fair to say that Kennedy's leadership was imperfect. The failed Bay of Pigs invasion and unresolved conflicts with Castro's government continue to trouble U.S. relations with Cuba to this day. Kennedy's stumbling performance in Vienna, where he was overpowered by Khrushchev, and his commitment of some sixteen thousand military advisers to Vietnam also stand as negative marks on his record. True, more than ever, we recognize that he managed the Cuban Missile Crisis brilliantly, averting a disastrous nuclear war that his military chiefs were ready to risk. In addition, the agreement with Moscow to a limited nuclear test ban and grudging Senate approval for what many saw as a controversial treaty are landmark moments in the struggle against the Communists. Despite those gains, the Cold War remained a post-Kennedy burden for almost thirty more years.

Revelations about Kennedy's cover-up of his health problems first described in this book, and the steady drum beat of stories about his reckless womanizing, also marred his White House tenure. His affair with a nineteen-year-old intern, which I briefly recounted in 2003, has now become more of a burden to his standing as a president worthy of our admiration: His execrable conduct in seducing Mimi Beresford (now Alford), which she has described in her 2012 book, *Once Upon a Secret*, provides disturbing details of his compulsive involvement with an impressionable and vulnerable young woman. Indeed, her book adds to the picture of a man and president more successful at image making than as a heroic leader notable for his honesty with the public and family values.

Why then the continued admiration for so flawed a man with so questionable a claim on presidential greatness?

Kennedy's enduring appeal has little to do with presidential achievements. In fact, the public approval of our most popular twentieth-century presidents — Theodore Roosevelt, Woodrow Wilson, FDR, Harry Truman, Dwight Eisenhower, Ronald Reagan, and Bill Clinton — rests less on great acts of leadership than on memories of them as appealing and inspiring figures.

Do people remember that TR founded the Food and Drug Administration or built the Panama Canal? Perhaps they associate him with the national parks and conservation, but that achievement is not what recommends him to most Americans. Do people recall that Wilson set up the Federal Reserve or established the Federal Trade Commission? Surely, they associate him with victory in World War I. But the unpopularity of that conflict in the 1920s and 1930s and subsequent convictions that the war was unnecessary and, worse, led to World War II largely undid Wilson's appeal as a war leader.

FDR is remembered as the president who led us through the Great Depression and World War II. But how many details of the New Deal — including Social Security, the National Labor Relations Act guaranteeing union rights, and the Fair Labor Law mandating minimum wages and maximum hours — do Americans recognize as his legacy? Truman is no doubt still identified with the Korean War and his defense of executive authority by dismissing General Douglas MacArthur. Yet it's hard to believe that many people seem to have forgotten Truman's reliance on containment, which was so central to winning the Cold War. And how many Americans can tell you anything about his Fair Deal, or defense of civil liberties against Senator Joseph McCarthy, or even specific elements of containment? Could many Americans say what the Truman Doctrine or Marshall Plan were?

For most people in this country, Eisenhower's presidency is pretty much a blank. They might recall his military leadership in World War II, but would they even know that he commanded allied forces in the 1944 D-Day invasion? Reagan's record as well, almost twenty-five years after he left office, is largely lost from view, except perhaps as a tax cutter. The very smart Stanford University and University of California students I have taught in recent years have no direct memory of Reagan and are hard-pressed to tell me anything he did in office. Bill Clinton had a robust 69 percent approval in the 2010 poll, but it hardly rests on any clear idea of what he accomplished or did as president, except perhaps to have presided over an expanding economy and for lying about his own sordid affair with a young White House staffer.

What sets Kennedy apart from these other presidents is his assassination. The murder of someone as young and full of promise as Kennedy has consistently made him an object of public regard. But this alone can't explain his hold on the public. What distinguishes him from William McKinley, whose considerable popularity in 1901 did not resonate at all fifty years after his assassination?

Kennedy's appeal, which he largely shares with other popular presidents, rests on attributes other than specific accomplishments or untimely death. All the popular presidents were well liked, and gave most Americans a sense of personal connection to them. They were and remain inspirational figures who make people feel better about the country and hopeful about the future.

Theodore Roosevelt was almost universally admired, if not adored, by millions of Americans. In his day, he was every boy's beau ideal — with toy companies naming a stuffed bear after him. His feats as a horseman, warrior, hunter, and moralist disciplining wrongdoers at home and abroad brought him a Nobel Prize and a celebrity that resonates almost a hundred years after he left the scene. His use of the White House as a Bully Pulpit to endear himself to citizens, advance his agenda, and promote national self-regard continue to make him a model president.

Woodrow Wilson never enjoyed TR's degree of hero worship, but he won his way into his countrymen's hearts as a man of unquestioned rectitude who made millions proud to be American. His command of English made his oratory a national treasure. (Some people said his speeches were so lyrical that you could have danced to them.) Moreover, despite falling short of realization, his vision of a war to end all wars and to make the world safe for democracy continues to echo the country's highest ideals — as evidenced by George W. Bush's assertion that the Iraq war would eventually spread democracy across the Middle East, and Barack Obama's backing of democracy in Libya.

No president had a stronger hold on Americans, and foreigners drawn to democratic governance, than Franklin Roosevelt. His Fireside Chats created an extraordinary tie to anyone who listened to him on the radio. Two anecdotes say it all: After Roosevelt died, a man stood sobbing by the railroad tracks as the funeral train traveled from Warm Springs, Georgia, to Hyde Park, New York, where he was laid to rest. Did you know the president? someone asked the crying man. No, the man replied, but he knew me. Someone stopped Eleanor Roosevelt on the street, not long after Franklin had died, to say, "I miss the way your husband used to talk to me about my government." It is difficult to imagine anyone saying that about any of our recent elected officials.

During his presidency, Harry Truman provoked the wrath of opponents and lost popular support over the stalemated Korean War that was costing the country so much blood and treasure without a foreseeable favorable end. Yet today, sixty years after the end of his term, Truman is a revered president. And nothing quite accounts for his popularity more than the remembered force of his personality. The most storied moment in his presidency was his 1948 upset election over New York Governor Thomas Dewey. Truman's cross-country whistle-stop campaign at small-town railroad crossings, where people warmed to his plain speaking, is etched in the minds of those who saw him and those who heard or read about his perform-ance then and now: listeners responded to his verbal broadsides against "the do-nothing, good-for-nothing Republicans" in the 80th Congress with shouts of "Give 'em hell, Harry!" Truman's enduring appeal also rests on memories of his ability to articulate the under-standable and ultimately realizable containment strategy for defeat-ing communism without a nuclear war.

Dwight Eisenhower had a different, but equally affectionate rela-tionship with the mass of Americans. The campaign buttons sup-porting him in 1952 defined his widespread appeal: "I like Ike." He was seen as an unassuming war hero — a reluctant politician who had never voted before he ran for president. He assumed the highest office not out of any overriding ambition or need for public affirma-tion but in order to serve the country in a time of Cold War peril. He was seen as a twentieth-century George Washington, the ideal citizen soldier, selflessly doing his duty in defense of the nation's highest ideals. His picture of an America with a smaller federal government, and diminished red tape impeding free enterprise, is never too far from the center of the country's political discourse.

During his time in office, Ronald Reagan was the most popular president since FDR. His ability to speak persuasively on television, radio, and in person to a majority of Americans gave him the envi-able title of the great communicator. One liberal columnist conde-scendingly described Reagan as "President Feel Good," but it was a description Reagan readily embraced as a surefire means to win pub-lic backing for his program of tax cuts and limited government. Although his promised reforms proved to be much less far reaching than advertised, people warmly endorsed his broad platform of change as the Reagan Revolution.

Bill Clinton had a number of stumbles as president, but no one could deny his similar skill at creating a bond with millions of Americans when he said, "I feel your pain." His ability to get into people's skins or create a sense of shared feelings allowed him to win two terms and achieve the considerable post-presidential standing reflected in his 69 percent approval rating. The prosperity of the nineties during his eight years spurred a belief in the country's future that people longed to recreate during the recent recession. And his role in the 2012 campaign was a potent reminder of the hold he still has on the voting public.

It is invaluable to compare Kennedy's popularity against that of other presidents. Like theirs, Kennedy's appeal largely rests on the sense of personal connection people feel to him. They identify with the tragic events that befell him and his family: his assassination and that of his brother, Bobby; the death of his only son, John Kennedy Jr., in a senseless accident; and Jacqueline Kennedy's death at a relatively young age. During his life, and as much since, Kennedy enjoyed the sort of affection the country reserves for its most popular celebrities. Visual images of him on television, especially, served his ability to make Americans feel that they knew and liked him. His good looks, charm, wit, and intelligence are captured and preserved in the taped news conferences he held during his thousand days in office. He is remembered, most of all, as an inspirational president, who encouraged young and old alike to serve their country in the reach for a "New Frontier," and the Peace Corps is a lasting expression of his call to service. He continues to inspire feelings of hope — that the country can meet any challenge, as it did in response to his call to put a man on the moon by the end of the 1960s.

However whimsical and romantic it seems, Kennedy is fixed in our minds at the age of 46 — a youthful war hero and political leader determined to bring out the best in his countrymen. His words asking Americans "to bear the long twilight struggle…against the common enemies of man: tyranny, poverty, disease, and war itself" are as relevant today as they were when he spoke them in 1961. In predicting that the battle to conquer these universal enemies would exceed all our lifetimes, he gave himself a kind of eternal hold on the nation and the world. Fifty years after his death, his appeal endures.

Acknowledgments

The research and writing of this book extended over five years and profited from the support of a number of institutions and people. The numerous books and articles on John F. Kennedy, which are reflected in my notes, are an indispensable starting point for a biographer. These works are particularly valuable for the authors' interviews with friends and associates of JFK, many of whom have since died or whose memories would now be made less precise by the passage of so much time.

The staffs of the various libraries and archives cited in the notes were uniformly helpful, but none was more essential to the study of Kennedy's personal life and public record than the exquisitely located John F. Kennedy Library at Columbia Point, overlooking Boston Harbor. The staff was consistently helpful, but I am particularly grateful to Megan Desnoyers, who worked so diligently to arrange my access to Joseph P. Kennedy's papers and, most important, the Janet Travell collection of medical records that had been unavailable to biographers until the donor committee agreed to open them to me in 2002.

I also wish to thank Kai Bird for access to Averell Harriman correspondence; the Clark Clifford executors for access to his oral history; Adam Clymer for sharing his interviews with Senator Edward M. Kennedy; George Eliades for providing transcripts of difficult to understand JFK tape recordings; Paul Fay for access to his papers and oral history; Barbara Gamarekian for opening previously closed pages in her oral history; Elizabeth Hadley and Geri Dallek for photo research; Nigel Hamilton for making the large collection of materials he assembled for his book *JFK: Reckless Youth*, available at the Massachusetts Historical Society; Maxwell Kennedy for opening Robert Kennedy's confidential files (and to Ted Widmer, who helped arrange this); Robert Kennedy Jr. for providing access to additional LeMoyne Billings letters supplementing those in the Hamilton collection; Christopher Matthews for use of taped interviews; Race Matthews for giving me a copy of Bruce Grant's book; Paul H. Nitze for his oral history; Kenneth O'Donnell Jr. for letting me listen to his father's taped recollections; and Abraham Ribicoff's executors for permitting me to read his Columbia University oral history.

Sven Dubie and Chrissy Kopp, graduate students studying for Ph.D.'s, helped by making copies of documents I identified in my research at the JFK Library. Chrissy also helped by checking some of my notes and by selecting photos for the book from the collection of visual materials at the library.

The many people who spoke with me about Kennedy have been cited at relevant points in the notes to the book, but I am particularly grateful to Elias P. Demetracopoulos, Philip J. Kaiser, and Marianne Means for sharing information with me, and to Peter Kovler for lending an ear and offering wise comments on my ideas.

Wayne Callaway, Robert Morantz, Judith Nowak, and David Schurman lent their medical expertise to the analysis of JFK's many health problems. No one, however, was more instrumental in helping me understand and formulate conclusions about Kennedy's ailments than Jeffrey Kelman. It is no exaggeration to say that I could not have made sense of JFK's complicated medical history without him. He read the Travell files with me at the JFK Library and checked my descriptions of Kennedy's medical woes to assure their accuracy. His contributions to this historical reconstruction were given as an act of friendship, for which I am most grateful.

Sheldon Stern, who served at the John F. Kennedy Library for twenty-three years, gave me the benefit of his expertise by reading the entire manuscript. He not only saved me from a number of errors, he also made excellent suggestions for additions and revisions, which significantly improved the manuscript.

Geoffrey Shandler at Little, Brown is as fine an editor as an author could hope to have. My hopes for the kind of thoughtful editing Geoff provided sank after the first two editors on the book moved on to other positions. But Geoff more than made up for their departure with two careful readings of the manuscript that confirmed me in the conviction that an author's best friend is a devoted editor insistent on making writers push to outdo themselves. Elizabeth Nagle, his assistant, also read the full manuscript and made several excellent suggestions, for which I am grateful. Peggy Leith Anderson, Peggy Freudenthal, Steve Lamont, Pamela Marshall, and Betsy Uhrig added greatly to the readability of the book with their super copyediting skills.

My agent, John W. Wright, has been an indispensable supporter of this book from its inception. He helped me formulate the proposal, arranged for publication, encouraged me along the way, read the entire manuscript, and made excellent suggestions for its improvement. He has been a wise adviser and friend. His courage and strength in response to the tragic loss of his son on September 11, 2001, have been an inspiration to everyone who knows him.

Matthew Dallek, Rebecca Dallek, and Michael Bender, my son, daughter, and son-in-law, cheered me on with words of encouragement and critical reviews of what I said and wrote. They helped me understand what young people born in the years after 1963 need to learn about Kennedy if his life and times are to have special meaning to them.

As with all my work over the last forty years, no one has been more instrumental in making this book a reality than my wife, Geraldine Dallek. She is my toughest, most constructive critic and my best friend. Her insistence on clearer, more felicitous prose and fuller explanations of events now obscured to general readers by the passage of time were essential in making this book comprehensible to that elusive character, "the general reader." She also suggested the title of the book. I cannot imagine writing anything produced for public consumption without her sensible judgments on my always imperfect drafts.

It goes without saying, but I'll say it anyway, any errors in this book are my sole responsibility.

Sources

The sources for the quotes and facts presented in the text rest on numerous manuscript collections, tape recordings, oral histories, interviews, conversations, and newspaper and magazine articles cited in the endnotes. Much of this material is housed in the John F. Kennedy Library in Boston, but several other libraries and archives contain essential documents for the study of Kennedy's life and presidency. Some of this material has not been available to earlier biographers and helped provide a fuller, more accurate picture of the man and his times. Additional materials will become available in the future and will attract other biographers to build upon the work in this book, as I have built on the invaluable research of predecessors who have told the Kennedy story during the last fifty years. Books I have drawn upon are cited in the notes by the author's name, and full publication details for these are provided in the Bibliography, which follows the notes. All the oral histories cited in the notes are from the John F. Kennedy Library unless otherwise indicated.

Notes

Abbreviations

AES	Adlai E. Stevenson
CEA	Council of Economic Advisers
CIA	Central Intelligence Agency
CR	*Congressional Record*
DDE	Dwight David Eisenhower
FBI	Federal Bureau of Investigation
FRUS	*Foreign Relations of the United States*, by U.S. Department of State
HST	Harry S Truman
JEH	J. Edgar Hoover
JFK	John F. Kennedy
JFKL	John F. Kennedy Library
KK	Kathleen Kennedy
KKH	Kathleen Kennedy Hartington
JPK	Joseph P. Kennedy
LBJ	Lyndon Baines Johnson
LBJA: CF	Lyndon B. Johnson Archives: Congressional File
LBJL	Lyndon B. Johnson Library
LBP	LeMoyne Billings Papers, at JFKL
LC	Library of Congress
MHS	Massachusetts Historical Society
NASA	National Aeronautics and Space Administration

NASM   National Security Action Memorandum

NHP   Nigel Hamilton Papers, at MHS

NSF   National Security Files

NSK   Nikita S. Khrushchev

O&C   Official and Confidential File, FBI

OH   Oral History

POF   President's Office Files, at JFKL

PP   Personal Papers, at JFKL

PPP   Pre-Presidential Papers, at JFKL

PPP: JFK   *Public Papers of the Presidents: John F. Kennedy*

RFK   Robert F. Kennedy

Chapter 1: Beginnings

p. 3: "good New Englander": Hugh Fraser OH.

p. 3: "Irishman": Collier and Horowitz, 7.

p. 3: "some disagreement": Notes for speeches for Irish trip, June 11, 1963, Speech Files, Box 45, POF.

p. 4: Lismore Castle and Kathleen's letter: Doris Goodwin, 729.

p. 4: Kathleen asked Jack: KKH to JFK, May 21, 1947, Box 4A, PP.

p. 4: Dress and appearance and the quotes: Burns, 57, 63, 71, 98, 122, 259; Lasky, 101–2; Parmet, *Jack*, 84–85, 170; Blair, 511.

p. 5: The quotes about his effect on women are from Lasky, 149, 205.

p. 5: "rather quietly": Doris Goodwin, 731.

p. 5: "Which Kennedys" and "looking just like": Ibid.

p. 6: "magic of the afternoon": Burns, 3–4; JFK to James M. Burns, Aug. 25, 1959, POF.

p. 6: "Did they have": Doris Goodwin, 732. For Kathleen's description of JFK visit, see KKH to JPK, Sept. 18, 1947, JPK Papers, JFKL.

p. 6: Kennedy great-grandparents: Collier and Horowitz, 7–11.

p. 6: Fitzgerald great-grandparents: Doris Goodwin, chap. 1.

p. 7: "Irishness": Davis, 54. Also see Tamara Plakins Thornton, "Timely Reminders," *Reviews in American History* (Dec. 1998), 795.

pp. 7–9: For the portrait of P. J. Kennedy, see Burns, 8–11; Collier and Horowitz, 11–17; Davis, 21–23, 27–32; Doris Goodwin, 226–32.

pp. 9–11: For the portrait of John F. Fitzgerald: Burns, 10–14; Collier and Horowitz, 18–20; Doris Goodwin, chaps. 4–7; Hamilton, 4–12.

p. 11: "a first hurrah": Collier and Horowitz, 20.

p. 11: Fitzgerald-Hannon marriage: Doris Goodwin, chap. 6.

p. 11: "There have been times": Rose Kennedy, 1.

p. 11: "a big, old rambling": Ibid., 11.

p. 11: "the absolute thrill": Doris Goodwin, 105.

p. 12: For the White House visit and horses and her own rig: Rose Kennedy, 33–34, 15–16.

p. 12: Old Orchard: Ibid., 17; Doris Goodwin, 123–25.

p. 12: "scrollwork porch": Collier and Horowitz, 28.

p. 12: "a hazy idea": Rose Kennedy, 24.

p. 12: "all manner" and Wellesley: Doris Goodwin, 130–33.

p. 13: For the Convent of the Sacred Heart, see Collier and Horowitz, 29.

p. 13: For the trip and schooling, see Doris Goodwin, 155–56, 158–59, 174–89; and Rose Kennedy, 29–33.

p. 13: Returned to Boston: Doris Goodwin, 197–98.

p. 13: Nothing more clearly: Ibid., 201–3.

p. 14: "mistrust" and "resentment" and other quotes in the paragraph: Rose Kennedy, 49–52.

p. 14: For social Darwinism, see Hofstadter, *Social Darwinism*.

p. 15: Joe's reading of Alger: Collier and Horowitz, 23.

p. 15: On rags to riches and mind power, see Weiss.

p. 15: Jobs: Collier and Horowitz, 23; Davis, 31.

p. 15: Assumptions and "If you can't be captain": Collier and Horowitz, 24; Davis, 32.

p. 15: For Joe at Boston Latin: Collier and Horowitz, 24; Davis, 31–33.

p. 16: "somehow seemed": Collier and Horowitz, 24–25.

p. 16: Special affection: Doris Goodwin, 227–28.

pp. 16–17: For Joe at Harvard: Ibid., chap. 13, especially 209 and 214.

p. 17: "basic profession": Collier and Horowitz, 26–28.

p. 17: For the power of the banks, see Brandeis.

p. 18: Joe's apprenticeship: Doris Goodwin, 237–41.

p. 18: Joe and Columbia Trust: Collier and Horowitz, 27–28; Doris Goodwin, 253–58.

p. 19: Courtship and wedding: Rose Kennedy, chap. 6; Doris Goodwin, 124, 258–59; Hamilton, 15–23.

pp. 19–20: Beals Street house: Rose Kennedy, 71–72, 75; Hamilton, 23–24.

p. 20: Joe Jr.'s birth: Ibid., 25; Collier and Horowitz, 32; Doris Goodwin, 261–62.

p. 20: JFK's birth: Hamilton, 30.

p. 21: Joe and the war: Doris Goodwin, 267–76.

p. 21: Joe's work for Bethlehem: Ibid., 276–81, 283–85.

p. 21: "for services rendered": Ibid., 292.

p. 22: Joe as stockbroker: Ibid., chap. 17; for Joe's fortune, 339.

p. 22: The family: Rose Kennedy, 75–76.

p. 22: Naples Road house: Ibid., 75; Doris Goodwin, 313–14.

p. 23: "Now, listen Rosie": Doris Goodwin, 392.

p. 24: "I hope you": Quoted in ibid., 303–4.

p. 24: "were another thing": Interview with Frank Kent Jr. in David E. Koskoff Papers, JFKL.

p. 24: "And the old man": Blair, 318.

p. 24: Affair with Swanson: See Collier and Horowitz, 47–55; "the largest private" is quoted on 53. Also see Doris Goodwin, 389–97, 415–18; Hamilton, 63–68, 73.

p. 24: "Your father again": Rose Kennedy to Children, Feb. 2, 1942, Box 4A, PP.

p. 25: Rose's return to her father's home: Doris Goodwin, 301–8.

p. 25: Rose's travels: Rose Kennedy, 94; Davis, 71; Doris Goodwin, 320–21.

Chapter 2: Privileged Youth

p. 26: And if Joe Kennedy were: "The Nine Kennedy Kids Delight Great Britain," *Life*, Apr. 11, 1938.

pp. 26–27: Early schooling: Rose Kennedy, 97; Doris Goodwin, 355–56; Hamilton, 52–53.

p. 27: Jack's first ten years: JFK childhood medical record, Box 1, and Report of Physical Exam, Oct. 20, 1943, Box 11A, PP; Burns, 32–33; Rose Kennedy, 84, 110–11; Parmet, *Jack*, 17, 19; Doris Goodwin, 353–54; Damore, 19–21.

pp. 27–28: "It was an easy" and Joe Jr.–Jack rivalry: Burns, 23, 28; Damore, 26–27; Collier and Horowitz, 59, 61.

p. 28: Jack's affection for Joe Jr.: Doris Goodwin, 355; John F. Kennedy, *As We Remember Joe*, 3.

p. 28: "When Joe came home": JFK to Dad, Dec. 9 (probably 1929), Box 1, PP.

p. 29: "was no place": McCarthy, 42.

p. 29: Rose's reaction: Doris Goodwin, 367–68; Rose Kennedy, 166.

pp. 29–30: Jack at Riverdale School and transfer to Canterbury, "Creditable": Upper School Scholarship Report, Box 1, PP; Notes on JFK's Canterbury Attendance, Dec. 8, 1988, in NHP; Hamilton, 81–85.

p. 30: "It's a pretty good place": JFK to Uncle Jack, n.d., Box 1, PP.

p. 30: "his average should be": Canterbury School, Record of JFK, Form II, Box 4B, PP.

p. 30: "a little worrying": JFK to Mother, n.d., Box 1, PP.

p. 30: Sports: Letter beginning, "I was certainly glad," JFK to Dad, n.d., Box 1, PP.

p. 30: "Please send me": Schoor, 37.

p. 30: Talk on India: JFK to Dad, n.d, Box 1, PP.

p. 30: "a desire to enjoy": Sorensen, 14.

pp. 30–31: "What do you remember": Hugh Sidey in Henderson, xxiv.

p. 31: "You watched these people": Charles Spalding quoted in Collier and Horowitz, 113.

p. 31: Arrogance: Damore, 20–21, 36–41.

pp. 31–32: Indifference to money: Ralph Horton OH; James Rousmaniere interview in NHP.

p. 32: "They really didn't have": Collier and Horowitz, 62.

p. 32: "Jack, I sent for you": Smith, 161.

p. 32: "Mind your own business": *Boston Globe,* Nov. 19, 1964.

p. 33: Jack's admission to Choate: Hamilton, 84, 88.

pp. 33–34: JFK medical record, including Rose Kennedy's card file on JFK's childhood illnesses; JFK undated letters to "Mother" and "Dad" in Box 1, PP; Doris Goodwin, 309–312; Hamilton, 87–88.

p. 34: "probably very homesick": "Notes on John Fitzgerald Kennedy's Canterbury Attendance" provided by the school, NHP.

p. 34: "a mild cold": Secretary to Mrs. Kennedy, Nov. 24, 1931; also see exchanges between Rose Kennedy and Mrs. St. John for Jan. 18, n.d., 19, 20, 21, 22, 1932, Box 1, PP.

p. 34: "quite a cough": Jan. 23, 25, 1932, Outline of JFK Choate Letters, Box 1, PP; JPK to Mr. St. John, Dec. 3, 1931, and Clara St. John to Mr. Massie and to Mrs. Kennedy, Feb. 8, April 28, 1932, NHP.

pp. 34–35: "flu-like symptoms" and "Jack's winter term": Quoted in Hamilton, 98. Also see Secretary to Mrs. Kennedy, Jan. 10, Feb. 14, 17, 18, Mar. 3, 9, 10, Apr. 13, 1933; Rose Kennedy to Mrs. St. John, Jan. 17, Mar. 9, 1933; Mrs. St. John to Mrs. Kennedy, Jan. 23, 1933; Mrs. St. John to Paul Murphy, Jan. 30, 1933; Paul Murphy to Mrs. Kennedy, Jan. 28, 1933, Outline of JFK Choate Letters, Box 1, PP.

p. 35: On his weight: George St. John to Mr. Maher, quoting JPK, Oct. 10, 1933, NHP.

p. 35: "We are still puzzled": Mrs. St. John to Mrs. Kennedy, Feb. 6, 1934, NHP.

p. 35: "I hope with all my heart": Mrs. St. John to Jack, Feb. 5, 1934, NHP.

p. 35: "It seems that I was": JFK to Billings, Feb. 1934, JFKL. Also see Mrs. St. John to Jack, Feb. 8, Mar. 6, 1934; George St. John to JPK, Feb. 8, 1934, NHP; George Steele to Masters, Feb. 14, 1934; Secretary to JPK, April 25, 1934, Outline of JFK Choate Letters, Box 1, PP; Maurice "Maury" Shea OH.

p. 35: "one of the 'big boys'": Clara St. John to Rose F. Kennedy, Oct. 7, 1931, NHP.

p. 35: Rose had already signaled: In letter to George St. John, July 3, 1931, NHP.

p. 36: "Jack sits at": G. St. John to JPK, Oct. 20, 1931, NHP.

p. 36: Rat Face: Meyers, 15.

p. 37: Jack told Billings: Doris Goodwin, 465–66.

p. 37: "stressed to his children": Ibid., 351.

p. 37: "Jack was sick," "Why don't you," and "Everybody wants to": Hersh, 16.

p. 37: "very frame": Quoted in Hamilton, 358–59.

p. 37: His schoolwork continued: JFK Choate School Records, Box 2, PP.

p. 37: "what concerned us": Rose Kennedy, 176–77.

p. 38: "conspicuously failed": Quoted in Hamilton, 107.

p. 38: *Information Please:* Horton OH. Reading the *New York Times:* Meyers, 15; Horton OH. On Churchill, Kay Halle OH.

p. 38: "most likely to succeed": Horton OH.

p. 38: "I'd like to take": John J. Maher Report of JFK, in Meyers, 14.

p. 38: "I can't tell you": JPK to G. St. George, Nov. 21, 1933; JPK to JPK Jr., Nov. 21, 1933; JPK to G. Steele, Jan. 5, 1935, NHP.

pp. 38–39: The Muckers episode is best recounted in Parmet, *Jack,* 34–38; Doris Goodwin, 486–89; Thomas C. Reeves, 42–43; and Hamilton, 119–27.

p. 39: For Tinker on St. John's anti-Catholicism, see Sheldon Stern to author, Mar. 25, 2002. Also, Meyers, 17; Parmet, *Jack,* 33.

p. 40: "the longer I live": Meyers, 15.

p. 40: "I never saw a boy": G. St. John to JPK, Nov. 24, 1933, NHP.

p. 40: "Jack is one": G. St. John to JPK, Feb. 8, 1934, NHP.

p. 40: "never lectured": Meyers, 16.

pp. 40–41: "My God": LeMoyne Billings recounted this to Doris Goodwin, 487–88.

p. 41: "To Boss Tweed": Horton OH.

p. 41: "a little wild": Doris Goodwin, 467.

p. 41: "If I were their age": Rose Kennedy, 172–73.

p. 41: "Jack has a clever": Meyers, 15.

p. 41: Harvard College: Principal's Report on Applicant, Box 2, PP.

pp. 41–42: Princeton decision: Rose Kennedy, 201. For the most detailed description of this interlude between fall 1935 and summer 1936, see Hamilton, 139–64.

p. 42: "Exam today": JFK to Billings, Jan. 27, 1937, LBP.

p. 42: "cram school": Torbert H. Macdonald OH. JFK's Harvard records, including tutor's report, are in Box 2, PP.

p. 43: On JFK at Harvard: Lawrence Lader, "Jack Kennedy at Harvard: A Fellow Student Tells About," which includes the quotes from the coach and the contemporary about Joe, Box 2, PP; also see Doris Goodwin, 505–6.

p. 43: "espoused their causes": Lasky, 74.

p. 43: "You are certainly": JFK to Billings, Nov. 9, 1936, NHP.

p. 43: The state of the university is described in Keller, chap. 1.

p. 44: Galbraith on Joe Jr.: Galbraith, A Life, 53.

p. 44: "When I become": Lasky, 75.

p. 44: For Joe Jr.'s career at Harvard, see Doris Goodwin, 504–5.

p. 44: For JFK's courses, see JFK, Harvard University Concentration Card, June 1940, Box 2, PP.

p. 44: "is planning to do work": Freshman Adviser's Report; the books are listed in Tutorial Record, 1937–38, Box 2, PP.

pp. 44–45: For the papers on Francis I and Rousseau, see Box 1, PP, and Hamilton, 168–71, 176–77.

p. 45: "A gangling": Lader, "Jack Kennedy at Harvard."

p. 45: a "Good boy" and other quotes in reports of house applications, April 1, 1937, Box 2, PP.

p. 45: "handsome . . . gregarious": Galbraith, A Life, 53.

p. 45: "We are having one hell": JFK to Billings, Sept. 29, 1936, NHP.

p. 45: "I am now known": JFK to Billings, Oct. 21, 1936, NHP.

p. 45: "very humorous": Blair, 49.

p. 45: "Anytime" and "Jack was more fun": Hamilton, 204.

p. 45: "I can't help it": JFK to Billings, July 25, 1934, NHP.

p. 46: "I had an enema": JFK to Billings, June 19, 1934, LBP.

p. 46: "The nurses here": JFK to Billings, June 27, 1934, NHP.

p. 46: "a bundle from": JFK to Billings, Oct. 21, 1936, NHP.

p. 46: "I can now get": JFK to Billings, Jan. 13, 1937, NHP.

p. 46: "dirty": See the JFK letters in Billings papers for 1934–1937, NHP.

p. 46: "He was interested": LeMoyne Billings OH.

p. 46: "brother John": Michaelis, 152.

p. 46: "because he was": Billings OH.

p. 47: His father's infidelities: Hamilton, 350–51.

p. 47: "went down to the Cape": JFK to Billings, Oct. 16, 1936, LBP.

p. 47: "locker room stories": Collier and Horowitz, 212.

p. 47: "needed female": Doris Goodwin, 724.

pp. 47–48: JPK's visits to Hollywood: Hersh, 27.

p. 48: go "down next week": JFK to Billings, Oct. 16, 1936, LBP.

p. 48: "little party": JFK to Billings, Oct. 21, 1936, in NHP.

p. 48: JFK's fascination with the Cecil book: Hellmann, 29–32; Hersh, 25.

p. 48: "didn't have to lift" and "Hello, kid": Hersh, 22–23.

p. 48: "Still can't get use to": JFK to Billings, Oct. 4, 1940, NHP.

pp. 48–49: The anecdotes about "only fifteen minutes" and "foreplay" were told to me respectively by a journalist and a colleague at Boston University, whose roommate dated JFK.

p. 49: "Slam, bam": Hellmann, 28.

p. 49: as "compulsive as Mussolini": Collier and Horowitz, 212.

p. 49: "a true count": William Walton Interview in NHP.

p. 49: The arrangement to pay Billings's way: Hamilton, 177.

pp. 49–53: The itinerary of the trip and most of the JFK quotes about what he saw are in JFK Diary, Box 1, PP. For other quotes, see LeMoyne Billings, *The New Yorker*, April 1, 1961, 126–27; Hamilton, 183, 185, 192–93; Collier and Horowitz, 85; Burns, 32.

p. 53: The Maryland mansion: Doris Goodwin, 450–51.

p. 53: The Spee and "It was a status symbol": Hamilton, 205–9.

p. 53: Appointment as ambassador: Dallek, *Franklin D. Roosevelt*, 533; Beschloss, *Kennedy and Roosevelt*, 123–28.

p. 53: "The moment the appointment": Quoted in Doris Goodwin, 509.

p. 54: "London is where": Arthur Krock OH.

p. 54: "You don't understand": Beschloss, *Kennedy and Roosevelt*, 126.

p. 54: "Don't go buying": Collier and Horowitz, 88.

p. 54: For Jack's summer: Doris Goodwin, 537, 539–40, 545; Hamilton, 233–37; Hugh Fraser OH; William Douglas-Home OH.

p. 54: Jack's 1938–39 academic record is in Box 2; his fall course list, grades, and tutorial record agreeing to the reading and thesis plan are in Box 3, PP.

p. 55: "a rather thin": A. Chester Hanford OH.

p. 55: For the Holcombe quotes, see Meyers, 23.

p. 55: The visit to New Orleans: Hamilton, 254.

pp. 55–56: Pro-Chamberlain speech and "It's pretty funny": JFK to Parents, n.d. (but probably Oct. 1938), Box 1, PP.

p. 56: "feeling very important": JFK to Billings, Mar. 1939, NHP.

p. 56: had had "a great time": JFK to Billings, Mar. 23, 1939, LBP.

p. 56: "graciously declined": Ibid.

p. 57: "living like a king": JFK to Billings, April 6, 1939, NHP.

p. 57: "Plenty of action": Postcard, April, n.d., 1939, NHP.

p. 57: "Things have been humming": JFK to Billings, April 28, 1939, NHP.

p. 57: "Jack sitting": Bullitt, 273. Offie remembers this as the summer of 1938, but other evidence suggests 1939.

p. 57: "The whole thing": JFK to Billings, May 1939, NHP. Also see JFK to Billings, April 28, July 17, and Aug. 20, 1939, and JFK to JPK, n.d., 1939, all in NHP; and Burns, 37–38.

p. 58: August travels: Meyers, 28; Kennan, 91–92.

p. 58: The Riviera: Dietrich, 182.

pp. 58–59: Visit to Parliament, JPK's reaction to the war, and the rescue mission: Hamilton, 279–86; Beschloss, *Kennedy and Roosevelt*, 163–64.

p. 59: Return to America: See undated 1939 letters from JFK to JPK, Boxes 1 and 4B, PP.

p. 59: "I saw the rock": CBS transcribed interview in the JFKL Audio-Visual Archive.

p. 59: "got this odd, hard look": Quoted in Collier and Horowitz, 102.

p. 59: Why the masses obey: Payson S. Wild OH.

p. 59: JFK editorial, Harvard *Crimson*, Oct. 9, 1939.

p. 59: "everyone here is ready": JFK to JPK, n.d., 1939, Box 1, PP.

p. 60: On JPK's appeal to Washington to mediate, see *Foreign Relations of the United States, 1939*, I (Washington, D.C.), 421–24.

p. 60: "He seemed to blossom": Wild OH.

p. 60: The editorial board: Parmet, *Jack*, 66.

p. 60: "I seem to be": Undated 1939 letters from JFK to JPK, Boxes 1 and 4B, PP.

p. 60: "The war clinched": Ed Plaut interview with JFK, n.d., in Ralph G. Martin Papers, Boston University.

p. 60: For JFK's courses, see JFK, Course List, Harvard University, Box 3, PP. Also see Wild OH and Hamilton, 297–302.

p. 61: On Lothian, see Hamilton, 306–7.

p. 61: "We used to": Ibid., 314–15.

pp. 61–62: On JFK's initial exchanges with Seymour, see JFK to Seymour, Jan. 11, 1940; Seymour to JFK, Jan. 11, 1940; JFK to Seymour, Jan. 30, Feb. 9, 1940; Seymour to Paul Murphy, Feb. 8, 1940; Seymour to JFK, Feb. 12, 1940; Murphy to Seymour, Feb. 27, 1940; all in Box 1, James Seymour Papers, JFKL.

p. 62: The unpublished thesis "Appeasement at Munich" is in the PP. The Yeomans and Friedrich Reports on Thesis for Distinction are in Box 2, PP.

p. 62: "a deep thinker": Wild OH.

p. 62: "imagination and diligence": Bruce C. Hopper, "Notes: Jack Kennedy as a Student at Harvard (Candidate for Honors)," July 1960, Box 2, PP.

p. 62: "again elated": Hopper to B. O'Riordan, Jan. 6, 1964, Box 2, PP.

p. 63: "a typical undergraduate": Burns, 40.

p. 63: JFK's argument is stated repeatedly throughout the thesis.

p. 63: "While Daddy Slept": Parmet, *Jack*, 70.

p. 64: "to give up their personal interests": JFK, "Appeasement at Munich," 91.

p. 64: "In this calm acceptance": Ibid., 146.

p. 64: "While it is the book": Quoted in Freedman, 590.

p. 65: "it was amateurish": Krock OH. Also see JFK to JPK, n.d., 1940, in Meyers, 33–34. The details of arranging publication, including "sales possibilities" and "things moving," are in Hamilton, 329–30.

p. 65: "as soon as possible": JFK to JPK, n.d., 1940, Box 4A, PP. For the revisions, see JFK to JPK, n.d., but clearly spring 1940, Box 1, PP; JPK to JFK, May 20, 1940, Box 129, POF; and Parmet, *Jack*, 72–76.

p. 65: For the reviews and sales, see Parmet, *Jack*, 74, 77; Parmet says sales amounted to 80,000 copies, but Nigel Hamilton says the figure was well below that (p. 380).

pp. 65–66: "I read Jack's book" and "The book will do you": Quoted in Rose Kennedy, 271, 261–62.

p. 66: "Jack was downstairs": Charles Spalding OH.

p. 66: On health problems and JFK's plans to attend Yale, see Blair, 91.

pp. 66–67: "I don't think": Quoted in ibid., 90.

p. 67: For JFK's term at Stanford, see ibid., 91–104.

p. 67: "He was fascinated": Quoted in Hamilton, 350.

p. 67: JFK conversation with Stanford student body president and "remote westerners": Harry Muheim, "Rich, Young, and Happy," *Esquire*, Aug. 1966.

p. 67: For JFK's counsel to his father, see JFK to JPK, Dec. 5, 1940, Box 4A, PP.

p. 67: On Lend-Lease: "a supplemental note," n.d., but Dec. 1940, Box 4A, PP; Hamilton, 393–97.

p. 68: For JFK's visit to Latin America, see Muheim, *Esquire*, 109–110; Hamilton, 403–5, and the notes for these pages on p. 841.

p. 68: On family requirements of a serious life purpose, see Doris Goodwin, 457.

Chapter 3: The Terrors of Life

p. 69: "was surprised": Collier and Horowitz, 212.

p. 69: "Gee, you're": Rose Kennedy, 93.

p. 69: Billings's recollections: Doris Goodwin, 353.

p. 69: Rose's insistence: Davis, 53.

p. 70: She "organized and supervised": Hellmann, 10.

p. 70: Billings quoted in Doris Goodwin, 353.

p. 70: Jack quoted in Burns, 21.

p. 70: Rose never told him: Hersh, 17.

p. 70: Spalding quoted in Hamilton, 690–91.

p. 70: "history made him": Interview with Jacqueline Kennedy, "The Camelot Papers, 1963–1964," Theodore H. White Papers, JFKL.

p. 70: Staged minor rebellions: Rose Kennedy, 93–94. Also see Hellmann, 10–11.

p. 70: "I enjoy your": Quoted in Doris Goodwin, 631.

p. 71: "I looked on": Rose Kennedy, 81. Some 200 of the 500 pages of Rose's book are devoted to a discussion of child rearing.

p. 71: Rose as mother: Also see Sheldon M. Stern's persuasive letter to Nigel Hamilton, June 10, 1994, describing Rose's behavior as a mother; Stern gave me a copy of his letter.

p. 71: The most thoughtful and sensitive discussion of Rosemary Kennedy is in Doris Goodwin, 356–63.

p. 72: "a marvelous capacity": William Walton interview in NHP.

p. 72: On Rosemary's lobotomy, Doris Goodwin, 639–44.

p. 73: " 'On your feet' ": Parmet, *Jack*, 16. On JFK's stoicism, see JPK to Paul B. Fay, Mar. 26, 1945, Paul B. Fay Papers, JFKL.

p. 73: "The Goddamnest hole": JFK to Billings, June 19, 1934, NHP.

p. 73: "We used to joke": LeMoyne Billings OH.

p. 73: The medical records with a diagnosis of colitis are from his naval service, in Box 11A, PP.

pp. 73–74: The initial diet and hopes to be at Mayo only a few days: JFK to JPK, n.d., but on Rochester hotel stationery, Box 4B, PP.

p. 74: "I am suffering": JFK to Billings, June 19, 1934, NHP.

p. 74: "God what a beating": JFK to Billings, June 21, 1934, LBP.

p. 74: "Shit!! I've got something wrong": JFK to Billings, June 27, 1934, NHP.

p. 75: "still in this": JFK to Billings, June 30, 1934, NHP.

p. 75: "diffuse duodenitis": Dr. Sara Jordan to Capt. Frederick L. Conklin,

July 14, 1944, Box 11A, PP; and JFK Navy Department Medical Record, Dec. 15, 1944, Box 11A, PP.

p. 75: Emotional stress: Choate report on JFK to Harvard University, Apr. 30, 1935, Box 2, PP.

p. 75: Colitis therapy: "Chronic Ulcerative Colitis: Progress in Its Management," *Proceedings of the Staff Meetings of the Mayo Clinic,* vol. 9 (Jan. 3, 1934), 1–5; "Illeosigmoidostomy for Chronic Ulcerative Colitis," *Proceedings,* vol. 11 (Dec. 9, 1936), 798; "Further Studies in Calcium and Parathyroid Therapy in Chronic Ulcerative Colitis," *American Journal of the Medical Sciences,* vol. 190 (Nov. 1935), 676–83. Mayo's pioneering work on adrenal-hormone extracts is discussed in Dr. Timothy Lamphier interview with Nigel Hamilton, May 1, 1991, NHP.

p. 75: "We always had": Dr. George Thorn interview with Nigel Hamilton, June 4, 1991, NHP.

p. 76: "Ordering stuff": JFK to JPK, "Early 1937," Box 1, PP. A parathyroid extract was available by 1935 and DOCA was available by 1937. See "Absorption of Desoxycorticosterone from Tablets Implanted Subcutaneously," *Lancet,* vol. 1 (Mar. 2, 1940), 406–7; and chap. 72, especially p. 1609, of *The Pharmacological Basis of Therapeutics.* There are listings of articles on DOCA in the 1939 *Index Medicus.*

p. 76: "a little knife": Paul B. Fay OH.

p. 76: It is also possible that the DOCA: Dr. Seymour Reichlin to author, Nov. 23, 2002.

pp. 76–77: Nevertheless by 1942: Goodman and Gilman, 1608.

p. 77: No one can say: Conversations with Dr. Jeffrey Kelman and Dr. Lawrence Altman.

p. 77: Celiac sprue: Dr. Peter Green to author, Nov. 21, 2002, and "What is Celiac Sprue?" Celiac Sprue Research Foundation, Palo Alto, Calif. Also, Richard J. Farrell and Ciaran P. Kelly, "Current Concepts: Celiac Sprue," *New England Journal of Medicine,* Jan. 17, 2002, 180–88. Dr. Jeffrey Kelman described to me why a diagnosis of celiac sprue could not be conclusive.

p. 77: Jack's blood count: See the numerous communications between October 1934 and June 1935 about monitoring JFK's blood count in Outline of Choate JFK Letters, Box 1, PP.

p. 77: Agranulocytosis: Dr. William Murphy to JPK, Box 4B, PP.

p. 77: Illness while in London: JFK to Billings, Oct. 1935, and Princeton records in NHP.

p. 78: "the most harrowing": JFK to Billings, Jan. 1936, LBP.

p. 78: "At 1500": JFK to Billings, Jan. 18, 1936, NHP.

p. 78: "Took a peak": JFK to Billings, Jan. 27, 1936, NHP.

p. 78: Letters to Billings: Jan. 1936, LBP; Jan. 18, Jan. 27, and Feb. 13, 1936, NHP.

p. 79: Enjoyed improved health: See JPK to Dean Delmar Leighton, Aug. 28, 1936, Box 2, PP.

p. 79: "Plunked myself down": JFK to Billings, May 15, 1936, NHP.

p. 79: "Jack broke out": Quoted in Hamilton, 196. See JFK Diary, Aug. 28, 29, 1937, Box 1, PP.

p. 80: The Mayo treatment: See "Chronic Ulcerative Colitis with Marked Deficiency State," *Proceedings of the Mayo Clinic,* vol. 14 (Oct. 25, 1939), 687.

Also see JFK to Billings, Jan. 21, Feb. 14, Mar. 15, June 1, June 15, Oct. 1938, Feb. 5, 1939, NHP. JFK to Mother, n.d. (but probably Feb. 1938), Box 4B, PP.

p. 80: "take my first liver injection": JFK to Dad & Mother, Nov. 1939, Box 4B, PP. Hamilton, 395.

p. 80: "For a man": JPK to JFK, Sept. 10, 1940, Box 4A, PP.

p. 81: "an occasional pain": JFK, Medical Record, Dec. 15, 1944, Box 11A, PP. Also see X rays for Nov. 8, 1944, in Dr. Janet Travell medical records, JFKL. Dr. Jeffrey Kelman suggested the possible connection between the adrenal extracts and JFK's back problem. David Schurman, M.D., an orthopedic surgeon at Stanford University, confirmed Kelman's analysis. The widely used text *The Principles of Internal Medicine*, edited by T. R. Harrison, relying on a 1943 article on "Ulcerative Colitis," in *Gastroenterology*, edited by H. L. Bockus (Philadelphia, 1943), p. 549, discussed the effects of "cortisone and ACTH on the course of the disease," saying things were "still in the experimental stages." In the late thirties the adrenal drug of choice was desoxycorticosterone acetate, known as DOCA. The 1939 and 1940 editions of the *Quarterly Cumulative Index Medicus* list numerous articles about the uses of DOCA.

p. 81: On Jack's draft status, see unidentified newspaper clipping with an AP photo of JFK, n.d., Box 4A, PP.

p. 81: "The only humorous thing": Torbert Macdonald to JFK, n.d., Box 4B, PP.

p. 81: "This draft": JFK to Billings, Nov. 14, 1940, NHP. Hamilton, 360–62.

p. 82: "I am having Jack": Quoted in Blair, 111–13. Also see Hamilton, 405–6.

p. 82: "usual childhood diseases": Report of Physical Exam, Aug. 5, 1941, Box 11A, PP.

p. 82: "exceptionally brilliant": Investigation Report, USNIS, Sept. 10, 1941, Box 11A, PP.

p. 83: "writing, condensing": Quoted in Hamilton, 424–25.

p. 83: "Isn't this a dull": JFK to Billings, Dec. 12, 1941, NHP.

p. 83: On JFK in Washington and Inga, see Doris Goodwin, 630; Hamilton, 420–23, 431.

p. 84: "He had the charm": Quoted in Hamilton, 422.

p. 84: The affair: Doris Goodwin, 627–35; Hamilton, 426–39. The FBI files on Inga are in the J. Edgar Hoover Official and Confidential File, Microfilm, JFKL.

p. 84: JFK's transfer: Chief of the Bureau of Navigation to JFK, Jan. 14, 1942, Box 11A, PP.

p. 84: "They shagged": Robert J. Donovan OH.

p. 84: "Jack finds": Rose Kennedy to Children, Feb. 16, 1942, Box 4A, PP.

p. 84: "just seemed": Billings quoted in Hamilton, 450. See Inga Arvad to JFK, Jan. 19, 20, 26, 27, 1942, Box 4A, PP.

p. 85: FBI wiretaps: D. M. Ladd to J. Edgar Hoover, Feb. 6, 1942; and J. R. Ruggles to Hoover, Feb. 23, 1942, O&C File, FBI Microfilm.

p. 85: "We are so well matched": Inga Arvad to JFK, Jan. 26, 1942, Box 4A, PP.

p. 85: On Joe's role in breakup, also see Doris Goodwin, 634–35.

p. 85: "There is one thing": Mar. 11, 1942; also KK to JFK, Mar., n.d., 1942, all in Box 4A, PP.

pp. 85–86: Back problems: See JFK to Billings, Mar. 11, April 9, 1942, NHP;

Rose Kennedy to Children, Mar. 27, 1942, Box 4A, PP; typed medical history and record, beginning April 13, 1942; and handwritten clinical record, May 21 to June 10, 1942; Chief of Bureau of Navigation to JFK, May 8, 1942, Box 11A, PP.

p. 86: "I have a feeling": Quoted in Doris Goodwin, 635; she also cites evidence of JFK's thoughts of renouncing Catholicism.

p. 87: "This goddamn place": JFK to Billings, Summer 1942, NHP.

p. 87: On the PTs, see Hamilton, 497–503.

p. 88: On Jack's entrance into the PT service and his medical concerns, including JPK's letter to Joe Jr., see Admiral John Harllee OH and Hamilton, 507.

p. 88: "He was in pain": Quoted in Hamilton, 517–18.

p. 88: "This job": JFK to Billings, Jan. 30, 1943, NHP.

p. 88: "his whole attitude": Rose Kennedy to Children, Oct. 9, 1942, Box 4A, PP; Doris Goodwin, 646–47.

p. 88: "causing his mother": Quoted in Goodwin, 647.

p. 89: "conscientious": JFK, Report on Fitness, Feb. 11, 1943, Box 11, PP.

p. 89: "Kennedy was extremely": Harllee OH.

p. 89: Meeting with Walsh and reassignment: Sen. David Walsh to John F. Fitzgerald, Dec. 21, 1942, Box 585, PPP. Harllee, in his OH, says he saw Walsh's letter to the Navy Dept. Commander, MTB Squadron Four, to JFK, Jan. 8, 1943, Box 11, PP.

p. 89: "way to war": Quoted in Schlesinger, *Robert Kennedy*, 51.

p. 89: "gastro-enteritis": JFK Navy Medical Record, Dec. 15, 1944, entries for Jan. 12–13, 1943, Box 11A, PP.

pp. 89–90: "Re my gut" and "be stuck in Panama": JFK to Billings, May 6, 1943, NHP.

p. 90: On JFK's transfers, see Orders for Feb. 11, 19, 20, Box 11, PP. Also, Hamilton, 521–22.

p. 90: "Your friend Jock": JFK to Billings, Jan. 30, 1943, NHP.

p. 90: "I'm extremely glad": Quoted in Hamilton, 537–38.

p. 91: "That slowed me": JFK to Billings, May 6, 1943, NHP.

p. 91: "to watch out": Macdonald quoted in Meyers, 38.

p. 91: "among the gloomier": Quoted in Hamilton, 535.

p. 91: "all the nuns": Quoted in Doris Goodwin, 651.

p. 91: "picture that I had": Quoted in ibid., 533; JFK to Dad & Mother, May 14, 1943, Box 5, PP; JFK to Billings, May 6, 1943, NHP.

p. 92: "It's not bad": JFK to Billings, May 6, 1943, NHP.

p. 92: "It's one of the": Quoted in Hamilton, 533.

p. 92: "I always like": JFK to Mother & Dad, Sept. 12, 1943, Box 5, PP.

p. 92: "He never said": Ibid.

p. 92: "If they do that": JFK to Dad & Mother, May 14, 1943, Box 5, PP.

p. 93: "Have been ferrying" and "Just had an inspection": Quoted in Hamilton, 539–41.

p. 93: "A great hold-up": JFK to Dad & Mother, May 14, 1943, Box 5, PP.

pp. 93–94: "that many Annapolis": Harllee OH.

p. 94: "this heaving puffing": Quoted in Sorensen, 19.

p. 94: On the PTs and "Let me be honest": Blair, 174, 156. JFK to KK, June 3, 1943: Quoted in Doris Goodwin, 650. Bulkley, *At Close Quarters*, with an Introduction by JFK.

p. 94: "When the showdown comes": JFK to Dad & Mother, May 14, 1943, Box 5, PP.

p. 94: "had become somewhat cynical": JFK to Mother & Dad, Sept. 12, 1943, Box 5, PP.

pp. 94–95: For the Guadalcanal, New Georgia, and Solomon Islands campaign in general, see Dear and Foot, 511–15, 791–96, 855–63, 918.

p. 95: On the failure of the PTs, see Blair, chap. 17, and 215–16 and 229 for the quotes.

p. 95: "least effective action": Cooper, 151.

pp. 95–96: Questions were raised: Hamilton, 554–72; the quotes are on 567–69. A controversy also erupted between the captain of the Japanese destroyer and his commanding officer, who was using the destroyer as a flagship, as to whether the collision with JFK's boat was accidental or on purpose. See Katsumori Yamashiro, the commander of the Japanese flotilla of August 1–2, 1943, to JFK, Nov. 15, 1958, Sept. 9, 1960, Jan. 20, 1961, Aug. 1, 1962, and the translated article by Kohei Hanami, the destroyer's captain, "The Man I Might Have Killed Was Kennedy," Nov. 2, 1960, all in Box 132, POF.

p. 96: "terrible thing": JFK to Mother & Dad, Sept. 12, 1943, Box 5, PP.

pp. 96–97: For the sinking and rescue, see Memorandum to Commander MTB Flotilla One: Sinking of PT 109 and Subsequent Rescue, Aug. 22, 1943, Box 6, PP; History of PT 109, n.d., Box 132, POF; Robert King Interview: The PT-109 Crew Rescue: The Scouts' Stories, MS 84-57, JFKL; *New York Times*, Aug. 20, 1943, June 4, 1961; Doris Goodwin, 654–57; and Hamilton, 577–602.

p. 97: "In human affairs": Dallek, *Franklin D. Roosevelt*, 378.

p. 98: JFK as hero: Hamilton, 598, 602, 605; *New York Times*, Aug. 20, 1943; *Boston Globe*, Aug. 19, 1943.

p. 98: "It certainly should occur": Quoted in Doris Goodwin, 658–59.

p. 98: "None of that hero": Quoted in Blair, 310–11.

p. 98: "It was easy": Quoted in Sorensen, 18.

p. 98: "Lieb, if I get": Quoted in Hamilton, 598–99. John Hersey, "Survival," *The New Yorker*, June 17, 1944.

p. 99: "God save this country": Sorensen, 19.

p. 99: "I'd like you to meet": Quoted in Hamilton, 592.

p. 99: "report to sick bay": Quoted in Blair, 179–81.

p. 99: "exactly what the Dr.": JFK to Dad and Mother, Aug. 10, 1943, JPK Papers, JFKL.

p. 99: "I imagine he's": Quoted in Doris Goodwin, 659.

p. 99: "It was a question": Quoted in Blair, 310.

p. 99: "he wanted to": Quoted in Hamilton, 608.

pp. 99–100: "symptoms of fatigue": JFK, Medical History, Aug. 9, 16, 1943, Box 11A, PP.

p. 100: For the gunboat combat, see JFK to Billings, Sept. 15, 1943, NHP; JFK to Dad, Oct. 30, 1943, and JFK to Family, Nov. 1, 1943, Box 5, PP; and Hamilton, 606–27.

p. 100: "just God damned": Quoted in Hamilton, 616–17.

p. 100: Health problems: See Report of Physical Exam, Oct. 20, 1943, Box 11A, PP.

p. 100: "I just took the physical": Quoted in Blair, 301.

p. 100: "I looked as bad": Quoted in Hamilton, 626.

pp. 100–101: His stomach pain: see [Medical] Report:-Kennedy, J. F., 11-23-43, G.I.; JFK Medical History, U.S. Naval Hospital, Chelsea, Mass., Nov. 25, 1944, Box 11A, PP; Commander A. P. Cluster to JFK, Dec. 21, 1943, and Chief of Naval Personnel to JFK, Jan. 7, 1944, Box 11, PP.

p. 101: "definitely not in good shape": Ron McCoy, Inga's son, to author, Dec. 10, 2002.

p. 101: "in reasonably good shape": Quoted in Blair, 315.

p. 101: "He is just the same": Rose Kennedy to Children, Jan. 31, 1944, JPK Papers.

p. 101: On his need for an operation, see JFK to Paul "Red" Fay, Feb. 21, 1944, quoted in Fay.

p. 101: "Once you get your feet": JFK to "Johnny" [Hersey], n.d., NHP.

p. 101: On his fevers and complexion, see Joseph Timilty interview with Nigel Hamilton, NHP.

p. 101: "with nothing more": JFK to Billings, May 3, 1944, NHP.

p. 102: For the Lahey surgeon's report, see Dr. James Poppen to Capt. Frederick Conklin, Aug. 1, 1944, Box 11A, PP.

p. 102: "an interesting complication": U.S. Naval Hospital, Neuro-Surgery, Dr. Heintzelman, Aug. 4, 1944, Box 11A, PP.

p. 102: Several medical problems: Dr. Sara Jordan to Captain Conklin, July 14, Aug. 1, 1944, Box 11A, PP. See Clinical Record, JFK, entries from Aug. 5 to Nov. 16, 1944, and Medical History, JFK, entries Aug. 4–Nov. 25, 1944, Box 11A, PP.

p. 103: "In regard to": Quoted in Sorensen, 44.

p. 103: "Am still in": JFK to Billings, Nov. 1944, NHP.

p. 103: "clearly indicate": Dr. B. H. Adams to MO in C, Nav. Hosp, Chelsea, Mass., Dec. 1, 1945, and to the Surgeon General, Dec. 1, 1944, Box 11A, PP.

p. 103: "present abdominal symptoms": Medical Record, JFK, Dec. 15, 1944, entry for Dec. 6, 1944, Box 11A, PP.

p. 103: Incapacity for naval service: R. T. McIntire, Chief of Bureau, to BUPers., Jan. 18, 1945, and Sec. of Navy James Forrestal to JFK, Mar. 16, 1945, Box 11, PP.

p. 104: "unstable back": Quoted in Interview with Dr. Elmer C. Bartels, n.d., NHP.

p. 104: The expert on steroids is Dr. Eugene Strauss, who described the problem with dosages in the early use of steroids to Dr. Jeffrey Kelman. Conversation with Dr. Kelman. Also see Jonathan D. Adachi and Alexandra Papaioannou, "Corticosteroid-Induced Osteoporosis: Detection and Management," *Drug Safety,* vol. 24, no. 8 (2001), 607–24, which demonstrates that osteoporosis can begin within three months after taking steroids.

p. 104: On the development and availability of DOCA by 1937, see Medvei, 476–78.

p. 104: "getting along well": JPK to Paul Fay, Mar. 26, 1945, Paul B. Fay Papers, JFKL.

p. 104: "he looked jaundiced": Quoted in Hamilton, 680.

p. 104: "so bad": JFK to Billings, Feb. 20, 1945, NHP.

pp. 104–5: On his health from May 1945 to November 1946, see Hamilton, 687, 703, 712, 721–22, 768–69, 793–94.

p. 105: "gastro-enteritis": Navy Medical History, JFK, entries for Aug. 3, 4, 5, 1945, Box 11A, PP.

p. 105: For the June 1946 medical crisis, see Blair, 560–62.

p. 105: On JFK's negligence about his medication, see Dr. Elmer C. Bartels Interview, n.d., NHP.

p. 105: "slow atrophy": Dr. Dorothea E. Hellman to Joan and Clay Blair, Mar. 31, 1977; and Dr. Elmer C. Bartels Interview, NHP. On Eunice Kennedy and whether JFK's Addison's disease was a primary or secondary form, I am grateful for the counsel of Dr. Wayne Callaway, a Washington, D.C., endocrinologist in a conversation on April 30, 2002.

p. 106: "much impressed": JK [Joe] Jr. to JFK, Aug. 10, 1944, Box 4A, PP. For the background to Joe's military service, see Doris Goodwin, 683–84.

p. 106: The mission and its dangers: Davis, 104–6.

p. 106: "intending to risk": JK Jr. to JFK, Aug. 10, 1944, Box 4A, PP.

p. 106: "If I don't come back": Quoted in Doris Goodwin, 688.

p. 107: The U.S. Air Force report, Aug. 14, 1944, JFKL.

p. 107: The 2001 explanation: William G. Penny to John F. Kennedy Library, Aug. 14, 2001, JFKL.

p. 107: "You know how much": Quoted in Doris Goodwin, 693.

p. 108: "defined his," "Forever in his," and "I'm shadowboxing": Quoted in Doris Goodwin, 698–99.

p. 108: "The pattern of life": KKH to JFK, Oct. 31, 1944, Box 4A, PP.

p. 108: "The news of": KKH to Family, Feb. 27, 1945, Box 4A, PP.

p. 108: "Luckily I am": KKH to Billings, Nov. 29, 1944, Box 4A, PP.

p. 108: "His sense of": Quoted in Sorensen, 14.

Chapter 4: Choosing Politics

p. 111: "The desire to enhance": Doris Goodwin, 500.

p. 112: "in the next generation": Collier and Horowitz, 75; and also 82.

p. 112: "for people to take": See Memo "About Nov. 10, 1941," in Speech and Book File, Nov. 11, 1941–Jan. 23, 1942; also Speech and Book Material, Oct. 1941–Jan. 1942. Both in Box 11, PP.

p. 112: "I never thought": JFK to Billings, Feb. 12, 1942, NHP. Also Memo, Feb. 14, 1942, Speech and Book Material, N.Y. office, 1937–1943, Box 11, PP; JFK to JPK, Feb. 25, 1942, Box 4A, PP; and JFK to KK, Mar. 10, 1942, also Box 4A, PP.

p. 113: "spent most of his time": Quoted in Blair, 191, and Hamilton, 543.

p. 113: "He made us all very conscious": Quoted in Hamilton, 629.

p. 113: "Let's Try an Experiment": In box of JFK Articles, 1941–1949, JFKL.

p. 114: For the response to JFK's article, see Blair, 364–65; Parmet, Jack, 128–30; Hamilton, 688.

p. 114: "labor was going to be": Quoted in Blair, 365–67.

p. 114: For JFK's newspaper work, see Blair, 371–72; Parmet, Jack, 131–32. Also see Louis Ruppel to Dr. Paul O'Leary, April 23, 1945, Box 11, PP, demonstrating JPK's part in arranging the assignment.

p. 114: "But if he's going": JPK to KK, May 1, 1945, Box 4A, PP.

p. 115: They received good value: Blair, 371–76; Hamilton, 692–95.

p. 115: "dressed for a black-tie evening": Krock, 350.

pp. 115–16: The dispatches are in a box containing JFK Articles, 1941–1949, JFKL. ["Cannot be overcome completely": April 3, 1945; "a skeleton":

May 4, 1945; "the world organization that will come": May 7, 1945.] They are also in POF, Box 129.

p. 116: "Things cannot be forced": Quoted in Schlesinger, *A Thousand Days*, 88.

p. 116: On England: May 28, June 24, July 10, 1945, articles in JFK Articles, 1941–1949, JFKL.

pp. 116–17: For JFK's travels with Forrestal, see Millis and Henderson.

p. 117: "the plane doors opened": Blair, 387.

p. 117: "I never thought at school:" JFK Tape 39: "Memoir entry concerning entrance into politics," Oct. 1960, Recordings, JFKL. On possible motives for the recordings, see Timothy Naftali, "The Origins of 'Thirteen Days,'" *Miller Center Report*, The University of Virginia, vol. 15, no. 2 (Summer 1999). I am indebted to Naftali for helping me clarify the date of the 1960 recording.

p. 117: "When the war is over": Fay, 152.

p. 118: "I got Jack" and "It was like being": Blair, 356.

p. 118: "Dad is ready": Fay, 152.

p. 118: "God! There goes": Collier and Horowitz, 172–73.

p. 118: "Yes. In fact" and "didn't want to": Blair, 356–57.

p. 118: "said he thought": Quoted in Blair, 367.

p. 118: "I take it that you": Billings to JFK, Jan. 1, 1946, Box 4A, PP.

p. 118: "I am returning": JFK to Billings, Feb. 20, 1945, NHP.

p. 118: "I am certain": George St. John Jr. to Rose Kennedy, Aug. 22, 1945, Choate Collection: Outline of Kennedy Letters, Box 1, PP.

p. 118: "Jack arrived home": Quoted in Doris Goodwin, 705–6.

p. 119: "terribly exposed and vulnerable": Quoted in ibid., 698–99.

p. 119: Joe Jr. "used to talk": McCarthy, 19.

p. 119: "to be built for politics": Mark Dalton OH.

p. 119: "He spoke very fast": James Reed OH.

p. 119: "A lot of people": Billings Interview, CBS Interviews, JFKL Audio-Visual Archive.

p. 119: "Knowing his abilities": Billings OH.

pp. 119–20: "He asked every sort of": Barbara Ward Jackson OH.

p. 120: "decisions of war and peace": JFK Tape 39: "Memoir entry concerning entrance into politics," Oct. 1960, Recordings, JFKL.

p. 120: "Legislation on": Ibid.

p. 120: "was drawn into politics": O'Donnell and Powers, 46.

p. 120: "Few other professions": JFK, *Harvard Alumni Bulletin*, May 19, 1956, 645–46.

p. 120: "The price of politics": Ed Plaut interview with JFK, n.d., in Ralph G. Martin Papers, Boston University.

p. 121: "a politician came up": Ibid.

p. 121: "smart and cunning" and "There is something": Quoted in Doris Goodwin, 699–700.

p. 121: "whatever success": Quoted in ibid., 713.

p. 121: "But a father": JPK interview, Martin Papers.

p. 121: "I just called people": Quoted in Martin and Plaut, 131.

pp. 121–22: "his reputation as": O'Donnell and Powers, 65.

p. 122: "became heated at": Parmet, *Jack*, 138.

p. 122: Joe made the front page: *Boston Globe*, April 15, 17, 29, 1945. Also see Collier and Horowitz, 177–79; Parmet, *Jack*, 143–44; Hamilton, 686–87.

p. 122: On Curley: Hamilton, 674, and Blair, 398–99.

p. 123: "the job Joe": *Look*, June 11, 1946, 32–36.

p. 123: "I'm just filling": Quoted in Martin and Plaut, 136.

p. 123: "If Joe had lived": JFK Interview, Martin Papers. Also John J. Droney OH.

p. 123: "I was as thin": Quoted in Blair, 461.

p. 123: JFK's urinary tract problems: Dr. Vernon S. Dick to Dr. William P. Herbst, Mar. 20, 1953, Dr. Janet Travell files on JFK's medical history, which include some pre-presidential medical records as well as a daily record of JFK's ills and medications during his presidency, JFKL. Dr. Gerald W. Labiner, who served as a Fellow at the Lahey Clinic from 1953 to 1955 and had discussed JFK's health problems with Dr. Elmer C. Bartels, told me that Kennedy had gonorrhea: Conversation, Oct. 31, 2002. This was confirmed by William Herbst Jr.: Conversation, Nov. 22, 2002.

p. 124: "As far as backslapping": Ed Plaut interview with JFK, n.d., in Martin Papers.

p. 124: "didn't think he" and "He wasn't a mingler": William F. Kelly OH; and Hamilton, 743–44.

p. 124: "I think it's more of a personal reserve": Plaut interview with JFK, n.d., in Martin Papers.

p. 124: "in a voice somewhat": Damore, 87.

p. 124: "'Eunice you made me'": Mary McNeely OH.

pp. 124–25: "many a night": Quoted in Doris Goodwin, 707.

p. 125: "You must organize": Drew Porter to JFK, Feb. 9, 1946, PPP.

p. 125: "Jack had a funny": Rose Kennedy, 317–18.

p. 125: "Like a boy": Daniel F. O'Brien OH.

pp. 125–26: "You're not going": O'Donnell and Powers, 49.

p. 126: He "would rather not": Blair, 442–43. Also Hamilton, 756.

p. 126: "a shot later on": O'Brien OH.

p. 126: "We have a very young": Boston City Councilor Joseph Russo radio speech, n.d., Box 74, PPP.

p. 126: "Congress seat for sale": *East Boston Leader*, n.d., Political Scrapbook No. 1, microfilm, JFKL. Also see Jeff Wylie, a reporter for *Time*, to JFK, April 30, 1946, Box 74, PPP, who tried unsuccessfully to excerpt part of the *Leader* column "as a sample of the below-the-belt tactics that you are running into."

p. 126: Mastering the political challenges: See Blair, 420–25.

p. 127: "The fascination about politics": Plaut interview with JFK, n.d., in Martin Papers.

p. 127: "Here's a millionaire's son": Rose Kennedy, 310.

p. 127: For JFK's challenge in getting out and winning votes, see J. Calvin Carpenter to JFK, May 30, 1946, Box 73, PPP.

p. 127: "With those two names": Quoted in Parmet, *Jack*, 182.

p. 127: "a new kind of Democrat": Hamilton, 742.

p. 127: "Compared to the Boston Irish": O'Donnell and Powers, 59.

pp. 127–28: Seeing Jack's amateur status: Martin and Plaut, 131, 136–37; O'Donnell and Powers, 58–60.

p. 128: He began going into: Martin and Plaut, 136.

p. 128: "I would have given odds": McCarthy, 20.

p. 128: "I seem to be": O'Donnell and Powers, 59.

p. 128: "I think I know": Ibid., 54–55.

p. 128: "hit the barbershops": Ibid., 63–64.

p. 129: Ride the trolleys: Parmet, *Jack*, 154.

p. 129: On the house parties, see Press Release, Bill McMorrow, May 2, 1946, Box 74, PPP; Burns, 66–67; O'Donnell and Powers, 64–65; Doris Goodwin, 716–17.

p. 129: Paid a heavy price: See Parmet, *Jack*, 154.

p. 129: "The New Generation": Quoted in Collier and Horowitz, 181.

p. 129: On the war record, see Martin and Plaut, 134–35; O'Donnell and Powers, 65–68; Doris Goodwin, 720; Hamilton, 755–56.

p. 130: For JFK's domestic agenda, see Martin and Plaut, 135–36; Parmet, *Jack*, 157–58.

p. 130: "You can never be too careful": Quoted in Evan Thomas, 48.

p. 130: "staggering sum" and "It was the equivalent": Quoted in Martin and Plaut, 133. Also see Paul E. Murphy to JFK, Feb. 18, 1946, Box 74, PPP, giving one instance of the money available for JFK to hire a campaign secretary.

p. 130: "With what I'm spending": Collier and Horowitz, 183.

p. 130: O'Neill's spending: O'Neill, 73–79.

p. 131: "Kennedy for Congress" and "There's our man": Parmet, *Jack*, 160. (Also see p. 133) and Doris Goodwin, 713–14.

p. 131: "Only way": Martin and Plaut, 140.

p. 131: On the tea, see Martin and Plaut, 144–45; Blair, 472–73; Doris Goodwin, 718–19.

p. 131: For the vote, see Blair, 478–79.

p. 132: "it was very, very quiet": Dalton OH.

p. 132: "In Brookline": JFK Speech, Choate School, Sept. 27, 1946, Box 94, PPP.

p. 132: "Why I Am a Democrat": Oct. 23, 1946, Ibid.

p. 132: VFW speech: "1946 National Encampment," Sept. 2, 1946, Ibid.

pp. 132–33: JFK Speech, "The Time Has Come," Oct. 1946, Ibid.

p. 133: For the vote, see Blair, 495.

Chapter 5: The Congressman

pp. 134–35: For current affairs and Truman's standing, see McCullough, 398, 520–24, 550–51.

p. 135: "*always* running for the next job": Quoted in Blair, 547.

p. 135: "I think from the time": Arthur Krock OH.

p. 135: "The life of the House": Burns, 99.

p. 136: "industrious, important": Donovan, 257–61.

p. 136: "Suppose you were": Quoted in Jay, 372.

p. 136: "the job as a congressman": Charles Spalding OH.

p. 136: "Well, I guess": Quoted in Collier and Horowitz, 209.

p. 136: "I never felt": JFK interview with James Burns, Mar. 22, 1959, JFKL.

p. 136: Swinging a golf club: Parmet, *Jack*, 166–67.

p. 136: "We were just worms": Quoted in Lasky, 117; also in JFK interview with Burns, Mar. 22, 1959, where he also said, "Congressmen get built up. . . ."

pp. 136–37: "found most of his": Quoted in Doris Goodwin, 725–26.

p. 137: On JFK's genuine idealism and view of public service, see the several letters between Jack and Choate faculty from October 1946 to December 1951, especially the Alumni Note, n.d., 1951, Outline of Kennedy Letters, and The Choate Alumni Bulletin, Jan. 1947, Box 1, PP.

p. 137: "I wasn't equipped": Ed Plaut interview with JFK in Ralph G. Martin Papers, Boston University.

p. 138: "freshman row" and "about as far": Blair, 509.

p. 138: "had a brain": Quoted in ibid., 512–13; also see p. 539.

p. 138: "It was good": Quoted in ibid., 513.

p. 138: Jack once encouraged him: William Sutton OH.

p. 138: "speechless indignation": Martin and Plaut, 149–50.

p. 138: "I can't do it": Grace Burke OH.

p. 138: "Mary Davis was unbelievable": Quoted in Blair, 510.

pp. 138–39: "never did involve himself": Quoted in ibid., 511.

p. 139: "No matter how many good things": Joseph Rosetti OH; Blair, 548–49.

p. 139: "She was very dedicated": Quoted in ibid., 488.

p. 139: JPK's commitment to pay: Ibid., 511.

pp. 139–40: Joe also put his money and influence: See Box 5, PP. For Joe's efforts with the media, see JPK to JFK, Oct. 1, 1946, JPK Papers, JFKL; and Parmet, *Jack*, 217–18.

p. 140: "Galahad": Clipping, *The Sign*, July 1950, in Box 4A, PP.

p. 140: "nice to meet": Quoted in Lasky, 101. Also see Burns interview with JFK, Mar. 22, 1959.

p. 140: "I wish you would tell": Kay Halle OH.

pp. 140–41: "I guess Dad": Quoted in Collier and Horowitz, 195.

p. 141: On efforts to hide Joe's role, see ibid., 192–94.

p. 141: On committee assignments, see James M. Burns OH; Blair, 508–9. Also see John McCormack to JFK, Mar. 30, 1946, Box 74, PPP, and Boston Archbishop to JFK, Jan. 18, 1947, Box 5, PP.

pp. 141–42: "His hair was tousled": Sutton OH.

p. 142: "An excellent political": Joe (?) to JFK, Mar. 11, 1947, Box 5, PP.

p. 142: "In 1946 I really knew nothing": Quoted in John Osborne, "The Economics of the Candidates," *Fortune*, Oct. 1960, 138.

p. 142: For his reaction to the tax cut proposal, see Statements and Speeches of JFK, July 8, 1947, in Box 93, PPP.

p. 143: "I do not see how": *CR*, April 20, 1950, 81st Congress, 2nd Session.

p. 143: "The scarlet thread": JFK, Commencement Address, University of Notre Dame, Jan. 29, 1950, Box 95, PPP.

p. 143: The Twenty-second Amendment: Burns, 89; Lasky, 100; William E. Leuchtenburg, *In the Shadow of FDR*, 75–76.

p. 143: JFK's support of housing legislation: Radio broadcast, Feb. 4, 1947, Box 94, PPP.

p. 144: "The only time that": Statements and Speeches of JFK, April 30, 1947, Box 93, PPP.

p. 144: "an investigation of": July 24, 1947, Box 93, PPP.

p. 144: "moral courage:" Clem Norton to Editor, May 23, 1947, Box 74, PPP.

p. 144: On the housing fight, see Burns, 73–76; O'Donnell and Powers, 74–75; and Blair, 537–41.

p. 144: "terribly important": Burns interview with JFK, Mar. 22, 1959, JFKL.

p. 145: JFK's view of unions: Alexander Christie OH.

p. 145: On the hearings and JFK's anticommunism, see Parmet, *Jack*, 175–82.

p. 145: "in their irresponsibility": Statements and Speeches of JFK, April 16, 1947, Box 93, PPP.

p. 145: JFK's call for a balanced law: Martin and Plaut, 151–52.

pp. 145–46: On Taft-Hartley, see Burns, 76–78; Collier and Horowitz, 197; and Blair, 541–46.

p. 146: JFK's voting record: C.I.O. Key Issues: Kennedy-Lodge, n.d., Box 100, PPP.

p. 146: "Now you don't mean": Quoted in Burns, 85–86.

p. 146: "acting as a trustee": Archbishop John Wright to JFK, Jan. 18, 1947, Box 5, PP.

p. 146: A Gallup poll: Gallup, 841.

p. 147: JFK's support of federal aid: "John F. Kennedy Record," n.d., Box 98, PPP. Also see Radio Broadcast, Feb. 4, 1947, Box 94; "Federal Aid to Education," n.d., Box 98, PPP; and Parmet, *Jack*, 201–6.

p. 147: "a white knight": Editorial, *Boston Pilot*, March 18, 1950.

pp. 147–48: On the Curley controversy, see Burns, 91–93; Martin and Plaut, 152–54; Blair, 550–52; Doris Goodwin, 726–29. Also see the oral histories at JFKL of James M. Burns, Garrett Byrne, Mark Dalton, Charles Murphy, and Daniel F. O'Brien.

p. 149: "not to dominate": JFK, speech at UNC, Mar. 27, 1947, in *CR*, April 1, 1947, 80th Congress, 1st Session.

p. 149: On JPK's opposition to Truman Doctrine, see Blair, 532–35; Parmet, *Jack*, 207–8.

p. 150: "a mixture of gaiety": Mrs. Christopher Bridge OH.

p. 150: On Jack's lifestyle, see Burns, 71–73; Collier and Horowitz, 189; Doris Goodwin, 722.

p. 150: "he would come by": Quoted in Goodwin, 521.

p. 150: "Kennedy never sits": Quoted in Burns, 98.

p. 151: "How's the Congressman": AP release, Nov. 8, 1949, Box 95, PPP.

p. 151: "Jack liked girls": Quoted in Blair, 523, 526. Also see George Smathers OH.

p. 151: "Palm Beach's": *New York World-Telegram*, Jan. 20, 1947.

p. 151: "playboy": William O. Douglas OH.

p. 151: "the girls just went": Quoted in Parmet, *Jack*, 167–68.

p. 151: "He was not a cozy" and "nice — considerate": Quoted in Collier and Horowitz, 212–13.

pp. 151–52: "A lovely-looking": Quoted in Blair, 516–17.

p. 152: "he was a very naughty": Interview with Priscilla Johnson McMillan.

p. 152: "less a self-assertion": Collier and Horowitz, 212.

p. 152: "I was one of the few": Quoted in ibid., 214.

p. 152: "The whole thing": Ibid.

p. 152: "a liking for women": Doris Goodwin, 725.

p. 153: "That young American friend": Quoted in Blair, 561.

p. 153: Extreme unction and "It's okay": Collier and Horowitz, 202–3.

p. 153: "His continual, almost heroic": Wills, 33.

p. 153: "mad, bad": Quoted in Collier and Horowitz, 214.

pp. 153–54: For the letters, see Box 4A, PP. On Fitzwilliam, see Collier and Horowitz, 200–205; and Doris Goodwin, 732–39, who relies on Lynne McTaggart, *Kathleen Kennedy: Her Life and Times* (New York, 1983), 129, 206–9, 219, 228, 230, 232–37.

p. 154: News of Kathleen's death and "How can there possibly be": Doris Goodwin, 739, 743.

p. 154: "The thing about Kathleen": Quoted in Burns, 54.

p. 154: "but there was no use": Joseph Alsop OH.

p. 154: "The point is" and "he always heard": Quoted in Collier and Horowitz, 207–9.

p. 155: "he was in terrible pain": Quoted in Doris Goodwin, 742–44.

p. 155: On plans for 1948, see Burns, 99–100; Blair, 546–49; Parmet, *Jack*, 197–98; and Burns interview with JFK, Mar. 22, 1959.

p. 155: For the speaking schedules, see Burns, 100; and Martin and Plaut, 156.

p. 156: "we usually ended up": O'Donnell and Powers, 77–79.

p. 156: For the X rays: See films of Dec. 14, 1944 and Nov. 6, 1950, in Dr. Janet Travell's medical records, JFKL.

p. 156: "he would lean": O'Donnell and Powers, 77–79.

p. 156: "When we've got": Ibid.

p. 156: "You young boys": Smathers OH.

pp. 156–57: On the speculation and the Progressive party support, see Blair, 555; and Parmet, *Jack*, 197–98.

p. 157: For the Roper poll, see "A Report on Political Sentiment in Massachusetts," June 1948, Box 81, PPP.

p. 157: For the election results: "Congressman John F. Kennedy's Election Count," 1948, Box 5, PP.

pp. 157–58: On Curley and Honey Fitz and for the quote, "It made him realize": Doris Goodwin, 745–49.

p. 158: For JFK's continuing focus on domestic issues, see the various documents on these matters in Boxes 81, 82, 83, 93, 95, 98, 99, and 100, PPP, especially the collection of JFK's House speeches in Box 93, and his speech to the Massachusetts state CIO, Dec. 7, 1951, Box 102, PPP.

p. 158: "Foreign policy today": JFK, Radio Speech, Nov. 14, 1951, Box 102, PPP.

p. 158: "perpetual, unending war": Address of JFK, n.d., 1948, Box 95, PPP.

pp. 158–59: On the communist fears, see Acheson, 250–52; McCullough, 521–22, 550–53, 742; Gallup, 788, 881.

p. 159: "the onslaught": JFK, "Aid to Italy," Nov. 20, 1947, *CR*, 80th Congress, 1st Session.

p. 159: "the opportunity": JFK Record, Box 98, PPP.

p. 159: "the betrayal": JFK, "Displaced Persons," June 11, 1948, *CR*, 80th Congress, 2nd Session; also, "Kennedy Raps Roosevelt Attitude Toward Russia," *Salem Evening News*, May 8, 1948.

p. 160: "The failure of our foreign policy": JFK, "Our Foreign Policy in Connection with China," Jan. 29, 1949; "China–Statement of JFK," Feb. 21, 1949, *CR*, 81st Congress, 1st Session.

p. 160: Anticommunism: Gallup, 808–809.

p. 160: On Smathers and Pepper, see Lasky, 102–3.

p. 161: "the lack of": Press Release, Oct. 7, 1949, Box 96, PPP; press release on JFK letter to HST, Oct. 10, 1949, and see letter to editors, Nov. 17, 1949, Box 7, PP.

p. 161: Kennedy worried: *NYT*, June 5, Sept. 1, 1950.

p. 161: "inexcusable delay": JFK, Remarks, July 13, 1950, *CR*, 81st Congress, 2nd Session.

p. 161: "sold like hot cakes": Names in the News, Aug. 26, 1950, Box 6, PP.

p. 161: "the inadequate state": JFK, Speech, n.d, Box 7, PP.

p. 161: Alsops' column: *CR*, Feb. 13, 1950, 81st Congress, 2nd Session.

p. 161: JFK on U.S. forces: JFK, Remarks, Aug. 25, 1950, *CR*, 81st Congress, 2nd Session.

pp. 161–62: For HST ratings, see Gallup, 800, 821, 834, 860, 903, 939, 953.

p. 162: For JFK's views at the Harvard seminar and dinner, see John P. Mallan, "Massachusetts: Liberal and Corrupt," *New Republic*, Oct. 13, 1952.

pp. 162–63: For JFK's ties to McCarthy and denial, see Parmet, *Jack*, 172–74, 211–14.

p. 162: "How dare you": Robert Amory Jr. OH.

p. 163: For fears about the cold war and favorable public opinion toward McCarthy's anticommunism, see Gallup, 897, 911–12, 924, 933–34.

p. 163: "a ballyhoo artist": Quoted in McCullough, 768.

p. 163: For JFK's views at the end of 1951 on communists in government, see "Meet the Press," Dec. 3, 1951, Box 105, PPP.

p. 163: For publicity about JFK's trip, see The Yankee Network News Releases, Jan. 7, 26, 30, 1951, and UPI, Feb. 6, 1951, Box 8, PP.

pp. 163–64: JFK's trip was recorded in a 149-page handwritten diary that became available to researchers in January 2000: Travel Journal, Jan.–Feb. 1951, JFKL. JFK, Radio Talk, Feb. 6, 1951; JFK Statement before Senate committees, Feb. 22, 1951, Box 95, PPP.

p. 164: Differences with his father: JFK Statement before Senate committees, Feb. 22, 1951, Box 95, PPP. Also JFK Travel Journal, Jan.–Feb. 1951, and JFK to JPK, Mar. 13, 1951, Box 6, PP.

p. 165: "nationalistic passions": JFK, Speech, April 21, 1951, Box 95, PPP; and document beginning, "Admits Briggs plan," n.d., in Asian Trip Folder, Box 11, PP.

p. 165: "I was anxious": JFK, Radio Broadcast, Nov. 14, 1951, Box 102, PPP.

p. 166: On Robert Kennedy, see Schlesinger, *Robert Kennedy*, 60–93; Collier and Horowitz, 217–22; Steel, 45.

p. 167: "It is tragic to report": JFK, Radio Broadcast, Nov. 14, 1951, Box 102, PPP.

p. 167: On the French regime: JFK, 182-page Travel Journal, Oct.–Nov. 1951, JFKL. Also see the document that begins "Admits Briggs plan," in Asian Trip Folder, Box 11, PP.

pp. 167–68: FDR Jr.: RFK Diary in Folder "Trips 1951, Mid & Far East," Box 24, Robert F. Kennedy Papers, JFKL.

p. 168: Dinner with Nehru: Ibid., and Schlesinger, *Robert Kennedy*, 91.

p. 168: French officials: Collier and Horowitz, 221; Lasky, 127.

p. 168: "Perhaps our next effort": Schlesinger, 93.

p. 168: "public service type": JFK to Patricia Kennedy, Sept. 12, 1951, Box 6, PP.

p. 168: "handing out sewer contracts": Quoted in Collier and Horowitz, 222.

p. 168: Limits of a governor's powers: Burns, 101.

pp. 168–69: Boston patronage, "to be on the take," "no standing": Interview with JFK, in Martin Papers.

p. 169: JPK's eagerness for a Senate race: Eunice Shriver quoting her father in Edward Kennedy, 237.

p. 169: JPK's confidence about winning: Joseph De Guglielmo OH.

p. 169: Chances 50-50: Anthony Galluccio OH.

p. 169: "the campaign against Lodge": Frank Morrissey, quoted in Edward Kennedy, 127.

p. 169: "if he was going to get anywhere": Spalding OH. Douglas OH.

p. 169: *Meet the Press*, Dec. 3, 1951, Box 105, PPP.

p. 169: Dever stood in the way: Dalton OH.

p. 169: "If you want to run": Byrne OH.

p. 170: "By the time": Douglas OH.

p. 170: Jack prepared a statement: Tommy O'Hearn, quoted in Collier and Horowitz, 631.

p. 170: "We got the race": O'Brien, 26.

p. 170: "had thought and questioned": Eunice Shriver, quoted in Edward Kennedy, 219.

p. 170: "was the distinct boss": Quoted in Martin and Plaut, 161.

p. 170: "The Ambassador worked": Quoted in ibid., 176. For good examples of Joe's efforts, see Leland Bickford to JPK, n.d., Box 6, PP, and Edward J. Dunn to JPK, Sept. 30, 1952, with Dunn to JFK, Sept. 30, 1952, attached, Box 103, PPP.

p. 170: Lodge had sent word: O'Donnell and Powers, 90.

p. 170: "All along, I always knew": Quoted in Doris Goodwin, 757–58. A student of the 1952 campaign found no evidence to refute Lodge's assertion: Thomas J. Whalen, "Evening the Score: John F. Kennedy, Henry Cabot Lodge, Jr., and the 1952 Massachusetts Senate Race," Ph.D. dissertation, History Department, Boston College, 1998, pp. 183–84; published by Northeastern University Press in 2001.

p. 170: Jack enlisted Gardner Jackson: Martin and Plaut, 174–75, and Parmet, *Jack*, 244–45, 250–51.

p. 171: "He is very popular": Quoted in Whalen, "Evening the Score," 262–63.

p. 171: On campaign finance, see Martin and Plaut, 182–83; Parmet, *Jack*, 255; and Whalen, "Evening the Score," who quotes the commentator and Eisenhower, 307–11. Lodge's complaint is recalled in Vincent J. Celeste OH.

pp. 171–72: The fullest discussion of the *Post* episode is in Whalen, "Evening the Score," 243–55, 285.

p. 172: "I've never doubted": Quoted in Doris Goodwin, 764–65.

p. 172: "Listen that was": Laura B. Knebel OH, and Sheldon Stern to author, Mar. 25, 2002.

p. 172: On JPK and Dalton, see Dalton OH; O'Donnell and Powers, 82–83; and Doris Goodwin, 760–61.

pp. 172–73: For RFK's role, see Robert Kennedy interview in Martin Papers; O'Donnell and Powers, 84–89; Schlesinger, *Robert Kennedy*, 94–95.

p. 173: "organization, organization": Martin and Plaut, 164. Also see the campaign organization chart set up under RFK in Box 103, PPP.

p. 173: "In each community": Quoted in "1952 Campaign," Political Notes, 1952–1958 Folder, Box 25, David Powers Papers, JFKL. Also see Dave Powers to Mark Dalton, April 9, 1952, Pre-Administration Political Files, Box 1, RFK Papers.

p. 173: "Black Book": Quoted in Collier and Horowitz, 227–28. See Boxes 98–105, PPP, for the many file folders publicizing the policy questions JFK tried to use against Lodge in the campaign. For just two examples, see the comparative charts on "Economy in Government," Box 98, and "Foreign Policy and Foreign Affairs," Box 100.

p. 174: For Lodge's loss of conservative support, see Whalen, "Evening the Score," 303–5.

p. 174: "voters in that election": O'Donnell and Powers, 91–92.

p. 174: "There's something about Jack": Quoted in Martin and Plaut, 178.

p. 174: For the vote, see Whalen, "Evening the Score," 292–307.

p. 174: "I felt rather like": Quoted in ibid., 295.

p. 175: On ethnic voting, see "Town Influence Up in Massachusetts Voter Shift"; and John P. McGrail to RFK, Nov. 5, 1952, Pre-Admin. Political Files, Box 1, RFK Papers.

p. 175: "I think that": Torbert H. Macdonald OH. Also see Boxes 108–111, PPP. The list of those endorsing JFK is in Box 104, PPP. Also see Parmet, *Jack*, 246–49, on the campaign's efforts to attract Jewish voters; and Whalen, "Evening the Score," 299, and Table One, Appendix A, on winning the women's vote, as well as Box 112, PPP.

p. 175: For the voting statistics, see Whalen, "Evening the Score," 299–303.

Chapter 6: The Senator

p. 177: "you will wonder": Quoted in McCullough, 214.

p. 177: "I've often thought": Quoted in Parmet, *Jack*, 260.

p. 177: "'What's it like'": John A. Carver Jr. OH.

p. 178: "Do you pray": Quoted in Van Wyck Brooks, 418. Also see John F. Kennedy, *Profiles*, 2.

p. 178: "I'd be very happy": Paul Healy, "The Senate's Gay Young Bachelor," *Saturday Evening Post*, June 13, 1953.

p. 178: "the fine art" and "realizes that once": JFK, *Profiles*, 5, 10.

p. 179: "A pleasant brunet": *Chicago Tribune*, Jan. 6, 1962.

p. 179: "If I had said": Quoted in Sorensen, 62.

p. 179: For Sorensen's background, see Martin and Plaut, 251–53; Sorensen, 12; Parmet, *Jack*, 262–64.

p. 180: "Jack Kennedy wouldn't hire": Sorensen, 11.

p. 180: Jack needed a liberal voice: Martin and Plaut, 251.

p. 180: "intellectual than emotional persuasion": Lasky, 165.

p. 180: "You couldn't write speeches": Sorensen, 33.

p. 180: "impressed by his 'ordinary' demeanor": Ibid., 11–12.

p. 180: "were going to throw in with him": Quoted in Martin and Plaut, 253.

pp. 180–81: "You've got to remember": Quoted in Collier and Horowitz, 243.

p. 181: The office: Burns, 119–20, 213–16.

p. 181: "devoted, loyal, and dedicated": Lincoln, 18.

p. 181: *Meet the Press*, Nov. 9, 1952, Box 920A, PPP.

p. 181: Developed forty proposals: Sorensen, 64–65; Burns, 120–22; Parmet, *Jack*, 265–69.

p. 181: "The Economic Problems of New England — A Program for Congressional Action," May 18, 25, June 1, 1953, Compilation of JFK Speeches, JFKL. Also see "Legislative Record of Senator John F. Kennedy in 83rd Congress, 1953–54, Box 781, PPP.

p. 182: "no great fireworks": T. J. Reardon to William L. Batt Jr., April 27, 1954, Box 509, PPP.

p. 182: 30,000 copies: "Memorandum of Progress of New England Program," Dec. 15, 1953, Box 552, PPP.

p. 182: The articles: Parmet, *Jack*, 269–70.

p. 182: "made some slurring": T. J. Reardon to Francis Morrissey, Mar. 18, 1954, Box 509, PPP.

pp. 182–83: For JFK's ruminations about the Seaway, see St. Lawrence Seaway File, Jan. 25, 1953–Jan. 8, 1954, Box 654, PPP. The speech, Jan. 14, 1954, is in Compilation of Speeches.

p. 183: For the *Boston Post* and two congressional supporters, see Parmet, *Jack*, 272.

p. 183: At least one Massachusetts newspaper: *New Bedford Standard Times*; see JFK to JPK, Jan. 29, 1954, Box 504, PPP.

p. 183: *Meet the Press*: Feb. 14, 1954, Box 920A, PPP.

p. 183: Worrisome issues to people: Gallup, 1113, 1118, 1125, 1142, 1162, 1194, 1225–26, 1230, 1241, 1255, 1277.

p. 184: "eager boyish": Charles Bartlett to JFK, n.d., Box 490, PPP.

p. 184: "on the weapons of subversion": JFK, Address, Wilmington, Del., May 14, 1953, Compilation of Speeches.

p. 184: "not see how": JFK Speech to American Legion, Oct. 16, 1953, ibid.

pp. 184–85: On defense spending, see Amendments of June 30, 1953 and July 1, 1953 to Mutual Security Act, 1951, Compilation of Speeches; and JFK to L. A. Weicker, Oct. 26, 1953, Box 479, PPP.

p. 185: For Johnson's report, see L. P. Marvin Jr. to Priscilla Johnson, April 17, 1953, Box 481; Johnson to JFK, April 22, 1953, Box 484, PPP.

p. 185: "the native populations": JFK to John F. Dulles, May 7, 1953, Box 481, PPP.

p. 185: State Department response: Thruston B. Morton to JFK, May 13, June 12, 1953, Box 481, PPP.

pp. 185–86: Case before Congress: JFK, Amendment to Mutual Security Act of 1951, June 30, 1953.

p. 186: "be administered in such a way": JFK, Amendment to Mutual Security Act of 1951, July 1, 1953, JFK, Compilation of Speeches.

p. 186: "how the new Dulles policy": JFK, Cathedral Club, Brooklyn, N.Y., Jan. 21, 1954, JFK, Compilation of Speeches.

p. 186: *Meet the Press*, Feb. 14, 1954, Box 920A, PPP.

pp. 186–87: "No amount of American military": "The War in Indochina," April 6, 14, 1954, JFK, Compilation of Speeches.

p. 187: Indochina "is lost": CBS, *Man of the Week*, May 9, 1954, Box 524, PPP.

p. 187: Attention and praise: See Holmes Alexander column "Capitol Comment," July 18, 1953, Box 481; George McT. Kahin to JFK, April 8, 1954, Box 488, PPP; and Parmet, *Jack*, 284–86.

p. 188: For polls about McCarthy, see Gallup, 1003, 1150, 1164, 1189, 1194, 1201, 1203, 1213, 1225, 1231–32, 1234–35, 1237, 1241–42, 1253, 1263.

pp. 188–89: On LBJ and McCarthy, see Dallek, *Lone Star Rising*, 451–57.

p. 189: "Not very much": Quoted in Burns, 141–42.

p. 189: "Oh, hell": Quoted in Collier and Horowitz, 248. Also see *Meet the Press*, Dec. 2, 1951, Feb. 14, 1954, Box 920A, PPP.

p. 189: On the confirmations, see Martin and Plaut, 207.

p. 190: "I don't think": Kenneth Birkhead OH.

p. 190: "is of such importance": Speech Prepared for Delivery on the Senate Floor, July 31, 1954, Box 12, Theodore Sorensen Papers, JFKL.

p. 190: McCarthy repudiated: Gallup, 1289.

p. 190: Schlesinger view: Martin and Plaut, 203.

p. 190: "certainly futile": Quoted in Parmet, *Jack*, 302.

p. 190: "Joe McCarthy is the only man": O'Donnell and Powers, 96.

p. 190: "What was I supposed to do": Martin and Plaut, 204. Also see Speech Prepared for Delivery, July 31, 1954, Box 12, Sorensen Papers.

p. 191: "I never said": JFK Interview, Martin Papers.

p. 191: "He liked McCarthy": Ibid.

p. 191: "I had never known": Quoted in Martin and Plaut, 204.

p. 191: For JFK's legalistic defense, see JFK appearance on Martin Agronsky's *Look Here*, NBC, Nov. 23, 1957, Box 12, Sorensen Papers; and Burns, 151–52.

p. 191: "I went into the hospital": JFK Interview, Martin Papers.

p. 192: Paul Healy, "The Senate's Gay Young Bachelor," *Saturday Evening Post*, June 1953.

p. 192: "Senate's Confirmed Bachelor": Parmet, *Jack*, 258.

p. 192: One close Kennedy friend: Burns, 127.

p. 193: "He saw her as a kindred": Quoted in Collier and Horowitz, 233.

p. 193: "They were so much alike": Quoted in ibid., 241.

p. 193: "Jack appreciated her": Quoted in ibid., 241–42.

p. 193: "I am a bit concerned": Smith, 662.

p. 193: "spasmodic courtship": Quoted in Burns, 127.

p. 194: "she wasn't sexually attracted": Collier and Horowitz, 236–37.

p. 194: For the wedding, see Burns, 128, and Parmet, *Jack*, 261–62.

p. 194: "At last I know": Smith, 663.

p. 194: "as well be in Alaska": Quoted in Burns, 131.

p. 194: "I was alone": Quoted in Doris Goodwin, 772.

p. 194: Jackie's spending and "like a transient": Collier and Horowitz, 240–41.

p. 194: Jack "insists": Rose Kennedy to Pat, June 2, 1954, JPK Papers, JFKL.

p. 194: "prepared for the humiliation": Quoted in Doris Goodwin, 774.

pp. 194–95: "I don't think" and "after the first year": Quoted in Collier and Horowitz, 242.

p. 195: "a bacchanal": Quoted in ibid., 258.

p. 195: "that being married": Clymer, 24.

p. 195: For JFK's health problems, see Dr. Walter B. Hoover to JFK, July 5, 1951, and JFK to Francis Morrissey, Sept. 27, 1951, both in Box 6, PP; and Dr.

Sara M. Jordan, RX, n.d., Box 73, PPP. Interviews with Dr. Elmer C. Bartels and Dr. Timothy Lamphier, NHP.

p. 195: "Senator Kennedy has been": Dr. Vernon S. Dick to Dr. William P. Herbst Jr., Mar. 20, 1953, Box 6, PP.

pp. 195–96: JFK's back problems: See X rays for Jan. 9, Jan. 22, Oct. 13, 1954, Dr. Janet Travell medical records, JFKL; Lincoln, 53–54; Parmet, *Jack*, 307–9; Goodwin, 774.

p. 196: "Jack was determined": Quoted in Goodwin, 774. The surgery is described in James A. Nichols, M.D., et al., "Management of Adrenocortical Insufficiency During Surgery," *Archives of Surgery*, Nov. 1955, 737–40.

p. 196: Postoperative problems: Nichols, "Management of Adrenocortical Insufficiency"; Parmet, *Jack*, 309–15. Arthur Krock OH.

p. 196: "His entire body shook": Quoted in Doris Goodwin, 775.

p. 197: Removal of the plate: X rays, Nov. 12, Dec. 16, 1954, Jan. 5, April 27, 1955, Travell medical records.

p. 197: "You know, when I get downstairs": Charles Spalding OH. Also see JFK's response to questions about McCarthy in JFK Interview, Martin Papers.

p. 198: "defying constituent pressures": Sorensen, 74.

p. 198: JFK, "What My Illness Taught Me," *The American Weekly*, April 29, 1956.

p. 199: "Jack Kennedy's involvement": Parmet, *Jack*, 323–33. For the tapes, Dictabelt Recordings 25A, 25B, 26, 27, JFKL. For Sorensen's part in the book, see Profiles in Courage Folders in Box 7, Sorensen Papers. For Jules David's involvement, see Professor William Gillette, a David student, to author, April 21, 2002. Also see Evan Thomas Sr. OH, Columbia University.

p. 199: The radio journalist and *New York Times* editor: Parmet, *Jack*, 330–31; Tifft and Jones, 388; John B. Oakes OH, Columbia University.

p. 199: For the Pearson controversy, see the Sorensen Profiles in Courage Folders, Box 7, Sorensen Papers. Abell, 420.

p. 199: "one of the most far-reaching": JFK, "Election of President and Vice President: Electoral College Reform," Mar. 20, 1956, Compilation of Speeches, JFKL.

p. 200: On the fight with Furcolo, see Burns, 147–48; O'Donnell and Powers, 85–86; Parmet, *Jack*, 291–95.

p. 201: "Leave it alone": Quoted in O'Donnell and Powers, 105.

p. 201: Speculation on JFK as Stevenson's VP: Fletcher Knebel, Feb. 23, 1956, Box 8, Sorensen Papers.

p. 201: Consequently, they urged Jack: Ibid., 103–5.

p. 201: "There is a great 'hassle'": Philip Philbin to JFK, Mar. 3, 1955, Box 503, PPP. JFK to O'Brien and O'Donnell, Mar. 8, 1955, Box 504, PPP.

p. 201: Jack persuaded and "So we can't let": O'Donnell and Powers, 106.

p. 202: For JFK's role in the primary, see Adlai Stevenson to Arthur Schlesinger Jr., Mar. 26, 1956, Box P-23, Arthur Schlesinger Jr. Papers, JFKL.

p. 202: For the fight, see "Burke Opposed: Kennedy Fight Gains Support," *Christian Science Monitor*, May 9, 1956.

p. 202: "I do not relish": Frank Morrissey to JFK, May 9, 1956, Box 31, POF. Also see Parmet, *Jack*, 346–54.

p. 202: For JFK's campaign, see the correspondence between May 2 and May 17, 1956, in Boxes 498, 523, 546, and 549, PPP.

p. 202: For the choice of Lynch, see O'Donnell and Powers, 110–16.

p. 203: "caught in a mud-slinging": Ibid., 110.

p. 203: The "nation's first great politicians": JFK, *Vogue*, April 1, 1956; and JFK, Harvard Commencement Address, June 14, 1956, Box 895, PPP.

p. 203: "The men who create power": *PPP: JFK, 1963*, 815–18, Oct. 26, 1963.

pp. 203–4: On LBJ, see Dallek, *Lone Star Rising*, 489–90.

p. 204: "unforgivably discourteous": "The Boston-Texas Axis," a chap. in Thomas G. Corcoran ms. memoir, Corcoran Papers, LC. Also see Dallek, *Lone Star Rising*, 490–91, and n. 61, 683.

p. 204: Start such a campaign: Senator Andrew P. Quigley to JFK, Jan. 25, 1956; JFK to Quigley, Jan. 31, 1956, Box 507, PPP.

p. 204: Keeping a low profile: See Irv Slomowitz to Ted Reardon, Jan. 26, 1956; Reardon to Slomowitz, Feb. 6, 1956, Box 509, PPP. John W. King to JFK, Feb. 18, 1956; JFK to King, Feb. 21, 1956, Box 549, PPP.

p. 204: Fletcher Knebel, column, Feb. 23, 1956, Box 8, Sorensen Papers. Sorensen to Knebel, April 6, 1956, Box 810, PPP. Knebel, "Can a Catholic Become Vice President?" *Look*, June 12, 1956.

p. 205: For Sorensen's comparison: "The Democratic Nominee for Vice President in 1956," n.d.; "Memorandum on Kennedy and the Vice-Presidency"; and Sorensen to Ken Hechler, Aug. 1, 1956, Box 810, PPP.

p. 205: For the endorsements and the Farley and Rayburn quotes, see Parmet, *Jack*, 354, 361–62.

p. 205: JPK's reluctance: JPK to JFK, May 25, 1956, Box 9, Sorensen Papers.

p. 205: A straw poll: Gallup, 1431.

p. 205: "while I think": JFK to JPK, June 29, 1956, Box 9, Sorensen Papers.

p. 205: "100% behind": Shriver to JPK, July 18, 1956, Box 810, PPP.

p. 206: "better known": Eunice Kennedy to JPK, Aug. 1, 1956, JPK Papers.

p. 206: Stevenson's decision: Parmet, *Jack*, 372–75.

p. 206: "looked like a thin year": Krock OH.

p. 206: "movie star," and set up a headquarters: *New York Times*, Aug. 12, 13, and 14, 1956.

p. 206: For JFK's belief that the invitation to nominate AES was a compensatory gesture, see JFK Interview, Martin Papers.

pp. 206–7: For the clash with JPK, see O'Donnell and Powers, 122, and Rose Kennedy, 328.

p. 207: "a sudden warmth": Quoted in Doris Goodwin, 783.

p. 207: a "realistic sense of futility": Parmet, *Jack*, 376–80.

pp. 207–8: "we lost because": RFK Interview and JFK Interview, Martin Papers. Also see John J. Mitchell to JFK, Aug. 22, 1956, Box 534, PPP; Mitchell shared RFK's view.

p. 208: On Eleanor Roosevelt's response to JFK, see Roosevelt, 164.

p. 208: "probably rates as": *Boston Herald*, Aug. 18, 1956.

p. 208: "out of the convention": Quoted in Doris Goodwin, 785.

p. 208: "you clearly emerged": Arthur Schlesinger Jr. to JFK, Aug. 21, 1956, Box 534, PPP. Also see Rep. Burr P. Harrison to JFK, Aug. 22, 1956, Box 534, PPP: "Your prestige has been enormously enhanced."

p. 208: Campaigned for Stevenson: Parmet, *Jack*, 384–86.

p. 209: "the most disastrous" and RFK's assessment: Schlesinger, *Robert Kennedy*, 133–36.

p. 209: For JFK's itinerary, see Compilation of Speeches, JFKL, for September–November, 1956. Also see JFK to Frank L. Dennis, July 9, 1958, Box 3, Sorensen Papers, and "Out of State Appearances of Sen. Kennedy, 1956 Campaign," Box 25, David Powers Papers, JFKL.

p. 209: "be prepared": JFK, Speech, Nov. 8, 1956, Box 896, PPP.

p. 210: "And, like me": Rose Kennedy, 329.

p. 210: The best account of how JFK won the Pulitzer, including Macdonald's telegram, is in Parmet, *Jack*, 394–97.

p. 210: Thomas's anecdote is in his OH, Columbia University.

p. 210: The FBI report: L. B. Nichols to Tolson, May 14, 1957, J. Edgar Hoover Official and Confidential File, FBI Microfilm, Folder 13, Reel 1.

p. 211: "this country is not" and "Well, Dad": Quoted in Goodwin, 787–88.

p. 211: "I'm forty-three": O'Donnell and Powers, 193.

pp. 211–12: JFK's hospitalizations were May 26–June 2, 1955, July 3, 1955, July 14–20, 1955, Jan. 11–13, 1956; Jan. 31–Feb. 1, 1957; July 18–19, 1957; Sept. 3–4, 1957; Sept. 13–Oct. 1, 1957; Oct. 28, 1957. The records of these admissions, with diagnoses and treatments, are in the Dr. Janet Travell medical records, JFKL. Also see Travell OH.

p. 213: The side effects of testosterone: Conversation with Dr. Jeffrey Kelman, April 22, 2002. Dr. Kelman read the records at the JFKL with me and helped me understand them.

p. 213: "I've learned that": Quoted in O'Donnell and Powers, 125–26. Immediately after the convention, JFK obtained a complete list of delegates with their home addresses as a prelude to courting them for 1960: See Sargent Shriver to Evelyn Lincoln, Sept. 5, 1956, Box 504, PPP.

p. 215: "all the credit for": Quoted in Dallek, *Lone Star Rising*, 517–18.

p. 215: "shaped primarily by": Quoted in Parmet, *Jack*, 409. For JFK and civil rights, also see JFK to Rep. Michael J. Kirwan, Nov. 1, 1956; JFK to Rep. Lenore K. Sullivan, Nov. 1, 1956; JFK to Gov. J. P. Coleman, Nov. 1, 1956, Box 781, PPP.

p. 215: "the balance of power": Doris Fleeson, "John Kennedy for President," *Washington Post*, Mar. 30, 1957.

p. 215: *Meet the Press*, Oct. 28, 1956, Transcript, Box 920A, PPP.

p. 216: "highly questionable": JFK, "Highly Questionable Legislative Course," June 20, 1957, *CR*, Compilation of Speeches, JFKL.

p. 216: "dangerous precedent": JFK to Roy Wilkins, July 10, 1957, Box 23, Powers Papers.

p. 216: On the vote and the four Western liberals, see Doris Fleeson, "Kennedy Looks to the South," *Washington Evening Star*, July 3, 1957; and Dallek, *Lone Star Rising*, 521–22.

p. 216: For attacks on JFK, see JFK to Roy Wilkins, July 10, 1957, Box 23, Powers Papers, and Parmet, *Jack*, 410.

p. 216: On Titles III and IV, see JFK, Civil Rights Act of 1957, July 23, 1957, *CR*, Compilation of Speeches; and Dallek, *Lone Star Rising*, 522–24.

p. 216: For the controversy over jury trials, see Dallek, *Lone Star Rising*, 524–26.

p. 217: For JFK's consultations, see Paul Freund to JFK, July 23, 1957; JFK to Freund, July 30, 1957; Arthur E. Sutherland to JFK, July 26, 1957; JFK to Sutherland, July 30, 1957; Robert Troutman to JFK, July 26, 1957; Mark Dewolf

Howe to JFK, Aug. 1, 1957; and conversation with Dean James Landis, n.d., Box 536, PPP.

p. 217: A vote against jury trials: JFK, Civil Rights Act of 1957, Aug. 1 and 7, 1957, *CR*, Compilation of Speeches.

p. 217: "impossible": JFK to Bill, the Chronicle, n.d., Box 536, PPP.

p. 217: Enactment of the law: Dallek, *Lone Star Rising*, 526–27.

p. 217: "Why not show" and "stout" bridge: Quoted in Parmet, *Jack*, 412.

p. 217: The tensions with Wilkins: "Wilkins Scores Kennedy for Vote on Civil Rights," *Berkshire Eagle*, April 28, 1958, clipping; JFK to Wilkins, May 6, June 6, July 18, 1958; Wilkins to JFK, May 29, 1958, Box 23, Powers Papers.

p. 218: "I think most of us agree": JFK, Speech, Oct. 17, 1957, Box 898, PPP.

p. 218: On RFK, see Schlesinger, *Robert Kennedy*, 119, 137–42, 162–63.

p. 218: "If the investigation": O'Donnell and Powers, 132.

p. 218: LBJ's warning: Schlesinger, *Robert Kennedy*, 143.

p. 218: JFK's decision: Martin and Plaut, 191.

p. 219: The Kennedys and Beck and Hoffa: Schlesinger, *Robert Kennedy*, chap. 8, and Thomas, 74–89.

p. 219: JFK's bill: "Disclosure of Financial Affairs of Labor Organizations," Mar. 11, 1958, Compilation of Speeches.

p. 220: Meany's response: *New York Times*, Mar. 28, 1958.

p. 220: NAM opposition: JFK, "National Association of Manufacturers Opposition to Kennedy-Ives Labor Bill," July 29, 1958, Compilation of Speeches.

p. 220: "Jimmy Hoffa can rejoice": *New York Times*, Aug. 19, 1958. Also see Parmet, *Jack*, 429–33.

p. 220: For JFK's 1959 labor reforms, see *Meet the Press*, Nov. 9, 1958, Box 920A, PPP.

p. 220: For Landrum-Griffin and "appalling public apathy," see Schlesinger, *Robert Kennedy*, 182–84.

p. 221: "Justice, Labor and": Quoted in Sorensen, 18.

p. 221: "Jesus, Jack": Quoted in Collier and Horowitz, 246–47.

p. 221: "My father is conservative": JFK Interview, Martin Papers.

p. 221: "I have never had": LBJ conversation with Kefauver, Jan. 11, 1955, LBJA/CF, LBJL.

p. 221: "bombarded me": Quoted in Doris Goodwin, 790.

p. 222: "The most powerful single force": JFK, "Imperialism — The Enemy of Freedom," July 2, 1957, Compilation of Speeches.

p. 222: JFK response to his critics: "Algeria," July 8, 1957, Compilation of Speeches.

p. 222: "You lucky mush": Quoted in Burns, 196.

pp. 222–23: JFK, "A Democrat Looks at Foreign Policy," *Foreign Affairs*, Oct. 1957, 1–16.

p. 223: "the Democratic party": JFK to J. K. Galbraith, Feb. 4, 1958, Box 691, PPP. Also see JFK to George Kennan, Feb. 13, 1958; Kennan to JFK, Feb. 19, 1958, Box 691, PPP. Also see JFK to Alton Hathaway, Mar. 6, 1958; and David C. Forbes, Mar. 6, 1958, Box 691, PPP. For examples of JFK's policy statements, see "Address at 50th Anniversary Dinner, Bnai Zion, NYC," Feb. 9, 1958, Box 563; "Social Science Foundation Lecture," Feb. 24, 1958, Box 811, PPP; "The Struggle Against Imperialism, Part II — Poland and Eastern Europe," Aug. 21, 1957; and "The Choice in Asia — Democratic Development in India," Mar. 25, 1958,

Compilation of Speeches; and Press Release, JFK and Sen. John Sherman Cooper, Mar. 25, 1958, Box 562, PPP.

pp. 223–24: On *Sputnik* and Gaither's committee, see Ambrose, *Eisenhower*, 423–35.

p. 224: JFK interview: "Kennedy Wants Us to Sacrifice," Dec. 8, 1957, *New York Times*. JFK, "Mutual Security Act of 1958," June 4, 1958, Compilation of Speeches.

p. 224: "dangerous period": JFK, "U.S. Military Power — Preparing for the Gap," Aug. 14, 1958, Compilation of Speeches. Also see Memo: "Foreign Policy Activities," in a Folder titled "Missiles, Sept. 5–23, 1958," Box 692, PPP.

p. 224: For the polls, see Gallup, 1523–24.

p. 225: "Seldom in the annals": Quoted in Doris Goodwin, 792.

p. 225: "Senator Kennedy, do you have" and "This man seeks": Quoted in Martin and Plaut, 461–62.

p. 225: "perfect politician," *American Mercury*, 1956.

p. 225: "Jack is the greatest": Quoted in Martin and Plaut, 461.

p. 225: The best discussion of the 1958 campaign is in Parmet, *Jack*, chap. 25.

p. 225: "direct and personal participation": Lawrence O'Brien to JFK, May 16, 1957, Box 527, PPP.

p. 225: "the flowering of another": Harold Martin, "The Amazing Kennedys," *Saturday Evening Post*, Sept. 7, 1957, 49.

Chapter 7: Nomination

p. 229: "terrible shapelessness": Quoted in the *New York Times*, Sec. 4, p. 21, May 16, 2000.

p. 229: Speaking invitations: Martin and Plaut, 462; O'Donnell and Powers, 129.

p. 229: some Massachusetts newspapers: *Lynn Sunday Telegram-News*, July 14, 1957; *Boston Globe*, July 29, 1957.

p. 229: Democratic state chairman: *New York Times*, Nov. 16, 1958. *Chicago Daily News* poll of 1,220 delegates: Box 25, David Powers Papers, JFKL.

p. 230: Democratic governors: Edward M. Edwin to JFK, Aug. 14, 1959, Box 549, PPP.

p. 230: "very smart": Gallup, 1623–24.

p. 230: "Month after month": William V. Shannon in the *New York Post*, Nov. 11, 1957.

p. 230: "clothes and hair-do": *New York Times*, Oct. 10, 1958.

p. 230: "on how to win": Ibid., Nov. 10, 1958.

p. 230: "looked at him": Peter Lisagor OH.

pp. 230–31: For Nixon's nomination prospects, see Gallup, 1602, 1607, 1616, 1625, 1631, 1641.

p. 231: For Eisenhower's popularity, see ibid., 1586, 1589, 1596–97, 1603, 1609, 1615, 1618, 1625, 1632, 1639.

p. 231: For Democratic-Republican matchups, see ibid., 1597, 1607, 1618–19, 1622, 1642, 1647–48; and Louis Harris, "An Analysis of a Trial Pairing of Vice President Richard Nixon vs. JFK," Oct. 1957, and "A Study of

Public Opinion on Candidates in Eight West Coast Cities," Feb. 1959, Box 819, PPP.

p. 231: Gridiron speech: Mar. 15, 1958, Box 1025, PPP.

p. 231: JFK's standing among Democrats, See Gallup, 1588, 1590, 1601, 1607, 1613, 1617, 1622–23, 1630, 1649.

p. 231: His standing with congressional Democrats: Parmet, *Jack*, 506.

pp. 231–32: "We've always been": Interview with JFK, Ralph G. Martin Papers, Boston University.

p. 232: "I'm not interested": Newton Minow OH, Columbia University.

p. 232: "If I don't make it": Interview with JFK, Martin Papers.

p. 232: "Catholic-baiting": Quoted in Martin and Plaut, 448. Also see Hofstadter, *The Paranoid Style*, 19–23.

p. 232: Twenty-four percent: Gallup, 1605–6.

p. 232: "Kennedy seemed too cool": Schlesinger, *A Thousand Days*, 14.

p. 233: "the effects upon this country": Memo, July 12, 1959, Box 123, Katie Louchheim Papers, LC.

p. 233: "youngsters he had summoned": White, *Making, 1960*, 48.

p. 233: Jack publicly denied: *Face the Nation*, Mar. 30, 1958, and Feb. 22, 1959, Box 779, PPP.

p. 233: "dodged the McCarthy issue": Quoted by John Madigan on *Meet the Press*, Mar. 30, 1958, Box 779, PPP.

p. 233: "not sure Kennedy": AP dispatch, May 8, 1958, Box 32, POF.

p. 233: TV appearance: ABC's *College News Conference, New York Times*, Dec. 8, 1958.

pp. 233–34: "father has been spending": JFK to Eleanor Roosevelt, Dec. 11, 1958, Box 32, POF.

p. 234: "gladly so state": Eleanor Roosevelt (ER) to JFK, Dec. 18, 1958, ibid.

p. 234: "accept the view": JFK to ER, Dec. 29, 1958. Also ER to JFK, Jan. 6 and 20, 1959; JFK to ER, Jan. 10 and 22, 1959; and ER telegram to JFK, Jan. 29, 1959, ibid.

p. 234: Spent an estimated $1.5 million: Doris Goodwin, 793.

pp. 234–35: "You do what you think" and other quotes: Wofford, 37–39.

p. 235: "knew instinctively," and O'Neill and Prendergast: Collier and Horowitz, 297–98, 646–47.

p. 235: "very vigorous" and "'I was so goddamn mad'": David Lawrence OH.

p. 235: Childs's column and the plane: Parmet, *Jack*, 512.

p. 235: "It's not the Pope": McCullough, 970. Also see "A vote for Jack is a vote for father Joe," in annotated ms. of Paul B. Fay, "The Pleasure of His Company," Paul B. Fay Papers, JFKL.

p. 236: "the Catholic issue": Quoted in Parmet, *Jack*, 469–70.

p. 236: Stevenson-Minow conversation: Minow OH; also see William Attwood OH, William Benton OH, and William McCormick Blair Jr., OH, all at Columbia University.

p. 236: Conversation with Steele and promises to remain neutral: Parmet, *Jack*, 470–71.

p. 236: "I don't think he'd be": Barbara Ward Jackson OH.

p. 236: "Do you think": *Face the Nation*, Mar. 30, 1958, Box 799, PPP.

p. 236: "independence from": James M. Burns to JFK, Nov. 1, 1959, Box 129, POF.

pp. 236–37: He believed that his votes: *Face the Nation*, Mar. 30, 1958, Box

779, PPP. Also see JFK interview, Martin Papers, and prenomination campaign speeches for 1958–60 in the PPP.

p. 237: "The key thing": Wofford, 36–37.

p. 237: JFK also gave voice: Though Burns and JFK had their differences about some of what Burns included in his book, there was substantial cooperation between them. See James M. Burns to JFK, Nov. 1, 1959, Box 129, POF.

pp. 237–38: "mixed voting record" and other quotes: Burns, 266–71.

p. 238: "his campaign identity": Schlesinger, *A Thousand Days*, 17–18.

p. 238: "This, I suppose": Schlesinger, *Robert Kennedy*, 203–4.

p. 239: "comprehensive housing": Burns, 268–73.

p. 239: As in Massachusetts: O'Donnell and Powers, 130.

p. 239: "We have to get organized": RFK Interview, Martin Papers.

p. 239: "citizen organizations" mounting a "grass roots appeal": "Preconvention Grass Roots Campaigning; Kennedy Clubs," Jan. 29, 1959, Box 26, David Powers Papers, JFKL.

pp. 239–40: Steve Smith's office: Burns, 233; White, *Making, 1960*, 51; Parmet, *Jack*, 507.

p. 240: "Where do we stand?": Sorensen to All "Summit Conference" Participants, April 1, 1959, Box 26, Powers Papers.

p. 240: "Regardless of whom": Gallup, 1633–39.

p. 241: For the fall schedule, see Burns, 231. For JFK's speeches along the way, see Box 1025, PPP. Also see Sorensen, 114.

p. 241: "certainly brilliant": Memo, July 12, 1959, Box 123, Louchheim Papers.

p. 241: "I'm getting a lot better": JFK Interview, Martin Papers.

p. 241: "he learned the art": Sorensen, 114.

p. 242: "The tone was tiredness": Martin and Plaut, 209–10.

p. 242: Meeting of seventeen principal people: Handwritten notes: "Oct. 28, 1959 — R.F.K. House — Hyannis Port." Also see "Summary of Talk of Kennedy Men," Summer 1959, Box 26, Powers Papers.

p. 242: "what has been done": Fay, 76–77.

p. 242: Six-page summary report to RFK: J. Miller, "Some Modest Realignment in the Kennedy Image," Oct. 20, 1959, Pre-Admin., Political Files, Box 39, RFK Papers, JFKL.

p. 243: "Check those things": Pierre Salinger OH; Salinger, 30.

p. 243: "hard-and-fast" and the quotes on JFK's performance: White, *Making, 1960*, 54–55.

p. 243: On Bowles and a southern strategy, see Minutes of Meeting, Oct. 28, 1959, Pre-Admin., Political Files, Box 39, RFK Papers; RFK to Files: Georgia and Virginia, Nov. 18, 1959, Box 26, Powers Papers; Chester Bowles OH; Parmet, *Jack*, 513–14.

p. 243: Announcement of candidacy: Jan. 2, 1960, Box 1025, PPP.

p. 244: "refuse the vice presidential": Ibid.

p. 244: Predictions: Sorensen, 139–40.

p. 244: "scored 100": Memo, July 12, 1959, Box 123, Louchheim Papers.

p. 244: Humphrey speech in Virginia: Adam Clymer interview with Sen. Edward M. Kennedy, Oct. 9, 1996, given to me by Clymer.

p. 245: "unpopular in some sectors": Lisagor OH. Also see "Summary of Talk of Kennedy Men."

p. 245: "I don't have to worry": JFK Interview, Martin Papers.

p. 245: "no Southerner can be nominated": "Summary of Talk of Kennedy Men," Box 26, Powers Papers.

p. 245: Joe Kennedy was more concerned: JPK Interview, Martin Papers.

p. 245: "a 'riverboat gambler'": Quoted in Schlesinger, *A Thousand Days*, 203.

p. 245: "has no very firm principles": Lisagor OH.

p. 245: "comes from the right state": "Summary of Talk of Kennedy Men," Box 26, Powers Papers.

p. 246: "I wish I could get Stu": JFK Interview, Martin Papers.

p. 246: Dirt on Symington: James Fahey to JPK, May 13, 1960, JPK Papers, JFKL.

p. 246: "sleeping candidacy": Schlesinger, *A Thousand Days*, 17.

p. 246: "But he still has": "Summary of Talk of Kennedy Men," Box 26, Powers Papers.

p. 246: "He is not a threat": JPK Interview, Martin Papers.

p. 246: "Look, when someone says": JFK Interview, Martin Papers.

p. 246: "definitely and categorically": Jan. 1960, Box 123, Louchheim Papers.

pp. 246–47: "conveyed an intangible": Schlesinger, *A Thousand Days*, 20.

p. 247: New Hampshire: Goodwin, 795–96; JFK, "The Presidential Primary and Your Vote," Jan. 25, 1960, Box 1025, PPP; "Results of Presidential Primaries in 1960: New Hampshire, Mar. 8, 1960," Box 26, Powers Papers.

p. 247: On Indiana, Nebraska, California, and Ohio, see "Results of the 16 Presidential Primaries in 1960," Box 26, Powers Papers. Also Sorensen, 144–50.

p. 247: For the discussions with Pat Brown, see "California," June 7, 1960, Box 26, Powers Papers.

p. 247: "Mike, it's time": Abraham Ribicoff OH, Columbia University.

p. 247: "a veteran politician": O'Donnell and Powers, 148–52. Also Sorensen, 145.

p. 248: "If we do not do very well": JPK to Count Enrico Galeazzi, Mar. 31, 1960, JPK Papers.

p. 248: JFK's 1958–59 appearances in Wisconsin: "Wisconsin", n.d., Box 26, Powers Papers. *Meet the Press*, Jan. 3, 1960, Box 920A, PPP.

pp. 248–49: "winter of cold winds": O'Donnell and Powers, 153–54.

p. 249: "You're too soon": Quoted in Collier and Horowitz, 294.

p. 249: "vicious falsehoods": Sorensen, 153.

p. 249: "Thank God": "Wisconsin Attacks," April 4, 1960, Box 989, PPP.

p. 249: "an element of": Humphrey, 208.

p. 250: "remained remarkably": James Reston, *New York Times*, April 4, 1960.

p. 250: "'Do you like'": Lisagor OH.

p. 250: "just an effective": Patrick J. Lucey OH.

p. 250: For the family's involvement and Humphrey's quotes, see O'Donnell and Powers, 157–59, and White, *Making, 1960*, 92–93.

p. 250: The vote: "Results of Presidential Primaries in 1960" and "Results of the 16 Presidential Primaries in 1960," Box 26, Powers Papers.

p. 251: "ashen" and "mighty uneasy": William Proxmire OH.

p. 251: "A shift of": "Analysis of the Wisconsin Returns," n.d., Box 27, Powers Papers.

p. 251: Jumped from his seat: Sheldon Stern to author, Mar. 25, 2002.

p. 251: "What does it all mean?": O'Donnell and Powers, 159–60.

p. 251: "The religious issue": Lucey OH; O'Donnell and Powers, 159.

p. 251: Cronkite: Schlesinger, *Robert Kennedy*, 295.

p. 251: On West Virginia, see West Virginia: Key Facts, Box 968, PPP; Robert McDonough OH; O'Donnell and Powers, 160.

pp. 251–52: The Harris poll: Jan. 1969, Box 818, PPP; and Bob Wallace to RFK, Jan. 5, 1960, Box 969, PPP.

p. 252: The Kanawha county poll: White, *Making, 1960*, 101.

p. 252: "public opinion had shifted": West Virginia Polls, n.d., Box 27, Powers Papers.

p. 252: "what are our problems?": O'Donnell and Powers, 160.

p. 252: "Bob Byrd is": ? to Dear Frank, April 12, 1960, Box 27, Powers Papers.

p. 252: "the reactionary element": Homer E. Bussa to Frank N. Hoffman, Jan. 22, 1960, Box 968, PPP.

p. 252: "bury the religious issue:" McDonough OH.

p. 252: "to meet the religious issue": "Meeting re West Virginia Primary — April 8, 1960," Pre-Admin., Political Files, Box 39, RFK Papers.

p. 252: "Four F's": Frank H. Fischer OH.

p. 253: "I am a Catholic": McDonough OH.

p. 253: "Nobody asked me": O'Donnell and Powers, 166–67.

p. 253: "He was the most": McDonough OH; also see James Haught OH.

p. 253: "I am the only": Sorensen, 158.

p. 253: "Over and over again": White, *Making, 1960*, 108.

p. 253: "a nice old man": "Jackie in West Virginia," n.d., Box 27, Powers Papers.

p. 254: "I have to confess": "West Virginia," May 10, 1960: "Highlights of JFK's Campaign in West Va.," Box 27, Powers Papers. On Jackie, also see Leaming, 16.

p. 254: "The Senator is still": Diary Notes, April 26, 1960, Box 2, Evelyn Lincoln Papers, JFKL.

p. 254: "Kennedy's shock": White, *Making, 1960*, 106.

p. 254: "By the pitiful": Sorensen, 158.

p. 254: "I assure you": "Memo from Lou Harris on the Last Week's Campaigning," n.d., Box 27, Powers Papers. "A Ten Point Program for West Virginia," April 25, 1960, Box 535, PPP.

p. 255: "Much more can": JFK to Fellow Democrats, April 18, 1960, Box 997, PPP.

p. 255: "And now it is time": Press Release, April 12, 1960, Box 989, PPP.

p. 255: FDR Jr.: O'Donnell and Powers, 165.

p. 255: "God's son": Charles Peters OH.

p. 255: "stop-Kennedy": "Memo from Lou Harris," n.d., Box 27, Powers Papers; Press Releases, April 30, May 1 and May 2, 1960, Box 968, PPP; O'Donnell and Powers, 161–62, 168–69.

p. 256: JFK discussion with LBJ: As recorded by Arthur Krock; quoted in Dallek, *Lone Star Rising*, 566–67.

p. 256: "millionaire 'money' candidates": "West Virginia Attacks," Box 994, PPP; Sorensen, 159–60.

p. 256: "personal abuse": Clipping, "Kennedy Asks Humphrey to End 'Personal Abuse'" n.d., Box 27, Powers Papers.

p. 256: "Poor little Jack": "West Virginia Attacks," Box 994, PPP.

p. 256: "I would suggest": Ibid.; also Schlesinger, *Robert Kennedy*, 201.

p. 256: "They believed me": Humphrey, 475.

pp. 256–57: "Any discussion": *New York Times*, May 7, 1960.

p. 257: "As I told you last time": ? to Frank, April 12, 1960, Box 27, Powers Papers.

p. 257: "Politics in West Virginia": White, *Making, 1960*, 99.

p. 257: Slates: Ibid., 99–100.

p. 257: "We would pay it": Told to me by Joe Galzer, who worked in Humphrey's campaign.

p. 257: Expenditures: White, *Making, 1960*, 110.

p. 257: O'Brien expenditures: O'Brien, 68.

p. 257: "Our highest possible contribution": Humphrey, 216–17.

p. 257: "the earthy and realistic people": O'Donnell and Powers, 169.

p. 257: The vote: "Results of Presidential Primaries in 1960," and "Results of the 16 Presidential Primaries in 1960," Box 26, Powers Papers.

pp. 257–58: Investigations and the *Gazette* quote: O'Donnell and Powers, 169; Sorensen, 165.

p. 258: "I have no complaints": HHH to Editor, May 26, 1960, Box 542, PPP.

p. 258: Beat Wayne Morse: "Results of Presidential Primaries in 1960, May 20 — Oregon," Box 26, Powers Papers.

p. 258: "the devil": Joseph Rauh OH.

p. 258: "She did not want": Humphrey, 221.

p. 259: "it would be most helpful": Undated memo attached to Schlesinger to AES, May 16, 1960, Box 33, POF.

p. 259: "which would nail down": Ribicoff OH.

p. 259: For the JFK-AES conversation and the quotes, "I guess there's nothing," and "Guess who": Schlesinger, *A Thousand Days*, 25–26. See Blair OH, which quotes JFK: "God, why won't he." Also see Schlesinger to AES, May 16, 1960, Box 33, POF; AES to Schlesinger, May 21, 1960, Box P23, Arthur Schlesinger Jr. Papers, JFKL.

p. 259: Anger toward AES: Lawrence Fuchs OH. Also see Collier and Horowitz, 289–90.

p. 259: JFK-Fritchey anecdote told to me by Marianne Means, who was recounting what Kay Graham had said at a memorial service for Fritchey.

pp. 259–60: LBJ on JFK, including conversations with Pearson, Krock, and Stevenson: Dallek, *Lone Star Rising*, 567–68.

p. 260: "I am not prepared": Ibid., 569.

p. 260: HST's comment and JFK's reply: *New York Times*, July 3 and 5, 1960.

p. 260: RFK vote count: RFK to Steve Smith, May 25, 1960, Box 535, PPP.

p. 260: "If we can get": Quoted in Goodwin, 800.

p. 260: "Well, that's it": Quoted in Collier and Horowitz, 299.

p. 260: "those wanting": Quoted in Dallek, *Lone Star Rising*, 571.

p. 261: LBJ's attack on JFK: Ibid., 569–73. Conversation with Dr. Gerald Labiner, October 31, 2002.

p. 261: Regarded Kennedy "as a mediocrity": Earl Mazo OH, Columbia University.

p. 261: "I knew he": Lisagor OH.

pp. 261–62: "You've got": Baker, 118.

p. 262: "despicable": Dallek, *Lone Star Rising*, 572.

p. 262: Report on JFK's health: Drs. Eugene J. Cohen and Janet Travell to JFK, June 11, 1960, Box 991, PPP.

p. 262: "the opportunity to carry out": Dr. Seymour Reichlin to author, Nov. 23, 2002.

p. 262: William Walton on the medical support: Parmet, *JFK*, 18.

p. 262: "There's a medical bag": Ribicoff OH.

p. 262: "far too fluid": Schlesinger, *A Thousand Days*, 33.

p. 263: *Meet the Press*, July 10, 1960, Box 920A, PPP.

p. 263: "We wanted to just try": Robert Kennedy OH.

p. 263: For the problems with Minnesota, see Sorensen to JFK, May 31, 1960, Box 547, PPP; New Jersey, Frank Thompson OH; and Pennsylvania, Lawrence OH.

p. 263: "never": Sorensen, 175.

p. 263: JPK's bet: Doris Goodwin, 800–801.

p. 263: "found thousands of supporters": Wofford, 50.

p. 263: "This was more": White, *Making, 1960*, 163.

pp. 263–64: "We've got to have": Robert Kennedy OH. Cohen and Taylor, 257–59.

p. 264: Fact sheet: "The Foreign Policy Experience of Senators Johnson and Kennedy," Box 740, PPP.

p. 264: "moods, questions": Sorensen, 174.

p. 264: "'I don't want'" and "Look, nobody asked you": Quoted in Schlesinger, *Robert Kennedy*, 205–6.

p. 264: JFK's every move: Democratic National Convention (From Saturday July 9–Friday July 15, 1960), Box 27, Powers Papers.

p. 264: "precise, taut, disciplined": White, *Making, 1960*, 157.

p. 265: For JFK's activities on July 10–12, see ibid.

p. 265: California, Kansas, and Iowa: Ibid., 163.

p. 265: "I wasn't any Chamberlain": Quoted in Dallek, *Lone Star Rising*, 573–74.

pp. 265–66: Stevenson demonstration: White, *Making, 1960*, 165–66.

p. 266: "Don't worry, Dad": Quoted in O'Donnell and Powers, 186–87.

p. 266: "Your man must be": Blair OH.

p. 266: "We can't miss a trick": Quoted in Schlesinger, *Robert Kennedy*, 206.

p. 266: JFK and RFK together: Hugh Sidey OH.

p. 266: "Not you nor anybody else": Quoted in Cohen and Taylor, 260.

Chapter 8: Election

pp. 267–68: VP candidates: Sorensen to JFK and RFK, June 29, 1960, Box 21, Theodore Sorensen Papers, JFKL. Sorensen, 184.

p. 268: Past problems with liberals: O'Donnell and Powers, 189.

p. 268: "No, absolutely not": Edward Morgan OH.

p. 268: "There was no respect": Quoted in Collier and Horowitz, 304.

p. 268: Civil rights plank: Schlesinger, *A Thousand Days*, 34.

p. 268: King and NAACP: G. Mennen Williams to JFK, June 25, 1960, Box 536; JFK speech to NAACP, July 10, 1960, Box 1027, PPP.

p. 269: Symington: Clark Clifford OH; John Seigenthaler OH; Sorensen,

186; Schlesinger, *Robert Kennedy,* 206–7; Cohen and Taylor, 260. Sorensen to JFK and RFK, June 29, 1960, Box 21, Sorensen Papers.

p. 269: RFK and LBJ: Dallek, *Lone Star Rising,* 490, 559.

p. 269: "the Democratic party owes": Quoted in ibid., 540–41.

p. 270: "immediately agreed": Quoted in White, *Making, 1964,* 407–9.

p. 270: "he supposed the same": Quoted in Dallek, *Lone Star Rising,* 574.

p. 270: "I wouldn't want to trade" and "Stop kidding": Quoted in ibid., 574–75.

p. 271: LBJ's interest in becoming VP: ibid., 574–78.

p. 271: "LBJ now means": Quoted in Wofford, 54.

pp. 271–72: "If you are sure," "This is the worst mistake," and "so upset": Quoted in O'Donnell and Powers, 190–92.

p. 272: "was very distressed": Schlesinger, *Robert Kennedy,* 208–9.

pp. 272–74: Jack and Bobby and other details of Johnson's nomination: Dallek, *Lone Star Rising,* 579–82.

p. 274: "I turned on television": Earl Mazo OH, Columbia University.

p. 274: "bland, vapid": Quoted in Leuchtenburg, *A Troubled Feast,* 111.

p. 274: The Podhoretz and Macdonald quotes are in Alan Ehrenhalt, "Are We as Happy as We Think?" *New York Times,* May 7, 2000.

p. 274: "With the supermarket": Quoted in Leuchtenburg, *A Troubled Feast,* 113.

pp. 274–76: JFK Acceptance Speech, July 15, 1960, Box 1027, PPP. And see Sorensen, 187–89.

p. 276: Initial polls: Political Analysis Assocs., Princeton, N.J., July 16–17, 1960, Box 27, POF.

pp. 276–77: "shining summer Saturday": Schlesinger, *A Thousand Days,* 62.

p. 277: "Had never seen": Ibid., 63.

p. 277: Meetings: Sorensen, 192–93.

p. 277: "run and fight": Quoted in Schlesinger, *Robert Kennedy,* 211–13.

p. 277: "Gentlemen," "absolutely strong," "Little Brother": Ibid.

p. 277: "Black Prince": Quoted in Parmet, *JFK,* 34.

p. 277: "Little Boy Blue" and "that little shit": Mazo OH.

p. 277: "I'm not running": Quoted in Schlesinger, *Robert Kennedy,* 213.

pp. 277–78: "This was a politician": Memo, June 13, 1960, Box 17, Henry Brandon Papers, LC.

p. 278: Meeting with Stevenson: Parmet, *JFK,* 34–35; Schlesinger, *A Thousand Days,* 64.

p. 278: Meeting with HST: O'Donnell and Powers, 202. Also see JFK to Clark Clifford, July 29, 1960, Box 29, POF.

p. 278: "I never liked": Abraham Ribicoff OH, Columbia University.

p. 278: JFK and Eleanor Roosevelt (ER): ER to JFK, Aug. 16, 1960, "the distinct feeling": ER to Mary Lasker, Aug. 15, 1960, Box 32, POF.

p. 279: "interest and concentration": Quoted in Parmet, *JFK,* 35.

p. 279: "Organization has an important": Arthur Schlesinger to JFK, Aug. 26, 1960, Box 32, POF.

p. 279: "who hardly qualifies": AS to JFK, Aug. 30, 1960, ibid.

p. 279: "I don't mind": JFK to Schlesinger, Sept. 2, 1960, ibid.

p. 279: Speech to the Liberal party: JFK, Sept. 14, 1960, Box 911, PPP.

pp. 279–80: On the Republican convention, see White, *Making, 1960,* chap. 7. The polls: Gallup, 1680–82.

p. 280: Nixon's advantage and "'What are you doing?'": White, *Making, 1960,* 249–51.

p. 280: "Counterattack Sourcebook:" Milton Gwertzman to Mike Feldman and Sorensen, Aug. 10, 1960, Box 991, PPP.

p. 280: "Senator Kennedy is": "Counterattack Sourcebook."

p. 281: "religion in the rural corn belt": John K. Galbraith to JFK, Aug. 25, 1960, Box 993, PPP.

p. 281: "the Catholic position": "Counterattack Sourcebook."

p. 281: FBI memos: DeLoach to Tolson, June 1, 1959; SAC, New Orleans, to Director, Mar. 23, 1960; and Memorandum, May 27, 1960, MF, Folder 13, Reel 1, O&C File, J. Edgar Hoover, FBI Papers.

p. 281: "to sit down with": Adlai Stevenson to Henry Van Dusen, Sept. 13, 1960, Box P 23, Arthur Schlesinger Jr. Papers, JFKL.

p. 282: "a pioneer of": Harold Evans, "Press Baron's Progress," review of *The Chief: The Life of William Randolph Hearst* by David Nasaw (Boston, 2000) in *New York Times Book Review,* July 2, 2000.

p. 282: Nixon's womanizing: Richard Bolling OH, Columbia University. Larry O'Brien unconvincingly claims that JFK had no womanizing problem; he says he was "totally unaware" of any "personal indiscretions" on JFK's part: Lawrence O'Brien OH, Columbia University.

p. 282: National Conference of Citizens for Religious Freedom: *New York Times,* Sept. 8, 1960. Also see Sorensen, 212–14.

p. 283: Community Relations division: James Wine OH; and Box 1015, PPP. Also see Sorensen, 198–99; Parmet, *JFK,* 40–41.

p. 283: Opposition to speaking and the quotes "They're mostly" and "I'm getting tired": O'Donnell and Powers, 205–8.

p. 283: Cogley: John Cogley OH.

p. 283: Kennedy went before the audience: Sept. 12, 1960; Box 1061, PPP.

p. 284: The response to him and "By God": O'Donnell and Powers, 209–10.

p. 284: Agreement to debate: Ambrose, *Nixon,* 558–59.

p. 285: JFK's preparation: White, *Making, 1960,* 283–85.

p. 285: Transcript of the first debate: Box 912, PPP.

p. 285: "That son of a bitch": Quoted in Matthews, 155.

p. 285: "calm and nerveless": White, *Making, 1960,* 288–90.

p. 286: "My God!": quoted in Summers, 208.

p. 286: Bored or amused: O'Donnell and Powers, 212–13.

p. 286: "put a stern expression": Ibid., 213.

p. 286: Polls: Gallup, 1685–87.

p. 286: Enthusiasm for JFK: Sorensen, 227–28; O'Donnell and Powers, 213–14.

p. 286 n.: Attempts to steal records: Dr. Janet Travell OH; Parmet, *JFK,* 120–21, which expands on the information in Travell's OH. According to Safire: William Safire, "Kennedy Agonistes," *New York Times,* Nov. 18, 2002. Refutations of the allegation: John Gizzi, "Historian Dallek Maligned Nixon's 1960 Campaign," *Human Events,* Jan. 6, 2003; John Taylor, "Dallek: Historian or Gumshoe?" Jan. 7, 2003, History News Network. "Dirty tricks": Ehrlichman, 30.

p. 287: "No matter how many": JBM, "Memo on Nixon," Sept. 30, 1960, John Bartlow Martin Papers, LC.

p. 287: "the large body": "Campaign Reflections," n.d., Box 535, PPP.

p. 287: "a nearly exhaustive": Nixon quotes and inconsistencies, n.d., Box 1024, PPP.

p. 287: "Dick Nixon stands": Quoted in O'Donnell and Powers, 217.

p. 287: "reigned rather than ruled," and "If you give me a week": Stephen Ambrose, "How Clinton Is Like Ike," *New York Times,* June 19, 2000. Ambrose believes Ike's remarks may have cost Nixon the election.

p. 287: "acting like": Quoted in Ambrose, *Nixon,* 564.

p. 287: no well-developed economic program: Walter W. Heller, Memo, Oct. 4, 1960, Box 4, Walter W. Heller Papers, JFKL; Walter Heller and Paul Samuelson, Council of Economic Advisers OH. "The Issues in 1960," Oct. 31, 1960, Box 992, PPP; and memos on the economy in Box 75, John B. Martin Papers.

p. 288: "I . . . think it would become": Quoted in Sorensen, 209.

p. 288: "Foreign policy for the first time": JFK to Dean Acheson, Aug. 1, 1960, Box 27, POF.

p. 288: 1958 *Foreign Affairs* article: *Foreign Affairs,* Oct. 1958.

p. 288: "the overwhelming majority": Gallup, 1676.

p. 288: U.S. prestige: Ibid., 1691. To bolster morale at home and prestige abroad and to discourage a possible Soviet first strike, the U.S. government in 1958–59 considered detonating a nuclear weapon on the moon "as a show of military and technical strength." The physicist in charge of the project said later that it was "a way to bolster national confidence." There was no clear scientific or military gain expected from the explosion. "It was a PR device, without question, in the minds of the people from the Air Force," the physicist said. Believing that "there were other ways to impress the public that we were not about to be overwhelmed by the Russians" than by "ruining the pristine environment of the moon," the planners scrapped the idea. See "U.S. Planned Nuclear Blast on the Moon, Physicist Says," *New York Times,* May 16, 2000.

p. 288: "our own offensive and defensive": JFK, "U.S. Military and Diplomatic Policies — Preparing for the Gap," Aug. 14, 1958, *CR,* 85th Congress, 2nd Session.

p. 289: Statements and speeches over the next two years: "Can Democracy Meet the Space Age Challenge?" CBS TV Symposium, Mar. 22, 1959, Box 568, PPP; "A Time for Decision," June 14, 1960, JFK, Compilation of Speeches, JFKL; JFK at Women's Democratic Luncheon, Sept. 14, 1960; and "Eight Years of Defense Programs and Budgets," Sept. 1960, Box 1028, PPP.

p. 289: "J.F.K. has made the point": J. K. Galbraith to Louis Harris, Sept. 27, 1960, Box 74, John K. Galbraith Papers, JFKL.

p. 289: Higher marks: Gallup, 1683.

p. 289: The Gaither report: Ambrose, *Eisenhower,* 434–35.

p. 289: DDE knowledge and briefings: Beschloss, *Crisis Years,* 25–26; DDE to JFK, Aug. 19, 1960, Box 29, POF, and Earle G. Wheeler OH. Also see James P. Warburg to JFK, Sept. 21, 1960; JFK to Warburg, Oct. 18, 1960, James P. Warburg Papers, JFKL; and Solis Horwitz OH, which emphasizes that DDE never refuted the missile gap and that "there was no question in anybody's mind that there was a missile gap." For the argument that JFK knew there was no missile gap: Beschloss, *Crisis Years,* 25–27, and Richard Reeves, 58–59, 671–72.

p. 289: Kennedy was in possession: "The Gap," "Notes," and "Weapons Evaluation," n.d., Box 771; Stuart Symington to JFK, Sept. 2, 1960, Box 733, PPP.

"National Defense," n.d., Box 75, John B. Martin Papers. Also see Deirdre Henderson to Sorensen, n.d., 1960, Box 1, Deirdre Henderson Papers, JFKL.

pp. 289–90: JFK-Dulles conversation: Beschloss, *Crisis Years*, 26.

p. 290: Democrats warned Kennedy: Walt W. Rostow OH; "Who Is Responsible for the Defense Lag?" n.d., Box 771, PPP. Also Eleanor Roosevelt to JFK, Oct. 24, 1960, Box 32, POF.

p. 290: "would be a very dangerous": Quoted in Beschloss, *Crisis Years*, 24–25.

p. 290: JFK on Cuba: Press Conference, Sept. 2, 1960, Box 1027, PPP; and "Kennedy Assails Nixon Over Cuba," *New York Times*, Oct. 7, 1960.

p. 290: "What are the Soviets'": Memo headed "Khrushchev" and subtitled "Cuba," n.d., Box 540, PPP.

p. 290: "stop talking about Cuba": Dean Acheson OH. The best discussion of the flap over Cuba is in Parmet, *JFK*, 45–49.

p. 291: "endorse and support": A. Willis Robertson to JFK, July 19, 1960, Box 535, PPP.

p. 291: "I understand": JFK to Robertson, July 27, 1960, ibid.

p. 291: "Now in five minutes": Wofford, 58; and see 58–65 for the campaign's civil rights activities.

pp. 291–92: On Adam Clayton Powell, see Thomas, 100. Also see "Appearance by JFK Before National Conventions of Negro Organizations," n.d., Box 536; Shriver to Sorensen, Aug. 8, 1960, and JFK Memo, Aug. 30, 1960, Box 543; and "Record of JFK on Civil Rights and Race Relations," n.d., Box 1061, PPP.

p. 292: "There are no Federal": *Meet the Press*, Oct. 16, 1960, Box 780, PPP.

pp. 292–93: The King episode is recounted in Wofford, 13–26, and Thomas, 100–103.

p. 293: Polls: Gallup, 1689–90.

p. 293: "the situation looks": James Farley to JFK, Oct. 20, 1960, Box 33, James Farley Papers, LC.

p. 293: "wearing the proper": Eric Sevareid, *Boston Globe*, Aug. 18, 1960.

p. 293: "lesser of two evils": Edward L. Bernays to John B. Martin, Sept. 15, 1960, Box 73, John B. Martin Papers.

p. 293: "an image of calm": Charles Kuralt, *Eyewitness to History*, Nov. 4, 1960, CBS TV, Freedom of Communications, Part III, JFKL.

p. 293: "The crowds tensed him up": Quoted in Summers, 204.

pp. 293–94: "the change in Kennedy": Ibid.

p. 294: "in our politics": Quoted in Schlesinger, *A Thousand Days*, 76.

p. 294: For JFK's response to the vote count and the vote itself: Sorensen, 238–40; Parmet, *JFK*, 56–59; White, *Making, 1960*, 350–51, 385–87; and Bernard Bailyn, xxii–xxiii.

p. 295: For analysis of the vote: See Louis Harris to Joseph Alsop, Nov. 16, 1960, "An Analysis of the 1960 Election for President," Joseph and Stewart Alsop Papers, LC; White, *Making, 1960*, 350–65; Sorensen, 238–51.

pp. 295–96: On fraud allegations: See Sen. Theodore F. Green to Attorney Gen. William P. Rogers, Nov. 12, 1960; James H. Duffy to JFK, Nov. 14, 1960, Box 110, POF. Also David Greenberg, "It's a Myth That Nixon Acquiesced in 1960," *Los Angeles Times*, Nov. 10, 2000.

p. 296: "Why, even our friend": William Benton OH, Columbia University.

Chapter 9: The Torch Is Passed

p. 299: "more perplexed": Schlesinger, *A Thousand Days*, 118.

p. 299: "jubilant:" Sorensen, 255.

p. 299: "hurt his self-confidence": Henry Brandon OH.

p. 299: "How did I": O'Donnell and Powers, 229.

p. 299: His hands trembled: White, *Making, 1960*, 348. Sheldon Stern says that films at the JFKL show other instances of JFK's trembling hands, which could have been caused by exhaustion, medications, or nervousness. Stern to Author, April 19, 2002.

p. 299: One reporter: Parmet, *JFK*, 59.

pp. 299–300: "still seemed tired": Sorensen, 268.

p. 300: "Jesus Christ": Quoted in Richard Reeves, 25.

p. 300: "I have been through": *New York Times*, Nov. 10, 1960.

p. 300: An article based: *New York Times*, Jan. 11, Jan. 17, 1961.

p. 300: Remain in the hands: For a revised view of DDE, see Greenstein.

pp. 300–01: Appointing prominent: See Dallek, *Flawed Giant*, 8–9.

p. 301: Dulles and Hoover: Schlesinger, *A Thousand Days*, 125.

p. 301: "I haven't the slightest": O'Donnell and Powers, 229.

p. 301: The *NYT* reported: *New York Times*, Nov. 15, 1960.

p. 302: For JFK's views of DDE, see Robert Kennedy OH; Charles Spalding OH.

p. 302: For DDE's view of JFK, see Earl Mazo OH, Columbia University. Also see Parmet, *JFK*, 72, and Ambrose, *Eisenhower*, 597.

p. 302: The HST-DDE meeting: Ambrose, *Eisenhower*, 14–15.

p. 302: "I was anxious": JFK undated notes, Box 29, POF.

p. 302: "the present national security": Informal List of Subjects to be Discussed at Meeting of President Eisenhower and Senator Kennedy, Dec. 5, 1960; John H. Sharon to JFK, Dec. 5, 1960; Briefing Memoranda for Meeting with President Eisenhower, Dec. 6, 1960, Box 29A, POF.

p. 302: "to avoid direct involvement" and DDE's topics for discussion: Sharon to JFK, Dec. 5, 1960, Box 29A, POF.

p. 303: For the Dec. 6 meeting and their views of each other, see *New York Times*, Dec. 7, 1960; Robert Kennedy OH; Guthman and Shulman, 54–55; John Sharon OH, Columbia University; Parmet, *JFK*, 73–74; Richard Reeves, 21–24.

pp. 303–4: JFK's topics: "Memorandum of Subjects for Discussion . . . Jan. 19, 1961"; "Mr. Kendall dictated," Jan. 17, 1961, Box 29A, POF.

pp. 304–5: For JFK's Jan. 19 meeting with DDE, see JFK memo: "I visited E. this morning"; Robert McNamara to JFK, Jan. 24, 1961; Clark Clifford to JFK, Jan. 24, 1961, Box 29A, POF; Clark Clifford OH; Sorensen, 649; Sidey, 37–38; Parmet, *JFK*, 80–81; Richard Reeves, 29–33.

p. 305: On Cuba, see Clifford and McNamara memos, Jan. 24, 1961, Box 29A, POF; and Pat Frank to Bob Kennedy, Aug. 6, 1960; Telephone Calls, Oct. 25, 1960, Pre-Admin., Political Files, RFK Papers, JFKL.

p. 306: "capacity to dominate": Schlesinger, *A Thousand Days*, 120.

p. 306: "If I am elected": Quoted in Clifford, 319.

p. 306: "except the right": Quoted in Sorensen, 258.

pp. 306–7: JFK and Neustadt: Richard Neustadt, "Organizing the Transition," Sept. 15, 1960, Box 31, POF; Richard Neustadt OH, Columbia University; Schlesinger, *A Thousand Days*, 122–23.

p. 307: The best discussion of JFK's transition is in Brauer, chap. 2.

p. 307: No women were considered: Sheldon Stern to Author, April 19, 2002.

p. 307: White House insiders: O'Donnell and Powers, 225.

p. 307: "The President was remarkably accessible": Sorensen, 419; also 293–96.

p. 308: "Jack has asked me": Wofford, 68.

p. 308: "appointing outstanding men" and "For the last four years": O'Donnell and Powers, 234.

p. 308: Schlesinger related his conversation with JFK to me, and told me that he saw the president two or three times a week. For the rest on Schlesinger, see Sorensen, 296–97.

p. 309: "If I string along": O'Donnell and Powers, 235.

p. 309: The economy: State of the Union Message, *PPP: JFK, 1961*, 19–20.

p. 309: The balance of payments: Roy Blough, et al., to JFK, Jan. 18, 1961, Box 1073. Conversations between Paul Nitze and Douglas Dillon, Nov. 18, 30, 1960; and Erik Blumenfeld to Ted Sorensen, Nov. 22, 1960, Box 1076, PPP. "The outflow of gold . . . interested and concerned the President more than any other matter over a longer period of time" (George Smathers OH). Also see Bernstein, 21–23.

pp. 310–11: Dillon's background and appointment: Schlesinger, *A Thousand Days*, 133–36; Dean Acheson OH; Clifford OH; Gore, 147; Parmet, *JFK*, 65–66; Bernstein, 127–28; Richard Reeves, 27–28; Guthman and Shulman, 40; *Time*, Jan. 2, 1961.

p. 311: On the CEA and Heller: Walter Heller OH; Walter Heller, "The Meeting with the President-elect," Dec. 23, 1960; and "Recollections of Early Meetings with Kennedy," Jan. 12, 1964, Box 5, Walter W. Heller Papers, JFKL; Parmet, *JFK*, 76; Bernstein, 123–25; Richard Reeves, 26–27.

p. 311: "I need you": Heller, "Recollections."

p. 312: McNamara's appointment: Shapley, chaps. 1–5, especially 82–86. McNamara, 13–17.

p. 313: For the RFK quote: Guthman and Shulman, 35–36.

p. 313: "The Ship of State": Myer Feldman OH.

p. 313: "I talked over the presidency": Richard Reeves, 666, n. 25.

p. 313: On AES: Abraham Ribicoff OH, William Atwood OH, John Sharon OH, all Columbia University. Charles Bartlett to JFK, n.d., but clearly after JFK's nomination ("I am given an extremely strong impression . . . that Adlai, when he meets you next week, intends to hit you hard for a commitment on the State Dept. Job"), Box 27, POF. AES to JFK, Nov. 11, 1960, Box 33, POF.

p. 314: "Fuck him": Ribicoff OH.

p. 314: "might forget": Quoted in Richard Reeves, 25.

p. 314: AES appointment to UN: William McCormick Blair Jr. OH, Columbia University; JFK-AES Press Conference, Dec. 8, 1960, Box 1060, PPP; Schlesinger, *A Thousand Days*, 138–39.

p. 314: "'a shit list'": Sharon OH.

p. 314: On Bowles and Bundy, see Brauer, 86.

p. 314: On Bruce, see Guthman and Shulman, 5.

p. 314: "thought he had some brains": Ibid., 36–37. Also see Schlesinger, *A Thousand Days*, 139–40; Parmet, *JFK*, 67–68.

p. 315: On JFK's appointment of Rusk: Schlesinger, *A Thousand Days*,

119–20, 140–41; Parmet, *JFK*, 67–69; Brauer, 88–90; Cohen. Dean Rusk, "The President," *Foreign Affairs*, April 1960.

p. 315: "hard-working, tough guy": RFK to O'Donnell, Jan. 4, 1961, Box 1066, PPP.

p. 316: On RFK: Schlesinger, *Robert Kennedy*, 228–32.

p. 316: "I have now watched you": Ribicoff OH.

p. 316: "he did not know": Acheson OH.

p. 316: "be a great mistake": Ibid.

pp. 316–17: "That would be impossible": Quoted in Schlesinger, *Robert Kennedy*, 228–29.

p. 317: "would not appoint": "Fletcher Knebel is reporting that you told him that if you were elected President, you would not appoint any relative to the White House staff." Notes, n.d., 1960, Box 7, Evelyn Lincoln Papers, JFKL.

p. 317: "It would be the 'Kennedy brothers'": Schlesinger, *Robert Kennedy*, 230. Acheson OH; Clifford, 335–36.

p. 317: Others reinforced: Schlesinger, *Robert Kennedy*, 229; Rayburn to JFK, Dec. 15, 1960, Box 32, POF; *New York Times*, Nov. 24, 1960.

p. 317: "just wanted to give": Quoted in Evan Thomas, 110–11.

pp. 317–18: "truly a strange assignment": Clifford, 336–37.

p. 318: "This will kill": Schlesinger, *Robert Kennedy*, 231–33. Evan Thomas, 109–10. John Seigenthaler OH.

p. 318: "I made up my mind": RFK to Drew Pearson, Dec. 15, 1960, Box 23, RFK Attorney General's Papers, JFKL. RFK said, "My father always told me never write it down" (RFK to John McCone, May 2, 1962, Personal Correspondence, RFK Attorney General's Papers). But in this instance, RFK did.

p. 319: "tried to persuade": Lincoln Diary, Dec. 15, 1960, Box 2, Lincoln Papers, JFKL. JFK and RFK also brought Philip Graham, the publisher of the *Washington Post*, into the discussion about the appointment. "Bobby came to my office for an hour and a half of good talk. I think we began to see some new light after much frank discussion. If you want to call me for a report, it might help you give him a little guidance." Philip L. Graham to JFK, Dec. 13, 1960, Box 30, POF.

p. 319: "'We did it.'": Helen Thomas, 22–23.

p. 319: Criticism: Schlesinger, *Robert Kennedy*, 233–36.

p. 319: "Dick Russell": Baker, 120–21.

p. 319: "Kennedy wanted": Sorensen, 284.

pp. 319–20: On the Hodges, Goldberg, Udall, and Ribicoff appointments, see Schlesinger, *A Thousand Days*, 130–31, 141–42. Also Ribicoff OH.

p. 320: "We are going down": Schlesinger, *A Thousand Days*, 143.

p. 320: "opening prayers": Ibid., 136.

p. 320: "could make or break": Sorensen, 285.

p. 320: He fell asleep: Ibid., 287.

p. 321: Cabinet selections and press conferences: Dec. 7, 8, 13, 15, 16, 20, 27, 31, 1960, and Jan. 1, 1961, Box 1060, PPP.

p. 321: Task force reports: See Boxes 1071–1074 and 1076–1077, PPP.

p. 321: "There is no evidence": Bartlett, "News Focus," Nov. 27, 1960, Box 30, POF.

p. 321: "Reporters are not": Quoted in Evan Thomas, 114–15.

p. 322: "a plethora of specifics": Louis Harris to JFK, Jan. 14, 1961, Box 30, POF.

p. 322: "Didn't you get the word?" *New York Times*, Jan. 21, 1961.

p. 322: On JFK's pills: Lincoln Diary, Jan. 2, 4, 11, 16, 20, 1961, Lincoln Papers.

p. 322: "My God": Lincoln Diary, Jan. 20, 1961, Lincoln Papers.

p. 322: "excellent" health: *New York Times*, Jan. 21, 1961.

p. 323: "the picture of health": Ibid.

p. 323: "He looked like": Lincoln Diary, Jan. 20, 1961, Box 4, Lincoln Papers.

p. 323: "grace under pressure": Mary McGrory, *Washington Evening Star*, Jan. 20, 1961.

p. 323: On Frost and JFK: Stewart Udall OH.

p. 324: The Inaugural speech: Sorensen, 269–73. Ted Sorensen told me that JFK wanted the speech to defuse rather than intensify the Cold War: Interview, Feb. 25, 2002. As one sample of the advice to JFK, see Louis Harris to JFK, Jan. 14, 1961, Box 30, POF.

p. 324: On the length, see *New York Times*, Jan. 21, 1961.

p. 324: "going over and over": Lincoln Diary, Jan. 20, 1961, Box 4, Lincoln Papers.

pp. 325–26: Inaugural Address: *PPP: JFK, 1961*, 1–3.

p. 326: "fine, very fine" and the other quotes are in the *New York Times*, Jan. 21, 1961.

p. 326: "You have truly": Emmet J. Hughes to JFK, Jan. 23, 1961, Box 30, POF.

p. 326: Krock told Kennedy: Arthur Krock OH.

p. 327: "impressed [n]or stirred": *The Reporter*, Feb. 2, 1961, 10.

p. 327: "disturbed": Evelyn Lincoln to JFK, n.d., 1961 ("Doug Cater called. Wanted me to bring this editorial to your attention, since you were disturbed over Ascoli's editorial on your inauguration speech"). Box 7, Evelyn Lincoln Papers.

p. 327: As good as Jefferson's: Parmet, *JFK*, 82.

p. 327: Burns told Jack: Burns told me this.

p. 327: JFK on Jefferson: *PPP: JFK, 1962*, 347.

p. 327: Public response to the Inaugural and to JFK: Gallup, 1707–8.

Chapter 10: The Schooling of a President

p. 328: "Well, because": *PPP: JFK, 1961*, 15–16.

p. 329: The House: White, *Making, 1960*, 361–62.

p. 329: On the Rules Committee: Bernstein, 227–28.

p. 329: "letting their judgments": *PPP: JFK, 1961*, 11.

p. 329: "Bullshit, buddy": Richard Bolling OH, Columbia University.

p. 330: Executive Order: *PPP: JFK, 1961*, 10.

p. 330: Expending political capital: JFK to Sen. A. Willis Robertson, Feb. 7, 1961, POF.

p. 330: On Weaver: Robert C. Weaver OH; Parmet, *JFK*, 77–78.

pp. 330–31: On the CEEO and LBJ, see Dallek, *Flawed Giant*, 11–12.

p. 331: On the Coast Guard and the Cabinet: Bernstein, 52–58.

p. 331: First black ambassador to a white nation: Sheldon Stern to Author, April 19, 2002.

p. 331: "It may be proper": JFK to Mike Feldman, Feb. 16, 1961, Box 63, POF.

pp. 331–32: Civil Rights Commission: Wofford, 130–33; Bernstein, 50–51; Richard Reeves, 59–63.

p. 332: "Look, Father": Quoted in Richard Reeves, 60.

p. 333: "We take office": PPP: JFK, 1961, 19–20.

p. 333: "With the seven percent": Robert Nathan OH.

p. 333: On interest rates and Martin: Bernstein, 131–32.

pp. 333–34: Feb. 2 message: PPP: JFK, 1961, 41–53.

p. 334: "second-stage": Walter Heller to JFK, Mar. 17, 1961, Box 73, POF.

p. 334: "The Secretary of Treasury": Gridiron speech, Mar. 11, 1961, Box 61, Theodore Sorensen Papers, JFKL.

p. 334: But liberal economists: Paul Samuelson to JFK and CEA, Mar. 21, 1961, ibid.

p. 334: "Kennedy never thought": Leon Keyserling OH, Columbia University.

p. 334: "The financial program": CEA, Memo: "The Administration's Financial Program Thus Far," April 6, 1961; Heller to JFK, May 27, 1961, Box 73, POF.

pp. 334–35: Administration proposals being enacted: Parmet, JFK, 97.

p. 335: The polls: Louis Harris to JFK, "A Word About This Report," Mar. 22, 1961, Box 105, POF; Gallup, 1708, 1715–16.

p. 335: "new, young": Newsweek, Mar. 13, 1961.

p. 335: The polls: Parmet, JFK, 98; Gallup, 1707, 1712.

p. 335: "I don't think": Joe Alsop to JFK, n.d., Box 27, POF.

p. 335: "the simple fact": Memorandum, n.d., 1961, Box 27, POF.

p. 335: Press conferences: Sorensen, 361–65.

p. 335: Dismissing fears: News Conference, Jan. 25, 1961, PPP: JFK, 1961, 10.

p. 335: "a superb show": Schlesinger, A Thousand Days, 717.

p. 336: "The 6 O'Clock": Sorensen, 362. Also see National Observer clipping, n.d., "Kennedy's Press Conferences: A Refined Tool in Skillful Hands," Box 28, POF.

p. 336: "we couldn't survive": Sorensen, 364.

p. 336: Public approval: Gallup, 1765–66.

p. 336: U.S. patrol plane: Ambrose, Eisenhower, 584–86.

p. 336: "step by step" and "cooperate with all": FRUS: Kennedy-Khrushchev Exchanges, 2–3.

pp. 336–37: Press Conferences, Jan. 25, and Feb. 8, 1961: PPP: JFK, 1961, 8–9, 70.

pp. 336–37: "he would set himself in right": Evelyn Lincoln to JFK, Feb. 25, 1961 ("Senator Gore called"), Box 125, POF.

p. 337: DDE speech, Jan. 17, 1961: Public Papers of the Presidents: Dwight D. Eisenhower, 1960, 1038.

p. 337: On Burke: Arthur Sylvester OH; PPP: JFK, 1961, 32, 73, 94; New York Times, Jan. 28, 1961. A Burke interview with Greek journalist Elias P. Demetracopoulos, in which the admiral freely expressed his views, got him into trouble with the White House. The interview also brought Demetracopoulos under CIA scrutiny: Demetracopoulos, "Muzzling Admiral Burke," U.S. Naval Institute Proceedings, Jan. 2000, and "Admirals Strike a Blow for the Press," Proceedings, May 2001; Demetracopoulos conversation with Author.

pp. 337–38: The missile gap: JFK to McGeorge Bundy, Feb. 8, 1961, Box 62, POF. U.S. News & World Report, Feb. 27, 1961, 43. Excerpts from Hearings of Defense Dept., April 6, 1961, Box 51, Sorensen Papers. Edward R. Murrow to

McGeorge Bundy, Mar. 8, 1961, Box 290, NSF. Beschloss, *Crisis Years*, 65–66; Shapley, 97–99. Gallup, 1662, 1704, 1705, 1721.

pp. 338–39: Origins of the Peace Corps: Wilbur Cohen OH, Columbia University; *PPP: JFK, 1961*, 134–36; Sorensen, 208; Schlesinger, *A Thousand Days*, 165, 605–7.

p. 339: Public response: Gallup, 1704, 1791.

pp. 339–40: On Shriver: Sargent Shriver OH, LBJL; Anthony Lewis, "Shriver Moves into the Front Rank," *New York Times Magazine*, Mar. 15, 1964; A. H. Raskin, "Generalissimo of the War on Poverty," ibid., Nov. 22, 1964; Schlesinger, *A Thousand Days*, 606–7.

p. 340: "wars of national liberation": Beschloss, *Crisis Years*, 60–61.

p. 340: "made clear": FRUS: *National Security Policy*, 240.

p. 340: "Latin America required": FRUS: *American Republics*, 880. Also see Stephen G. Rabe, "John F. Kennedy and Latin America," *Diplomatic History* (Summer 1999), 545.

p. 340: More documents: Stephanie Fawcett, Senior Foreign Policy Archivist, JFKL, remarks at Cold War Documentation Conference, National Archives, II, College Park, Md., Sept. 25, 1998.

p. 340: "that, with all its pretensions": Schlesinger, *A Thousand Days*, 201.

p. 341: "Never in the long history": *PPP: JFK, 1961*, 170–75.

p. 341: JFK's Spanish: Richard Goodwin, 156–59.

p. 342: On the Latin reaction, see Thomas Mann OH; Schlesinger, *A Thousand Days*, 205; and Schlesinger to JFK, Feb. 6, 1961, Box 65, POF.

p. 342: Khrushchev's views: FRUS: *Soviet Union*, 39–46.

p. 342: Feb.11, 1961 meeting: Ibid., 63–67.

p. 342: "a mentality": Charles Bohlen OH.

p. 342: "a sustained offensive": Barbara Jackson to JFK, Mar. 5, 1961, and "Outline for a Possible Address," Box 33, POF.

p. 343: "find another forum": JFK to Jackson, n.d., ibid.

p. 343: "greatest nightmare": White House Staff OH, LBJL.

p. 343: "I have been greatly": JFK to DDE, Mar. 30, 1960, Box 29A, POF.

p. 343: "in the overall interest": John J. McCloy to JFK, Mar. 8, 1961, Box 100, POF.

p. 343: "stand at Geneva": JFK-Macmillan talks, April 6, 1961, 3:45 P.M., Box 175, POF.

p. 343: "every approach": Roswell L. Gilpatric OH.

p. 343: "only in the light": JFK-Adenauer Talks, April 13, 1961, 10:30 A.M., Box 255A, NSF.

p. 343: "a war-fighting capability": Rand Research Memorandum, "Political Implications of Posture Choices," Dec. 1960, Box 64, POF.

p. 344: "a subordinate commander": McGeorge Bundy to JFK, Jan. 30, 1961, Box 313, NSF.

p. 344: "whether he was not": Brandon Diary, Jan. 16, 1961, Box 5, Henry Brandon Papers, LC.

p. 344: "We became increasingly": Gilpatric OH. Memorandum, Feb. 24, 1961; JFK conference with military chiefs, Feb. 27, 1961, Box 345, NSF.

p. 344: "might trigger": Five Interviews with Glen T. Seaborg, Box 11, Closed Deposit, NHP.

p. 344: "the lead in bringing": Gilpatric OH.

p. 344: "is a nuclear war man": McGeorge Bundy to JFK, Oct. 3, 1961, Box 103, POF.

p. 345: "Would things be": Quoted in Kaplan, 43–44, 256.

p. 345: "unreconstructable": Gilpatric OH.

p. 345: "was always troubled": Paul Nitze OH.

pp. 345–46: "The plan that he inherited": White House Staff OH.

p. 346: "a truly monstrous": Walt W. Rostow OH.

p. 346: Lemnitzer presentation and JFK's tension: White House Staff OH.

p. 346: "And we call ourselves": Quoted in Richard Reeves, 229–30.

p. 346: "not so happy": JFK-Adenauer conversation, April 13, 1961, Noon, Box 79, NSF.

p. 346: "the threshold for": April 12, 1961, Box 79, NSF.

p. 346: "stop Soviet forces": Dean Acheson to JFK and Rusk, April 20, 1961, Box 70, NSF.

p. 346: "these plans might lessen": April 12, 1961, Box 79, NSF.

pp. 346–47: "have left the United States": Nitze OH. Also see Robert Komer to Dean Acheson, Feb. 20, 1961, and Komer to JFK, Mar. 6, 1961, Box 4339, NSF.

p. 347: "'repeat to the point'": Kaplan, 285.

p. 347: "That son of a bitch": White House Staff OH.

p. 347: On a nuclear first strike: Fred Kaplan, "JFK's First Strike Plan," *The Atlantic*, Oct. 2001, though Kaplan makes clear that JFK was highly skeptical of any first-strike plan.

p. 347: "I never met a man": Quoted in Hersh, 253.

p. 347: Kennedy announced increases: *PPP: JFK, 1961*, 229–40, 658–59.

p. 348: "charges that": Ibid., 658–59.

p. 348: "They don't get it": Quoted in Richard Reeves, 245.

p. 348: "would have been profoundly": Parmet, *JFK*, 132. JFK's view of Khrushchev's speech: Schlesinger, *A Thousand Days*, 302; Kalb and Abel, 110.

p. 348: "brutally torn": *PPP: JFK, 1961*, 23.

p. 349: "I find it difficult": Ibid., 91.

p. 349: "massive unilateral intervention": Ibid., 99.

p. 349: "the U.N. could not": Quoted in Schlesinger, *A Thousand Days*, 575.

p. 349: "used to oppress": FRUS: Congo Crisis, 99–101.

pp. 349–50: For LBJ's African trip and "Cadillac diplomacy," see Dallek, *Flawed Giant*, 12–16.

p. 350: "counter-guerrilla forces": National Security Action Memorandum No. 2, Feb. 3, 1961; JFK to Mac Bundy, Feb. 6, 1961; Robert McNamara to Bundy, Feb. 23, 1961, Box 328, NSF. Robert Komer to Walt W. Rostow, Feb. 28, 1961, Box 414, NSF. Also see Schlesinger, *A Thousand Days*, 320, 340–42.

p. 351: "It is, I think": *PPP: JFK, 1961*, 213. Also see 16, 23, 34, 71, 74–75, 122, 149, 154, 185, and 1–120 of *FRUS: Laos Crisis*.

p. 351: "I don't think there are probably": Kenneth P. O'Donnell taped interview with Sander Vanocur, MR 91-27:49, JFKL.

p. 351: "any satisfactory solution": FRUS: Laos Crisis, 45.

p. 351: "Laos was hopeless": Winthrop G. Brown OH.

p. 351: "These jungle regimes": Galbraith, *Letters*, 70.

p. 351: "We must never": Brown OH.

pp. 351–52: "Laos is far away": *PPP: JFK, 1961*, 214.

p. 352: He "said that": Memo of conversation, April 7, 1961, Chalmers

Roberts Papers, JFKL. *New York Times,* Mar. 21, 1961; Richard Reeves, 75; O'Donnell Tapes, MR 91-27:49.

p. 352: "But I need not tell you": Harold Macmillan to DDE, April 9, 1961, Box 29A, POF.

p. 352: "That boy doesn't know": Earl Mazo OH, Columbia University.

p. 352: Ambassador Brown: *FRUS: Laos Crisis,* 139–41.

p. 353: NSC meeting, April 27, 1961, Box 313, NSF.

p. 353: "You start using": Guthman and Shulman, 248.

p. 353: "if we are given": Schlesinger, *A Thousand Days,* 338.

p. 353: "general agreement among" and congressional leaders: *FRUS: Laos Crisis,* 142–43, 146–47. JFK and congressional leaders, April 27, 1961, Box 345, NSF.

p. 353: "It would be a mistake": Lincoln Diary, April 28, 1961, Box 9, Evelyn Lincoln Papers, JFKL.

p. 353: Neutrality agreement: Gibbons, 112.

p. 353: "dribbled to a conclusion": O'Donnell Tapes, MR 91-27:49.

pp. 353–54: "critical condition" and "for the first time": *FRUS: Vietnam, 1961,* 12–19.

p. 354: "the worst one": Rostow OH.

p. 354: "the entire western": Quoted in David Kaiser, 73.

p. 354: LBJ trip and troop commitment: *PPP: JFK, 1961,* 354, 356.

pp. 354–55: LBJ's visit to Saigon: Dallek, *Flawed Giant,* 13–14.

p. 355: "a series of joint": *FRUS: Vietnam, 1961,* 128.

p. 355: "We have not become": Quoted in David Kaiser, 73.

p. 355: "I cannot stress too strongly": Quoted in Dallek, *Flawed Giant,* 17–18.

p. 355: "our billions": John K. Galbraith to JFK, Mar. 2, 1961, Box 29, POF.

p. 356: "nearly always": Laura B. Knebel to James Ellison, n.d., in Box 5, "Closed Deposit," NHP. Also see Laura B. Knebel OH.

p. 356: Refusing to comment: *FRUS: Cuba, 1961–1962,* 5.

p. 356: "a rapprochement": John Sharon OH, Columbia University.

p. 356: The Lens report: AES to JFK, Jan. 13, 1961, Box 33, POF.

p. 356: CIA plan: Schlesinger, *A Thousand Days,* 233.

pp. 356–57: January 22 meeting: *FRUS: Cuba, 1961–1962,* 46–53.

p. 357: During the last week: January 25 and 28 meetings and follow-ups, ibid., 54–58, 61–65; JFK to Bundy, Feb. 6, 1961, Box 35A, POF.

pp. 357–58: The February 8 discussions: *FRUS: Cuba, 1961–1962,* 89–91.

p. 358: "appeaser": O'Donnell Tape 49.

p. 358: "However well disguised": *FRUS: Cuba, 1961–1962,* 92–93.

p. 358: "be landed gradually": Ibid., 90.

p. 359: "the small invasion force": Ibid., 119–20.

p. 359: "will have": Ibid., 135.

p. 359: "The Cuban paramilitary": Ibid., 142.

p. 359: "willing to take": Ibid., 143–44.

p. 359: "small-scale World War II": Ibid., 145–48.

p. 359: "A slight danger": Ibid., 156–57.

p. 360: "[has] done a remarkable job": Ibid., 158.

p. 360: "in order to make this appear" and "reserved the right": Ibid., 159–60.

p. 360: "the plan was dependent on": Ibid., 160.

p. 360: "What do you think": Schlesinger, *A Thousand Days*, 246.

p. 360: "U.S. strike forces": *FRUS: Cuba, 1961–1962*, 177.

p. 360: "If you fail": Quoted in Johnson, 67.

pp. 360–61: "If the operation": *FRUS: Cuba, 1961–1962*, 178–81.

p. 361: "No one": Schlesinger, *A Thousand Days*, 247.

p. 361: CIA paper: *FRUS: Cuba, 1961–1962*, 213–16.

p. 361: "Are you serious?": Dean Acheson OH. For the Schlesinger, Rusk, and Fulbright dissents, see *FRUS: Cuba, 1961–1962*, 185–89, 191, 196–203, and Schlesinger, *A Thousand Days*, 250–56.

p. 362: "Mr. President": Theodore Sorensen OH; Sorensen, 332.

p. 362: Schlesinger remembered: *A Thousand Days*, 258.

pp. 362–63: "appear as an internal": *FRUS: Cuba, 1961–1962*, 185.

p. 363: "everything possible": Ibid., 191–92, 213.

p. 363: Newspaper stories: For examples of the newspaper leaks: "Regime to Fight Castro Being Formed Here," *New York Herald Tribune*, Mar. 22, 1961, and Schlesinger to JFK, April 7, 1961, Box 65, POF.

p. 363: Castro "doesn't need": Quoted in Wyden, *Bay of Pigs*, 155.

p. 363: "in helping": *PPP: JFK, 1961*, 258.

p. 363: "play down the magnitude": Bissell, 183.

p. 363: "one of those rare events": Quoted in Peter Kornbluh, 2.

p. 363: On the bombing raids and Stevenson's response: *FRUS: Cuba, 1961–1962*, 226–30; Schlesinger, *A Thousand Days*, 268–72; Richard Reeves, 90–91.

p. 364: "the room in evident concern": Schlesinger, *A Thousand Days*, 272–73.

p. 364: "failure to make": *FRUS: Cuba, 1961–1962*, 235–37.

p. 364: "the situation in Cuba": Ibid., 272. For the details of the defeat, see 273 ff.

p. 364: "nobody knew": Ibid., 274–75.

pp. 364–65: Meeting in the Cabinet Room: Richard Reeves, 93–95.

p. 365: "were sure": O'Donnell and Powers, 274.

p. 365: "an incident, not a disaster": Schlesinger, *A Thousand Days*, 275–76.

pp. 365–66: "Under a parliamentary": Quoted in Powers, 115.

p. 366: "the chief cause" and other quotes: See Kornbluh, 13–14, 45–46, 113–14.

p. 366: "was so upset": Smith, 697–98.

p. 366: "within the privacy": O'Donnell and Powers, 274.

p. 366: The Rose Garden: Ibid., 272, and Salinger, 195.

p. 366: Messed hair: Richard Reeves, 95 and 677.

pp. 366–67: Henry Raymont: Interview with author.

p. 367: Ill-timed health problems: See Dr. Janet Travell medical records, Jan.–Apr. 1961, JFKL.

p. 367: "quite shattered": *FRUS: Cuba, 1961–1962*, 305.

p. 367: "How could I" and the meeting with the Cubans: Richard Reeves, 94, 96–99; Schlesinger, *A Thousand Days*, 279–85.

p. 367: "the worst experience": Nixon, 234–35.

p. 367: "I was thinking about": O'Donnell and Powers, 274–75.

pp. 367–68: "President Kennedy has stated," and "an old saying": Schlesinger, *A Thousand Days*, 289–90.

p. 368: "the testimony": JFK to Henry Luce, Aug. 29, 1961, Box 9, Evelyn Lincoln Papers.

p. 368: "I have felt": Sept. 12, 1961, ibid.

p. 368: "the military and intelligence": Schlesinger, *A Thousand Days*, 258.

p. 368: "never to rely": Ibid., 296.

p. 368: "The first advice": Bradlee, *Conversations*, 122.

p. 369: "Well for the time being": Brandon Diary, May 2, 1961, Box 5, Brandon Papers.

p. 369: Cynical complaint, especially in western Europe: *FRUS: Cuba, 1961–1962*, 423–28. Also see Stevenson's depressing analysis from the UN: Ibid., 295–97.

p. 369: "Not much time": Quoted in Richard Reeves, 108.

p. 369: Nixon and Republican opposition: Ambrose, *Nixon*, 632.

p. 369: "It is doubtful": RCC Newsletter, April 27, 1961, Box 18, Arthur Schlesinger Jr. Papers, JFKL.

p. 369: "look pretty good": Schlesinger, *A Thousand Days*, 289.

p. 369: "When he disagreed": Guthman and Shulman, 264–65.

p. 369: The White House and NSC meetings: *FRUS: Cuba, 1961–1962*, 304–7, 313–14. RFK memo: Ibid., 302–4.

p. 370: "That's the most": Richard Goodwin, 187.

p. 370: "I knew it!": Quoted in Ambrose, *Nixon*, 632.

p. 370: "It really is true": Nixon, 233–35.

p. 370: "There is only one thing": Quoted in Richard Reeves, 102–3.

p. 370: Gallup, 1717, 1721.

p. 371: "It's just like": Schlesinger, *A Thousand Days*, 292.

p. 371: The Taylor committee: Taylor, 180–84; *FRUS: Cuba, 1961–1962*, 318–24.

p. 371: "reoriented": Guthman and Shulman, 11–13.

p. 371: "agreed that": *FRUS: Cuba, 1961–1962*, 482–83.

p. 371: "There can be no": Ibid., 605–6.

p. 371: With only 44 percent: Gallup, 1721.

pp. 371–72: *Time*, May 5, 1961.

p. 372: Liked it better and "always on the edge": JFK on Presidency, Box 23, David Powers Papers, JFKL.

p. 372: "Sons of bitches": Quoted in Richard Reeves, 116.

Chapter 11: A World of Troubles

p. 373: "If the self-discipline": *PPP: JFK, 1961*, 304–6.

p. 374: Steel production: Arthur Goldberg to JFK, Mar. 21, 1961, Arthur Goldberg Papers, LC.

p. 374: Williard Mathias, "evolution," and "suspected of being": Bird, 177, 431, n74.

p. 374: "the Soviets have no": Walter Heller to JFK, June 27, 1961, Box 125A, POF.

p. 375: "in the interest": *PPP: JFK, 1961*, 334–38.

p. 375: "Maybe if you": Quoted in Tifft and Jones, 314–15.

p. 375: "intended to examine": *PPP: JFK, 1961*, 335.

p. 375: Philandering: Conversation with Robert Novak. Other journalists, Haynes Johnson, James Kilpatrick, Nick Kotz, Marianne Means, Bruce Morton, and Don Oberdorfer, echoed Novak's assertion.

p. 375: Ultra-right-wing press stories: Conversation with Ronald Whalen, JFKL.

p. 375: "underground market": Parmet, *JFK*, 114.

p. 375: LBJ's womanizing: Dallek, *Lone Star Rising*, 189–91, 637, n13; and *Flawed Giant*, 186–87.

p. 376: People around the president worried: Confidential source.

p. 376: "Once every two": Evan Thomas, 116.

p. 376: JFK-NSK Messages between November and February: *FRUS: Kennedy-Khrushchev Exchanges*, 1–6.

p. 376: "It is a secret": NSK to JFK, April 18, 1961; JFK to NSK, April 18, 1961, ibid., 7–10. Also see Nixon, 234–35, and Beschloss, *Crisis Years*, 120–21.

p. 377: Khrushchev answered Kennedy: NSK to JFK, April 22, 30, May 16, 1961; also see JFK to NSK, April 12, 1961: *FRUS: Kennedy-Khrushchev*, 10–16, 18–21.

p. 377: His dilemma: *PPP: JFK, 1961*, 288.

p. 377: Department of urban affairs and housing: Ibid., 285.

pp. 377–78: On political opposition: Lee C. White to JFK, Aug. 21, 1961, Box 30, POF.

p. 378: On the bill's secondary priority: Legislative Items Recommended by the President, May 15, June 30, 1961, Box 49, POF.

p. 378: On the economy, see Walter Heller to JFK, April 6, 27, and May 10, 1961, Box 5, Walter W. Heller Papers, JFKL; Schlesinger, *A Thousand Days*, 630; and Bernstein, 126–27.

p. 378: Tax reform bill: *PPP: JFK, 1961*, 290–303.

p. 378: Business leaders' opposition: Schlesinger, *A Thousand Days*, 631.

p. 378: LBJ: Dallek, *Flawed Giant*, 11.

p. 378: Gains in domestic affairs: *PPP: JFK, 1961*, 220, 282, 344, 353, 365, 486, 488, 524, 552.

p. 379: "highest-priority items": Legislative Items Recommended by the President, May 15, June 30, 1961, Box 49, POF.

p. 379: On defeat of the education and health insurance bills: Bernstein, chaps. 7 and 8.

p. 380: "Phase Two": Lou Harris to JFK, June 22, 1961, Box 63A, POF.

p. 380: Vow to renew his efforts in 1962: See the undated 8-page memo headed: "Is the Kennedy Administration financially responsible?" Box 50, POF.

pp. 380–81: "the limited goal," "quick-talking," and "the smartest politician": Quoted in Schlesinger, *A Thousand Days*, 315.

p. 381: "This is the way": Bayard Rustin OH, Columbia University.

p. 381: Executive Order: Bernstein, 51–52.

p. 381: "kept muttering": Wofford, 169–70.

p. 381: "timid and reluctant": Louis Martin to Sorensen, May 10, 1961, Box 66, Gen. Corresp., RFK Papers, JFKL.

pp. 381–82: Polls: Gallup, 1705, 1713, 1723–24.

p. 382: Burke Marshall: Branch, 405.

p. 382: The Charleston incident: Ibid., 399–400.

pp. 382–83: "King's name," O'Donnell's response, and the Mayflower meeting: Ibid., 404–7. Martin Luther King OH.

p. 383: "Summary of Civil Rights Progress," Box 63, POF.

pp. 383–84: Freedom Riders: Burke Marshall OH; Guthman and Shulman, 82–84, 92–93; Branch, 412–30; Richard Reeves, 122–25.

p. 384: "Can't you get": Quoted in Richard Reeves, 125.

p. 384: "What sort of help": Branch, 428.

p. 384: Gallup, 1723.

pp. 384–85: Nashville students: Burke Marshall OH; John Patterson OH; Guthman and Shulman, 84–86; Branch, 429–44.

p. 385: "Do you know": Schlesinger, *Robert Kennedy*, 296.

p. 385: "I never recovered": Guthman and Shulman, 93.

p. 385: "Oh, there are fists": Quoted in Guthman, *We Band*, 170–71. For the rest, Branch, 444–50.

p. 386: The response to King's decision: Ibid., 451–54.

p. 386: JFK statement: *PPP: JFK, 1961*, 391.

p. 386: Bobby consulted him constantly: Guthman and Shulman, 95–96.

p. 386: Riots at Abernathy's church: Branch, 454–65.

p. 386: "If they don't get here": Ibid., 460.

pp. 386–87: "Now, Reverend": Wofford, 154.

p. 387: "destroying us politically": Quoted in Branch, 464–65.

p. 387: "They had made their point": Guthman and Shulman, 97–98.

p. 387: "Negroes have been," "Man, we've been," and "You know": Wofford, 155–57.

p. 387: "Wait means 'Never!'": *Time*, June 2, 1961.

p. 387: "could say something": Wofford, 125–26.

p. 388: "Eisenhower never did": Harris Wofford to JFK, May 29, 1961, Box 68, Gen. Corresp., RFK Attorney General's Papers, JFKL.

p. 389: Speech to Canadian Parliament: *PPP: JFK, 1961*, 380–88.

p. 389: Conflict with Diefenbaker: Sorensen, 648; Memo, April 7, 1961, Chalmers Roberts Papers, JFKL; Guthman and Shulman, 29; Lawrence Martin, 180–91; Bradlee, *Conversations*, 167, 181–85.

p. 389: Special message: *PPP: JFK, 1961*, 396–402. And see Memo on Defense Posture, to JFK, n.d., Box 84A, POF.

p. 390: Act for International Development: George Ball to JFK, Mar. 16, 1961, Box 87; Chester Bowles to JFK, May 22, 23, 1961, Box 28, POF. Gallup, 1700–1701.

pp. 390–91: "apathy, indifference": *PPP: JFK, 1961*, 402–3. Gallup, 1724–25, 1732, 1734, 1741, 1745.

p. 391: "What should I do": Quoted in Sorensen, 691.

p. 391: Civil defense meetings: David Bell to Files, Mar. 20, 1961, Box 283A; McGeorge Bundy, "Civil Defense Meeting," May 9, 1961, Box 295, NSF.

p. 391: "great fears": Marc Raskin to Bundy, May 19, 1961, Box 295, NSF.

p. 391: Considerations governing expanded civil defense: David Bell to JFK, Mar. 18, 1961, Box 70; McGeorge Bundy to Sherley Ewing, April 26, 1961, Box 295, POF.

p. 391: "would show the world": "Some Issues Relating to a Fallout Shelter Program," n.d., but clearly before JFK's May 25 State of the Union speech; Box 295, NSF.

p. 391: "which we could never": *PPP: JFK, 1961*, 402.

pp. 391–92: Rockefeller: Sorensen, 692.

p. 392: Landing a man on the moon: *PPP: JFK, 1961*, 403–5.

p. 392: Only time he departed from his text in speaking to Congress: Sorensen, 592.

p. 392: Arguments against manned spaceflights: Michael R. Beschloss, "Kennedy and the Decision to Go to the Moon," in Launius and McCurdy, 51–55.

p. 392: A majority of Americans agreed: Gallup, 1702–3, 1720.

p. 392: "that we shall": *PPP: JFK, 1961*, 404.

p. 393: "clearly one of the great": Sorensen, 591.

p. 393: "But why": *PPP: JFK, 1962*, 669.

p. 393: Advantages of manned mission: JFK to Brook Overton, Mar. 22, 1961, Box 82, POF; Robert Dallek, "Johnson, Project Apollo, and the Politics of Space Program Planning," in Launius and McCurdy, 72–74.

p. 393: JFK-LBJ exchange: JFK to LBJ, April 20, 1961; LBJ to JFK, April 28, 1961, Box 28, POF. McDougall, 320; Dallek, "Johnson, Project Apollo," 70–72.

p. 394: The president "is afraid": Lincoln Diary, May 1, 1961, Box 4, Evelyn Lincoln Papers, JFKL.

p. 394: "You know, Lyndon": Newton Minow OH, LBJL.

pp. 394–95: Discussions with de Gaulle: *PPP: JFK, 1961*, 405–6, 413.

p. 395: "a great captain": *PPP: JFK, 1961*, 405. De Gaulle and FDR: Dallek, *Franklin D. Roosevelt*, 376–79.

p. 395: De Gaulle's attitude: *FRUS: Laos Crisis*, 22.

p. 395: De Gaulle and JFK's shared views: C. L. Sulzberger, "De Gaulle — How Splendid the Day Was," *New York Times*, April 29, 1961; President's Visit to De Gaulle: Talking Points, May 27, 1961, Box 116A, POF.

pp. 395–96: Tensions with de Gaulle: R. W. Komer to JFK, Mar. 6, 1961, Box 220, NSF; President's Visit: Talking Points, May 27, 1961, Box 116A, POF; *FRUS: Laos Crisis*, 115; *FRUS: Vietnam, 1961*, 254.

p. 396: "seemed to prefer": Sorensen, 633.

p. 396: "Even when": Nicholas Wahl to McGeorge Bundy, May 1961, Box 331, NSF. Also see Abram Chayes OH.

p. 396: Kennedy read de Gaulle's: Sorensen, 631.

p. 396: "behind his patrician": De Gaulle, *The War Memoirs*, 78–84.

p. 396: The only topic: President's Visit to De Gaulle, May 27, 1961, Box 116A, POF. JFK's arrival in Paris: *New York Times*, June 1, 1961; *Time*, June 9, 1961; Charles de Gaulle, *Memoirs of Hope*, 254, including "suffering the drawbacks"; Richard Reeves, 145–46.

p. 397: De Gaulle's formal dinner toast: *PPP: JFK, 1961*, 424–25.

p. 397: "somewhat fumbling": De Gaulle, *Memoirs of Hope*, 254.

p. 397: Memorized quotes: Beschloss, *Crisis Years*, 183.

p. 397: The gift: Sorensen, 633.

p. 397: "You've studied": Charles Bohlen OH.

p. 397: The conversations: De Gaulle, *Memoirs of Hope*, 254–59; *FRUS: Berlin Crisis, 1961–1962*, 80–86; *FRUS: Laos Crisis*, 214–20; Talking Points Reviewing Conversations between Pres. Kennedy and Pres. De Gaulle, May 31–June 2, 1961, Box 116A, POF.

p. 397: Told an English friend: Sir Alec Douglas-Home OH.

pp. 398–99: Medical problems: Dr. Janet Travell medical records, JFKL. Dr. Max Jacobson, "John F. Kennedy," in NHP. Parmet, *JFK*, 120–21; Beschloss, *Crisis Years*, 189–91.

p. 399: "I don't care": Reeves, *President Kennedy*, 36.

p. 399: "was in overall charge": Beschloss, *Crisis Years,* 191.

p. 399: "doctors came and went": Richard Reeves, 146–47.

p. 399: Jacobson and Jackie: Dr. Max Jacobson, "John F. Kennedy," in NHP; Richard Reeves, 146–47.

p. 399: Jackie and de Gaulle: Schlesinger, *A Thousand Days,* 349.

p. 399: Jackie's impact on the French: Leaming, 112–13.

p. 399: "Charm": Ibid., 425.

p. 399: The French press: Quoted in Richard Reeves, 154.

p. 400: "I do not think": *PPP: JFK, 1961,* 429.

p. 400: JFK resented: Interview with Marianne Means.

p. 400: Contingency planning for the Dominican Republic and Haiti: *FRUS: American Republics, 1961–1963,* 614, 616–18, 623–24, 629–33; the report of the assassination plot is on 629n. *FRUS: Cuba, 1961–1962,* 472–73, 478, 481. Salinger, 225–26.

pp. 400–401: The Bowles-RFK clash: *FRUS: American Republics,* 634–41.

p. 401: "gutless bastard" and Bowles conversation with JFK: Halberstam, *Best and Brightest,* 88–89.

p. 401: British Guiana: *FRUS: American Republics,* 513–19.

p. 402: "I hear there is something": Halberstam, *Best and Brightest,* 94–95.

p. 402: JFK and de Gaulle on Khrushchev: *FRUS: Berlin Crisis,* 80–81. Also see Halberstam, *Best and Brightest,* 96–97.

pp. 402–3: The quotes in the documents preceding the summit are in *FRUS: Soviet Union,* 130–33, 135–37, 153, 161, 163, 168.

p. 403: Kennan's analysis: Ibid., 168–70.

p. 403: The initial reception: *New York Times,* June 4, 1961; Kenneth O'Donnell Tapes, Tape 51, JFKL; Beschloss, *Crisis Years,* 191–92.

p. 403: "You make a hell": Quoted in Schoenbaum, 335.

p. 405: For the opening exchanges: Richard Reeves, 159; *FRUS: Soviet Union,* 172–73.

p. 405: "ways and means": Ibid., 173–74.

pp. 405–6: Additional JFK-Khrushchev exchanges in the first conversation: Ibid., 174–78.

p. 406: The luncheon exchanges: Ibid., 178–81.

pp. 406–7: The stroll in the garden: O'Donnell and Powers, 296; *FRUS: Soviet Union,* 182; Beschloss, *Crisis Years,* 198–99.

p. 407: The afternoon meeting: *FRUS: Soviet Union,* 183–96.

p. 407: Khrushchev's exhilaration: Sergei Khrushchev, 106.

p. 407: "He's very young": Quoted in Richard Reeves, 166.

p. 408: "to connect the questions": *FRUS: Soviet Union,* 196–97.

p. 408: For the JFK, Thompson, Bohlen reactions: Beschloss, *Crisis Years,* 205; Richard Reeves, 165–67.

pp. 408–9: The competition for international prestige: "John F. Kennedy, USIA, and World Public Opinion," *Diplomatic History,* Winter 2001, 63–84.

pp. 409–10: The dinner party: *New York Times,* June 4, 1961; Rose Kennedy, 404–5; Schlesinger, *A Thousand Days,* 367; Nikita Khrushchev, 498–99; Beschloss, *Crisis Years,* 207–9.

p. 410: The second day opening exchanges: *FRUS: Soviet Union,* 206–11.

p. 410: "Look, Mr. Chairman": Richard Reeves, 167. This exchange is not in the *FRUS* memo for June 4 at 10:30 A.M., but Reeves cites it as in a memcom at the National Security Archive, George Washington University, Washington, D.C.

pp. 410–11: Exchanges over the test ban and disarmament: *FRUS: Soviet Union*, 211–16.

pp. 411–12: Discussion of Germany and Berlin: Ibid., 216–25.

p. 412: Exchanges over lunch: Ibid., 225–28.

p. 412: "I can't leave here": O'Donnell and Powers, 297.

p. 412: "I'm not going": *Time*, Jan. 5, 1962.

p. 412: "This is the nut-cutter": Quoted in Bradlee, *Conversations*, 126.

p. 413: Kennedy began by saying: *FRUS: Soviet Union*, 229–30.

p. 413: "Then Mr. Chairman:" Quoted in Richard Reeves, 171, which is based on a Reeves interview with, and letter from, Rusk.

p. 413: With James Reston: *New York Times*, June 5, 1961; Halberstam, *Best and Brightest*, 95–97.

p. 413: On *Air Force One*: O'Donnell Tapes, Tape 53; O'Donnell and Powers, 298; Press Panel OH.

pp. 413–14: Conversation with O'Donnell: O'Donnell Tapes, Tape 53; O'Donnell and Powers, 297–99.

p. 414: "somebody with whom": Guthman and Shulman, 28–29, 262–63.

Chapter 12: Crisis Manager

p. 415: On initial contact between JFK and Macmillan, see Memo of Meeting, April 6, 1961, Box 175, NSF.

p. 415: "so old": Guthman and Shulman, 30–31, 262.

p. 415: "in the bosom": Brandon Diaries, June 9, 1961, Henry Brandon Papers, LC.

p. 415: "It was the gay things": Schlesinger, *A Thousand Days*, 374–77.

pp. 415–16: Macmillan meeting: Macmillan, 355–59. *FRUS: Berlin Crisis, 1961–1962*, 98–102.

p. 416: Meeting with congressional leaders: *FRUS: Soviet Union*, 232–37.

pp. 416–17: JFK TV address, June 6: *PPP: JFK, 1961*, 441–46.

p. 417: "a widespread feeling": *Time*, June 30, 1961.

p. 417: "I 'feel in my bones'": Horne, *Macmillan*, 310. See *The Times* of London, which complained that JFK "has not exercised proper and effective leadership": Sen. Albert Gore to Editor, The Times, June 28, 1961, Box 27, POF.

p. 417: "this problem": *FRUS: Berlin Crisis*, 107–8.

p. 417: "There are limits": Quoted in Wofford, 379.

p. 418: Khrushchev's dilemma: Vladislav M. Zubok, "Khrushchev and the Berlin Crisis, 1958–1962," Cold War International History Project, Woodrow Wilson International Center for Scholars, Washington, D.C., May 1993.

p. 418: Aide-mémoires and Khrushchev speech: *New York Times*, June 12, 16, and 17, 1961.

p. 418: "dropped all pretense": *FRUS: Soviet Union*, 249–50.

p. 418: Hans J. Morgenthau, "The Trouble with Kennedy," *Commentary*, Dec. 1961, 51–55.

p. 418: But behind the scenes: *FRUS: Berlin Crisis*, 265.

p. 418: "He's imprisoned": Sidey, 218.

pp. 418–19: Highest priority: *FRUS: Berlin Crisis*, 106–38. Also see NSAM No. 41, April 25, 1961, Box 329, NSF; Henry Kissinger to McGeorge Bundy,

June 1, 1961, Box 31, POF; JFK-Finletter meeting, June 14, 1961, and JFK-Stikker meeting, June 16, 1961, Box 220A, NSF; Amb. David Bruce to Rusk, June 25, 1961, Box 170, NSF.

p. 419: "The need for re-establishing": *FRUS: Berlin Crisis*, 135–36, and 138–59.

p. 419: "Look at this": Quoted in Richard Reeves, 188–89.

pp. 419–20: The Nixon dig and the news conference: *PPP: JFK, 1961*, 476–84. 644: Also see ibid., 455–56, 458–59, 460–64.

p. 420: "more than military men": NSAM No. 55, June 28, 1961, Box 330, NSF.

p. 420: June 29 meeting with Acheson and others: *FRUS: Berlin Crisis*, 160–62.

p. 421: JFK meeting with Soviet journalists: *FRUS: Soviet Union*, 264–66.

p. 421: The leak and Khrushchev's response: *Newsweek*, July 3, 1961; Beschloss, *Crisis Years*, 244–45.

p. 421: Schlesinger delivered a memo: Schlesinger to JFK, July 7, 1961, in *FRUS: Berlin Crisis*, 173–76; also see Schlesinger to Bundy, July 13, 1961, Box WH 3, Arthur Schlesinger Jr. Papers, JFKL; and *A Thousand Days*, 385–88.

pp. 421–22 : While they cruised: Richard Reeves, 192–93.

p. 422: Asked McNamara and Bundy: NASM No. 58, June 30, 1961, in *FRUS: Berlin Crisis*, 162–65. Explanations from the Pentagon: Bundy to McNamara, July 10, 1961, Box 273, NSF. Directed Sylvester: Arthur Sylvester to JFK, July 13, 1961, with Sylvester to Hearst, July 13, 1961, attached, Box 77, POF.

p. 422: July planning: *FRUS: Berlin Crisis*, 176–226.

p. 422: "the only alternatives" and "If Khrushchev wants": Schlesinger, *A Thousand Days*, 390–91.

p. 422: Press conference, July 19, 1961: *PPP: JFK, 1961*, 513–21.

pp. 422–23: "didn't amount to very much": Guthman and Shulman, 276–77. Also see *PPP: JFK, 1961*, 520.

p. 423: "Gentlemen, you might as well": Quoted in Catudal, 182. Also see *FRUS: Berlin Crisis*, 218.

pp. 423–24: Kennedy's speech on the 25th: Report to American People on the Berlin Crisis, July 25, 1961. *PPP: JFK, 1961*, 533–40.

p. 424: Response to the speech: Donald M. Wilson to JFK, Aug. 1, 1961, Box 290, NSF.

p. 424: Press reaction: Schlesinger, *A Thousand Days*, 392. Congress: *New York Times*, Aug. 4, 1961. Nixon: *Dallas Morning News*, July 29, 1961.

p. 424: Sixty percent: Gallup, 1726, 1729–30.

p. 424: Leaked suggestions: Beschloss, *Crisis Years*, 262.

p. 424: Khrushchev was unhappy: *FRUS: Berlin Crisis*, 231–34.

p. 425: The "twin tactics": Thomas Hughes, "August 7 Khrushchev Speech on Berlin," n.d., Box 82, NSF.

p. 425: Closing the border: *FRUS: Berlin Crisis*, 325; Beschloss, *Crisis Years*, chap. 11.

p. 425: Fulbright quote: Schlesinger, *A Thousand Days*, 394.

p. 425: JFK to Rostow: Rostow, 231; Walt W. Rostow OH.

p. 425: JFK, "I can get": Schlesinger, *A Thousand Days*, 394.

p. 425: Kennedy had no advance knowledge: Lawrence Freedman, 73–75.

p. 425: Frustrated and angry: Parmet, *JFK*, 199.

p. 425: "With this weekend's": JFK to McNamara, Aug. 14, 1961, Box 273, NSF.

pp. 425–26: "What steps": *FRUS: Berlin Crisis*, 332.

p. 426: Stayed at the Cape: Richard Reeves, 211.

p. 426: State Dept. statement: Ibid., 325.

p. 426: "Why would Khrushchev": O'Donnell and Powers, 303.

p. 426: "can and should be": *FRUS: Berlin Crisis*, 339–41.

p. 426: Willy Brandt: *FRUS: Berlin Crisis*, 345–46.

p. 426: "Look at this!": Quoted in Wyden, *Wall*, 230.

p. 426: Aug. 17 meeting: *FRUS: Berlin Crisis*, 347–49.

p. 427: JFK reply to Brandt: Ibid., 352–53.

p. 427: "There'll be a lot": O'Donnell and Powers, 303. Also see Walter Jenkins OH, LBJL.

p. 427: Norstad to Chiefs: *FRUS: Berlin Crisis*, 350–51.

pp. 427–28: On LBJ in Bonn and Berlin: Dallek, *Flawed Giant*, 19–20; Schlesinger, *A Thousand Days*, 396–97. Also see Wyden, *Wall*, 227–34.

p. 428: Wanted fresh proposals: JFK to Rusk, Aug. 21, 1961, in *FRUS: Berlin Crisis*, 359–60.

p. 428: De Gaulle to JFK, Aug. 26, 1961, in ibid., 377–78.

p. 428: Neutralism and threats to civil air and road access: Ibid., 380–85.

p. 428: Nuclear testing and "Khrushchev intends": *FRUS: Soviet Union*, 284, 392.

p. 428: Khrushchev-Pearson: *Washington Post*, Aug. 28, 1961.

p. 428: Kennan reported: *FRUS: Berlin Crisis*, 387.

pp. 428–29: JFK to Adenauer, Sept. 4, 1961: Ibid., 389–91.

p. 429: JFK reply to Rusk, Sept. 5, 1961: Quoted in Schlesinger, *A Thousand Days*, 398.

p. 429: Clay appointment: *PPP: JFK, 1961*, 573.

p. 429: Nuclear testing: Ibid., 580–81, 584–85, 587, 589–90.

p. 429: "Fucked again": Halberstam, *Best and Brightest*, 84.

p. 429: "The bastards": Quoted in Richard Reeves, 223.

p. 429: Khrushchev-Sakharov: Sakharov, 215–17.

p. 430: Sept. 5 conversation: *FRUS: Berlin Crisis*, 393.

p. 430: Thompson and Gromyko: Ibid., 388–89, 394–95.

p. 430: Reston: *New York Times*, Sept. 6, 1961.

p. 430: Wechsler: *New York Post*, Sept. 21–22, 1961.

p. 430: "spark a Western": "The End of the Berlin Crisis, 1961–1962," *Cold War International History Project Bulletin*, Winter 1998, 218–220.

p. 430: Message carried by Sulzberger: *FRUS, Kennedy-Khrushchev*, 24–25.

p. 430: Rusk-Gromyko talks: *FRUS: Berlin Crisis*, 431–33, 439–41.

pp. 430–31: Message from NSK to JFK, Salinger, 191–94.

p. 431: JFK speech: *PPP: JFK, 1961*, 618–26.

p. 431: "The United States and the Soviet Union": RFK interview, Oct. 24, 1961, Box 2, Personal Papers, RFK Papers, JFKL.

pp. 431–32: NSK to JFK, Sept. 29, 1961: *FRUS: Kennedy-Khrushchev*, 25–38.

p. 432: "This is really": O'Donnell and Powers, 304.

p. 432: JFK greeted Gromyko: *FRUS: Berlin Crisis*, 468–80.

p. 432: JFK's view of Gromyko: Walter Lippmann OH.

p. 432: JFK to NSK, Oct. 16, 1961: *FRUS: Kennedy-Khrushchev*, 38–44.

p. 432: NSK announcement: Schlesinger, *A Thousand Days*, 400.

pp. 432–33: JFK and Dealey: Manchester, 48–49, 85. Dealey Plaza in Dallas, where JFK was killed, was named for the publisher.

p. 433: JFK to Norstad, Oct. 20, 1961: *FRUS: Berlin Crisis*, 520–23.

p. 433: The Gilpatric speech: Beschloss, *Crisis Years*, 329–31.

pp. 433–34: Soviet reaction: Ibid., 331–36. NSK to JFK, Nov. 9, 1961: *FRUS: Kennedy-Khrushchev*, 45–57.

p. 434: "a time of": Bundy, 363, 681.

p. 434: Rusk cable: *FRUS: Soviet Union*, 308–10.

p. 434: JFK and Adzhubei, Nov. 25, 1961: Ibid., 320–34.

pp. 434–35: JFK and AES: John B. Martin, 661.

p. 435: Ten-year plan, Berle, and Schlesinger to JFK, June 27, 1961: *FRUS: American Republics*, 19–25, 29–30.

p. 436: Mann to Rusk, Oct. 19, 1961: Ibid., 66–70.

p. 436: Bowles agreed: Ibid., 44–45, 70–72.

p. 436: Bowles and the State Department bureaucracy: Schlesinger, *A Thousand Days*, 437–45.

pp. 436–37: "The question" and other Bowles quotes: Halberstam, *Best and Brightest*, 88, 112.

p. 437: "a true believer": Evan Thomas, 141–42.

p. 437: NSAM: NSAM No. 88, Sept. 5, 1961; Bowles to JFK, Sept. 30, 1961, Box 331, NSF.

p. 438: "The Cuba matter": Quoted in Schlesinger, *A Thousand Days*, 473.

p. 438: Discussions foundered and JFK asked Burke: *FRUS: Cuba, 1961–1962*, 620–21, 631–33, 635.

p. 438: JFK told Goodwin and ignoring Castro: Ibid., 640–41, 645–47, 654–58.

p. 438: Goodwin and Che: Ibid., 642–45; Richard Goodwin, 190–208; Goodwin, "President Kennedy's Plan for Peace with Cuba," *New York Times*, July 5, 2000.

p. 438: Renewed concern: *FRUS: Cuba, 1961–1962*, 659–60.

pp. 438–39: Goodwin urged JFK: Ibid., 664–65.

p. 439: Mongoose and RFK quote: Ibid., 666–67.

p. 439: Nov. 21 meeting: Ibid., 684–86, 688–89.

p. 439: Eight schemes: U.S. Senate, Select Committee on Intelligence Activities, *Interim Report: Alleged Assassination Plots Involving Foreign Leaders* (Washington, D.C., 1975), 142.

p. 439: "people would be gratified": George Smathers OH.

p. 439: His 1988 recollection: Beschloss, *Crisis Years*, 139.

p. 439: "on the very same day": Evan Thomas, 157–58. U.S. Senate, *Interim Report*, 83–84, 128–36.

p. 439: "We were hysterical": U.S. Senate, *Interim Report*, 142. Also see *FRUS: Cuba, 1961–1962*, 659–60.

pp. 439–40: On JFK, RFK, and assassination plots, see Lawrence Freedman, 150–51; Central Intelligence Agency, *CIA Targets Fidel*, 25, 108; and Arthur Schlesinger Jr. to Editor, Dec. 21, 1997, *New York Times Book Review*.

pp. 440–41: On Jagan and British Guiana: *FRUS: American Republics*, 519–40; Schlesinger, *A Thousand Days*, 773–79.

Chapter 13: Reluctant Warrior

p. 442: For discussions on Vietnam between March and LBJ's trip in May: *FRUS: Vietnam, 1961*, 58–157.

p. 443: For a concise history of Indochina, see Roy Jumper and Marjorie Weiner Normand, "Vietnam: The Historical Background," in Gettleman.

p. 443: Kissinger had it right: Kissinger, 226.

p. 443: "There is no clearer example": *FRUS: Vietnam, 1961*, 84.

pp. 443–44: Muting U.S. involvement: Gibbons, 34–36.

p. 444: Rostow to JFK, May 26, 1961: *FRUS: Vietnam, 1961*, 157–58.

p. 444: Assurance on MAAG, limited appropriations, and Diem's resistance: Ibid., 85–86, 166–68, 174.

p. 444: Special Financial Group: Ibid., 179, 198–203, 221–23.

p. 444: "emphasized the reluctance": Ibid., 253–54.

p. 445: "you would wish": Quoted in Gibbons, 61–62.

p. 445: JFK to Diem, Aug. 5, 1961, *FRUS: Vietnam, 1961*, 263–66.

p. 445: "specifically conditioned": Ibid., 260.

p. 446: U.N. speech: *PPP: JFK, 1961*, 624.

p. 446: Rostow to JFK, Sept. 15, 1961; Taylor to JFK, Sept. 18, 1961: *FRUS: Vietnam, 1961*, 298–99, 304–5.

p. 446: In his U.N. address: *PPP: JFK, 1961*, 624.

p. 446: Bowles to Rusk, Oct. 5, 1961: *FRUS: Vietnam, 1961*, 322.

p. 447: "any investment": Theodore White to JFK, Oct. 11, 1961, Box 128, POF.

p. 447: "Concept for": Quoted in Gibbons, 69–70.

p. 447: White House meeting, Oct. 11, 1961: *FRUS: Vietnam, 1961*, 343–44.

p. 447: Preferred alternatives: *PPP: JFK, 1961*, 656, 660.

p. 447: Press conference: Ibid.

p. 447: Responded to press reports: *New York Times*, Oct. 14, 1961; Gibbons, 71.

p. 448: Rusk to Bell, Oct. 12, 1961; Lemnitzer to Adm. Felt, Oct. 13, 1961: *FRUS: Vietnam, 1961*, 359, 362–63. Felt's reply: Gibbons, 72.

p. 448: JFK's message to Taylor, Oct. 28, 1961: *FRUS: Vietnam, 1961*, 443.

p. 448: Taylor report: Ibid., 477–532. The quotes are on 477–79.

pp. 448–49: Taylor proposals: Ibid.

p. 448: "Only the Vietnamese": Ibid., 489. Gibbons, 73–78.

p. 449: Military coup: *FRUS: Vietnam, 1961*, 493–94, 512–14.

p. 449: McNamara recommendations: Ibid., 538–40, 559–61.

p. 449: The compromise recommendations: Ibid., 561–66, 576; Gibbons, 89–91.

p. 450: "United States troops": Krock, *Memoirs*, 332–33.

p. 450: "They want a force": Schlesinger, *A Thousand Days*, 547.

p. 450: "had many questions": *FRUS: Vietnam, 1961*, 532–33.

p. 451: Opposed the suggestion: Ibid., 467–70, 474–76, 580–82.

p. 451: Ball was as emphatic: Ball, 366–67.

p. 452: Armed himself with eight questions: *FRUS: Vietnam, 1961*, 576.

p. 452: Nov. 11 meeting: Ibid., 577–78.

p. 452: William Bundy believed: Gibbons, 91–92.

pp. 452–53: Kennedy approved a recommendation: *FRUS: Vietnam, 1961*, 591–94, 603–4.

p. 453: NSC meeting, Nov. 15, 1961: Ibid., 607–10.

p. 454: Rostow's warning: Ibid., 601–2.

p. 454: Rusk to Nolting, Nov. 13, 1961: Ibid., 583.

p. 454: The sense of urgency: Ibid., 477, 479, 486, 490, 511–12, 524.

pp. 454–55: JFK's message of Nov. 15, 1961, to Diem: Ibid., 656–57; Gibbons, 99–100.

p. 455: Diem's ghosted letter: *PPP: JFK, 1961*, 801–2.

p. 455: JFK's speeches: *PPP: JFK, 1961*, 724–28, 735–36.

p. 455: Implemented JFK's directives: Gibbons, 137.

pp. 455–56: Opposition from Diem: *FRUS: Vietnam, 1961*, 643, 689–91.

p. 456: John K. Galbraith to JFK, Nov. 21, 1961: Galbraith, *Letters*, 89–94.

p. 456: "I've told the Secretary": *FRUS: Vietnam, 1961*, 612–14.

p. 456: "considerable discussion": Ibid., 673–74, 675–76. Gibbons, 106–7.

p. 456: Drawn into firefights and lacked the training: Edward G. Lansdale OH, Columbia University; *FRUS: Vietnam, 1961*, 741, 754.

p. 457: Rusk cable, Nov. 28, 1961: Ibid., 679.

p. 457: JFK news conference, Jan. 15, 1962: *PPP: JFK, 1962*, 17.

p. 458: "we seem headed": *FRUS: Vietnam, 1962*, 129–32.

p. 458: "now involved in": James Reston, *New York Times*, Feb. 14, 1962. Salinger, 394, 398.

p. 458: "maximum feasible": Rusk to Saigon Embassy, Feb. 21, 1962. *FRUS: Vietnam, 1962*, 158–60.

p. 458: February 14 press conference: *PPP: JFK, 1962*, 136–37.

p. 458: Ongoing problems with the press: *FRUS: Vietnam, 1962*, 194–95, 206–7, 279–81.

p. 459: Harriman to Embassy, April 4, 1962: Ibid., 305–6.

p. 459: Rusk to Embassy, April 11, 1962: Ibid., 323–24.

p. 460: Galbraith to JFK, April 4 and 5, 1962: Galbraith, *Letters*, 100–103. David Kaiser, 131–32, 518 n. 37.

p. 460: JFK-Harriman discussion, April 6, 1962: *FRUS: Vietnam, 1962*, 309–10.

p. 460: "subterranean war": *PPP: JFK, 1962*, 199.

p. 460: "we are going to win": *New York Times*, Feb. 19, 1962. In March, the White House told Sen. Wayne Morse of Oregon that RFK's remarks "reflect the policy of the Administration toward Viet-Nam": *FRUS: Vietnam, 1962*, 230.

p. 461: White House conversation, May 1, 1962: Ibid., 366–67.

p. 461: For JFK's dilemma on testing, see Seaborg, 63–86. Also see *FRUS: Arms Control and Disarmament, 1961–1963*, 38–40, and Memo, April 7, 1961, Chalmers Roberts Papers, JFKL.

p. 462: Soviets' fifty atmospheric tests: Seaborg, 89–90.

p. 462: Nov. 2 NSC meeting: *FRUS: Arms Control*, 217–22.

p. 462: The president announced: *PPP: JFK, 1961*, 692–93.

p. 462: "we now entered": Seaborg, 111.

p. 462: "We could not get": Ibid., 126–27.

pp. 462–63: "considerably more in favor": Ibid., 129–30. Also *FRUS: Arms Control*, 272–81.

p. 463: Repeatedly sought assurances: Seaborg, 132. News conference, Jan. 15, 1962: *PPP: JFK, 1962*, 18.

p. 463: "Who would want": Quoted in Richard Reeves, 274.

p. 463: Decision to test: NSC Meeting., Feb. 27, 1962: *FRUS: Arms Control*, 331–37.

pp. 463–64: JFK address, Mar. 2, 1962: *PPP: JFK, 1962*, 186–92.

pp. 464–65: Civil defense: *PPP: JFK, 1961*, 536–37; JFK to McNamara, Aug. 20, 1961, Box 295, NSF; Jerome Wiesner to JFK, Sept. 27, 1961, Box 67, POF; Kaplan, 309–10.

p. 465: JFK to governors, Oct. 7, 1961, and news conference, Oct. 11, 1961: *PPP: JFK, 1961*, 648–49, 657.

pp. 465–66: The pamphlet and the response to it and the program: Kaplan, 310–12; Galbraith to JFK, Nov. 9, 1961, Box 295, NSF; Schlesinger to JFK, Nov. 22, 1961, Box 63, POF; Sorensen to JFK, Nov. 23, 1961, Box 30, Theodore Sorensen Papers, JFKL.

p. 466: Meetings with Teller: Bundy to JFK, Dec. 1, 1961, Box 295, NSF; Kaplan, 313–14.

p. 466: JFK's backtracking on civil defense: Schlesinger, *A Thousand Days*, 748–49; Kaplan, 314.

p. 466: JFK news conference, July 5, 1962: *PPP: JFK, 1962*, 543.

p. 467: Anti-Castro planning: *FRUS: Cuba, 1961–62*, 689–700, 703, 710, 719–20, 746, 767, 771, 786–91.

p. 467: Mary Hemingway: *The Nation*, Mar. 26, 2001, 17.

p. 468: Dominican Republic: *FRUS: American Republics*, 623–24, 642–44, 679–93.

p. 468: Visits to Venezuela and Colombia: *PPP: JFK, 1961*, 803–15. Also see Angello M. Novello to RFK, July 27, 1961, General Correspondence, Box 2, RFK Papers, JFKL.

p. 469: "I too found": JFK to James Farley, Jan. 5, 1962, Box 33, James Farley Papers, LC.

p. 469: JFK's reception: Schlesinger, *A Thousand Days*, 767

Chapter 14: The Limits of Power

p. 470: "the fix that he was in": Theodore C. Sorensen, "Judgment and Responsibility: John F. Kennedy and the Cuban Missile Crisis," in Lobel, 27.

p. 470: "I know that": Lincoln Diary, n.d., Box 4, Evelyn Lincoln Papers, JFKL.

p. 471: "He and I continued": Sorensen, 294.

p. 471: "He was tired": Lincoln Diary, May 18, 1961, Box 2, Evelyn Lincoln Papers.

p. 471: "So much depends": "JFK on Presidency," Box 23, David Powers Papers, JFKL.

p. 471: "less tense": Memorandum for the Files, Aug. 23, 1961, Box 479, Averell Harriman Papers, LC.

p. 471: "Do you think": RFK interview, Oct. 23, 1961, Box 2, RFK Personal Papers, JFKL.

p. 471: Medical problems in Aug. 1961: Dr. Janet Travell medical records, JFKL.

p. 472: The lectern: Janet Travell to Evelyn Lincoln, July 10, 1961, Box 67, POF.

p. 472: Diet: Charles Bartlett to JFK, n.d., Box 28, POF.

p. 472: Dr. Janet Travell's care: RFK to George McGovern, June 26, 1961, Box 2, RFK Personal Papers. Also see Travell, 5–7, 358.

pp. 472–73: JFK's back problems and treatment: Dr. Janet Travell OH; Dr. George Burkley OH; Parmet, *JFK*, 120–24; Richard Reeves, 242–44, 273–74; Leamer, 544–45. For the quotes describing JFK's improvement, see Travell medical records.

p. 473: Kenneth O'Donnell to Dr. Travell and Dr. Burkley, April 10, 1962, document provided by Virginia P. Street, Travell's daughter.

p. 473: "so totally inadequate": Elizabeth Carpenter OH, LBJL.

p. 474: "As little as possible": Richard Reeves, 154.

p. 474: "I don't think": Cass Canfield OH, Columbia University.

p. 474: "sorry for Jackie": Hersh, 238.

p. 474: Jacqueline Kennedy to William Walton, June 8, 1962, Box 1, William Walton Papers, JFKL.

pp. 474–75: Jacqueline's spending: Pierre Salinger OH; Parmet, *JFK*, 109–10; Bradlee, *Conversations*, 118–19.

p. 475: JPK's illness: Parmet, *JFK*, 124–25.

pp. 475–76: Kennedy's womanizing: A number of books in recent years have catalogued Kennedy's sexual escapades, but none more fully and probably more accurately than Hersh's *Dark Side of Camelot*. As scholars Ernest May and Philip Zelikow wrote in an otherwise persuasive critical assessment of the book, "Hersh has accumulated new evidence that Kennedy's womanizing became increasingly more abandoned and more reckless as he became older, more famous, and more powerful. Hersh has amassed convincingly detailed testimony to this effect from numerous confidantes, four Secret Service agents talking on the record, and many others, some of it buttressed by contemporaneous FBI records." Ernest R. May and Philip D. Zelikow, "Camelot Confidential," *Diplomatic History,* Fall 1998, 642. Also see Giglio, 267.

p. 476: The nineteen-year-old: Barbara Gamarekian OH, to which she gave me access, including 17 pages blacked out at the JFKL.

p. 476: He told Macmillan: Horne, 290.

p. 476: Mary Meyer: Parmet, *JFK*, 305–7.

p. 476: "Mary would be rough": Bradlee, *Conversations*, 54.

p. 476: "heard stories about": Bradlee, *A Good Life,* 216–17.

p. 477: Jacqueline Kennedy's response to the affairs: Confidential source.

p. 477: "This is the girl": Barbara Gamarekian OH.

p. 477: Keeping JFK's staff informed: Hersh, 390 n.

p. 477: The story about JFK's married aide and press hypocrisy: Gamarekian Interview, April 19, 2001.

p. 477: Press sleeping around: Barbara Gamarekian, "My Turn: History in the Making," *Newsweek,* June 16, 1997.

p. 478: JFK called Sidey to the White House: *Time,* Feb. 23, 1962; Hugh Sidey OH; Richard Reeves, 287–88.

p. 478: On Marilyn Monroe: Richard Reeves, 315–16; and see a *Village Voice* clipping, attached to Schlesinger to JFK, May 31, 1962, Box 65A, POF.

p. 478: JFK's relations with the media: Salinger, 34–35, 49–50, 121, 124–25, 127, 141–42.

p. 478: "You can't go": Quoted in Richard Reeves, 279.

p. 479: After Hoover made clear: "Judith E. Campbell, Associate of Hoodlums," Mar. 20, 1962, JEH O&C, FBI microfilm. Richard Reeves, 288–90.

p. 479: Telephone calls: May and Zelikow, "Camelot Confidential," 643, n. 2.

p. 479: Have JFK "by the balls": Richard Reeves, 288–90.

p. 479: Some historians: May and Zelikow, "Camelot Confidential," 652–53.

p. 479: Vietnam as a priority: Ibid., 652.

p. 480: "took less time": Richard Reeves, 291.

p. 480: Heller and Martin: James Tobin Memo, Aug. 28, 1961, Box 6, Walter W. Heller Papers, JFKL.

p. 480: JFK instructions to Heller, Bell, and Dutton: Notes on conversations with JFK, Sept. 2, 1961, Box 6; Sept. 5, 1961, Box 5, Heller Papers. Evelyn Lincoln to Fred Dutton, Sept. 5, 1961, Box 62; Dave Bell to *Life* Editor, Sept. 8, 1961, Box 70, POF.

p. 480: Kennedy's courting of business: Meeting with JFK, Oct. 17, 1961, Box 6, Heller Papers.

p. 481: Economic worries: JFK to Sen. Joseph Clark, Aug. 7, 1961; James Tobin to Sec. Fowler, Sept. 6, 1961, Box 73, POF; meetings with JFK, Oct. 17, 19, 1961, Box 6, Heller Papers.

p. 481: "upward price": Bernstein, 134–36.

p. 481: "'I know everyone'": Sorensen, 457–58.

p. 481: For an excellent summary of the balance-of-payment problem, see Naftali, *Presidential Recordings*, vol. I, 385–88.

p. 481: "The pressures to grasp": Heller to JFK, Nov. 28, 1961, Box 29, Theodore Sorensen Papers, JFKL.

p. 481: "cloud on the horizon": James Tobin Memo, Aug. 28, 1961, Box 6, Heller Papers.

p. 482: JFK request for reports on gold losses: Lincoln Diary, Oct. 3, 1961, Box 3, Evelyn Lincoln Papers.

p. 482: Draconian reforms: Memo of meeting with JFK, Oct. 17, 1961, Box 6, Heller Papers.

p. 482: Stopgap measures and restricting Jacqueline's travel: Sorensen, 458–60.

p. 482: Reduced gold losses: The Kennedy Record in Domestic Affairs, Dec. 29, 1961, Box 57, Sorensen Papers.

p. 482: Jokes about JPK's travel: Gridiron speech, Mar. 11, 1961, Box 61, Sorensen Papers.

p. 482: Trade Expansion Act: *PPP: JFK, 1962*, 13–15.

p. 482: Tax increase: Dillon to Sorensen, July 21, 1961; Mike Mansfield to JFK, July 24, 1961, Box 40, Sorensen Papers; *PPP: JFK, 1961*, 537.

p. 482: The steel industry bulked: Heller to JFK, Aug. 2, 1961, Box 39, Sorensen Papers.

p. 482: Armed with statistics: "The Case Against a Steel Price Increase," Aug. 2, 1961, Box 39, Sorensen Papers. Heller to JFK, Sept. 8, 1961; Kermit Gordon to JFK, Sept. 16, 20, 1961, Box 73, POF. JFK Letters: *PPP: JFK, 1961*, 592–94, 604–5. Steel companies agreed: *Wall Street Journal*, Sept. 15, 1961.

pp. 482–83: Reactions from labor and business to pressure: Bernstein, 136–37.

p. 483: Negotiations: Ibid., 140–41. Arthur Goldberg to JFK, Mar. 6, April 3, 1962, Box 27, Arthur Goldberg Papers, LC.

p. 483: "After your speech": Goldberg to JFK, Dec. 12, 1961, ibid.

p. 483: JFK's reaction to the settlement: *PPP: JFK, 1962*, 272, 284.

p. 484: The meeting with Blough and JFK's reaction: Tape 56, Kenneth O'Donnell Tapes, JFKL. Bradlee, *Conversations*, 75–77, 81; Bernstein, 142–43; Richard Reeves, 296–97.

pp. 484–85: JFK's news conference: *PPP: JFK, 1962*, 315–17.

p. 485: Public opinion: Gallup, 1767–68, 1771.

p. 485: "I can't go make a speech": Bradlee, *Conversations*, 77.

p. 485: "bad for the country": Guthman and Shulman, 333.

pp. 485–86: JFK's directives and RFK's actions pressuring the steel companies: Angie Novello to Evelyn Lincoln, April 12, 1962; RFK to JFK, May 31, 1962, May 31, 1962, with Lee Loevinger to RFK attached, Box 80, POF.

p. 486: "Their expense accounts": Guthman and Shulman, 333; Bernstein, 143; Richard Reeves, 298–99.

p. 486: "Can't you just see:" Manuscript, Paul Fay, "The Pleasure of His Company," Box 12, Martin Land Papers, Boston University.

pp. 486–87: On the rollback: Bernstein, 143–45; Richard Reeves, 300–301.

p. 487: Private joking: Schlesinger, *A Thousand Days*, 637; Bradlee, *Conversations*, 111–12.

pp. 487–88: Press conference and speech: *PPP: JFK, 1962*, 331–32, 348–52.

p. 488: Attacks on JFK: Schlesinger, *A Thousand Days*, 637–40; Parmet, *JFK*, 239; Richard Reeves, 302–304, 316; Bernstein, 145.

p. 488: News conferences: *PPP: JFK, 1962*, 334–35, 376; Guthman and Shulman, 354–55.

p. 489: "an enormous asset": Richard Neustadt to Douglas Cater, Dec. 14, 1961, Box 64, POF.

p. 490: State of the Union: *PPP: JFK, 1962*, 5–8.

pp. 490–91: Civil rights, etc.: Ibid., 8–9.

p. 491: Polls: Gallup, 1749, 1751–52.

p. 491: Document stamped "Propaganda": Box 57, Sorensen Papers.

p. 491: Journalists' skepticism: Edward F. Woods article, "President Said to Think . . . ," *St. Louis Post-Dispatch*, Sept. 16, 1961.

p. 491: Briefing paper: "Notes for Congressional Session, Jan. 17–18, 1962," Box 36, Sorensen Papers.

p. 491: Focus on international affairs: *PPP: JFK, 1962*, 9–15.

p. 492: Civil rights surveys: Gallup, 1764, 1769.

p. 492: Plans for Progress: *New York Times*, July 12, Nov. 25, 1961; *PPP: JFK, 1962*, 117–18, 505–7; Dallek, *Flawed Giant*, 28–30; Bernstein, 58–61.

pp. 492–93: Substantive and symbolic initiatives: RFK to JFK, Dec. 29, 1961, Box 96; Adam Yarmolinsky to Fred Dutton, Oct. 25, 1961; Dutton to JFK, Nov. 3, 1961, Box 63, POF. Carl Rowan to RFK, Sept. 23, 1961, Box 9; Berl Bernhard Statement, Oct. 9, 1961; Clipping, "8 Owners Persuaded," n.d., Box 13, Gen. Corresp., RFK Papers. *PPP: JFK, 1962*, 23, 508.

p. 493: Executive Order on housing: Wofford to JFK, Oct. 10, 1961, Box 68, Gen. Corresp., RFK Papers; Roy Wilkins to JFK, n.d., Box 30, Sorensen Papers; James A. Wechsler, "As JFK Said . . . ," *New York Post*, Dec. 27, 1961; *PPP: JFK, 1962*, 21, 324; Evelyn Lincoln to Lee White, Aug. 30, 1962, with White to JFK, Aug. 28, 1962, attached, Box 96, POF.

pp. 493–95: Judicial appointments: Presidential Judicial Appointments, 1961; Lifetime Judges Appointed by President Kennedy, Jan. 15, 1964, Box 13, Personal Papers, RFK Papers; Roy Wilkins OH; Schlesinger, *Robert Kennedy*, 307–10, 376–78; Bernstein, 70–71; Guthman and Shulman, 108–9, 112.

p. 495: "gained anything": Wilkins OH.

p. 495: "the passage of any": Abraham Ribicoff to JFK, Oct. 6, 1961, Box 30, Sorensen Papers. Taking a bold stand: *PPP: JFK, 1962*, 9, 110–17.

pp. 495–96: Medicare: *PPP: JFK, 1962,* 8–9, 165–73, 213, 269, 416–20, 449–50, 560–61; Bernstein, 255–57; *Los Angeles Times,* July 22, 1962.

p. 496: Would tend "to inhibit": *PPP: JFK, 1962,* 576.

p. 496: Transportation problems: *PPP: JFK, 1962,* 292–306.

p. 497: "I'm putting someone in": Quoted in Clymer, 32.

p. 497: "He just felt": Guthman and Shulman, 328.

p. 497: "I'll hear whether": Quoted in Clymer, 31–32.

p. 497: "He felt that": Guthman and Shulman, 328–29.

p. 497: "Your brother": *PPP: JFK, 1962,* 63.

p. 498: "Well, in part": Ibid., 226.

p. 498: "administration aid": Ibid., 407.

p. 498: JFK and White House involvement in Ted's campaign: Evelyn Lincoln to Staff, April 27, 1962, Box 62, POF.

p. 498: "number 99 on your list": Told to me by James MacGregor Burns.

p. 498: Ted joked: Clymer, 35.

p. 498: "my brother pointed out": *PPP: JFK, 1962,* 514.

p. 498: "made it clear" and *Meet the Press:* Clymer, 35, 37.

p. 499: The cheating scandal: Ibid., 18–22, 36–37; *Boston Globe,* Mar. 30, 1962.

p. 499: "It won't go over": Bradlee, *Conversations,* 67–68.

pp. 499–500: JFK's defense of Ted: *PPP: JFK, 1962,* 514.

pp. 500–501: Estes scandal: *PPP: JFK, 1962,* 400–401, 404, 407. Guthman and Shulman, 354–55; Bradlee, *Conversations,* 79–80, 105–6; Salinger, 129; Dallek, *Flawed Giant,* 39. Also see Jayne Lahey to Evelyn Lincoln, June 11, 1962, with JEH to RFK, June 4, 1962: Billy Sol Estes, Box 80, POF. On LBJ and Estes, see Dallek, *Flawed Giant,* 39–40, and 651 nn. 78, 79, 80.

pp. 501–2: The orbital flights: *PPP: JFK, 1962,* 139–40, 150, 439, 450. Richard Reeves, 285–87.

p. 502: JFK-NSK exchanges on cooperative space exploration: *FRUS: Kennedy-Khrushchev,* 96, 116–18, 127–31.

p. 502: "awarding these contracts": Guthman and Shulman, 153.

p. 502: "the distribution of contracts": *PPP: JFK, 1962,* 229–32. Also see James Webb to JFK, May 7 and June 1, 1962, Box 84, POF.

p. 503: LBJ and NASA: Dallek, "Johnson and Project Apollo," in Lanius and McCurdy, 73–74.

p. 503: Rumors about LBJ: *PPP: JFK, 1962,* 380.

p. 503: "after seeing": *PPP: JFK, 1962,* 276.

Chapter 15: Frustrations and "Botches"

p. 504: "There is always": *PPP: JFK, 1962,* 259–60.

p. 505: Approval ratings: Gallup, 1771–72, 1780, 1786.

p. 505: JFK response to Tuchman book: Sorensen, 577–78.

pp. 505–6: Installation of the tape recorders and reliability of the tapes: Naftali, *Presidential Recordings,* vol. I, xi, xvii–xxiv.

pp. 506–7: Economic problems: Memo, May 5, 1962, Box 5, Walter W. Heller Papers, JFKL.

p. 507: Responses to the market tumble: JFK-Douglas Dillon telephone conversations, May 28, 1962, Box 38, Douglas Dillon Papers, JFKL. Walter Heller to JFK, May 28, 1962, Box 63A; J. K. Galbraith to JFK, May 29, 1962; McGeorge Bundy to JFK, May 29, 1962, Box 107, POF.

p. 507: Tax cut proposal: CEA to JFK, May 29, 1962, Box 107, POF; see "The Current Economic Situation," June 6, 1962, Box 33, Dillon Papers; Paul Samuelson to JFK, June 6, 1962, Box 5, Heller Papers; *PPP: JFK, 1962*, 456–58, 462–63; Gallup, 1777.

p. 507: "a very large part": John K. Galbraith to JFK, July 10, Aug. 20, 1962, Box 62A, POF.

p. 508: Address at Yale: Notes on JFK's Yale speech, Box 4, Heller Papers. Commencement address: *PPP: JFK, 1962*, 470–75.

p. 508: "storm signals": Heller to JFK, June 27, 1962.

p. 508: "millions of stockholders": Heller to JFK, July 4, 1962, Box 5, Heller Papers.

p. 508: Economy remained sluggish: *PPP: JFK, 1962*, 575, 593.

p. 508: Congressional opposition: See David Bell's comments: Naftali, *Presidential Recordings*, vol. I, 61–62.

p. 508: "rigged data": Heller meeting with JFK, Aug. 15, 1962, Box 6, Heller Papers.

p. 508: "It is clear": Sorensen Memo, Aug. 9, 1962, Box 40, Theodore Sorensen Papers, JFKL. Also see *PPP: JFK, 1962*, 637.

p. 508: August unemployment: Heller to JFK, Sept. 4, 1962, Box 38, Kermit Gordon Papers, JFKL.

p. 508: Political resistance: Seymour Harris to JFK, Sept. 27, 1962, Box 90, POF.

pp. 508–9: See conversations with Mills and a Cabinet Room meeting on the economy: Naftali, *Presidential Recordings*, vol. I, 233–59, 361–84.

p. 509: "running out of gas": Heller to JFK, Oct. 8, 1962; Gordon to JFK, Oct. 10, 1962, Box 38, Gordon Papers. AFL-CIO: Heller to JFK, Oct. 17, 1962, Box 36, Gordon Papers.

p. 509: Series of meetings: Heller to JFK, July 12, 14, 1962, Box 5, Heller Papers. Heller to Sorensen, July 19, 1962; Ted Reardon to Cabinet, July 29, 1962, Box 29, Sorensen Papers. "The Administration and Business," July 26, 1962, Box 92, POF. Naftali, *Presidential Recordings*, vol. I, 335–61. *PPP: JFK, 1962*, 709–16.

p. 509: Doing some good: Heller meeting with JFK, Aug. 15, 1962, Box 6, Heller Papers.

p. 509: "fully aware": Thomas Lamont to JFK, July 30, 1962, Box 62A, POF.

p. 509: "Whenever I say": Schlesinger, *A Thousand Days*, 639–40.

p. 509: Gallup poll: *Washington Post*, Aug. 19, 1962.

pp. 509–10: Balance of payments: Heller to JFK, May 5, 1962, Box 29, Sorensen Papers; Seymour Harris to Dillon, June 7, 1962, Box 89, POF; Gardner Ackley Memo, July 26, 1962, Box 6, Heller Papers.

p. 510: Trade Expansion Bill: *PPP: JFK, 1962*, 14–15, 17, 510, 614, 632, 636–37.

p. 510: Opposition to the law: JFK-Dillon telephone conversation, Mar. 30, 1962, Box 38, Dillon Papers; Naftali, *Presidential Recordings*, vol. I, 566–69.

p. 510: Distinguished columnist: Schlesinger, *A Thousand Days*, 846–48.

p. 510: "a suit made in Britain": Bill, 66.

p. 510: "the most important": *PPP: JFK, 1962*, 759–60.

pp. 510–11: Taping: Naftali, *Presidential Recordings*, vol. I, JFK-LBJ conversation, Aug. 21, 1962, 541–44.

p. 511: "proper groundwork": Unsigned, undated memorandum in the Mar. 21–31, 1962, Folder, Box 50, POF.

p. 511: Clash between the White House and Civil Rights Commission: Wofford, 159–61. Guthman and Shulman, 157–58.

p. 512: Publication of the Commission's report and "You're making my life difficult": Guthman and Shulman, 162–65; and Berl Bernhard OH.

p. 512: "could do more": *PPP: JFK, 1962*, 572.

p. 513: The Albany Movement: Branch, chap. 14.

p. 513: JFK's response: *PPP: JFK, 1962*, 592–93.

p. 513: Troutman's resignation and Taylor's appointment: Naftali, *Presidential Recordings*, vol. I, 541–44; *PPP: JFK, 1962*, 642; Dallek, *Flawed Giant*, 28–30.

p. 513: "The Kennedy civil rights": Schlesinger, *Robert Kennedy*, 317.

pp. 513–14: "asking for" and "I don't know any more": *PPP: JFK, 1962*, 676–77.

p. 514: Meredith and the Mississippi crisis: "Mississippi Chronology," n.d., Box 15, Arthur Schlesinger Jr. Papers, JFKL. RFK-Barnett conversations, Box 11, RFK Attorney General's Papers, JFKL. Bernstein, 73–79; Schlesinger, *Robert Kennedy*, 317–20.

pp. 514–15: Potential federal pressure on Mississippi: Schlesinger to RFK, Sept. 27, 1962, Box 97, POF; Memo on Gov. Coleman's advice, Sept. 28, 1962; Bell Memorandum for the President, Sept. 28, 1962, Box 11, RFK Attorney General's Papers; Sorensen to JFK, Sept. 28, 1962, Box 40, POF.

p. 515: "I won't agree": Quoted in Schlesinger, *Robert Kennedy*, 319.

p. 515: The events of Sept. 25–27: Bernstein, 80–81.

p. 516: JFK-Barnett conversations: Naftali and Zelikow, *Presidential Recordings*, vol. II, 222–30, 232–36, 239–47; Guthman and Shulman, 159–61; JFK telegram to Barnett, and White House Press Release on the call-up, Sept. 29, 1962, Box 97, POF.

p. 516: JFK and Schlei: Schlesinger, *Robert Kennedy*, 321.

p. 516: RFK and Barnett: Ibid.

p. 516: JFK speech: *PPP: JFK, 1962*, 726–28.

p. 516: On Barnett's betrayal: Press Release, Oct. 1, 1962, Box 11, RFK Attorney General's Papers.

pp. 516–17: On the night's events: Pierre Salinger news conferences, Oct. 1, 1962, Box 98, POF; Bernstein, 82–84.

p. 517: "President Kennedy had": Guthman and Shulman, 162–64.

p. 517: "They always give you": Quoted in Richard Reeves, 363.

p. 517: "Imagine that": Naftali and Zelikow, *Presidential Recordings*, vol. II, 272.

p. 517: "I haven't had": Ibid., 274.

p. 517: "We are going to have": Ibid., 303–5.

p. 517: Bobby later remembered: Guthman and Shulman, 165.

p. 517: "Forget the Monday morning": Graham to RFK, Oct. 9, 1962, Box 80, POF.

p. 517: LBJ sent word: Ralph Dungan to JFK, Oct. 3, 1962, Box 30, POF.

pp. 517–18: Polls of northern: Gallup, 1789. Harris poll: Lou Harris to JFK, Oct. 4, 1962, Box 105, POF.

p. 518: Foreign press: Donald M. Wilson to JFK, Oct. 19, 1962, Box 98, POF. Also see Lincoln Diary, April 5, 1962, Box 4, Evelyn Lincoln Papers, JFKL.

p. 519: Concerns about Alliance for Progress: William Haddad to JFK, Mar. 9, 1962; T. Graydon Upton to JFK, Mar. 16, 1962; "Why We Have not Made Satisfactory Progress, n.d., Box 95, POF. Richard Goodwin to Schlesinger, n.d., Box 63, POF.

p. 519: Argentina: *FRUS: American Republics,* 368–75.

p. 519: Schlesinger on IMF: Ibid., 373.

p. 519: Teodoro Moscoso to JFK, May 4, 1962, Box 290A, NSF.

p. 519: JFK continued to speak: *PPP: JFK, 1962,* 495, 597.

p. 519: Worries about funding: JFK to Edward Martin, July 3, 1962, Box 68, POF.

pp. 519–20: Peru: *FRUS: American Republics,* 863–79. *PPP: JFK, 1962,* 571–72, 597. Naftali, *Presidential Recordings,* vol. I, 34–35, 38–41, 287–88, 290–94.

p. 520: British Guiana: *FRUS: American Republics,* 540–83. Stephen G. Rabe, "JFK and Latin America," *Diplomatic History,* Summer 1999, 542–43, 546.

pp. 520–21: Brazil in 1961: Schlesinger, *A Thousand Days,* 178–80; *FRUS: American Republics,* 444.

p. 521: "a matter which": *PPP: JFK, 1961,* 578.

p. 521: "suspected of being": *FRUS: American Republics,* 450–52.

p. 521: Expropriation: Ibid., 456–57.

p. 521: JFK agreed to release funds: Ibid., 458–67.

p. 521: JFK meeting with Gordon: Naftali, *Presidential Recordings,* vol. I, 5–25.

p. 521: "$5 million": Rabe, "JFK and Latin America," 544.

p. 522: Cuban training of guerrillas: Fursenko and Naftali, 167–68. Also see a meeting with Kubitschek and Camargo: *FRUS: American Republics,* 117–25.

p. 522: December meeting with Alessandri: *PPP: JFK, 1962,* 860, 872.

p. 522: "virtually nothing": William E. Brubeck to McGeorge Bundy, Aug. 10, 1962, Box 290A, POF. Special Group (Counter Insurgency), NSAM No. 124, in *FRUS: Vietnam, 1962,* 48–50.

p. 522: "sufficiently threatened": NSAM No. 165, June 16, 1962, Box 337, NSF. Rabe, *"The Most Dangerous Area."*

p. 523: For the Laos crisis: Gibbons, 112–17; Lawrence Freedman, 345–50.

p. 523: "The morale": Gibbons, 115.

p. 523: "provoke the Viet Minh": *FRUS: Laos Crisis,* 734–35.

p. 523: "he might make a public statement": Ibid., 741–42.

pp. 523–24: "indicated both his support": Ibid., 760–61.

p. 524: "to maintain vis-a-vis": Ibid., 758–60, 767.

p. 524: JFK-NSK messages: *FRUS: Kennedy-Khrushchev,* 134–36.

p. 524: RFK and Bolshakov: Guthman and Shulman, 258–59, 337; Beschloss, *Crisis Years,* 152–53.

p. 525: NSK message to JFK: RFK to JFK, June 19, 1962, Box 80, POF.

p. 525: The *Times* report and JFK response: Salinger to JFK, May 24, 1962, Box 65A, POF.

p. 525: JFK hoped that Hanoi: *FRUS: Vietnam, 1962,* 543–46; Gibbons, 120–21.

p. 525: McNamara and U.S. optimism: *FRUS: Vietnam, 1962,* 546–56; Gibbons, 121–22; Neil Sheehan, 289–91; Shapley, 159–61.

p. 526: Taylor reported: *FRUS: Vietnam, 1962*, 660–63. Also Naftali, *Presidential Recordings*, vol. I, 165, and Gibbons, 104–5.

p. 526: "tremendously encouraged": *FRUS: Vietnam, 1962*, 655–57.

p. 526: JFK told Thuan: Ibid., 667, 671–72.

p. 526: "made clear": Roswell L. Gilpatric OH. Also see Bird, 223; NSAM No. 182, Aug. 24, 1962, in *FRUS: National Security Policy, 1961–1963*, 381–83; and David Kaiser, 139–40.

p. 526: McNamara's withdrawal plan: Gibbons, 125–26.

p. 527: "thought very highly": Guthman and Shulman, 46, 418, 421.

p. 527: "symbolized the idea": Halberstam, *Best and Brightest*, 264.

p. 527: JFK himself said: Quoted in Beschloss, *Crisis Years*, 402.

p. 527: "Men can't understand": Bradlee, *Conversations*, 230.

p. 527: "Why is it": Halberstam, *Best and Brightest*, 269.

p. 527: "unnecessary trips": Memo of the President's Instructions at the Laos/Vietnam Briefing, May 2, 1962, Box 320, NSF.

p. 527: "formally involved": Memo of JFK Meeting with Congressional Leaders, Feb. 21, 1962, Box 345, NSF.

p. 527: Concession to Joint Chiefs: Memo for Bundy, Oct. 4, 1962, Box 320, NSF.

p. 528: "What can we do": Naftali and Zelikow, *Presidential Recordings*, vol. II, 166.

p. 528: "The closer one gets": Quoted in Lawrence Freedman, 360–61.

p. 528: "adjunct of a dictatorship": Quoted in Schlesinger, *A Thousand Days*, 984.

p. 528: The press: *FRUS: Vietnam, 1962*, 656, 661–62, 671–72. Also, Naftali and Zelikow, *Presidential Recordings*, vol. II, 165; C. V. Clifton to McGeorge Bundy, Mar. 6, 1962, Box 320, NSF.

p. 528: *Time*'s coverage: Henry Luce to JFK, Sept. 15, 21, 1962; JFK to Luce, Oct. 2, 1962, Box 31, POF.

p. 529: JFK sympathized: See Halberstam, chap. 11.

p. 529: Response to the Baldwin story: Naftali, *Presidential Recordings*, vol. I, 186–201.

p. 529: Directives about the press: Joe Alsop to Evelyn Lincoln, Oct. 3, 1962; "Joe Alsop called," n.d.; Alsop to JFK, Nov. 24, 1962; McGeorge Bundy to Alsop, Nov. 27, 1962, Box 27, POF. Sorensen, 360.

p. 530: JFK to NSK, Mar. 5, 1962: *FRUS: Kennedy–Khrushchev*, 115.

p. 530: JFK's numerous exchanges and differences with Moscow: Ibid., 362–65, 369–72, 401–3, 405–6, 411–14, 425–26, 438–41; Naftali, *Presidential Recordings*, vol. I, 86–88, 162. Also see NSK, *Khrushchev Remembers*, 536.

p. 530: Public relations setback: Seaborg, 164–66; *FRUS: Arms Control*, 510–14; JFK to Rusk and McNamara, July 19, 1962, Box 88, POF; Naftali, *Presidential Recordings*, vol. I, 117.

p. 530: "I just see": Naftali, *Presidential Recordings*, vol. I, 47–51.

p. 531: "Domestic policy": Schlesinger, *A Thousand Days*, 426.

p. 531: "Creative governments": Schlesinger to Orvil Dryfoos, July 5, 1962, with a note to JFK, July 5, 1962, attached, Box 65A, POF.

pp. 531–32: JFK's proposals and response to the Soviets: *PPP: JFK, 1962*, 649–50, 652–55; Seaborg, 167–71.

p. 532: JFK's search for a Berlin formula: Lawrence Freedman, 112–16. Also see conversations with Adzhubei in *FRUS: Soviet Union*, 356–60; *FRUS: Berlin Crisis, 1961–1962*, 780–84; and JFK-NSK exchanges in *FRUS: Kennedy-Khrushchev*, 81–84, 92–95, 118–26.

p. 532: "Matters relating to": *FRUS: Kennedy-Khrushchev*, 133 and 137–47.

p. 532: "consistent failure": Ibid., 143.

p. 532: Incidents at the Wall: Lawrence Freedman, 118–19.

pp. 532–33: NSK's fears and Bolshakov conversation with RFK: RFK to JFK, Mar. 16, 1962, Box 80, POF; Salinger, 248; Fursenko and Naftali, 155, 185.

p. 533: NSK's response: Fursenko and Naftali, 185–86, and Schlesinger, *Robert Kennedy*, 512.

p. 533: Conversation with Udall: *FRUS: Berlin Crisis, 1962–1963*, 308–10.

pp. 533–34: Sorensen told Dobrynin: *FRUS: Cuba, 1961–62*, 1045–47.

p. 534: JFK's view of NSK: Guthman and Shulman, 27–28, 311. Sulzberger, 808–13.

p. 534: Thompson told JFK: Naftali, *Presidential Recordings*, vol. I, 270.

Chapter 16: To the Brink — and Back

p. 535: For an up-to-date review of the missile crisis literature, see Mark J. White, "New Scholarship on the Cuban Missile Crisis," *Diplomatic History*, Winter 2002, 147–53.

p. 535: Cardona asked Bundy: *FRUS: Cuba, 1961–62*, 777–78.

p. 535: JFK told Cardona: Richard Goodwin to JFK, April 14, 1962; and "Topics Discussed During Meeting of Dr. Cardona with the President," April 25, 1962, Box 45, NSF.

p. 535: NSK's worries about Cuba: Fursenko and Naftali, 166–79.

pp. 535–36: NSK's decision to deploy missiles: Ibid., chaps. 9 and 10; Raymond L. Garthoff, "New Evidence on the Cuban Missile Crisis: Khrushchev, Nuclear Weapons, and the Cuban Missile Crisis," *Cold War International History Project*, Winter 1998, 251–61.

p. 536: Fursenko and Naftali took the phrase "one hell of a gamble" from JFK, who used it at an Oct. 22 meeting with congressional leaders about invading Cuba. See May and Zelikow, 264, for the quote, and 35–39.

p. 537: For the 1959 Soviet missile deployment, see Matthias Uhl and Vladimir I. Ivkin, "'Operation Atom': The Soviet Union's Stationing of Nuclear Missiles in the German Democratic Republic, 1959," *Bulletin: Cold War History Project*, Fall/Winter 2001, 299–306. Soviet expert Raymond Garthoff, who was a member of the National Board of Intelligence Estimates, remembers the deployment in East Germany. He knew of no evidence that JFK or anyone else high in his administration, including John McCone, knew about this earlier deployment. Conversation with Garthoff, Mar. 19, 2002.

p. 537: "but there is no evidence": *FRUS: Cuba, 1961–62*, 1002–10, especially 1004 and 1007.

p. 537: "We have no": *FRUS: Kennedy-Khrushchev*, 12.

pp. 537–38: "for the sake of" and "Nothing will be": Fursenko and Naftali, 194–97.

p. 538: "Now, as to Cuba": *FRUS: Cuba, 1961–62*, 1047–48.

pp. 538–39: Pressures on JFK: *FRUS: Cuba, 1961–62*, 923–24, 947–58, 968,

1033–34; Fursenko and Naftali, 198–206; and three Sept. 4, 1962, conversations about Cuba in Naftali and Zelikow, *Presidential Recordings*, vol. II, 19–80.

p. 539: Preparation of the statement: Naftali and Zelikow, *Presidential Recordings*, vol. II, 33–51.

p. 539: "The major danger": Ibid., p. 42.

p. 539: The statement: *FRUS: Cuba, 1961–62*, 1038.

pp. 539–40: "What is our policy?": Naftali and Zelikow, *Presidential Recordings*, vol. II, 61–62, 71.

p. 540: Robert Frost: *New York Times*, Sept. 10, 1962.

p. 540: JFK's reaction: Stewart Udall OH.

p. 540: Democratic senators: Mike Mansfield to JFK, Sept. 12, 1962, Box 31, POF.

pp. 540–41: JFK news conference, Sept. 13, 1962: *PPP: JFK, 1962*, 674–75.

p. 541: CIA assessment: Special National Intelligence Estimate, Sept. 19, 1962, in *FRUS: Cuba, 1961–62*, 1070–80.

p. 541: NSK to JFK, Sept. 28, 1962: *FRUS: Kennedy-Khrushchev*, 152–61.

p. 541: Senate resolution: *New York Times*, Sept. 21, 1962.

p. 541: Schlesinger urged: Schlesinger Memo, Sept. 24, 1962, in *FRUS: Cuba, 1961–62*, 1084–86.

p. 541: "The question is": William Jordan to W. W. Rostow, Oct. 10, 1962, Box 415, NSF.

p. 542: Kennedy further instructed and Khrushchev canceled: *FRUS: Cuba, 1961–62*, 1081; *FRUS: Cuban Missile Crisis*, 6–7, 10–13; Fursenko and Naftali, 206–17; Richard Reeves, 366–67.

pp. 542–43: "a first-hand sighting": *FRUS: Cuba, 1961–62*, 1083–84.

p. 543: U-2 flights: Ibid., 1054; Fursenko and Naftali, 212.

p. 543: Bundy and McCone: *FRUS: Missile Crisis*, 14.

p. 543: Bolshakov carried: Fursenko and Naftali, 219.

p. 543: JFK Oct. 9 decision and weather conditions: *FRUS: Missile Crisis*, 17; Fursenko and Naftali, 220–21.

p. 543: Dobrynin-Bowles conversation: *FRUS: Missile Crisis*, 26–29.

p. 544: Leak to Reston: *New York Times*, Oct. 12, 1962; Richard Reeves, 367.

p. 544: Results of the U-2 mission and Bundy's decision to wait until morning: *FRUS: Missile Crisis*, 29–30.

p. 544: The 8:45 A.M. meeting and JFK's response: Richard Reeves, 368.

pp. 545–47: The 11:45 Ex Comm meeting: For participants and seating: May and Zelikow, 39–43; Naftali and Zelikow, *Presidential Recordings*, vol. II, 397. The initial discussion: Naftali and Zelikow, 397–403.

p. 547: Oct. 16, morning discussion: Ibid., 404–27.

pp. 547–48: Ad lib remarks: O'Donnell and Powers, 315–16.

p. 548: Evening meeting: Naftali and Zelikow, *Presidential Recordings*, vol. II, 427–68.

p. 549: RFK and JFK on Pearl Harbor: Schlesinger, *Robert Kennedy*, 507; Brinkley, 154–74; Chace, 398–99.

p. 550: For an overview of activities on Oct. 17, see May and Zelikow, 118–21.

pp. 550–51: Summaries of the meetings, including McCone's with JFK, AES to JFK, and RFK's memo: *FRUS: Missile Crisis*, 94–106.

pp. 551–53: Thursday, Oct. 18, meeting: Naftali and Zelikow, *Presidential Recordings*, vol. II, 516–72.

p. 553: JFK-Gromyko conversation: *FRUS: Missile Crisis*, 110–14.

p. 553: JFK-Lovett conversation: Naftali and Zelikow, *Presidential Recordings*, vol. II, 573–74.

p. 553: Gromyko's reaction: Fursenko and Naftali, 231–32.

p. 553: Lovett's advice and RFK's agreement: Naftali and Zelikow, *Presidential Recordings*, vol. II, 573–74.

pp. 553–54: Late-night meeting: Ibid., 576–77. The JFK quote is on 512.

p. 554: Considered canceling the trip: O'Donnell and Powers, 315; and *PPP: JFK, 1962*, 797–805.

pp. 554–55: Meeting with Joint Chiefs: Naftali and Zelikow, *Presidential Recordings*, vol. II, 578–98.

p. 555: "Can you imagine": O'Donnell and Powers, 318.

p. 555: After JFK left the room: Naftali and Zelikow, *Presidential Recordings*, vol. II, 597–98.

p. 555: JFK told Bundy: *FRUS: Missile Crisis*, 117.

p. 555: Told RFK and Sorensen: Sorensen, 780.

p. 556: Afternoon meeting: *FRUS: Missile Crisis*, 116–22.

p. 556: RFK urged JFK: Brugioni, 303–4.

p. 556: Oct. 20 meeting: *FRUS: Missile Crisis*, 126–36. Also see JFK conversation with Omsby-Gore, Zelikow and May, *Presidential Recordings*, vol. III, 5.

p. 556: "that we would accept nothing": Ibid., 148.

p. 556: JFK asked the *Times*: JFK to Orvil Dryfoos, Oct. 25, 1962, Box 29, POF; Zelikow and May, *Presidential Recordings*, vol. III, 4.

p. 557: JFK told Taylor: Naftali and Zelikow, *Presidential Recordings*, vol. II, 614.

p. 557: For calls to the former presidents: *FRUS: Missile Crisis*, 153.

p. 557: For the National Security Council meeting: Ibid., 152–56, and Zelikow and May, *Presidential Recordings*, vol. III, 42–57.

p. 557: Meeting with congressional leaders: Zelikow and May, *Presidential Recordings*, vol. III, 60–90.

p. 557: Joked with Humphrey: Richard Reeves, 393.

pp. 557–58: JFK comment to Donald: Donald, 13.

p. 558: DDE to JFK: Zelikow and May, *Presidential Recordings*, vol. III, 12.

p. 558: "the most difficult meeting": Robert Kennedy, 53, 55.

p. 558: JFK to NSK, Oct. 22, 1962: *FRUS: Kennedy-Khrushchev*, 165–66.

pp. 558–59: JFK speech: *PPP: JFK, 1962*, 806–9.

p. 559: "We have won": Quoted in Richard Reeves, 397. NSAM No. 196, in *FRUS: Missile Crisis*, 157.

p. 559: Ex Comm meeting, 10 A.M., Oct. 23: Zelikow and May, *Presidential Recordings*, vol. III, 102–140.

p. 560: NSK to JFK, Oct. 23, 1962: *FRUS: Kennedy-Khrushchev*, 166–67.

p. 560: JFK and Clay: Zelikow and May, *Presidential Recordings*, vol. III, 146–47.

p. 560: Enforce the blockade: Ibid., 148–49.

p. 560: Evening Ex Comm meeting: Ibid., 150–73.

p. 560: JFK to NSK, Oct. 23, 1962: *FRUS: Kennedy-Khrushchev*, 168. Soviet shipment of warheads by plane also worried JFK. Because Moscow would need landing rights in West Africa for this shipment, JFK won agreement from the presidents of Guinea and Senegal not to allow it. See Philip Kaiser, 197–99.

p. 560: JFK and RFK: Zelikow and May, *Presidential Recordings*, vol. III, 177.

pp. 560–61: RFK initiative and meeting with Dobrynin: Fursenko and Naftali, 251–53; *FRUS: Missile Crisis,* 175–77; Zelikow and May, *Presidential Recordings,* vol. III, 178–82.

p. 561: Ex Comm meeting, Oct. 24, 10 A.M.: Zelikow and May, *Presidential Recordings,* vol. III, 183–205.

p. 561: The MRBMs and Soviet knowledge of SAC's nuclear alert: Fursenko and Naftali, 256, 258.

p. 561: "This was the moment": Quoted in Schlesinger, *Robert Kennedy,* 514.

pp. 561–62: State Dept. report, report to McCone, and JFK worried: Zelikow and May, *Presidential Recordings,* vol. III, 188, 191–92, 196–98.

p. 562: "We're eyeball": Rusk, 237.

pp. 562–63: McNamara and Anderson: Roswell L. Gilpatric OH; Shapley, 176–77; Brugioni, 415–17.

p. 563: Afternoon meetings, Oct. 24, 1962: Zelikow and May, *Presidential Recordings,* vol. III, 206–26.

p. 563: JFK told Macmillan, Ibid., 226–28.

p. 563: NSK to JFK, Oct. 24, 1962: *FRUS: Kennedy-Khrushchev,* 169–70.

pp. 563–64: Knox-Khrushchev meeting: William E. Knox OH.

p. 564: JFK to NSK, Oct. 25, 1962: *FRUS: Kennedy-Khrushchev,* 171. "He could not go to war": Fursenko and Naftali, 259–62.

p. 564: NSK's proposal: Fursenko and Naftali, 259.

p. 564: JFK's temporizing: Zelikow and May, *Presidential Recordings,* vol. III, 232–69.

p. 564: "a sense of euphoria": Ibid., 253.

p. 564: U Thant, JFK, and Macmillan: Ibid., 261–62, 280. Also, *FRUS: Missile Crisis,* 183, 191–97, 199, 203–4, 210–12.

pp. 564–65: AES and Zorin: *New York Times,* Oct. 26, 1962.

p. 565: "I never knew": O'Donnell and Powers, 334.

p. 565: Lebanese ship boarding: Zelikow and May, *Presidential Recordings,* vol. III, 284.

p. 565: For quotes from the Oct. 26 meetings: Ibid., 287–88, 293, 295, 302, 309–10, 312, 328, 345.

pp. 565–66: NSK's letter: Llewellyn Thompson OH. *FRUS: Kennedy-Khrushchev,* 172–77.

p. 566: Scali-Fomin meeting: Fursenko and Naftali, 263–65. Fursenko and Naftali believe that Fomin took this initiative on his own. But it so closely reflected two of NSK's proposals as to make it doubtful that Fomin acted without instructions. Indeed, would any KGB operative have taken the initiative on so large a matter?

p. 566: Ex Comm meeting, Oct. 27, 10 A.M.: Zelikow and May, *Presidential Recordings,* vol. III, 356–57, 380, 382.

pp. 566–67: NSK's revised Oct. 26 letter: *FRUS: Kennedy-Khrushchev,* 178–81.

p. 567: Response to the revised proposal: Zelikow and May, *Presidential Recordings,* vol. III, 363–64, 366, 377, 385–86.

pp. 567–68: The afternoon–evening Oct. 27 Ex Comm meeting: Ibid., 387–482. The JFK quotes are on 398–400, 417, 419, 421.

p. 568: JFK to NSK, Oct. 27, 1962: *FRUS: Kennedy-Khrushchev,* 181–82.

pp. 568–69: RFK's record of conversation with Dobrynin: *FRUS: Missile Crisis,* 270–71.

p. 569: The meeting on the Turkish pledge: Bundy, 432–33.

p. 569: JFK instruction to Rusk: Blight and Welch, 83–84.

p. 569: "the most depressing": O'Donnell and Powers, 341.

pp. 569–70: State Dept. cable: *FRUS: Missile Crisis*, 276–77.

p. 570: RFK and McNamara: Zelikow and May, *Presidential Recordings*, vol. III, 509.

p. 570: The presidium meeting: Fursenko and Naftali, 283–87.

p. 570: NSK's replies to JFK, Oct. 28, 1962: *FRUS: Kennedy-Khrushchev*, 183–87, 189–90.

p. 570: On LeMay: Fursenko and Naftali, 287. JCS to JFK, Oct. 28, 1962, in Zelikow and May, *Presidential Recordings*, vol. III, 517.

pp. 570–71: Meeting with the Chiefs: Beschloss, *Crisis Years*, 544.

p. 571: JFK's view of the agreement and future difficulties: Zelikow and May, *Presidential Recordings*, vol. III, 517–23.

p. 571: JFK could not assume: *PPP: JFK, 1962*, 814. The CIA saw little danger that the Soviets would delay dismantling the missiles: "Implementation of Khrushchev's Message of Oct. 28," CIA, Memo, Oct. 29, 1962, Box 415, NSF.

p. 571: "We've given K.": Komer to McGeorge Bundy, Oct. 29, 1962, Box 322, NSF.

p. 571: "We must operate": JFK to Robert McNamara, Nov. 5, 1962, Box 274, NSF.

p. 571: "I am sure": JFK to McCone, Dec. 15, 1962, Box 68, POF.

p. 572: On the negotiations: May and Zelikow, 663–65.

p. 572: The news conference: *PPP: JFK, 1962*, 830–31.

p. 572: "Considering the size": JFK to McNamara, Nov. 5, 1962, Box 274, NSF.

p. 572: "An invasion would have been": Schlesinger, *A Thousand Days*, 831.

p. 572: Continued covert opposition to Castro: May and Zelikow, 665; *FRUS: Missile Crisis*, 586–90, 668–87. JFK, Background Briefing for the Press, Dec. 31, 1962, Box 415, NSF. JFK continued to worry about Cuban subversion in the hemisphere; see JFK to John McCone, Feb. 9, 1963, Box 68, POF.

pp. 572–73: JFK's performance: Bird, 242–46.

p. 573: "unimaginative and sterile": Arthur Schlesinger to JFK, Nov. 17, 1962, Box 5, Arthur Schlesinger Jr. Papers, JFKL.

p. 573: "a different president": Barton J. Bernstein, "Reconsidering the Missile Crisis: Dealing with the Problems of the American Jupiter Missiles in Turkey," in Nathan, 106–7. Cf. Beschloss, *Crisis Years*, 564.

pp. 573–74: NSK's motives: May and Zelikow, 668–71.

Chapter 17: New Departures: Domestic Affairs

p. 575: JFK's image: Dean Acheson to JFK, Oct. 29, 1962, Box 27, POF; Harriman memo of conversation with James Reston, Oct. 30, 1962, Box 588, Averell Harriman Papers, LC; Pierre Salinger to JFK, Oct. 30, 1962, Box 65, POF; Gen. Lauris Norstad to JFK, Nov. 1, 1962, Box 103, POF; *Newsweek*, Nov. 12, 1962.

p. 576: For JFK's medications during the crisis, see Dr. Janet Travell medical records, October 1962, JFKL. For the Stelazine, see the Dec. 11–13, 1962, records.

p. 576: JFK on physical fitness: *PPP: JFK, 1963*, 624–25.

pp. 576–77: On the Stevenson flap: Stewart Alsop and Charles Bartlett, "In Time of Crisis," *Sat. Eve. Post*, Dec. 8, 1962; *PPP: JFK, 1962*, 873; *FRUS: Missile Crisis*, 134, 137–38, 145, 567; Schlesinger, *A Thousand Days*, 835–38; Lawrence Freedman, 220. Also see JFK to AES, Dec. 5, 1962; AES to JFK, Dec. 8, 1962, Evelyn Lincoln Papers, JFKL; Clayton Fritchey to Salinger, Dec. 10, 1962; Stevenson to Salinger, Dec. 10, 1962; Stevenson to John Steele, Dec. 10, 1962, Box 65A, POF.

p. 577: Legislative record: Henry H. Wilson Jr. to Larry O'Brien, July 9, 1962; "Kennedy Legislative Boxscore," *Congressional Quarterly*, Nov. 14, 1962, Box 31, POF. Larry O'Brien to JFK, Sept. 10, 1962, Box 64, POF. James M. Burns letter to Editor, *New York Times*, dated July 30, 1962, published Aug. 5, 1962.

pp. 577–78: "were talking quite honestly": McGeorge Bundy to JFK, Aug. 20, 1962, Box 405, NSF.

p. 578: "The President is just": HST to JFK, Aug. 11, 1962, Box 33, POF.

p. 578: Worked behind the scenes: JFK to Charles Bartlett, Aug. 21, 1962; Martin S. Ochs to JFK, Aug. 30, 1962, Box 27, POF.

p. 578: Speak "over and over": Lou Harris to JFK, July 26, 1962, Box 30, POF.

pp. 578–79: For JFK's campaign speeches, see *PPP: JFK, 1962* for May–Oct., and specifically 414–16, 643–44, 722, 734–35, 739–40, 745, 763–64, 799–800.

p. 579: JFK's hold on the public: Schlesinger, *A Thousand Days*, 664.

pp. 579–80: The congressional elections: Gallup, 1786–88; TCS [Sorensen], "It looks as though we might gain in the Senate and lose in the House," Nov. 6, 1961, Box 66A, POF; Lou Harris to JFK, "Analysis of the 1962 Elections," Nov. 19, 1962, Box 30, POF; *PPP: JFK, 1962*, 834–35, 891; Richard Reeves, 429.

p. 580: Approval rating: Gallup, 1793.

p. 580: hailed as "your excellent": Lou Harris to JFK, Nov. 19, 1962, Box 30, POF.

p. 580: The housing order: *PPP: JFK, 1962*, 831–32, 835.

p. 580: "see the editors": Quoted in Richard Reeves, 316.

p. 581: On Monroe and the Kennedys: Thomas C. Reeves, 317–27; and Schlesinger, *A Thousand Days*, 590–91, who quotes Lawford.

p. 581: JFK's health care: Parmet, *JFK*, 120–24.

p. 581: "physically impaired": Statement of Dr. George Burkley, Mar. 2, 1964, Box 14, Lincoln Papers.

p. 581: "that if I ever": *New York Times*, Dec. 4, 1972.

p. 581: "that if Dr. Travell": Lincoln Diary, Dec. 29, 1962, Box 4, Lincoln Papers.

p. 581: "potential threat": Quoted in Leamer, 545.

p. 582: Jacobson made occasional: Richard Reeves, 242, 364, 684–85, 689–99.

p. 582: Her records indicate: Travell medical records.

p. 582: According to Dr. James M. Young: Conversation with Dr. Young, Nov. 27, 2002.

p. 582: "robust health": Dr. James M. Young, handwritten memoir, Nov. 23, 1963, which he allowed me to read.

pp. 582–83: "The Congress looks": *PPP: JFK, 1962*, 892–94.

p. 583: Heller asked him: Heller memo to JFK, Oct. 16, 1962, Box 6, Walter W. Heller Papers, JFKL.

p. 583: "The economic conditions": Philip L. Graham to JFK, Oct. 17, 1961, Box 30, POF.

pp. 583–84: "The lesson": *PPP: JFK, 1962*, 879.

p. 584: Mills's opposition to a tax cut: Henry H. Fowler, Conference with Mills, Nov. 15, 1962, Box 88; Larry O'Brien to JFK, Dec. 5, 1962, Box 64, POF. Douglas Dillon, Notes of conversation with Mills, Dec. 6, 1962, Box 38, Douglas Dillon Papers, JFKL. "Why a Tax Cut Is Unlikely in '63," *U.S. News & World Report*, Dec. 17, 1962, 42–45.

p. 584: "a reduction in revenue": Sen. Albert Gore to JFK, Nov. 15, 1962, Box 90, POF.

p. 584: "we are in serious danger": Robert G. Baker to Sen. Mansfield, Dec. 27, 1962, Box 52, POF.

p. 585: State of the Union Message: *PPP: JFK, 1963*, 11–15.

p. 585: "not going to pass": Naftali and Zelikow, *Presidential Recordings*, vol. II, 337.

p. 585: JFK on educational needs: *PPP: JFK, 1963*, 38–39, 69–70, 105–16, 238, 877–79.

pp. 585–86: Education spending: Ibid., 215–16.

pp. 586–87: JFK and health reforms: Ibid., 140–47, 188–204, 338–39, 823, 849; JFK to Anthony Celebrezze, May 6, 1963, Box 68, POF; Bernstein, *Promises Kept*, 257–58.

p. 587: On the tax cut: M. J. Rossant, "The Economic Education of John F. Kennedy," *The Reporter*, Feb. 14, 1963, 22–25.

p. 587: "a lot of willingness": Heller to JFK, Dec. 21, 1962, Box 5, Heller Papers.

p. 587: Dillon to JFK, Nov. 20, 1962, Box 34, Dillon Papers.

p. 587: "highly desirable": DDE Statement, Sept. 8, 1963, Box 29, POF; also see Charles S. Murphy to JFK, Sept. 10, 1963, Box 33, POF, for HST's view.

pp. 587–89: Wilbur Mills and federal spending: Tel. Convs., Dillon and Kermit Gordon and Dillon and Larry O'Brien, both February 1, 1963, Box 38, Dillon Papers. *PPP: JFK, 1963*, 27, 57, 59–60, 68, 210–212, 332, 351, 384, 393, 403–4, 576, 637–38, 662–63, 822, 863. JFK-Walter Heller, July 25, 1963, Audiotape 101.3; JFK-Wilbur Mills, July 29, 1963, Audiotape 101.4; JFK-Martha Griffiths telephone conversation, Aug. 7, 1963, 25A6, 25B1; JFK-Douglas Dillon, etc., Sept. 12, 1963, Audiotape 110.3; JFK-Dillon, Fowler, Sept. 30, 1963, Audiotape 113.5, JFKL. Bernstein, 157–59.

p. 589: "the most precious": *PPP: JFK, 1963*, 14.

p. 589: "an end to racial": Ibid., 71.

p. 589: "legal, economic": Ibid., 159–60.

pp. 589–90: Special Message to the Congress on Civil Rights, Feb. 28, 1963, *PPP: JFK, 1963*, 221–30.

p. 590: Had been "appointing": Ibid., 239.

p. 591: JFK-Katzenbach telephone conversation, Mar. 7, 1963, Audiotape 11A.5, JFKL.

p. 591: "Could you discuss": *PPP: JFK, 1963*, 347–48.

p. 591: JFK's civil rights record: Dallek, *Flawed Giant*, 30–31.

pp. 591–92: The voting rights bill: Berl I. Bernhard to Lee C. White, Feb. 21, 1963, Box 30, Theodore Sorensen Papers, JFKL.

p. 592: RFK and LBJ: *Flawed Giant*, 30, 32–33, 35–36.

p. 592: "fussed and interfered": Burke Marshall OH. Guthman and Shulman, *Robert Kennedy*, 150–53.

pp. 592–93: May and July CEEO meetings: Dallek, *Flawed Giant*, 35–36.

p. 593: RFK-LBJ personal differences: Schlesinger, *Robert Kennedy*, 623.

p. 594: Birmingham demonstrations: Bernstein, 85–90.

p. 595: Hoover's allegations: Schlesinger, *Robert Kennedy*, 352–54; David J. Garrow, "The FBI and Martin Luther King," *Atlantic Monthly*, July/August 2002, 80–88.

p. 595: JFK press conference: *PPP: JFK, 1963*, 372–73, 378.

p. 595: "It seems clear to me": Quoted in Richard Reeves, 490–91.

p. 596: King's letter: Branch, 737–40.

p. 596: took issue with JFK's assertion: Ibid., 787.

p. 596: The negotiated compromise: Bernstein, 90–92.

p. 597: The explosions and rioting: Ibid., 92–93; Branch, 791–96.

p. 597: "The passivity": Quoted in Schlesinger, *Robert Kennedy*, 330.

pp. 597–98: Wallace: Carter, chap. 3.

p. 598: JFK's discussion of the dilemma: JFK conversation with RFK, Burke Marshall, Nicholas Katzenbach, Ed Guthman, McNamara, Army Sec. Cyrus Vance, and Gen. Earle Wheeler, May 12, 1963, JFK Tape 86.2, JFKL.

p. 598: On King's intentions: Ibid.; Branch, 796–800.

p. 598: "leaned too much": Quoted in Branch, 800.

p. 598: JFK statement and telegram: *PPP: JFK, 1963*, 397–98.

pp. 598–99: RFK survey: RFK to JFK, June 4, 1963, and Lee White to JFK, June 4, 1963, Box 97, POF.

p. 599: RFK and Wallace: Carter, 117–23; Guthman and Shulman, 185–86.

p. 599: JFK and Wallace: Carter, 128–29. Pierre Salinger memo of conversation between JFK and Wallace, n.d., given to me by Sheldon Stern with Stern to Author, April 19, 2002.

pp. 599–600: The prospect of race wars: Burke Marshall OH.

p. 600: May 20 and 21, 1963, meetings: JFK, RFK, John Macy, Marshall, O'Brien, O'Donnell, Sorensen, and Lee White, JFK Tapes 88.4 and 88.6.

p. 600: Reporter asked: *PPP: JFK, 1963*, 423.

pp. 600–601: RFK meeting in New York: Guthman and Shulman, 223–26; Schlesinger, *Robert Kennedy*, 330–35.

p. 601: "How long": Guthman and Shulman, 64–65.

p. 601: JFK and Gov. Jimmie Davis, June 3, 1963, tel. conv., JFK Tape 21A.

p. 601–2: Conversations with Davis and Thompson: JFK Tapes 21A.1, 22A.3 and 4; 22B.1 and 3.

p. 602: On LBJ and the civil rights bill: Dallek, *Flawed Giant*, 36–37; LBJ-Sorensen tel. conv., June 3, 1963, Vice Presidential Papers: Civil Rights, LBJL.

p. 602: RFK request to Harriman: TELCON, May 29, 1963, and RFK to Harriman, June 17, 1963, Box 479, Harriman Papers.

pp. 602–3: The confrontation with Wallace: Guthman and Shulman, 185–98; Carter, 142–51.

p. 603: Preparation of the televised evening speech: Guthman and Shulman, 198–201.

pp. 603–4: Televised evening speech: *PPP: JFK, 1963*, 468–71.

p. 604: The civil rights bill: Ibid., 483–94. On Evers: Carter, 153–54.

pp. 604–5: Bipartisan support: JFK to DDE, June 10, 1963; DDE to JFK, June 14, 1963, Box 29A, POF.

p. 605: "He always felt": Guthman and Shulman, 176.

p. 605: "I suppose that civil rights": JFK-Carl Albert telephone conversation, June 12, 1963, JFK Tape 22A2.

p. 605: Dirksen quoting Hugo: Dallek, *Flawed Giant*, 119.

p. 605: JFK told Hodges: Luther Hodges OH.

p. 605: More than moral considerations: Guthman and Shulman, 392.

pp. 605–6: "Kennedy will lose": Fred R. Travis to Charles Bartlett, May 20, 1963, Box 28, POF.

p. 606: "the most sweeping": Martin Luther King, June 20, 1963, Box 97, POF.

Chapter 18: New Departures: Foreign Affairs

pp. 607–8: December 17 interview: *PPP: JFK, 1962*, 896–903. Also see Schlesinger to JFK, Dec. 15, 1962, Box 62A, POF.

p. 609: On Berlin: Beschloss, *Crisis Years*, 549; *FRUS: Berlin Crisis*, 510–11, 544–46.

p. 609: JFK's view of alliances: Theodore Sorensen, Foreword, in Brinkley and Griffiths, xiii.

p. 609: On Skybolt and the Bermuda meeting: Schlesinger, *A Thousand Days*, 856–66; JFK, Background Briefing of the Press, Dec. 31, 1962, Box 415, NSF.

p. 610: "the riot act": Lincoln Diary, Dec. 22, 1962, Box 4, Evelyn Lincoln Papers.

p. 610: Richard E. Neustadt's report was later published as *Alliance Politics* (New York, 1970).

pp. 610–11: Relations with France and Germany: John Newhouse, "De Gaulle and the Anglo-Saxons," 32–48, and Roger Morgan, "Kennedy and Adenauer," 16–31, in Brinkley and Griffiths.

p. 611: "if Germany developed": *PPP: JFK, 1961*, 751.

p. 611: "What is your judgment": JFK-Macmillan tel. conv., Jan. 19, 1963, Box 127A, POF.

p. 611: "There is always the argument": JFK, Background Briefing of the Press, Dec. 31, 1962, Box 415, NSF.

p. 611: "Well, I am going": Quoted in Schlesinger, *A Thousand Days*, 870–71.

p. 611: "not possible to persuade": Dean Acheson to JFK, Feb. 20, 1963, Box 27, POF.

p. 612: Malraux and JFK remarks at the National Gallery: *PPP: JFK, 1963*, 4–6. Also see *FRUS: Western Europe and Canada*, 485.

p. 612: On defense spending, see *PPP: JFK, 1963*, 15–16, 18–19; JFK, Background Briefing of the Press, Dec. 31, 1962, Box 415, NSF.

pp. 612–13: Rename foreign aid: David Bell Memo, Dec. 22, 1962, Box 28, Theodore Sorensen Papers, JFKL.

p. 613: NSK to JFK, Nov. 12, Dec. 14 and 19, 1962: *FRUS: Kennedy-Khrushchev*, 205–6, 233–34.

p. 613: On Israel, see Cohen and chap. 6 of Bass.

p. 614: "achieved much": Seaborg, 158.

p. 614: On JFK's request for an assessment of the tests: *FRUS: Arms Control*, 599–601.

p. 614: JFK to NSK, Nov. 21, Dec. 14, 22, 1962: *FRUS: Kennedy-Khrushchev*, 223, 231–33, 237.

p. 614: Differences between JFK and NSK: Ibid., 238–42; Seaborg, 178–81.

p. 614: NSK's agreement to talks in New York, and continuing differences: *FRUS: Kennedy-Khrushchev,* 247–49, 250–62; Seaborg, 183–85.

p. 615: "Well, my hopes": *PPP: JFK, 1963,* 80.

p. 615: "And so once again": Cousins, 95–110.

p. 615: "Any negotiations": *FRUS: National Security Policy,* 462.

p. 615: Other pressures on NSK and JFK: Lawrence Freedman, 264–65; *FRUS: Arms Control,* 683–85; and "Meeting of Soviet and Chinese Communist Party Delegations, July 8, 1963," *Cold War International History Bulletin,* March 1998, 178.

pp. 615–16: "Who did we think": *FRUS: Kennedy-Khrushchev,* 262–65.

p. 616: "an unofficial": NSK to Leo Szilard, Nov. 4, 1962, Box 369, NSF. Also see Szilard to NSK, Oct. 9, 1962, and Szilard to Dr. Robert Livingston, Dec. 29, 1962, in ibid., and *FRUS: Arms Control,* 655–56.

p. 616: "had been helpful": *FRUS: Kennedy-Khrushchev,* 264.

p. 616: Hot line: *FRUS: Soviet Union,* 708.

p. 616: For the JFK-Macmillan proposals to NSK: *FRUS: Arms Control,* 659–61, 663–67, 670–78.

p. 617: "almost entirely negative": Ibid., 685–86.

p. 617: NSK to JFK, April 29, May 8, 1963; JFK to NSK, May 13, 30, 1963: *FRUS: Kennedy-Khrushchev,* 271–87, 290–92.

p. 617: Thompson analysis: *FRUS: Arms Control,* 687.

p. 618: "This challenge by the ChiComs": Averell Harriman, Memo concerning the Soviet Union, n.d., Averell Harriman Papers, Kai Bird Collection.

p. 618: Press conferences: *PPP: JFK, 1963,* 377–78, 424.

p. 618: JFK meeting with Cousins, April 22, 1963: Cousins, 111–20.

p. 618: "the most important speech": Cousins to JFK, April 30, 1963, Box 36, Sorensen Papers.

p. 618: JFK reply to Cousins: Richard Reeves, 476.

p. 619: "'This is not propaganda'": Seaborg, 204–5.

pp. 619–21: The "peace speech," its timing, and preparation: *FRUS: Arms Control,* 710–14; Schlesinger, *A Thousand Days,* 899–900; Sorensen, 822–23; *PPP: JFK, 1963,* 459–64.

p. 621: Reactions to the speech: Gallup, 1837, 1842.

p. 621: "hardly electrified": Lawrence Freedman, 268.

p. 621: The mail, and "with disgust": Schlesinger, *A Thousand Days,* 909–10.

p. 621: Congressional Republicans: Sorensen, 825–26.

p. 621: Soviet reaction: Beschloss, *Crisis Years,* 601.

p. 621: "an atmosphere of détente": Chester L. Cooper to Averell Harriman, Aug. 22, 1963, Harriman Papers, Kai Bird Collection.

p. 621: "the best statement": *FRUS: Arms Control,* 862.

p. 621: "It was as though": Seaborg, 218.

p. 622: "a direct communications link": *PPP: JFK, 1963,* 495.

p. 622: Test message: Beschloss, *Crisis Years,* 602.

pp. 622–23: The struggle to find a realistic agenda: Naftali, *Presidential Recordings,* vol. I, 172–73; *FRUS: Arms Control,* 719–20, 762–63, 768–69, 783–90, 801; *FRUS: Northeast Asia, 1961–1963,* 339–40, 370–71. Seaborg, chap. 17, 239; Lawrence Freedman, 270–74. Schlesinger, *A Thousand Days,* 902–3. Also see Carl Kaysen to Mayor Willy Brandt, July 5, 1963, Box 539; Harold Macmillan to JFK,

July 10, 1963, Box 540; "Points to Be Covered by Governor Harriman in the Forthcoming July 15 Mission to Moscow," Box 539, Harriman Papers.

p. 622: "I regard the Chiefs": JFK-Mansfield telephone conversation, Aug. 12, 1963, JFK Tapes 25B2, 25C1, JFKL.

p. 622: Excluded military officers and control of cables: Bernard J. Firestone, "Kennedy and the Test Ban," in Brinkley and Griffiths, 83–84.

p. 623: Harriman appointment: *FRUS: Arms Control*, 656; Cousins, 114.

p. 623: On the goals of JFK's Europe trip: Schlesinger, *A Thousand Days*, 881–84; Morgan, "Kennedy and Adenauer," in Brinkley and Griffiths, 25–31; Beschloss, *Crisis Years*, 603–4, 609–10.

pp. 624–26: For the speeches and JFK's reception in Germany and trip to Ireland: *PPP: JFK, 1963*, 497–530.

p. 624: "put more money": Memo of Conf. with JFK, Dec. 27, 1962, Box 345, NSF.

p. 624: Reception in Berlin: Schlesinger, *A Thousand Days*, 884–88; Sorensen, 677–78; O'Donnell and Powers, 358–59; Beschloss, *Crisis Years*, 604–8.

p. 625: JFK remark to McHugh: Confidential source.

p. 626: "on desirability": *FRUS: Arms Control*, 799.

p. 626: "make a 'big thing' out of": Memo to Harriman, July 16, 1963, Harriman Papers, Kai Bird Collection.

p. 627: Khrushchev-Harriman exchanges: *FRUS: Arms Control*, 799–801.

p. 627: "glad to see": NSK-Harriman conversation, July 20, 1963, Box 587, Averell Harriman Papers, LC.

p. 627: "Gospodin Garriman": NSK-Harriman conversation, July 26, 1963, ibid.

p. 627: Completion of the treaty: *FRUS: Arms Control*, 802–55.

pp. 628–30: The battle for treaty approval and the treaty's impact: Sorensen, 829–33; Seaborg, chaps. 19–21. Firestone, "Kennedy and the Test Ban," 88–94. Carl Kaysen, "The Limited Test Ban Treaty of 1963," in Brinkley and Griffiths, 108–113.

p. 628: JFK's July 26 speech: *PPP: JFK, 1963*, 601–6.

p. 629: "Maybe we can save": JFK-HST telephone conversation, July 26, 1963, JFK Tape 24A1.

p. 629: Fulbright had worried: JFK-Fulbright tel. conv. Aug. 23, 1963, JFK Tape 26C1.

p. 629: Harris poll and "I don't see any": Firestone, "Kennedy and the Test Ban," 91.

p. 630: For the Mar., June, and Sept. polls, see Gallup, 1700, 1734, 1738, 1808, 1826.

Chapter 19: An Unfinished Presidency

p. 631: The decor: "As I Remember J.F.K.," Nov. 21, 1963, Box 15, David Powers Papers, JFKL.

pp. 631–32: "loved being President": Schlesinger, *A Thousand Days*, 671–72, 676, 679. "Kennedy enjoyed being President": "As I Remember J.F.K.," Nov. 21, 1963, Box 15, Powers Papers; O'Donnell and Powers, 375.

p. 632: Remarks to Sorensen and to Jackie and Lee Radziwill: Lincoln Diary, Jan. 16, 19, 1963, Evelyn Lincoln Papers, JFKL.

p. 632: The Cannon interview notes, April 5, 1963, Box 1, James M. Cannon Papers, JFKL.

p. 632: European opinion of JFK: John L. Steele to Gen. Chester V. Clifton, Mar. 6, 1963, Box 62A, POF.

p. 633: JFK's wit: "Remarks for Gala," Box 36, Theodore Sorensen Papers, JFKL.

p. 633: Turned aside criticism: Notes on briefing session with JFK, Sept. 12, 1963, Box 6, Walter W. Heller Papers, JFKL.

p. 633: Patrick Bouvier Kennedy: O'Donnell and Powers, 375–79.

pp. 633–34: E. B. White poem, New Yorker, Oct. 12, 1963.

p. 634: JFK on the presidency: Schlesinger, A Thousand Days, 676, 679.

pp. 634–35: Profumo affair: JFK and Schlesinger, Mar. 22, 1963, tel. conv., JFK Tape 15B, JFKL.

p. 635: Gallup poll: Schlesinger to JFK, June 21, 1963, Box 66, POF.

p. 635: "devoured every word": Bradlee, Conversations, 230.

p. 635: "You've read about": Quoted in Garrow, 61–63; Branch, 837–38.

pp. 635–36: The Journal-American story: Hersh, 390–98; Evan Thomas, 254.

p. 636: "Gratitude stirred": Charles Bartlett, "News Managing?" clipping, Feb. 28, 1963, Box 28, POF.

pp. 636–37: Ellen Rometsch: Hersh, 387–90, 398–400; Evan Thomas, 255–56.

pp. 637–38: On Mollenhoff's story and the JFK-RFK response to it: Lincoln Diary, Oct. 28, 1963, Lincoln Papers; Guthman and Shulman, 129–30; Hersh, 400–406; Evan Thomas, 263–68.

pp. 638–39: Baker, LBJ, and the vice presidency: Dallek, Flawed Giant, 40–44.

p. 639: The country's concerns: McGeorge Bundy to JFK, May 16, 1963, Box 62A, POF; Gallup, 1818, 1823–29.

p. 639: Democrats' focus: O'Brien and Sorensen to JFK, April 30, 1963, and two undated memos attacking the Republicans, Box 53; Senate policy committee meetings, Mansfield to JFK, April 30, May 16, 1963, Box 31, POF.

pp. 639–40: The tax cut: Heller to JFK, Mar. 21, 1963, Box 5; Aug. 7, Sept. 4, 1963, Box 6, Heller Papers. Leadership breakfast, Nov. 5, 1963, Box 53; CEA Draft Statement, Nov. 10, 1963, Box 76, POF. O'Brien and Sorensen to JFK, Nov. 20, 1963; Henry H. Fowler to Sec. Dillon, Nov. 29, 1963, Box 59, Sorensen Papers. New York Times, Oct. 31, 1963.

p. 640: The war on poverty: Schlesinger, A Thousand Days, 1010; Isserman; Notes on meetings with JFK, Oct. 21, Nov. 19, 1963, Box 6, Heller Papers; Heller to Sorensen, Nov. 20, 1963, Box 31, Sorensen Papers.

pp. 640–41: Civil Rights and Congress: Sen. Mike Mansfield to JFK, June 18, 1963, Box 30, Sorensen Papers; Bernstein, 105–6.

p. 641: "A leading southern Senator": Schlesinger to RFK, July 1, 1963, Box 80, POF.

p. 641: LBJ on the Senate vote: Schlesinger, A Thousand Days, 970.

p. 641: Kennedy remained uncertain: Charles A. Horsky to JFK, two memos of July 9, 1963; Lee White to JFK, July 11, 1963, Box 97, POF.

pp. 641–42: The June 22 meeting: Schlesinger, A Thousand Days, 968–71; Schlesinger, Robert Kennedy, 350; Branch, 839–41.

p. 642 The Aug. 1 news conference: *PPP: JFK, 1963*, 615.

pp. 642–44: Preparations for the march and the march: Schlesinger, *A Thousand Days*, 972–73; Schlesinger, *Robert Kennedy*, 350–52; Branch, chap. 22.

pp. 645–46: The post-march White House meeting: Audiotape 108.2, Aug. 28, 1963, JFKL; Branch, 883–86.

p. 646: JFK Interv. with Cronkite, Sept. 2, 1963, Box 14, Powers Papers.

pp. 646–47: Sept. 19 meeting: Audiotapes 111.7, 112.1, JFKL; "King and Kennedy Discuss Birmingham," *Miller Center Report*, Winter 2000, 22–27.

pp. 647–48: JFK meeting with white Birmingham leaders, Sept. 23, 1963, Audiotapes 112.6 and 113.1, JFKL.

pp. 648–50: JFK and the fight over civil rights: Ibid. Audiotapes, Sept. 30, 1963, 113.2; Oct. 23, 1963, 116.6, 116.7, 117.1; Oct. 29, 1963, 118.2. Tel. Convs. Oct. 29, 1963, 28A.3; Oct. 30, 1963, 28A.4. Lincoln Diary, Oct. 23, 28, 29, 1963, Lincoln Papers. RFK Press Conf., Oct. 15, 1963, Box 30, Sorensen Papers; O'Brien and Sorensen to JFK, Nov. 20, 1963, Box 59, Sorensen Papers. *PPP: JFK, 1963*, 762–65. "JFK and the South," *Arkansas Gazette*, Oct. 6, 1963. Brooks Hays to JFK, Oct. 20, 1963, Box 63A, POF. Bonnie Faugus Salcido to JFK, Aug. n.d., 1963, Box 31, RFK Confidential File RFK Papers, JFKL. Bernstein, 108–13.

pp. 651–52: JFK and space: June 14 press conf., *PPP: JFK, 1962*, 485. Edward R. Murrow to JFK, Aug. 13, 1962, Box 91; JFK to Dave Bell, Aug. 23, 1962, Box 125A, POF. NSAM, No. 183, Aug. 27, 1962, Box 338, NSF. LBJ to JFK, Jan. 14, 1963, Box 30; James Webb to JFK, Oct. 29, Nov. 30, 1962, Box 84, POF. Tape 63, Nov. 21, 1962, JFKL. Dec. 31, 1962, background briefing, Box 415, NSF.

pp. 652–53: Criticism of moon program: McDougall, 389–94. Also see Vannevar Bush to James Webb, April 11, 1963, Box 84, POF.

p. 653: Asked Johnson: JFK to LBJ, April 9, 1963, Box 84, POF.

p. 653: "the desirability of": *PPP: JFK, 1963*, 349–50.

p. 653: JFK wanted Johnson: JFK to LBJ, July 29, 1963; LBJ to JFK, July 31, 1963, Box 30, POF.

p. 653: Soviet second thoughts and pressure on JFK: Obituary of Vasily Mishin, *New York Times*, Oct. 29, 2001; *PPP: JFK, 1963*, 568, 831–32; McDougall, 395; JFK to Albert Thomas, Sept. 23, 1963, Box 38, Sorensen Papers.

p. 653: USIA survey: Donald Wilson to JFK, June 11, 1963, Box 91, POF.

p. 654: Sept. 20 U.N. speech: *PPP: JFK, 1963*, 693–98.

p. 654: JFK instructed Webb: NSAM No. 271, Nov. 12, 1963, Box 342, NSF.

p. 655: A 1965 survey: Maria Carosa to John Stewart, n.d., Box 14, Powers Papers.

p. 655: JFK-NSK exchanges: *FRUS: Kennedy-Khrushchev*, 215–23, 226–33.

p. 656: "we must assume": JFK conference with Chiefs, Dec. 27, 1962, Box 345, NSF.

p. 656: Feb. and Apr. exchanges about invasion plans: *FRUS: Missile Crisis*, 711–12, 791, 802–3.

p. 656: "the situation could develop": JFK to McNamara, Oct. 4, 1963, Box 68, POF.

p. 656: Political pressures on JFK over Cuba: McGeorge Bundy to JFK, Dec. 30, 1962, Box 215A, NSF; Lincoln Diary, Feb. 5, 1963, Lincoln Papers; Richard Goodwin, "President Kennedy's Plan for Peace with Cuba," *New York Times*, July 5, 2000; Lawrence Freedman, 225.

p. 656: JFK speech, Dec. 29, 1962: *PPP: JFK, 1962*, 911–13; O'Donnell and Powers, 276–77; Evan Thomas, 238.

p. 656: Soviet troops: *FRUS: Missile Crisis*, 681–83, 715–18; Lawrence Freedman, 224.

p. 656: Subversion: *FRUS: Missile Crisis*, 359, 433, 648, 662, 696–97, 726–27, 867–68, 888. JFK to McCone, Feb. 9, 1963; Marshall S. Carter to JFK, Feb. 13, 1963; JFK to Rusk, McNamara, McCone, Feb. 15, 1963; Bundy to McCone, Mar. 14, 1963, Box 72, POF. RFK to JFK, Mar. 14, 1963, Box 35, Sorensen Papers. JFK to Rusk, May 31, 1963, Box 68, POF.

p. 657: Replace failed Mongoose: Evan Thomas, 233–35.

p. 657: Ousting Castro: *FRUS: Missile Crisis*, 670–75, 780–81, 804, 821–23, 828–38, 852–53; U.S. Policy Toward Cuba, Feb. 19, 1963, Box 49, Sorensen Papers; Cabinet Meeting, Mar. 1, 1963, Box 7, RFK Attorney General's Papers, JFKL; "Backstage with Bobby," *Miami News*, July 14, 1963; "U.S. Builds Up Underground's Support in Cuba," *Washington Post*, Aug. 13, 1963; John McCone to RFK, Mar. 22, 1962, Box 1, RFK Confidential File; Lawrence Freedman, 228, 232, 238–39. Also see Evan Thomas, 234.

p. 657: "Kennedy was maintaining": Lawrence Freedman, 227.

p. 658: Cuban-Soviet tensions and Castro's demands on the U.S.: Fursenko and Naftali, 290–91.

p. 658: NSC staffer urged: *FRUS: Missile Crisis*, 699–700.

p. 658: Kennedy had told newsmen, and the shrimp boat incident: *PPP: JFK, 1963*, 177–78, 202–4; "'Soft' Cuba Reply Expected by U.S. in Firing on Boat," *New York Times*, Feb. 25, 1963.

p. 658: March NSC meeting and RFK pressure for more action: *FRUS: Missile Crisis*, 715–18; RFK to JFK, Mar. 14, 1963, Box 35, Sorensen Papers; Evan Thomas, 233–39.

pp. 658–59: JFK's unresponsiveness: Evan Thomas, 239.

p. 659: The exile raids: *FRUS: Missile Crisis*, 728, 738–40, 745–46.

p. 659: JFK was willing to consider: Ibid., 739. Also see Robert A. Hurwitch to RFK, April 6, 1963, Box 30; "Miami to Sec. of State," April 14, 1963, Box 11; CIA reports, May 15 and 22, 1963, Box 8, RFK Confidential File.

pp. 659–60: Donovan and Castro: JFK to RFK and Rusk, April 4, 1963, Box 34, RFK Confidential File; McCone to JFK, April 10, 1963, in *FRUS: Missile Crisis*, 755–56 and n. 1; M. C. Miskovsky to McCone, April 13, 1963, Box 47, NSF; Gertrude Samuels, "James Donovan and Castro," *The Nation*, April 13, 1963.

p. 660: On Castro's Moscow visit: CIA Memo, May 18, 1963, Box 1, RFK Confidential File; *FRUS: Missile Crisis*, 820–24, 838–44.

pp. 660–61: The raids, Soviet protests, and JFK's response: *FRUS: Missile Crisis*, 828–38, 866–68, 875–77.

pp. 661–63: Attwood's initiative: Ibid., 868–70, 877–83, 888–89; Lawrence Freedman, 240–43; Audiotape /A55, Nov. 5, 1963, conversation between JFK and Bundy about Attwood and Cuba.

pp. 661–62: The Daniel-JFK meeting: Schlesinger, *Robert Kennedy*, 552–53.

p. 662: Castro surprised the Americans: Charles O. Porter to Arthur Schlesinger, Jr., Oct. 11, 1963, Box 36, RFK Confidential File.

p. 663: JFK's Nov. 18 Miami speech: *PPP: JFK, 1963*, 872–77.

p. 663: "expressions of willingness": Richard Helms Memo, Nov. 21, 1963, Box 1, RFK Confidential File.

p. 663: Still intense pressure: *FRUS: Missile Crisis*, 871–72, 874, 883–88.

pp. 663–64: JFK asked whether the sabotage program: Ibid., 884.

p. 664: The assassination plot: Lawrence Freedman, *Kennedy's Wars*, 232–33.

pp. 664–65: JFK and comments on Vietnam in 1962: *PPP: JFK, 1962*, 17, 93, 136–37, 199, 228, 322, 360, 362, 453, 493, 500, 502, 537, 592–93, 651, 690, 703.

pp. 665–66: Debate about strategic hamlets, and reports to JFK: *FRUS: Vietnam, 1962*, 727–29, 736–41, 763–65, 779–87, 797–98; Forrestal to RFK, Nov. 7, 1962, RFK Confidential File.

p. 666: December 1962 press conference: *PPP: JFK, 1962*, 870.

p. 666: JFK's reaction to Mansfield: David Kaiser, 180; O'Donnell and Powers, 15.

p. 666: Sylvester comment: Quoted in *The Nation*, April 22, 2002.

p. 667: JFK meeting with Wheeler: *FRUS: Vietnam, Jan.–Aug. 1963*, 94–95, 97–98.

p. 667: Hilsman, Forrestal report and CIA: Ibid., 7, 22, 50, 52.

pp. 667–68: JFK public statements on Vietnam between January and March: *PPP: JFK, 1963*, 11, 20, 34, 243–44, 294–96, 303.

p. 668: JFK call to Hilsman: *FRUS: Vietnam, Jan.–Aug., 1963*, 63. CIA director John McCone said in 1988 that Kennedy saw the "folly" of escalation in Vietnam and was determined to withdraw U.S. advisers: "Conversation with John A. McCone," Spring 1988, Institute of International Studies, Univ. of California, Berkeley.

p. 668: JFK-Mansfield conversation and JFK to O'Donnell: O'Donnell and Powers, 16; Newman, 321–25.

p. 669: On the civil strife in Vietnam and reports of it in the U.S, see the documents for May, June, and July in *FRUS: Vietnam, Jan.–Aug. 1963*. Also see JFK news conference: *PPP: JFK, 1963*, 569.

p. 669: On July 17, a reporter asked: *FRUS: Vietnam, Jan.–Aug. 1963*, 294–96; Lawrence Freedman, 363; *PPP: JFK, 1963*, 421.

p. 669: 107 taped meetings: Logs of Presidential Recordings, JFKL.

p. 669: Warning to Diem and JFK embargo: *FRUS: Vietnam, Jan.–Aug. 1963*, 381–83 n., 386–87; David Kaiser, 215–16.

pp. 669–70: Frankel: *New York Times*, July 3, 1963.

p. 670: Kattenburg: *FRUS: Vietnam, Aug.–Dec. 1963*, 69–74; Lawrence Freedman, 372.

p. 670: Lodge's appointment: Lawrence Freedman, 367–68; *FRUS: Vietnam, Jan.–Aug. 1963*, 413–14.

pp. 670–71: July 4 meeting: *FRUS: Vietnam, Jan.–Aug. 1963*, 451–53.

p. 671: July 8 meeting: Ibid., 486 n.

p. 671: Urging of State Dept. officials: 531–43, 559–60.

p. 671: Request of Aug. 15: Ibid., 589, n.

p. 671: Krulak's response to Halberstam: Ibid., 584.

p. 671: Krulak's meeting with JFK: Tape 106/A41, Aug. 21, 1963.

p. 672: Mansfield to JFK, Aug. 19, 1963: *FRUS: Vietnam, Jan.–Aug. 1963*, 585–88.

p. 672: Taylor to McNamara, Aug. 20, 1963: Ibid., 590–91.

pp. 672–73: Attack on pagodas and U.S. response: Ibid., 560–66, 597–99, 625–31, 634–35.

p. 673: JFK's second thoughts: Schlesinger, *A Thousand Days*, 991.

p. 673: Aug. 26 meeting: *FRUS: Vietnam, Jan.–Aug. 1963*, 638–41.

p. 673: Aug. 27 meeting: Ibid., 659–65.

pp. 673–74: CIA analysis: Ibid., 671.

p. 674: Aug. 28 meeting: *FRUS: Vietnam, Aug.–Dec. 1963*, 1–9.

p. 674: The acrimony between advocates and opponents of a coup: Schlesinger, *Robert Kennedy*, 713–14; Gibbons, 155–56.

pp. 674–75: Exchanges with Lodge: *FRUS: Vietnam, Aug.–Dec., 1963*, 20–21, 26–31, 35–36.

p. 675: The aborted coup: Ibid., 55, 63, 64, 66, 70–74, 76.

p. 675: Kattenburg's views: Gibbons, 160–61.

pp. 675–76: JFK interviews: *FRUS: Vietnam, Aug.–Dec., 1963*, 81–82, 93–94; *PPP: JFK, 1963*, 658–59.

p. 676: JFK told Manning: *FRUS: Vietnam, Aug.–Dec. 1963*, 103–4; also see 111–12.

p. 676: "We should wait": Ibid., 103.

p. 676: Sept. 6 meeting: Ibid., 117–21.

pp. 676–77: Reports on and response to the Nhus: Ibid., 135.

p. 677: JFK facetiously suggested: Briefing Session with JFK, Sept. 12, 1963, Box 6, Heller Papers.

p. 677: CIA also reported: CIA reports, Sept. 5 and 12, 1963, Box 199A, NSF.

p. 677: Conflicting assessments: *FRUS: Vietnam, Aug.–Dec. 1963*, 137–40, 146, 161–62.

pp. 677–78: JFK's frustration: Ibid., 162–67.

p. 678: Continuing divisions among JFK's advisers: Ibid., 190–93, 209, 235.

p. 678: New coup plans: CIA reports, Sept. 16, 20, 21, 28, Oct. 3, 1963, Boxes 199A and 200, NSF; *FRUS: Vietnam, Aug.–Dec. 1963*, 291–92.

p. 678: McNamara-Taylor mission and stage managing it: *FRUS: Vietnam, Aug.–Dec. 1963*, 255–57, 278–81.

pp. 678–79: McNamara-Taylor report: Ibid., 336–46.

p. 679: JFK Oct. 9 statement: *PPP: JFK, 1963*, 770.

pp. 679–80: Response to the report and follow-up announcements and actions: *FRUS: Vietnam, Aug.–Dec. 1963*, 350–54, 368–71, 395–96, 407–9, 467; McNamara, 77–81; Tapes 114/A49 and A50.

p. 679: JFK and Halberstam: *FRUS: Vietnam, Aug.–Dec., 1963*, 277–78, 281; Tifft and Jones, 388–89.

p. 680: Salinger publicly announced: Salinger news conference and statement, Oct. 2, 1963, 6:52 P.M., following JFK meeting, Box 14, Powers Papers.

p. 680: Taylor said, "Well, goddammit": Quoted in Gibbons, 186.

p. 680: Oct. 31 news conference: *PPP: JFK, 1963*, 828.

p. 681: Minh told Taylor, and discussions about a coup: *FRUS: Vietnam, Aug.–Dec. 1963*, 326–27, 365–67, 379, 393.

p. 681: "We certainly would not": Quoted in Gibbons, 190.

p. 681: Bundy to Lodge, Oct. 25, 1963: *FRUS: Vietnam, Aug.–Dec. 1963*, 437.

p. 681: Lodge's response: Ibid., 454–55.

p. 682: If the coup failed: Ibid., 468–75; Audiotape 118/A54, and transcripts of these meetings given to me by George Eliades.

p. 682: The coup and the JFK-Lodge-Rusk responses: Conference with JFK, Nov. 1, 1963, Box 317, NSF; Audiotape 118/A54, and Eliades transcript; *FRUS: Vietnam, Aug.–Dec. 1963*, 502, 505, 513, 519–20, 525–26.

pp. 682–83: The assassinations and JFK response: Ibid., 527; Audiotape /

A55, and Eliades transcript; Gibbons, 200–202; Taylor, 301; Schlesinger, *A Thousand Days*, 997–98.

p. 683: Diem had a million: Described in a cable from Lodge to Rusk, May 1964, in the Gerald Ford Library, cited by Douglas Brinkley, who suggests the CIA involvement: "Of Ladders and Letters," *Time*, April 24, 2000, 40–41.

pp. 683–84: JFK taped statement, Nov. 4, 1963, Cassette M (Side 2).

p. 684: JFK's official and public statements: *FRUS: Vietnam, Aug.–Dec. 1963*, 579–80; *PPP: JFK, 1963*, 846.

p. 685: Honolulu conference: *FRUS: Vietnam, Aug.–Dec. 1963*, 593–94, 625.

p. 685: Newspaper editorials and administration opposition to neutralization: Ibid., 581, 592, 594–95, 599–600. Only 37 percent of the public was paying attention to Vietnam as late as April of 1964: Gallup, 1882.

p. 685: For the unsigned memo, see David Kaiser, 258.

pp. 685–86: JFK request to Forrestal: Rust, 3–5.

p. 686: JFK's popularity: Gallup, 1796, 1800, 1807, 1810–11, 1815, 1818, 1820, 1827, 1829, 1835–36, 1840–42, 1844–45, 1847, 1850.

p. 686: North Dakota: Joseph F. Kraft Analysis, April 1963, Box 104, POF.

pp. 686–87: Pennsylvania: Public Opinion Surveys, April 1963, Box 105, POF.

p. 687: Journalists echoed: Charles Bartlett, "The Waiting Game," April 7, 1963; Fred Travis to Bartlett, May 20, 1963, Box 28, POF. David Beetle, "Kennedy Holding Fast to '60 Voters," *Rochester Democrat and Chronicle*, Sept. 12, 1963, Box 31, Sorensen Papers.

p. 687: JFK's view of 1964: Comment to George Brown, Oct. 24, 1963, Audiotape 117/A53; "JFK—on Re-election," Jan. 1963, Box 27, Powers Papers.

p. 687: Westchester chairman: William Luddy to Ken O'Donnell, Nov. 7, 1963, Box 1, Kenneth O'Donnell Papers, JFKL.

p. 688: Doubts about winning the southern black vote: Guthman and Shulman, 106.

p. 688: Start of the campaign: O'Donnell and Powers, 379; "Notes on JFK Meetings," Nov. 20, 1963, Box 6, Heller Papers.

p. 688: New Jersey: Walter Pozen to O'Donnell, Nov. 6, 1963, Box 1, O'Donnell Papers.

pp. 688–89: The South: JFK TV Interview, Sept. 2, 1963, Box 14, Powers Papers; Louis Harris to JFK, Sept. 3, 1963, Box 30, POF; "Farley Predicts JFK Victory," *Atlanta Journal*, Oct. 21, 1963.

p. 689: The hard right: Meyer Feldman to JFK, Aug. 15, 1963, Box 63, POF.

pp. 689–90: JFK on Goldwater: O'Donnell and Powers, 13; *PPP: JFK, 1963*, 828.

p. 690: Rockefeller and JFK: Roswell L. Gilpatric OH; Bradlee, *Conversations*, 121; Gallup, 1810, 1820, 1826, 1830–36.

pp. 690–91: The Nov. 13 meeting: O'Donnell and Powers, 386–87; Guthman and Shulman, 343, 388, 390–93; Schlesinger, *Robert Kennedy*, 603–4; Richard Reeves, 655–57.

p. 691: The trip to Florida: *PPP: JFK, 1963*, 860–77.

pp. 691–92: Origins of the Texas trip and JFK's affinity for campaigning: Ibid., 443–44; O'Donnell and Powers, 3–5, 11–13, 386–87; Guthman and Shulman, 344; Dallek, *Flawed Giant*, 46.

p. 692: JFK the morning of Nov. 21: Powers Diary, Nov. 21, 1963, Box 15, Powers Papers.

p. 692: JFK's Nov. 21 schedule in Texas is described in ibid., and by O'Donnell and Powers, 20–23.

p. 693: Doubts about wisdom of visiting Texas: Byron Skelton to RFK, Nov. 4, 1963, Box 36, RFK Confidential File; O'Donnell and Powers, 18–20, 23–25.

pp. 693–94: For Oswald's movements, see Posner.

p. 695: "I do not wish": Isaiah Berlin to Schlesinger, Nov. 28, 1963, Box 36, RFK Confidential File.

p. 695: "I never knew": Reinhold Niebuhr to Schlesinger, Nov. 29, 1963, ibid.

p. 695: "America now": Earl Warren to Mrs. Jacqueline Kennedy, Dec. 1963, Box 104, Earl Warren Papers, LC.

p. 696: Jacqueline Kennedy on the secret service, JFK's doctors, and spoke lovingly: Dr. James M. Young to author, Dec. 21, 2002, and telephone conversation with Young, Dec. 30, 2002.

pp. 696–97: Jacqueline Kennedy and JFK's funeral and burial: Manchester, 490–91, 541–42, 550; Hamilton, xix–xxiv. Leaming, 345–50.

p. 697: "needed the myth": Evan Thomas, 285.

p. 697: Describing Kennedy's death: Theodore White, "For President Kennedy an Epilogue," *Life*, Dec. 6, 1963.

p. 697: "would have provoked": Schlesinger, *Robert Kennedy*, 632.

p. 697: On Joe and Rose: Hamilton, xx; Rose Kennedy, 442–46.

pp. 697–98: On RFK: Schlesinger, *Robert Kennedy*, 611–20; and Evan Thomas, chap. 15.

p. 698: On LBJ, the assassination, the Warren Commission, and public opinion, see Dallek, *Flawed Giant*, 50–53. Anthony Lewis is quoted on 53.

pp. 698–99: The best study of the Warren Commission will be in a forthcoming book on the subject by Max Holland. In the meantime, see Max Holland, "After Thirty Years: Making Sense of the Assassination," *Reviews in American History*, vol. 22 (1994), 191–209; Max Holland, "The Key to the Warren Report," *American Heritage*, Nov. 1995, 50–64, and Posner, *Case Closed*.

pp. 698–99: The polls: Gallup, 1854, 2044; *New York Times*, Jan. 5, 1992; *New York Times Book Review*, Feb. 2, 1992.

pp. 699–702: JFK's hold on public's imagination and assessments by critics: Thomas C. Reeves, especially 3, 6–7, 10–11, 418–19; Hersh, xi, 5–6, 10; Mike Feinsilber, "The Kennedy Legend," Associated Press release, Jan. 7, 1998; Alvin S. Felzenberg, "JFK: not one for the (history) books: Historians give him a B–, though to many people he earned an A+," *Boston Sunday Globe*, Nov. 15, 1998; "Ranking the Presidents, results of a study released by the Federalist society for law and public policy studies," Nov. 16, 2000, *Wall Street Journal*; Gallup polls, Presidents Day, 1999, 2000, 2001.

Epilogue

p. 705: Autopsy notes and Bobby persuaded Burkley: Conversation with Dr. James Young, Nov. 25, 2002.

p. 705: Burned his files: Conversation with William Herbst Jr., Nov. 22, 2002.

pp. 707–8: On Byron White, see Hutchinson, and White's obituary: *New York Times*, April 16, 2002.

Bibliography

Abell, Tyler, ed. *Drew Pearson Diaries, 1949–1959*. New York: Holt, Rinehart and Winston, 1974.

Acheson, Dean. *Present at the Creation*. New York: Norton, 1969.

Ambrose, Stephen E. *Eisenhower: The President*. New York: Simon & Schuster, 1984.

———. *Nixon: The Education of a Politician, 1913–1962*. New York: Simon & Schuster, 1987.

Bailyn, Bernard, et al. *The Great Republic: A History of the American People*. Lexington, Mass.: D. C. Heath, 1992.

Baker, Bobby. *Wheeling and Dealing: Confessions of a Capitol Hill Operator*. New York: Norton, 1978.

Ball, George W. *The Past Has Another Pattern*. New York: Norton, 1982.

Bass, Warren. *Support Any Friend: JFK's Middle East and the Making of the U.S.-Israel Alliance*. New York: Oxford University Press, 2003.

Bernstein, Irving. *Promises Kept: John F. Kennedy's New Frontier*. New York: Oxford University Press, 1991.

Beschloss, Michael R. *The Crisis Years: Kennedy and Khrushchev, 1960–1963*. New York: HarperCollins, 1991.

———. *Kennedy and Roosevelt: The Uneasy Alliance*. New York: Norton, 1980.

Bill, James A. *George Ball: Behind the Scenes in U.S. Foreign Policy*. New Haven, Conn.: Yale University Press, 1997.

Bird, Kai. *The Color of Truth: McGeorge Bundy and William Bundy: Brothers in Arms*. New York: Simon & Schuster, 1998.

Bissell, Richard M., Jr. *Reflections of a Cold Warrior*. New Haven, Conn.: Yale University Press, 1996.

Blair, Joan and Clay, Jr., *The Search for JFK*. New York: Putnam, 1974.

Blight, James G., and David A. Welch. *On the Brink: Americans and Soviets Reexamine the Cuban Missile Crisis*. New York: Hill & Wang, 1989.

Bradlee, Benjamin C. *Conversations with Kennedy*. New York: Norton, 1975.

———. *A Good Life*. New York: Simon & Schuster, 1995.

Branch, Taylor. *Parting the Waters: America in the King Years, 1954–1963.* New York: Simon & Schuster, 1988.

Brandeis, Louis D. *Other People's Money and How the Bankers Use It.* New York: Stokes, 1914.

Brauer, Carl M. *Presidential Transitions: Eisenhower Through Reagan.* New York: Oxford University Press, 1986.

Brinkley, Douglas. *Dean Acheson: The Cold War Years, 1953–1971.* New Haven, Conn.: Yale University Press, 1992.

Brinkley, Douglas, and Richard T. Griffiths. *John F. Kennedy and Europe.* Baton Rouge, La.: Louisiana State University Press, 1999.

Brockus, H. L., ed. *Gastroenterology.* Philadelphia: Saunders, 1943.

Brooks, Van Wyck. *New England: Indian Summer, 1865–1915.* New York: Dutton, 1940.

Brugioni, Dino. *Eyeball to Eyeball: The Inside Story of the Cuban Missile Crisis.* New York: Random House, 1991.

Bulkley, Robert. *At Close Quarters.* Washington, D.C.: U.S. Government Printing Office, 1962.

Bullitt, Orville H., ed. *For the President: Personal and Secret. Personal and Secret Correspondence Between Franklin D. Roosevelt and William C. Bullitt.* Boston: Houghton Mifflin, 1972.

Bundy, McGeorge. *Danger and Survival: Choices About the Bomb in the First Fifty Years.* New York: Random House, 1988.

Burns, James MacGregor. *John Kennedy.* New York: Harcourt, Brace, 1959.

Carter, Dan T. *The Politics of Rage: George Wallace, the Origins of the New Conservatism, and the Transformation of American Politics.* New York: Simon & Schuster, 1995.

Catudal, Honore M. *Kennedy and the Berlin Wall Crisis.* Berlin: Berlin Verlag, 1980.

Chace, James. *Acheson.* New York: Simon & Schuster, 1998.

Clifford, Clark. *Counsel to the President.* New York: Random House, 1991.

Clymer, Adam. *Edward M. Kennedy: A Biography.* New York: William Morrow, 1999.

Cohen, Adam, and Elizabeth Taylor. *American Pharaoh: Richard J. Daley: His Battle for Chicago and the Nation.* Boston: Little, Brown, 2000.

Cohen, Avner. *Israel and the Bomb.* New York: Columbia University Press, 1998.

Cohen, Warren I. *Dean Rusk.* Totowa, N.J.: Rowman & Littlefield, 1980.

Collier, Peter, and David Horowitz. *The Kennedys: An American Drama.* New York: Summit Books, 1984.

Cooper, Bryan. *The Battle of the Torpedo Boats.* New York: Stein and Day, 1970.

Cousins, Norman. *The Improbable Triumvirate: John F. Kennedy, Pope John, Nikita Khrushchev.* New York: Norton, 1972.

Dallek, Robert. *Flawed Giant: Lyndon Johnson and His Times, 1961–1973.* New York: Oxford University Press, 1998.

———. *Franklin D. Roosevelt and American Foreign Policy, 1932–1945.* New York: Oxford University Press, 1979, 1995.

———. *Lone Star Rising: Lyndon Johnson and His Times, 1908–1960.* New York: Oxford University Press, 1991.

Damore, Leo. *The Cape Cod Years of John Fitzgerald Kennedy.* Englewood Cliffs, N.J.: Prentice Hall, 1967.

Davis, John H. *The Kennedys: Dynasty and Disaster, 1848–1983.* New York: McGraw-Hill, 1984.

Dear, I.C.B., and M.R.D. Foot, eds. *The Oxford Companion to the Second World War.* New York: Oxford University Press, 1995.

De Gaulle, Charles. *Memoirs of Hope: Renewal and Endeavor, 1958–1962.* New York: Simon & Schuster, 1971.

———. *The War Memoirs of Charles de Gaulle: Unity, 1942–1944.* New York: Viking, 1959.

Dietrich, Marlene. *Marlene.* New York: Grove/Atlantic, 1987.

Donald, David Herbert. *Lincoln.* New York: Simon & Schuster, 1995.

Donovan, Robert J. *Conflict and Crisis: The Presidency of Harry Truman, 1945–1948.* New York: Norton, 1977.

Ehrlichman, John. *Witness to Power.* New York: Simon & Schuster, 1982.

Fay, Paul B., Jr. *The Pleasure of His Company.* New York: Harper & Row, 1966.

Freedman, Lawrence. *Kennedy's Wars: Berlin, Cuba, Laos, and Vietnam.* New York: Oxford University Press, 2000.

Freedman, Max, ed. *Roosevelt and Frankfurter: Their Correspondence, 1928–1945.* Boston: Little, Brown, 1967.

Fursenko, Aleksandr, and Timothy Naftali. *"One Hell of a Gamble": Khrushchev, Castro, and Kennedy, 1958–1964.* New York: Norton, 1997.

Galbraith, John K. *Letters to Kennedy.* Edited by James Goodwin. Cambridge, Mass.: Harvard University Press, 1998.

———. *A Life in Our Times.* Boston: Houghton Mifflin, 1981.

Gallup, George. *The Gallup Poll: Public Opinion 1935–1971.* New York: Random House, 1972.

Garrow, David J. *The FBI and Martin Luther King, Jr.* New York: Penguin Books, 1983.

Gettleman, Marvin, ed. *Viet Nam.* New York: Fawcett, 1965.

Gibbons, William C. *The U.S. Government and the Vietnam War, Part II, 1961–1964.* Washington, D.C.: U.S. Government Printing Office, 1984.

Giglio, James N. *The Presidency of John F. Kennedy.* Lawrence, Kans.: University of Kansas Press, 1991.

Goodman, Louis S., and Alfred Gilman. *The Pharmacological Basis of Therapeutics.* London: Macmillan, 1969.

Goodwin, Doris Kearns. *The Fitzgeralds and the Kennedys.* New York: Simon & Schuster, 1987.

Goodwin, Richard. *Remembering America.* Boston: Little, Brown, 1988.

Gore, Albert. *Let the Glory Out: My South and Its Politics.* New York: Viking, 1972.

Grant, Bruce. *A Furious Hunger: America in the Twenty-first Century.* Melbourne, Australia: Melbourne University Press, 1999.

Greenstein, Fred. *The Hidden Hand Presidency.* Princeton, N.J.: Princeton University Press, 1982.

Guthman, Edwin O. *We Band of Brothers: A Memoir of Robert F. Kennedy.* New York: Harper & Row, 1971.

Guthman, Edwin O., and Jeffrey Shulman, eds. *Robert Kennedy: In His Own Words.* New York: Bantam Books, 1988.

Halberstam, David. *The Best and the Brightest.* New York: Random House, 1972.

———. *The Making of a Quagmire: America and Vietnam During the Kennedy Era.* New York: Knopf, 1988.

Hamilton, Nigel. *JFK: Reckless Youth*. New York: Random House, 1992.

Harrison, T. R. *The Principles of Internal Medicine*. New York: McGraw-Hill, 1950.

Hellmann, John. *The Kennedy Obsession: The American Myth of JFK*. New York: Columbia University Press, 1997.

Henderson, Deirdre, ed. *Prelude to Leadership: The European Diary of John F. Kennedy, Summer 1945*. Chicago: Regnery, 1995.

Hersh, Seymour. *The Dark Side of Camelot*. Boston: Little, Brown, 1997.

Hofstadter, Richard. *The Paranoid Style in American Politics*. New York: Alfred A. Knopf, 1967.

———. *Social Darwinism in American Thought*. New York: Columbia University Press, 1945.

Holt, L. Emmett. *The Care and Feeding of Children*. New York: D. Appleton, 1934.

Horne, Alistair. *Macmillan, 1957–1986*. Vol. 2. New York: Viking Penguin, 1989.

Humphrey, Hubert H. *The Education of a Public Man*. Garden City, N.Y.: Doubleday, 1976.

Hutchinson, Dennis J. *The Man Who Once Was Whizzer White*. New York: Free Press, 1998.

Isserman, Maurice. *The Other America: The Life of Michael Harrington*. New York: Public Affairs, 2000.

Jay, Anthony, ed. *The Oxford Dictionary of Political Quotations*. New York: Oxford University Press, 1996.

Johnson, Haynes. *The Bay of Pigs*. New York: Norton, 1964.

Kaiser, David. *American Tragedy: Kennedy, Johnson, and the Origins of the Vietnam War*. Cambridge, Mass.: Harvard University Press, 2000.

Kaiser, Philip M. *Journeying Far and Wide*. New York: Scribners, 1992.

Kalb, Marvin, and Elie Abel. *Roots of Involvement: The U.S. in Asia, 1784–1971*. New York: Norton, 1971.

Kaplan, Fred. *The Wizards of Armageddon*. New York: Simon & Schuster, 1983.

Keller, Morton and Phyllis. *Making Harvard Modern*. New York: Oxford University Press, 2001.

Kennan, George F. *Memoirs, 1925–1950*. Boston: Little, Brown, 1967.

Kennedy, Edward M. *Fruitful Bough*. Privately published, 1969.

Kennedy, John F. *Profiles in Courage*. New York: Harper, 1956.

———. *The Strategy of Peace*. New York: Harper and Brothers, 1960.

———, ed. *As We Remember Joe*. Privately printed, 1945.

———. *Why England Slept*. New York: Wilfred Funk, 1940.

Kennedy, Robert F. *Thirteen Days: A Memoir of the Cuban Missile Crisis*. New York: Norton, 1969.

Kennedy, Rose Fitzgerald. *Times to Remember*. Garden City, N.Y.: Doubleday, 1974.

Kern, Montague, Patricia W. Levering, and Ralph B. Levering. *The Kennedy Crises: The Press, the Presidency, and Foreign Policy*. Chapel Hill, NC: University of North Carolina Press, 1983.

Khrushchev, Nikita S. *Khrushchev Remembers: The Last Testament*. Boston: Little, Brown, 1974.

Khrushchev, Sergei N. *Khrushchev on Khrushchev: An Inside Account of the Man and His Era*. Boston: Little, Brown, 1990.

Kissinger, Henry. *White House Years*. Boston: Little, Brown, 1979.

Kornbluh, Peter, ed. *Bay of Pigs Declassified: The Secret CIA Report on the Invasion of Cuba*. New York: New Press, 1998.

Krock, Arthur. *Memoirs: Sixty Years on the Firing Line*. New York: Funk & Wagnalls, 1968.

Lasky, Victor. *J.F.K.* New York: Macmillan, 1963.

Launius, Roger D., and Howard E. McCurdy, eds. *Space Flight and the Myth of Presidential Leadership*. Urbana, Ill.: University of Illinois Press, 1997.

Leamer, Lawrence. *The Kennedy Men, 1901–1963*. New York: William Morrow, 2001.

Leaming, Barbara. *Mrs. Kennedy*. New York: Free Press, 2001.

Leuchtenburg, William E. *In the Shadow of FDR*. Ithaca, N.Y.: Cornell University Press, 1983.

———. *A Troubled Feast: American Society Since 1945*. Boston: Little, Brown, 1973.

Lincoln, Evelyn. *My Twelve Years with John F. Kennedy*. New York: David McKay, 1965.

Lobel, Aaron. *Presidential Judgment: Foreign Policy Decision Making in the White House*. Cambridge, Mass.: Hollis, 2001.

Logevall, Fredrik. *Choosing War: The Last Chance for Peace and the Escalation of War in Vietnam*. Berkeley, Calif.: University of California Press, 1999.

McCarthy, Joe. *The Remarkable Kennedys*. New York: Dial Press, 1960.

McCullough, David. *Truman*. New York: Simon & Schuster, 1992.

McDougall, Walter A. . . . *The Heavens and the Earth: A Political History of the Space Age*. New York: Basic Books, 1985.

Macmillan, Harold. *Pointing the Way, 1959–1961*. New York: Harper & Row, 1972.

McNamara, Robert S. *In Retrospect: The Tragedy and Lessons of Vietnam*. New York: Times Books, 1995.

Manchester, William. *The Death of a President*. New York: Harper & Row, 1967.

Martin, John Bartlow. *Adlai Stevenson and the World*. Garden City, New York: Doubleday, 1977.

Martin, Lawrence. *The Presidents and the Prime Ministers*. Toronto: Doubleday, 1982.

Martin, Ralph G., and Ed Plaut. *Front Runner, Dark Horse*. Garden City, N.Y.: Doubleday, 1960.

Matthews, Christopher. *Kennedy and Nixon*. New York: Simon & Schuster, 1996.

May, Ernest R., and Philip D. Zelikow, eds. *The Kennedy Tapes: Inside the White House During the Cuban Missile Crisis*. Cambridge, Mass.: Harvard University Press, 1997.

Medvei, Victor C. *A History of Endocrinology*. Lancaster, England: 1982.

Meyers, Joan, ed. *John Fitzgerald Kennedy — As We Remember Him*. New York: Atheneum, 1965.

Michaelis, David. *The Best of Friends: Profiles of Extraordinary Friendships*. New York: William Morrow, 1983.

Millis, Walter, ed. *James Forrestal Diaries*. New York: Viking, 1951.

Naftali, Timothy, ed. *The Presidential Recordings: John F. Kennedy: The Great Crises*, vol. I: *July 30–August 1962*. Philip D. Zelikow and Ernest R. May, gen. eds. New York: Norton, 2001.

Naftali, Timothy, and Philip D. Zelikow, eds. *The Presidential Recordings: John F. Kennedy: The Great Crises*, vol. II: *September–October 21, 1962*. New York: Norton, 2001.

Nathan, James, ed. *The Cuban Missile Crisis Revisited*. New York: St. Martin's, 1992.

Neustadt, Richard E. *Alliance Politics.* New York: Columbia University Press, 1970.

———. *Presidential Power: The Politics of Leadership from FDR to Carter.* New York: John Wiley, 1980.

Newman, John M. *JFK and Vietnam.* New York: Warner, 1992.

Nixon, Richard M. *RN: The Memoirs of Richard Nixon.* New York: Grosset & Dunlap, 1978.

O'Brien, Lawrence. *No Final Victories.* Garden City, N.Y.: Doubleday, 1974.

O'Donnell, Kenneth P., and David F. Powers. *"Johnny, We Hardly Knew Ye."* Boston: Little, Brown, 1970.

O'Neill, Thomas P. *Man of the House.* New York: Random House, 1987.

Parmet, Herbert. *Jack: The Struggles of John F. Kennedy.* New York: Dial, 1980.

———. *JFK: The Presidency of John F. Kennedy.* New York: Penguin Books, 1984.

Perrault, Geoffrey. *Jack: Nothing Like Him in the World.* New York: Random House, 2001.

Posner, Gerald. *Case Closed: Lee Harvey Oswald and the Assassination of JFK.* New York: Random House, 1993.

Powers, Thomas. *The Man Who Kept the Secrets: Richard Helms and the CIA.* New York: Knopf, 1979.

Public Papers of the Presidents: Dwight D. Eisenhower, 1960. Washington, D.C.: U.S. Government Printing Office, 1961.

Public Papers of the Presidents: John F. Kennedy, 1961–1963. Washington, D.C.: U.S. Government Printing Office, 1962–1964.

Rabe, Stephen G. *"The Most Dangerous Area in the World": John F. Kennedy Confronts Communist Revolution in Latin America.* Chapel Hill, N.C.: University of North Carolina Press, 1999.

Reeves, Richard. *President Kennedy: Profile of Power.* New York: Simon & Schuster, 1993.

Reeves, Thomas C. *A Question of Character: A Life of John F. Kennedy.* New York: Macmillan, 1991.

Roosevelt, Eleanor. *On My Own.* New York: Harper and Bros., 1958.

Rostow, Walt W. *The Diffusion of Power.* New York: Macmillan, 1972.

Rusk, Dean. *As I Saw It.* New York: Norton, 1990.

Rust, William J. *Kennedy in Vietnam.* New York: De Capo Press, 1985.

Sakharov, Andrei. *Memoirs.* New York: Knopf, 1990.

Salinger, Pierre. *With Kennedy.* New York: Doubleday, 1966.

Schlesinger, Arthur, Jr. *Robert Kennedy and His Times.* Boston: Houghton Mifflin, 1978.

———. *A Thousand Days.* Boston: Houghton Mifflin, 1965.

Schoenbaum, Thomas J. *Waging Peace and War: Dean Rusk in the Truman, Kennedy, and Johnson Years.* New York: Simon & Schuster, 1988.

Schoor, Gene. *Young John Kennedy.* New York: Harcourt, Brace & World, 1963.

Seaborg, Glenn T. *Kennedy, Khrushchev, and the Test Ban.* Berkeley, Calif.: University of California Press, 1981.

Shapley, Deborah. *Promise and Power: The Life and Times of Robert McNamara.* Boston: Little, Brown, 1993.

Sheehan, Neil. *A Bright Shining Lie: John Paul Vann and America in Vietnam.* New York: Random House, 1988.

Sidey, Hugh. *John F. Kennedy, President.* New York: Atheneum, 1964.

Smith, Amanda, ed. *Hostage to Fortune: The Letters of Joseph P. Kennedy.* New York: Viking, 2001.

Sorensen, Theodore C. *Kennedy.* New York: Bantam Books, 1966.

Steel, Ronald. *In Love with Night: The American Romance with Robert Kennedy.* New York: Simon & Schuster, 2000.

Sulzberger, Cyrus L. *The Last of the Giants.* New York: Macmillan, 1970.

Summers, Anthony. *The Arrogance of Power: The Secret World of Richard Nixon.* New York: Viking, 2000.

Taylor, Maxwell D. *Swords and Ploughshares.* New York: Norton, 1972.

Thomas, Evan. *Robert Kennedy: His Life.* New York: Simon & Schuster, 2000.

Thomas, Helen. *Thanks for the Memories, Mr. President.* New York: Scribner, 2002.

Tifft, Susan E., and Alex S. Jones. *The Trust: The Private and Powerful Family Behind the New York Times.* New York: Little, Brown, 1999.

Travell, Janet. *Office Hours: Day and Night. The Autobiography of Janet Travell, M.D.* New York: World, 1968.

U.S. Central Intelligence Agency and Fabian Escalante. *CIA Targets Fidel: Secret 1967 CIA Inspector General's Report on Plots to Assassinate Fidel Castro.* Melbourne, Australia: Ocean Press, 1996.

U.S. Congress. *Congressional Record.* Washington, D.C.: U.S. Government Printing Office, 1947–1960.

U.S. Department of State. *Foreign Relations of the United States, 1939,* vol. I. Washington, D.C.: U.S. Government Printing Office, 1950.

———. *Foreign Relations of the United States, 1961–1963.* 25 vols. Washington, D.C.: U.S. Government Printing Office, 1988–2001.

———. *Foreign Relations of the United States, Vietnam, 1961–1963.* 4 vols. Washington, D.C.: U.S. Government Printing Office, 1988–1991.

U.S. Senate Select Committee on Intelligence Activities. *Interim Report: Alleged Assassination Plots Involving Foreign Leaders.* Washington, D.C.: U.S. Government Printing Office, 1975.

Weiss, Richard. *The American Myth of Success.* Urbana, Ill.: University of Illinois Press, 1988.

Whalen, Thomas J. *Kennedy and Lodge: The 1952 Massachusetts Senate Race.* Boston: Northeastern University Press, 2001.

White, Theodore H. *The Making of the President, 1960.* New York: Atheneum, 1961.

———. *The Making of the President, 1964.* New York: Atheneum, 1965.

Wills, Garry. *The Kennedy Imprisonment: A Meditation on Power.* Boston: Little, Brown, 1981.

Wofford, Harris. *Of Kennedys and Kings.* New York: Farrar, Straus & Giroux, 1980.

Wyden, Peter. *The Bay of Pigs: The Untold Story.* New York: Simon & Schuster, 1979.

———. *Wall: The Inside Story of Divided Berlin.* New York: Simon & Schuster, 1989.

Zelikow, Philip, and Ernest May, eds. *The Presidential Recordings: John F. Kennedy: The Great Crises,* vol. III: *October 22–28, 1962.* New York: Norton, 2001.

Index